FEDERAL CIVIL PRACTICE

EDITOR-IN-CHIEF
PROFESSOR GEORGENE M. VAIRO

New York State Bar Association
Albany, New York
1989
Cosponsored by
COMMERCIAL AND FEDERAL LITIGATION SECTION

FEDERAL CIVIL PRACTICE

EDITOR-IN-CHIEF
PROFESSOR GEORGENE M. VAIRO

Copyright 1989
by
New York State Bar Association
All rights reserved
Library of Congress Catalog Card Number: 89-061058
ISBN Number: 0-942954-23-8

FEDERAL CIVIL PRACTICE

Editor-in-Chief
Professor Georgene M. Vairo

Chairman, Commercial and Federal Litigation Section
Robert L. Haig, Esq.

Editorial Board
David A. Harland, Esq.
Mitchell A. Lowenthal, Esq.
Francis R. Matera, Esq.
Thomas J. McNamara, Esq.

Contributing Authors

Walter Barthold, Esq.
Frederic Block, Esq.
Peter E. Calamari, Esq.
Alexander C. Cordes, Esq.
Martin L. Feinberg, Esq.
Honorable James C. Francis, IV
Richard D. Greenfield, Esq.
Honorable Sharon E. Grubin
Frank Gulino, Esq.
Robert L. Haig, Esq.
E. Stewart Jones, Jr., Esq.
Edward W. Keane, Esq.
Deborah E. Lans, Esq.
Bernice K. Leber, Esq.
Philip H. Magner, Jr., Esq.
Alan E. Mansfield, Esq.
Denis McInerney, Esq.
Colleen McMahon, Esq.
Richard G. Menaker, Esq.
Barbara A. Mentz, Esq.
Lawrence Mentz, Esq.
James A. Moss, Esq.
Lawrence W. Newman, Esq.
Loretta A. Preska, Esq.
L. Donald Prutzman, Jr., Esq.
John J. Quinn, Esq.
Leonard L. Rivkin, Esq.
John F. Scheffel, Esq.
Michael P. Tierney, Esq.
Harry P. Trueheart, III, Esq.
Professor Ettie Ward
Jon O. Webster, Esq.
David Zaslowsky, Esq.
Jeffrey R. Zuckerman, Esq.

FOREWORD

Law Libraries of large New York law firms are stocked with multivolume treatises on Federal Procedure such as Wright & Miller, *Civil Practice and Procedure* (1988) and Moore's *Federal Practice* (1988). Smaller law firms, particularly those with primarily a New York State court practice, may not want to spend the substantial sums to maintain such treatises. Moreover, individual lawyers may often find the multivolume treatises an inappropriate source of information for quick reference. It is increasingly difficult for lawyers to obtain the expertise needed to be comfortable in federal courts.

Thus, there is a need for a single volume handbook on the subject of Federal Civil Practice with an emphasis on practice in the New York Federal Courts. The New York State Bar Association Committee on Federal Courts (now the Commercial and Federal Litigation Section), under the able leadership of its Chair, Robert L. Haig, undertook the project.

Federal Civil Practice, the result of the project, is designed to serve as a basic guide for new or inexperienced federal court practitioners, and as a resource tool and refresher for more experienced federal practitioners. The aim of the editors and authors is to make the vast and complex subject of federal practice accessible to every practicing attorney.

The project began a year ago. Various lawyers were asked to volunteer to write a chapter for the book. There was an enthusiastic response, making the Board of Editors' job of selecting the authors for the thirty projected chapters exceedingly difficult. *Federal Civil Practice* is thus fortunate to have an outstanding group of some of the finest federal practitioners, federal magistrates, and law professors as its authors.

As the Editor-in-Chief, I was impressed by the excellence, dedication and commitment of the authors. We were able to complete *Federal Civil Practice* in record time. At the same time, however, quality has not suffered. The chapters are concise, informative, and readable. Each of the chapters provides the reader with an overview of the topics presented, practical advice, and a clear exposition of legal principles. Many of the chapters contain "how to do it" checklists and samples of forms, or suggestions as to where forms can be located and where further legal authority may be found. The authors have also emphasized the local rules, alerting the readers to the sometimes inconsistent practices of the four federal districts in New York.

The book's scope is broad. Chapters 1, 2, 3, and 4 cover choice of forum considerations, subject matter and personal jurisdiction, service, venue and removal. Chapters 5, 6, 7 and 8 cover the myriad issues involved in investigating a case, drafting pleadings, and choosing provisional remedies. Joinder of party questions are addressed in Chapters 10 and 11. Pretrial management and discovery are covered in Chapters 12 through 15; pretrial resolution of a case and motion practice are the subjects of Chapters 16, 17 and 18.

Trials and trial practice, including direct and cross-examination strategy, motions, openings and summations, and alternatives to trial are treated in Chapters 19 through 24. Chapters 25, 26, and 27 cover judgments, appeals and preclusion.

Specialized chapters have been prepared on choice of law (Chapter 9), cases involving foreign parties (Chapter 28), jurisdiction and procedure in bankruptcy (Chapter 29), and multidistrict litigation (Chapter 30).

I am indebted to the individuals who took time out from their busy law, law school, or judicial business and from their weekends and leisure time to contribute chapters to this book. Their efforts are sincerely appreciated and I consider it a distinct honor to have been able to work with them on this project. I refer the reader to the biographical notes at the end of *Federal Civil Practice*.

A number of other individuals made this book possible: Robert L. Haig, Chair of the Committee on Federal Courts, for giving me the opportunity to work on this project, for providing advice and two chapters, and for helping insure that the project was completed before schedule; (Mr.) Jean Nelson, Associate Director, Continuing Legal Education, New York State Bar Association, for organizing and supporting the project in its initial stages; Daniel J. McMahon, CLE Publications Manager, New York State Bar Association, for his advice, organizational ability and supervision of the process of putting the book together; Professor Mary Daly for her superb help in editing one of the chapters;

and finally, David Harland, Mitchell Lowenthal, Francis Matera and Thomas McNamara, all members of the Committee on Federal Courts, each of whom edited a group of chapters. I thank them all.

In this "New Era of Sanctions," as a judge of the United States Court of Appeals for the Second Circuit has put it, it is increasingly important for litigators *not* to step lightly into federal court. Good federal practice, like any good practice, requires lawyers to come to court prepared. It is the aim of *Federal Civil Practice* to facilitate their preparation.

Georgene M. Vairo
Editor-in-Chief

New York, New York
March 31, 1988

ABOUT THE AUTHORS

THE EDITOR-IN-CHIEF

PROFESSOR GEORGENE M. VAIRO

Ms. Vairo is an Associate Dean and Professor at Fordham University School of Law. Her primary areas of teaching and practice are Federal Procedure, Complex Litigation, and Federal Jurisdiction. She received her law degree from Fordham University.

Ms. Vairo is a member of the American Bar Association (Section of Litigation, Subcommittee on Rule 11; Judicial Administration Division, Federal Courts Committee), the New York State Bar Association (Federal Courts Committee), the Association of the Bar of the City of New York (Federal Courts Committee), and the Women's Bar Association of the State of New York. She has served as a lecturer for the American Law Institute/American Bar Association Federal Practice Program since 1983 and for various Practising Law Institute programs and videotapes since 1986. Ms. Vairo has also been a lecturer for the Federal Judicial Center, for seminars for newly appointed federal judges, and for various Federal Judicial conferences and workshops. She has served as a panelist at various Federal Bar Council programs for the NAACP Legal Defense and Education Fund, and for Legal Aid Society programs. Ms. Vairo is the author of numerous articles on federal practice and procedure, including *Rule 11: A Critical Analysis*, "Through the Prism: Summary Judgment and the Trilogy," and *MultiTort Cases: Cause For More Darkness On The Subject, Or A New Role For Federal Common Law?*

Mr. Matera is a member of the New York State Bar Association (Committee on Commercial and Federal Litigation; Sub-committee for publication *Individual Judges' Rules*) and the Maritime Law Association of the United States. He is the author of "The Enforcement of an Arbitration Award," Association of Ford Industries, 1985 and "Time Bar Limitation in the Carriage of Goods," Association of Food Industries, 1986.

THOMAS J. McNAMARA, ESQ.

Mr. McNamara is the head of the Litigation Department in the firm of Wingate and Cullen. He specializes in commercial and banking litigation. He received his law degree from New York University.

Mr. McNamara is a member of the New York State Bar Association (Commercial and Federal Litigation Section; Committee on CPLR), the Nassau County Bar Association (Federal Courts Committee), and the Brooklyn Bar Association (Banking Law Committee). He served as an Adjunct Instructor of Legal Research and Writing at New York Law School, 1982-83. He is also the author of "The Constitutionality of Maritime Attachment" (1980).

EDITORIAL BOARD

DAVID A. K. HARLAND, ESQ.

Mr. Harland is an Associate Attorney in the New York City firm of Fried, Frank, Harris, Shriver & Jacobson. He specializes in commercial and securities litigation. He received his law degree from the London School of Economics and Political Science.

Mr. Harland is a member of the New York State Bar Association (Commercial and Federal Litigation Section), the Association of the Bar of the City of New York (Special Committee on Public Education and Service), the District of Columbia Bar (International Law and Litigation Divisions), and the American Bar Association, as well as the Honourable Society of the Inner Temple (London, England). Mr. Harland has coauthored two articles: "Sanctions and Attorneys' Fees," Report of the Committee on Federal Courts, New York State Bar Association and "Debarment and Suspension Practices at the General Services Administration," American Bar Asssociation.

MITCHELL A. LOWENTHAL, ESQ.

Mitchell A. Lowenthal (Cornell A.B. 1978, J.D. 1981) is associated with Cleary, Gottlieb, Steen & Hamilton in New York City. He served as Note Editor of the *Cornell Law Review* and as law clerk to the Honorable Edward Weinfeld of the United States District Court for the Southern District of New York. He also served as an Adjunct Associate Professor at the Cornell Law School in 1987, and is a member of the Board of Directors of the Legal Action Center for the Homeless. He is a coauthor of *Time Bars in Specialized Federal Common Law: Federal Rights of Action and State Statutes of Limitations*, 65 Cornell Law Review 1011-1105 (1980).

FRANCIS R. MATERA, ESQ.

Mr. Matera is a partner in the New York City firm of Crowell, Rouse & Matera. He specializes in commercial, negligence, maritime, insurance, aviation, and family law. He received his law degree from New York Law School.

THE AUTHORS

WALTER BARTHOLD, ESQ.

Mr. Barthold is counsel to Leaf Sternklar & Drogin, New York City. He received the degree of LL.B. from Yale Law School. He specializes in civil litigation. In the New York State Bar Association, he has chaired the Antitrust Law Section and served as a member of the House of Delegates and the Committee on Professional Ethics. He also belongs to the American Bar Association and to the Association of the Bar of the City of New York. In the latter organization, he has served as a member of the Committee on the Judiciary, the Committee on State Courts of Superior Jurisdiction, and the Committee on Professional Discipline. As a Fellow of the American College of Trial Lawyers, he heads that body's Committee on Attorney-Client Relationships. He is also a Fellow of The New York Bar Foundation. Mr. Barthold is the author of *Attorney's Guide to Effective Discovery Techniques* and coauthor of *Depositions and Other Disclosure*.

FREDERIC BLOCK, ESQ.

Mr. Block is a partner in the Smithtown law firm of Block, Amelkin & Hamburger. He is a graduate of Cornell Law School and has been President of the Suffolk County Bar Association and Vice President of the New York State Bar Association. Mr. Block is the founder of the Suffolk Academy of Law and has served throughout the years on many New York State Bar Association committees, including Chair of NYSBA's Conference of Bar Leaders and its Special Committee on Association Meetings. He has authored articles for the *New York State Bar Journal* and the *New York Law Journal*, and has been a frequent lecturer for the New York State Bar Association and other institutions on federal practice. He has been counsel in many cases of statewide and national significance as an active litigator in the areas of civil rights, municipal, and constitutional law.

PETER E. CALAMARI, ESQ.

Mr. Calamari is a member of the firm of Hertzog, Calamari & Gleason in New York City. He specializes in litigation (securities and general commercial). He received his law degree from Fordham University.

Mr. Calamari is a member of the American Bar Association (Litigation Section), the New York State Bar Association, the New York City Bar Association, the Federal Bar Council, and the Securities Industry Association (Compliance and Legal division). He was an Adjunct Professor of Law at Fordham Law School from 1976 to 1985.

ALEXANDER C. CORDES, ESQ.

Mr. Cordes practices trial law with the Buffalo law firm of Phillips, Lytle, Hitchcock, Blaine & Huber. Between graduating from the University of Buffalo Law School and becoming a member of his present firm, he was Assistant U.S. Attorney, W.D.N.Y., and a member of the Erie County Board of Supervisors. Mr. Cordes is a Fellow of the American College of Trial Lawyers, the American Bar Foundation, and the New York State Bar Foundation. He is also a member of the Erie County, New York State and American Bar Associations, the Erie County Trial Lawyers Association, and the American Judicature Society. Mr. Cordes has taken part in New York State Bar Association programs on "Trial of a Personal Injury Case," "Federal Court Practice," and "Complex Product Liability."

MARTIN L. FEINBERG, ESQ.

Martin L. Feinberg is a staff attorney in the Enforcement Division of the Securities and Exchange Commission's New York Regional Office. He received a J.D. from Catholic University Law School in 1983 and an LL.M. in corporation law from New York University Law School in 1988. Before joining the SEC in 1988, he was in private practice. He is a member of the ABA sections of Litigation, Business Law, and Criminal Justice.

HONORABLE JAMES C. FRANCIS, IV

Mr. Francis has been a United States Magistrate in the Southern District of New York since 1985. After graduating from the Yale Law School in 1978, he served as law clerk to U.S. District Judge Robert L. Carter. Mr. Francis then joined the Civil Appeals & Law Reform Unit of the Legal Aid Society in New York City where he conducted complex civil litigation in the fields of housing, education, and the rights of disabled persons.

RICHARD D. GREENFIELD, ESQ.

Mr. Greenfield is a senior partner in the Haverford, Pennsylvania firm of Greenfield & Chimicles. He specializes in securities and consumer litigation. He received his law degree from Cornell Law School.

Mr. Greenfield is a member of the American Bar Association (Litigation Section, Class and Derivative Action and Securities Litigation Subcommittees), the Philadelphia Bar Association (Federal Courts Committee), Complex Litigation Subcommittee, the Philadelphia chapter of the Federal Bar Association, and the Federal Bar Council of New York City. He has served as a lecturer for numerous programs, seminars, and conventions. Mr. Greenfield has also made many contributions to and been quoted in major national and international business publications.

HONORABLE SHARON E. GRUBIN

Sharon E. Grubin has been a United States Magistrate for the Southern District of New York since March 1984, previously having practiced law with the firm of White & Case. She has lectured on various litigation topics for the New York State Bar Association, Association of the Bar of the City of New York, New York County Lawyers' Association, Practising Law Institute, and various law schools. She is a member of the Committee on Second Circuit Courts of the Federal Bar Council, Committee on Professional and Judicial Ethics, and the Council on Judicial Administration of the Association of the Bar of the City of New York, and formerly served on the Judiciary Committee and Nominating Committee of the Association of the Bar.

FRANK GULINO, ESQ.

Mr. Gulino is counsel to the firm of Stockfield & Fixler. His primary area of practice is litigation. He is a graduate of the Fordham University School of Law.

Mr. Gulino is a member of the New York State Bar Association, the American Bar Association, the Federal Bar Council, and the Federal Bar Association. He has served as a guest lecturer in trial advocacy at Fordham University School of Law and was an Adjunct Associate Professor of Law from 1983 to 1988. In addition, Mr. Gulino has contributed in numerous capacities to the *Fordham Urban Law Journal* and Fordham Urban Law Journal Alumni Association.

ROBERT L. HAIG, ESQ.

Mr. Haig is a partner in the New York City law firm of Kelley Drye & Warren, where he specializes in civil litigation. He is the current Chair of NYSBA's Commercial and Federal Litigation Section and a former Chair of its Committee on Federal Courts. As a representative of the NYSBA, he served on the Democratic Party Independent Judicial Screening Panels for candidates for the Civil Court and the Supreme Court in New York County. He is an Elected Delegate from the First Judicial District to NYSBA's House of Delegates and a member of NYSBA's Committee on Judicial Selection. Mr. Haig is currently a vice president of the New York County Lawyers' Association, and serves on its Executive Committee and Board of Directors. He is the current Chair of its Finance Committee, former Chair of its Committee on the Supreme Court, and is also a member of the Board of Directors of the New York County Lawyers' Association Foundation, Inc. Mr. Haig is currently a member of the Executive Council of the New York State Conference of Bar Leaders; Network of Bar Leaders; and Committee for Modern Courts, Legislative Committee. He has been a member of the Committee on the Judiciary of the Association of the Bar of the City of New York and the Committee on Second Circuit Courts of the Federal Bar Council. He is a Fellow of the American Bar Foundation. He has lectured on various federal and New York State litigation issues for the Practising Law Institute, NYSBA, and New York County Lawyers' Association. His articles, chapters, and outlines on litigation issues have been included in various publications.

E. STEWART JONES, JR., ESQ.

Mr. Jones, of the E. Stewart Jones Law Offices in Troy, has served as Assistant District Attorney, then Special Prosecutor, for Rensselaer County. He is a member of the New York State Bar Association, the New York State Trial Lawyers Association, the Association of Trial Lawyers of America, and the National Association of Criminal Defense Lawyers. He is also a Fellow of the American College of Trial Lawyers, the Amercian Bar Foundation, and the American Board of Criminal Lawyers. Mr. Jones has lectured on criminal trial and practice techniques and civil trial techniques for the New York State Trial Lawyers Association and the Capital District Trial Lawyers Association. His published works include a chapter on negligence which appears in a multi-volume work on forensic medicine and a chapter on cross-examination which appears in NYSBA's work on civil lawsuits.

EDWARD W. KEANE, ESQ.

Mr. Keane is a partner in the firm of Sullivan & Cromwell in New York City. His wide-ranging civil litigation practice has included corporate, securities, antitrust, tax, regulatory, takeover, and many other kinds of business-related cases in both trial and appellate courts. He is a former Chairman of the New York State Bar Association's Committee on the Federal Constitution. He graduated in 1957 from the Harvard Law School, where he was an editor and later the President of the *Harvard Law Review*. He was a law clerk to a Justice of the United States Supreme Court before commencing practice with Sullivan & Cromwell.

DEBORAH E. LANS, ESQ.

Ms. Lans is a partner and head of the litigation department of the firm of Morrison Cohen & Singer. She practices primarily in the areas of securities and commercial law. She graduated *cum laude* from Boston University School of Law in 1974. She is a member of the Executive Committee of the Association of the Bar of the City of New York; a past delegate to the New York State Bar Association House of Delegates; past chair of the Young Lawyers Committee of the Association of the Bar and past member of its Judiciary and Membership Committees. She is also a member of the American Arbitration Association's panel of arbitrators for commercial disputes.

BERNICE K. LEBER, ESQ.

Bernice K. Leber is a partner in the firm of Summit Rovins & Feldesman, specializing in litigation and international law. She graduated from Columbia University Law School in 1978. She is a member of the Federal Courts Committee of the New York State Bar Association and the Civil Court Committee of the Association of the Bar of the City of New York. She has coauthored the article "Using Rule 9(b) to Challenge Securities Fraud Actions" in *The National Law Journal* and serves as an arbitrator to the United States District Court for the Eastern District of New York.

PHILIP H. MAGNER, JR., ESQ.

Mr. Magner is President of Magner, Love & Morris, P.C. of Buffalo, New York and Sarasota, Bradenton and Venice, Florida, and practices law actively in both states. He is a Fellow of the American College of Trial Lawyers, and a past President of the Bar Association of Erie County, the Western New York Trial Lawyers Association and the Erie County Bar Foundation. He has been a Governor of the American Trial Lawyers Association and Founding Chairman of its Judicial Administration Section. A Fellow of the American Bar Foundation and a member of the Amercian Law Institute, he presently serves also on the Governor's Judicial Nominating Committee for the Court of Claims and the Fourth Department. Mr. Magner has lectured for and been published frequently by the Amercian Bar, the American Medical Association, the New York State Bar Association and many other bar and medical groups. He has been the recipient of the Distinguished Lawyer of the Year Award from the Bar Association of Erie County and the Distinguished Alumnus Award from the State University of New York at Buffalo Law School.

ALAN MANSFIELD, ESQ.

Mr. Mansfield is a partner in the firm of Phillips, Nizer, Benjamin, Krim & Ballon, New York City, where he specializes in civil litigation and white-collar criminal defense. He received his law degree from the Duke Law School.

Mr. Mansfield is a member of the New York State and local Bar Association. He was a member of the Committee on Federal Courts, Commercial and Federal Litigation Section. He served as Secretary of the Criminal Courts Committee from 1985 to 1988. Mr. Mansfield published *Lawyers' Admissions* in the fall of 1985. He was an Adjunct Instructor of Law at the Cardoza Law School from 1982-1985.

DENIS McINERNEY, ESQ.

Mr. McInerney is a partner in the firm of Cahill Gordon & Reindel. He has authored a number of legal articles and coauthored Practitioners' Handbooks on Appeals to the Court of Appeals and to the Appellate Divisions of the State of New York, both of which were published by the New York State Bar Association. He is past president of the New York County Lawyers' Association and of the Fordham Law Alumni Association, a Fellow of the American College of Trial Lawyers, and has been a lecturer and panelist on trial advocacy programs sponsored by various bar associations and law schools.

COLLEEN McMAHON, ESQ.

Ms. McMahon is a partner in the firm of Paul Weiss Rifkind Wharton & Garrison, where she specializes in state and federal litigation. She received her law degree from Harvard University.

Ms. McMahon is a member of the American, New York State and local Bar Associations. She served as Chairman of the Committee on State Courts of Superior Jurisdiction from 1984-1987. Presently she is a member of the Council on Judicial Administration and the Committee on the Profession. Ms. McMahon has published two articles—on copyright and libel—in *Law and the Arts* (formerly known as *Art and the Law*).

RICHARD G. MENAKER, ESQ.

Mr. Menaker is a practicing commercial trial lawyer in New York City, where he is a member of the firm of Menaker & Herrmann. He holds degrees from Columbia College (A.B. 1969) and the University of Virginia School of Law (J.D. 1974), as well as a D. Phil. in legal history from Oxford (1972). Mr. Menaker is a member of the Committee on Continuing Legal Education of the Trial Lawyers Section of the New York State Bar Association and a member of the panel of commercial arbitrators of the American Arbitration Association. He is the author of *Sanctions for Frivolous Litigation: Should New York Have a Counterpart to Federal Rule 11?* 59 New York State Bar Journal 31 (November 1987).

BARBARA A. MENTZ, ESQ.

Ms. Mentz specializes in accounting law litigation as an associate general counsel to Deloitte Haskins & Sells in New York City. She received her law degree from the University of Notre Dame. Ms. Mentz is a member of the American and local Bar Associations. She served on the Committee on Section 7 of the Clayton Act and the Professional Discipline Committee from 1983 to 1986. Presently she serves on the Antitrust and Trade Regulation Committee.

LAWRENCE MENTZ, ESQ.

Mr. Mentz is a partner in the firm of Condon & Forsyth, New York City. He specializes in commercial litigation, aviation, products liability and insurance law. He received his law degree from the University of Notre Dame.

Mr. Mentz is a member of the American and the New York State and local Bar Association. He has served on the Section of Antitrust Law—Industry Regulation Committee; the American Bar Association Litigation Section—Aviation

Committee, the Commercial and Litigation Section; the Committee on Supreme Courts and the Aeronautics Law Committee. Mr. Mentz is also a member of the Federal Bar Council.

Mr. Mentz has lectured on the U.S. Constitution for the Second Circuit Committee on the Bicentennial of the U.S. Constitution.

JAMES A. MOSS, ESQ.

Mr. Moss is a partner in the firm of Herrick, Feinstein in Manhattan. He graduated from Columbia Law School in 1973. He is a member of the Trial Lawyers Section of the Circuit Courts of the Federal Bar Council. He is also a member of the Attorneys' Panel Of the Grievance Committee for the U.S. District Court for the Southern District of New York, where he served as Deputy Chief of the Criminal Division and Chief of the Narcotics Unit. For many years, Mr. Moss has been an instructor in trial practice for the National Institute of Trial Advocacy and at numerous law schools throughout the country, including Harvard's Trial Advocacy Workshop. He is also a contributing author and lecturer for the RICO Litigation Seminars sponsored annually by the Law Journal Seminars-Press. Mr. Moss specializes in commercial litigation and white-collar criminal defense.

LAWRENCE W. NEWMAN, ESQ.

Mr. Newman is a partner in the Litigation Department of the New York office of the international law firm of Baker & McKenzie. He is a graduate of Harvard College and Harvard Law School (1960). He was an Assistant United States Attorney for the Southern District of New York for five years prior to joining Baker & McKenzie in 1969. He has lectured frequently before law school and bar association groups on international litigation, international commercial arbitration and claims against the government of Iran. He and his partner Michael Burrows are regular contributors to the *New York Law Journal*, for which they write a column on international litigation. Mr. Newman is also a contributing columnist on legal matters for a business publication, *Northeast International Business*. He is the coauthor of portions of *International Commercial Arbitration in New York* (1986) (published by the American Arbitration Association) and of a chapter in *Judicial Enforcement of International Debt Obligations* (1987) (published by the International Law Institute).

LORETTA A. PRESKA, ESQ.

Ms. Preska is a partner in the firm of Hertzog, Calamari & Gleason, where she specializes in litigation, with particular expertise in securities and defamation. She received her law degree from Fordham University.

Ms. Preska is a member of the American Bar Association (Litigation, Corporate Counsel), the Association of the Bar of the City of New York, the Federal Bar Counsel, and the New York State Bar Association (Federal Litigation, Litigation).

L. DONALD PRUTZMAN, JR., ESQ.

Mr. Prutzman is a partner in the firm of Stecher Jaglom & Prutzman in New York City. He received his law degree from N.Y.U.

Mr. Prutzman is a member of the American, New York State and Pennslyvania Bar Associations. He has served on the Economics Committee of Antitrust Section and the Committee on Children and Law. He is a member of the Federal Bar Counsel and the Committee on Second Circuit Courts.

JOHN J. QUINN, ESQ.

Mr. Quinn is a member of the New York City firm of Kelley Drye & Warren, where he specializes in civil and white-collar criminal litigation. Formerly, he was an Assistant District Attorney for New York County. He is a graduate of Albany Law School and received an LL.M. in Corporation Law from New York University in 1982. Mr. Quinn has served as a guest faculty member for the Practising Law Institute's workshop on Direct and Cross Examination. He is also the author of *Preparing and Trying Civil Lawsuit*.

LEONARD L. RIVKIN, ESQ.

Leonard L. Rivkin is the founding partner of the national law firm of Rivkin, Radler, Dunne & Bayh. He received his law degree from the University of Virginia Law School. He served in the U.S. Army and was awarded two Purple Hearts and the Silver Star.

He is a member of the American, New York State, and local Bar and Trial Lawyer Associations; the International Academy of Law and Science; the Federation of Insurance and Corporate Counsel (chairman of the Environmental Law and Toxic Tort Committee); the American Judicature Society; Director of the Nassau and Suffolk Inns of the Court; and the Federal Bar Counsel. He is a former Special Professor of Law at Hofstra University School of Law.

Mr. Rivkin has been a lecturer and author for the American and New York State Bar Associations, the Defense Research Institute, Federation of Insurance and Corporate Counsel, Practicing Law Institute, National Environmental Enforcement Council Journal, National Association of Attorneys General, and many other local and national trial groups. He was the Editor-in-Chief of the *Hazardous Waste and Toxic Tort* national monthly newsletter published by Leader Publications.

JOHN F. SCHEFFEL, ESQ.

John F. Scheffel has specialized in bankruptcy law for over 15 years. He maintains offices in Manhattan and Westchester. A partner of Bigham Englar Jones & Houston, he graduated from the Cornell University School of Law in 1972. He is cochairman of the New York State Bar Association's Committee on Multinational Insolvency and Reorganization. He most frequently represents debtors, creditors, trustees and examiners in commercial Chapter 11 reorganization matters in New York State as well as many other jurisdictions of the United States.

MICHAEL P. TIERNEY, ESQ.

Mr. Tierney is a partner in the firm of Cahill Gordon & Reindel. He graduated from Columbia University School of Law in 1969. He has been involved in complex commercial litigation in both state and federal courts in New York and around the country.

HARRY P. TRUEHEART, III, ESQ.

Mr. Trueheart is a partner in the firm of Nixon, Hargrave, Devans & Doyle where he is principally involved in the litigation of business, commercial, securities and antitrust litigation in state and federal courts.

Mr. Trueheart received his B.A. and J.D. degrees from Harvard University. He is a member of the Commercial and Federal Litigation section of the New York State Bar Association and has been Chairman of the Continuing Legal Education Committee. He is a member of the Antitrust and Corporation Banking and Business Law Sections of the American Bar Association. He is a commercial arbitrator for the American Arbitration Association and a member of the panel of Special Counsel and Adjudicators for the ADR Service of the Federal Bar Council. He is a regular lecturer and program chairman for the New York State Bar Association programs on federal litigation.

PROFESSOR ETTIE WARD

Ms. Ward is on the faculty of St. John's University School of Law. She attended Columbia Law School and practiced general commercial and securities litigation after graduation. Ms. Ward is the Reporter to the Second Circuit Standing Committee on the Improvement of Civil Litigation. She is a member of the Federal Practice Section of the New York State Bar Association, the American Bar Association (Discovery and Rule 11 Subcommittees), the Association of the Bar of the City of New York (Legal Education and Admissions Committee), the Federal Bar Council and the New York Women's Bar Association.

JON O. WEBSTER, ESQ.

Mr. Webster is an Associate in the firm of Nixon, Hargrave, Devans and Doyle. He specializes in litigation, with a concentration in antitrust, commercial, and intellectual property. He received his law degree from the State University of New York at Buffalo.

Mr. Webster is a member of the American Bar Association (Antitrust Section), the New York State Bar Association, and the Monroe County Bar Association. He is the author of *Copyright Protection of Systems Control Software Stored in Read Only Memory Chips: Into the World of Gulliver's Travels*, 33 Buffalo L. Rev. 193.

DAVID ZASLOWSKY, ESQ.

Since graduating from the Yale Law School in 1984, Mr. Zaslowsky has worked in the New York office of the international law firm of Baker & McKenzie. He is an associate in the litigation department of the firm. Mr. Zaslowsky's primary areas of practice are international litigation and arbitration, and he has participated in arbitrations before the American Arbitration Association, International Chamber of Commerce and Iran-United States Claims Tribunal. Mr. Zaslowsky is a member of the American Bar Association and the Association of the Bar of the City of New York.

JEFFREY R. ZUCKERMAN, ESQ.

Mr. Zuckerman is an Assistant Regional Administrator in the Enforcement Division of the Securities & Exchange Commission, New York Regional Office. He previously served as a Special Trial Counsel and a Senior Trial Counsel with the SEC. Mr. Zuckerman graduated from NYU Law School in 1980 where he was a staff member and editor of NYU's *Annual Survey of American Law* and coauthored an article on *Administrative Law* (1979 Annual Survey). Before joining the SEC, he was a litigation associate at Guggenheimer & Untermyer (9/80 to 3/85) and Rosenman Colin, Freund, Lewis & Cohen (3/85 to 5/86). Mr. Zuckerman specializes in securities litigation. He is a member of the American Bar Association (Litigation Section), the Association of the Bar of the City of New York, the New York State Bar Association, and the New York County Lawyers' Association. He is a member of the New York County Lawyers' Committee on the Supreme Court and Chair of that committee's Subcommittee On Continuing Legal Education. Mr. Zuckerman cochaired the Association's six-part lecture series on *Commercial Litigation in the New York State Courts* in the Fall of 1988.

TABLE OF CONTENTS

Chapter Number	Title and Author	Page

Foreword ix

About the Authors xiii

1. Federal Subject-Matter Jurisdiction
   by Michael P. Tierney, Esq. 1

2. Personal Jurisdiction and Service
   by L. Donald Prutzman, Jr., Esq 25

3. Venue
   by Colleen McMahon, Esq 61

4. Removal
   by Hon. Sharon E. Grubin and Deborah E. Lans, Esq. 79

5. Investigation of the Case and Use of Experts
   by Robert L. Haig, Esq., and John J. Quinn, Esq. 103

6. Commencement of the Action—The Complaint
   by Richard G. Menaker, Esq. 139

7. Provisional Remedies
   by Denis McInerney, Esq 164

8. Responding to the Complaint
   by Peter E. Calamari, Esq. 181

9. Choice of Law
   by Barbara A. Mentz, Esq 191

10. Parties
   by James A. Moss, Esq 253

11. Class Actions and Other Representative Litigation
   by Richard D. Greenfield, Esq. 277

12. Pretrial Management
   by Hon. James C. Francis, IV. 299

13. Discovery
   by Alexander C. Cordes, Esq.. 323

14. Depositions
   by Jeffrey R. Zuckerman, Esq., and Martin L. Feinberg, Esq. 347

15. Other Methods of Discovery
   by Prof. Ettie Ward 425

16. Motion Practice and Dismissal Without Trial
   by Robert L. Haig, Esq..471

17. Summary Judgment Under Rule 56
   by Harry P. Trueheart, III, Esq., and Jon O. Webster, Esq 503

18. Settlement
   by Alan Mansfield, Esq. 545

19. Trials
   by Frederic Block, Esq..561

20. Opening Statement
   by E. Stewart Jones, Jr., Esq..................................603

21. Summation
   by Philip H. Magner, Jr., Esq..................................631

22. Direct and Cross-Examination
   by Walter Barthold, Esq. 643

23. Alternatives to Trial
   by Loretta A. Preska, Esq.....................................663

24. Trial and Post-Trial Motions
   by Lawrence Mentz, Esq.......................................681

25. Judgments
   by Frank Gulino, Esq...703

26. Appellate Review
   by Edward W. Keane, Esq. 725

27. Preclusion: *Res Judicata* and Collateral Estoppel; Recent Developments in the United States Supreme Court; What Practitioners Can Expect
    by Bernice K. Leber, Esq. 749

28. Special Considerations in Cases Involving Foreign Parties
    by Lawrence W. Newman, Esq., and David Zaslowsky, Esq. 779

29. Jurisdiction and Procedure in Bankruptcy
    by John F. Scheffel, Esq 829

30. Multidistrict Litigation
    by Leonard L. Rivkin, Esq................................871

Index 891

Table of Authorities 991

	A.	Issuance of the Summons—Rule 4(a)...............27
	B.	The Form of the Summons—Rule 4(b) 28
	C.	Service of the Summons and Complaint—Rule 4(c) and (d) 29
	D.	Time Limit for Service 45
	E.	Return of Service 45
	F.	The Remedy for Improper Service—Dismissal of the Action or Quashing of Service....................46
III.	Amenability to Federal District Court Jurisdiction 47
	A.	Introduction 47
	B.	Statutory Authorization for Exercise of Federal Court Personal Jurisdiction..........................47
	C.	New York Federal Court Extraterritorial Jurisdiction Under New York Law........................50
	D.	Constitutional Limitations on the Exercise of Extraterritorial Jurisdiction—The Due Process Clause 53
IV.	Quasi-In-Rem Jurisdiction—A Possible Substitute for Personal Jurisdiction 56
V.	Raising Lack of Personal Jurisdiction as a Defense........58

CHAPTER THREE: Venue

I.	General Considerations 61
II.	The Key to Venue is Convenience 62
III.	How to Choose Venue in a Particular Case..............63
	A. What Is a Party's Residence?.....................64
	B. How to Determine Where the Claim Arose..........67
	C. Special Venue Statutes..........................68
IV.	Objections to Venue—Motions for Transfer or Dismissal ...71
	A. Transfer for Improper Venue.....................72
	B. Transfer for Convenience 73
	C. *Forum Non Conveniens*.........................76

CHAPTER FOUR: Removal

| I. | Overview ....79 |
| II. | What Actions May be Removed: 28 U.S.C. § 1441.......80 |

DETAILED TABLE OF CONTENTS

		Page
CHAPTER ONE: Federal Subject-Matter Jurisdiction		
I.	Introduction: Article III Courts and Congress	2
	A. Federal Courts are Courts of Limited Jurisdiction and Their Jurisdiction is Conferred only by Act of Congress	2
	B. The Requirement of a "Case" or "Controvery"	3
	C. Bases of Federal Subject-Matter Jurisdiction	4
	D. Current Make-up of the Inferior Federal Courts	4
	E. Practice Pointers	6
II.	The Basic Statutes	8
	A. 28 U.S.C. § 1331—Federal Question Jurisdiction	8
	B. 28 U.S.C. § 1332—Diversity Jurisdiction	10
	C. Other Statutes	16
III.	Special Problems in Federal Subject-Matter Jurisdiction	17
	A. Pendent Jurisdiction	17
	B. Pendent Parties	19
	C. Ancillary Jurisdiction	20
	D. Pre-emption and Abstention	21
	E. Implied Rights of Action	23
	F. Anti-Injunction Statute	23
IV.	Bibliography	24
CHAPTER TWO: Personal Jurisdiction and Service		
I.	Introduction	25
II.	Proper Service of the Summons and Complaint	27

	A.	Federal Question Cases 82
	B.	Diversity Cases 83
	C.	Separate and Independent Claims 86
III.	Provisions Permitting or Prohibiting Removal in Specialized Cases 88
	A.	Removal Permitted 88
	B.	Removal Prohibited 90
IV.	Procedure for Removal 91
	A.	Who May Remove 91
	B.	Place of Filing 92
	C.	Time for Filing the Petition 93
	D.	Contents of the Notice of Removal 94
	E.	Waiver by the Defendant of the Right to Remove 95
	F.	Requirement of a Bond 95
	G.	Requirement of Notice of Removal 96
	H.	When Removal is Effective 96
V.	Procedure After Removal 96
	A.	Process, §§ 1447(a) and 1448 96
	B.	Transfer of State Court Record, §§ 1447(b) and 1449 ..97
	C.	Case is Governed by Federal Rules, Rule 81(c) 97
	D.	Orders Issued by State Court Remain Effective, § 1450, But Federal Rules Apply; the Granny Goose Doctrine ..98
VI.	Remand 99
VII.	Appeal of Orders Granting or Denying Remand 100

CHAPTER FIVE: Investigation of Case and Use of Experts

I.	Introduction 103
II.	Interviews 104
	A.	Client, Nonparties, and Parties 104
	B.	Eyewitness Interviews 105
III.	Governmental and Institutional Records and Information ... 107
	A.	Freedom of Information Requests 108
	B.	Medical Records 109
	C.	Accident Reports 111

	D.	Death Certificates 112
	E.	School and Employment Records 112
	F.	Workers' Compensation and Social Security Records ..113
	G.	Corporate Filings 113
	H.	Court Records.................................114
	I.	Violations of Government Regulations..............115
	J.	Common Carrier Reports 116
	K.	Public Facility Maintenance Records...............117
	L.	Government Funding Records....................117
	M.	Product Information 117
	N.	United States Postal Service 118
	O.	Weather Information 118
	P.	Government Standards and Statistical Information.....118
	Q.	Computer Records 119
IV.	Private Investigators................................120
V.	The Investigation of Particular Types of Cases 122
	A.	Products Liability 122
	B.	Medical Malpractice 123
	C.	Workers' Compensation 125
	D.	Contracts 125
VI.	The Retention and Proper Use of an Expert 127

Appendix A: Directory of Selected Federal Government Agencies...133

Appendix B: Sources for Medical Information 137

CHAPTER SIX: Commencement of the Action—The Complaint

I.	Introduction......................................139
II.	Laying the Groundwork............................140
	A. The Goals and the Obstacles......................140
	B. Determining the Grievance 140
	C. Identifying the Client's Objectives 141
	D. Satisfying Rule 11.............................141
	E. Reconstituting the Case.........................141
	F. Checklist of Predrafting Preparation 142

III.	Drafting the Complaint—General Considerations	142
	A. Modern Pleading, the Theory	142
	B. Modern Pleading, the Reality	143
	C. Comparison with New York's CPLR	144
IV.	Drafting the Complaint—The Particulars	145
	A. Appearance and Format	145
	B. Pleading Jurisdiction	146
	C. Pleading the Claim for Relief	148
	D. Pleading the Demand for Judgment	149
	E. Checklist for Drafting the Complaint	151
V.	"Particularity" in Pleading	152
	A. The Requirements of Rule 9	152
	B. Particularity of State-Law-Claims in Diversity Actions	155
	C. Special Requirements for Class Actions and Shareholder Suits	156
	D. Court-Imposed Particularity	156
	E. Checklist for Particularity in Pleading	158
VI.	Filing the Complaint	159
	A. The Civil Cover Sheet	160
	B. General Rule 9 Statement	160
	C. The Summons	161
	D. Fees	161
VII.	Effect of Filing on Statutes of Limitations	161
	A. Federal Question Claims	161
	B. Diversity Cases	162

CHAPTER SEVEN: Provisional Remedies

I.	Introduction	164
II.	Preliminary Injunctions and Temporary Restraining Orders	164
	A. Commencing the Action and Bringing On the Motion	164
	B. Appeals	168
III.	Attachment and Garnishment	172
	A. Grounds and Showing for Attachment	172

	B.	Debt or Property Subject to Attachment 174
	C.	Bringing On the Motion 174
	D.	Appeals 176
IV.	Receiverships. 176
	A.	Appointing a Receiver. 177
	B.	Suits By and Against Receivers 179
	C.	Jurisdiction 179
	D.	Appeals 179

CHAPTER EIGHT: Responding to the Complaint

I.	The Answer 181
	A.	General 181
	B.	Timing 182
	C.	Responding to the Individual Averments of the Complaint. 183
	D.	Affirmative Defenses 185
II.	Counterclaims, Cross-Claims and Third-Party Complaints . . 186
	A.	Counterclaims. 186
	B.	Cross-Claims 188
	C.	Third-Party Claims 188
III.	Amended and Supplemental Answers. 189

CHAPTER NINE: Choice of Law

I.	The *Erie* Doctrine 191
	A.	Introduction 191
	B.	Constitutional Considerations 192
	C.	Substantive Versus Procedural Test 194
	D.	Applicability to Actions Involving Federal Questions. . . 196
	E.	Applicability of Federal Common Law 196
	F.	Applicability to the Federal Rules of Civil Procedure and the Federal Rules of Appellate Procedure 198
	G.	Applicability to Federal Procedural Statutes. 201
	H.	Applicability to the Federal Rules of Evidence. 201
II.	Modern Choice of Law Methods 202

		A.	Introduction 202
		B.	Threshold Consideration in Choosing the Best Forum 202
		C.	Choice of Law Methods in Specific Types of Actions ..222

CHAPTER TEN: Parties

I.	Capacity 253
	A. Capacity to Sue or Be Sued 253
	B. Representations of the Interested Party 255
	C. Citizenship 256
II.	Permissive and Compulsory Joinder...................256
	A. Permissive Joinder 257
	B. Compulsory Joinder 258
	C. Jurisdiction and Venue........................260
III.	Intervention 261
	A. Absolute Right of Intervention....................261
	B. Permissive Intervention........................262
	C. Procedure and Jurisdiction 262
IV.	Impleader 265
	A. Type of Claim Allowed to be Impleaded 266
	B. Rights of Each Party 267
	C. Procedure.................................267
	D. Jurisdiction 268
	E. Service of Process; Venue......................269
	F. Judgment and Appeal 269
	G. Admiralty Practice 269
V.	Interpleader 270
	A. Statutory Interpleader 271
	B. Rule Interpleader.............................272
	C. Conduct of an Interpleader Action.................273
	D. Interpleader and the United States 276

CHAPTER ELEVEN: Class Actions and Other Representative Litigation

I.	The Applicable Rules	277
II.	Introduction	280
III.	Deciding Whether Claims Should be Asserted on a Class Basis	283
	A. Arguments in Favor	283
	B. Arguments Opposed	286
IV.	A Defendant's Perspective	289
V.	Class Certification	290
	A. The Class Representative	290
	B. Pleading	290
	C. Class Certification Motion	291
	D. Certification Standards	292
	E. Notice to Absent Class Members	293
	F. Exclusions	294
VI.	Settlement of Class Actions	295
	A. Stipulation of Settlement	295
	B. Preliminary Hearing	295
	C. Notice of Settlement and Hearing Date	296
	D. Briefs in Support of Settlement	296
	E. The Settlement Hearing	296
	F. Attorneys' Fees	297
VII.	Other Representative Litigation	298
	A. Rule 23.1	298
	B. Rule 23.2	298

CHAPTER TWELVE: Pretrial Management

I.	Introduction	299
II.	Pretrial Proceedings	299
	A. Pretrial Conferences	300
	B. Scheduling Orders	301
	C. Final Pretrial Orders	302
III.	Complex Litigation	304

	A.	Coping with Multiple Issues 305
	B.	Coping with Multiple Parties....................307
	C.	Coping with Multiple Cases 307
IV.	Amendment of Pleadings 308
	A.	Procedural Requirements 308
	B.	Standards for Permitting Amendment 309
	C.	Amendments to Conform to the Evidence 311
	D.	Relation Back 312
	E.	Supplemental Pleadings..........................314
V.	Magistrates and Special Masters......................314
	A.	Magistrates' Jurisdiction 315
	B.	Review of Magistrate Decisions 316
	C.	Procedures for Objection.........................317
	D.	Trial Before a Magistrate........................318
	E.	Special Masters................................320

CHAPTER THIRTEEN: Discovery

I.	Introduction 323
II.	Discovery Methods 323
	A. Depositions Upon Oral Examination 324
	B. Depositions Upon Written Questions 325
	C. Interrogatories to Parties 325
	D. Production of Documents and Things and Entry Upon Land for Inspection and Other Purposes 326
	E. Physical and Mental Examination of Persons.........326
	F. Requests for Admissions 326
III.	Scope of Discovery 326
	A. In General....................................326
	B. Insurance Agreements..........................327
	C. Limitations on Discovery 327
IV.	Discovery of Experts 328
	A. Purposes 328
	B. Discovery of Experts Under the Federal Rules 329

V.	International Discovery 331	
	A. The Provisions of the Federal Rules of Civil Procedure .331	
	B. The Hague Evidence Convention 333	
VI.	Protective Orders, Including Problems Involving Access by Nonparties...336	
	A. The Applicable Rules 336	
	B. Grounds for Protective Orders 337	
	C. Access to Discovery Materials by Nonparties 339	
VII.	Motion Practice 339	
	A. Orders Compelling Discovery...................340	
	B. Orders Imposing Sanctions 342	
VIII.	Discovery Strategy.................................343	
	A. Order of Discovery Among Parties 343	
	B. Sequence Among Discovery Devices 344	
	C. Nonparty Discovery 346	

CHAPTER FOURTEEN: Depositions

I.	Preliminary Matters................................347	
	A. Introduction 347	
	B. Purpose of a Deposition 348	
	C. Stipulations Regarding Depositions 350	
	D. Who May Take a Deposition or be Deposed 351	
	E. When to Take a Deposition 354	
	F. Where to Take the Deposition 358	
	G. Persons Before Whom The Deposition May be Taken ..360	
	H. How to Record the Deposition 361	
	I. Costs of the Deposition 362	
	J. Production of Documents in Connection with Depositions 363	
	K. Notice and Service 364	
	L. Seeking Judicial Intervention Prior to Deposition......368	
II.	Preparation for Deposition 372	
	A. Preparing to Take a Deposition 372	
	B. Preparing the Deponent........................378	

xlii

	C.	Administrative Matters 383
III.	Conduct of Depositions 384	
	A.	Who May Attend the Deposition 384
	B.	Administrative Matters Preceeding Deposition Testimony 386
	C.	Failure to Attend or to Serve Subpoena 387
	D.	"Usual" Stipulations 388
	E.	Oaths and Other Preliminaries 390
	F.	Examining the Witness 391
	G.	Defending Depositions—Objections 403
	H.	Adjourning and Concluding the Deposition 411
	I.	Judicial Intervention/Supervision of Depositions 412
IV.	After the Deposition 413	
	A.	Correcting and Signing 413
	B.	Certifying, Sealing and Filing the Deposition 414
	C.	Obtaining a Copy of the Deposition 414
V.	Conclusion 414	

CHAPTER FIFTEEN: Other Methods of Discovery

I.	Interrogatories 425	
	A.	Purposes, Advantages, Disadvantages and Abuses 425
	B.	Requirements Under Federal Rule of Civil Procedure 33 and Local Rules 426
	C.	Form of Interrogatories 431
	D.	Responses to Interrogatories 434
	E.	Compelling Responses to Interrogatories 440
	F.	Use Made of Interrogatories 441
II.	Production of Documents and Things and Entry Upon Land for Inspection 442	
	A.	Purposes, Advantages, Disadvantages and Abuses 442
	B.	Requirements Under Federal Rule of Civil Procedure 34 and the Local Rules 444
	C.	Form of Rule 34 Requests 449
	D.	Responses to Rule 34 Requests 450

		E. Document Production 453
		F. Compelling Responses 456
		G. Use Made of Documents and Things.............456
III.	Physical or Mental Examinations 457
	A. General Procedural Requirements Under Federal Rule of Civil Procedure 35(a) 457
	B. Terms of the Order of Examination 459
	C. Exchange of Reports........................461
	D. Sanctions 463
IV.	Requests for Admission 463
	A. Purposes, Advantages, Disadvantages and Abuses 463
	B. Requirements under Fed. R. Civ. P. 36............465
	C. Form of Rule 36 Requests for Admission 466
	D. Responding to Rule 36 Requests for Admissions 467
	E. Motion to Determine the Sufficiency of Answers or Objections 469
	F. Use Made of Admissions 469

CHAPTER SIXTEEN: Motion Practice and Dismissal Without Trial

I.	General Strategy and Factors in Motion Practice 471
	A. Whether to Make a Motion....................471
	B. Timing 472
	C. Affidavits 473
	D. Memoranda of Law 475
	E. To Argue or Not to Argue.....................476
II.	Rules Governing Motion Practice....................477
	A. Sources of Rules 477
	B. Form of Motion 480
	C. Service, Notice and Filing of Papers 481
	D. Orders to Show Cause.......................482
	E. Oral Argument 482
	F. Form and Submission of Orders 483
III.	Motions Directed to the Pleadings 483

xliv

	A.	"Corrective" Motions.....................483
	B.	"Dispositive" Motions 486
IV.		Motions *In Limine* 489
	A.	Introduction 489
	B.	Legal Authority...............................489
	C.	Purposes and Advantages 490
	D.	Disadvantage 490
	E.	Recent Examples of Motions *in Limine* Granted and Denied by Federal Courts...................491
	F.	Procedure for Motion *in Limine* 493
V.		Voluntary or Involuntary Dismissal Under Rule 41........494
	A.	Voluntary Dismissal 494
	B.	Involuntary Dismissal 497
	C.	Dismissal of Counterclaims, Cross-Claim or Third-Party Claim.......................................497
	D.	Costs of Previously Dismissed Claims..............498
VI.		Default Judgments Under Rule 55 498
	A.	When and Against Whom Entry of Default is Appropriate......................................498
	B.	Granting of Judgment by Default..................498
	C.	Setting Aside an Entry of Default 499
	D.	Setting Aside a Default Judgment 500

CHAPTER SEVENTEEN: Summary Judgment Under Rule 56

I.		Introduction......................................503
	A.	Nature of Summary Judgment....................503
	B.	Overview of Fed. R. Civ. P. 56...................504
	C.	The Second Circuit's View of Summary Judgment 505
II.		Basic Procedural Requirements 506
	A.	Federal Civil Practice 506
	B.	Local Rules in New York Federal Courts............512

III.	Contents of the Motion Papers	515
	A. The Motion	515
	B. Statement of Uncontested Material Facts	516
	C. Supporting Evidence	517
IV.	Contents of Opposition Papers	524
	A. Statement of Contested Material Facts	524
	B. Opposing Evidence	525
	C. Obtaining Unavailable Evidence Via Rule 56(f)	529
V.	Standards for Granting or Denying Summary Judgment	531
	A. The Basic Standard for Deciding the Summary Judgment Motion	531
	B. Determining What Constitutes a Genuine Issue of Material Fact	533
	C. Weighing the Evidence	534
	D. Expert Evidence	535
VI.	Appealability and Standard of Review on Appeal of Summary Judgment Motions	536
	A. Appeal From an Order Granting Summary Judgment	536
	B. Appeal From an Order Denying Summary Judgment	537
	C. Standard of Review on Appeal	537
VII.	Some Strategic and Tactical Considerations Regarding Summary Judgment	538
	A. Considerations in Bringing the Motion	538
	B. When to Bring the Motion	539
	C. Planning for the Motion	540
	D. Presentation of the Motion	541
	E. Partial Summary Judgment	541
	F. Opposing the Motion	541
Appendix: Rule 56. Summary Judgment		543

CHAPTER EIGHTEEN: Settlement

I.	Introduction	545
II.	Evaluating the Case	545

III.	Judicial Involvement in the Settlement Process	547
	A. Summary Jury Trials	550
	B. Minitrials, Arbitration, Masters and Experts	551
IV.	The Negotiation Process	551
V.	Substantive Law Governing Settlements	552
	A. Evidentiary Issues	552
	B. Agency Issues	553
VI.	Procedural Law Governing Settlements	554
	A. Judicial Approval	554
	B. Formal Matters	555
VII.	Ethical Issues	557
	A. Responsibilities to Client	557
	B. Responsibilities to Adversary Counsel	558
	C. Responsibilities to the Tribunal	559

CHAPTER NINETEEN: Jury Trials

I.	Introduction	561
II.	The Origin and Right of Jury Trial	561
III.	The Joining of Legal and Equitable Issues in One Litigation	564
	A. Mixing of Legal and Equitable with a Single Claim	565
	B. Defenses and Counterclaims	565
	C. Procedural Devices at Variance with Relief	566
	D. Facts Affecting Jurisdiction and Venue	567
	E. Impact of State Law	567
IV.	Asserting, Protecting and Regulating the Right to Jury Trial	568
	A. The Demand	568
	B. Waiver	575
	C. Relief from Waiver	577
	D. Jury Demand Chart	579
	E. Advisory Jury	582
V.	Selecting the Jury	582
	A. Creating the Jury Pool	582
	B. Determining the Size of the Jury	583

		C. Examining the Jury: The *Voire Dire* 584
		D. Challenges 585
VI.	Instructing the Jury................................ 586
		A. The Jury Charge 588
		B. Eliciting the Verdict........................... 594
VII.	The Rendering of the Verdict 601
		A. The Need for Unanimity 601
		B. Polling the Jury.............................. 601

CHAPTER TWENTY: Opening Statements

	I.	Introduction 603
II.	The Psychology of the Opening Statement 604
		A. The Principles of Primacy and Recency............. 604
		B. Order of Information........................... 605
		C. The "Halo" Effect 606
		D. Simplicity 606
III.	The Purpose of the Opening Statement................. 606
IV.	The Structure of the Opening Statement 607
		A. Introduction 607
		B. Brevity 607
		C. Transitions 607
		D. Construction 608
		E. The Story Order 608
		F. Elements of the Opening 608
V.	The Presentation of the Opening..................... 616
		A. Be Positive 616
		B. Be Specific 616
		C. Develop Psychological Identification Between the Jury and You, Your Client and the Client's Case 616
		D. Personalize Your Client........................ 617
		E. Use the Courtroom 617
		F. Use of Physical Space......................... 617
		G. Use of Pleadings and Exhibits 618

	H.	Depositions................................618
	I.	Make the Jurors "Experts"......................618
	J.	Word Choice................................619
	K.	Do Not Overreach 619
	L.	Emotion 620
	M.	Vocal Tone 620
	N.	Use Transitions.............................620
	O.	Maintain Eye Contact 621
	P.	Levity 621
	Q.	Avoid Objections............................621
	R.	Do Not Promise a Witness by Name or Link Precise Details of Testimony to a Specific Witness...........622
	S.	Opening the Opening 622
	T.	Use Contrast...............................623
	U.	Use Rhetorical Questions 623
	V.	Do Not Tell the Jury that What You are Telling Them is Not Evidence 624
	W.	Pre-Empt the Defense........................624
	X.	Concluding the Opening 625
	Y.	Do Not Present the Jury with Too Many Dominant Themes or Alternative Theories 626
	Z.	Notes 627
VI.		The Law of Opening Statements.....................627
	A.	Avoiding Mistrials and Reversals.................627
	B.	The Need to Object..........................628
Selected Bibliography..629

CHAPTER TWENTY-ONE: Summation

I.	Purely Practical Aspects............................631
II.	Immediate Legal Preparation 632
III.	Immediate Physical Preparation 633

IV.	Philosophy of Trial and Psychology of Summation—The Plaintiff	634
V.	Philosophy of Trial and Psychology of Summation—Defendant	635
VI.	Prerequisites to Effective Final Argument	638
VII.	Preparing the Argument	638
VIII.	Credibility	639
IX.	Matters of Style and Technique	640

CHAPTER TWENTY-TWO: Direct and Cross-Examination

I.	Introduction	643
II.	Direct Examination	643
	A. Non-Leading Questions	643
	B. Laying the Foundation	645
	C. Introducing Exhibits	646
	D. Offers of Proof	648
	E. Expert Witness	650
	F. The Forgetful or Mistaken Witness	651
	G. Redirect	653
III.	Cross-Examination	655
	A. "Whether," a Crucial Question	655
	B. Leading Questions	656
	C. Blanket Cross: A Blunder	657
	D. Selectivity: The Right Way	658
	E. The Sequence of Cross	659
	F. The Witness	660
	G. Prior Inconsistent Statements	660
IV.	Concluding Observations	661

CHAPTER TWENTY-THREE: Alternatives to Trial

I.	Consent to Trial Before Magistrates	663
	A. Consent	663
	B. Appeals	664
II.	Summary Trials	666

	A.	Procedure 666
	B.	Basis in the Federal Rules 667
III.	Advisory Juries 667
	A.	Availability 667
	B.	Effect of Verdict 668
IV.	Arbitration 668
	A.	Introduction 668
	B.	Agreements to Arbitrate 669
	C.	Pleadings 671
	D.	Discovery 673
	E.	Hearing 673
	F.	Advantages and Disadvantages to Arbitration 677
	G.	Open Issues 678
	H.	Other 679

CHAPTER TWENTY-FOUR: Trial and Post-Trial Motions

I.	Introduction 681
II.	Jury Trial 682
	A.	Motions for Consolidation or for Separate Trials—Rule 42 682
	B.	Involuntary Dismissal—Rule 41(a)(2) 684
	C.	Motion to Amend Pleadings to Conform to Evidence—Rule 15(b) 685
	D.	Motion for Directed Verdict—Rule 50(a) 687
	E.	Motion for Judgment Notwithstanding the Verdict—Rule 50(b) 690
	F.	Motion for New Trial—Rule 59(a)(1) 693
	G.	Motion to Alter or Amend Judgment—Rule 59(e) 697
III.	Nonjury Trial 698
	A.	Motion for Involuntary Dismissal—Rule 41(b) 698
	B.	Motion to Amend Findings or Make Additional Findings—Rule 52(b) 700
	C.	Motion to Amend Pleadings to Conform to the Evidence—Rule 15(b) 701
	D.	Motion for New Trial—Rule 59(a)(2) 701

CHAPTER TWENTY-FIVE: Judgments

I. Definition; Requirement of "Separate Document" 703
II. Form and Entry of Judgment 704
    A. Preparation of the Judgment 704
    B. Sample Forms 705
    C. Entry by the Clerk 707
    D. Multiple Claims and Parties 707
    E. Notice of Entry 708
    F. Registration of Judgments 708
III. Declaratory Judgments 708
    A. Statutory Basis 708
    B. When Declaratory Relief Appropriate 709
    C. Procedure 710
IV. Enforcement of Judgments 711
    A. Enforcement of the Money Judgment: The Writ of Execution 711
    B. Enforcement of Judgments for Specific Acts 714
    C. Enforcement Against Nonparties 714
    D. Discovery in Aid of Execution 715
    E. Stay of Enforcement of Judgments 715
V. Relief from Judgments 717
    A. Overview 717
    B. Harmless Error 718
    C. Obtaining Relief from Clerical Mistakes 718
    D. Motion to Alter or Amend a Judgment 719
    E. Obtaining Relief from Final Judgments: Rule 60(b) Motion 720
    F. Other Methods of Obtaining Relief from Judgments to Rule 60(b) 723

CHAPTER TWENTY-SIX: Appellate Review

I. Whether to Seek Appellate Review 725
II. What District-Court Decisions are Reviewable by the Court of Appeals 727

	A.	Review as of Right 727
	B.	Review by Permission...............................729
III.		When District-Court Decisions are Reviewable 730
IV.		How an Appeal to a Court of Appeals is Taken...........731
	A.	Appeals as of Right................................731
	B.	Appeals by Permission under 28 U.S.C. § 1292(b) 732
	C.	Extraordinary Writs...............................733
V.		Civil Appeals Management Plan 734
VI.		The Record on Appeal 735
VII.		The Appendix 736
VIII.		The Briefs 737
	A.	Formal Requirements 738
	B.	Contents 738
	C.	Length of Brief 739
	D.	Importance of the Brief 740
IX.		Oral Argument.....................................741
X.		Temporary Relief Pending Appeal 742
XI.		Motion Practice 743
XII.		Decision 743
XIII.		Petitions for Rehearing.............................744
XIV.		Hearings and Rehearings *In Banc*...................744
XV.		Supreme Court Review 745
	A.	Review by Certiorari..............................745
	B.	Review on Certified Questions 747
	C.	Review by Appeal................................747

Selected Bibliography.......................................748

CHAPTER TWENTY-SEVEN: Preclusion: *Res Judicata* **and Collateral Estoppel; Recent Developments in the United States Supreme Court; What Practitioners Can Expect**

I. Introduction 749
   A. Policies Underlying Preclusion and Terminology 750
II. Application of Doctrines 754
   A. Effect of State Court Judgment in Federal Court 754
   B. The Effect of Failure to Raise Exclusively Federal Claims in State Court 761
   C. Effect of State Court Agency Judgment in Federal Court 768
   D. Effect of Unreviewed State Agency Decision in Federal Court 773
   E. How Does the Government Fare? 775
III. Conclusion 777

CHAPTER TWENTY-EIGHT: Special Considerations in Cases Involving Foreign Parties

I. Introduction 779
II. Motions to Dismiss 780
   A. Service of Process 780
   B. Jurisdiction Over Foreign Parties 784
   C. *Forum Non Conveniens* 789
III. Discovery Aboard 792
   A. Enforceability of the Hague Evidence Convention 795
   B. Depositions Abroad 799
   C. Blocking Legislation 802
IV. Judgments and Prejudgment Attachments 803
   A. Prejudgment Attachments 803
   B. Enforcement of Judgments 810
V. Cases Involving Foreign Sovereigns 813
   A. Jurisdiction 814
   B. Service of Process 821
   C. Attachment and Execution 824

CHAPTER TWENTY-NINE: Jurisdiction and Procedure in Bankruptcy

I. Introduction 829
II. Bankruptcy Jurisdiction 830
    A. Bankruptcy Reform Act/*Northern Pipeline Construction Co. v. Marathon Pipe Line Co.* 830
    B. 28 U.S.C. § 1334 830
    C. Venue 834
    D. Jury Trials 835
    E. Power of the Court in Bankruptcy Cases 836
III. Bankruptcy Procedure 836
    A. Appeals 836
    B. United States Trustee 839
    C. Bankruptcy Rules and Forms 841
    D. Title II—The Chapters Defined; *i.e.*, Types of Bankruptcy Cases 848
    E. Commencing a Case 852
    F. Trustees 858
    G. Chapter II Plans and Disclosure 860
    H. Creditors 860
    I. Automatic Stay 865
    J. Executory Contracts and Leases 869
IV. Conclusion 869

CHAPTER THIRTY: Multidistrict Litigation

I. Introduction 871
II. The Statute 871
III. Transfer of Actions 872
    A. Criteria for Transfer 872
    B. Motions to Transfer 873
    C. Orders to Show Cause 874
    D. Papers: Format, Filing and Service 875
    E. Panel Hearings and Decisions 875
    F. Tag-Along Actions 877

IV.		After the Panel Decision...........................877
	A.	Appellate Review of the Panel....................877
	B.	Proceedings in the Transferee Court 878
	C.	Power of the Transferee Court....................878
	D.	Choice of Law After Transfer 880
	E.	Law of the Case 880
	F.	The Anti-Injunction Act 881
	G.	Appeals in Transferred Actions 882
	H.	Transfer for All Purposes—28 U.S.C. §§ 1404(a), 1406..882
I.		Termination and Remand 882
V.		Conclusion......................................883

Selective Bibliography 884

Appendix A 885

Appendix B 888

Index 891

Table of Authorities 991

CHAPTER ONE

FEDERAL SUBJECT-MATTER JURISDICTION

by Michael P. Tierney, Esq.

Before beginning a discussion of the jurisdictional underpinnings of civil litigation in federal courts, a few very basic questions should be addressed:

— Do you want the case to be in federal court? Why?

— If the case is presently in federal court, do you want it to stay there? Why?

— If the case is presently in state court, do you want it to stay there? Why?

Your initial responses to these questions will tend to determine your interest in the various topics presented in this chapter and in the remainder of this book. However, it is also hoped that exposure to the materials discussed herein will not only make you more comfortable with practice in the federal courts but will help you to avoid some of the common pitfalls encountered by practitioners unfamiliar with federal civil practice.

The emphasis placed on subject-matter jurisdiction in federal practice is easily demonstrated by reference to the numerous provisions of the Federal Rules of Civil Procedure[1] that deal therewith, many of which will be discussed in the ensuing sections of this chapter. Among the more significant rules are the requirement that the grounds for federal jurisdiction be ex-

---

[1] Complete familiarity with and diligent reference to the Federal Rules of Civil Procedure, 28 U.S.C. Appendix (1982), which are available, *inter alia*, in pamphlet form from West Publishing Company, is absolutely critical for both the new practitioner and one who is generally familiar with practice in the federal courts. I still recall the statement of my federal civil procedure professor, who was then a sitting federal court of appeals judge, that the Federal Rules are intended to and usually do provide the answers to procedural questions and the numerous reported decisions on federal procedure are attributable in large measure to counsel's failure to consult and comply with the Rules. My own experience in federal litigation has borne out this sage advice.

pressly pleaded[2] and the provision that the absence of subject-matter jurisdiction may be raised at any time in the course of a federal court litigation.[3] These procedural rules are rooted in the limitations upon the federal judicial power contained in Article III of the United States Constitution.

I. INTRODUCTION: ARTICLE III COURTS AND CONGRESS

A. Federal Courts are Courts of Limited Jurisdiction and Their Jurisdiction is Conferred only by Act of Congress

There is no more fundamental principle of federal jurisdiction than that the inferior federal courts are courts of limited jurisdiction whose jurisdiction may be expanded (within Constitutional limits) or reduced or eliminated by act of the Legislative Branch.[4] If you come away from this chapter with nothing else, an appreciation of this fact will have made the effort worthwhile.

We begin, therefore, with the United States Constitution. Section 1 of Article III provides that the

> judicial Power of the United States, shall be vested in one supreme Court, and in such inferior Courts as the Congress may from time to time ordain and establish.

Section 2 of Article III goes on to define that judicial power:

> The judicial Power shall extend to all Cases, in Law and Equity, arising under this Constitution, the Laws of the United States, and Treaties made, or which shall be made, under their Authority;—to all Cases affecting Ambassadors, other public Ministers and Consuls;—to all Cases of admiralty and maritime Jurisdiction;—to Controversies to which the United States shall be a Party;—to Controversies between two or more States;—between a State and Citizens of another State;—between Citizens of different States;—between Citizens of the same State claiming Lands under the Grants of different States, and between a State, or the Citizens thereof, and foreign States, Citizens or Subjects.

---

[2] Fed. R. Civ. P. 8(a).

[3] Fed. R. Civ. P. 12(h)(3).

[4] *See, e.g., Turner v. Bank of North America*, 4 U.S. (4 Dall.) 7, 11 (1799) (An inferior federal court "is of limited jurisdiction: and has cognisance, not of cases generally, but only of a few specially circumstanced, amounting to a small portion of the cases which an unlimited jurisdiction would embrace. And the fair presumption is . . . that a cause is without its jurisdiction, until the contrary appears.").

FEDERAL SUBJECT-MATTER JURISDICTION

Apart from certain classes of cases expressly reserved for the Supreme Court's original jurisdiction,[5] Congress is empowered to vest Article III judicial power in such inferior federal courts as it chooses. Congress need not—initially it did not—confer full Article III jurisdiction on the inferior courts it created.[6] Equally, Congress is free to—and has—reduced the federal courts' jurisdiction it had previously granted.[7] A detailed examination of the historic development of the federal courts' jurisdiction is beyond the scope of this chapter, and the reader is referred to commentators like Professor Moore[8] and Professors Wright, Miller and Cooper[9] for a fuller treatment of this subject.

B. The Requirement of a "Case" or "Controversy"

A second critical threshold limitation on federal jurisdiction arises from the explicit extension of judicial power in Section 2 of Article III to "all Cases" of the types enumerated and to "Controversies" between specified parties. This Constitutional requirement of a "case or controversy" has very real and practical effects on the actions that may be brought in federal court, principally in the area of "standing to sue." The Supreme Court has insisted upon a real dispute between the parties, failing which the action will be dismissed regardless of the importance of the issues involved or the strength of the convictions whose clash led to the filing of the lawsuit.[10] A unanimous Supreme Court very recently confirmed in *United States Catholic Conference v. Abortion Rights Mobilization, Inc.*, 108 S. Ct. 2268 (1988), that a federal district court has an affirmative obligation to rule upon an objection to

---

[5] Essentially cases involving ambassadors or where a State is a party. U.S. Const. art. III, § 2, cl. 2.

[6] *See, e.g., Kline v. Burke Construction Co.*, 260 U.S. 226, 234 (1922) ("[t]he Constitution simply gives to the inferior courts the capacity to take jurisdiction in the enumerated cases, but it requires an act of Congress to confer it"). Until 1875, Congress did not give to the inferior federal courts jurisdiction in all cases arising under the Constitution, laws and treaties of the United States, but left such federal questions as might arise in the course of litigation to be finally determined by the Supreme Court upon appeal from, or writ of error to, the State courts.

[7] Thus the McCarran-Ferguson Act, 15 U.S.C. §§ 1011, *et seq.* (1982), was passed by Congress in response to the Supreme Court's decision in *United States v. South-Eastern Underwriters Ass'n*, 322 U.S. 533 (1944), to remove cases involving "the business of insurance" from federal regulation. The interplay of McCarran-Ferguson and federal jurisdiction is discussed in the special case study, *infra*.

[8] 1 J.W. Moore, *Federal Practice* ¶0.2 [1] (2d ed. 1988).

[9] 13 Wright, Miller & Cooper, *Federal Practice & Procedure* §§ 3501-05 (2d ed. 1984).

[10] *See, e.g., Schlesinger v. Reservists Committee To Stop The War*, 418 U.S. 208, 226 (1974).

its subject-matter jurisdiction on the grounds of lack of standing before proceeding with pretrial discovery and other aspects of the litigation.

C. Bases of Federal Subject-Matter Jurisdiction

As will be discussed in detail in Section II, *infra*, Article III specifies two principal grounds for the exercise of federal judicial power: what is loosely called "federal question" jurisdiction (*i.e.*, "all Cases, in Law and Equity, arising under this Constitution, the Laws of the United States, and Treaties") and "diversity" jurisdiction (*i.e.*, "Controversies . . . between Citizens of different States").[11] Congress has provided different conditions for the exercise of these jurisdictions by the inferior federal courts, and careful study of the basic statutes is crucial to a successful understanding of practice in the federal courts. The fact that the inferior federal courts are courts of limited jurisdiction and the specific ways in which Congress has chosen to confer that jurisdiction affects not only whether a case may be brought in or removed to federal court, but equally impacts the timing and nature of initial motion practice and discovery efforts in federal cases.

D. Current Make-up of the Inferior Federal Courts

Subject to the final appellate jurisdiction of the United States Supreme Court over the inferior federal courts,[12] the primary trial courts in the federal system are the district courts, which are currently divided into 90 judicial districts[13] New York has four districts[14] and from which appeals may be taken

---

[11] A third category of cases specified in Article III—"all Cases of admiralty and maritime Jurisdiction"—have dwindled in importance as the United States has declined as a maritime nation, but still occupy a significant amount of judicial time in the federal districts containing large commercial seaports. Perhaps one-third of the business of the district courts involves another enumerated Article III jurisdiction—"Controversies to which the United States shall be a Party"—but these are over one-third criminal in nature, since the federal courts have exclusive jurisdiction in enforcing the federal criminal law. *See* Annual Report of the Director of the Administrative Office of the United States Courts 6 - 15 (1987).

[12] Article III, Section 2, cl. 2 provides that the Supreme Court's appellate jurisdiction is subject to "such Exceptions, and under such Regulations as Congress shall make."

[13] *See* 28 U.S.C. §§ 81-131 (1982 & Supp. IV 1986).

[14] *See* 28 U.S.C. § 112 (1982 & Sup. IV 1986).

FEDERAL SUBJECT-MATTER JURISDICTION

of right to the circuit courts of appeal,[15] which are now divided into thirteen circuits,[16] the four New York district courts and the Connecticut and Vermont district courts are in the Second Circuit.[17]

There are also several permanent courts with specialized jurisdictions: the United States Claims Court,[18] which is *not* an Article III court[19] and principally tries contractual claims against the United States; the Court of International Trade,[20] which is an Article III court[21] and replaced the old Customs Court; and the United States Tax Court,[22] which is also *not* an Article III court[23] and tries contested deficiency assessments by the Internal Revenue Service. In contrast, the bankruptcy courts[24] are not separate courts in the federal judicial system, but are "a unit of the district court" in each judicial district.[25] There is also a Judicial Panel on Multidistrict Litigation, which is discussed in Chapter 30 of this book.

Two temporary courts also presently exist: the Temporary Emergency Court of Appeals, which hears appeals from the district courts in cases arising under the Economic Stabilization Act of 1970 and three other stat-

---

[15] There are today a limited number of cases where Congress has provided a right of direct appeal to the Supreme Court. *See, e.g.*, 28 U.S.C. § 1252 (1982) (appeals in civil actions in which the United States is a party where a federal statute is held unconstitutional); 28 U.S.C. § 1253 (1982) (appeals in remaining three-judge court cases).

[16] *See* 28 U.S.C. § 41 (1982). The United States Court of Appeals for the Federal Circuit hears all appeals from the Court of International Trade and the claims court and certain appeals from the district courts. 28 U.S.C. § 1295 (1982 & Supp. IV 1986).

[17] *See* 28 U.S.C. § 41 (1982).

[18] *See* 28 U.S.C. §§ 171-77 (1982).

[19] *See* 28 U.S.C. § 171(a) (1982) ("a court established under Article I of the Constitution of the United States").

[20] *See* 28 U.S.C. §§ 251-57 (1982).

[21] *See* 28 U.S.C. § 251(a) (1982) ("a court established under article III of the Constitution of the United States").

[22] *See* I.R.C. § 7441 (1982).

[23] *Id.*

[24] *See* 28 U.S.C. §§ 151-58 (Supp. IV 1986).

[25] *See* Pub. L. No. 91-379, 28 U.S.C. § 151 (Supp. IV 1986).

utes[26] and a Special Court that hears cases involving the reorganization of the Eastern Railroads and two other railway reorganization statutes.[27] Finally, Congress has provided for a special three-judge court to be constituted when necessary in each judicial district[28] to hear constitutional challenges to federal and state legislative apportionment and "when otherwise required by Act of Congress."[29]

E. Practice Pointers

1. Threshold Decision—Do You Want to Bring Your Claim in Federal Court?

Often the plaintiff will have some measure of choice in the specific causes of action which may be pleaded and the parties against which a claim may be asserted (subject in the latter case to "real party in interest" and "indispensable party" requirements).[30] In such circumstances the plaintiff will have the option of instituting an action in either state court or federal court. Moreover, as will be discussed in Part III, D of this chapter (Pre-emption and Abstention) and in Chapter 4 of this book (Removal), the plaintiff's initial decision to opt for one forum over the other may not be final.

Some of the risk of losing the jurisdiction of choice, however, can be removed by considering in advance the requirements for remaining in (or avoiding removal to) federal court. For example, where no federal question is involved and the plaintiff opts for state court, identification and joinder of a nondiverse necessary party will generally defeat removal to federal court. Where remaining in federal court is desired, finding and pleading a substantial federal claim can avoid a discretionary declination of jurisdiction. In

---

[26] See Pub. L. No. 91-379, 84 Stat. 796, tit. 2; see also Emergency Petroleum Allocation Act of 1973, 15 U.S.C. §§ 751, et seq. (1982); Energy Policy & Conservation Act of 1975, Pub. L. No. 94-163, 89 Stat. 871; and Emergency Natural Gas Act of 1977, Pub. L. No. 95-2, 91 Stat. 4.

[27] See Regional Rail Reorganization Act of 1973, 45 U.S.C. §§ 701 et seq. (1982 & Supp. IV 1986); Northeast Rail Service Act of 1981, 45 U.S.C. §§ 159a, 581, et seq. (1982 & Supp. IV 1986); and Conrail Privatization Act, 45 U.S.C. §§ 1301, et seq. (Supp. IV 1986).

[28] See 28 U.S.C. § 2284 (1982 & Supp. IV 1986).

[29] Id. Prior to 1976, three-judge courts were also required where a suit sought to enjoin enforcement of a federal or state statute on U.S. Constitutional grounds, although the procedure was invoked sparingly. See, e.g., Swift & Co. v. Wickham, 382 U.S. 111 (1965).

[30] See Fed. R. Civ. P. 17(a) (Real Party In Interest); see also Fed. R. Civ. P. 19 (Joinder of Persons Needed for Just Adjudication). Rule 19 excepts from the persons to be joined "if feasible" a person whose joinder will deprive the court of subject-matter jurisdiction. For a discussion of these rules, see Chapter 10 of this book.

FEDERAL SUBJECT-MATTER JURISDICTION

either case, pre-complaint investigation of the pertinent facts and applicable substantive law and careful drafting of the initial pleading is essential to maintaining the plaintiff's choice of jurisdiction.

2. The Grounds for Federal Jurisdiction Must be Affirmatively Pleaded

Since, as noted above, federal courts are courts of limited jurisdiction, it is not surprising that the grounds for federal jurisdiction must be expressly pleaded. Thus, Rule 8(a) of the Federal Rules of Civil Procedure provides that a

> pleading which sets forth a claim for relief, whether an original claim, counterclaim, cross-claim, or third-party claim, shall contain (1) a short and plain statement of the grounds upon which the court's jurisdiction depends, unless the court already has jurisdiction and the claim needs no new grounds of jurisdiction to support it, . . .

In most cases to be brought in federal court, the grounds for jurisdiction will be either a claim based on a federal statute which expressly confers either exclusive or concurrent jurisdiction on the federal district courts, *see* Part II, A, *infra*, or a dispute between parties that are not citizens of the same state, *see* Part II, B, *infra*. Failure to properly plead federal jurisdiction will result in unnecessary delay and expense, and where the applicable statute of limitations has run in the meanwhile, the risk that the right to assert the claim may be lost. Forms for pleading various jurisdictional grounds are given in the ensuing sections of this chapter.

3. Lack of Subject-Matter Jurisdiction May be Raised at Any Time

Unlike the numerous defences and objections that are waived if not raised by inclusion in a motion in advance of filing a responsive pleading or in a responsive pleading,[31] the absence of subject-matter jurisdiction may be raised at any time. Thus, Rule 12(h)(3) of the Federal Rules of Civil Procedure provides that "[w]henever it appears by suggestion of the parties or otherwise that the court lacks jurisdiction of the subject matter, the court shall dismiss the action." However, the Federal Rules encourage this defense to be determined at a preliminary hearing prior to trial.[32]

---

[31] *See* Fed. R. Civ. P. 12(b)(1)-(7). Pursuant to Fed. R. Civ. P. 12(h)(1), the defenses enumerated in Rule 12(b)(2), (3), (4) and (5) are waived if not joined in any motion filed under Rule 12.

---

[32] *See* Fed. R. Civ. P. 12(d). Under the Rule the court is free to defer such a determination until trial.

II. THE BASIC STATUTES

A. 28 U.S.C. § 1331—Federal Question Jurisdiction

The Judicial Code provides that the

> district courts shall have original jurisdiction of all civil actions arising under the Constitution, laws, or treaties of the United States. 28 U.S.C. § 1331 (1982).

This grant of the federal judicial power derived from in the first clause of section 2 of Article III is, of course, always subject to such limitation on its exercise as Congress provides in particular statutes. Moreover, whether there is jurisdiction under § 1331 does not depend merely on whether in the course of a given case it will be necessary to refer to or give a construction to the United States Constitution or to a federal statute, regulation or treaty.

1. The Decision of the Case Must Turn on a Federal Question

While it is not necessary that every issue in the case, or issue relating to a specific claim, turn on a federal question, jurisdiction under § 1331 requires that the decision substantially involves interpretation or the enforcement of some federal right.[33] Moreover, it is insufficient that the defendant may be expected to raise some defense to plaintiff's claim that implicates a federal right, since it is plaintiff's claim that must be shown to arise under federal law.[34] As pointed out above, the failure properly to plead federal question jurisdiction will result in dismissal of the action.

---

[33] This question was considered by Chief Justice Marshall in *Osborn v. Directors of Bank of United States*, 22 U.S. (9 Wheat.) 737, 821-23 (1824):

A cause may depend on several questions of fact and law. Some of these may depend on the construction of a law of the United States; others on principles unconnected with that law. . . . We think, then, that when a question to which the judicial power of the Union is extended by the Constitution, forms an ingredient of the original cause, it is in the power of Congress to give the Circuit Courts jurisdiction of that cause, although other questions of fact or of law may be involved in it.

---

[34] *See Louisville & Nashville R.R. v. Mottley*, 211 U.S. 149, 152-53 (1908).

2. Federal Question Jurisdiction is Not Dependent upon the Amount in Controversy

Although at one time required for both federal question and diversity jurisdiction, a case arising under the Constitution, laws and treaties of the United States does not now require a minimum amount in controversy as a condition to jurisdiction.[35]

3. Cases Arising Under Constitution, Laws and Treaties

In order for a case to be found to "arise under" one of the bases enumerated in § 1331, the federal right or immunity claimed to be involved must be an essential element of plaintiff's cause of action.[36] Thus, vague and general allegations that a plaintiff's constitutional rights have been denied fails to invoke federal question jurisdiction.[37] Similarly, federal question jurisdiction is not invoked merely on the strength of some reference to federal law in the case.[38] However, it is equally clear that federal question jurisdiction may in an appropriate case attach on the basis of a right created by the federal common law.[39]

4. Practice Pointers

As noted above, Rule 8(a) requires a plain and concise statement of the jurisdictional grounds for the action. With respect to federal question jurisdiction, this will normally require specific reference to the particular statutory or constitutional provision on which the claim for relief is based, as well as to § 1331, unless there is another section of the Judicial Code granting jurisdiction over specified controversies. *See* Part II, C, *infra*, for a discus-

---

[35] For over 100 years, federal question jurisdiction, except pursuant to specific statutory enactments, was subject to the requirement of a minimum jurisdictional amount. In 1976, Congress eliminated the jurisdictional amount where the action was brought against the United States, an agency of the United States or an officer or employee thereof in their official capacity. Act of Oct. 21, 1976, Pub. L. No. 94-574, § 2, 90 Stat. 2721. In 1980, the jurisdictional amount was eliminated in all federal question cases. Act of Dec. 1, 1980, Pub. L. No. 96-486, § 2 (a), 94 Stat. 2369.

[36] *See, e.g., Phillips Petroleum Co. v. Texaco Inc.*, 415 U.S. 125, 127-28 (1974) (*per curiam*). In order to base federal jurisdiction on a treaty, the plaintiff's right must be expressly created thereunder. *Dreyfus v. Von Finck*, 534 F.2d 24, 29-30 (2d Cir.), *cert. denied*, 429 U.S. 835 (1976).

[37] *See Pilkinton v. Pilkinton*, 389 F.2d 32, 33 (8th Cir.), *cert. denied*, 392 U.S. 906 (1968).

[38] *See Prescription Plan Service Corp. v. Franco*, 552 F.2d 493, 495 (2d Cir. 1977).

[39] *See Illinois v. City of Milwaukee*, 406 U.S. 91 (1972).

sion of a number of these sections. The following jurisdictional allegation was included in a private treble damage complaint alleging a horizontal price-fixing conspiracy by component suppliers:

> The jurisdiction of this Court is based upon 28 U.S.C. 1337 (1982), which grants to this Court original jurisdiction of any civil action or proceeding arising out of any Act of Congress regulating commerce or protecting trade or commerce against restraints and monopolies. This action is brought under Section 4 of the Clayton Antitrust Act, 15 U.S.C. 15 (1982), to seek redress for defendants' violation of Section 1 of the Sherman Antitrust Act, 15 U.S.C. 1 (1982).

However, it must be stressed that such a general allegation of federal question jurisdiction, while sufficient to satisfy Rule 8(a), is not of itself effective to maintain federal subject matter jurisdiction unless a claim for relief pleaded in the complaint raises a federal question.[40]

In order to obtain federal question jurisdiction, the following considerations arise:

— On what federal constitutional, statutory or common law right does the claim depend?

— Is there a specific statute granting jurisdiction to the district courts?

— What are the substantive elements of the federal cause of action?

— Have you pleaded both the general federal question jurisdictional allegation and the required elements of the federal claim for relief?

B. 28 U.S.C. § 1332—Diversity Jurisdiction

The Judicial Code provides that the

> district courts shall have original jurisdiction of all civil actions where the matter in controversy exceeds the sum or value of $50,000,[40a] exclusive of interest and costs, and is between—
>
> (1) citizens of different States;
>
> (2) citizens of a State and citizens or subjects of a foreign state;

---

[40] *See* the Advisory Committee Note to Official Form 2, 28 U.S.C., Appendix (1982). As stated in Fed. R. Civ. P. 84, the "forms contained in the Appendix of Forms are sufficient under the rules." *See Watters v. Ralston Coal Co.*, 25 F. Supp. 387 (M.D. Pa. 1938); *Connecticut General Life Insurance Co. v. Cohen*, 27 F. Supp. 735, 736 (E.D.N.Y. 1939).

[40a] In 1988, Congress enacted a bill amending 28 U.S.C. § 1332(a) which increased the jurisdictional amount form $10,000 to $50,000.

(3) citizens of different States and in which citizens or subjects of a foreign state are additional parties; and

(4) a foreign state, defined in section 1603(a) of this title, as plaintiff and citizens of a State or of different States. 28 U.S.C. § 1332(a).

Here, unlike federal question jurisdiction, Congress has chosen to continue the amount in controversy restriction on its grant of Article III judicial power.

1. The Jurisdictional Amount Must be Pleaded

It is clear that the jurisdictional amount requirement is strictly construed by the courts, such that an even $50,000 is not sufficient.[41] Whether the minimum amount is satisfied is determined as of the time that the complaint is filed.[42] The plaintiff's claims against a single defendant, exclusive of interest and costs, may be aggregated in order to meet the test,[43] but where there are multiple plaintiffs with separate distinct claims, each plaintiff must independently satisfy the jurisdictional amount.[44] Similarly, in a diversity case involving multiple defendants, the aggregatable claims against each defendant must exceed $50,000 where their alleged liability is several, while aggregation is proper where their alleged liability to plaintiffs is joint or integrated.[45] Where the claim is for injunctive, equitable or declaratory relief, the "matter in controversy" still must exceed "the sum or value" of $50,000,[46] and it is preferable that the pleading clearly allege that the requirement is met. The requirement does not apply to compulsory counterclaims or cross-claims.[47]

---

41 *See, e.g., Elfand v. Widman*, 284 F. Supp. 498, 500 (S.D.N.Y. 1968); *P.H. Glatfelter Co. v. Thomas A. Galante & Sons, Inc.*, 236 F. Supp. 1022, 1023 (N.D.N.Y. 1964).

42 *See, e.g., Smithers v. Smith*, 204 U.S. 632 (1907).

43 *See, e.g., Hales v. Winn-Dixie Stores, Inc.*, 500 F.2d 836 (4th Cir. 1974).

44 *Zahn v. International Paper Co.*, 414 U.S. 291 (1973); *Clark v. Paul Gray, Inc.*, 306 U.S. 583 (1939); *Sarnoff v. American Home Products Corp.*, 798 F.2d 1075 (7th Cir. 1986).

45 *See* 1 J.W. Moore, *Federal Practice* ¶ 0.97[2] (2d ed. 1988).

46 *See* 1 J.W. Moore, *Federal Practice* ¶¶ 0.95-0.96 (2d ed. 1988).

47 *See* 1 J.W. Moore, *Federal Practice* ¶ 0.98 [1]-[3] (2d ed. 1988). However, the requirement does apply to permissive counterclaims where not asserted by way of set-off. *Libby, McNeill, & Libby v. City National Bank*, 592 F.2d 504 (9th Cir. 1978).

Although diversity jurisdiction, once properly invoked, is not lost if the plaintiff ultimately fails to recover more than $50,000,[48] the Judicial Code provides that

> [e]xcept when express provision therefor is otherwise made in a statute of the United States, where the plaintiff who files the case originally in the Federal courts is finally adjudged to be entitled to recover less than the sum or value of $[5]0,000, computed without regard to any setoff or counterclaim to which the defendant may be adjudged to be entitled, and exclusive of interest and costs, the district court may deny costs to the plaintiff and, in addition, may impose costs on the plaintiff. 28 U.S.C. § 1332(b).

Whether to deny costs to or impose costs on plaintiff is within the discretion of the district court, and ordinarily will not be exercised where the plaintiff has pleaded the jurisdictional amount in good faith.[49]

2. Actions Between Citizens of Different States

For purposes of Article III diversity jurisdiction, a natural person who is a native or naturalized citizen of the United States is a citizen of the State in which he or she is domiciled.[50] Mere residence is not enough and a person may have no more than one domicile at any given time.[51] In representative party cases, the citizenship of the "represented" party, *i.e.*, the infant, estate or incompetent, is controlling, not the citizenship of the legal representative.[51a] The Judicial Code expressly provides that "States" include "the Territories, the District of Columbia, and the Commonwealth of Puerto

---

48 *See, e.g., Griffin v. Red Run Lodge, Inc.*, 610 F.2d 1198 (4th Cir. 1979).

49 *See, e.g., Dr. Franklin Perkins School v. Freeman*, 741 F.2d 1503 (7th Cir. 1984).

50 *See* 1 J.W. Moore, *Federal Practice* ¶ 0.74 [1] (2d ed. 1988).

51 *See* 1 J.W. Moore, *Federal Practice* ¶ 0.74 [3.-2] (2d ed. 1988).

51a Congress amended 28 U.S.C. § 1332(c) to eliminate the confusion as to whose citizenship controlled in representative cases. Section 1332 (c)(2) now provides: "The legal representative of the estate of a decedent shall be deemed to be a citizen only of the same state as the decedent, and the legal representative of an infant or an incompetent shall be deemed to be a citizen only of the same state as the infant or incompetent." S.1482, 100th Cong. 2d Sess. (1988).

Rico." 28 U.S.C. § 1332(d) (1982).[52] However, neither a State nor a state-created entity found to be an *alter ego* of the State are citizens of a State for diversity purposes.[53]

In cases where there are multiple joint plaintiffs and/or multiple joint defendants, each plaintiff must be diverse from each defendant.[54] The only exception to the "complete diversity" rule appears to be in representative actions like class action, where diversity is tested by the citizenship of the representative parties.[55]

3. Alienage

Congress has specified in 28 U.S.C. § 1332(a)(2)-(4) (1982) the circumstances in which the federal courts are permitted to exercise Article III jurisdiction over "Controversies . . . between a State, or the Citizens thereof, and foreign States, Citizens or Subjects."[56] Mere inclusion of a non-United States citizen as a party is not enough—the dispute must be between United States citizens and aliens, or the aliens must be additional parties to an otherwise diverse action among citizens or a foreign state must be the plaintiff in a suit against citizens. Moreover, for diversity or alienage jurisdiction purposes, a permanent resident alien is now deemed to be a citizen of the state in which that alien is domiciled.[56a] In addition, the Judicial Code provides for jurisdiction over actions involving aliens in two instances without regard to diversity.[57]

---

[52] The Supreme Court early on held that for Article III purposes "States" did not refer to Territories or the District of Columbia. *Corporation of New Orleans v. Winter*, 14 U.S. (1 Wheat.) 91 (1816); *Hepburn v. Ellzey*, 6 U.S. (2 Cranch) 445 (1805).

---

[53] *See Postal Telephone Cable Co. v. Alabama*, 155 U.S. 482, 487 (1894) (State); *Gibson-Homans Co. v. New Jersey Transit Corp.*, 560 F. Supp. 110, 112-13 (D.N.J. 1982) (State Transit Authority).

---

[54] *See Strawbridge v. Curtiss*, 7 U.S. (3 Cranch) 267 (1806); *Treinies v. Sunshine Mining Co.*, 308 U.S. 66 (1939).

---

[55] *See Supreme Tribe of Ben-Hur v. Cauble*, 255 U.S. 356 (1921); *but see* Justice Brennan's dissenting opinion in *Zahn v. International Paper Co.*, *supra*, n. 44, 414 U.S. at 308-09.

---

[56] U.S. Const. art. III, § 2.

[56a] Congress amended the judiciary act to curtail the use of § 1332 in cases involving permanent resident aliens. Accordingly, under amended § 1332(a), federal courts would not have jurisdiction over a case between a citizen of New York and a permanent resident alien domiciled in New York.

---

[57] *See* 28 U.S.C. § 1350 (1982) (tort actions in violation of international law or treaty); and 28 U.S.C. §1351 (1982) (actions against consuls).

4. Citizenship of Corporations

Congress has provided with respect to diversity jurisdiction that a corporation

> shall be deemed a citizen of any State by which it has been incorporated and of the State where it has its principal place of business. . . . 28 U.S.C. § 1332(c) (1982).

This "dual citizenship" of corporations can create special problems for the federal litigant seeking to invoke diversity jurisdiction, and care must be taken to ascertain the facts with respect to where a corporate party has its principal place of business, so that it can be properly alleged. Thus, the plaintiff must expressly allege that a corporate defendant's place of incorporation and principal place of business are different from the plaintiff's state or states of citizenship,[58] and a corporate plaintiff must plead its own state of incorporation and principal place of business.[59]

The legal fiction of corporate personality has not been extended to partnerships and unincorporated associations, and thus each of the members of the group must be diverse from each opposing party.[60] In direct actions against liability insurers in which the insured is not named as a defendant, the Judicial Code specifies that each defendant insurer is also deemed to have the citizenship of its insured.[61]

5. Maintaining or Defeating Diversity Jurisdiction

Diversity jurisdiction cannot be invoked by the creation of a sham corporation[62] nor by the fictitious assignment of a claim for relief.[63] However, where, for example, a claim is transferred for consideration, diversity jurisdiction will attach even though the assignment was for the express purpose of creating jurisdiction.[64]

---

[58] *See, e.g., Rush Presbyterian St. Luke's Medical Center v. Safeco Insurance Co.*, 825 F.2d 1204 (7th Cir. 1987).

[59] *See, e.g., Guerrino v. Ohio Casualty Insurance Co.*, 423 F.2d 419, 421 (3d Cir. 1927).

[60] *See, e.g., Great Southern Fire Proof Hotel Co. v. Jones*, 177 U.S. 449 (1900).

[61] *See* 28 U.S.C. § 1332(c) (1982).

[62] *See* 1 J.W. Moore, *Federal Practice* ¶ 0.76[6] (2d ed. 1988).

[63] *See* 28 U.S.C. § 1359 (1982).

[64] *See, e.g., Prudential Oil Corp. v. Phillips Petroleum Co.*, 546 F.2d 469 (2d Cir. 1976).

FEDERAL SUBJECT-MATTER JURISDICTION 15

Where the liability of multiple defendants is joint and several, a plaintiff can validly obtain diversity jurisdiction by bringing the action against only diverse defendants, since such a plaintiff is not required to join all potentially liable parties.[65] Similarly, a plaintiff cannot be compelled to join a nonparty whose presence is necessary to grant complete relief where to do so would defeat diversity jurisdiction,[66] although there is the risk that considerations of fairness would lead the court to dismiss the action.[67] Again, proper pleading here can alleviate a potential problem—indeed, Rule 19(c) mandates it.[68]

Where a claimant desires to avoid removal to federal court on diversity grounds, the simple expedient of joining a non-diverse party (if one is available) usually will do the job. *See* Chapter 4. On the other hand, if a plaintiff has invoked diversity jurisdiction by declining to name non-diverse potentially liable parties, a named defendant not only may move under Rule 19 but also may seek dismissal on *forum non conveniens* grounds.[69]

6. Practice Pointers

Again, Rule 8(a) requires a plain and concise statement of the grounds where federal diversity jurisdiction is invoked. This requires that both the diversity of citizenship between each plaintiff and each defendant and that a claim in excess of $50,000 is involved must be expressly pleaded. Satisfactory forms for pleading diversity jurisdiction are found in Fed. R. Civ. P. Official Form 2(a):[70]

> Plaintiff is a [citizen of the State of Connecticut] [corporation incorporated under the laws of the State of Connecticut having its principal place of business in the State of Connecticut] and defendant is a corporation incorporated under the laws of the State of

---

[65] *See, e.g., Austin v. Unarco Industries, Inc.*, 705 F.2d 1 (lst Cir.), *cert. dismissed*, 463 U.S. 1247 (1983).

[66] Fed. R. Civ. P. 19(a) ("person . . . whose joinder will not deprive the court of jurisdiction over the subject matter of the action shall be joined").

[67] Fed. R. Civ. P. 19(b). *See Niles-Bement-Pond Co. v. Iron Moulders' Union Local 68*, 254 U.S. 77, 80 (1920).

[68] Fed. R. Civ. P. 19(c) provides that a
  pleading asserting a claim for relief shall state the names, if known to the pleader, of any persons as described in subdivision (a)(1)-(2) hereof who are not joined, and the reasons why they are not joined.

[69] *See, e.g., Piper Aircraft Co. v. Reyno*, 454 U.S. 235 (1981).

[70] *See* 28 U.S.C. Appendix (1982).

New York having its principal place of business in a State other than the State of Connecticut. The matter in controversy exceeds, exclusive of interest and costs, the sum of ten thousand dollars. [Footnote omitted.]

Obviously, such generalized allegations are unavailing if contradicted elsewhere in the pleading.

In order to obtain federal diversity jurisdiction, the following considerations arise:

— What is the domicile of all individual plaintiffs and defendants?

— If a corporation is to be a party, what is its place of incorporation and principal place of business?

— If a partnership or unincorporated association is to be a party, what is the citizenship of each of its members?

— Have you pleaded the fact of diversity as between each plaintiff and each defendant?

— Have you pleaded that the amount in controversy exceeds $50,000 exclusive of interest and costs?

— Have you pleaded the existence of any known interested parties not joined and the reasons for non-joinder?

C. Other Statutes

As noted in Point II, A above, there are many sections of the Judicial Code that confer original jurisdiction on the district courts with respect to particular controversies, subjects or statutes. These Article III jurisdictional grants are found at 28 U.S.C. §§ 1330, 1333-1340, and 1343-1365 (1982 & Supp. IV 1986). Certain of these statutes confer exclusive jurisdiction on the federal courts,[71] while others by their silence confer only parallel jurisdiction with the state courts.[72]

---

[71] *See, e.g.*, 28 U.S.C. § 1333 (1982), granting to the district courts "original jurisdiction, exclusive of the courts of the States" over admiralty, maritime and prize cases; *see also* 28 U.S.C. § 1334(a) (Supp. IV 1986), granting to the district courts "original exclusive jurisdiction" of bankruptcy cases and proceedings, except as to those cases where Congress has granted exclusive jurisdiction to another court, in which case the jurisdiction of the district courts is "original but not exclusive." *Id.* § 1334(b).

[72] *See, e.g.*, 28 U.S.C. § 1335 (1982) (Interpleader); 28 U.S.C. § 1337(a) (1982) (Commerce and antitrust regulations); 28 U.S.C. § 1343(a) (1982) (Civil rights and elective franchise).

III. SPECIAL PROBLEMS IN FEDERAL SUBJECT-MATTER JURISDICTION

Considerations of fairness, finality of judicial decisions and the avoidance of multiplicity of suits have led the federal courts to develop doctrines that allow certain claims which do not directly satisfy the tests for attaching federal jurisdiction. These doctrines may present special problems to the federal litigant.

A. Pendent Jurisdiction

In a federal question case, when the parties are not diverse, joinder of state law claims, while permitted under Fed. R. Civ. P. 18(a),[73] requires application of the doctrine of pendent jurisdiction. This doctrine found its first expression in *Hurn v. Oursler*, 289 U.S. 238 (1933), where the Supreme Court held that where both state law and federal law theories supported a single claim for relief and the federal ground was substantial, the district court could decide the merits of the state law claim even if plaintiff did not prevail on the federal ground. However, the Court also held that a purely state law claim that was not part of a federal law claim was not within the district court's jurisdiction.

1. *United Mine Workers v. Gibbs*

The relatively limited expansion of federal jurisdiction over state law claims involved in *Hurn v. Oursler, supra*, received a significant new scope in *United Mine Workers v. Gibbs*, 383 U.S. 715 (1966). Again requiring as a condition precedent the presence of a substantial federal claim, the Supreme Court held that the district court has the power to entertain a state law claim if the relationship between that claim and the federal claim

> permits the conclusion that the entire action before the court comprises but one constitutional "case." The federal claim must have substance sufficient to confer subject matter jurisdiction on the court. . . . The state and federal claims must derive from a common nucleus of operative fact. But if, considered without regard to their federal or state character, a plaintiff's claims are such that he would ordinarily be expected to try them all in one judicial

---

[73] Rule 18(a) provides:
   A party asserting a claim to relief as an original claim, counterclaim, cross-claim, or third party claim, may join, either as independent or alternative claims, as many claims . . . as the party has against an opposing party.

proceeding, then, assuming substantiality of the federal issues, there is *power* in federal courts to hear the whole. 383 U.S. at 725 [citation and footnotes omitted].

However, the Court also stressed that "pendent jurisdiction is a doctrine of discretion, not of plaintiff's right" and that it should be exercised with respect to traditional considerations of judicial economy, convenience and fairness to the parties. 383 U.S. at 726. Moreover, to avoid unnecessary decisions by federal courts of state law questions, the Court stated that

> if the federal claims are dismissed before trial even though not insubstantial in a jurisdictional sense, the state claims should be dismissed as well. Similarly, if it appears that the state issues substantially predominate . . . the state claims may be dismissed without prejudice and left to resolution by state tribunals. . . . Finally, there may be reasons independent of jurisdictional considerations, such as the likelihood of jury confusion in treating divergent legal theories of relief, that would justify separating state and federal claims for trial. . . . If so, jurisdiction should ordinarily be refused. *Id.* at 726-27.

A detailed consideration of the issues raised by the requirements of substantiality of the federal question and that the federal and state claims arise out of the same nucleus of operative fact are beyond the scope of this chapter, and the reader is respectfully referred to the discussion of these issues by Professor Moore[74] and Professors Wright, Miller and Cooper.[75]

2. Practice Pointers

Since pendent jurisdiction is not a separate source of statutory jurisdiction, it is not required to be pleaded.[76] However, prudence suggests that later difficulties can be avoided by stating in the complaint the pendent basis for jurisdiction, particularly since the determination to exercise pendent jurisdiction is made on the facts presented in the pleadings.[77] Finally, since pendant jurisdiction is discretionary, consideration should be given in drafting to pleading matters which tend to militate in favor of its exercise.

---

[74] *See* 3A J.W. Moore, *Federal Practice* ¶ 18.07 [1.-3] (2d Ed. 1988).

[75] *See* 13B Wright, Miller & Cooper, *Federal Practice & Procedure* § 3567.1 (2d ed. 1984).

[76] *See, e.g.*, *Leather's Best, Inc. v. S.S. Mormaclynx*, 451 F.2d 800, 809 n. 10 (2d Cir. 1971) ("Pendent jurisdiction is not a matter which must be pleaded since the court already has jurisdiction over the case").

[77] *See* 3A J.W. Moore, *Federal Practice* ¶ 18.07 [1.-5] (2d ed. 1988).

B. Pendent Parties

Fed. R. Civ. P. 20(a) provides that all persons may join as plaintiffs and all persons may be joined as defendants in one action where the right to relief sought by or against them is joint, several or alternative and arises

> out of the same transaction, occurrence, or series of transactions or occurrences and if any question of law or fact common to all these persons will arise in the action.

As is the case with Fed. R. Civ. P. 18(a), the Rule itself does not confer jurisdiction, which must independently attach to the claim by or against each party. However, following the Supreme Court's decision in *United Mine Workers v. Gibbs*, *supra*, courts of appeals in the Second and Eighth Circuits began to apply the *Gibbs* analysis of a "case" for federal jurisdictional purposes to permit pendent claims against parties not the subject of the federal claim.[78]

1. Federal Question Cases—the *Moor* and *Aldinger* Decisions

In *Moor v. County of Alameda*, 411 U.S. 693 (1973), the Supreme Court affirmed a district court's dismissal of claims against a county under state law which were pleaded as pendent to federal law claims against county officials, holding that the district court had not abused its discretion under *United Mine Workers v. Gibbs*, *supra*. Although the Court stated that it was not necessary to reach the "subtle and complex" question of whether the state law claims against the county could be pendent to the federal claims against county officials,[79] the decision was read by many courts as endorsing the decisions in the Second and Eighth Circuits in favor of pendent party jurisdiction.[80]

The question avoided in *Moor* was more directly presented in *Aldinger v. Howard*, 427 U.S. 1 (1976), in which the Court gave some indication that the pendent party doctrine being developed in the lower courts is not precluded by its affirmance in *Aldinger* of the district court's dismissal of pendent claims against a municipal corporation.[81] However, the Court indicated that the question required the courts to determine whether Congress had expressly or by implication negated the exercise of jurisdiction.

---

[78] *See* 3A J.W. Moore, *Federal Practice*, ¶20.07 [5.-1] (2d ed. 1988).

[79] 411 U.S. at 715.

[80] *See* 3A J.W. Moore, *Federal Practice*, *supra*, at 20-67 n. 25.

[81] 427 U.S. at 18; *see* 3A J.W. Moore, *Federal Practice*, *supra*, at 20-68 to 20-76.

Given the Supreme Court's failure to revisit this issue, the federal practitioner must carefully review the pertinent precedents in his or her circuit. Obviously, there is a greater risk of dismissal where the complaint seeks to assert pendent claims against parties as to which no federal claim can be asserted.

2. Diversity Cases

As discussed in Section II, B, 1, *supra*, multiple plaintiffs with separate and distinct claims must each meet the jurisdictional amount requirement. Moreover, each plaintiff must be diverse from each defendant, and, therefore, the pendent party doctrine does not appear to reach federal diversity jurisdiction.[82]

3. Class Actions

In light of the Supreme Court's decision in *Zahn v. International Paper Co.*, 414 U.S. 291 (1973), it is questionable whether the pendent party doctrine applies to class actions, although this was the pre-*Zahn* holding of the Second Circuit in *Almenares v. Wyman*, 453 F.2d 1075 (2d Cir. 1971), *cert. denied*, 405 U.S. 944 (1972). Professor Moore concludes that

> at the discretionary level the pendent jurisdiction doctrine as applied to the joinder of parties can be expected to play very little role in the class action setting.[83]

C. Ancillary Jurisdiction

As noted above in connection with the jurisdictional amount in diversity cases, compulsory counterclaims—and permissive counterclaims involving set-off—may be entertained without requiring an independent federal jurisdictional basis. *See* Section II, B, 1, at n. 47. Cross-claims and third-party claims, since they must arise out of the transaction or occurrence that is the subject matter of the original claim over which the court already has jurisdiction, are deemed "ancillary" to that claim and do not require an independent federal jurisdictional ground.[84]

---

[82] *See* 3A J.W. Moore, *Federal Practice*, ¶ 20.07 [5.-2] (2d ed. 1988). *See Owen Equipment & Erection Co. v. Kroger*, 437 U.S. 365 (1987).

[83] *See* 3A J.W. Moore, *Federal Practice*, ¶ 20.07 [5.-3] at 20-86 (2d ed. 1988).

[84] *See, e.g., Executive Financial Services, Inc. v. Heart Chec, Inc.*, 95 F.R.D. 383 (D. Colo. 1982); *see also* Fed. R. Civ. P. 13 and 14.

D. Pre-emption and Abstention

1. The Supremacy Clause—Has Congress Pre-empted the Field?

The determination of whether a particular state law claim has been preempted by a Congressional enactment is usually a matter of reviewing the language of the pertinent federal statute, since in the absence of a clear expression of Congressional intent to pre-empt the field, the presumption is that our federal and state court systems will continue to each retain the power to adjudicate disputes within their respective jurisdictions.[85] A more complex question is raised where there is no federal pre-emption, but a federal court is asked to defer to the state courts which also have jurisdiction to entertain the matter.

2. Should a Federal Court Abstain?

The Supreme Court has enunciated four distinct situations in which a federal court, although properly seized of subject-matter jurisdiction, should abstain from exercising its jurisdiction and defer to state court proceedings. The first abstention doctrine, established in *Railroad Commission of Texas v. Pullman*, 312 U.S. 496 (1941), counsels abstention in favor of state courts where state law is uncertain and its resolution may avoid the need for the federal court to decide a federal constitutional question. The second abstention doctrine was announced in *Burford v. Sun Oil Co.*, 319 U.S. 315 (1943), where the Court held that federal courts should abstain from interfering with specialized, ongoing state regulatory schemes.

A somewhat related doctrine was established in *Younger v. Harris*, 401 U.S. 37 (1971), where the Court held that a federal court should not entertain suits challenging state action where the state has already instituted proceedings in state court in which the plaintiff can assert its federal claims. The recent *Pennzoil Co. v. Texaco Inc.*, 481 U.S. 1 (1987), litigation expanded the reach of *Younger* abstention.

Finally, in *Colorado River Water Conservation District v. United States*, 424 U.S. 800, 817 (1976), the Court enunciated an "exceptional circumstances" doctrine based on "considerations of '[w]ise judicial administration,' " under which a federal court should abstain where (a) the state court obtained jurisdiction over the matter prior to commencement of the federal action and (b) piecemeal litigation can be avoided by permitting all claims to be determined on the prior state action. This fourth abstention doctrine was further elucidated in *Moses H. Cone Memorial Hospital v. Mercury Con-*

---

85 *See, e.g., Merrell Dow Pharmaceuticals, Inc. v. Thompson*, 478 U.S. 804 (1986); *Metropolitan Life Insurance Co. v. Massachusetts*, 471 U.S. 724 (1985).

struction Corp., 460 U.S. 1 (1983), where the Court adverted to additional factors favoring abstention, including the absence of any uniquely federal law issues and the adequacy of the prior state court proceedings to protect the claimant's rights.[86] It is therefore obvious that where the federal rights invoked in the case are substantial, a plaintiff can better sustain the threat to losing the federal forum. As noted above, thorough pre-complaint investigation of facts and law and careful pleading will maximize the ability to sustain federal jurisdiction.

3. Case Study—Enforcement of Arbitration Clauses in State Insurance Liquidations

The interplay of state and federal jurisdiction and the application of the federal abstention doctrines discussed above has recently been the subject of several decisions in the Southern District of New York and the Second Circuit in the context of attempts by creditors to enforce arbitration clauses to avoid adjudication of claims in state court liquidation proceedings.[87] An important aspect of the issues raised in such litigation is the fact that Congress has in the McCarran-Ferguson Act[88] expressly committed the regulation of the business of insurance to the several states.[89] At the same time, Congress has provided in the Federal Arbitration Act that arbitration clauses are enforceable in state or federal court pursuant to a policy to encourage the private resolution of contractual disputes.[90]

This apparent clash between competing federal policies has been resolved by the federal courts by exercise of abstention. Thus, in *Law Enforcement Insurance Co. v. Corcoran*, 807 F.2d 38, 43-44 (2d Cir. 1986), *cert. denied*, 107 S. Ct. 1896 (1987), the Court upheld the district court's dismissal of a suit to enforce an arbitration clause, relying upon the *Burford* abstention

---

86 460 U.S. at 23-27.

87 N.Y. Ins. Law §§ 7401-36 (McKinney 1985 & Supp. 1987), provides a comprehensive scheme for the liquidation of insolvent insurance companies domiciled in New York with the Superintendent of Insurance to be appointed as statutory liquidator. One of the principal assets on an insolvent insurer's estate is its reinsurance contracts which traditionally contain arbitration clauses.

88 15 U.S.C. §§ 1011-1015 (1982).

89 The Act provides, *inter alia*, that
No Act of Congress shall be construed to invalidate, impair, or supersede any law enacted by any state for the purpose of regulating the business of insurance . . . unless such Act specifically relates to the business of insurance. . . . 15 U.S.C. § 1012(b) (1982).

90 *See* 9 U.S.C. §§ 1-14 (1982).

doctrine. A similar result has been reached in other cases.[91] Arguably, where a matter of greater federal concern is involved, federal jurisdiction might not be so easily relinquished. Therefore, if maintaining federal jurisdiction is important, a substantial federal claim should be identified.

E. Implied Rights of Action

Federal courts are generally reluctant to create implied rights of private action under federal statutes that do not expressly provide therefor. *See Touche Ross & Co. v. Redington*, 442 U.S. 560 (1979). However, where such a right of action is implied from the United States Constitution or a federal statute, it is plain that jurisdiction attaches under 28 U.S.C. § 1331.[92] Obviously, federal question jurisdiction should be pleaded as "arising under" the Constitutional provision or statute from which the private right of action is to be implied.

F. Anti-Injunction Statute

The concern of Congress to avoid unnecessary conflicts between federal and state courts also finds expression in 28 U.S.C. § 2283 (1982):

> A court of the United States may not grant an injunction to stay proceedings in a State court except as expressly authorized by Act of Congress, or where necessary in aid of its jurisdiction, or to protect or effectuate its judgments.

While § 2283 technically does not go to the jurisdiction of the federal courts,[93] it is a binding limitation on their exercise of jurisdiction.[94] Its prohibition applies not only to direct restraints of state courts, but equally to parties to state court proceedings.[95] Unless one of the three enumerated exceptions are applicable, it is an absolute bar to claims for injunctive relief or declaratory relief in the nature of an injunction.

---

[91] *See, e.g., Corcoran v. Ardra Insurance Co.*, 842 F.2d 31 (2d Cir. 1988); *Levy v. Lewis*, 635 F.2d 960 (2d Cir. 1980); *cf. Washburn v. Corcoran*, 643 F. Supp. 554 (S.D.N.Y. 1986) (holding that McCarran-Ferguson bars an order under the Federal Arbitration Act enforcing an arbitration clause).

[92] *See, e.g., Herman & MacLean v. Huddleston*, 459 U.S. 275 (1983); *Owen v. City of Independence*, 560 F.2d 925, 932-33 (8th Cir. 1977), *vacated & remanded on other grounds*, 438 U.S. 902 (1978).

[93] *See, e.g., Smith v. Apple*, 264 U.S. 274, 278 (1924).

[94] *See, e.g., Atlantic Coast Line R. R. v. Brotherhood of Locomotive Engineers*, 398 U.S. 281, 286-87 (1970).

[95] *See, id.*, 398 U.S. at 287.

IV. BIBLIOGRAPHY

J.W. Moore, *Federal Practice* (2d ed. 1988).

Wright, Miller & Cooper, *Federal Practice & Procedure* (2d ed. 1984).

Frumer & Waxner, *Bender's Federal Practice Forms* (1988).

Meisenholder, *West's Federal Forms: District Courts Civil* (3d ed. 1983).

CHAPTER TWO

PERSONAL JURISDICTION AND SERVICE

by L. Donald Prutzman, Jr., Esq.*

I. INTRODUCTION

Chapter 1 discussed the federal district court's subject matter jurisdiction—jurisdiction to adjudicate the type of controversy before it. This chapter considers personal jurisdiction and its cousin, quasi-in-rem jurisdiction, a personal jurisdiction substitute based on attachment of property.[1] Personal jurisdiction refers to a court's power over a party. If the court has personal jurisdiction, it can render orders and judgments that others will recognize as binding.

---

* The valuable assistance of Josiah Greenberg and Andrea Galbo in the preparation of this chapter is gratefully acknowledged.

[1] Unless expressly noted, in this chapter the term "personal jurisdiction" includes jurisdiction quasi-in-rem.

The simplest way a court obtains personal jurisdiction is through a party's consent.[2] Absent consent, a court may exercise personal jurisdiction over a party only when two elements are satisfied. First, a summons and complaint must be served on the party in a manner authorized by the Federal Rules of Civil Procedure ("Fed. R. Civ. P."). Second, the party must be "amenable" to the court's personal jurisdiction. " 'Amenability to jurisdiction means that defendant is within the substantive reach of a forum's jurisdiction under applicable law. Service of process is simply the physical means by which that jurisdiction is asserted.' " *DeMelo v. Toche Marine, Inc.*, 711 F.2d 1260, 1264 (5th Cir. 1983), *quoted in Soltex Polymer Corp. v. Fortex Indus., Inc.*, 590 F. Supp. 1453, 1456 (S.D.N.Y. 1984), *aff'd*, 832 F.2d 1325 (2d Cir. 1987).

Part II of this chapter discusses the mechanics of making the proper service necessary to obtain jurisdiction. The intricate and somewhat confusing structure of the rule governing service of process, Fed. R. Civ. P. 4, can often make it difficult to determine the correct procedure.

Part III discusses the concept of amenability to jurisdiction. As will be seen, amenability has two dimensions. First, the Fed. R. Civ. P. must authorize the exercise of personal jurisdiction over a defendant. Second, exercise of that authorized jurisdiction must be consistent with due process of law. Again, both of these elements—statutory authorization and due process—must be satisfied.

Part IV discusses quasi-in-rem jurisdiction and certain considerations unique to its exercise. Where the ability to get personal jurisdiction over a defendant is absent or uncertain, it may still be possible to bring that defendant into court by invoking quasi-in-rem jurisdiction. To do so, a plaintiff must first attach the defendant's property within the court's jurisdiction.

Part V considers the procedural aspects of raising lack of personal jurisdiction as a defense. If not timely raised, the defense is waived.

---

2 Unlike subject matter jurisdiction, which cannot be conferred by consent, any party who appears before the court voluntarily, or contractually agrees to submit to jurisdiction, becomes subject to that court's jurisdiction. The plaintiff consents to personal jurisdiction by commencing the action. Personal jurisdiction is a two-way street. It applies not only to the claim plaintiff asserts, but also to claims for relief that other parties may assert against the plaintiff during the course of the litigation, *e.g.*, compulsory counterclaims.

Defendants can also confer jurisdiction by consent—advertently or inadvertently. When a defendant responds to a complaint without contesting personal jurisdiction, *e.g.*, by answering or by moving against the complaint on grounds other than lack of personal jurisdiction, the court obtains jurisdiction by consent even if a challenge to jurisdiction would have been successful if made.

II. PROPER SERVICE OF THE SUMMONS AND COMPLAINT

Service of a summons "is the procedure by which a court having venue and jurisdiction of the subject matter of the suit asserts jurisdiction over the person of the party served." *Mississippi Publishing Corp. v. Murphree*, 326 U.S. 438, 444-45 (1946). One important purpose of the summons is to notify the defendant—unmistakably—that he or she is being sued and had better take some action. The often out of the ordinary impact of the procedures for service of process assists this notice function.

Fed. R. Civ. P. 4, captioned "Process," governs issuance and service of the summons and complaint in federal courts. Rule 4 is complex. It liberally incorporates the law of the state where the district court sits and other provisions of federal law. The convoluted structure of Rule 4 makes it particularly difficult to determine the proper method of serving the summons and complaint. One court's description of the Rule's service provisions as "somewhat baroque," *United States v. Union Indem. Ins. Co.*, 109 F.R.D. 153, 156 (E.D.N.Y. 1986) (Weinstein, C.J.), is entirely too kind. Indeed, Rule 4's service provisions are often misleading and contain some dangerous traps for the unwary.

A. Issuance of the Summons—Rule 4(a)

Fed. R. Civ. P. 4(a) governs issuance of the summons. Although Rule 4(a) states that upon filing the complaint, "the clerk shall forthwith issue a summons"[3] and "deliver" it to the plaintiff for service, the practice in New York federal courts is for plaintiff's counsel to prepare the form of summons and submit it to the clerk at the time the complaint is filed. The clerk's "issuance" of the summons consists of signing and sealing it and stamping the assigned docket number and judge on it. The practice can be different in federal districts outside New York. For example, in the District of New Jersey, the clerk prepares the complete summons and mails it to the plaintiff's counsel subsequent to the filing of the complaint.

Rule 4(a) allows a plaintiff to request "separate or additional summonses . . . against any defendants." However, in practice, one form of summons addressed to all defendants is usually prepared. After "issuance," sufficient copies are made for service on each defendant.

Typically, in New York federal courts the complaint and form of summons are given to the clerk at the same time. The clerk accepts the complaint

---

[3] Note that the federal requirement that the clerk "issue" the summons differs from New York state court practice in which the plaintiff's attorney "issues" the summons.

for filing and hands the "issued" summons back to plaintiff's counsel who is then responsible for arranging for its service with a copy of the complaint. The summons and complaint must *always* be served together. Fed. R. Civ. P. 4(d). The New York state court option of commencing an action by serving a summons with notice, CPLR §§ 304, 305(b), is not available in federal court.[4]

After making sufficient copies for service (either photocopies or conformed copies), plaintiff's counsel retains the original summons to be filed with proof of service once service has been made. *See* Fed. R. Civ. P. 4(g). Theoretically, the process server should have the original summons to display at the time of service if the served party requests to see it. In practice, most attorneys do not give the original to the process server because requests for its display are extremely rare.

B. The Form of the Summons—Rule 4(b)

Fed. R. Civ. P. § 4(b) specifies the content of the summons. A form meeting the Rule's requirements, "Form AO 440 (Rev. 5/85)," is available free from the district court clerk's office. It is ordinarily most convenient to use this form and practitioners should keep a supply on hand.

If for some reason the form is not available, or is not suitable, *e.g.*, defendants are too numerous to be listed in the space provided, a summons conforming to the rules can easily be drafted by following "Form 1," in the Appendix of Forms to the Fed. R. Civ. P. These forms are always sufficient. Fed. R. Civ. P. 84.

As provided in Rule 4(b), the summons must:

1. be signed and sealed by the clerk;
2. name the court and the parties;
3. state the name and address of the plaintiff's attorney;
4. advise the defendant that in case of failure to respond, judgment for the relief demanded in the complaint will be rendered; and
5. specify the time within which the defendant must "appear and defend" in response to the complaint.

Fed. R. Civ. P. 12(a) governs how much time after service the defendant has to "appear and defend." This period is ordinarily 20 days, but there are

---

[4] It is also vital for the practitioner to understand that although filing a complaint commences a federal court action, Fed. R. Civ. P. 3, while service of a summons commences a New York state court action, CPLR § 304, filing a federal court complaint does not toll the statute of limitations on a New York state law claim based on diversity of citizenship. Only service on the defendant can do so because that is what New York law requires. *See Walker v. Armco Steel Corp.*, 446 U.S. 740 (1980).

two exceptions. First, when either the United States or a foreign sovereign is a defendant, the period for answering is 60 days as to such party only. Fed. R. Civ. P. 12(a) (U.S. as defendant); 28 U.S.C. § 1608(d) (foreign sovereign as defendant). Second, where extraterritorial service is made as permitted under Fed. R. Civ. P. 4(e),[5] the time to respond is as specified in the applicable federal statute or state law permitting the out-of-state service. Where New York law applies to service under Rule 4(e), the applicable period for response is ordinarily 30 days. CPLR §§ 313, 320(a).

In three situations, the form of summons may vary from that specified in Rule 4(b). First, when a state law service provision is borrowed, pursuant to Fed. R. Civ. P. 4(e), and the applicable state law specifies some different form of summons or notice-giving document, Fed. R. Civ. P. 4(b) provides that the document "shall correspond as nearly as may be to that required by the [state] statute or rule." Second, when a state law procedure that uses some other document to obtain jurisdiction over a nonparty, such as a garnishee or stakeholder, is "borrowed" pursuant to the Fed. R. Civ. P. or local custom, a "notice," "order to show cause" or "rule to show cause" may perform the notice-giving function of a summons. In such cases, the notice-giving document should correspond as nearly as possible to that required by the applicable state law. Finally, in a time-critical situation where a judge issues a temporary restraining order but no clerk is available to "issue" a summons, the Second Circuit has held that the TRO is an adequate substitute for the summons so that service of the TRO and complaint will confer personal jurisdiction on the court. *Backo v. Local 281, United Bhd. of Carpenters & Joiners*, 438 F.2d 176 (2d Cir.), *cert. denied*, 404 U.S. 858 (1971).

C. Service of the Summons and Complaint—Rule 4(c) and (d)

1. Who Serves the Summons and Complaint?

Fed. R. Civ. P. 4(c)(1), (2) specifies who must serve federal court process, including the summons and complaint. The Rule makes the plaintiff's attorney responsible for seeing that service is made. In all but a few specific situations, process will be served by a private individual under the attorney's direction.

Generally, a summons and complaint may be served on behalf of a private litigant by "any person who is not a party" to the action and "is not less than 18 years of age." Fed. R. Civ. P. 4(c)(2)(A). The only potential exception is where service is made on a *sui juris* individual or a corporation in accordance with a state law provision pursuant to Fed. R. Civ. P.

---

[5] *See* Part II.C.2.b., *infra*.

4(c)(2)(C)(i) and the state law specifies different requirements for the person making service. In such a case, state law must be followed. For federal courts sitting in New York, this is a non-issue. New York law, like the Fed. R. Civ. P., provides that any nonparty 18 or over can make service. CPLR 2103(a). For non-New York federal courts, the law of the state where the court sits must be consulted.

Prior to an extensive set of amendments to the Fed. R. Civ. P. in 1983, the United States Marshal's office played a large role in service of civil process including summonses. This is no longer true. The Marshal is basically out of the business of serving any process for private litigants.

The Marshal may be used for service only in limited circumstances. These include (1) service on behalf of a person authorized to proceed in *forma pauperis* under 28 U.S.C. § 1915, or a seaman in a suit filed without payment of fees under 28 U.S.C. § 1916, and (2) service on behalf of the United States, its offices or agencies.

Service by the Marshal is also permitted when ordered by the court "in order that service be properly effected" in a particular action. Such an order might be appropriate where, perhaps because of time constraints, it is necessary to use an official with law enforcement powers to get access to a defendant, or possibly where service of a summons is to be made in conjunction with a search or seizure, as in a trademark or copyright infringement case. Even in these situations, the practitioner is well advised to consider the alternative of service by a person "specially appointed" by the court, which the rules always permit. Fed. R. Civ. P. 4(c)(1).[6] Use of a "specially appointed" person is preferable because the Marshal's office has other pressing responsibilities that often dictate that civil litigants' problems get less urgent attention there than they would from someone specially hired to deal with them. If it is, nevertheless, decided to seek an order requiring the Marshal to serve process, and time is at all critical, the practitioner should draft the order to include a provision directing the Marshal to make service within a specified time.

2. How the Service is Made

Fed. R. Civ. P. 4(c), (d) governs how, technically, service of the summons and complaint must be made on various types of defendants. These subsections establish a partially overlapping dual system using methods described directly in Fed. R. Civ. P. 4 ("Federal Rules Methods") and methods borrowed from the law of the state where the district court sits ("State Law

---

6 Fed. R. Civ. P.4(c)(3) directs the court to issue such special appointments "freely."

PERSONAL JURISDICTION AND SERVICE 31

Methods").[7] Although most defendants can be effectively served by following the law of the forum state, it would be a misleading oversimplification to say that all defendants can. The careful practitioner should always consult the Rules. Also, practitioners who habitually follow state law for service rather than exploring Federal Rules Methods may be wasting a lot of effort, since Federal Rules Methods are sometimes simpler than State Law Methods.

a. Service by Mail

The clearest example of how simple service can be under the Fed. R. Civ. P. is its mail service provision, introduced in 1983. However, despite its simplicity, this procedure has some limitations and dangerous pitfalls that seriously detract from its utility.

Fed. R. Civ. P. 4(c)(2)(C)(ii) permits service by first class mail on *sui juris* individuals, corporations, partnerships and unincorporated associations. To make mail service, the summons, complaint, two copies of a notice and acknowledgement form conforming substantially to Fed. R. Civ. P. Form 18-A,[8] and a stamped, self addressed return envelope must be mailed first class (not registered or certified) to the defendant.

The defendant is then supposed to return a signed and notarized acknowledgement of receipt to plaintiff's counsel within 20 days of mailing. Upon return, this "Notice and Acknowledgement" form is filed with the clerk as proof of service. Fed. R. Civ. P. 4(g).

Unfortunately, mail service will only be as cheap and easy as it sounds where the adversary chooses to acknowledge service cooperatively and litigate the merits. Defendants, never anxious to make the plaintiff's job easy,

---

[7] Under the prevailing precedent in the Second Circuit, Federal Rules Methods are not generally valid outside the borders of the state where the district court sits, unless service is being made pursuant to a federal statute that specifically permits extraterritorial service of process. State Law Methods (or the alternative methods for service in a foreign country specified in Fed. R. Civ. P. 4(i)) must be used to serve any extraterritorial defendant. *Davis v. Musler*, 713 F.2d 907, 913-14 (2d Cir. 1983). This rule has been justly called an "unfortunate reading" of Rule 4, D. Siegel, Practice Commentaries, 28 U.S.C.A. Rule 4, at 53 (West Supp. 1988), but seems to be gaining acceptance by the majority of courts. Only the Eleventh Circuit has disagreed. *McDougald v. Jenson*, 786 F.2d 1465, 1487 (11th Cir.), *cert. denied*, 107 S. Ct. 207 (1986).

[8] Form 18-A, printed in the Appendix of Forms to the Fed. R. Civ. P., contains the requisites for the Notice and Acknowledgement. The practitioner should customize this form to meet each particular situation.

often do not timely return the Notice and Acknowledgement forms. The only sanction is the possibility of being required to pay the cost of conventional service.[9]

In the Second Circuit, a defendant's failure to return the Notice and Acknowledgement form is, at least theoretically, irrelevant because mail service is considered effective upon receipt. Return of the Notice and Acknowledgement is not required to validate jurisdiction, but merely serves as proof of service. *Morse v. Elmira Country Club*, 752 F.2d 35, 39-41 (2d Cir. 1984). However, the cost of proving receipt of the mailing in the absence of an acknowledgement is, even if possible, likely to exceed substantially the cost of conventional service in the first instance.

Further, the emerging majority view, in conflict with the Second Circuit's, is that a defendant can frustrate mail service by withholding the Notice and Acknowledgement form. *E.g.*, *Del Raine v. Carlson*, 826 F.2d 698, 705 (7th Cir. 1987); *Combs v. Nick Garin Trucking*, 825 F.2d 437 (D.C. Cir. 1987); *Green v. Humphrey Elevator & Truck Co.*, 816 F.2d 877 (3d Cir. 1987); *Armco, Inc. v. Penrod-Stauffer Bldg. Sys., Inc.*, 733 F.2d 1087 (4th Cir. 1984). That can obviously be disastrous if the statute of limitations runs before an alternative method of service is used.

The practitioner must also be aware that if Federal Rules mail service is attempted but fails, Rule 4(c)(2)(C)(ii), read literally, restricts subsequent service to the Federal Rules Methods stated in Fed. R. Civ. P. 4(d)(1) or (3).[10] A State Law Method (including state law mail service, if available where the district court sits), although valid *ab initio* under Fed. R. Civ. P. 4(c)(2)(C)(i), may thus be ineffective following an attempted Federal Rules mail service. Some courts have so held. *Delta S.S. Lines, Inc. v. Albano*, 768 F.2d 728 (5th Cir. 1985); *Armco, Inc. v. Penrod Stauffer Bldg. Sys., Inc.*, 733 F.2d 1087, 1089 (4th Cir. 1984); *Billy v. Ashland Oil, Inc.*, 102 F.R.D. 230 (W.D. Pa. 1984). One circuit has, however, disagreed, following a less literal reading of the Rule. *Humana, Inc. v. Jacobson*, 804 F.2d 1390, 1393 (5th Cir. 1986).

---

[9] One New York federal court has held that these costs include attorney's fees. *C.I.T. Leasing Corp. v. Manth Machine & Tool Corp.*, Civ-85-261C (W.D.N.Y. September 3, 1985). However, other courts to address the issue have given cost awards too minimal to serve as a serious inducement to return the Notice and Acknowledgement form. *Eden Foods, Inc. v. Eden's Own Prods., Inc.*, 101 F.R.D. 96 (E.D. Mich. 1984); *Sally Beauty Co. v. Nexxus Prods. Co.*, 578 F. Supp. 178 (N.D. Ill. 1984).

[10] Fed. R. Civ. P. 4(c)(2)(c)(ii) provides that if the Notice and Acknowledgement form is not returned within 20 days of mailing, service of the summons and complaint "shall be made . . . in the manner prescribed by subdivision (d)(1) or (d)(3)."

Another important limitation on Federal Rules mail service is its general unavailability in New York federal courts for service on out-of-state defendants—exactly where it would maximize the cost savings it is designed to foster. In *Davis v. Musler*, 713 F.2d 907, 913-14 (2d Cir. 1983), the Second Circuit interpreted Fed. R. Civ. P. 4(e) to require a state law method of service on an out-of-state defendant served pursuant to a state "long-arm" statute. New York, of course, does not permit mail service.

Several New York federal court decisions applying *Davis v. Musler* have held Federal Rules mail service on extraterritorial defendants invalid. *Catalyst Energy Dev. Corp. v. Iron Mountain Mines, Inc.*, 108 F.R.D. 427 (S.D.N.Y. 1985); *Olympus Corp. v. Dealer Sales & Serv., Inc.*, 107 F.R.D. 300 (E.D.N.Y. 1985); *Daley v. ALIA*, 105 F.R.D. 87 (E.D.N.Y. 1985); *William B. May Co. v. Hyatt*, 98 F.R.D. 569 (S.D.N.Y. 1983).[11] However, some federal courts outside the Second Circuit disagree. *E.g., McDougald v. Jenson*, 786 F.2d 1465, 1487 (11th Cir.), *cert. denied*, 107 S. Ct. 207 (1986); *Scarton v. Charles*, 115 F.R.D. 567 (E.D. Mich. 1987); *Boggs v. Darr*, 103 F.R.D. 526 (D. Kan. 1984); *Chronister v. Sam Tanksley Trucking, Inc.*, 569 F. Supp. 464 (N.D. Ill. 1983).

The two caveats described above can gang up on the unwary practitioner with disastrous results. For example, a plaintiff who attempts Federal Rules mail service on an out-of-state defendant may find not only that the mail service is invalid, but that under the language of Fed. R. Civ. P. 4(c)(ii), he is now restricted to the Federal Rules Methods of service in Fed. R. Civ. P. 4(d)(1) or (3). Since these methods are not valid on an out-of-state defendant either, the erroneous initial mail service attempt would cost plaintiff the ability to invoke "long-arm" jurisdiction in the case. The defendant could no longer be served. *Pittsburgh Terminal Corp. v. Mid Allegheny Corp.*, 110 F.R.D. 4 (S.D.W. Va. 1985), reached exactly that Kafkaesque result. Although one New York federal court reached a more sensible conclusion in *United States v. Union Indem. Ins. Co.*, 109 F.R.D. 153 (E.D.N.Y. 1986) (Weinstein, C. J.), the potential trap for the unwary cannot be ignored.

The practitioner must also be aware that a defendant's return of a signed Notice and Acknowledgment form establishes only that the mailing was received. It is neither an "appearance" nor an admission of due and timely service, and no jurisdictional defenses are waived. Technical defects in the summons, the validity of mail service in the particular case, or any other attack on the exercise of jurisdiction can still be raised. *Epstein v. Wilder*, 596 F. Supp. 793, 797 (N.D. Ill. 1984); *William B. May Co. v. Hyatt*, 98

---

11 *Accord Reno Distrib., Inc. v. West Texas Oil Field Equip., Inc.*, 105 F.R.D. 511 (D. Kan. 1985); *San Miguel & Compania, Inc. v. International Harvester Export Co.*, 98 F.R.D. 572 (D.P.R. 1983).

F.R.D. 569 (S.D.N.Y. 1983); D. Siegel, Practice Commentaries 28 U.S.C.A. Rule 4, at 71-72 (West Supp. 1988); 4A Wright & Miller § 1092.1, at 59 (1987).

Thus, unless the Federal Rules mail service provisions are revised to eliminate some of the above problems, one must question whether the potential savings in process server fees justifies risking the potential mischief the current provision can work. In any case where time is critical, mail service is a poor choice.

b. Conventional Service

The practitioner planning to make conventional service must be sure to choose a technically correct method. Use of a method not authorized by the Fed. R. Civ. P. will not confer jurisdiction even if it adequately performs the notice-giving function of the summons. See *Wuchter v. Pizzutti*, 276 U.S. 13 (1924); *Leab v. Streit*, 584 F. Supp. 748 (S.D.N.Y. 1984). Unfortunately, the convoluted and confusing interplay among Fed. R. Civ. P. 4(c), (d), (e) and (f) can make identification of the proper technical method of making service on a particular defendant difficult. The Rule badly needs clarifying revisions. Until the revisions are made, the practitioner must pay close attention to the structure of Rule 4 and to applicable court decisions construing the Rule in the circuit and district where the action is pending. Failure to do so may be disastrous for a plaintiff and may cause a defendant to waive a potentially dispositive non-merits defense.

To identify the proper method, or alternative methods, of service, it is first necessary to understand that Fed. R. Civ. P. 4(f), captioned "Territorial Limits of Effective Service" makes the state where the district court sits the basic jurisdictional unit within which a summons may be served and personal jurisdiction may be exercised.[12] Under Rule 4(f), effective service may be made beyond the territorial limits of that state only when authorized by a federal statute or by "these rules"— *i.e.*, the Fed. R. Civ. P. Rule 4(e), captioned "Summons: Service Upon Party Not Inhabitant of or Found Within State," contains the authorization in "these rules" for service of process outside the state where the district court sits.

Rule 4(e) also, at least in the Second Circuit, exclusively specifies the proper method of service on defendants found outside the state ("extraterritorial defendants"). This means that the methods of service specified in Rule 4(c) and (d) are *not* applicable to extraterritorial defendants unless Rule 4(e) specifically allows them.

---

[12] Fed. R. Civ. P. 4(f) is more fully discussed at Part III.B. below.

Rule 4(e) *does* allow them with respect to extraterritorial defendants served pursuant to federal statutes permitting extraterritorial service of process. It provides that where a federal statute permits extraterritorial service, service of the summons and complaint may be made in the manner specified in the statute, "or, if there is no provision therein prescribing the manner of service, in a manner stated in this rule." Many federal statutes allowing extraterritorial service do not specify their own methods of service. Thus, the Federal Rules Methods of service detailed in Rule 4(c)(2)(C)(ii) and (d) and the State Law Methods allowed by Rule 4 (c)(2)(C)(i) will often be available.

In addition to allowing extraterritorial service pursuant to federal law, Rule 4(e) also allows extraterritorial service to the extent available under the law of the state where the district court sits, *i.e.*, it incorporates the state "long-arm" provisions. It also provides that service on defendants amenable to jurisdiction under the state "long arm" statute or court rule "may . . . be made under the circumstances and in the manner prescribed in the statute or rule." As previously noted, under the Second Circuit's interpretation, this provision specifies the exclusive method of service on extraterritorial defendants amenable to jurisdiction under state "long-arm" provisions. Accordingly, such defendants *must* be served according to state law. Use of Federal Rules Methods is technically ineffective.

In summary, to determine the proper method of service of the summons and complaint on a given defendant, it is first necessary to identify the statutory basis for the exercise of jurisdiction over that defendant. If the basis is either presence within the state where the district court sits, or extraterritorial service pursuant to a federal statute, then Rule 4(c) and (d) specify the proper method of service. If the basis for jurisdiction is a state "long-arm" provision, then service "under the circumstances and in the manner prescribed" by state law is required. There is, of course, some overlap in the Rules' dichotomy for determining service method since Rule 4(c)(2)(C)(i) also allows the state law service methods.

The next sub-section will describe the proper method of service under Rule 4(c) and (d) on various types of defendants found within the state or amenable to extraterritorial jurisdiction under federal statutes that do not themselves specify a service method. The following sub-section will address service under Rule 4(e) on defendants amenable to jurisdiction pursuant to state "long-arm" principles.

3. Service Pursuant to Rule 4(c) and (d)

In-state defendants or defendants amenable to extraterritorial jurisdiction under federal statutes may be served by complying with the Federal Rules Methods specified in Fed. R. Civ. P. 4(d), or the State Law Methods incorporated by Fed. R. Civ. P. 4(c)(2)(C)(i), if applicable. Note that the

State Law Methods may be used only to serve *sui juris* individuals and corporations, partnerships or unincorporated associations. Fed. R. Civ. P. 4(c)(2)(C)(i), 4(d)(1), (3). Other types of defendants must be served by the Fedral Rules Methods specified in Rule 4(d).

a. Service Upon a *Sui Juris* Individual

Fed. R. Civ. P. 4(d)(1) provides three methods of serving an individual:

(i) Personal delivery to the individual. In hand personal delivery is not essential in the face of evasion or refusal to accept. Touching the party with the papers or leaving them in his or her proximity upon refusal to accept is generally sufficient. *See Novak v. World Bank*, 703 F.2d 1305, 1310 n.14 (D.C. Cir. 1983); *Errion v. Connell*, 236 F.2d 447 (9th Cir. 1956); 4A Wright & Miller § 1095 at 71 (1987).

(ii) Leaving the summons and complaint "at the individual's dwelling house or usual place of abode with some person of suitable age and discretion then residing therein." Note that unlike the New York service procedure under CPLR § 308(2), no subsequent mailing is required and service is complete upon delivery. However, the person of suitable age and discretion must reside with the defendant. Under New York law, the recipient of the summons can be anyone of suitable age and discretion who answers the door.

(iii) Delivering the summons and complaint to an agent "authorized by appointment or by law" to receive service of process. The agent must be explicitly or implicitly appointed to receive service of process. Ordinary agency is not enough. *See* 4A Wright & Miller § 1097 at 84 (1987). Agents appointed by law may also be validly served, *e.g.*, the New York Secretary of State for a nonresident motor vehicle owner. Veh. & Traf. Law § 253.

State Law Methods of service incorporated by Rule 4(c)(2)(C)(i) add additional flexibility. In New York, these include all the familiar CPLR § 308 methods:

(i) "Leave & Mail" service. CPLR § 308(2). This method may be used to serve an individual by leaving the papers with a person of suitable age and discretion at his or her actual place of business, if more convenient than service at the home or if the home address is unknown, or at the home when the process server is unable to confirm that the person receiving the papers "resides" there. Note that leave and mail service is not complete until 10 days after filing of proof of service, and that the follow-up mailing must be made.

(ii) "Nail & Mail" service. CPLR § 308(4). Under this method, the papers are affixed to the door of the individual's home or business and are also mailed. Reliance on this method requires a showing that personal service or leave and mail service could not be made with due diligence. Nail and mail service is not complete until 10 days after filing proof of service.

(iii) An individually prescribed method of service where the usual methods are "impracticable." CPLR § 308(5). This can be an important tool in an "oddball" case or where a defendant is evading service, is a fugitive or is otherwise difficult or expensive to serve. The individually prescribed methods might include publication, service on an attorney for the party, service on an agent not expressly authorized to receive process, or a combination of these. A CPLR § 308(5) order can be obtained *ex parte* by application based on an affidavit showing what methods of service have been attempted, what the results were, why an individually prescribed method is necessary in the particular case and how the method proposed is calculated to give actual notice.

The chief constraint on the CPLR § 308(5) method of service is that the method devised must comport with due process. *See, e.g., Peralta v. Heights Medical Center, Inc.*, 108 S. Ct. 896 (1988); *Mullane v. Central Hanover Bank & Trust Co.*, 339 U.S. 306 (1950). The one significant risk in using this method is that a default judgment based on such service will be subject to later collateral attack for failure to afford due process.

b. Service Upon an Infant or Incompetent

Fed. R. Civ. P. 4(d)(2) provides for service on an infant or incompetent "in the manner prescribed by the law of the state in which the service is made." Thus, for an in-state defendant, the law of the forum state specifies the method. If the infant or incompetent is located in another state, that state's law governs the method of service. Note that Rule 4(c)(2)(C)(i) does not incorporate state law methods for service on an infant or incompetent; rather, Rule 4(d)(2) specifies state law, but it specifies the law of the state where service is made, not the law of the state where the district court sits.

In New York, CPLR § 309 governs service on an infant or incompetent. Section 309(a) provides that when the infant is under 14, personal service must be made within the state on the infant's parent, guardian, person having legal custody or adult spouse with whom the infant resides. If none of these is in the state, then service may be made on any other person with whom the infant resides or by whom he is employed. If the infant is 14 or older, he or she must also be personally served.

Service on an incompetent under CPLR § 309(b) is made by personally serving the incompetent's committee, *see* Mental Hygiene Law Art. 78, or conservator, *see* Mental Hygiene Law Art. 77, and also the incompetent, but the court may dispense with the latter.

c. Service Upon a Corporation or Partnership

Fed. R. Civ. P. 4(d)(3) specifies the Federal Rules Method for service on a domestic or foreign corporation or a partnership. A copy of the summons and complaint must be delivered to "an officer, a managing or general agent, or to any other agent authorized by appointment or by law to receive service of process." If the agent is one authorized by statute to receive service, and the statute so requires, a copy of the papers must also be mailed to the defendant.

This last provision is aimed at, for example, state statutes designating state officials to receive process on behalf of domestic and foreign corporations. These sometimes require a plaintiff to mail the papers to the defendant. New York's provisions designating the Secretary of State as agent for service of process, BCL §§ 304, 306(b), 307, do not, except that where the Secretary of State is served on behalf of a foreign corporation not authorized to do business in New York, either personal delivery to the corporation or registered mailing is required.

Fed. R. Civ. P. 4(c)(2)(C)(i) also allows State Law Methods for service on corporations or partnerships. In New York federal courts, this adds some flexibility. Under CPLR § 311, a domestic or foreign corporation may be served by personal delivery to a director or to a cashier or assistant cashier, in addition to the officials designated in Fed. R. Civ. P. 4(d)(3). In addition, under New York law, all corporations are deemed to have appointed the Secretary of State as an agent for service of process, BCL § 304, and may be served by service on the Secretary in accordance with the procedures stated in BCL § 306(b) (domestic or authorized foreign corporation) or § 307 (unauthorized foreign corporation).

There are also some special New York statutes that appoint public officials as agents to receive process for corporations in particular businesses. These statutes include Insurance Law § 1212 (b) (service on an insurance company by delivery to the Superintendent of Insurance) and General Business Law § 686 (service on a franchisor or franchisor sales agent by delivery to the Secretary of State).

New York law also makes service on a partnership easier than under the Federal Rules Method. Any partnership may be served by personal service on any partner. CPLR § 310.

d. Service on an Unincorporated Association Subject to Suit Under a Common Name

Suits against unincorporated associations (other than partnerships), which include business trusts, many trade associations and special interest groups, pose some special problems. The first problem is whether the unincorporated association is subject to suit under a common name at all, *i.e.*, has the capacity to sue or be sued. Fed. R. Civ. P. 17(b) governs questions of such capacity in federal court. Pursuant to Rule 17(b), the capacity of an unincorporated association

> to sue or be sued shall be determined by the law of the state in which the district court is held, except . . . that a[n] . . . unincorporated association, which has no such capacity by the law of such state, may sue or be sued in its common name for the purpose of enforcing for or against it a substantive right existing under the Constitution or laws of the United States.

Thus, if an unincorporated association has capacity under the law of the forum state, then the Federal Rules Method of Service—delivery to an officer, managing agent or any other agent authorized by appointment or by law, Fed. R. Civ. P. 4(d)(3)—or a State Law Method, Fed. R. Civ. P. 4(c)(2)(c)(i), may be used. If, under the law of the forum state, an unincorporated association lacks capacity, then it may nevertheless, under Rule 17(b), be sued on a federal claim. For such a claim, service must be made by the Federal Rules Method since, presumably, there is no State Law Method.

New York law relating to the capacity of an unincorporated association to sue or be sued is unique. In New York, an unincorporated association may be sued only by suing and serving its president or treasurer (except that a labor union may be served through a number of additional officers). Gen. Ass'ns Law § 13.

Thus, in a New York federal court, an unincorporated association may be sued in its own name on a federal claim and service may be made on any officer or managing agent. However, for a state law claim, the organization must be sued by naming its president or treasurer and serving such officer as an individual. *See Markewich v. Adikes*, 422 F. Supp. 1144, 1147-48 (E.D.N.Y. 1976). Note that such an action may be subject to Fed. R. Civ. P. 23.2 relating to the adequacy of the person through whom the association is sued to represent the association's members.

Although they are unincorporated associations, labor unions are an exception to the above rules. They are expressly granted capacity to sue and be sued as entities by § 301(b) of the Labor Management Relations Act ("LMRA"), 29 U.S.C. § 185(b). In addition, under the LMRA, service may be made on a labor union by serving any officer or agent. LMRA § 301(d), 29 U.S.C. § 185(d). Although it might be argued that the capacity and service provisions of § 301 were intended to apply only to suits under § 301 or other federal labor laws, nothing in the statute supports that conclusion. Thus, it would appear that even for state law claims, cumbersome state law capacity and service requirements such as New York's Gen. Ass'ns Law § 13 are not applicable to suits against labor organizations. *See S. & H. Grossinger, Inc. v. Hotel & Restaurant Employees & Bartenders Int'l Union*, 272 F. Supp. 25, 29-30 (S.D.N.Y. 1967); *Isbrandtsen Co. v. National Marine Eng'rs Beneficial Assoc.*, 9 F.R.D. 541 (S.D.N.Y. 1949); *Wilson & Co. v. United Packinghouse Workers*, 83 F. Supp. 162 (S.D.N.Y. 1949) (Kaufman, J.).

e. Service Upon the United States

Fed. R. Civ. P. 4(d)(4) specifies a two, and in some cases three, step procedure for service on the United States. First, the summons and complaint must be delivered to the United States attorney for the district where the action is brought, an assistant United States Attorney, or a clerical employee designated to receive service of process. (Most United States Attorney's offices have designated such an employee.) Second, the summons and complaint must be sent by registered or certified mail to the United States Attorney General in Washington. Finally, if the action attacks the validity of an order of an officer or agency of the United States that is not made a party, the summons and complaint must be sent by registered or certified mail to the officer or agency. Note that Rule 4(c)(2)(C)(i) does not authorize service on the United States by a State Law Method.

f. Service Upon a Federal Officer or Agency

Fed. R. Civ. P. 4(d)(5) governs service on a federal officer or agency. It requires a two-step procedure. First, service must be made on the United States as specified above. Second, a copy of the summons and complaint must be sent by registered or certified mail to the officer or agency. However, if the defendant federal agency is a corporation, instead of mailing, the summons and complaint must be delivered to a person specified in Fed. R. Civ. P. 4(d)(3), *i.e.*, an officer, a managing or general agent, or an appointed or statutory agent for service of process.

g. Service Upon a State or Local Governmental Organization

Fed. R. Civ. P. 4(d)(6) allows service to be made on a state, a municipal corporation or a state or local government organization by two methods. First, the summons and complaint may be delivered to the chief executive officer of the entity. For actions against states or large cities, this method is not very practical since governors or mayors are not personally served so easily. Fortunately, Rule 4(d)(6) also permits service in the manner prescribed by the law of the state being served or which created the state governmental entity. In New York, the CPLR's provisions for service on state governmental entities offer many alternatives to service on the chief executive officer.

PERSONAL JURISDICTION AND SERVICE

CPLR § 307 allows service on the State of New York or its agencies

by delivering the summons [and complaint] to an assistant [New York State] attorney-general at an office of the attorney-general or to the attorney general within the state.

However,

in the event any provision of law shall also require personal service upon a specified officer of a state to effect service on such agency, personal service shall then also be made by delivering the summons [and complaint] to such officer or to the chief executive officer of such agency or to a person designated by such chief executive officer to receive service. The chief executive officer of every such agency shall designate at least one person, in addition to himself, to accept service on behalf of the agency. For purposes of this subdivision the term state agency shall be deemed to refer to any agency, board, bureau, commission, division, tribunal or other entity which constitutes the state for purposes of service under subdivision one of this section.

CPLR § 311 governs service upon state governmental subdivisions by delivery of the summons and complaint as follows:

[U]pon the City of New York, to the corporation counsel or to any person designated by him to receive process in a writing filed in the office of the clerk of New York county;
[U]pon any other city, to the mayor, comptroller, treasurer, counsel or clerk; or, if the city lacks such officers, to an officer performing a corresponding function under another name;
[U]pon a county, to the chairman or clerk of the board of supervisors, clerk, attorney or treasurer;
[U]pon a town, to the supervisor or the clerk;
[U]pon a village, to the mayor, clerk, or any trustee;
[U]pon a school district, to a school officer, as defined in the education law; and
[U]pon a park, sewage or other district, to the clerk, any trustee or any member of the board.

CPLR § 312 governs service upon courts, boards or commissions. It provides,

Personal service upon a court consisting of three or more judges may be made by delivering the summons [and complaint] to any one of them. Personal service upon a board or commission having a chairman or other presiding officer, secretary or clerk, by whatever official title he is called, may be made by delivering the summons [and complaint] to him. Personal service upon a board or commission of a town or village may also be made by delivering the summons [and complaint] to the clerk of the town or village. Personal service upon any other board or commission shall be made by delivering the summons [and complaint] to any one of the members.

h. Service Upon a Foreign State or its Political Subdivision, Agency or Instrumentality

The Fed. R. Civ. P. do not specify the manner of service upon foreign states or their constituent parts. The proper method for such service is, however, specified in detail in the Foreign Sovereign Immunities Act, 28 U.S.C. § 1608. The practitioner considering suit against a foreign government or governmental entity should study this rather complex section carefully. *See* 4A Wright & Miller § 1111 (1987). A full exposition is beyond the scope of this chapter.

4. Service Upon Defendants Outside the Forum State Pursuant to Rule 4(e) and State Law

As previously explained, Fed. R. Civ. P. 4(e) governs service on defendants found outside the forum state. Under this provision, the proper method of service depends on whether the basis for the court's exercise of extraterritorial jurisdiction is federal or state law.

Where the basis for jurisdiction is federal law, service is made as provided in Rule 4(c) and (d), noted above, except where the particular federal law involved specifies its own method of service.

However, where state law is the basis for exercise of federal court extraterritorial jurisdiction, Rule 4(e) provides that service "may" be made "under the circumstances and in the manner prescribed in" the state statute or court rule permitting extraterritorial service. Ambiguity in the use of the word "may" has spawned a dispute over the relationship between subdivisions (c)(2)(C) and (d) of Rule 4, and subdivision (e) of Rule 4. Some believe, relying on the use of "may," that they are overlapping provisions and that service on any defendant over which a district court may exercise jurisdiction may be made by either the Federal Rules or State Law Methods. Others, reading "may" as "must," maintain that the provisions have separate purposes—that subdivision (c)(2)(C)(i) applies to service within the forum state, while subdivision (e) applies to service outside the forum state.

The arguments for and against both interpretations are well summarized in 4A Wright & Miller §§ 1114, 1115 at 240-253 (1987). However, the Second Circuit has chosen the more restrictive alternative. *Davis v. Musler*, 713 F.2d

907 (2d Cir. 1983). Thus, in New York federal courts, out-of-state service based on state law must be made in accordance with state law. The most significant effect of this rule is that Fed. R. Civ. P. 4(c)(2)(C)(ii) mail service is not valid outside the forum state unless there is a federal law basis for extraterritorial jurisdiction.

Fortunately, under New York law, service is made outside the state the same way as within the state. Because these methods are set forth above, further discussion is unnecessary. However, New York does have a provision governing who may serve a defendant out-of-state. It requires that service be made by any 18 year-old New York resident not a party to the action, any person authorized to serve process in the jurisdiction where service is made, or any "duly qualified attorney, solicitor, barrister, or equivalent in such jurisdiction." CPLR §§ 313, 314(3).

5. Service in Foreign Countries

Fed. R. Civ. P. 4(i), captioned "Alternative Provisions for Service in a Foreign Country," appears to provide some inexpensive and simple-to-arrange methods for service on parties outside the United States. The Rule states that in addition to the methods of service Rule 4(e) allows,

> it is also sufficient if service of the summons and complaint is made (A) in the manner prescribed by the law of the foreign country for service in that country in an action in any of its courts of general jurisdiction; or (B) as directed by the foreign authority in response to a letter rogatory, when service in either case is reasonably calculated to give actual notice; or (C) upon an individual, by delivery to the individual personally, and upon a corporation or partnership or association, by delivery to an officer, a managing or general agent; or (D) by any form of mail, requiring a signed receipt, to be addressed and dispatched by the clerk of the court to the party to be served; or (E) as directed by order of the court.

The mail service provision sounds particularly inviting.

Unfortunately, the unwary practitioner who relies on Rule 4(i) will find that international agreements to which the United States is a party severely circumscribe its benefits in most cases. The availability of Rule 4(i) service methods is subject to a number of bi-lateral treaties between the United States and foreign countries concerning service of judicial documents, and, most importantly, to a multi-lateral treaty known as the "Hague Convention."[13] The Supreme Court's recently-expressed view is that, despite Rule 4(i), compliance with the procedure of the Hague Convention is mandatory for service in signatory nations. *Volkswagenwerk Aktiengesellschaft v. Schlunk*, 108 S. Ct. 2104 (1988); *Societe Nationale Industrielle Aerospatiale v. United States Dist. Court*, 107 S. Ct. 2542, 2550 n.15 (1987).

The Hague Convention procedures can be cumbersome, time consuming, and expensive. For example, translation of the summons and complaint is often required. The procedures also must be individually determined for a specific country because each signatory designates a different official through whom service is made and can specify certain Hague Convention service methods that it will not recognize. For those who must make service under the Hague Convention, 1 Ristau, *International Judicial Assistance*, Part IV, at 118-76, published by the International Law Institute at Georgetown University, is a useful guide.

Fortunately there are some alternatives to Hague Convention service on nationals of signatory countries. The Supreme Court recently held that the Hague Convention is mandatory only where the summons and complaint must actually be served abroad. *Volkswagenwerk Aktiengesellschaft v. Schlunk*, 108 S. Ct. 2104 (June 15, 1988). Thus, if the foreign defendant can be served in the United States, the Convention does not apply. Service might be made, for example, on an officer or agent found in the United States. In *Schlunk*, the Court upheld service on the foreign defendant's American subsidiary where, under state law, a subsidiary can be served as agent for the parent. This method of avoiding Hague Convention service is available in New York federal courts if the subsidiary constitutes a "mere department" of the parent. *Volkswagenwerk Aktiengesellschaft v. Beech Aircraft Corp.*, 751 F.2d 117 (2d Cir. 1984); *Larball Publishing Co. v. CBS Inc.*, 664 F. Supp. 704 (S.D.N.Y. 1987); *Taca Int'l Airlines, S.A. v. Rolls-Royce, Ltd.*, 15 N.Y.2d 97, 204 N.E.2d 239, 256 N.Y.S.2d 129 (1965). However, its use invites motion practice over the "mere department" classification.

A practical "back-door" method of avoiding Hague Convention service where time is not critical may be to attempt mail service under Rule 4(i)(1)(D) in the first instance. The defendant may appear without challenging service. If not, then subsequent Hague Convention service can be made.

---

13 Convention On The Service Abroad of Judicial and Extrajudicial Documents in Civil or Commercial Matters, Nov. 15, 1965, 20 U.S.T. 361; T.I.A.S. No. 6638. The text of the Hague Convention is conveniently available to most practitioners in the Martindale-Hubbell Law Directory, or in the material following the text of Fed. R. Civ. P. 4 in 28 U.S.C.A., at 121-36 (West Supp. 1988).

D. Time Limit for Service

Fed. R. Civ. P. 4(j) requires that if service is not made within 120 days of filing the complaint, the action as against the unserved defendant is subject to dismissal without prejudice, *sua sponte*[14] or on motion, unless good cause for not making the service can be shown. Although the rule applies, by its term, to "defendants," it applies as well to third-party claims, cross-claims and counterclaims. 4A Wright & Miller § 1137 at 383 (1987); *see Montalbano v. Easco Hand Tools, Inc.*, 766 F.2d 737 (2d Cir. 1985).

Rule 4(j) expressly exempts service in a foreign country pursuant to Rule 4(i) (or presumably the Hague Convention or a relevant treaty) from the 120-day rule. However, the benefit of this exception is available only where service has actually been initiated within 120 days. *Montalbano v. Easco Hand Tools*, 766 F.2d 737 (2d Cir. 1985).

Where "good cause" is shown, the court can enlarge the 120-day period pursuant to its power under Rule 6(b) to enlarge most of the Fed. R. Civ. P.'s time limits. *Williams v. Allen*, 616 F. Supp. 653, 655-56 (E.D.N.Y. 1985). Although the definition of "good cause" is relatively flexible, lack of familiarity with federal procedure and "law office failure" have generally been held not to constitute "good cause." *E.g., Townsel v. County of Contra Costa*, 820 F.2d 319 (9th Cir. 1987); *Reynolds v. United States*, 782 F.2d 837 (9th Cir. 1986); *Winters v. Teledyne Movible Offshore, Inc.*, 776 F.2d 1304 (5th Cir. 1985); *Delicata v. Bowen*, 116 F.R.D. 564 (S.D.N.Y. 1987); *Barco Arroyo v. Federal Emergency Management Agency*, 113 F.R.D. 46 (D.P.R. 1986). Whether an extension of time for service will prejudice defendant is a relevant factor for the court to consider in determining whether "good cause" has been shown. *Gordon v. Hunt*, 116 F.R.D. 313, 321 (S.D.N.Y.), *aff'd*, 835 F.2d 452 (2d Cir. 1987), *cert. denied*, 108 S. Ct. 1734 (1988).

E. Return of Service

Fed. R. Civ. P. 4(g) requires that proof of service be filed "promptly and in any event within the time during which the person served must respond to" the summons and complaint. However, the Rule also provides that "[f]ailure to make proof of service does not affect the validity of the service." No cases address whether the provisions of Rule 4(g) supersede state law time limits

---

[14] A *sua sponte* dismissal may only be made on notice to the plaintiff. *Ruiz Varela v. Sanchez Velez*, 814 F.2d 821 (1st Cir. 1987).

for filing proof of service where service is made pursuant to state law.[15] However, where such time limits might arguably apply, the practitioner is wise to adhere to them.

Where mail service pursuant to Rule 4(c)(2)(C)(ii) is made, Rule 4(g) specifies that the acknowledgement form signed by the recipient be filed as the return. Where service in a foreign country by a form of mail requiring a signed receipt is made, Rule 4(i)(2) requires that the return include the "receipt signed by the addressee or other evidence of delivery to the addressee satisfactory to the court." In all other cases, Rule 4(g) provides that proof of service be made by "affidavit." Although the content of the affidavit is not specified, it should, of course, contain sufficient information to show that service was made in accordance with the service provision relied upon. In addition, where service is made on an individual, it is good practice to include "facts showing that the defendant is not in military service" so that, if necessary, a default judgment may be entered consistent with the Soldiers' and Sailors' Civil Relief Act of 1940, 50 U.S.C. App. § 520.

F. The Remedy for Improper Service—Dismissal of the Action or Quashing of Service

Defects in the summons and complaint or in the manner of their service support the affirmative defenses of lack of personal jurisdiction, insufficiency of process (*i.e.*, the summons is somehow defective) or insufficiency of service of process *(i.e.,* the manner of service is somehow improper). These defenses may be raised initially in a motion pursuant to Fed. R. Civ. P. 12(b)(1), (4), (5), or merely preserved for later adjudication by inclusion in the Answer, Fed. R. Civ. P. 7. If a defendant takes the latter course, and the plaintiff wishes to test the validity of the defenses before proceeding further, the plaintiff may move to strike these affirmative defenses pursuant to Rule 12(f) within 20 days of service of the Answer.

If the Court finds the summons, or its service, defective, it may choose either to quash the service or dismiss the action. If service is quashed, the action remains pending and subsequent proper service may be attempted. If the action is dismissed, subsequent service without filing a new action will not be valid. However, the dismissal must be without prejudice, Fed. R. Civ. P. 41(b), so that the action can be refiled in the same, or a different, court.

---

[15] For example, in New York, proof of substituted service on a natural person under CPLR § 308 must be filed within 20 days.

The court's choice of remedy can have a significant impact if the statute of limitations expires after a defective service. Quashing of service preserves the cause of action if proper service can be made, but dismissal may be its death knell.[16]

Although courts have broad discretion in choosing between quashing service or dismissal, quashing is ordinarily preferred where there is a reasonable prospect that proper service can be made. Where proper service is impossible or unlikely, courts will dismiss. *Montalbano v. Easco Hand Tools, Inc.*, 766 F.2d 737 (2d Cir. 1985); *Alexander v. Unification Church of Am.*, 634 F.2d 673 (2d Cir. 1980); *Rankel v. Town of Greenburgh*, 117 F.R.D. 50 (S.D.N.Y. 1987).

III. AMENABILITY TO FEDERAL DISTRICT COURT JURISDICTION

A. Introduction

The prior section of this chapter discussed how, mechanically, a federal court summons and complaint are properly served on a party anywhere in the world. As noted in the Introduction, however, proper service alone is not sufficient to give a court personal jurisdiction over the served party. That party must also be amenable to jurisdiction. This section now turns to the separate question of when a party is amenable to the federal district court's jurisdiction.

No party can be amenable to federal court jurisdiction unless two necessary conditions are satisfied. First, exercise of jurisdiction must be authorized by some applicable statute, either the Fed. R. Civ. P. or a federal statute expressly permitting the exercise of jurisdiction. Second, exercise of such authorized jurisdiction must be consistent with due process of law. *Omni Capital Int'l v. Rudolf Wolff & Co.*, 108 S. Ct. 404 (1987).

B. Statutory Authorization for Exercise of Federal Court Personal Jurisdiction

Fed. R. Civ. P. 4(f), captioned "Territorial Limits of Effective Service," governs where, geographically, service of a summons and complaint, if properly made, can be "effective" to confer personal jurisdiction. Rule 4(f) provides generally that service is "effective" (a) "anywhere within the terri-

---

[16] In New York federal courts, however, a plaintiff's claims may be saved by CPLR § 205(a), which allows an extra six-month window for refiling after a non-merits dismissal, even if the statute of limitations has run. However, § 205(a) may not be available if the action is dismissed for lack of personal jurisdiction. *See Mankoff v. South Nassau Community Hospital*, 61 N.Y.2d 283, 473 N.Y.S.2d 766 (1984); *Parker v. Mack*, 61 N.Y.2d 114, 472 N.Y.S.2d 882 (1984).

torial limits of the state in which the district court is held," and (b) beyond the territorial limits of that state when authorized (1) "by a statute of the United States," or (2) by "these rules," *i.e.*, the Fed. R. Civ. P.

Rule 4(f) has one important exception to the general rule, which permits "effective" service to be made outside the forum state, but within 100 miles of the federal courthouse (and within the United States) on two classes of parties. These classes are (a) additional parties brought into an action as (1) third party defendants pursuant to Fed. R. Civ. P. 14, or (2) additional defendants on counterclaims or cross-claims pursuant to Fed. R. Civ. P. 19, and (b) "persons required to respond to an order of commitment for civil contempt." Where this "100-mile bulge" rule is invoked, Rule 4(f) requires that service be made pursuant to the Federal Rules Methods of Fed. R. Civ. P. 4(d)(1)-(6). State Law Methods or Federal Mail Service are ineffective.[17]

Thus, rule 4(f) makes the boundaries of the state where the district court sits the basic jurisdictional unit of the federal district court. All parties found within that state are amenable to its jurisdiction. Parties outside the state are, as discussed above, amenable to jurisdiction (1) when authorized by a federal statute, and (2) when authorized by "these rules," a reference to state "long-arm" jurisdiction principles, which Fed. R. Civ. P. 4(e) makes applicable to federal district courts sitting in the state.

Significantly, the territorial limitations Rule 4(f) imposes are not constitutionally mandated. They represent a Congressional choice. So far as the Constitution is concerned, Congress could, by legislation, authorize federal district court process to run throughout the nation in all cases. *Mississippi Publishing Corp. v. Murphree*, 326 U.S. 438 (1946).

1. United States Statutes Authorizing Extraterritorial Service

A number of federal statutes expressly provide for service of process on, and thus exercise of personal jurisdiction over, parties found outside the state where the district court sits in particular types of actions. Those most often invoked govern actions under the federal securities laws, § 22(a) of the Securities Act of 1933, 15 U.S.C. § 77v(a) and § 27 of the Securities Exchange Act of 1934, 15 U.S.C. § 78aa; the Racketeer Influenced and Corrupt Organizations Act ("RICO"), 18 U.S.C. § 1965; the Federal Interpleader Act, 28 U.S.C. § 2361; the Patent Act, 35 U.S.C. § 293; and the Antitrust Laws, 15 U.S.C. §§ 5, 10, 25 (applicable only to bringing in additional parties).

---

17 Of course, in many cases, parties within the exception who can be found inside the "100-mile bulge" will also be amenable to jurisdiction under the Fed. R. Civ. P. without the regard to the exception pursuant to state "long-arm" provisions. In such cases, State Court Methods of service may be effective.

Other federal statutes authorizing extraterritorial service are scattered throughout the United States Code. These include statutes relating to enforcement of Interstate Commerce Commission Orders, 28 U.S.C. § 2321; actions against federal officers or agencies, 28 U.S.C. § 1391(e); Federal Labor Law actions, National Labor Relations Act § 11, 29 U.S.C. § 161(5); actions on government insurance policies issued to members of the armed forces, 38 U.S.C. § 784; and actions requiring service on the heirs of members of the Five Civilized Tribes, 25 U.S.C. § 375. The precise terms of these statutes differ. Each must be consulted to determine its applicability to a particular situation.

The exact scope of the extraterritorial jurisdiction that each federal statute authorizes depends on its wording. For example, a statute authorizing service "in any district" is likely to permit nationwide, but not worldwide, service. A statute authorizing service "wherever defendant may be found," would likely authorize worldwide service. *See, e.g., Soltex Polymer Corp. v. Fortex Indus., Inc.*, 590 F. Supp. 1453 (E.D.N.Y. 1984), *aff'd*, 832 F.2d 1325 (2d Cir. 1987).

At present, the authorities remain split over whether extraterritorial service under a federal statute permits the court to exercise "pendant personal jurisdiction," *i.e.*, jurisdiction with respect not only to a claim for relief under that federal statute, but also pendant state law claims asserted in the action. Although contrary authority exists, and the Second Circuit has vacillated in the past, all circuits to consider the issue recently, including the Second, have approved "pendant personal jurisdiction." *Hargrave v. Oki Nursery, Inc.*, 646 F.2d 716 (2d Cir. 1980); *International Controls Corp. v. Vesco*, 593 F.2d 166, 175 n.5 (2d Cir.), *cert. denied*, 442 U.S. 941 (1979); *Loveridge v. Dreagoux*, 678 F.2d 870, 876 (10th Cir. 1982); *Oetiker v. Jurid Werke, G.M.B.H.*, 556 F.2d 1, 4-5 (D.C. Cir. 1977); *Robinson v. Penn Cent. Co.*, 484 F.2d 553, 555-56 (3d Cir. 1973).

2. Service Under Federal Statutes that do not Expressly Authorize Extraterritorial Service—The Supreme Court's "Omni" Decision

In a recent landmark decision, *Omni Capital Int'l v. Rudolf Wolff & Co.*, 108 S. Ct. 404 (1987), the Supreme Court made it clear that if a federal statute does not expressly authorize extraterritorial service of process, then a federal court's exercise of extraterritorial jurisdiction in a federal question case must be grounded in the law of the state where the district court sits. This principle was always analytically sound, but the Supreme Court had never expressly articulated it.

Prior to *Omni*, some courts had in fact held that in federal question cases, federal courts were not limited by state "long-arm" principles, but could exercise personal jurisdiction to the limits of the fifth amendment's Due Process clause. *E.g., Handley v. Indiana & Michigan Elec. Co.*, 732 F.2d 1265 (6th Cir. 1984); *Lapeyrouse v. Texaco, Inc.*, 693 F.2d 581 (5th Cir. 1982); *Terry v. Raymond Int'l, Inc.*, 658 F.2d 398 (5th Cir. 1981), *cert. denied*, 456 U.S. 928 (1982). The Supreme Court rejected that notion in *Omni*, holding that a federal court's exercise of extraterritorial jurisdiction must be supported by statutory authorization for extraterritorial service of process. If that statutory authorization does not come from federal law, then state law, applicable through Fed. R. Civ. P. 4(e), is its only potential source.

In reaching this result, the Court considered whether federal courts might possibly have a common law power to create service of process rules extending their jurisdiction in situations where Congress did not authorize service. While expressing doubt that such power exists, the Court noted that even if it did, its exercise would be "unwise." 108 S. Ct. at 412.

The Court also considered whether in some circumstances authorization for extraterritorial service of process might be "implied" from the nature of the federal remedy granted. Although it did not foreclose the possibility of "implied" extraterritorial service authorization, the Court declined to find it in *Omni*, 108 S. Ct. at 410-11, and, indeed, no court has ever found it.

C. New York Federal Court Extraterritorial Jurisdiction Under New York Law

As noted above, unless an action arises under a federal statute that authorizes extraterritorial service, state law governs all out-of-state defendants' amenability to jurisdiction for federal or state claims. Thus, in New York federal courts, New York's "long-arm" principles, applicable through Fed. R. Civ. P. 4(e), govern.

Unlike many states, New York has chosen not to permit its courts to exercise personal jurisdiction to the full reach of the due process clause. Its statutes authorize something less. *Kreutter v. McFadden Oil Corp.*, 71 N.Y.2d 460, 471, 522 N.E.2d 40, 527 N.Y.S.2d 195, 201 (1988); *Banco Ambrosiano v. Artoc Bank & Trust Ltd.*, 62 N.Y.2d 65, 464 N.E.2d 432, 476 N.Y.S.2d 64 (1984); *Longines-Wittnauer Watch Co. v. Barnes & Reinecke, Inc.*, 15 N.Y.2d 443, 209 N.E.2d 68, 261 N.Y.S.2d 8, *cert. denied*, 382 U.S. 905 (1965). This self-imposed limitation also limits the extraterritorial reach of federal courts sitting in New York.

CPLR §§ 301 and 302 provide the basic statutory framework of New York's "long-arm" jurisdiction. CPLR § 301, which, by its terms, simply authorizes the exercise of jurisdiction as developed through court decisions prior to the CPLR's enactment in 1963, incorporates a body of New York case law that permits exercise of jurisdiction over an out-of-state entity if its

PERSONAL JURISDICTION AND SERVICE 51

activities in New York are sufficiently regular and systematic to justify a finding that the entity is "doing business" in New York. As the Court of Appeals has put it, to satisfy this "doing business" test a foreign corporation must conduct business in New York "not occasionally or casually, but with a fair measure of permanence and continuity." *Tauza v. Susquehanna Coal Co.*, 220 N.Y. 259, 267, 115 N.E. 917 (1917); *see also Bryant v. Finnish Nat'l Airline*, 15 N.Y.2d 426, 208 N.E.2d 439, 260 N.Y.S.2d 625 (1965); *Simonson v. International Bank*, 14 N.Y.2d 281, 200 N.E.2d 427, 251 N.Y.S.2d 433 (1964). Satisfying the "doing business" test is simply one way of being constructively "present" in New York for jurisdictional purposes. It is important to note that if a foreign corporation is "doing business" in New York, it is subject to jurisdiction for any cause of action, even one completely unrelated to its New York operations.

CPLR § 302, New York's "long-arm" statute, does not require as high a threshold of New York activity to permit exercise of jurisdiction, but does require that the cause of action arise from the New York activity. The section provides:

> As to a cause of action arising from any of the acts enumerated in this section, a court may exercise personal jurisdiction over any non-domiciliary, or his executor or administrator, who in person or through an agent:
>
> 1. transacts any business within the state or contacts anywhere to supply goods or services in the state; or
>
> 2. commits a tortious act within the state, except as to a cause of action for defamation of character arising from the act; or
>
> 3. commits a tortious act without the state causing injury to person or property within the state, except as to a cause of action for defamation of character arising from the act, if he
>
>> (i) regularly does or solicits business, or engages in any other persistent course of conduct, or derives substantial revenue from goods used or consumed or services rendered, in the state, or
>>
>> (ii) expects or should reasonably expect the act to have consequences in the state and derives substantial revenue from interstate or international commerce; or
>
> 4. owns, uses or possesses any real property situated within the state.

A complete discussion of the cases interpreting CPLR § 302 would fill volumes and is beyond the scope of this chapter. However, the main highlights of this body of law are:

— "Transaction" of business for § 302(a)(1) purposes requires considerably less in-state activity than "doing business" under § 301. *Simonson v. International Bank*, 14 N.Y.2d 281, 200 N.E.2d 427, 251 N.Y.S.2d 433 (1964).

— Telephone, telex or mail communications sent into New York to place or solicit orders generally do not constitute "transaction" of business for CPLR § 302(a)(1) purposes, no matter how high the volume. *Agrashell, Inc. v. Bernard Sirotta Co.*, 344 F.2d 583, 587 (2d Cir. 1965); *Lichtenstein v. Jewelart, Inc.*, 95 F.R.D. 511, 514 (E.D.N.Y. 1982); *but see Parke-Bernet Galleries, Inc. v. Franklin*, 26 N.Y.2d 13, 308 N.Y.S.2d 337 (1970).

— The "substantial revenue" criterion of § 302(a)(3)(i) and (ii) can be satisfied by a showing of either absolute (*i.e.*, large *vel non*) or relative (*i.e.*, a large proportion) substantiality. *Allen v. Canadian Gen. Elec. Co.*, 65 A.D.2d 39, 410 N.Y.S.2d 707 (3d Dep't 1978).

— Section 302 applies generally to one who performs any of the enumerated acts in New York "through an agent." Recently, the New York Court of Appeals significantly expanded this agency aspect of state "long-arm" jurisdiction by rejecting the so-called "fiduciary shield doctrine," which lower courts and some federal courts had imposed on CPLR § 302. This doctrine generally forbade the exercise of jurisdiction over nonresident individuals in actions arising from acts performed in their capacity as corporate officers or directors. These individuals are now subject to New York jurisdiction. *Kreutter v. McFadden Oil Corp.*, 71 N.Y.2d 460, 522 N.E.2d 40, 527 N.Y.S.2d 195 (1988).

— In one respect, however, New York still significantly restricts the application of CPLR § 302 to the actions of an agent. New York refuses to allow the agent's own in-state activities to support jurisdiction in an action by the agent against the principal. *Haar v. Armendaris Corp.*, 31 N.Y.2d 1040, 294 N.E.2d 855, 342 N.Y.S.2d 70 (1972). The *Haar* rule is illogical and has been severely criticized, but it remains the law. *Celton Man Trade, Inc. v. Utex, S.A.*, No. 84 Civ. 8179 (WCC) (S.D.N.Y. 1986).

In addition to *the* "long-arm" statute, CPLR § 302, New York also has several special purpose "long-arm" provisions scattered throughout the consolidated laws. These include Vehicle and Traffic Law § 253, an "owner consent" statute subjecting the owner of any motor vehicle operated with consent in New York to jurisdiction in New York, General Business Law

§ 686,[18] permitting service on franchisors who sell franchises in New York and their principals, by service on the secretary of state, and Insurance Law § 1213, permitting similar service on insurance companies.

D. Constitutional Limitations on the Exercise of Extraterritorial Jurisdiction—The Due Process Clause

In addition to having state or federal statutory authorization, a federal court's exercise of extraterritorial jurisdiction must also comport with due process requirements. U.S. Const. amend. XIV. As interpreted by the Supreme Court in *International Shoe v. Washington*, 326 U.S. 310, 316 (1945), "due process requires only that in order to subject a defendant to a judgment in personam, if he be not present within the territory of the forum, he have certain minimum contacts with it such that the maintenance of the suit does not offend 'traditional notions of fair play and substantial justice.' "

In many states, but not New York, "long-arm" statutes are expressly, or by court decision, co-extensive with the "minimum contacts" standard of *International Shoe*. In such states, the issues of statutory authorization for, and constitutionality of, extraterritorial jurisdiction collapse into one inquiry.

In states like New York, however, a federal court exercising state "longarm" jurisdiction under Fed. R. Civ. P. 4(e) must, if jurisdiction is challenged, inquire into both statutory authorization and constitutionality. The absence of one of the two defeats jurisdiction.

To determine whether the exercise of extraterritorial jurisdiction is constitutional in a particular case, a federal court must weigh the defendant's contacts with the forum against *International Shoe*'s "minimum contacts" standard. Although each case is *sui generis*, in the four decades since *International Shoe*, decided cases have left some helpful guide posts. The most significant are (1) that the defendant must have "purposefully avail[ed] itself of the privilege of conducting activities within the forum State, thus invoking the benefits and protections of its laws," *Hanson v. Denckla*, 357 U.S. 235, 253 (1958), and (2) that it be "foreseeable" that the defendant might be haled into court in the forum in connection with the transaction or occurrence in issue, *World-Wide Volkswagen v. Woodson*, 444 U.S. 286, 297 (1980).

In recent years, particularly in cases involving the sale of goods, courts have focused on the "foreseeability" issue. A number of courts adopted a so-

---

18 Curiously, one federal court has held that Gen. Bus. L. § 686 merely provides a method of service of process on franchisors, but does not itself authorize the exercise of extraterritorial jurisdiction. *Retail Software Services, Inc. v. Lashlee*, 84 CV 4506 (JMcL) (E.D.N.Y.), *rev. on other grounds*, 854 F.2d. 18 (2d Cir. 1988). Ordinarily, however, providing a method for service of process is the way a legislature authorizes extraterritorial jurisdiction. *See Omni Capital Int'l v. Rudolf Wolff & Co.*, 108 S. Ct. 404 (1987).

called "stream of commerce" theory under which litigation in the forum was "foreseeable" if defendant placed goods in the "stream of commerce" anywhere in the world with a reasonable likelihood that the goods would find their way to consumers in the forum.

The concept of "foreseeability" is changing, however, and the current viability of the "stream of commerce" theory is doubtful. Mere likelihood that the goods will reach the forum in the course of commerce is no longer the standard; rather the defendant must have expressly intended to serve the forum market, directly or indirectly. *E.g., Montalbano v. Easco Hand Tools, Inc.*, 766 F.2d 737, 742 (2d Cir. 1985), quoting *World-Wide Volkswagen v. Woodson*, 444 U.S. 286 (1980).

Recently, in *Asahi Metal Indus. Co. v. Superior Court*, 480 U.S. 102 (1987), four justices expressly rejected the "stream of commerce" theory in favor of such a "purposeful direction" theory under which a seller is amenable to suit only in markets he affirmatively sought to serve. This "purposeful direction" concept is also being incorporated into the "minimum contacts" analysis outside the sale of goods context. *Burger King Corp. v. Rudzewicz*, 471 U.S. 462 (1985). At present, where any defendant's acts were "purposefully directed" toward residents of the forum, litigation in the forum arising from these acts is "foreseeable," and jurisdiction likely constitutional, even if there was little or no physical contact between the defendant and the forum. *See Keeton v. Hustler Magazine, Inc.*, 465 U.S. 770 (1984); *Calder v. Jones*, 465 U.S. 783 (1984); *Retail Software Services, Inc. v. Lashlee*, 854 F.2d 18 (2d Cir. 1988).

In analyzing "minimum contacts" for purposes of federal law claims brought in a federal court against an alien, there is currently some uncertainty about the relevant "forum" with which the defendant must have such contacts. Is it the United States as a whole, or the state where the district court sits?

It can be cogently argued that since a federal court is a court of the United States, in considering whether an alien has "minimum contacts" with the forum for purposes of a federal law claim, the relevant "forum" is the nation as a whole. Some courts have accepted such a "national contacts" theory and permitted aggregation of an alien's United States contacts for jurisdictional purposes. *E.g., Laker Airways Ltd. v. Sabena, Belgian World Airlines*, 731 F.2d 909 (D.C. Cir. 1984); *Honeywell, Inc. v. Metz Apparatewerke*, 509 F.2d 1137 (7th Cir. 1975); *Centronics Data Computer Corp. v. Mannesmann, A.G.*, 432 F. Supp. 659 (D.N.H. 1977); *Cryomedics, Inc. v. Spembly, Ltd.*, 397 F. Supp. 287 (D. Conn. 1975).

The problem with the "national contacts" theory is that, however fair and reasonable it may seem from a due process standpoint, unless a case arises under one of the federal statutes authorizing nationwide service of process, there is no statutory authorization for aggregation of contacts. Federal courts are only authorized to exercise the extraterritorial jurisdiction permitted by the states where they sit. Such jurisdiction requires contacts with that state. Many courts have rejected the "national contacts" theory for this reason. *E.g., Max Daetwyler Corp. v. R. Meyer*, 762 F.2d 290 (3d Cir.), *cert. denied*, 474 U.S. 980 (1985); *Wells Fargo & Co. v. Wells Fargo Express Co.*, 556 F.2d 406 (9th Cir. 1977); *Superior Coal Co. v. Ruhrkohle, A.G.*, 83 F.R.D. 414 (E.D. Pa. 1979); *Amburn v. Harold Forster Indus., Ltd.*, 423 F. Supp. 1302 (E.D. Mich. 1976); *Graham Eng'g Corp. v. Kemp Prods., Ltd.*, 418 F. Supp. 915 (N.D. Ohio 1976).

Although rejection appears to be the current trend, recent Supreme Court decisions have expressly left the viability of the "national contacts" theory an open question. In *Omni Capital Int'l v. Rudolf Wolff & Co.*, 108 S. Ct. 404, 408-09 n.5 (1987), although the Court held that there must be a state law statutory basis for exercise of federal court extraterritorial jurisdiction, it declined to reach the question of whether, if such a basis exists, the "minimum contacts" necessary to support its constitutionality may be national in scope. *Asahi Metal Indus. Co. v. Superior Court*, 480 U.S. 102 (1987), which considered state court jurisdiction, similarly adverted to the "national contacts" theory, but did not address its validity.

The Supreme Court recently granted certiorari in a case that discussed the debate over the "national contacts" theory but took no position because it found ample contacts with both the forum state and the United States as a whole. *In re Chase & Sanborn Corp.*, 835 F.2d 1341 (11th Cir.), *cert. granted sub nom. Granfinanciera, S.A. v. Nordberg*, 108 S. Ct. 2818 (1988). Although the Court may wish to use this case to rule on the "national contacts" theory, it should not be necessary to reach the issue because jurisdiction was based on a federal authorization for nationwide service rather than a state "long-arm" statute.

In contrast to actions that depend on state "long-arm" provisions for jurisdiction, in actions based on federal statutes that authorize extraterritorial service of process, it is already fairly well established that jurisdiction over an alien may be based on contacts with the United States as a whole. *E.g., Securities Investor Protection Corp. v. Vigman*, 764 F.2d 1309 (9th Cir. 1985); *Texas Trading & Milling Corp. v. Federal Republic of Nigeria*, 647 F.2d 300 (2d Cir.), *cert. denied*, 454 U.S. 1148 (1981); *Mariash v. Morrill*, 496 F.2d 1138 (2d Cir. 1974). This should not mean that an alien may be sued in a federal court far from the locus of its United States activities. Because the venue statute, which permits an alien to be sued in any district, 28 U.S.C. § 1391(d), does not protect an alien from potential abuse, courts should consider the locus of United States contacts in relation to the federal district selected for suit in assessing overall fundamental fairness.

IV. QUASI-IN-REM JURISDICTION—A POSSIBLE SUBSTITUTE FOR PERSONAL JURISDICTION

Quasi-in-rem jurisdiction, personal jurisdiction's close relative, is based on attachment of a defendant's property within the territorial limits of the court's process. The attachment is said to give the court power to adjudicate personal claims against the defendant up to the value of the attached property. Although a judgment in excess of that value will not be enforceable, the controversy involved in the action need not be over rights in the attached property.

Thus, the practitioner should consider the possibility of exploiting quasi-in-rem jurisdiction where the defendant has few contacts with the forum that relate to the action, but does have an interest in some property in the forum. The property can be real or personal, tangible or intangible, but, of course, intangible property raises situs issues. Quasi-in-rem jurisdiction is particularly useful in New York federal courts because individuals and businesses located world-wide with few New York contacts will often have bank deposits or a securities account in New York City, or will be owed an attachable debt by a New York entity.

The Fed. R. Civ. P. do not directly provide for the exercise of quasi-in-rem jurisdiction, or for the attachment of property to support it. However, Fed. R. Civ. P. 4(e) incorporates the quasi-in-rem jurisdiction, if any, of the state in which the district court sits, and Fed. R. Civ. P. 64 incorporates that state's attachment procedures. Thus, a federal court can exercise quasi-in-rem jurisdiction to the extent available in the forum state.

In New York, although the CPLR does not specifically mention quasi-in-rem jurisdiction, it is available pursuant to CPLR § 301, which permits a court to "exercise such jurisdiction over persons, property, or status as might have been exercised heretofore" (*i.e.*, before the effective date of the CPLR in 1963). *Banco Ambrosiano, S.p.A. v. Artoc Bank & Trust Ltd.*, 62 N.Y.2d 65, 71, 464 N.E.2d 432, 476 N.Y.S.2d 64, 66 (1984). CPLR § 6201 authorizes attachment of property in New York where, *inter alia*, "the defendant is a nondomiciliary residing without the state, or is a foreign corporation not qualified to do business in the state," exactly the type of defendant that may not be subject to personal jurisdiction.

CPLR Article 62 details the procedure for attachment. Plaintiff must obtain an order of attachment from the court and then levy on specific property by serving the order on the proper garnishee. Article 62 contains proce-

PERSONAL JURISDICTION AND SERVICE

dures for obtaining the Order of Attachment *ex parte*, CPLR § 6211, or by noticed motion, CPLR § 6210. Where anything movable is involved, it is obviously critical to proceed *ex parte* and federal courts ordinarily issue attachment orders on that basis.

Once the order is obtained, levy can be made by having the United States Marshal serve the order on the garnishee, but the wise practitioner can avoid delay in the Marshal's office and the Marshal's fees (1.5 percent of the sum attached, 28 U.S.C. § 1921) by drafting the attachment order to include a paragraph specially appointing one or several individuals to serve the process. Fed. R. Civ. P. 4(c)(1) permits such special appointments, and Rule 4(c)(3) directs federal courts to make them "freely."[19]

The exercise of quasi-in-rem jurisdiction must, like personal jurisdiction, satisfy the "minimum contacts" test of due process discussed at Part III.D., above. *Schaffer v. Heitner*, 433 U.S. 186 (1977). The mere presence of a property interest in the state is not alone sufficient to support jurisdiction. It is, however, a contact to be weighed in the balance.

The New York Court of Appeals held that due process requires the attached property supporting quasi-in-rem jurisdiction to have some relationship to the claim asserted. Its presence in New York cannot be merely incidental. *Banco Ambrosiano, S.P.A. v. Artoc Bank & Trust Ltd.*, 62 N.Y.2d 65, 464 N.E.2d 432, 476 N.Y.S.2d 64 (1984). Prior to this decision, New York federal courts had not imposed that limitation. *Intermeat, Inc. v. American Poultry, Inc.*, 575 F.2d 1017 (2d Cir. 1978); *Drexel Burnham Lambert, Inc. v. D'Angelo*, 453 F. Supp. 1294 (S.D.N.Y. 1978); *Feder v. Turkish Airlines*, 441 F. Supp. 1273 (S.D.N.Y. 1977). At present, it is unclear whether New York federal courts are bound by New York's interpretation of the federal due process limitations on quasi-in-rem jurisdiction when exercising New York's quasi-in-rem jurisdiction pursuant to Fed. R. Civ. P. 4(e).

Finally, quasi-in-rem jurisdiction is particularly useful in New York federal courts because, unlike "long-arm" jurisdiction under CPLR § 302, its exercise is limited only by the Constitution's due process clause. *Banco Ambrosiano v. Artoc Bank & Trust Ltd.*, 62 N.Y.2d 65, 464 N.E.2d 432, 476 N.Y.S.2d 64 (1984). One important ramification of this broader scope is freedom from the much-maligned *Haar* rule, which bars an agent from

---

19 The availability of special appointments to serve attachment orders under the Fed. R. Civ. P. makes federal court the clear choice for the New York practitioner in any action involving attachment in which federal subject matter jurisdiction is available. In the New York Supreme Court only the sheriff can serve attachment orders, and the sheriff's poundage fees are steep—in New York City 5 percent of the amount attached; elsewhere, 5 percent of the first $250,000 and 3 percent of the rest. Although theoretically the defendant, if liable, must pay these fees, practically they will be a substantial issue in settlement discussions.

relying on his own in-state activities to support "long-arm" jurisdiction under CPLR § 302 in an action against his principal. *Haar v. Armendaris Corp.*, 31 N.Y.2d 1040, 294 N.E.2d 855, 342 N.Y.S.2d 70 (1973). For due process purposes, the plaintiff-agent's in-state activities *can* provide "minimum contacts" with the state. *Drexel Burnham Lambert, Inc. v. D'Angelo*, 453 F. Supp. 1294 (S.D.N.Y. 1978).

V. RAISING LACK OF PERSONAL JURISDICTION AS A DEFENSE

A practitioner who concludes that a federal court has no jurisdiction over his or her client has three ways of raising a jurisdictional defense:

1. Move to dismiss for lack of jurisdiction within the time to respond to the complaint;

2. Plead lack of personal jurisdiction as an affirmative defense in the answer, Fed. R. Civ. P. 8; or

3. Ignore the complaint and assert lack of jurisdiction as a collateral attack in subsequent efforts to enforce the resulting default judgment.

If a defendant responds to the complaint by motion or answer without raising lack of personal jurisdiction, then the defense is waived and jurisdiction is conferred by consent.

Whichever method of jurisdictional attack a party chooses, plaintiff always bears the burden of proof as to whether jurisdiction exists. *Cutco Indus., Inc. v. Naughton*, 806 F.2d 361 (2d Cir. 1986); *Hoffritz for Cutlery, Inc. v. Amajac, Ltd.*, 763 F.2d 55 (2d Cir. 1985). However, plaintiff is entitled to discovery of defendant on that issue, and defendant cannot refuse to comply with discovery requests based on the asserted lack of jurisdiction. A federal court has power to enforce its discovery orders by appropriate sanctions even before its jurisdiction is adjudicated. *Insurance Corp. of Ireland v. Compagnie des Bauxites de Guinee*, 456 U.S. 694 (1982).

Where lack of jurisdiction is raised by motion, under Second Circuit precedent plaintiff need make only an initial prima facie showing of jurisdiction, usually by affidavit. If plaintiff does so, the court has discretion to hold a preliminary hearing on the jurisdictional issues at any point, or to try them jointly with the merits. *Cutco Indus., Inc. v. Naughton*, 806 F.2d 361 (2d Cir. 1986); *Hoffritz for Cutlery, Inc. v. Amajac, Ltd.*, 763 F.2d 55 (2d Cir. 1985); *Marine Midland Bank, N.A. v. Miller*, 664 F.2d 899 (2d Cir. 1981); Fed. R. Civ. P. 12(d). At a preliminary hearing or at trial, plaintiff must demonstrate jurisdiction by a preponderance of the evidence.

Where lack of jurisdiction is raised as an affirmative defense in the answer, either party can apply for a preliminary hearing to determine the

PERSONAL JURISDICTION AND SERVICE

jurisdictional issues. The court can hold the hearing or defer the issues to trial on the merits. Fed. R. Civ. P. 12(d). Alternatively, if jurisdiction may depend solely on issues of law, plaintiff can move to strike the jurisdictional defense within 20 days of service of the pleading asserting it. Fed. R. Civ. P. 12(f).

A plaintiff who chooses simply to ignore a complaint had better be quite certain that there is no arguable basis for jurisdiction. If jurisdiction is upheld in a subsequent collateral attack on a resulting default judgment, litigation of the merits is likely foreclosed. It will be difficult for a defendant who decided to ignore a complaint to convince the court that rendered the default judgment that it should be set aside. The requirements of Fed. R. Civ. P. 60(b) would apply to such an application. Fed. R. Civ. P. 55(c).

CHAPTER THREE

VENUE

by Colleen McMahon, Esq.*

I. GENERAL CONSIDERATIONS

Venue is the forum where a lawsuit should be heard. Venue should not be confused with jurisdiction. The latter is the power of a particular court to adjudicate a given case. Venue specifies which court among those that have jurisdiction may exercise that jurisdiction.

Venue is a creature of statute, and except in extremely limited circumstances, venue in federal cases—even diversity cases—is governed by federal law. In most cases, venue is governed by the general federal venue statute, 28 U.S.C. §§ 1391-1392. However, numerous other provisions of federal law, including such substantive laws as the antitrust, banking, securities and admiralty laws, contain special venue provisions that override the general statute. *Bruns, Nordeman & Co. v. American National Bank & Trust Co.*, 394 F.2d 300 (2d Cir.), *cert. denied*, 393 U.S. 855 (1968). Thus, in selecting a forum in which to bring suit, the practitioner must make sure that his case does not fall within one of the special venue statutes before relying on § 1391.

The only exception to the rule that federal law controls venue in federal actions is where an action is purely local in nature. "Local" actions are those in which the court needs (or is thought to need) jurisdiction over a particular *res* in order to grant relief. Examples of such actions include those to fore-

---

* The author thanks John F. O'Sullivan, who helped prepare this chapter while a summer associate at Paul, Weiss, Rifkind, Wharton & Garrison.

close a mortgage, quiet title, to evict a tenant or to abate a nuisance. In local actions, state law, which generally provides that the action may be brought only where the subject property is located, controls the question of venue. In actions of a local nature involving the United States, special venue statutes govern where the action can be prosecuted. *See* "Local Actions Involving the United States" *infra*.

II. THE KEY TO VENUE IS CONVENIENCE

Many texts and treatises have been written about venue, but all stress that the key to venue is convenience. This is overly simplistic, however, since what is convenient for one party may not be convenient for an opponent.

In most cases, venue statutes are designed to protect the defendant against the risk that the plaintiff will select an unfair or inconvenient place of trial. *Leroy v. Great Western United Corp.*, 443 U.S. 173 (1979). Because venue statutes exist for their protection, defendants can waive their right to challenge the plaintiff's choice of venue, even if that choice is improper or, while technically proper, inconvenient. 28 U.S.C. § 1406(b); *Olberding v. Illinois Cent. R.R. Co.*, 346 U.S. 338, 340 (1953); *Concession Consultants, Inc. v. Mirisch*, 355 F.2d 369 (2d Cir. 1966). Some commentators thus refer to venue as a "personal privilege" of defendants, which they can stand on or surrender as they see fit. *See, e.g.*, Wright, Miller & Cooper—*Federal Practice and Procedure* (1986 ed.), § 3826.

Because venue is a personal privilege, parties may agree that a dispute between them will be heard in a particular forum. Such agreements, which are known as choice of forum clauses, are presumptively valid, even though the venue selected is not one of those provided by statute. Choice of forum clauses will be enforced by federal courts unless "trial in the contractual forum will be so gravely difficult and inconvenient that the party opposing enforcement of the clause will for all practical purposes be deprived of his day in court." *M/S Bremen v. Zapata Off-Shore Co.*, 407 U.S. 1, 18 (1972).

There are two caveats to this rule. First, a choice of forum clause cannot confer jurisdiction on a court that has no power to decide a particular controversy. *Cf. Neirbo Co. v. Bethlehem Shipbuilding Corp.*, 308 U.S. 165, 167 (1939). Second, while an action brought in accordance with a choice of forum clause will not be dismissed for improper venue, it may still be transferred to a more convenient forum under 28 U.S.C.§ 1404(a). *Walter E. Heller & Co. v. James Godbe Co.*, 601 F. Supp. 319 (N.D. Ill. 1984). Indeed, in a recent diversity case, the United States Supreme Court ruled that a court faced with a motion to transfer an action to the forum specified by the parties in their contract should give the forum-selection clause "neither dispositive consideration nor no consideration," but rather had to weigh that factor with others in deciding the transfer motion. *Stewart Organization v. Ricoh*, 108 S. Ct. 2239, 2245 (1988).

III. HOW TO CHOOSE VENUE IN A PARTICULAR CASE

The general rules for laying venue in a federal action are found in 28 U.S.C. §§ 1391-1392. Most cases, however, are governed by the rules set forth in §§ 1391(a) and (b). The former section controls venue in diversity question cases and the latter in federal question cases.

The two governing concepts in choosing a forum under Sections 1391(a) and (b) are *residence of the parties* and *where the claim arose*.

The principal difference between venue in cases based solely on diversity of citizenship and venue in cases that raise a federal question is whether the plaintiff may choose to sue in its own backyard. The rule is very simple: in a diversity case, the plaintiff's residence is a proper venue, but in a federal question case it is not. The defendant's residence is always a proper venue, whether the action is brought under diversity or federal question principles.

The residence rule is simple enough to follow when there is only one plaintiff and/or one defendant. However, where there are multiple parties the matter becomes more complicated, since an action may only be sited in the district where "all plaintiffs" or "all defendants" reside. Historically, the "all plaintiffs/all defendants" rule meant that there were some cases where no venue was proper, because there was no district in which all the parties on one side or the other resided. The option of suing *where the claim arose* was added to the general venue statute to close this loophole and to ensure that there would be some court where venue could be laid. In both diversity and federal question cases that fall within the general venue statute, venue is proper in the district where the claim arose.

In diversity cases, where plaintiff's residence can be used as the basis for choosing venue, it is important to note that the statutory requirement is that suit be brought where "all plaintiffs *or* all defendants" reside, not where "all plaintiffs *and* all defendants" reside. Thus, the plaintiff can select venue by looking solely to the residence of all plaintiffs or solely to the residence of all defendants. It does not matter if the plaintiffs and defendants reside in different districts.

In multi-party cases, venue must be proper as to each party. However, if the venue selected by the plaintiff is improper with regard to some of the parties, the case need not be dismissed as to all parties. If there is a district in which venue would be proper as to all parties and where jurisdiction can be obtained over all defendants, the suit can be transferred there. And if there is no such district, the court can either dismiss any party as to whom venue is improper, *Champion Spark Plug Co. v. Karchmar*, 180 F. Supp. 727, 730 (S.D.N.Y. 1960)—unless that party is "indispensable" within the meaning of Rule 19(b), *see Camp v. Gress*, 250 U.S. 308 (1919)—or sever the party as to whom venue is improper and transfer the severed portion to a proper forum. *United Nations Korean Reconstruction Agency v. Glass Production Meth.*, 143 F. Supp. 248 (S.D.N.Y. 1956).

The residence of nominal parties or "sham" parties will be ignored in determining the propriety of venue. This makes it virtually impossible to defeat a case by the collusive joinder of parties as to whom the venue otherwise selected is not proper.

A. What Is a Party's Residence?

1. Individuals

In general, the test used to determine an individual's "residence" for venue purposes is the same as that used to determine "citizenship" for jurisdictional purposes. *Kahane v. Carlson*, 527 F.2d 492 (2d Cir. 1975); *Smith v. Murchison*, 310 F. Supp. 1079 (S.D.N.Y. 1970). Thus, in this Circuit, an individual is a resident of the place where he is legally domiciled, even if he lives elsewhere. That is not the rule in all circuits, however. *See, e.g., Arley v. United Pacific Ins. Co.*, 379 F.2d 183 (9th Cir. 1967), *cert. denied*, 390 U.S. 950 (1968).

Federal officials who are sued in their official capacities are deemed to be residents of the place where they perform their duties rather than the place where they are domiciled. *Butterworth v. Hill*, 114 U.S. 128 (1885). Some courts consider state (as opposed to federal) officials to be residents of both the place where they work and the place where they are domiciled, but others question that view. *Compare Cheeseman v. Carey*, 485 F. Supp. 203 (S.D.N.Y.), *remanded on other grounds*, 623 F.2d 1387 (2d Cir. 1980) *with Procario v. Ambach*, 466 F. Supp. 452, 454 (S.D.N.Y. 1979).

For purposes of selecting venue, a natural person's residence is the place where he is domiciled at the time the action is commenced, not at the time the claim arose.

2. For a Corporation

Before the Judicial Improvements and Access to Justice Act of 1988 was inacted, Section 1391(c) provided that a corporation may be sued in, and shall be deemed a resident of, "any judicial district in which it is incorporated or licensed to do business or is doing business." The 1988 amendment to

Section 1391(c) settled various problems associated with this statute. The statute now provides that a "defendant that is a corporation" resides for venue purposes "in any judicial district in which it is subject to personal jurisdiction at the time the action is commenced." Thus, amended § 1391(c) settled two issues that the prior version of the statute did not address: whether "doing business" under the statute meant the same thing as "doing business" for personal jurisdiction purposes, and whether the time for determining corporate defendant venue was at the time the cause of action arose, or when the action was commenced.

The amended statute also provides that in states with more than one district, corporate venue lies in any district with which it has contacts sufficient for personal jurisdiction. If there is no such district, but the corporation is subject to personal jurisdiction in that state, venue is proper in the district within which it has "the more significant contacts."

3. For a Partnership or Other Unincorporated Association

No provision of the general venue statute specifically addresses the question of venue for an unincorporated association, including a partnership. In general, an unincorporated association is treated like a corporation; while it obviously does not have a state of incorporation, its residence is deemed to be any district in which it does business. *Denver & Rio Grande Western R.R. Co. v. Brotherhood of R.R. Trainmen*, 387 U.S. 556 (1967). There is a split of authority on whether this rule applies only when the unincorporated association is a defendant or whether a plaintiff association in a diversity case can sue in any district in which it does business. The better view appears to be that an unincorporated association or partnership does not have a residence for purposes of laying venue if the association is the plaintiff.

4. Aliens

The rule of venue for suits against an alien is simple: an alien may be sued in any district. 28 U.S.C. § 1391(d). This is true for foreign corporations as well as individuals.

Since aliens have no "residence" in any district for venue purposes, they cannot lay venue with reference to their own residence in diversity cases, even if they are domiciled in a particular district. They must sue either where all defendants reside or where the claim arose. *Brunett Machine Works, Ltd. v. Kockum Industries, Inc.*, 406 U.S. 706 (1972).

One particular class of aliens—foreign states—are treated specially under the general venue statute. A civil action against a foreign state may be brought (i) in any judicial district in which a substantial part of the events or omissions giving rise to the claim occurred, or where a substantial part of the property that is the subject of the action is situated; (ii) in any judicial district in which the vessel or cargo of a foreign state is situated, if the claim is in admiralty; (iii) in any district in which an agency or instrumentality of the foreign state is licensed to do business or is doing business if the action is brought against such agency or instrumentality (for example: a separately incorporated national tourist board of a foreign state); or (iv) in the District of Columbia. 28 U.S.C. § 1391(f).

5. The United States

The United States has no residence. Thus, in the absence of a special venue statute, a suit brought by the United States must be brought where all defendants reside or where the claim arose.

Suits brought against the United States are governed by a special venue statute. 28 U.S.C. § 1402. Actions against the United States other than tort actions can only be brought where the plaintiff resides. 28 U.S.C. § 1402(a). Since aliens have no residence, they may only sue the United States in the Court of Claims. Tort actions against the United States may be brought where the plaintiff resides or where the act or omission complained of occurred. 28 U.S.C. § 1402(b).

Except as otherwise provided by law, federal officers and agents who are sued in their official capacities may be sued (1) in the district in which they perform their official duties, (2) in any district where the cause of action arose, (3) in any district in which real property involved in the action is situated, or (4) in the district in which any plaintiff resides if no real property is involved in the action. 28 U.S.C. § 1391(e). These general provisions are overridden by special venue statutes that provide for other forums in particular actions against government officials. For these rules to apply, the defendant must be an employee of the executive branch as of the date the action is brought. Employees of the legislature are not encompassed by this statute. *Liberation News Service v. Eastland*, 426 F.2d 1379, 1384 (2d Cir. 1970).

6. Special Rules for Residence

a. Class Actions

In class actions, the court looks only to the residence of the named parties to determine the propriety of venue. *U.S. ex rel. Sero v. Preiser*, 506 F.2d 1115, 1129 (2d Cir. 1974), *cert. denied*, 421 U.S. 921 (1975).

b. Shareholder Derivative Suits

Although the corporation on whose behalf a derivative suit is brought is always named as a defendant, the corporation's residence is not considered in determining where "all defendants reside" for venue purposes. This is but a variant on the rule that the residence of nominal or sham parties will not be considered in laying venue.

c. Subsequently Added Parties

The propriety of venue is determined at the time the original complaint is filed. Adding parties at a later date will neither create nor defeat proper venue.

7. How Judicial Divisions and Multiple Districts within a State Affect the Concept of "Judicial District"

A number of states contain several judicial districts. A non-local civil action against multiple defendants who reside in different judicial districts of the same state may be brought in any district where one defendant resides, 28 U.S.C. § 1392(a), and local civil actions involving property that is located in different districts of the same state may be brought in any district where a portion of the subject property lies. 28 U.S.C. § 1392(b).

In many states, judicial districts are further subdivided into divisions. The Judicial Improvements and Access to Justice Act of 1988 repealed 28 U.S.C. § 1393 which provides that civil actions against a single defendant in a district containing more than one division must be brought in the division where the defendant resides, and that actions brought against two or more defendants who reside in different divisions within a district, or different districts in the same state, may be brought in the division where any one of them resides.

B. How to Determine Where the Claim Arose

As noted above, the concept of laying venue where the claim arose was added to the general venue statute to avoid a "venue gap" in multi-party cases—i.e., the inability to sue anywhere because there was no district where all defendants (or, in a diversity case, all plaintiffs) resided.

As with all other venue-related questions, determining where the claim arose is governed by federal law. *Jaffe v. Dolan*, 264 F. Supp. 845, 848 (E.D.N.Y. 1967). However, it is possible that a suit cannot be maintained in the district where the claim arose because one or more defendants cannot be served with process in that district. Plaintiffs must look to state law to determine whether a foreign defendant is amenable to process under the long-arm statute of the state where the claim arose. *See* Chapter 2.

For many years, there was considerable dispute about whether a claim could arise in more than one district. Some courts held that a literal reading of the phrase *"the* judicial *district* . . . where the claim arose" precluded such a result. Others, supported by respected commentators like the American Law Institute, thought that a claim arose in any district where "a substantial part of the events or omissions giving rise to the claim occurred. . . ." ALI, *Study of the Division of Jurisdiction between State and Federal Courts*, Official Draft 1969, §§ 1301(a)(1), 1314(a)(1) and 1326(a)(1).

In 1979, the United States Supreme Court finally addressed the question. In *Leroy v. Great Western United Corp.*, 443 U.S. 173, the Supreme Court decided that a plaintiff did not have unfettered discretion to bring suit in any district that arguably had some contact with the matter. While the court refused to decide whether a claim could only arise in one district (although Justice Stevens called that an "occasionally fictive assumption"), it did rule that

> the broadest interpretation of the language of § 1391(b) that is even arguably acceptable is that in the unusual case in which it is not clear that the claim arose in only one specific district, a plaintiff may choose between those two (or conceivably even more) districts that with approximately equal plausibility—in terms of the availability of witnesses, the accessibility of other relevant evidence, and the convenience of the defendant (but *not* of the plaintiff) may be assigned as the lower of the claim.

Thus, the Court ruled that only in those unusual cases where two or more districts have approximately equal contact with the matter could a claim be said to arise in more than one district, that the convenience of litigants and witnesses is paramount in evaluating the contacts question, and that, in close cases, the convenience of the defendant outweighs that of the plaintiff.

Leroy gives plaintiffs little guidance in determining where the claim arose. In tort cases, the place where the injury is suffered is often thought to be where the claim arose, but if the activities giving rise to the injury occurred outside that judicial district, it would seem that venue more properly lies in the place where the activities took place. (That, in fact, was the result in *Leroy*.) In contract cases, courts often look to the place where negotiations took place or where performance occurred—tests that seem more suitable given the type of analysis stressed in *Leroy*. Only one thing is clear: where the claim arose will be decided on a case-by-case basis.

C. Special Venue Statutes

As noted above, venue cannot always be determined with reference to 28 U.S.C. § 1391. There are many specific or special venue statutes, some of which are found in Title 28 of the United States Code and some of which are found in the particular substantive laws to which they relate. While special venue provisions often supersede the general statute, the provisions of

§ 1391 may supplement special venue provisions in special cases. In those instances, one may lay venue with reference to either the special or the general statute. For example, the definition of a corporation's "residence" contained in the general venue statute has been held to supplement the reference to residence in the venue provision of the Jones Act, 46 U.S.C. § 688; therefore, in a Jones Act case, the plaintiff can lay venue in accordance with either statute. *Pure Oil Co. v. Suarez*, 384 U.S. 202 (1966). But where Congress has specifically indicated that it intended a special venue statute to be read restrictively—for example, in patent infringement cases—general venue provisions (such as the definition of a corporation's "residence") do not supplement the special statute. *Fourco Glass Co. v. Transmirra Products Corp.*, 353 U.S. 222 (1957). Regrettably, in most cases one can only guess whether Congress intended that a special venue statute be read restrictively or broadly.

Some examples of special venue statutes:

1. Local Actions Involving the United States

Under 28 U.S.C. § 1403, eminent domain actions brought by the United States must be commenced in the judicial district where the land is located. The same is true of a partition action involving the United States. 28 U.S.C. § 1399. These rules, while statutory, are but an extension of the rule that local actions must be brought in the judicial district where the *res* is located.

2. Actions Against National Banks

Historically all actions against national banks had to be brought in the district where the bank was "established" or "located"—i.e., the site of its principal place of business. 12 U.S.C. § 94. However, in 1982, that special venue provision was restricted to suits brought against banks under FDIC receivership. All other actions against national banks, as well as all actions brought by national banks, may be brought pursuant to the general venue statute.

3. Admiralty Actions

That admiralty actions are not "civil actions" is an enduring legal fiction. Over the years, admiralty cases have developed their own relatively liberal venue rules. An admiralty action (a "libel") may be brought as follows:

— if jurisdiction is *in rem*, in any district where the ship can be attached

— if jurisdiction is *in personam*, wherever the ship is, or, if it is not within any district, wherever valid service can be made on the defendant. Supplemental Civil Rule F(9).

4. Copyright and Patent Infringement Actions

Pursuant to 28 U.S.C. § 1400(a), actions arising under the copyright laws may be brought wherever the defendant or his agent resides or may be "found"—i.e., where they may be served with process.

Pursuant to 28 U.S.C. § 1400(b), patent infringement actions may be brought in any judicial district where the defendant resides (in case of a corporation, this is *only* the state of incorporation), or where the defendant has committed infringement and has a regular and established place of business. The "regular and established place of business" rule means more than merely doing business in the district; it requires that the defendant maintain a permanent physical location under its control in that district.

All other actions arising under the patent laws are governed by the general venue statutes.

5. Jones Act Actions

Suits under the Jones Act must be brought where the defendant resides or has its principal place of business. 46 U.S.C. § 688.

6. Securities Actions

Suits brought under the Securities Exchange Act of 1934 may be brought in any district where the challenged transaction occurred or where the defendant is an inhabitant, transacts business or may be found (i.e., can be served). 15 U.S.C. § 78aa.

7. Antitrust Actions

Suits brought under either the Sherman or Clayton Acts may be brought in any district where the defendant resides, is found (i.e., can be served) or has an agent. Corporate defendants may be sued in any district in which they transact business, are inhabitants or may be found. 15 U.S.C. §§ 15, 22.

8. Employment Discrimination Actions

Suits brought under Title VII may be prosecuted where the challenged employment practice was committed, where the relevant records are maintained or where the plaintiff would have been employed in the absence of any discrimination, if the defendant can be found (i.e., served) in such districts. Otherwise, suit must be brought in the district where defendant's principal office is located. 29 U.S.C. § 2000e-5(f)(3).

9. ERISA Actions

Suits brought under the Employee Retirement Income Security Act of 1974 must be brought in the district where the pension plan is administered,

VENUE

where the breach of trust took place, or anywhere the defendant resides or may be found (i.e., can be served). 29 U.S.C. § 1132(e)(2).

10. Collective Bargaining Agreements

Suits brought under collective bargaining agreements may be brought in any district court that has jurisdiction over the parties. 29 U.S.C. § 185(a).

11. Actions Against the Internal Revenue Service

Civil actions for the collection of taxes may be brought in the district where the liability for the tax accrued, where the taxpayer resides or where the return was filed. 28 U.S.C. § 1396.

12. Interpleader

Suits in interpleader may be brought in the district where any one claimant resides. 28 U.S.C. § 1397.

13. Stockholder Derivative Suits

Derivative suits may be prosecuted in any judicial district where the corporation might have sued the same defendants. 28 U.S.C. § 1401.

14. Cases Removed From State Courts

In cases that are removed from state courts under 28 U.S.C. § 1441, venue is always proper in the district to which the case is removed—even if the action could not have been filed in that district if it had originally been brought in a federal court. 28 U.S.C. § 1441(a); *Polizzi v. Cowles Magazine, Inc.*, 345 U.S. 663 (1953).

IV. OBJECTIONS TO VENUE—MOTIONS FOR TRANSFER OR DISMISSAL

Once the plaintiff has chosen a forum and commenced an action, objections may be raised to the trial of the action in that forum. Where an action is brought "laying venue in a wrong division or district," 28 U.S.C. § 1406(a) empowers a court to, in its discretion, transfer or dismiss the action.

Where an action is brought in a district where venue is proper, but a more convenient forum exists, a motion may be made to transfer or dismiss the action. Where the more convenient forum is another federal court, 28 U.S.C. § 1404(a) provides for the transfer of the action to that court. If the alternative forum is a state court, or a court in a foreign state, the common law doctrine of *forum non conveniens* allows the action to be dismissed, so that it can be commenced in the more convenient forum.

A. Transfer for Improper Venue

If an action is brought in the wrong division or district, a party may make a motion to have the action dismissed, or, in the alternative, to have the case transferred to a proper venue. 28 U.S.C.A. § 1406(a) provides:

> The district court of a district in which is filed a case laying venue in the wrong division or district shall dismiss, or if it be in the interest of justice, transfer such case to any district or division in which it could have been brought.

When a case is brought in a district in which venue is improper and an alternative forum where the action may properly proceed is available, the "interest of justice" will generally favor transfer over dismissal. This is especially true where the statute of limitations has run on an action while it was pending in the improper forum. *See Burnett v. New York Cent. R.R. Co.*, 380 U.S. 424, 430 & n.7 (1965); *Goldlawn, Inc. v. Heiman*, 369 U.S. 463 (1962) (statute is an attempt to alleviate injustice that resulted to plaintiffs that had "made an erroneous guess with regard to the existence of some elusive fact of the kind upon which venue provisions often turn"); *Corke v. Sameiet M.S. Song of Norway*, 572 F.2d 77 (2d Cir. 1978). If venue is properly objected to under § 1406(a) the court must transfer or dismiss the action. The court will consider judicial economy and convenience of the parties and witnesses in determining whether to transfer or dismiss an action.

In order to avoid waiving his right to object to an improper venue, a defendant must make "timely and sufficient objection." 28 U.S.C.§ 1406(b).

Objections to venue may be raised by answer or by motion. Fed. R. Civ. P. 12(b). If a defendant neither moves to dismiss for improper venue and nor asserts the impropriety of venue as an affirmative defense in his answer, any objection will be waived. Fed. R. Civ. P. 12(h). Thus, it is incumbent on the defendant to object to venue at the earliest possible moment.

To transfer an action under § 1406(a), the district court must have subject matter jurisdiction. *Leroy v. Great Western United Corp.*, 443 U.S. 173 (1979). The transferor court need not have personal jurisdiction over defendant to transfer an action. *Goldlawn, Inc. v. Heiman*, 369 U.S. 463 (1962); *Corke v. Sameiet M.S. Song of Norway*, 572 F.2d 77 (2d Cir. 1978).

Under § 1406(a), an action may be transferred only to a district where "it might have been brought." Essentially, the statute requires the transferee court to have subject matter jurisdiction over the action, and to be a proper venue for the action, in which service of process may be obtained over defendant. *Hoffman v. Blaski*, 363 U.S. 335 (1960); *AT&T v. Milgo Electronic Corp.*, 428 F. Supp. 50 (S.D.N.Y. 1977).

In addition to the power to transfer actions brought in a wrong district or division, § 1406(a) gives courts the power to dismiss such actions. Because dismissal is a somewhat harsh penalty, it is generally reserved for cases where a plaintiff has brought an action in bad faith. For example, a plaintiff would not be allowed to "backdoor" a defendant by bringing an action in an improper venue to obtain personal jurisdiction, and then transferring the action to a district where personal jurisdiction could not originally have been obtained. Such a result would not be in the interest of justice. *See Hoffman v. Blaski*, 363 U.S. 335 (1960); *Harry Rich Corp. v. Curtiss-Wright Corp.*, 308 F. Supp. 1114 (S.D.N.Y. 1969); *Foster-Milburn Co. v. Knight*, 181 F.2d 949 (2d Cir. 1950).

When an action is transferred pursuant to a § 1406(a) motion, the transferee court will apply the law of the state in which it sits, since the transferor court was not a proper forum.

A court's decision granting or denying a motion to transfer an action under § 1406(a) is interlocutory, and thus not immediately appealable. Under certain, very narrow, circumstances set forth in 28 U.S.C. § 1292(b), a permissive appeal is available. In addition, in exceptional cases, writs of mandamus and prohibition are available. *See A. Olinick & Sons v. Demster Bros.*, 365 F.2d 439 (2d Cir. 1966).

B. Transfer for Convenience

Where an action is brought in a proper district or division, a federal district court may nonetheless transfer the case to another forum. 28 U.S.C. § 1404(a) provides:

> (a) For the convenience of the parties and witnesses, in the interest of justice, a district court may transfer any civil action to any other district or division where it might have been brought.

A motion to transfer for convenience is to be made in the district court in which the action is pending and may be made by either the plaintiff or the defendant. The seminal discussion of transfer of venue under § 1404(a) in this circuit is Judge Weinfeld's opinion in *Schneider v. Sears*, 265 F. Supp. 257 (S.D.N.Y. 1967).

Generally, it is the defendant who moves for transfer. A plaintiff would probably have to show changed circumstances to prevail on a motion for transfer from the forum initially chosen. The court need not have personal jurisdiction over the defendant to enter a transfer order. However, subject matter jurisdiction would probably be required to bind defendant. *See Leroy v. Great Western United Corp.*, 443 U.S. 173 (1979).

The language in the statute, "any civil action," means just what it says. Section 1404(a), if otherwise applicable, applies to all civil actions, regardless of which venue statute they arise under. *Ex Parte Collett*, 337 U.S. 55 (1949).

Unlike an objection to improper venue, a motion to transfer for convenience may be made at any time. However, unnecessary delay will weigh against transfer. *See Pesin v. Goldman, Sachs & Co.*, 397 F. Supp. 92 (S.D.N.Y. 1975).

The decision to deny or grant a motion to transfer is entirely within the discretion of the trial judge. However, a necessary precondition to any transfer is the existence of an alternative forum where the action "might have been brought." 28 U.S.C. § 1406(a). While there had been some confusion as to where an action "might have been brought," and consequently could be transferred to, it is now clear that transfer can be only to a court with subject matter jurisdiction over the action in question, where venue is proper, and where the power to issue process over the defendant is available. *See Hoffman v. Blaski*, 363 U.S. 335 (1960); *Foster-Milburn Co. v. Knight*, 181 F.2d 949 (2d Cir. 1950). *See also AT&T v. Milgo Electronic Corp.*, 428 F. Supp. 50 (S.D.N.Y. 1977).

Assuming the above conditions exist, the court will then decide whether transfer of the action is mandated by the convenience of the parties and witnesses and whether such transfer is in the "interest of justice." *See generally Heyco, Inc. v. Heyman*, 636 F. Supp. 1545, 1548-51 (S.D.N.Y. 1986). Specific factors considered by a court in deciding a § 1404(a) motion include:

1. Relative ease of access to sources of proof. *See Y^4 Design, Ltd. v. Regensteiner Publishing Enterprises, Inc.*, 428 F. Supp. 1067 (S.D.N.Y. 1977).

2. Availability of process to compel presence of reluctant witnesses and the cost of obtaining the presence of willing witnesses. *See Vaughn v. American Basketball Ass'n*, 419 F. Supp. 1274 (S.D.N.Y. 1976) (it is the importance of the witness and the proposed testimony, not the number of witnesses, that controls). *See also Castillo v. Shipping Corp. of India*, 606 F. Supp. 497 (S.D.N.Y. 1985).

3. Calendar congestion. *See Foster v. Litton Industries*, 431 F. Supp. 86 (S.D.N.Y. 1977).

4. Ability of defendant to implead necessary third party in transferred district. *See Vasallo v. Neidermeyer*, 495 F. Supp. 757 (S.D.N.Y. 1980).

5. The ability to consolidate the action with a closely related action. *See Pesin v. Goldman, Sachs & Co.*, 397 F. Supp. 392 (S.D.N.Y. 1975); *Unico Industrial Corp. v. S.S. Andros City*, 323 F. Supp. 896 (S.D.N.Y. 1971).

6. The desirability of having cases decided by a court familiar with the substantive law to be applied in the case. *See Heyco, Inc. v. Heyman*, 636 F. Supp. 1545, 1550 (S.D.N.Y. 1986); *Kreisner v. Hilton Hotel Corp.*, 468 F. Supp. 176 (E.D.N.Y. 1979).

The party seeking to transfer an action under § 1404(a) has the burden of making a clear showing that the above factors militate in favor of a change in venue. *See Factors, Etc., Inc. v. Pro Arts, Inc.*, 579 F.2d 215 (2d Cir. 1978), *cert. denied*, 440 U.S. 908 (1979). The motion for transfer should include detailed fact statements that support the factors listed above. *See Riso Kagaku Corp. v. A.B. Dick Co.*, 300 F. Supp. 1007 (S.D.N.Y. 1969). Where grounds for change of venue include the convenience of witnesses, movant should provide precise information, in affidavit form, about witnesses to be called and the anticipated areas of their testimony. *See Saminsky v. Occidental Petroleum Corp.*, 373 F. Supp. 257 (S.D.N.Y. 1974).

Where the parties to an action have entered into an agreement providing that disputes will be litigated in a certain forum, the enforcement of such a forum selection clause must be accomplished within the constraints of § 1404(a). Thus, as noted earlier, an action might be transferred from the agreed upon forum, despite a forum selection clause, if the convenience of parties or witnesses and the interest of justice so required. However, forum selection clauses are probably determinative as to the convenience of the *parties*. *See General Electric Credit Corp. v. Toups*, 644 F. Supp. 11 (S.D.N.Y. 1985). As recently stated by the Supreme Court, forum selection clauses are to be given "neither dispositive consideration nor no consideration," in the court's decision. *Stewart Organization, Inc. v. Ricoh*, 108 S. Ct. 2239, 2245 (1988).

A denial of a motion to transfer under § 1404(a) is not immediately appealable, except under the very limited circumstances permitted by 28 U.S.C.A. § 1292(b). Writs of mandamus and prohibition are available in a proper case. *See A. Olinick & Sons v. Dempster Bros.*, 365 F.2d 439 (2d Cir. 1966). Mandamus review is conducted pursuant to the "clearly erroneous" standard. *Id*.

Following the transfer of an action under § 1404(a) the transferor court loses all jurisdiction over the case. For claims based on state law, the transferee court must continue to apply the law of the transferor state, at least where the motion to transfer is made by the defendant. *VanDusen v. Barrack*, 376 U.S. 612 (1964). The theory behind this rule is that a change in courtrooms simply for the convenience of witnesses and parties should not change the substantive law that applies to the case. It remains unsettled which district's law will apply when the plaintiff has successfully moved for transfer. *See VanDusen v. Barrack*, 376 U.S. 612, 640 (1964).

C. *Forum Non Conveniens*

In the leading case on the common law doctrine of *forum non conveniens, Gulf Oil Corp. v. Gilbert*, 330 U.S. 501 (1947), the Supreme Court affirmed the dismissal by a New York district court of a tort action which arose out of events that took place in Virginia. Technically, New York was a proper venue in which to bring the action, but many of the witnesses and much of the evidence was in Virginia. Mr. Justice Jackson, writing for the court, noted:

> The principle of *forum non conveniens* is simply that a court may resist imposition upon its jurisdiction even when jurisdiction is authorized by the letter of a general venue statute.

Id. at 507.

The application of the common law doctrine of *forum non conveniens* has been greatly restricted in federal court by the implementation of the transfer statutes, § 1404(a) and § 1406(a). Nonetheless, where the federal court in which an action is brought is an inconvenient forum, and the more convenient forum is not one the federal court could transfer to, i.e., the appropriate forum is a state court or the court of a foreign state, dismissal on the ground of *forum non conveniens* may be the proper action.

Dismissal under the doctrine of *forum non conveniens* requires the existence of an alternative forum. This alternative forum need not be a forum where the action "might have been brought." In a motion for dismissal under *forum non conveniens*, it is irrelevant whether an alternative forum existed at the time the action was brought. As long as jurisdiction over all parties can be obtained in the alternative forum at the time of the motion to dismiss, the alternative forum requirement is met. *Schertenleib v. Traum*, 589 F.2d 1156 (2d Cir. 1978).

Less favorable treatment for the plaintiff under the substantive law of the alternative forum does not preclude dismissal, assuming that plaintiff will not be "deprived of any remedy [at all] or treated unfairly." *Piper Aircraft Co. v. Reyno*, 454 U.S. 235, 255 (1981); *see also In re Union Carbide Corp. Gas Plant Disaster*, 809 F.2d 195 (2d Cir. 1987).

The burden of proving that a case should be dismissed when *forum non conveniens* is applicable rests with the defendant. The court will give substantial weight to plaintiff's choice of forum. *See Gulf Oil Co. v. Gilbert*, 330 U.S. at 508; *Overseas Programming Companies, Ltd. v. Cinematographische Commerz-Anstalt*, 684 F.2d 232 (2d Cir. 1982); *Ford Motor Co. v. Ryan*, 182 F.2d 329, 330 (2d Cir.), *cert. denied*, 340 U.S. 851 (1950). However, the presumption in favor of plaintiff's forum choice is less strong where

VENUE

plaintiff is not a resident of the United States. *See Piper Aircraft Co. v. Reyno*, 454 U.S. 235 (1981); *In re Union Carbide Corp. Gas Plant Disaster*, 809 F.2d 195 (2d Cir. 1987).

The factors a New York federal court will consider in deciding whether or not to dismiss a motion on *forum non conveniens* grounds are essentially those set forth in *Gulf Oil v. Gilbert*. The inquiry focuses on the same public and private interests that are considered in a § 1404(a) motion to transfer. *See* p. 73. However, a greater showing of inconvenience is required to have a case dismissed.

The grant of a motion to dismiss on *forum non conveniens* grounds should be accompanied by conditions to be imposed on the defendant in order to preserve the viability of the action in the alternate forum. For example, a dismissal order may require defendant to subject himself to personal jurisdiction in another forum or to waive any statute of limitations defenses he might have raised. *See In re Union Carbide Corp. Gas Plant Disaster*, 809 F.2d 195 (2d Cir. 1987). Note, however, that the Second Circuit recently struck down district court imposed conditions that (1) required defendant to consent to enforcement in the United States of an Indian judgment against it, and (2) required defendant to be subject to discovery under the Federal Rules of Civil Procedure while not requiring the same of the plaintiff. *Id.*

In the Second Circuit, an order denying a motion to dismiss on *forum non conveniens* grounds is considered interlocutory and thus is not immediately appealable. *Carlenstolpe v. Merck & Co.*, 819 F.2d 33 (2d Cir. 1987). The United States Supreme Court recently adopted the Second Circuit's approach. *See Van Cauwenberghe v. Biard*, 108 S. Ct. 1945 (1988). Where the district court has considered the appropriate factors in ruling on the motion, mandamus will issue only upon a showing of clear-cut abuse of discretion. *Carlenstolpe*, 819 F.2d at 35.

Dismissal of an action on *forum non conveniens* grounds is a final judgment and may be appealed. The Second Circuit standard of review on appeal requires a "clear showing of an abuse of discretion" by the district court. *Maria Victoria Naviera, S.A. v. Cementos Del Valle*, 759 F.2d 1027 (2d Cir. 1985) (Timbers, J.).

CHAPTER FOUR

REMOVAL

by Honorable Sharon E. Grubin
Deborah E. Lans, Esq.*

I. OVERVIEW

"Removal" simply refers to the process whereby an action commenced in a state court is transferred by a defendant into a federal district court. Congress has expressly provided by statute that defendants may remove certain cases from state courts to federal courts and thereby override a plaintiff's choice of forum. Sections 1441-1445 of Title 28 of the Unites States Code define the right to remove, and Sections 1446-1450 set forth the procedures to follow in removing the case and after removal. Other federal statutes expand or limit the basic removal right in specified circumstances. This chapter will discuss both the removal jurisdiction of the federal courts and the procedures for removal. We will also point out some of the practical and strategic aspects of removal.

The procedures for removal are generally quite simple. If the case is one that meets the criteria of the statute, the defendant simply, in effect, refiles the state action in the federal district court by means of a pleading known as a "notice of removal," and the defendant notifies the plaintiff and the state court of the removal. The state court is then automatically divested of the case. It is to be noted that what is removed is the entire action, not issues or separate claims.

The Constitiution vests Congress with the inherent power to prescribe the jurisdiction of the federal courts. The removal statutes have been passed pursuant to that inherent power, and thus the federal courts apply federal law

---

* The valuable assistance of Jill Israeloff, currently a student in the Harvard Law School, in the preparation of the chapter is gratefully acknowledged.

when determining removability. *Shamrock Oil & Gas Corp. v. Sheets*, 313 U.S. 100 (1941). For the last century, these statutes have been strictly construed against expanding the removal right, as a result of the Supreme Court's view of Congress' intention to limit the jurisdiction of the federal courts. *American Fire & Casualty Co. v. Finn*, 341 U.S. 6, 9-10 (1951). Because removal is a federal right, a state cannot restrict the right to remove a case. The federal courts will, however, enforce the parties' elimination of the right by a forum selection clause in a contract. *See M/S Bremen v. Zapata Off-Shore Co.*, 407 U.S. 1011 (1972). A plaintiff cannot thwart the removal of a case which meets the statutory criteria. A plaintiff's only remedy is to challenge removal in those cases where it may have been improper by making a motion to the federal court to remand the case. *See* Section VI, below.

II. WHAT ACTIONS MAY BE REMOVED: 28 U.S.C. § 1441

Section 1441 sets out the principal grounds for removal. It provides:

(a) Except as otherwise expressly provided by Act of Congress, any civil action brought in a State court of which the district courts of the United States have original jurisdiction, may be removed by the defendant or the defendants, to the district court of the United States for the district and division embracing the place where such action is pending. For the purposes of removal under this chapter, the citizenship of defendants sued under fictitious names shall be disregarded.

(b) Any civil action of which the district courts have original jurisdiction founded on a claim or right arising under the Constitution, treaties or laws of the United States shall be removable without regard to the citizenship or residence of the parties. Any other such action shall be removable only if none of the parties in interest properly joined and served as defendants is a citizen of the State in which such action is brought.

(c) Whenever a separate and independent claim or cause of action, which would be removable if sued upon alone, is joined with one or more otherwise non-removable claims or causes of action, the entire case may be removed and the district court may determine all issues therein, or, in its discretion, may remand all matters not otherwise within its original jurisdiction.

(d) Any civil action brought in a State court against a foreign state as defined in Section 1603(a) of this title may be removed by the foreign state to the district court of the United States for the district and division embracing the place where such action is pending. Upon removal the action shall be tried by the Court without jury. Where removal is based upon this subsection, the time limitations of section 1446(b) of this chapter may be enlarged at any time for cause shown.

(e) The court to which such civil action is removed is not precluded from hearing and determining any claim in such civil action because the State court from which such civil action is removed did not have jurisdiction over that claim.

In a nutshell, any action which could have been brought in federal district court in the first place generally may be removed there, *i.e.*, a "federal question" or "diversity" case, except that if it is a diversity case it can only be removed if none of the defendants is a citizen of the state where the action has been brought.[1] As section 1441(a) states, generally only civil actions are removable.[2] A criminal, mandamus or administrative proceeding cannot be removed under section 1441(a) (although a statutory proceeding in state court to review an administrative decision is a "civil action" and thus is removable). *Range Oil Supply Co. v. Chicago, Rock Island & P.R. Co.*, 248 F.2d 477, 479 (8th Cir. 1957).

The federal court ultimately decides whether a proceeding is a "civil action." Suits which seek to vindicate a private, common law or statutory right and to redress a wrong in violation of such a right are "civil," not criminal, actions. Proceedings to compel arbitration or confirm or vacate an award are considered civil actions within the meaning of the statute. *Heifetz v. Tugendrajch*, 542 F. Supp. 1207, 1208 (S.D.N.Y. 1982); *Minkoff v. Budget Dress Corp.*, 180 F. Supp. 818, 822-23 (S.D.N.Y. 1960).[3]

Proceedings which are ancillary or supplementary to a state court action and inseparably connected with it cannot be removed. The distinction can be illustrated by the difference between a suit to enjoin a sale of land pursuant to an execution, which is not removable, *Lawrence v. Morgan's L.&T. R.R. &*

---

[1] Special provisions allow removal of cases which do not meet the "federal question" or "diversity" criteria, and other provisions limit the right to remove cases even though the cases are "federal question" or "diversity" ones. *See* Section III, below.

[2] Certain criminal prosecutions against federal officers or involving civil rights may be removed. *See* Section III.A.2. and 3. below.

[3] An arbitration proceeding is not a civil "action," however, unless a state court has been asked to participate in the proceeding, such as by a motion to compel or stay arbitration. *See, e.g., Davenport v. Proctor & Gamble Mfg. Co.*, 241 F.2d 511, 514 (2d Cir. 1957).

S.S. Co., 121 U.S. 634 (1887), and a garnishment proceeding against a third party which is generally considered an independent suit and, therefore, removable, *Butler v. Polk*, 592 F.2d 1293, 1295 (5th Cir. 1979). *See also Graef v. Graef*, 633 F. Supp. 450, 453 (E.D. Pa. 1986).

A. Federal Question Cases

Any case arising under the federal Constitution or a federal statute or treaty may be removed. The citizenship of the parties is irrelevant. Whether a case is a so-called federal question "is governed by the 'well-pleaded complaint rule,' which provides that federal jurisdiction exists only when a federal question is presented on the face of the plaintiff's properly pleaded complaint." *Caterpillar v. Williams*, 107 S. Ct. 2425, 2429 (1987). The complaint should establish "either that federal law creates the cause of action or that the plaintiff's right to relief necessarily depends on resolution of a substantial question of federal law." *Franchise Tax Bd. of Cal. v. Construction Laborers Vacation Trust for S. Cal.*, 463 U.S. 1, 27-28 (1983).

When removal is challenged, *see* Section VI, below, the federal court must examine the complaint as it existed at the time the removal petition was filed. *Great N. Ry. Co. v. Alexander*, 246 U.S. 276, 281 (1918). Thus, the federal question on which removal by the defendant is sought to be based cannot be an anticipated defense, part of the answer, cross-claim or counter-claim, or a cause of action on which a plaintiff could have, but did not, plead. *See, e.g., Pan American Petroleum Corp. v. Superior Court of Del.*, 366 U.S. 656, 663 (1961). If removal is challenged and the ground for removal is not apparent from the face of the complaint, the court may consult the removal petition, but only to "understand the real nature of the complaint rather than to add extraneous elements to it"[4] or to determine the federal status of the item at issue, such as a trademark or copyright if removal turns on a question of such federal status.[5]

The converse of this rule is also true. If the case necessarily will involve a federal question, it is removable, regardless of how the plaintiff has presented the claims in the complaint. Thus, a plaintiff may not defeat removal "by clothing a federal claim in state garb" by artful pleading. *Travelers Indemnity Co. v. Sarkisian*, 794 F.2d 754, 758 (2d Cir.), *cert. denied*, 107 S. Ct. 277 (1986). However, the plaintiff is master of the complaint and may rely on any law of its choosing. *The Fair v. Kohler Die & Specialty Co.*, 228

---

[4] *See, e.g., Puerto Rico v. Cordeco Dev. Corp.*, 534 F. Supp. 612, 617 (D.P.R. 1982).

[5] *See, e.g., Ulichny v. General Electric Co.*, 309 F. Supp. 437 (N.D.N.Y. 1970) (federal trademark). *Contra La Chemise Lacoste v. The Alligator Co.*, 506 F.2d 339 (3rd Cir. 1974), *cert. denied*, 421 U.S. 937, *reh'g denied*, 42 U.S. 1006 (1975) (declining to follow *Ulichny*).

U.S. 22, 25 (1913). Thus, if a cause of action can fairly be based either on state or federal law, the plaintiff may draft the complaint to assert only state law claims and thereby avoid federal removal jurisdiction. *Caterpillar Inc. v. Williams*, 107 S. Ct. 2424, 2429 (1987).[6]

B. Diversity Cases

Because § 1441(a) permits removal of any action over which the district courts have original jurisdiction, diversity actions can be removed, *i.e.*, actions in which defendants and plaintiffs have complete diversity of citizenship and the amount in controversy exceeds $10,000. However, unlike original diversity jurisdiction, removal of diversity cases is subject to the limitation expressed in § 1441(b) that a defendant cannot remove a case based on diversity if it or any of the other defendants is a citizen of the state in which the action is pending.[7] Congressional fear of bias against out-of-state defendants, one of the motivating policies behind the removal statutes, is eliminated if a defendant is sued in its home state. As a result, a plaintiff can avoid the possibility of removal by naming a citizen of the state in which the action is brought as a defendant. However, the courts will look behind a joinder, and a defendant who is "fraudulently," *i.e.*, improperly, joined need not be considered for purposes of diversity. *See, e.g., New York Shipping Ass'n v. Int'l Longshoremen's Ass'n, AFL-CIO*, 276 F. Supp. 51, 53 (S.D.N.Y. 1967) (a defendant is "fraudulently" joined if plaintiff does not really intend to obtain a judgment against that defendant).

The citizenship of individuals is based on domicile, not residence. A corporation is deemed a citizen of both its place of incorporation and its principal place of business. Unincorporated associations have no citizenship for diversity purposes. The citizenship of individual partners determines the

---

[6] The issue of the right to removal in situations involving federal pre-emption of state law was recently discussed by the Supreme Court in *Caterpillar Inc. v. Williams*, 107 S. Ct. 2425 (1987). As a general rule, if the area is one in which federal law has clearly pre-empted state law and the plaintiff's claim is exclusively governed by federal law so that federal law must be applied to the merits of the case, the case is removable. If, however, as will usually be the situation, pre-emption is really only a defense that a defendant may raise and argue in the state action, the action is not removable. Complete pre-emption has been found in actions involving § 301 of the Labor Management Relations Act of 1947, 29 U.S.C. § 185 (actions to enforce a collective bargaining agreement), and §§ 502(a)(1)(b) and 502(f) of the Employee Retirement Income Security Act of 1974, 29 U.S.C. § 1132 (contract and tort actions for denial of benefits under an employee benefit plan). *See Avco Corp. v. Aero Lodge No. 735, Int'l Ass'n of Machinists and Aerospace Workers*, 390 U.S. 557, *reh'g denied*, 391 U.S. 929 (1968) (LMRA § 301 pre-emption), and *Metropolitan Life Ins. Co. v. Taylor*, 481 U.S. 58 (1987) (ERISA § 502 pre-emption).

---

[7] The limitation applies only to defendants who have been properly joined and served. The naming of an unserved defendant in the caption of the action who resides in the forum therefore will not bar removal.

citizenship of a partnership.[8] A nominal party's presence can be ignored. *Salem Trust Co. v. Manufacturers' Finance Co.*, 264 U.S. 182, 189 (1924).[9]

Diversity must have been complete both at the time the state court action was commenced and at the time the notice of removal is filed. *Stevens v. Nichols*, 130 U.S. 230, 231 (1889).[10] However, if a plaintiff voluntarily dismisses a non-diverse defendant, removal is permitted even though diversity did not exist when the action was commenced.[11] *Powers v. Chesapeake & O. Ry. Co.*, 169 U.S. 92, 98 (1898). However, section 1441 was amended in 1988 to provide that "a case may not be removed on the basis of jurisdiction conferred by section 1332 of this title more than 1 year after commencement of the action."

Traditionally, a plaintiff could not force a remand by joining a non-indispensable, diversity-destroying defendant after removal because of the general rule that "[w]here a case has been properly removed, jurisdiction over it will not be defeated by later changes or developments in the suit, such as changes in citizenship, [or] in parties." *Southern P. Co. v. Haight*, 126 F.2d 900, 903 (9th Cir.), *cert. denied*, 317 U.S. 676 (1942).[12] However, in 1988, section 1447 was amended to provide: "If after removal the plaintiff seeks to join additional defendants whose joinder would destroy subject matter jurisdiciton, the court may deny joinder, or permit joinder and remand the action to State court."

Prior to 1988, difficult questions arose when "John Doe" defendants were joined but not sufficiently identified so that citizenship could be ascertained. Utilization of Doe defendants is disfavored by the federal courts, and some

---

8 In *Colonial Realty Corp. v. Bache & Co.*, 358 F.2d 178 (2d Cir.), *cert. denied*, 385 U.S. 817 (1966), the Second Circuit held that unnamed limited partners were not to be considered for purposes of citizenship of the partnership.

9 A party is nominal if no claim is or could be stated by it or against it based on the substantive law of the state where the federal courts sits. *Saxe, Bacon & Bolan, P.C. v. Martindale-Hubbell, Inc.*, 521 F. Supp. 1046 (S.D.N.Y. 1981). The burden of proving the nominal nature of the non-diverse party is on the removing party. *Id.*

10 This rule is intended to prevent a defendant from changing residence after commencement of the suit in order to remove the action.

11 By contrast, however, an involuntary dismissal of a non-diverse defendant by the state court (by, for example, grant of a motion to dismiss) does not make an action removable, at least until the time to appeal has run, because otherwise there is the risk that if the dismissal is reversed and the non-diverse defendant rejoined, lack of complete diversity will again be present. *Quinn v. Aetna Life & Casualty Co.*, 616 F.2d 38, 40 n.2 (2d Cir. 1980).

12 However, if jurisdiction is based solely on diversity, joinder of an indispensible, non-diverse party will compel a remand. *Encoder Communications, Inc. v. Telegen, Inc.*, 654 F.2d 198, 203 (2d Cir. 1981).

courts have held that Doe defendants are not permitted in a diversity complaint. *See Applegate v. Top Assocs., Inc.*, 300 F. Supp. 51 (S.D.N.Y. 1969, Weinfeld, J.), *aff'd*, 425 F.2d 92 (2d Cir. 1970). Where a fictitious defendant's joinder is permitted and such joinder is not merely nominal or fraudulent, some courts held that a defendant's failure to affirmatively show diversity between plaintiff and the Doe defendant would defeat removal. *See, e.g., Pecherski v. General Motors Corp.*, 636 F.2d 1156, 1160 (8th Cir. 1981). The Ninth Circuit, in *Bryant v. Ford Motor Co.*, 844 F.2d 602, 605-06 (9th Cir. 1987) (en banc), *cert. granted sub nom. Ford Motor Co. v. Bryant*, 109 S. Ct. 54 (Oct. 4, 1988), *cert. denied as moot Ford Motor Co. v. Bryant*, ___ S. Ct. ___ ( ), held that the naming of any Doe defendants will preclude removal of a diversity action until all Doe defendants are either named, unequivocally abandoned by the plaintiff or dismissed by the state court. That decision relied on a California civil practice rule allowing a plaintiff three years from the commencement of an action to discover the identity of Doe defendants, amend the complaint accordingly and effect service. In the very recent decision in *Block v. First Blood Assocs.*, 691 F. Supp. 685 (S.D.N.Y. 1988), a district judge allowed removal in a Doe case, rejecting the *Bryant* rule.[13] The problem has been resolved by Congress. In 1988, section 1441(a) was amended to provide: "For the purposes of removal . . ., the citizenship of defendants sued under fictitious names shall be disregarded."

No special rules apply for removal jurisdiction concerning the requirement of an amount in controversy. Thus, the claim must exceed $50,000, exclusive of interest and costs. This requirement pertains only to a case wherein federal jurisdiction is based on diversity of citizenship. *See* 28 U.S.C. § 1332. This jurisdictional amount is determined from the plaintiff's complaint at the time the petition for removal is filed by the defendant. *St. Paul Mercury Indemnity Co. v. Red Cab Co.*, 303 U.S. 283, 291 (1938).[14] The removing defendant has the burden of pleading that the amount exceeds $50,000. *McNutt v. General Motors Acceptance Corp.*, 298 U.S. 178, 189 (1936). Class action claims cannot be aggregated in order to meet the juris-

---

[13] The court reasoned, first, that the state procedural rule for joinder of Doe defendants is pre-empted by the Federal Rules of Civil Procedure; second, that the rules for removal should be nationwide and uniform and, therefore, not dependent on state procedures; and, third, that a district court in New York is not bound by a Ninth Circuit ruling.

[14] However, there is some authority that where a counterclaim is compulsory under state practice, and the amount involved in the counterclaim is over $50,000 although the plaintiff's original claim was less, the removing defendant may utilize its counterclaim for purposes of satisfying the requirement because otherwise a plaintiff with a small claim, who is subject to a large counterclaim, could race to state court to deprive defendant of access to the federal court. *See National Upholstery Co. v. Corley*, 144 F. Supp. 658 (M.D.N.C. 1956); *Lange v. Chicago, R.I. & P.R. Co.*, 99 F. Supp. 1 (S.D. Iowa 1951).

dictional amount; each plaintiff's share of the potential recovery must fulfill the requirement. *Zahn v. International Paper Co.*, 414 U.S. 291, 301 (1973). Later reduction of a claim by amendment does not require remand, nor does the inability of the plaintiff to recover the stated amount, as long as the plaintiff did not act in bad faith in seeking a high damage award. *See St. Paul*, 303 U.S. 283.

C. Separate and Independent Claims

Where an action is brought asserting both removable and nonremovable claims or causes of action, the entire action may be removed under § 1441(c). The federal district court then has the discretion to determine all the issues presented or to remand those claims not within its original jurisdiction to the state court.

Section 1441(c) requires, however, that the removable claim be "separate and independent" from the nonremovable claims for removal to be permitted. If a sole plaintiff sues multiple defendants alleging a single wrong that arose from a series of related transactions, the claims are not separate, and removal will not be permitted. In *American Fire & Casualty Co. v. Finn*, 341 U.S. 6 (1951), the Supreme Court gave a restrictive interpretation to the "separate and independent claim or cause of action" language in the statute. Plaintiff, a Texan, sued two out-of-state insurers and their Texas insurance broker in a Texas state court to recover for a fire loss. Plaintiff's complaint pleaded in separate claims that the diverse insurers were liable on policies they issued, or, in the alternative, that the nondiverse Texas broker was liable to the plaintiff for failing to obtain proper coverage. The insurers removed. The Supreme Court ruled that there was no removal jurisdiction because "where there is a single wrong to plaintiff [failure to pay compensation for the loss] for which relief is sought, arising from an interlocked series of transactions, there is no separate and independent claim or cause of action under § 1441(c)." *Id.* at 14. Thus, a cause of action brought against a diverse defendant will permit removal only if it is wholly separate from the claims against nondiverse defendants.[15] Because most state rules do not allow joinder of claims unless there is a common question of law or fact,[16] under *Finn* there will exist few diversity cases where removal will be proper under

---

15 For example, if in *Finn* plaintiff had added a claim against one of the out-of-state insurers arising under a different policy and related to a different loss from that which was the subject of the property claims, removal would have been permissible. *See Breslerman v. American Liberty Ins. Co.*, 169 F. Supp. 531 (E.D.N.Y. 1959). The Second Circuit, however, strictly construes § 1441(c). *See Gardner and Florence Call Cowles Found. v. Empire, Inc.*, 754 F.2d 478 (2d Cir. 1985).

16 *See* N.Y. C.P.L.R. § 1002(a) and (b) permitting joinder where claims arise "out of the same transaction, occurrence, or series of transactions or occurrences. . . ."

§ 1441(c). If multiple plaintiffs sue one defendant and each asserts separate and independant damage claims arising from a single wrong, the claims are considered separate even though a common question of law or fact is involved. *Stokes v. Merrill, Lynch, Pierce, Fenner & Smith, Inc.*, 523 F.2d 433, 438 (6th Cir. 1975).

A case may not be removed if the claim on which removal is purportedly based is collateral or incidental to the central claim. *See, e.g.*, *Eisenhardt v. Coastal Indus., Inc.*, 324 F. Supp. 550 (M.D. Pa. 1971). Although the Supreme Court has not yet decided whether third-party claims, cross-claims and counterclaims are removable under § 1441(c), the majority of lower court cases have concluded that they are not.[17] Although there is some authority that to avoid an unjust result, a defendant can remove an otherwise nonremovable state action based on a compulsory counterclaim which is within the exclusive federal jurisdiction,[18] district courts in the Second Circuit and the weight of authority elsewhere prohibit removal in such circumstances. *See, e.g.*, *Harris v. G.C. Servs. Corp.*, 651 F. Supp. 1417 (S.D.N.Y. 1987); *White v. Hughes*, 409 F. Supp. 1005 (W.D. Tenn. 1975); *Sequoyah Feed & Supply Co. v. Robinson*, 101 F. Supp. 680 (W.D. Ark. 1951). *See also Shamrock Oil & Gas Corp. v. Sheets*, 313 U.S. 100, 107-08 (1941) (a "plaintiff" who is a "defendant" on a counterclaim is not a defendant for purposes of removal).

As should be clear from the foregoing, when a case is removed under § 1441(c), all of the causes of action go to the federal district court, whether or not they would have been within the district court's original jurisdiction. *See, e.g.*, *Breslerman v. American Liberty Ins. Co.*, 169 F. Supp. 531 (E.D.N.Y. 1959). The district court then has the discretion to remand some or all of the nonfederal pendent claims to the state court. The courts will consider factors such as the similarity of issues and relatedness of facts, convenience of parties and witnesses and conserving the time of the courts and witnesses. *See Baltimore Gas & Electric Co. v. United States Fidelity & Guaranty Co.*, 159 F. Supp. 738, 741 (D. Md. 1958).

---

17 *See, e.g.*, *Luebbe v. Presbyterian Hosp.*, 526 F. Supp. 1162 (S.D.N.Y. 1981); *Verschell v. Fireman's Fund Ins. Co.*, 257 F. Supp. 153 (S.D.N.Y. 1966); *Harper v. Sonnabend*, 182 F. Supp. 594 (S.D.N.Y. 1960). As to counterclaim, generally, the cases reason that only a defendant may remove a case, and a plaintiff sued on a counterclaim is not a defendant. A few courts have permitted removal of a third-party claim which meets the "separate and independent" test. *First Nat'l Bank & Trust Co. of Okla. City v. Port Lavaca Vending Mach., Inc.*, 334 F. Supp. 375, 376-77 (S.D. Tex. 1971). Courts in the Second Circuit are to the contrary. *See, e.g.*, *Harris v. G.C. Servs. Corp.*, 651 F. Supp. 1417 (S.D.N.Y. 1987); *Knight v. Hellenic Lines, Ltd.*, 543 F. Supp. 915 (E.D.N.Y. 1982).

---

18 *See, e.g.*, *Electronic Data Systems Corp. v. Kinder*, 360 F. Supp. 1044 (N.D. Texas 1973), *aff'd*, 497 F.2d 222 (5th Cir. 1974).

If a case is removed and the removable claim is later dismissed, the federal court may then remand all, some or none of the pendent state law claims. In *Carnegie-Mellon Univ. v. Cohill*, 108 S. Ct. 614 (1988), the Supreme Court, in affirming the remand of pendent claims after plaintiff amended early in the action to delete the federal claim, resolved a split in the Circuits by holding that the federal court could relinguish its jurisdiction by a remand even though no statute explicitly provides for remand after the court has accepted jurisdiction over the pendent claims. The Court also discussed under what circumstances such a remand by the district court would be more appropriate than dismissal.

III. PROVISIONS PERMITTING OR PROHIBITING REMOVAL IN SPECIALIZED CASES

Various provisions in the removal statutes and in other statutes expressly permit removal in certain cases where it otherwise might be improper under the general statute or expressly prohibit it where it otherwise might be proper.

A. Removal Permitted

1. Actions Against Foreign States

Section 1441(d) allows a foreign state (as defined in the Foreign Sovereign Immunities Act, 28 U.S.C. § 1603) to remove any action brought against it in a state court. *See also* 28 U.S.C. § 1330.

2. Actions Against Federal Officers

28 U.S.C. § 1442 provides for removal of civil *or criminal* proceedings against any "officer of the United States or any agency thereof, or person acting under him" for acts committed under color of office.[19] This section was enacted to maintain the supremacy of federal laws by protecting officers acting under federal authority from possible undue punishment by a state court for violation of a state law which might conflict with his federal authority. The provision is read broadly. *Colorado v. Symes*, 286 U.S. 510, 517 (1932). The Supreme Court has interpreted the "color of office" requirement to mean a "causal connection between the charged conduct and asserted official authority" and has declared it sufficient if the acts occurred at the place of employment and during the performance of defendant's official duties. *Willingham v. Morgan*, 395 U.S. 402, 409 (1969) (suit against war-

---

[19] Some circuits have held that a government corporation cannot remove under this section. *See, e.g., Lovell Mfg. v. Export-Import Bank*, 843 F.2d 725, 733 (3d Cir. 1988).

den and medical officer of federal penitentiary). The defendant must aver in the removal petition facts necessary to justify application of this section.

A member of the armed forces is expressly permitted to remove a civil or criminal prosecution brought on account of an act done under color of office by a separate statute. 28 U.S.C. § 1442a.

3. Certain Civil Rights Actions

28 U.S.C. § 1443 provides that a civil *or criminal* action brought in state court may be removed by a defendant who (1) is denied or cannot enforce in the state courts "a right under any law providing for the equal civil rights of citizens of the United States, or of all persons within the jurisdiction thereof" or (2) is charged with having committed an act "under color of authority derived from any law providing for equal rights, or for refusing to do any act on the ground that it would be inconsistent with such law."

It is important to note that the subsection (1) defendant must claim the protection of a civil rights law promising *racial* equality, not other forms of equality generally protected by the Constitution or federal statutes, *Georgia v. Rachel*, 384 U.S. 780, 792 (1966), and the removal petition must demonstrate by specific allegations that the defendant is "denied or cannot enforce" the civil rights law in the state court, *Johnson v. Mississippi*, 421 U.S. 213, 219 (1975). Additionally, the petitioner must show that the denial of the right may be firmly predicted by virtue of a state law or similar enactment and is not merely anticipated as the illegal or corrupt act of a state official. *Georgia v. Rachel*, 384 U.S. at 800; *City of Greenwood, Miss. v. Peacock*, 384 U.S. 808, 828 (1966); *Kentucky v. Powers*, 201 U.S. 1 (1906).

It further has been held that subsection (2), allowing a defendant to remove any action or prosecution for an act taken *under color of authority* derived from a civil rights law, applies only to federal officers or their agents who have acted affirmatively under a federal law which specifically provides for equal civil rights. *City of Greenwood, Miss. v. Peacock*, 384 U.S. at 814.

4. Other Miscellaneous Actions

There are various other statutes permitting removal in specialized cases concerning the areas listed below. You should refer to the statutes cited if you are involved in such a case:

a. Claims within the exclusive federal bankruptcy jurisdiction. 28 U.S.C. § 1452.

b. Actions against federal employees sued under the Federal Tort Claims Act. 28 U.S.C. § 2679.

c. Quiet title or foreclosure actions brought against the United States under 28 U.S.C. § 2410 in a state court. 28 U.S.C. § 1444.

d. Actions relating to arbitration agreements or awards covered by the Foreign Arbitral Awards Convention. 9 U.S.C. § 205.

e. Actions in which the Federal Deposit Insurance Corporation is a party may be removed by it. 12 U.S.C. § 1819(4).

f. Medical malpractice claims against certain federal governmental employees. See 10 U.S.C. § 1089, 22 U.S.C. § 2699, 38 U.S.C. § 4116, 42 U.S.C. § 233, and 42 U.S.C. § 2458a.[20]

B. Removal Prohibited

1. Actions Against Railroads and Common Carriers

28 U.S.C. § 1445(a) prohibits removal of an action brought under Sections 51-60 of the Federal Employers' Liability Act (45 U.S.C.) (railroad employee's action for injury) against a railroad, its receiver or trustee. Section 1445(b) prohibits removal of any case under the Interstate Commerce Act (49 U.S.C. § 11707) (damages for delay, loss or injury to shipments) against a common carrier, its receiver or trustee, if the amount in controversy does not exceed $10,000.

Some courts have held that these provisions will prohibit removal even if the § 1445 nonremovable claim is joined with a "separate and independent claim" which would otherwise be removable under § 1441(c). See Gamble v. Central of Ga. Ry. Co., 486 F.2d 781, 785 (5th Cir. 1973) (remanding the § 1445 claim but allowing the district court to retain the separate claim). The Second Circuit permits removal but has underscored that the "separate," removable § 1441(c) claim must be markedly independent of the nonremovable § 1445 claim. Gonsalves v. Amoco Shipping Co., 733 F.2d 1020, 1026 (2d Cir. 1984). Accord Hages v. Aliquippa & So. R.R. Co., 427 F. Supp. 889, 892 (W.D. Pa. 1977).

2. Actions Under Section 12 of the Securities Act of 1933

Suits for misrepresentation under 15 U.S.C. § 77l of the Securities Act of 1933 (prospectus fraud) cannot be removed even though the state and federal courts have concurrent original jurisdiction. 15 U.S.C. § 77v. Note, however, that separate and independent claims joined with a nonremovable Securities Act claim will render the action removable under § 1441(c). *Milton R. Barrie Co. v. Levine*, 390 F. Supp. 475, 477 (S.D.N.Y. 1975); *U.S. Industries, Inc. v. Gregg*, 348 F. Supp. 1004, 1014-16 (D. Del. 1972), *rev'd on other grounds*, 540 F.2d 142, *cert. denied*, 433 U.S. 908 (1977).

---

[20] These statutes should be consulted for special procedural requirements applicable to removal.

3. Actions Against Employers Under State Workers' Compensation Laws

No action brought under a state workers' compensation law of the forum state may be removed. 28 U.S.C. § 1445(c).

4. Actions Under the Jones Act

Claims under the Jones Act, 46 U.S.C. § 688 (injury or death to seaman) cannot be removed. This is so because the Jones Act incorporates by reference the Federal Employers' Liability Act, and 28 U.S.C.§ 1445(a) precludes removal of FELA actions. In the Second Circuit, a Jones Act case which also pleads a "markedly" separate and independent cause of action may be removed under § 1441(c), although a claim for maintenance and cure is not considered so distinct as to permit removal. *See Gonsalves v. Amoco Shipping Co.*, 733 F.2d at 1021-22.

5. Actions Challenging State Taxes

Actions to enjoin, suspend or restrain the assessment, levy or collection of any state or local tax are not removable (unless an adequate remedy is unavailable in the state courts). This is so because the Tax Injunction Act, 28 U.S.C. § 1341, requires the federal courts to abstain from such cases. *See Soo Line R.R. Co. v. City of Harvey*, 424 F. Supp. 329, 330-31 (D.N.D. 1976).

IV. PROCEDURE FOR REMOVAL

Removal is accomplished by the defendant's filing a pleading called a "notice of removal." No order of the federal court granting removal is required for it to become effective. *See* Section IV.H., below. 28 U.S.C. § 1446 governs the procedures for removal, defining the parties entitled to remove, the place of filing and time within which the petition must be filed, the contents of the petition and the papers which must accompany the petition.

A. Who May Remove

Generally, only defendants on the original claim may remove a case, not parties who are "defendants" on a counterclaim, third-party defendants or intervenors (unless the court severs the third-party claim from the main action). 28 U.S.C. § 1446(a).[21] The federal court will make the final determination of the real parties in interest and may realign the parties. *Chicago v. Stude*, 346 U.S. 574, 579-80 (1954).

In the usual case, all served defendants must sign the petition for removal. *See Chicago R.I. P. Ry. Co. v. Martin*, 178 U.S. 245, 248 (1900); *Bradford v. Harding*, 284 F.2d 307, 309 (2d Cir. 1960); *McKay v. Point Shipping Corp.*, 587 F. Supp. 41, 42 (S.D.N.Y. 1984). However, if removal is based on 28 U.S.C. § 1441(c), only the defendant(s) to the separate and independent claim need sign the petition. *Reiken v. Nationwide Leisure Corp.*, 458 F. Supp. 179, 182 (S.D.N.Y. 1978). If the removal is based on § 1441(d), as the foreign state has the sole an individual right to remove, it is the only defendant which would sign the petition. Similarly, if removal is based on § 1442, only the federal officer need sign the petition because the officer alone has the right to remove, and if removal is based on § 1444, only the United States need sign, as it is the only party which can remove. Nominal or fraudulently joined defendants need not join in the petition, *see Pullman Co. v. Jenkins*, 305 U.S. 534 (1939), although the petition should then allege that the party who has failed to sign the petition is a nominal or fraudulently joined party. *See, e.g., Northern Ill. Gas Co. v. Airco Indus. Gases*, 676 F.2d 270, 273 (7th Cir. 1982). Parties who are named but have not been served and whose presence in the suit would not disturb diversity jurisdiction can be ignored both for the purpose of jurisdiction and for the purpose of joining the petition. *See, e.g., Browne Bros. Cypen Corp. v. Carner Bank of Miami Beach Fla.*, 287 F. Supp. 700, 702 (S.D.N.Y. 1968).

B. Place of Filing

Section 1446(a) requires that the removal petition be filed "in the district court of the United States for the district and division within which such

---

[21] Some statutes do permit certain nondefendants to remove. *See, e.g.*, 12 U.S.C. § 1819 (Federal Deposit Insurance Corporation). And, in *Yonkers Racing Corporation v. City of Yonkers*, Nos. 88-6140, 6146, slip op. (2d Cir. September 22, 1988), the Second Circuit held that an Article 78 proceeding brought by two condemnees of land intended to be used to provide public housing in compliance with a consent decree approved by the federal court could be removed by the condemnor to the federal court, even though it was debatable whether the condemnor was properly classified as a defendant for purposes of the removal statutes. (In *Mason City & Fort Dodge R.R. v. Boynton*, 204 U.S. 570 (1907), and *Chicago, Rock Island & Pac. R.R. v. Stude*, 346 U.S. 574 (1954), the Supreme Court held that under Iowa eminent domain statutes which required the condemnee to initiate a proceeding to contest the assessment of the condemned property's value determined by a sheriff's jury, the condemnor remained the plaintiff for purposes of removal.) The *Yonkers* Court held that, regardless of whether the condemnor was a defendant for purposes of the general and civil rights action removal statutes, 28 U.S.C. §§ 1441 and 1443, the All Writs Act, 28 U.S.C. § 1651, provided authority for removal because "removal was necessary to protect the integrity of the Consent Decree and because the issues raised by the Article 78 petitions cannot be separated from the relief provided by the Consent Decree." Slip op. at 6436.

action is pending." Thus, venue can be proper in the federal court, even if it were not proper in the original state court. Likewise, the venue provisions controlling actions originally brought in district court do not apply to removed actions. *Polizzi v. Cowles Magazines, Inc.*, 345 U.S. 663 (1953). The failure to fulfill the venue requirements is not a fatal defect requiring dismissal.

C. Time for Filing the Petition

Section 1446(b) prescribes a thirty-day period for filing the removal petition, and the period essentially runs from the defendant's receipt of notice of the nature of the claims, not service of the complaint. The thirty-day period expires on the *earlier* of: (a) defendant's *receipt* (by service *or* "otherwise") of the initial state court pleading setting forth the claim (not necessarily the complaint), or (b) service of the summons (if the pleading has been filed *and* is not required to be served under state law). However, service on a statutory agent (for example, the Secretary of State designated under a nonresident motorist statute) does not commence the period. *Percell's Inc. v. Central Tel. Co.*, 493 F. Supp. 156, 157 (D. Minn. 1980).[22] The thirty-day limit will be strictly construed and it cannot be enlarged by stipulation or order. *Biscup v. New York*, 129 F. Supp. 765, 767 (W.D.N.Y. 1955). However, the time limit is not jurisdictional; failure to object timely to the late filing of a petition will waive the defect. *See Ayers v. Watson*, 113 U.S. 594, 598-99 (1885); *Green v. Zuck*, 133 F. Supp. 436, 438 (S.D.N.Y. 1955). In New York, a summons with notice served pursuant to C.P.L.R. §§ 304 and 305(b) constitutes an initial pleading for purposes of § 1446(b). *Universal Motors Group of Cos. v. Wilkerson*, 674 F. Supp. 1108, 1113 (S.D.N.Y. 1987); *DiMeglio v. Italia Crociere Internazionale*, 502 F. Supp. 316, 318 (S.D.N.Y. 1980).

In a case with multiple defendants, the thirty-day period expires for all defendants when it expires for the first served/notified defendant. *See, e.g., Ortiz v. General Motors Acceptance Corp.*, 583 F. Supp. 526, 529 (N.D. Ill. 1984); *Balestrieri v. Bell Asbestos Mines, Ltd.*, 544 F. Supp. 528, 530 (E.D. Pa. 1982).[23] But, even if the time period has expired for the first-served defendant, a later-served defendant who has a § 1441(c) ("separate and independant") claim has thirty days from his or her receipt of the initial pleading to file for removal under § 1441(c). With respect to a foreign state's

---

[22] Note, however, that service on other authorized agents, such as attorneys, has in some cases been held sufficient. *Davis v. Baer*, 599 F. Supp. 776, 778-79 (E.D. Pa. 1984) (service on defendant's insurance company).

---

[23] This result is logical. Since all defendants must join in the petition for removal, the refusal of any one defendant to join would bar removal. Therefore, the failure of the first-served defendant timely to file a petition is construed as its refusal to remove which precludes *any* defendant from removing.

removal under § 1441(d), the court may enlarge the thirty-day period for "good cause," which requires an "unusual set of circumstances." *Boland v. Bank Sepah-Iran*, 614 F. Supp. 1166, 1169 (S.D.N.Y. 1985).

The second paragraph of § 1446(b) governs the filing of a petition in an action which was not initially removable but becomes so during the course of the case. A case may be so transformed for any number of reasons, such as plaintiff's service of an amended pleading, addition of a federal claim, increase in the amount in controversy or voluntary dismissal of a diversity-destroying defendant. The statute provides that a new thirty-day period starts to run when the defendant receives notice of the amended pleading *or other paper* from which it appears that the case has become removable. However, if the action was one which had been removable initially, a later change will not revive the period unless the plaintiff adds a new cause of action which gives rise to a new basis for removal. *Hearst Corp. v. Shopping Center Network, Inc.*, 307 F. Supp. 551, 555 (S.D.N.Y. 1969); *Gerety v. Inland Newspaper Representatives, Inc.*, 152 F. Supp. 31, 32-33 (S.D.N.Y. 1957). In addition, cases may not be removed on the basis of diversity jurisdiction more than one year after the commencement of the action.

The practitioner who would prefer for some reason to have the case in federal rather than state court, but has no basis for getting it there, should always be alert to amendments by the plaintiff or court rulings which may have the effect of turning the case into a removable one. Often, in anticipation of trial, pleadings are amended and parties dropped. Note that if a case becomes removable before the trial, but the thirty-day period has not expired when the trial is ready to begin, the defendant will waive the right to remove by commencing the state court trial without filing the petition. *See Waldron v. Skelly Co.*, 101 F. Supp. 425 (E.D. Mo. 1951). *See also Fugard v. Thierry*, 265 F. Supp. 743 (N.D. Ill. 1967). *See* Section IV.E., below.

D. Contents of the Notice of Removal

The notice of removal should normally be a simple, brief document, containing "a short and plain statement of the facts which entitle" the defendant(s) to remove the case. It must be accompanied by copies of "all process, pleadings and orders served upon him or them" in the state court. The notice must be signed pursuant to Rule 11 of the Federal Rules of Civil Procedure. Section 1446(a).

The defendant-petitioner carries the burden of pleading and, if challenged, proving adequate removal grounds. *R.G. Barry Corp. v. Mushroom Makers, Inc.*, 612 F.2d 651, 655 (2d Cir. 1979). Accordingly, the notice should include the statutory basis for removal, the date of receipt by the defendant(s) of the initial pleading, the facts relied upon in seeking removal, the fact that the necessary bond has been filed, and the citizenship of the parties if diversity is the basis for removal. The "pleading" requirements have been construed liberally; failure to allege all necessary facts will not make the notice fatally defective as long as the removal court can ascertain an adequate basis for removal. *See, e.g., Harlem River Produce Co. v. Aetna Casualty & Surety Co.*, 257 F. Supp. 160, 163-164 (S.D.N.Y. 1965).[24]

The notice of removal can be amended freely before the thirty-day removal period expires, and it can be amended thereafter with leave of court to set out more specifically the jurisdictional basis for removal, *see* 28 U.S.C. § 1653, or to correct a defect in a formality, but at that point the amendment cannot change the grounds for removal or make any other substantive changes. *See Kinney v. Columbia Savings & Loan Ass'n*, 191 U.S. 78 (1903).[25]

E. Waiver By the Defendant of the Right to Remove

Apart from watching the time limit for removal, a defendant must be careful not to take an action in state court which is inconsistent with removal because it may waive the right to remove. For example, filing a permissive counterclaim in state court constitutes waiver because the defendant has voluntarily submitted to the jurisdiction of the state court. *In re Harris*, 560 F. Supp. 940, 942 (S.D.N.Y. 1983). However, entering a general appearance, answering a complaint, filing a compulsory counterclaim or serving a notice to examine a plaintiff are all examples of pre-removal steps which a defendant can take without waiving the removal right. *See Dri Mark Products, Inc. v. Meyercord Co.*, 194 F. Supp. 536, 537-38 (S.D.N.Y. 1961) (stipulating to an adjournment); *Minkoff v. Scranton Frocks*, 172 F. Supp. 870, 875-76 (S.D.N.Y. 1959) (request for adjournment and extension of time to file papers); *Markantonatos v. Maryland Drydock Co.*, 110 F. Supp. 862, 864 (S.D.N.Y. 1953) (filing appearance, answering complaint, and serving notice to examine plaintiff).

F. Requirement of a Bond

Formerly, defendants removing an action were required to post a bond. That provision was repealed in 1988, and thus the bond is no longer required.

---

24 The defendant should also consult the federal district court's local rules to determine any additional requirements. *See, e.g.*, Rule 25 of the Civil Rules of the Southern and Eastern Districts of New York.

25 The Second Circuit has allowed a petitioner to amend the removal petition where the federal cause of action was dropped from the case along with a diversity-destroying defendant because diversity became a new ground for removal. *Naylor v. Case and McGrath, Inc.*, 585 F.2d 557, 562 (2d Cir. 1978).

G. Requirement of Notice of Removal

Under 28 U.S.C. § 1446(d), removing defendants are required to give prompt written notice to all adverse parties and are required to file a copy of the notice in the state court. The state court then may proceed no further in the case, unless and until the case is remanded to it. *See* Section VI, below. Failure to follow the notice requirement is not a jurisdictional defect. *Manufacturers & Traders Trust Co. v. Hartford Accident & Indemnity Co.*, 434 F. Supp. 1053, 1055 (W.D.N.Y. 1977).

H. When Removal is Effective

Removal is automatically effected when the notice is filed in federal court, a copy of the notice is filed in court, and notice is given to adverse parties.[26] No court order is necessary to effect removal. *See* 28 U.S.C. § 1446(e); *United States ex. rel. Echevarria v. Silberglitt*, 441 F.2d 225 (2d Cir. 1971). Once removal has become effective, any later state court proceedings will be void, because the state court no longer has jurisdiction over the case. *National S.S. Co. v. Tugman*, 106 U.S. 118, 122 (1882). Any orders issued by the state court thereafter will be vacated even if removal is later found to have been improper and the case is remanded.

V. PROCEDURE AFTER REMOVAL

28 U.S.C. §§ 1447-1450 and Rule 81(c) of the Federal Rules of Civil Procedure pertain to proceedings in a removed case: section 1447 deals generally with post-removal procedures; section 1448 with service of process; section 1449 with supplying the state court record to the district court; and section 1450 with the effect of orders issued by the state court prior to removal. Rule 81(c) concerns the applicability of the Federal Rules to a removed action.

A. Process, §§ 1447(a) and 1448

That the federal court gains subject matter jurisdiction over a removed action does not mean it has personal jurisdiction over the defendants, and if service has not been completed on all defendants by the time removal occurs, it must be done as in any other case pending in federal court. Filing a notice of removal is not a consent by a defendant to personal jurisdiction, *Goldey v. Morning News*, 156 U.S. 518, 526 (1895), nor a waiver of the right to the sufficiency of process, *Bomze v. Nardis Sportswear, Inc.*, 165 F.2d 33, 35

---

26 *See McGoldrick v. ICS Sales & Leasing Inc.*, 412 F. Supp. 268 (E.D.N.Y. 1976) (removal not effected until copy of removal petition filed with the state court).

(2d Cir. 1948); *Stimler v. Yoshida Shoji Co.*, 195 F. Supp. 671 (S.D.N.Y. 1961). State law governs the substantive inquiry as to the sufficiency of pre-removal service of process. *See Bomze v. Nardis Sportswear*, 165 F.2d at 35. Although the removal court must remand the case to the state court if it fails to secure personal jurisdiction, a defect in the service of process at the state level will not necessarily force the federal court to dismiss the case. The federal court can re-serve process, issue new process or transfer the case to another forum which has personal jurisdiction over the defendant.

B. Transfer of State Court Record, §§ 1447(b) and 1449

The federal district court has the power to order the removal petitioner to file with the clerk copies of all records of proceedings before the state court or to issue a writ of certiorari to the state court to cause the transfer of the file. 28 U.S.C. § 1447(b). If the clerk of the state court, upon demand by a party entitled thereto and the payment or tender of appropriate fees, fails to deliver certified copies of the state court record, the district court may provide that copies of the record be supplied by affidavit of the parties or in another manner, and the case will proceed as if certified copies from the state court had been filed.

C. Case is Governed by Federal Rules, Rule 81(c)

After removal is complete, *see* Section IV.H., above, the federal court has full and exclusive jurisdiction over the subsequent litigation. *See French v. Hay*, 89 U.S. 238 (1875). Rule 81(c) states that the Federal Rules of Civil Procedure govern the action after removal, and the court will treat the case just as if it had been commenced originally in federal court. Plaintiff need not replead according to federal form, *see Frank B. Hall & Co. v. Rushmore Ins. Co.*, 92 F.R.D. 743, 745 (S.D.N.Y. 1981),[27] but plaintiff can amend, adding, for example, a claim which is within the federal court's exclusive jurisdiction. *See Freeman v. Bee Mach. Co.*, 319 U.S. 448 (1943), *reh'g denied*, 320 U.S. 809 (1943).

If the defendant has not answered the complaint before removing, Rule 81(c) gives the defendant the longer of twenty days from receipt of the plaintiff's initial pleading or five days after filing the removal notice to answer or to move against the complaint or other pleading.

Rule 81(c) also details the mechanism for demanding a jury trial in a removed action. If issue had already been joined before the action was re-

---

[27] Further, if the state action were commenced by a motion for summary judgment in lieu of complaint under N.Y. C.P.L.R. § 3213, the motion can be entertained by the federal court without the filing of a formal complaint, although federal summary judgment standards will apply. *Miller v. Steloff*, 686 F. Supp. 91, 92 n.1, 93 (S.D.N.Y. 1988).

moved, a removing defendant who is entitled to a jury trial must demand it within ten days after filing the notice; each other party has ten days after service of the removal notice upon it. If a party demanded a jury trial prior to removal, it need not repeat the demand. If the applicable state law does not require an express jury trial demand, the parties do not need to make the express demand in the removal court unless the district court directs that they do so. *See Leve v. General Motors Corp.*, 248 F. Supp. 344 (S.D.N.Y. 1965). However, the right to a jury trial may be waived unless a timely demand, when required, is made. Because New York state law allows discretionary relief from a waiver, *see* N.Y. C.P.L.R. § 4002, the Second Circuit has read such relief into the language of Rule 81(c). *See, e.g., Higgins v. Boeing Co.*, 526 F.2d 1004 (2d Cir. 1975). *See also Cascone v. Ortho Pharmaceutical Corp.*, 702 F.2d 389 (2d Cir. 1983) (affirming district court's grant of untimely request for jury trial in removed case).

D. Orders Issued by State Court Remain Effective, § 1450, But Federal Rules Apply; the Granny Goose Doctrine

A federal district court recognizes all the prior pleadings, orders, injunctions and other proceedings in the state court action and presumes they are valid. *Istituto per lo Sviluppo Economico Dell' Italia Meridionale v. Sperti Prods., Inc.*, 47 F.R.D. 310, 312 (S.D.N.Y. 1969). Interlocutory orders entered by the state court (such as attachments, sequestrations and injunctions) and security filed (such as bonds) do not lapse upon removal, but under 28 U.S.C. § 1450 remain in effect. *See Rorick v. Devon Syndicate, Ltd.*, 307 U.S. 299 (1939), *reh'g denied*, 307 U.S. 650 (1939). However, because the district court may dissolve or modify prior orders issued in the state court, the removal court is not bound by any "law of the case" rendered by the state court. *See, e.g., Quinn v. Aetna Life & Casualty Co.*, 616 F.2d 38, 40 (2d Cir. 1980) (affirming dismissal of the action by the district court although an earlier motion in the state court for dismissal had failed).

In spite of the presumptive validity of the state court orders, their efficacy will be governed in accordance with applicable federal rules. In *Granny Goose Foods, Inc. v. Brotherhood of Teamsters & Auto Truck Drivers*, 415 U.S. 423 (1974), the Supreme Court held that an *ex parte* temporary restraining order issued by the state court prior to removal would remain in effect in the district court only for the period permitted by Rule 65 of the Federal Rules of Civil Procedure (or the period permitted by the applicable state rule, if that were shorter). Thus, the prompt hearing requirement of Rule 65 applies to a temporary restraining order issued by the state court, and absent the holding of such a hearing, the restraint will be a nullity. *Frank B. Hall & Co. v. Rushmore Ins. Co.*, 92 F.R.D. 743 (S.D.N.Y. 1981).

VI. REMAND

The grounds and procedures pertaining to a remand of the action to the state court are provided by 28 U.S.C. § 1447(c). Either party can move for remand at any time during the litigation if it appears that the court lacks subject matter jurisdiction. Motions to remand based on defects in the removal procedure, however, must be made within 30 days after the filing of the notice of removal. The federal court may also remand on its own motion, if it questions its removal jurisdiction. *See Gardner and Florence Call Cowles Found. v. Empire, Inc.*, 754 F.2d 478, 480 (2d Cir. 1985).

The federal court may remand the case only if it lacks jurisdiction or the case was removed "improvidently." "Improvident" removal has been defined to mean removal made "wrongfully or without legal basis." *Haelan Laboratories, Inc. v. Topps Chewing Gum, Inc.*, 131 F. Supp. 262, 263 (E.D.N.Y. 1955). Administrative convenience or procedural defects in the notice are not grounds for remand. *Thermtron Products, Inc. v. Hermansdorfer*, 423 U.S. 336, 344 (1976) (over-crowded federal court docket is not a basis for remand). Although a party can waive a procedural defect in removal, because a federal court cannot obtain subject matter jurisdiction by consent of the parties, the right to move to remand for lack of jurisdiction cannot be waived. *In re Winn*, 213 U.S. 458, 469 (1909).

The federal court looks at the complaint as it existed at the time of removal to determine whether it must remand the case. *See* Section II, above. The federal court decides all factual issues bearing on removability without a jury. The burden of proof is on the party seeking to preserve the removal. *Video Connection of America, Inc. v. Priority Concepts, Inc.*, 625 F. Supp. 1549, 1550 (S.D.N.Y. 1986). If federal jurisdiction seems doubtful, the doubts usually will be resolved in favor of a remand because the removal statutes are strictly construed. *Id. Deats v. Joseph Swantak, Inc.*, 619 F. Supp. 973, 977 n.12 (N.D.N.Y. 1985).

If the plaintiff tries to amend the complaint so as to force a remand, the district court may prohibit the amendment. Thus, because an amendment to join a diversity-destroying defendant would require a remand for lack of jurisdiction if diversity were the sole ground for removal, the court may refuse it rather than be forced to remand. *McIntyre v. Codman & Shurtleff, Inc.*, 103 F.R.D. 619 (S.D.N.Y. 1984).[28] However, a 1988 amendment to

---

[28] Before the removal statute was amended in 1988, many district courts would not allow joinder of a party which is not "indispensable." One recent New York district court decision allowed joinder of a non-indispensable party, because the joinder was sought for the legitimate purpose of avoiding multiplicity of litigation. *McIntyre v. Codman & Shurtleff, Inc.*, 103 F.R.D. 619 (S.D.N.Y. 1984).

section 1447 makes clear that the court now has discretion to deny joinder, or permit joinder and remand the action. If the sole federal claim in an action is dismissed by the court at some point during the litigation, the court then has discretion whether to retain the remaining pendent state law claims, remand them or dismiss them. *Carnegie-Mellon University v. Cohill*, 108 S. Ct. 614, 619 n.7. (1988). On June 19, 1986, Congress passed § 1441(e), eliminating the anomalous "derivative" jurisdiction doctrine that had existed.

Previously, if, upon removal, the federal court determined that the state court could not have had subject matter jurisdiction over the action (*e.g.*, a fraud action under the Securities Exchange Act of 1934 over which the federal courts have exclusive jurisdiction), the federal court was held to have gained no new jurisdiction to hear the case, and it was obliged to dismiss the case, even if the case was within the federal court's original jurisdiction. The plaintiff was then required to file a new action in federal court. Now, however, if the federal court has subject matter jurisdiction, the case is not dismissible on the ground that the state court where it was originally brought did not have jurisdiction. Note that § 1441(e) only applies to claims filed after June 19, 1986. *Nordlicht v. New York Tel.*, 799 F.2d 859, 863 (2d Cir. 1986), *cert. denied*, 107 S. Ct. 929 (1987).

A remand order ends the federal court's jurisdiction. The removal court sends a certified copy of the remand order to the clerk of the state court, and the state court is thereupon entitled to proceed with the case. 28 U.S.C. § 1447(c).[29] If a new ground for removal arises with subsequent developments in the state case, the defendant can file a new notice of removal. *Fritzlen v. Boatmen's Bank*, 212 U.S. 364, 372 (1909).

VII. APPEAL OF ORDERS GRANTING OR DENYING REMAND

An order of remand is not reviewable by appeal or otherwise, except in civil rights cases removed under § 1443. 28 U.S.C. § 1447(d). The purpose of this rule is to avoid undue delay and interruption of litigation. The Supreme Court has created a narrow exception to this rule in *Thermtron Products, Inc. v. Hermansdorfer*, 423 U.S. 336, 352, by authorizing mandamus as a proper remedy for review of a remand order entered by the district court on a ground not permitted by § 1447(c). Orders entered prior to remand are,

---

[29] Some courts have stayed a remand order for a short period of time where there existed a right to appeal the remand order. *See*, *e.g.*, *Board of Educ. of N.Y. v. City-Wide Comm. for Integration of Schools*, 342 F.2d 284, 286 (2d Cir. 1965).

however, subject to review, including an order which because it dismissed a claim caused the remand. *See Waco v. United States Fidelity & Guaranty Co.*, 293 U.S. 140 (1934).

If a remand motion is denied, the denial is reviewable, either on appeal from a final judgment or, permissively, by interlocutory appeal pursuant to 28 U.S.C. § 1292(b).[30] On appeal from a final judgment, if the Circuit Court of Appeals holds that removal had been improper and directs a remand of the case, this remand is not within the prohibitions of § 1447(d) and may be reviewed by the Supreme Court because § 1447(d) only prohibits review of *district* court orders. *Aetna Casualty & Surety Co. v. Flowers*, 330 U.S. 464, 466-67 (1947).

VIII. PRACTICAL CONSIDERATIONS IN DECIDING WHETHER TO REMOVE

A defendant's attorney must, of course, weigh the benefits and disadvantages to the client of proceeding in the state or federal forum, and the decision whether to remove must be made in a relatively short period of time. Although many factors will play a role in this decision, we set forth the following not to be overlooked:

(a) Whether the applicable procedural or evidentiary rules will be more favorable in the state or federal court. For example, in a products liability action, evidence of subsequent repairs might be admissible in one forum but not the other.

(b) Which forum will have greater familiarity with the substantive law.

(c) Where there is an application pending for preliminary relief, what form of disposition is preferred. For example, the federal court will require an expeditious injunction hearing and will allow witnesses to testify under Rule 65. The state court, on the other hand, at least in New York, usually decides such motions on papers.

(d) Whether orders have been issued by the state court of which reconsideration by the federal court is desirable since the federal court is not bound by the "law of the case."

(e) Which court's dockets are more congested and in which forum may a speedier (or slower) disposition of the case be secured for other reasons.

---

30 If a motion to remand is denied and permission to appeal that denial is not granted, but a later interlocutory appeal is permitted, some circuit courts have held that review of the denial of the remand motion may be had. *See, e.g., Beech-Nut, Inc. v. Warner-Lambert Co.*, 480 F.2d 801 (2d Cir. 1973); *contra Sheeran v. General Elec. Co.*, 593 F.2d 93 (9th Cir.), *cert. denied*, 444 U.S. 868 (1979).

The attorney must also consider the possibility of a federal judge's levying sanctions. If the federal judge believes the removal has been taken on frivolous grounds, he or she may assess expenses, including attorney's fees, to be paid by the removing party, and these would be enforceable against the removal bond. *See, e.g., Four Keys Leasing & Maintenance Corp. v. Simithis*, 849 F.2d 770, 774 (2d Cir. 1988); *Baas v. Elliot*, 71 F.R.D. 693, 694 (E.D.N.Y. 1976). Further, proceedings in federal court after removal will generally be subject to the various statutes and rules permitting the award of sanctions such as Fed. R. Civ. P. 11, which may be more severe than those available in New York state courts. Thus, besides considering whether you might be in danger of sanctions being imposed upon you for unwarranted removal, you should consider whether you might desire to seek to have sanctions awarded in favor of your client at the conclusion of an action you believe meritless.

CHAPTER FIVE

INVESTIGATION OF CASE AND USE OF EXPERTS

by Robert L. Haig, Esq.*
John J. Quinn, Esq.

I. INTRODUCTION

The first part of this chapter describes techniques that enable the trial lawyer to investigate the case before the start of formal discovery. The formal discovery process is discussed elsewhere in this book. The purpose of this section is to identify many of the sources of information that can assist the practitioner in the early, often pre-pleading, investigatory stages of the case.

As this chapter illustrates, numerous sources of information are useful in helping counsel learn about the subject matter of a case before the start of discovery. It is at this stage that the lawyer can often determine whether his client has a viable cause of action or defense. If the investigative steps discussed are taken, the pleadings and the discovery that follow will be more effective and ultimately produce either a stronger case at trial or, alternatively, put the case in a better posture for a favorable settlement.

The second part of this chapter explores the use of experts generally and provides illustrations of cases in which experts can be particularly helpful. Rather than focus on the traditional use of an expert as a witness at trial, this section will show how the expert can provide technical assistance to the practitioner from the earliest stages of the litigation. The expert can help

---

* The valuable assistance of Warren N. Stone in the preparation of this chapter is gratefully acknowledged.

direct the attorney's thinking about the technical aspects of the case and assist counsel to avoid erroneous or ill-founded theories of recovery or defense. This section also describes ways in which a practitioner can avoid some of the common pitfalls in the use of an expert.

It would be impossible in one chapter to discuss all aspects of case investigation and the use of experts. The reader is encouraged to look to cases similar to the one he is handling to learn from the experiences of others. The beginning practitioner should read news accounts and reports of cases, particularly those which attract continuing media attention, to learn about the evolution of a case and the investigative effort which went into the trial preparation. One should also read books about trials, which frequently detail the investigation that preceded the trial process. To paraphrase Professor Irving Younger, the books, usually written by the winning attorney, may not be good literature but are valuable learning tools that help the lawyer to confront the "recurrent problems" all trial practitioners face.[1]

II. INTERVIEWS

A. Client, Nonparties, and Parties

Personal interviews are an important component of nearly any investigation. An interview with one's own client is usually the starting point. The lawyer should encourage the client to give a detailed and fair statement of all of the facts in the case. At the outset, many experienced interviewers prefer to let the client tell his version of the facts with as few interruptions as possible. Then, after listening to the client's narrative, the attorney should ask for clarifications and additional details. It is imperative that the client be made to understand that to be an effective advocate, the lawyer must be aware of all of the facts. A particular effort should be made to elicit any facts that the client feels may weaken his position.

Rumor has it that some lawyers first tell their clients what the law is and then seek to elicit the facts. The theory behind this approach apparently is that an astute client will not burden the lawyer with facts inconsistent with the legal position most favorable to the client. Therefore, according to this theory, the lawyer may go off and do battle on behalf of his client without his conscience being troubled by awareness of the inconsistent facts. Such an approach is not only ethically questionable, it is likely to result in unpleasant surprises at trial and in an inability to evaluate the case realistically.

---

[1] Speech given by Professor Irving Younger at the American Bar Association's Annual Meeting in Montreal, Canada, August 12, 1975, entitled "The Art of Cross Examination," No. 1 in the A.B.A. Section of Litigation Monograph Series, at 32 (1976).

INVESTIGATION OF CASE AND USE OF EXPERTS

Nonparty witnesses are sometimes willing to talk about the facts of the case before suit is filed. In many instances, the lawyer's best approach to a witness interview is to emphasize that he is merely seeking to better understand what took place at the time in question. A telephone call, or an on-site visit in a personal injury case, is a useful approach with many witnesses. A letter to a prospective witness may be less effective because it allows time for reflection and because the frequent response is no reply.

Various ethical questions are presented by interviews with potential adverse parties. A lawyer who conducts such an interview runs the risk of criticism and possibly a rejection of the evidence he obtains on the ground that he has taken advantage of an adverse party not represented by counsel. Although there may be no blanket prohibition against communicating with potential adverse parties, the better course is to advise the witness, preferably in writing, that he may become a party and that he may wish to be represented by counsel during any interview which may take place. Perhaps not surprisingly, the result of such advice may be a refusal of the requested interview.

Counsel should avoid interviewing a potentially adverse party under circumstances that suggest that counsel and the party enjoy a cooperative or neutral relationship. Even if the party is represented by an attorney during such an interview, a court may later determine that counsel obtained an unfair advantage from the interview and may disqualify him from the case.

The lawyer should take notes of what he has been told during the interview. These notes, which should be treated as work product, should be made immediately after the interview, if possible. Taking notes during the interview may distract both the attorney and the person being interviewed, and perhaps intimidate or inhibit the latter. This is a question which can only be decided in the particular situation depending on counsel's observation of the witness.

Counsel should be aware that there are ethical considerations which limit the attorney's participation in the tape recording of interviews or telephone conversations with witnesses. Counsel should indicate to the witness that counsel wishes to tape record the conversation and allow the witness the option of not having the interview recorded. As a safeguard to the lawyer, the consent to the recording should be either in writing or on the tape itself.

B. Eyewitness Interviews

In the investigatory phase of any case involving a particular event, such as an automobile accident or a fall, interviewing eyewitnesses often provides valuable information. Eyewitnesses, because of their proximity to the event in question, can give details that may not be available through any other means.

The first step in obtaining an interview with an eyewitness is to identify the individual as an eyewitness. Often, the client may be an important source of such information. For instance, in the case of an injury at work, both the injured employee-plaintiff and the employer-defendant will frequently know the names of any other persons present. In the case of an accident involving complete strangers, such as an auto accident, the client may, or may not, know the names of any eyewitnesses, depending on his condition at the time of the injury and on whether any eyewitnesses came forward in his presence. In many situations, the police report will contain the names of any eyewitnesses interviewed by police at the accident scene and should be consulted for this information. Accident reports identifying eyewitnesses may also be available from adverse parties or other persons or entities.

Do not rely entirely on the police report, however. It is often more productive to visit the scene and do a house-to-house or store-to-store canvass. In addition, visiting the scene at the same time as the incident will sometimes disclose witnesses who travel that route on a regular basis and who may have helpful information.

Once an eyewitness is located, the attorney should give the eyewitness an opportunity to recount what he witnessed. The attorney may want to permit the witness to tell his complete story before asking questions. This may help the witness feel more comfortable and willing to talk. If the eyewitness appears biased against his client at the outset, however, the best strategy for an attorney may be to interrupt the witness in order to focus his attention on details that may call into question the soundness of his conclusions. For instance, if the eyewitness states that he is positive that he observed the client fleeing from the auto accident scene, counsel may wish to call his attention to the lighting conditions, distracting noises, and the assembled onlookers, all of which may have severely limited the witness' ability to accurately identify the client.

The accuracy of eyewitness observation varies in certain circumstances. It is widely recognized that stress or fear can severely limit an eyewitness' ability to perceive. Thus, an eyewitness standing on a sidewalk who may have believed he was in danger of being hit by one of the cars in a nearby collision may perceive events less clearly than one who witnessed the accident from a safer place. The presence of violence may also impair a witness' ability to perceive events.

Another significant variable in witness recall is time. It is not uncommon for two or more people to witness the same event and have widely divergent recollections of how long the event lasted. It is often helpful to do a reenactment, even simply in the office, and time how long it takes. Without telling the witness how long the reenactment actually took, the attorney should have the witness tell him how long the witness believed it took. By comparing the witness' estimate with the actual elapsed time, it is often possible to obtain a more accurate and credible accounting from the witness.

Counsel should ask the eyewitness whether there is any objective data to aid his testimony. For example, in a civil assault case where the defendant is charged with beating counsel's client when the client was already on the ground, if the witness says that the beating continued through two series of red lights at the nearby intersection, counsel can independently establish that period of time. The result is a more effective and credible presentation than saying "it lasted about three to five minutes."

The attorney conducting an eyewitness interview should also be aware of the eyewitness' prior expectations and subsequent exposures that may alter the witness' perception and ability to recall the event. A witness who believed that one of the people he observed in a fight was a violent individual may be predisposed to believe that this individual threw the first punch. If, after observing the event in question the eyewitness has been exposed to a great deal of information concerning the event, the witness' memory may be altered. In the example above, if the witness learns after the event that one of the individuals observed was known to have a hot temper, the witness may reassess what he saw. An awareness of these types of factors influencing the accuracy of a witness' observation can improve the lawyer's ability to assess the quality of eyewitness testimony.

If eyewitness testimony is favorable to his client, the lawyer may wish to ask the eyewitness to write a report of what he saw. The lawyer may also wish to ask the witness to sign the report before a notary public. Such a report may provide an important tool for eliciting the same information at trial or for impeaching the witness in the event that he changes his story at trial.

III. GOVERNMENTAL AND INSTITUTIONAL RECORDS AND INFORMATION

Records and information available from government agencies and other institutions, such as hospitals, are often critical to an attorney's investigation of a case. The types of records and information that one can obtain from these sources vary widely. The following discussion is not intended to provide an exhaustive survey but rather to illustrate, by example, the different kinds of information available from these sources.

Not all of the information discussed in this section will be available to all parties in the litigation during the pre-discovery stage. For instance, while counsel for the defendant in a personal injury case will need to obtain authorizations from the plaintiff to obtain the plaintiff's medical records, plaintiff's counsel can obtain these records immediately. Similarly, counsel for the products liability defendant can obtain company documents concerning the product at this stage while plaintiff's counsel can only obtain these documents after discovery begins.

A. Freedom of Information Requests

Much of the following information is available through either the federal Freedom of Information Act ("FOIA"), 5 U.S.C. § 552 (1977), or the New York State Freedom of Information Law ("FOIL"), N.Y. Pub. Off. Law § 84-90 (McKinney Supp. 1988). Although privacy laws do make some types of government information unavailable, the diligent investigator can obtain a substantial amount of information. FOIA and FOIL are similar. They each provide that government information will be made available to the public except where a specific enumerated exemption applies. 5 U.S.C. § 552(a), (b); N.Y. Pub. Off. Law § 87. The exemptions are intended to prevent such abuses as invasion of privacy and exploitation of government information to either obtain unfair advantage over the government in civil litigation or avoid criminal prosecution.

Use of FOIA or FOIL has several advantages over use of formal discovery. First, information can be obtained before filing suit and thus before the other party is on notice of the request (note, however, that the identity of the person making the request is not kept confidential and may be published in certain journals). One is no less entitled to information through FOIA because the information is to be used in litigation. *Canadian Javelin, Ltd. v. Securities and Exchange Commission*, 501 F. Supp. 898 (D.D.C. 1980). Second, use of these freedom of information laws does not entail having to satisfy a relevancy standard, such as in the case of a discovery request. *Firestone Tire and Rubber Co. v. Coleman*, 432 F. Supp. 1359 (N.D. Ohio 1976). Third, assuming the requesting party has exhausted the appropriate administrative remedies, an unsuccessful federal freedom of information request is appealable to the district court as a final decision. By contrast, an unsuccessful discovery motion in federal court is reviewable only by either obtaining a writ of mandamus or appealing an adverse final decision on the merits. Furthermore, the standard of appealability for unsuccessful FOIA requests is more advantageous. Instead of the "abuse of discretion" standard used with discovery, freedom of information requests are reviewed de novo. 5 U.S.C. § 552(a)(4)(B).

The exemptions under FOIA and FOIL are not mandatory. An agency might provide information even where it could have withheld the same information under an enumerated exemption. *FTC v. Owens-Corning Fiberglas Corp.*, 626 F.2d 966 (D.C. Cir. 1980). Furthermore, these exemptions are narrowly construed. *New England Apple Council v. Donovan*, 725 F.2d 139

(1st Cir. 1984). In any event, even if information is withheld based on an exemption, it may still be obtainable later in discovery proceedings. *Association for Women in Science v. Califano*, 566 F.2d 339 (D.C. Cir. 1977).[2]

In addition to FOIA and FOIL, one may also request information with a Civil Investigation Demand ("CID") set out in the Antitrust Civil Process Act. 15 U.S.C. §§ 1311-14 ("Act") However, § 1312(c)(1) of the Act exempts from production documents, answers to interrogatories or oral testimony that "would be protected from disclosure under (A) the standards applicable to subpoenas or subpoenas duces tecum issued by a Court of the United States in aid of a grand jury investigation, or (B) the standards applicable to discovery requests under the Federal Rules of Civil Procedure . . ."

The following discussion is intended to provide a sampling of the different types of records and other information that might be helpful to the lawyer's investigation.

B. Medical Records

Hospital, physician, and pharmacy records are essential to the lawyer involved in litigation involving medical evidence.

Hospital records are an invaluable source of information about the patient's condition and treatment when hospitalized. While the quality of recordkeeping varies among hospitals, many hospitals maintain similar types of records. To make the most effective use of available records, an attorney should be familiar with the many categories of information contained in hospital records.

The hospital record includes information concerning both the patient's medical history and current treatment. The chart usually contains progress notes that reveal the patient's progress in the hospital. These are completed by a treating physician or sometimes a resident if the hospital is a teaching facility. Prescription and treatment orders are usually dated and signed by a physician when recorded on the chart (which is occasionally done by a nurse).

Usually, it is the practice to obtain the patient history and conduct a physical examination as soon after admission as possible. If a lawyer is representing the defendant, the medical history can be especially helpful as a source of alternative explanations for a disease or injury. For instance, although a plaintiff claims he has cancer because of the client's product, his medical

---

[2] *Califano* was superseded by the Amendment of Federal Rule 26(b)(1) as stated in *Hammemran v. Peacock*, 108 F.R.D. 66 (1986). However, this is not the proposition for which *Califano* is cited herein.

history may reveal that cancer is very common in his family. Thus, the history may identify alternative genetic explanations for the disease.

Usually, specialized records are kept when surgery is performed. Surgical records reveal when and how a patient has been prepared for scheduled surgery and the nature of the surgical procedure used. Many hospitals employ a surgery preparation record to ensure that any necessary pre-surgical procedures are performed. Surgical records should list the name of the primary surgeon and all personnel present. The hospital record frequently will also contain a note prepared by the lead surgeon or an assistant summarizing the operation. In addition, during surgery, detailed anesthesia records are usually kept which indicate the length of time and the type of anesthesia that was administered. In most instances, the patient's pulse, blood pressure, and respiration will also be recorded by the anesthesiologist as a means of monitoring the patient's response to both the surgery and the anesthesia.

Consent forms often provide useful information to the lawyer. Consent forms, which vary from one institution to another, usually contain information about the procedure to be performed. The hospital record also may contain information about advice to the patient relating to risks of the procedure and the availability of alternative treatments. Obviously, a consent form is of greatest significance if a patient's consent is a major issue in the litigation.

Nurses' notes can also be a good source of information. Comments about the patient's progress, eating habits, attitudes, actions during the course of treatment (*e.g.*, did the individual follow all instructions or did he try to determine his own treatment), emotional and physical reactions to medication, and, finally, the patient's comments about his medical history or the "cause" of his illness may be recorded by a nurse. Patients often speak more candidly to nurses who usually spend the most time with patients before and after surgery. The nurse's notes may also provide useful information about the patient's visitors and events in the patient's room (such as the signing of documents). In many hospitals, nurse's notes are kept separately from doctor's notes. The hospital record may also include sections on checks by hospital personnel of blood pressure, pulse, fluid balances, and medications.

Hospital test reports can be of value in documenting or disproving claims concerning a particular condition and in determining if the course of treatment undertaken was adequate and correct.

A discharge summary is completed at the termination of hospitalization. This form, which is usually completed by the treating physician, summarizes what was done during the patient's stay and may contain instructions given to the patient when discharged. It often includes a diagnosis, prognosis, and a plan for future treatment.

Finally, when a patient returns to the hospital for a check-up subsequent to an illness for which he was hospitalized, outpatient records are generally kept which indicate the patient's post-hospitalization progress.

While hospital records are often the most comprehensive medical records available, the records kept by the client's personal physician, pharmacist, and medical laboratory before and after hospital treatment should not be overlooked. These records often contain evaluations of a disease or condition over a longer period of time. Thus, they often contain information not found elsewhere. For instance, a pharmacy is an excellent source of information regarding the prescription drug intake of an individual during the time that he has patronized the pharmacy. Its records should include a list of all medications used and how often refills were obtained, as well as any medical equipment that was purchased. The records of a private medical laboratory, like those of a hospital laboratory, can provide objective data about the patient's condition as revealed in any test results.

C. Accident Reports

Police reports of accidents are available through requests for "aided/accident" reports. In New York State, Public Officers Law § 66-a provides that interested persons may inspect accident reports kept by police authorities. Also, tape recordings of 911 emergency calls are available. However, 911 tapes, like many computer tapes, are recycled.[3] The original tape may have only a limited retention period, *e.g.*, 90 days, and must be requested as soon as possible. Although in some instances transcripts of recordings are available, they may be objected to on grounds of the best evidence rule and are not always complete.

The United States Coast Guard keeps Search And Rescue (SAR) incident reports. These reports, as well as tapes of voice communications during search and rescue operations, are available from the search and rescue branch of the Coast Guard's Operations Division. While part of New York State is within the Third District of the Coast Guard, which covers the Atlantic coast, the Great Lakes area of the state is part of the Ninth District. Accident reports, including mishaps involving the Coast Guard's own vessels, are available from the Marine Inspection Office.

Public transportation accident reports are available from the relevant public transportation organization, such as the Metropolitan Transportation Authority, or the relevant government-subsidized transportation company, such

---

[3] Similarly, Air Traffic Control tapes are recycled. Unless a major incident occurs, in which the Federal Aviation Administration becomes immediately involved, the request for an Air Traffic Control tape must be made promptly.

as the Long Island Railroad or Conrail. Regulatory agencies may also compile accident reports. For example, the Bureau of Motor Carrier Safety investigates accidents involving common carriers and transportation of hazardous materials. Aircraft accidents are investigated by both the National Transportation Safety Board and the Federal Aviation Administration. These accident reports contain detailed information such as photographs, statistical reviews, and safety recommendations which are prepared by both general aviation experts and experts in aircraft accident reconstruction.

D. Death Certificates

Details concerning a person's death are contained in a death certificate. Usually, a death certificate is filled out by a medical doctor and states the date, time, and cause of death. In a suspicious death, the appropriate Medical Examiner's office may prepare the death certificate. This death certificate specifies the time and place that death occurred and contains the doctor's opinion as to whether death occurred as a result of natural causes, accident, suicide, homicide, or undetermined circumstance, or whether the opinion is pending further investigation. The medical examiner also renders his opinion as to the immediate, underlying, and contributory causes of death. In New York City, death certificates are kept in a centralized file at the Bureau of Vital Records, Department of Health, 125 Worth Street, New York, New York 10013. Outside New York City, county health officials should be contacted to determine where death certificates are filed. If the location of the death is unknown, counsel should contact the State Department of Health, where death certificates are computerized according to last name.

E. School and Employment Records

School and employment records are often very useful in an investigation. While these records are usually available with the consent of the individual student or employee, they may be difficult to obtain without formal discovery if the lawyer does not represent the individual who is the subject of these records.

Employment records often include birthdate, addresses during the time of employment, education, job performance, absenteeism from work, health problems during the time of employment, evaluations by superiors, and salary records. If the person about whom counsel is inquiring has served in the military, the lawyer should consider obtaining his military records. One should be able to obtain the rank, serial number, duty assignments, duty office address, pay, marital status, education, and promotion history. It may be more difficult to obtain the reason for discharge.

Employment records should be closely scrutinized because people sometimes misrepresent previous experience, training or education to improve their prospects for being hired. Resumes in particular are occasionally more fiction than reality and a fertile source for impeachment.

School records may also contain valuable information. Information contained in school records includes birthdate, address, schools previously attended, academic performance, absenteeism, and teacher evaluations.

F. Workers' Compensation and Social Security Records

Files relating to an individual's workers' compensation claim include the medical reports of personal or consulting physicians, hospital records, and correspondence with the individual, his employer, or physicians. However, this information is generally unavailable without the claimant's authorization unless the requesting party is the claimant's employer or insurance carrier. To request the information under FOIL, one should provide the claimant's name, authorization, and if possible, the date of the accident. A successful request will enable the requesting party to examine the files at the workers' compensation office and to photocopy desired portions. Copies of the files are not normally sent out of the office.

The Social Security Administration maintains medical and correspondence files for those individuals who are disabled and receive Social Security assistance. The Administration also maintains correspondence files for people who receive survivor benefits from the Administration. These records are generally unavailable without the authorization of the individual in question unless the requesting party is the individual's legal representative. An employer, however, may receive verification of an employee's social security number. Also, as is often the case with freedom of information requests, social security information normally unavailable without an individual's authorization may be obtained if the individual is deceased.

FOIA requests, with an accompanying authorization, should be made to the claimant's local social security office. Other requests should be made to the Director of the Office of Information, Social Security Administration, 6401 Security Boulevard, Baltimore, Maryland 21235. The requesting party should provide the individual's social security number or, if the social security number is unknown, as much other identifying information as possible including name, and date and place of birth.

G. Corporate Filings

Many important facts about public companies that trade on the New York Stock Exchange, American Stock Exchange or Over-The-Counter are contained in documents filed with the Securities and Exchange Commission (SEC). SEC filings include information regarding a company's directors and officers, auditors, debt structure, depreciation practices, earnings per share, labor contracts, legal agreements, portfolio operations, securities structure, unregistered securities, and relevant tender offers. A private service, known as Disclosure, can obtain most filings. Disclosure can be written to at 61 Ann Street, New York, N.Y. 10038 and can be called at (212) 732-5955.

In New York, much corporate and financing information is filed with the Secretary of State. Available information includes a corporation's status, classes of shares, and identification of the corporation's registered agent. In addition, Uniform Commercial Code financing statements are filed with the Secretary of State. These statements identify the debtor, the secured party, the types of property or collateral covered, and any assignees of the secured party. This financing information is often useful in determining a party's solvency when attempting to satisfy a judgment against it. Filings with the Secretary of State are diverse; information as varied as whether a notary public is validly licensed, whether a charity is actually authorized, or whether trademarks are registered may be available through the Secretary of State.

Land records indicating the ownership of and encumbrances on land are filed with the county clerk where the property is located. In New York City, this information is at the City Register. The county clerk's files also contain partnership records which identify the principals of the partnership and indicate whether the partnership is doing business under a trade name.

City and town building departments possess original blue prints and modification plans for buildings within their jurisdiction. It is often essential to examine these filed plans to compare them with the actual structure when a construction accident occurs or a real estate dispute such as a disagreement about a party wall arises.

To determine whether a professional is licensed, one should contact the applicable regulatory agency. A list of different government agencies that license different occupations is provided in the Green Book, an official directory of the City of New York.

H. Court Records

Information regarding prior litigation in federal court may be obtained through the party index in the relevant district courts. The New York County Supreme Court has a plaintiff index but not a defendant index so one can learn whether the adversary has previously commenced a suit in that County but not the number of times it has been sued. Counsel may also be advised to research prior litigation through the appropriate county clerk's office. At the time of this publication, at least one county clerk's office[4] was preparing to

---

4 Westchester County.

establish a computerized file indexed according to both plaintiff and defendant. The Criminal Court of New York City has computerized records of all summonses and all convictions.

Briefs and records on appeal are available from a variety of sources, though there is no complete and comprehensive collection of these documents. The Association of the Bar of the City of New York maintains a collection which covers not only the Second Circuit and New York State's appellate courts but also the United States Supreme Court and the other federal circuits. Other sources include the New York County Lawyers' Association, the New York Law Institute, and either the relevant appellate court or the lower court from which appeal was taken.

Bankruptcy filings are available from the U.S. Bankruptcy Court. The Southern District has locations in Manhattan and White Plains and the Eastern District has locations in Brooklyn and Long Island. These filings contain information regarding the initial and follow-up schedule of creditors, notices of claims, and the proceedings in the case.

I. Violations of Government Regulations

It is often helpful to know whether an opposing party has previously violated government regulations. Generally, agencies which enforce government regulations retain records of past violations. These records may take the form of dockets, claim letters, or, if the party settled, settlement letters. Even if there is no record of actual violations, the agency may have a record of past complaints concerning the prospective opposing party's, activities or products. For instance, health, building, and fire departments usually maintain records of past violations. Similarly, agencies responsible for the investigation and completion of accident reports sometimes keep records of any violations.

The Coast Guard maintains a record of violations of boating safety laws. Records of past violations are available from the legal department of the appropriate Coast Guard district. These records are referenced to the name of either the owner or the user, and to the boat number.

Enforcement of safety regulations regarding interstate carriers and the transportation of hazardous materials is carried out by the United States Department of Transportation, Federal Highway Administration, Bureau of Motor Carrier Safety. The Department of Transportation's National Highway Traffic Safety Administration ("NHTSA") enforces safety regulations regarding the manufacturing of automobiles and automobile parts. NHTSA has a toll free auto safety hotline ((800) 424-9393) for consumer complaints and sends complainants a vehicle owner questionnaire. Complainants can receive computer printouts indicating other complaints about the same automobile problem.

The Environmental Protection Agency (EPA) inspects plants and responds to citizens' complaints regarding violations of environmental regulations. These regulations pertain to virtually every aspect of the environment, encompassing air, water, and noise pollution, toxic substances and pesticides, radiation, solid waste and sewage treatment plants. The EPA may become involved in the investigation of any incident which may have a substantial effect on the environment.

Records of EPA investigations (*e.g.*, samples, photographs, graphs, transcripts of conversations with individuals in the area of the problem) are kept on file in the regional offices of the EPA. The first step toward obtaining these files is to contact the EPA's Information Office in Washington (*see* Appendix B) which will direct the attorney to the appropriate Regional Office. A request should be submitted in writing. The more detailed the request, the more complete the information counsel is likely to receive.

Information concerning violations of wage and hour laws are available from the U.S. Department of Labor, Employment Standards Administration.

J. Common Carrier Reports

Public and government-subsidized transportation organizations maintain reports of unusual delays or incidents. Such information can be helpful not only if the primary issue of the potential litigation arose as a consequence of the transportation, but also if it is important to establish why or whether a person was or was not at a particular place at a particular time.

Ascertaining a person's whereabouts when he is traveling by automobile is far more difficult. However, there is always the possibility that the person received a traffic ticket or more likely a parking ticket during the period of time at issue. Records of traffic violations are kept by the New York State Department of Motor Vehicles. In New York City, records of parking violations are kept by the Department of Transportation. Outside New York City, most municipalities also have an office that records parking violations.

By providing a license plate number and the approximate time the parking ticket may have been issued, one can find out if a ticket was in fact issued. The notorious "Son of Sam" was located by a detective who traced the defendant through a parking ticket issued to his car parked near the murder scene at the time of the crime.

K. Public Facility Maintenance Records

If the physical condition of government-owned premises is an issue, investigation of public maintenance records may be helpful. For example, New York City's Department of Transportation is responsible for maintaining highways and city streets. Its records can be helpful in a case involving a highway or street accident in which a defective condition, such as a pothole, is relevant. New York City's Department of Transportation is also responsible for the maintenance of traffic lights and traffic signs. In addition, it is responsible for inspecting sidewalks and repairing a defective sidewalk if the owner fails to do so. Requests for Department of Transportation records should be addressed to the Records Access Officer, New York City Department of Transportation, 44 Worth Street, New York, New York 10013.

In some cases, the amount or absence of street lighting is important. In New York City, the Department of General Services is responsible for maintaining the street lighting and possesses records indicating when street lighting was replaced at a particular location.

L. Government Funding Records

Government organizations often give grants to other government entities or private organizations. Information accompanying the grant of such funds may be helpful to a party interested in the project for which those funds were provided. For example, the EPA grants funds for the construction of waste disposal plants. A contractor hired by the local government or a subcontractor hired by the general contractor may want specific information available from the EPA regarding the construction of the plant if litigation arises from that construction.

M. Product Information

The federal government inspects and tests many types of products. Perhaps the most important agency for product information is the Consumer Products Safety Commission, which handles simple information requests through a hotline open from 8:30 a.m. to 8:30 p.m. weekdays. The number is (800) 638-2772. Foreign and domestic automobiles and automobile parts are tested by the National Highway Traffic Safety Administration.

The Food & Drug Administration inspects and tests foods, drugs, cosmetics, and medical devices. Its regulations require manufacturers, packers, and distributors to report unexpected adverse experiences associated with the use of their products. 21 C.F.R. of §§ 310.300, 310.305 (1987) (expanding scope of requirement). These regulations recently received publicity when a major drug manufacturer pleaded guilty to charges that it failed to report adverse effects regarding one of its products.

An attorney should find out whether this type of filing requirement is involved in his case. Failure to meet the requirement might indicate possible concerns about the safety of the product. If the requirement was met, the resulting information may indicate that the defendant was or should have been on notice regarding the cause of the client's injury.

N. United States Postal Service

With a one dollar fee and a written FOIA request, the postal service can provide a postal patron's current address from an old address. There is, however, no standard directory matching names to addresses. The post office's information about a patron's address derives from filed change of address forms. Moreover, the street address of a post office box holder can only be obtained under the requirements listed in 39 C.F.R. § 265(6)(d). A FOIA request should be sent to the post office where the address is located or where counsel believes the individual may maintain a postal address.

O. Weather Information

Weather information may constitute valuable evidence in a variety of cases. In maritime and aviation cases, weather conditions are often an important issue. Weather information can also be helpful even when the weather itself is not a significant issue. For instance, it may be important to know when the last rainfall occurred to determine if wet leaves may have caused someone to fall.

General weather information for the New York City vicinity for a particular day, including temperature, rainfall, and humidity, is available from the New York City office of the National Weather Service, located at 30 Rockefeller Plaza in New York City, if the request is made in person. Written requests should be addressed to the National Climatic Data Center, NOAA, Federal Building, Asheville, N.C. 28801 ((704) 259-0682), which provides weather information for the entire country. More detailed information, such as weather maps, radar photographs, and notices of severe weather conditions, may be obtained by contacting either the General Counsel's Office of the National Weather Service, Department of Commerce, Washington, D.C., or the National Climatic Data Center.

P. Government Standards and Statistical Information

Government statistical data and standards may also be helpful when investigating a claim. For instance, in determining whether a landlord was negligent for providing too little lighting above his stairway, an attorney can consult the information contained in Guidelines For Stair Safety, one of the myriad publications of the National Bureau of Standards. This kind of information can be useful not only for preparing for litigation but also for negotiat-

INVESTIGATION OF CASE AND USE OF EXPERTS

ing a settlement. Showing the other party that its conduct was inconsistent with an established government standard may convince the adversary that it would not prevail in litigation.

The government produces an almost infinite amount of statistical data and standards. However, locating the right information may be difficult. Fortunately, the National Technical Information Service ("NTIS") exists. This is the source of federal publications which have been declassified and made available for public use. NTIS maintains a bibliography of the titles available from the various federal departments and their affiliated administrations, commissions and boards, as well as those from outside sources which were contracted or funded by the federal government. If counsel supplies NTIS with a title, it will provide the order number and price of the publication. At that point, a credit card order can be placed by phone or a check in the proper amount with the title and stock order number can be sent and the item will be forwarded.

If the attorney does not have a title, but does have a topic, NTIS is capable of doing a search for publications which might be of interest, for a modest fee.

In addition, there are a few indexes which are helpful in locating government information. Among them is the "Guide to Sources of Information on Auto Defects," by the Center for Auto Safety, 1223 DuPont Circle Building, Washington, D.C. 20036 and "Federal Motor Vehicle Safety Standards and Procedures," publication No. DOT-HS-805674, April, 1985, U.S. Department of Transportation, National Highway Traffic Safety Administration, Washington, D.C. Also, a "Guide to Freedom of Information Indexes" is published in the Federal Register Index for January to March 1988. This guide lists the agency or subagency name, describes the information index it maintains, and includes information regarding how to order, inspect, or obtain further information about the index.

Q. Computer Records

While any detailed discussion of computerized recordkeeping is beyond the scope of this chapter, it may be useful to note a basic observation about computer records since many records are stored on computers. Computers store information that usually begins in a written document. For instance, in a computerized accounting system, the invoice or written record is merely transferred to the computer at some stage. The lawyer should inquire whether any supporting "back up" documentation is available to determine whether there are any errors in the computerized information and whether the original documents contain any additional information not contained on the computer record.

IV. PRIVATE INVESTIGATORS

Any practitioner experienced in the handling of tort suits has probably had occasion to use private investigators. Private investigators, depending on their ability, can be an invaluable aid to counsel in the preparation of a case. Private investigators can be useful in obtaining witness statements from people who may be frightened by an approach made by an attorney. An experienced private investigator is often better able to approach the witness on the witness's home territory and obtain valuable information. While in the witness's mind the attorney is on a particular "side" of a controversy, such a distinction may not be drawn when an investigator appears at the door to inquire about certain events. In addition, investigators are experts at getting information and, as such, have often had extensive experience in obtaining information from witnesses.

A good investigator will also provide ideas and insights into sources of information about which counsel may not be aware. Private investigators are often knowledgeable about the types of information that can be obtained from governmental agencies and sometimes have relationships with the agencies that can facilitate the gathering of information.

A common use of a private investigator is to observe the plaintiff at times when the plaintiff would not expect to be under observation to determine whether claims of permanent injury or limitation of mobility are credible. Thus, for example, private investigators are commonly used to film a plaintiff walking, mowing the lawn, or engaging in athletic activity inconsistent with claims of a debilitating injury. Similarly, in this surveillance role, investigators are useful in matrimonial actions where the fidelity of one party is at issue and the spouse wishes to confirm that adultery is in fact taking place.

The single most important point to remember in using private investigators is that the attorney must, in all instances, control the efforts of the private investigator. Surveillance, if sufficiently overzealous, may constitute an unlawful invasion of privacy or grounds for a claim of intentional infliction of mental distress. *See Nader v. General Motors Corporation*, 25 N.Y.2d 560, 255 N.E.2d 765, 307 N.Y.S.2d 647 (1970). Therefore, the attorney should review beforehand all steps to be taken by the investigator to obtain the information.

The popular media has aggrandized the role of the private investigator. In many instances, the private investigator is shown in illegal or, at least, unethical acts which ultimately end up "winning" the case. One example of such improper conduct is that depicted in the recent movie "The Verdict," in which Paul Newman, an attorney whose client apparently could not afford the cost of a private investigator, took it upon himself to break into the mail

INVESTIGATION OF CASE AND USE OF EXPERTS

box of a witness to obtain a copy of a telephone bill which would give him the telephone number of a potentially helpful witness. Such conduct constitutes a federal felony, which is not mentioned in the movie. Needless to say, this type of conduct by an investigator should never be sanctioned or tolerated by an attorney.

An important area of potential abuse by an investigator is the telephone. Wiretaps or any means of electronic eavesdropping violate federal and state statutes. Counsel should in all instances expressly advise the investigator not to use such techniques.

Wiretaps and electronic eavesdropping are, however, to be contrasted with the use of "consensual" recordings. Under § 250.05 of the New York State Penal Law, a consensual recording is one in which one party to the conversation is aware of the fact that the conversation is being recorded.[5] Thus, the individual, non-attorney investigator may use a tape recorder to record a conversation with an individual even though the other party to the conversation is not aware that the conversation is being recorded. However, though such recording breaks no law, both Federal Communications Commission regulations and New York administrative rules generally require that the recording party install an automatic device which beeps at 15 second intervals to warn the other party that the conversation is being recorded. The penalty for failing to activate the beeper is loss of telephone service. 11 F.C.C. 1033 (1947); 12 F.C.C. 1005; 86 F.C.C.2d 313 (1981) (FCC rule); P.S.C. No. 900-Telephone, General Tariff in New York State—New York Telephone, § 1 B. 1.1.d.1. (New York rule). In addition, an attorney should keep in mind that there are ethical constraints relating to involvement of attorneys in some types of recordings.

There is no litmus test to determine whether an investigator is a good investigator and appropriate in a particular case. The investigator must be licensed by New York State under Article 7 of the General Business Law. Even when an investigative firm is licensed, the licensed principals in the firm may employ non-licensed investigators. It is important in those circumstances that the attorney insist that the work of the junior investigator be supervised by the licensed investigator so that all rules of investigator conduct are observed.

In some instances, a client may have a relationship with a particular investigator. For instance, insurance companies frequently use investigators to investigate claims. If neither the attorney nor the client has experience with a particular investigator, other attorneys who use investigators are probably

---

[5] Many jurisdictions do not follow the New York Rule and prohibit all recordings unless the party being recorded is informed of and consents to the recording.

the best sources for the names of reputable investigators. It is also frequently helpful to speak to law enforcement personnel to seek the names of reputable investigators. Many of the best private investigators are retired or former employees of law enforcement agencies.

The attorney should look for certain qualities in a private investigator. First, the investigator should be experienced in cases of the kind for which you are seeking assistance. Second, the investigator should have actual courtroom experience in testifying. Although not essential if the investigator will not testify, such experience is valuable because the investigator will have a greater appreciation for the fact that what happens in the field will likely be subjected to the scrutiny of cross-examination. As a result, his work may be more thorough and effective. Private investigators who do not have sufficient testimonial experience are frequently not comfortable when they appear in court.

A private investigator is a professional and should appear to be such when your case goes to trial. Without significant previous experience testifying, the investigator may not project the confidence and professionalism which the attorney seeks for his case. The more experience in testifying that an investigator has, the less likely it is that mistakes will be made in the investigation that will prove detrimental on the witness stand.

V. THE INVESTIGATION OF PARTICULAR TYPES OF CASES

Although there is no single "correct" approach to the investigation of any claim, it may be useful to show how various investigative techniques can be helpful in certain types of cases. This section discusses products liability, medical malpractice, and workers' compensation cases. These cases, which frequently involve many of the same types of tort issues and medical evidence, illustrate how the exact nature of the action will focus the investigative efforts. I have also described a contracts investigation because it will illustrate that investigation is also important in commercial cases.

A. Products Liability

In handling a product liability case, the first step is frequently for the lawyer to obtain a basic knowledge of the product and its uses. At the outset, the lawyer should understand the proper use and handling of the product. A detailed account of the client's use of the product should then be obtained. As early as possible, counsel should gather relevant product documents. These may include advertising materials, labels, warnings, manuals, warranties, bills of sale, and invoices regarding repairs or maintenance. It is important to evaluate the plaintiff's use of the product against any guidelines for use that the plaintiff may have received. There are many instances in which people use products in entirely improper ways.

The lawyer should try to locate the actual product used to determine if it had any deficiencies. Counsel should try to obtain the product's brand name, model number, serial number, and batch and lot number, if the product is produced in batches, such as a chemical or drug. Counsel should also determine if the product or its container had any manufacture or expiration dates. It should be determined whether any component parts were made by other manufacturers who should be sued. An attempt should be made to understand the distribution method the manufacturer uses to determine if the product may have been altered by any transportation processes or by the mishandling of a wholesaler or retailer. If any accessories have been added, information about the accessories should be obtained.

Statements should be obtained from witnesses who may have observed a client's handling of the product. In speaking with witnesses, counsel should focus on whether the witness noticed anything unusual about the client's use of the product.

The plaintiff should also be asked for any information he has regarding his or anyone else's prior use of the same product. If the client has altered the product before or after the incident, the exact alteration made should be reviewed. Finally, if the client had any conversations concerning the product's condition or the incident, these may be important, particularly if he made any damaging statements.

The product information available from the applicable governmental agencies should be sought to determine whether the client's problem with the product is common. Moreover, information about competitors' products should be obtained to assess whether this product and its warning labels conformed to prevailing safety standards.

B. Medical Malpractice

At the outset, the lawyer should recognize that because the applicable limitations period in New York for malpractice suits is two years and six months, the lawyer must move somewhat quickly when investigating malpractice claims. An awareness of the relatively short limitations period is helpful in developing an appropriate investigation schedule.

There are, however, special circumstances in which the statute of limitations for medical malpractice actions will be extended. Perhaps the most significant of these circumstances occurs when there has been continuous treatment and when a foreign object has been left in the patient's body. If there has been continuous treatment of the same illness, injury or condition that gave rise to the alleged malpractice, the statute generally does not run until the date of the last treatment. Continuous treatment, however, does not include examinations requested by the patient for the sole purpose of ascertaining his condition.

When the malpractice claim is based on the discovery of a foreign object in the body, the action must be brought within one year of either the date the object was discovered or of the date the patient learned of facts which would reasonably lead to such discovery, whichever is earlier. Plaintiff's counsel should view these rules as beneficial because they increase the likelihood that he can file suit in a timely manner. He should not, however, allow them to operate as an excuse for delaying the commencement of the action.

As a first step, it is vital to obtain all of the client's medical records. As a rule, the lawyer should ask the client to try to obtain these records or promptly sign authorizations so that counsel may obtain them. The First and Second Departments of the New York Supreme Court have special authorizations forms for this purpose. Complete physician, hospital, pharmacy, and laboratory records should be obtained.

Interview family members and relatives who may have talked with the doctors and who accompanied the client. They may have heard conversations between the doctor and patient and they may recall any unusual circumstances. If the event occurred in a hospital, one may ask a neighboring patient for the same type of information.

The lawyer should confirm that any doctor who treated the patient is properly licensed and qualified to give the treatment in question. Counsel should also investigate whether the doctor has been the subject of prior malpractice actions or other complaints. The Office of Professional Medical Conduct of the State Department of Health, which investigates complaints lodged against doctors, will inform a requesting party whether a particular doctor has been the subject of a formal hearing and what the outcome was of that hearing.

An important step in preparing for a medical malpractice case is to review the records obtained with a physician. The physician should be a competent judge of medical care in the particular medical area in question. In reviewing the material with the physician, an effort should be made to trace the patient's progress. If there are hospital records, they should be closely scrutinized. Nurses' and doctors' notes should be compared as well as the surgical report and anesthesia and recovery records. Pharmacy order sheets should be compared with the record to see if medication ordered was administered as directed. Any conflicting evaluations should be noted. In addition, any substantial changes in the treatment should be studied to determine whether a mistake may have been made that necessitated a substantial change.

C. Workers' Compensation

The attorney who is not familiar with the type of injury or disease of which the client complains should consult one of the many treatises on occupational diseases to more fully understand the symptoms and etiology of the particular occupationally related disease. A widely recognized publication of the United States Public Health Service, *Occupational Diseases: A Guide To Their Recognition,* is often a good place to start learning about the particular disease. Obtaining background information on the disease in question prior to a detailed interview with the client may be productive as it can focus attention on the facts that are relevant to the particular disease.

Many important sources of information can be uncovered through your own client in the investigative phase of a workers' compensation case. As in a malpractice case, the plaintiff can provide his attorney with the names and addresses of any physicians who may have treated him and can sign authorizations enabling the lawyer to obtain medical records. Similarly, the plaintiff can provide access to military and employment records that may be of use.

Counsel for the plaintiff should press the plaintiff for as many details as he can provide concerning the workplace. The plaintiff can frequently draw a sketch of the plant, identify any hazardous areas in the plant, and provide information concerning any hazardous materials used in the plant. Sometimes the plaintiff can provide safety information given to him by the employer. The plaintiff may also be able to provide access to other plant workers who have suffered similar illnesses and/or who could provide additional information about the plant. If another employee is receiving compensation or is on disability, the records of the relevant proceedings should be obtained as they may provide useful information.

Frequently, valuable information concerning the plant, plant conditions, and health conditions in the plant can be obtained from the Occupational Safety and Health Administration ("OSHA"). For instance, if an employee has complained to OSHA about a plant condition that may violate applicable laws, 29 U.S.C. § 657 requires that the complaint be investigated if the Secretary determines that there are reasonable grounds to believe a violation exists. The results of this investigation can sometimes be obtained from the employee making the complaint, because he should receive a copy of the report, or it can be obtained from OSHA. Although an OSHA report is not binding on the State Workers' Compensation Board, it may prove useful in both investigating and presenting the claim.

D. Contracts

Contract cases arise out of either a written or oral contractual agreement. In any contract case, it is thus essential that the practitioner familiarize himself thoroughly with the entire agreement. If the contract is written, the lawyer should obtain all drafts of the contract. In addition, sales proposals, order forms, invoices, checks, or bills of lading should be obtained. Careful reading of all of the provisions of the contract is almost always time well spent. In addition, notes of telephone conversations, meetings, correspondence, and internal memoranda concerning the contract should be obtained.

If the contract is oral, it may be helpful to imagine that you were retained to prepare a written contract based on the oral agreement. In reviewing the terms of the contract in this manner, an oral contract can become clearer.

At the start of a contract investigation, the lawyer should also inquire into the general history of the relationship of his client and the other party. Usually, this history can be obtained by interviewing the client. Witnesses to, or participants in, the transaction should be interviewed. This is especially vital if your client is a large company in which many people act in the company's behalf. In addition, the files of relevant individual employees should be examined. Each employee may have committed valuable thoughts or impressions to writing. Handwritten notes can be especially informative.

When a corporation is involved, the lawyer should inquire about the corporate structure so that he can determine if representations were made or other actions were taken by persons with the apparent or actual authority to bind the corporation.

Needless to say, the lawyer should ask his client to be objective regarding the case. If the issue is one of defective goods, the lawyer should know what problems, if any, exist in similar goods sold to other parties. In some cases, the attorney must learn the standards of the industry to determine whether a particular level of performance is generally considered to be acceptable. Trade associations and other independent industry groups can often provide a wide range of useful information about the industry standards.

In many contract actions, a defendant can raise valid defenses or counterclaims. The defendant's attorney's investigation of the case should be with that goal in mind. If the defendant did not perform completely as a result of plaintiff's own breach, defendant should counterclaim for his damages. Any documents or conversations which support defendant's claim for damages should be sought. Obviously, the plaintiff's lawyer should investigate such defenses and counterclaims before even filing a complaint to determine whether the action may be counter to his client's best interests.

VI. THE RETENTION AND PROPER USE OF AN EXPERT

Although experts are frequently misused by lawyers during the preparation and trial of a lawsuit, an expert can be of invaluable assistance to the trial practitioner at various stages of a lawsuit. The lawyer who skillfully uses experts to assist him can add greatly to the strength and clarity of the case he is seeking to present.

Perhaps the most frequent error lawyers make when employing experts is that they wait to employ the expert until after much discovery is completed and a trial date is approaching. By delaying the hiring of a competent expert, the lawyer loses an important ally in the preparation of the case and places the expert in the difficult position of having to review the case in a hurried and sometimes haphazard way. Just as the lawyer may need time to explore the case and live with it for a while in order to most effectively represent the client, the expert needs time to fully develop a persuasive and comprehensive theory of the case. The lawyer should make it a standard practice to focus on whether an expert is needed at the outset. If an expert is needed, the lawyer should retain one promptly.

In many cases it may appear an unjustified expense to hire an expert in the investigative, pre-complaint, or pre-answer periods in a litigation. If an expert will ultimately be necessary, however, the cost of the expert's services is simply a reality of the expense of litigation which may ultimately be saved many times over in the result.

Often one need look no further than the client to learn about the kind of expert needed. Where the client is a company engaged in a technical area, individuals with useful technical backgrounds are frequently employed by the company and can provide the preliminary education counsel requires to intelligently select an expert and proceed with the case.

Another common misuse of an expert occurs because counsel hires the wrong expert. In this age of complexity and specialization, any notion of a jack-of-all-trades expert is fanciful. The most highly skilled and multi-degreed neurosurgeon may be incompetent to testify about disorders that do not involve the brain and central nervous system. In fact, even for certain issues involving the brain or central nervous system, such as the incidence of brain cancer in a particular population, an epidemiologist may be the more useful expert.

The lawyer should promptly determine the precise type of expert that is needed. One must, as discussed below, look beyond merely the degrees and certifications an individual possesses. In fact, formal credentials are merely the starting point in the search for an expert. It is vital that the expert not merely be well educated; he must be familiar with the precise issues with which he will be asked to deal.

In a complex case involving numerous issues, it may be necessary to hire a number of experts. There are instances, however, in which you may be surprised to find that a multi-disciplinary expert may have just the skills needed. For instance, in a case involving fraud by a restaurant manager, one may not need to hire an accountant and a restaurant manager to serve as experts on the handling of money in a restaurant. There are accountants who specialize in restaurant accounting. Focusing at the outset on the type of expert needed is critically important to insure that the expert selected can provide the needed assistance.

Once an expert is chosen, it is vital for the lawyer to remember that the expert is not trained in law and legal thinking. However much experience the expert may have as a witness, the lawyer must always retain control of the case. Just as when employing the services of a private investigator, the lawyer must direct the expert's efforts. The expert must be made to fit into the litigation; he should not be given control of the litigation.

A principal advantage of retaining an expert early is that an expert can help the lawyer determine the strengths and weaknesses of a case at the outset. The expert can help the lawyer develop a clearer picture of the types of facts that are important. For instance, an accident reconstruction expert, by looking at police photographs of the accident scene, may provide clues as to whether the driver of a car may have been distracted, was the victim of a faulty mechanism, or was speeding. The lawyer should provide the expert with as much information as is available so that the expert has a complete picture of the litigation.

A word of caution is needed here. Under the Federal Rules of Civil Procedure, as well as under some state counterparts, broad discovery of experts is permitted. If the expert is expected to testify, his opinions and conclusions are discoverable. If he is not expected to testify, they are discoverable only under "exceptional circumstances." Fed. R. Civ. P. 26(b)(4)(B). "Exceptional circumstances" generally arise when the other party cannot obtain the desired information through reasonable diligence, such as when opposing counsel has retained the only available expert on a topic or the opposing counsel's expert has inspected something that has changed in a way that makes subsequent inspection fruitless.

Documents given to the expert by the attorney may also become discoverable. Although a lawyer may seek to convey information to the expert as protected work product, the lawyer should be warned that the work product doctrine may not always be asserted successfully. For this reason, some lawyers try to keep many of their preliminary sessions with experts on an oral basis.

The expert should not produce a written report until directed to do so by the lawyer. If the preparation of a formal report is delayed until the expert has had the time to reach all of his conclusions, the lawyer and expert will both be better prepared to present and defend the findings. This avoids the problem of any premature discovery of an expert's work which may contain preliminary findings that are later changed.

Experts can provide assistance in drafting discovery requests. For instance, an expert in a particular kind of manufacturing business will often know the types of documents that such a manufacturer may have in its files and can thus provide assistance in drafting meaningful document requests. Similarly, an expert can assist in drafting interrogatories and in formulating deposition questions because of his technical competence. Once an attorney identifies his adversary's expert, the attorney's own expert can be an invaluable aid in assessing the strengths and weaknesses of the other side's expert.

Again, however, the lawyer must remember that an expert is not a lawyer. However many times an expert may have testified, he still needs to be advised by the lawyer as to what the lawyer perceives to be the critical issues in the case. In addition, some lawyers mistakenly take the view that experts need little preparation for a deposition because of their prior testimonial experience. In reality, the expert needs as much preparation as any witness and sometimes, because of the importance and technical nature of his testimony, he may warrant even more preparation. Experts, too, must be taught how to answer the precise question asked and how to avoid rambling, as well as how to avoid the use of too many highly technical terms.

The selection of an expert can be a difficult process, but there are certain guidelines that, if followed, will help avoid the retention of an unqualified expert. While the experienced trial lawyer who handles many of the same types of cases will probably have a number of experts he regularly employs, in many instances, a lawyer must give substantial thought to the process of expert selection. Even when a lawyer has successfully used an expert before, he should give careful consideration to whether it may be dangerous to use the same expert in a similar case where the expert's prior testimony may be useful to the present adversary. The lawyer must weigh the risk that an adversary may be tipped off from the expert's prior direct testimony as to the lawyer's thinking about this sort of case. In addition, if the lawyer uses the same expert too frequently, he runs the risk that the jury will perceive the expert to be a "professional witness" who will testify to virtually anything for a fee.

Perhaps the best resolution is for the lawyer to follow a rule of moderation in selecting an expert. That is, he should seek an expert who has testified previously, but not one who is exclusively engaged in the business of being an expert witness. Moreover, a witness the lawyer has successfully used before can usually be used again so long as he is not used so often that he may appear to be in the lawyer's debt.

If the lawyer is retaining an expert with whom he is not familiar and who has not been recommended by another lawyer, the lawyer should first obtain the potential expert's resume or curriculum vitae. Once this is done, the lawyer must begin to sort the wheat from the chaff to determine both the quality and applicability of the expert's experience to the particular case at bar.

To illustrate this process, it may be helpful to examine the process of determining whether a particular medical doctor is competent to testify.

First, one should determine if the candidate has successfully completed a residency training program. Such programs, which generally last from three to five years depending on the particular specialty, are usually a prerequisite to specialist certification. Any physician who has not completed a residency program in a specialty field should be considered a questionable expert in that field. No matter how much practical experience he may possess, he will almost certainly be attacked on cross-examination because of his failure to complete this training.

Second, counsel must determine if the expert is certified by the appropriate national specialty board. This is the single most important criteria for qualifying a medical expert witness. Each of the recognized medical specialties has an organized board which gives examinations and certifies that a particular physician is a specialist by training and experience to treat patients in that particular field. If it is unclear what medical specialty is appropriate for a particular disease, the American Board of Medical Specialties, which was organized with the cooperation of the American Medical Association, may be contacted to determine the medical specialty that is appropriate.

Experience is also an important factor. Experience should be measured not merely by the length of time spent in a specialty, but also by the quality of exposure. One must decide whether the experience was obtained at a first-rate medical facility or at a small and less sophisticated facility. A burns expert who spends time in the burn facility of a major teaching hospital is likely to have had a greater extent and quality of experience with serious burns than a dermatologist in a small town. In addition, one should also consider whether the doctor has dealt with the particular illness at issue in the case. Thus, if an expert is needed to testify about burns, there is little sense in hiring as an expert a specialist in psoriasis.

One should also evaluate whether the doctor is generally respected by his peers. A physician who is recognized as a researcher and author in the specialty field will often make a strong witness. For instance, a doctor who has written for a respected journal with peer review of the published articles by other specialists, such as the *New England Journal of Medicine,* is often an appropriate witness.

Local, state, and national professional societies can be important in evaluating the expert witness. Calling the particular associations on the doctor's resume can sometimes provide valuable insights. When asking whether a doctor is a member of the association, one can ask how active he is in the association. It is sometimes possible to obtain valuable information about his reputation and degree of involvement with the group. In the surgical field, membership or lack of membership in the American College of Surgeons is perhaps especially indicative of a surgeon's expertise.

Other types of experts can also provide valuable assistance to the lawyer. Economists and accountants are often useful in damage determinations and in working out the division of assets in a divorce. An economic expert can provide attorneys with a precise assessment of the damages sustained while accountants can determine the various tax implications of a property division. By relying on such expertise, it is often possible to avoid either the understatement or overstatement of the damages sustained.

To qualify as an economic expert, an individual should have earned a doctorate in economics. Evidence of formal research such as research grants and the publication of research results can be an important source of help in assessing the expert's qualifications. One should also consider whether the economist has been appointed to any governmental positions. In addition, if he is an academic, one should consider both his position at the university and the quality of the university with which he is affiliated.

An economist's testimony, like that of many experts, can be enhanced by the use of graphs and charts. One should always be sure that expert testimony is made as simple as possible for the sake of the trier of fact.

In the case of an accountant, it should be considered at the outset whether the accountant is a Certified Public Accountant. His experience and familiarity with the particular type of case should also be considered. For instance, in a tax shelter case, only a Certified Public Accountant with substantial tax shelter experience should be consulted.

One interesting, though less well known, category of expert is the human factors expert. Human factors experts deal with man's operation of machines. These experts are especially helpful in machine injury and product liability cases. They can analyze the contribution of the machine's operation or design to the cause of the injury. Their analysis is based upon the specific facts of an accident and their knowledge of normal human behavior and capabilities. Such an expert can study the design of the product to determine if ordinary consumer expectations were considered in analyzing the risks to which use of the product would expose the consumer. Although there are now doctorate programs at the university level, most human factors experts are psychologists or engineers. In the years ahead, it is likely that human factors experts will become an increasingly important source of expert assistance to the trial lawyer.

APPENDIX A
DIRECTORY OF SELECTED FEDERAL GOVERNMENT AGENCIES

This Directory is intended to provide a current listing of the addresses and phone numbers of some of the federal agencies that can be especially useful sources of information.

A. Consumer Product Safety Commission
   5401 Westbard Avenue
   Bethesda, Maryland 20207

   1. Procurement Information   301-492-6444
   2. Freedom of Information/
      Privacy Act   301-492-5785

B. Department of Health and Human Services
   200 Independence Avenue, S.W.
   Washington, D.C. 20201

   1. Public Information   202-475-0257
   2. Freedom of Information/
      Privacy Act   202-472-7453

C. Department of Justice
   Tenth Street and Constitution Avenue, N.W.
   Washington, D.C. 20530

   1. Procurement Information   202-272-8444
   2. Public Information   202-633-2007
   3. Freedom of Information/
      Privacy Act   202-633-3642

D. Department of Transportation (Main Address)
   Nassif Bldg.—400 Seventh Street, S.W.
   Washington, D.C. 20590

   1. Procurement Information   202-366-4952
   2. Public Information   202-366-5580
   3. Freedom of Information/   202-366-4542
      Privacy Act   202-366-1887

E. Environmental Protection Agency
   401 M Street, S.W.
   Washington, D.C. 20460

1. Procurement Information — 202-382-5020
2. Public Inquiries — 202-382-2080
3. Freedom of Information/
   Privacy Act — 202-382-4048

F. Federal Aviation Administration
   800 Independence Avenue, S.W.
   Washington, D.C. 20591

   1. FAA Records Center Facility
      P.O. Box 437
      Martinsburg, West Virginia 25401

   2. Operational Test and Evaluation Staff
      FAA Technical Center
      Atlantic City Airport, New Jersey 08405 — 609-484-4000

G. Food and Drug Administration
   Department of Health and Human Services
   Parklawn Building
   5600 Fishers Lane
   Rockville, Maryland 20857

   1. Medical Staff Chief—Robert V. Veiga — 301-443-5470
   2. Health Science Administrators — 301-443-4480
   3. Freedom of Information Inquiries — 301-443-6310

H. National Climatic Data Center, NOAA
   Federal Building,
   Asheville, N.C. 28801

   1. Public Inquiries — 704-259-0682

I. National Highway Traffic Safety Administration
   Department of Transportation
   Nassif Building—400 Seventh Street, S.W.
   Washington, D.C. 20590

   1. Public Inquiries — 202-366-5972

J. National Injury Information Clearing House
   U.S. Consumer Product Safety Commission
   Room 625—5401 Westbard Avenue
   Washington, D.C. 20207

   1. Public Inquiries — 301-492-6424

K. National Technical Information Service
    5285 Port Royal Road
    Springfield, Virginia 22161

    Att: Sales Desk or Order by Phone w/ Credit Card

    1. General Orders   703-487-4650
    2. General Information   703-487-4600
    3. Customer Service   703-487-4660

L. National Transportation Safety Board
    800 Independence Avenue, S.W.
    Washington, D.C. 20594

    1. Procurement Information   202-382-6731
    2. Public Information   202-382-6600
    3. Freedom of Information/
       Privacy Act   202-382-6546

M. Occupational Safety and Health Administration
    Department of Labor
    200 Constitution Avenue, N.W.
    Washington, D.C. 20210

    1. Office of Information & Consumer Affairs
       Director James F. Foster (N3637)   202-523-8148
    2. Public Information   202-523-8151

N. Office of Workers' Compensation Programs
    Department of Labor
    200 Constitution Avenue, N.W.
    Washington, D.C. 20210

    1. Office of Director, Lawrence W. Rogers, Jr.
       (S3524)   202-523-7503
    2. Medical Standards & Rehabilitation Branch
       Medical Director
       Virginia Miller (S3522)   202-523-7497

O. Securities and Exchange Commission
    450 Fifth Street, N.W.
    Washington, D.C. 20549

    1. Procurement Information   202-272-7010
    2. Public Information   202-272-7450
    3. Consumer Complaints   202-272-7440

4. Freedom of Information/
   Privacy Act   202-272-7420

P. Social Security Administration
   Baltimore, Maryland 21235

   1. Public Information   301-965-2738

Q. United States Postal Service
   475 L'Enfant Plaza West, S.W.
   Washington, D.C. 20260

   1. Procurement Information   202-268-4100

   2. Public Information   202-268-2145

   3. Freedom of Information/
      Privacy Act   202-268-2924

R. Veterans Administration
   810 Vermont Avenue, N.W.
   Washington, D.C. 20420

   1. Public Information   202-233-2817

   2. Freedom of Information/
      Privacy Act   202-233-3616

APPENDIX B

SOURCES FOR MEDICAL INFORMATION

1. MEDICAL ASSOCIATIONS

For each of the recognized medical specialties, there is a professional association that can be an excellent source of information about diseases treated by the particular specialty. Telephone numbers and addresses for these associations can be obtained from the Encyclopedia of Associations. This multi-volume encyclopedia also contains valuable information on foreign associations.

2. NATIONAL LIBRARY OF MEDICINE (NLM)

The most complete collection of medical information in the country is at the National Library of Medicine, based in Washington, D.C. This national library has regional branches including the New York Academy of Medicine. This library system has a medical database which allows for extensive computer searches, an excellent interlibrary loan system that allows for circulation of materials between all branches and the National Library, and research and medical staff who are available for consultation. The National Library of Medicine can be contacted at:

Office of Inquiries and Publications Management, Room 2515

>National Library of Medicine
>8600 Rockville Pike, Building 38
>Bethesda, Maryland 20894
>(301) 496-6308

The New York Academy of Medicine can be contacted at:

>New York Academy of Medicine
>Medical Library
>2 East 103rd Street
>New York, New York 10029
>(212) 876-8200

3. CENTERS FOR DISEASE CONTROL (CDC)

Based in Atlanta, the Centers For Disease Control is an excellent source of disease information. As the national research facility handling the study of many diseases, the CDC is an invaluable source of information about diseases that it is studying. The Centers For Disease Control has regional and branch offices throughout the country. Centers for Disease Control (CDC) is located in Atlanta, Georgia. Telephone inquiries can be made to the main number, (404) 639-3311 or to public information at (404) 639-3534.

4. ASSOCIATIONS RELATED TO DISEASE

Disease oriented associations, such as the American Cancer Society and the Multiple Sclerosis Society, can provide much useful information. If an attorney thinks there is an association for the disease he is investigating, he should consult the Encyclopedia of Associations. These associations are often set up with the express purpose of supplying the most comprehensive information available on the disease to anyone who wants such information. It is usually best to contact one of these associations by telephone or in person, as written requests for information tend to take longer to process. Also, these associations can be an excellent starting place for contacting medical experts who deal with the disease being researched.

CHAPTER SIX

COMMENCEMENT OF THE ACTION —THE COMPLAINT

by Richard G. Menaker, Esq.

I. INTRODUCTION

The phrase "commencement of the action" is a term of art in federal civil litigation that means both more and less than it might seem. Like the "commencement" at the close of an academic year, an action's commencement is really an intermediate step in a much longer process—in one sense the conclusion of much preparatory work, in another sense the beginning of a new stage of activity.

While the rules and concepts associated with commencing an action through drafting and filing a complaint seem simple and straightforward, much more is involved than the rules superficially suggest. The procedure has more than its share of twists and misnomers.

For example, filing the document known as the "complaint" in a strict sense "commences" the action under Federal Rule, and it ordinarily stops the running of the statute of limitations, at least as to a claim brought under the court's federal question jurisdiction. But the action is otherwise meaningless and has not truly begun until the complaint has been duly served on the defendant. And in some instances, where the claim is predicated on state law, the statute of limitations may continue to run until the complaint is served. *See* Section VII, B, *infra*.

As another example, Rule 8(a) requires the complaint to consist of a "short and plain statement of claim" and the official Forms would seem to confirm this. But few experienced practitioners would dare to rely exclusively upon those forms, and an enormous number of complaints are dismissed for pleading deficiencies notwithstanding Judge Clark's famous dictum that "special pleading cannot be made to do the service of trial and . . .

live issues between active litigants are not to be disposed of or evaded on the paper pleadings." C. Clark, Special Pleading in the "Big Case," 21 F.R.D. 45, 49 (1957).

The entire subject is mined through with traps for the unwary, many potentially fatal to the prosecution of the action. One of the purposes of this chapter is to alert practitioners to some of the more significant of these traps. In the following discussion, we describe the requirements of the Federal Rules of Civil Procedure ("Fed. R. Civ. P.") governing complaints, compare and contrast federal pleading practice with New York practice under the Civil Practice Law and Rules ("CPLR"), and offer hints on the drafting of complaints in several of the kinds of actions frequently brought in federal court.

II. LAYING THE GROUNDWORK

A. The Goals and the Obstacles

The function of the federal civil complaint is to give notice to the defendant of the claim being asserted—a requirement of due process—and to place that claim before the district court so that it can be considered on the merits.

The plaintiff faces a number of obstacles in achieving these goals. Some of the obstacles have already been discussed in connection with service of process and other jurisdictional issues. *See* Chapters 1 and 2, *supra*. But there are additional obstacles that relate to the formulation of the complaint itself, including the risk of dismissal on grounds unrelated to the merits of the plaintiff's cause, or dismissal on the merits based upon deficiencies in the drafting of the complaint, Fed. R. Civ. P. 12(b),(c), 56. Moreover, the power of the courts to impose monetary sanctions for "frivolous claims" under Fed. R. Civ. P. 11, increasingly yet unpredictably exercised, creates further risks and anxieties for the draftsmen of complaints.

There are thus powerful reasons for the plaintiff's attorney to take great care in preparing the complaint. The success of the action and the security of the attorney's own pocketbook may depend heavily on the groundwork laid before the complaint is filed.

B. Determining the Grievance

The first steps involve active consultation with the client. *See* Chapter 5, *supra*. The attorney must listen carefully to the client's description of his or her grievance. This may take more time than the busy attorney would like, because the client's thinking may not be well organized and the client's attempts to explain the problem may not be completely articulate.

The attorney should nevertheless be careful not to interject unduly, to make assumptions about the facts, or to suggest facts that seem to fill in gaps in the client's account. Such gaps should instead serve as red flags, inducements to additional investigation that will ferret out the real facts. To this end, the client should be asked to turn over, and the attorney must carefully review, all relevant documents, photographs and other evidence as a precondition to the attorney's accepting any engagement to commence proceedings. A client's tale sometimes acquires new perspective in the light of the applicable documentation.

C. Identifying the Client's Objectives

The attorney must also develop with the client a clear understanding of objectives. A lawsuit must have a goal; yet the courts (and this includes the federal courts) are limited in the kinds of relief they can provide. They can award damages; they can enjoin injurious conduct; they can declare the parties' rights. How the complaint is formulated will be substantially affected by the relief the client seeks. Determining objectives is an interactive process and may only emerge from diligent questioning by the attorney.

D. Satisfying Rule 11

The requirements of Fed. R. Civ. P. 11, referred to above, make independent investigation of the facts essential. The attorney's inquiry should not end with the client's account of the facts or even with a review of the documents. The client should be asked to identify sources of corroborating evidence, and these should then be pursued unless it would jeopardize the client's case. Considerations of the need for speed or to avoid telegraphing an impending action may limit outside inquiry, but in most cases it should be pursued.

Equally mandated by Rule 11 is appropriate legal research prior to drafting the complaint. Nothing is more critical, not even understanding the facts, because if the facts are not presented in terms that the courts recognize as constituting valid sources for awarding relief, the claim may be turned away without ever being considered on the merits. Among the best initial source for developing appropriate legal theories based on the facts are updated editions of the standard legal encyclopedias such as *New York Jurisprudence* and *Corpus Juris Secundum*, as well as specialized treatises. For diversity cases presenting potential claims under New York law, Carmody-Wait 2d, *Cyclopedia of New York Practice* provides useful checklists of the requisite elements of traditional theories.

E. Reconstituting the Case

The federal courts generally continue to follow the legal formalism that has characterized the common law adjudicative process throughout much of this nation's history. This means that grievances must be molded to fit in legalistic cubbyholes previously established by legislatures, government agencies or, most often, the courts themselves. Sometimes the facts will not fit the theory the client and attorney originally anticipated. It then becomes the task of the attorney to reconstruct the case by accommodating its theory to the facts and the law. This should always include appropriate explanations to and approval of the client.

Where it becomes clear that the existing law simply will not support relief upon the facts involved, and there seems no reasonable basis to try to extend the law, the client must be so advised and the project should cease.

F. Checklist of Predrafting Preparation

____ 1. Fact session with the client.

____ 2. Request for and review of documents and other evidence.

____ 3. Delineation of client's objectives in bringing action.

____ 4. Independent investigation.

____ 5. Legal research to determine theories of claim.

____ 6. Constructing outline of case by applying law to facts.

____ 7. Reviewing proposed case with the client.

III. DRAFTING THE COMPLAINT—GENERAL CONSIDERATIONS

A. Modern Pleading, the Theory

Pleading in the early days of the federal courts, as in state practice, was concerned with the formulation of issues from which proof at trial could not deviate. The intricacies of such pleading are notorious and led in 1848 to the enactment of New York State's Field Code, the model for procedural reform for many generations thereafter. The Field Code eliminated the distinction between actions at law, suits in equity and introduced the concept of a single form of action—"for the enforcement or protection of private rights and the readers or prevention of private wrongs." L. Friedman, *A History of American Law* at 340-347 (1973).

The Field Code's progeny include the Federal Rules of Civil Procedure, by way of the Federal Equity Rules, whose pleading provisions are the direct model for the counterpart provisions in the current Rules. The crux of the modern theory of pleading is "notice," not formulation of issues. Fed. R. Civ. P. 8(a). As stated by the Supreme Court in *Conley v. Gibson*, 355 U.S. 41, 47 (1957), "all the Rules require is 'a short and plain statement of the claim' that will give the defendant fair notice of what the plaintiff's claim is and the grounds upon which it rests." If more detail is needed, it may be obtained through discovery under Fed. R. Civ. P. 26. Under the modern theory, the pleadings are not where one finds the proof on which the adversary will rely.

The Appendix of Forms annexed to the Rules seems to reinforce the principle of simplicity and notice. Federal Rule 84 emphasizes that the forms "are sufficient under the rules and are intended to indicate the simplicity and brevity of statement which the rules contemplate." The forms set out claims under traditional theories in two or at most three paragraphs. For example, a complaint for goods sold and delivered would consist of nothing more than an allegation of jurisdiction, an allegation that:

> [d]efendant owes plaintiff _____ dollars for goods sold and delivered by plaintiff to defendant between June 1, 1936 and December 1, 1936,

and a demand for relief. Official Form 5.

B. Modern Pleading, the Reality

It may be true that the most elementary common law claims would today be deemed sufficiently pleaded if phrased in line with the Appendix of Forms. Few experienced federal practitioners, however, will have seen or submitted such concise complaints in the district courts. The reality is that the courts pay lip service to the concept of notice pleading, but in many instances they require much more.

Pleading practice, which Rule 8 was aimed at abolishing, has not vanished. Defendants continue to make motions to dismiss, and the courts continue to grant them with frequency. The phenomenon has sparked much recent commentary. *See, e.g.*, R. Marcus, *The Revival of Fact Pleading under the Federal Rules of Civil Procedure,* 86 Column. L. Rev. 433, 434 n.12 (1986). In the words of Professor Marcus, "*Conley* is not taken literally." And again: "Although they rarely acknowledge the shift, federal courts are insisting on detailed factual allegations more and more often." *Id.* at 435-436.

The environment is fluid. Much turns on the temperaments of individual judges and certain fashions regarding the claims at issue. As of this writing, state law claims brought in federal court on diversity grounds are not in favor; nor are civil RICO claims, antitrust claims or civil rights claims. On the other hand, claims for securities fraud seem to be finding a more favorable reception than a decade ago when the limits of the substantive law were not yet settled. Claims in connection with employees' benefits now have the advantage of the pre-emptive effect of ERISA: the federal courts must hear them. Claims under the admiralty and patent jurisdictions have long escaped excessive scrutiny at the pleadings stage.

The pretrial significance of these fashions or trends in judicial attitude towards different kinds of claims is that the practitioner must make exceptional efforts to meet, and even surpass, the governing legal standards for pleading claims that are out of favor. Special attention must be paid to the rules relating to pleading with particularity, a subject discussed more fully below. *See* Part V, *infra*.

C. Comparison with New York's CPLR

The theory of pleading in New York State practice follows the same principle of notice. *See* CPLR 3013. Like the federal approach, New York has endorsed the reduced importance of pleadings and the enhanced role of discovery. D. Siegel, *New York Practice* 245 (1978) (hereinafter, "Siegel"). In both systems, there are no prohibitions against pleading legal conclusions as well as factual allegations. But there are a few differences in approach that at least in theory seem to affect the way the complaints in each system should be formulated.

In New York practice, the predicate for obtaining relief from a court is establishing a "cause of action," a concept with roots in the Field Code. CPLR 3013. The federal rule, in contrast, has replaced that concept with the expression "claim showing that the pleader is entitled to relief." The intent of the draftsmen was to eliminate the "unfortunate rigidity and confusion surrounding the words 'cause of action' that had developed under the codes," while furthering the modern emphasis on notice pleading. 5 C. Wright & A. Miller *Federal Practice and Procedure* § 1216 at 115 (1969) (hereinafter "Wright & Miller").

The significance of the distinction is less practical than theoretical. In theory, a properly pleaded "cause of action" under the CPLR should give the defendant notice of the respects in which the "transactions" or "occurrences" complained of have given rise to each element required for liability. Thus, a cause of action for breach of contract should recite the existence of the contract, the relevant provision that was breached, how the breach occurred, and the resulting injury to plaintiff. In federal practice, the "claim for relief" supposedly need only give notice of "claim" sued on, without setting forth the requisite legal elements. *E.g.*, Official Form 3. Yet an attorney who neglected to allege any of the elements in the breach of contract example described above would run the same risk of dismissal in federal court as in state court.

The only practical effect of the distinction is in the physical layout of the complaint. A pleading for state court should separately label each "cause of action," and under each label the requisite elements should be fully laid out. Incorporation by reference from other separately labeled causes of action is permitted, but it should be explicit in each instance.

The federal complaint, on the other hand, need not separately label each claim for relief that arises from the same transaction or occurrence. Fed. R. Civ. P. 10(b). A single recital of facts in a group of numbered paragraphs encompassing multiple claims is permitted. Unlike in state court, where the assertion of more than one theory under a single label may result in dismissal for "duplicity" (meaning "doubleness," not dishonesty), an unlimited number of claims may be comprehended by a single statement of facts. This does not mean that organization of the complaint under headings (labeled "counts" or "claims for relief") is undesirable. To the contrary, it is to be encouraged, and some district courts have even required it notwithstanding Rule 10(b). 5 Wright & Miller § 1324 at 471-472. But it is necessary in federal practice only to the extent the claims arise out of separate occurrences or transactions.

To sum up, the shibboleth of "notice pleading" provides an uncertain standard for actual formulation of a complaint, and the prudent draftsman will not rely upon it. As a rule of thumb, the attorney writing a complaint for a federal court should plead enough factual detail to show every legally required element of each "claim for relief" as if it were being presented as a "cause of action" under state law. Prolixity should certainly be avoided. But rare is the complaint that is dismissed because of ample, literately phrased detail.

IV. DRAFTING THE COMPLAINT— THE PARTICULARS

A. Appearance and Format

The attorney should look both to Federal Rules and to the relevant local rules for guidance as to format. Every complaint must carry on the first page a caption setting forth the name of the court, the title of the action, the file or "docket" number and a designation that it is a complaint. Fed. R. Civ. P. 10(a). The complaint is the only pleading whose caption must set forth the names of all parties; all subsequent pleadings may state the name of the first party on each side, followed by an "et al." to indicate that other parties have been named. *Id.*

The local rules in the four New York district courts require that all pleadings be "plainly and legibly written, typewritten, printed or reproduced." E.D. and S.D.N.Y. Civ. R. 1; N.D.N.Y. Gen. R. 7; W.D.N.Y. Local R. 13. In the Eastern and Southern Districts the caption must carry the initials of the judge assigned to the action. Civil Rule 1(a). All four courts require covers (*i.e.*, "backs") setting forth the name, office and post office address and telephone number of the attorney for the filing party.

Accompanying the caption, usually just below the title of the pleading, is the jury demand if the plaintiff seeks a trial by jury. As a general matter, claims at law (*e.g.*, for damages) may be tried by a jury. U.S. Const. amend. VII. The joinder of legal with equitable claims will not preclude a jury trial. *See* 9 Wright & Miller § 2306 at 37. The demand consists simply of the phrase "Jury Trial Demanded"; that alone preserves the right. The demand may also be made separately, no later than ten days after service of the last responsive pleading, which ordinarily will be the defendant's answer, Fed. R. Civ. P. 38(b), with three extra days added if the responsive pleading is served by mail. Fed. R. Civ. P. 5(b), 6(e).

Every complaint must be manually signed by an attorney of record and show that attorney's address and telephone number (except in *pro se* circumstances, where the party must sign). Fed. R. Civ. P. 11; E.D. and S.D.N.Y. Civ. R. 1(b); N.D.N.Y. Gen. R. 7. The procedure of verification by the client provided for in state practice, CPLR 3021, exists in the Federal Rules only for shareholders' derivative actions under Rule 23.1.

In the Western District all complaints must be dated, Local Rule 13, which is a good practice to follow with court papers in any jurisdiction.

Immediately below the caption and title of the paper, there should appear a brief introductory sentence such as: "Plaintiff X, by his attorneys Y, for his complaint against defendant alleges as follows:". Thereafter, the complaint must contain three substantive components—a statement of jurisdiction, a statement of claim, and a demand for judgment. Fed. R. Civ. P. 8(a). We consider each of these in turn.

B. Pleading Jurisdiction

1. Subject Matter Jurisdiction

Federal courts are courts of limited jurisdiction. It is the duty of the party who comes to such court for relief to show at the outset that it has the authority to hear the case. Fed. R. Civ. P. 8(a)(1). The principal grounds for federal jurisdiction are presence of a federal question, 28 U.S.C. § 1331, diversity of citizenship of the parties, 28 U.S.C. § 1332, admiralty or maritime jurisdiction, 28 U.S.C. § 1333, or jurisdiction expressly conferred by a substantive federal statute—*e.g.*, the antitrust laws, 15 U.S.C. § 4, or the securities laws, 15 U.S.C. § 77V. *See generally* Chapter 1, *supra*.

Form 2 of the Appendix of Forms contains a useful model of each of the principal grounds for invoking the federal court's subject matter jurisdiction. Rule 8(a)(1) requires only a "short and plain statement" of the grounds for subject matter jurisdiction. Federal question jurisdiction ("arising under" the constitution or a federal statute) and admiralty and maritime jurisdiction may be alleged in a single paragraph, usually the first in the complaint.

COMMENCEMENT OF THE ACTION—THE COMPLAINT 147

It is essential in admiralty cases that the substantive allegations of fact make it clear that the case is indeed within the admiralty jurisdiction as traditionally exercised by the federal courts. Inclusion of a $50,000 amount in controversy is desirable, if it can be done in good faith because of a division of view among the courts as to whether it is necessary. 5 Wright & Miller § 1211 at 101.

In diversity cases, the complaint should introduce each party in a separate paragraph and state the party's citizenship, showing it to be different from that of each adverse party. A further paragraph must allege that "the matter in controversy exceeds, exclusive of interest and costs, the sum of ten thousand dollars." 28 U.S.C. § 1332(a).

Claims based upon state law may be asserted in a complaint that also asserts a federal question claim, where the state and federal claims "derive from a common nucleus of operative fact." *United Mine Workers v. Gibbs*, 383 U.S. 715, 725 (1966). Such "pendent" state claims, will be governed by state substantive law. 383 U.S. at 726. An amount in controversy is no longer required for general federal question jurisdiction, although the pleader should be alert to the requirements of particular statutes. *E.g.*, Consumer Product Safety Act, 15 U.S.C. § 2072 (requiring allegation of $10,000 matter in controversy).

2. Personal Jurisdiction, Venue and Capacity

Rule 8(a)(1) only covers subject matter jurisdiction. The complaint need not set forth any basis for jurisdiction over the person of the defendant, nor need it justify venue. 5 Wright & Miller § 1206 at 81. Separate paragraphs identifying each party are customary, and while not always legally required, it is desirable to include such information early in the complaint.

Where the right to assert a particular kind of claim is limited to persons suing in a certain capacity, the complaint should affirmatively plead capacity to show that the court has jurisdiction. Fed. R. Civ. P. 9(a). Thus a corporation should be designated as such and its place of incorporation expressly averred to show diversity. *See* Official Form 2(a). Union officials suing on behalf of employees must allege their authority to sue under the Fair Labor Standards Act. 29 U.S.C. §§ 201 *et seq.*; 5 Wright & Miller § 1239 at 208. On the other hand, appointment of a plaintiff as administrator, executor, guardian, receiver, or similar representative should be indicated, but it is sufficient to do so in the caption. *E.g.*, "John Smith an Executor of the Estate of William Clarence Jones, Deceased, Plaintiff v. Richard Roe, Defendant." 2A J. Moore, *Federal Practice* ¶ 9.02 at 9-16 to 17 (1987) (hereinafter "Moore").

C. Pleading the Claim for Relief

1. Separation of Paragraphs and Counts

Under Fed. R. Civ. P. 10(b), all averments of claim should be made in separately numbered paragraphs. While it is rarely possible to limit each paragraph to the allegation of a single fact, the attorney should plan what kind of an answer he or she hopes to get from the defendants. Where a paragraph of the complaint has sharply focused upon a single fact or narrow set of facts, the defendant's denial or statement of lack of information is likely to be of greater value later in the case than a similar response to a more expansive paragraph.

As stated above, the presentation of claims is less strictly governed in federal practice than it is under the CPLR, although it is ordinarily required that claims based on separate occurrences or transactions be stated in separate counts. Fed. R. Civ. P. 10(b). The attorney should organize the claims in a manner that "facilitates the clear presentation of the matters set forth." *Id*. Separately labeling all claims, even if several arise from the same occurrence or transaction, is the safest practice.

2. Adoption by Reference

Undue repetition can be avoided through adopting by reference statements from one court in subsequent courts. Fed. R. Civ. P. 10(c). Where references must be made to lengthy contractual or other documentary language, the relevant document may be attached as an exhibit at the end of the complaint and expressly incorporated in a single phrase—*e.g.*, "which is fully incorporated by reference in the complaint and is made a part hereof for all purposes." *Id*.

3. Alternate or Hypothetical Pleading

The Federal Rules explicitly permit a complaint to set forth claims "alternatively or hypothetically" and "regardless of consistency." Fed. R. Civ. P. 8(e)(2). Such leniency arises from the general principle discussed above that pleadings are not vehicles for defining issues to be tried but means of providing notice to one's adversary. It is presumed that discovery will enable the plaintiff to hone down the party's theory of the case, and that inconsistent claims will be discarded by the time of the trial.

Alternate or hypothetical pleading can allow the plaintiff to avoid being bound to a single scenario when all the facts are not yet known. For example, on questions of causation in a personal injury case, the complaint may allege separate negligence counts against the maker, the owner and operator of the offending equipment on hypothetical grounds that are mutually inconsistent. Similarly, in an action to recover assets of a bankrupt, a plaintiff has been

COMMENCEMENT OF THE ACTION—THE COMPLAINT

permitted to assert alternatively that either certain funds were transferred while the bankrupt was insolvent or that the transfer of the funds rendered the bankrupt insolvent. 5 Wright & Miller § 1282 at 369, citing *Shaw v. Gaurdy*, 11 F.R.D. 145 (N.D. Ohio 1950).

The alternative or hypothetical pleading of action must conform to the requirements of Rule 11, requiring a legal and factual basis for asserting each claim. On the other hand, Rule 11 does not compel an election of remedies. If the attorney has complied with the pre-filing reasonable inquiry of Rule 11 and has a basis for believing a claim exists, but has a doubt concerning the facts that would narrow it to a simple theory, the attorney will be free to plead alternatively or hypothetically without offending Rule 11. 2A Moore ¶ 833 at 8-230.

4. Pleading on Information and Belief

Both attorney and client may encounter factual matters needed for adequate pleading of a claim which cannot be confirmed firsthand at the time the complaint is drafted. This is especially a problem where relevant information is exclusively in the possession of the defendant. Although the Federal Rules do not expressly provide for it, practice in the federal courts permits a party to plead elements of a claim "on information and belief," subject to the constraints of Rule 11. Such pleading is appropriate where the party's information is secondhand or derived by reasonable inference from facts known to the party. *See* 5 Wright & Miller § 1224 at 156157.

Pleading on information and belief is not appropriate where the matter is in fact within the personal knowledge of the pleader. Moreover, as noted below, the particularity requirements of Rule 9(b) make it desirable for a complaint pleaded on information and belief to set forth the facts upon which the belief is derived. *Odette v. Shearson, Hamill & Co.*, 394 F. Supp. 948 (S.D.N.Y. 1975). Even where such supporting facts need not be pleaded, the practitioner should be sure to keep a record in the files of what facts were relied upon for any information and belief allegations so that an appropriate response can be made to discovery requests from the adversary at a later date.

D. Pleading the Demand for Judgment

1. Form of the Demand

The final component required in a federal complaint is a "demand for judgment for the relief the pleader seeks." Fed. R. Civ. P. 8(a)(3). For this there is no required form other than a short statement identifying the remedies sought and the parties as to whom each item of relief should be applied. 5 Wright & Miller § 1255 at 250. In that respect the demand for judgment in a federal complaint may be shorter than the demand for relief or "wherefore" clause (sometimes referred to as the "*ad damnum*" in money actions) in state practice. CPLR 3017(a). Because there are state-law causes of action where damage is a substantive element of the claim, Siegel § 217 at 259, state-law practitioners often separately enumerate each item of relief as to each cause of action. That approach is unnecessary in a federal complaint.

The demand for judgment appears at the end of the pleading. As in state practice, it usually begins with the word "wherefore" and thereafter lists the items of relief sought. The demand may seek traditional legal relief—such as money damages, replevin or restitution—as well as equitable remedies—such as an injunction, specific performance, accounting and rescission. *See generally* D. Dobbs, *The Law of Remedies*. Relief may be demanded in the alternative or of several different types. Fed. R. Civ. P. 8(e)(2).

2. Subsequent Modification

Federal practice is somewhat more flexible than the CPLR with respect to the extent to which a plaintiff will be bound by amount or character of the relief demanded. Not only is amendment liberally permitted, Fed. R. Civ. P. 15, but perhaps more important, Rule 54(c) permits the granting of the relief to which the plaintiff is entitled "even if the party has not demanded such relief in the party's pleadings."

In state practice, in contrast, such modification after verdict rests with the discretion of the trial court. *Loomis v. Civetta Corinno Const. Corp.*, 54 N.Y.2d 18, 429 N.E.2d 90, 444 N.Y.S.2d 571 (1981).

An exception to the federal court's flexibility arises in the case of a default judgment, which must adhere precisely to the demand for relief. Fed. R. Civ. P. 54(c). If there seems any likelihood of a default, it is desirable to specify maximum appropriate damages.

3. Particularity in Demanding Money Damages

The rules plainly contemplate that the complaint may set forth the specific dollar amount of damages the plaintiff is claiming, *see* Official Form 9, and indeed failure to do so in a default context may deprive the plaintiff of any right of enforcement. Fed. R. Civ. P. 54(c). On the other hand, a complaint will not be deemed defective for failure to specify damages; some district courts (not in New York) have even deemed it the better practice to omit a specific demand where the complaint requests a jury trial. 5 Wright & Miller § 258-259.

Nevertheless, particularity is required in the pleading of "special damages," a trap for the unwary. Fed. R. Civ. P. 9(g). Special damages, as distinguished from general damages (which need not be specifically pleaded), are "those elements of damages that are the natural, but not the necessary, consequences of defendant's conduct." 5 Wright & Miller § 1310 at 443. Thus in a personal injury case, pain and suffering result in general damages, while medical expenses and loss of earnings are items of special damages that must be pleaded. 36 N.Y. Jur. 2d, "Damages" §§ 187-188, 193-198 (1984). In an action for breach of contract, any consequential damages such as loss of profits must be specifically pleaded. *Id.* § 199.

The mode of particularized pleading required for special damages depends on the nature of the case. Where the special damages are simply sought as a supplement to general damages, it is sufficient to identify them in the relevant counts and list them in the demand for judgment. However, certain claims for relief such as defamation make special damages an essential element of liability itself. As to those claims, the complaint should allege with particularity the circumstances giving rise to the special damages under the relevant count, as well as itemizing such damages in the demand for judgment. 5 Wright & Miller § 1311 at 448-449.

4. Declaratory Relief

A federal complaint may seek a judgment from the district court declaring the rights of the parties, as authorized by the Declaratory Judgment Act, 28 U.S.C. § 2201. Such relief may be requested in addition to whatever other legal or equitable relief is available, Fed. R. Civ. P. 57., and the rules of pleading are the same as for other federal civil actions. 5 Wright & Miller § 1238 at 202.

The Declaratory Judgment Act does not independently constitute a jurisdictional basis for coming into federal court; it therefore need not be recited in the complaint. *See* Official Form 18. Instead there must be an independent basis of subject matter jurisdiction, but the court has the discretionary power to decline to hear the case. 28 U.S.C. § 2201(a) (providing that the court "may" declare rights and other legal relations). Moreover, the action must present an "actual controversy" with the court's jurisdiction, since the federal courts may not issue advisory opinions. *Id.* The complaint must therefore frame the plaintiff's claim in terms of an actual dispute with the defendant, and should also emphasize considerations of equity and policy that warrant an exercise of discretion in favor of hearing the case.

E. Checklist for Drafting the Complaint

____ 1. Prepare the caption.

    ____ a. Name of court.

    ____ b. Names of all parties, properly designated as plaintiff or defendants.

    ____ c. Space to insert case number and judge's initials (after filing).

    ____ d. Title of pleading.

    ____ e. Jury demand.

____ 2. Draft introductory sentence.

____ 3. Assert basis for subject matter jurisdiction.

____ 4. Identify parties, showing capacity where necessary for jurisdiction.

____ 5. In separately numbered paragraphs, allege the occurrences or transactions upon which claims for relief are based.

____ 6. Organize claims into separate counts, incorporating by reference prior allegations where appropriate.

    ____ a. All elements of each claim set forth.

    ____ b. Particularized pleading where necessary (*see infra*).

    ____ c. Special damages where necessary.

____ 7. Draft demand for judgment.

    ____ a. All items of relief identified.

    ____ b. Special damages quantified.

    ____ c. Maximum supportable damages quantified where default is anticipated or possible.

____ 8. Enter date.

____ 9. Manually sign and include address and telephone of attorney.

V. "PARTICULARITY" IN PLEADING

A. The Requirements of Rule 9

Rules 8 and 9 are the Jekyll and Hyde of the Federal Rules of Civil Procedure. While Rule 8(a) stresses the simplicity contemplated in modern pleading theory, and Rule 8(e) mandates that each averment "shall be simple, concise, and direct," Rule 9 identifies certain matters that must nevertheless be "stated with particularity." Reconciling the two rules has been left to the courts. The pleader must be prepared to struggle with the uncertain guidelines that have emerged.

COMMENCEMENT OF THE ACTION—THE COMPLAINT

1. Pleading Fraud

Rule 9(b) requires that "in all averments of fraud, or mistake, circumstances constituting the fraud or mistake shall be stated with particularity." This requirement derives from the view of the draftsmen of the Federal Rules and of many courts that fraud allegations are frequently asserted with little foundation or as a catch-all where a more precise theory of claim seems unavailable. As Judge Carter put it, "[t]he irreparable damage to reputations and goodwill, which inevitably results from charges of fraud, and the threat of baseless strike suits are ample reasons for careful judicial review of claims alleging fraud." *Somerville v. Major Exploration, Inc.*, 576 F. Supp. 902, 909 (S.D.N.Y. 1983).

The traditional elements of fraud are generally (i) a representation of a material existing or pre-existing fact, (ii) falsity, (iii) scienter (knowledge a belief as to truth or falsity by the person making the representation), (iv) deception and (v) injury to the claimant. 60 N.Y. Jur. 2d, "Fraud and Deceit" § 11 at 445-446 (1987). All of these elements should be alleged, although they are not "circumstances" as referred to in the rule. Indeed, pleading only the elements of fraud will not be sufficient. *Hunter v. H.D. Lee Co., Inc.*, 563 F. Supp. 1006, 1012 (S.D.N.Y. 1983). The circumstances that must be pleaded in addition are matters such as the time, place and contents of the false representation, the identity of the person making it, and what that person gained as a result. 5 Wright & Miller § 1297 at 403.

Rule 9(b) has provided the courts with an open door through which they have been able to boot disfavored complaints. Only state of mind—*i.e.*, "malice, knowledge, intent"—need be stated generally under the rule. Otherwise, the degree of detail required can be extraordinarily subjective. The example given in Official Form 13 is by no means an adequate indication of what some courts have required. As a result, any complaint alleging fraud faces the risk of dismissal depending upon the intensity with which the court chooses to scrutinize the pleading "circumstances."

Certain kinds of cases are more vulnerable than others under Rule 9(b). A decade ago actions for alleged securities fraud were prime targets for intense scrutiny. *E.g.*, *Blue Chip Stamps v. Manor Drug Stores*, 421 U.S. 723 (1975). As of this writing, the civil liability provisions of the Racketeer Influenced and Corrupt Organizations Act, 18 U.S.C. §§ 1961 *et seq.* ("civil RICO") have led to an extraordinary amount of pleading practice, based upon many plaintiffs' allegations of mail fraud and wire fraud to meet the "predicate acts" element of the statute.

Fraud by its very nature may involve covert activity and deception; thus facts needed to plead with particularity may be exclusively in the possession of the defendant or third parties. The only solution to this quandary is diligence. The attorney preparing to draft a claim for fraud must be prepared to shoulder a greater than usual pleading burden. Thorough investigation is essential. The paragraphs of each fraud count should tell the story of the deception, answering the questions who, what, where, when, how and why. Where a missing link remains, the pleading should briefly identify it, indicate why it is missing and suggest what it will take to discover it.

The goal in pleading fraud should be more than just giving notice of the claim; it should be to satisfy a court that there is merit to the claim. If the attorney determines that he or she cannot accomplish that on the facts available, the client should be so advised and consideration given to not asserting the claim.

2. Pleading Mistake

Claims of mistake ordinarily arise out of circumstances where the plaintiff's own conduct has resulted in the injury which he or she alleges. Examples may include a contract, deed or obligation which the plaintiff seeks to abrogate or reform because of a mistake in drafting or in understanding relevant facts, 55 N.Y. Jur. 2d "Equity" §§ 8385 (1986), or a default judgment which the plaintiff seeks to set aside under Federal Rule 60(b).

Some of the same considerations applicable to the pleading of fraud with particularity likewise relate to claims of mistake. The claim is easily stated even when altogether without foundation. Moreover, the basic principles of notice pleading should require a plaintiff to advise a defendant of the circumstances of an act or omission that was largely or entirely of the plaintiff's own doing.

Therefore, the complaint should recite in detail the circumstances of the mistake, again providing answers to the who, what, when, where, how and why questions that a defendant or court may be expected to ask. In the case of an instrument that the plaintiff seeks to reform, the mistake must be shown to be "material"—that is, affecting the substance of the transaction. 55 N.Y. Jur. 2d, "Equity" at 516. Where the complaint seeks to vacate a default judgment, the mistake or neglect must be shown to be "excusable." Fed. R. Civ. P. 60(b).

3. Other Pleading Provisions of Rule 9

With the exception of special damages (discussed above), Fed. R. Civ. P. 9(g), the other pleading provisions of Rule 9 are intended to liberalize pleading practice over common law requirements.

Rule 9(c) eliminates the need to allege in detail the performance or occurrence of a condition precedent, placing the burden on the defendant to deny that element "specifically and with particularity." The rule still requires a general averment of compliance with the contract, but that is all. Doing more, in fact, creates the risk that the detailed allegations will not adequately show compliance, thereby paradoxically rendering the complaint legally insufficient. 5 Wright & Miller § 1303 at 431.

General allegations are likewise sufficient in pleading compliance with law in the issuance of an official document or doing of a public act. Fed. R. Civ. P. 9(d). Similarly, it is sufficient to allege the existence of a judgment or a judicial decision without showing the court's jurisdiction to render it. Fed. R. Civ. P. 9(e).

In response to the allegation of "time and place," the Federal Rules are stricter than practice under the common law, which regarded such matters as immaterial. As a matter of substantive law, certain claims must include an allegation of time or place, and are insufficient if the pleading omits them. Claims in which time must be alleged include those based upon fraud (as noted above), for payment on commercial paper and under certain statutes, such as the securities laws. Allegations of "fraudulent concealment," an equitable doctrine tolling the statute of limitations, should also specify time. Both time and place should be alleged in claims for defamation and for personal injury based upon the defendant's negligence. Rule 9 does not compel such particularity—the substantive law does. The rule does provide, however, that where time and place are alleged, they become "material." Fed. R. Civ. P. 9(f). Therefore, an error in specifying the relevant time may render the claim vulnerable to dismissal under the statute of limitations.

Rule 9(h) permits a plaintiff asserting a claim within the admiralty and maritime jurisdiction to have the benefit of the Supplemental Rules for Certain Admiralty and Maritime Claims by stating at the outset: "This is an admiralty or maritime claim within the meaning of Rule 9(h)." *See* Official Form 15. As noted above, pleading that language does not eliminate the need to set forth allegations in each count sufficient to state a cognizable admiralty or maritime claim. 5 Wright & Miller § 1313 at 454.

B. Particularity of State-Law Claims in Diversity Actions

The provision governing particularity of pleading in state actions in New York, CPLR 3016, covers many more kinds of claims than Fed. R. Civ. P. 9. The only direct overlap is CPLR 3016(b), which parallels Rule 9(b)'s requirements for the pleading of fraud and mistake with particularity. As a general matter, the Federal Rules supersede the CPLR when a state-law cause of action is pleaded as a federal claim. *Hanna v. Plumer*, 380 U.S. 460 (1965). Nevertheless, the attorney who is preparing a federal complaint that includes one or more claims required to be pleaded with particularity in state practice will find it useful to consult CPLR 3016. A federal judge is likely to regard a state-law claim that meets the requirements of CPLR 3016(b) as well-pleaded even if, or perhaps especially because, it carefully lays out matters required under the state rule.

Such extra effort is not just desirable but necessary in claims of defamation. Although the federal rules do not contain a counterpart to CPLR 3016(a) requiring that the particular words complained of be set forth in the complaint, there is authority in the New York federal courts that pleading the substance of the defamatory language is desirable. *Liguori v. Alexander*, 495 F. Supp. 641 (S.D.N.Y. 1980).

C. Special Requirements for Class Actions and Shareholder Suits

A class action or a shareholders' derivative suit does not ordinarily require greater particularity in pleading than other civil actions. But under Rule 23.1, the complaint in a derivative suit must be verified. Moreover, it must expressly state (1) that the plaintiffs were shareholders (or in the case of an association, members) at the time of the transaction complained of and (2) that the suit is not a collusive effort to obtain federal jurisdiction. The complaint must also allege "with particularity" the plaintiffs' efforts to obtain redress by the organization and the reasons why this proved unsuccessful. Fed. R. Civ. P. 23.1.

Under Rule 23, a complaint bringing suit on behalf of a class must contain a section alleging that (1) the class is so numerous that joinder of all members is impracticable, (2) there are questions of law or fact common to the class, (3) the claims of the representative parties are typical of the claims of the class, and (4) the representative parties will fairly and adequately protect the interests of the class. Fed. R. Civ. P. 23(a). In addition, the pleader should consult the conditions concerning when a class action is appropriate, as set forth in Rule 23(b), and allege the condition that is applicable to the case at hand.

Finally, the pleader should consult the local rules of the district in which the class action is being brought. The Eastern, Southern and Western Districts require the complaint to bear a "Class Action" designation next to the caption and to include the requisite allegations in a separate section headed "Classification Allegations." E.D. and S.D.N.Y. Civ. R. 4; W.D.N.Y. Local R. 8. These rules also require the pleading of particularized averments supporting the presence of each element of Federal Rule 23.

D. Court-Imposed Particularity

Anyone who has followed the federal courts closely over the past decade will have noticed their frequently stated concern about heavy caseloads and the various proposals advanced to remedy the problem. One by-product has been an enhanced receptivity to summary adjudication prior to trial, including especially dismissals of complaints for legal insufficiency, sometimes without leave to replead.

Part of this trend is what one commentator has described as "the revival of fact pleading" in certain kinds of cases in which courts "refuse to accept 'conclusory' allegations as sufficient under the Federal Rules." R. Marcus, *supra*, 86 Colum. L. Rev. at 435. Professor Marcus has identified securities fraud, civil rights cases, and conspiracy cases as especially vulnerable.

1. Securities

Securities complaints are vulnerable not only for failure to allege fraud with particularity under Rule 9(b), but also for failure to specify any basis for alleging guilty knowledge or wrongful intent. *Id.* at 448. Civil rights complaints have failed for lack of any specific delineation of the facts claimed to show a violation of the plaintiff's civil rights, including discriminatory intent. *Id.* at 449. Claims predicated upon "conspiracy" have been held insufficient for failure to list the overt acts that supposedly evidenced the illegal agreement. *Id.* at 450.

2. Antitrust

Antitrust complaints have occasioned controversy in the context of whether stricter pleading standards are required for a "big case" than for more conventional cases. That question seems generally to have been answered in the negative. *Id.* at 445. Still, a claim for restraint of trade under Section 1 of the Sherman Act should allege in detail the "conspiracy" or "concert of action" complained of, including overt acts, as well as the nature of the injury to the plaintiff's business or property that is a precondition to suit. 9 U.S.C. §§ 1, 4. Moreover, if the currently hostile environment for monopolization cases should change, it will still be essential for the pleader to allege carefully the offending acts of monopolization or attempt to monopolize, together with a description of the relevant market in which the monopolization occurred and the nature of the resulting injury to the plaintiff's business or property. 9 U.S.C. § 2.

3. Civil RICO

Civil RICO, currently one of the most popular and controversial predicates for liability in commercial tort cases, now functions under a thick overlay of judicially created pleading requirements. The statute authorizes a treble damages suit for any person injured by the misconduct of an enterprise engaged in a "pattern of racketeering activity." 18 U.S.C. § 1964(c). To show such a pattern, the complaint must allege the occurrence of two or more criminal acts recognized by the statute, within a ten-year period, with sufficient "continuity plus relationship" that the acts cannot be regarded as isolated events. *Sedima, S.P.R.L. v. Imrex Co., Inc.*, 473 U.S. 479, 496 n.14 (1985).

The substantive law governing pleading of "pattern" and "enterprise" is rapidly developing, and differences in standards among the circuits have emerged. Any pleader contemplating a civil RICO claim should carefully study the most recent cases before drawing up the complaint.

4. Constitutional Rights

Claims based upon violations of constitutional rights present special problems for the courts, since such a large portion of them are in the context of *habeas corpus* applications. A set of general Rules has been promulgated governing cases under 28 U.S.C. sections 2254 and 2255. In addition, three of the four district courts in New York have local rules regulating the contents of petitions for *habeas corpus*. E.D. and S.D.N.Y. Civ. R. 32, N.D.N.Y. Gen. R. 31; *see also* W.D.N.Y. Local R. 21. The petition must recite all prior applications for relief, if any, identifying the court and judge, the determination in each case, and any new facts on the present petition that were not previously shown. Full detail in the presentation of the facts is essential.

The "state action" precondition to a valid claim under the Constitution adds to the difficulty in persuading a court to grant such claims. Institutional considerations make the courts hesitant to invoke the Constitution against the other branches of government. Thus even in a non-habeas context, the complaint should provide a detailed account of the Constitutional violation and show the respect in which the plaintiff has been injured. 5 Wright & Miller § 1234 at 184-185.

5. Intellectual Property

Pleading in intellectual property cases requires similar attention to particularity. The Official Forms for infringement of copyright, unfair competition and patent infringement are among the few models in the Appendix of Forms that call for real detail. *See* Official Forms 16, 17. As to patents, the complaint must identify the patent that has been infringed and the respects in which it occurred. A trademark infringement claim must not only identify the infringed trademark but also allege its registration. 5 Wright & Miller § 1237 at 201. Ownership by the plaintiff should be pleaded in all intellectual property cases. *Id.* at 200, 239.

E. Checklist for Particularity in Pleading

    ____ 1. Fraud claims should recite

        ____ a. all traditional elements,

COMMENCEMENT OF THE ACTION—THE COMPLAINT

    ____ b. time, place and content of false representation,

    ____ c. identity of person making representation.

____ 2. Mistake claims should recite

    ____ a. detailed statement of circumstances,

    ____ b. materiality (with respect to instruments),

    ____ c. excusability (with respect to default judgment).

____ 3. Allegation of time and/or place required by substantive law for

    ____ a. fraud claims,

    ____ b. fraudulent concealment (tolling statute of limitations),

    ____ c. commercial paper and similar contract claims,

    ____ d. certain statutory claims,

    ____ e. personal injury claims based on negligence,

    ____ f. defamation claims.

____ 4. Class actions—follow Rule 23 and applicable local rule.

____ 5. Shareholders' derivative suits—follow Rule 23.1.

____ 6. Requiring special attention—court-imposed particularily in claims under

    ____ a. antitrust laws,

    ____ b. civil RICO,

    ____ c. civil rights laws,

    ____ d. Constitution,

    ____ e. intellectual property laws,

    ____ f. securities laws.

____ 7. Be alert to pleading requirements for state-law claims even where not strictly required under the Federal Rules.

____ 8. Be alert to elements of claim under any federal statute relied upon as basis for claim.

VI. FILING THE COMPLAINT

It is often said that a client needs an attorney "who knows his (or her) way around the courthouse." This is literally true when the time comes for filing the complaint. The pleader's learning, industry and hours of labor are worthless unless the complaint is duly filed. Prompt filing may be particularly critical if the statute of limitations is about to expire.

A. The Civil Cover Sheet

The attorney must know before submitting the complaint for filing what the clerk's office will require in order to accept the pleading and issue a summons. All four districts require submission of an information sheet with the complaint, the form of which is available from the clerk's office. The Southern District specifies that the "civil cover" sheet be submitted in triplicate and requires that eight items of information be supplied for civil cases. *See* Rules for Division of Business, Rule 4(a). Of these items, only those requiring indications of "the nature of the action and amounts involved" and "the category of the case" need give the practitioner pause.

As to the "nature of the action," one need simply set out a brief statement of the complaint's principal theories, with appropriate reference to any federal statute under which the claims arise. It is perhaps advisable to add the phrase "and related claims" so that an adversary can make no argument based upon what is set forth on the cover sheet.

The form then lists a number of categories of claims with a box beside each and requires the attorney to "place an X in one box only." The box marked will guide the clerk in determining which "wheel" will be turned for the purposes of assigning the case to a judge. Where the complaint contains multiple claims based on different theories, the practitioner is free to select any one of them for designation on the cover sheet. This may create an opportunity to affect which judge is assigned. It is generally known that certain judges are regularly assigned to certain kinds of cases, particularly admiralty, labor, securities and intellectual property cases. If a preferred judge is among those assigned to handle any of the claims alleged in the complaint, the practitioner should check the relevant claim box likely to lead to an assignment to that judge.

The "demand" line on the Southern District's information sheet is ambiguous. It could be filled in with a dollar figure or with a "yes." Ordinarily, one cannot err by inserting "greater than $50,000" or "not less than" the amount set forth in the demand of relief. The line that says "other," if applicable, can be filled in with either "equitable relief" or a more particular designation such as "injunction" or "declaratory judgment."

B. General Rule 9 Statement

The Eastern and Southern Districts both require that the complaint be accompanied at the time of filing by a certificate of identification of any corporate parents, subsidiaries or affiliates of any corporate plaintiff. General Rule 9. This enables the judges and magistrates of the court to evaluate possible disqualification or refusal.

C. The Summons

The practitioner should obtain a blank form of summons and fill it out prior to filing the complaint. The clerk will then "issue" the summons when the fee is paid and the pleading submitted. General Rule 9(h) of the Northern District makes submission of a previously prepared summons a precondition to acceptance of the complaint for filing.

D. Fees

A further precondition to filing is payment of the requisite filing fee. The amount should be confirmed in advance by review of an up-to-date schedule of fees or by a call to the clerk's office. Fees have increased several times in recent years and are currently $100 in the Eastern and Southern Districts. Ordinarily the fee must be paid in cash or money order or by check with the printed indication on it that the drawer is an attorney.

VII. EFFECT OF FILING ON STATUTES OF LIMITATIONS

The effect of filing the complaint on the running of the applicable statutes of limitations is a complex and in some respects controversial matter. The original Advisory Committee for the Federal Rules was not of one mind on the subject, and the issue continues to generate conflicting court decisions and debate in the professional and academic journals. The following outlines the generally applicable principles, but the practitioner should consult the latest cases for guidance if any doubt arises.

A. Federal Question Claims

The basic rule seems to be that as to all federal question claims, Federal Rule 3 governs the tolling of the statute of limitations, *except* those for which a directly applicable federal statute provides a different rule. *West v. Conrail*, 481 U.S. 35 (1987). This means that unless Congress has provided explicitly to the contrary, Rule 3's simple statement that a civil action "is commenced by filing a complaint with the court" makes such filing sufficient to stop the running of the limitations period.

The Supreme Court's decision in *West* reversed both the district court and a unanimous panel of the Third Circuit, which had held that under Section 10(b) of the National Labor Relations Act, 29 U.S.C. § 160(b), a complaint against an employer pursuant to the Railway Labor Act, which had been filed within but served after the requisite six months, was time barred. In reinstating the action, the Supreme Court held that

> when the underlying cause of action is based on federal law and the absence of an express federal statute of limitations makes it neces-

sary to borrow a limitations period from another statute, the action is not barred if it has been "commenced" in compliance under Rule 3 within the borrowed period. 481 U.S. at 37 (footnote omitted).

Certain 1983 amendments to Rule 4 have added a further wrinkle to this situation. Rule 4(a) was modified to shift responsibility for service of the summons and complaint from the court clerks and the United States marshals to the plaintiff's attorney. A new Rule 4(j) has provided for dismissal without prejudice if the summons and complaint are not served within 120 days after filing.

Thus, the filing of the complaint commences a federal question case for statute of limitations purposes, but only conditionally. If service is not effected within the next 120 days, the complaint is dismissed, and the plaintiff is left in the same position as if the action had never been commenced. If the statute of limitations has expired in the meantime, the action is barred. *See* 4 Wright & Miller § 1056 at 187.

Nevertheless, if the plaintiff can show "due diligence" in attempting to serve the complaint, the statute of limitations may still be held to have been tolled. Rule 4(j) contains a provision that the complaint will not be dismissed if the plaintiff can show "good cause why such service was not made" within the 120-day period. The alert practitioner will take these words to heart by undertaking service immediately after filing the complaint and by meticulously documenting every effort to make service upon the process-evading defendant.

B. Diversity Cases

Federal Rule 3 does not furnish the tolling rule in a diversity action where the claim in question is based upon state law. *Walker v. Armco Steel Corp.*, 446 U.S. 740 (1980). Under the principles of *Erie R. R. Co. v. Tompkins*, 304 U.S. 64 (1938), when the claim is based on a right created by state law, the state's provisions governing commencement of the action and their effect on the statute of limitations control in the federal court. *Ragan v. Merchants Transfer & Warehouse Co.*, 337 U.S. 530, 533534 (1949).

The provisions of Rule 4, discussed above, apply in diversity as well as federal question cases. Therefore an attorney pursuing an action as to which state law requires service of process for commencement must accomplish such service both (a) before the state statute of limitations runs and (b) within 120 after filing the complaint. 4 Wright & Miller § 1057 at 206. While some state laws contain grace periods for recommencement after a "voluntary" dismissal, New York law is not among them. *See* CPLR 205(a); Siegel § 232 at 281. With service or process, as with so much else relating to the complaint, diligence is rewarded, its opposite punished.

CHAPTER SEVEN

PROVISIONAL REMEDIES

by Denis McInerney[*]

I. INTRODUCTION

In theory, the so-called "provisional" remedies (preliminary injunctions and temporary restraining orders, attachment and garnishment, and receiverships) are designed, as their name implies, to meet only a temporary need—that is, to maintain the *status quo* or protect the interests of one of the parties during the pendency of the action. In fact, a provisional remedy application is frequently not just a preliminary skirmish; it is the whole war. In tender offer cases, for example, a preliminarily enjoined tender offer is often a dead letter; on the other hand, if the offer is not enjoined and succeeds, the ousted incumbents rarely pursue their permanent injunction action. In these and other cases, a request for a provisional remedy is not merely a pretrial motion; it is *the* trial and there is no subsequent trial. The whole litigation may be over in a matter of days, and there may be no effective appeal—either because of time constraints or the discretionary nature of the remedy.

Accordingly, this is not an area that lends itself to "on the case" learning as the need arises. While it is always possible to learn from defeat, the prudent practitioner will become acquainted with provisional remedy procedures well before using them under a tight time deadline. The material that follows, while obviously not a comprehensive treatment of legal issues, is intended to provide a roadmap for those who prefer to become familiar with dangerous territory before entering it.

---

[*] The author gratefully acknowledges the assistance of his associate, David R. Scheidemantle, in preparing this chapter.

Before considering each of these remedies, it should be stressed that each of them is not only extraordinary but equitable in nature, and therefore subject to the usual requirements (*e.g.*, no adequate remedy at law, no unfair prejudice to the opponent) and defenses (*e.g.*, laches, unclean hands) applicable in equity.

II. PRELIMINARY INJUNCTIONS AND TEMPORARY RESTRAINING ORDERS

A. Commencing the Action and Bringing On the Motion

1. General Requirements

To obtain a preliminary injunction ("PI") a distict court within the Second Circuit, the movant must demonstrate two elements: "(a) irreparable harm [if the PI does not issue] and (b) *either* (1) likelihood of success on the merits *or* (2) sufficiently serious questions going to the merits to make them a fair ground for litigation and a balance of hardships tipping decidedly toward the party requesting the preliminary relief." *Jackson Dairy Inc. v. H.P. Hood & Sons, Inc.*, 596 F.2d 70, 72 (2d Cir. 1979) (*per curiam*; emphasis added); *see Stormy Clime Ltd. v. Progroup, Inc.*, 809 F.2d 971, 973 (2d Cir. 1987); *Church of Scientology International v. Elmira Mission of the Church of Scientology*, 794 F.2d 38, 41 (2d Cir. 1986).

The essential element of irreparable harm has been defined to mean injury for which a monetary award cannot be adequate compensation. Therefore, "it has always been true . . . that where money damages is adequate compensation a preliminary injunction will not issue." *See Jackson Dairy Inc. v. H.P. Hood & Sons, Inc.*, *supra*, 596 F.2d at 72.

Bearing this in mind, the applicant should consider the possibility that precise allegations of money damages in the complaint could undermine a claim that a preliminary injunction is the exclusive means of protecting the plaintiff from irreparable harm. *See, e.g., Weinberger v. Romero-Barcelo*, 456 U.S. 305, 312 (1982); *Sampson v. Murray*, 415 U.S. 61, 88-92 (1974); *Jackson Dairy, Inc. v. H.P. Hood & Sons, Inc.*, *supra*, 596 F.2d at 72-73. A PI " 'is not a remedy which issues as of course,' " *Weinberger v. Romero-Barcelo, supra*, 456 U.S. at 311 (*quoting Harrisonville v. W.S. Dickey Clay Manufacturing Co.*, 289 U.S. 334, 337-38 (1933)); it can be awarded only upon a clear showing that the movant is entitled to the relief. *See, e.g., Buffalo Forge Co. v. Ampco-Pittsburgh Corp.*, 638 F.2d 568, 569 (2d Cir. 1981); *Medical Society v. Toia*, 560 F.2d 535, 538 (2d Cir. 1977); *New York v. Nuclear Regulatory Commission*, 550 F.2d 745, 750 (2d Cir. 1977). *See generally* 11 C. Wright and A. Miller, *Federal Practice and Procedure* §§ 2942, 2944 (1973). Thus, the importance to the movant of demonstrating

PROVISIONAL REMEDIES

clearly and convincingly exactly why money damages are inadequate cannot be overstated. *See, e.g., Rondeau v. Mosinee Paper Corp.*, 422 U.S. 49, 57-65 (1975).

2. The Motion and Related Papers

Since prompt relief is usually important, the movant will often want to shorten the period before the return date by proceeding by order to show cause ("OTC") rather than by notice of motion. The proposed OTC should recite the preliminary injunctive relief sought and leave blanks for the return date of the motion.

If the movant also seeks a temporary restraining order ("TRO"), the nature of the temporary restraint sought ("pending hearing on the motion for a preliminary injunction") should be recited as well. Counsel should be aware, however, that as a general rule, district judges will not grant a TRO or similar relief *ex parte*, but will insist that the other side be given at least telephonic notice and an opportunity for argument.

The motion must be supported by an affidavit showing the need for each item of relief requested. If the motion is by OTC, there must be a "clear and specific showing by affidavit of good and sufficient reasons why procedure other than by notice of motion is necessary." S.D.N.Y. & E.D.N.Y. Civ. R. 3(c)(4). The PI affidavit should specify the injunction sought and the grounds for it, addressing with particularity each prong of the PI standard described above. *See* 11 C. Wright and A. Miller, *supra*, § 2949, at 468. The affidavit must recite (typically in the final numbered paragraph) that "no prior application for this or similar relief has previously been sought in any court" or explain why it is not possible to so state.

Pertinent law and facts, corresponding to the two-pronged PI standard, should be set out in a legal memorandum. Civil Rule 3(b) of the Local Rules for the Southern and Eastern Districts of New York requires service and filing of memoranda of law "[u]pon any motion"; failure to comply with the Rule "may be deemed sufficient cause for the denial of the motion or the granting of the motion by default." S.D.N.Y. & E.D.N.Y. Civ. R. 3(b). *Accord* N.D.N.Y. Gen. R. 10(c), (g).

A proposed order containing the PI should also be appended as an exhibit to the affidavit or brief. Fed. R. Civ. P. 65 is quite specific regarding the form and scope of the order:

> Every order granting an injunction and every restraining order shall set forth the reasons for its issuance; shall be specific in terms; shall describe in reasonable detail, and not by reference to the complaint or other document, the act or acts sought to be restrained; and is binding only upon the parties to the action, their officers, agents,

servants, employees, and attorneys, and upon those persons in active concert or participation with them who receive actual notice of the order by personal service or otherwise.

Fed. R. Civ. P. 65(d); *see also* Fed. R. Civ. P. 52(a).

The plaintiff-movant may also wish to file a companion motion for expedited discovery (prior to the 30-day waiting period imposed by Fed. R. Civ. P. 30(a)), including a proposed discovery schedule, attaching notices of depositions and requests for production of documents as exhibits. Conversely, the defendant-respondent should consider serving notices of depositions immediately after being notified (by the court, the client or otherwise) that a complaint and motion have been filed. Since the Federal Rules do not restrict the timing of defendant's discovery, when defense counsel knows the caption and the nature of the claim, it may be appropriate to notice key depositions even before reading the complaint.

Finally, although it is not necessary to address the issue at this stage, consideration should be given to Fed. R. Civ. P. 65(c), which states that security, in the amount deemed proper by the court, must be given before a TRO or PI shall issue. In certain limited circumstances, the court may dispense with this requirement. *See, e.g., International Controls Corp. v. Vesco*, 490 F.2d 1334, 1356 (2d Cir.), *cert. denied*, 417 U.S. 932 (1974) (no showing of likelihood of harm to the party enjoined); *Clarkson Co. v. Shaheen*, 544 F.2d 624, 632 (2d Cir. 1976) (no request for security made).

3. Where to File and Who to See

The complaint is filed, docket fee paid, docket number assigned and judge assigned in Room 14 in the S.D.N.Y.; in Room 130, E.D.N.Y.; in Room 304, W.D.N.Y.; and in Room 443, N.D.N.Y.

Where a TRO, OTC or expedited discovery is sought, before proceeding to the judge's chambers, in the S.D.N.Y. the movant must see the Orders and Appeals Clerk (Room 14A) who reviews the form of the papers. In the E.D.N.Y., the movant should go to Room 130; in the W.D.N.Y., Room 304, and Room 443 in the N.D.N.Y.

If the judge to whom the case is assigned is not available in S.D.N.Y., contact the Part I clerk. In E.D.N.Y., call (718) 330-7671 to determine the Part I Miscellaneous Judge for that day, and proceed accordingly. In the W.D.N.Y., if the assigned judge is not available, call (716) 846-4211 for instructions; call (518) 472-5651 in the N.D.N.Y.

Fed. R. Civ. P. 65(a)(1) states that "[n]o preliminary injunction shall be issued without notice to the adverse party." A number of judges also have individual rules regarding notice. Be sure to consult individual rules of the assigned judge (found in N.Y.L.J. and New York State Bar Association

PROVISIONAL REMEDIES

Committee on Federal Courts, *Individual Judges' Rules, Procedures and Forms in U.S. District Courts for Southern, Eastern, Northern and Western Districts of N.Y.* (1986)). In the absence of a rule, telephone the judge's courtroom deputy (or, if judge permits, chambers) in advance.

4. TRO Applications

A TRO may be entered without notice under Fed. R. Civ. P. 65(b), but the following conditions must be met:

(1) it clearly appears from specific facts shown by affidavit or by the verified complaint that immediate and irreparable injury, loss, or damage will result to the applicant before the adverse party or that party's attorney can be heard in opposition, and (2) the applicant's attorney certifies to the court in writing the efforts, if any, which have been made to give the notice and the reasons supporting the claim that notice should not be required.

If a TRO is entered without notice, Rule 65(b) provides for a hearing at "the earliest possible time"; meanwhile, on two days' notice to the party who obtained the TRO without notice, or on such shorter notice to that party as the court may prescribe, the adverse party may appear and move for dissolution or modification of the TRO. The court should rule as expeditiously as the ends of justice require. *Ex parte* TRO's have the limited function of preserving the *status quo* and preventing irreparable harm for only so long as may be required to hold a hearing on the motion for preliminary injunctive relief. *See Granny Goose Foods, Inc. v. Brotherhood of Teamsters & Auto Truck Drivers*, 415 U.S. 423 (1974).

Professors Wright and Miller suggest that the procedures outlined in Fed. R. Civ. P. 5(b) for service on attorneys should suffice for notice of an application for a TRO, and that the more formal procedure for serving process on parties under Rule 4 need not be followed. *See* 11 C. Wright & A. Miller, *supra*, § 2952, at 513. However, any such service should be (and most judges will require that it be) supplemented by telephonic notice to opposing counsel.

At the TRO hearing, the essential question for the applicant is: Assuming a PI hearing can be promptly scheduled, what harm will befall applicant until then? For the opposing party, the other side of the question is: What harm will befall you if the *status quo* is maintained until the PI hearing? After obtaining these respective positions, courts will often try to resolve the TRO application on consent using the following variables: (i) date of the PI hearing; (ii) discovery in the interim; (iii) opposing party's representation to refrain from engaging in certain of the acts covered by the proposed TRO.

If granted, a TRO cannot extend beyond ten days unless, within that initial period fixed by the court (10 days or less), "for good cause shown, [the TRO] is extended for a like period [not to exceed 10 days] or unless the party against whom the order is directed consents. . . ." Fed. R. Civ. P. 65(b); *see generally* 11 C. Wright & A. Miller, *supra*, § 2953.

5. The Preliminary Injunction Hearing

Depending on the nature of the case and the preference of the court, on the return day the parties may be required to put on live testimony to supplement the written record prior to argument. Alternatively, pursuant to Fed. R. Civ. P. 65(a)(2), "the court may order the trial of the action on the merits to be advanced and consolidated with the hearing of the application."

Since sharply contested factual issues are common, evidentiary hearings are usually required. *See, e.g.*, *SEC v. Frank*, 388 F.2d 486, 490-93 (2d Cir. 1968); *see also Forts v. Ward*, 566 F.2d 849, 851-54 (2d Cir. 1977). Because it gives the trial court the opportunity to observe witnesses' demeanor, there is a strong judicial preference for live oral testimony. *See generally Dopp v. Franklin National Bank*, 461 F.2d 873, 879 (2d Cir. 1972). As Judge Friendly put it: "where there are disputed issues of fact . . . a temporary injunction should not issue on the basis of affidavits save in cases of extreme urgency." *Carter-Wallace, Inc. v. Davis-Edwards Pharmacal Corp.*, 443 F.2d 867, 872 n.5 (2d Cir. 1971).

B. Appeals

1. Appealability

An order granting or denying injunctive relief is appealable prior to the entry of a final judgment. *See* 28 U.S.C. § 1292(a)(1) (1982), which explicitly grants jurisdiction to courts of appeals to review interlocutory orders "granting, continuing, modifying, refusing or dissolving injunctions, or refusing to dissolve or modify injunctions." *See generally* 11 C. Wright & A. Miller, *supra,* § 2962.

On the other hand, the granting or denial of a TRO is ordinarily not appealable. *See, e.g.*, *Office of Personnel Management v. American Federation of Government Employees*, 473 U.S. 1301 (1985) (Burger, C.J., in chambers); *Clarkson Co. v. Shaheen, supra,* 544 F.2d at 627 n.4; *Hoh v. Pepsico, Inc.*, 491 F.2d 556, 560 (2d Cir. 1974); *Morning Telegraph v. Powers*, 450 F.2d 97, 99 (2d Cir. 1971), *cert. denied*, 405 U.S. 954 (1972). There are a few possible exceptions, all quite limited. First, if (despite being styled a TRO) the order is in substance a granting or denial of a request for a preliminary or permanent injunction, the order may be appealable. *See Sampson v. Murray, supra,* 415 U.S. at 86-88 & n.58; *Truck Drivers Local*

Union No. 807 v. Bohack Corp., 541 F.2d 312, 316 (2d Cir. 1976); *Morning Telegraph v. Powers, supra*, 450 F.2d at 99; *Belknap v. Leary*, 427 F.2d 496, 498 (2d Cir. 1970); *Grant v. United States*, 282 F.2d 165, 167-68 (2d Cir. 1960). Secondly, if the denial of the TRO is effectively the "death knell" of the movant's claim, the decision may be appealable pursuant to 28 U.S.C. § 1291 (1982), under *Cohen v. Beneficial Industrial Loan Corp.*, 337 U.S. 541, 545-47 (1949). Third, a TRO that is continued beyond the period prescribed by Rule 65(b) may be treated as a preliminary injunction appealable pursuant to 28 U.S.C. § 1292(a)(1). *See, e.g., Telex Corp. v. International Business Machines Corp.*, 464 F.2d 1025 (8th Cir. 1972) (*per curiam*); *see generally* 11 C. Wright & A. Miller, *supra*, § 2953.

The denial of a request for a TRO may also (but even more rarely) be appealable if denial comes after a full adversarial hearing and if, without appellate review, appellant would be effectively precluded from seeking further injunctive relief. *See Environmental Defense Fund, Inc. v. Andrus*, 625 F.2d 861, 862 (9th Cir. 1980).

2. Procedure for Appeals

The rules applicable to ordinary appeals also govern appeals from rulings granting or denying preliminary injunctive relief, but often on a more expedited schedule.

Although the losing party will usually appeal the grant or denial of a PI immediately, there are the usual outside time limits set out in Fed. R. App. P. 4(a)(1). Note that the notice of appeal must be *received* by the Clerk of the district court (not mailed) by the due date. Late filing of a notice of appeal is permitted only upon application to the district court made within 30 days of the due date, *see* Fed. R. App. P. 4(a)(5). Such an application must be made upon a convincing showing of "excusable neglect or good cause." *See generally In re O.P.M. Leasing Services, Inc.*, 769 F.2d 911 (2d Cir. 1985).

Unless the normal procedures are preempted by a motion for an expedited appeal (see below), pursuant to paragraph 3 of the Civil Appeals Management Plan ("CAMP") of the Second Circuit, within 10 days of the filing of the Notice of Appeal, a Civil Appeal Pre-Argument Statement ("Form C"), as well as a Transcript Information Form ("Form D"), must be filed by the appellant with the Clerk of the Court of Appeals, with copies served on all parties.

As soon as practicable thereafter, staff counsel will issue a scheduling order and direct attendance at a pre-argument conference to consider settlement possibilities and/or any other matter which may aid in expediting the disposition of the case. *See* Fed. R. App. P. 31(c), 39(a); 2d Cir. R. § 38; CAMP ¶ 7(b).

3. Stays of Injunctions; Expedited Appeals

The filing of a notice of appeal does not automatically stay the operation of the judgment, order or decision appealed from. An application for a stay or an injunction pending appeal should be made to the district court whose decision is being reviewed in the first instance. *See* Fed. R. App. P. 8(a). The district court "may suspend, modify, restore, or grant an injunction during the pendency of the appeal upon such terms as to bond or otherwise as it considers proper for the security of the rights of the adverse party." *See* Fed. R. Civ. P. 62(c).

After the initial application to the district court, or upon a showing that it is "not practicable" to do so, a motion for interim relief may be made to the Court of Appeals. *See* Fed. R. App. P. 8(a). Such a motion must comply with the motion rules of the Court (*e.g.*, use of Form T1080, accompanied by an affidavit and a separately identified exhibit containing the lower court opinion dealing with the moving party's request for relief), as well as the general requirements for motions. *See* Fed. R. App. P. 27; 2d Cir. R. § 27. Counsel must submit an original and three copies of the motion, accompanied by proof of service. *See* Fed. R. App. P. 25(d), 27(d). In every case, the motion should state the grounds for the relief sought, furnish supporting materials, and describe any previous application for relief and its outcome. Pursuant to Fed. R. App. P. 8(b), "[r]elief available in the court of appeals under this rule may be conditioned upon the filing of a bond or other appropriate security in the district court."

The application for a stay or injunction pending appeal necessarily is addressed to the court's discretion and should be based on a showing: (a) of substantial likelihood of success on the appeal; (b) that irreparable injury will result if the requested relief is not entered before the appeal is decided; (c) that other parties will not suffer substantial harm if the relief is granted; and (d) that the requested relief will not interfere with the public interest. *See, e.g., Jean v. Nelson*, 683 F.2d 1311, 1312 (11th Cir. 1982); *James River Flood Control Ass'n v. Watt*, 680 F.2d 543, 544 (8th Cir. 1982) (*per curiam*); *Long v. Robinson*, 432 F.2d 977, 979 (4th Cir. 1970).

While the court's desire to maintain the *status quo* pending the outcome of the appeal is an important consideration, in certain circumstances keeping the *status quo* can have irreparable consequences. For example, in takeover cases, courts of appeals are reluctant to grant injunctions or stays pending appeal that in effect would moot the controversy. Instead, expedited appeals are usually permitted. *See, e.g., Martin-Marietta Corp. v. Bendix Corp.*, 690 F.2d 558, 567-69 (6th Cir. 1982). The Second Circuit motions clerk will often seek to negotiate withdrawal of the stay motion in exchange for early hearing date of the appeal.

The usual procedure in obtaining an expedited appeal involves moving simultaneously (a) in the court of appeals for a preference under 2d Cir. R. §§ 27(b) and (f); and (b) in the district court or the court of appeals for a stay of the injunction appealed from under Fed. R. App. P. 8. The appellant may move, on whatever notice is feasible, on the same day the judgment or order is entered in the district court, but only after the notice of appeal has been filed. The preference motion will usually be referred by the clerk to the panel then sitting or to a single judge pursuant to 2d Cir. R. § 27(f). If an expedited appeal is granted, the court may at the same time set a briefing schedule and argument date, waive the pre-argument conference, permit an abbreviated record, and take other action to expedite the matter.

4. Standard of Review

The standard of appellate review in injunction actions is more easily stated than understood. Generally speaking, the district court's decision granting or denying injunctive relief can be overturned only where there is an "abuse of discretion." *See Doran v. Salem Inn, Inc.*, 422 U.S. 922, 932 (1975). However, the precise meaning of "abuse of discretion" leaves much room for argument.

The Second Circuit's review of injunction decisions entails much more than perfunctory approval of the district court's decision. *See, e.g., Hanson Trust PLC v. ML SCM Acquisition, Inc.*, 781 F.2d 264, 281 (2d Cir. 1986); *Hanson Trust PLC v. SCM Corp.*, 774 F.2d 47, 54, 60-61 (2d Cir. 1985). It has expressed "dissatisfaction with contentions that would render the review of the grant or denial of temporary injunctions [a] largely meaningless ritual." *See Buffalo Courier-Express, Inc. v. Buffalo Evening News, Inc.*, 601 F.2d 48, 59 (2d Cir. 1979). *See generally Donovan v. Bierwirth*, 680 F.2d 263, 269-70 (2d Cir., Friendly, J.), *cert. denied*, 459 U.S. 1069 (1982) (discussing the various formulations of the standard of review imposed by the Second Circuit, and stating, "[w]e would ill perform our duties by a decision affirming the district court because of limitations on the scope of review, thereby necessarily implying that we would equally have upheld a contrary ruling"). *Accord Omega Importing Corp. v. Petri-Kine Camera Co.*, 451 F.2d 1190, 1197 (2d Cir. 1971) (Friendly, J.).

At the same time, the Court of Appeals adheres to the general principle that whether the district court grants or refuses injunctive relief, its findings of fact, which are made pursuant to Fed. R. Civ. P. 52(a), will not be set aside unless those findings are clearly erroneous. *See, e.g., Unicon Management Corp. v. Koppers Co.*, 366 F.2d 199, 203 (2d Cir. 1966). The appellate court's review is quite different, of course, when it considers the district court's interpretation of law. *See, e.g., Empresa Hondurena de Vapores, S.A. v. McLeod*, 300 F.2d 222, 231 (2d Cir. 1962), *vacated on other grounds sub nom. McCulloch v. Sociedad Nacional de Marineros de Honduras*, 372 U.S. 10 (1963). Procedural errors are reviewable. *See Dopp v. Franklin National Bank, supra*, 461 F.2d at 878-79 (reversing district court's error in resolving a factual dispute without an evidentiary hearing).

III. ATTACHMENT AND GARNISHMENT

Rule 64 of the Federal Rules of Civil Procedure generally defers to state procedures for the provisional remedies of attachment and garnishment except that (1) any applicable federal statute will govern and (2) the action must be commenced and prosecuted pursuant to the Fed. R. Civ. P. 64:

> At the commencement of and during the course of an action, all remedies providing for seizure of person or property for the purpose of securing satisfaction of the judgment ultimately to be entered in the action are available under the circumstances and in the manner provided by the law of the state in which the district court is held, existing at the time the remedy is sought, subject to the following qualifications: (1) any existing statute of the United States governs to the extent to which it is applicable; and (2) the action in which any of the foregoing remedies is used shall be commenced and prosecuted or, if removed from a state court, shall be prosecuted after removal, pursuant to these rules. The remedies thus available include arrest, attachment, garnishment, replevin, sequestration, and other corresponding or equivalent remedies, however designated and regardless of whether by state procedure the remedy is ancillary to an action or must be obtained by an independent action.

Thus, unlike State practice, attachment is not permitted prior to commencement of the action by filing a complaint.

In New York State practice, attachment and garnishment are governed by Article 62 of the New York Civil Practice Law and Rules ("CPLR"), and, by virtue of the above Rule, that Article governs use of those remedies in federal court.

A. Grounds and Showing for Attachment

Under CPLR § 6201, attachment may be ordered if the plaintiff is seeking a money judgment (but not necessarily only a money judgment) and at least one of the following applies:

> (1) the defendant is a nondomiciliary residing without the state, or is a foreign corporation not qualified to do business in the state; or

> (2) the defendant resides or is domiciled in the state and cannot be personally served despite diligent efforts to do so; or

(3) the defendant, with intent to defraud his creditors or frustrate the enforcement of a judgment that might be rendered in plaintiff's favor, has assigned, disposed of, encumbered or secreted property, or removed it from the state or is about to do any of these acts; or

(4) the cause of action is based on a judgment, decree or order of a court of the United States or of any other court which is entitled to full faith and credit in this state, or on a judgment which qualifies for recognition under the provisions of article 53 [governing recognition of foreign country money judgments].

CPLR Rule 6212 requires the plaintiff to show by affidavit that:

(a) there is a cause of action;

(b) it is probable that the plaintiff will succeed on the merits;

(c) one or more of the above grounds for attachment (in CPLR § 6201) exist; and

(d) the amount demanded from the defendant exceeds all counterclaims known to the plaintiff.

See *Merrill Lynch Futures Inc. v. Kelly*, 585 F. Supp. 1245, 1249 (S.D.N.Y. 1984).

Although a verified complaint can be treated as an affidavit, *American Jerex Co. v. Universal Aluminum Extrusions, Inc.*, 340 F. Supp. 524 (E.D.N.Y. 1972), the movant should take care to state details of the cause of action that ordinarily might not appear in the complaint. See *Tampimex Oil Ltd. v. Latina Trading Corp.*, 558 F. Supp. 1201 (S.D.N.Y. 1983). The facts set forth should be " 'such that a person of reasonable prudence would be willing to accept and act upon [them].' " *Swiss Bank Corp. v. Eatessami*, 26 A.D.2d 287, 290, 273 N.Y.S.2d 935, 938 (lst Dep't 1966). "While there must be a sufficient showing that the ultimate facts stated in the pleading can be substantiated . . . the truth of the facts stated may be assumed" (*id.*, citations omitted); and statements may be made upon information and belief, so long as " 'that information and belief . . . [are] competently derived.' " *Id.*, 273 N.Y.S.2d at 938; see also *Worldwide Carriers, Ltd. v. Aris S.S. Co.*, 301 F. Supp. 64, 66 (S.D.N.Y. 1968). The plaintiff should disclose the sources of the hearsay evidence, and conclusory allegations will not suffice. *Gitlin v. Stone*, 262 F. Supp. 500, 501 (S.D.N.Y. 1967); *Merrill Lynch Futures Inc. v. Kelly, supra*, 585 F. Supp. at 1259.

The court will give the plaintiff the benefit of all legitimate inferences. *National Bank & Trust Co. of North America, Ltd. v. J.L.M. International, Inc.*, 421 F. Supp. 1269, 1272 (S.D.N.Y. 1976).

In addition to showing a cause of action, the movant should allege one of the grounds in CPLR § 6201 with " 'some probative force and not . . . hearsay alone.' " *Swiss Bank Corp. v. Eatessami, supra,* 26 A.D.2d at 290, 273 N.Y.S.2d at 938. If, for example, attachment is sought under section 6201(3), "a plaintiff must not only show that a defendant is about to assign, encumber, secrete or remove property from the state, it must also show that one of these acts will be done with the intent to defraud. Moreover, the moving papers must contain evidentiary facts as opposed to conclusions establishing the fraud." *Marina B. Creation S.A. v. de Maurier,* 1988 U.S. Dist. LEXIS 1096, at 4-5 (S.D.N.Y. Feb. 8, 1988) (citations omitted). Courts will not infer an act of fraud merely from the fact that defendant is transferring or disposing of assets. *Computer Strategies, Inc. v. Commodore Business Machines, Inc.,* 105 A.D.2d 167, 483 N.Y.S.2d 716 (2d Dep't 1984).

Although CPLR Rule 6212(d) also requires the plaintiff to state that he is entitled to recover money greater than all known counterclaims, the court need only consider those counterclaims that the plaintiff is willing to concede as just. *Shearson Hayden Stone, Inc. v. Scrivener,* 480 F. Supp. 256, 259 (S.D.N.Y. 1979); *American Jerex Co. v. Universal Aluminum Extrusions, Inc., supra.*

Plaintiff should also allege that attachment is necessary for security, *Burt Printing Co. v. Middle East Media Corp.,* 80 F.R.D. 449 (S.D.N.Y. 1978), especially where attachment is not necessary to obtain jurisdiction, *Incontrade, Inc. v. Oilborn International, S.A.,* 407 F. Supp. 1359, 1361 (S.D.N.Y. 1976).

B. Debt or Property Subject to Attachment

CPLR § 6202 provides that any debt or property against which a money judgment may be enforced, *see* CPLR § 5201, is subject to attachment. The plaintiff need not identify the property to be attached, or even allege its existence within the state, *see ABKCO Industries, Inc. v. Apple Films, Inc.,* 39 N.Y.2d 670, 350 N.E.2d 899, 385 N.Y.S.2d 511 (1976), although Professor Siegel counsels that a court may more likely grant attachment if it is made aware of the defendant's significant local property. D. Siegel, *New York Practice* § 316, at 379 (1978).

C. Bringing On the Motion

New York permits attachment by motion on notice or by *ex parte* application followed by a confirmation hearing. CPLR § 6210 governs the procedure for obtaining an order of attachment by motion on notice; it also empowers the court, *without* notice to the defendant, to grant a temporary restraining order prohibiting the transfer of assets by a "garnishee" (as

PROVISIONAL REMEDIES 175

provided by CPLR § 6214 (b)). Although the statute uses the term "garnishee," Judge McLaughlin suggests that the section should not be read narrowly, and "that what is intended to bind a garnishee should also bind the defendant." McLaughlin, *Practice Commentaries to CPLR § 6210*, C6210:1, at 58 (McKinney 1980).

The more common practice is for the plaintiff to move by OTC for an *ex parte* order of attachment. If the action has not already been commenced, the first step will be to obtain an index number and file the complaint and civil cover sheet. In S.D.N.Y., this is done at the cashier's window in Room 14. In E.D.N.Y., go to Room 130; in W.D.N.Y., Room 304; in N.D.N.Y., Room 443. After filing the complaint, take the OTC and supporting papers (affidavit, memorandum of law) to the Orders and Appeals Clerk—Room 14A, S.D.N.Y.; Room 130, E.D.N.Y.—who will inspect the OTC as to form. In W.D.N.Y., go to Room 304; in N.D.N.Y., to Room 443.

CPLR § 621(a) sets forth the requisite contents of the OTC; it must:

specify the amount to be secured by the order of attachment including any interest, costs and sheriff's fees and expenses, be endorsed with the name and address of the plaintiff's attorney and shall be directed to the sheriff of any county or of the city of New York where any property in which the defendant has an interest is located or where a garnishee may be served. The order shall direct the sheriff to levy within this jurisdiction, at any time before final judgment, upon such property in which the defendant has an interest and upon such debts owing to the defendant as will satisfy the amount specified in the order of the attachment.

Upon making a motion for an order of attachment, the plaintiff must give a bond (minimum of $500) to cover the defendant's costs should the defendant recover judgment or if it is determined that the plaintiff was not entitled to the attachment. CPLR Rule 6212 (b). Ordinarily, the amount of the bond should not be less than 5 percent of the amount of defendant's property plaintiff seeks to attach. The bond (if prepared in advance as it should be to save time) should be presented for review to the orders and appeals clerk, who, if all is in order, will direct counsel to the assigned judge or the Part I emergency judge.

Under CPLR Rule 6212(c) within ten days after an order of attachment is granted, the plaintiff must file it and the affidavit and any other papers on which it was based with the clerk of the court. In federal court, this should be done before leaving the courthouse after the judge has signed the order.

If the order was granted *ex parte,* within no more than five days after *levy* on the defendant's property (or ten days if the attachment is based on CPLR § 6201 (1), *see* D. Siegel, *supra,* § 316, at 380), the plaintiff must move on notice (*i.e.*, serve the motion papers) for an order confirming the attachment. CPLR § 6211 (b). If the plaintiff fails to do so, the order and the levy become void and may be vacated on motion, with costs to the defendant.

The defendant can present arguments in opposition to the attachment at the confirmation hearing, or, alternatively, the defendant can move at any time to vacate or modify the attachment order, *see* CPLR § 6223(a), or to "discharge" the attachment by replacing the levied property with something of equal value, *see* CPLR § 6222. *See generally* D. Siegel, *supra,* § 325 at 392-95. The plaintiff, under CPLR § 6223(b), has the burden of "establishing the grounds for the attachment, the need for continuing the levy and the probability that he will succeed on the merits." *Merrill Lynch Futures Inc. v. Kelly, supra* 585 F. Supp. at 1249. The Appellate Division, First Department, recently held that a foreign corporation that files a post-attachment, preconfirmation application to do business in New York, cannot, by that act alone, cause an order of attachment to be vacated. *Elton Leather Corp. v First General Resources Co.*, 138 A.D.2d 132, 529 N.Y.S.2d 769 (1st Dep't 1988) (rejecting contrary holding in *Brastex Corp. v. Allen International, Inc.*, 702 F. 2d 326 (2d Cir. 1983)).

D. Appeals

The Second Circuit has permitted appeals when an attachment has been denied or vacated, but not from decisions granting or continuing orders of attachment. *See Brastex Corp. v. Allen International, Inc., supra,* 702 F.2d at 329 n.8, *rejected in part on other grounds, Elton Leather Corp. v. First General Resources Co., supra,* 138 A.D.2d 132, 529 N.Y.S.2d 769. The cases have been treated differently because the vacating or denial of an attachment order may result in the disposition or destruction of the property at issue, rendering any subsequent appeal meaningless, while there is no commensurate risk when the trial court grants or continues the order of attachment. *See* 7 J. Moore, *Moore's Federal Practice* ¶ 64.10, at 104 (Supp. 1987-88). The continuing validity of this disparate treatment was questioned in *Dayco Corp. v. Foreign Transactions Corp.*, 705 F.2d 38, 40 (2d Cir. 1983), in which the Second Circuit held that an order refusing to confirm "what otherwise would be an invalid attachment" is not appealable under *Cohen v. Beneficial Industrial Loan Corp.*, 337 U.S. 541 (1949), because that doctrine "generally involve[s] unusual circumstances, serious and unsettled questions. . . ."

IV. RECEIVERSHIPS

An equity receiver has been defined as:

> a person specially appointed by the court to take control, custody, or management of property that is involved in or is likely to become

involved in litigation for the purpose of preserving the property, receiving rents, issues, or profits, and undertaking any other appropriate action with regard to the property pending its final disposition by the suit.

12 C. Wright & A. Miller, *Federal Practice and Procedure* § 2981, at 5 (1973).

Receivership should not be the objective of litigation; rather, it "is only a means to reach some legitimate end." *Gordon v. Washington*, 295 U.S. 30, 37 (1935); *see also Kelleam v. Maryland Casualty Co.*, 312 U.S. 377 (1941). Accordingly, a receiver's appointment is incidental to the other proceedings in which relief is sought. *Zittman v. McGrath*, 341 U.S. 446 (1951); *see also SEC v. Republic National Life Insurance Co.*, 378 F. Supp. 430, 438 (S.D.N.Y. 1974).

Equity receiverships, which are governed by federal law, are provided for in 28 U.S.C. § 959(b) (1982) and Fed. R. Civ. P. 66, neither of which applies to trustees in bankruptcy. Section 959(b) sets forth the rights, duties and liabilities of federal equity receivers:

> [A] trustee, receiver or manager appointed in any cause pending in any court of the United States, including a debtor in possession, shall manage and operate the property in his possession as such trustee, receiver or manager according to the requirements of the valid laws of the State in which such property is situated, in the same manner that the owner or possessor thereof would be bound to do if in possession thereof.

Fed. R. Civ. P. 66 provides:

> An action wherein a receiver has been appointed shall not be dismissed except by order of the court. The practice in the administration of estates by receivers or by other similar officers appointed by the court shall be in accordance with the practice heretofore followed in the courts of the United States or as provided in rules promulgated by the district courts. In all other respects the action in which the appointment of a receiver is sought or which is brought by or against a receiver is governed by these rules.

A. Appointing a Receiver

Any person with an interest in property that is protectible by the remedy of receivership may petition the court to have a receiver appointed. Appropriate parties to petition for receivers include, among others, secured creditors, lienholders, mortgagees, stockholders in a corporation and judgment creditors. The party seeking appointment must demonstrate a legally recognized right in the property possessed by the defendant; it is also necessary (but not sufficient) that the applicant has a claim against the defendant for which there is no adequate remedy at law. *SEC v. Republic National Life Insurance Co., supra*, 378 F. Supp. at 437.

A plaintiff whose claim is essentially one for damages, rather than for equitable relief, may not have the defendant's property placed in receivership before the claim is reduced to judgment and all legal remedies have been exhausted. *See Piambino v. Bailey*, 757 F.2d 1112, 1131 n.46 (11th Cir. 1985), *cert. denied*, 476 U.S. 1169 (1986). At least when the appointment of a receiver is sought at the commencement of the action, the complaint should be verified.

The appointment of a receiver "lies in the discretion of the court and the applicant bears a heavy burden to establish an actual need therefor." *SEC v. Republic National Life Insurance Co., supra*, 378 F. Supp. at 438. The elements that establish need are:

(1) "imminent danger of the loss of the property" at issue, *SEC v. Republic National Life Insurance Co., supra*, 378 F. Supp. at 438, or the danger that the property will be "concealed, injured, diminished in value or squandered," 12 C. Wright & A. Miller, *supra*, § 2983, at 23; *Republic of the Philippines v. Marcos*, 653 F. Supp. 494, 497 (S.D.N.Y. 1987);

(2) inadequacy of available legal remedies, *Leighton v. One William Street Fund, Inc.*, 343 F.2d 565 (2d Cir. 1965);

(3) probability that harm to the plaintiff caused by a denial of the appointment would outweigh the injury to the parties opposing the appointment;

(4) plaintiff's probability of success on the merits; and

(5) irreparable injury to his interests in the property should the appointment be denied. *Meineke Discount Muffler Shops, Inc. v. Noto*, 603 F. Supp. 443, 445 (E.D.N.Y. 1985).

Just as the appointment of a receiver is in the court's discretion, so too is the manner of presenting evidence, the requirement of a bond, and the setting of its terms and conditions. *Ferguson v. Tabah*, 288 F.2d 665, 675 (2d Cir. 1961).

Notice of the application for the appointment of a receiver must be sent to all interested parties, except that in a clear emergency the appointment of a receiver may be done on an *ex parte* basis. *Argonaut Insurance Co. v. Halvanon Insurance Co.*, 545 F. Supp. 21, 23 (S.D.N.Y. 1981).

The court has continuing power to vacate the appointment of a receiver, and can also condition the receivership—*e.g.*, on plaintiff's timely prosecution of the action. *Levin v. Ruby Trading Corp.*, 352 F.2d 508 (2d Cir. 1965).

B. Suits By and Against Receivers

A receiver may sue or be sued in any federal district court. Since a receiver "stands in the shoes of the person for whom he has been appointed," however, the receiver can "assert only those claims which that person could have asserted." *Armstrong v. McAlpin*, 699 F.2d 79, 89 (2d Cir. 1983). Thus, any defenses that "might have been interposed against persons represented by a receiver may be interposed against the receiver." *Id.* (citations omitted). As distinguished from such matters of defense, court approval is needed to sue a receiver on claims arising out of acts or transactions by the property's owner or prior custodian, or suits involving the receivership property itself. *See* Advisory Committee notes to 1948 amendments to Fed. R. Civ. P. 66, *reprinted in* 12 C. Wright & A. Miller, *supra*, App. C at 514-15. However, under 28 U.S.C. § 959(a), leave of court is unnecessary when the receiver is sued arising out of a transaction connected with acts as a receiver.

C. Jurisdiction

The district court is empowered to appoint a receiver whether its jurisdiction over the underlying suit rests on a federal question or diversity jurisdiction, and whether or not the action was commenced in state court and removed to federal court. In separate actions by or against the receiver, the citizenship of the receiver, rather than that of the debtor or creditor, is controlling for purposes of diversity. However, ancillary jurisdiction exists in the appointing court when the receiver brings suit to accomplish the ends sought by the appointment or when the receiver is sued over his or her conduct as the receiver.

Under 28 U.S.C. § 754 (1982), the court and the receiver have jurisdiction and control over *all* of the defendant's property covered by the receivership, irrespective of its location, so long as the receiver files copies of the complaint and order in each district in which the property is located. When the receiver finds it necessary to sue in another district court, no ancillary appointment is necessary. 28 U.S.C. § 754 (1982).

D. Appeals

Under 28 U.S.C. § 1292(a)(2) (1982), interlocutory orders appointing receivers or refusing orders to wind up receiverships are appealable. These orders have been defined as "executions before judgment" that either remove parties from the possession of property or control the management and disposition of property. 12 C. Wright & A. Miller, *supra*, § 2986, at 48.

Other orders involving receivers, however, are not appealable. *Id*. On appeal, review is limited to determining whether the district court abused its discretion. *See SEC v. American Board of Trade, Inc.*, 830 F.2d 431, 436 (2d Cir. 1987), *cert. denied*, 108 S. Ct. 1118 (1988).

CHAPTER EIGHT

RESPONDING TO THE COMPLAINT

by Peter E. Calamari, Esq.

I. THE ANSWER

A. General

The form of the answer in federal practice is much the same as in New York State practice. The answer must contain a caption setting forth the "name of the court, the title of the action, the file number" and a designation of the nature of the pleading. Fed. R. Civ. P. 10(a). In the Southern and Eastern Districts, the caption must also contain the initials of the assigned judge. Rule 1(a) of the Civil Rules of the S.D.N.Y. and E.D.N.Y.

The caption is generally followed by an introductory paragraph providing the identity of the party and counsel submitting the answer.

Following this material is a series of individualized responses to the averments of the complaint. These may be followed with one or more affirmative defenses, counterclaims, cross-claims and/or third-party claims. The answer concludes with a "wherefore" clause setting forth a demand for judgment in favor of the party submitting the answer together with any affirmative relief sought by that party. The answer must be signed in accordance with Fed. R. Civ. P. 11 and, for convenience of future reference, it is advisable to date the document as of the date of service. Unlike New York State practice, the answer must be filed with the clerk of the court with proof of service. Fed. R. Civ. P. 5(d).

As with the complaint, the answer should be organized in separately numbered paragraphs, Fed. R. Civ. P. 10(b), which may be incorporated by reference in other parts of the answer or in other pleadings or motions, Fed. R. Civ. P. 10(c).

Although it is not necessary to include a jury demand with the answer (assuming one is desirable), it has become common practice to do so because of the relatively tight time constraints (generally 10 days from the close of pleadings) involved. *See* Fed. R. Civ. P. 38(b).

In cases where there are actual or threatened parallel criminal proceedings, care should be taken to avoid inadvertent waiver of the defendant's fifth amendment privilege. In such instances, a motion for stay of all proceedings would seem to be the safest course of action.[1]

B. Timing

The answer is due 20 days after service of the summons and complaint except (i) when service is made on an out-of-state defendant under Fed. R. Civ. P. 4(e); (ii) when the defendant is the United States or an officer or agency thereof; or (iii) when a motion addressed to the complaint is made under Fed. R. Civ. P. 12. Fed. R. Civ. P. 12(a). If the complaint is amended, the answer is due within the original period or within 10 days after service of the amended complaint, whichever is longer. Fed. R. Civ. P. 15(a).

1. Timing When Service is Made under Fed. R. Civ. P. 4(e)

Fed. R. Civ. P. 4(e) provides for service on a party not an inhabitant of or found within the state in which the district court is located. Under such circumstances, the defendant is entitled to respond to the complaint within the time permitted under the statute (federal or state) or court order providing for service of process. If resort is made to service of process on the out-of-state defendant in a manner permitted under New York State law, then the defendant will generally have a minimum of 30 days to respond to the complaint. *See* CPLR 320(a).

2. Timing When the Government is the Defendant

The Government, its officers and agencies are entitled to respond to the complaint within 60 days of service of the summons and complaint. Fed. R. Civ. P. 12(a).

---

[1] *See, e.g., Spevack v. Klein*, 385 U.S. 511, 515 (1967); *Wehling v. Columbia Broadcasting System*, 608 F.2d 1084, 1088-89 (5th Cir. 1979), *reh'g denied*, 611 F.2d 1026 (1980) (per curiam); *Brock v. Tolkow*, 109 F.R.D. 116, 120-21 (E.D.N.Y. 1985); *Clark v. United States*, 481 F. Supp. 1086, 1099-1100 (S.D.N.Y. 1979), *appeal dismissed*, 624 F.2d 3 (2d Cir. 1980); *Corbin v. Federal Deposit Ins. Corp.*, 74 F.R.D. 147, 149-50 (E.D.N.Y. 1977); *Dienstag v. Bronsen*, 49 F.R.D. 327, 329 (S.D.N.Y. 1970).

3. Timing When a Motion Has Been Addressed to the Complaint

The answer is due 10 days after a motion addressed to the complaint is denied and 10 days after a motion for a more definite complaint is served if a motion for a more definite statement is granted. *Id.* Care should be taken regarding these deadlines as, unlike New York State practice, deadlines generally run from the date of the court's order, not from service of notice of entry thereof.

An interesting question arises as to the appropriate practice regarding dispositive motions addressed to only a portion of the complaint. While a literal reading of Fed. R. Civ. P. 12(a) would imply that the time to respond to the entire complaint is extended, some lower court cases have held to the contrary[2] and the better practice is to either answer the unchallenged portion of the complaint or obtain an order of the court providing for a stay. This seems in direct contrast to New York State practice. *See* CPLR 3214(b).

The deadlines set forth above may only be extended by court order. Fed. R. Civ. P. 6(b). Thus, in obtaining adjournments, the practitioner should be careful to request the court to "so order" stipulations between the parties.

C. Responding to the Individual Averments of the Complaint

As in New York State practice, individual averments of the complaint may be responded to by admissions, denials or a statement that the party is "without knowledge or information sufficient to form a belief as to the truth of an averment." Fed. R. Civ. P. 8(b). The latter being generally referred to as a "dki." Portions of a particular averment which are true should be admitted with other portions of the same averment treated accordingly. *Id.*

Although the most common practice is to include a separate paragraph in the answer for each one in the complaint,[3] it is acceptable to lump all paragraphs in the complaint treated in the same manner in a single paragraph of the answer.[4] In addition, the federal rules specifically permit general denials but point out that such a pleading is subject to the obligations imposed under Fed. R. Civ. P. 11.

---

2 *See, e.g., Gerlach v. Michigan Bell Telephone Co.*, 448 F. Supp. 1168 (E.D. Mich. 1978).

3 *E.g.*, "defendant denies the averments of paragraph 1 of the answer."

4 *E.g.*, "defendant states that it is without knowledge or information sufficient to form a belief as to the truth of the averments of paragraphs 1, 3, 4, 5, 7 and 11 of the complaint" or "defendant denies the averments of the complaint except admits the averments of paragraphs 2, 4, 6 and 8 thereof."

1. Effect of Failure to Deny

Failure to deny an averment in the answer constitutes an admission (except as to the amount of damages). Fed. R. Civ. P. 8(d). Thus, in situations where a portion of an averment in the complaint is to be denied, the safest procedure is to deny the entire averment "except" specifically identified passages.

Often the complaint pleads legal conclusions and the defendant responds with a statement such as "Paragraph ____ is a conclusion of law to which no responsive pleading is required." Pursuant to Fed. R. Civ. P. 8(d), such a response should be treated as a denial, but to avoid any confusion, the practitioner should go on to deny (or dki) the conclusion.

2. Multiple Parties

When responding to averments addressed to multiple parties it may be necessary to distinguish between the pleader's knowledge insofar as the averment is addressed to him and his knowledge insofar as the averment is addressed to another party.[5]

3. Excess Matter in the Response

Often the practitioner deviates from a clear, unequivocal statement and resorts to such language as "denies the *material* allegations of the complaint." This surplusage is, at best, ambiguous and should be avoided. *See* discussion in J. Moore's *Federal Practice and Procedure* ¶ 8.24 (hereinafter "J. Moore's *Fed. Prac. & Proc.*").

4. Specificity

While affirmative statements in response to the complaint's averments (*e.g.*, "denies the averments in paragraph 1 and states that . . .") should be avoided unless absolutely necessary for clarity, in one instance the Federal Rules mandate specificity. Fed. R. Civ. P. 9(c) provides that compliance with conditions precedent may be averred generally but that "[a] denial of performance or occurrence shall be made specifically and with particularity." Thus, the response to a pleading that plaintiff performed all required conditions precedent should itemize each and every condition which plaintiff

---

5 *E.g.*, "denies the averments of paragraph ____ thereof except denies knowledge or information sufficient to form a belief as to the truth of those averments insofar as they relate to (co-defendant)."

failed to perform.[6] This provision is not intended to alter the burden of proof which, assuming appropriate pleading, remains on plaintiff. *See generally* J. Moore's *Fed. Prac. & Proc.* ¶ 9.04 at 9-63.

D. Affirmative Defenses

Fed. R. Civ. P. 8(b) provides that "[a] party shall state in short and plain terms his defenses to each claim asserted. . . . " Fed. R. Civ. P. 8(e) goes on to provide: "[a] party may set forth two or more statements of a claim or defense alternately or hypothetically." While a party may set forth as many defenses as the party has "regardless of consistency," the rule goes on to remind the pleader of his obligations under Fed. R. Civ. P. 11.

Fed. R. Civ. P. 8(c) provides the following examples of matters to be pled as affirmative defenses:

> accord and satisfaction, arbitration and award, assumption of risk, contributory negligence, discharge in bankruptcy, duress, estoppel, failure of consideration, fraud, illegality, injury by fellow servant, laches, license, payment, release, res judicata, statute of frauds, statute of limitations, waiver.

The rule makes clear that the list is not exclusive concluding with the catch-all:

> any other matter constituting an avoidance or affirmative defense.

1. Burden of Proof

As a rule of thumb, the party that bears the burden of proof on an issue also bears the burden of pleading; however, this rule is subject to many exceptions and care should be taken to avoid both the erroneous assumption of the burden of proof and the inadvertent waiver by failing to properly plead. *See* discussion at 5 C. Wright & A. Miller, *Federal Practice and Procedure* §§ 1276, 1278 (1969).

2. Specificity

When pleading affirmative defenses which involve fraud or a judgment, care should be taken to comply with Fed. R. Civ. P. 9.

---

6 *E.g.*, "denies the allegation of paragraph # and states that plaintiff failed to perform at least the following conditions:
    (a) - -
    (b) - -
    (c) - - -"

3. Waiver

Failure to plead an affirmative defense in the answer or a timely amendment thereof may constitute a waiver of that defense. In addition, certain defenses (lack of personal jurisdiction, improper venue, insufficiency of process) can be waived if a motion is made pursuant to Fed. R. Civ. P. 12 which does not raise these defenses. Unlike state practice, if such a motion is made, the waiver would occur even if defendant raises the defense in the answer.

II. COUNTERCLAIMS, CROSS-CLAIMS AND THIRD-PARTY COMPLAINTS

Fed. R. Civ. P. 13 provides for the assertion of counterclaims and cross-claims.[7] As in New York State practice, these are usually, but not necessarily, included in the answer.

A. Counterclaims

Any request for relief against the opponent should be set forth in a counterclaim which, in form, corresponds to a complaint.

Fed. R. Civ. P. 13(c) provides that the complaint does not limit the counterclaim in amount, or in the nature of the relief sought. Thus, the counterclaiming defendant may seek to recover damages in excess of those sought in the complaint or may seek equitable relief (or damages) in response to a claim for damages (or equitable relief) as the case may be.

The counterclaim may add additional parties, Fed. R. Civ. P. 13(h); however, in such instances, service of a summons in a permissible manner is necessary.

1. The Compulsory/Permissive Distinction

Counterclaims fall into two categories: "compulsory" and "permissive." A compulsory counterclaim is one which the pleader has at the time of service of the pleading that "arises out of the transaction or occurrence that is the subject matter of the opposing party's claim and does not require for its adjudication the presence of third parties of whom the Court cannot acquire jurisdiction." Fed. R. Civ. P. 13(a). A permissive counterclaim is any other claim the pleader may have against the opposing party. Fed. R. Civ. P. 13(b).

The phrase "transaction or occurrence" is broadly construed and usually defined by such standards as "(1) identity of facts between original claim and

---

[7] Counterclaims and cross-claims should be clearly designated as such. This is especially so in the case of counterclaims, as Fed. R. Civ. P. 7(a) only requires a reply to a counterclaim "denominated as such."

counterclaim; (2) mutuality of proof; (3) logical relationship between original claim and counterclaim." *Federman v. Empire Fire and Marine Ins. Co.*, 597 F.2d 798, 812 (2d Cir. 1979).[8]

If the pleader fails to assert a compulsory counterclaim prior to judgment then the claim will be extinguished by the judgment. *See, e.g., Harris v. Steinem*, 571 F.2d 119, 122 (2d Cir. 1978). Consequently, if there is any doubt as to whether a counterclaim is compulsory or permissive it should be resolved in favor of inclusion in the pleading.

Fed. R. Civ. P. 13(a) provides two exceptions to the compulsory counterclaim rule: (a) claims which are the subject of another pending action at the time the action was commenced; and (b) *in rem* claims, unless the pleader nevertheless asserts a counterclaim in which case he must assert all counterclaims which would otherwise be compulsory.

Additionally, Fed. R. Civ. P. 13(c) provides that a claim which matures or is acquired after a pleading may be asserted by supplemental pleading with the permission of the court.

Fed. R. Civ. P. 13(f) is designed to avoid a harsh application of these rules. It provides:

> When a pleader fails to set up a counterclaim through oversight, inadvertence, or excusable neglect, or when justice requires, the pleader may by leave of court set up the counterclaim by amendment.

2. Jurisdictional Issues

Compulsory counterclaims generally need not be supported by a separate basis of federal jurisdiction, as the courts have ancillary jurisdiction to entertain such claims. *Harris v. Steinem*, 571 F.2d 119, 121 (2d Cir. 1978). In order to assert a permissive counterclaim, however, the pleader must have an independent basis for federal subject matter jurisdiction. *Id.* at 122.

In asserting a counterclaim, care must be taken to avoid a waiver of any defense based on a lack of personal jurisdiction. *Merz v. Hemmerle*, 90 F.R.D. 566, 569 (E.D.N.Y. 1981) and cases cited therein. If the counterclaim is compulsory, the better rule is that the defense is not waived, C. Wright and A. Miller, *Federal Practice and Procedure* ¶ 1416 (1971), although district courts in the Second Circuit have gone both ways on the

---

[8] For a detailed discussion of what constitutes a "transaction or occurrence that is the subject matter of the opposing party's claim," *see* J. Moore's *Federal Practice and Procedure* § 13.12 *et seq.*

issue.[9] If the counterclaim is permissive, the defense will usually be deemed waived.[10] Given the lack of a definitive opinion by the Second Circuit, the safest course would be to move for dismissal for lack of personal jurisdiction prior to answering and asserting counterclaims. This is the procedure outlined in *Beaunit Mills, Inc. v. Industrias Reunidas F. Matarazzo*, 23 F.R.D. 654 (S.D.N.Y. 1959). Should the district court decline to rule on such a motion prior to trial, the defense should then be preserved. *Id.*

3. Counterclaims Against the Government

Fed. R. Civ. P. 13(d) provides that the Rules do not enlarge the ability of the pleader to assert counterclaims against the United States or its officers and agencies "beyond the limits fixed by law."

B. Cross-Claims

Cross-claims "arising out of the transaction or occurrence that is the subject matter either of the original action or of a counterclaim therein or relating to any property that is the subject matter of the original action" may be asserted against a co-party. Fed. R. Civ. P. 13(g).

The cross-claim must be against a co-party to the litigation. The most common cross-claims are those seeking contribution and/or indemnity and the Rule specifically permits the assertion of such claims. The "transaction or occurrence" test is the same employed in analyzing compulsory counterclaims.[11] Also like compulsory counterclaims, cross-claims are supported by the court's ancillary jurisdiction. However, unlike compulsory counterclaims, if the claim is not asserted, it is not necessarily waived.

C. Third-Party Claims

Fed. R. Civ. P. 14 specifically permits the service of a third-party complaint on a person who "is or may be liable" to the pleader "at any time after commencement of the action." Leave of court, however, is necessary if service of the third-party complaint takes place more than 10 days after service of the answer. In addition, pursuant to Rule 3 of the local civil rules

---

[9] *Compare Keil Lock Co., Inc. v. Earle Hardware Manufacturing Co.*, 16 F.R.D. 389 (S.D.N.Y. 1954) (no waiver) *with Beaunit Mills, Inc. v. Industrias Reunidas F. Matarazzo*, 23 F.R.D. 654 (S.D.N.Y. 1959) (waiver).

[10] *Merz v. Hemmerle, supra*; C. Wright and A. Miller, *supra*, ¶ 1424; *but see Cargill, Inc. v. Sabine Trading & Shipping Co., Inc.*, 756 F.2d 224, 229-30 (2d Cir. 1985) (assertion of non-compulsory counterclaim did not waive jurisdictional defense when counterclaim was for damages arising out of attachment proceeding to gain *in rem* jurisdiction and state law would permit counterclaim without waiver of jurisdictional defense).

[11] *See Federman v. Empire First and Marine Ins. Co.*, 597 F.2d 798, 811 (2d Cir. 1979).

for the Southern and Eastern Districts of New York, a motion for leave to bring a third-party action under Fed. R. Civ. P. 14 must be made within six months from the date of service of the moving party's responsive pleading, *i.e.*, answer or the reply to counterclaim. This six-month limitation may be avoided if the moving party can demonstrate special circumstances and the necessity of such relief in the interest of justice.

While Rule 14 limits third-party practice to contribution or indemnity claims, Fed. R. Civ. P. 18(a) would permit joinder of any other claim which the pleader has against the third-party defendant, assuming he has pled an appropriate third-party claim in the first instance.

In admiralty cases the Rule permits a third-party action *in rem*, Fed. R. Civ. P. 14(a), and allows the third-party plaintiff to assert a claim against a person who may be liable in whole or in part to plaintiff, Fed. R. Civ. P. 14(c).

The third-party defendant may assert any defenses and counterclaims he has against the third-party plaintiff as well as any he has against plaintiff provided that counterclaims against plaintiff are restricted to claims "arising out of the transaction or occurrence that is the subject matter of the plaintiff's claim against the third-party plaintiff." A third-party defendant or plaintiff responding to a counterclaim, Fed. R. Civ. P. 14(b), may in turn resort to the same procedures against anyone who "is or may be liable to the third party plaintiff for all or part of the claim."

The court has ancillary subject matter jurisdiction over an appropriately pled third-party claim; however, personal jurisdiction over the third-party defendant must be acquired. *Security Nat'l Bank v. Ubex Corp.*, 404 F. Supp. 471 (S.D.N.Y. 1975).

III. AMENDED AND SUPPLEMENTAL ANSWERS

Fed. R. Civ. p. 15(a) provides for an amendment of right any time before a responsive pleading is served, or if no responsive pleading is permitted (and the action is not on the trial calendar) then within 20 days after service of the pleading.

Otherwise, amendments are permitted only by stipulation or with leave of a court. However, the Rule provides that "leave shall be freely given when justice so requires," and this Rule has been liberally interpreted.[12] The Rule also provides for liberal amendments of pleadings to conform to evidence at trial.

---

12 *Reiter's Beer Distributors, Inc. v. Christian Schmidt Brewing Co.*, 657 F. Supp. 136 (E.D.N.Y. 1987); *Leone v. Advest, Inc.*, 624 F. Supp. 297 (S.D.N.Y. 1985); *Index Fund, Inc. v. Hagopian*, 609 F. Supp. 499 (S.D.N.Y. 1985).

The practitioner should review pleadings in light of motions and early developments in the litigation to avoid inadvertent waivers since factors considered in deciding a motion for leave to amend are undue delay, bad faith and, most importantly, prejudice to the opponent. *See, e.g., Fustok v. Conticommodity Services Line, Inc.*, 103 F.R.D. 601 (S.D.N.Y. 1984).

Fed. R. Civ. P. 15(c) provides that amendments relate back to the date of the original pleading if the claim or defense asserted "arose out of the conduct, transaction or occurrence set forth or attempted to be set forth in the original pleading." Thus, if an amendment to the pleading asserts a counterclaim, so long as that claim is sufficiently related to the original answer, the counterclaim will relate back.[13]

If necessary the answer may be supplemented, for example, to add an after acquired counterclaim or other new material. Motions for permission to supplement pleadings are given the same liberal treatment as motions to amend. *Soler v. G & U, Inc.*, 103 F.R.D. 69 (S.D.N.Y. 1984).

---

[13] *See American Tel. & Tel. Co. v. Delta Communications Corp.*, 114 F.R.D. 606 (S.D. Miss. 1986).

CHAPTER NINE

CHOICE OF LAW

by Barbara A. Mentz, Esq.

The choice of law analysis and the ultimate decision where to file a claim can affect such far ranging and dispositive issues as statutes of limitations, enforceability of forum and choice of law selection clauses, applicability of privileges and defenses, and recoverability of compensatory and punitive damages, interest, and attorney fees. Choice of law considerations should be carefully analyzed before any action is filed in a particular state, or before removing an action to federal court. Unfortunately there are few, if any, concrete rules, nor are there any bright line tests.

I. THE *ERIE* DOCTRINE

A. Introduction

In 1938, the Supreme Court decided *Erie R.R. Co. v. Tompkins*, 304 U.S. 64 (1938), which continues to govern choice of law issues in federal court today. The *Erie* doctrine and its progeny mandate that, as a general rule, a federal court where an action is filed is required to apply the substantive law of the state in which the federal court is sitting, including that state's choice of law rules, except where the subject matter of the action involves the Constitution of the United States, an Act of Congress, a treaty, international law, domestic law of another country, or federal common law.

The purpose of the *Erie* doctrine was to avoid forum shopping and to provide uniformity of substantive results to a litigant whether that litigant was in a federal court sitting in a particular state or in the state court. It is primarily applicable to actions based upon diversity of citizenship.

B. Constitutional Considerations

Two basic aspects of the *Erie* doctrine are the Constitutional basis for the decision, and the Constitutional restraints which have been placed upon its application.

The *Erie* decision involved a construction of the Rules of Decision Act which provided in pertinent part that except where the constitution, treaties or Acts of Congress otherwise require or provide, the "laws of the several states . . . shall be regarded as rules of decision in civil actions . . . " in federal courts in cases where they apply. 28 U.S.C. § 1652 (1966). The *Erie* decision rejected the prior decisional law in *Swift v. Tyson*, 41 U.S. 1, 16 Pet. (1842), and its progeny which had interpreted the Rules of Decision Act to mean that state law was to be followed in a federal court in diversity actions only if a state statute was applicable to the situation. According to the *Swift* doctrine, if no state statute was applicable, the case was to be governed by federal common law rather than state decisional law.

Justice Brandeis noted in *Erie* that because state courts each rendered their own opinions "on questions of common law [this] prevented uniformity." *Erie R.R. Co. v. Tompkins*, 304 U.S. at 74. Moreover, it resulted in unfair discrimination against residents who could not sue in federal courts by non-resident plaintiffs, who could sue in federal court and possibly avoid unfavorable state court decisional law in favor of more favorable federal common law. *Id*. at 74-75. This, of course, had the effect of fostering forum shopping. *Id*. Justice Brandeis held that *Swift* and its progeny thus "rendered impossible equal protection of the law." *Id*. at 75.

He further held that the *Swift* doctrine had "invaded rights which in our opinion are reserved by the Constitution to the several states," *id*. at 80, and "except in matters governed by the Federal Constitution or by Acts of Congress, the law to be applied in any case is the law of the State. And whether the law of the State shall be declared by its Legislature in a statute or by its highest court in a decision is not a matter of federal concern." *Id*. at 78. The *Erie* opinion itself does not refer to any specific section of the Constitution as having been violated by *Swift* and its progeny. However, references to an "invasion of rights" and to "equal protection" are considered to be references to the tenth, fifth and fourteenth amendments, respectively.

The Constitutional basis of *Erie* was not mentioned in subsequent Supreme Court decisions for almost twenty years. In 1956, the Supreme Court made reference to *Erie*'s constitutional basis in *Bernhardt v. Polygraphic Co. of America*, 350 U.S. 198, 202 (1956). In *Bernhardt*, the court skirted the constitutional issue by finding that the matter of whether *Erie* required that a federal court sitting in diversity stay the action and enforce an arbitration clause under the Federal Arbitration Act need not be decided because the contract in question involved only intrastate commerce and the Federal Arbitration Act did not apply to such contracts. In passing, Justice Douglas noted that had the Federal Arbitration Act been applicable, a Constitutional question "might have been raised." *Id.* at 202.

Byrd v. Blue Ridge Rural Elect. Coop., 356 U.S. 525 (1958), was a diversity case in which the Court was faced with a question whether a particular affirmative defense was to be decided by a judge as dictated by state law or by a jury pursuant to federal practice. The Court determined that federal law would be applied. While the opinion is not a model of clarity, the Court referred to the fact that an essential characteristic of the federal system "under the influence—if not the command of the Seventh Amendment" was the distribution of functions between judge and jury which outweighed the "policy of uniform enforcement of state created rights and obligations."*Id.* at 537. At least one commentator has suggested that the *Byrd* decision points out the weakness of *Erie*'s constitutional underpinnings which will cause it to give way in face of a constitutional provision such as the seventh admendment. *See* D. Siegel, *Conflicts in a Nutshell* § 104 (1982).

In *Hanna v. Plumer*, 380 U.S. 460, 471-472 (1965), the Court discussed the Constitutional underpinnings of *Erie*, by way of suggesting its limitations. In *Hanna*, Chief Justice Warren noted that federal courts are free to fashion rules if supported by a grant of federal authority contained in Article I or some other section of the Constitution and that the Constitutional provision for the federal court system, as augmented by the Necessary and Proper Clause, carried with it Congressional power to make rules governing practice and procedure in the courts, including the power to regulate matters rationally capable of being classified as either substantive or procedural. *Id.* The Court thus appears to be narrowly confining *Erie*'s Constitutional underpinnings to leave room to maneuver when the need arises as in the case of the Federal Rules of Civil Procedure.

The second Constitutional aspect to *Erie* is the extent to which the Constitution restrains a federal court sitting in diversity from applying a particular state's substantive law if such application would violate any article of the Constitution. Even before *Erie* was decided, the Supreme Court held that state courts in applying their laws to those who were outside of their borders could not do so in a constitutionally impermissible manner and must provide such non-citizens with due process as required by the Constitution. *Home Ins. Co. v. Dick*, 281 U.S. 397, 407 (1930). In *Dick*, Justice Brandeis for the Court held that a state "may not abrogate the rights of parties beyond its borders having no relation to anything done or to be done within them." *Id.* at 410. The plaintiff in *Dick* was a Texas domiciliary who had been assigned an insurance policy. The policy was issued in Mexico to a Mexican for coverage of a Mexican vessel only in Mexican waters. The policy provided a one-year statute of limitations. An action was brought in a Texas state court after the one-year statute had expired. The Texas state court had applied its two-year limitations statute to save the action, arguing that the statute was procedural not substantive. The Court held that Texas was too lacking in contacts to apply its own law which would violate the Constitutional guaranty against deprivation of property without due process.

Subsequent to the *Erie* decision, numerous Supreme Court cases have made clear that federal courts are constrained by various Constitutional provisions, such as the Due Process Clause, the Full Faith and Credit Clause, the Equal Protection Clause, the Privileges and Immunities Clause, and the Supremacy Clause, when making choice of law decisions. Other limitations on *Erie*'s application are discussed below in the context in which they have arisen in the decisional law.

C. Substantive Versus Procedural Test

The principle result of the *Erie* doctrine is that a federal court sitting in diversity actions must apply state law to all substantive issues while applying federal procedural rules. There is no bright line test as to what constitutes a substantive issue as opposed to a procedural issue. The label itself when applied to a specific issue in a specific context can also shift. In *Guaranty Trust Co. v. York*, 326 U.S. 99, 108, 109 (1945), the Court recognized that the substantive/procedural labeling was too amorphous and that determinations made by trying to pigeonhole issues by substantive or procedural labels might result in failure to apply a state law when the underlying policies of the *Erie* doctrine would suggest a different result. In *Guaranty Trust*, the Court tried to formulate a more realistic test as to what law should apply. This is known as the "outcome determinative" test. Under this formulation, if it can be shown that the outcome of the action would change or would not be substantially the same if federal rather than state law were applied to an issue, *Erie* requires that state law be used. *Id.*

Guaranty Trust arose in the context of the statute of limitations which has been characterized in many states as procedural. However, if the statute were labeled procedural, the result would have been different if the action had been filed in state court rather in federal court. The Court, therefore, avoided the typical substantive/procedural characterizations in favor of what it considered to be a clearer test.

In *Byrd v. Blue Ridge Rural Elec. Coop.*, 356 U.S. 525 (1958), the Court recognized that whether a judge or a jury tried the case could affect the outcome, but that this was not the only consideration. The Court formulated a test that if an issue is "bound up [with] the rights and obligations of the parties" under the particular state law that it is to be governed by state law. *Id.* at 536. However, when the issue did not fall within that scope, the Court was to analyze "countervailing considerations" that may favor application of federal rules over otherwise applicable state court rules, because of the federal courts' independent system for "administering justice." *Id.* at 537. The Court, however, provided no specific guidance for determining when an issue was bound up with the rights and obligations of the parties under state law and this "test" has not been relied upon heavily by other courts.

More recent Supreme Court cases have suggested another more workable test. *See, e.g., Hanna v. Plumer*, 380 U.S. 460 (1965); *Stewart Org., Inc. v. Ricoh Corp.*, 108 S. Ct. 2239 (1988).

In *Hanna*, the Court considered the appropriate test for determining the validity and applicability of the Federal Rules of Civil Procedure. Chief Justice Warren discussed various shortcomings of *Erie*'s substantive/procedural and outcome determinative tests, noting that there is no "automatic litmus paper" test and terming *Erie*'s choice "unguided." *Hanna v. Plumer*, 380 U.S. at 466-472.

According to Chief Justice Warren, a determination that the Massachusetts rule in question, which required in hand service, was applicable, rather than Fed. R. Civ. P. 4 (d) which allowed service on a person of suitable age and discretion, would be outcome determinative because the failure to have been served by hand would require an immediate dismissal of the action thereby altering the outcome. *Id.* at 469. But this fact, standing alone, would be insufficient to determine that the *Erie* doctrine should apply. Chief Justice Warren noted that "[a]n outcome determinative test could not be read without reference to the twin-aims of the *Erie* rule: discouragement of forum-shopping and avoidance of inequitable administration of the laws." *Id.* at 468. If further analyzed under the "twin aims of *Erie*," clearly the test had not been met in *Hanna*: for in choosing her forum, plaintiff was not forum shopping because application of the Massachusetts rule would not have wholly barred recovery at the outset. Rather, it would have simply altered the way process was served. Chief Justice Warren concluded that it was difficult to argue "the mode of enforcement of state created rights was in a fashion sufficiently 'substantial' to raise the sort of equal protection problems to which the *Erie* opinion alluded." *Id.* at 469.

The Supreme Court decision in *Walker v. Armco Steel Corp.*, 446 U.S. 740 (1980), further illustrates the "twin aims of *Erie*" analysis. *Walker* involved the issue of whether a state statute of limitations barred an action brought in federal court in that state or whether Fed. R. Civ. P. 3 served to toll the state statute. The state statute provided that the action was not "commenced" for purposes of the statute of limitations until service of summons on defendant was made, and if the complaint was filed in court within the limitations period, *service* of summons had to be made within sixty days thereafter, if such service was outside of the limitation period, or the action was barred. The complaint had been filed within the two-year limitations period, but service was not made within sixty days after the limitations period ran. The question was whether Fed. R. Civ. P. 3, which provides that the action is *commenced* upon the filing of the complaint, served to toll the state statute.

In *Walker*, the application of the state statute would have wholly barred plaintiff's action if filed in state court, but would not have barred it if Fed. R. Civ. P. 3 were applied as defendant had argued. As in *Hanna*, the outcome would have been different if the state statute were applied; but unlike *Hanna*, such a result would do violence to the twin aims of *Erie*. Although it might not encourage forum shopping, the result would be an "inequitable administration of the law." Justice Marshall noted there was no reason why an action based on state law which would be barred at the outset by the statute of limitations if in state court "should proceed through litigation to judgment in federal court solely because of the fortuity that there is diversity of citizenship between litigants. . . . Erie and its progeny do not permit it." *Id.* at 753.

The substantive/procedural test or "outcome determinative" test, further analyzed in light of *Erie*'s twin aims, although not a bright line test, is somewhat more definitive. The time for this analysis for plaintiff's counsel is before litigation is commenced, and if in doubt, to the extent possible, state and federal law should both be followed.

D. Applicability to Actions Involving Federal Questions

While the *Erie* doctrine particularly applies to diversity actions, it also has application to federal question cases. Since the *Erie* doctrine is the Supreme Court's construction of the Rules of Decision Act, it applies to all situations where federal law does not govern. "The scope of a federal right is, of course, a federal question but that does not mean that its content is not to be determined by state law rather than federal law." *See, e.g., DeSylva v. Ballentine*, 351 U.S. 570, 580-581 (1956) (in a dispute involving the Federal Copyright Act, the word "children" is defined in accordance with state law); *Abraham v. Volkswagen of America, Inc.*, 795 F.2d 238, 248-249 (2d Cir. 1986) (in action commenced under the Magnuson-Moss Act, the implied warranty claims were held to be subject to state law privity rules); 19 C. Wright, A. Miller & E. Cooper, *Federal Practice and Procedure* § 4515 (1982).

E. Applicability of Federal Common Law

Justice Brandeis announced in *Erie* that: "There is no federal general common law." *Erie R.R. Co. v. Tompkins*, 304 U.S. at 78. While this is a true statement, there are a limited number of situations in which the governing rule of law in diversity actions is in fact "federal common law," rather than state law. Federal common law is not expressly authorized by the Constitution or any Act of Congress, it is fashioned by the court and limited to areas in which Congress has power to legislate. Unfortunately, "[w]hatever definition of federal common law one uses, the area cannot be delimited by any clear-cut line." Field, *Sources of Law: The Scope of Federal Common Law*, 99 Harv. L. Rev. 883, 894 (1986).

Matters involving federal common law appear to share the following characteristics: (a) it is supported by some express or implied affirmative grant of power to the federal government; (b) it displaces state law and is binding upon the states, even in diversity cases; (c) it can be overridden by an act of Congress; and (d) an action arising under federal common law may present a federal question which is within the original jurisdiction of the federal courts and is not dependent upon diversity of citizenship. *Cf. City of Milwaukee v. Illinois*, 451 U.S. 304, 312-315 (1981); 19 C. Wright, A. Miller & E. Cooper, *supra*, § 4514 at 217-222.

There are three contexts in which federal common law has been developed in diversity actions: (a) where there is a significant conflict between some legitimate federal policy or interest and the use of state law, *D'Oench, Duhme & Co. v. Federal Deposit Ins. Corp.*, 315 U.S. 447, 459 (1942) (protection of Federal Deposit Insurance Corp.); *Clearfield Trust Co. v. United States*, 318 U.S. 363, 366-367 (1943) (protection of federal government commercial paper and strong need for national uniformity); (b) "those areas of judicial decision within which the policy of the law is so dominated by the sweep of federal statutes that legal relations which they affect must be deemed governed by federal law," *see, e.g., Sola Elec. Co. v. Jefferson Elec. Co.*, 317 U.S. 173, 176 (1942); *Textile Workers Union of Am. v. Lincoln Mills of Alabama*, 353 U.S. 448, 456-457 (1957) (Labor Management Relations Act); and (c) matters implicating the Constitution, Congressional legislation or national necessity such as controversies between the states, admiralty matters and foreign relations, *see, e.g., U.S. v. Reliable Transfer Co., Inc.*, 421 U.S. 397 (1975).

Other examples of federal common law can be found in: (a) contracts to which the federal government is a party; *see, e.g., United States v. Allegheny County*, 322 U.S. 174, 182 (1944); (b) cases involving whether a tortfeasor who injured a U.S. soldier was liable to the federal government for hospital bills; *United States v. Standard Oil Co.*, 332 U.S. 301, 305, 311 (1947); *but see In re "Agent Orange" Prod. Liab. Litig.*, 635 F.2d 987 (2d Cir. 1980), *cert. denied sub nom. Chapman v. Dow Chem. Co.*, 454 U.S. 1128 (1981) (the Second Circuit refused to apply federal common law to products liability cases affecting millions of veterans); (c) cases involving a government contractor and the United States; *see, e.g., Boyle v. United Technologies Corp.*,

108 S. Ct. 2510 (1988). *See* Vairo, *Multi-tort Cases: Cause For More Darkness on the Subject, or a New Role for Federal Common Law?*, 54 Fordham L. Rev. 167 (1985). It is clear that the presence or absence of the United States as a party does not in itself dictate whether federal common law can be applied. *See, e.g., U.S. v. Yazell,* 382 U.S. 341 (1966); *Bank of America v. Parnell,* 352 U.S. 29, 34 (1956).

Federal courts generally exercise restraint in fashioning federal common law. Moreover, even though an area of law is an appropriate one in which to apply federal common law, a court is not required to exercise its power to do so. 19 C. Wright, A. Miller & E. Cooper, *supra,* § 4514. However, as noted above, when a court does exercise its power to make federal common law or when there is existing federal common law, it displaces state law in diversity actions.

F. Applicability to the Federal Rules of Civil Procedure and the Federal Rules of Appellate Procedure

1. The Federal Rules of Civil Procedure

The Federal Rules of Civil Procedure ("Federal Rules") are designed to govern practice and procedure in the United States District Courts in all actions, including diversity actions with the exception of those stated in Fed. R. Civ. P. 81. Fed. R. Civ. P. 1. They were promulgated pursuant to the Rules Enabling Act, 28 U.S.C. § 2072, which empowers the Supreme Court to make general rules of practice and procedure for the United States District Courts with the restriction that "such rules shall not abridge, enlarge or modify any substantive right."

The main purpose of Congress in authorizing the development of a uniform and consistent system of rules governing federal practice and procedure suggests that rules which incidentally affect litigants' substantive rights do not violate the Rules Enabling Act, if they are necessary to maintain the integrity of the system. The Federal Rules have presumptive validity under both constitutional and statutory constraints. If a Federal Rule regulates a matter that is indisputably procedural, it is *a priori* constitutional. If a Federal Rule regulates matters which fall between the areas of substance and procedure and is rationally capable of classification as either, it also satisfies the constitutional standard. *Hanna v. Plumer,* 380 U.S. at 471-472.

The *Erie* doctrine does not constitute the appropriate test for the validity and applicability of the Federal Rules. *Id.* at 470; *Walker v. Armco Steel Corp.,* 446 U.S. at 747.

As Chief Justice Warren explained in *Hanna, Erie* has never been invoked to void a Federal Rule. Where the Court has held that a state court rule was

CHOICE OF LAW

applicable instead of one of the Federal Rules, it is not because *Erie* required its displacement by an inconsistent state court rule, but rather that the scope of the Federal Rule was not broad enough to cover the situation and, there being no Federal Rule which covered the point, *Erie* required the application of state rules. *Hanna v. Plumer*, 380 U.S. at 470. When there is a direct conflict between a state rule that is inconsistent with a Federal Rule, the initial step is to determine whether the scope of the Federal Rule in question is sufficiently broad to control the issue before the Court, leaving no room for the operation of state law. *Id.* at 470; *Walker v. Armco Steel Corp.*, 446 U.S. at 749-750.[1]

The Federal Rule *must* be applied if it was within the scope of the Rules Enabling Act in that it does not abridge, enlarge or modify a substantive right and if so, if it was within a Constitutional grant of power such as the Necessary and Proper Clause of Article I. *Hanna v. Plumer*, 380 U.S. at 470-472; *Walker v. Armco Steel Corp.*, 446 U.S. at 748. The test is whether the Federal Rule really regulates procedure, the judicial process for enforcing right and duties recognized by sustantive law, and for administering the remedy. Although rules of practice and procedure often affect litigants' rights, Congress' prohibition was not addressed to incidental effects as necessarily follow from the procedural rules. And this incidental effect does not modify, enlarge or abridge the rules of decision by which the courts adjudicate those rights. *Id.* at 464-465.

As noted earlier, in *Hanna*, the Court was faced with the question whether, in a diversity action, state law governed the manner of service of process or whether Fed. R. Civ. P. 4(d)(1) governed. The state law in question required *in-hand* service, while Fed. R. Civ. P. 4(d)(1) provided service could be made upon a person of suitable age and discretion, which was the method by which service was effected in *Hanna*. The Court concluded that Fed. R. Civ. P. 4(d)(1) was designed to control the practice and procedure of service of process in diversity actions and neither exceeded the Congressional mandate in the Rules Enabling Act, nor transgressed Constitutional bounds. Therefore, it should govern service of process in federal court actions. The Court concluded that to hold that a Federal Rule must cease to function whenever it alters the mode of enforcing state-created rights would be to disembowel either the Constitution's grant of power over federal procedures or Congress' attempt to exercise that power in the Rules Enabling Act. *Id.* at 473-474.

---

[1] The court in *Walker* noted that the Federal Rules are not to be narrowly construed to avoid a direct collision with state law and they should be given their plain meaning. However, if such a direct collision arises, then the *Hanna* analysis governs. *Walker v. Armco Steel Co.*, 446 U.S. at 750 n.9.

The rationale for the decision was that while the method of service would have an effect on the outcome, because service would be invalid under state law, the difference in the two rules did not alter, abridge or modify plaintiff's substantive rights, because application of the state court rule would not have barred recovery at the outset and affected only the manner of service. *Id.* at 468-470.

Similarly, in *Walker*, the question was whether Fed. R. Civ. P. 3 acted to toll the state statute of limitations which required service of the summons within sixty days after expiration of the statute of limitations if the complaint had been filed before the expiration of the statutory period, as a condition for tolling the statute. The Court in *Walker* noted that the function of the statute of limitations was to provide a deadline after which a defendant "may legitimately have peace of mind." *Id.* at 751. As such, the service of summons requirement of the state statute was an integral part of the statute of limitations. The Court held the scope of Fed. R. Civ. P. 3 was not sufficiently broad to control the issue, because Fed. R. Civ. P. 3 merely governs the date from which various timing requirements of the Federal Rules began to run. There was no indication that Rule 3 was intended to displace the state statute of limitations or to act as a tolling mechanism for such statutes. *Id.* at 751-752. Fed. R. Civ. P. 3 was therefore held not broad enough to cover the tolling of a state statute of limitations. *Id.*

2. The Federal Rules of Appellate Procedure

The applicability of the Federal Rules of Appellate Procedure ("Fed. R. App. P.") to diversity actions is governed by the same analysis as the Federal Rules of Civil Procedure. *Burlington Northern R.R. Co. v. Woods*, 480 U.S. 1, n.3 (1987). *Burlington* involved the question whether a state's mandatory 10 percent penalty statute, imposed on appellants who obtain stays of judgments pending unsuccessful appeals, should have been applied to a judgment entered by a federal court sitting in diversity, instead of Fed. R. App. P. 38 which allows the court to exercise discretion in assessing a penalty. The Court noted that the discretionary nature of Fed. R. App. P. 38 conflicts with the mandatory 10 percent penalty required by state law and that the purposes of the rules were sufficiently co-extensive that Fed. R. App. P. 38 occupies the state court's field of operation so as to preclude the state statute's application in federal diversity actions. However, the Court concluded that Fed. R. App. P. 38 regulates matters that can reasonably be classified as procedural, because it affects only the process of enforcing litigants rights and not the rights themselves, thereby satisfying the Constitutional standard for validity. *Id.* at 970-971. Therefore, in *Burlington*, Fed. R. App. P. 38 was applicable, not the state court rule.

G. Applicability to Federal Procedural Statutes

The same analysis has been applied with respect to 28 U.S.C. § 1404(a) in *Stewart Org., Inc. v. Ricoh*, 108 S. Ct. 2239 (1988). In *Stewart*, the Court relied on the *Hanna* and *Walker* analysis to determine whether § 1404(a) controlled defendants' request to transfer to another federal district court pursuant to a forum selection clause in a contract, or whether a state policy invalidating such a forum selection clause overrode § 1404(a).[2]

The Court noted that § 1404(a) occupied the same field of operation as the state policy disfavoring forum selection clauses and, citing to *Burlington*, the Court held that when two choices operate in a single field of operations, the "instructions of Congress are supreme" and § 1404(a) was applicable. *Id.*

H. Applicability to the Federal Rules of Evidence

The Federal Rules of Evidence ("Fed. R. Evid.") are applicable in actions pending in federal courts based upon diversity of citizenship without regards to the *Erie* doctrine.[3] State evidentiary rules are applicable in diversity cases only in two instances. First, they are applicable to the extent that the Federal Rules of Evidence specifically make them applicable. *See, e.g.*, Fed. R. Evid. 302 (effect of presumptions of fact where state substantive law provides the rule of decision); Fed. R. Evid. 501 (privileges where state substantive law provides the rule of decision); Fed. R. Evid. 601 (competency of witnesses where state law provides the rule of decision); Fed. R. Evid. 901 (testimony of subscribing witness); Fed. R. Evid. 902(9) (commercial paper, signatures thereon, and documents relating thereto to the extent provided by *general commercial law* are self-authenticating).

Second, they are applicable to the extent the Federal Rules of Evidence require supplementation from external sources of law. In those instances where state substantive law provides the rule of decision, it is necessary to look to state law. *See, e.g.*, Fed. R. Evid. 401 (definition of relevant evidence as "evidence having any tendency to make the existence of any fact that is of consequence to the determination of the action more or less probable than it would be without the evidence." Where an issue is governed by

---

[2] In *Stewart*, the Court noted that if no Federal Rule covers the point in dispute, the Court must then evaluate whether the application of a federal judge-made law would disserve the twin aims of *Erie* and if it would, the Court should apply state law. *Stewart Org., Inc. v. Ricoh*, 108 S. Ct. at n.6.

---

[3] The Federal Rules of Evidence are not subject to the *Erie* doctrine because they were enacted by Congress in 1975, Act of Jan. 2, 1975, Pub. L. 93-595, 88 Stat. 1926. In this respect, they differ from the Federal Rules of Civil Procedure which were not enacted by Congress and unlike the Federal Rules of Civil Procedure, they are not subject to the Rules Enabling Act, 28 U.S.C. § 2072, or the Rules of Decision Act, 28 U.S.C. § 1652. For a discussion, of the Federal Rules of Evidence, *see* 19 C. Wright, A. Miller & E. Cooper, *Federal Practice and Procedure* § 4512 (1982).

state law, to decide whether it is relevant under Fed. R. Evid. 401, it may be necessary to analyze whether it is of consequence to the determination of the action which is answered in the context of the applicable state law.); Fed. R. Evid. 803(8)-803(12), 803(14), 803(15) (involving various hearsay exceptions); Fed. R. Evid. 902(1)-902(5), 902(8) (dealing with self-authentication); Fed. R. Evid. 1005 (best evidence exemptions). *See generally* Wellborn, *The Federal Rules of Evidence and the Application of State Law in Federal Courts*, 55 Tex. L. Rev. 371, 442-448 (1977).

II. MODERN CHOICE OF LAW METHODS

A. Introduction

A federal court adjudicating an action governed by the *Erie* doctrine must apply the choice of law rules of the forum state in which the district court is sitting. *Klaxon Co. v. Stentor Elec. Mfg. Co.*, 313 U.S. 487, 496 (1941). This is, however, only the beginning of the inquiry. Where there is a choice of forums, how to determine the best forum in which to commence an action is not only desirable, but is critical in many instances to what, if any, recovery can be had.

B. Threshold Considerations in Choosing the Best Forum

1. How to Determine Which State Law Can Apply

As a threshold consideration, a list of all possible forums which could entertain personal and subject matter jurisdiction[4] should be made. The list should include both state courts which have such jurisdiction and federal courts. If consideration is given to bringing the action in state court, the question whether a defendant could remove the action and transfer it should also be given. Questions of *forum non conveniens* and public policy issues should also be considered.

Second, once it is determined where the action could be brought, a list should be made of each state whose law might be applied to the situation. It might well be that the best case analysis from the plaintiff's standpoint would be the application of the law of a place where the plaintiff cannot obtain personal jurisdiction. The next step may be helpful in this regard. It requires

---

[4] The subjects of personal and subject matter jurisdiction are covered elsewhere in this book. *See* Chapters 1 and 2. However, certain restrictions on personal jurisdiction, including constitutionally mandated minimum contacts, *Phillips Petroleum Co. v. Shutts*, 472 U.S. 797, 806-07 (1985), *forum non conveniens* and public policy principles can affect the ability to choose a forum. The "minimum contacts" necessary to obtain jurisdiction should not be confused with, and are not analogous to, the "grouping of contacts," "counting of contacts," "interest analysis" or any other discussion involving actual choice of law methods employed in torts, contracts or other cases discussed in this chapter.

an analysis of the internal law of each state where jurisdiction can be obtained *and* an analysis of each such state's choice of law principles. The analysis may suggest that one of the appropriate forums would, under its choice of law principles, apply the substantive law of the state which plaintiff originally desired, but for reasons of lack of personal jurisdiction, could not bring suit. The analysis may also show that no true conflict exists and the law of only one state could possibly apply. The application of the doctrines of depecage[5] and renvoi should be considered at this stage, as well as the applicable statutes of limitations of each state, whether desired causes of action are viable in each state, and any limitation on damages each state would apply. An unthinking decision to litigate "at home" could result in an unnecessary loss to plaintiff. *Cf. Fort Howard Paper Co. v. William D. Witter, Inc.*, 787 F.2d 784 (2d Cir. 1986) (demonstrating a successful strategy of not litigating "at home").[6] While choice of forum is in effect a form of forum shopping, it is permissible and should be well thought out in advance of bringing suit.

2. Recognizing Whether There is a True Conflict

A true conflict exists where the laws of the relevant states would produce different results and the policies underlying the laws demonstrate that they were designed to cover exactly the same situation. A false conflict exists if the law of all relevant states when examined are: (a) the same; (b) would produce the same result; or (c) even though not producing the same result, upon analysis the policies underlying one state's laws are not designed to cover the situation involved in the action and the other state's laws are designed to cover the situation. If there is a false conflict, the court will not proceed further with the choice of law analysis. A neutral or unprovided for case exists when the laws of all relevant states are examined and an anaylsis of their underlying policies indicates that none of the state's laws were designed to cover the situation. Siegel, *supra* §§ 81-83.

---

5 New York's choice of law rules require an issue by issue choice of law analysis. *See, e.g., James v. Powell*, 19 N.Y.2d 249, 225 N.E.2d 741, 279 N.Y.S.2d 10 (1967); *Hutner v. Greene*, 734 F.2d 896, 901 (2d Cir. 1984). This could result in application of the law of different states to different issues based upon the same underlying facts.

---

6 The Wisconsin company sought a declaratory judgment against an individual employed in New York and his company headquartered in New York that the defendants were not entitled to a finder's fee. The federal district court sitting in New York had determined that New York law would apply and the breach of contract action for an oral finders' fee was barred by the New York statute of frauds, even though it would have been valid under Wisconsin law. This part of the decision was affirmed by the Second Circuit. Obviously, the Wisconsin plaintiff correctly analyzed that it had a better chance of having a New York court apply New York law to bar the claim than it had of a Wisconsin court ignoring its own law validating oral finder's fee agreements in favor of New York law.

a. Example of a True Conflict

Bader v. Purdom, 841 F.2d 38 (2d Cir. 1988) was a negligence action which involved a dog bite injury received by a minor New York resident while vacationing with parents in Ontario, Canada. The Canadian resident filed a third-party complaint against the parents for negligent supervision of the child. This cause of action was viable in Ontario, but not in New York. The district court in the Eastern District of New York applied New York law and dismissed the third-party action, but the Second Circuit reversed. The court first analyzed whether there was a "true conflict." The court looked to the underlying purpose of New York's rule barring an action for negligent supervision. The Second Circuit concluded that the underlying purpose of the New York rule was to protect the interest of New York children and their parents over the interests of nonparent tortfeasors.[7] The court next analyzed the underlying purpose of Ontario's rule which holds dog owners strictly liable for injuries caused by their dogs, but which mitigates such strict liability by allowing contribution or indemnification for comparative fault. Since the underlying purpose was to protect Ontario dog owners from strict liability in the event of contributory fault by others, the Second Circuit held that this case was a "true conflict" because "application of the New York rule would undermine Ontario's interest, while application of the Ontario rule would undermine New York's interest." Thus, the court had to resolve the true conflict by moving to the next step in the analysis to determine whose state's law should govern.

b. Example of a False Conflict

In *Babcock v. Jackson*, 12 N.Y.2d 473, 191 N.E.2d 279, 240 N.Y.S.2d 743 (1963), a New York passenger in a car licensed and insured in New York and driven by a New York driver had a one-car accident in Ontario. New York's law would allow the passenger to recover. New York's interest was in requiring a tortfeasor to compensate a New York guest for injuries caused by negligence even if the injury occurred in another state which had rules that prevent recovery. Ontario's laws barred recovery. Upon analysis, it was clear that the purpose of Ontario's statute was to prevent fraudulent claims against Ontario defendants and their insurers. *Id.* at 482-83, 191 N.E.2d 279, 284, 240 N.Y.S.2d 743. Since, under the facts in *Babcock*, the purpose of Ontario's statute was not thwarted (because no Ontario defendant or Ontario insur-

---

[7] The underlying reasons for the rule were that: (1) if parents were vulnerable to suits for contribution, they might not assert their child's rights against third parties; (2) family tension might increase if parents sue and are later held liable for negligent supervision; (3) allowing recovery for contribution could effectively reduce the child's compensation given the fact that a typical family is a "single economic unit"; and (4) the state should preserve a sphere of parental autonomy. *Bader v. Purdom*, 841 F.2d. at 39-40.

ance carrier was involved), this was a false conflict. *See also Phillips Petroleum Co. v. Shutts*, 472 U.S. 797, 838 (1985) (the Court described the action as a "classic 'false conflicts' case" because Phillips had not demonstrated that any significant conflict existed merely because two relevant states' statutes "suggest that those State's would 'most likely' reach different results . . . The Court's heavy reliance on the characterizations of the law provided by Phillips is not an adequate substitute for a neutral review."); *Norlin Corp. v. Rooney, Pace Inc.*, 744 F.2d 255, 263-64 (2d Cir. 1984).

c. Example of a Neutral or Unprovided For Case

Where the underlying policies of neither relevant state is truly in issue, this is a neutral or unprovided for case. *Neumeier v. Keuhner*, 31 N.Y.2d 121, 286 N.E.2d 454, 335 N.Y.S.2d 64 (1972). In *Neumeier*, the defendant was a New York driver with an Ontario passenger when an accident occurred in Ontario. As noted above, New York's scheme would allow recovery, but its purpose was to insure for recovery by a New Yorker for injuries received through negligent acts. The person injured was not a New Yorker and New York's rule therefore was neutral. Ontario's guest-host statute's purpose was to prevent false claims against Ontario defendants and insurers, also facts which were not present in the action. Thus, Ontario's law was also neutral. The forum in that circumstance is free to apply the law of one of the states involved. New York often applies *lex loci* to these situations. *Id.*

3. How to Determine the Substance of Applicable State Law

Under the *Klaxon* rule, a federal court in an action governed by the *Erie* doctrine must apply the choice of law rules of the state in which the district court is sitting and cannot exercise its independent judgment or apply general principles of law. *Klaxon v. Stentor Mfg. Co.*, 313 U.S. at 496.

The *Klaxon* rule is to be applied, absent exceptional circumstances, even though it allows for elements of forum shopping and even though a mechanical application of *Klaxon* might require a federal court to apply the choice of law rules of a state that has little or no interest in the dispute before the Court. *Day & Zimmermann, Inc. v. Challoner*, 423 U.S. 3 (1975) (*per curiam*). The exception to such mechanical application is if the state's choice of law rules are Constitutionally prohibited under the Full Faith and Credit Clause and other Constitutional restrictions. *See Wells v. Simonds Abrasive Co.*, 345 U.S. 514, 516 (1953). A federal court need not give effect to a state statute that violates the United States Constitution or to adopt a state court's interpretation of United States Constitutional principles as applied to the state's statute. *Industrial Consultants, Inc. v. H. S. Equities, Inc.*, 646 F.2d 746 (2d Cir.), *cert. denied*, 454 U.S. 838 (1981).

There is little difficulty in applying state law if the state's choice of law principles are clear because there is a statute in point or there is clear decisional law on point from the state's highest court. However, if the above circumstances do not exist, the court must determine the content of applicable state law by reference to other means.

New York has a certification procedure permitting the federal courts to obtain an advisory opinion on state law from the Court of Appeals. *See* N.Y. Rules of Court § 500.17 (N.Y. Ct. App.) (McKinney 1987); *DeWeerth v. Baldinger*, 836 F.2d 103, 108 n.5. (2d Cir. 1987), *U.S. appeal pending* (certification of issues should be limited "to issues likely to recur with some frequency"). However, where an advisory opinion is either not available or not sought, the following general rules can be used in finding the content of applicable state law.

A federal court may look to and give proper regard for an intermediate appellate level decision which is binding unless the court is convinced by other persuasive data that the highest court of the state would come to a different result. *See, e.g., Entron, Inc. v. Affiliated FM Ins. Co.*, 749 F.2d 127, 132 (2d Cir. 1984). In *Entron*, the Second Circuit rejected an intermediate appellate court's decision finding the reasoning wrong and stating the highest state court would reach a different conclusion. Thus, where there is no case in point from the highest state court, there is room for the advocate's position that the highest court would decide otherwise.[8]

If the state's highest court has not decided an issue, a federal court sitting in New York should defer to a decision of a federal circuit court encompassing that state within its territory, unless the federal circuit court had disregarded clear signals from the state's highest court that would point toward a different rule. *Factors Etc., Inc. v. Pro Arts, Inc.*, 652 F.2d 278, 283 (2d Cir. 1981), *cert. denied*, 456 U.S. 927 (1983).

The federal court must apply state law as it exists at the time of decision. Therefore, if there has been a change in state law between the time of the lower court's decision and the time of review by the circuit court, the circuit court must apply the state law as changed. *Vandenbark v. Owens-Illinois Glass Co.*, 311 U.S. 538 (1941).

In the event that there appears to be confusion about a state court's decision, or a developing line of decisional or legislative authority places doubt

---

[8] Decisions by courts below the intermediate state court appellate level are not controlling. In that case, a court may proceed to make its own determination of what it believes the highest court in the state would do. *See King v. Order of United Commercial Travelers of Am.*, 333 U.S. 153 (1948); *Competex, S.A. v. LaBow*, 783 F.2d 333, 340, n.16 (2d Cir. 1986) (not required to accept a state trial court's view of state law if federal court believes the state's highest court would disagree).

over established decisions, federal courts should be sensitive to such changes, but are not free to change established decisions of the highest court without more. *Bernhardt v. Polygraphic Co. of Am., Inc.*, 350 U.S. 198 (1956). This is a fine line, for while the federal court should not mindlessly follow a state court rule, but must consider all the data the state's highest court would use, it cannot simply abandon a decision of the highest state court merely because it is unwise, antiquated or anomolous unless there are very persuasive grounds for believing the state's highest court would no longer adhere to it. *Compare Krauss v. Manhattan Life Ins. Co. of New York*, 643 F.2d 98, 102 (2d Cir. 1981), *with Hausman v. Buckley*, 299 F.2d 696, 704 (2d Cir.), *cert. denied*, 369 U.S. 885 (1962).

If there are no state court decisions, the federal court must make an estimate of what the state's highest court would rule. *DeWeerth v. Baldinger*, 836 F.2d at 108. The federal court can look to the following types of evidence for guidelines: (1) state court *dicta*; (2) opinions of the state's attorney general; (3) determinations of state agencies; and (4) all other available legal sources such as treatises, law review commentaries, and the law of other jurisdictions. *Cf. id.*

When the federal court's application of the forum's choice of law rules requires that the law of another state be applied and that state's law is silent on the issue, the federal court can turn for guidance to the state law of the forum. *Sagamore Corp. v. Diamond West Energy Corp.*, 806 F.2d 373, 377 (2d Cir. 1986). Moreover, if the state court would presume that the other state's laws were the same as its own, under the given circumstances, a federal court could make the same presumption, especially if the forum's laws are consistent with the laws of most other jurisdictions. *Aetna Casualty & Sur. Co. v. General Time Corp.*, 704 F.2d 80, 82 (2d Cir. 1983).

4. Renvoi

As noted above, *Klaxton* requires the federal court to look to the whole state law of the forum, including the state's choice of law rules. Since the federal court is required to look at the state's choice of law rules, the doctrine of renvoi must be considered.

When a true conflict arises and the forum determines that it is necessary to apply the law of another jurisdiction, the question arises as to whether the forum applies only the other jurisdiction's internal law or its whole law, including that jurisdiction's choice of law rules. If the forum were to apply the other jurisdiction's whole law, that jurisdiction's choice of law rules might dictate that it look to the law of the original forum. This is known as "remission" and its result could be a never-ending circle, unless the forum then determined to apply its own internal law. If the other jurisdiction's choice of law rules would refer instead to the law of a third forum, this is known as "transmission."

The doctrine of renvoi has very limited application in most jurisdictions.[9] New York courts have not been either totally consistent nor absolutely clear on the application of renvoi. But, it appears that renvoi is primarily limited to cases involving title to land, divorce actions or where statutorily mandated. *Cf. Reger v. Nat'l Ass'n of Bedding Mgf. Group Ins. Trust Fraud*, 83 Misc. 2d 527, 372 N.Y.S.2d 97, 117-18 (S. Ct. 1975); *In re Schneider's Estate*, 198 Misc. 1017, 96 N.Y.S.2d 652 (Sur. Ct. 1950), *adhered to on rehearing*, 100 N.Y.S.2d 371 (Sur. Ct. 1950) (In *Schneider*, a New York domicilary left real property in Switzerland. The New York court looked to whole law of Switzerland including its choice of law principles. Switzerland's choice of law principles applied the law of the state of domicile to title to property and the New York court then returned to its own law as limited to its internal law.); *Competex, S.A. v. Labow*, 783 F.2d 333, 340-41 and n.18 (2d Cir. 1986); *Neal v. Butler Aviation Int. Inc.*, 460 F. Supp. 98, 102-103 (E.D.N.Y. 1978). Renvoi is statutorily mandated in New York in various sections of the Uniform Commercial Code §§ 2-402 (rights of creditors); § 4-102 (bank deposits and collections); § 6-102 (bulk transfers); § 8-106 (investment securities); § 9-103 (perfection of secured transactions). N.Y.U.C.C. §§ 2-402, 4-102, 6-102, 8-106, 9-103 (McKinney 1964 & 1988 Supp.). It is also mandated by the Federal Tort Claims Act, 28 U.S.C. § 346(b).

5. Statutes of Limitations Issues—Borrowing Statutes

Traditionally, statutes of limitations have been classified as procedural for choice of law purposes. Under this view, the statutes of limitations of the forum may constitutionally be applied even though the forum's choice of law rules may require that the substantive law of another jurisdiction be applied. *Sun Oil Co. v. Wortman*, 108 S. Ct. 2117 (1988). The rationale is the forum's interest in protecting against stale claims and in providing defendants with peace of mind. There are generally two exceptions to this traditional rule: when borrowing statutes are involved or when the foreign state's statute would not only bar the remedy, but would extinguish the right, in which case the statute is deemed to be substantive not procedural.

---

9 For a discussion of renvoi, including an argument for its broader application, *see* E. F. Scoles and P. Hay, Conflict of Laws, §§ 3.13-3.14 (L.ed. 1984). *See also* the Restatement (Second) of Conflict of Laws § 8(2) and (3) which advocates the use of renvoi "[w]hen the objective of the particular choice-of-law rule is that the forum reach the same result on the very facts involved as would the courts of another state . . . subject to considerations of practicality and feasibility," or "[w]hen the state of the forum has no substantial relationship to the particular issue or to the parties" and all interested states would concur in selecting the local law rule applicable to the issue.

The traditional view that statutes of limitations are procedural and the forum's law should be applied has recently been eroded. The April 15, 1986, draft revisions of the Restatement (Second) of Conflict of Laws uses the "more significant relationship" test in determining the applicable statute of limitations. Restatement (Second) of Conflict of Laws § 142 (draft April 15, 1986). These revisions are in draft only and the Section should be checked before relying upon it. The approach of the Restatement (Second) requires an issue by issue analysis. This could lead to application of a limitations period governed by the law of a state that is different than the law governing the underlying claim. There is also a Uniform Conflict of Laws-Limitations Act, 12 U.L.A. Pocket Part at 54 (1988), which adopts a substantive characterization of the statute of limitations and in general would apply the limitations period of the state whose law governs the underlying claim.

a. New York State Courts

New York does not follow the Restatement (Second) approach, nor has it adopted the Uniform Conflict of Laws Limitation Act. Under New York law, actions that accrue within New York are governed by New York's statutes of limitations, while actions that accrue outside of New York are governed by the rules set forth in N.Y. Civ. Prac. Law § 202 (McKinney 1972). See *Martin v. Julius Dierck Equip. Co.*, 43 N.Y.2d 583, 588-589, 374 N.E.2d 97, 99, 403 N.Y.S.2d 185, 187-188 (1978).

CPLR § 202 provides that in a choice of law situation where the cause of action accrues outside New York, but to one who at the time was a New York resident, only the New York statute of limitations applies and the foreign state's limitations period is disregarded. Only if the foreign claim accrued to a nonresident, including a nonresident foreign corporation, will New York look to the foreign state's limitation period. Then, the two limitations periods are compared and the *shorter* one is applied. N.Y. Civ. Prac. L. § 202.

The term "resident" as used in § 202 does not have the same meaning as the term "domicile." *Antone v. General Motors Corp.*, 64 N.Y.2d 20, 26, 30, 473 N.E.2d 742, 744-746, 484 N.Y.S.2d 514, 516-518 (1984). In *Antone* the shorter limitations period of the state of plaintiff's residence was borrowed and applied to bar plaintiff's claim. The plaintiff had a New York post office box, but did not actually live in New York. The court defined "residence" for purposes of CPLR § 202 as a "significant connection with some locality in the State as a result of living there for some length of time during the course of the year." *Id.* at 30, 473 N.E.2d at 746, 484 N.Y.S.2d at 518. The court also noted that each state's limitations period carried its own tolling provisions, which is to be computed into the formula to obtain the "shorter" period. *Id.* at 31, 473 N.E.2d at 747, 484 N.Y.S.2d at 519.

If a claim accrued to a New York resident, but was subrogated to a foreign carrier, the foreign carrier stands in the shoes of the New York resident for statute of limitations purposes. *U.S. Fidelity & Guar. Co. v. Smith Co.*, 46 N.Y.2d 498, 504, 387 N.E.2d 604, 606-607, 414 N.Y.S.2d 672, 674-675 (1979).

A defendant who asserts that a foreign statute of limitations is applicable and admits he was not a resident of the foreign jurisdiction must prove his presence in the foreign state to avoid the tolling provisions pursuant to New York rules of evidence, because questions of burden of proof are procedural. *Childs v. Brandon*, 60 N.Y.2d 927, 459 N.E.2d 149, 471 N.Y.S.2d 40 (1983).

The second exception, when a foreign limitations period is intended not only to bar the remedy but also to extinguish the right, applies only to statutorily created causes of actions, not common law ones. The presence of a limitations period within a statute is not necessarily conclusive as to the substantive nature of the limitations period. In that event, the right must be found outside of the statute itself. Examples of this type of statute are wrongful death statutes or shareholder liability act statutes. *See Bournias v. Atlantic Maritime Co.*, 220 F.2d 152, 154-156 (2d Cir. 1955); *Chartener v. Kice*, 270 F. Supp. 432 (E.D.N.Y. 1967); E. F. Scoles and P. Hays, *supra* § 3.10; Restatement (Second) of Conflict of Laws § 143 comment c (1969).

b. Federal Courts Sitting in New York

A federal court sitting in New York is bound to apply New York's law with respect to the statute of limitations issue, including its borrowing statute. *See, e.g., DeWeerth v. Baldinger*, 836 F.2d at 106.

In a federal action, based upon diversity, the claim is deemed "interposed" for statute of limitations purposes as governed by state law, not by Rule 3 of the Federal Rules of Civil Procedure. *Walker v. Armco Steel Corp.*, 446 U.S. 740 (1980). Therefore, a summons and complaint in a federal action has to be served within the New York state statute of limitations. Filing of the complaint in federal court before the expiration of the New York limitations period and service after the expiration of the limitations period will not save the action if it would otherwise be barred by the applicable New York statute of limitations.

c. Laches

In New York, the law of the forum determines whether the action is barred by laches. *See DeWeerth v. Baldinger*, 836 F.2d at 107-108; *cf.* Restatement (Second) of Conflict of Laws § 142 comment b; *accord* Restatement (Second) of Conflict of Laws (April 15, 1986, draft revisions § 142 comment d).

CHOICE OF LAW

This Section of the Restatement (Second) is under revision and should be checked to see if the final version when adopted holds to this position.

6. Matters Involving Public Policy

Every state may have a different interpretation of public policy and it is impossible to quantify. However, mere differences in a rule of law, including substantive rights or the measure of damages, is insufficient to constitute a policy of the forum which would cause a state to reject another state's law on public policy grounds. *Loucks v. Standard Oil Co.*, 224 N.Y. 99, 110-113, 120 N.E. 198 (1918).

In New York, before a court will invoke the public policy exception, it must first find that: (a) another state's law is applicable; (b) the party invoking the doctrine has satisfied the "heavy burden" of showing that the other state's law is repugnant to New York's public policy as found in New York's Constitution, statutes and judicial decisions; and (c) there are sufficient *important* contacts with New York for the court to invoke the doctrine. *Schultz v. Boy Scouts of Am.*, Inc., 65 N.Y.2d 189 at 202-03, 480 N.E.2d 679 at 687-688, 491 N.Y.S.2d 90 at 98-100 (1985). *Schultz* was an action against a religious order and the Boy Scouts by parents of two children who had been sexually molested by one of the religious order's clerics. Some of the wrongful acts took place in New York, while others took place in New Jersey. The court had determined that under New York's choice of law rules, New Jersey law should apply, thus, barring the action under New Jersey's charitable immunity doctrine. The plaintiff argued that since New York had discarded the doctrine of charitable immunity, New York should reject New Jersey's charitable immunity statute as repugnant to New York's public policy. *Schultz v. Boy Scouts of Am.*, Inc., at 202, 480 N.E.2d 679, 687-688, 491 N.Y.S.2d at 98-99.

The court ultimately refused to decide the public policy issue[10] because, even though several acts of molestation took place in New York, the court determined that "there are not sufficient contacts between New York, the parties and the transactions involved to implicate our public policy and call for its enforcement." *Id.* at 203, 480 N.E.2d at 688-689, 491 N.Y.S.2d at 100.

Following *Schultz*, New York courts will first determine if the law of another jurisdiction is applicable. Then it will examine the contacts under an

---

[10] A forum could also invoke the doctrine of public policy and either dismiss the action on this ground or consider it as one of the reasons to grant a *forum non conveniens* motion. If there is a dismissal, the plaintiff would be free to bring the action in another jurisdiction, if there is an alternative forum available.

interest analysis test to determine whether there are "sufficient important contacts" with New York for it to invoke the doctrine. If there are no such contacts, the court will never reach the next prong of the public policy exception test as to whether the policy is repugnant enough to be invoked.

Federal courts sitting in New York essentially apply New York's rules with respect to the public policy exception. *See, e.g., Bader v. Purdom*, 841 F.2d 38, 40-41 (2d Cir. 1988) (refusal to apply New York law which bars counterclaim for negligent parental supervision, even though New York domiciliaries were plaintiffs, as not violating fundamental principles of justice).

However, federal courts sitting in New York cannot invoke the public policy exception of New York unless it is done in a "constitutionally permissible manner," which requires that New York must have significant contacts or significant aggregation of contacts creating state interests, such that the choice is neither "arbitrary nor fundamentally unfair." *Allstate Ins. Co. v. Hague*, 449 U.S. 302, 307-313 (1981); *see Schultz v. Boy Scouts of Am., Inc.*, 65 N.Y.S.2d at 202 n.4, 480 N.E.2d at 688 n.4, 491 N.Y.S.2d at 99 n.4 (where the court noted that it might not be constitutionally permissible for New York to apply its own law, given the lack of sufficiently important contacts); *cf. Farmland Dairies v. Barber*, 65 N.Y.2d 51, 478 N.E.2d 1314, 489 N.Y.S.2d 713 (1985). A state, however, is not required by the Full Faith and Credit Clause to apply another state's law in violation of its own legitimate public policy. *Nevada v. Hall*, 440 U.S. 410, 422 (1979); *cf. Travelers Indem. Co. v. Sarkisian*, 794 F.2d 754, 762, *cert. denied*, 479 U.S. 885 (1986).

7. Effect of Choice of Law on Damage Issues—Interest—Attorneys' Fees

Choice of law determinations can have a devastating effect upon the recovery of compensatory and punitive damages, interest and attorneys' fees. Such issues should be considered by plaintiff before commencing an action, and by a defendant as early as possible. Early determination of which state's law applies and of that state's measure of damages, recoverability of interest and attorneys' fees could set the stage for settlement and the perimeters of discovery, if settlement is not achieved.

Which state law applies and the nature of the claim may determine the recoverability of such items of potential damages as (a) loss of decedent's prospective earnings; (b) mental pain and suffering of survivor; (c) out of pocket rule vs. benefit of the bargain rule in contract claims; (d) intentional infliction of emotional distress; (e) loss of consortium; (f) effect of income tax on award; (g) reduction of recovery to present value; (h) contributory or comparative fault; and (i) recoverability of punitive damages.

CHOICE OF LAW

a. New York State Courts

When the issue involves compensatory damages, the measure of damages is determined by the same law under which the cause of action arose because it depends upon the existence of the wrongdoing. *See, e.g., James v. Powell,* 19 N.Y.2d 249, 258-259, 225 N.E.2d 741, 746, 279 N.Y.S.2d 10, 17-18 (1967); *Long v. Pan Am. World Airways,* 16 N.Y.2d 337, 343, 213 N.E.2d 796, 799, 266 N.Y.S.2d 513, 517 (1965); *Davenport v. Webb,* 11 N.Y.2d 392, 183 N.E.2d 902, 230 N.Y.S.2d 17 (1962). The issue of the allowance of prejudgment interest is determined by the law of the state whose law determined liability on the main claim. *Davenport v. Webb,* 11 N.Y.2d at 395, 183 N.E.2d at 904-905, 230 N.Y.S.2d at 20. Where a remedy under one state's law carries with it an award of attorneys' fees, attorneys' fees will also be awarded once a choice of law determination as to liability has been made. *See, e.g., Thorpe v. Erb,* 255 N.Y. 75, 174 N.E. 67 (1931).

However, where the issue involves punitive damages, the choice of law determination depends upon the "*object* or *purpose* of the wrongdoing" and on this issue the New York courts "look to the 'law of the jurisdiction with the strongest interest in the resolution of the particular issue presented.' " *James v. Powell,* 19 N.Y.2d at 259, 225 N.E.2d at 746-747, 279 N.Y.S.2d at 17-18 (citations omitted) (emphasis in original). *James* involved a fraudulent conveyance of property in Puerto Rico. The underlying liability and compensatory damages were to be determined by the situs of property in accordance with traditional New York choice of law rules. However, as to the issue of punitive damages, the Court of Appeals applied New York law because the fraudulent conveyance was done to frustrate satisfaction of a New York judgment and New York had the "strongest interest" in protecting its judgments.

In some instances, application of the law of one state rather than another would result in no recovery of damages because the state does not recognize a claim for relief. *See, e.g., Schultz v. Boy Scouts of Am., Inc.,* 65 N.Y.2d 189, 480 N.E.2d 679, 491 N.Y.S.2d 90 (1985).

b. Federal Courts Sitting in New York

Federal courts sitting in New York are bound to apply choice of law rules of New York and as such will apply the above rules regarding compensatory and punitive damages, attorneys' fees and interest. *See, e.g., Entron, Inc. v. Affiliated FM Ins. Co.,* 749 F.2d at 131 (pre-judgment interest); *Bader v. Purdom,* 841 F.2d 38 (2d Cir. 1988) (application of Ontario law allowing a counterclaim for negligent supervision of parents, in effect a contributory negligence claim, which New York would not recognize, allows possible damage recovery); *Victrix S.S. Co., S.A. v. Salen Dry Cargo, A.B.,* 825 F.2d

709, 716 (2d Cir. 1987) (in affirming the vacating of an attachment obtained under New York state court procedures, the Second Circuit held where New York state court could award attorneys' fees for wrongful attachment, district court's award of attorneys' fees was appropriate);[11] *Fort Howard Paper Co. v. William D. Witter, Inc.*, 787 F.2d at 792-95 (demonstrating exactly how in a case involving breach of contract and fraud claims, depending upon whose law applies to the issue of liability, the issue of damages is dramatically affected); *Dobelle v. National R.R. Passenger Corp.*, 628 F. Supp. 1518, 1528-1529 (S.D.N.Y. 1986) (punitive damages).

8. Choice of Law in Transferred Actions

28 U.S.C. § 1404(a) provides that: "For the convenience of parties and witnesses, in the interest of justice, a district court may transfer any civil action to any other district or division where it might have been brought." When an action is transferred pursuant to § 1404(a), the district court to which the action is transferred must apply the law of the state in which the transferor district court was sitting. *Van Dusen v. Barrack*, 376 U.S. 612 (1964); *Lehman v. Dow Jones & Co.*, 783 F.2d 285, 289 (2d Cir. 1986).

Under the *Barrack* rule, the whole law of the transferor forum is to be applied, including that forum's choice of law rules. Thus, if a diversity action is transferred from a federal district court in New York to a federal district court outside of New York, the substantive law of the state of New York, including its choice of law principles, is applicable to the action. As with other choice of law rules, there are exceptions to the *Barrack* rule. The principle exceptions involve actions commenced against the United States under the Federal Tort Claims Act ("FTCA") and the Foreign Sovereign Immunities Act ("FSIA") (at least in New York).

In addition, there are three other instances where it has been suggested that the law of the transferee forum, rather than the law of the transferor forum, should apply. First, if the transferor court lacked jurisdiction or venue was improper; second, even if there was jurisdiction and venue was proper, if the state court of the transferor state might have dismissed for *forum non conve-*

---

[11] *But see Burlington Northern R.R. Co. v. Woods*, 480 U.S. 1 (1987), where the Supreme Court reversed the Eleventh Circuit's imposition of a 10% penalty as required by an Alabama statute upon any unsuccessful appellant who had obtained a stay of judgment pending appeal. The purpose of the statute was to penalize those who filed frivolous appeals and delayed execution of judgments. The Supreme Court held that Fed. R. App. P. 38, which allows a discretionary grant of such an award, and Fed. R. App. P. 37, which allows for postjudgment interest in the event of an unsuccessful appeal, are procedural. Since they conflict with Alabama's "mandatory" statute, Fed. R. App. P. 38 is applicable, not Alabama's statute. It is unlikely that the result in *Victrix*, which was decided after *Burlington*, should change as a result of *Burlington*, because Fed. R. Civ. P. 64 provides that state court procedures are to be followed in cases of attachment.

niens; and, third, if the transfer is effected on plaintiff's motion. If the law of the transferor state were to be automatically applied in these situations, forum shopping might be encouraged. Therefore, it has been suggested that in the above situations, the transferee court be allowed to make its own choice of applicable law. For a discussion of these possible exceptions to the *Barrack* rule, *see* E. F. Scoles and P. Hay, *supra* § 3.46 (1986 Supplement at 11); *but see Stewart Org., Inc. v. Ricoh Corp.*, 108 S. Ct. 2239 (1988).

In *Stewart Organization* the court held that § 1404(a) governed transfers in federal court diversity actions, not state law. *Stewart Organization* involved a case of blatant forum shopping. Plaintiff had filed an action in federal district court in Alabama, in breach of a forum selection clause in an agreement designating New York as the forum, in order to try to take advantage of Alabama's law which disfavored such clauses. The defendant moved to transfer under 28 U.S.C. § 1404(a) based upon the forum selection clause. The Court did transfer the action, although it did not automatically apply the forum selection clause. The Court did not hold that venue had been technically improper, and noted that the venue statute had been classified as a procedural housekeeping rule by the Court's holding in *Barrack* and that the transfer does not carry with it a change in applicable law. *Id.* However, if the transfer under these circumstances does not carry with it a change of applicable law to the transferee state and, if Alabama law also disfavors choice of governing law provisions, and after transfer, the transferee court in New York has to apply Alabama law, the party's clear choice of law provision of New York law could be defeated because of the filing of the action in Alabama in violation of the forum selection clause.

9. Choice of Law in Multidistrict Litigation

28 U.S.C. § 1407(a) provides in pertinent part that: "When civil actions involving one or more common questions of fact are pending in different districts, such actions may be transferred to any district for coordinated or consolidated pretrial proceedings." The district court to which the cases have been transferred from several different district courts pursuant to § 1407(a) is required to apply the law of the transferor courts to substantive issues, and different substantive state laws may govern claims of class members residing in different states. *See In re "Agent Orange" Prod. Liab. Litig.*, 635 F.2d 987 (2d Cir. 1980), *cert. denied sub nom. Chapman v. Dow Chem. Co.*, 454 U.S. 1128 (1981);[12] The Manual for Complex Litigation (Second) citing to

---

[12] The Second Circuit noted in a multidistrict action involving agent orange claims that "it is possible that the law of every state and Australia and New Zealand, including choice of law rules, will at some point come into play." *In re Diamond Shamrock Chemicals Co.*, 725 F.2d 858, 861 (2d Cir.), *cert. denied*, 465 U.S. 1067 (1984).

the *Barrack* rule suggests that immediate consideration be given to choice-of-law consequences in cases consolidated for pretrial proceedings pursuant to 1407(a). Manual for Complex Litigation (Second) § 30.15.

If the differences are so substantial as in most mass tort actions, class certification may not be appropriate. Advisory Committee Note to the 1966 Revision of Rule 23(b)(3), *reprinted in* 39 F.R.D. 69, 103 (1966); *cf. In re "Agent Orange" Prod. Liab. Litig.*, 818 F.2d 145, 164-165 (2d Cir. 1987), *cert. denied sub nom. Pinkney v. Dow Chem. Co.*, 108 S. Ct. 695 (1988). *See also* Manual for Complex Litigation (Second) § 30.16. [13]

Early determination of which law governs, particularly in an action brought as a result of some mass disaster, is preferable as an understanding of the differences in substantive law governing liability and damages may substantially facilitate discovery strategy, settlement or trial. Moreover, certification of one of the earliest cases may avoid statute of limitations problems. *Id.* at § 30.15; *see also id.* at § 33.23 n. 36.

10. Arbitration

Generally, whether a dispute is subject to arbitration arises in the context of a contract which provides for arbitration. When an action in a federal district court is based upon diversity of citizenship, the law of the forum state as to the enforceability of an arbitration agreement applies, rather than the Federal Arbitration Act, 9 U.S.C § 1, unless the contract is one involving interstate or foreign commerce or admiralty, in which case the Federal Arbitration Act applies, *Bernhardt v. Polygraphic Co. of Am.*, 350 U.S. 198 (1956).[14]

---

[13] Even if only one nationwide class action has been brought, pursuant to Fed. R. Civ. P. 23, and no individual actions have been transferred under § 1407(a), different state laws may govern the claims of class members residing in different states. *See Phillips Petroleum Co. v. Shutts*, 472 U.S. 797, 821-823 (1985). The Court held that if a forum applies its law to claims unrelated to the forum it is "sufficiently arbitrary and unfair as to exceed constitutional limits." *Id.* 427 U.S. at 822. This applies to class actions pending in state and federal courts and suggests that if there are sufficient differences in the applicable law, the class may not be certified as the requirement of "common questions of law" could not be satisfied. *Cf. id.* 472 U.S. at 821-822.

[14] *Bernhardt* involved a claim for breach of an employment agreement which contained a provision that all disputes were to be referred to arbitration. The action had been filed in a Vermont state court and removed by defendant to federal court based upon diversity. The defendant moved to stay the court proceedings pending arbitration pursuant to the agreement of the parties. If Vermont law were to be applied, plaintiff could revoke the agreement to arbitrate anytime before an award. The defendant argued that once removed to federal court, the Federal Arbitration Act was applicable and the arbitration clause was enforceable. The Supreme Court disagreed and held that enforceability of an arbitration clause was governed by state law, unless the transaction involved interstate or foreign commerce or admiralty.

CHOICE OF LAW

When drafting or reviewing an agreement that contains a provision to arbitrate that does not involve interstate or foreign commerce or maritime transactions, the agreement should provide a choice of law selection designating a state which will enforce such an arbitration agreement, and which will have a sufficient relationship with the parties or the transaction under general choice of law principles that the forum where the action is brought will enforce the parties' choice of law provision.

When litigating in a federal court, the issue of arbitration should be raised pursuant to the Federal Rules of Civil Procedure and the local rules of the federal district court governing motions or for declaratory relief.

New York, by statute, generally enforces arbitration agreements. N.Y. C.P.L.R. § 7501 (McKinney 1980). However, if New York has no other nexus with the transaction, New York's choice of law provisions might dictate that the New York court look to another state's law for the validity and enforceability of the arbitration provision. McLaughlin, Practice Commentaries, C7501:3.[15]

If an action is brought in a state court in New York, or in any other state court, and the matter involves interstate or foreign commerce, the state court must apply the Federal Arbitration Act. *Southland Corp. v. Keating*, 465 U.S. 1 (1984); *A/S J. Ludwig Mowinckels Rederi v. Dow Chem. Co.*, 25 N.Y.2d 576, 255 N.E.2d 774, 307 N.Y.S.2d 660, *cert. denied*, 398 U.S. 939 (1970). State court procedures should be used to raise the applicability of the Federal Arbitration Act.

11. *Forum Non Conveniens*

Even though a court may have jurisdiction over the parties and the subject matter, it may exercise its discretion, out of considerations of justice, fairness and convenience of the court and the parties, to stay or dismiss the action. This is known as the doctrine of *forum non conveniens*.

a. New York State Courts

When the parties to an agreement, not involving consumer contracts or personal service agreements, designate New York as the forum and choose to

---

[15] The Restatement (Second) of Conflict of Laws § 218 provides that the parties may stipulate to the governing law in an agreement which will be enforced in accordance with § 187 of the Restatement (Second) unless the state chosen has no significant relationship to the parties or the transaction, or application of that state's law would violate a fundamental policy of a state with a materially greater interest than the state chosen. Restatement (Second) § 187 currently under revision and the April 15, 1986, draft revisions contain substantially different provisions than are currently adopted. Therefore, before relying upon § 187 one should verify whether it has been changed. Absent such a choice of a governing law provision, the validity of the agreement to arbitrate will be measured by the law of the state with the most significant relationship to the transaction. *Id.* § 188.

have New York law applied, and the value of the agreement is more than one million dollars, New York courts cannot dismiss the action on *forum non conveniens* grounds if there is personal jurisdiction either by consent of the parties or through normal means. N.Y. Gen. Oblig. Law § 5-1401, 02; CPLR § 327 (McKinney 1988).

If the choice of forum provision does not fall within the above statutory provisions, a New York court may exercise its discretion to stay or dismiss on *forum non conveniens* grounds, although the contract's provisions constitute a substantial factor to be considered by the court in exercising its discretion. Generally, when there is a forum selection clause, the courts will give little weight to any argument that the forum is inconvenient to the parties or the witnesses as those "factors should have been considered by the parties in arriving at their choice of forums. Therefore, those factors will be obviated in making the court's determination because contracts are made to be enforced." *See, e.g., Arthur Young & Co. v. Leong*, 53 A.D.2d 515, 516, 383 N.Y.S.2d 618, 619 (lst Dep't), *appeal dismissed*, 40 N.Y.2d 984, 359 N.E.2d 435, 390 N.Y.S.2d 927 (1976). Of course, the court also weighs inconvenience and burden to the court and the availability of an alternative forum.[16]

If there is no choice of forum provision in an agreement or, if the action does not involve a contract claim, CPLR § 327 (McKinney 1988 Supp.) provides:

> The domicile or residence in this state of any party to the action shall not preclude the court from staying or dismissing the action.

In other words, the mere fact that one of the parties is domiciled or has its residence in New York does not preclude the court from dismissing or staying an action on the grounds of *forum non conveniens*. Rather, the court will examine the relevant public or private interest factors which militate against accepting the action and weigh the various competing factors to determine whether to retain jurisdiction.[17] The rule rests upon justice, fairness and convenience and no one factor is controlling. The factors to be considered are:

---

[16] In *Arthur Young & Co.*, the court did not dismiss on *forum non conveniens* grounds even though the following facts were apparent: (a) there was no nexus with New York (except the choice of forum provision); (b) no witnesses were in New York; (c) the dispute arose in Hawaii; (d) voluminous records were in Hawaii; (e) defendant was a resident of Hawaii; (g) Hawaii was an alternate viable forum. This case indicates that New York courts demonstrate a strong preference for validating the parties' express choice of a New York forum.

[17] The burden rests upon the one challenging a forum. It is a heavy burden which must be based upon more than a showing of inconvenience. *Islamic Republic of Iran v. Pahlavi*, 62 N.Y.2d 474, 467 N.E.2d 245, 478 N.Y.S.2d 597 (1984).

CHOICE OF LAW

(a) nexus between New York and the cause of action;

(b) convenience of parties;

(c) convenience of witnesses;

(d) domicile of the parties;

(e) effectiveness of any judgment rendered;

(f) availability of alternative suitable forum;

(g) any other potential hardship to the parties; and

(h) administrative and financial burden to the court.

When the lower court takes all of these various factors into consideration, the appellate courts will not disturb the ruling as an abuse of discretion. *See Islamic Republic of Iran v. Pahlavi*, 62 N.Y.2d 474, 479-480, 467 N.E.2d 245, 247-248, 478 N.Y.S.2d 597, 599-600 (1984), *cert. denied*, 469 U.S. 1108 (1985). Indeed, in *Islamic Republic*, the Court of Appeals held that the lack of availability of an alternative forum does not require the court to entertain jurisdiction. *Id.* at 481-483, 467 N.E.2d at 248-250, 478 N.Y.S.2d at 600-602.

b. Federal Courts Sitting in New York

Federal courts sitting in New York will apply, as a matter of federal law, the following considerations in determining whether to dismiss or stay on *forum non conveniens* grounds:

(a) Private interests of the litigants, including:

  i. relative ease of access to the source of proof;

  ii. availability of compulsory process for attendance if unwilling, and the cost of obtaining attendance if willing, witnesses;

  iii. possibility of view of premises, if appropriate to action;

  iv. all other practical problems which make trial of a case easy, expeditious and inexpensive;

  v. enforceability of judgment obtained.

(b) Factors of public interest:

  i. administrative difficulties where there are congested court dockets;

  ii. jury duty burden imposed upon people with no relation to litigation;

    iii. if case involves affairs of many people, desirability of holding trial where they can have actual access to process rather then read reports of it;

    iv. local interest in having local controversies decided at home;

    v. in diversity cases, having case in state where that state's law must govern where federal court is more familiar with local state law; and

    vi. availability of an adequate alternative forum.[18]

The court will weigh the relative advantages and disadvantages to a fair trial and unless the forum was picked by plaintiff to vex, harass or oppress defendant, "plaintiff's choice of forum should rarely be disturbed." *Gulf Oil Corp. v. Gilbert*, 330 U.S. 501, 508 (1947); *Piper Aircraft Co. v. Reyno*, 454 U.S. 235, 247-249 (1981). Dismissal will be appropriate only where there is a heavy burden on the defendant or the court and where the plaintiff is unable to give any specific reasons for convenience. A showing that the law of the alternative forum was less favorable is not enough. *Id.*

    Since every *forum non conveniens* decision is fact intensive, it is impossible to set forth a bright line test. However, the Second Circuit has expressed its willingness to allow a plaintiff its choice of forum even though there may not be any substantial nexus with New York. *Cf. Carlenstolpe v. Merck & Co.*, 819 F.2d. 33 (2d Cir. 1987)[19] (where the court determined a dismissal if a *forum non convenience* motion was nonappealing but the court noted that New York not inconvenient forum for negligence, products liability and breach of warranty action against a New Jersey producer of vaccine by a Swedish consumer, where alleged injury occurred in Sweden, and producer developed and tested the vaccine in New Jersey and Pennsylvania, Pennsylvania law was applicable to suit, and public interest existed in having United States court decide issues of tortious conduct occurring in United States, Swedish interest not sufficiently weighty to require dismissal). It is clear

---

[18] The availability of a "more appropriate" forum is a requirement of the Restatement (Second) before a *forum non conveniens* motion can be granted. Restatement (Second) § 84. It is not, however, a requirement under New York law. *Islamic Republic of Iran v. Pahlavi*, 62 N.Y.2d 474, 467 N.E.2d 245, 478 N.Y.S.2d 597 (1984). The Supreme Court in *Gulf Oil Corp. v. Gilbert*, 330 U.S. 501 (1947), states in *dicta* that it is a factor which should be considered, but does not make it mandatory. *See also Piper Aircraft Co. v. Reyno*, 454 U.S. 235 (1981) (suggesting the importance of the existence of an alternative forum).

[19] This matter came before the court on a writ of mandamus challenging an order denying a motion to dismiss on *forum non conveniens* grounds. The Second Circuit dismissed the appeal as a *forum non conveniens* motion was interlocutory and nonappealable and mandamus would only issue if there was a clear abuse of discretion and the court below had failed to consider all of the appropriate factors. The Supreme Court has adopted this approach. *Van Cauwenberghe v. Biard*, 108 S. Ct. 1945 (1988).

CHOICE OF LAW 221

from the district court's opinion that there was no connection with New York except the possibility of potential expert witnesses located there and location of plaintiff's "unusually qualified lawyer." *Carlenstolpe v. Merck & Co. Inc.*, 638 F. Supp. 901, 907 (S.D.N.Y. 1986); *compare In re Union Carbide Corp. Gas Plant Disaster*, 634 F. Supp. 842 (S.D.N.Y. 1986), *modified sub nom. Plaintiffs v. Union Carbide Corp.*, 809 F.2d 195 (2d Cir.), *cert. denied*, 108 S. Ct. 199 (1987) (dismissed on *forum non conveniens* on factual pattern similar to *Carlenstope* citing exclusively to federal *forum non conveniens* cases, as basis for decision); *AVC Nederlands B.V. v. Atrium Inv. Partnership*, 740 F.2d 148 (2d Cir. 1984) (upholding a *forum non conveniens* dismissal noting that the court could retain jurisdiction over securities fraud action brought by Dutch citizen against other Dutch companies involving building in New York, but in view of forum selection/choice of law of Holland, the court determined to dismiss; "[t]here can be nothing 'unreasonable and unjust' in enforcing such an agreement; what would be unreasonable and unjust would be to allow one of the [parties] to disregard it;" *id.* at 156; the court noted that if there had been a claim that the clause had been induced by fraud, a different result might have ensued. It also seems apparent that if any Americans had been involved, the result might be different because Holland would not enforce federal securities laws).

In *Stewart Org., Inc. v. Ricoh Corp.*, 108 S. Ct. 2239 (1988), the majority refused to give conclusive weight to the existence of a forum selection clause and noted that a motion pursuant to 28 U.S.C. § 1404(a) required a court to weigh a number of case specific factors, of which a forum selection clause was a central, but not dispositive factor. The other factors were: (a) convenience of the forum chosen given the parties expressed venue preference; (b) fairness of the transfer in light of the forum selection clause; (c) parties relative bargaining power; (d) convenience of witness; (e) interests of justice. The decision is, however, a mixed blessing as far as New York law is concerned.

On the one hand, if an action has been brought in a federal court sitting in a state other than New York and that state's law will not honor a forum selection clause, the federal court cannot automatically apply that state's law to invalidate the forum selection clause. On the other hand, the decision makes clear that the federal courts do not have to give conclusive effect to a choice of forum selection clause, thereby undercutting to a certain extent the value of New York's forum selection statute.

The decision makes it clear that a federal district court sitting in New York need not give conclusive effect to a forum selection clause even if it falls within the statutory parameters of Gen. Obli. Law § 5-1402. As the court noted, "[i]t is conceivable in a particular case . . . a District Court acting under § 1404(a) would refuse to transfer a case notwithstanding the counterweight of a forum-selection clause, whereas the coordinate state rule might dictate the opposite result." *Id.*

C. Choice of Law Methods in Specific Types of Actions

1. Tort Actions

a. Basic Methods

There are five methods employed by courts in deciding choice of law questions in tort actions, and as many permutations of those methods as courts have deemed useful depending upon the facts of the case or the desired result. While the basic methods are discussed below, the focus is on the method used by the state and federal courts in New York.

(1) *Lex Loci Delicti*

The traditional choice of law method in a tort action was *lex loci delicti*. The *lex loci delicti* method requires a court to apply the law of the place of the wrong. The method was adopted by the Restatement (First) of Conflict of Laws. *See* R. Leflar, *American Conflicts Law* § 132 (3d. ed. 1977). This method has the advantage of simple mechanical application and predictability of results. Of course, the place of the wrong may have absolutely no contacts with the parties, except through the fortuitous circumstance that an accident or injury occurred in that jurisdiction.

At one time, New York adhered to the *lex loci delicti* method, but this approach was abandoned in the 1963 landmark decision *Babcock v. Jackson*, 12 N.Y.2d 473, 191 N.E.2d 279, 240 N.Y.S.2d 745 (1963).

Babcock involved an action for injuries sustained by a passenger against a driver arising out of an automobile accident in Ontario, Canada. If the court had applied the traditional *lex loci delicti* method, the passenger would not have recovered because the place of the tort, Ontario, had a guest-host statute which would bar recovery. However, instead of mechanically applying the law of the locus of the tort, the Court of Appeals held that "controlling effect" must be given to the law of the jurisdiction where the "relationship or contact with the occurrence or the parties, has the greatest concern with the specific issues raised in the litigation." *Id.* at 481, 191 N.E.2d at 283, 240 N.Y.S.2d 743.

In grouping the contacts, the Court noted several factors which should be considered: (1) the parties' domicile; (2) where the automobile was garaged; (3) where the automobile was licensed; (4) where the automobile was insured; (5) where the guest-host relationship arose; (6) where the trip was to begin and end; and (7) the locus of the tort. The answer to each of the above, except for item 7, was New York. Next, the Court looked at whether Ontario's laws would be thwarted if the law of New York were to be applied. The Court noted that New York's interest in requiring a tortfeasor to compensate a guest for injuries caused by his negligence would be thwarted if Ontario law would be applied, but application of New York's law would not threaten the policy underlying Ontario's statute which was Ontario's interest in preventing fraudulent claims against its defendants and their insurers. *See id.* at 482-83, 191 N.E.2d at 284, 240 N.Y.S.2d 743. The *Babcock* "grouping of contacts" method was criticized for placing too much emphasis on mere contact-counting without specifying the relative significance of the contacts.[20]

In the twenty-five years since the *Babcock* decision, there have been several Court of Appeals decisions which have refined the indiscriminate grouping of contacts of the *Babcock* court to an interest analysis method based upon two significant criteria.

(2) The "Interest Analysis" Method

(a) New York State Courts

The interest analysis method involves application of the law of the jurisdiction having the greatest interest in the litigation. Under New York decisional law, the significant contacts which the courts are to consider are: (1) the parties' domicile, and (2) the locus of the tort. *Schultz v. Boy Scouts of Am., Inc.*, 65 N.Y.2d 189, 480 N.E.2d 679, 491 N.Y.S.2d 90 (1985). In *Schultz*, the New York Court of Appeals, after reviewing the historical evolution of New York's choice of law methods in tort actions, stated:

> Interest analysis became the relevant analytical approach to choice of law in tort actions in New York. [T]he law of the jurisdiction having the greatest interest in the litigation will be applied and . . . the [only] facts or contacts which obtain significance in defining State interests are those which relate to the purpose of the particular law in conflict. . . . Under this formulation, the significant contacts are, almost exclusively, the parties' domiciles and the locus of the tort.

Id. at 197, 480 N.E.2d at 684, 491 N.Y.S.2d at 95 (citations omitted).

As noted earlier, the *Schultz* case was a tort action by domiciliaries of New Jersey who were parents of two boys who had been sexually molested a number of times both in New York and New Jersey by a cleric who was a

---

[20] *See, e.g., Schultz v. Boy Scouts of Am., Inc.*, 65 N.Y.2d 789, 480 N.E.2d 679, 491 N.Y.S.2d 90 (1985).

member of a religious order of Franciscan Brothers, a not-for-profit organization. Since some of the alleged acts took place while the cleric was a scoutmaster of a boy scout troop, which was also a not-for-profit organization, the Boy Scouts of America was also a defendant.

The choice-of-law issue was key. If New Jersey law applied, the action would have been barred as New Jersey recognized the doctrine of charitable immunity. If New York law applied, New York did not recognize the charitable immunity doctrine and plaintiffs were not barred from recovery.

Once the court established the principle that the elements to be examined are domicile and locus,[21] the court stated that which state's laws apply when these two elements are not the same jurisdiction depends upon the particular tort in question. If the conflicting rules involve a standard of conduct, *i.e.*, the rules of the road, the place of the wrong will usually have a "predominant, if not exclusive, concern" because of that jurisdiction's interest in protecting the reasonable expectation of the parties who rely on its standards to govern their conduct and the prophylactic effect that applying its law will have on similar conduct in future, outweighs any interest of common-domicile jurisdiction. *Id.* at 198, 480 N.E.2d 684-685, 491 N.Y.S.2d at 95-96. Where defendant's negligent conduct occurred in one jurisdiction and plaintiff's injuries are suffered in another, the place of the wrong is considered to be where the last event necessary to make the actor liable occurred. *Id.* at 195, 480 N.E.2d at 683, 491 N.Y.S.2d at 94. If the rule is a loss-distribution rule, the common domicile would normally apply to domiciliaries who must accept the burdens as well as the benefits of associating with the forum.

The *Schultz* court relied on the earlier analysis in *Neumeier v. Kuehner*, 31 N.Y.2d 121, 286 N.E.2d 454, 335 N.Y.S.2d 64 (1972), an action involving a guest-host statute.

A chart of the elements in *Schultz* demonstrates the New York "interest analysis" method.

The facts relevant to the interest analyses in *Schultz* were as follows:

(1) The Plaintiffs were New Jersey residents.

(2) The Boys Scouts of America ("BSA") was federally chartered by Act of Congress for educational and charitable purposes with its National headquarters, at the time of the events, in New Jersey.

---

[21] The Court noted that such items as where a guest-host relationship arose, where the journey began and was to end, which had been counted as contacts in *Babcock*, were no longer of any significance in tort actions involving guest-host statutes, although some importance may still be placed upon where the automobile is insured in recognition that the insurer is often the real party in interest.

CHOICE OF LAW 225

(3) The Franciscan Order was incorporated in Ohio and was domiciled in Ohio.

(4) New York would allow recovery under its loss-distribution rules as it had no charitable immunity doctrine.

(5) New Jersey would not allow recovery under its loss-distribution rules as it had a charitable immunity doctrine.

(6) Ohio would not allow recovery under its loss distribution as it had a charitable immunity doctrine, but the doctrine did not apply to actions based upon negligent hiring and supervision. No one argued that Ohio law should be applied.

(7) The acts of negligent hiring and failure to dismiss (after prior incidents of sexual abuse by the same individual defendant) occurred in New York.

If New Jersey's loss distribution rule applied to bar the claim, the issue of whether New York's substantive law would be applied to determine whether there had been negligent hiring and negligent failure to dismiss was irrelevant to any claims.

Therefore, the analysis focused upon whose law should govern the loss-distribution rules.

Cause of Action	Domicile of Parties	Locus of Tort	Analysis
Wrongful Death	Pls-NJ; BSA-NJ; FO-Ohio	NJ	NJ law applied. No choice need be made between NY/NJ as NY has no sufficient interest in the cause of action.
Psychological Injury to parents	Pls-NJ; BSA-NJ; FO-Ohio	NJ	NJ law applied. No choice need be made between NY/NJ NY has no sufficient interest in the cause of action.
Psychological injury to children	Pls NJ; BSA-NJ; FO-Ohio	NY/NJ	Analysis necessary as New York had sufficient interest to require resolution of choice of law problem.
Physical injury to children	Pls-NJ; BSA-NJ; FO-Ohio	NY/NJ	Analysis necessary as New York had sufficient interest to require resolution of choice of law problem.

With respect to the claims against the BSA, both plaintiffs and defendant BSA were domiciliaries of New Jersey at the time of the events. The court found New Jersey had weighed the interest of charitable tortfeasors and their victims and decided to retain the defense of charitable immunity. The underlying policy of New Jersey was to encourage growth of charitable work in New Jersey. Given the fact of common domiciliaries of plaintiffs and BSA, they must, according to the *Schultz* court, be bound by the burdens as well as the benefits of that choice of domicile and New Jersey law applied.

In determining the applicable law with respect to plaintiffs' claims against the Franciscan Brothers, the parties were not common domiciliaries, the loss-distribution rules were different in New Jersey and Ohio and the locus of the wrong was New York. In this situation, the law of the place of the tort normally applied, unless displacing it "will advance the relevant substantive law purposes without impairing the smooth working of the multi-system or producing great uncertainty for litigants" citing *Neumeier*.

Based upon the same analysis used to conclude that New Jersey law applies to bar the claims against the BSA, the Court concluded that New Jersey law applied to bar claims against the Franciscan Brothers because it:

> would further that State's interest in enforcing the decision of its domiciliaries to accept the burdens as well as the benefits of that State's loss-distribution tort rules and its interest in promoting the continuation and expansion of defendant's charitable activities in that State. Conversely, although application of New Jersey's law may not affirmatively advance the substantive law purposes of New York, it will not frustrate those interests because New York has no significant interest in applying its own law to this dispute. Finally, application of New Jersey law will enhance "the smooth working of the multi-state system" by actually reducing the incentive for forum shopping and it will provide certainty for the litigants whose only reasonable expectation surely would have been that the law of the jurisdiction where plaintiffs are domiciled and defendant sends its teachers would apply, not the law of New York where the parties had only isolated and infrequent contacts as a result of Coakeley's position as Boy Scout leader.

Id. at 201-202, 480 N.E.2d at 687; 491 N.Y.S.2d at 98.

While the interest analysis method is not capable of the same mechanical application as the *lex loci* method, an examination of the *Schultz* decision leads to certain definitive elements which lend some predictability to New York's choice of law methods in tort actions.

(1) Only two elements are, as a general rule, to be examined: locus of the wrong and domicile of the parties. In certain cases involving insured matters, where the liability insurance is in force, such fact may be considered. In determining locus of the wrong, if the negligence took place in one jurisdiction and the injury happened in another, the locus of the wrong is the place where the last event necessary to make the defendant liable occurred.

(2) If the locus of the wrong and the parties common domicile are the same, no choice of law decision is necessary, as that jurisdiction's law governs.

(3) If the locus of the wrong and the common domicile of the parties is not the same, the next step is to examine whether there is a true conflict as discussed in Section 2, b, *supra*. Only if there is a true conflict, need the court proceed with any further analysis. If there is a false conflict, because the laws of the relevant states are the same or, if not the same, the underlying policies of only one law show that it was intended to cover that situation, then that is the law which applies. If the underlying policies of neither law was intended to apply, the law of the situs of the wrong applies, unless there are exceptional circumstances which dictate otherwise.

(4) If there is a true conflict, then the relative interests of the common domicile and locus jurisdictions in having their laws apply will depend upon the particular tort issue in conflict in the case:

(a) If the conflicting rules involve the appropriate standards of conduct, such as rules of the road, or negligent supervision, the laws of the locus of the wrong as above defined, "will usually have a predominant, if not exclusive concern."

(b) If the conflicting rules involve loss distribution rules, such as immunity from suit, wrongful death, guest-host statutes, vicarious liability, "considerations of the state's admonatory interest and party reliance are less important. Under those circumstances, the locus jurisdiction has at best a minimal interest in determining the right of recovery or extent of the remedy in an action by a foreign domiciliary for injuries resulting from the conduct of a domiciliary that was tortious under the law of both jurisdictions. . . . Analysis then favors the jurisdiction of common domicile because of its interest in enforcing the decisions of both the benefits

CHOICE OF LAW

and the burdens of identifying with that jurisdiction and to submit themselves to its authority."[22]

(c) In the event that there is no common domicile among plaintiffs and defendants and the place of the wrong is a separate jurisdiction, the law of the place of the wrong will normally apply, "unless displacing it will advance the relevant substantive law purposes without impairing the smooth working of the multi-state system or producing great uncertainty for litigants."

Following the above guidelines can lead to some predictability in choice of law in tort actions in New York.

(b) Federal Courts Sitting in New York

In *Bader v. Purdom*, 841 F.2d 38, the Second Circuit reversed a decision from the Eastern District of New York which had dismissed a third-party complaint by residents of Ontario, Canada based upon the lower court's decision that New York would apply its own substantive law, rather than the law of Ontario. The decision that the law of Ontario should apply is based upon the Court's application of the *Schultz* Court's "interest analysis" test and by analogizing to *Neumeier*'s three-pronged analysis in guest-host situations.

Bader was a negligence action by New York domiciliaries against Canadian residents arising out of injuries sustained by a minor child of the New York domiciliaries when that child was bitten by defendants' dog at defendants' home in Ontario. The Ontario residents had filed a third-party complaint against the parents of the child seeking indemnification and contribution for negligent supervision of the child. The Second Circuit first determined that there was a true conflict. The Court noted that to resolve the particular conflict, New York courts would apply the law of the place of the

---

[22] The contrasting reasons to apply the two rules are:
   Reasons to apply forum/locus rules
   (a) Protect medical creditors who provided services to injured party in locus state.
   (b) Prevent injured victim from becoming public ward of locus state.
   (c) Deterrent effect on future tortfeasors in locus state.
   Reasons to apply rule of parties common domicile
   (a) Reduces forum shopping between common domicile and locus jurisdictions.
   (b) Rebuts inference of forum-locus bias in favor of its own laws and in favor of permitting recovery.
   (c) Concepts of mutuality and reciprocity support *consistent* application of common domicile law. Thus, applicable law would not change depending on status of parties being common domicile of one state or other state.
   (d) Produces a rule easy to apply and brings a degree of predictability and certainty to this area of the law.

wrong, citing the *Neumeier* rule, unless special circumstances existed. However, the Second Circuit determined that this was not a case where special circumstances existed, that New York's interest analysis test as applied to this action required application of Ontario law. The Court rejected the public policy argument and refused to bar the negligent supervision claims under the facts of the action, where New York domiciliaries voluntarily vacationed in Ontario and all of the tortious conduct took place there. The dissent agreed with the results, but said the court applied the wrong *Neumeier* test.

In *Machleder v. Diaz*, 801 F.2d 46 (2d Cir. 1986), *cert. denied sub nom. Machleder v. CBS, Inc.*, 107 S. Ct. 1294 (1987), the court was called upon to review whether the lower court had correctly determined that New Jersey law, not New York law, applied to an action for defamation and false light invasion of privacy. The action had been brought in the Southern District of New York by a New Jersey resident against a Manhattan television station which was an affiliate of CBS, Inc. The broadcast had emanated in New York, but involved an interview conducted in New Jersey on the property of a corporation owned by plaintiff which was plaintiff's principal place of business, prepared by the station's New Jersey reporter as part of a series which aired in New Jersey as well as New York.

As a threshold matter, the court reviewed the correctness of the lower court's decision that New Jersey law applied. The court noted that as New York was the forum state, it was to New York's law that the court must look to in making its analysis. Then the court determined that a New York Court "must apply the substantive tort law of the state that had the most significant relationship with the occurrence and the parties" citing *Babcock*. The court did not mention either the *Neumeier* or the *Schultz* decisions. The court noted that CBS had correctly asserted that New York had a strong interest in regulating the conduct of a television station's broadcast which emanated in New York and the daily activities of professionals' activities. However, the court noted New Jersey had "superior contacts" in that (1) plaintiff was interviewed there; (2) the news report was part of a series on New Jersey; (3) the report aired in New Jersey as well as elsewhere; (4) plaintiff is a resident of New Jersey and plaintiff's corporation has its principle place of business in New Jersey. *Id.* at 52.

The court adopted the rationale of the lower court that despite the interest of New York in establishing a standard of fault for its news media, New Jersey also had an important compelling interest in protecting its citizens from defamation and an additional interest in governing the fault of the those who come within its boundaries to investigate the news and later broadcast it there. The court never analyzed whether New York and New Jersey had competing laws which would create a "true conflict," but that appears to be implicit in the decision. This particular panel of the Second Circuit ignored

Neumeier and *Schultz*, and seemed to be counting the contacts. The court also used the "most significant contacts" verbiage rather the "interest analysis" verbiage used by *Schultz* and *Bader* Courts.

In light of the *Schultz* decision in which the New York Court of Appeals fashioned rules of more general applicability than the more limited *Neumeier* guest-host decision, the *Schultz* analysis should be used in federal courts in New York to resolve choice of law questions in tort actions.

(3) The "Most Significant Relationship" Method

This method also requires an issue by issue analysis for choice of law and with respect to each such issue, the law of the state having the "most significant relationship" to the particular issue be applied. This is the method used by the Restatement (Second) of Conflicts of Laws §§ 6, 145.

The Restatement (Second) lists several factors that a court should generally consider in determining the choice of law as follows:

 i) the needs of the interstate and international systems;

 ii) the relevant policies of the forum;

 iii) the relevant policies of other interested states and the relative interests of those states in the determination of the particular issue;

 iv) the protection of justified expectations;

 v) the basic policies underlying the particular field of law;

 vi) certainty, predictability and uniformity of result; and

 vii) ease in the determination and application of the law to be applied.

Restatement (Second) of Conflict of Laws § 6.

The Restatement (Second) § 145 sets forth general principles regarding choice of law decisions in tort actions as follows:

(1) The rights and liabilities of the parties with respect to an issue in tort are determined by the local law of the state which, with respect to that issue, has the most significant relationship to the occurrence and the parties under the principles stated in [Section] 6;

(2) Contacts to be taken into account in applying the principles of [Section] 6 to determine the law applicable to an issue include:

 (a) the place where the injury occurred;

 (b) the place where the conduct causing the injury occurred;

(c) the domicile, residence, nationality, place of incorporation and place of business of the parties; and

(d) the place where the relationship, if any, between the parties is centered.

These contacts are to be evaluated according to their relative importance with respect to the particular issue.

As is readily apparent, not every one of these elements will be given the same weight in every case or be of significance in every case. This injects some uncertainty in the outcome in those jurisdictions which use this method.

(4) The "Better Rule of Law"/"Choice Influencing Considerations" Method

A similar method is Professor Leflar's "choice-influencing considerations," also known as the "better rule of law." Professor Leflar has formulated five "choice influencing considerations":

i) predictability of results;

ii) maintenance of interstate and international order;

iii) simplication of the judicial task;

iv) advancement of the forum's governmental interests; and

v) application of the better rule of law.

Leflar, *supra* § 96.

Many of these considerations overlap with the Restatement (Second's) factors. The "better rule of law" element of the analysis is determined by the "superiority of one rule of law over another in terms of socio-economic jurisprudential standards." *See* E. F. Scoles & P. Hay, *supra* § 17.18.

(5) "Comparative Impairment" Method

Under this method, once the court determines there is a true conflict, it must determine which jurisdiction's policies and interests will be most impaired if its law is not applied. The court is, therefore, called upon to weigh competing state interests. *See, e.g.*, E. F. Scoles & P. Hay, *supra* §§ 2.6 n.20, 17.17. California courts have applied this method, commencing with a 1976 decision in *Bernhard v. Harrah's Club*, 16 Cal. 3d 313, 546 P.2d 719, 128 Cal. Rptr. 215, *cert. denied*, 429 U.S. 859 (1976). In *Bernhard*, the court first determined that a true conflict existed. It concluded that the method which should be applied in resolving true conflicts is the application of "the law of the state whose interest would be more impaired if its law were not applied."

CHOICE OF LAW

The court in *Bernhard* held a Nevada bar civilly liable to a California plaintiff injured in California by a Californian to whom the Nevada bar had served drinks when the Californian had been intoxicated. California law provided for civil liability against a California bar under the same circumstances. However, Nevada law did not provide for such civil liability, but imposed only criminal sanctions. The California Supreme Court held that California's policy would be more impaired than Nevada's were California law not chosen. Since Nevada forbade the conduct, the net result of a choice of California law would only be to add civil liability in Nevada to a criminal violation, an extension less painful to Nevada than the total denial of a civil recovery to the plaintiff would be to California.

b. Federal Tort Claims Act

In an action commenced against the United States under FTCA, 28 U.S.C. § 1346, the liability of the United States is determined "in accordance with the law of the place where the act or omission occurred." 28 U.S.C. § 1346(b). *Richards v. United States*, 369 U.S. 1 (1962).

In *Richards*, an airplane, which had taken off in Tulsa, Oklahoma enroute to New York City, crashed in Missouri. The alleged negligence of the United States, through the negligence of an air traffic controller, took place in Oklahoma. There were two issues presented to the Supreme Court for review:

a) In cases where the act of negligence and injury occur in different states, which is the law of the place where the "act or omission occurs" under 28 U.S.C. § 1346(b); and

b) Once a determination as to what state's law constitutes the place where the "act or omission occurs," is only the internal law of the state applied, or is the state's whole law applied, including the state's choice of law rules?

The Supreme Court held that in FTCA actions, the law of the state where the actual negligence of the United States took place governs, rather than the law of the state where the injury occurred and the state where the negligent acts occurred is to apply its whole law, including that state's choice of law rules.

2. Contract Actions

a. Express Choice of Law Provision in a Contract

(1) Introduction

The parties to a contract often include a provision selecting the law which is to govern their contractual obligations. In drafting a contract which has a choice of law provision, it is important to insure that the provision adequately provides for all of the choice of law issues which may arise.

If a choice of law provision[23] does not specify that all issues arising out of the agreement, including its validity, construction, interpretation, breach, and damages for breach, are to be governed by the law of a particular state, a court is free to determine that the issue of validity is to be determined by the law of the state of the making of the contract and other issues according to the law of the state designated in the agreement, if it is different than the law of the place of the making.

If a choice of law provision does not specify whether the designated state's laws to be applied refers only to the internal laws of the state, without reference to that state's conflicts of law or vice-a-versa, the court may be free to determine that issue either way, if the forum's choice of law rules on that issue are not clear. In the event a court applies the state's choice of law principles, the result could be the application of the law of a state other than the state designated in the agreement.

If the choice of law provision does not also provide for a choice of forum,[24] the litigation could be commenced in a forum which may be hostile to a choice of law provision, have different procedural rules for such important items as attachment, injunction rules, or provision for attorneys' fees, rules of construction or interpretation that is different than that of the designated choice of law state (*i.e.*, what constitutes fraud, duress, void as against public policy, internal law of state applicable rather than law of state, including its choice of law rules).

If a choice of forum provision has been included, but not a choice of law provision, the choice of forum provision may not be interpreted to include by implication a choice of law provision that the internal law of that state should also govern, and the courts would be free to apply the state's choice of law principles and interpret the agreement in accordance with the laws of another state.

If certain issues are subject to arbitration and other issues are not, the agreement should make clear in the choice of law/choice of forum provisions exactly what choices are being made to avoid the same types of problems that are discussed above. *See, e.g., Cutco Industries, Inc. v. Naughton*, 806 F.2d

---

23 A plain vanilla choice of law provision, lacking in specificity, might read: "This agreement is to be governed by the law of the state of New York." This could be subject to varying interpretations.

24 A plain vanilla choice of forum provision, which could be subject to varying interpretations, might read: "Any action arising under or relating to this agreement may only be brought in any court of the State of New York or any federal court of the United States located in any city of the state of New York." It would be wise to include in any choice of forum provision an irrevocable consent to such jurisdiction and to jurisdiction over the person.

361 (2d Cir. 1986).[25] Even if there is a detailed choice of law/choice of forum provision in the agreement, it may not be enforced due to fraud, unequal bargaining positions, no reasonable relationship to the parties or the agreement, *forum non conveniens*, or similar issues.

New York provides by statute for mandatory acceptance in certain instances of choice of law/choice of forum provisions.

(2) New York State Courts

New York courts must give effect to a choice of law designation in an agreement that New York law governs, "whether or not such contract, agreement or undertaking bears a reasonable relation to this state" if the transaction in the aggregate is not less than two hundred and fifty thousand dollars and it is not a contract for personal services or a consumer contract. The statute also covers actions under § 1-105 of the Uniform Commercial Code. N.Y. Gen. Oblig. Law § 5-1401 (McKinney 1988).

Further, if an agreement provides that New York law governs and the value of the transaction is not less than one million dollars, New York courts must entertain jurisdiction and cannot dismiss or stay the action on *forum non conveniens* grounds, provided that a foreign corporation or a nonresident, not otherwise subject to the jurisdiction of the New York courts, has agreed to submit to the jurisdiction of the New York courts.[26] N.Y. Gen. Oblig. Law § 5-1402; CPLR § 327 (McKinney 1988). These statutes have retroactive effect and apply to contracts made prior to their enactment.

In the event that there is such a choice of law or choice of forum clause, a race to the courthouse could ensue. If a party to the agreement did not want either or both provisions enforced, that party could try to bring suit for declaratory judgment, rescission or breach in another jurisdiction which bears some relationship to the transaction and argue that the provision should

---

25 In *Cutco Industries*, a written agreement provided that should disputes of a certain nature arise, the parties agreed to arbitration in New York. The Second Circuit noted that "an agreement to arbitrate in New York in a contract is irrelevant when the cause of action being sued upon does not constitute an arbitrable dispute." *Id.* at 366.

26 Presumably a party could still attack a choice of law/choice of forum provision in an agreement on the grounds of fraud or unequal bargaining positions, or as contrary to public policy. More importantly, if the choice of law provision does not contain an express statement that the law of New York is to govern the validity of the agreement, as well as other aspects of it, a New York court might determine, assuming New York bears no reasonable relation to the transaction, that validity (statute of frauds, capacity of the parties to contract, or other issues of execution) must be determined by application of the law of a state that has a reasonable relation to the agreement. *Cf. Freedman v. Chemical Const. Corp.*, 43 N.Y.2d 260, 372 N.E.2d 12, 401 N.Y.S.2d 176 (1977).

not be enforced as against public policy, does not bear a reasonable relation, due process or other similar grounds which that jurisdiction might be willing to hear.[27]

In the event that there is a choice of law/choice of forum provision in an agreement which does not fall within the statutory mandates of the General Obligations Law, New York courts generally honor such clauses if the parties or the transaction bears a reasonable relation with New York, if it is not contrary to public policy, fraud, unequal bargaining power. *Gilbert v. Burnstine*, 255 N.Y. 348, 354, 357, 174 N.E. 706 (1931); *Arthur Young & Co. v. Leong*, 53 A.D.2d at 516, 383 N.Y.S.2d at 619 (The Appellate Division, citing *Gilbert* noted: "In the absence of a showing of contrary public policy, or fraud, or mistake, the meetings of the minds expressed in the contract should ordinarily be enforced."). Such provisions are enforceable when the parties or the transaction bear a reasonable relation to the chosen state. *Accord A. S. Rampell, Inc. v. Hyster Co.*, 3 N.Y.2d 369, 381, 144 N.E.2d 371, 379, 165 N.Y.S.2d 475, 486 (1957). If they do not, it may well be that New York courts would not apply that state's law.[28] The choice of law provision is deemed to carry with it only substantive law, not procedural law which will be governed by the law of the forum. *See Sears, Roebuck & Co. v. Enco Associates, Inc.*, 43 N.Y.2d 389, 397, 372 N.E.2d 555, 560, 401 N.Y.S.2d 767, 772 (1977).

(3) Federal Courts Sitting in New York

Where an agreement provides for a choice of New York law, federal courts in New York will give such a provision great deference, and, if New York has "sufficient" contact with the parties or the transaction, the choice

---

27 The Restatement (Second) provides that while courts will generally honor choice of law provisions, an exception applies if the law chosen would violate a "fundamental policy" of a state with a "materially greater interest than the chosen state." Restatement (Second) § 187. The Restatement (Second) also provides that if only one state has any relationship with the parties and the agreement and that state's law would hold the agreement invalid, that the parties cannot validate the agreement by stipulating that the issue of validity is governed by the law of another state having no relationship with the parties or the agreement. *Id.* However, if several states bear some relation to the transaction, the Restatement (Second) would uphold a choice of law provision as to validity. *Id.* § 187, comment on Subsection 2. The law in the federal courts in New York also pose potential problems for the New York statutes and will be discussed in the text at 3.b(1)(c). It should be noted that this Section of the Restatement (Second) is under revision and the April 15, 1986, draft revision differs radically from the current Section. There is no "fundamental" policy exception, no requirement for any relation to the parties, the chosen forum's law can validate an agreement invalid under the laws of all states having a relation to the transaction. Before relying on this Section, one should check to ensure that it is still in effect.

28 Choice of forum provisions falling outside of the General Obligations Law's provisions are generally enforced in the court's discretion absent fraud, unequal bargaining power or public policy considerations. However, such choice of forum provisions are also subject to *forum non conveniens* considerations.

CHOICE OF LAW

will be given determinative effect. *Woodling v. Garrett Corp.*, 813 F.2d 543, 551-552 (2d Cir. 1987); *Zerman v. Ball*, 735 F.2d 15, 20 (2d Cir. 1984). In *Zerman*, the court found that New York had a reasonable relation with the transaction: a securities account, where E. F. Hutton, the securities dealer, was headquartered, and where the margin loan was payable.

This general statement is subject to two caveats. First, if the issue involves the validity of the agreement, it appears that the federal courts will not honor the parties' choice of New York law if New York bears no relation to the parties or the transaction, if the agreement would be invalid under the law of all jurisdictions having any relationship to the parties or the transaction. *Cf. Siegelman v. Cunard White Star, Ltd.*, 221 F.2d 189, 195 (2d Cir. 1955). With the enactment of the General Obligations Law, the question arises whether a federal court sitting in New York must now honor an express choice New York law provision in a contract without regard to whether New York bears any relation to the parties or the transaction, particularly if the issue involves the validity of the contract. The principles of *Erie* and its progeny suggest that the federal courts must recognize the express choice. On the other hand, the result in *Stewart Org., Inc. v. Ricoh*, 108 S. Ct. 2239 (1988), suggests that, at least where a motion to transfer is made, the federal court may be free to refuse to enforce the provision.

Second, if the court finds that another state has an "overriding interest" in the transaction, the court may give weight to the choice of New York law, as one factor to consider, but refuse to honor the choice of New York law given the other state's "overriding interest." *Southern Int'l Sales Co. v. Potter & Brumfield Div. of AMF, Inc.*, 410 F. Supp. 1339, 1342-1343 (S.D.N.Y. 1976).

Where there is no choice of law provision in an agreement, the New York courts and federal courts sitting in New York apply a different test.

b. No Express Choice of Law Provision in a Contract

(1) Introduction

Where there is no choice of law provision in a contract, the traditional methods for deciding what law governs involved three different methods: (a) the law of the place where the contract was made; (b) the law of the place of performance; or (c) the intent of the parties. At one time or another New York courts have employed each of these three methods. New York presently employs the law of the place which has the most significant contacts or the paramount interest in the matter in dispute. This has also been referred to as the "center of gravity" or "grouping of contacts" method. Before discussing the modern methods, the traditional methods will be briefly discussed.

(2) The Law of the Place of Making of the Contract

The validity of a contract was traditionally governed by the law of the place where it was made. It was the rule adopted by the Restatement of Conflict of Law. *See* R. Leflar, *supra* § 145. While it afforded predictability of results, like the *lex loci* rule in torts, the place where the contract was made[29] often was adventitious, and had no connection with the contemplated place of performance. The law of the place of making is now one of the contacts that is considered in New York's modern analysis.

(3) The Law of the Place of Performance

Some courts have employed the law of the place of performance if it is different than the law of the place of making. Obvious difficulties arise with this method when performance is to be rendered in two or more states. Should the law of each jurisdiction apply only to that part of the contract to be performed only in that jurisdiction, or should the law of one jurisdiction apply to the entire contract? Moreover, if the law of the place of performance is different than the law of the place of making, the parties may not have been aware that the applicable law would be the law of the place of performance. Some jurisdictions allow the place of performance to govern issues involving performance such as breach, termination, rescission and payment and the law of the place of making to govern validity. *Id.* § 146.

(4) The Presumed Intent of the Parties

If the intent has not been expressed, the "presumed" intention of the parties as to which law they intended to apply to a particular agreement, has also been utilized by the courts. The courts followed a rule of validation in that the parties could not be presumed to contemplate application of a law which would defeat their contract. *Pritchard v. Norton*, 106 U.S. 124, 136 (1882). This law of validation is also applicable as a factor in modern choice of law methods.

(5) New York's Modern Choice of Law

(a) New York State Courts

New York's modern method was first adopted in the landmark decision of *Auten v. Auten*, 308 N.Y. 155, 124 N.E.2d 99 (1954). *Auten* involved the issue of whose law governed a separation agreement made in New York by an

---

[29] In the event that the law of the place of making of the contract is unclear, the contract is deemed made at the time and place "where the last act necessary to the completion of the contract was done—that is, where the contract first created a legal obligation." R. Leflar, *American Conflicts Law* § 145 (3d ed. 1977).

English couple. After making the agreement in New York, the wife returned to England and brought suit against the husband in England for failure to perform. The suit was unsuccessful. An action was subsequently brought in New York to recover under the agreement. The Court of Appeals held that the issues of rescission and repudiation were governed by the law of England. Before analyzing which jurisdiction's law should apply, Judge Fuld revisited the then current state of New York choice of law rules in contractual transactions involving different jurisdictions, terming it "a matter not free from difficulty. The New York decisions evidence a number of different approaches to the question." *Id.* at 159-160, 124 N.E.2d 101.[30] With respect to the applicable method which should be applied, Judge Fuld noted:

> Under this theory, the courts, instead of regarding as conclusive the parties intention or the place of making or performance, lay emphasis rather upon the law of the place 'which has the most significant contacts within the matter in dispute.'

Id. at 160, 124 N.E.2d 101-102 (citations omitted).

The contacts to be examined, in light of the relevant facts, were set forth by Judge Fuld as follows:

a) *Type of Agreement* - Agreement effecting a separation between British subjects who had been married in Britain, had children there and lived there as a family for 14 years;

b) *Place of Making of the Contract* - New York, which Judge Fuld characterized as fortuitous;

c) *Place of Domicile* - Wife and children - England. Husband temporary visa for U.S. at time of execution of contract;

d) *Place of Performance* - Monies to be paid to New York trust "for the account" of wife and children in England. Court determined this in effect meant England was the place of performance;

e) *Intentions of Parties* - Since both parties knew the wife and children would be living in England, the court presumed that "both parties necessarily realized that any action which the wife took would necessarily be in England";

---

30 Judge Fuld noted that most New York courts at that time applied the law of the place where the contract was made to issues bearing upon execution, interpretation and the validity of contracts, while matters of performance including what constitutes a breach or what excuses a breach were generally determined by the law of the place of performance. Many New York courts, Judge Fuld noted, had treated the above rules as conclusive, while others had treated the intention of the parties as controlling and the general rule as presumptions or guideposts to be considered with other facts.

f) *Jurisdiction which had the Greater Interest or Concern* - The court determined that there was no question that England had the greatest concern in prescribing and governing obligations under the agreement in order to secure for the wife and children essential support and maintenance. England was the jurisdiction of the marital domicile and the place where the wife and children were. England, therefore, had the greatest concerns in defining and regulating those rights and duties including the effect of any termination or repudiation of it.

Judge Fuld did not discuss the relative weight which these elements should have. The method has been referred to variously as the "grouping of contacts," "center of gravity" and "most significant contact" method. This, of course, adds an element of uncertainty in trying to determine how any given factual situation will be decided. The analysis should be a qualitative, not a quantitative approach.

More recently, New York's choice of law method in contract actions has been described as the "predominant" or "paramount" interest test which refers to the law of the jurisdiction having the greatest interest in the particular issue. *See, e.g., Downs v. Am. Mut. Liab. Ins. Co.*, 14 N.Y.2d 266, 271, 200 N.E.2d 204, 206, 251 N.Y.S.2d 19, 22 (1964); *Intercontinental Planning Ltd. v. Daystrom, Inc.*, 24 N.Y.2d 372, 382, 248 N.E.2d 576, 582, 300 N.Y.S.2d 817, 825 (1969). In *Intercontinental Planning, Ltd.*, the court described the paramount interest test as requiring the application of the jurisdiction having the greatest interest in the litigation and the facts or contacts which have significance in defining the jurisdiction's interest are those which relate to the particular law in conflict. *Id.*

(b) Federal Courts Sitting in New York

The Second Circuit applies New York's "paramount interest" test in resolving choice of law issues in contract actions where the parties have not expressed a choice of law. *See, e.g., Hutner v. Greene*, 734 F.2d 896, 899-900 (2d Cir. 1984). In *Hutner*, Justice Winter applied the *Intercontinental* test to conclude that New York law would apply to an express contract claim where plaintiff was a California resident and defendants were New York residents, the limited partnership was a New York limited partnership, the contract was negotiated in New York and the stock purchase agreements were to be governed by New York law. Judge Winter concluded that such contacts implicate New York's interest in protecting its position as a national business capital, attractive as a location for negotiating the type of acquisition transaction involved in the action. *Id.* at 899-900.

New York's method is very similar, if not identical, to the other modern method frequently used, the law of the state with the "most significant relationship."

CHOICE OF LAW

(6) The "Most Significant Relationship" Method

This is the method of the Restatement (Second), which lists five elements the court should consider in applying the principles set forth in Section 6 of the Restatement (Second) in determining the law of the state with the most significant relationship to the parties and the transaction.

The contacts to be taken into account are:

(a) the place of contracting;

(b) the place of negotiation of the contract;

(c) the place of performance;

(d) the location of the subject matter of the contract; and

(e) the domicile, residence, nationality, place of incorporation and place of business of the parties.

Restatement (Second) of Conflict of Laws § 188.

These contacts are to be evaluated on an issue by issue basis according to their relative importance with respect to the particular issue in the particular action. Restatement (Second) of Conflict of Laws § 188. This, of course, leads to wide discretion in application, and, therefore, lack of predictability in result. The internal law of the place chosen by this method is to be applied without regard to its choice of law rules. The capacity to contract, formalities and validity are to be determined using the same analysis. Restatement (Second) of Conflict of Laws §§ 198-200. In addition, the Restatement (Second's) approach is supplemented by a number of rules for specific types of contracts. Restatement (Second) §§ 189-197.

(7) Other Modern Methods

The other major modern choice of law method in contracts is Professor Leflar's "Better Rule of Law" method which has been previously discussed in the section on modern choice of law methods in torts. For a detailed discussion and a state by state analysis of choice of law methods, as well as a subject matter analysis, *see* E. F. Scoles and P. Hay, *supra* §§ 18.21-18.29.

c. Actions Involving the Uniform Commercial Code

The Uniform Commercial Code, Section 1-105(1) specifically addresses choice of law considerations as follows:

> Except as provided hereafter in this section, when a transaction bears reasonable relation to this state and also to another state or nation the parties may agree that the law either of this state or of

such other state or nation shall govern their rights and duties. Failing such agreement this Act applies to transactions bearing an appropriate relation to this state.

N.Y.U.C.C. § 1-105(1) (McKinney 1964 & 1988 Supp.).

This choice of law provision applies to all Articles of the Uniform Commercial Code not just to Article 2, except as set forth in § 1-105(2).[31]

While most states have adopted the Uniform Commercial Code, some states adopted variations, and before proceeding in another state the specific state's Uniform Commercial Code should be checked.[32] There is a question as to whether the language stating that the Act applies to "transactions bearing an appropriate relation to this state" means that the forum state should apply its substantive law as to the Uniform Commercial Code or its whole law, including its choice of law rules which could direct it to another state. *See* Siegel, *supra* § 71. When dealing with perfection of a security interest in secured transactions, perfection should be made in all states which could fall within the choice of law provisions of § 9-103. *See* Siegel, *supra* § 72.

(1) New York State Courts

As noted earlier, Section 1-105(1) of the Uniform Commercial Code has been modified by the General Obligations Law §§ 5-1401-1402. In the event that the agreement does not fall within the General Obligations Law's statutory guidelines, the Uniform Commercial Code § 1-105(1) and (2) applies. Under New York law, a "reasonable relation" where the parties have chosen a forum means that the relation "should not be an adventitious relationship, but one that bears upon the facts involved in the transaction itself." Denoun Practice Commentary McKinney's § 1-105. Where the parties do not choose the forum, the court must determine the applicable law based upon a test of "appropriateness" which appears to be a more circumscribed test than that of reasonableness, but again its application will turn on the facts themselves. *Id.* The test of what state bears an "appropriate" relation suggests that the *Auten* test be adopted. New York Annotations (1). Thus, what is an "appropriate"

---

[31] Section 1-105(2) provides exceptions to § 1-105(1)'s choice of law provision, and a contrary agreement is effective only to the extent permitted by law (including the conflict of law rules). The exceptions relate to rights of creditors against goods sold, § 2-402; bank deposits and collections, § 4-102; bank transfers, § 6-102; investment securities, § 8-106; secured transactions relating to perfection of security interests, § 9-103. § 9-103 provides for separate choice of law determinations depending upon the category of security interest: documents, instruments, ordinary goods; certificates of title; accounts, general intangibles and mobile goods; chattel paper, minerals; uncertified securities.

[32] This is particularly true with respect to § 9-102 which had a choice of law provision, but has been revised to exclude it. Some states have not adopted the revision.

relation is left to judicial decision and the court is not bound by common-law conflict-of-law rules developed in other contexts. New York Annotations, Historical Note.

The official comment to Section 1-105 also provides that where there is "no agreement as to governing law . . . the mere fact that suit is brought in a state does not make it appropriate to apply the substantive law of the state."

New York does not automatically apply its substantive law in these situations. New York has interpreted the official comments to be legislative approval of the Restatement (Second's) "most significant contacts" or New York's "grouping of contacts approach." *Martin v. Julius Dierck Equip. Co.*, 52 A.D.2d 463, 468, 384 N.Y.S.2d 479, 483 (2d Dep't 1976), *aff'd*, 43 N.Y.2d 583, 374 N.E.2d 97, 403 N.Y.S.2d 185 (1978).

(2) Federal Courts Sitting in New York

Where there is an express choice of law provision, federal courts in New York will follow New York's rule honoring a choice of law provision as long as it bears a "reasonable relationship" to the state whose law is chosen. *Associated Metals & Minerals Corp. v. Sharon Steel Corp.*, 590 F. Supp. 18, 20 (S.D.N.Y. 1983), *aff'd without opinion*, 742 F.2d 1431 (2d Cir. 1983). Where there is no express choice of law provision, the federal courts in New York apply New York state court's choice of law method governing contracts to determine whose law governs. *Windsor Indus., Inc. v. EACA Int'l Ltd.*, 548 F. Supp. 635, 638 (E.D.N.Y. 1982); *Bache & Co., Inc. v. Int'l Controls Corp.*, 339 F. Supp. 341, 347-348 (S.D.N.Y.), *aff'd*, 469 F.2d 696 (1972).

One should be careful where there is a "battle of the forms" that the choice of law provision is incorporated in such a way and in a place in a contract or form that it is considered to be part of the contract. The courts are free to determine that such a choice of law provision under given circumstances does not form part of the contract and need not be honored. *See, e.g., Trans World Metals, Inc. v. Southwire Co.*, 769 F.2d 902, 910 (2d Cir. 1985).

d. General Considerations

(1) Statute of Frauds

The Statute of Frauds arises in the context of an oral contract or an oral agreement. Where two or more states are involved with the transaction and the parties and one state's law recognizes such oral agreements, but the other state's law does not, for choice of law purposes, the question is whose state law applies to the question of the enforceability of the oral agreement? The Restatement (Second) of Conflict of Laws § 141 states that the enforceability of the contract is determined in accordance with the principles set forth in §§ 187-188, which have been previously discussed herein. This is the "most significant relationship" test.

(a) New York State Courts

New York has treated the issue of the Statute of Frauds as a separate issue and has analyzed its applicability for choice of law purposes by applying the law of the jurisdiction which has the "paramount interest" in the Statute of Frauds issue. *See, e.g., Andover Realty, Inc. v. Western Elec. Co.*, 64 N.Y.2d 1006, 478 N.E.2d 193, 489 N.Y.S.2d 52 (1985); *Intercontinental Planning, Ltd. v. Daystrom*, 24 N.Y.2d 372, 248 N.E.2d 576, 300 N.Y.S.2d 817 (1969). Thus, an underlying contract, such as a merger agreement, or a real estate contract, could be analyzed under the laws of one jurisdiction, while a finder's fee or broker's fee with respect to such agreement could be governed by the laws of another jurisdiction. *Id.*

While the New York courts have refused to classify the Statute of Frauds as substantive or procedural, *id.*, the use of the paramount interest test effectively gives the Statute of Frauds a substantive classification requiring New York to apply its choice of law rules.

In *Freedman v. Chemical Constr. Corp.*, 43 N.Y.2d 260, 372 N.E.2d 12, 401 N.Y.S.2d 176 (1977), the court noted in *dicta* that even if the parties had agreed orally that the law of a particular jurisdiction applied that "where, as with the Statute of Frauds, the issue arguably cannot be controlled by voluntary agreement, there is some question whether, in the absence of a reasonable basis for choosing the law of the jurisdiction designated by the parties, their choice of law will be honored. *Id.*, at n.265, 372 N.E.2d at n.15, 401 N.Y.S.2d at n.179-180.

In *Intercontinental Planning, Ltd.*, the Court of Appeals applied a "governmental interest" analysis to the issue of whether a New York statute requiring business finders' contracts to be in writing should be applied to an oral agreement made in New Jersey, to be performed by a New York firm. The court looked at the underlying purpose of the statute and applied New York law. In *Andover Realty*, the action involved New Jersey/New York brokers who had been solicited by a corporation that had offices in New York, but which wanted to sell some of its New Jersey real property. Relying on *Intercontinental Planning*, the Court of Appeals held that brokers could not recover a claim for commissions which were barred by New Jersey, but not by New York law. Although the brokers had dealings with New York in relation to the sale, the court felt in part that New Jersey as the situs of the property had the paramount interest. *Id.* at 1008, 478 N.E.2d at 194, 489 N.Y.S.2d at 53.

CHOICE OF LAW

The *Andover* case seems to turn in part on choice of law concepts applicable to real property, *i.e.*, the law of the situs of the property and the "presumed" intent of the parties rather than on the *Intercontinental Planning* paramount interest test.

(b) Federal Courts Sitting in New York

The federal courts sitting in New York apply *Intercontinental Planning, Ltd.*'s paramount interest test and New York's depecage doctrine to choice of law issues involving the Statute of Frauds. *Hutner v. Greene*, 734 F.2d at 899-901; *Fort Howard Paper Co. v. William D. Witter, Inc.*, 787 F.2d at 789; *Lehman v. Dow Jones & Co.*, 783 F.2d 285, 289 (2d Cir. 1986); *Holding Capital Group, Inc. v. A.P. and Co.*, 673 F. Supp. 1274 (S.D.N.Y. 1987).

(2) Actions Involving Usurious Interest Rates Under One State's Law

As noted above, under New York law if there is an express choice of law designation in a contract and, if the state selected has sufficient contacts with the transaction, New York will honor the choice of law provision. *Zerman v. Ball*, 735 F.2d at 19-20. Such choice of law provision will apply even if there is a rate of interest applicable that is usurious under the laws of another relevant state.

Zerman involved an action by a securities broker's customer against the broker and others. One of the questions on appeal was whether the customer who signed an agreement with a choice of New York law provision had expressly waived her right to challenge a margin interest rate, lawful under New York law, as usurious under the laws of the other relevant state. The complaint alleged that plaintiff had purchased securities from E.F. Hutton at one of Hutton's Florida offices. One of the allegations was that the margin interest rate violated Florida's usury law, a fact which apparently had not been disclosed to plaintiff. In affirming the grant of partial summary judgment on the usury claim, the court relied upon New York's law that an express choice of law designation in a contract is determinative if the state selected has sufficient contacts with the transaction. The court noted that the present transaction had a reasonable relationship to New York because E.F. Hutton was headquartered there *and* the margin loan was payable there. It is clear from the decision, that even if New York law had been chosen, if New York did not have a "reasonable relationship" with the transaction, New York law would not have been used to uphold the usurious interest rate.

In the event that there is no express choice of law provision and several states are involved in the transaction, The Restatement (Second) of Conflict of Laws provides that the interest rate will generally be sustained against the validity of the contract if it provides for a rate of interest that is permissible in a state to which the contract has a substantial relationship (not necessarily the most significant contact) and is not greatly in excess of the rate permitted by the general usury law of the state otherwise applicable under general choice of law rules. Restatement (Second) of Conflict of Laws § 203. "To have a substantial relationship" as to a particular issue, a state must have "a normal and natural relationship to the contract and the parties." Numerous examples of the types of relationships that are considered substantial and those that are not are set forth in Restatement (Second) of Conflict of Laws § 203, comment C. The rationale for the use of a "substantial relationship" test rather than a "most significant relationship" test is that the parties will expect upon entering a contract that the provisions of the contract will be binding upon them. Courts, therefore, will not invalidate a contract unless the value of protecting the expectation of the parties is outweighed in a particular case by the interest of the state with the invalidating rule. Usury is an area where the "policy of validation" is particularly strong. Restatement (Second) of Conflict of Laws § 203 comment B.

Under New York law, if a contract is usurious under the laws of all states having any relation to the parties or the transaction, and one state would invalidate the agreement while another state hold recovery to the legal interest rate, New York will choose the law of the later state or the state with the lightest penalty, under the rule of validation theory. *Crisafuli v. Childs*, 33 A.D.2d 293, 307 N.Y.S.2d 701, 705 (4th Dep't 1970).

(3) Actions Involving Property Interests

(a) Real Property

The general rule is that title to real property that is located within a particular state, and all aspects of acquisition or disposition with regard thereto, are governed by the laws of that state. *Knox v. Jones*, 47 N.Y. 389 (1872). All instruments affecting such title are also governed by the law of the state where the real property is located. Contracts relating to real property, including its transfer, are governed by the law of the state where the property is located. *See, e.g., James v. Powell*, 19 N.Y.2d at 256-259, 225 N.E.2d 741, 279 N.Y.S.2d at 15-17; *El Cid, Ltd. v. N.J. Zinc Co.*, 575 F. Supp. 1513, 1517 (S.D.N.Y. 1983), *aff'd without opinion*, 770 F.2d 157 (2d Cir. 1985), *cert. denied*, 474 U.S. 1021 (1985). *Cf.* Restatement (Second) of Conflict of Laws §§ 189-190 (contractual duties arising out of transfer of land, including validity of contract, governed by local law of state where land located, unless some other state has a "more significant relationship" as defined by the Restatement (Second) test in which event its local law governs).

CHOICE OF LAW

Where title to property is being litigated in one state, and the property is located in another state, New York will refer to the laws of the state where the land is located including its choice of law rules. *In re Schneider's Estate*, 198 Misc. 1017, 96 N.Y.S. at 657-660.

The choice of law rules relating to wills and intestate estates, with respect to real and personal property, where more than one state may have an interest, is governed in New York by the Section 3-5.1 of the EPTL (McKinney 1981).

(b) Personal Property Interests

Personal property interests are classified as tangible and intangible.

(i) Tangible Personal Property

Tangible personal property, that which "adheres" to the owner and has no locality of its own, was traditionally generally governed by the law of the domicile of the owner, no matter where the property was physically located. *Cross v. United States Trust Co.*, 131 N.Y. 330, 30 N.E. 125 (1892). However, under present rules in New York the law of the place where the property is kept and used is generally applied. *Wyatt v. Fulrath*, 16 N.Y.2d 169, 211 N.E.2d 637, 264 N.Y.S.2d 233 (1965); *Kunstsammlungen Zu Weimar v. Elicofon*, 536 F. Supp. 829, 845-846 (E.D.N.Y. 1981), *aff'd*, 678 F.2d 1150, 1160 (1982); *Severnoe Sec. Corp. v. London & Lancashire Inc., Co.*, 255 N.Y. 120, 174 N.E. 299, *modified*, 255 N.Y. 631, 175 N.E. 345 (1931).

The law of the state where the tangible personal property is located determines the validity of the formalities to execution of a conveyance of such property. *In re Bulova's Will*, 14 A.D.2d 249, 220 N.Y.S.2d 541, 545-546 (1st Dep't 1961). A transfer of an interest in tangible personal property is valid and effective if it was valid under the laws of the state where it was located at the time of transfer, even if the laws of the state of domicile of the owner would hold such transfer ineffective. *Cf. Weissman v. Banque De Bruxelles*, 254 N.Y. 488, 494, 173 N.E. 835 (1930). The exception to this rule is if the property was brought into a state without the owner's permission. *Id.*

A state where the tangible personal property is located may regulate by its own laws the creation, transfer or enforcement of rights in such property. *Goetschius v. Brightman*, 245 N.Y. 186, 190, 191, 156 N.E. 660 (1927). An exception exists where the parties have expressed their intent in a contract to be bound by the laws of a state other than where the property is located. *Wyatt v. Fulrath*, 16 N.Y.2d 169, 264 N.Y.S. 637, 211 N.E.2d 233 (1965). In *Wyatt* the parties had no relation with New York and had never even been to New York, but their choice of law provision was upheld, even though Spanish law which otherwise would clearly have been applicable would have strongly disfavored the transaction, since New York was an important commercial and financial center, and parties had a right to rely upon their expectations that their express intentions would be honored.

(ii) Intangible Property

The law of the place of transfer will generally govern the validity of the transfer of intangible personal property. *In re Liebl's Estate*, 201 Misc. 1102, 105 N.Y.S.2d 715 (Sur. Ct. 1951); *cf. Severnoe Sec. Corp. v. London Lancashire Inc. & Co.*, 255 N.Y. 120, 174 N.E. 299, *modified*, 255 N.Y. 631, 175 N.E. 345 (1981). If the property is located in a state other than the state of transfer, such transfer is not valid in the other state if the transfer conflicts with the interests of the state and its citizens. *In re Liebl's Estate*, 201 Misc. 1102, 105 N.Y.S.2d 715 (1951); *Capital Nat'l Bank of N.Y. v. McDonald's Corp.*, 625 F. Supp. 874, 878 (S.D.N.Y. 1986).

If the intangible property is in the form of a documents such as a bill of exchange, promissory note or stock certificate, the law of the situs of the document at the time of transfer would govern. *See, e.g., Hutchinson v. Ross*, 262 N.Y. 381, 389-391, 187 N.E. 65, *reh'g denied*, 262 N.Y. 643, 188 N.E. 102 (1933).

Determining the situs of intangible property has been described by Justice Cardozo as a "legal fiction. . . . [t]he locality selected is for some purposes, the domicile of the creditor; for others, the domicile or place of business of the debtor, the place, that is to say where the obligation was created or was meant to be discharged; for others, any place where the debtor can be found. . . . At the root of the selection is generally a common sense appraisal of the requirements of justice and convenience in particular conditions." *Severnoe Sec. Corp. v. London & Lancashire Ins. Co.*, 255 N.Y. at 123-124, 174 N.E. 299. *Severnoe* involved the validity of an assignment of a cause of action of a Russian Company arising out of a transaction in Britain to a subsidiary whose situs was New York. The assignment apparently would not have been valid under New York law if the situs were deemed to be New York. Justice Cardozo held that the situs was England or Russia, but not New York. "The debtor is solvent, and is subject to suit in the place of its corporate life, which is also the place of the creation of the debt. No emergency exists, and no excuse for the implication of extraordinary powers. The powers of conservators should be exercised where there are assets to be conserved." *Id.* at 124, 174 N.E. at 299.

Thus, the situs is a moving target and depending upon the situation the "situs" and, thus, the governing law may be different depending upon the specific type of property. For a general discussion of the choice of law rules with respect to intangible personal property, *see* E. F. Scoles and P. Hays, *supra* §§ 19.27-19.32. The Uniform Commercial Code should also be consulted where applicable.

(4) Special Corporate Considerations

As a general rule, when a corporation is a party to an action, the choice of law considerations are no different than in any other choice of law context. Restatement (Second) Conflict of Laws §§ 301-302.

However, when an action involves the internal affairs of a corporation, including its organization and structure, the law of the state of incorporation as a general rule governs with few exceptions. *Id.* §§ 296-300, 303-313. Internal matters of a corporation which are generally governed by the law of the state of incorporation include: the validity of incorporation, *id.* §§ 296-298; termination, dissolution and winding-up, *id.* §§ 299-300; rights and liabilities of shareholders, *id.* §§ 303-308 (with exceptions noted therein); and rights and liabilities of directors, *id.* §§ 309-310. Qualification to do business is generally governed by the law of the state where qualification is sought. *Id.* § 312. The Restatement (Second) provides that any court having jurisdiction may handle an action involving the internal affairs of a foreign corporation unless it is inappropriate or an inconvenient forum. *Id.* § 313.

(a) New York State Courts

New York's choice of law rules generally provide that the internal affairs of a corporation are governed by the law of the state of incorporation. However, the Court of Appeals apparently has rejected any automatic application of the so-called "internal affairs" choice of law rule in an action involving a challenge by holders of beneficial shares of a real estate investment trust against the trustees for excessive management fees. The court noted that the action was the equivalent of a shareholders' derivative action. The court applied Massachusetts law where the trust was formed. *Greenspun v. Lindley*, 36 N.Y.2d 473, 477-478, 330 N.E.2d 79, 369 N.Y.S.2d 123, 126 (1975). The court expressly left open the question what law might apply if the business trust involved were "so 'present' in our State as perhaps to call for the application of New York law." In that sense, the court rejected the automatic application of the internal affairs rule, "under which the relationship between shareholders and trustees of a business trust by strict analogy to the relationship between shareholders and directors of a business corporation would be governed by the law of the state in which the business entity was formed." *Id.* By contrasting the automatic application of the internal affairs rule with respect to a corporation, the court by implication suggested that New York has an automatic rule with respect to the internal affairs of a corporation, but that the court will not extend the rule to a real estate investment trust. This distinction is supported by case law in both the state and federal courts in New York. *See, e.g., Galef v. Alexander*, 615 F.2d 51, 58 (2d Cir. 1980); *Russian Reinsurance Co. v. Stoddard*, 240 N.Y. 149, 154, 147 N.E. 703 (1925); *cf. Hart v. General Motors Corp.*, 129 A.D.2d 179, 517 N.Y.S.2d 490 (1st Dep't 1987); Herzog, *Conflict of Laws*, 34 Syracuse L. Rev. 113, 115 (1983).

(b) Federal Courts Sitting in New York

However, in *Norlin Corp. v. Rooney, Pace, Inc.*, 744 F. 2d. at 263-264, the Second Circuit interpreted *Greenspun* to say that there is no automatic application of the law of the state of incorporation, in effect looking to a test that would use the law of another state if there were a legitimate and substantial interest of that state to do so. In *Norlin*, the court did not need to resolve the issue, because it found New York and Panamanian law, the state of incorporation, to be the same. Further, the court noted that Panama did not choose to apply its own law to the transaction. Thus, as with other areas of choice of law, there is some uncertainty, however, that *Norlin* might have overstated New York law in this regard,[33] and while there may not be an automatic rule in situations where shareholders are involved, if the only nexus with the state of incorporation is the fact that it was incorporated there, certainly other automatic rules such as validity of incorporation, and dissolution or winding up are still automatically governed by the law of the state of incorporation.

(5) Special Considerations Involving Foreign Law, Foreign Sovereigns, Citizens of Foreign Countries

Whenever foreign law, a foreign sovereignty, or citizens of foreign states are involved, consideration should be given to whether a treaty, statute or federal policy governs choice of law considerations. A few of the more frequent situations that arise in this context are set forth below.

(a) Foreign Arbitral Awards

With respect to issues of enforcement of arbitration provisions involving citizens of different countries, one must determine at the outset whether there is a treaty between the United States and the country of citizenship of the foreign litigant or litigants. The United States is a signatory to the Conven-

---

[33] Section 1319 of New York Business Corporation Law makes a number of provisions of that law applicable to foreign corporations authorized to do business in New York and should be kept in mind in any suit involving foreign corporations. N.Y. Bus. Corp. Law § 1319 (McKinney 1986); *see also* N.Y. Bus. Corp. Law §§ 1315, 1317, 1318 (McKinney 1986). *Cf. Lewis v. Dicker*, 118 Misc. 2d 28, 459 N.Y.S.2d 215 (S. Ct. 1982) (applying center of gravity analysis to interpret § 1319).

CHOICE OF LAW

tion on the Recognition and Enforcement of Foreign Arbitral Awards ("Convention") which applies to both the enforcement of arbitration provisions and the enforcement of arbitration awards in commercial transactions. The Federal Arbitration Act, 9 U.S.C. §§ 201-08, governs enforceability whether the action is pending in *state* or *federal* court. If the subject matter of an action pending in state court relates to an arbitration agreement falling under the Convention, the defendant may remove the action to a federal court *at any time before trial.* 9 U.S.C. § 205.

The Convention preempts state law and the entire subject is governed by the Convention's terms. *Victrix Steamship Co., S.A. v. Salem Dry Cargo A.B.*, 825 F.2d 709, 712-713 (2d Cir. 1987).

(b) Foreign Sovereign Immunities Act

When an action is brought against a "foreign state," defined as a political subdivision or an "agency or instrumentality of a foreign state," [34] the Foreign Sovereign Immunities Act ("FSIA"), 28 U.S.C. §§ 1602-1611 (1976), provides that the law of "the place where the act or omission occurred" must be applied. FSIA must be applied when such an action is brought. Although there are conflicting views on the interpretation of "the place where the act or omission occurred," one federal court in New York has interpreted this provision to be consistent with the FTCA. *In re Air Crash Disaster at Warsaw, Poland, on March 14, 1980*, 19 Avi. Cas. ¶ (CCH) 17, 966 (E.D.N.Y. 1985) (the place where the negligence occurred governed and the whole law of that jurisdiction, including its choice of law provision applied). *See* Barry, *Solving Choice of Law Problems in Foreign Sovereign Immunities Act Cases*, 55 Defense Counsel Journal 255 (July 1988), for a discussion of the conflicting decisions.

(c) Warsaw Convention

The Warsaw Convention, 49 U.S. Stat. § 3014-3023, is a treaty of the United States which is applicable to international air flights. It provides essentially for strict liability against air carriers in tort cases subject to comparative or contributory negligence, but the amount of damages is limited to $75,000 per passenger if the flight involves the United States. If one seeks to recover more than the damage limits, it is necessary to prove willful misconduct on the part of the airline. Almost all foreign countries whose carriers fly into or out of the United States are signatories.

---

34 An "agency of instrumentality of a foreign state" means any entity "(1) which is a separate legal person, corporate or otherwise, and (2) which is an organ of a political subdivision thereof, or a majority of whose shares or other ownership interest is owned by a foreign state or political subdivision thereof, and (3) which is either a citizen of a state of the United States . . . nor created under the laws of any third country."

The statute has certain choice of law provisions which should be reviewed before bringing an action. In the event that the action involves a foreign carrier which constitutes "an agency or instrumentality of a foreign state" as defined by FSIA, the choice of law provision for damages is dictated by the FSIA test of the law of the place where the act or omission occurred." *In re Air Crash Disaster at Warsaw, Poland on March 14, 1980*, 19 Avi. 17, 966.

(d) The "Act of State" Doctrine

The "Act of State" doctrine precludes both federal and state courts from examining the acts of a foreign sovereign which effects property within that sovereign's territory. *Banco Nacional de Cuba v. Sabbatino*, 376 U.S. 398, 416 (1964); *French v. Banco Nacional de Cuba*, 23 N.Y.2d 46, 52, 242 N.E.2d 704, 295 N.Y.S.2d 433 (1968). For a discussion of the recent cases in New York state and federal courts dealing with the Act of State doctrine, *see* Herzog, *Conflict of Laws*, 37 Syracuse L. Rev. 362, 407-411 (1986).

CHAPTER TEN

PARTIES

by James A. Moss, Esq.*

I. CAPACITY

A. Capacity To Sue or Be Sued

An action shall be prosecuted only in the name of the party who, by the substantive law, has the right sought to be enforced. That party is known as the "real party in interest."[1]

When an action is incorrectly commenced by a person who is not a "real party in interest," the complaint is subject to dismissal under Fed. R. Civ. P. 17(a), unless the true "real party in interest" steps forward within a reasonable time after defendant's objection is lodged and ratifies or joins in the action.[2]

---

* The valuable assistance of Ellen Casey and Howard Singer in the preparation of this chapter is gratefully acknowledged.

[1] See, e.g., American Optical Co. v. Curtiss, 56 F.R.D. 26 (S.D.N.Y. 1971) (in diversity case, whether a party is a real party in interest as required by federal rule is to be determined by the substantive law of the forum state). See also Yonkers Comm'n on Human Rights v. City of Yonkers, 654 F. Supp. 544 (S.D.N.Y. 1987) (a municipal commission's capacity to sue had to be determined by substantive state law).

[2] See American Optical Co. v. Curtiss, supra (court allows 10 days for assignor of claim to join or be substituted as party plaintiff, where assignment of claims on which action was based is contrary to public policy of forum state); American Dredging Co. v. Federal Ins. Co., 309 F. Supp. 425 (S.D.N.Y. 1970) (court determined that plaintiff's insurer was the real party in interest and ordered the insurer joined as a plaintiff within 30 days); Supine v. Compagnie Nationale Air France, 100 F. Supp. 214 (E.D.N.Y. 1952) (in executors' wrongful death suits, court granted leave to amend to add dependents and next of kin as plaintiffs).

Real parties in interest can derive their claims from others. For example, where the substantive law permits, a claim may be completely or partially assigned to another person, who then becomes a real party in interest.[3] Where the assignment is partial, the assignor remains a real party in interest with respect to so much of the claim as has not been assigned. The same principles apply to the subrogation of a claim, since subrogation is viewed as an assignment by operation of law.[4] However, the courts have held that an attorney-in-fact (*i.e.*, an agent for the sole purpose of the suit) is *not* a real party in interest and may not maintain an action on behalf of his or her principal.[5]

Just as the named plaintiff must have the legal capacity to commence the lawsuit, so too must each defendant have the legal capacity to be sued.[6] Absent such capacity, a defendant is entitled to be dismissed from the lawsuit.

What body of substantive law should a litigant consult to determine whether a named party has the capacity to sue or be sued? The answer to that question is found in a series of rules set forth in Fed. R. Civ. P. 17(b). Those rules are summarized as follows:

CAPACITY TO SUE OR BE SUED

STATUS OF PARTY	DETERMINATIVE LAW
Individual not acting in a representative capacity[7]	Law of the individual's domicile
Corporation[8]	Law under which it was organized
All other parties*	Law of state in which district court sits

---

3 *See Staggers v. Otto Gerdau*, 359 F.2d 292 (2d Cir. 1966) (an assignee for collection may sue as the real party in interest); *Rosenblum v. Digfelder*, 111 F.2d 406 (2d Cir. 1940).

---

4 *See, e.g., Liberty Mut. Ins. Co. v. Tel-Mor Garage Corp.*, 92 F. Supp. 445 (S.D.N.Y. 1950) (a subrogee who has paid the full amount of a subrogor's loss is the only real party in interest and must bring suit in his own name).

---

5 *See Photometric Products Corp. v. Radtke*, 17 F.R.D. 103 (S.D.N.Y. 1954).

---

6 *See O'Connor v. Western Freight Ass'n*, 202 F. Supp. 561 (S.D.N.Y. 1962).

---

7 *See D'Ippolito v. Cities Service Co.*, 374 F.2d 643 (2d Cir. 1967).

---

8 *See Gonzalez v. Progressive Tool & Die Co.*, 455 F. Supp. 363 (E.D.N.Y. 1978).

* *Except* that (1) a partnership or other unincorporated association shall always have the capacity to sue or defend in its common name when a federal right is being enforced, and (2) the capacity of a federally-appointed receiver to sue or be sued is governed by Title 28, U.S.C. §§ 754 and 959(a).

B. Representatives of the Interested Party

Rule 17(a) makes it clear that certain kinds of representatives are to be accepted as the "real parties in interest" and may bring actions in their own names, even though they seek benefits not for themselves, but for the persons they represent. The categories of representatives enumerated in Rule 17(a) are:

- executors and administrators
- guardians
- bailees
- trustees of an express trust
- parties to a contract made for the benefit of others

Rule 17(a) also allows a party to sue without joining the person for whose benefit the action is brought whenever a statute authorizes that party to do so. In particular, when a federal statute so provides, an action for the benefit of another may be brought in the name of the United States.[9]

Whenever a person involved in the underlying dispute is an infant or incompetent, he or she *must* have a representative in the action. Rule 17(c) provides that representatives such as general guardians, guardians *ad litem*, next friends, committees and conservators are entitled to appear in an action on behalf of an infant or incompetent. Where none exists, the court must appoint a guardian *ad litem* or take some other appropriate action for the protection of the infant or incompetent.[10]

---

[9] This clause is limited in application because there are few statutes that permit private parties to sue in the name of the United States. One of the most important of these statutes is the Miller Act, which authorizes suit in the name of the United States by labor or material claimants against contractors for federal public buildings and works. See, e.g., *United States ex rel. United Brotherhood of Carpenters & Joiners Local Union No. 2028 v. Woerfel Corp.*, 545 F.2d 1148 (8th Cir. 1976).

[10] See, e.g., *Swift v. Swift*, 61 F.R.D. 595 (E.D.N.Y. 1973) (where daughter was named beneficiary of a trust which her father, the settlor, sought to cancel, her interest could not be adequately represented by her father, and an independent guardian *ad litem* was appointed for her). See *Von Bulon v. Von Bulon*, 634 F. Supp. 1284 (S.D.N.Y. 1986).

C. Citizenship

Issues about who should or should not be named in the complaint often arise in diversity cases, where the citizenship of the parties determines whether the action can be brought in federal court. Where the action is brought by a representative party, who is a real party in interest under Rule 17(a), diversity jurisdiction is now determined by the citizenship of those represented.[11] In a diversity case brought on behalf of a partnership or unincorporated association, the residence of the individual general partners of the partnership (or members of an unincorporated association) is determinative of the "residence" of the entity, and their residence must be wholly diverse from that of the opposing parties.[12]

Although the assignee of a claim for collection is generally recognized to be the real party in interest,[13] an assignment may not be collusively used to manufacture jurisdiction in the federal courts.[14]

II. PERMISSIVE AND COMPULSORY JOINDER

It is not uncommon for a plaintiff and defendant in an action to be joined by additional parties in the original complaint or as the lawsuit progresses. The addition of a new party at the request of an existing party is known as joinder; when the additional party is added at his own request, this is known as intervention.[15] The proposed joinder or intervention of an additional party often raises questions of jurisdiction and venue, and requires the court to examine the interests of the additional party, so as to determine whether the joinder or intervention is appropriate.

This section explores the topic of joinder—both permissive and compulsory. The related topic of intervention is addressed in the succeeding section.

---

[11] In the Fall of 1988, Congress amended § 1332(c) to provide: "(2) the legal representative of the estate of a decedent shall be deemed to be a citizen only of the same state as the decedent, and the legal representative of an infant or incompetent shall be deemed to be a citizen only of the same state as the infant or incompetent." This amendment eliminates the prior confusing law in the area.

[12] See Lewis v. Odell, 503 F.2d 445 (2d Cir. 1974); Bamco 18 v. Reeves, 675 F. Supp. 826 (S.D.N.Y. 1987). But see Carlsberg Resources Corp. v. Cambria Sav. & Loan Ass'n, 554 F.2d 1254 (3d Cir. 1977) (in determining existence of diversity of citizenship in action by limited partnership, the court must look to citizenship of limited as well as general partners).

[13] Supra note 3.

[14] 28 U.S.C. § 1359.

[15] New York Ass'n for Retarded Children v. Carey, 438 F. Supp. 440, 445 (E.D.N.Y. 1977).

A. Permissive Joinder

Fed. R. Civ. P. 20(a) provides that a court may, but need not, permit additional parties to be joined in an action if:

* a right to relief is asserted by (or against) them jointly,[16] severally,[17] or in the alternative;[18]

* the right to relief arises out of the same transaction or series of transactions;[19] and

* there is at least one question of law or fact common to all parties sought to be joined.[20]

Generally, courts are liberal when applying the three enumerated criteria.[21] A plaintiff joined in the action may seek relief that is separate or joint from that being sought by other plaintiffs. It is not necessary that each plaintiff be interested in every cause of action or in all the relief prayed for, so long as the relief each seeks arises out of the "same transaction." A claim is deemed to have arisen out of the "same transaction" if there is any factual relationship to the claims joined. The "common question" requirement is satisfied if there is a single question of law or fact common to all parties joined.[22]

---

[16] *See Hess v. Gray*, 85 F.R.D. 15 (N.D. Ill. 1979).

[17] *See General Inv. Co. of Conn., Inc. v. Ackerman*, 37 F.R.D. 38 (S.D.N.Y. 1964) (claims under securities laws by twelve plaintiffs defrauded in single course of dealing were several in nature).

[18] *See Amalgamated Packaging Indus., Ltd. v. National Container Corp.*, 14 F.R.D. 194, 196 (S.D.N.Y. 1953) (where complaint states claim in the alternative by two plaintiffs, "a right to a single recovery is stated so that permissive joinder is appropriate").

[19] *See, e.g., Abraham v. Volkswagen of America, Inc.*, 795 F.2d 238 (2d Cir. 1986) (in a Magnuson-Moss Warranty Act suit brought by owners of Volkswagen Rabbit, district court abused its discretion in refusing to permit joinder of 75 plaintiffs where amended complaint alleged that faulty valve stem seal was single defect that caused various damages to all plaintiffs, thus satisfying same transaction or series of transactions requirement).

[20] *See Abraham v. Volkswagen of America, Inc., supra.*

[21] *See, e.g., Hercules Inc. v. Dynamic Export Corp.*, 71 F.R.D. 101 (S.D.N.Y. 1976) (rule governing joinder of additional parties should be construed liberally to foster judicial economy and avoid multiplicity of litigation).

[22] *See United States v. Yonkers Bd. of Educ.*, 518 F. Supp. 191 (S.D.N.Y. 1981).

A party who wishes to object to the joinder of an additional plaintiff or defendant must raise this objection at the outset by appropriate motion.[23] Failure to do so waives that party's right to object later on.[24]

Of course, the court can always entertain a motion (or act *sua sponte*) to sever an action for trial at any time prior to or during the trial. Such a severance may be granted pursuant to Fed. R. Civ. P. 20(b) in order to curb any extra expense, delay or other prejudice that might result from the joinder of numerous parties asserting numerous separate claims against each other.[25]

B. Compulsory Joinder

Under Fed. R. Civ. P. 19(a), the court should require the joinder of any party who has a material interest in the case, and whose absence would result in substantial prejudice, either to that person or to the other parties already before the court (a so-called "conditionally necessary" party).[26]

A necessary party is one who has a joint interest in the subject matter of the action and, therefore, ought to be joined if possible. The interest of a conditionally necessary party in the action is severable from the interests of other parties, however, so the court can still proceed to determine the rights and liabilities of the parties before the court, even if the necessary party cannot be joined for some reason.[27] Two criteria are to be used to determine whether an absent person is conditionally necessary (that is to say, whether the absent person should be joined if feasible). A person is necessary if:

---

23 *See* Fed. R. Civ. P. 21.

24 *See, e.g., Celanese Corp. of America v. Vandelia Warehouse Corp.*, 424 F.2d 1176 (7th Cir. 1970) (proper remedy for misjoined party is timely notice to drop improper party; failure to raise timely objection constitutes waiver of objection to improper party's continued presence in proceeding).

25 *See, e.g., Vulcan Society v. Fire Dept. of City of White Plains*, 82 F.R.D. 379 (S.D.N.Y. 1979) (court ordered separate trial of issues not common to all defendants); *cf. United States v. Anchor Line, Ltd.*, 232 F. Supp. 379 (S.D.N.Y. 1964) (severance of claims would lead to delay, inconvenience and added expense, results which Rule 20 seeks to prevent). *See also McNally v. Simons*, 29 F. Supp. 926 (S.D.N.Y. 1939) (joinder of defendants is permissible if such joinder results in no substantial prejudice to defendant and if delay, expense and inconvenience to witnesses will be lessened by such joinder).

26 *See, e.g., Gramatan-Sullivan, Inc. v. Koslow*, 143 F. Supp. 641 (S.D.N.Y. 1956) (parties necessary under Rule 19 are parties jointly interested in the subject of the action), *aff'd*, 240 F.2d 523 (2d Cir.), *cert. denied*, 353 U.S. 958 (1957).

27 *Gramatan-Sullivan, Inc. v. Koslow, supra; Jones Knitting Corp. v. A.M. Pullen & Co.*, 50 F.R.D. 311 (S.D.N.Y. 1970) (a "necessary party" is one who must be joined but whose nonjoinder will not result in dismissal, if there is adequate excuse for his nonjoinder).

* in the person's absence complete relief cannot be accorded among those who are already parties;[28] or

* the person claims an interest in the subject of the action and an adjudication in his absence will either (1) impede his ability to protect that interest, or (2) leave someone, who is already a party, in risk of incurring multiple or inconsistent obligations by reason of the claimed interest.[29]

If a person determined to be conditionally necessary under Fed. R. Civ. P. 19(a) cannot be joined as a party, then the factors of Fed. R. Civ. P. 19(b) should be considered to determine whether the absent party is "indispensable." The failure to join an indispensable party under Rule 19 will lead to dismissal of the lawsuit.[30]

An indispensable party is one whose interests are so directly and unavoidably involved that "a final decree cannot be made without either affecting that interest, or leaving the controversy in such a condition that its final determination may be wholly inconsistent with equity and good conscience."[31] Rule 19(b) lists four factors to be considered in determining if a person is indispensable:

* the extent to which a judgment rendered in the person's absence might be prejudicial to him or those already parties;

* the extent to which, by protective provisions in the judgment, by shaping of relief, or other measures, the prejudice can be lessened or avoided;

* whether a judgment rendered in the person's absence will be adequate; and

* whether the plaintiff will have an adequate remedy if the action is dismissed for nonjoinder.

A motion to dismiss on the ground that an indispensable party has not been joined can be made prior to answering under Fed. R. Civ. P. 12(b)(7), or as late as the trial on the merits under Fed. R. Civ. P. 12(h)(2).

---

[28] Fed. R. Civ. P. 19(a)(1).

[29] Fed. R. Civ. P. 19(a)(2).

[30] *See* Fed. R. Civ. P. 19(b).

[31] *Shields v. Barrow*, 58 U.S. 130 (1855). *See also Grace v. Carroll*, 219 F. Supp. 270 (S.D.N.Y. 1963).

C. Jurisdiction and Venue

General principles of subject matter jurisdiction are fully applicable to compulsory joinder[32] and permissive joinder.[33] Problems of jurisdiction may restrict the Court's ability to join parties. A serious limitation on the joinder of parties often arises in diversity cases from the requirement that there be complete diversity of citizenship between all plaintiffs on one hand and all defendants on the other[34]—although some courts have held that a conditionally necessary party can be joined under the doctrine of ancillary jurisdiction, regardless of his citizenship.[35] It is undisputed, however, that the court lacks jurisdiction in a diversity action if the citizenship of an *indispensable* party would defeat complete diversity.[36]

While a conditionally necessary party will generally not be joined in an action if that would destroy the court's jurisdiction, such a party will be allowed to join the action at his request under Fed. R. Civ. P. 24(a) as an intervenor as of right. Professor Wright points out that courts have offered no explanation for this anomaly.[37]

Before the joinder of a party will be permitted, statutory venue requirements must be met. A court will not join a party if to do so will defeat venue—unless the party consents to being joined.[38] If the joinder of an indispensable party will defeat venue, the court cannot permit the joinder and must instead dismiss the action.[39]

---

[32] *Felix Cinematografica S.r.l. v. Penthouse Intern, Ltd.*, 99 F.R.D. 167 (S.D.N.Y. 1983).

[33] 3A Moore's Federal Practice, ¶20.05 (2d ed. 1987). *But see Shaw v. Munford*, 526 F. Supp. 1209, 1213 (S.D.N.Y. 1981) (where there is no showing that plaintiff seeks to join additional defendants solely to effectuate a remand from federal court to state court by destroying diversity, court in exercise of sound discretion may permit new parties to be added even though diversity jurisdiction is thereby destroyed).

[34] *Wasserman v. Perugini*, 173 F.2d 305, 306 (2d Cir. 1949).

[35] *New York State Ass'n for Retarded Children v. Carey*, 438 F. Supp. at 445 (E.D.N.Y. 1977).

[36] *See Carlton v. Bawn, Inc.*, 751 F.2d 781, 786 (5th Cir. 1985) (indispensable party cannot be joined unless his presence in action is consistent with statutory limitation on subject matter jurisdication).

[37] 7 Wright, Miller, & Kane § 1610 at 150 (2d ed. 1986).

[38] *Smith v. Am. Fed'n of Musicians of United States & Canada*, 47 F.R.D. 152, 154 (S.D.N.Y. 1969).

[39] *Id.* at 154.

III. INTERVENTION

Intervention is the process by which an additional party is joined in an action at the request of that party. Intervention is governed by Fed. R. Civ. P. 24. The Rule allows for two types of intervention: intervention as of right and permissive intervention.

A. Absolute Right of Intervention

1. Statutory Right

Fed. R. Civ. P. 24(a)(1) recognizes a party's absolute right to intervene whenever a federal statute unconditionally confers such a right. It is sometimes difficult to determine, however, whether a statute is bestowing an unconditional right to intervene under 24(a)(1) or a conditional right to intervene under 24(b)(1). Only the *un*conditional grant of such a right will entitle the party to intervene as of right.

Statutory authority exists granting an unconditional right of intervention to the United States (or a state) whenever the constitutionality of a federal (or state) law is called into question.[40] Other statutes also allow the United States to intervene, either expressly or by interpretation, in various other types of disputes.[41]

Private parties have been held to have an absolute right to intervene under such statutes as the Fair Labor Standards Act, the National Labor Relations Act, and the Civil Rights Act of 1964, among others.[42]

2. Non-Statutory Right

Fed. R. Civ. P. 24(a)(2) confers an absolute right of intervention when an applicant can demonstrate an interest which may be adversely affected by an adjudication of the action in his absence. An application for intervention under this section must:

    1. be timely;

---

[40] 28 U.S.C. § 2403.

[41] *See In re Transvision, Inc.*, 217 F.2d 243 (2d Cir. 1954) (SEC has right to intervene in proceedings brought under Chapter XI of Bankruptcy Act for purpose of urging dismissal of proceeding if it was brought improperly); *Rivoli Trucking Corp. v. New York Shipping Ass'n*, 167 F. Supp. 943 (S.D.N.Y. 1957) (Federal Maritime Board has right to intervene in action under Shipping Act of 1916, 46 U.S.C.A. § 801 *et seq.*, to protect its own jurisdiction).

[42] 33 U.S.C. § 1365(b)(1)(B); 29 U.S.C. § 160(f); 42 U.S.C. § 2000e - 5(f)(1).

2. establish the applicant's interest in the subject matter of the action;

3. show that the applicant's ability to protect this interest may be impaired by a disposition of the action; and

4. show that this interest is not adequately represented or protected by the existing parties.[43]

Rule 24(a) no longer requires the applicant to establish that judgment in his absence will bind him under the doctrine of *res judicata*.

B. Permissive Intervention

Fed. R. Civ. P. 24(b) permits, but does not require, intervention when (a) a permissive right to intervene is provided by a federal statute, or (b) the applicant's claim or defense has a question of law or fact in common with the main action. The rule is intended to reduce court congestion and undue delay and expense to all parties by encouraging the consolidation of claims.

Intervention under Rule 24(b) is within the court's discretion. In the exercise of its discretion, the court may limit the intervention to certain issues, or place other conditions on it (*e.g.*, the court may allow intervention on condition that it not affect any orders already entered in the case).[44]

Rule 24(b) also provides for permissive intervention by federal or state officials or agencies when a statute, regulation or executive order is being relied upon by a party as the basis of a claim or defense. If the government intervenes, it waives sovereign immunity and submits to the jurisdiction of the court.[45] Some courts have refused to recognize this waiver, however, and therefore have denied the government leave to intervene.[46]

C. Procedure and Jurisdiction

1. General Requirements

All applications for leave to intervene must be made in a timely fashion. The determination of whether an application is timely is left to the sound discretion

---

[43] *E.g., LaRouche v. Federal Bureau of Investigation*, 677 F.2d 256, 257 (2d Cir. 1982).

[44] *E.g., SEC v. Everest Management Corp.*, 75 F.2d 1236 (2d Cir. 1972). *See Spirt v. Teachers Ins. and Annuity Ass'n*, 93 F.R.D. 627, 636 (S.D.N.Y. 1982) (trial court may condition intervention by requiring intervenor to abide by court's previous decisions or by limiting issues that intervenor is permitted to contest).

[45] *Rank v. Krug*, 142 F. Supp. 1, 67 (S.D. Cal. 1956).

[46] *Humble Oil & Ref. Co. v. Sun-Oil Co.*, 190 F.2d 191 (5th Cir. 1951), *cert. denied*, 342 U.S. 920 (1952).

of the trial court.[47] Leave of the court is not required in order to file the motion for intervention. The motion to intervene must be served on all parties as provided by Fed. R. Civ. P. 5 and must be accompanied by a pleading and a statement of the grounds upon which intervention should be granted.[48]

The district court shall notify the Attorney General whenever the constitutionality of an act of Congress affecting the public interest is drawn into question, unless the United States is already a party to the action.[49]

2. Subject Matter Jurisdiction

When leave to intervene is granted as of right, the intervention generally is deemed ancillary to the main proceedings. Therefore, no independent grounds of jurisdiction are required.[50]

On the other hand, when intervention is permissive only, it is, in effect, a new claim. Therefore it is permitted only if an independent basis of jurisdiction exists as to the intervenors.[51]

3. Venue

When intervention is granted as of right, no objection to venue can be made by *any* party.[52] An intervening party waives all objections to venue whether intervening under Fed. R. Civ. P. 24(a) or 24(b).[53]

4. Intervenor's Rights

An intervening party has the right to challenge the court's subject matter jurisdiction. An intervenor may also contest the merits of any claim or de-

---

47 *E.g., Spirt v. Teachers Ins. and Annuity Ass'n*, 93 F.R.D. at 637. Timeliness is judged not merely by the calendar, but also by reference to (1) the purpose for which intervention is sought, (2) the length of time the applicant knew of its interest in the suit, and (3) whether the intervention will delay the litigation or prejudice a party to the action. *Id.*

---

48 Fed. R. Civ. P. 24(c).

---

49 *Id.*

---

50 *E.g., Nelson v. Greenspoon*, 103 F.R.D. 118 (S.D.N.Y. 1984).

---

51 *E.g., Nat'l Am. Corp. v. Fed. Republic of Nigeria*, 597 F.2d 314 (S.D.N.Y. 1977).

---

52 *See Stewart-Warner Corp. v. Westinghouse Electric Corp.*, 325 F.2d 822 (2d Cir. 1963), *cert. denied*, 376 U.S. 944 (1964) (where plaintiff brought suit with full knowledge that third party would intervene, destroying venue, plaintiff waived any objection to venue).

---

53 *Trans World Airlines, Inc. v. Civil Aeronautics Board*, 339 F.2d 56, 64 (2d Cir. 1964).

fense.[54] However, intervention will not be allowed for the purpose of impeaching a decree already made. Prior orders in the case should not be set aside unless it is clear that they would deprive the intervening party of substantial rights which the intervenor has not been remiss in pursuing.[55]

Intervening parties have the right to assert counterclaims, cross-claims, and third-party claims pursuant to Fed. R. Civ. P. 13 and 14 as long as the court has not prohibited such claims as a condition of granting permissive intervention.[56] Counterclaims asserted by an intervenor are supported by ancillary jurisdiction when the intervention was allowed as of right.[57] However, there must exist an independent basis for federal jurisdiction over the counterclaim when intervention is merely permissive.[58]

5. Appeal

The decision of a district court must generally be final in order to be appealable. Because an order allowing a party to intervene is not a final order, it is not appealable.[59] An order denying permissive intervention is also generally not appealable, unless it is argued that the district court abused its discretion.[60] However, an order denying intervention as of right is appealable.[61]

Once intervention is allowed, intervenors may appeal from all interlocutory and final orders which affect them as they were original parties to the action.[62]

---

[54] *E.g.*, *In re Oceana Int'l, Inc.*, 49 F.R.D. 329 (S.D.N.Y. 1969).

[55] *In re First Colonial Corp. of America*, 544 F.2d 1291 (5th Cir.), *cert. denied*, 431 U.S. 904 (1977).

[56] *See Stewart-Warner Corp. v. Westinghouse Electric Corp.*, 325 F.2d at 827 (reversing district court order denying intervenor right to assert counterclaims and defenses against plaintiff).

[57] *See* note 50, *supra*.

[58] *See* note 51, *supra*.

[59] *Ionian Shipping Co. v. British Law Ins. Co.*, 426 F.2d 186, 188 (2d Cir. 1970).

[60] *Lipsett v. United States*, 359 F.2d 956, 959 (2d Cir. 1966); *Brotherhood of R.R. Trainmen v. Baltimore & Ohio R.R.*, 331 U.S. 519, 524-25 (1947).

[61] *Stringfellow v. Concerned Neighbors in Action*, 107 S. Ct. 1177 (1987); *Ionian Shipping Co. v. British Law Ins. Co.*, 426 F.2d at 188 (*quoting Sam Fox Publishing Co. v. United States*, 366 U.S. 683, 688 (1961)).

[62] *See Fishgold v. Sullivan Drydock & Repair Corp.*, 328 U.S. 275 (1946) (allowing intervening party to appeal from adverse judgment against original defendant).

IV. IMPLEADER

Third-party practice in the Federal Courts is governed by Fed. R. Civ. P. 14. That Rule allows a defendant to bring into the action another party who is or may be liable for all or a part of the plaintiff's claim against the defendant, a process also known as impleader. The purpose of impleader is to protect the defendant from inconsistent verdicts and from delay in determining proportionate shares of liability. The party utilizing this procedure is designated a third-party plaintiff. The impleaded party is designated the third-party defendant.

When a counterclaim is asserted against a plaintiff, the plaintiff becomes a defendant within the counterclaim and is entitled to implead a third party in the same manner as any other defendant may utilize impleader.[63]

Impleader is confined to those situations in which the defending party has an actual or potential right to indemnity, subrogation, or contribution from the impleaded third-party defendant.[64] Whether the impleading party has such a right is a question of substantive law and, under the *Erie* doctrine, the federal court must consult the appropriate state law in cases where jurisdiction is based on diversity of citizenship.[65] Impleader under Rule 14 is merely a procedural device and creates no substantive rights.

Impleader is available to a defendant even though liability to the plaintiff may rest upon a different theory than the one asserted against the third-party defendant.[66] In fact, no legal relationship between the plaintiff and the third-party defendant need exist. The only nexus required between the original complaint and the third-party complaint is that the third-party plaintiff must be seeking to hold the impleaded third party liable for plaintiff's claim against him.

---

[63] Fed. R. Civ. P. 14(b).

[64] *See generally Index Fund, Inc. v. Hagopian*, 417 F. Supp. 738, 22 Fed. R. Serv. 2d 1273 (S.D.N.Y. 1976).

[65] *Paone v. Aeon Realty Corp.*, 58 F.R.D. 531, 533 (S.D.N.Y. 1973).

[66] *Gardner v. United States*, 36 F.R.D. 453, 454 (S.D.N.Y. 1964). *See generally Stratton Group, Ltd. v. Sprayregen*, 466 F. Supp. 1180 (S.D.N.Y. 1979) (once third-party action is brought, liability of third-party defendant requires independent substantive basis).

Where the United States is a defendant, it is allowed to implead a third party under Fed. R. Civ. P. 14, subject to jurisdictional limitations.[67] The United States may also be impleaded as a third-party defendant under the Federal Tort Claims Act.[68]

A. Type of Claims Allowed to be Impleaded

Impleader is permissive and not compulsory. An original party is permitted, but not obliged, to implead a third party. Neither the failure to do so nor the court's refusal to permit impleader will affect any substantive rights.[69]

Although the type of claim that may be asserted by impleader is to be broadly defined under Rule 14, there must exist some attempt to pass on, to the third party, all or part of the liability asserted against the defendant.[70] An entirely separate claim may not be asserted against a third party even though it arises out of the same set of facts as the main claim.

Traditional tests employed under Rule 14(a) allow impleader of claims which:

* "must depend upon the outcome of the main claim,"[71]

* are "derivative of the outcome of the main claim,"[72] or

* represent an attempt to pass on liability.[73]

---

[67] *See Hipp v. United States*, 313 F. Supp. 1152 (E.D.N.Y. 1970) (United States allowed to implead motorist under Federal Tort Claims Act).

[68] 28 U.S.C. § 1346(b); *see Berger v. Winer Sportswear, Inc.*, 394 F. Supp. 1110 (S.D.N.Y. 1975) (United States may be impleaded under Fed. R. Civ. P. 14(a) when jurisdiction is asserted under Federal Tort Claims Act and claim raised is one which might have been made against it in independent suit).

[69] *See Stratton Group Ltd. v. Sprayregen*, 466 F. Supp. at 1186 (Rule 14 does not provide substantive theory of recovery but stands merely as procedural device).

[70] *Patrick v. Beasley*, 15 F.R.D. 204, 205 (S.D.N.Y. 1953).

[71] *Index Fund, Inc. v. Hagopian*, 22 Fed. R. Serv. 2d at 1278.

[72] *Id.*

[73] *See United States v. Joe Grasso & Sons, Inc.*, 380 F.2d 749 (5th Cir. 1967) (discussing traditional tests for type of "claim" allowable under Rule 14(a)).

B. Rights of Each Party

1. Third-Party Defendant

Fed. R. Civ. P. 14(a) gives the third-party defendant a permissive right to assert against the plaintiff a claim arising out of the transaction or occurrence that is the subject matter of plaintiff's claim against the original defendant (a so-called "permissive claim"). A permissive claim is generally considered ancillary to the main action and therefore has no effect on jurisdiction and venue requirements.[74]

The third-party defendant has the right to participate in the trial of the main claim and is bound by its adjudication whether he chooses to participate or not.[75] The third-party defendant may assert against the plaintiff any defenses which the third-party plaintiff has to plaintiff's claim.[76] This right protects him where the third-party plaintiff neglects to assert a proper defense to the plaintiff's action.

The procedures for bringing counterclaims and cross-claims under Fed. R. Civ. P. 13 are expressly incorporated into third-party practice under Fed. R. Civ. P. 14.

2. Plaintiff

The plaintiff's right to amend the complaint so as to assert a claim directly against the third-party defendant is limited by the requirements that there exist federal jurisdiction over that claim and that the claim be timely brought.[77] The plaintiff may choose instead to bring a separate action against the third-party defendant.

C. Procedure

When the defendant files a third-party complaint within ten days after serving his original answer, it is unnecessary for him to obtain permission from the court to do so. Otherwise, leave of the court is required before a third-party complaint may be filed.[78]

---

[74] *Dery v. Wyer*, 265 F.2d 804, 807 (2d Cir. 1959).

[75] *Horton v. Moore-McCormack Lines, Inc.*, 326 F.2d 104, 108 (2d Cir. 1964).

[76] Fed. R. Civ. P. 14(a).

[77] *See Owen Equip. & Erection Co. v. Kroger*, 437 U.S. 365, 367 (1978); *Monarch Indus. Corp. v. American Motorists Ins. Co.*, 276 F. Supp. 972 (S.D.N.Y. 1967) (plaintiff's amendment of complaint bringing action against third-party defendant is subject to applicable statute of limitations).

[78] Fed. R. Civ. P. 14(a).

The third-party complaint can only be used to assert claims which the third-party plaintiff possesses against the third-party defendant, except in maritime cases, where the defendant may also assert a claim which the plaintiff possesses against the third-party defendant.[79]

In answering the third-party complaint, the impleaded party may assert objections and defenses, pursuant to Fed. R. Civ. P. 12, either to the third-party complaint or to the original complaint.[80] The answer must be served on both the plaintiff and the third-party plaintiff.[81]

The court has discretion to refuse to entertain a third-party claim.[82] Any party may make a motion to strike the third-party claim, or sever it from the main action.

D. Jurisdiction

Even where no diversity of citizenship exists between the defendant and the impleaded party and there is no other basis for asserting federal jurisdiction, courts will permit impleader on the basis of ancillary jurisdiction.[83] Courts are in disagreement as to whether jurisdiction over the third-party claim continues after the main action has been settled where the third-party claim was supported only by ancillary jurisdiction.[84]

No independent basis of jurisdiction is required to permit a third-party defendant to raise defenses to the plaintiff's claims or to assert "permissive claims" against the plaintiff.[85]

When the plaintiff does not amend the complaint to assert claims directly against the third-party defendant, no independent ground of jurisdiction need

---

[79] Fed. R. Civ. P. 14(a),(c).

[80] Fed. R. Civ. P. 14(a).

[81] Fed. R. Civ. P. 5(a).

[82] *E.g.*, *Olympic Corp. v. Societe Generale*, 462 F.2d 376, 379 (2d Cir. 1972).

[83] *Dery v. Wyer*, 265 F.2d at 807.

[84] For law of New York federal courts, *see Dery v. Wyer*, 265 F.2d at 808, and *McDonald v. Blue Jeans Corp.*, 183 F. Supp. 149, 151 (S.D.N.Y. 1960) (allowing for jurisdiction to continue after main action was settled).

[85] *Dery v. Wyer*, 265 F.2d at 807.

exist between the two.[86] Where the plaintiff amends his complaint to assert a claim against the third-party defendant, an independent basis for subject-matter jurisdiction over that claim is required.[87]

E. Service of Process; Venue

The territorial limits of third-party process are governed by Fed. R. Civ. P. 4(f). Because a third-party claim is deemed ancillary to the main action, no objections to venue may be made by any party.[88]

F. Judgment and Appeal

The dismissal of a third-party complaint while the main action is pending is an interlocutory order that is not appealable unless the district court determined it to be final under Fed. R. Civ. P. 54(b).[89] An order denying leave to file a third-party complaint is not a final order and, therefore, is also not appealable.[90] Nor may the plaintiff take an immediate appeal from a court's decision to allow the impleader of a third party.[91]

Courts are in disagreement as to whether a third-party defendant has the right to appeal from a judgment entered only against the defendant where the plaintiff did not join the third-party defendant in the original claim.[92]

G. Admiralty Practice

The unification of civil and admiralty practice was accomplished in 1966. The impleader procedures of Fed. R. Civ. P. 14(a) apply to maritime actions as well as all other civil actions. In addition, Fed. R. Civ. P. 14(c) preserves the special admiralty procedure allowing third-party claims based on the liability of the third-party defendant directly to the original plaintiff.

---

86 *E.g.*, *Peter Pan Fabrics, Inc. v. Kay Windsor Frocks, Inc.*, 187 F. Supp. 763, 765 (S.D.N.Y. 1959).

87 *E.g.*, *Owen Equip. & Erection Co. v. Kroger*, 437 U.S. 365, 367 (1978).

88 *ABCKO Music, Inc. v. Beverly Glen Music, Inc.*, 554 F. Supp. 410, 412 (S.D.N.Y. 1983).

89 *Luckenbach Steamship Co. v. H. Muehlstein & Co., Inc.*, 280 F.2d 755, 757 (2d Cir. 1960). *See also Paliaga v. Luckenbach Steamship Co.*, 301 F.2d 403 (2d Cir. 1962) (dismissal of third-party complaint held appealable where original action had already been dismissed).

90 *State of Minnesota v. Pickands Mather & Co.*, 636 F.2d 251, 255 (8th Cir. 1980).

91 *Skelly Oil Co. v. Zimmerman*, 332 F.2d 618, 619 (10th Cir. 1964).

92 *See Kicklighter v. Nails by Jannee, Inc.*, 616 F.2d 734 (5th Cir. 1980) (third-party defendant who actively participated in trial of main case but did not present defense to original claim was entitled to assert on appeal errors in main case).

1. Jurisdiction under Rule 14(c)

Most courts apply the traditional admiralty rule requiring that there be admiralty jurisdiction or some other basis for federal jurisdiction to sustain a third-party claim under Rule 14(c).[93] However, the Second Circuit has permitted impleader under Rule 14(c) based on ancillary jurisdiction, even when the third-party complaint asserts a state law claim.[94]

2. Right to Jury Trial

Under traditional admiralty practice, the plaintiff is allowed to choose whether the trial shall be to a jury or to the court. That practice has been continued under the 1966 unification.[95]

V. INTERPLEADER

Fed. R. Civ. P. 22 allows a party, against whom are asserted several mutually exclusive claims regarding the same debt or property, to join all adverse claimants in one action, requiring them to litigate among themselves to determine which has a valid claim to the debt or property. This procedure, known as interpleader, protects stakeholders against multiple judgments resulting from inconsistent determinations of liability to different claimants in separate suits.[96]

Traditionally, interpleader was used to protect a stakeholder against two or more mutually exclusive claims in which only one party would be successful on the merits of that claim. More recently, it has been used to assure a fair distribution among claimants where all claims may have merit.[97]

An interpleader action must be brought by the stakeholder and not the claimant. A stakeholder must have a *bona fide* fear of adverse claimants to warrant the use of interpleader.[98] Claimants are "adverse" to one another (1) when each claimant asserts a right to the debt or property as sole benefi-

---

[93] *Bernard v. U.S. Lines, Inc.*, 475 F.2d 1134 (4th Cir. 1973).

[94] *Leather's Best, Inc. v. S.S. Mormaclynx*, 451 F.2d 800, 810-11 n.12 (2d Cir. 1971).

[95] *Harrison v. Flota Mercante Grancolombiana, S.A.*, 577 F.2d 968 (5th Cir. 1978).

[96] *A/S Krediit Pank v. Chase Manhattan Bank*, 155 F. Supp. 30, 33 (S.D.N.Y. 1957).

[97] *State Farm Fire & Cas. Co. v. Tashire*, 386 U.S. 523 (1967).

[98] *See generally New York Life Ins. Co. v. Connecticut Dev. Auth.*, 700 F.2d 91 (2d Cir. 1983) (discharge of stakeholder may be delayed or denied if stakeholder acted in bad faith).

ciary,[99] (2) when one claimant asserts a claim as superior to that of another claimant by virtue of attachment or garnishment,[100] or (3) when all claims exceed the limit of the stakeholder's liability and all claimants cannot be fully compensated.[101]

There are two essential types of interpleader actions: interpleader by statute, and rule interpleader. Each stakeholder should consider carefully the form of interpleader because the choice of one form over the other will affect the jurisdiction, venue and service of process requirements in the case.

A. Statutory Interpleader

The first federal interpleader statute was passed in 1917 and amended in 1925, 1926 and 1936. Provisions of the 1936 statute have been substantially preserved and now appear in Title 28 of the United States Code in three sections:

> 28 U.S.C. § 1335 - jurisdiction
> § 1397 - venue
> § 2361 - process and procedure

Fed. R. Civ. P. 22(2) preserves statutory interpleader, but mandates that such actions be subject to the provisions of the Federal Rules of Civil Procedure.

1. Jurisdiction

Section 1335(a) of Title 28 confers original jurisdiction on the federal district courts. Statutory interpleader has always been based on diversity of citizenship among claimants—diversity between *any* two adverse claimants being sufficient. The citizenship of the stakeholder is irrelevant.[102]

2. Jurisdictional Amount

The amount in controversy must be at least $500.[103] This requirement may be met by an aggregate of the adverse claims.[104]

---

[99] *Metropolitan Life Ins. Co. v. Dumpson*, 194 F. Supp. 9 (S.D.N.Y. 1961).

[100] *Loew's, Inc. v. Hoyt Management Corp.*, 83 F. Supp. 863 (S.D.N.Y. 1949).

[101] *State Farm Fire & Cas. Co. v. Tashire*, 386 U.S. 523 (1967).

[102] *Id.* at 530.

[103] 28 U.S.C. § 1335(a).

[104] *Metropolitan Life Ins. Co. v. Dunne*, 2 F. Supp. 165, 166 (S.D.N.Y. 1931).

3. Venue

Venue is proper so long as any of the claimants reside in the district in which the action is brought.[105] This rule affords a remedy to the stakeholder who cannot obtain service on all claimants in any one state.

4. Service of Process

Nationwide service of process is allowed in statutory interpleader actions.[106]

5. Deposit in Court Registry

The deposit of funds or the giving of a bond by the plaintiff is a condition precedent to obtaining statutory interpleader jurisdiction.[107] The court has flexibility in shaping the order for such deposit or bond.[108]

B. Rule Interpleader

Fed. R. Civ. P. 22(1) liberalizes the old equity practice of interpleader by employing the notion of joinder in the alternative, as is provided in Fed. R. Civ. P. 20. Rule interpleader under Fed. R. Civ. P. 22(1) is the more modern method of obtaining interpleader relief; most of the technical restrictions of former bills of interpleader have been eliminated.

1. Jurisdiction

Under rule interpleader, the jurisdictional requirements are the same as in any other civil action. Unlike statutory interpleader, no subject matter jurisdiction is granted under Rule 22(1); therefore, some other basis for jurisdiction must exist (either diversity of citizenship or the existence of a federal question).[109]

If jurisdiction is based upon diversity of citizenship, complete diversity must exist between the plaintiff and all of the adverse claimants. However, all claimants need not be diverse from one another.[110] Litigation among the claimants themselves has been held to be ancillary to the original suit.[111]

---

[105] 28 U.S.C. § 1397.

[106] 28 U.S.C. § 2361.

[107] 28 U.S.C. § 1335(a)(2).

[109] *Cowan v. United States*, 172 F. Supp. 291 (S.D.N.Y. 1959).

[110] *Baron Bros. Co. v. Stewart*, 182 F. Supp. 893, 895 (S.D.N.Y. 1960).

[111] *Republic of China v. American Express Co.*, 195 F.2d 230, 234 (2d Cir. 1952).

PARTIES

2. Amount in Controversy

The threshold amount in controversy must be the same as in any other civil action (*i.e.*, in excess of $50,000).

3. Venue

The action must be brought in the district court in which plaintiff resides or in which all defendants reside.[112]

4. Service of Process

Service of process requirements are the same as in any other civil action.[113]

5. Deposit in Court Registry

There is no requirement in a rule interpleader action that the "stake" be deposited into court. However, the court has equitable power to require or accept such a deposit or a bond.[114]

C. Conduct of an Interpleader Action

1. Discharge of the Stakeholder

In statutory interpleader actions, the district court may discharge the plaintiff from further liability and make permanent its injunction barring claimants from bringing suit in another court.[115] Although not expressly provided for under Rule 22(1), the district court holds the same powers in a rule interpleader action.[116]

2. Litigation Among the Claimants

After a determination has been made that interpleader is appropriate, the district court will proceed as in any other civil case to adjudicate the respective claims of each claimant.

---

[112] 28 U.S.C. § 1391.

[113] *See* Fed. R. Civ. P. 4.

[114] *United States v. Coumantaros*, 146 F. Supp. 51, 53 (S.D.N.Y. 1956).

[115] 28 U.S.C. § 2361.

[116] 3A Moore's Federal Practice, ¶ 22.14[1] (2d ed. 1987).

3. Claim of Indecendent Liability

The traditional rules of interpleader did not allow one of the claimants to assert a claim against the stakeholder which was independent of any question of title to the stake. Generally, this rule has been disregarded by modern courts, which usually permit interpleader and independent claims to proceed simultaneously.[117]

4. Power to Enjoin Other Proceedings

In any statutory interpleader action, the district court may issue an injunction to stay state and federal court proceedings.[118] An injunction to stay such proceedings in a rule interpleader action may be allowed if the case falls within one of the exceptions under 28 U.S.C. § 2283.[119]

5. Jury Trial

The determination of whether interpleader should be allowed is properly made by the court, not a jury.[120] There is disagreement as to whether interpleaded claimants have a right to a jury trial of their claims to the interpleader fund.[121]

6. Applicable Law

The *Erie* doctrine dictates that state law will determine the applicable substantive law of torts/contracts/property in interpleader actions based on diversity of citizenship.[122]

Under the *Klaxon* doctrine, the choice of applicable substantive law is to be made in accordance with the conflict of laws rule of the state in which the

---

[117] *Poland v. Atlantis Credit Corp.*, 179 F. Supp. 863 (S.D.N.Y. 1960).

[118] 28 U.S.C. § 2361.

[119] A federal court may not grant an injunction to stay proceedings in a state court except where expressly authorized by Congress, or where necessary in aid of its jurisdiction, or to protect or effectuate its judgments. 28 U.S.C. § 2283.

[120] *Jefferson Standard Ins. Co. v. Craven*, 365 F. Supp. 861, 863 (M.D. Pa. 1973).

[121] *See generally Beacon Theatres, Inc. v. Westover*, 359 U.S. 500 (1959).

[122] *Erie Railroad v. Tompkins*, 304 U.S. 64 (1938). *See Prudential Ins. Co. v. Glasgow*, 208 F.2d 908 (2d Cir. 1953) (state law of New York applied in statutory interpleader action).

federal court sits.[123] This doctrine applies in all statutory interpleader actions.[124] Most courts hold that the doctrine applies as well in rule interpleader actions.[125]

7. Appeal

If an action for either statutory or rule interpleader is dismissed, the dismissal is ordinarily a final order and, therefore, appealable.[126] If the action contains other unresolved claims (such as where interpleader is sought by way of counterclaim), the dismissal would be interlocutory (and therefore *not* appealable absent a Rule 54(b) order).[127] An order granting interpleader is also interlocutory in the absence of a Rule 54(b) determination.[128] The granting or denial of interlocutory injunctive orders is appealable under 28 U.S.C § 1292(a).[129]

8. Equitable Doctrines

Neither the federal interpleader statutes nor Fed. R. Civ. P. 22 expressly addresses such issues as laches, estoppel, general lack of equity, or award to the stakeholder of costs and attorneys' fees out of the interpleader fund. Drawing on the history of interpleader as an equitable device, the federal courts have generally incorporated these principles into federal interpleader practice.[130]

---

123 *Klaxon Co. v. Stentor Electric Mfg. Co.*, 313 U.S. 487 (1941).

124 *See Griffin v. McCoach*, 313 U.S. 498 (1941) (extending *Klaxon* doctrine to statutory interpleader actions).

125 3A Moore's Federal Practice, ¶22.14[5] (2d ed. 1987).

126 *Republic of China v. American Express Co., supra.*

127 Fed. R. Civ. P. 54(b) allows the district court to direct immediate entry of a final judgment disposing of fewer than all of the claims or parties upon a determination that there is "no just reason for delay."

128 *Guy v. Citizens Fidelity Bank & Trust Co. v. Byrne*, 429 F.2d 828, 830 (6th Cir. 1970).

129 *Id.* at 831; *John Hancock Mut. Life Ins. Co. v. Kraft*, 200 F.2d 952, 953 (2d Cir. 1953).

130 *See United Artists Corp. v. Fields Productions, Inc.*, 363 F. Supp. 903 (S.D.N.Y. 1973); *Royal School Laboratories, Inc. v. Town of Watertown*, 358 F.2d 813, 817 n.3 (2d Cir. 1966) (discussing doctrine that interpleader may not be invoked by plaintiff with unclean hands); *Travelers Indem. Co. v. Israel*, 354 F.2d 488 (2d Cir. 1965).

D. Interpleader and the United States

1. Statutory Interpleader by the United States

38 U.S.C. § 445 allows the United States to commence an interpleader action when it acknowledges its indebtedness upon a contract of National Service Life Insurance or U.S. Government life insurance, and when there is a dispute as to the persons entitled to payment.

2. United States as Adverse Claimant

The doctrine of sovereign immunity precludes the United States from being named as a party in an interpleader action without its consent. Neither 28 U.S.C. § 1335 nor Rule 22 provides such consent. However, in an interpleader action to quiet title to real property, 28 U.S.C. § 2410(a) permits the stakeholder to name the United States as one of the claimants.

CHAPTER ELEVEN

CLASS ACTIONS AND OTHER REPRESENTATIVE LITIGATION

by Richard D. Greenfield, Esq.

I. THE APPLICABLE RULES

Three of the Federal Rules of Civil Procedure, amended Rules 23, 23.1 and 23.2, provide the procedural foundation for representative litigation in the Federal Courts. These rules are set forth below in their entirety for the convenience of the reader. The Rules Advisory Committee Notes to Amended Rule 23 are set forth at 39 F.R.D. 69, 98 (1966).

1. *Rule 23. Class Actions.*

(a) Prerequisites to a Class Action. One or more members of a class may sue or be sued as representative parties on behalf of all only if (1) the class is so numerous that joinder of all members is impracticable, (2) there are questions of law or fact common to the class, (3) the claims or defenses of the representative parties are typical of the claims or defenses of the class, and (4) the representative parties will fairly and adequately protect the interests of the class.

(b) Class Actions Maintainable. An action may be maintained as a class action if the prerequisites of subdivision (a) are satisfied, and in addition:

(1) the prosecution of separate actions by or against individual members of the class would create a risk of

(A) inconsistent or varying adjudications with respect to individual members of the class which would establish incompatible standards of conduct for the party opposing the class, or

(B) adjudications with respect to individual members of the class which would as a practical matter be dispositive of the interests of the other members not parties to the adjudications or substantially impair or impede their ability to protect their interests; or

(2) the party opposing the class has acted or refused to act on grounds generally applicable to the class, thereby making appropriate final injunctive relief or corresponding declaratory relief with respect to the class as a whole; or

(3) the court finds that the questions of law or fact common to the members of the class predominate over any questions affecting only individual members, and that a class action is superior to other available methods for the fair and efficient adjudication of the controversy. The matters pertinent to the findings include: (A) the interest of members of the class in individually controlling the prosecution or defense of separate actions; (B) the extent and nature of any litigation concerning the controversy already commenced by or against members of the class; (C) the desirability or undesirability of concentrating the litigation of the claims in the particular forum; (D) the difficulties likely to be encountered in the management of a class action.

(c) Determination by Order Whether Class Action to be Maintained; Notice; Judgment; Actions Conducted Partially as Class Actions.

(1) As soon as practicable after the commencement of an action brought as a class action, the court shall determine by order whether it is to be so maintained. An order under this subdivision may be conditional, and may be altered or amended before the decision on the merits.

(2) In any class action maintained under subdivision (b)(3), the court shall direct to the members of the class the best notice practicable under the circumstances, including individual notice to all members who can be identified through reasonable effort. The notice shall advise each member that (A) the court will exclude him from the class if he so requests by a specified date; (b) the judgment, whether favorable or not, will include all members who do not request exclusion; and (C) any member who does not request exclusion may, if he desires, enter an appearance through his counsel.

(3) The judgment in an action maintained as a class action under subdivision (b)(1) or (b)(2), whether or not favorable to the class, shall include and describe those whom the court finds to be members of the class. The judgment in an action maintained as a class action

under subdivision (b)(3), whether or not favorable to the class shall include and specify or describe those to whom the notice provided in subdivision (c)(2) was directed, and who have not requested exclusion, and whom the court finds to be members of the class.

(4) When appropriate (A) an action may be brought or maintained as a class action with respect to particular issues, or (B) a class may be divided into subclasses and each subclass treated as a class, and the provision of this rule shall then be construed and applied accordingly.

(d) Orders in Conduct of Actions. In the conduct of actions to which this rule applies, the court may make appropriate orders: (1) determining the course of proceedings or prescribing measures to prevent undue repetition or complication in the presentation of evidence or argument; (2) requiring, for the protection of the members of the class or otherwise for the fair conduct of the action, that notice be given in such manner as the court may direct to some or all of the members of any step in the action, or of the proposed extent of the judgment, or of the opportunity of members to signify whether they consider the representation fair and adequate, to intervene and present claims or defenses, or otherwise to come into the action; (3) imposing conditions on the representative parties or on intervenors; (4) requiring that the pleadings be amended to eliminate therefrom allegations as to representation of absent persons, and that the action proceed accordingly; (5) dealing with similar procedural matters. The orders may be combined with an order under Rule 16, and may be altered or amended as may be desirable from time to time.

(e) Dismissal or Compromise. A class action shall not be dismissed or compromised without the approval of the court, and notice of the proposed dismissal or compromise shall be given to all members of the class in such manner as the court directs. (As amended Feb. 28, 1966, eff. July 1, 1966.)

2. Rule 23.1. Derivative Actions by Shareholders.

In a derivative action brought by one or more shareholders or members to enforce a right of a corporation or of an unincorporated association, the corporation or association having failed to enforce a right which may properly be asserted by it, the complaint shall be verified and shall allege (1) that the plaintiff was a shareholder or member at the time of the transaction of which he complains or that his share or membership thereafter devolved on him by operation of law, and (2) that the action is not a collusive one to confer jurisdiction on a court of the United States which it would not otherwise have. The complaint shall also allege with particularity the efforts, if any, made by the plaintiff to obtain the action he desires from the directors or comparable authority and, if necessary, from the shareholders or members, and the reasons for his failure to obtain the action or for not making the effort. The derivative action may not be maintained if it appears that the plaintiff does not fairly and adequately represent the interests of the shareholders or members similarly situated in enforcing the right of the corporation or association. The action shall not be dismissed or compromised without the approval of the court, and notice of the proposed dismissal or compromise shall be given to shareholders or members in such manner as the court directs. (Added Feb. 28, 1966, eff. July 1, 1966.)

3. Rule 23.2. Actions Relating to Unincorporated Associations.

An action brought by or against the members of an unincorporated association as a class by naming certain members as representative parties may be maintained only if it appears that the representative parties will fairly and adequately protect the interests of the association and its members. In the conduct of the action the court may make appropriate orders corresponding with those described in Rule 23(d), and the procedure for dismissal or compromise of the action shall correspond with that provided in Rule 23(e). (Added Feb. 28, 1966, eff. July 1, 1966.)

II. INTRODUCTION

This chapter deals with the various types of representative actions that may be litigated in federal court. For reasons of space, the primary emphasis here will be upon class actions and, even in this regard, no "in depth" analysis can be provided when volumes have been written on the subject. No reference is made to relatively rare defendant class actions and, although some consideration is given to defense perspectives, these too are only given modest attention. For a comprehensive approach to virtually every "nook and cranny" of class actions, the reader is directed to Prof. Herbert B. Newberg's authoritative five-volume treatise, *Newberg on Class Actions—Second Edition* (Shepard's/McGraw-Hill 1985).

For all its mystique, a class action is nothing more than a simple procedural device which permits one or more persons or entities to conduct litigation on behalf of the plaintiff or against a defendant and all others similarly situated. As with any individual suit, a class action can seek injunctive or other equitable relief, damages, or some combination thereof. With the amendments to the Federal Rules in 1966, Rule 23 became an important part of the litigant's procedural arsenal, permitting the aggregation of claims and causes of action that were, previously, practically impossible to accomplish. The Hon. John P. Fullam, Chief Judge of the U.S. District Court in Philadelphia, has observed: "Rule 23 is an undoubtedly useful tool in handling complex litigation that may ultimately prove to have been one of the most significant procedural developments of the century."[1]

Although some practitioners are thought to be class action specialists, such a view mistakenly implies that there is something that is more substantive than procedural about class litigation. In fact, although specialists in certain substantive areas of the law tend to employ Rule 23 more than not (*e.g.*, securities, civil rights), there is wide applicability of this procedural framework for many forms of substantive claims including antitrust, employment discrimination, environmental and tort litigation.

It must be recognized that fundamental due process considerations are brought into play by the invocation of the representative status conferred by Rule 23. As will be discussed below, the primary consideration given by many courts in making a determination as to whether litigation should be "certified" as a class action is whether the representative party and his counsel will fairly and adequately represent the absent members of the class. Such requirement has been engrafted to Rule 23 since the traditional rule, as set forth by the Supreme Court in *Pennoyer v. Neff*, is "that one is not bound by a judgment *in personam* in a litigation in which he has not been made a party by service of process."[2] In *Hansberry v. Lee*, the Supreme Court spoke to the binding effect of class actions on nonparties:

> To these general rules is a recognized exception that, to an extent not precisely defined by judicial opinion, the judgment in a "class" or "representative" suit, to which some members of the class are parties, may bind members of the class of those represented who were not made parties to it.
>
> The class suit was an invention of equity to enable it to proceed to a decree in suits where the number of those interested in the subject of the litigation is so great that their joinder as parties in conformity to the usual rules of procedure is impracticable. Courts are not frequently called upon to proceed with causes in which the number of those interested in the litigation is so great as to make difficult or impossible the joinder of all because some are not within the jurisdiction or because their whereabouts is unknown or where if all were

---

[1] Fullam, *Federal Rule 23 - An Exercise in Utility*, 38 J. Air L & Com 369, 388 (1972).

[2] *Pennoyer v. Neff*, 95 U.S. 714 (1878).

made parties to the suit its continued abatement by the death of some would prevent or unduly delay a decree. In such cases where the interests of those not joined are of the same class as the interests of those who are, and where it is considered that the latter fairly represent the former in the prosecution of the litigation of the issues in which all have a common interest, the court will proceed to a decree.[3]

The Supreme Court went on to say that so long as there was adequate representation by the plaintiff (and, presumably, his counsel), he could bind those similarly situated who were not present:

It is familiar doctrine of the federal court that members of a class not present as parties to the litigation may be bound by the judgment where they are in fact adequately represented by parties who are present, or where they actually participate in the conduct of the litigation in which members of the class are present as parties, [citations omitted] or where the interest of the members of the class, some of whom are present as parties is joint, or where for any other reason the relationship between the parties present and those who are absent is such as legally to entitle the former to stand in judgment for the latter.

In all such cases, so far as it can be said that the members of the class who are present are, by generally recognized rules of law, entitled to stand in judgment for those who are not, we may assume for present purposes that such procedure affords a protection to the parties who are represented though absent, which would satisfy the requirements of due process and full faith and credit.[4]

It should be noted that Rule 23 cannot be used to broaden the Court's subject matter jurisdiction. Because of the limitations imposed on the procedural rules by Rule 82, a Class Action can be maintained as such only if jurisdiction exists by virtue of statutory authority or pursuant to the Court's pendent jurisdiction. In any event, jurisdiction of the Court cannot properly be "bootstrapped in" by claims possessed by absent class members which the plaintiff does not also possess.

---

[3] *Hansberry v. Lee*, 311 U.S. 32, 41-42 (1940).

---

[4] *Id.* 42-43 (citations omitted).

III. DECIDING WHETHER CLAIMS SHOULD BE ASSERTED ON A CLASS BASIS

From the practitioner's point of view, this basic question must always be asked since the assertion of claims pursuant to Rule 23 is not a step that should be taken lightly. While frequently litigation can be justified in terms of time and cost only if brought representatively rather than individually, a third alternative may be no litigation at all. By embarking upon a class action, a lawyer will be adding at least one additional dimension to litigation that may already be complex and costly. Further, by taking on responsibility to absent class members, a plaintiff and his counsel cannot readily dismiss litigation or settle to benefit the plaintiff but not others on whose behalf claims were asserted. One should also anticipate that, despite the supposed *in terrorem* effect of class actions and the mistaken belief on the part of some lawyers that the assertion of class claims will make the defendants settle quickly, such litigation can be protracted, costly and frustrating. Since the choices between unjustifiable individual litigation and complicated, expensive class litigation may be as unacceptable as no litigation, a decision must be made as to the appropriate litigation strategy. To enable the reader to make an informed decision as to whether or not to commence suit on a class basis, set forth below are a number of factors to consider.

A. Arguments in Favor

1. Individual Claims Too Small

Most class actions are commenced as such because they cannot be economically justified on any other basis. For example, a purchaser of 25 shares of artificially high priced XYZ common stock with maximum damages of $250, a purchaser of 10 bottles of adulterated apple juice, or a consumer who pays $29 more for a camera because of a price-fixing conspiracy between manufacturer and retailer cannot possibly obtain relief for their respective individual claims standing by themselves. Even if an effective "small claims" procedure existed to adjudicate such claims, the costs of investigation and development of a factual record would preclude the claimant from doing anything. More significantly, such a victim could not hope to retain competent legal counsel to pursue such claims, even if the lawyer were to receive as much as 50 percent of the amount recovered.

By aggregating the claims of all persons similarly situated (*i.e.*, those whose claims are typical and arise out of a common cause of action) and suing on a class-wide basis, a plaintiff can turn what would be an unjustifiable or marginally justifiable economic claim into one for tens of millions of dollars, or more. In the case of injunctive relief, where the plaintiff would seek, for example, the termination of an illegal or otherwise socially undesirable practice, the beneficiaries of such litigation would include not only the plaintiff but a whole class of persons affected by the wrongful actions of the defendant. By so escalating the litigation to one where a significant economic or other result can be obtained for the benefit of a class, the claim becomes transformed into one more likely to attract a competent lawyer to take on the victims' representation on a contingent-fee basis. *See Newman v. Piggie Park Enterprises*[5] (civil rights case in which statutory attorneys' fees may be awarded). In the traditional "common fund" class action, plaintiff's counsel has the incentive to apply for a fee award out of a hoped-for class-wide recovery. *See Boeing v. Van Gemert.*[6] Put simply, unless the prospect of reasonable, and even generous, attorneys' fees is on the horizon, there may be no lawyer ready, willing and able to take the victim's representation.[7]

2. Credibility of the Claimant

Putting it rather bluntly, a plaintiff and his counsel are more likely than not to be "taken seriously" if a claim is asserted on a properly pleaded class-wide basis. Because of the aggregation of claims, a well-founded cause of action prosecuted competently will create a level of enhanced credibility on the part of the plaintiff and/or his lawyer, both with the defendant and the Court. It is important to avoid creating the impression, however, that the class device has been used for its *in terrorem* impact so as to extort a settlement from the defendant. While there is absolutely nothing wrong with escalating a small claim into a multimillion dollar one if that is the only legitimate means to obtain recourse for the victim of wrongdoing, care must be exercised to avoid implying any coercive aspect of doing so.

Although some courts simply do not like class actions, the fact remains that most will apply a "smell test" to the allegations of class-wide injury. If the complaint passes that test, most courts, although remaining objective, tend to put up a protective umbrella over the absent members of the class, especially if they are perceived to be truly victims of circumstances beyond their control. Ultimately, the credibility of plaintiff and the class represented by him is manifested in a defendant's greater willingness to settle. If the plaintiff and his counsel have successfully pretried the case and put together a

---

[5] *Newman v. Piggie Park Enterprises*, 390 U.S. 400 (1968).

[6] *Boeing Co. v. Van Gemert*, 444 U.S. 472 (1980).

[7] *Deposit Guaranty National Bank v. Roper*, 445 U.S. 326, 339 (1980) "Where it is not economically feasible to obtain relief within the traditional framework of a multiplicity of small individual suits for damages, aggrieved persons may be without any effective redress unless they may employ the class action device."

persuasive demonstration of liability, that together with the defendant's exposure to a significant damage verdict should bring that defendant to the bargaining table. By contrast, in individual litigation, with a relatively smaller amount at stake, the defendant may more rationally force the case to trial.

3. Tolling of the Statute of Limitations

The proper commencement of a timely-filed class action will serve to toll the statutes of limitations applicable to those claims asserted on behalf of plaintiff and the members of the class.[8] Thus, as a practical matter, even if class certification is not granted ultimately, the applicable statutes of limitations will have been suspended from the filing of suit until denial of class certification.[9] By so acting, a plaintiff can properly "buy time" for others similarly situated so long as the claim of class status can satisfy the standards of Rule 11.

4. Extensive Discovery Rights

Although it should not make any practical difference and the potential scope of discovery should be the same for class actions as for individual litigation, courts typically permit much broader discovery to be conducted by the parties in class litigation.[10]

The evidence that a plaintiff will want to compile with respect to, for example, the dissemination of false and misleading information to the investing public, patterns of employment discrimination or price-fixing conspiracies should be as readily reachable in discovery by the individual plaintiff as to a class plaintiff. However, courts routinely permit greater latitude to class plaintiffs. The credibility afforded to a class-wide claim of wrongdoing ultimately is a potent argument for allowing the plaintiff to search for the proverbial "needle in a haystack," even if it means setting aside claims of attorney-client privilege and work product.[11]

5. Expense Allocation

Much the same as the problem facing the plaintiff seeking competent legal counsel, the expenses of prosecuting litigation on behalf of an individual plaintiff create a disproportionate burden on any potential recovery. If such

---

[8] *American Pipe & Construction Co. v. Utah*, 414 U.S. 538 (1974).

[9] *Chardon v. Soto*, 462 U.S. 650 (1983); *United Airlines v. McDonald*, 432 U.S. 385 (1977).

[10] *Hoffman v. Charnita, Inc.*, 17 Fed. R. Serv. 2d 1215 (M.D. Pa. 1973); *Branch v. Reynolds Metals Co.*, 17 Fed. R. Serv. 2d 494 (E.D. Va. 1972); *Duke v. University of Texas*, 729 F.2d 994 (1984).

[11] *Cohen v. Uniroyal*, 77 F.R.D. 685 (E.D. Pa. 1977).

expenses, whether they be in the thousands or hundreds of thousands of dollars are thought of as the "overhead" of the litigation, it is clear that by allocating them among the many members of the class, the individual proportionate burden to any one of them is relatively small. If there is an eventual recovery for the class, by spreading this litigation "overhead," including the fees awarded to plaintiff's counsel, no individual recovery will be so burdened as to eliminate it entirely. By contrast, the costs attributed to experts, transcripts and the like, if chargeable to an individual plaintiff, may wipe out any recovery.

B. Arguments Opposed

1. Cost Burdens

Except in a Rule 23(b)(2) class action, where notice is not required, plaintiffs have the obligation to notify the members of the class, after the action has been certified, of the pendency of the litigation on a class-wide basis and to afford such absent class members of the right to exclude themselves from the binding effect of the litigation pursuant to Rule 23(c)(1). In this regard, *see Eisen v. Carlisle & Jacquelin,* where the Supreme Court laid out fundamental rules regarding responsibility for notice, costs and, in particular, the necessity of individual notice even when the number of class members is in the millions.[12]

The plaintiff, or most typically, his lawyer, must agree unequivocally to be responsible for these notice costs, which can be many thousands of dollars. Further, since individual mailed notice may not be "the best notice practicable under the circumstances," the Court may require published notice, including relatively expensive advertisements in national publications.

Since the failure to fulfill the notice requirement of Rule 23(c)(2) may result in noncertification or the dissolution of a previously certified class, this cost burden must be addressed at the outset with financial provision therefor.

2. Added Complexity

The sad fact of litigation is that its complexity increases exponentially with each added issue. This is particularly so with class actions. Since very few judges will certify a class at the outset without the benefit of discovery and/or briefing, this aspect of the litigation frequently gets out of hand and takes on a life of its own, particularly if there is poor judicial control. In this regard, aggressive defense counsel will frequently turn the focus of the litigation on the plaintiff and his counsel, purportedly to test their adequacy to represent

---

[12] *Eisen v. Carlisle & Jacquelin,* 417 U.S. 156 (1974).

the putative class. Class certification motions and related discovery can provide defense counsel with an opportunity to "paper plaintiff to death" since significant issues may arise during the course of class determination, all of which may regrettably lead to delay, obfuscation and motion practice.

Further, it is not unusual for defendants to argue that discovery on the merits be deferred until the class is certified or denied, a process which may take up to several years with slow-moving judges. Unless the plaintiff has the resources and state of mind necessary to "ride out" this potential delay, it is wise to consider something other than a class action to resolve the matter in dispute.

As will be discussed below, issues such as class notice and determination of class-wide injury or damages will further complicate the proceedings, as will potential issues which may arise out of attempts by the defendants to take discovery of absent members of the class or to prevent plaintiff or his counsel from communicating with such persons.

3. Added Delay

From a plaintiff's personal perspective, all litigation takes too long to be resolved. The added complexity of class litigation, by itself, will further delay resolution. Unlike individual litigation, where once settlement agreements and releases are signed, monetary or other relief can be delivered and the matter concluded. In a class action, the execution of a settlement agreement merely ends one phase of the litigation and commences another.

Before a class action can be concluded, Rule 23(e) provides that it "shall not be dismissed or compromised without the approval of the court, and notice of the proposed dismissal or compromise shall be given to all members of the class." In the typical situation, identifying the members of the class and providing them with legally sufficient notice and time to object will take as little as two months and as long as six before a settlement hearing. Even if the settlement is approved from the bench, the matter cannot even remotely be regarded as concluded.

First, the order or judgment of dismissal must be allowed to become "final" and no longer subject to appeal by absent class members or others. Thus, at least thirty additional days must expire and, in the event of an appeal, an indeterminate amount of time can expire before the matter is resolved finally.

Second, if the resolution of the litigation on behalf of the class involves a so-called "common fund," against which plaintiff and the members of the class may claim, the process by which claims are made and the fund administered may take anywhere from a few months to a few years. While such a delay may be of no great moment to absent class members who have invested nothing of themselves in the litigation, it is frustrating, indeed, for the plaintiff who assumes the case to be over and anticipates receiving his share of the recovery.

4. Responsibility to Class Members

In a class action, the plaintiff and his counsel serve as fiduciaries to the absent members of the class. Indeed, assuming the plaintiff's claim is typical of and not antagonistic to those of the other members of the class, it is the plaintiff's counsel who ultimately has the responsibility for carrying on the litigation.[13]

In its most simplistic form, this responsibility is one that requires plaintiff's counsel to act as if each of the members of the class are his clients, to prosecute the litigation vigorously for all of them and not seek to settle the case for the benefit of the plaintiff without seeking a comparable benefit for all others similarly situated. Whereas in individual litigation, a plaintiff's counsel may get little attention from the court, the conduct of a class action by a plaintiff's counsel is subject to great scrutiny "at every turn."[14]

5. Subordination of Individual Claims

As stated above, an individual case can be resolved quickly and with a minimum of paperwork and delay. Not so with a class action which requires court approval and occasionally notice in the event of a dismissal and, in the event of a settlement, notice, a hearing and court approval. Even with a Rule 23(b)(2) class action, court approval is required for dismissal of the litigation to be dismissed with prejudice.

There are very real economic consequences that may befall a plaintiff who asserts a class claim. Whereas an individual claim may be more readily settleable by means of a repayment of the claimant's damages plus counsel fees, such a recovery is rare in cases brought to recover class-wide damages. Indeed, although the gross recovery to the class may be a high multiple of the plaintiff's individual damages, his proportionate recovery as an individual member of the class may be relatively low. While this may not be a serious issue for one with minimal damages, for whom "economic reality dictates that [the] suit proceed as a Class Action or not at all,"[15] a plaintiff with

---

[13] *Wetzel v. Liberty Mutual Co.*, 508 F.2d 239 (3d Cir.), *cert. denied,* 421 U.S. 1011 (1975).

[14] *Clark v. South Central Bell Tel. Co.*, 419 F. Supp. 697, 701 (W.D. La. 1976); *Foster v. Boise-Cascade, Inc.*, 420 F. Supp. 674, 682 (S.D. Tex. 1976), *aff'd,* 577 F.2d 335 (5th Cir. 1978); *Greenfield v. Villager Industries,* 483 F.2d 824 (3d Cir. 1973).

[15] *Eisen v. Carlisle & Jacquelin,* 417 U.S. 156, 161 (1974).

substantial individual damages has a difficult decision to make. In any event, the plaintiff's choice may be dictated more by the willingness of an attorney to take the case on a contingent basis than upon what he wants to do in ideal circumstances.

IV. A DEFENDANT'S PERSPECTIVE

Many defendants and their counsel react to the commencement of a class action in "knee-jerk" fashion and regard such an event as undoubtedly negative. Although it can hardly be said that any defendant wishes to be sued, many class actions arise out of circumstances that make them a desirable alternative to a multiplicity of individual suits.

The principal advantage to a defendant in litigating a single case in a single forum, as compared to multiple litigations, is the ability to avoid inconsistent results or being held to incompatible standards of conduct.[16]

Additionally, a defendant can realize significant cost savings as a result of litigating a single class action, even if it involves a multiplicity of individual plaintiffs. It goes without saying that uniform pretrial discovery and a single trial is not only more economical than many individual cases being litigated on an uncoordinated basis, but the class action will reduce the personal burdens on the defendant.

Although some defense lawyers will prefer denying the various plaintiffs the credibility that follows from class status, there is one overriding benefit that can be obtained from class certification of a case the defendant believes it can win. If a well-represented class action is taken to trial by the plaintiff and lost, the defendant not only has the benefit of his individual victory but the ability to have the result binding on all members of the class.

Even where the defendant's position is not one where a victory can be envisioned, the class action provides the means to resolve finally a controversy in one forum with one order that, except for "opt-outs," can bring the matter at issue to a close. The *res judicata* effect of such a final judgment, whether after settlement or otherwise, enables the defendant to put a "cap" on its liability exposure to claims and, as such, eliminate future clouds to its continued existence.

---

[16] *Sierra Club v. Hardin,* 325 F. Supp. 99 (D. Ark. 1971); Rules Advisory Committee Notes to 1966 Amendments to Rule 23, 39 F.R.D. 69, 100 (1966).

V. CLASS CERTIFICATION

A. The Class Representative

In an ideal circumstance, a plaintiff's lawyer will be able to choose among a multiplicity of ready, willing and able members of a putative class to select one who is best suited to be the representative plaintiff in a class action. However, this is not usually a luxury that is presented. More typically, it is a single potential plaintiff who approaches the lawyer with a claim which may be justifiable to assert only if prosecuted on a class-wide basis. If the plaintiff possesses a claim cognizable as a class-wide claim and no other alternative litigation format is appropriate, a class action may be the end result. In such circumstances, plaintiff's counsel will not have the benefit of choosing his ideal plaintiff to be class representative, but utilizing the client who walked through the door. However imperfect that plaintiff may be, the more enlightened courts have allowed such a person to proceed in his self-annointed capacity, so long as certain prerequisites are met.

B. Pleading

Although there is no particular language required, the complaint must set forth sufficient affirmative allegations to the effect that the action is a class action and that specified paragraphs of the Rule have been satisfied. Sample class action allegations from a complaint based upon the alleged securities fraud of defendants are set forth below:

> 1. Plaintiff brings this action as a Class Action under Rules 23(a) and 23(b)(3) of the Federal Rules of Civil Procedure. The Class is defined as all persons who purchased the common stock of XYZ during the period of May 22, 1987, through April 26, 1988, inclusive (the "Class Period") and who sustained damages as a result of such purchases. Excluded from the Class are the defendants herein, members of their immediate families and any subsidiary, affiliate or controlled person of any such person entity. The Class Period may be modified or expanded as further facts come to light.
>
> 2. The Class is so numerous that joinder of all members is impractical. There are more than 28 million shares of XYZ common stock outstanding and trading in XYZ common stock during the Class Period has been substantial. There are over 5,000 shareholders of record of XYZ and the Class clearly consists of at least several thousand persons.

CLASS ACTIONS AND OTHER REPRESENTATIVE LITIGATION

3. Plaintiff's claims are typical of the claims of the members of the Class, as plaintiff and all members of the Class sustained damages arising out of defendants' conduct in violation of federal law as complained of herein.

4. Plaintiff will fairly and adequately protect the interests of the members of the Class and has retained counsel competent and experienced in class and securities litigation.

5. A Class Action is superior to other available methods for the fair and efficient adjudication of this controversy since joinder of all members is impracticable. Further, as the damages ordered by individual members of the Class may be relatively small, the expense and burden of individual litigation make it impossible for the members of the Class individually to redress the wrongs done to them. There will be no difficulty in the management of this action as a Class Action.

6. Common questions of law and fact exist as to all members of the Class and predominate over any questions affecting solely individual members of the Class. Among the questions of law and fact common to the Class are:

(a) Whether the federal securities laws were violated by defendants' acts as alleged herein;

(b) Whether defendants participated in and pursued the conspiracy and common course of conduct complained of;

(c) Whether documents, Offering Circulars and financial statements disseminated to the investing public and the shareholders of XYZ during the Class Period omitted and/or misrepresented material facts about the business and financial condition of XYZ;

(d) Whether the defendants acted willfully, recklessly or with gross negligence in omitting and/or misrepresenting material facts or in aiding and abetting the making of such misstatements;

(e) Whether the initial offering prices and market prices of XYZ securities during the Class Period were artificially inflated due to the non-disclosures and/or misrepresentations complained of herein; and

(f) Whether the members of the Class have sustained damages and, if so, what is the proper measure of damages.

C. Class Certification Motion

Rule 23(a)(4) provides that a class action can be maintained only if "the representative parties will fairly and adequately protect the interests of the class." Plaintiff's counsel has the burden of demonstrating to the court that at least the minimal standards of representative status can be satisfied. The plaintiff indicates to the court by way of affidavit that he is a member of the putative class he seeks to represent and that his claim is typical of that of all members of the class defined by him. Although enlightened defense counsel are increasingly stipulating to the existence of a class and the adequacy of plaintiff as representative of the class, as often as not, certification is likely to be a contested issue. By local rule in many district courts, if class certification is to be contested, plaintiff must seek certification by motion, which must be filed within a specified time after commencement of the action.

The opening motion papers will consist of a memorandum of law setting forth the arguments why the case before the court warrants class certification and why the plaintiff and his counsel should be designated to represent the class. This brief is frequently "boilerplate"-laden since the action, presumably, is colorably a proper class action and plaintiff's counsel will not know what grounds a defendant will assert to the contrary. Plaintiff's counsel will accompany the initial brief with his affidavit or declaration and/or a similar one from the plaintiff setting forth their respective qualifications for representative status.

In opposing class certification, defendants frequently attack plaintiff's alleged failure to satisfy one or more of the prerequisites to the Rule, *i.e.*, numerosity, typicality or numerosity and/or a real or imagined infirmity of the plaintiff or his counsel that might serve as a basis for disqualification. These arguments may be gleaned from plaintiff's responses to interrogatories and/or document requests or from his testimony at a deposition taken in connection with the class certification motion.

It is in plaintiff's reply brief and any supplemental affidavits and/or declarations that he can truly address the issues before the court. Until the defendant has made known its arguments in opposition to class certification and the purported basis thereof, plaintiff is not in a position to rebut them. As a matter of good practice, it is thus more important to obtain ample time to submit these reply papers than for the intial brief which, as stated, will be largely a routine citation of general principles of law adapted to the case *sub judice*.

D. Certification Standards

It is a fact of life that some judges almost always certify a properly pleaded class action and some will bend over backward not to do so. As such, although the applicable law and general principles may be well known, it is wise to research the trial judge's prior rulings in connection with class certification motions. Ultimately, the district courts apply Rule 23 as written and, almost without exception, make an almost unavoidable incursion into the merits of the litigation although this is proscribed by the Supreme Court.[17] It is the rare case which, properly pleaded as a class action, should not be certified as such. The standards for certification, while theoretically unitary, vary from court to court, even within the same circuit. Further, some types of causes of action are more certifiable if plead one way than another. For example, a nondisclosure of a material fact common to all customers of a brokerage firm may give rise to the certification of a class action, but an oral misrepresentation to all such customers may not, the argument being that the latter involved thousands of separate and differing oral communications, thus destroying commonality, typicality and predominance.[18]

E. Notice to Absent Class Members

1. When Required

Rule 23(b)(3) requires that notice be provided to members of the class under subdivision (c)(2) of the Rule under some circumstances and Rule 23(d)(2) under others. Rule 23(e) also requires that any compromise or dismissal of a class action be preceded by notice to the members of the class and ultimate court approval. By comparison, class actions brought under Rule 23(b)(1) and (b)(2) do not require notice and it is for this reason, if no other, that great care must be exercised in pleading. If, for example, a class action is commenced to seek some uniform type of relief, such as a declaratory judgment or an injunction, it would be wise to steer clear of Rule 23(b)(3) allegations, which requires the plaintiff to provide notice to the members of the class, "including individual notice to all members who can be identified through reasonable effort."

2. Identifying Class Members and Paying for Notice

In *Eisen v. Carlisle & Jacquelin*,[19] the Supreme Court required the representative plaintiff in a Rule 23(b)(3) class action to initially bear the costs of providing notice to the members of the class. It was not until *Oppenheimer Fund, Inc. v. Sanders*[20] that the Supreme Court set guidelines for the district courts to allocate responsibility for the role of identifying the class members. Although the plaintiff remains primarily responsible for all costs related to

---

17 *Eisen v. Carlisle & Jacquelin*, 417 U.S. 156 (1974).

18 *Shapiro v. Merrill Lynch Pierce Fenner & Smith, Inc.*, [1975-1976 Transfer Binder] Fed. Sec. L. Rep. (CCH) ¶ 95,377 (S.D.N.Y. 1975).

19 *Eisen v. Carlisle & Jacquelin*, 417 U.S. 156 (1974).

20 *Oppenheimer Fund v. Sanders*, 437 U.S. 340 (1978).

the provision of notice, in practice, where the defendant can provide information from its own records or from those under its control (*e.g.*, stock transfer agents), the courts have not hesitated to appropriately allocate the various burdens to a defendant or others.

3. Form of Notice

Whenever possible, individual mailed notice is most desirable since all parties have the greatest degree of assurance that notice will be received. If, however, a list of class members cannot be compiled or, if compiled, will be out-of-date or incomplete, published notice may also be required. Additionally, notice may be tailored to the unique circumstances of the case and the membership in the class. As such, notices have appeared on the sides of milk containers, on tear-off coupons in supermarkets and otherwise adapted to the needs of the moment.

The precise form of the notice provided under Rule 23(c)(2) is flexible so long as it shall

> advise each member that (A) the court will exclude him from the class if he so requests by specific date; (B) a judgment whether favorable or not will include all members who do not request exclusion; and (C) any member who does not request exclusion may, if he desires, enter an appearance through his counsel.

The notice must be sufficiently clear and must contain appropriate language set forth neutrally so that a member of the class, upon receipt, will be able to make an intelligent decision about whether, *inter alia*, to exclude himself from the class, enter an appearance or to take some other course of action.

In general, the notice should describe, *inter alia*, the stage of the litigation (*i.e.*, what has taken place to date); the precise definition of the class; the nature of the allegations made by the plaintiff and the defendants' responses thereto; a disclaimer of any judicial position with respect to the allegations; the identity of plaintiff's counsel; the obligations and rights of absent class members; the binding nature of the litigation; and the opt-out procedures. Notice under Rule 23(e) will also set forth the details of any proposed settlement or compromise, the scope of any releases or final judgment that will follow from the dismissal of the action and, if appropriate, claims or similar instructions.

F. Exclusions

Class members in Rule 23(b)(3) actions, typically brought to recover damages, have a right to exclude themselves from the binding effect of the litigation. Although rarely permitted by district courts, pursuant to Rule 23(d), a right to exclude can be permitted in Rule 23(b)(1) and (b)(2) class actions.

The right to exclusion (or "opt out") is to be set forth in the notice provided to members of the class. Clear instructions must be provided so that an informed decision can be made. Further, the period in which the class member can exercise his right of exclusion must be "a reasonable time for those interested to choose whether to appear or default, acquiesce or contest."[21]

In the ordinary case, very few class members elect to opt out of the class. There is rarely a justifiable reason for doing so unless the class member wishes to pursue litigation individually. More frequently, people exclude themselves from the class because of a mistaken belief that they will be "involved in litigation" if they do not opt out. Occasionally, because of principle and/or some affinity to a defendant, a request for exclusion will be submitted.

VI. SETTLEMENT OF CLASS ACTIONS

A. Stipulation of Settlement

Once the terms of a settlement have been negotiated and, perhaps, set forth in a so-called "agreement in principle," the parties set to work drafting a definitive stipulation of settlement or settlement agreement.

Unlike an individual case, resolving a class-wide litigation requires a comprehensive agreement which, in its body or by means of exhibits, provides, *inter alia*, the scope of the claims asserted and released; the payment to be made or relief provided; the manner in which the payment and/or relief is to be allocated to class members; the scope of a final judgment and release language to be included therein; provisions for claims administration, notice; and fees and reimbursement of expenses for plaintiff's counsel. Typically, the exhibits thereto include a "hearing order" which establishes a notice and claims procedure and sets a final settlement hearing date; forms of individual notice and summary published notice; escrow agreements; and a proposed final judgment.

B. Preliminary Hearing

Once the stipulation of settlement has been executed by all the parties, it is typically presented to the district court for a preliminary review or hearing. At this time, the parties use the occasion to briefly describe the settlement to

---

21 *Mullane v. Central Hanover Bank*, 339 U.S. 306, 314 (1950).

the presiding judge and to set forth counsels' proposal for notice and a hearing date. The court is not asked to evaluate the substance of the proposed settlement but, rather, to preliminarily satisfy itself that what has been negotiated represents an arm's-length result that should be set down for a hearing pursuant to Rule 23(e) after notice is provided to members of the class.

C. Notice of Settlement and Hearing Date

Assuming the Court has preliminarily approved the settlement, it will order notice to be provided forthwith. In the ordinary case, the defendants will be required to produce any lists of class members either for plaintiff's counsel or to the party who will be mailing notice. Provision also will be made for any other manner of notice thought by the parties or the court to be necessary and/or appropriate.

The settlement hearing must be set for a date sufficiently in the future so as to permit mail (and any other) notice to be received and acted upon. Since notice procedures utilized in class actions are of constitutional significance and must be viewed in due process terms, the notice must not only convey the required information but it must afford a reasonable time to act thereupon.[22] In the ordinary case, where a class list has not been compiled, a two-month period between preliminary hearing and settlement hearing would appear to be the minimum time needed to satisfy due process requirements.

D. Briefs in Support of Settlement

Although there is no legal requirement that a brief be submitted, one or more of the proponents of a settlement will do so. The purposes of such briefs are to educate any class members who require information beyond that provided in the notice in making a decision whether or not to opt out or object and to "flesh-out" the docket generally so that the trial judge will have at his disposal an ample record upon which to question the proponents and, ultimately, make a decision as to the fairness and reasonableness of the proposed settlement.

Typically, such briefs will set forth the nature of the claims asserted; the defenses thereto; the stage of the proceedings and, in particular, the extent of discovery; the strengths and weaknesses of the plaintiff's case; and the law applicable to the various issues.

E. The Settlement Hearing

Notice may bring out many or no objectors or spectators. The hearing can last five minutes if the trial judge is well familiar with the facts of the case, its

---

[22] *Greenfield v. Villager Industries*, 483 F.2d 824, 834 (3d Cir. 1973).

progress and the applicable law, or many hours or days, if the settlement is contested. The hearing may consist of argument only or it may turn into a full-blown evidentiary hearing. The nature and scope of such hearing will be determined by the circumstances of the case and the preferences of the trial judge.

If the proposed settlement is approved, a final order or judgment will be signed. If the court does not approve the settlement, the typical settlement agreement provides that the parties will, effectively, turn the clock back to their presettlement positions.

F. Attorneys' Fees

There are several basic means for a plaintiff's counsel to be compensated (or for a plaintiff to be repaid if he has previously paid his counsel on a current or noncontingent basis). In "common fund" cases, the attorney will apply to the court to be compensated out of the fund created for plaintiff and the members of the class. Most typically, the fees to be awarded are based upon, *inter alia*, the amount of time expended by plaintiff's counsel, the value of that time and the value of the benefit obtained for the class. A body of law has developed that has set down a series of guidelines for district courts to follow in awarding fees in common fund class actions.[23] More recently, there has been a movement away from "lodestar," or hours-driven fee awards, to those which award plaintiff's counsel a flat percentage of the fund created.[24]

In statutory fee cases, where the enabling legislation provides for fees to be paid by a governmental entity or other defendant if the plaintiff prevails, the court will typically make an award to plaintiff's counsel based upon the value of the time expended to obtain the result, sometimes with a multiplier attached to reward a noteworthy and/or efficiently-obtained result.[25] In such cases, plaintiff's counsel can anticipate an opposed fee petition since the award will be paid not by the members of the class, as in a "common fund" case, but by the defendant. In some cases, the fee dispute and subsequent appeals have consumed more time and cost than litigating the underlying cause of action.

---

[23] *City of Detroit v. Grinnell Corp.*, 560 F.2d 1093 (2d Cir. 1977); *Lindy Bros. Builders, Inc. v. American Radiator & Standard Sanitary Corp.*, 540 F.2d 102 (3d Cir. 1976) ("Lindy I") and *Lindy Bros. Builders, Inc. v. American Radiator & Standard Sanitary Corp.*, 341 F. Supp. 1077 (E.D. Pa. 1972), settlement aff'd, 487 F.2d 161 (3d Cir. 1973) ("Lindy II").

[24] *Court Awarded Attorneys Fees-Report of the Third Circuit Task Force*, 108 F.R.D. 237 (1985).

[25] *Blum v. Stenson*, 465 U.S. 886 (1984); *Hensley v. Eckerhart*, 461 U.S. 424 (1983).

VII. OTHER REPRESENTATIVE LITIGATION
A. Rule 23.1
This rule deals solely with derivative suits by shareholders of corporations. Although such suits are representative in nature, they are not brought for the direct benefit of the plaintiff or any other shareholder but in the name and for the benefit of a corporation which will not act to protect itself or recover damages to which it is entitled. The most typical of such suits are commenced against an entrenched management and board of directors, who cannot be expected to sue themselves.

B. Rule 23.2
This rule is, in essence, an offshoot of Rule 23 and was adopted to clarify the right for class actions to be commenced by or against representatives of the membership of an unincorporated association.

CHAPTER TWELVE

PRETRIAL MANAGEMENT

by Hon. James C. Francis IV

I. INTRODUCTION

This chapter deals with four aspects of the pretrial phase of civil litigation in the federal courts: pretrial proceedings, including scheduling conferences and development of a final pretrial order; pretrial problems specific to complex litigation; the amendment of pleadings; and the use of magistrates and special masters. Wherever possible, citation is made to decisions of the Second Circuit Court of Appeals and to opinions of the district courts within this circuit.

II. PRETRIAL PROCEEDINGS

In the federal courts the pretrial phase—where the vast majority of attorney time is expended—is shaped by a number of formal and informal procedures. The basic outline for pretrial proceedings is set forth in Rule 16 of the Federal Rules of Civil Procedure. This rule sets out a list of objectives for pretrial conferences[1] as well as subjects that may be discussed.[2] It includes the requirement that a scheduling order be established within 120 days after filing of the complaint.[3] It provides for the issuance of pretrial directives, including the final pretrial order, and sets the standards for modification of

---

1 Fed. R. Civ. P. 16(a).

2 Fed. R. Civ. P. 16(c).

3 Fed. R. Civ. P. 16(b).

such orders.[4] Finally, Rule 16 authorizes sanctions against a party or its attorney who fails to participate in established pretrial proceedings or abide by pretrial orders.[5]

Prior to 1983, Rule 16 was substantially less comprehensive. It merely authorized the conduct of a pretrial conference and formulation of a final pretrial order. According to the Advisory Committee on Civil Rules, the 1983 amendments were designed to make the rule more adaptable to the needs of individual cases, encouraging regulation of complex litigation while permitting simpler cases to progress without time-consuming judicial intervention.[6] Despite this avowed goal of flexibility, the amendment's creation of absolute requirements, such as the establishment of an initial scheduling order, evinces the drafters' intent to stimulate greater judicial involvement in pretrial management.[7] Accordingly, the district courts as well as individual judges have promulgated procedures supplementing Rule 16.

A. Pretrial Conferences

The purposes served by any particular pretrial conference will depend in part on when it is held during the course of pretrial preparation. An initial conference generally will be concerned with establishing a scheduling order and familiarizing both the court and counsel with the legal and factual issues raised in the litigation. Subsequent conferences may be devoted to schedule revision, resolution of discovery disputes,[8] or settlement negotiations.[9] Pretrial conferences can be particularly helpful in eliminating extraneous issues and focusing on the legal contentions in a case. Indeed, stipulations entered into by counsel in the course of a pretrial conference have binding effect.[10] Thus, the scope of the pretrial conference is broad, but it is not unlimited: the

---

[4] Fed. R. Civ. P. 16(e).

[5] Fed. R. Civ. P. 16(f).

[6] Fed. R. Civ. P. 16 Advisory Committee's note.

[7] The committee explicitly relied on one study which found that early judicial intervention results in more efficient disposition of cases. *See* Flanders, *Case Management and Court Management in the United States District Courts*, Federal Judicial Center (1977).

[8] *See* Chapters 13-15, *infra*.

[9] *See* Chapter 18, *infra*.

[10] *See, e.g., Risher v. United States*, 465 F.2d 1, 5 (5th Cir. 1972); *Neiger v. Sheet Metal Workers Int'l Ass'n*, 470 F. Supp. 622, 628 (W.D. Mo. 1979).

court may not, for example, "direct" a verdict on the basis of evidence proffered during pretrial discussions. It may, however, dispose of claims summarily at a pretrial conference where it is apparent that no factual disputes exist.

In view of the importance of the pretrial conference to efficient case management, courts will enforce the obligation of counsel to participate meaningfully. The trial court has no obligation to define a case unilaterally[11] and must rely on the parties and their attorneys to narrow issues. Thus, if counsel fails to appear at a pretrial conference, the court may assess as a sanction the costs and attorneys' fees incurred by the adversary.[12] Moreover, mere presence is insufficient: sanctions may be imposed if counsel is unprepared to participate fully at the conference. Finally, if counsel is unable to articulate the theory of a claim or defense at a pretrial conference, the court may preclude that issue from being raised at trial.

A relatively new and growing subspecies of the pretrial conference is the pre-motion conference. Many district judges are now requiring counsel to present apparent disputes in a conference prior to submitting a formal motion. This process serves several purposes. It sharpens the issues to be resolved and alerts counsel to those questions of greatest concern to the court. Furthermore, through such conferences the court may deter frivolous motions or, at least, create a record for the subsequent issuance of sanctions where counsel persist in advancing futile contentions. Of course, even if counsel's arguments at a pre-motion conference appear unpersuasive, the court may not ultimately deny a party the right to submit a motion.[13]

B. Scheduling Orders

Two types of orders—scheduling orders and final pretrial orders—are uniquely related to pretrial conferences and are directly addressed by Rule 16. A scheduling order must be entered in each case, except for those types of actions exempted by local rule.[14] Failure of a party to seek a scheduling order may be considered a failure to prosecute, potentially leading to dismissal of

---

[11] *See United States v. International Business Machines Corp.*, 68 F.R.D. 358, 359 (S.D.N.Y. 1975).

[12] *See Yannitelli v. Navieras de Puerto Rico*, 106 F.R.D. 42 (S.D.N.Y. 1985).

[13] *See Richardson Greenshields Securities, Inc. v. Mui-Hin Lau*, 825 F.2d 647, 652 (2d Cir. 1987).

[14] In the Eastern District of New York, for example, no scheduling order need be filed in matters involving *habeas corpus* petitions, social security disability determinations, motions to vacate sentences, forfeitures, or review of administrative decisions. E.D.N.Y. Civ. R. 45.

the action.[15] According to Rule 16(b), the scheduling order must contain deadlines for joining parties, amending pleadings, filing motions, and completing discovery, and it may also include dates for pretrial conferences, trial, and other matters.

As with any court order, the violation of a scheduling order can lead to sanctions. Most commonly, the failure to meet a deadline results in the offending party being precluded from taking the action that would otherwise have been permitted. Thus, a party may be barred from taking a deposition after the discovery cut-off[16] or from making a motion after the deadline for such submission has passed. Occasionally, however, a party's pattern of noncompliance with scheduling orders is so pervasive that the court will dismiss the action or strike the answer. But to be enforceable, a scheduling order must be explicit, and no sanctions can be imposed for failure to abide by an "implied" schedule.[17]

Scheduling orders are, of course, mutable, and a court can modify them for "good cause." Although this standard is a generous one, it is not without limit. For example, a deadline for discovery need not be extended where the case is not complex and where a lengthy period of inactivity by counsel is unexplained. Likewise, a motion to amend a complaint may be denied where, without good cause, it is filed after the date for submission of all motions.

C. Final Pretrial Orders

The culmination of the pretrial process is the final pretrial order. This document serves several critical functions. It provides a roadmap for the court to follow in trying the case: a preview of the issues to be contested and of the relation of the evidence to the legal questions raised. Furthermore, the final pretrial order aids the court in anticipating problems that will arise at trial regarding such issues as the admissibility of evidence and the qualification of expert witnesses. Finally, the process of formulating the order forces counsel to focus on all aspects of the case, and this can result in the narrowing of issues through stipulation and even the abandonment of some claims.[18]

---

15 *See C.E. Bickford & Co. v. M.V. "Elly,"* 116 F.R.D. 195 (S.D.N.Y. 1986).

16 *See, e.g., Dolgow v. Anderson*, 53 F.R.D. 661, 664 (E.D.N.Y. 1971).

17 *See Salahuddin v. Harris*, 782 F.2d 1127, 1133 (2d Cir. 1986).

18 *See* Pollack, *Pretrial Procedures More Effectively Handled*, 65 F.R.D. 475, 480 n.1 (1974).

Despite these advantages, final pretrial orders are not absolutely mandatory,[19] and some judges do not require them, especially in simple cases.

The process of creating the final pretrial order generally involves each party submitting lists of disputed and undisputed facts, exhibits, witnesses, and so forth.[20] The contents of the order are generally determined by the rules of individual judges. The final pretrial order is expected to reflect the views of all parties, and it is therefore improper for one party to submit its draft without notice to its adversaries. Agreement should be attainable since the order need not resolve all disputes but may simply identify them for subsequent determination by the court.

Once the final pretrial order is approved by the court, it supercedes the pleadings. Consequently, claims or defenses not set forth in the order are precluded, and in order to preserve for appeal an issue that the district court omits from the final pretrial order, the aggrieved party must record an objection to the order. Although these principles are easily applied in most cases, there are some situations where a claim raised at trial is similar but not identical to that embodied in the pretrial order, and the court must then determine whether justice will best be served by permitting the related claim to be tried.

The binding nature of the final pretrial order also applies to any factual stipulations that it contains. However, upon a showing of manifest injustice, a party may be relieved of a pretrial stipulation. For example, agreed upon facts may be set aside where substantial contrary evidence is proffered at trial.

Lastly, the final pretrial order may dictate the scope of evidence to be presented at trial. The court may require parties to disclose the documents or witnesses that they intend to offer, and counsel may not use the pretrial order to seek a tactical advantage by either withholding such information or burying it in masses of "evidence" never intended to be presented. Evidence not identified in a pretrial order may be precluded,[21] but courts tend to apply this principle leniently where the opposing party will not be prejudiced.

Although "final," the final pretrial order can be modified. In evaluating any request for modification, the court must balance the need to do justice

---

19 *See United States v. International Business Machines Corp.*, 68 F.R.D. 358 (S.D.N.Y. 1975).

20 For a detailed description of a recommended procedure for creating a final pretrial order, *see* Pollack, *supra* n.31 at 481-83.

21 *See Napolitano v. Compania Sud Americana de Vapores*, 421 F.2d 382, 385-86 (2d Cir. 1970); *Goldbaum v. Bank Leumi Trust Co. of New York*, 545 F. Supp. 1008, 1013 (S.D.N.Y. 1982).

against the interest in preserving an orderly and efficient procedure.[22] Pursuant to Rule 16, modification of the final pretrial order may be permitted "only to prevent manifest injustice." Thus, a court will consider such factors as the impact on the moving party if modification is not permitted, prejudice to the adversary if it is,[23] any reason for failing to include the new material in the original order, and any delay in resolution of the case that would result from the proposed change. Modification can affect a party's claims, the evidence to be presented, or stipulations of fact: indeed, any aspect of the final pretrial order.

III. COMPLEX LITIGATION

It has become increasingly apparent that techniques of pretrial management should be adapted to meet the special needs of complex cases.[24] One impetus for this movement has been the perception that complicated cases clog judicial dockets. As one commentator has observed:

> It was in the 1950's that courts and commentators first became alarmed at the disturbing effect the increasing number of protracted cases was having on judicial calendars. In too many instances years would pass between commencement of an action and its final adjudication.[25]

It is questionable whether judicial delays have in fact increased over time.[26] Furthermore, it is doubtful that the pretrial phase of most protracted cases—which until recently attracted little judicial involvement—adversely affects the progress of other litigation. But there remain important reasons to encourage the efficient resolution of complex cases: the reduction of time and cost to the litigants so that resources may be devoted to more socially useful endeavors.

---

[22] *See Laguna v. American Export Isbrandtsen Lines, Inc.*, 439 F.2d 97, 101 (2d Cir. 1971).

[23] *See McFadden v. Sanchez*, 710 F.2d 907, 911-12 (2d Cir. 1983).

[24] An invaluable resource of advice on all aspects of complex litigation is the *Manual for Complex Litigation, Second*, published by the Federal Judicial Center.

[25] Wright & Miller, *Federal Practice and Procedure* § 1530 at 624 (1971).

[26] Delays in the judicial system can hardly be attributed exclusively to the advent of complex corporate litigation. In pre-Revolutionary Virginia, for example, a typical case in the General Court took approximately eight years from filing to verdict. If an appeal was taken, another two or three years would elapse before the appellate court rendered a determination. *See* F.L. Dewey, *Thomas Jefferson: Lawyer* 21-22 (1986).

Since a case can be "big" in a variety of respects, it is helpful to define the attributes of complex litigation in order to find means for coping with it. First, litigation can be complicated because it raises multiple issues. A single transaction may give rise to many legal claims, or an action may be based on a series of interconnected transactions. A related, but not identical, issue is the problem of massive evidentiary preparation. Cases that involve many legal issues often require extended discovery, with numerous depositions and exchange of large quantities of documents, accompanied by many opportunities for disagreement among counsel. Next, even a case raising few legal issues may be complicated if there are multiple parties and, of course, multiple counsel. Finally, complex litigation may actually consist of multiple cases arising out of the same events but proceeding in various forums. Each of these factors complicates litigation and each requires a different strategy to facilitate efficient resolution.

A. Coping with Multiple Issues

Litigation is often unnecessarily complicated because issues are not well defined. This difficulty is magnified when a case involves numerous issues. Therefore, it is useful in complex litigation for counsel to list all the elements of each claim and defense, thus identifying the interrelationship of some issues and permitting the elimination of duplicative claims. When counsel resist this exercise, the court can require it. Indeed, where a specific issue is particularly complicated, or its evidentiary foundation appears tenuous, counsel may be directed to outline the factual support for the party's contentions. This enables the parties to focus discovery on the critical factual questions and to prepare any dispositive pretrial motions. Finally, the party faced with an adversary who relies on vague, general assertions can flush out the nature of the issues through the use of contention interrogatories. Although generally most appropriate at the completion of discovery,[27] such interrogatories should be utilized at an earlier stage in complex litigation in order to avoid aimless discovery and motion practice.

Multiple issues are frequently accompanied by massive discovery. The first step in dealing with such discovery is to understand its goal. To do this, counsel should identify each party's claims and "map" them first to the facts which, if proven, would support the claim, and then to the sources from

---

27 *See* S.D.N.Y. Civ. R. 46.

which such facts may be obtained through discovery.[28] Counsel can then begin to rationalize the discovery process by sequencing it in a manner that, for example, permits disclosure on potentially dispositive issues to take place first. The order in which discovery proceeds will depend on the needs of each specific case. For instance, in one case disclosure should focus first on some narrow issue of jurisdiction or liability so that a dispositive motion can be made, while in another action discovery should dwell initially on damages to aid in negotiation of a settlement. The principle, then, is not that all discovery in complex litigation should follow a particular pattern, but rather that it should have *some* pattern, dictated by the nature of the case.

The form of discovery instrument used, like the order in which discovery is taken, depends on the unique needs of the complex case. For example, a local rule in the Southern District of New York creates a presumption that most substantive discovery shall be taken through depositions and document production and that interrogatories will primarily serve to identify potential witnesses.[29] However, in many complex cases, the cost of deposing all potential witnesses would be overwhelming, and it is more fruitful to begin by serving all of them with limited substantive interrogatories in order to identify those whose depositions are most critical.

Finally, counsel engaged in complex litigation must confront the logistical problem of assembling discovery materials and making them accessible. A rational identification and indexing system is obviously critical, and in some cases computerization of the index may be helpful. Where documents are numerous but may not need repeated access, counsel may choose to use a single document depository and avoid the costs of massive photocopying.

As discovery progresses, the issues in a complex case come into sharper focus, and counsel should anticipate the course of trial. Even if a case will not be finally resolved by dispositive motion, motions for partial summary judgment can eliminate some claims and defenses and thus make the trial less costly and more comprehensible. Just as pretrial motions may narrow the issues for trial, so may they resolve evidentiary problems. For example, by motion *in limine*, a party can seek a determination whether evidence prof-

---

[28] A partial evidentiary "map" in a simple tort case might look like this:

Claim	Element	Fact	Sources of Evidence
Negligence	Proximate Cause (other elements would follow)	Defendant's vehicle struck plaintiff's vehicle, etc.	—Plaintiff's deposition —Defendant's deposition —Police report —Witness X's deposition, etc.

---

[29] *See* S.D.N.Y. Civ. R. 46.

fered by an adversary will be considered germane to the litigation. Similarly, the court may hold preliminary hearings with respect to admissibility pursuant to Rule 104 of the Federal Rules of Evidence.

B. Coping with Multiple Parties

Litigation is generally noisy, and as the number of parties and their counsel multiplies, the cacophony increases. Two approaches facilitate communication among counsel and with the court in complex litigation. First, the court may appoint lead or liaison counsel to deal with the court and with opposing counsel on issues where the positions within each camp are relatively uniform. This approach not only reduces the number of voices competing in court, but it also encourages counsel on the same side to resolve minor differences. Second, multiple parties need not all be individually represented in each court proceeding. Instead, the court may hold conferences on specific, limited issues, and excuse from attendance those parties with no interest in the agenda.

A more structured approach to the problem of multiple parties takes place in those cases where class certification is appropriate.[30] Because the conduct of pretrial proceedings will vary substantially depending on whether a class is certified, early resolution of this issue is desirable. Therefore, in complex cases, it is often important to direct initial discovery efforts to issues related to class certification.

C. Coping with Multiple Cases

An action in federal court may be closely related to actions pending in a variety of forums, including other federal district courts,[31] bankruptcy court, state courts, administrative agency proceedings, or arbitrations. Strategies for dealing with such situations might be separated into three categories characterized as "beat 'em," "join 'em" or "cooperate with 'em."

The first approach involves any effort to halt litigation in one or more of the competing forums. Under some circumstances, one court may be persuaded to abstain in favor of resolution of the issues before another tribunal. For example, a federal constitutional challenge to state law may be dismissed from federal court where the state courts have not definitively construed the law under attack.[32] Likewise, a federal court may abstain where identical

---

30 *See generally* Chapter 11, *supra.*

31 If related cases are pending in several federal district courts, they may be subject to supervision by the Panel on Multidistrict Litigation. *See* Chapter 29, *infra.*

32 *See Railroad Commission v. Pullman Co.*, 312 U.S. 496 (1941). *See generally* Chapter 1, *supra.*

issues are raised by the same parties in another district court.[33] Where the prerequisites for abstention are not available, a court may nevertheless reach the same result by informally staying the action before it while the parallel case proceeds to judgment elsewhere.

If this tactic fails, efficiency may still be achieved by consolidating two or more related cases in the same district for pretrial purposes or for trial.[34] If cases are pending in separate districts, it may be possible to transfer them to the same district.[34a]

Nevertheless, problems such as the ability to subpoena witnesses and the need to establish personal jurisdiction may preclude the joining of related actions in the same forum. In such cases, counsel should still consider coordinating pretrial management. For example, it may be possible to agree on a common discovery schedule or to stipulate that discovery obtained in one action will be available in another. In complex litigation, even this minimal degree of coordination may reduce costs and enhance efficient pretrial management.

IV. AMENDMENT OF PLEADINGS

In the course of refining the issues to be tried, it is often necessary to amend the pleadings. The procedure for amending or supplementing pleadings is governed by Rule 15 of the Federal Rules of Civil Procedure, and each of the rule's four subsections deals with a discrete aspect of the process. Rule 15(a) sets the time limits for amending a pleading as of right, after which leave of court must be sought. Subsection (b) establishes the standard for allowing amendments to conform to the evidence presented at trial. Rule 15(c) defines the circumstances under which an amendment will "relate back," that is, when it will be treated as if it had been included in the original pleading. Finally, Rule 15(d) creates the procedure for supplementing pleadings to account for events occurring after the prior pleading was filed.

A. Procedural Requirements

A party may amend its pleading once without leave of court if it does so prior to service of a responsive pleading. Thus, for example, the plaintiff has a right to amend the complaint before the answer is served. The timeliness of such an amendment is determined in relation to actual service of the respon-

---

[33] *See Colorado River Water Conservation District v. United States*, 424 U.S. 800 (1976). *See generally* Chapter 1, *supra.*

[34] *See* Fed. R. Civ. P. 42(a).

[34a] *See* 28 U.S.C. § 1404(a). *See generally* Chapter 3, *supra.*

sive pleading, not its theoretical due date. Therefore, a party filing a responsive pleading early cuts off his opponent's opportunity to amend as of right.[35] Similarly, a stipulation extending time to file a responsive pleading extends the time to amend the initial pleading until a response is served.[36] Finally, the filing of a pre-answer motion does not preclude amendment of the complaint, since such a motion is not considered a responsive pleading.[37]

A problem arises when several parties are required to file responses to the same pleading. As soon as any of those parties files its response, the opportunity to amend the original pleading as to that party is lost, and subsequent amendments will only be effective as to those parties that have not yet responded.[38] This problem is more theoretical than real, however, since the party seeking to amend can always request leave of the court to amend as to all parties.

Once a party has missed the opportunity to amend as of right, it can still move for permission to amend at virtually any time. Certainly a motion is timely at any time prior to trial,[39] and even after trial to conform the pleadings to the evidence. However, counsel should be wary since, as discussed below, delay in making the motion will influence the court's decision whether to permit amendment.

B. Standards for Permitting Amendment

Courts will permit amendment of pleadings for virtually any purpose. For example, a pleading that was originally defective may be amended to cure the flaw.[40] Similarly, a party may seek to add claims, alter its legal theories, or request different or additional relief.[41] From the defendant's perspective,

---

35 Wright & Miller, *supra* n.25 at § 1480, p. 406.

---

36 *Id.*

---

37 *See Chodos v. F.B.I.*, 559 F. Supp. 69, 70 n.2 (S.D.N.Y.), *aff'd mem.*, 697 F.2d 289 (2d Cir. 1982), *cert. denied*, 459 U.S. 1111 (1983).

---

38 *See* 3 *Moore's Federal Practice* ¶ 15.07 [2] at 15-53 (2d ed. 1982).

---

39 *See, e.g., Matarazzo v. Friendly Ice Cream Corp.*, 70 F.R.D. 556, 559 (S.D.N.Y. 1976).

---

40 *See World Arrow Tourism Enterprises, Ltd. v. Trans World Airlines, Inc.*, 582 F. Supp. 808, 812 (S.D.N.Y. 1984).

---

41 *See Jones v. New York City Human Resources Administration*, 539 F. Supp. 795, 801 (S.D.N.Y. 1982) (add claim for attorneys' fees); *Sadowy v. Sony Corp.*, 93 F.R.D. 450, 454 (S.D.N.Y. 1982) (increased damages requested).

amendments may be utilized to add defenses or counterclaims.[42] An amendment may not be used, however, to defeat the court's jurisdiction with respect to an issue upon which it has already ruled.[43]

Rule 15(a) states that leave to amend "shall be freely given when justice so requires." In discussing the application of this principle in *Foman v. Davis*,[44] the Supreme Court held:

> In the absence of any apparent or declared reason—such as undue delay, bad faith, or dilatory motive on the part of the movant, repeated failure to cure deficiencies by amendments previously allowed, undue prejudice to the opposing party by virtue of allowance of the amendment, futility of amendment, etc.—the leave sought should, as the rules require, be "freely given." [45]

As some courts have observed, the Supreme Court's articulation can be viewed as a mandate to weigh the harm to the moving party if amendment is denied against the prejudice to the non-moving party if it is allowed.[46]

Thus, a factor favoring amendment is a change in the law affecting the movant's claims.[47] Similarly, if new claims could be asserted in a separate action, then amendment is appropriate, since the non-moving party is not prejudiced. On the other hand, amendment may be denied if it would unduly increase the complexity and expense of a trial or cause confusion for the jury.[48] Likewise, a party demonstrating bad faith—as by failing to amend after being given a sufficient opportunity or by moving long after the relevant facts are known—may be precluded from amending.[49] Finally, some factors,

---

[42] *See Sullivan v. American Airlines, Inc.*, 613 F. Supp. 226, 230 (S.D.N.Y. 1985); *Blossom Farm Products Co. v. Amtraco Commodity Corp.*, 64 F.R.D. 424, 427 (S.D.N.Y. 1974).

[43] *See Smiga v. Dean Whitter Reynolds, Inc.*, 766 F.2d 698, 703 (2d Cir. 1985).

[44] 371 U.S. 178 (1962).

[45] *Id.* at 182.

[46] *See, e.g., Pollux Marine Agencies, Inc. v. Louis Dreyfus Corp.*, 455 F. Supp. 211, 215 (S.D.N.Y. 1978).

[47] *See Davis v. Smith*, 431 F. Supp. 1206, 1208-09 (S.D.N.Y. 1977), *aff'd*, 607 F.2d 535 (2d Cir. 1978).

[48] *See Triangle Industries, Inc. v. Kennecott Copper Corp.*, 402 F. Supp. 210, 212 (S.D.N.Y. 1975); *Data Digests, Inc. v. Standard & Poor's Corp.*, 57 F.R.D. 42, 45 (S.D.N.Y. 1972).

[49] *See Sanders v. Thrall Car Mfg. Co.*, 582 F. Supp. 945, 952 (S.D.N.Y. 1983), *aff'd mem.*, 730 F.2d 910 (2d Cir. 1984); *Dow Corning Corp. v. General Electric Co.*, 461 F. Supp. 519, 520 (N.D.N.Y. 1978); *Roorda v. American Oil Co.*, 446 F. Supp. 939, 947-48 (W.D.N.Y. 1978).

such as possible exposure to greater liability and the cost of simply filing a response, are not considered prejudicial and therefore play no role in determining whether to allow amendment.[50]

Two factors influencing decisions whether to permit amendment deserve special mention. The first is delay: an unexplained and prejudicial delay in seeking relief will result in denial of leave to amend.[51] Although delay is not in itself a basis for denying amendment, it shifts the burden to the moving party to explain the lapse of time since the filing of the original pleading.[52] The moving party may carry that burden by showing, for example, that the claim sought to be added is a novel one.[53]

The second factor is the sufficiency of the proposed amendment. Where the amendment raises a colorable claim, and especially when the validity of the claim is based on disputed facts, amendment should be allowed and any comprehensive legal analysis deferred to a subsequent motion to dismiss or motion for summary judgment.[54] But if a proposed amendment raises a claim that is frivolous or insufficient on its face, it may properly be denied.[55] For example, if *res judicata* would bar the proposed claim, amending the pleading would be an exercise in futility.[56]

C. Amendments to Conform to the Evidence

Under Rule 15(b), pleadings may be amended to include issues that have been tried with the express or implied consent of the parties. Although the language of this subsection differs from that found in Rule 15(a), the standard for permitting amendment is essentially the same: amendments are to be freely allowed unless the non-moving party is prejudiced. In addition, provision is made for granting a continuance to allow the non-moving party to defend against the newly raised issues.

---

50 *See In re Osage Oil Exploration Co.*, 104 F.R.D. 45, 49 (S.D.N.Y. 1984); *Gutierrez v. Vegari*, 499 F. Supp. 1040, 1045 (S.D.N.Y. 1980).

51 *See Evans v. Syracuse City School District*, 704 F.2d 44, 47-48 (2d Cir. 1983).

52 *See Sanders v. Thrall Car Mfg. Co.*, 582 F. Supp. at 952.

53 *See Employee Savings Plan of Mobil Oil Corp. v. Vickery*, 99 F.R.D. 138 (S.D.N.Y. 1983).

54 *See Madison Fund, Inc. v. Denison Mines, Ltd.*, 90 F.R.D. 89, 91 (S.D.N.Y. 1981); *EEOC v. Sage Realty Corp.*, 87 F.R.D. 365, 371-72 (S.D.N.Y. 1980); *WIXT Television, Inc. v. Meredith Corp.*, 506 F. Supp. 1003, 1010 (N.D.N.Y. 1980).

55 *See Valdan Sportswear v. Montgomery Ward & Co.*, 591 F. Supp. 1188, 1190-92 (S.D.N.Y. 1984).

56 *See Klein v. Spear, Leeds & Kellogg*, 309 F. Supp. 341, 345 (S.D.N.Y. 1970).

Amendments to conform to the evidence serve two functions. First, they prevent the injustice that would result from the dismissal, on purely technical grounds, of issues that have actually been tried. Second, they facilitate appellate review by providing the reviewing court with pleadings that reflect the reality of the trial.

Despite the *post hoc* nature of such amendments, they violate neither procedural fairness nor the sanctity of the pretrial order. Due process principles are preserved because Rule 15(b) allows conforming amendments only when there has been notice to the non-moving party of the issues raised and an opportunity to cure any potential prejudice.[57] At the same time, any independent interest that the court may have in an orderly procedure based on the pretrial order is accounted for, since the court has acquiesced in trial of the additional issues.[58]

D. Relation Back

An amendment raising a new allegation may "relate back," so that it is treated as if it had been included in the original pleading. In order to relate back, the new allegations must satisfy two criteria: they must arise out of the conduct, transaction, or occurrence set forth in the original pleading,[59] and the original pleading must have given the adversary general notice of the new allegations.[60] The function of the relation back doctrine is to avoid the statute of limitations and permit the new allegations to be litigated, even if they would be time-barred if raised in a separate lawsuit.

Of course, new allegations may implicate additional parties, and Rule 15(c) therefore establishes a standard for determining whether claims relate back as against the newly added party. In addition to meeting the requirement that the new allegations arise out of the events underlying the original pleading, the moving party must show both that the new party received notice of the original action such that his defense will not be prejudiced and that it knew or should have known that it was an intended target of the original pleading.

---

[57] *See* Wright & Miller, *supra* n.25 at § 1491, p. 455.

[58] To avoid confusion, the pretrial order as well as the pleadings should be amended to conform to the evidence.

[59] *See* Fed. R. Civ.P. 15(c).

[60] *See Rosenberg v. Martin*, 478 F.2d 520, 526 (2d Cir.), *cert. denied*, 414 U.S. 872 (1973); *Oliner v. McBride's Industries, Inc.*, 106 F.R.D. 9, 12 (S.D.N.Y. 1985).

PRETRIAL MANAGEMENT

The notice requirement incorporates two issues: the form that the notice must take, and the time within which it must be provided. Certainly, service of the original pleading itself on the prospective party or its agent is adequate,[61] but it is not necessary, and less formal notice will suffice. The timing requirement is better defined: the Supreme Court recently held that the relation back doctrine will only apply where the newly added party had notice of the original pleading prior to the running of the statute of limitations; it is not sufficient for notice to have been provided after the limitations period but before the time for service of the original pleading on the new party would have elapsed under Rule 4 of the Federal Rules of Civil Procedure.[62]

The second requirement—that the added party have known that it was supposed to have been named in the original pleading—is closely related to the first, since it ensures that notice of the original action was effective. However, a party receiving notice of an action mistakenly brought against another cannot simply claim ignorance of the plaintiff's intention to have sued him in the first instance. Instead, the courts apply a reasonable person test, and if a party should reasonably have understood that the original claim was directed at him, the subsequent amendment will relate back.[63]

Some courts have applied an "identity of interest" test to aid the determination whether the two aspects of the notice requirement are met. That is, if there is an identity of interests between the party originally named and the added party—as between a parent company and its wholly-owned subsidiary—the notice requirement is satisfied.[64] But this standard is often more misleading than helpful since it deviates from the language of Rule 15. Hence, while some courts treat the identity of interest test as equivalent only to the actual notice requirement, others also equate it with the requirement that the new party know that it was an intended target of the original suit.[65]

Rule 15(c) eliminates this type of confusion with respect to amendments affecting federal agencies or officers. Under the rule, service of the complaint on the United States Attorney, the U.S. Attorney General or a federal agency or officer who would have been a proper defendant satisfies both

---

[61] See Volvo v. M/V Atlantic Saga, 534 F. Supp. 647 (S.D.N.Y. 1982).

[62] Schiavone v. Fortune, 477 U.S. 21, 106 S. Ct. 2379, 2384-85 (1986).

[63] See Davis v. Buffalo Psychiatric Center, 613 F. Supp. 462, 467 (W.D.N.Y. 1985); Sounds Express International, Ltd. v. American Themes & Tapes, Inc., 101 F.R.D. 694, 697 (S.D.N.Y. 1984).

[64] Id. at 697.

[65] Id.

prongs of the notice requirement for relation back of claims against the United States or another federal officer or employee.

The relation back doctrine can apply to amendments that add plaintiffs as well as to those that add defendants. In such circumstances, as long as the new plaintiffs' claims arise from the same transaction, the defendant has presumably been on notice of the potential claims and is not prejudiced.[66] The defendant is, of course, exposed to greater possible liability, but, as in other contexts, that is an insufficient reason for rejecting amendment.[67]

Finally, the question arises whether state or federal relation back principles apply in diversity cases. Because strong federal policies underlie the relation back doctrine, the Second Circuit has held that Rule 15(c) applies in such cases even if the applicable state law might be more restrictive.[68]

E. Supplemental Pleadings

In contrast to amendments, which address matters that could have been raised in the original pleadings, supplemental pleadings relate to occurrences that have taken place after the original pleadings were filed. Pursuant to Rule 15(d) supplemental pleadings may only be filed by leave of court.

The substantive rules for granting leave to file supplemental pleadings are substantially similar to those for permitting amendment. Permission is granted freely,[69] and courts balance the potential prejudice to each party as they would in considering a motion to amend. Finally, the relation back doctrine applies to supplemental pleadings as it does to amendments.[70]

V. MAGISTRATES AND SPECIAL MASTERS

The role of magistrates and special masters in the federal courts is defined by statute and rule. The primary source of authority for United States Magistrates is found in the Federal Magistrates' Act ("the Act"), 28 U.S.C. § 631,

---

[66] *See Cunningham v. Quaker Oats Co.*, 107 F.R.D. 66, 72 (W.D.N.Y. 1985); *Employees Savings Plan of Mobil Oil Corp. v. Vickery*, 99 F.R.D. 138, 143 (S.D.N.Y. 1983).

[67] *See Cunningham v. Quaker Oats Co.*, 107 F.R.D. at 72.

[68] *Ingram v. Kumar*, 585 F.2d 566, 570 n.5 (2d Cir. 1978), *cert. denied*, 440 U.S. 940 (1979). Whether the Second Circuit's holding is still good law, however, is seriously in doubt. *See Schiavone v. Fortune*, 477 U.S. 24 (1986).

[69] *See Soler v. G. & U. Inc.*, 103 F.R.D. 69, 73 (S.D.N.Y. 1984).

[70] *See id.* at 75.

et seq. The guidance provided in that statute is further refined by Rules 72-76 of the Federal Rules of Civil Procedure and by local court rules.[71] Rule 53 of the Federal Rules of Civil Procedure and applicable local rules outline the role of the special master.

A. Magistrates' Jurisdiction

The Act identifies a variety of purposes for which the district court may refer a case to a magistrate. For example, certain types of motions may be generically characterized as "dispositive." Under the Act,[72] these include motions to dismiss, motions for summary judgment or judgment on the pleadings, motions for injunctive relief, and motions for class certification. A magistrate may not make a final determination of such motions but may issue a report and recommendation to the district court, following an evidentiary hearing, if appropriate.[73]

On the other hand, magistrates may make determinations in the context of general pretrial supervision as well as with respect to motions not identified by the Act as "dispositive." For example, in ruling on discovery motions, magistrates have the authority to issue sanctions, including imposition of attorneys' fees and costs,[74] preclusion of evidence, and dismissal of claims or defenses.[75] Similarly, a magistrate can determine miscellaneous pretrial motions as diverse as motions to disqualify counsel or requests for a gag order.

The Act further designates three specific types of cases in which the district court may utilize a magistrate.[76] First, magistrates may review *habeas corpus* petitions, hold evidentiary hearings if appropriate, and submit recommendations to the district court. Next, as will be discussed in more detail below, magistrates may serve as special masters. Finally, magistrates may consider prisoner petitions challenging conditions of confinement. This last category has created conflict, since it is not clearly defined and could impinge on the rights of inmates. For example, the reference of such cases to

---

[71] *See* Rules for Proceedings Before Magistrates, S.D.N.Y. and E.D.N.Y.; N.D.N.Y. Gen. R. 43.1-44; W.D.N.Y. Loc. R. Pract. 35-37.

[72] *See* 28 U.S.C. § 636(b)(1).

[73] 28 U.S.C. § 636(b)(1)(B) & (C).

[74] *See Merritt v. International Brotherhood of Boilermakers*, 649 F.2d 1013, 1016-17 (5th Cir. 1981); *McHan v. Grandbouche*, 99 F.R.D. 260, 268-69 (D. Kan. 1983).

[75] *See DeVore & Sons, Inc. v. Aurora Pacific Cattle Co.*, 560 F. Supp. 236, 238-39 (D. Kan. 1983).

[76] 28 U.S.C. § 636(b)(1)(B).

a magistrate cannot serve to deprive the prisoner of the right to a jury trial presided over by the district court. Although pretrial hearings may be conducted by the magistrate, the trial itself must proceed before the district judge unless the parties have consented to trial before a magistrate.[77]

Finally, "[a] magistrate may be assigned such additional duties as are not inconsistent with the Constitution and laws of the United States."[78] Accordingly, a variety of additional responsibilities are often assigned to magistrates, ranging from conducting *voir dire* and selecting the jury for cases to be tried by the district court[79] to presiding over inquests to determine damages following the granting of a default judgment.

B. Review of Magistrate Decisions

The referral of judicial responsibility to magistrates is constitutional because the ultimate responsibility for each decision remains with the district judge,[80] and the standard of review applied by the district court depends upon the nature of the referral. When the magistrate has submitted a report and recommendation, as is always the case when a dispositive motion has been referred, the district court engages in *de novo* review.[81] Such broad review is required when a party objects to a magistrate's report, and it is permitted even in the absence of objections. However, when no party has objected or when the objections are vague and general, courts have generally confined their review to a search for clear error on the face of the record.[82]

In response to objections to a magistrate's report, "the district court has the duty to conduct a careful and complete review."[83] This may include further evidentiary hearings at which additional testimony is solicited. Indeed, if there is an indication that the district court failed to review the full record, adoption of the magistrate's report may be vacated.

---

[77] *See Hall v. Sharpe*, 812 F.2d 644 (11th Cir. 1987); *Wimmer v. Cook*, 774 F.2d 68, 74 (4th Cir. 1985); *Ford v. Estelle*, 740 F.2d 374 (5th Cir. 1984). *But see Lugenbeel v. Schutte*, 600 F. Supp. 698 (D. Md. 1985).

[78] 28 U.S.C. § 636(b)(3).

[79] *See United States v. Garcia*, No. 87-1243, slip op. at 3507-19 (2d Cir. June 1, 1988).

[80] *See United States v. Raddatz*, 447 U.S. 667, 680-81 (1980).

[81] Fed. R. Civ. P. 72(b); *see Bayersdorfer v. Secretary of Health and Human Services*, 578 F. Supp. 131, 132 (S.D.N.Y. 1983).

[82] *See Nelson v. Smith*, 618 F. Supp. 1186, 1189 (S.D.N.Y. 1985).

[83] *Nettles v. Wainwright*, 677 F.2d 404, 408 (5th Cir. 1982) (*en banc*).

PRETRIAL MANAGEMENT

A lesser standard of review applies to a magistrate's decision with respect to discovery matters and other nondispositive motions. The district court will modify such rulings only upon a showing that the magistrate's decision was clearly erroneous or contrary to law.[84] In resolving discovery disputes, a magistrate has broad discretion, and an aggrieved party bears a heavy burden in seeking to reverse such rulings.[85]

C. Procedures for Objection

A party wishing to file objections to either a magistrate's decision on a nondispositive motion or to a report and recommendation has ten days in which to do so.[86] The point at which this period starts to run is somewhat ambiguous. With respect to reports on dispositive motions, Rule 72(b) of the Federal Rules of Civil Procedure requires objections "[w]ithin 10 days after being served with a copy of the recommended disposition," and the Advisory Committee notes indicate that service of the report by mail extends the period for objecting by three days, consistent with Rule 6(e). On the other hand, Rule 72(a) requires that a party object within ten days of *entry* of an order on a nondispositive motion. Local court rules add to the confusion by adopting still different language. For example, Rule 7 of the Rules for Proceedings Before Magistrates in the Southern and Eastern Districts of New York requires objections to both determinations and recommendations to be filed within ten days of the date that the order or report is mailed.[87]

Under limited circumstances, failure to file objections in a timely fashion may be excused. For example, some adequate explanation, such as the illness of counsel, may justify an enlargement of the time allowed for objection. Similarly, a *pro se* litigant may be excused from strict compliance if he has not been notified of the time limits. However, a party may not avoid timeliness requirements simply by couching objections as a motion for reargument.[88]

---

[84] Fed. R. Civ. P. 72(a); see *Detection Systems, Inc. v. Pittway Corp.*, 96 F.R.D. 152, 154 (W.D.N.Y. 1982).

[85] See *Citicorp v. Interbank Card Ass'n*, 87 F.R.D. 43, 46 (S.D.N.Y. 1980).

[86] Fed. R. Civ. P. 72.

[87] Similar confusion surrounds the time limits for a party to respond to objections. Rule 72(b) requires responses within ten days of receipt of the objections to a report, but Rule 72(a) is silent with respect to responding to objections to a determination.

[88] *National Automotive Publications, Inc. v. United States Lines, Inc.*, 486 F. Supp. 1094, 1102 (S.D.N.Y. 1980).

Where the failure to file timely objections is unexcused, tardy objections may be rejected.[89] Although the district court may review and modify a report that has not been objected to, it is not required to do so.[90] Moreover, an issue that was not previously raised before the magistrate may not be used as the basis for objecting to a report. Thus, to preserve all arguments, counsel must present them first to the magistrate and then file timely and complete objections with the district court.

A magistrate's report is not directly appealable to the Court of Appeals; rather, it must first be adopted by the district court. The appellate courts have taken divergent positions on the treatment of appeals raising issues that were not first presented to the district court as objections to the magistrate's report. Some courts have held that such issues are waived, others have considered them appealable. Still other courts have taken a middle ground, holding that appeals on issues of law may be heard in such circumstances, but that arguments based on factual findings are barred. Most recently, in *Thomas v. Arn*,[91] the Supreme Court held that it is within the supervisory power of the courts of appeal to decline to hear appeals of cases—whether legal or factual issues are raised—where the aggrieved party failed to object to a magistrate's report.

D. Trial Before a Magistrate

Pursuant to 28 U.S.C. § 636(c), magistrates may try civil cases—jury or nonjury—upon the consent of the parties. Indeed, a magistrate may "conduct any or all proceedings" in civil cases, so that a preliminary injunction motion, for example, might be heard by a magistrate upon consent, while the full trial on the merits would later be conducted by the district court. Constitutional challenges to consent trials have consistently been rejected.[92]

Only magistrates specially designated by the district court may conduct consent trials. Such designations are generally accomplished by local rule and are applicable to all full-time magistrates in the district.[93] However, part-time magistrates may exercise such jurisdiction only if the chief judge of the district court certifies that no full-time magistrate is reasonably available.

---

[89] *See McCarthy v. Mason*, 554 F. Supp. 1275, 1286 n.11 (D. Conn. 1982), *aff'd*, 714 F.2d 234 (2d Cir. 1983).

[90] *See McCarthy v. Mason*, 714 F.2d at 237 n.2.

[91] 474 U.S. 140 (1985).

[92] *See, e.g., Collins v. Foreman*, 729 F.2d 108, 111-20 (2d Cir. 1984).

[93] *See* Rule 1 of the Rules for Proceedings Before Magistrates, S.D.N.Y. and E.D.N.Y.

Consent to trial before a magistrate must be voluntary, and the Act forbids both the district court and the magistrate from attempting to persuade or induce any party to consent.[94] Nevertheless, advising the parties both by telephone and by letter of the opportunity to consent is permissible.[95] Indeed, one court has found it not to be intrinsically coercive for the magistrate to have scheduled a hearing and then required the parties on the same day to decide whether they would consent to his jurisdiction.[96]

In form, consent to a magistrate's jurisdiction must be clear and unambiguous. Generally, this means that a written consent form will be executed, but the absence of such a form is not fatal if the parties' intent is clear. Although consent will not be lightly implied from the conduct of the parties alone, a party that fails to object to a trial being conducted by a magistrate until after a verdict has been rendered may be found to have waived any objection.[97]

After a case has been referred to a magistrate for trial under section 636(c), "the reference can be withdrawn only by the district court and only 'for good cause shown on its own motion, or under *extraordinary circumstances* shown by any party.' 28 U.S.C. § 636(c)(6) [emphasis added]."[98] Absent a showing that there was no valid consent at the outset, circumstances justifying withdrawal of consent are rare. For example, a substantial change in the relief sought does not warrant withdrawal of the reference. Similarly, judicial economies that might be achieved if the district court were to try the case are not "extraordinary circumstances."

Pursuant to 28 U.S.C. § 636(c)(3), appeal from a judgment entered by a magistrate is generally taken directly to the court of appeals. However, if the parties consent, appeal may instead be taken to the district court, which then utilizes normal standards of appellate review.[99] In that instance, further appeal may be taken only by permission of the court of appeals.[100] Leave to appeal is then granted only if the case presents substantial novel questions of law or there is a substantial likelihood that the decision violates precedent in

---

94 28 U.S.C. § 636(c)(2).

95 *See Collins v. Foreman*, 729 F.2d at 111.

96 *See Adams v. Heckler*, 794 F.2d 303, 307 (7th Cir. 1986).

97 *See Archie v. Christian*, 808 F.2d 1132, 1135-37 (5th Cir. 1987) (*en banc*).

98 *Fellman v. Fireman's Fund Insurance Co.*, 735 F.2d 55, 58 (2d Cir. 1984).

99 28 U.S.C. § 636(c)(4).

100 28 U.S.C. § 636(c)(5).

the circuit.[101] However, even if the magistrate decided a question of law contrary to circuit precedent, the court of appeals need not grant leave if this error has been corrected by the district court.

E. Special Masters

Pursuant to Rule 53 of the Federal Rules of Civil Procedure, the district court may appoint private attorneys to serve as special masters to take evidence, hear argument, and submit reports to the court. Local court rules also address the appointment and function of masters.[102] Special masters differ from magistrates in three significant respects.[103] First, as will be discussed below, the circumstances in which a master may be appointed are far more limited than those in which the court may refer a case to a magistrate. Second, while magistrates, like other judicial officers, are "generalists," a master may be chosen precisely because of his or her expertise in a particular subject area. Finally, magistrates are salaried government employees, while arrangements must be made in each case for compensating special masters.

Rule 53 states that "[a] reference to a master shall be the exception and not the rule." The rule further distinguishes between references in jury and nonjury cases. When a case is to be tried before a jury, a special master may be appointed "only when the issues are complicated." Although the rule does not specify at what stage in a complex case the master may be utilized, there are two situations in which appointment is most common. In cases with massive discovery, the district court may appoint a master to hear and report on disputes over document production, depositions, and the like.[104] Similarly, in cases involving systemic change, such as desegregation cases, the court may employ a special master to help develop and then oversee implementation of the decree effectuating such change.[105]

In nonjury cases, there must be exceptional circumstances justifying appointment of a special master unless the subject of the referral is an account-

---

[101] *See Adams v. Heckler*, 794 F.2d at 309-10; *Wolff v. Wolff*, 768 F.2d 642, 647-48 (5th Cir. 1985).

[102] *See* S.D.N.Y. and E.D.N.Y. Civ. R. 19; N.D.N.Y. Gen. R. 21.

[103] Magistrates may be appointed as special masters, *see* 28 U.S.C. § 636(b)(2), though how this authority differs from that of a magistrate receiving a referral under § 636(b)(1) or (3) is not readily apparent.

[104] *See United States v. International Business Machine Corp.*, 76 F.R.D. 97, 98 (S.D.N.Y. 1977); *Fisher v. Harris, Upham & Co.*, 61 F.R.D. 447, 449 (S.D.N.Y. 1973).

[105] *See, e.g., Powell v. Ward*, 487 F. Supp. 917 (S.D.N.Y. 1980), *aff'd and modified*, 643 F.2d 924 (2d Cir.), *cert. denied*, 454 U.S. 832 (1981).

ing or a difficult computation of damages. Congestion of the district court's docket is not such an exceptional circumstance.[106] On the other hand, no special showing is required to appoint a magistrate as special master.

The function of the special master's report also differs depending on whether the case is tried to the court or to a jury. In jury cases, the report is simply one piece of evidence. As such, it is subject to challenge on grounds of inadmissibility and to rebuttal by other forms of evidence. By contrast, in nonjury cases, the special master's report is generally adopted by the court unless it is clearly erroneous or contrary to law. Objections to a special master's report must be submitted within ten days of the report, but the court may reject or modify a report even if it receives no objections.[107] However, the parties may stipulate that the report is "final," in which case the factual determinations of the master are unreviewable and any objections must be based on legal error.[108]

The court determines the compensation to be received by a special master, often with the stipulation of the parties. After setting the rate for compensation, the court may require one or more parties to pay if, for example, the master has found them guilty of discovery abuses. Alternatively, the court may establish a formula for apportioning this obligation among all parties. Finally, compensation for the special master may be withdrawn from some fund that exists in connection with the litigation.

---

106 *See LaBuy v. Howes Leather Co.*, 352 U.S. 249, 259 (1957).

107 *See Mitchell v. All-States Business Products Corp.*, 250 F. Supp. 403 (S.D.N.Y. 1965).

108 Fed. R. Civ. P. 53(e)(4).

CHAPTER THIRTEEN

DISCOVERY
by Alexander C. Cordes, Esq.*

I. INTRODUCTION

As its name suggests, perhaps the principal purpose of discovery is to discover—learn about—the evidence underlying the opposing party's claims or defenses prior to trial. However, learning about the other party's case—and thus eliminating surprise as a trial tactic—is not the only purpose of discovery. It also helps you find out what evidence is available to support your own case and preserve it so that it will be available at trial.

Discovery, used effectively, should define and narrow the issues, and when this happens, shorter trials are likely. Moreover, in an appropriate case, it may enable you to make a successful summary judgment or partial summary judgment motion. Finally, discovery permits each party to assess his own and his adversary's strengths and weaknesses, enhancing the chance of early settlement.

There are numerous methods that may be utilized in conducting discovery. They are discussed at II, *infra*. The scope of permissible discovery is extremely broad, although there are some specific limitations to it. Both the breadth of discovery and its limitations are analyzed at III, *infra*. The remaining portions of the chapter review the discovery of experts, IV, *infra*, international discovery, V, *infra*, protective orders, VI, *infra*, motion practice, VII, *infra* and discovery strategy, VIII, *infra*.

II. DISCOVERY METHODS

Rule 26(a), Fed. R. Civ. P., lists the six basic methods of discovery:

Parties may obtain discovery by one or more of the following methods: depositions upon oral examination or written questions; written

---

*The author is a partner in the firm of Phillips, Lytle, Hitchcock, Blaine & Huber and he gratefully acknowledges the assistance of his partners, Paul F. Jones, Joseph Ritzert, Paul K. Stecker, Thomas S. Wiswall and Paul B. Zuydhoek in the preparation of this chapter.

interrogatories; production of documents or things or permission to enter upon land or other property, for inspection and other purposes; physical and mental examinations; and requests for admission.

The use of each of these methods is further delineated in the rules.

A. Depositions Upon Oral Examination

While each discovery method has its particular role, oral depositions, which are detailed in Fed. R. Civ. P. 30, enjoy a special place in the discovery arsenal. The oral deposition is best calculated to give you the witness's own answers to questions rather than those of counsel (as happens in the case of answers to interrogatories). Moreover, oral depositions let you see the opposing party or witness in action and may also give you a chance to preview trial counsel's manner and methods. In addition, the oral deposition may catch the adverse deponent in some careless or willfully false testimony.

Rule 30(b)(1), Fed. R. Civ. P., requires that the party desiring to take the deposition of any person upon oral examination give "reasonable notice" in writing to every party to the action. The deposition notice should identify the deponent by name and address, if known, and otherwise should contain a general description sufficient to describe him or the class or group to which he belongs. If the deponent is a nonparty, he must also be subpoenaed. A notice to take the deposition of a corporate party should designate "with reasonable particularity" the matters on which the deposition is sought. The corporation then selects "one or more officers, directors, or managing agents, or other persons who consent to testify in its behalf" who "shall testify as to matters known or reasonably available to the organization." Fed. R. Civ. P. 30(b)(6). The deposition notice may also require the deponent to produce books, papers and things within his possession, custody and control to be marked as exhibits and used in the examination. Fed. R. Civ. P. 30(b)(5). Such a request must comply with the notice requirements of Fed. R. Civ. P. 34, discussed below.

Ordinarily, oral depositions are recorded by a stenographer. However, increasingly, use is being made of videotaped depositions. While they are more costly, in certain circumstances they may be worth the expense. Such may be the case where the objective is to preserve the testimony of some key witness whose demeanor and appearance are especially important but who will be unable to testify in court because of distance, illness or age. Similar considerations may arise in the case of (i) an expert whose schedule precludes a commitment to a later trial court appearance or (ii) the party or witness who should be deposed while examining certain property or demonstrating the use of some particular tool or piece of equipment. A stipulation or court order is required to conduct a videotaped deposition. Fed. R. Civ. P. 30(b)(4). The same subsection also contemplates that an oral deposition may be recorded by audio tape alone. Experience has shown, however, that while this may save money, the savings will probably be at the expense of accuracy when voices drop or several people speak at once.

Finally, Fed. R. Civ. P. 30(b)(7) authorizes a deposition by telephone if the parties so stipulate or there is a court order. The principal advantages of this method are economy and convenience for the deponent. On the other hand, a telephone deposition precludes observing the deponent's demeanor. It is, and should be, used sparingly.

A thorough discussion of depositions is contained in Chapter 14.

B. Depositions Upon Written Questions

Rule 31, Fed. R. Civ. P., sets forth the procedures to be followed in this method of discovery, which is actually a blend of interrogatories and depositions. It is seldom used; its principal advantage is said to be economy. In fact, however, there may be few, if any, economies as the parties follow the detailed procedures for preparing and serving written questions, followed by cross questions, followed by re-direct questions, re-cross questions, etc. Understandably, the cross-examining attorney is at a disadvantage as he tries to draft a cross question without knowledge of the answer to the previous, direct question. In sum, the exercise can be time-consuming and, in the end, ineffectual in all but limited situations.

C. Interrogatories to Parties

Interrogatories are authorized by Fed. R. Civ. P. 33. As already noted, interrogatories do not give examining counsel the chance to see the opposing party—or for that matter his counsel—in action. Moreover, because the answers are almost always prepared by opposing counsel, there is essentially no chance of catching the opposition in some careless or willfully false testimony. On the other hand, interrogatories can play an important role in discovery. When used as an evidence gathering device they should be precisely phrased, narrow in scope and used to obtain discrete, particular items of information. Broadly phrased interrogatories that seek information which need not be stated in precise, objective terms will almost certainly yield little but opposing counsel's subjective responses.

Rule 33(b), Fed. R. Civ. P., also envisions the use of "contention" or "issue" interrogatories that can be useful in narrowing and defining the issues. A more complete discussion of interrogatories and the other methods of discovery outlined below is contained in Chapter 15.

D. Production of Documents and Things and Entry Upon Land for Inspection and Other Purposes

This method of discovery is detailed in Fed. R. Civ. P. 34. While requests for documents frequently appear in deposition notices where a substantial volume of materials is involved, it is ordinarily better to serve a separate request that calls for production well in advance of the deposition. This is further discussed under VIII, "Discovery Strategy," *infra*.

E. Physical and Mental Examination of Persons

When the mental or physical condition or blood group of a party is at issue, physical and mental examinations are available by order under Fed. R. Civ. P. 35. The rule also provides for the exchange of examining physicians' reports.

F. Requests for Admission

Under Fed. R. Civ. P. 36, a request may be made for admission "of the truth of any matters within the scope of Rule 26(b), . . . that relate to statements or opinions of fact or of the application of law to fact, including the genuineness of any documents. . . ." It should be borne in mind that a party responding to a request for admission "who considers that a matter of which an admission has been requested presents a genuine issue for trial may not, on that ground alone, object to the request. . . ."

III. SCOPE OF DISCOVERY

A. In General

The very broad scope of permissible discovery is set forth in Fed. R. Civ. P. 26(b). Discovery may be had of everything that is "relevant to the subject matter involved in the pending action," providing it is not privileged or material prepared for trial.

It is important to recognize that discovery is not limited to that which would be admissible at trial. Rule 26(b)(1), Fed. R. Civ. P., expressly provides that "[i]t is not ground for objection that the information sought will be inadmissible at the trial if the information sought appears reasonably calculated to lead to the discovery of admissible evidence."

Nor is discovery limited to that which is relevant to the *issues*. The standard is whether the material sought is "relevant to the *subject matter*." Indeed, suggestions that the scope of discovery should be narrowed to the "issues" in the case (as a means of limiting discovery abuse) have been rejected. Instead, provision has been made for increased judicial supervision of discovery under Fed. R. Civ. P. 26(f), and, in addition, counsel both making and responding to discovery requests must, in effect, certify that what they have asked and answered is reasonable. *See* Fed. R. Civ. P. 26(g).

B. Insurance Agreements

Rule 26(b)(2), Fed. R. Civ. P., provides for the discovery of "the existence and contents of any insurance agreement under which any person carrying on an insurance business may be liable to satisfy part of all of the judgment. . . ." Recognizing that insurance is "created specifically to satisfy" claims against the insured, it was the view of the Advisory Committee on the Rules that disclosure of this type of information would lead to realistic settlement negotiations. It should be noted that while information concerning the insurance agreement is discoverable, the rule explicitly provides that "the insurance agreement is not by reason of disclosure admissible in evidence at trial."

C. Limitations on Discovery

Despite the breadth of permissible discovery, it is subject to certain specific limitations. Most notably, privileged information is protected and work product is conditionally protected.

It is no surprise that the "collision" between a policy of broad disclosure on the one hand, and privilege and work product exceptions on the other, has generated extensive litigation. A review of the cases is beyond the scope of this chapter, but no discussion of privilege from discovery would be complete without reference to *UpJohn Co. v. United States*, 449 U.S. 383 (1981), which deals with the scope of the attorney-client privilege in respect of corporate employees.

1. Privileged Information

Rule 26(b)(1), Fed. R. Civ. P., in defining the general scope of discovery, specifically excludes matters that are "privileged." The Federal Rules of Evidence specify that privileges may arise under the United States Constitution (*e.g.*, the privilege against self-incrimination in the fifth amendment), federal statutes and common law, or, in civil proceedings where state law applies, under state law. Fed. R. Evid. 501. For practitioners in New York, the state privileges are found in Article 45 of the CPLR. In addition to the familiar attorney-client privilege, CPLR 4503, others listed in Article 45 include: self-incrimination, CPLR 4501, spouse, CPLR 4502, physician/dentist/nurse-patient, CPLR 4504, clergy-penitent, CPLR 4505, eavesdropping evidence, CPLR 4506, psychologist-patient, CPLR 4507, and social worker-client, CPLR 4508.

2. Work Product

While privileged materials are immune from discovery, work product or trial preparation materials are only conditionally privileged: a party can obtain an opponent's trial preparation materials if he makes "the required showing," *i.e.*, shows "substantial need" and that he "is unable without undue hardship to obtain the substantial equivalent of the materials by other means." Fed. R. Civ. P. 26(b)(3). The rule balances the need to know against the important considerations justifying work product protection described in *Hickman v. Taylor*, 329 U.S. 495, 510 (1947):

> In performing his various duties . . . it is essential that a lawyer work with a certain degree of privacy, free from unnecessary intrusion by opposing parties and their counsel.

According to the Advisory Committee on the Rules, "[m]aterials assembled in the ordinary course of business, or pursuant to public requirements unrelated to litigation, or for other nonlitigation purposes are not under the qualified immunity provided by this subdivision." The cases identifying what is—or is not—work product are legion.

Two other points deserve mention concerning the work product limitation: (1) a party or witness can obtain a copy of any statement he has made without "the required showing," and (2) even when trial preparation materials are disclosed "the court shall protect against disclosure of the mental impressions, conclusions, opinions, or legal theories of an attorney or other representative of a party concerning the litigation."

IV. DISCOVERY OF EXPERTS

A. Purposes

Several purposes can be served through discovery of experts. Such discovery, including interrogatories and depositions, can narrow the issues significantly, as to both contentions and factual predicates for the claims of each party. Expert discovery enables each party to avoid ambush at trial and better prepare the case, particularly in the cross-examination of the opponent's experts.

Finally, depositions (and, increasingly, videotaped depositions) are being utilized to preserve the testimony of experts in the event of unavailability for trial.

B. Discovery of Experts Under the Federal Rules

1. Testifying Experts

Rule 26(b)(4)(A)(i), Fed. R. Civ. P., permits a party, through interrogatories, to discover the name of the adversary's expert witness along with the subject matter, substance of facts and opinions and the grounds for the opinions.

> A party may through interrogatories require any other party to identify each person whom the other party expects to call as an expert witness at trial, to state the subject matter on which the expert is expected to testify, and to state the substance of the facts and opinions to which the expert is expected to testify and a summary of the grounds for each opinion.

The local rules of practice of many of the district courts in New York also contain provisions concerning expert discovery and should be consulted. *See, e.g.*, Rule 46(c) of the Civil Rules of the Southern District, Rule 19 of the Rules of the Northern District and Rules 16(d)(3) and (e) of the Rules of the Western District.

2. Non-Testifying Experts

Where exceptional circumstances can be shown, Fed. R. Civ. P. 26(b)(4)(B), permits discovery of non-testifying experts retained by the adversary.

> A party may discover facts known or opinions held by an expert who has been retained or specially employed by another party in anticipation of litigation or preparation for trial and who is not expected to be called as a witness at trial, only as provided in Rule 35(b) or upon a showing of exceptional circumstances under which it is impracticable for the party seeking discovery to obtain facts or opinions on the same subject by other means.

The rule itself does not state what "exceptional circumstances" must be shown. For a discussion of the cases, *see generally* 4 *Moore's Federal Practice* ¶ 26.66[4], n.2 (2d ed. 1987); 8 C. Wright and A. Miller, *Federal Practice and Procedure* § 2032 (1970).

The courts are split as to whether "exceptional circumstances" must be shown in order to discover only the name of a non-testifying expert. One position is that a special showing is not necessary because Fed. R. Civ. P. 26(b)(4)(B) does not contain the word "identify" with the result that the issue is controlled by Fed. R. Civ. P. 26(b)(1), which permits discovery of "the identity and location of persons having knowledge of any discoverable matter." *Baki v. B. F. Diamond Constr. Co.*, 71 F.R.D. 179, 181 (D. Md. 1976). Other cases reaching the same conclusion but for somewhat different reasons include *Sea Colony, Inc. v. Continental Ins. Co.*, 63 F.R.D. 113 (D. Del. 1974); *Martin v. Easton Publishing Co.*, 85 F.R.D. 312 (E.D. Pa. 1980); *Weiner v. Bache Halsey Stuart, Inc.*, 76 F.R.D. 624 (S.D. Fla. 1977).

This position has been rejected by the only Court of Appeals to consider the issue, as well as numerous other District Courts. In *Ager v. Jane C. Stormont Hospital & Training School for Nurses*, 622 F.2d 496 (10th Cir. 1980), the court held that a showing of exceptional circumstances must precede discovery of the name as well as the facts and opinion of a nontestifying expert. In reaching this result, the court relied upon the Advisory Committee notes as well as several policy considerations, including a concern that once identified, the adverse party might contact the expert and obtain information which would not normally be discoverable. Such discovery has been denied by several district courts: *Puerto Rico Aqueduct and Sewer Auth. v. Clow Corp.*, 108 F.R.D. 304 (D.P.R. 1985); *In re Sinking of Barge "Ranger I" etc.*, 92 F.R.D. 486 (S.D. Tex. 1981); *Guilloz v. Falmouth Hospital Ass'n, Inc.*, 21 Fed. R. Serv. 2d 1367 (D. Mass. 1976). There do not appear to be any reported decisions in the Second Circuit. The identity of an expert who has been informally contacted but who was not retained by a party may not be discovered.

3. Depositions of Experts

Pursuant to Fed. R. Civ. P. 26(b)(4)(A)(ii), depositions of experts are permitted only by order of the court. There is no requirement that any special or exceptional circumstances be shown. As a result, depositions of experts are frequently conducted by agreement of counsel, without any order of the court, so long as the party requesting the deposition is willing to pay the expenses. District court judges, of course, have very broad discretion to order the deposition of an opposing party's expert and will generally permit the deposition where the testimony would be important to the case or where it will permit trial counsel to better assess the value of the case or avoid trial by surprise. *See, e.g., United States v. Hooker Chemicals & Plastics Corp.*, 112 F.R.D. 333 (W.D.N.Y. 1986); *Dennis v. BASF Wyandotte Corp.*, 101 F.R.D. 301 (E.D. Pa. 1983).

4. Treating Physicians in Personal Injury Actions

A treating physician is subject to discovery not only as an expert pursuant to Rule 26(b)(4), but also as a fact witness pursuant to Rule 30(a). It is recognized that a treating physician may be not only a retained expert, but also a fact witness whose testimony may be taken as any other nonparty witness. *Quarantillo v. Consolidated Rail Corp.*, 106 F.R.D. 435 (W.D.N.Y. 1985).

V. INTERNATIONAL DISCOVERY

A. The Provisions of the Federal Rules of Civil Procedure

1. In General

Once the court acquires *in personam* jurisdiction over a party, it has the power to require the party to produce evidence within its control, even though the evidence is located in a foreign country. *United States v. First Nat'l City Bank*, 396 F.2d 897, 900-01 (2d Cir. 1968); *see Societe Internationale Pour Participations Industrielles et Commerciales, S.A. v. Rogers*, 357 U.S. 197 (1958). The rules discussed below govern the exercise of that power, as well as enabling parties to obtain discovery from nonparties abroad.

2. Rule 29, Fed. R. Civ. P.

Probably the most flexible and convenient method for obtaining discovery abroad—whether from parties or nonparties—is for counsel simply to stipulate as to when, where, and how the evidence will be taken. Rule 29 allows the parties to modify the discovery procedures established by other rules, and specifically contemplates "that depositions may be taken before any person, at any time or place, upon any notice, and in any manner" as the parties may stipulate in writing. As with any other method of discovery, however, an attorney intending to obtain discovery abroad by stipulation should be sure that his proposed method does not violate the law of the host country. *See* V, A, 5, *infra*.

3. Rule 28(b), Fed. R. Civ. P.

Rule 28(b) sets forth three methods by which a deposition may be taken in a foreign country for use in the federal court: (1) by notice; (2) by commission; and (3) by letter rogatory. If a party proceeds by notice, he simply serves the notice required by Fed. R. Civ. P. 30 or 31, and proceeds to take the deposition at the designated time and place and before the designated person, provided the law of the foreign country permits it. The deposition must be taken before a person authorized to administer oaths *in the place in which the examination is held*, by the laws of either the United States or the foreign country. The notice may designate that person either by name or by descriptive title. 22 U.S.C. §§ 4221 and 4215 authorize U.S. consular officers to administer oaths and take depositions in the consulates to which they are assigned, and subjects the witness at any such deposition to penalties of perjury under the laws of the United States. 22 C.F.R. Part 92 sets out the procedures followed by foreign service officers in taking depositions. The notice method is suitable when the witness will appear voluntarily, but will not be sufficient if the foreign country's compulsory process will be required.

If the party chooses to proceed by commission, he applies to the court for the issuance of a commission, which designates a person to administer the oath and take the testimony, either by name or by descriptive title. The commission by its own terms confers the authority to administer the oath and take the testimony. If the party proceeds by letter rogatory, then he essentially applies to the court to request a foreign tribunal to cause the testimony to be taken, following its own customary procedure and using its compulsory process. *See* Notes of Advisory Committee on Rules. Forms for commission and letters rogatory are set out in 4 Moore's *Federal Practice* ¶¶ 28.04, 28.05 (2d Ed. 1987). The advantage of using letters rogatory lies in the availability of compulsory process in the foreign jurisdiction. The disadvantage lies in the foreign tribunal's lack of familiarity with American concepts of due process. In some legal systems, testimony is taken by a judge, attorneys are not permitted to question, witnesses do not testify under oath or are not subject to cross-examination, and no verbatim transcript is made. *See* Bishop, *Service of Process and Discovery in International Tort Litigation*, 23 Tort & Ins. L.J. 70, 71-2 (1987). An attorney should take steps to determine what practices are followed in the foreign country and whether they can be varied on request.

28 U.S.C. § 1781 authorizes the U.S. Department of State to act as a conduit for letters rogatory and requests for discovery to and from foreign or international tribunals. The section expressly contemplates that letters rogatory and requests may be transmitted directly from foreign or international tribunals to "tribunals, officers, or agencies" in the United States and vice versa. The issuance or denial of letters rogatory rests upon principles of international comity, and is in that sense discretionary with the issuing American court. *In re Anschuetz & Co., GmbH.*, 754 F.2d 602 (5th Cir. 1985), *vacated sub nom. Anschuetz & Co., GmbH. v. Mississippi River Bridge Auth.*, 483 U.S., 107 S. Ct. 3223 (1987), *on remand*, 838 F.2d 1362 (1988). 28 U.S.C. §§ 1696 and 1782 permit the district court to reciprocate the courtesy of the foreign tribunal by executing its letters rogatory and requests for discovery.

4. Rule 45(e)(2), Fed. R. Civ. P.

If the witness abroad is a citizen or resident of the United States, the court can compel him to return and give testimony. 28 U.S.C. § 1783, incorporated into the Federal Rules of Civil Procedure at Rule 45(e)(2), authorizes the district court to issue a subpoena to a United States national or resident who is in a foreign country. The subpoena may require the witness to appear before the district court or to produce a specified document or thing, but will be issued only in extraordinary circumstances. The court must find the testimony or document to be "necessary in the interest of justice" and must further find "that it is not possible to obtain his testimony in admissible form without his personal appearance or to obtain the production of the document or other thing in any other manner." The subpoena must be served pursuant to the Federal Rules, and must be accompanied by a tender of travel and attendance expenses, as determined by the issuing court. 28 U.S.C. § 1784 authorizes the court to punish disobedience of its subpoena served in a foreign country by a fine of up to $100,000.

5. Importance of Foreign Law

In some civil law countries, the taking of evidence is an act reserved to the sovereign, and an attempt by a private attorney to do so would be seen as a violation of judicial sovereignty. Bishop, *supra*, at 71-72. Non-disclosure laws or "blocking statutes" sometimes prohibit a foreign party from producing documents located abroad. *See, e.g.*, *In re Uranium Antitrust Litigation*, 480 F. Supp. 1138, 1144-45 (N.D. Ill. 1979); *United States v. Vetco, Inc.*, 644 F.2d 1324, 1326, 1330-33 (9th Cir.), *modified*, 691 F.2d 1281, *cert. denied*, 454 U.S. 1098 (1981); *In re Grand Jury Subpoenas Duces Tecum Addressed to Canadian Int'l Paper Co.*, 72 F. Supp. 1013, 1018-22 (S.D.N.Y. 1947); *In re Equitable Plan Co.*, 185 F. Supp. 57, 58-59 (S.D.N.Y.), *modified*, 282 F.2d 149 (2d Cir. 1960); *American Indus. Contracting, Inc. v. Johns-Manville Corp.*, 326 F. Supp. 879, 880 (W.D. Pa. 1971). It may also be necessary to obtain a work permit to allow a court reporter to work for hire abroad.

B. The Hague Evidence Convention

The so-called "Hague Evidence Convention"—The Convention on the Taking of Evidence Abroad in Civil and Commercial Matters, *opened for signature* March 18, 1970, 23 U.S.T. 2555, TIAS No. 7444 entered into force for the United States October 7, 1972 (118 Cong. Rec. 20,623)—is intended to facilitate procedures for the taking of evidence abroad. It is set out at 28 U.S.C.A. § 1781 (West Supp. 1988); at U.S.C.S. Administrative Rules of Procedure and Conventions at page 523 (1983); and at VIII Martindale-Hubbell Law Directory Part VII, p. 13 (1988). The Convention has seventeen signatories: Barbados, Cyprus, Czechoslovakia, Denmark, Finland, France, Federal Republic of Germany, Israel, Italy, Luxembourg, The Netherlands, Norway, Portugal, Singapore, Sweden, the United Kingdom, and the United States.

1. Provisions of the Hague Evidence Convention

The Hague Evidence Convention provides for three methods of obtaining evidence abroad: by Letter of Request, Arts. 1-14; by diplomatic officers and consular agents, Arts. 15 and 16; and by commissioner, Art. 17.

a. Letters of Request

The Convention requires each contracting state to designate a Central Authority, through which a "judicial authority" may transmit Letters of Request, requesting the "competent authority" of the receiving country to obtain evidence. The required contents of the Letter of Request are set out in Article 3. Signatory countries may require that the Letter of Request be accompanied by a translation (*see* Art. 4 and the declarations of the contracting countries). The receiving state applies its own law as to the methods and procedures for executing the Letter of Request, but will comply with a request for a special method or procedure unless that is incompatible with its own internal law or otherwise impossible of performance, Art. 9. The executing authority is required to use "appropriate measures of compulsion" to the same extent as it would for parties in its own proceedings, Art. 10.

b. Diplomatic and Consular Officers, and Commissioners

Articles 15 through 22 of the Convention allow signatory countries to specify the conditions under which diplomatic officers, consular agents, and persons appointed as commissioners may take evidence in their territory for use in proceedings abroad. Where one of those officials takes the evidence, Article 21 requires that the notice to the witness be drawn up in the language of the receiving country, notify the witness that he may be legally represented, and in some cases inform him that he is not compelled to appear or to give evidence.

2. Limitations of the Hague Evidence Convention

Article 12(b) of the Convention permits the receiving state to refuse to execute a Letter of Request if it "considers that its sovereignty or security would be prejudiced thereby." Article 21(d) restricts consular officers and commissioners from taking evidence in a manner forbidden by the law of the receiving state, and Article 23 permits signatories to declare that they "will not execute Letters of Request issued for the purpose of obtaining pre-trial discovery of documents as known in Common Law countries." A significant number of signatories have filed declarations limiting the pretrial discovery of documents.

3. Applicability of the Hague Evidence Convention

In *Societe Nationale Industrielle Aerospatiale v. United States District Court for the Southern District of Iowa*, 482 U.S. 522 (1987), the Supreme Court in a five-to-four decision held (1) that the Hague Evidence Convention does not provide the exclusive means for obtaining evidence abroad from a foreign party subject to the court's jurisdiction, (2) that a domestic party need not in all cases resort to the Hague Convention before pursuing the normal methods of the Federal Rules, but (3) that when evidence is sought abroad, the district court "must supervise pretrial proceedings particularly closely" and "should exercise special vigilance to protect foreign litigants from the danger that unnecessary, or unduly burdensome, discovery may place them in a disadvantageous position." 482 U.S. at ____. The court held that a particularized analysis of the facts, sovereign interests, and likelihood of success in each case would be necessary to determine whether international comity required resort to the Hague Convention in the first instance.

In *In re Anschuetz & Co., GmbH*, 838 F.2d 1362, 1363 (5th Cir. 1988), *on remand from* 107 S. Ct. 3223, the Court interpreted *Societe Nationale* to hold "that the district court has complete discretion to determine the most appropriate manner of producing evidence in the cases before it," and declined to set guidelines for resolving conflicts between the Federal Rules and the Hague Convention. Several courts both before and after *Societe Nationale* have held as a matter of international comity that parties should resort first to the Convention before proceeding under the discovery rules of American courts. *Pierburg GmbH & Co. KG v. Superior Court*, 137 Cal. App. 3d 238, 186 Cal. Rptr. 876, 878 (1982); *Hudson v. Hermann Pfauter GmbH & Co.*, 117 F.R.D. 33 (N.D.N.Y. 1987); *Philadelphia Gear Corp. v. American Pfauter Corp.*, 100 F.R.D. 58 (E.D. Pa. 1983); *Schroeder v. Lufthansa German Airlines*, 18 Aviation L. Rep. (CCH) § 17,222 (N.D. Ill. Sept. 15, 1983); *Goldschmidt v. Smith*, 676 S.W.2d 443 (Tex. App. 1984); *Vincent v. Ateliers de la Motobecane, S.A.*, 193 N.J. Super. 716, 475 A.2d 686, 690 (1984); *but see Benton Graphics v. Uddeholm Corp.*, 118 F.R.D. 386 (D.N.J. 1987); *Haynes v. Kleinwefers*, 119 F.R.D. 335 (E.D.N.Y. 1988).*

---

*For a detailed discussion of discovery abroad and other problems arising in international litigation see Chapter 28.

VI. PROTECTIVE ORDERS, INCLUDING PROBLEMS INVOLVING ACCESS BY NONPARTIES

A. The Applicable Rules

1. Rule 26(c), Fed. R. Civ. P.

Rule 26(c) provides the statutory basis for the motion for a protective order. A brief outline of its provisions follows:

Who may move:	"a party" or "the person from whom discovery is sought."
On what basis:	"for good cause shown," such as protection from "annoyance, embarrassment, oppression, or undue burden or expense."
Where to move:	where the action is pending or, "alternatively, on matters relating to a deposition, the court in the district where the deposition is to be taken."
Available relief:	the court "may make any order which justice requires" including eight enumerated, but non-exclusive examples.

As respects the "good cause" element, the burden is on the party seeking to limit discovery. *United States v. Hooker Chemicals & Plastics Corp.*, 90 F.R.D. 421, 425 (W.D.N.Y. 1981). The movant must make "a particular and specific demonstration of fact as distinguished from stereotyped and conclusory statements." *Cooper v. Welch Foods, Inc.*, 105 F.R.D. 4, 6 (W.D.N.Y. 1984). The burden has been characterized as "heavy." *CBS, Inc. v. Ahern*, 102 F.R.D. 820, 822 (S.D.N.Y. 1984).

Unlike state practice, *see* CPLR 3103(b), there is no automatic stay under the Federal Rules merely because a Rule 26(c) motion is made. Only a court order has the effect of staying noticed discovery. *Federal Aviation Administration v. Landy*, 705 F.2d 624, 634 (2d Cir. 1983), *cert. denied*, 464 U.S. 895 (1983). If one fails to move in timely fashion, a waiver may be found. *United States v. International Business Machines*, 70 F.R.D. 700 (S.D.N.Y. 1976).

The granting or denial of a protective order is within the discretion of the district court. The exercise of that discretion will be reversed "only on a clear showing of abuse." *Galella v. Onassis*, 487 F.2d 986 (2d Cir. 1973). The granting of a protective order has been held to be non-appealable. *Bridge C.A.T. Scan Associates v. Technicare Corp.*, 710 F.2d 940 (2d Cir. 1983). As

DISCOVERY

respects the non-exclusivity of the eight enumerated types of protective orders, *see Quaker Chair Corp. v. Litton Business Sys., Inc.*, 71 F.R.D. 527, 533 (S.D.N.Y. 1976).

2. Local Court Rules

The local rules of each District Court in New York also must be consulted in connection with a Rule 26(c) motion. They all require preliminary attempts to resolve disputed discovery matters prior to involving the court. *See* Rule 3(f) of the Civil Rules for the Southern and Eastern Districts; Sec. I(1) of the Standing Order on Effective Discovery in Civil Cases, Eastern District; Rule 10(k)(1) of the Rules of the Northern District; Rule 17 of the Rules of the Western District. Rule 3(f) is typical:

> No motion [under Rules 26 through 37, Fed. R. Civ. P.] . . . shall be heard unless counsel for the moving party files with the court at or prior to the argument an affidavit certifying that said counsel has conferred with counsel for the opposing party in an effort in good faith to resolve by agreement the issues raised by the motion without the intervention of the court and has been unable to reach such an agreement. If part of the issues raised by motion have been resolved by agreement, the affidavit shall specify the issues so resolved and the issues remaining unresolved.

In *Quaker Chair Corp. v. Litton Business Sys., Inc., supra*, after discussing the purpose of the local rule, the court (1) excused the failure to comply as respects that aspect of a motion which it found could not have been resolved in any event, but (2) referred the matter to the magistrate for an assessment of costs and reasonable attorneys' fees as to that portion of the motion which should have been resolved. *See also Yates v. Buscaglia*, 87 F.R.D. 139, 142-43 (W.D.N.Y. 1980) ("Discovery is a matter far more expeditiously and efficiently resolved by negotiation and compromise of counsel than by the court.")

B. Grounds for Protective Orders

1. Confidentiality and Trade Secrets

Issues relating to the need to protect confidential and trade secret information commonly arise in patent, commercial and products liability litigation. The problems are particularly sensitive where the parties, or one of the parties and a nonparty witness, are competitors. The drafters of Fed. R. Civ. P. 26(c) obviously had these concerns in mind when enumerating the following examples of proper protective orders:

> (4) that certain matters not be inquired into, or that the scope of the discovery be limited to certain matters;

(5) that discovery be conducted with no one present except persons designated by the court;

(6) that a deposition after being sealed be opened only by order of the court;

(7) *that a trade secret or other confidential research, development, or commercial information not be disclosed or be disclosed only in a designated way;*

(8) that the parties simultaneously file specified documents or information enclosed in sealed envelopes to be opened as directed by the court. [Emphasis supplied.]

While only subparagraph (7) relates expressly to trade secret and confidential data, subparagraphs (4), (5), (6) and (8) also pertain to those issues. Typical protective orders may include the following provisions: (1) a designation by the producing party of discovery materials to be protected as "confidential, protected by court order"; (2) a limitation of access to confidential materials to "designated persons"; (3) a restricted definition of designated persons, such as, in the competitive context, to attorneys, employees of attorneys and independent experts retained by attorneys; (4) a written undertaking by each designated person that he has read the protective order and will be bound by it; (5) a procedure by which any party may question in court the legitimacy of a confidential designation; (6) a commitment to use the confidential information solely in the pending litigation; (7) a sealing of any confidential documents filed with the court; and (8) a provision requiring the return or destruction of confidential information upon the termination of the action. A form containing many such provisions can be found in the Appendix to *In re "Agent Orange" Prod. Liab. Litig.*, 96 F.R.D. 582 (E.D.N.Y. 1983).

2. Undue Burden or Expense

Another ground for a protective order is undue burden or expense. The arguments over what may constitute an undue burden or expense are legion; however, a few examples may be illustrative.

The courts have granted relief from discovery where the information sought would be easily obtainable elsewhere. *ACLI Int'l Commodity Services, Inc. v. Banque Populaire Suisse*, 110 F.R.D. 278, 288 (S.D.N.Y. 1986). Similarly, the courts express opposition to a "fishing expedition" where the plaintiff's complaint does not define clearly the nature of the claim for relief. *Strait v. Mehlenbacher*, 526 F. Supp. 581, 584 (W.D.N.Y. 1981). A corporate defendant should normally be examined at its principal place of business. *Buryan v. Max Factor & Co.*, 41 F.R.D. 330 (S.D.N.Y. 1967); 4 *Moore's Federal Practice* ¶ 26.70. In the case of pleadings containing allegations of fraud, the courts are especially careful to require that the mandate of specificity in Rule 9(b), Fed. R. Civ. P., be followed before opening the door to discovery. *Segal v. Gordon*, 467 F.2d 602, 607 (2d Cir. 1972); *Goldman v. Belden*, 98 F.R.D. 733 (W.D.N.Y. 1983).

C. Access to Discovery Materials by Nonparties

Rule 5(d), Fed. R. Civ. P., provides that the court "may on motion of a party or on its own initiative order that depositions . . . interrogatories, requests for documents, requests for admission, and answers and responses thereto not be filed unless on order of the court or for use in the proceeding." The Southern, Eastern and Western Districts have local rules which ordinarily prohibit the filing of such materials. Rule 18(a) of the Southern and Eastern Districts; Rule 14(a)(1) of the Western District. Thus, except in the Northern District, discovery materials are not directly available to the public.

A more serious question arises as to whether the public may have access to discovery materials that are the subject of a protective order. Ordinarily the courts will not modify such an order upon application of a nonparty absent extraordinary circumstances. *Palmieri v. State of New York*, 779 F.2d 861 (2d Cir. 1985) (protective order granted in civil antitrust action prohibited nonparty Attorney General from access to discovery materials); *Federal Deposit Ins. Corp. v. Ernst & Ernst*, 677 F.2d 230, 232 (2d Cir. 1982); *but see American Tel. & Tel. Co. v. Grady*, 594 F.2d 594, 597 (7th Cir. 1978), *cert. denied*, 440 U.S. 971 (1979) (permitting modification of protective order despite "higher burden on the movant to justify modification" because the information would otherwise have to be obtained through wasteful duplication).

Some recent cases discussing the right of access to discovery materials by nonparties in product liability cases include *Liggett Group Inc. v. Public Citizen*, No. 88-1195 (1st Cir. September 28, 1988); *Littlejohn v. BIC Corp.*, 851 F.2d 673 (3rd Cir. 1988); *Wyeth Laboratories v. United States District Court*, 851 F.2d 321 (10th Cir. 1988).

VII. MOTION PRACTICE

There are many different types of discovery motions that can arise in the course of a civil lawsuit. Although one thinks first of Fed. R. Civ. P. 37 in connection with discovery motions, there are other provisions that authorize motions relating to particular aspects of discovery. These include Rule 26(c) (motions for protective orders, discussed above in Part VI), Rule 26(d) (motions to establish priority in discovery), Rule 26(b)(4)(A)(ii) (motions for discovery concerning expert witnesses by means other than interrogatories),

Rule 26(g) (motions to impose sanctions for improper signing of a discovery request or response), Rule 30(d) (motions to terminate or limit depositions), Rule 30(g) (motions for expenses and attorneys' fees in appearing for a deposition that does not take place due to the fault of the party scheduling the deposition), Rule 11 (motions to impose sanctions for improper signing of discovery papers), and 28 U.S.C. § 1927 (motions to impose costs, expenses and attorneys' fees on attorneys who multiply proceedings unreasonably and vexatiously).

In addition to the foregoing provisions, the local rules applicable in each district court must be consulted. *See* the discussion at VI, A, 2, *supra*. For example, it is now typically required that before any discovery motion can be brought, counsel must attempt to resolve the dispute and, where those attempts fail, must describe such efforts in the affidavits supporting the motion. Failure to provide an adequate description can lead to summary denial of the motion.

Due to the time, effort and expense consumed in motion practice, the requirement of a good faith effort to resolve the dispute must be taken seriously. There are many occasions on which a discovery dispute cannot be compromised even after good faith efforts to do so. In those cases, the party seeking discovery must make a motion for an order compelling the discovery requested and, if necessary, make a second motion thereafter for sanctions. Those motions are discussed below.

A. Orders Compelling Discovery

1. General Procedures

The procedures to be followed in making a motion for an order compelling discovery are set forth in Fed. R. Civ. P. 37(a). The motion must be made on notice to the other parties (and any nonparties that are affected) and is usually made in the court where the action is pending. In the case of depositions, such a motion may also be made in the district where the deposition is being taken, and indeed must be made there if the deponent is a nonparty.

A motion to compel discovery may be made in connection with any of the discovery devices described in the Federal Rules. It may be made on the ground that no discovery was made at all, that the disclosures that were made were evasive or incomplete, or that the objections asserted were improper.

Rule 37 does not set forth any requirement concerning the time within which the motion must be made. However, this subject is frequently covered by scheduling orders under Fed. R. Civ. P. 16. The more promptly a party moves, the more seriously his position is likely to be taken by the court.

2. Grounds for a Motion to Compel Discovery

The necessary grounds to be set forth in support of a motion to compel discovery under Fed. R. Civ. P. 37(a), are described in Rule 37(a)(2). In general, the moving party must establish by its supporting affidavits that (1) a proper request for discovery was served; (2) the deadline for responding to the request has passed; (3) either the response was not provided at all or, if provided, was insufficient, and (4) the other party rejected the moving party's efforts to obtain a proper response. The moving party should attach to its supporting affidavits copies of the discovery request, the response (if any), and any written communications reflecting efforts to resolve the dispute by agreement (to the extent that those papers are not already in the court file).

Although the moving party has the initial burden of showing he is entitled to the discovery, the burden may shift depending upon the particular objections asserted by the other party. For example, if an objection is based on attorney-client privilege or undue burden and expense, the objecting party will normally have to present facts establishing its applicability. On the other hand, if the objection challenges the relevance of the request, the moving party should be prepared to convince the court that the requested material is relevant to the subject matter of the action within the meaning of Rule 26(b)(1).

3. Available Relief

A successful motion to compel discovery will result in an order directing the other party to make various disclosures. Due to the potential for sanctions for a violation of the order, everyone involved in the motion must pay close attention to the precise language used in the order. For example, if it simply directs the party "to make the discovery requested" (or other words that, in effect, simply adopt the language in the moving party's request), each vague, ambiguous, or indefinite phrase in the request can lead to later argument that the order was violated. It is in the interest of the losing party to insist upon an exact identification of the disclosures to be made.

Where the motion to compel discovery is denied, Fed. R. Civ. P. 37(a)(2) specifically permits the court to enter a protective order in favor of the non-moving party.

Finally, whichever party prevails, Fed. R. Civ. P. 37(a)(4) states that the court "shall" require the losing party (or his attorney) to pay the expenses, including attorneys' fees, of making or opposing the motion as the case may be, unless the court finds that the losing party's position was substantially justified or that such an award would be unjust.

4. Responding to Motions to Compel Discovery

The opposition to a motion to compel discovery will normally include some or all of the following positions: (1) the disclosures that were made in response to the request were sufficient; (2) the request was objectionable and objections were asserted timely in accordance with the rules; (3) the requested disclosures are not yet due as a result of, for example, a court-approved, see Fed. R. Civ. P. 29, agreement to extend the deadline; or (4) the moving party failed to make good faith efforts to resolve the matter prior to making the motion. The opposing party may also request that a protective order be entered, to the extent that the party's objections are sustained.

Where the party receiving the motion does not have a sufficient basis for opposing it, he should consider making the requested disclosures before the motion is heard so that an award of attorneys' fees to the moving party can be reduced or avoided.

B. Orders Imposing Sanctions

If an order compelling discovery has been violated, a variety of sanctions can be imposed under Fed. R. Civ. P. 37(b). The party moving for sanctions should establish in the supporting papers the following elements: (1) an order was entered compelling discovery; (2) the time provided for compliance has expired; (3) the party directed to provide the discovery has not done so; and (4) the movant's efforts to resolve the matter prior to motion were rejected.

Like Rule 37(a), Rule 37(b) does not provide any time period within which a motion for sanctions must be brought. However, it is generally prudent to make the motion while the matters leading to the order compelling discovery are still fresh in the court's mind.

With regard to the relief available on a motion for sanctions, the district courts have wide latitude, making it wise for the moving party to request several alternative forms of relief from which the court may choose. Rule 37(b)(2) authorizes the court to "make such orders in regard to the failure as are just" and then lists the following nonexclusive possibilities:

> (A) An order that the matters regarding which the order was made or any other designated facts shall be taken to be established for the purposes of the action in accordance with the claim of the party obtaining the order;
>
> (B) An order refusing to allow the disobedient party to support or oppose designated claims or defenses, or prohibiting that party from introducing designated matters in evidence;

(C) An order striking out pleadings or parts thereof, or staying further proceedings until the order is obeyed, or dismissing the action or proceeding or any part thereof, or rendering a judgment by default against the disobedient party;

(D) In lieu of any of the foregoing orders or in addition thereto, an order treating as a contempt of court the failure to obey any orders except an order to submit to a physical or mental examination;

(E) Where a party has failed to comply with an order under Rule 35(a) requiring that party to produce another for examination, such orders as are listed in paragraphs (A), (B), and (C) of this subdivision, unless the party failing to comply shows that that party is unable to produce such person for examination.

In addition to those listed sanctions, the rule also expressly authorizes the imposition of expenses, including attorneys' fees, against the party violating the order.

Of particular importance is the authority granted in subparagraph (C) to enter an order "dismissing the action . . . or rendering a judgment by default." It must also be noted in connection with the sanction of dismissal that under Fed. R. Civ. P. 41(b) such a dismissal will be considered "upon the merits" unless the dismissal order specifies otherwise.

VIII. DISCOVERY STRATEGY

A. Order of Discovery Among Parties

Except as is implicit in the provisions discussed in the next paragraph, neither plaintiff nor defendant has priority in conducting discovery. This is embodied in Fed. R. Civ. P. 26(d), which provides: "the fact that a party is conducting discovery, whether by deposition or otherwise, shall not operate to delay any other party's discovery." Civil Rule 14 of the Southern and Eastern Districts applies this rule specifically to depositions, providing:

Neither the service of a notice to take the deposition upon oral examination of party or witness, nor the pendency of any such deposition, shall prevent another party, adverse or otherwise, from noticing or taking the deposition upon oral examination of party or witness concurrently with the taking of such deposition noticed or commenced earlier.

Notwithstanding these provisions, a limited priority can sometimes be achieved through early service of discovery requests because the sooner a discovery request is served, the sooner a response is due.

During the period immediately following commencement of the action, the rules, in effect, afford the defendant a limited priority. Rule 30(a), Fed. R. Civ. P., generally requires the plaintiff, but not the defendant, to obtain leave of court "to take a deposition prior to the expiration of 30 days after service of the summons and complaint upon any defendant. . . ." Similarly, Fed. R. Civ. P. 33(a), 34(b) and 36(a) provide that a defendant need not respond to interrogatories, requests for production and requests for admission until 45 days after service of the summons and complaint. On the other hand, a plaintiff may sometimes obtain a *de facto* discovery priority by virtue of the fact that interrogatories, requests for production and requests for admission may be served before the defendant has appeared—even with the summons and complaint. *See* Fed. R. Civ. P. 33(a), 34(b) and 36(a).

B. Sequence Among Discovery Devices

Rule 26(b)(1), Fed. R. Civ. P., permits the court to limit the frequency or extent of use of the various discovery devices if the discovery sought is duplicative or unduly burdensome. In all other respects, the Federal Rules permit use of the various discovery devices in any sequence (unless otherwise ordered by the court, *see* Fed. R. Civ. P. 26(d)). While the sequence used is a matter of strategy, the following principles should be considered in determining the appropriate sequence in a particular case.

1. Initial Discovery

The deposition of the opposing party is, in most cases, the most important discovery event. Preparation for this and other depositions is facilitated if they are preceded by some preliminary discovery consisting of a request for production of all relevant documents and, where appropriate, limited interrogatories to develop basic facts that will assist in structuring the deposition questioning. Interrogatories concerning the identity and anticipated testimony of experts, *see* Fed. R. Civ. P. 26(b)(4)(A)(i), should be included in the first interrogatories served, if only so that the need to serve such interrogatories will not be overlooked as the case progresses. Extensive interrogatories concerning factual details should be avoided at the predeposition stage, as they will simply elicit counsel's carefully-phrased responses and may unintentionally provide opposing counsel with a preview of the proponent's planned deposition questioning.

2. Timing of Interrogatories

Factually-oriented interrogatories are generally most effective when used in the predeposition discovery described above and to clarify or develop points raised during deposition testimony. For example, interrogatories requesting itemization and description of claimed special damages are helpful

DISCOVERY

if not essential when the deposition testimony concerning damages has been generalized or unsubstantiated. So-called "contention interrogatories" (*i.e.*, those inquiring as to a party's claims and contentions) are generally effective, if at all, following fairly complete factual discovery (*e.g.*, preliminary to trial or summary judgment motion).

Southern District Civil Rule 46 restricts the content of interrogatories that may be served at various stages of the case. Rule 46(a) provides:

> At the commencement of discovery, interrogatories will be restricted to those seeking names of witnesses with knowledge or information relevant to the subject matter of the action, the computation of each category of damage alleged, and the existence, custodian, location and general description of relevant documents, including pertinent insurance agreements, and other physical evidence, or information of a similar nature.

Rule 46(b) permits interrogatories other than those described in Rule 46(a) "[d]uring discovery . . . only . . . if they are a more practical method of obtaining the information sought than a request for production or a deposition." Rule 46(c) permits "[a]t the conclusion of each party's discovery . . . interrogatories seeking the claims and contentions of the opposing party. . . ."

3. Depositions

While depositions may be taken at any stage of discovery, "discovery depositions" (*i.e.*, those seeking discovery of the factual bases of the opposing party's case) are best taken early, and notices should be served with the preliminary discovery requests described above (leaving sufficient time for responses prior to the depositions). Depositions intended not for discovery purposes, but to preserve the testimony of witnesses who may be unavailable at trial, *see* Fed. R. Civ. P. 32(a)(3), are best deferred (absent impending death or other special circumstances) until discovery is sufficiently complete that the questioner can determine all of the subject areas as to which the witness should be questioned.

4. Requests for Admission

Rule 36, Fed. R. Civ. P., permits service of requests for admission "that relate to statements or opinions of fact or of the application of law to fact, including the genuineness of any documents described in the request." While such requests may be served at any stage of discovery, they are best used as a form of "clean-up" discovery to eliminate the need to prove at trial facts which prior discovery has revealed to be indisputable and to resolve evidentiary issues (*e.g.*, by establishing the genuineness of documents).

C. Nonparty Discovery

While Fed. R. Civ. P. 30 authorizes depositions of both parties and nonparties, unless there is a pressing need to preserve testimony, nonparty depositions should generally be deferred until the subject areas requiring nonparty testimony have been clarified by other discovery. Counsel should use discretion in noticing nonparty depositions: often there is no reason to preview for opposing counsel the testimony of a "friendly" nonparty witness who will be available for trial.

CHAPTER FOURTEEN

DEPOSITIONS

by Jeffrey R. Zuckerman, Esq.*
Martin L. Feinberg, Esq.*

I. PRELIMINARY MATTERS

A. Introduction

The deposition is the most powerful weapon in the litigator's discovery arsenal. It is the only formal discovery device by which the attorney can elicit information directly from an adverse party, test his credibility, observe his demeanor, and assess his jury appeal—all without the sanitizing intervention of opposing counsel. It is the only formal discovery device by which a party can obtain information from a nonparty. And it is the only formal discovery device by which counsel can obtain information before the action is filed. But for all of its strengths, the deposition is no more effective than the person employing it. This chapter covers the rules and the practices governing depositions upon oral examination and how to employ them effectively.[1]

---

* Mr. Zuckerman is an Assistant Regional Administrator and Mr. Feinberg is a Staff Attorney in the Enforcement Division of the U.S. Securities and Exchange Commission, New York Regional Office. The authors thank Carmen J. Lawrence, Esq. and Jason R. Gettinger, Esq. for their thoughtful comments.
The U.S. Securities and Exchange Commission, as a matter of policy, disclaims responsibility for any private statement by any of its employees. The views expressed here are those of the authors and do not necessarily reflect the views of the Commission, or of their colleagues on the staff of the Commission.

B. Purpose of a Deposition

Counsel can achieve four main objectives using depositions. First, he can educe the facts of the case. Second, he can uncover additional sources of information. Third, he can learn about the witness. Each witness is unique. Each witness has his own perception of the facts, and each will vary in honesty, credibility and jury appeal. Through the deposition, counsel can determine what facts the deponent knows and evaluate the deponent as a potential witness at trial.

Finally, and especially important, counsel can use the deposition to pin down the witness's testimony for motion practice[2] and for trial.[3] Any party can use the deposition testimony of a witness—party or nonparty—to contradict or impeach that witness if he testifies at trial,[4] for any purpose when the witness is unavailable for trial,[5] or for any other purpose allowed by the

---

[1] There are two kinds of depositions: the deposition upon oral examination, which is the subject of this chapter, and the rarely used deposition upon written questions. Depositions upon written questions are governed by Rule 31 of the Federal Rules of Civil Procedure, which clearly lays out the procedure for taking them. The examining party prepares written questions to be asked the deponent. Before the deposition, he serves them on the other parties (including a party deponent) and presents them to the officer who will take the witness's oral testimony. Cross, redirect, and recross questions may also be propounded and should be served on all the parties.

Depositions upon written questions are rarely used because they are a poor substitute for depositions upon oral examination. In most cases the deponent's counsel will have the questions before the deposition and will prepare the witness to answer them. Moreover, counsel is not able to ask the witness follow up questions. As a result, this method of discovery is not much more effective than interrogatories.

It does have at least two advantages over interrogatories. First, interrogatories cannot be propounded to nonparties while depositions upon written questions can. Second, if a party is not an individual but, for example, a corporation, the corporation determines which one of its officers, directors or managing agents will swear to the accuracy of the information contained in response to an interrogatory. On the other hand, counsel can direct the deposition upon written questions to a particular individual, and in this way counsel can determine that individual's actual knowledge.

[2] See Fed. R. Civ. P. 43(e) (motions generally) & 56(c) (summary judgment).

[3] See Fed. R. Civ. P. 32. The deposition can also be used to authenticate documents for use at trial.

[4] Fed. R. Civ. P. 32(a)(1). Generally, whenever any deposition testimony is used against a party, the party must have either attended the deposition or been represented at the deposition, or had reasonable notice of the deposition. Fed. R. Civ. P. 32(a).

[5] See Fed. R. Civ. P. 32(a)(3) (listing circumstances when the witness is considered unavailable).

DEPOSITIONS

Federal Rules of Evidence.[6] Moreover, an adverse party[7] may offer a deponent's testimony as original evidence—even when the deponent is present in court[8]—if the deponent is a party; someone who was an officer, director or managing agent[9] of a party when the deposition was taken; or someone designated by a party pursuant to Rule 30(b)(6) or 31(a).[10]

Thus, many important discovery goals can be achieved through depositions. However, success requires considerable planning and preparation, since not all of these goals are compatible with each other. Indeed, two primary goals—discovery of facts and pinning down testimony—often conflict. When counsel seeks to discover the facts, he tries to extract from the deponent everything he knows about the case. Conversely, when counsel wants to pin down evidence, he seeks to elicit admissions or other useful facts from the deponent without eliciting exculpatory explanations.

For example, suppose in his case-in-chief, plaintiff's counsel chooses to offer into evidence admissions the defendant made in his deposition testimony. Counsel can do so merely by reading the testimony into evidence. The defendant cannot respond until he testifies in his own case-in-chief, which can be days or even weeks later. This, of course, is the desired effect from the plaintiff's perspective—especially in a jury trial. But if the plaintiff asked too many questions at the deposition, the defendant may have explained away the admission, and if he did, the plaintiff may be required to offer the exculpatory explanation at the trial along with the admission.[11]

---

6 Fed. R. Civ. P. 32(a)(1). The Federal Rules of Evidence are broader than the Federal Rules of Civil Procedure in at least two respects. Federal Rule of Evidence 801(d) permits the use of a trial witness's prior inconsistent statement made "under oath subject to the penalty of perjury at a trial hearing, or other proceeding, or in a deposition" as substantive evidence. Federal Rule of Evidence 801(d)(2) provides in part that a statement made "by a party's agent or servant concerning a matter within the scope of the agency or employment, made during the existence of the relationship . . ." is admissible in evidence. *See* 8 C. Wright, A. Miller & F. Elliott, *Federal Practice and Procedure*, § 2144 (Supp. 1988).

---

7 An adverse party is one "whose interest in the case is adverse to that of another party, even though they may be both nominally aligned as co-parties." 4A J. Moore, J. Lucas & D. Epstein, *Moore's Federal Practice* ¶ 32.04 at 32-18 to 32-19 (2d ed. 1981).

---

8 *See* Fed. R. Civ. P. 32(a)(2); *Pfotzer v. Aqua Systems, Inc.*, 162 F.2d 779, 785 (2d Cir. 1947); 4A J. Moore, J. Lucas & D. Epstein, *Moore's Federal Practice* ¶ 32.04 at 32-17 (2d ed. 1981).

---

9 Who is a managing agent is discussed *infra* Section I, D, 2, b.

---

10 Citations to the Rules are to the Federal Rules of Civil Procedure unless otherwise noted.

---

11 Fed. R. Civ. P. 32(a)(4) provides that if "only part of a deposition is offered in evidence by a party, an adverse party may require the offeror to introduce any other part which ought in fairness to be considered with the part introduced, and any party may introduce any other parts."

Ideally, trial strategy will govern deposition strategy. Accordingly, before taking the deposition, counsel should consider whether he plans to use the deposition testimony at trial, and if so, he should carefully construct his examination to avoid conflicting results.

Besides possible conflicting results, depositions have other disadvantages. First, they are very expensive. Second, they not only educate the examining counsel, they educate opposing counsel. Opposing counsel will learn about the case from preparing the witness before the deposition and from the examiner's questions during the deposition. Opposing counsel may also learn about the examiner's theory of the case, including its strengths and its weaknesses. Moreover, by noticing the deposition of a nonparty, counsel identifies the existence of a witness of whom opposing counsel may otherwise have been unaware.

Third, the deposition educates the witness as well as opposing counsel. It gives the witness a preview of the questions counsel may ask at trial and gives the witness a chance to adjust to them. Finally, just as the deposition preserves testimony favorable to the client, it preserves testimony that may be used against the client.

Despite these drawbacks, the deposition remains the most powerful formal discovery device available. Sometimes, however, an informal discovery device can be equally effective. For example, instead of deposing a nonparty, consider interviewing him when it is ethical and practical.[12] Interviews are less expensive, and counsel can learn—without educating the opponent— what the witness knows and whether it favors his client. If it does, counsel can decide whether to preserve the person's testimony by deposing the witness (because, for example, the person is old, infirm, or located outside the court's jurisdiction), or whether he wants to avoid alerting the opposition to the witness or his testimony until trial. In any case, remember that when you are dealing with nonparties anything you discuss is *not* privileged and is subject to discovery.

C. Stipulations Regarding Depositions

Nearly half of the Federal Rules of Civil Procedure regarding discovery are devoted solely to depositions. But parties can supersede many of the rules by stipulation.[13] Rule 29 provides that the parties may stipulate:

---

[12] *See* New York Code of Professional Responsibility EC 7-18 & DR 7-104, N.Y. Jud. Law Appendix (McKinney 1975). *See also* Model Rules of Professional Conduct 4.2 & 4.3.

[13] Although Rule 29 refers to stipulations by parties, The Eastern District expressly permits stipulations with nonparty witnesses when appropriate. E.D.N.Y. Standing Order 2.

DEPOSITIONS

(i) Before whom the deposition may be taken, *cf.* Fed. R. Civ. P. 28 and *infra* Section I, G;

(ii) When the deposition will be taken, *cf.* Fed. R. Civ. P. 26(d) & 30(a) and *infra* Section I, E;

(iii) Where the deposition will be taken, *cf.* Fed. R. Civ. P. 45(d)(2) and *infra* Section I, F;

(iv) How the deposition will be taken, *cf.* Fed. R. Civ. P. 30(b)(4) (deposition may be taken by non-stenographic means) and *infra* Section I, H; and

(v) Upon what notice the deposition will be taken, *cf.* Fed. R. Civ. P. 30(b)(1) & 45(d)(1) and *infra* Section I. K.

The stipulation must be in writing, and Professor Moore suggests that it be filed with the court.[14] The Western District of New York expressly requires that such stipulations be filed with the court.[15] In these matters as in all others regarding discovery, counsel should check the local rules, as well as any rules of the judge before whom the case is pending.

Often, at the beginning of the deposition, someone will ask whether you agree to the "usual stipulations." Stipulations regarding the conduct of the examination are covered *infra* Section III, D.

D. Who May Take a Deposition or be Deposed

1. Who May Take a Deposition

Generally, only a party may take a deposition.[16] However, under certain circumstances, someone who is not a party but expects to be a party in a future action may take depositions.[17] This topic is discussed *infra* Section I, E, 1, a.

2. Who May be Deposed

a. Party or Nonparty

Either a party or a nonparty may be deposed, and "an allegation that a deponent knows little concerning a matter sought to be inquired into does not

---

14 4A J. Moore, J. Lucas & D. Epstein, *Moore's Federal Practice* ¶ 29.02 at 29-3 (2d ed. 1982).

15 W.D.N.Y. Local R. 25(a).

16 Fed. R. Civ. P. 30(a).

17 Fed. R. Civ. P. 27(a)(1).

prohibit the taking of the deponent's deposition."[18] Whether the proposed deponent is a party or nonparty will affect the type of notice and service required,[19] where counsel can take the deposition,[20] and how counsel can use the deposition testimony at trial.[21]

For example, suppose counsel deposes the employee of a corporate party. Is the employee deemed to be a party? If he is an officer, director or managing agent (discussed in the next section) of the corporation, he is treated as a party. In such a case, anything he says at the deposition can be used for any purpose at the trial, including, for example, as an admission of the party corporation that employs him.[22] If, however, the employee is not an officer, director or managing agent of the corporation, he is not considered a party, and his deposition testimony may only be used for limited purposes such as contradicting or impeaching his trial testimony.[23]

If the issue is raised, the party seeking testimony bears the burden of showing whether the witness is a party or nonparty.[24]

b. Corporations, Partnerships, and Associations

Corporations, partnerships, and associations testify through their officers, directors, or managing agents.[25] Who is a managing agent for these purposes varies with the facts of the case, and the test is not based on the person's title, but on his function.[26] In *Krauss v. Erie R. Co.*, Judge Weinfeld described the managing agent as follows:

---

[18] *Cooper v. Welch Foods, Inc.*, 105 F.R.D. 4, 6 (W.D.N.Y. 1984) (citing *Transcontinental Motors, Inc. v. NSU Moterenwerke Aktiengesellschaft*, 45 F.R.D. 37, 37 (S.D.N.Y. 1968)). *Cf.* E.D.N.Y. Standing Order 10 (discussed in the next section of the text).

[19] *See infra* Section I, J.

[20] *See infra* Section I, F.

[21] *See supra* Section I, B.

[22] *See* Fed. R. Civ. P. 32(a)(2); Fed. R. Evid. 801(d)(2).

[23] *See* Fed. R. Civ. p. 32(a)(1); Fed. R. Evid. 801(d)(1). *But see supra* n.6.

[24] *E.g., Sugarhill Records, Ltd. v. Motown Record Corp.*, 105 F.R.D. 166, 170 (S.D.N.Y. 1985); *Proseus v. Anchor Line, Ltd.*, 26 F.R.D. 165, 167 (S.D.N.Y. 1960).

[25] *See* Fed. R. Civ. P. 30(b)(6) & 37(d).

[26] *Transcontinental Motors, Inc. v. NSU Moterenwerke Aktiengesellschaft*, 45 F.R.D. 37, 38 (S.D.N.Y. 1968).

A managing agent, as distinguished from one who is merely "an employee" is a person invested by the corporation with general powers to exercise his judgment and discretion in dealing with corporate matters; he does not act "in an inferior capacity" under close supervision or direction of "superior authority." He must be a person who has "the interests of the corporation so close to his heart that he could be depended upon to carry out his employer's direction to give testimony at the demand of a party engaged in litigation with the employer."

Each situation is governed by its own facts.[27]

In the Eastern District of New York, if a particular officer, director or managing agent of a corporation or a government official is served with a notice of deposition to testify about a particular subject as to which he has no knowledge, the proposed deponent may submit to the noticing party "reasonably before the date" set for the deposition an affidavit stating he has no knowledge and identifying someone in the corporation or the government entity who does. The noticing party may proceed with the deposition in accordance with the original notice if he chooses, but the proposed deponent may seek a protective order.[28]

If the party seeking testimony is unable to identify the particular individual who has the information he seeks in conjunction with the deposition of a public or private corporation, a partnership, an association or a governmental agency, he may describe the information he seeks in either the notice of deposition or the subpoena[29] "with reasonable particularity" and the entity to be deposed must then designate a representative to testify.[30] The subpoena should notify the nonparty organization of its duty to designate a representative to testify.[31]

---

27 *Krauss v. Erie R. Co.*, 16 F.R.D. 126, 127 (S.D.N.Y. 1954) (citations omitted).

---

28 E.D.N.Y. Standing Order 10.

---

29 For a discussion of notices of deposition and subpoenas, see *infra* Section I, K.

---

30 Fed. R. Civ. P. 30(b)(6).

---

31 *Id.*

c. Person Confined to Prison

A court order is required to depose someone in prison.[32] Counsel should therefore allow sufficient time between the time he moves for authority to depose the prisoner and the time he wants to take the deposition.

E. When to Take a Deposition

1. When a Deposition May be Taken

A deposition may be taken at three times: before commencement of the action,[33] after commencement of the action,[34] and during the pendency of an appeal.[35]

a. Before Commencement of an Action

Before the commencement of an action, an expected party to the action may take the deposition of an expected party (including himself) or a non-party in order to perpetuate testimony, but only pursuant to a court order.[36] The court may order additional discovery of expected parties pursuant to Fed. R. Civ. P. 34 ("Production of Documents and Things and Entry Upon Land for Inspection and Other Purposes") and Fed. R. Civ. P. 35 ("Physical and Mental Examination of Persons").[37] Anyone who expects to be a party to a federal action may seek such discovery before the action is commenced.

b. After Commencement of the Action

The rules governing the plaintiff and the defendant differ. The defendant may notice and take depositions immediately after the complaint is filed with the court.[38] In general, the plaintiff must wait until the expiration of 30 days "after service of the summons and complaint upon any defendant or service

---

[32] Fed. R. Civ. P. 30(a).

[33] Fed. R. Civ. P. 27(a).

[34] Fed. R. Civ. P. 30(a).

[35] Fed. R. Civ. P. 27(b).

[36] Fed. R. Civ. P. 27.

[37] *See* Fed. R. Civ. P. 27(a)(3). At least one court has stated that in the proper circumstances an order authorizing discovery under Rule 34 prior to the commencement of an action need not be in conjunction with a deposition taken pursuant to Rule 27. *See Martin v. Reynolds Metal Corp.*, 297 F.2d 49, 55-56 (9th Cir. 1961). *But see United States v. Morelock*, 124 F. Supp. 932, 948 (D. Md. 1954).

[38] Fed. R. Civ. P. 3 & 30(a).

DEPOSITIONS

made under Rule 4(e)" before taking any depositions.[39] This gives the defendant an opportunity to retain counsel.[40] The plaintiff may serve the notice of deposition before the expiration of the 30 days so long as the date set for the deposition is subsequent to the 30-day period.[41]

If the plaintiff is interested in receiving documents from the defendant before the deposition, he should coordinate the dates he sets for the document production and the deposition carefully.[42] For example, the defendant has 30 days after the service of the document request or 45 days after the service of the summons and complaint, whichever is longer, before responding to the document request.[43] Thus, if the plaintiff serves the defendant with the summons, complaint, notice of deposition, and document request on March 31, the earliest he can depose the defendant is May 1, but the defendant need not respond to the document request until as late as May 15.

The plaintiff may take depositions prior to the expiration of the 30 days after service of the summons and complaint:

(i) If a defendant has sought discovery (including by service of a notice of deposition) during the 30 day period; or

(ii) By court order obtained with or without notice to the other parties; or

(iii) By serving a notice of deposition[44] upon the parties stating:

— the person to be deposed "is about to go out of the district where the action is pending and more than 100 miles from the place of trial, or is about to go out of the United States, or is bound on a voyage to sea,"[45]

---

39 Fed. R. Civ. P. 30(a).

40 Fed. R. Civ. P. 30(a) advisory committee note to 1970 amendment.

41 Fed. R. Civ. P. 30(a) advisory committee note to 1970 amendment.

42 *See* E.D.N.Y. Standing Order 14.

43 Fed. R. Civ. P. 34(b). For a more detailed discussion of document requests, see Chapter 15.

44 Discussed below, Section I, K.

45 Fed. R. Civ. P. 30(a) & (b).

— the person to be deposed "will be unavailable for examination unless the person's deposition is taken before expiration of the 30-day period,"[46] and

— the facts supporting the above statement.[47]

The plaintiff's attorney must sign the notice, and the sanctions of Rule 11 of the Federal Rules of Civil Procedure apply.

A deposition cannot be used against a party if he is deposed before the expiration of the 30-day period pursuant to the special notice provisions and he demonstrates that when he was served with the notice he "was unable through the exercise of diligence to obtain counsel to represent" him at the deposition.[48]

c. Pending Appeal

Depositions and discovery under Rules 34 and 35 may be taken to perpetuate testimony for future proceedings in the district court when an appeal is taken from a district court judgment or the time for taking such an appeal has not expired.[49] The party seeking the deposition must move before the district court that rendered the judgment for leave to take the deposition. The motion should include:

(i) The names and addresses of the persons to be deposed;

(ii) The substance of the testimony to be elicited; and

(iii) The reasons for perpetuating the testimony.

The court will grant the motion if "the perpetuation of the testimony is proper to avoid a failure or delay of justice."[50]

2. When the Deposition Should be Taken—Strategy

Except as discussed above, no hard and fast rule governs the timing of a particular deposition. However, when counsel considers taking a deposition, he should consider (1) whether to take it early in the discovery process and (2) whether to depose other people first.

---

[46] Id.

[47] Id.

[48] Fed. R. Civ. P. 30(b)(2).

[49] See Fed. R. Civ. P. 27(b).

[50] Fed. R. Civ. P. 27(b).

DEPOSITIONS

Deposing someone early in the discovery process has a number of advantages. Opposing counsel and his client will not have responded to a document request or interrogatories and will not have had the benefit of reading earlier testimony. They will probably know less about the facts and issues of the case, and counsel will not be able to prepare the deponent as well as he could later. The deponent's testimony will be more nearly spontaneous, less influenced by his counsel's theory of the case (which may not yet have crystallized), and if taken properly, locked-in for the remainder of the case. On the other hand, early in the discovery process, the examining attorney may also know less about the facts and the issues, which limits his ability to educe the information he needs and to test the witness's veracity.

Taking the deposition later in the discovery process solves this problem. The examining attorney has access to all the discovery educed and is able to prepare properly for the deposition. This, of course, is also true of the deponent, but in a complex case, taking the deposition later in the discovery process (i.e., after documents are produced and interrogatories are answered) may be the more effective strategy.

Another possible tactic is to start the deposition early in discovery, examine the deponent with regard to the issues conducive to early examination, adjourn the deposition, and complete it later in the discovery process.

In what order should the witnesses be deposed? Again, there is no hard and fast rule. In more complex cases, it may be advisable to depose witnesses who have the basic facts before deposing, for example, the high level policy makers of large organizations, who may know less about the day-to-day operations of the organization.

3. Priorities in the Taking of Depositions

The federal rules expressly reject priorities in discovery, including depositions (unless, of course, the court sets priorities).[51] Counsel may stipulate to the sequence in which the depositions will be taken. If counsel must take a particular deposition first (and counsel does not want to move for a protective order), he should consider noticing the deposition first and scheduling it for the shortest reasonable period after service of the notice.

---

51 Fed. R. Civ. P. 26(c); *see* S.D.N.Y. & E.D.N.Y. Local Civ. R. 14.

F. Where to Take the Deposition

1. Requirements

a. Party

The rules provide no guidance regarding where a party's deposition should be taken, and the party noticing the deposition can choose the place of the examination subject, of course, to a motion for a protective order pursuant to Rule 26(c). Generally, if the plaintiff's deposition is noticed for the place where the action is pending, he must usually present himself there, since he selected the forum.[52] However, the court has discretion pursuant to Rule 26(c) to order that the deposition be taken at another site:

> [N]ot in every case is a party seeking pretrial discovery entitled as of right to a deposition on oral examination at the situs of the forum. His preference therefor, if opposed under Rule 30(b) [currently Rule 26(c)], must be weighed both against his actual, as distinguished from his supposed, need for oral examination at the forum and against the resulting burden to his opponent.[53]

When the issue has arisen, the courts have usually ordered that a defendant's deposition be taken in the jurisdiction of his residence, place of business or employment.[54] A corporation's deposition is usually taken in the jurisdiction of its principal office and place of business.

b. Nonparty

A nonparty may be deposed at any convenient place the court may order, or within 100 miles of:

(i) The nonparty's residence;

(ii) The nonparty's place of employment or where the nonparty personally transacts business; or

(iii) Where the nonparty is served.[55]

---

[52] *E.g., Clem v. Allied Van Lines Int'l Corp.*, 102 F.R.D. 938, 939-40 (S.D.N.Y. 1984) (citing cases); *Slade v. Transatlantic Fin. Corp.*, 21 F.R.D. 146, 146 (S.D.N.Y. 1957).

[53] *Hyam v. American Export Lines, Inc.*, 213 F.2d 221, 222 (2d Cir. 1954).

[54] *Kurt M. Jachmann Co. v. Hartley, Cooper & Co.*, 16 F.R.D. 565, 565 (S.D.N.Y. 1954); *see Haymes v. Columbia Pictures Corp.*, 16 F.R.D. 118 (S.D.N.Y. 1954) (Weinfeld, J.). *But see Sugarhill Records, Ltd. v. Motown Record Corp.*, 105 F.R.D. 166, 171-72 (S.D.N.Y. 1985).

[55] Fed. R. Civ. P. 45(d)(2).

DEPOSITIONS

A nonparty served with a subpoena may volunteer to be deposed where the subpoena is not enforceable. In such a case, if he does not appear, the party noticing the deposition may be required to pay the expenses of the other parties or their attorneys who do appear.[56]

2. Other Considerations

Once the general site of the deposition is determined, the specific site of the deposition should be determined. Some possibilities include:

  (i) *The examining attorney's office.* The examining attorney has the advantage since he is on his home turf, and he is familiar with the surroundings. Moreover, he does not waste time traveling to the site of the deposition or suffer the burden of carrying the potential deposition exhibits to the site of the deposition.

  (ii) *Office of the examining attorney's local counsel.* The examining counsel is usually more familiar with the office than the opposition and will therefore feel more comfortable there than the deponent.

  (iii) *Court reporter's office.* A neutral site that may serve as a good compromise if counsel cannot agree upon a site and the parties want to avoid court intervention.

  (iv) *Courthouse.* May intimidate the deponent. If necessary, counsel may obtain immediate rulings on objections that impede the conduct of the deposition.

  (v) *Deponent's office.* May sometimes be considered, especially if the deponent will have ready access to documents the examining attorney may want. Also, the examining attorney may learn about the deponent by observing the surroundings. For these reasons, the defending attorney may want to avoid the deponent's office and suggest someplace nearby.

  (vi) *Opposing counsel's office.* The deponent may feel too comfortable in these familiar surroundings, and the examining counsel may want to avoid taking the deposition there.

3. Deposition by Telephone

Counsel may also consider taking the deposition by telephone. Rule 30(b)(7) expressly provides for telephone depositions pursuant to a stipulation of the parties or an order of the court. In the Eastern District of New

---

[56] 4A J. Moore, J. Lucas & D. Epstein, *Moore's Federal Practice* ¶ 30.57[7] at 30-96 (2d ed. 1987). *See* Fed. R. Civ. P. 30(g)(2).

York, "the motion of a party to take the deposition of an *adverse party* by telephone will be presumptively granted."[57] The deposition is considered taken in the jurisdiction where the deponent answers the questions.[58]

The main advantage of the telephone deposition, of course, is its relatively low cost, since counsel need not travel to the site of the deposition. Its greatest disadvantage is counsel's inability to observe the deponent's demeanor, which reduces counsel's ability to evaluate the deponent's credibility.

If counsel requests documents from the deponent, he should leave sufficient time to obtain and review them and to send those documents to be used as exhibits to the site of the deposition. Consider using the telephone deposition when the deposition will be relatively short and will have few exhibits, and you need relatively simple, objective information. If counsel seeks to depose a nonparty, remember that any documents he requests may be produced at the time and place of the deposition, and it may be difficult to examine the witness about them.

Counsel should also consider using telephone depositions in lieu of depositions upon written questions (discussed *supra* n.1). Although it is slightly more expensive, the telephone deposition has all the advantages of the written deposition, plus the deponent does not get a preview of the questions and the examining attorney is able to ask follow-up questions.

Also consider having the examining counsel depose the witness in person while counsel for some or all of the other parties participate by telephone.[59] In this way, the examining counsel may evaluate the deponent's demeanor, while counsel for parties whose interests do not require that they attend the deposition personally may provide adequate representation at a fraction of the cost.

G. Persons Before Whom the Deposition May be Taken

The person before whom the deposition may be taken (the "officer") is not necessarily, but usually is, the same person who records the deposition. When the deposition is taken in the United States,[60] this person must be:

---

57 E.D.N.Y. Standing Order 8 (emphasis added).

---

58 Fed. R. Civ. P. 30(b)(7).

---

59 *See* 4A J. Moore, J. Lucas & D. Epstein, *Moore's Federal Practice* ¶ 30.57[15] at 30-127 to 30-128 (2d ed. 1981).

---

60 For the rules on taking depositions outside the United States, *see* Fed. R. Civ. P. 28(b). *See* Chapter 28.

(i) "an officer authorized to administer oaths by the laws of the United States or of the place where the examination is held,"[61]

(ii) "a person appointed by the court in which the action is pending,"[62] or

(iii) a person "designated by the parties under Rule 29 [Stipulations Regarding Discovery Practice]."[63]

The officer administers the oath and must be present throughout the deposition even if he is not the person recording the testimony. When calling the reporting service to hire a reporter, make sure you tell the service you need a reporter who is authorized to administer the oath.

A deposition may not be taken before "a person who is a relative or employee or attorney or counsel of any of the parties, or is a relative or employee of any such attorney or counsel, or is financially interested in the action."[64] Presumably, if the parties stipulate to the taking of the deposition before a particular individual (with full disclosure of any disqualifying attributes), then there is no disqualification. Objection to the qualifications of an individual is waived unless "made before the taking of the deposition begins or as soon thereafter as the disqualification becomes known or could be discovered with reasonable diligence."[65]

H. How to Record the Deposition

The deposition is usually recorded in one of three ways: by a stenographer, by audio tape, or by video tape. The most common method is by stenographer. Indeed, this is the method by which the Rules presume the deposition will be recorded, since the use of any other method requires an order of the court or a stipulation of the parties.[66] If the deposition is taped electronically pursuant to a stipulation, the stipulation must designate "the person before whom the deposition shall be taken, the manner of recording, preserving and

---

61 Fed. R. Civ. P. 28(a).

62 *Id.*

63 *Id.*; *see* Fed. R. Civ. P. 29 & 30(c).

64 Fed. R. Civ. P. 28(c).

65 Fed. R. Civ. P. 32(d)(2). *See also infra* Section III, G, 1.

66 *See* Fed. R. Civ. P. 30(b)(4). In the Eastern District of New York motions to record depositions by non-stenographic means are presumptively granted, and the audio or video taped deposition must be transcribed if one of the parties requests it. E.D.N.Y. Standing Order 7.

filing the deposition, and may include other provisions to assure that the recorded testimony will be accurate and trustworthy."[67]

Video taped depositions are especially useful to memorialize the testimony of important witnesses who may not be available for trial.[68] Nearly everyone under the age of 40 grew up watching television, and if the witness looks attractive and credible on the television screen, his "T.V. testimony" will have a greater impact on the trier of fact than will counsel reading the deposition testimony.

Electronically recorded depositions are fraught with traps for the unwary, ranging from the failure of recording equipment at the deposition to the doctoring of the taped testimony after the deposition. Much has been written about the pros and cons of the electronic recording of depositions and the possible problems that may arise from taking them.[69] To assure that he protects his client's interests, counsel should read some of the literature before committing himself to an electronically recorded deposition.

I. Costs of the Deposition

Who pays for the costs of the deposition is not always clear. The party noticing the deposition pays for the officer. The deposition is not transcribed unless one of the parties requests it,[70] and who pays the cost of transcribing the deposition is left to the discretion of the court, with a relevant factor being who requested that the deposition be transcribed.[71] The general rule, however, is that "the party noticing and conducting the deposition is the proper

---

[67] Fed. R. Civ. P. 30(b)(4).

[68] *See, e.g.*, *In re Agent Orange Prod. Liab. Litig.*, 96 F.R.D. 587 (E.D.N.Y. 1983).

[69] *See, e.g.*, R. Haydock & D. Herr, *Discovery Practice* §§ 3.3.2 & 3.3.3 (1982); McElhaney, *Presenting Depositions*, 74 A.B.A. J. 84, 85 (1988); Murray, Jr., *Using Video in Litigation*, in Deposition Techniques in Commercial Litigation 299 (P.L.I. 1987); Supplee, *Depositions: Objectives, Strategies, Tactics, Mechanics, and Problems*, 2 Rev. of Litigation 255, 314 18 (1982).

[70] Fed. R. Civ. P. 30(b)(4).

[71] Fed R. Civ. P. 30(c) advisory committee note to 1970 amendment.

DEPOSITIONS

party to bear the transcription costs" unless there are extenuating circumstances.[72] The deponent and the parties pay for their own copies of the deposition.[73]

At the end of the litigation, the prevailing party may recover some of his deposition costs.[74] In the Southern and Eastern Districts of New York, for example, the following deposition costs are allowed:

> The original transcript of a deposition, plus one copy is taxable if the deposition was received in evidence whether or not it was read in its entirety. Costs for depositions are also taxable if they were used by the court in ruling on a motion for summary judgment. Costs for depositions taken solely for discovery or used only for impeachment purposes are not taxable. Counsel's fees and expenses in attending the taking of a deposition are not taxable except as provided by statute, rule or order of the court. Fees, mileage, and subsistence for the witness at the deposition are taken at the same rate for attendance at trial if the deposition taken is received in evidence.[75]

J. Production of Documents in Connection with Depositions

In conjunction with the deposition, the examining party can require the deponent to produce documents. If the deponent is a party, the examining party need only attach a Rule 34 document request to the notice of deposition, and the procedures of Rule 34 apply.[76] If the deponent is a nonparty, the *only* way to obtain documents by means of formal discovery procedures is in

---

[72] *Melton v. McCormick*, 94 F.R.D. 344, 346 (W.D.N.Y. 1982); *accord Caldwell v. Wheeler*, 89 F.R.D. 145, 147, 148 (D. Utah 1981).

[73] Fed. R. Civ. P. 30(f)(2) ("Upon payment of reasonable charges therefor, the officer shall furnish a copy of the deposition to any party or to the deponent."). For a discussion of the apparent conflict between a deponent's right to a copy of the transcript and the necessity that a party request that the deposition be transcribed, *see* 4A J. Moore, J. Lucas & D. Epstein, *Moore's Federal Practice* ¶ 30.59 (2d ed. 1981).

[74] *See* Fed. R. Civ. P. 54(d).

[75] S.D.N.Y. & E.D.N.Y. Local Civ. R. 11(c)(2).

[76] *See* Fed. R. Civ. P. 30(b)(5). Of course a party may also serve a separate Rule 34 document request. For a discussion of notices of deposition and subpoenas, *see infra* Section I, K.

conjunction with a deposition[77] and pursuant to a Rule 45(d) subpoena.[78] The subpoena "may command the person to whom it is directed to produce and permit inspection and copying of designated books, papers, documents, or tangible things. . . ."[79]

The examining counsel should assure that the witness produces the documents before the date of the deposition. He can do this by agreement with the witness's attorney or by use of formal discovery methods. If the witness is a party, the examining counsel can serve him with a Rule 34 document request that requires the production of documents prior to the date of the deposition. If the witness is a nonparty, no formal procedure appears to exist. Some counsel serve the nonparty with a deposition subpoena that commands him to appear for a deposition but to produce documents in advance of the deposition. Other counsel serve a subpoena that commands the nonparty to appear for a deposition and produce documents at the same time, while in a transmittal letter, they adjourn the witness's appearance until after the documents are produced.

In the Eastern District, the rule is that the notice of deposition and the request for documents to a party should be made so that the party produces documents before the deposition in light of the requirements of Rule 34.[80]

K. Notice and Service

1. Parties

All parties must receive "reasonable notice in writing" of the deposition,[81] regardless of whether the person to be deposed is a party or a nonparty. The form of notice is almost the same whether or not the party happens to be the person being deposed. *See* Exhibits 1 & 2 to this chapter. The notice may be served by mail. Be sure to prepare a proof of service and, when appropriate, file it with the court.

---

[77] *See, e.g., Turner v. Parsons*, 596 F. Supp. 185, 186 (E.D. Pa. 1984) (citing cases); *United States v. International Business Machines*, 71 F.R.D. 88, 90 (S.D.N.Y. 1976); *Newmark v. Abeel*, 106 F. Supp. 758, 759 (S.D.N.Y. 1952).

[78] *See infra* Section I, K, 1, b. This is not to be confused with a Rule 45(e) subpoena ("Subpoena for a Hearing or Trial"), which, unlike a Rule 45(d) subpoena, does not require notice to the parties before the clerk of the court issues it.

[79] Fed. R. Civ. P. 45(d)(1). For a discussion of quashing the subpoena or objecting to the production of documents, see *infra* Section I, L, 2, a.

[80] *See* E.D.N.Y. Standing Order 14.

[81] Fed. R. Civ. P. 30(b)(1).

a. Reasonable Notice

(1) Number of Days in Advance

Professor Moore suggests that five days notice in advance of the deposition constitutes "reasonable notice."[82] It would follow from Rule 6(e) that if the notice is served by mail that "reasonable notice" is eight days.

(2) Enlarging or Shortening Time

For "good cause shown," the time between the notice and the deposition may be enlarged or shortened by motion pursuant to Rules 26(c) or 30(b)(3). The plaintiff may also move *ex parte* pursuant to Rule 30(a) to take a deposition within the first 30 days after the summons is served.[83]

b. Contents of Notice

The notice should contain the following information:[84]

(i) *The time the deposition will be taken*—date and hour. *See* discussion *supra* Section I, E.

(ii) *The place the deposition will be taken*—provide as much detail as possible including the number of the room in which the deposition will take place. *See* discussion *supra* Section I, F.

(iii) *The name and address of deponent*—if the name and/or address are not known, "a general description sufficient to identify the person or the particular class or group to which the person belongs" is sufficient.[85]

If the deponent is a corporation, partnership, association or government agency, then the party seeking testimony may describe in the notice "with reasonable particularity" the information sought and the entity must designate someone with the information.[86]

---

82 4A J. Moore, J. Lucas & D. Epstein, *Moore's Federal Practice* ¶ 30.57[3] at 30-89 to 30-90 (2d ed. 1981). *Cf. Radio Corp. of Am. v. Rauland Corp.*, 21 F.R.D. 113 (N.D. Ill. 1957) (one day's notice was reasonable under the circumstances of the case).

---

83 *See* discussion *supra* Section I, E, 1, b, (2).

---

84 *See* Fed. R. Civ. P. 30(b)(1).

---

85 Fed. R. Civ. P. 30(b)(1).

---

86 *See* Fed. R. Civ. P. 30(b)(6) and *supra* Section I, D, 2, b.

(iv) The signature of at least one attorney of record in the attorney's individual name and the attorney's address. If the party is not represented by counsel, then the party must sign the notice and provide his address.[87]

If a plaintiff wishes to take a deposition within 30 days following the commencement of the action, special requirements for the contents of the notice may apply. *See supra* Section I, E, 1, b, (2).

2. Nonparties

Nonparties do not receive notices of deposition. A nonparty who is to be deposed is served with a subpoena pursuant to Rule 45(d)(1). *See* Exhibit 3. The procedure for obtaining and serving the subpoena is as follows:

(i) Serve a notice of deposition of the nonparty upon all parties. *See* Exhibit 2. Attach to the notice any document request that you are making to the intended witness.

(ii) File the original notice of deposition and the "proof of service" of the notice of deposition with the clerk of the court in the district in which the deposition will be taken.

The usual certificate of service certifying that the notice of deposition has been served upon each party's counsel and listing the date and manner of service and the names of those served is adequate proof of service. If the deposition will be taken in a jurisdiction with which you are not familiar, it is usually a good idea to call the clerk in advance to confirm exactly what procedures they follow.

If the district in which the deposition will be taken is *not* the district in which the action is pending, file the notice of deposition and the certificate of service with the clerk of the court in the district in which the action is pending, obtain a certified copy of the certificate of service from the clerk and file it with the clerk of the court in the district in which the deposition will be taken.[88]

You may want to take three copies of the certificate of service to the clerk of the court in which the action is pending. One copy should be filed. The other two should be certified by the clerk. Retain one for your records and file the other one with the clerk in the court from which the subpoena will be issued.

---

[87] Fed. R. Civ. P. 26(g).

[88] 5A J. Moore & J. Lucas, *Moore's Federal Practice* ¶ 45.07[1] at 45-54 (2d ed. 1986).

(iii) The clerk will issue to you a signed and sealed subpoena. It will be blank otherwise.

(iv) Fill in the subpoena and attach to it any document request you have. (Refer to the attachment in the appropriate place in the body of the subpoena.)

(v) Have a *copy* of the subpoena served on the intended witness with *fees* for round trip mileage for the trip to the place of the deposition and for *one* day's attendance at the deposition. If you do not serve the fees with the subpoena, the subpoena may be quashed.[89] Moreover, if service is improper, the subpoena can be ignored.[90] If the subpoena is issued on behalf of the United States, or an officer or agency of the United States, the fees need not be tendered when the subpoena is served.[91] The fees will, however, be paid at a later date.

The person serving the subpoena should fill out the back of the *original* subpoena (including the affidavit of service) and return it to you for filing with the clerk of the court from which the subpoena was issued.

The witness fee is currently $30 for each day's attendance.[92] The mileage fee is currently $.20 per mile for a privately-owned motorcycle, $.25 per mile for privately-owned automobile, and $.45 per mile for a privately-owned plane.[93]

---

89 *CF & I Steel Corp. v. Mitsui & Co.*, 713 F.2d 494, 496 (9th Cir. 1983); *Bowers v. Buchanan*, 110 F.R.D. 405, 406 (S.D. W. Va. 1986).

90 *In re Tracy*, 106 F.2d 96 (2d Cir.), *cert. denied*, 308 U.S. 597 (1939).

91 Fed. R. Civ. P. 45(c).

92 28 U.S.C.A. § 1821(b).

93 28 U.S.C.A. § 1821(c)(2) & 5 U.S.C.A. § 5704.

The subpoena must be served personally on the intended witness[94] "by the marshall, a deputy marshall, or by any other person who is not a party and is not less than 18 years of age."[95] The subpoena cannot be served by mail.[96]

With few exceptions, "witnesses, suitors and their attorneys, while in attendance in connection with the conduct of one suit are immune from process in another."[97]

L. Seeking Judicial Intervention Prior to Deposition

1. Party

a. Type of Protection Available

A party seeking protection from a deposition must seek protection from the court pursuant to Rule 26(c).[98] The court will grant protection for "good cause shown" to protect a "party or person from annoyance, embarrassment, oppression, or undue burden or expense. . . ."[99] The types of protection the court may grant include:

(i) That the deposition not be taken;

(ii) That the deposition be taken only at a designated time or place;

(iii) That another form of discovery be substituted for the deposition;

(iv) That the examination be limited only to certain matters;

(v) That the examination not include certain matters;

(vi) That only certain people be present at the deposition;

(vii) That a sealed deposition be opened only by the court;

---

[94] *FTC v. Compagnie de Saint-Gobain-Pont-a-Moussan*, 636 F.2d 1300, 1312-13 (D.C. Cir. 1980); *Harrison v. Prather*, 404 F.2d 267, 273 (5th Cir. 1968). *But see FTC v. Carter*, 636 F.2d 781, 790-91 (D.C. Cir. 1980).

[95] Fed. R. Civ P. 45(c).

[96] *FTC v. Compagnie de Saint-Gobain-Pont-a-Moussan*, 636 F.2d 1300, 1312 (D.C. Cir. 1980).

[97] *Ferguson v. Ford Motor Co.*, 92 F. Supp. 868, 869 (S.D.N.Y. 1950) (quoting *Lamb v. Schmitt*, 285 U.S. 222, 225 (1932)). For a discussion of the exceptions, *see Ferguson*, 92 F. Supp. at 869-70.

[98] In the United States District Courts in New York, counsel must satisfy certain preliminary requirements first. *See infra* Section I, L, 1, b.

[99] Fed. R. Civ. P. 26(c).

(viii) That the deposition transcript and information elicited from the deposition not be disclosed to anyone or only to certain people (*e.g.*, those who have signed a confidentiality agreement);

(ix) That certain kinds of information (*e.g.*, trade secrets or other confidential, research and development or commercial information) not be disclosed or be disclosed only to certain people or in a certain manner; and

(x) That a *Martindell* order be entered.[100]

b. Procedure

Motions under Rule 26(c) are filed like other motions; however, in New York certain preliminary requirements must be met. All four district courts in New York require that counsel first confer with counsel for the opposing party in good faith to resolve their differences and file an affidavit with the court reporting such conference.[101] The time for filing and the contents of the affidavit vary with the court, and counsel should refer to the local rules for guidance.

In addition to requiring counsel to confer, the Southern District of New York requires counsel to seek an informal conference with the court to resolve the issues before moving for relief.[102] In the Eastern District of New York, counsel must contact the court by telephone or by a letter not exceeding

---

[100] A *Martindell* order is a protective order requiring that deposition testimony be treated as confidential and used solely by the parties in the litigation in question. Without the *Martindell* order, the deponent is more likely to assert his fifth amendment rights in fear that his testimony may be discovered by the government and used in a criminal matter against him.
In *Martindell* the government sought (as part of a criminal investigation) transcripts of depositions taken in a private litigation in which the parties agreed—pursuant to a court-approved stipulation—to treat the depositions as confidential and to use them solely for the purposes of the litigation. The court found that the stipulation "so ordered" by the trial court
   should not be vacated or modified merely to accommodate the Government's desire to inspect protected testimony for possible use in a criminal investigation, either as evidence or as the subject of a possible perjury charge.
Martindell v. International Tel. and Tel. Corp., 594 F.2d 291, 296 (2d Cir. 1979). *See also Palmieri v. New York*, 779 F.2d 861, 864-65 (2d Cir. 1985) (citing *Martindell* with approval).

---

[101] S.D.N.Y. & E.D.N.Y. Local Civ. R. 3(f); W.D.N.Y. Local R. 17; N.D.N.Y. Local R. 10(k)(2).

---

[102] S.D.N.Y. & E.D.N.Y. Local Civ. R. 3(1).

three pages describing the dispute.[103] Opposing counsel may reply with a three page letter.[104] Counsel should consult the local rules for additional procedures in the Eastern District.

2. Nonparty

The nonparty has the same remedies under Rule 26(c) as a party.[105] The nonparty may also move before the court issuing the subpoena for an order quashing or modifying the subpoena "if it is unreasonable and oppressive."[106]

a. Documents

If a nonparty objects to producing documents, he should consider—in lieu of moving for an order to quash or modify the subpoena with regard to the document production—objecting to their production and placing the burden of going to court on the party seeking discovery. The objection can be "to inspection or copying of any or all of the designated materials,"[107] must be in writing, and served on the "attorney designated in the subpoena."[108] The objection need not include a reason for the objection.[109] Service should be within 10 days of the service of the subpoena on the nonparty or before the date set for the deposition if the time between service of the subpoena and the date of the deposition is less than 10 days. Once he properly objects, the nonparty need not produce the documents.

Counsel should not object lightly. The party serving the subpoena is entitled to move to compel discovery,[110] and the court will not likely look kindly upon someone who capriciously objects to complying with its process. In

---

[103] E.D.N.Y. Standing Order 6(b)(i).

[104] *Id.*

[105] Fed. R. Civ. P. 45(d)(1); *see* Fed R. Civ. P. 26(c) ("Upon motion by a party or by the *person* from whom discovery is sought . . . the court . . . may make any order . . . to protect a party or *person*. . . ." (emphasis added)).

[106] Fed. R. Civ. P. 45(b).

[107] Fed. R. Civ. P. 45(d)(1).

[108] *Id.*

[109] *Compare* Fed. R. Civ. P. 45(d)(1) *with* Fed. R. Civ. P. 34(b).

[110] Fed. R. Civ. P. 45(d)(1).

DEPOSITIONS

general, counsel should consider objecting to the production of the documents only if he has sufficient reason to move to quash or to modify the subpoena.

b. Testimony

The nonparty can also move to quash or modify the subpoena with respect to testimony. A number of courts have held that once the motion is filed, the nonparty need not appear for the deposition until the court rules on the motion.[111] In any event, counsel should try to convince the party serving the subpoena to adjourn the deposition until after the court rules on the motion. Otherwise, the court may still consider citing the nonparty for contempt for failure to obey the subpoena "without adequate excuse."[112]

3. Appeals

Generally, counsel may not appeal discovery orders immediately, because they are not final orders.[113] However, in most of the circuits, "orders denying discovery of nonparties in suits pending in other jurisdictions are immediately appealable."[114] Thus, if an action is pending in the Third Circuit, for example, and a district court in the Second Circuit denies discovery, counsel can immediately appeal the ruling to the United States Court of Appeals for the Second Circuit. In the Second and Ninth Circuits, an appeal may not be

---

111 *Ghandi v. Police Dep't*, 74 F.R.D. 115, 118 n.4 (E.D. Mich. 1977) ("a witness may not disregard a subpoena he has not challenged by a motion to quash, . . . but may refuse to comply with a subpoena until his motion to quash has been ruled upon."), *aff'd in non-relevant part and rev'd in non-relevant part*, 747 F.2d 338 (6th Cir. 1984); *Sullivan v. Sturm, Ruger & Co.*, 80 F.R.D. 489, 491 (D. Mont. 1978); *Shawmut, Inc. v. American Viscose Corp.*, 11 F.R.D. 562, 564 (S.D.N.Y. 1951) ("inequitable to hold deponents in contempt for refusing to comply with the subpoenas before a ruling on the motion"); 5A J. Moore & J. Lucas, *Moore's Federal Practice* ¶ 45.03[6] (2d ed. 1986); 9 C. Wright & A. Miller, *Federal Practice and Procedure* § 2462 at 448-49 (1971); *see In re Certain Complaints Under Investigation by an Investigating Comm.*, 783 F.2d 1488, 1495 (11th Cir.) ("If a witness disregards the subpoena and fails to comply without filing a timely motion to quash, the witness may be found in contempt of court . . . ."), *cert. denied*, 477 U.S. 904 (1986).

---

112 Fed. R. Civ. P. 45(f).

---

113 *E.g., United States v. Nixon*, 418 U.S. 683, 690-91 (1974); *Corporation of Lloyd's v. Lloyd's U.S.*, 831 F.2d 33, 34 (2d Cir. 1987).

---

114 *Id.*; *accord National Life Ins. Co. v. Hartford Accident and Indem. Co.*, 615 F.2d 595 (3d Cir. 1980); *Carter Products, Inc. v. Eversharp, Inc.*, 360 F.2d 868 (7th Cir. 1966); *Gladrow v. Weisz*, 354 F.2d 464, 466 (5th Cir. 1965); *Westinghouse Electric Corp. v. City of Burlington*, 351 F.2d 762 (D.C. Cir. 1965); *Horizons Titanium Corp. v. Norton Co.*, 290 F.2d 421 (1st Cir. 1961). *See also Westmoreland v. CBS, Inc.*, 770 F.2d 1168, 1172 (D.C. Cir. 1985).

taken from a discovery order of a district court that is in the same circuit as the district court in which the action is pending.[115]

A nonparty cited for contempt for disobeying a discovery order may appeal the contempt citation immediately.

II. PREPARATION FOR DEPOSITION

A. Preparing to Take a Deposition

Like every aspect of successful litigation practice, the key to taking an effective deposition is *preparation*. Sound preparation requires an unwavering commitment to four basic rules: (1) know the law; (2) know the facts; (3) know the deponent; and (4) know what you need to accomplish at the deposition. Adherence to these principles will facilitate the preparation of an appropriate deposition outline, the main purpose of which is to insure that all matters of importance to your case are covered with the witness. This is the first critical step to taking an effective deposition.

1. Know the Law

Knowing the applicable law is the starting point in preparing to depose any witness. Presumably, the plaintiff's lawyer will have mastered the relevant law and developed a theory of the case *before* commencing the action. The defendant's lawyer will have gone through the same preparations *before* serving an answer, particularly where affirmative defenses or counterclaims are alleged.[116] The day before the deposition is *not* the time to begin your legal research.

The legal theories of the prosecution and defense provide a framework for discovery. They define the essential elements of each cause of action, affirmative defense, counterclaim and third-party claim. Knowing these elements and how they can be proved or negated is the job of every examiner. Overlooking any item can be costly, if not fatal, at a later stage of the case. Whether your goal is to ascertain the facts, obtain admissions, lock-in the witness's testimony, use it at trial or on a motion for summary judgment or

---

[115] *See Barrick Group, Inc. v. Mosse*, 849 F.2d 70, 74 (2d Cir. 1988) (expressly adopting the Ninth Circuit rule and rejecting the Eleventh Circuit and Federal Circuit rule); *Southern California Edison Co. v. Westinghouse Elec. Corp.*, 813 F.2d 1473 (9th Cir. 1987).
The Eleventh Circuit has expressly ruled that it has jurisdiction over an appeal from a discovery order issued by a district court in its circuit when the action is pending in another district court in its circuit. *Ariel v. Jones*, 693 F.2d 1058 (11th Cir. 1982). *See also Heat and Control, Inc. v. Hester Indus., Inc.*, 785 F.2d 1017 (Fed. Cir. 1986). It does not appear that the other circuits have addressed this issue.

[116] Under Fed. R. Civ. P. 11, an attorney's signature on a pleading is a certificate by him that "he has read the pleading" and that it is "warranted by existing law or a good faith argument for the extension, modification or reversal of existing law...."

eliminate the witness as a factor in the case altogether, the only way of assuring that *all* the right questions will be asked is knowing *in advance* precisely what proof is required as a matter of law.

Knowing what proof is required is not always obvious from the face of the pleadings. Under the liberal notice pleading requirements of the Federal Rules of Civil Procedure, generally all that need be alleged is a "short and plain statement" of the claim or defense, the grounds upon which jurisdiction is based and a demand for the relief sought.[117] In contrast, the legal and evidentiary requirements for proving many claims and defenses are far more complex. For example, to state a claim for relief for trademark infringement under Section 32(a) of the Lanham Act, the complaint need allege little more than that defendant's use of a similar name or mark in commerce is creating a "likelihood of confusion" among reasonably prudent consumers as to the source of the defendant's product.[118] But the question of whether defendant's use is creating a likelihood of confusion itself depends upon a multi-factor legal test which counsel should be familiar with before deposing the witness.[119] To state an affirmative defense of statute of limitations to a federal securities fraud claim, an answer may be sufficient if it alleges that plaintiff's claim is "barred by the applicable statute of limitations." But this defense may turn upon the date when plaintiff learned or had reason to know of the alleged fraud.[120] Counsel may need to develop this issue through deposition testimony. Knowing the relevant law is thus essential to insuring that all appropriate lines of proof are developed and tested.

2. Know the Facts

Knowing the facts is as crucial a part of preparing to take a deposition as knowing the law. But the examiner is seldom in a position to know *all* the facts before the deposition. Indeed, a primary goal of most depositions is to discover the facts.

---

117 Fed. R. Civ. P. 8. *See also Conley v. Gibson*, 355 U.S. 41, 47-48 (1957).

118 *See* 15 U.S.C. § 1114; *Miss Universe, Inc. v. Patricelli*, 753 F.2d 235 (2d Cir. 1985); *Standard & Poor's Corp. v. Commodity Exch.*, 683 F.2d 704, 708 (2d Cir. 1982).

119 *20th Century Wear, Inc. v. Sanmark-Stardust, Inc.*, 747 F.2d 81, 87 (2d Cir. 1984), *cert. denied*, 470 U.S. 1052 (1985); *Spring Mills, Inc. v. Ultracashmere House, Ltd.*, 689 F.2d 1127, 1129 (2d Cir. 1982); *Polaroid Corp. v. Polarad Electronics Corp.*, 287 F.2d 492, 495 (2d Cir.), *cert. denied*, 368 U.S. 820 (1961).

120 *Phillips v. Levie*, 593 F.2d 459, 462 (2d Cir. 1979); *ITT v. Cornfield*, 619 F.2d 909, 928 (2d Cir. 1980).

The examiner's ability to "know the facts" is a function of many variables, including the type of case, the specificity of the pleadings, the quantity and quality of the information provided by the client, the amount of discovery obtained to date and the nature and extent of any independent investigation conducted by or for the benefit of counsel. Knowing the facts means knowing what facts you have; knowing what facts you need to investigate, corroborate and/or clarify; and knowing what witnesses, documents and/or tangible proof support the claims and defenses at issue. At a minimum, this requires a *comprehensive* review and analysis of the following items:

(i) The pleadings in the case;

(ii) Interrogatory answers, especially any that relate to the witness or which the witness verified or supplied information for;

(iii) Documents produced by the witness;

(iv) Documents obtained from any source that the witness generated, received, sent or signed;

(v) Documents obtained from any source that concern the witness or relate to any subject to be covered at the deposition;

(vi) Any other relevant documents;

(vii) Prior statements and testimony of the witness;

(viii) Prior statements and testimony of others that concern the witness or relate to any subject to be covered at the deposition; and

(ix) All other relevant information and data, including client interview notes, motion papers, physical evidence (*e.g.*, the allegedly defective product in a product liability case), expert reports, relevant news events (*e.g.*, reports of subsequent design changes to the allegedly defective product) and background information about the subject matter of the lawsuit and the parties involved.

Obviously, the more facts the examiner knows about a case *before* the deposition, the better prepared he will be. Accordingly, counsel will often prefer to proceed with document discovery and/or interrogatories before taking depositions. *See* E.D.N.Y. Standing Order 14, suggesting that counsel "schedule the deposition to allow for the production of documents in advance of the deposition." This is particularly important in complex commercial litigation involving sophisticated parties and/or multiple transactions, where there is apt to be a substantial paper trail. In these cases, often the documents can be used as a road map for the deposition.

Avoid document production *at the deposition* whenever possible. Not only does it use up valuable deposition time, but it creates logistical nightmares (*e.g.*, copying and keeping track of documents produced at the deposition).

More important, it places the examiner at a strategic disadvantage; it leaves little or no time for the examiner to absorb, analyze and organize the materials for use at the deposition. This is a prescription for mistake, inefficiency and duplication (the examiner will no doubt want the witness to return; opposing counsel may resist).

There are certain circumstances where counsel may prefer to proceed with depositions before taking other discovery. *See supra* Section I, E, 2.

3. Know the Deponent

Knowing the deponent is a special subset of "knowing the facts" that deserves separate mention. The well-prepared examiner will make every effort *before* the deposition to know what the deponent has done, said and written on all relevant subjects. It is equally important to investigate the deponent's background. Does the deponent have any prior convictions? Has the deponent ever been sued before? Has the deponent previously testified under oath? Was the deponent's testimony credible? Has the deponent published any books, articles or papers on a subject relevant to the deposition? Was the deponent ever quoted on a subject relevant to the deposition? Is there anything in the deponent's background that reflects favorably or adversely upon the deponent's character or qualifications as a witness (*i.e.*, capacity or propensity to tell the truth). These are some of the things to consider in preparing for the deposition.

In addition to searching traditional sources of information (*e.g.*, pleadings, documents, interrogatories, etc.), it may be useful to consult other resources. These may include:

   (i) Lexis and Nexis searches for cases and news items in which the deponent is mentioned or quoted.

   (ii) Interviews with persons who know the deponent.

   (iii) Discussions with lawyers who examined the deponent previously.

   (iv) Information available to the public through freedom of information requests of federal, state and local governmental agencies.[121]

Two notes of caution are in order. First, there are substantial risks involved in interviewing persons who know the deponent. Word of the interviews may get back to the deponent; this may facilitate the deponent's preparation, eliminate the element of surprise and defeat the examiner's goal of

---

[121] 5 U.S.C. § 552; N.Y. Pub. Off. Law § 84 *et seq.* (McKinney's 1988).

obtaining an informational advantage. Another risk to be avoided is saying or doing anything which may damage the deponent (*e.g.*, cause a loss of employment, reputational injury, etc.).

Second, requests for information from governmental agencies must be calculated to allow sufficient time for a response.

The nature and extent of your investigation may depend upon whether the deponent is hostile or friendly, where the deponent fits into your case and what you hope to accomplish at the deposition.

4. Know What You Need to Accomplish

Your goals in noticing a deposition in the first place will dictate the nature and extent of the preparation required. If, for example, your primary purpose is to have a custodian of the records authenticate documents, the preparation involved will be different than where the primary purpose is to elicit facts. Keeping in mind what you *need* to accomplish (*i.e.*, the reasons why you are deposing the witness) will insure that your preparation remains on track.

Your preparation should take into account any known limitations on the witness's knowledge. If the witness is an accounts payable clerk, you are likely to get nowhere inquiring about corporate policy; on the other hand, valuable information may be obtained about accounting and bookkeeping procedures. If the witness is the Chairman of the Board of a Fortune 500 company, the opposite may be true. There are no fixed rules for what to cover or not cover in preparing to depose a witness; very rarely will you know in advance exactly what the witness knows on every relevant subject. But your preparation should bear some rational relationship to what the witness *reasonably can be expected to know*, given his position, responsibilities and role in the case.

5. Outlines

A goal in preparing to depose any witness is the preparation of an *appropriate* deposition outline. What is appropriate will depend upon the examiner's experience and skills, the number and complexity of the topics to be covered and the examiner's current knowledge of the case.

The outline is a working document. It should be *organized*, but *flexible*. It should be tailored to the examiner's style, as well as the requirements of the case. And, it should include a *preliminary* check list of all topics to be covered with the witness. The check list is *preliminary* because items may be added or deleted as the deposition proceeds.

How should the outline be organized? The most common ways of organizing a deposition outline are chronologically and by subject matter. Often, some combination of the two will work best. Where a primary purpose of the deposition is to elicit facts, you want the witness to tell a full and coherent story. You want to make sure that nothing of importance is overlooked. The best way of insuring this is to cover the material chronologically, even if you do it one subject at a time. In some cases, an outline can be organized around the salient documents; one example is where the events in question are recounted in periodic reports or minutes of directors' meetings.

How detailed should the outline be? This, too, depends upon the needs of the examiner and the requirements of the case. In general, it is recommended that the outline not recite each and every question verbatim. *First*, as is discussed more fully *infra*, one of the examiner's goals at the deposition is to establish control. To the extent that the examiner appears to be wholly dependent upon a rigid, deposition outline of verbatim questions, this may be perceived as a lack of control. Indeed, the witness and opposing counsel may make a conscious effort to confuse the examiner by getting him to stray from the script. *Second*, it is impossible to anticipate with 100 percent certainty every question that ought to be asked at a deposition or the order in which to ask them. Written questions tend to inhibit flexibility: examiners may be apt to forget to follow-up on significant answers in their zeal to deliver the next line. This, of course, is to be avoided. *See infra* Section III, F, 3, d. *Third*, a useful outline is one which enables the examiner to pick information off the page at glance. A list of wordy questions does not lend itself to this; a list of relevant subjects, conversations, meetings, events, transactions and documents does.

Some examiners may feel more secure at a deposition having a list of written questions to fall back on. There is nothing wrong with this, provided that the examiner is not wedded to it. In fact, in some situations it may be absolutely essential to word the questions with extreme precision to satisfy certain legal requirements. In these situations it is advisable to write the questions out in advance.

With outlines of any size, it is useful to organize the material around topical headings and sub-headings. The headings can serve as a check list to help insure that all areas of interest are covered fully.

In conjunction with the preparation of a deposition outline, determine what documents should be taken to the deposition and what documents should be marked as exhibits. Each document to be marked should be referred to in the outline at the appropriate place. It is also useful to have a separate check list of all exhibits to be marked.

In addition to making copies of documents to be used as exhibits (originals should not be marked), copies should be made for each counsel and the examiner. The examiner may want to annotate his own copy to facilitate the questioning.

B. Preparing the Deponent

1. Lawyer's Preparation

Just as preparation is the key to taking an effective deposition, preparation is essential to defending one effectively. The lawyer defending a deposition should know the law, know the facts and know the deponent. *See* Section II, A, 1-3, *supra*. He should determine at an early stage where the deponent fits into the case. Whether the deponent is a party or a nonparty, the deponent's potential exposure to civil and/or criminal liability should be considered. If there is even the slightest possibility that the deponent may be subject to criminal liability, fifth amendment issues should be addressed; specifically, the attorney must determine whether there is any reason or basis for recommending that the deponent assert his fifth amendment privilege against self-incrimination. Also, counsel should consider making a motion for a *Martindell* order. *See supra* Section I, L, 1, a.

Attorneys representing a nonparty witness should obtain copies of all relevant legal documents, especially the pleadings. This will broaden their understanding of the case as a whole and of why the witness is being deposed. In this connection, it may be useful for the deponent's lawyer to speak with counsel for one or more of the parties involved (the deponent should never do this). In some cases, the client's interests may be aligned more or less with the interests of a party. Counsel for that party may be helpful in providing documents, information and insights. Where the client is truly a disinterested fact witness, *all* counsel may be helpful. A word of caution, however: always look out for your own client's interests; do not rely on others to do this, even ostensibly "friendly" counsel.

2. Client Preparation

It is best to speak with the client early on about the deposition—namely, what preparation will be required and how and when this should be done. When the deponent is a party, an important fact witness or a person who may have exposure to civil or criminal liability, the need for adequate preparation must be emphasized all the more. Although preparation is no doubt time-consuming and costly, it is time and money well spent.

Instruct the client not to speak with anyone but counsel about the case. Every conversation outside the presence of counsel is potentially a subject of questioning at the deposition. For similar reasons, the client should be instructed not to create any documents other than those prepared for counsel for the sole purpose of obtaining legal advice.

Once these preliminaries are covered, two steps remain: (a) case review; and (b) a review of deposition procedures and etiquette. It is also useful to conduct a dress rehearsal with the client.

a. Case Review

(1) The Law

A deponent who is a party or a key employee of a party should have at least some familarity with the legal claims and defenses set forth in the pleadings. This is particularly so if the deponent has verified a pleading.

Although it is not proper form for the examiner to ask questions which call for legal conclusions, *see infra* Section III, G, if your witness has a fundamental understanding of the legal concepts involved this may help him prepare for the deposition. It may help explain why certain lines of questioning will likely be pursued. It may help put the facts in proper perspective and focus the witness on critical areas of the case. It may help put a nervous witness at ease.

Care should be taken in discussing the legal aspects of a case with any witness. Certain witnesses may be apt to slant the facts to meet the legal burden of proof. This cannot be tolerated, and it is the principal reason why legal discussions with many fact witnesses should be kept to a minimum or avoided altogether.

(2) The Facts

In preparing the witness for testimony, counsel should exhaust the witness's knowledge on all relevant subjects (*e.g.*, events, transactions, meetings, conversations, etc.). It is useful to do this in the first instance without showing the witness any documents. It will then be clear exactly what the witness has an independent recollection of and exactly what the witness does not know or remember.

What documents should be shown to the witness? In general, the witness should review and be familiar with all documents he prepared or signed. A witness who does not know his own documents is often *not credible*, absent a good explanation to the contrary (*e.g.*, a document was signed under duress; someone else signed the witness's name without his consent).

In general, every witness should have some familiarity with the documents he received, especially memoranda and correspondence addressed to him, documents which indicate he received a carbon copy and documents he works with in the ordinary course of his business. This does not mean that the witness is required to learn or memorize every document. But at the very least, the witness should be prepared to respond to the question, "Did you receive this document?" If the document came from the witness's own files, the answer should be obvious.

It is generally not a good idea to show a witness documents he has never seen before. Doing this creates a risk that the witness will be unable to distinguish between what he knows based upon independent recollection and what he learned as a result of having reviewed otherwise *unfamiliar* documents in preparing for the deposition. This may tend to distort the fact-finding process.

In some cases, however, it may be essential to review the contents of an unfamiliar document with the witness in preparation for his deposition (*e.g.*, a contemporaneous memorandum written by the plaintiff to the file summarizing purported conversations or meetings with the witness on the subject matter of the lawsuit). In these cases, it is generally recommended that the subject matter be reviewed through a series of objective questions, without showing the witness the document itself (*e.g.*: Did you meet with the plaintiff on February 1, 1987? What was discussed? Did you discuss the board of directors' decision to reject the plaintiff's offer?).

In *exceptional* cases, counsel may prefer not to show a witness certain of his own documents. A witness who sees or signs hundreds of documents every day most likely will *not* have a specific recollection of each and every one of them. Indeed, even when the documents are not so voluminous, the witness may have little or no recollection due to the passage of time. Should an attempt be made to refresh the witness's recollection before the deposition? This will depend upon many factors. Is the witness a party? Are the documents an essential part of his case or defense? Will he be required to testify about the documents or authenticate them at trial? Can he credibly assert a lack of recollection or knowledge of the documents? Is there another witness who is more familiar with them? Will the deponent perform better at the deposition as a result of having reviewed the documents in preparation for his testimony? These are some of the questions to consider. In general, though, it is recommended that counsel err on the side of showing the witness all *relevant* documents he signed, prepared or received, even in exceptional situations.

b. Deposition Procedure and Etiquette

As counsel for the witness you want the witness to be relaxed but on guard at the deposition. You want a clear record. You want the witness to perform well. If the witness is a party, you want him to help his case (if a plaintiff) or limit his exposure (if a defendant on a claim, counterclaim or third-party claim).

To accomplish these goals, the witness should be made aware of proper deposition procedure and etiquette. The starting point is explaining what a deposition is, why the witness's deposition is being taken, who is taking it, who else will be present (*e.g.*, a stenographer who will record the questions and answers), where it is being taken and what is likely to occur after the witness arrives. In addition, the following themes should be emphasized:

CREDIBILITY AND DEMEANOR

(a) *Tell the truth.* It is a crime to give perjured testimony. The examiner is a professional. The truth will come out eventually. You will only hurt yourself and your case by lying or shading the truth.

(b) *Take the deposition seriously.* Do not make jokes, use foul language or be sarcastic.

(c) *Do not argue with the examiner.* If necessary, that is my job, not yours. Just answer the questions.

(d) *Be yourself,* consistent with the solemnity of the proceeding. *See supra* paragraph (b).

(e) *Do not be condescending.* It is not good form and the examiner may know more than you think.

(f) *Treat the examiner with respect.* A rule of thumb is treat the examiner with the same respect as you would want if you were asking the questions.

(g) *Dress appropriately.* No dungarees, shorts, etc.

(h) *Be business-like.*

(i) *Do not fidget.* This means, for example, do not shake your feet, tap your hands, snap your fingers or play with rubber bands or paper clips. The examiner may misconstrue this as a sign of nervousness, guilt or personality disorder.

(j) *Do not make faces, gestures or hand signals.* You are not there to offend anyone.

FIELDING QUESTIONS PROPERLY

(k) *Listen to the question carefully.*

(l) *Let the examiner finish the entire question before responding.*

(m) *Give me time to object before responding* (but do not pause for an inordinate amount of time after every question). Also, *listen to the objections.* They may provide a clue as to how the question should be handled.

(n) *Think about your answer before responding.*

(o) *If your answer requires you to disclose any conversation you had with me or with any other counsel, ask to consult with me before disclosing it.* In general, such conversations are privileged.

(p) *Answer only the question asked—nothing more, nothing less.*

(q) *Do not try to convince the examiner of the righteousness of your position.* You will fail in any such attempt. You will have more than ample opportunity to tell your side of the story in your own way before the case is over.

(r) *Do not speculate.* In general, you only know what you saw, heard or did. If you believe something to be true and you have a factual basis for believing it, you may answer. But be careful and consult with me first.

(s) *It is perfectly acceptable to say "I don't recall" if it is the truth.*

(t) *It is perfectly acceptable to say "I don't know" if it is the truth.*

(u) But if you answer "I don't recall" or "I don't know" to questions which you ought to know or remember (*e.g.*, who do you report to?; do you keep any files?; what are your job responsibilities?) you are going to have credibility problems.

(v) *Do not repeat the questions aloud.*

(w) *If you did not hear the question or any part of it, say so.* The examiner will repeat the question or have it read back.

(x) *If you do not understand the question or any part of it, say so.* It is important that you understand fully what it is you are responding to.

(y) *Do not ramble.* Try to organize your answers, make your point and stop.

(z) *If you want to amend or supplement an answer, ask to consult with me or speak with me during a break.* You will be afforded an opportunity to clarify your testimony.

(aa) *Do not make notes during the deposition.* They may wind up as an exhibit to your testimony.

(bb) *Do not take any documents with you into the deposition room* (*e.g.*, pocket calenders, diaries, notes). They may wind up as exhibits to your testimony.

MAKING A RECORD

(cc) *Nothing is "off the record."* Even if not recorded by a stenographer, examining counsel may summarize your words on the record and ask you to confirm them. Moreover, you may eventually see your words repeated in an attorney's affidavit.

(dd) *Only the record counts, but a solid performance will help your case.* Unlike testimony at trial, there is no trier of fact to observe your demeanor and assess your credibility (absent video-taping). All that is left in the end is a written record. Therefore, making a stellar record is the primary objective. However, everyone in the room will be assessing your credibility, your performance as a witness and how it is likely to impact on the outcome of the case. A solid performance might conceivably lead to a quick or more favorable settlement.

(ee) *Speak clearly, in sentences, in a normal tone and at a normal speed.* Someone has to transcribe your testimony. Others have to read and understand it later on.

(ff) *Finish your answer.* If the examiner interrupts before you finish, let him complete his statement but politely indicate that you have not finished your answer to the previous question and ask for an opportunity to finish.

TAKING BREAKS

(gg) *There is nothing wrong with asking for a break.* Breaks will be taken at regular intervals. If you are tired, hungry, thirsty or need to use the rest room, speak with me privately. It is best to do this when there is no question pending. Also, when a break is taken, follow me to a place where we can talk in private.

The witness should be taken through a mock deposition before the day of his testimony arrives. This will provide another opportunity for the witness to review the relevant subject matter. It will also afford an opportunity for counsel to assess the witness's performance. All of the "hard" questions should be asked, and the witness should be told when he strays from the rules of procedure you have outlined (*e.g.*, "do not ramble," etc.).

C. Administrative Matters

The logistics of setting up the time, manner and place of the deposition should be taken care of well in advance of the deposition date. Counsel who noticed the deposition is responsible for reserving an appropriate conference room, hiring a reporter, specifying in the first instance the type of service required (*e.g.*, daily, expedited or ordinary copy) and reminding the deponent's counsel of the time and place of the deposition.

Most depositions are taken on weekdays during business hours. The deponent must set aside all personal business to attend. Typically, the parties are represented by counsel who are compensated on the basis of time charges. It is therefore costly, unprofessional and embarrassing if the party who noticed the deposition has forgotten to reserve a conference room or order a reporter.

Rule 28 of the Federal Rules identifies the persons before whom a deposition may be taken within the United States, Rule 28(a), and in foreign countries, Rule 28(b). *See supra* Section I, G.

III. CONDUCT OF DEPOSITIONS

A. Who May Attend the Deposition

There are no express limitations in the Federal Rules on who may attend a deposition. Obviously, the witness, any counsel who represent the witness and counsel who noticed the deposition are essential participants. So too are counsel who represent other parties to the action. In certain cases, counsel may desire that other law office personnel (*e.g.*, a paralegal) or experts (*e.g.*, an accountant) be present to assist. In general, there should be no objection to having law office personnel present to assist the examiner in handling documents or taking notes, provided equal treatment is afforded every other party. In reality, this is no different than having two lawyers present from the same firm: one to ask questions and another to observe, consult or assist.

A different situation may be perceived in the case of experts, particularly those who are not employed in the ordinary course of the attorney's business. There is an element of unfairness inherent in having an expert assist in taking the deposition of a lay witness who has no expert present to assist in his own defense. Also, at some point a line must be drawn on the number and type of attendees so as to prevent the proceeding from becoming unwieldy.

While there is no express prohibition under the Federal Rules to having experts or anyone else present to assist the attorney in taking or defending a deposition, it is best to work these matters out ahead of time. If they are not worked out ahead of time, the objecting party's remedy is a Rule 26(c) motion.

Under Rule 26(c), upon motion by a party or the person from whom discovery is sought, the court where the action is pending or where the deposition is being taken may for good cause shown order "that discovery be conducted with no one present except persons designated by the court."[122]

---

[122] Fed. R. Civ. P. 26(c). This provision was adopted in 1970 and substituted for former Rule 30(b) which permitted the Court to order that discovery be conducted "with no one present except the parties to the action and their officers or counsel. . . ."

This has been interpreted to mean that "the Court has the power to exclude even a party, although such an exclusion should be ordered rarely indeed."[123] Thus, a party may be excluded to prevent harassment of another party;[124] protect against disclosure of confidential information;[125] or sequester witnesses.[126]

At least one federal court has held that neither the general public nor members of the press have a right to be present at a deposition.[127] The same limitation applies under New York law.[128]

Should all of the parties attend each deposition? At the deposition, each party is afforded an opportunity to examine or cross-examine the witness "as

---

[123] *Galella v. Onassis*, 487 F.2d 986, 997 (2d Cir. 1973). *See also* 4 Moore's *Federal Practice* ¶ 26.73, at pp. 26-481 to 26-482 (2d ed. 1987). *Cf.* 8 C. Wright and A. Miller, *Federal Practice and Procedure* § 2041, at 295-96 (1970).

[124] *Galella*, 487 F.2d at 997 (holding that order excluding plaintiff was not clearly erroneous because at time of order plaintiff "had already been charged with violation of the court's temporary restraining order which was entered to protect the defendant from further harassment. Such conduct could be deemed to reflect both an irrepressible intent to continue plaintiff's harassment of defendant and complete disregard for judicial process. Anticipation of misconduct during the examination could reasonably have been founded on either").

[125] 4 *Moore's Federal Practice* ¶ 26.73, at 26-481 & n.2 (citing *Carr v. Monroe Mfg. Co.*, 431 F.2d 384 (5th Cir. 1970), *cert. denied*, 400 U.S. 1000 (1971), and *Metal Foil Prods. Mfg. Co. v. Reynolds Metal Co.*, 55 F.R.D. 491 (E.D. Va. 1970)).

[126] *E.g.*, *Milsen Co. v. Southland Corp.*, 16 F.R. Serv. 2d 110, 111 (N.D. Ill. 1972) (granting defendants' motion in antitrust action for order "excluding each of plaintiffs from the deposition of co-plaintiffs which precede that plaintiff's deposition" in order to secure *independent* recollection of each deponent); *Beacon v. R. M. Jones Apartment Rentals*, 79 F.R.D. 141 (N.D. Ohio 1978) (granting plaintiff's motion in Title VIII housing discrimination action for order requiring that deposition be conducted "with no person present other than the party to be deposed, counsel and court reporter" and further prohibiting disclosure of plaintiff's deposition, if taken first, to "any of the other persons to be deposed until after their deposition . . ."). *But see Kerschbaumer v. Bell*, 112 F.R.D. 426, 427 (D.D.C. 1986) (denying plaintiff's motion for order barring non-deposed parties from attending deposition of other parties on the basis of "some inchoate fear that perjury would otherwise result"). *See also Shephard v. Swatling*, 36 Misc. 2d 881, 234 N.Y.S. 2d 370 (Sup. Ct. Rens. Co. 1981) (reaching similar result under New York State law).

[127] *Times Newspapers, Ltd. (Gr. Brit.) v. McDonnell Douglas Corp.*, 387 F. Supp. 189 (C.D. Cal. 1974) (in suit for declaratory judgment that plaintiff newspaper is entitled to have its representatives "present at all depositions and to publish their reports of what occurred," *held* that "deposition before a qualified officer in an equity or law case is not a judicial trial, nor a part of a trial and neither the public nor representatives of the press have a right to be present at such taking").

[128] *Westchester Rockland Newspapers, Inc. v. Marbach*, 66 A.D.2d 335, 413 N.Y.S.2d 411 (2d Dep't 1979). Indeed, the New York courts have gone further than the federal courts in restricting attendance at depositions in general. *See, e.g.*, *Cavuoto v. Smith*, 108 Misc. 2d 221, 437 N.Y.S. 2d 234 (Sup. Ct. Mon. Co. 1981) (holding that in general no one but the parties, officers of the court and counsel may be present without being invited).

permitted at trial under the provisions of the Federal Rules of Evidence."[129] The deposition is binding upon *all* parties who are "present or represented at the taking of the deposition or *who had reasonable notice thereof...*" (emphasis added).[130] To avoid prejudice, it is therefore recommended that every party be *represented* at every deposition.

B. Administrative Matters Preceding Deposition Testimony

1. Where to Sit

There are no fixed rules governing where to sit at a deposition. Typically, the deposition is taken at a rectangular conference table. The reporter sits at the head of the table, facing the side where the witness is seated. The witness sits near the head of the table with his counsel one seat over on the same side. The examining attorney sits opposite the witness and opposing counsel.

When the deposition is taken in the examining attorney's office, the examining attorney should decide upon a seating arrangement *before* the witness arrives. This can be easily done by placing an object (*e.g.*, a book or papers) on the seat the examiner wants to use.

In general, where the witness sits will have little impact on the deposition itself. But it is a tool that can be used to help the examiner establish control. For example, an examiner who knows that the witness has a short attention span may desire that the witness face a wall, not a window.[131] In general, though, the accommodations should be equally amenable to all participants.

2. Instructing the Reporter and Confirming Service

Before the deposition begins, counsel should confirm the type of service required (*e.g.*, daily, expedited or ordinary copy). Also, examining counsel should consider giving instructions in the following areas:

(i) How the exhibits are to be identified (*e.g.*, Exhibit 1 vs. Defendant's Exhibit 1 vs. Jones' Exhibit 1, etc.).

(ii) Where and how the exhibits should be listed (*e.g.*, separately, with page citations, at the front or back of the transcript).

---

[129] Fed. R. Civ. P. 30(c).

[130] Fed. R. Civ. P. 32(a). This Rule provides that deposition testimony may be used against any such party at the trial or upon the hearing of a motion or any interlocutory proceeding "so far as admissible under the rules of evidence." *See, e.g.*, Fed. R. Evid. 613; Fed. R. Civ. P. 56(e).

[131] *See* Supplee, *Depositions: Objectives, Strategies, Tactics, Mechanics and Problems*, 2 The Rev. of Litigation, 255, 282 (1982) for a good discussion of other relevant considerations.

(iii) Whether and how other lists should be compiled at the back of the transcript, referencing:

— Documents requested at the deposition.

— Questions to which opposing counsel objected.

— Questions the witness was directed not to answer.

— Questions in response to which the witness asserted privilege, including fifth amendment and attorney-client.

(iv) Noting the time of breaks.

(v) Noting when the witness consults with counsel.

Some of these instructions are better omitted unless and until a problem arises. For example, if counsel improperly instructs the witness not to answer a question and persists in refusing to back down from this position, it may be helpful *there and then* to instruct the reporter to compile a separate list of questions (with page citations) that the witness is directed not to answer. When accompanied by an unequivocal statement that you intend to get a ruling from the court at the appropriate time, this will send a message to counsel that you are serious about obtaining this discovery. Although counsel may adhere to his original direction not to answer the particular question (his credibility with the client is on the line), he may be more hesitant to direct the witness not to answer the next time around. Indeed, if the witness is able to answer and the answer will not involve disclosure of any privileged information, the witness himself may insist upon answering, if only to avoid the costs of motion practice or the possibility of a return engagement.

C. Failure to Attend or to Serve Subpoena

Suppose you have prepared the witness for a deposition, you and the witness travel to the place where the deposition was noticed to be taken but the examining attorney does not show up or is not prepared to go forward. Suppose, in the alternative, that you represent the defendant, the plaintiff has noticed the deposition of a nonparty witness, and you travel to the place where the deposition was noticed to be taken but the witness does not show up because the plaintiff failed to serve a subpoena pursuant to Rule 45.[132] In these circumstances, Rule 30(g) permits the court to order "the party giving the notice to pay to such other party the reasonable expenses incurred by him

---

[132] Fed. R. Civ. P. 30(a), 45(d).

and his attorney in attending, including reasonable attorney's fees."[133] The moving party need not show that attorney's fees were actually paid: absent proof to the contrary, payment will be presumed.[134] Rule 30(g) may be invoked where a nonparty witness who was not subpoenaed is *physically present* but unwilling to testify.[135]

At least one court has held that it is beyond the scope of Rule 30(g) for a court to restrain a party from taking further depositions until costs assessed against that party are deposited with the court.[136] The same court also found that even if it were within the scope of the Rule, such a sanction would be "unnecessarily severe under the circumstances. . . ."[137]

D. "Usual" Stipulations

Before the deposition gets underway the reporter typically turns to the attorneys and asks expectantly, "The usual stipulations?" Resist any temptation to give an unqualified "yes" to this question. Whether you are taking your first deposition or your fiftieth, there should be a clear understanding from the very outset as to what stipulations, if any, will govern the deposition. What is "usual" to the reporter may differ from what is "usual" to you or the other counsel present. Indeed, it may even vary from reporter to reporter.

Having said this, however, it is generally understood that the usual stipulations include the following:

(i) Waiver of the filing, sealing and certification of the deposition transcript.

---

133 Fed. R. Civ. P. 30(g). *See, e.g., Detsch & Co. v. American Products Co.*, 141 F.2d 662, 663 (9th Cir. 1944) (upholding award of expenses to appellee where appellant noticed two depositions but went forward with only one, appellant's counsel arrived two hours late and appellee's counsel travelled from San Francisco to Los Angeles for both depositions); *Greenwood v. Dittmer*, 776 F.2d 785 (8th Cir. 1985) (upholding award of fees and expenses to defendant whose counsel travelled to Des Moines on short notice and appeared at the appropriate time, only to find that the witness had not been subpoenaed and was unwilling to be deposed at that time); *Fino v. McCullum Mining Co.*, 93 F.R.D. 455 (N.D. Tex. 1982) (imposing award of at least $7,000 costs against plaintiff where parties travelled to Quito, Equador for 10 depositions, but only 4 witnesses actually appeared and testified and the trip produced no relevant evidence).

---

134 *Detsch & Co.*, 141 F.2d at 663.

---

135 *Greenwood*, 776 F.2d at 790-91.

---

136 *Id.* at 864.

---

137 *Id.* at 863-65.

(ii) Reservation to the time of trial of all objections, except as to the form of the questions.[138]

Waiver of the signing of the deposition transcript is occasionally included among the usual stipulations. When signing and certification are not waived, it is often stipulated that the deposition may be signed before any notary public. Each of the usual stipulations has a counterpart in the Federal Rules.[139] *See infra* Section IV for a detailed discussion of the relevant provisions.

Stipulations which provide that all objections except as to the form of the questions are reserved to the time of trial, obviate the need for making certain objections to avoid a waiver.[140] A more detailed discussion of this subject is contained in Section III, G, *infra*.

It is recommended that counsel *not* stipulate at the deposition to waiving the examination, reading or signing of the transcript. From the examiner's point of view, if the witness signs the transcript without making corrections, the witness will be hard-pressed to claim at trial that the deposition is inaccurate in any respect. If the witness signs the transcript after making corrections or submits corrections without signing it,[141] the examiner will have notice of any potential problems. From the witness's perspective, there is no incentive to sign; but it is absolutely essential that the transcript be reviewed for mistakes, particularly if the witness is a party, has an interest or has exposure to civil or criminal liability. The examiner will want to undertake a similar review of both the questions and the answers.

---

[138] As set forth in Section I, C, 2, *supra*, Fed. R. Civ. P. 29 permits the parties to stipulate as to deposition procedure "[u]nless the Court orders otherwise." Waiver of the filing of deposition transcripts in New York is rendered unnecessary by Rule 18 of the Civil Rules for the Southern and Eastern Districts. This Rule provides that "depositions . . . shall not be filed with the Clerk's office except by order of the Court." *Cf.* Fed. R. Civ. P. 30(f)(1), which otherwise directs the officer before whom the deposition was taken to "promptly file it with the Court in which the action is pending or send it by registered or certified mail to the Clerk thereof for filing."

---

[139] *See* Fed. R. Civ. P. 30(e), 30(f).

---

[140] *See infra* Section III, G, 1, a.

---

[141] The witness has 30 days to sign the transcript after it is submitted to him. Fed. R. Civ. P. 30(e). Thereafter, the officer before whom the deposition was taken "shall sign it and state on the record the fact of the waiver or of the illness or absence of the witness or of the fact of the refusal to sign together with the reason, if any, given therefor. . ." *Id.* The deposition may then be used as fully as though signed "unless on a motion to suppress" under Rule 32(d)(4), the court holds that the "reasons given for the refusal to sign require rejection of the deposition in whole or in part." *Id.* Under Rule 32(d)(2), "[e]rrors and irregularities in the manner in which the testimony is transcribed or the deposition is prepared, signed, certified, sealed, indorsed, transmitted, filed or otherwise dealt with under Rules 30 and 31 are waived unless a motion to suppress . . . is made with reasonable promptness after such defect is, or with due diligence might have been, ascertained." Fed. R. Civ. P. 32(d)(4).

Although the requirement in Rule 30(f) that the officer "securely seal the deposition" would appear to have nothing to do with confidentiality, special attention should be paid to stipulations regarding the sealing of the transcript when confidential or otherwise sensitive information is involved. In cases of this kind (*e.g.*, cases involving trade secrets, patents, customer lists, etc.), the party concerned should seek to enter into a confidentiality stipulation with the other parties before discovery begins. The stipulation should be "so ordered" by the court. If the parties cannot agree, a protective order may be sought. Where an appropriate order is in place, it should be referred to at the deposition and incorporated into the proceeding by exhibit or reference. If the witness is not a party, it may be required or desirable that he and his counsel agree to be bound by the confidentiality order.

When in doubt, the safest course is to consult the Federal Rules and the local rules before stipulating to anything. Indeed, some attorneys prefer to stipulate that "the deposition shall be governed by the Federal Rules of Civil Procedure." While this will seldom prejudice any party whose counsel is familiar with the applicable Rules, due consideration must always be given to the unique circumstances of the case and the client.

E. Oaths and Other Preliminaries

After the parties reach an understanding as to what, if any, stipulations are to govern the deposition, the officer will administer the oath to the witness.[142] If the witness objects to taking an oath, an affirmation will do.[143] Once the witness is sworn in, it is customary to go over certain ground rules with the witness, particularly if the witness has never been deposed. In this connection, it is advisable for the examining attorney to identify himself, his firm and the party he is representing; to explain that the witness will be asked a series of questions that should be answered to the best of his knowledge and recollection; and to point out that if the witness does not hear or understand a question he should say so. The latter instruction will be helpful at a later time if the witness attempts to back away from his testimony on the grounds that he either did not hear or did not understand the question, especially where the instruction was accompanied by a statement that the examiner will presume the witness heard and understood absent any indication to the contrary.

Instructions pertaining to breaks in the testimony for food, drink, rest and/or consultations with counsel are unnecessary unless the witness is appearing *pro se*. While the examiner should always be cordial to the witness and make

---

[142] Fed. R. Civ. P. 30(c): "The officer before whom the deposition is taken shall put the witness on oath."

[143] Fed. R. Civ. P. 43(d).

every effort to honor reasonable requests, it is important to stay in control of the examination. Breaks when a question is pending, though sometimes unavoidable, should be kept to a minimum, if not resisted altogether. The examiner should always be reasonable, but it is best to deal with these situations *when they arise* in the ordinary course.

Between the time the witness enters the deposition room and the time preliminary instructions are given, the examining attorney should begin sizing up the witness. Does the witness appear to be friendly or hostile? Does the witness appear to be taking the proceeding seriously? Does the witness appear to be nervous? Is the witness able to look the examiner in the eyes? Observing the witness's demeanor and speech at this early stage of the proceeding will aid the examiner in setting a proper tone for the deposition.

In general, the examiner should set a tone which is most conducive to eliciting complete and direct answers. In some cases, this can be achieved by making an extra effort to make the witness feel at ease. In other cases, a firmer tone is required. The examiner's goal is always to get the witness to give full and candid responses.

F. Examining the Witness

1. Scope of Examination: Relevancy; Privilege

As with all other civil discovery, depositions may be used to "obtain discovery of any matter, not privileged, which is relevant to the subject matter involved in the pending action. . . ."[144] This specifically includes information which is "reasonably calculated to lead to the discovery of admissible evidence."[145]

Though, in general, counsel is not permitted to inquire into privileged matters, he is entitled to test whether there is a valid basis for the assertion of privilege.[146] For example, if a witness refuses to answer on grounds of attorney-client privilege, counsel may properly ascertain:

(i) The identity of the client.

(ii) The identity of the lawyer.

(iii) The date when the lawyer was retained, how long the representation continued and whether any fees were billed or paid.

---

144 Fed. R. Civ. P. 26(b)(1).

145 *Id.*

146 *See, e.g., Securities and Exch. Comm'n v. Kingsley,* 510 F. Supp. 561, 563 (D.D.C. 1981). Privileged matter may, of course, be inquired into if no objection is interposed and a waiver occurs.

(iv) The general purpose of the retention.

(v) Where and how (*e.g.*, by phone or in person) the allegedly privileged conversation took place.

(vi) The identity of anyone else who was present when it took place or told thereafter. (If a third party was present or told, the privilege may have been waived.)

(vii) The general subject matter of the communication.

(viii) Any other matters which tend to show whether the communication was made for the purpose of obtaining legal advice and with an expectation that it would be kept confidential.[147]

When privilege is asserted with respect to a document, the examining attorney should ascertain the following *additional* information:

(i) Who prepared the document (*e.g.*, wrote it, signed it, compiled it, reviewed it or provided information in connection with its preparation).

(ii) The date or period of time over which it was prepared.

(iii) The date of the document itself.

(iv) Whether and to whom it was sent.

(v) The nature of the document (*e.g.*, letter, memorandum, notes, etc.).[148]

These same matters should be covered when the privilege asserted is the work product doctrine.[149] Because the work product doctrine is a *qualified* privilege whose application depends upon whether "the party seeking discovery has substantial need of the materials in the preparation of his case and . . . is unable to obtain the substantial equivalent of the materials by other means,"[150] the examining attorney may want to explore whether the items involved or their substantial equivalent are available elsewhere.

---

[147] *See* S.D.N.Y. & E.D.N.Y. Civ. R. 46(e)(2)(ii); *Kingsley*, 510 F. Supp. at 563-64.

[148] *See* E.D.N.Y. Standing Order 21(a)(2)(i).

[149] *See Hickman v. Taylor*, 329 U.S. 495 (1947), for a discussion of this doctrine.

[150] *See* Fed. R. Civ. P. 26(b)(3), regarding the discovery of documents and tangible things "prepared in anticipation of litigation or for trial by or for another party's representative . . . ."

2. Mode of Examination

In general, the best deposition, from the examining attorney's standpoint, is one where the examiner stays in *control* of the conduct of the examination, is *methodical* and *persistent* in covering the areas required, *listens carefully* to the witness's answers and *follows-up* on all relevant testimony.

a. Staying in Control

Staying in control does not mean the examiner has a license to bully the witness. Rather, it is a function of being well prepared (*e.g.*, knowing the law, the facts and the deponent),[151] being well organized, establishing a flow to the questions, fielding objections properly and always bearing in mind the goals of the deposition.[152] A deposition outline, particularly one prepared by examining counsel himself,[153] will be of *some* assistance in accomplishing this objective. By itself, it is not enough, however. It is only the *first* critical step to taking an effective deposition.[154] The *second* critical step lies in the *execution* of the deposition.

Proper execution is learned by observing other examiners (both their virtues and vices) and through personal experience (your own successes and failures). A few elemental rules are worth noting here:

(i) *Speak loudly, clearly and slowly enough for everyone to hear you. In the end, only the record will count.*

(ii) *Use simple sentences.* Long-winded sentences tend to frustrate witnesses and opposing counsel, inject confusion into the proceeding and slow down the pace of the deposition. If the question is too long, there is a good likelihood it will have to be repeated. There is also a good likelihood it is prone to other defects (*e.g.*, it is a compound question, it assumes facts not in the record, it mischaracterizes the witness's prior testimony, etc.).

(iii) *Use simple words.* The deposition is not the place to show-off your "lexicon." Everyday words with everyday meanings insure against ambiguity. There should be no possibility of any misunderstanding as to what it is you are asking and what it is the witness is responding to. There are exceptions to this rule. If the

---

151 *See supra* Section II, A, 1-3.

152 *See supra* Section II, A, 4.

153 *See supra* Section II, A, 5.

154 *See supra* Section II, A.

witness is an accountant, for example, he may reasonably be expected to understand the technical terms of his profession (*e.g.*, income recognition; accrual method; last-in, first-out (LIFO); etc.). The same is true of other professionals (*e.g.*, lawyers, doctors, construction engineers): they are presumed to know the terms of their trade. In practice, though, you will find this is not always true.

(iv) *Do not repeat the witness's prior testimony, except to the extent it is reasonably necessary to put your question in context or clarify an ambiguous record.* Repeating the witness's testimony invariably leads to objections that the examiner is mischaracterizing the testimony. If possible, therefore, references to prior testimony should be minimized. If they cannot be minimized, every effort should be made to get the testimony right. In general, there are two situations where some repetition is required. The first is where the witness refers to a series of items, each of which requires follow-up. By the time the examiner reaches the last or even the second or third item, many questions may have intervened. In this situation, it may be necessary to refer back to the prior testimony (*e.g.*, "Mr. Jones, you mentioned before our lunch break that a second factor you considered in deciding to terminate Ms. Robert's employment was her inability to get along with co-workers. What did you mean by that?"). The second situation is where the examiner finds it necessary to return to a subject previously covered, either because it was not covered exhaustively or the record is unclear. Indeed, where a witness's testimony is disjointed it is sometimes useful to summarize the testimony for later use on a motion or at trial.

(v) *Do not engage in extended colloquy with opposing counsel. Make your point and move on.* You are there to examine the witness, not to converse with counsel. Be wary of being trapped into using up valuable deposition time on unimportant matters.

(vi) *Do not let opposing counsel rush you.* You are entitled to at least one full opportunity to depose the witness. Some opposing counsel make a habit of showing up late to the deposition, taking extended breaks, checking the time expectantly and asking when the deposition will be over. In some cases, opposing counsel is simply being inconsiderate. In other cases, this behavior is calculated to frustrate the examiner, *i.e.*, throw the examination off schedule or cause the examiner to race through the deposition with the attendant risk of doing an incomplete job. The examiner should resist all pressure to adopt opposing counsel's schedule. If everything cannot be covered in one session, there is always another day.

(vii) *Do not let opposing counsel interrupt your examination.* Sometimes, opposing counsel, under the guise of being "helpful," will seek to question the witness in the middle of *your* examination. This should not be permitted. Counsel should be advised immediately that he will be afforded an opportunity to cross-examine the witness after you are finished.

(viii) *Do not let opposing counsel "coach the witness" during your examination.* You want the witness's *own* recollection, not answers prompted by counsel. Counsel may attempt to suggest answers to the witness in the guise of objections. This is improper. *See, e.g.*, E.D.N.Y. Standing Order 12 ("objections in the presence of a witness which are used to suggest an answer to the witness are presumptively improper"). Some common examples are:

A. *Prompting lack of knowledge*:

Q. Why was Mr. Jones fired?

A. The company felt —

Opposing Counsel: If you know. Don't speculate.

Witness: I really don't know for certain.

B. *Prompting lack of recollection*:

Q. Who else was at the meeting?

A. The meetings were always attended by —

Opposing Counsel: If you remember. Do you have a specific recollection of every single person who attended this particular meeting?

Witness: I really don't remember who attended the meeting.

Q. Do you recall the names of *anyone* who attended?

Opposing Counsel: The witness already answered he doesn't remember. Asked and answered.

This type of behavior is difficult to deal with because the damage is done before the examining attorney has a chance to counter it. In general, there are two ways to deal with situations like these. Where the witness began to give a substantive response before being stopped by his counsel, it may be fruitful to go back to the initial response:

Q. Mr. Woods, you began to say in your previous answer that "the meetings were always attended by" certain individuals. Which individuals always attended the meetings?

A. Mr. Green, Mrs. White, Mrs. Black and Dr. Blue.

Q. Can you think of any meeting which any of them didn't attend?

A. No.

Q. Do you have reason to believe any of them did not attend the meeting in question?

A. No.

Q. Do you have reason to believe that anyone else attended that meeting?

A. I don't remember one way or the other.

In addition to going back to the original response, the examining attorney should remind the witness and opposing counsel of his original instruction:

> As I stated at the outset of this deposition, all questions are to be answered to the best of the witness's knowledge and recollection. There is no need to keep repeating this. Do you [the witness] understand the procedure?

(vii) *Do not let opposing counsel testify for the witness.* As soon as you perceive that this is occurring, cut it off:

Q. Why did you purchase 50 March 1987 call options in XYZ Corporation on February 1, 1987?

A. I believed it was a takeover candidate. I discussed —

Opposing Counsel: I think what Mr. Arbitrage means, and this is corroborated by his earlier testimony, is that based upon his research of the company, his belief that it was undervalued relative to other companies in the industry and the market activity in the stock, he surmised that it might be a takeover candidate, discussed it with his broker and decided to invest. Is that right Mr. Arbitrage?

Witness: Exactly.

This bald-faced type of interference should be stopped right after the phrase "I think what Mr. Arbitrage means . . . ." This can be accomplished by advising opposing counsel "I appreciate your help but we are here to obtain the witness's testimony in his own words." Then turn to the witness and say "Can you answer the question, please?"

(viii) *Do not let the witness begin to answer until you have finished your question.* Some witnesses will attempt to anticipate your questions and blurt out responses before the questions are stated fully. This makes for a poor record. The witness should be entreated to let you finish your questions and reminded that the reporter cannot record two voices at the same time.

(ix) *If you lose your place or forget the question, ask the reporter to read it back.* There is no need to be embarrassed about doing this. On the contrary, it is a sign you will not be diverted from your course.

b. Being Methodical and Persistent

(1) Sequence of Questions: Go From General to Specific

There are no fixed rules governing the sequence in which questions should be asked at a deposition. It is customary, though, to start with background questions and build upon this foundation. In general, the topics to be covered include the witness's education, employment and history as a witness. In some cases, it may be necessary to identify the witness's bank accounts, brokerage accounts and business affiliations. In other cases, the witness's medical history may be relevant. It all depends upon the nature of the case and the issues involved.

It is usually best to move from the *general* to the *specific*, particularly with a hostile witness. General questions concerning duties and responsibilities, policy and practice or habit and routine set the stage for more specific questions and responses. A witness who testifies that for eight years her practice was to take notes at board of directors' meetings will be hard-pressed to deny taking notes at any particular meeting. A witness who testifies that his responsibility was to report *all* complaints to the manager of customer service will find it difficult to deny having reported any particular customer complaint. A denial will imply he did not do his job. In essence, the general testimony serves to lock the witness into a specific response, absent an adequate explanation to the contrary.

(2) Exhaust the Witness's Knowledge and Recollection

To prepare adequately for trial, the examiner needs to know exactly what the witness's story will be. The deposition is an effective tool for accomplishing this objective, but *only if* the witness is locked-in to his deposition testimony. In general, the examiner should leave no room for the witness to change his story at trial without creating a prior inconsistent statement.[155] To do this, the examiner must exhaust the witness's knowledge and recollection of every relevant subject.

---

155 *See* Fed. R. Evid. 801(d), which defines prior inconsistent statements made under oath at a deposition as non-hearsay.

The starting place, of course, is an appropriate deposition outline setting forth a preliminary list of topics to be covered with the witness. *See supra* Section II, A, 5. This, by itself, is not enough, however. At the deposition, the examiner must pin down the *who, what, when, where, how* and *why* of every important meeting, communication and event. The following example illustrates the technique:

Q. Did you discuss the proxy statement with anyone before it was filed?

A. Yes.

Q. *Who* did you discuss it with?

A. I discussed it with the other members of the Board.

Q. *Anyone else*?

A. I discussed it with Mr. York, the Chief Executive Officer.

Q. *Anyone else*?

A. Not that I can think of.

Q. *Which members* of the Board did you discuss the proxy statement with?

A. Mr. Ryan and Ms. Sims only.

Q. *How many times* did you discuss it with Mr. Ryan?

A. Two or three times.

Q. *How many times* did you discuss it with Ms. Sims?

A. Twice, at Board meetings.

Q. *When* did the first conversation with Mr. Ryan take place?

A. Over the phone. I called Mr. Ryan at the office on November 5, a Saturday; I was at home.

Q. Was *anyone else* on the line?

A. Not that I know of.

Q. *Why* did you call Mr. Ryan on November 5?

A. To discuss a number of matters, including the proxy statement.

Q. *Any other reason*?

A. No.

Q. *What* did you say to Mr. Ryan and what did he say to you?

A. I told Mr. Ryan that I had reviewed the proxy statement and noted a number of inaccuracies.

Q. *What* inaccuracies?

A. My name was spelled wrong.

Q. *Anything else?*
A. The financials overstated the company's sales by $25 million.
Q. *Any other inaccuracies?*
A. No.
Q. *What* did Mr. Ryan say?
A. He said don't worry about it.
Q. *Anything else?*
A. No.
Q. *What other matters* did you discuss with Mr. Ryan?
A. I don't remember.
Q. Did you make *any notes* of your conversation with Mr. Ryan?
A. No.
Q. *Have you now told us everything* you recall about your conversation with Mr. Ryan on November 5?
A. Yes.
Q. *When did you next discuss* the proxy statement with Mr. Ryan? [continue until each discussion is covered fully].

As the foregoing example illustrates, despite appearances, the witness will not always give a complete and forthright answer to every question. The only way of assuring that you have the whole answer is by asking "lock-in" questions such as "who else," "what else," "anyone else," "anything else," "any other conversations," "any other factors that you considered" and "have you now told us everything concerning . . . ?" With some witnesses, particularly those who purport to have little or no knowledge or recollection of anything, it is useful to test their memory with more specific questions:

Q. What other matters did you discuss with Mr. Ryan?
A. I don't remember.
Q. Did you discuss the inventory figures in the proxy statement?
A. Yes.
Q. What was said?
A. I don't *specifically* remember.

When a witness claims to have no "specific" recollection, this usually is a clue that the witness has at least some recollection. In this situation, always ask the question, "Do you have a general recollection?" The general recollection may become fairly specific through methodical questioning.

In some cases, the examiner may be content to ask a series of questions that establish the witness's lack of recollection. One example is where the case turns upon a key conversation between the examiner's client and the witness. The client remembers the conversation; the witness does not. In this situation, a deposition establishing the witness's lack of recollection may ripen the case for summary judgment.[156]

It is occasionally useful to ask the witness if there are any documents that would refresh his recollection. More often than not, this results in nothing new. But if at trial the witness suddenly has a flawless recollection, he will have difficulty explaining this inconsistency away on the basis of having later reviewed documents not referred to at the deposition.

Very often, a witness who is asked a question which calls for a numerical answer will have no specific recollection. The questions may range from the size of an object, to the number of conversations the witness had with the plaintiff, to the time of an event. When the witness in fact appears to have no specific recollection, an effort can be made to define the parameters of an answer:

Q. How many times did you meet with Mr. Mars in 1985?

A. I don't recall.

Q. Was it more than 10 times?

A. Yes.

Q. Was it more than 20?

A. No, somewhere between 10 and 15 times sounds about right. I don't recall the exact number.

Q. When was the first meeting?

A. I don't recall.

Q. Was it after the partnership was dissolved on March 19, 1985?

A. No, it was before then, sometime in January or February.

(3) Do not Permit Ambiguities to Remain

Exhausting the witness's knowledge and recollection will never serve to lock-in the witness's testimony if the testimony is unclear. Every effort should be made, therefore, to clarify the record as the deposition proceeds. As the context requires, words such as *this, that, those, these, his, hers* and

---

[156] Fed R. Civ. P. 56.

theirs, may require explanation. If the witness points to a paragraph of an exhibit or describes the size or shape of an object with his hands, this too may require clarification:

Q. How long was the knife?

A. About this long (gesturing).

Q. You are holding your hands about one foot apart indicating a length of about one foot?

A. Yes.

If you ask the question, "Do you remember whether the knife was about a foot long?" and the witness responds in the affirmative, you have not locked-in the witness's testimony concerning the length of the knife; you have only established that the witness has a recollection. You must still ask the question, "How long was it?" For this reason, the better question in the first instance is, "How long was the knife?"

Make sure there are no ambiguities in the transcription of the deposition. Difficult names should be spelled for the reporter.

(4) Make the Witness Answer Your Question

Subject to any legitimate objection (*e.g.*, attorney-client privilege), you are entitled to an answer to *your* question, even if the answer is "I don't know" or "I don't recall." Occasionally, a witness will give a wholly unresponsive answer or respond to a related but different question, either because the question was not understood or because the witness wants to be evasive:

Q. Did you take any steps to determine whether the product was safe before it was marketed?

A. The product is a safe product. I have used it hundreds of times; we have thousands of satisfied customers. Until the plaintiff brought this lawsuit, the company had not received one complaint; and even the plaintiff told me he was satisfied with the product just a week before the suit was filed.

It is quite obvious from the foregoing response that the witness has not answered the question. In a situation such as this, the examiner may respond as follows:

> That was not my question. The question was did you take any steps to determine whether the product was safe before it was marketed. Please answer that question.

In addition, the examiner may move to strike the answer as nonresponsive. If necessary, the reporter can repeat the question. Once you have an answer to *your* question, it may then be appropriate to follow-up on the witness's gratuitous remarks.

c. Listen Carefully to the Answers and Follow-up

This is one of the most important techniques to master. Typically, a witness's initial response to your question will not provide a complete answer. Often, however, it will prompt other questions, identify other witnesses or suggest additional lines of inquiry. If you are thinking about the next question on your outline while the witness is answering the pending one, you are likely to miss some critical follow-up questions. If in response to the question "did you speak with the police at the scene of the accident" the witness mentions that the police took statements from "me and the other eyewitnesses," at a minimum the witness should be asked about his own statement as well as the statements of the other witnesses (*e.g.*, "who are the other eyewitnesses" and "what did they say"). If the witness mentions a series of events, communications or meetings in a single answer, each of these items may require follow-up. The examiner should keep track of these items by jotting down key words and phrases and methodically reviewing each one with the witness once his answer to the pending question is completed. Some examiners prefer to take no notes at all while the witness is answering; if the answer is important they will have it read back when the witness is through or rely completely on recollection. This technique can be cumbersome (if too many answers are repeated) and dangerous (if the attorney's recollection is imperfect). In general, limited note taking will not impair the examiner's ability to hear and comprehend the entire answer.

While it is crucial to follow-up on matters of relevance to the examiner's case, it is equally important not to interrupt the witness's answer in midstream (even if it does not respond in whole or part to the question asked). The only notable exception is where immediate clarification is required (*e.g.*, "By 'this' you mean the December 22, 1987, letter, marked as defendant's Exhibit 3?"). The witness may lose track of the thought he was about to communicate or never have a chance to get back to it. As a result, relevant testimony may be lost forever.

3. Using Documents at the Deposition

In general, any documents the witness is shown at the deposition should be marked as exhibits. Care should be taken in handling exhibits. The examiner or his assistant should keep a separate list of exhibits as they are marked. If exhibits have been pre-marked (a technique which saves time but sometimes causes confusion; occasionally, it may be necessary to use exhibits out of order), a list should be maintained to keep track of what exhibits have been shown to the witness for identification.

In some cases, counsel may want to exhaust a witness's recollection before showing him a document. In other cases, the document itself may require clarification (*e.g.*, ambiguous terms, gaps in the narrative, questions prompted by the narrative, etc.). In still other cases, counsel may desire to have the witness qualify the document as a business record.[157]

In general, it is not fruitful to examine the witness about a document he has never seen before. When the witness *can* authenticate a document, he should be asked to describe it (*e.g.*, "Is this a copy of the letter you sent to Ms. Collins on March 1, 1987?") and, where applicable, to identify his signature (*e.g.*, "Did you sign the letter at the bottom of p. 3?"). There is no need to read the document into the record.

When a party being examined has served and/or verified a pleading or a set of interrogatory answers, these documents often serve as a good source for deposition questions (*e.g.*, "What is the factual basis for the allegation in paragraph 24 of the verified complaint that plaintiff sustained $500,000 in damages?"). The witness's counsel may attempt to prevent this sort of inquiry where the witness himself, though a party to the action, did not sign or verify the document. At a minimum, however, the examiner should insist upon getting an answer to the question or establishing that the witness has no knowledge of the contents of the document.

G. Defending Depositions—Objections

Much of what is involved in the actual defense of a deposition is embodied in the instructions given the witness in preparing for it.[158] The goals of the attorney defending the deposition are to insure that the examiner stays within the bounds of the Federal Rules, that all objections that matter are preserved to the time of trial, that the witness testifies truthfully and only with regard to what he knows and recalls, and that the witness suffers minimum damage as a result of his deposition testimony.

The attorney defending a deposition is permitted to make objections. The objections, in general, fall into two categories:

(1) Those that must be made in order to preserve the issue and avoid a waiver; and

---

157 *See* Fed. R. Evid. 803(c).

---

158 *See supra* Section II, B, 2, a (iii).

(2) Those that by Rule or stipulation are preserved without objection.

1. Object or Waive

The following objections, unless timely made, are waived by the attorney defending the deposition:

   (i) Errors and irregularities in the notice for taking a deposition—"waived unless written objection is *promptly* served upon the party giving the notice."[159]

   (ii) Disqualification of the officer before whom the deposition is taken—waived unless made before the deposition begins or "as soon thereafter as the disqualification becomes known or could be discovered with reasonable diligence."[160]

   (iii) Objections to the competency of a witness or to the competency, relevancy or materiality of his testimony—waived by failure to object "before or during the taking of the deposition" *if and only if* "the ground of the objection is one which might have been obviated or removed if presented at that time."[161]

   (iv) Errors and irregularities in the manner of taking the deposition, the form of the questions or answers, the oath or affirmation or the conduct of the parties—waived "unless seasonable objection thereto is made at the taking of the deposition."[162]

   (v) Other errors and irregularities "of any kind" which occur at the deposition and "might be obviated, removed or cured if promptly presented"—waived "unless seasonable objection is made thereto at the taking of the deposition."[163]

---

[159] Fed. R. Civ. P. 32(d)(1).

[160] Fed. R. Civ. P. 32(d)(2).

[161] Fed. R. Civ. P. 32(d)(3)(A).

[162] Fed. R. Civ. P. 32(d)(3)(B).

[163] *Id*. Though not the focus of this chapter, objections to questions propounded in connection with a deposition upon written questions pursuant to Fed. R. Civ. P. 31 are waived "unless served in writing upon the party propounding them within the time allowed for serving the succeeding cross or other questions and within 5 days after service of the last questions authorized." Fed. R. Civ. P. 32(d)(3)(C).

2. Preserved Without Objection

The following defects in general are *not* waived by reason of the attorney's failure to object before or during the deposition:

> objections to the competency of a witness or to the competency, relevancy or materiality of his testimony—not waived unless "the ground of the objection is one which might have been obviated or removed if presented at that time."[164]

3. Typical Grounds for Objection

While it is impossible to catalogue every objection that will be required at a given deposition, the following objections are encountered frequently:

(i) *The question seeks irrelevant information or is immaterial.* As noted above, these objections need only be made if the defect might be obviated or removed before or during the taking of the deposition, absent a stipulation preserving them to the time of trial. It is rarely possible to obviate or remove an objection to relevancy or materiality; such objections usually reflect a fundamental disagreement over the proper scope of discovery. In general, the Rules provide that "evidence objected to shall be taken subject to the objections."[165] *But see infra*, Section III, G, 2, regarding when and under what circumstances it may be proper to direct a witness not to answer or to terminate the examination and seek a ruling or protective order.

(ii) *The question is a leading question.* In general, at a deposition of a hostile witness or adverse party, leading questions are permitted. *See* Fed. R. Civ. P. 32(a): depositions may be used at a trial or hearing against a person who was present or represented "so far as admissible under the rules of evidence. . . ." Under Fed. R. Evid. 611(c), ordinarily "leading questions should be permitted on cross examination." They are also permitted "[w]hen a party calls a hostile witness or adverse party, or a witness identified with an adverse party. . . ." They are even permitted on direct examination if "necessary to develop the witness's testimony." Leading questions are always objectionable if they misstate the facts or mischaracterize the witness's testimony.

---

[164] Fed. R. Civ. P. 32(d)(3)(A).

[165] Fed. R. Civ. P. 30(c).

(iii) *The question misstates the facts or mischaracterizes the witness's prior testimony*:

Q. After you received the letter you called Mrs. Blue on the phone, correct?

Witness's Counsel:

Objection. The witness just testified that he received a memo, not a letter, that after receiving it he called Ms. Green not Mrs. Blue, and that he has never even heard of Mrs. Blue, let alone spoken with her about any memo. Please rephrase the question.

(iv) *The question lacks a proper foundation.* At times, an examiner will ask questions that assume facts, which though correct in every respect, were not yet testified to by this witness at this deposition or are misleading standing alone. In fairness to the witness, and to insure an accurate record, counsel may object:

Q. When you met with the labor union officials about the issue of a pay increase, what did they say their reason was for rejecting the company's offer?

Witness's Counsel:

I object to the form of the question. This witness has not yet been asked or testified about whether he met with the union officials, he discussed the issue of a pay increase with them or they rejected all or part of any company offer.

Q. Did you meet with the union officials on November 4, 1987?

A. Yes.

Q. At that meeting, did you discuss a pay increase with them?

A. There were two proposals on the table. At the meeting, we only discussed management's proposal for a 7% cost of living increase. The union rejected out of hand and refused to discuss the company's proposal for a 3% pay increase.

(v) *The question is beyond the scope of the witness's knowledge or expertise.* In general, most witnesses can handle these questions by indicating a lack of knowledge. Some witnesses, however, will try to answer every question, even ones they do not know anything about. Conversely, some examiners will persist in asking questions about subjects the witness has already indicated he has no knowledge of. In these situations, counsel should object.

(vi) *The question is a compound question*:

Q. Did you write to or speak with the insurance company representative?

Witness's Counsel:

Objection. The question is a compound question. Please break it down.

Q. Did you write to the insurance company representative?
A. No.
Q. Did you speak with her?
A. Yes.

(vii) *The question is hypothetical or calls for the witness to speculate.* Questions with words such as "if," "were" and "had" often call for speculation. Also, questions which ask about someone else's state of mind are sometimes objectionable (*e.g.*, "what did Mr. Lemon mean when he wrote . . ."). In general, this objection may be cured by asking the witness if he has "any understanding of what Mr. Lemon meant when he wrote. . . ." The examiner should make sure that the basis for any such "understanding" is stated in the record.

(viii) *The question calls for a legal conclusion* (*e.g.*, was plaintiff's conduct toward the defendant fraudulent?; was the defendant negligent in his treatment of the patient?; was the defendant denied due process of law?).

(ix) *The question was asked and answered.*

(x) *The question is unintelligible, vague or ambiguous.* Some examples are questions that contain double negatives, questions that include terms which the witness or counsel do not understand and questions that are so lengthy or contain so many thoughts that they are difficult to follow or answer. In these situations, if there is any basis for the objection, the examiner should rephrase the question. Some witnesses or their counsel may ask the examining attorney to define his terms (*e.g.*, "What do you mean by the term 'file'?") The examiner should avoid defining terms. The best approach is to ask the witness if *he* understands the question or if *he* has any understanding of what the term means. If he does not, rephrase the question.

(xi) *The question seeks information which is protected by the attorney-client privilege or by some other applicable privilege.*

4. When and How to Object at the Deposition

The safest course of action is to object to all defects that would otherwise be waived if not objected to promptly. Most frequently, this means objecting to (1) any defect in "the manner of taking the deposition, or the form of the questions or answers, in the oath or affirmation or in the conduct of the parties," or (2) any defect that can be obviated, removed or cured if promptly presented.[166] Other considerations may obtain, however. Too many objections may have a negative impact upon the witness, disrupt the flow of the testimony or unduly prolong the examination. Certain objections, while technically correct, may in essence be frivolous. There may be times when counsel chooses not to object, provided the question is free of ambiguity and the witness is able to field it. This is a judgment call; but out of an abundance of caution, it may be preferable to preserve *all* objections.

How should an objection be interposed? Counsel should wait for the question to be stated fully, say "I object" or "objection" and, in general, *briefly* state the grounds for the objection (*e.g.*, asked and answered; compound question; the question calls for the witness to divulge a confidential communication that is protected by the attorney-client privilege; etc.). The primary reason for stating the grounds is to make a record; it also affords examining counsel an opportunity to cure the defect by modifying, rephrasing or withdrawing the question. Finally, it may bring to light certain difficulties with the question that the witness will pick up on in his answer.

5. Directing the Witness Not to Answer

When counsel defending a deposition objects to a question, several scenarios may develop:

(i) The question may be withdrawn or modified to meet the objection;

(ii) Having stated the objection and made a record, counsel may permit the witness to answer (*e.g.*, "I object to the form of the question. It calls for the witness to speculate about the defendant's state of mind. The witness can answer only *if he knows* why the defendant wrote the letter"); or

(iii) Counsel may object and instruct the witness not to answer the question (*e.g.*, "I object on grounds of attorney-client privilege and direct the witness not to answer.")

When, if at all, is it appropriate for counsel to instruct the witness not to answer? Despite the apparent mandate of Rule 30(c) that "[e]vidence objected to shall be taken subject to the objection,"[167] many courts permit an

---

166 Fed. R. Civ. P. 32(d)(3).

167 Fed. R. Civ. P. 30(c).

instruction not to answer in "exceptional situations" (*e.g.*, those involving trade secrets or privileged information), where "some serious harm is likely to result" from responding to a given question.[168] Some courts go even further: they hold that a witness may be directed not to answer questions that seek *irrelevant* information.[169] The more prevalent view appears to be that a witness must answer even irrelevant questions or move for an order to terminate or limit the examination.[170] In *Shapiro v. Freeman*[171] the Court explained:

> It is not the prerogative of counsel, but of the court, to rule on objections. Indeed, if counsel were to rule on the propriety of

---

[168] *E.g., International Union of Elec., Radio and Mach. Workers, AFL/CIO v. Westinghouse Elec. Corp.*, 91 F.R.D. 277, 280 (D.D.C. 1981); *Paparelli v. Prudential Ins. Co. of Am.*, 108 F.R.D. 727, 730-31 (D. Mass. 1985); *First Tennessee Bank v. Federal Deposit Ins. Corp.*, 108 F.R.D. 640, 640-41 (E.D. Tenn. 1985).

[169] *E.g., Kamens v. Horizon Corp.*, 81 F.R.D. 444 (S.D.N.Y. 1979) (denying motion to redepose defendant and rejecting contention that Rule 30(c) "mandates that a deponent answer all questions"); *In re Folding Carton Antitrust Litigation*, 83 F.R.D. 132 (N.D. Ill. 1979); *accord* 4A *Moore's Federal Practice* ¶ 37.02[2], at 37-33 to 37-34 ("when a deponent wishes to assert an objection that the question seeks information that . . . is not relevant to the subject matter of the pending action, his only course is to decline to answer"; according to Professor Moore, the *examining party* then "has the option of suspending the examination and moving immediately for a court order compelling an answer, or of completing the examination as to other matters and then moving for such an order"). *See also Westinghouse Electric Corp.*, 91 F.R.D. at 280 n.5 (exceptional situations where direction not to answer is appropriate may include questions concerning irrelevant information "directed to a sensitive part of the witness' past").

[170] *E.g., Ralston Purina Co. v. McFarland*, 550 F.2d 967, 973-74 (4th Cir. 1977) ("action of plaintiff's counsel in directing the deponent not to answer was highly improper"; the appropriate remedy "[i]f counsel felt the procedures were being conducted in bad faith or abused was to move to terminate or limit the examination pursuant to Rule 30(d)"); *Westinghouse Electric Corp.*, 91 F.R.D. at 279-80 (it is ordinarily improper to direct witness not to answer on grounds of relevancy); *Shapiro v. Freeman*, 38 F.R.D. 308, 311 (S.D.N.Y. 1965) ("even if the plaintiffs' attorney believed the questions to be without the scope of the [court's] . . . order, he should have done nothing more than state his objection"). The same is true of questions which go beyond the scope of a Rule 30(b)(6) document notice, *Paparelli v. Prudential Ins. Co. of Am.*, 108 F.R.D. 727 (D. Mass. 1985), or which are objected to on the ground that they were "asked and answered." *First Tennessee Bank v. FDIC*, 108 F.R.D. 640, 640-41 (E.D. Tenn. 1985).
A motion to terminate or limit the examination is made pursuant to Fed. R. Civ. P. 30(d), which provides in relevant part that:
> At any time during the taking of the deposition, on motion of any party or of the deponent and upon a showing that the examination is being conducted in bad faith or in such manner as unreasonably to annoy, embarrass, or oppress the deponent or party, the court in which the action is pending or the court in the district where the deposition is being taken may order the officer conducting the examination to cease forthwith from taking the deposition, or may limit the scope and manner of the taking of the deposition as provided in Rule 26(c).

[171] 38 F.R.D. at 311-12.

questions, oral examinations would be quickly reduced to an exasperating cycle of answerless inquiries and court orders. Alternatively, if the [witness's] . . . attorney believed the examination was being conducted in bad faith, that the information sought was privileged, or that the deponents were being needlessly annoyed, embarrassed, or oppressed, he should have halted the examination and applied immediately to the *ex parte* judge for a ruling on the questions, or for a protective order, pursuant to Rule 30(d). He had no right whatsoever to impose silence or to instruct the witness not to answer, especially so when the witnesses were not even his clients.[172]

Just as a witness may move pursuant to Rule 30(d) to terminate or limit the examination in the face of improper questioning, the examining attorney may move pursuant to Rule 37(a)(2)[173] to compel answers in the face of an improper refusal to answer. In the latter case, the examining attorney has the option of adjourning the deposition for the purpose of making the motion or completing the examination before seeking relief.[174] In either case, the losing party may be assessed "the reasonable expenses incurred" on the motion by the prevailing party, including attorney's fees, unless the losing party's position was "substantially justified or . . . circumstances make an award of expenses unjust."[175]

Sometimes counsel for the witness will prevent the witness from answering without actually instructing the witness not to answer. If counsel persists, the examiner should force him to take position: either give a direction not to answer or permit the witness to respond:

Q. Have you ever before been named as a defendant or respondent in a proceeding alleging medical malpractice?

---

172 Nor may the witness's counsel unilaterally terminate the examination without moving to limit or terminate it. *Hanlin v. Mitchelson*, 623 F. Supp. 452, 455 (S.D.N.Y. 1985), *aff'd in part, rev'd in part*, 794 F.2d 834 (2d Cir. 1986).

173 Fed. R. Civ. P. 37(a)(2) provides in relevant part:
If a deponent fails to answer a question propounded or submitted under Rules 30 or 31, . . . the discovering party may move for an order compelling an answer . . . "

174 Fed. R. Civ. P. 37(a)(2). *See generally* 8 Wright & Miller, *Federal Practice and Procedure* § 2113, at 419-20 (1970).

175 Fed. R. Civ. P. 30(d), 37(a)(4). *See, e.g., Westinghouse Electric Corp.* 91 F.R.D. at 280 (granting motion for costs and attorneys' fees); *Shapiro*, 38 F.R.D. at 312-13 (granting costs and expenses of bringing motion, together with reasonable attorneys' fees to be paid by plaintiffs' attorneys without recourse to their clients).

DEPOSITIONS

Witness's Attorney: Objection. I don't see how that's even remotely relevant to this case.

Examiner: [To the witness] Can you answer the question?

Witness's Attorney: I think we are entitled to an explanation of why you think the question is relevant.

Examiner: Are you directing the witness not to answer the question?

Witness's Attorney: No, not yet. I'll let him answer this one but the questioning is beginning to get out of line. If it continues this way, I'll terminate the examination and seek a court order.

Examiner: [To the witness] You can answer.

Witness: No.

H. Adjourning and Concluding the Deposition

Counsel may seek to adjourn the deposition for a number of reasons. It may not be possible to cover all matters of relevance in one session. The witness may have identified documents which should be requested and reviewed by examining counsel before concluding the deposition. Indeed, counsel may need to examine the witness about these documents. It may be necessary to adjourn the deposition pending a motion to terminate or limit the examination[176] or to compel answers.[177]

If there is any possibility that examining counsel will want to continue the examination (often and preferably these matters have been worked out in advance), this should be made clear "on the record" before the examination is adjourned. Counsel defending the deposition may agree to an adjournment, object to an adjournment or take the matter under advisement. If during the course of the examination documents were requested, examining counsel should reiterate his request for documents. Counsel for the witness should agree to search for and/or produce the documents, object or take the matter under advisement.

Once the examination is concluded, the next step is to review and sign the transcript, noting any corrections on an errata sheet. Unless the parties have stipulated otherwise, Rules 30(e) and 30(f) set forth the procedures for reviewing, changing, signing, sealing and certifying the transcript. *See infra* Section IV for a more detailed discussion of this subject.

---

176 Fed. R. Civ. P. 30(d).

177 Fed. R. Civ. P. 37(a)(2); "when taking a deposition upon oral examination, the proponent of the question may complete or adjourn the examination before he applies for an order."

I. Judicial Intervention/Supervision of Depositions

As has been noted throughout this chapter, there are a number of points at which one or more parties or the witness may apply to the court for assistance. A person may seek leave of court to take his own deposition or that of another person prior to commencement of an action.[178] Prior to the deposition, a party or witness may move to quash the deposition notice or subpoena, or for a protective order limiting the scope or manner of discovery.[179] During or after the deposition, a motion can be made to terminate or limit the examination[180] to compel discovery[181] and for sanctions.[182]

Courts do not relish expending limited judicial resources on petty discovery disputes. Indeed, the local Rules for the Southern and Eastern Districts place a premium on the parties making a good faith effort to resolve their own disagreements.[183] While the resolution of discovery disputes without court intervention will not always be possible, unreasonable conduct on the part of any counsel may be met with the imposition of severe sanctions.

Under Rule 37(a), if a deponent fails to answer a question propounded at a deposition, the party seeking discovery may move for an order compelling an answer.[184] For purposes of this Rule, "an evasive or incomplete answer is to be treated as a failure to answer."[185] If the deponent then fails to be sworn or to answer after being directed to do so by the court in the district where the deposition is being taken, this failure "may be considered a contempt of that court."[186] In addition, sanctions may be imposed, including but not limited to

---

[178] Fed. R. Civ. P. 27. *See supra* Section I, E.

[179] Fed. R. Civ. P. 26(c); 45(d). *See supra* Section I, K.

[180] Fed. R. Civ. P. 30(d).

[181] Fed. R. Civ. P. 37(a).

[182] Fed. R. Civ. P. 37(b).

[183] *E.g.*, S.D.N.Y. & E.D.N.Y. Local Civ. R. 3(f), (1).

[184] Fed. R. Civ. P. 37(a)(2).

[185] Fed. R. Civ. P. 37 (a)(3).

[186] Fed. R. Civ. P. 37(b)(1).

the striking of a party's pleading, the entry of a default judgment, the entry of a preclusion order and the payment of reasonable expenses engendered by the failure.[187]

IV. AFTER THE DEPOSITION

A. Correcting and Signing

After the deposition is transcribed, it is given to the witness through his counsel to review, make any changes to the form or substance of the testimony, and to sign.[188] Neither the witness nor the witness's counsel should write on the transcript. Instead, the changes should be made on a separate sheet of paper and presented to the officer along with the reasons for the changes.[189] The officer then enters the changes upon the original pages of the deposition or at the end of the deposition accompanied by the reasons, and the witness then signs the deposition.[190]

Although the witness is entitled to make whatever changes he considers necessary,[191] courts have reopened depositions if the changes are substantial and the reasons inadequate.[192]

At trial the original testimony, the changes, and the reasons for the changes are admissible[193] and have been required in the interest of fairness.[194]

---

[187] Fed. R. Civ. P. 37(b)(2).

[188] Fed. R. Civ. P. 30(e).

[189] It has been held that the changes written upon the deposition by the witness and unaccompanied by the reasons for the changes are inoperative. *Architectural League of New York v. Bartos*, 404 F. Supp. 304, 311 (S.D.N.Y. 1975). *But see Allen & Co. v. Occidental Petroleum Corp.*, 49 F.R.D. 337 (S.D.N.Y. 1970); *Usiak v. New York Tank Barge Co.*, 299 F.2d 808 (2d Cir. 1962).

[190] If the deposition is taken by non-stenographic means, the changes, the reasons for the changes, certification, and witness's signature are in writing and accompany the deposition. Fed. R. Civ. P. 30(b)(4).

[191] *See* Fed. R. Civ. P. 30(e) ("*Any changes* in form or substance which the witness desires to make *shall be entered* upon the deposition by the officer with a statement of the reasons given by the witness for making them." (emphasis added)).

[192] *See, e.g., De Seversky v. Republic Aviation Corp.*, 2 F.R.D. 113, 115 (E.D.N.Y. 1941).

[193] Fed. R. Civ. P. 32(a)(4); *Allen & Co. v. Occidental Petroleum Corp.*, 49 F.R.D. 337, 341 (S.D.N.Y. 1970).

[194] *Rogers v. Roth*, 477 F.2d 1154, 1159 (10th Cir. 1973); *see Usiak v. New York Tank Barge Co.*, 299 F.2d 808, 810 (2d Cir. 1962).

If the witness does not sign the deposition within 30 days of submission of the deposition to him, the officer signs the deposition and provides the reasons why the witness did not sign it.

B. Certifying, Sealing and Filing the Deposition

After the deposition is signed, the officer certifies (unless waived) that "the witness was duly sworn by the officer and that the deposition is a true record of the testimony given by the witness."[195] The officer then seals the deposition and files it with the court.[196] In the Eastern, Southern and Western Districts of New York, the deposition is not filed with the court.[197]

C. Obtaining a Copy of the Deposition

The parties and the deponent may obtain a copy of the deposition from the officer. However, the officer may withhold the deposition unless a reasonable payment is received.[198]

V. CONCLUSION

In 1987 Senior United States District Judge Milton Pollack sanctioned an attorney under 28 U.S.C. § 1927[199] and the inherent power of the court for "contentious, abusive, obstructive, scurrilous, and insulting conduct in a court ordered deposition."[200] Counsel's misconduct pervaded the deposition and included such *ad hominem* attacks on the examiner as "[y]ou are being an obnoxious little twit. Keep your mouth shut. . . . You are a very rude and impertinent young man."[201] Judge Pollack found counsel acted in bad faith, intended to harass and delay the examiner, and disregarded the orderly process of justice. Accordingly, he ordered that a new deposition be taken in his

---

[195] Fed. R. Civ. P. 30(f)(1).

[196] *Id.*

[197] S.D.N.Y. & E.D.N.Y. Local Civ. R. 18(a); W.D.N.Y. Local R. 14(a)(1).

[198] *See* Fed. R. Civ. P. 30(f)(2).

[199] 28 U.S.C. § 1927 provides that "[a]ny attorney or other person admitted to conduct cases in any court of the United States . . . who so multiplies the proceedings in any case unreasonably and vexatiously may be required by the court to satisfy personally the excess costs, expenses, and attorney's fees reasonably incurred because of such conduct."

[200] *Unique Concepts, Inc. v. Brown*, 115 F.R.D. 292, 294 (S.D.N.Y. 1987).

[201] *Id.* at 292.

presence, that counsel pay a $250 fine, and that counsel pay for the first deposition transcript "without reimbursement from his client."[202]

The deposition is the most powerful weapon in the litigator's discovery arsenal. But it must not be abused.

---

[202] *Id.* at 294.

EXHIBIT 1

UNITED STATES DISTRICT COURT
SOUTHERN DISTRICT OF NEW YORK

——————————————— x
ABBIE RODE, :
                            :
  Plaintiff,   :
                                                92 Civ. 2419 (MLF)
     against -
                            :
                                                NOTICE OF DEPOSITION
LUCY S. DIAMOND,   :
                            :
  Defendant.   :
——————————————— x

SIRS:

PLEASE TAKE NOTICE that pursuant to Rule 30 of the Federal Rules of Civil Procedure, the undersigned will take the deposition upon oral examination of the plaintiff, Abbie Rode, 162 Long and Winding Road, New York, New York 10016, before an officer or other person authorized to administer oaths, at the offices of Jon, Pawl, George & Richard, 280 Maiden Lane, Suite 3600, New York, New York 10038, at 10:00 a.m., on November 10, 1992, and from day to day thereafter until completed. You are invited to attend and cross-examine.

Dated: New York, New York
       October 15, 1992

                                 Jon, Pawl, George & Richard
                                 By: Leticia I. Bee
                                     A Member of the Firm

                                 Attorneys for Defendant
                                   Lucy S. Diamond
                                 280 Maiden Lane

DEPOSITIONS 417

New York, New York 10038

(212) 264-4177

To:

Dewey, Suem & Howe

350 Wall Street

New York, New York 10001

EXHIBIT 2

ABBIE RODE,

    Plaintiff,

        against -

LUCY S. DIAMOND,

    Defendant.

92 Civ. 2419 (MLF)

NOTICE OF DEPOSITION

SIRS:

PLEASE TAKE NOTICE that pursuant to Rules 30 and 45 of the Federal Rules of Civil Procedure, the undersigned will take the deposition upon oral examination of Walter Russ, 360 South End Avenue, New York, New York 10280, before an officer or other person authorized to administer oaths, at the offices of Jon, Pawl, George & Richard, 280 Maiden Lane, Suite 3600, New York, New York 10038, at 10:00 a.m., on November 9, 1992, and from day to day thereafter until completed. You are invited to attend and cross-examine.

PLEASE TAKE FURTHER NOTICE that pursuant to Rules 30 and 45 of the Federal Rules of Civil Procedure, the witness is directed to produce at the deposition for inspection and copying all documents requested in the attached schedule.

Dated: New York, New York
       October 15, 1992

                Jon, Pawl, George & Richard

                By: *Leticia I. Bee*
                A Member of the Firm
                Attorneys for Defendant
                  Lucy S. Diamond
                280 Maiden Lane
                New York, New York 10038

(212) 264-4177

To:
Dewey, Suem & Howe
350 Wall Street
New York, New York
Attorneys for Plaintiff
Abbie Rode

SCHEDULE A

[Counsel should include the definitions, the instructions and the list of documents he wishes produced. *Note*: Under Local Civil Rule 47, the Southern and the Eastern District of New York have adopted uniform definitions that are deemed incorporated by reference into all discovery requests.]

EXHIBIT 3

AO 89 (Rev 5 85) Subpoena

United States District Court

_____ DISTRICT OF _____

V.

SUBPOENA

CASE NUMBER:

| TYPE OF CASE ☐ CIVIL ☐ CRIMINAL | SUBPOENA FOR ☐ PERSON ☐ DOCUMENT(S) or OBJECT(S) |

TO:

YOU ARE HEREBY COMMANDED to appear in the United States District Court at the place, date, and time specified below to testify in the above case.

PLACE	COURTROOM
	DATE AND TIME

YOU ARE ALSO COMMANDED to bring with you the following document(s) or object(s): *

☐ *See additional information on reverse*

This subpoena shall remain in effect until you are granted leave to depart by the court or by an officer acting on behalf of the court.

U.S. MAGISTRATE OR CLERK OF COURT	DATE
(BY) DEPUTY CLERK	

This subpoena is issued upon application of the:

☐ Plaintiff ☐ Defendant ☐ U.S. Attorney

QUESTIONS MAY BE ADDRESSED TO:

ATTORNEY'S NAME, ADDRESS AND PHONE NUMBER

*If not applicable, enter "none"

EXHIBIT 3

AO 90 (Rev. 11/87) Deposition Subpoena

United States District Court

_____ DISTRICT OF _____

V.

DEPOSITION SUBPOENA

CASE NUMBER:

TYPE OF CASE ☐ CIVIL ☐ CRIMINAL	SUBPOENA FOR ☐ PERSON ☐ DOCUMENT(S) or OBJECT(S)

TO:

YOU ARE HEREBY COMMANDED to appear at the place, date, and time specified below to testify at the taking of a deposition in the above case.

PLACE	DATE AND TIME

YOU ARE ALSO COMMANDED to bring with you the following document(s) or object(s):*

☐ *Please see additional information on reverse*

Any subpoenaed organization not a party to this suit is hereby admonished pursuant to Rule 30(b)(6), Federal Rules of Civil Procedure, to file a designation with the court specifying one or more officers, directors, or managing agents, or other persons who consent to testify on its behalf, and setting forth, for each person designated, the matters on which he will testify or produce documents or things. The persons so designated shall testify as to matters known or reasonably available to the organization.

U.S. MAGISTRATE OR CLERK OF COURT	DATE
(BY) DEPUTY CLERK	

This subpoena is issued upon application of the:

☐ Plaintiff ☐ Defendant ☐ U.S. Attorney

QUESTIONS MAY BE ADDRESSED TO:

ATTORNEY'S NAME, ADDRESS AND PHONE NUMBER

DEPOSITIONS

AO 90 (Rev. 11/87) Deposition Subpoena

RETURN OF SERVICE (1)

RECEIVED BY SERVER	DATE	PLACE
SERVED	DATE	PLACE

RVED ON (NAME)	FEES TENDERED
	☐ YES ☐ NO AMOUNT $
ERVED BY	TITLE

STATEMENT OF SERVICE FEES

RAVEL	SERVICES	TOTAL

DECLARATION OF SERVER (2)

I declare under penalty of perjury under the laws of the United States of America that the foregoing information contained in the Return of Service and Statement of Service Fees is true and correct.

Executed on _____   _____
                    Date   Signature of Server

                                    _____
                                         Address of Server

ADDITIONAL INFORMATION

As to who may serve a subpoena and the manner of its service see Rule 17(d), Federal Rules of Criminal Procedure, or Rule 45(c), Federal Rules of Civil Procedure.

"Fees and mileage need not be tendered to the deponent upon service of a subpoena issued on behalf of the United States or an officer or agency thereof (Rule 45(c), Federal Rules of Civil Procedure; Rule 17(d), Federal Rules of Criminal Procedure) or on behalf of certain indigent parties and criminal defendants who are unable to pay such costs (28 USC 1825, Rule 17(b) Federal Rules of Criminal Procedures)".

SCHEDULE A

[Counsel should include the definitions, the instructions and the list of documents he wishes produced. *Note*: Under Local Civil Rule 47, the Southern and the Eastern District of New York have adopted uniform definitions that are deemed incorporated by reference into all discovery requests.]

CHAPTER FIFTEEN

OTHER METHODS OF DISCOVERY

by Professor Ettie Ward

I. INTERROGATORIES

A. Purposes, Advantages, Disadvantages and Abuses

Interrogatories can be useful for obtaining certain limited types of information fairly cheaply and quickly. In many cases, interrogatories may be the only discovery a party can afford. Yet, interrogatories have come under a great deal of criticism in recent years by practitioners and judges alike because of the ease with which they can be abused and overused. Voluminous and repetitive sets of interrogatories, boilerplate questions and forays into subject areas in which useful responses are unlikely are among the most common complaints. Interrogatories serve a useful function in a discovery plan in *many* cases but not in *every* case nor are interrogatories an appropriate or efficacious means of obtaining certain types of information. For example, information based upon subjective material or dependent on the demeanor or credibility of the respondent would best be obtained by depositions rather than interrogatories. Interrogatories are probably most useful early in the litigation to obtain general information to focus the claims and defenses and discovery. Interrogatories may help in determining who to depose, the availability of documents and areas for further inquiry.

First among the advantages of interrogatories is their cost. Interrogatories are relatively inexpensive to draft and serve; no court appearances are required and no court reporter is needed. Additionally, interrogatories draw on the collective knowledge of the responding party and his attorney. It will not suffice, as it would at a deposition, for the respondent to answer "I do not recall" if the information is available in the party's files or known to someone under his control. If the information must be assembled from a variety of sources, the responding party is required to gather the information. Interrogatories can be a particularly useful method for identifying and locating potential deponents and documents, for locating the proper spokesperson within a corporation and for gathering objective data regarding, for example, specific transactions or events, damage calculations and claims, and statistical and accounting records. On occasion, interrogatories may successfully narrow the issues and focus subsequent discovery by identifying the substantive claims and contentions and by particularizing the factual and legal bases for the pleading.

There are a number of disadvantages in using interrogatories. Interrogatories may be directed only to parties whereas the rules allow document discovery and depositions from nonparties. Thoughtful interrogatories may educate one's opponent concerning the propounding lawyer's theories and strategy and can force one's opponent to develop his own theories and strategy in order to respond. Nor do interrogatories permit spontaneity; there is no give-and-take as in depositions, no immediate opportunity for follow-up or to correct an ill-drafted question and no way to use the element of surprise to obtain a candid, spontaneous response. Although interrogatories must be signed by the party to whom they are directed, the answers are drafted by his attorney, who is much more likely to read the questions narrowly and avoid making damaging admissions.

Artfully drafted responses are even more likely to frustrate the proponent who has not carefully drafted his questions; good, clear and simple interrogatories are difficult to draft. The economic advantage of interrogatories may be lost if the responses are evasive, nonresponsive, self-serving or lead to extensive discovery disputes.

B. Requirements Under Federal Rule of Civil Procedure 33 and the Local Rules

1. Procedure

Rule 33(a) of the Federal Rules of Civil Procedure answers the basic procedural questions as to who may serve interrogatories and when they can be served. Interrogatories are a device for the discovery of *parties*. Rule 33(a) Fed. R. Civ. P., provides that "any party may serve any other party written interrogatories." This makes it explicit that interrogatories may be used to obtain discovery from co-parties, third-party plaintiffs or defendants or intervening parties, and not merely from adversaries.

The intention of the drafters was that interrogatories, like most discovery in the federal courts, should generally proceed without court intervention. Accordingly, Fed. R. Civ. P. 33(a) provides that "written interrogatories may, without leave of court, be served upon the plaintiff after commencement of the action and upon any other party with or after service of the summons and complaint upon that party." The Advisory Committee specifically rejected the view that defendants should be given any sort of priority in serving interrogatories or that service of interrogatories with a complaint should be discouraged.

Answers and objections to interrogatories must be served within 30 days after service of the interrogatories, except that a defendant has 45 days after service of the summons and complaint to respond. Although the court may allow for shorter or longer periods of time to respond, the parties cannot agree to extend or limit the time periods without court approval. In practice parties routinely agree by letter or stipulation to extend the time periods and such agreements are routinely "so ordered" by the court.

2. Scope

The permissible scope of Rule 33(b) interrogatory discovery is the same as for other discovery and "[i]nterrogatories may relate to any matters which can be inquired into under Rule 26(b)."

3. Types of Interrogatories

Rule 33 does not otherwise limit the use of interrogatories or the types of questions which may be asked. The only specific type of interrogatory mentioned in the rule is the "opinion or contention" interrogatory. Although an interrogatory "is not necessarily objectionable merely because an answer to the interrogatory involves an opinion or contention that relates to fact or the application of law to fact," special protection is provided for the respondent who may request that such an interrogatory be answered at a designated time later in the proceedings.

Opinion or contention interrogatories have always been troublesome, in part as a result of the legacy from early code pleading where efforts were made to distinguish between facts and law and facts and opinion. Opinion or contention interrogatories tend to generate discovery disputes. The Advisory Committee recognized that interrogatories that call for the application of law to fact can be very useful in narrowing and sharpening issues. Yet because it is still inappropriate to ask a party "pure law" questions unconnected to the facts of the case,[1] drawing the line between a proper and improper question can be difficult. It is difficult to articulate specific criteria, but a few examples should highlight the problems.

Proper: Does defendant contend that the defense of laches applies in this case?

---

[1] *See* Fed. R. Civ. P. 33(b) advisory committee note (1970) ("interrogatories may not extend to issues of 'pure law', *i.e.*, legal issues unrelated to the facts of the case").

Improper: Is the defense of laches dispositive of the claim asserted by plaintiff?
[Improper as calling for a pure legal conclusion.]

Proper: Do you contend that the person operating defendant's crane at the time of the accident was your agent, an independent contractor, or a trespasser?
[Proper in calling for application of law to facts of particular case even though it requires making a legal determination as to how the jurisdiction defines agent, contractor and trespasser.]

There are different schools of thought as to the efficacy of opinion and contention interrogatories. Some believe that a clever attorney will reveal little useful information in response to such questions and if one wants to probe trial theory, a request for admissions under Fed. R. Civ. P. 36 is more useful because that response will be binding at trial. Others feel that if used selectively to delve into specific issues, opinion and contention interrogatories can be fruitful. There is a great deal of variation in judicial attitudes toward opinion and contention interrogatories. Local rules and standing orders in certain federal district courts have attempted to address the issue directly.[2] In any event, opinion and contention interrogatories do not provide an avenue of obtaining the "mental impressions, conclusions, opinions, or legal theories" developed by an attorney in preparation for trial and subject to work-product protection.[3] Interrogatories seeking the opinions of expert witnesses are governed by Fed. R. Civ. P. 26(b)(4).

Contention interrogatories are more likely to generate useful information if phrased so as to elicit yes/no answers rather than narrative responses and if the questions are specifically derived from statements in the pleadings or in other documents.

The Eastern District Committee that drafted the Standing Orders which became effective in 1984 classified interrogatories into three categories:

(1) identification interrogatories which request the identity of knowledgeable witnesses, the location and availability of relevant documents, organizational structures, and the extent of applicable insurance;

(2) substantive interrogatories which seek a description of events or discussion at a meeting or computation of damages; and

---

[2] *See, e.g.*, S.D.N.Y. Civil Rule 46 and prefatory comments to E.D.N.Y. Standing Order 15.

[3] *See* Fed. R. Civ. P. 26(b)(3).

(3) contention interrogatories.

The Eastern District Committee concluded that identification interrogatories were least likely to be abused, whereas substantive interrogatories often led to objections or self-serving responses which did not advance the discovery process and contention interrogatories too often were used to harass the opposition. The prefatory comments to Standing Orders 15 through 17 suggested:

> In many cases identificaiton interrogatories *early* in the litigaiton are useful . . . . Substantive and contention interrogatories are better used, if at all, near the completion of discovery and after utilization of other discovery devices.

The Southern District of New York took a different approach in Civil Rule 46 and set specific guidelines regarding the stage of the litigation at which different types of interrogatories may be used.[4] At the commencement of discovery, Civil Rule 46 restricts the use of interrogatories to those seeking such items as the names of witnesses with knowledge or information relevant to the subject matter, computation of damages and the existence, custodian, location and general description of relevant documents. Other types of interrogatories can only be served "if they are a more practical method of obtaining the information sought than a request for production or a deposition."[5] In other words, although no absolute bar is imposed, a party who wishes to serve substantive or opinion or contention interrogatories must make an affirmative showing to the court that using such interrogatories is more practical—that is, cheaper, more efficacious and more likely to yield the desired results—than other methods of discovery.[6] Opinion or contention interrogatories may be served only at the conclusion of discovery and prior to the discovery cut-off date, unless the court has ordered otherwise.[7] At that

---

[4] The Eastern District of New York Discovery Oversight Committee in its 1986 Report declined to adopt a rule similar to S.D.N.Y. Civil Rule 46 on the grounds that the Southern District rule was better suited for large complex cases, that it threw out permissible as well as impermissible interrogatories and that it might encourage litigation on the issue.

[5] S.D.N.Y. Civil Rule 46(b).

[6] In a decision which appears to be one of first impression, a Southern District judge in *Underwriters at Interest v. Federal Express Corp.*, 88 Civ. 0266 (S.D.N.Y. May 19, 1988) has interpreted S.D.N.Y. Civil Rule 46(b) to allow the service of interrogatories seeking information other than the names of witnesses, the computation of damages or the existence, custodian, location and general description of relevant documents, without leave of court. The district court concluded that "the determination whether interrogatories are a more practical method of obtaining the information sought than a request for production must lie with the party propounding the interrogatories."

[7] S.D.N.Y. Civil Rule 46(c).

point in the litigation, a party may also serve questions seeking the names of expert witnesses and the substance of their opinions, if that information has not been previously obtained.[8] This type of limitation is permissible under the Federal Rules of Civil Procedure because it does not prohibit any particular type of interrogatory but merely regulates the timing of its use; a party who makes the requisite showing may be permitted to adjust the timing to the needs of a particular case. S.D.N.Y. Civil Rule 46 tries to take advantage, as well, of the proportionality requirement written into Fed. R. Civ. P. 26(b) in 1983 to limit repetitive, duplicative and cumulative discovery.

Districts outside New York have imposed various types of other restrictions on the use of interrogatories. For example, approximately forty districts restrict the number of interrogatories a party may ask.[9] The allowable number varies, depending on the district, from between twenty and fifty questions. Some judges in districts without such local rules have done the same thing by individual standing orders. To date, the Advisory Committee has declined to amend Rule 33 to impose such numerical limits and there are no such limits in any of the federal districts in New York. However, even in the absence of a rule imposing numerical limits, an excessive number of interrogatories may be a basis for obtaining relief from the court.[10] Other types of restrictions include requiring court approval before serving interrogatories in certain types of lawsuits or with regard to particular issues in a lawsuit. Although not formally a restriction, some districts by local rule or standing order require all parties to respond to the court's interrogatories.[11] This approach attempts to advise the court early as to the nature of the litigation and to encourage the early exchange of basic information without formal discovery initiated by the parties.

---

[8] S.D.N.Y. Civil Rule 46(d).

---

[9] A recent Federal Judicial Center Study determined that lawyers in districts with such rules expressed satisfaction with the numerical limitation. J. Shepard and C. Seron, *Attorney's Views of Local Rules Limiting Interrogatories* (Federal Judicial Center 1986). Wright & Miller take the position that such restrictions are inappropriate and inconsistent with Fed. R. Civ. P. 26(b)(1), and 33, and thus in violation of Fed. R. Civ. P. 83 which permits the promulgation of local district-wide or judge-made rules "not inconsistent" with the federal rules. 8 C. Wright & A. Miller, *Federal Practice and Procedure* § 2168 (1988 Supp.).

---

[10] *But see Compagnie Francaise d' Assurance Pour Le Commerce Exterieur v. Phillips Petroleum Co.*, 105 F.R.D. 16 (S.D.N.Y. 1984) (while lengthy interrogatories may be stricken on the basis of irrelevancy, sheer numerosity is not a valid objection).

---

[11] *See, e.g.*, District of South Carolina Local Rule 7.05 (implementing Rule 16 and establishing "standard interrogatories" to be answered by parties in every civil action except those exempted from application of Rule 16(b)).

Even in the absence of a local rule, the court has authority to modify a party's abusive or excessive use of interrogatories in response to a motion for a protective order pursuant to Fed. R. Civ. P. 26(c), as part of its routine discovery scheduling responsibilities under Fed. R. Civ. P. 16, in formulating a Fed. R. Civ. P. 26(f) discovery conference plan at a party's request or on its own initiative, or by imposing appropriate sanctions under Fed. R. Civ. P. 26(g).

C. Form of Interrogatories

Like other papers filed in federal court, interrogatories should include a caption, title, docket number and signature line, in addition to the particular questions.[12] The signature of the attorney on a Rule 33 request now carries with it the certification required under Fed. R. Civ. P. 26(g) that counsel has read the interrogatories and, after reasonable inquiry, believes that they are consistent with the discovery rules, warranted by existing law or a good faith argument for extension, modification or reversal of existing law, not interposed for an improper purpose, and not unreasonable, unduly burdensome or expensive within the context of the litigation and given the discovery already had.

Local rules or an individual judge's standing orders may impose additional requirements or supplement the requirements of the Federal Rules. For example, although Fed. R. Civ. P. 5(d) provides generally that all papers served upon a party be filed with the court unless the court orders otherwise, many district courts by local rules have ordered that discovery materials *not* be filed.[13]

In addition, most interrogatories include some or all of the following: a preface, instructions and definitions, in addition to the body of the request. The rules do not require it but the prefatory material is often included as a matter of tradition and professional custom.

The purpose of a preface is simply to advise the recipient of the applicable rule governing the request and, particularly in multi-party cases, to make explicit who is requesting the information and who is required to respond to it.

Instructions and definitions are often included to advise the responding party of particular information or conditions to be satisfied in answering interrogatories. Instructions and definitions may be important in preventing

---

[12] Fed. R. Civ. P. 7(b)(2) provides that the rules applicable to captions and other matters of form of pleadings apply to all papers, including discovery requests.

[13] *See, e.g.*, S.D.N.Y. and E.D.N.Y. Joint Civil Rule 18(a).

evasion of questions or an overly narrow construction of questions or for reminding a party of his obligations in responding, but if overdone these sections may be a source of discovery abuse and lead to additional objections and delay. In most cases instructions merely paraphrase or emphasize the requirements of Fed. R. Civ. P. 33 or the case law interpreting it.[14] An instruction may also specify the time period relevant to the questions or require specified disclosure if work product or attorney-client privilege is claimed.

Civil Rule 46 of the Southern District of New York and the Eastern District Standing Orders now pre-empt some of the items traditionally included in instructions. For example, S.D.N.Y. Civil Rule 46(d) makes explicit that no part of an interrogatory shall be left unanswered merely because an objection is interposed to another part of the interrogatory and Civil Rule 46(e)(2) specifies the information which must be furnished where a claim of privilege is asserted.[15] E.D.N.Y. Standing Order 21(b), which is made applicable to interrogatories by Standing Order 15, requires the party claiming privilege to disclose the same information. The purpose of these local rules is to reduce the number of questions asked and to eliminate erroneous instructions while clarifying the respondent's obligations and minimizing discovery disputes engendered by evasive or disingenuous answers and objections.

Definitions are particularly useful for specifying the exact meaning of words or phrases likely to recur in the questions or which may mean different things to different people. Technical terms or "words of art" may be defined as well. The use of definitions may simplify and shorten questions by elimi-

---

[14] For example, a typical instruction might remind the responding party of his obligation to furnish all information, however obtained, including hearsay, known to the party, his agents or attorneys or appearing in his records. This paraphrases Rule 33(a) and, in any event, case law requires such disclosure even in the absence of a specific instruction. Other typical instructions include an explanation of the Rule 33(c) alternative to providing a detailed, written answer; a request for supplementation of answers (either co-extensive or more extensive than that required by Rule 26(e)); or a reminder to the respondent of his obligation to investigate and the duty to disclose the information available and efforts taken to obtain additional information.

[15] S.D.N.Y. Civil Rule 46(e)(2)(ii) provides that the following information shall be provided in the objection, unless divulgence of such information would cause disclosure of the allegedly privileged information:
(A) for documents: (1) the type of document; (2) general subject matter of the document; (3) the date of the document; (4) such other information as is sufficient to identify the document for a subpoena *duces tecum*, including, where appropriate, the author of the document, the addressee of the document and, where not apparent, the relationship of the author and addressee to each other;
(B) for oral communications: (1) the name of the person making the communication and the names of persons present while the communication was made and, where not apparent, the relationship of the persons present to the person making the communication; (2) the date and place of communication; (3) the general subject matter of the communication.
See also E.D.N.Y. standing Order 21(b)(2).

nating the need to repeat the meaning of such terms as "document" or "occurrence" or "contract" each time they are used in a particular set of questions. Proper use of definitions may help the parties avoid misunderstandings that will delay or extend discovery and require court intervention. It is not appropriate, however, to use definitions and instructions as a substitute for well-drafted interrogatories and an overly-long set of definitions and instructions can render an otherwise reasonable set of questions unduly burdensome.[16]

Civil Rule 47, which has been adopted in the Eastern and Southern Districts of New York, establishes uniform definitions and construction rules to be incorporated by reference in all discovery requests, including interrogatories. By implication, the parties are free to frame narrower definitions, but not broader ones. There is no prohibition against framing definitions of terms or short-hand references specific to a particular litigation. Civil Rule 47 thus defines such commonly-used terms as "communication," "document," "identify" and "parties." The intent is to reduce the need for court intervention to resolve disputes.

Careful drafting of interrogatories and tailoring them to address the issues, claims and defenses in the particular matter reduces, but does not eliminate, the likelihood of obtaining responsive answers without the need for extensive motion practice. E.D.N.Y. Standing Order 16(a) makes the point that interrogatories should be drafted "reasonably, clearly and concisely, be limited to matters discoverable pursuant to Fed. R. Civ. P. 26(b), and shall not be duplicative or repetitious." The use of form interrogatories not tailored to the particular case is a bad and inappropriate practice which may lead to sanctions under Fed. R. Civ. P. 26(g) and may violate local rules.[17] E.D.N.Y. Standing Order 15, for example, imposes an affirmative obligation on a party serving interrogatories to have reviewed them to determine their applicability to the case. Wholesale use of form interrogatories makes it less likely that the interrogating party will obtain useful information in the answers.

---

16 The Commentary to E.D.N.Y. Standing Order 15 makes the point succinctly: "Use of overly complex definition and instruction sections should rarely be necessary if the interrogatories are prepared and responded to in a reasonable manner."

---

17 *See, e.g., Blank v. Ronson Corp.*, 97 F.R.D. 744 (S.D.N.Y. 1983) (interrogatories served by defendants in connection with a pending motion for class certification and purported answers would be stricken, where "there was no indication that any lawyer (or even moderately competent paralegal) ever looked at the interrogatories or at the answers," rather it was "obvious that they had all been produced by some word processing machine's memory of prior litigation").

D. Responses to Interrogatories

1. General Comments

Rule 33(a) Fed. R. Civ. P., establishes certain basic guidelines for responding to interrogatories:

(1) each interrogatory shall be answered separately and fully in writing under oath, unless objected to;[18]

(2) if objected to, reasons for the objection shall be stated;[19]

(3) answers are to be signed by the person making them; and

(4) objections are to be signed by the attorney.[20]

Under Rule 33(a) the responding party has the same time period whether he answers or objects or does both. Each interrogatory or part thereof must be answered or objected to; it is never appropriate to simply ignore a question. If a party fails to respond to interrogatories within 30 days[21] and no court-approved extension has been obtained, objections, even as to privilege or work product, to any interrogatories are waived.[22]

2. Objections

Proper grounds for objections to interrogatories include:

(1) not within the scope of discovery as defined in Fed. R. Civ. P. 26(b), *i.e.*, that the information sought is not relevant to the sub-

---

[18] *See also* S.D.N.Y. Civil Rule 46(d); E.D.N.Y. Standing Order 17.

[19] S.D.N.Y. Civil Rule 46(e) further clarifies that *all* grounds of an objection be stated and are waived if *not* stated.

[20] The attorney of a represented party or an unrepresented party must also sign the response pursuant to Fed. R. Civ. P. 26(g) and thereby certify that he has read it, and that after a reasonable inquiry, he believes it to be consistent with the discovery rules, warranted by existing law or a good faith argument for extension, modification or reversal of existing law, not interposed for an improper purpose, and not unreasonable, unduly burdensome or expensive within the context of the litigation and given the discovery already had.

[21] A defendant has 45 days after service of the summons and complaint.

[22] *See Turick v. Yamaha Motor Corp.*, 121 F.R.D. 32, 36 (S.D.N.Y. 1988); S.D.N.Y. Civil Rule 46(e). The court does, however, have discretion to ignore an unintentional waiver and refuse to compel an answer to an interrogatory which is grossly improper. Most courts hold that privilege objections can be waived for failure to respond in a timely fashion. *See, e.g., Davis v. Fendler*, 650 F.2d 1154 (9th Cir. 1981); *In re Shopping Carts Antitrust Litigation*, 95 F.R.D. 299 (S.D.N.Y. 1982); *United States v. 58.16 Acres of Land*, 66 F.R.D. 570 (E.D. Ill. 1975); *Bollard v. Volkswagen of America, Inc.*, 56 F.R.D. 569 (W.D. Mo. 1971); 8 C. Wright & A. Miller, *Federal Practice and Procedure* § 2173 (1970 and 1988 Supp.).

ject matter involved in any claim or defense in the action, and does not appear to be reasonably calculated to lead to the discovery of admissible evidence (because the scope of discovery under Rule 26(b) is so broad, this is a difficult objection to successfully advance);

(2) attorney-client privilege or work product immunity;

(3) annoyance, embarrassment, oppression, or undue burden or expense (these generally would provide grounds for a motion for a protective order under Fed. R. Civ. P. 26(c));

(4) the information sought is obtainable from other less expensive and more convenient sources or the discovery sought is duplicative or disproportionate to the needs of the case and the parties' resources (Fed. Civ. P. 26(b)(1) as amended in 1983 adds this proportionality requirement and is meant to "encourage jduges to be more aggressive in identifying and discouraging discovery overuse" as well as to reflect the "existing practice of many courts in issuing" Rule 26(c) protective orders);[23]

(5) overbreadth or excessive detail and number;

(6) vague and ambiguous;

(7) requests pure legal conclusions;

(8) inapplicable boilerplate or form interrogatories.

A number of other objections commonly interposed should be considered improper and may subject the respondent to sanctions. That the information is already known to the requesting party is not a proper ground for objection,[24] although it may be some evidence that the discovery is unnecessary or duplicative. Nor may a respondent object to providing answers which would be inadmissible at trial; the information sought must only be reasonably calculated to lead to the *discovery* of admissible evidence. Although some courts have held otherwise, many courts will sustain objections that the information is equally available to the requesting party.[25] It is not an objection that the interrogatory seeks opinions, conclusions, or legal contentions un-

---

[23] Advisory committee note to Fed. R. Civ. P. 26 (1983).

[24] *See, e.g., Weiss v. Chrysler Motors Corp.*, 515 F.2d 449 (2d Cir. 1975).

[25] *See, e.g., United States v. 58.16 Acres of Land*, 86 F.R.D. 570 (E.D. Ill. 1975).

less the claim is that such discovery is premature.[26] Even if some information sought by interrogatories might be better disclosed by other means of discovery, unless the objection is based upon the Rule 26(b)(1) "proportionality" requirements it is generally within the proponent's discretion to select the form of discovery.

The responding party may either object to an improper interrogatory or seek a protective order pursuant to Fed. R. Civ. P. 26(c). Although seeking a protective order is usually the more costly alternative, it may be the preferable avenue if the basis of the objection is redundancy, undue burdensomeness or expense. The court may find such a motion to be more persuasive of a genuine need for protection.

An objection based on privilege or work product requires that the respondent provide sufficient information to permit the interrogating party and the court to assess the validity of the claim. E.D.N.Y. Standing Order 17(a) and S.D.N.Y. Civil Rule 46(e)(2) both specify the kind of detail generally required to support such an objection. In the absence of a local rule, similar information may be sought by specific interrogatory question or instruction or pursuant to procedure established by stipulation or court order.

3. Answers

In responding to interrogatories, a party shall furnish such information as is available to the party.[27] A party has a duty to conduct a reasonable investigation to obtain information to respond to interrogatories and must reveal not only what the party itself knows, but also what it or its employees, officers or agents know, have learned through hearsay, believe to be true, have in their records or documents or have in their possession or control.[28] As distinct from a deposition question which only tests the deponent's recall at the moment of interrogation, the interrogatory requires the responding party to go beyond immediate recall and conduct a reasonable investigation unless it has a good faith basis for declining to do so.[29]

---

26 In the Southern District of New York, Civil Rule 46 postpones contention interrogatories until the cost of discovery. *See* notes 4 though 8 above and accompanying text.

---

27 Fed. R. Civ. P. 33(a).

---

28 *United States v. 216 Bottles*, 36 F.R.D. 695, 702 (E.D.N.Y. 1965).

---

29 The required Fed. R. Civ. P. 26(g) certification further bolsters the duty of the responding party and his attorney. Although "Rule 26(g) does not require the signing attorney to certify the truthfulness of the client's factual responses to a discovery request," the signature "certifies that the lawyer has made a reasonable effort to assure that the client has provided all the information and documents available to him that are responsive to the discovery demand." Advisory Committee note to Rule 26(g)(1983).

A party is usually only required to present requested data in the form in which it is routinely maintained and need not create statistical compilations or financial statements not kept in the ordinary course of business so long as the same basic data is supplied in existing form.[30]

Interrogatories should be read reasonably to avoid expensive and time-consuming motion practice caused by overly-narrow construction of questions. Such construction to avoid giving meaningful answers is a form of discovery abuse addressed by the Eastern District of New York in Standing Order 16(b), which provides that:

> Interrogatories shall be read reasonably in the recognition that the attorney serving them generally does not have the information being sought and the attorney receiving them generally does have such information or can obtain it.

If counsel is unsure about the meaning of an interrogatory, he should give it a reasonable interpretation or seek clarification.

Answers must be full and complete. If an objection is made to part of an interrogatory, the remainder of the interrogatory must be answered.[31] It is permissible to incorporate a previous response to answer an interrogatory where the answer or objection incorporated is responsive and the meaning is clear. It is not proper to avoid responding by stating that the information is known to the requesting party or that discovery is continuing. If the interrogatory calls for disclosure of information not yet obtained or computed by the respondent, it should be answered to the extent that any information is then available, reserving the right to revise or supplement the answer in the future. For example, an interrogatory may ask for details of plaintiff's damage computations which have not been completed or which cannot be completed until additional information becomes available. Yet prior to filing a complaint, the plaintiff must have had some information with respect to damages in order to frame the relevant allegations and the *ad damnum* clause. Whatever information the party has available or can obtain should be disclosed.

Answers are generally prepared by the attorney with information supplied by the client or pulled from the client's files. Interrogatories are answered "under oath" and "signed by the person making the answer"; objections are

---

30 If documents have been created for the purposes of the litigation and would support a claim of work product, the party seeking discovery can only obtain them by making the requisite showing of need under Fed. R. Civ. P. 26(b)(3).

31 *See* S.D.N.Y. Civil Rule 46(d); E.D.N.Y. Standing Order 17.

signed by the attorney.[32] The response must also be signed by an attorney for the party pursuant to Fed. R. Civ. P. 26(g). The attorney's certification does not verify the truth of the client's responses; the client's verification serves that purpose. The person signing the verification need not have personal knowledge of all the information in the answers and may sign based on information provided by others.[33] The person signing the verification will, however, be subject to being deposed on the answers and cross-examined on them.

The form in which answers are submitted may be affected by local rules. For example, W.D.N.Y. Local Rule 13(c) requires that "[p]apers containing responses to written questions or demands, including answers to interrogatories . . . shall set forth each question or demand *verbatim* with the party's response set forth immediately thereafter." This accords with the practice followed by many litigators.

4. Rule 33(c) Option to Designate and Produce Business Records

Fed. R. Civ. P. 33(c) gives the responding party the option to specify records from which the answer to an interrogatory may be derived and afford the proponent of the interrogatory a reasonable opportunity to examine, audit or inspect such records and to make copies: (1) where the answer may be obtained from the responding party's business records, and (2) the burden of deriving or ascertaining the answer is substantially the same for the proponent as for the respondent.

This option was added by the 1970 amendments to the Federal Rules of Civil Procedure to cover the situation where the party served would otherwise have to engage in burdensome or expensive research to answer the interrogatory. The intent is to shift the burden of such research without foreclosing essential discovery.

The interrogating party is protected from improper response tactics by the responding party such as dumping a mass of records on the proponent or offering to make all the respondent's records available because the burden must be substantially the same for both parties and, the specification of records must be "in sufficient detail to permit the interrogating party to locate and to identify, as readily as can the party served, the records from

---

[32] Fed. R. Civ. P. 33(a). If the party is a corporation, partnership, association or government agency, the answers may be verified by an appropriate officer or agent.

[33] *See* 8 C. Wright & A. Miller, *Federal Practice and Procedure* § 2177 at 561-2 (1970).

OTHER METHODS OF DISCOVERY

which the answer may be ascertained."[34] The Advisory Committee designated such practices an "abuse of the option." If only a party familiar with the records could locate the answer, the burden is not substantially the same.[35] The Advisory Committee notes also clarify that "if the information sought exists in the form of compilations, abstracts or summaries then available to the responding party, those should be made available to the interrogating party."[36]

The interrogating party may still be held responsible for out-of-pocket costs to the responding party such as computer time, employee time or other "expense of assembling his records and making them intelligible,"[37] although as a general matter the cost of discovery or the relative financial resources of the litigants does not determine whether the Rule 33(c) option may be exercised. In any event, even if the burden is not substantially the same and the Rule 33(c) option is unavailable, the responding party may still seek a protective order pursuant to Rule 26(c) against oppressive or unduly burdensome or expensive interrogatories.

5. Supplementing and Amending Responses

There is no general duty to supplement or amend interrogatory responses except to the limited extent required by Fed. R. Civ. P. 26(e). A party is under a duty seasonably to supplement the response to include information acquired thereafter with respect to any question regarding: (1) the identity and location of persons having knowledge of discoverable matters, and (2) the identity of persons expected to be called as expert witnesses at trial and the subject matter and substance of such expert testimony. A party must seasonably amend a prior response if the party obtains information such that the party knows (1) the response was incorrect when made, or (2) the response is no longer true and failure to amend would amount to a knowing concealment.[38]

Although instructions to interrogatories demanding additional or more extensive supplementation are common, such requests are probably unenforceable. A duty to supplement or amend answers that is more extensive

---

34 Fed. R. Civ. P. 33(c). The final sentence of Rule 33(c) was added to cut down the abusive use of the business records option.

35 Advisory Committee note to Fed. R. Civ. P. 33(c) (1980).

36 Advisory Committee note to Fed. R. Civ. P. 33(c) (1980). *See also* S.D.N.Y. Civil Rule 46(f).

37 Advisory Committee note to Fed. R. Civ. P. 33(c) (1970).

38 Fed. R. Civ. P. 26(e)(1) and (2).

than that specified in the rule can be imposed only by stipulation or order.[39] An interrogating party can also serve new interrogatories later in the litigation which seek updates of prior answers or new information acquired since the service of the prior answers.

E. Compelling Responses to Interrogatories

The discovering party may move for an order pursuant to Fed. R. Civ. P. 37(a) to compel an answer to its interrogatories whether the respondent has objected or simply failed to answer adequately or at all. Although the burden is on the objecting party to justify its objection or the adequacy of its answer, the discovering party has the burden of going forward.

The Federal Rules do not require that the parties consult informally to resolve their differences, but the Advisory Committee note to Fed. R. Civ. P. 33(a) states that the procedure "should encourage consultation, and the court may by local rule require it."[40] Each of the districts in New York by local rule mandates that the parties confer and make good faith efforts to resolve the discovery dispute prior to bringing on any discovery motion under Rules 26 through 37.[41] Outside New York, most courts require, either by local rule or by individual judge's order, similar attempts to confer and certification of good faith efforts. In the absence of an express requirement, judges will still expect lawyers to attempt to resolve differences among themselves prior to seeking judicial relief. Some courts and judges encourage the parties to attempt to resolve the disputes by informal conference with the judge or magistrate, including telephone conferences and imposing restrictions on the length or type of motion papers to be submitted.[42]

The procedure for obtaining relief by formal motion and the sanctions available to a successful movant are discussed in Chapter 13, *supra*.

---

[39] A broad, general obligation to supplement by stipulation or order is cumbersome to monitor and difficult to comply with, particularly for corporate entities. Much new information acquired may be of only marginal relevance or importance. Reliance on compliance can be dangerous to the party seeking discovery. Fed. R. Civ. P. 26(e).

---

[40] Advisory Committee note to Fed. R. Civ. P. 33(a) (1970).

---

[41] *See* N.D.N.Y. General Rule 10(k) (the certification of good faith efforts requires that the discovering party detail the names of participants and the dates and length of meetings to resolve the disputed matters); W.D.N.Y. Local Rule of Practice 17 (similar certification required); S.D.N.Y./E.D.N.Y. Civil Rule 3(f); E.D.N.Y. Standing Order 6. The commentary to E.D.N.Y. Standing Order 16 states:

> [I]t is desirable for the attorneys to communicate directly with each other and thereby seek to avoid disputes as to the intended scope of particular interrogatories, burden, inadvertant duplication or repetition, and like matters.

---

[42] *See, e.g.*, E.D.N.Y. Standing Order 6(b)(ii).

F. Use Made of Interrogatories

Fed. R. Civ. P. 33(b) provides that interrogatory answers "may be used to the extent permitted by the rules of evidence." The Advisory Committee note to Rule 33(b) further clarifies that under ordinary circumstances, use of interrogatories does not limit proof, although in exceptional circumstances, a party's reliance on an answer may cause such prejudice that the court will hold the answering party bound to its answer. Additionally, the court can bar use of certain material at trial as a sanction for withholding information from interrogatory answers. Rule 33(b) does not affect the power of the court to permit withdrawal or amendment of answers to interrogatories.

Neither interrogatories nor the responses are part of the pleadings; they are not a proper subject for judicial notice. Before an interrogatory answer can be used at trial, it must be offered and received into evidence. Because interrogatories are not limited to admissible evidence, objection can be made to the introduction of answers on the grounds of relevancy and materiality or on any other appropriate basis. Interrogatory answers are generally inadmissible as substantive evidence by the responding party; the answers would be considered hearsay, *i.e.*, self-serving statements not subject to cross-examination. The interrogating party can, however, make use of interrogatory answers of an adverse party at trial if they qualify as admissions of a party or for impeachment purposes.[43] If some of a party's answers are properly introduced, the responding party is entitled to read any other answer that tends to explain or correct the answer already introduced, even though such material would otherwise be inadmissible as self-serving statements.[44]

Simply because answers are admissible against a party does not make them binding judicial admissions. If a party amends its answers prior to trial, the answer cannot be used without the amendment. Even if there is no amendment, at trial a party may introduce inconsistent evidence and contentions. The responding party may be questioned about the amendment and is subject to impeachment by the prior answers.

Use of interrogatory answers is not limited to use at trial. Answers to interrogatories may be submitted and can be taken into consideration by the

---

[43] Answers to interrogatories served in a prior action may be used in a subsequent litigation as admissions of an opposing party if there is "substantial identity of issues and parties in the two actions." *Rule v. International Ass'n of Bridge, Structural and Ornamental Ironworkers, Local Union No. 396*, 568 F.2d 558 (8th Cir. 1977). Under Fed. R. Evid. 801(d)(2)(C), interrogatory answers in other cases may be admissible as *some* evidence on the points involved whether or not there is an identity of parties and issues.

[44] *Grace & Co. v. City of Los Angeles*, 278 F.2d 771 (9th Cir. 1960).

court in ruling on a motion for summary judgment.[45] Interrogatory responses may also aid the parties in assessing their claims and defenses for the purpose of settlement, making other substantive motions or developing trial strategy.

II. PRODUCTION OF DOCUMENTS AND THINGS AND ENTRY UPON LAND FOR INSPECTION

A. Purposes, Advantages, Disadvantages and Abuses

Rule 34, Fed. R. Civ. P, is most commonly used to obtain access to the documents of a party for inspection and copying, but the rule also extends to (1) the inspection, copying, testing and/or sampling of a party's *tangible things*; (2) gaining entry to a party's land or other property to inspect, measure, survey, photograph, test or sample the land or property; and (3) gaining entry to a party's land or other property to inspect, measure survey, photograph, test or sample something *or* the land or property. For example, a Rule 34 request may seek permission to inspect and test equipment or products which allegedly fail to meet contract specifications or to inspect the specific location on a party's property where an injury occurred. A Rule 34 request may be made to give a party's expert the opportunity to inspect, measure, photograph and otherwise test "things" belonging to an adverse party.

Most of the time Rule 34 requests seek the production of documents. There are few cases that do not involve at least some documents and many more cases that involve the production and distillation of large volumes of documents. Obtaining relevant documents is the primary way that parties develop the information required and uncover facts necessary to resolve a matter, whether by agreement or adjudication. Documents are used extensively as a basis for probing for additional information using other discovery tools. Documents may be used fruitfully to identify prospective deposition and trial witnesses. It is almost always beneficial to have obtained and reviewed a party's documents prior to taking the party's deposition. Document review can aid the preparation of more pointed interrogatories or permit a party to make better use of requests for admissions. Document requests often seek the production of documents identified in interrogatories and can be served in conjunction with a Rule 33 request. Often document exchanges can be done informally, but if done outside Rule 34 there is no enforcement mechanism to deal with inadequate compliance.

"Document" is broadly defined by the discovery rules to include "writings, drawings, graphs, charts, photographs, phono-records, and other data

---

[45] Fed. R. Civ. P. 56(c).

OTHER METHODS OF DISCOVERY

compilations from which information can be obtained."[46] The rule clearly includes computer-readable data and other information producible in some form other than a writing. The breadth of the "document" definition expands the usefulness of a Rule 34 request by extending its reach to more extensive types of information. The disadvantages of document discovery derive from the ease of requesting enormous amounts of material; there is an unfortunate tendency to forgo careful drafting in favor of inclusiveness to insure that no stone is left unturned or, more likely, that no file drawer is left unopened. Unless the case is one in which few documents exist, the expense of production, review and copying easily becomes a significant one for both sides.

Document requests generate a significant number of complaints about discovery abuse, although not as many as interrogatories. Although either side has the potential to engage in abusive behavior, with respect to document requests it is more likely that the respondent will be called to task. Serious abuses range from the destruction of documents to the over-zealous deletion of sensitive material from documents or "sanitizing" documents. A respondent may also simply fail to produce certain documents. Other abuses are more "mischievous" and appear to be done in the hope that maybe something will slip by the other side or that one's opponent will be worn down. Favorite techniques include (1) burying key documents in the midst of a sea of irrelevancy; (2) overproducing;[47] (3) shuffling documents so that the requester must put them together like a jigsaw puzzle; or (4) producing illegible or barely legible copies.

The most common abusive request is one that overreaches or seeks the production of far more documents than are needed or seek to impose an impossible burden on the respondent to locate all the information requested. A large corporate entity with far-flung offices is particularly vulnerable to such requests. Careful drafting to request documents that are likely to be material and useful requires a thorough understanding of the issues and the parties in the case as well as the purposes of document requests; it is much easier to draft a blunderbuss request than one that is finely honed to extract only relevant information. At the same time an abusive request is likely to ricochet to the detriment of the requesting party—when objections to production are sustained or the response is only of minimal relevance or there is significant delay occasioned by motion practice or a similar request is returned to the requester. Such discovery abuse by either side is more likely to

---

46 Fed. R. Civ. P. 34(a). *See also* S.D.N.Y. and E.D.N.Y. Joint Civil Rule 47 which defines "document" as "synonymous in meaning and equal in scope to the usage of the term" in Rule 34(a).

---

47 This technique has been variously referred to as the "warehouse ploy," the "Hiroshima defense" or the "boxcar response."

generate sanctions since the 1983 amendment to Fed. R. Civ. P. 26(g). Even if neither side engages in abusive behavior, controlling the flow of paper can be a major administrative and expense item.

B. Requirements Under Federal Rule of Civil Procedure 34 and the Local Rules

1. Procedure

Rule 34 requests are made *by* parties *to* parties in a pending action.[48] A Rule 34 request can be made only *after* commencement of the action.[49] Requests for production and inspection directed to nonparties must be made pursuant to Fed. R. Civ. P. 45.

A request under Rule 34 must be served on all parties; no motion, affidavit, good cause showing or court order is required. A proper Rule 34(b) request must set forth the items to be inspected either by individual item or by category and must describe each item and category "with reasonable particularity."[50] What that means in any given request and the amount of detail required will vary depending on the case, the nature of the request, the parties involved and the particular judge assigned to the matter—in other words, there are no established guidelines. For example, if you are aware of the existence of specific documents or are knowledgeable about your adversary's recordkeeping, your request may be required to be more specific. On the other hand, there is no obligation to take depositions or serve interrogatories before making a Rule 34 request in order to improve specificity. As a general rule, the designation should be of sufficient specificity to apprise a person of ordinary intelligence what documents are required and to allow the court to determine if all requested documents have been produced.[51] The bottom line is that one should make the clearest and most specific request possible. The more specific the request, the greater the likelihood that the documents called for will be produced or, in the event of a dispute, that the court will enforce the request or preclude the use of such documents by the responding party at trial.

Examples of specific requests include:

---

[48] Fed. R. Civ. P. 34(a).

[49] Fed. R. Civ. P. 34(b).

[50] Fed. R. Civ. P. 34(b).

[51] 8 C. Wright & A. Miller, *Federal Practice & Procedure* § 2211 at 631 (1970). *See, e.g.*, *In re Folding Carton Antitrust Litigation*, 76 F.R.D. 420 (N.D. Ill 1977).

(1) (In a contract case): "All documents which formed the basis for or source of the 'General Conditions' contained in plaintiff's specifications dated November 12, 1987 for the purchase and sale of the equipment designated for Plant No. 1."

(2) (In a securities fraud case): "Each document referring to a complaint filed by the Securities and Exchange Commission on or about March 23, 1988 in the United States District Court for the District of Columbia against defendant and others alleging violations of certain provisions of the Federal Securities Laws."

(3) (In an action for unpaid services): "Each bill sent to defendant by plaintiff for services rendered and each document referring or evidencing each such bill."

(4) (In a personal injury case): "Each document referring or reflecting expenditures for any physical or mental injury, condition or treatment resulting from the accident on May 20, 1988."

A Rule 34 request must also specify a reasonable *time*, *place* and *manner* of making the inspection and performing the related acts.[52] The usual practice is to request production at the offices of the attorneys for the requesting party, although that might be inappropriate or inconvenient in a particular case. For example, if the production involves large quantities of documents which are part of respondent's ordinary business records and to which respondent must have continuous access, production may be arranged upon agreement of the parties at respondent's premises or the place where the documents are maintained in the ordinary course of business. The requesting party has no right to demand that production be made at respondent's premises. Although more common in state court practice, production at the courthouse is rarely an option in federal court. Where and when production will be made is usually resolved by the parties and, if necessary, the court will resolve any dispute. For this reason it is not unusual to see a Rule 34 request that specifies production "at a time, place and manner to be agreed upon by the parties."

2. Scope

There are three basic limitations on the permissible scope of Rule 34 discovery:[53]

---

[52] Fed. R. Civ. P. 34(b).

[53] Fed. R. Civ. P. 34(a).

(1) It covers only the inspection and copying of "documents," as broadly defined by the rule and caselaw, or the inspection and copying, testing or sampling of "any tangible thing" or the entry upon land or other property to inspect, measure, test or sample the property or "any designated object or operation thereon."

(2) The documents, tangible things, property or designated objects must "constitute or contain matters within the scope of Rule 26(b)."33(a)

(3) The documents, tangible things, property or designated objects must be "in the possession, custody or control" of the party upon whom the request is served.

The Rule 34 definition of "document" expressly applies to "electronic data compilations from which information can be obtained only with the use of detection devices"[54] to include any type of computer-generated or stored information, and the respondent may be required to translate the data into usable form, including providing hard copies, disks, or printouts. The Advisory Committee notes recognize that the burden on respondent will vary from case to case and that the court may need to exercise its power under Rule 26(c) to protect the respondent against undue burden or expense by restricting discovery or shifting costs, and to take additional care to ensure the preservation and confidentiality of the records or of nondiscoverable material contained within them.[55] For example, the translation into intelligible form of certain computer-generated data might disclose a highly secretive and competitive programming system or contain nondiscoverable matter. In some cases a responding party might have to revise its programming or create a new program to avoid such issues, but a new program and the information generated thereby is not a document within the responding party's possession, custody or control. Similarly, work product protection issues may arise if the particular program or compilation was created in anticipation of litigation even though the raw data was derived from records maintained in the ordinary course of business. Many of the difficulties associated with new forms of data collection and storage are resolved by agreement between the parties.

Rule 26(b) permits discovery of any nonprivileged matter which is relevant and reasonably calculated to lead to the discovery of admissible evidence. Unless the court on motion orders otherwise, and subject to the

---

[54] Advisory Committee note to Fed. R. Civ. P. 34(a).

[55] Advisory Committee note to Fed. R. Civ. P. 34(a).

OTHER METHODS OF DISCOVERY

portion of Rule 26(b) that limits the frequency or extent of use of discovery methods if discovery is unreasonably cumulative or duplicative or unduly burdensome or expensive in relation to the parties' resources and the issues, a Rule 34 request may be used at any point in the discovery process and successive requests may be made.

The restriction that the document, thing, land or property must be in the responding party's possession, custody or control is based on the practical consideration that a party cannot be required to produce materials he does not have or control. The meaning of "possession" is obvious; even if the document is not the respondent's, if it is in its possession it must produce it if it is within the scope of Rule 26(b). If a party has custody or control of any responsive materials, they too must be produced. It is not permissible to insulate from production responsive materials by physically putting them in another's possession if custody or control is retained. If a document or thing is under a party's control then that party has the right to get it. For example, documents given to an attorney,[56] accountant or insurer,[57] copies of statements made in a litigation or documents held by a corporate subsidiary[58] of a party must be produced. If a party has possession, custody or control of responsive materials they must be produced even if they are outside the court's jurisdiction.[59] The Supreme Court and a number of lower courts have held that the court has power to order a party to produce foreign documents even though such production might subject the party to criminal sanctions in the foreign country; the effect of the foreign laws is to be considered in determining the appropriate sanction for noncompliance.[60]

3. Types of Rule 34 Information Obtainable

Three types of information are generally available using Rule 34: (1) inspection and copying of documents; (2) inspection, copying, testing or

---

[56] *In re Ruppert*, 309 F.2d 97, 98 (6th Cir. 1962).

[57] *Parrett v. Ford Motor Co.*, 47 F.R.D. 22, 24 (W.D. Mo. 1968).

[58] *In re Uranium Antitrust Litigation*, 480 F. Supp. 1138 (N.D. Ill. 1979).

[59] *See, e.g., Cooper Industries, Inc. v. British Aerospace, Inc.*, 102 F.R.D. 918 (S.D.N.Y. 1984).

[60] *See Societe Internationale Pour Participations Industrielles et Commerciales, S.A. v. Rogers*, 357 U.S. 197 (1958); *In re Westinghouse Electric Corp. Uranium Contracts Litigation*, 563 F.2d 992 (10th Cir. 1977); *Compagnie Francaise d'Assurance Pour le Commerce Exterieur v. Phillips Petroleum Co.*, 105 F.R.D. 16 (S.D.N.Y. 1984); *SEC v. Banca Della Svizzera Italiana*, 92 F.R.D. 111 (S.D.N.Y. 1981).

sampling tangible things; and (3) entry on land or property to inspect, measure, test, or sample the property or any designated object or operation thereon.[61]

The types of documents discoverable under Rule 34 and the broad range of items encompassed in the inclusive definition of "document" have been discussed above. Relevant documents may be obtained if they (a) relate to the claim or defense of the requesting party; (b) relate to the claim or defense of any other party; (c) may lead to the discovery of admissible evidence; (d) assist in the examination of witnesses; or (e) assist in the preparation of witnesses.

Rule 34 discovery involving tangible things most commonly involves testing or examination by the requesting party's expert. Testing, and particularly destructive testing, poses special problems and consideration. Tests, particularly those that may alter the properties of a thing or affect its operation will usually require a stipulation or court order detailing exactly what will be done and how, when and by whom. The testing protocols, test records and results are generally available to all parties. For this reason it is necessary for the requesting party to be sure that the benefits override the risks. A result unfavorable to the requesting party may be devastating to that party's litigation position; alternatively, if the physical evidence will clearly contradict a party's contentions it may be more economical to discover it sooner. Tests may also alter evidence. Before risking one's case in a test, the tactical impact should be considered and detailed planning and consultation with experts should take place. Such planning can help insure the admissibility of test results and their usefulness for trial preparation. Sometimes the potentially adverse effects of testing will require the court to protect the party against whom the request is made by barring particular tests or imposing conditions on the test. For example, in a contract litigation in which the plaintiff, a utility, claimed that a generator manufactured by defendant could not operate at its contract-specified capacity, defendant sought to test the equipment by running it at the specified capacity; plaintiff had been operating the equipment at a reduced load. If the defendant's test was successful, some of plaintiff's claims would be effectively refuted, but if plaintiff was correct and the generator "blew," plaintiff would stand to lose additional millions of dollars. Absent an indemnification from defendant against such an occurrence, testing was initially limited to a visual and physical inspection of the non-operating generator by the parties' experts.

Entry and inspection on property also requires special consideration as to whether less intrusive and expensive alternatives are available, such as pro-

---

[61] Fed. R. Civ. P. 34(a).

OTHER METHODS OF DISCOVERY

ducing photographs, samples, surveys or maps. As with testing of tangible things, testing of property or designated objects or their operation must be carefully worked out in a stipulation or court order in advance. Entry and inspection on property might be appropriate in many different type cases. For example, in an environmental case the defendant may want to inspect the property and measure pollutants; in a personal injury action a party may want to inspect the premises where the accident occurred and take appropriate measurements.

C. Form of Rule 34 Requests

Like other papers filed in federal court, Rule 34 requests should include a caption, title, docket number and signature line in addition to the substantive request.[62] The signature of the attorney on a Rule 34 request now carries with it the certification required under Fed. R. Civ. P. 26(g) that counsel has read the request and, after a reasonable inquiry, believes that it is consistent with the discovery rules, warranted by existing law or a good faith argument for the extension, modification or reversal of existing law, not interposed for an improper purpose, and not unreasonable, unduly burdensome or expensive within the context of the litigation and given the discovery already had.

Local rules or an individual judge's standing orders may impose additional requirements or supplement the requirements of the Federal Rules. For example, although Fed. R. Civ. P. (5)d provides that all papers served upon a party shall be filed with the court unless the court orders otherwise, many district courts by local rules have ordered that such materials *not* be filed.[63]

Most Rule 34 requests include a preface which indicates the governing rule, the party required to respond and the time, place and manner designated for production; instructions; and definitions, in addition to the body of the request. The rules do not require it, but the prefatory material is often included as a matter of tradition and professional custom.

Instructions are useful to inform the responding party of certain conditions. Setting time period constraints, for example, may limit the scope and burdensomeness of requests. Instructions may also be used to remind a party of its obligations in responding or to require specified identification of materials withheld from production on the grounds of work product protection or attorney-client privilege.

---

[62] Fed. R. Civ. P. 7(b)(2) provides that the rules applicable to captions and other matters of form of pleading apply to all papers, including discovery requests.

[63] *See, e.g.*, S.D.N.Y. and E.D.N.Y. Joint Civil Rule 18(a).

Definitions are particularly useful for specifying the exact meaning of recurring or ambiguous words or phrases or to clarify technical terms or words of art. Definitions can also operate as a welcome "shorthand" to simplify and shorten questions by eliminating the need to repeat the meaning of recurring terms or phrases, such as "document" or "occurrence" or "contract." For example, a definition can clarify that "contract" means the agreement signed by A and B on October 23, 1987. Proper use of definitions may help the parties avoid misunderstandings that will delay or extend discovery and may require court intervention. But definitions and instructions are not a substitute for a well-drafted Rule 34 request and an overly-long and cumbersome set of instructions and definitions can convince a court that an otherwise reasonable set of requests is unduly burdensome.

To avoid some of the abusive uses of instructions and definitions to expand what appears otherwise to be a reasonable set of requests and Eastern and Southern Districts of New York have adopted Joint Civil Rule 47 which establishes uniform definitions and construction rules to be incorporated by reference in all discovery requests, including Rule 34 requests. The local rule does not preclude (i) the definition of any terms specific to the specific litigation; (ii) the use of abbreviations; or (iii) a more narrow definition of any term defined in the rule. By defining the most common terms, including "communication," "document," "identify" and "parties," and including basic rules of construction normally included in discovery requests, the skirmishing over discovery requests can be limited to issues involving the body of the request.

The request should be tailored to the specific case. Form requests should not be used without reviewing them and making whatever changes are necessary. E.D.N.Y. Standing Order 18 prohibits the use of a request "not directed to the facts and contentions of the particular case." In any event, a generic request is less likely to uncover crucial documents or encompass the particular records available in the case.

Official Form 24 of the Federal Rules of Civil Procedure is an illustrative request for production.

D. Responses to Rule 34 Requests

1. Timing

Rule 34, Fed. R. Civ. P, requires written responses to requests to be served within 30 days after service of the request, except that a defendant has 45 days from service on it of the summons and complaint. Rule 34 does not require *production* within that time frame, but merely the written responses; production is usually made within a "reasonable" time as worked out by agreement of the parties. Pursuant to Fed. R. Civ. P. 29(2), parties cannot stipulate to extend the time to respond without court approval. In practice parties routinely agree by letter or stipulation to extend the time periods and such agreements are routinely "so ordered" by the court.

2. Objections

A responding party may object to all or part of a request. Whether a party objects involves tactical and strategic considerations as well as legal concerns. If an objection is made, the reasons for the objection must be stated. Objections must be signed and certified pursuant to Rule 26(g). Possible valid objections include:

(1) Not within the scope of discovery as defined in Fed. R. Civ. P. 26(a), *i.e.*, that the information sought is not relevant to the subject matter involved in any claim or defense in the action, and does not appear to be reasonably calculated to lead to the discovery of admissible evidence.

(2) Attorney-client privilege or work product immunity.

(3) Annoyance, embarrassment, oppression or undue burden or expense. (These generally would provide the basis for a motion for a protective order under Fed. R. Civ. P. 26(c).)

(4) The information sought is obtainable from other less expensive and more convenient sources or the discovery sought is duplicative or disproportionate to the needs of the case and the parties' resources. (Federal Rule of Civil Procedure 26(b)(1) as amended in 1983 adds this proportionality requirement and is meant to "encourage judges to be more aggressive in identifying and discouraging discovery overuse" as well as to reflect the "existing practice of many courts in issuing" Rule 26(c) protective orders.)[64]

(5) The material requested is not in the responding party's possession, custody or control or is no longer in existence. (But, if not, then the respondent is not obligated to produce it in any event.)

(6) Information is contained in public records available as easily to requester as respondent.

(7) Response would disclose confidential business information or trade secrets, or with respect to property or things, compliance would invade privacy, extensively disrupt respondent's business or would be dangerous. (These generally would be the basis for a motion for a protective order under Fed. R. Civ. P. 26(c).)

---

[64] Advisory Committee note to Fed. R. Civ. P. 26 (1983).

(8) The request is vague and ambiguous.

(9) The request is overbroad.

Before serving objections, a party should consider making informal efforts to modify requests and eliminate objectionable matter by negotiating with the requesting party.[65] Because each side generally has outstanding requests at the same time, "horsetrading" is possible at such meetings. Valid objections can be traded as a *quid pro quo* for obtaining an adversary's documents or used as a basis for limiting a discovery request. In any event, "turn about is fair play" when it comes to discovery and similar objections are likely to be parroted back when the objector becomes the requesting party. Additionally, the objecting attorney's Rule 26(g) certification requires that he has read the objections and, based on a reasonable inquiry, believes them to be consistent with the discovery rules and warranted by existing law or a good faith argument for the extension, modification, or reversal of existing law and not interposed for any improper purpose, such as to harass or cause needless increase in litigation costs. Boilerplate or unjustified objections may subject an attorney and his client to sanctions.

E.D.N.Y. Standing Order 19(b) also mandates that document requests "be read reasonably" to counter the practice of some attorneys who narrowly construe the request to avoid production, thereby leading to expensive and time-consuming motion practice. Failure to read a request reasonably or to solve the matter informally is likely to antagonize the judge or magistrate assigned to referee the dispute. Assuming that respondent has a valid objection, if the material is harmless and production is inexpensive, pressing for a Rule 26(c) protective order or defending against a Rule 37(c) motion to compel production may, in many cases, be more expensive, time-consuming and counter-productive than simply responding to the request.

Another consideration is whether the respondent will need to use the objected-to materials at trial. If the requesting party does not compel production or the objections to production are sustained by the court, any effort by the objecting party to offer the documents or information at trial is likely to be blocked.

Respondent has the option to make a motion pursuant to Rule 26(c) for a protective order instead of of serving objections or, if amicable resolution is

---

[65] The commentary to E.D.N.Y. Standing Order 19 reminds attorneys that it is "desirable" for them "to communicate directly with each other and thereby seek to avoid disputes as to the volume of documents called for by a particular request, burden, and like matters."

not possible, to seek the court's assistance in establishing the time, place and other conditions of production so as to reduce the burdensomeness of a request.

An objection based on privilege or work product requires that the respondent provide sufficient identifying information to permit the requesting party and the court to assess the validity of the claim.

3. Responses

The response must state, with respect to each request, that inspection and related activities will be permitted as requested, unless an objection has been made.[66] The response should also state the time and place where production will be made and any specified conditions. As a general matter, the logistics will be worked out in advance by the parties.

With respect to the production of documents for inspection, two options are available under Rule 34(b): (1) produce them as they are kept in the usual course of business, or (2) organize and label them to correspond with the categories in the request. This requirement was added in 1980 in recognition that "[i]t is apparently not rare for parties deliberately to mix critical documents with others in the hope of obscuring significance."[67] Although the production of copies is usually sufficient, inspection of originals may be required if requested.

4. Supplementing Responses

There is no general obligation to supplement an earlier production with later-discovered material. Supplementation is required pursuant to Rule 26(e) if failure to do it would amount to a knowing concealment. It is good practice to produce voluntarily any later-discovered responsive documents.

E. Document Production

1. Obligations of the Responding Party

a. Locating Documents

A respondent should make good faith efforts to locate responsive material. Good faith compliance with production requests may involve an extensive search at considerable cost and require substantial amounts of time and manpower. More often than not, the difficulties are compounded because a par-

---

[66] Fed. R. Civ. P. 34(b).

[67] Advisory Committee note to Fed. R. Civ. P. 34(b) (1980) quoting from *Report of the Special Committee for the Study of Discovery Abuse*, Section of Litigation of the American Bar Association 22 (1977).

ty's records are not organized so as to readily retrieve materials sought in discovery. For example, a straight-forward request for copies of invoices for certain services rendered might be filed in several places within a company, including the accounting department, the department requesting the service or individual project files. A request for documents reflecting equipment failures similar to those experienced by a party may be similarly scattered. In situations such as these, and in many others, a balance needs to be struck between the need for the documents and the cost of locating them. Various alternatives can be tried, including obtaining the information from other sources or from prepared summaries, stipulating as to certain information so as to obviate the need for production, agreeing to produce a sample of relevant records or deferring discovery until some later date. Often there is no alternative to production but, in some cases, the court may exercise its discretion to shift or spread the costs of the search and production.

The search may be conducted by the attorney representing the responding party, by paralegal or clerical personnel under the attorney's direction or, to save costs, by the client. Whoever does the actual search should do so in accordance with a plan provided by or approved by the attorney and an appropriate record of the steps taken should be made. At minimum, the respondent must take reasonable steps to locate responsive documents from persons likely to have them and from locations where it is likely that they would be kept. Whether discovery disputes arise as to the adequacy of the production or not, witnesses for the respondent are likely to be asked at deposition about the completeness of the production and the adequacy of the search. In addition, the attorney will be held to his Rule 26(g) obligation to insure that a reasonable investigation has been made and responsive materials produced. It is a good practice for the attorney to make the initial inquiries of the client as to where responsive documents are likely to be found. Written instructions issued to the persons doing the actual search will help avoid misunderstandings and misconstruction of requests, as well as set the standard for what a reasonable search entails. Adequate supervision of the persons conducting the search is necessary as well.

If unfavorable documents turn up later, the attorney may not only be embarrassed but subject to a monetary sanction as well if no adequate explanation is supplied. If it appears that a failure to produce was intentional, additional sanctions may be imposed, including preclusion orders prejudicial to the responding party.

b. Segregation and Production of Documents

As a general proposition, it is preferable to segregate responsive documents for production at the responding attorney's office rather than at the client's facilities, unless the volume of responsive documents is too great or

OTHER METHODS OF DISCOVERY 455

removal of the documents would be too disruptive to the client. The responding attorney can maintain better control over the inspection and copying phase at his own office and can avoid the danger of leaving the adversary to rummage at the client's offices and ask questions informally of the client.

Documents should generally be reviewed by the producing attorney or a paralegal at his direction both with regard to litigation preparation and to cull nonresponsive, privileged and confidential documents. Disclosure of privileged documents, even if inadvertent, can result in waiver not only of the particular document but also the entire subject matter. If done properly, this initial review can aid trial and deposition preparation. Lists and/or numbering of documents should be undertaken to provide a record of production as well as to permit later identification of documents.

If prior review is not possible, usually because of the volume of materials involved and time constraints, the producing party can protect against inadvertent disclosure by stipulating with opposing counsel that production will not constitute a waiver of any privilege or of certain objections. An appropriate review may then be done prior to copying.

All the logistics which are involved in a document production should be discussed and arranged in advance to avoid on-site disputes, delay and extra expense. For example, exactly how the production will be made should be determined, including whether originals will be produced, where production will occur, at what time and date, during what hours, how many representatives of requesting counsel will be permitted to review the materials, how copies will be made (*i.e.*, what process) and by whom, and who will pay for the copies. Special restrictions or arrangements may be necessary depending on where production is made. If the production is at the client's facilities, the facilities for viewing the documents or the hours for viewing them may be limited to permit normal business operations to proceed or outside copying services may be required. The producing party will usually want to arrange for copying to maintain control of the production, but it is not obligated to do so.

2. Review by the Requesting Party

As indicated above, the review will proceed much more smoothly if the logistics are worked out in advance. The requesting party should make sure that sufficient personnel are available to review the production. Although the requesting party might prefer to review the documents in its own offices, that usually does not occur unless the volume of documents is small and a set of copies is provided. The producing party is required to make the documents available for "inspection and copying" but the rules do not specify where, and the producing party will usually seek to maintain control.

The requesting party may, however, specifically demand to see originals, rather than copies, and raw files to ensure seeing, for example, enclosed scraps with notations, handwritten additions and attachments. The particular order of documents in a file may be of interest in a particular case. If reviewing raw files, the requesting party may have to agree that no work product or attorney-client waiver will occur.

Part of the review should include the preparation of a list and description of documents produced as well as a list of those to be copied.

F. Compelling Responses

If a respondent fails to respond at all, the requesting party can move for sanctions pursuant to Rule 37(d) without first making a Rule 37(a) motion to compel. The respondent cannot excuse its failure to respond on the ground the request is objectionable; the respondent must serve a response, including objections, or make a Rule 26(c) motion for a protective order.

If a respondent answers, but objects and the parties cannot amicably resolve the matters in dispute, the requesting party can make a motion to compel production under Rule 37(a) which will test the objections.[68] The requesting party may also seek relief if the production appears to be inadequate or incomplete and no explanation or supplementation is offered.

Prior to making a motion, however, each of the federal districts in New York by local rule mandates that the parties confer and make good faith efforts to resolve the discovery dispute.[69] Outside New York, most courts require, either by local rule or by individual judge's order, attempts to resolve disputes informally and a certification that a good faith effort to do so was made.

G. Use Made of Documents and Things

Documents produced or tests on property or things conducted pursuant to Rule 34 are not necessarily admissible at trial unless they qualify under the

---

68 For a more detailed discussion of the procedure for obtaining relief by formal motion and the sanctions available, *see* Chapter 13, *supra*.

69 *See* N.D.N.Y. General Rule 10(k) (the certification of good faith efforts requires that the discovering party detail the names of participants and the dates and length of meetings to resolve the disputed matters); W.D.N.Y. Local Rule of Practice 17 (similar certification required); S.D.N.Y. and E.D.N.Y. Joint Civil Rule 3(f); E.D.N.Y. Standing Order 6. In addition, the commentary to E.D.N.Y. Standing Order 19 states:
 [I]t is desirable for the attorneys to communicate directly with each other and thereby seek to avoid disputes as to the volume of documents called for by a particular request, burden and like matters.

rules of evidence. A proper foundation must be laid through discovery or stipulations and the documents must qualify, for example, as business records or other exceptions to the hearsay rule.

Use of documents or test results is not limited to use at trial; they may be submitted and can be taken into consideration by the court in ruling on a motion for summary judgment. Documents and test results may also aid the parties in assessing their claims and defenses for the purpose of settlement, making other substantive motions or developing discovery and trial strategy.

III. PHYSICAL OR MENTAL EXAMINATIONS

A. General Procedural Requirements Under Federal Rule of Civil Procedure 35(a)

An examination under Fed. R. Civ. P. 35(a) is appropriate when the mental or physical condition of a person who is a party, or under the legal control or custody of a party, is "in controversy." Rule 35(a) refers generally to physical examination by a physician or mental examination by a physician or psychologist, but also expressly includes blood examinations among the kinds of examinations that can be ordered under the rule. The scope of Rule 35(a) is thus not coextensive with Rule 26.[70] Although the vast majority of actions in which examinations are sought are personal injury actions, an examination may be sought in any type of action, including but not limited to, paternity actions, citizenship actions and any matter in which incompetence or undue influence of a party is an issue.

The party seeking the examination must file a motion, on notice, seeking a court order. The motion must include a showing of good cause to conduct an examination. The rule thus creates two standards in obtaining an examination of an adverse party: (1) the party's physical, mental or blood condition must be "in controversy," and (2) good cause must be shown for the examination. In other words, a physical or mental examination is not a routine discovery request and the trial court is to apply the rule discriminately, exercising broad discretion in considering and acting on the Rule 35(a) motion. In many cases, a physical or mental examination will be arranged by stipulation, thereby avoiding the requirements of Rule 35(a) for a motion and an order. The courts recognize that Rule 35(a) is a device which should be used only if the parties fail to agree on an examination. As the Supreme Court stated in *Schlagenhauf v. Holder*, the rule prohibits "sweeping examinations . . .

---

[70] *See In re Mitchell*, 563 F.2d 143 (5th Cir. 1977); 8 C. Wright & A. Miller, *Federal Practice and Procedure* § 2231 (1988 Supp.).

automatically ordered merely because the person has been involved in an accident . . . and a general charge of negligence lodged."[71]

1. Who May Be Examined

Rule 35(a) states that a party or a person in the party's legal custody or control may, if appropriate, be ordered to submit to a physical or mental examination. Prior to 1970, Rule 35(a) only required a *party* to submit to an examination. The 1970 amendment to Rule 35(a) extended the rule to cover also a person in the party's "legal custody or control." The amendment was intended to settle "beyond doubt" that a parent or guardian suing to recover for injuries to a minor may be ordered to produce the minor for examination.[72] The Advisory Committee notes recognize that an order to "produce" the third person imposed only an obligation to use good faith efforts to produce that person. The rule is so limited in recognition of the intrusive nature of this form of discovery.

2. The "In Controversy" Requirement

Rule 35(a) Fed. R. Civ. P, permits an examination only when the mental or physical condition of a party, or a person in the party's legal custody or control, is "in controversy." In cases in which a party alleges physical or mental injury, the condition is clearly "in controversy," but examinations are not restricted to personal injury actions in which a party claims damages. For example, in a defamation action where the alleged defamatory remarks concern plaintiff's physical, mental or blood condition, a Rule 35 examination may be justified to establish the defense of truth. Similarly, in an automobile accident case, a *defendant's* physical or mental condition might be placed in controversy by a plaintiff who alleges that defendant was impaired.[73]

In cases in which a party alleges physical or mental injury, the condition is clearly "in controversy" but if an adverse party calls into question a party's physical or mental condition, the court must determine if it is actually in controversy and whether there is good cause for an examination or whether the requesting party is merely seeking to harass or intimidate his opponent.

---

71 379 U.S. 104, 121 (1964).

---

72 Advisory Committee note to Fed. R. Civ. P. 35(a) (1970).

---

73 *See, e.g.*, *Schlagenhauf v. Holder*, 379 U.S. 104 (1964) (bus/trailer accident in which bus passenger sued).

3. The "Good Cause" Showing

The "good cause" showing required by Fed. R. Civ. P. 35(a) is not a mere formality and is warranted by the intrusive nature of the examination. The standard is a dual one: (1) the moving party must establish that the prospective information meets the relevancy standard of Rule 26; (2) the moving party must establish that he needs the information and that it is not possible to obtain the same information using other discovery techniques.[74]

If an examination is painful or dangerous, a higher standard may be imposed. A determination of good cause in such cases involves a balancing approach: weighing the pain or danger of an examination against the adverse party's need for, or the usefulness of, the information to be gained.

4. Conditions for Examinations

A party's Rule 35(a) motion must specify the time, place, manner, conditions and scope of the requested examination as well as the person or persons by whom it is made. The party whose examination is sought may oppose the motion or may make a separate motion for a protective order pursuant to Fed. R. Civ. P. 26(c). In either event, the court may limit the scope or conditions of the proposed examination by order. In many cases the conditions for examination will be agreed upon the by the parties. Rule 35(a) does not set any additional criteria for the Rule 35(a) order for examination.

B. Terms of the Order of Examination

1. What Kind of Examination May be Made

In a routine personal injury case, the kind of examination required to produce findings relevant to the issues in dispute will generally be apparent. In other cases, there will be some disagreement as to the kind of examination appropriate or necessary because, for example, a party's justification for the examination seems dubious or somewhat tenuous or the procedure sought is painful, intrusive or experimental or because additional avenues of inquiry are suggested by an initial examination.

As a general matter, the least intrusive form of examination and fewest number of examinations should be requested. A court will be far more reluctant to order an intrusive test, such as a biopsy, or any test that is painful or subjects the examinee to risk of injury. To avoid controversy during the examination process, it is essential to have established the parameters of any examination beforehand.

---

[74] *See, e.g., Marroni v. Matey*, 82 F.R.D. 371 (E.D. Pa. 1979).

The number of examinations is not expressly limited by the rule, but can be resolved within the "in controversy" and "good cause" framework. Sometimes an injury involves several distinct medical specialties and more than one examination may be necessary. In other cases, a party's condition may change during the course of the litigation. A request for a follow-up examination will usually require some changed circumstances. Although courts prefer to keep the number of examinations to a minimum, judges are often influenced by a need to "balance" the parties' positions. For example, if the plaintiff's mental and physical condition is "in controversy" and the plaintiff is being treated by a dozen doctors, all of whom may testify, the court is more likely to find that the defendant has established good cause to conduct a comparable set of examinations. Other factors which might persuade a court to order multiple examinations include: (1) the length of time since the initial examination; (2) the examinee's lack of cooperation during the first examination; (3) the inability of the examining physician to testify; or (4) amendments to the pleadings or newly discovered information which highlight different contentions and claims.

2. Who May Conduct the Examination

The Rule 35(a) order or the parties' stipulation should identify the person to conduct the examination. The person conducting the examination must be a physician or psychologist qualified to perform the procedures, and should also be a competent witness available to testify at a deposition and at trial.[75] The examiner need not be, and should not be expected to be, a neutral expert, but he may have to be qualified as an expert to express an opinion as part of the good cause showing. The examiner is usually designated by the party seeking to obtain an examination, but if the examination is arranged by stipulation, the examinee may be able to negotiate on this issue as well.

3. Where is the Examination Conducted

The issue as to where the examination will take place is often contested. A court will often require a plaintiff to appear for a medical examination where the action is pending in view of the fact that plaintiff chose that forum. Using a physician or psychologist from the forum state makes it easier for the examiner to testify at trial. The particular condition of the examinee or the need for special test facilities and equipment may affect the court's choice of venue for the examination.

---

[75] Effective November 18, 1988, Fed. R. Civ. P. 35 was amended to permit mental examinations by licensed or certified psychologists as well as by physicians.

4. Who May be Present During the Examination

Fed. R. Civ. P. 35(a) does not indicate who may attend the examination. Other than the examiner and the examinee, anyone else usually must be identified in the court order or stipulation.

Although the examinee's attorney might want to be present to protect his client from making damaging admissions, generally he has no right to attend.[76] An examinee should, therefore, be prepared adequately by counsel in advance. A physical or mental examination is not intended to be a deposition without benefit of counsel or an opportunity to extract damaging or embarrassing testimonial admissions. The Rule 35(a) order or the parties' stipulation can limit the scope of questioning, prohibit nonmedical questions entirely or preclude the introduction into evidence of statements made during the course of the examination which are not necessary to the examiner's opinion.

Whether the examinee's physician may attend is a matter for the court's discretion or for agreement by the parties and may depend on a showing of need. If the examination requires a painful or intrusive procedure, the presence of physicians for both sides may avoid unnecessary duplication and costs and reduce the examinee's discomfort.[77] For other types of examinations, particularly examinations of a person's mental state, the presence of additional parties might affect the results or disrupt the proceedings.[78] In some situations, particularly if a minor or incompetent is being examined, the presence of a third party may be necessary or, at least, desirable.

C. Exchange of Reports

Rule 35(b) Fed. R. Civ. P, governs the exchange of medical reports prepared after an examination of parties. The premise of Fed. R. Civ. P. 35(b) is that, insofar as possible, it is desirable for each side to have access to all medical reports on the condition in controversy. Rule 35(b) applies to exami-

---

[76] *See, e.g.*, *Brandenberg v. El Al Israel Airlines*, 79 F.R.D. 543 (S.D.N.Y 1978); *Warrick v. Brode*, 46 F.R.D. 427 (D. Del. 1969); *Dziwanoski v. Ocean Carriers Corp.*, 26 F.R.D. 595 (D. Md. 1960).

[77] *See, e.g.*, *Warrick v. Brode*, 46 F.R.D. 427 (D. Del. 1969); *Klein v. Yellow Cab Co.*, 7 F.R.D. 169 (N.D. Ohio 1944) (tests of a drastic nature). *But see Sanden v. Mayo Clinic*, 495 F.2d 221 (8th Cir. 1974) (no abuse of discretion to deny attendance).

[78] *See Swift v. Swift*, 64 F.R.D. 440 (E.D.N.Y. 1974) (plaintiff's physician barred from examination to determine plaintiff's mental capacity to maintain action).

nations made by agreement of the parties as well as to examinations conducted pursuant to a Rule 35(a) order, unless the parties' agreement expressly provides otherwise.[79]

Pursuant to Rule 35(b)(1), an examinee, or the party against whom a Rule 35(a) order is made, has the right to obtain a copy of a detailed written report of the examining physician or psychologist setting out his findings, including the results of all tests made, diagnoses and conclusions, as well as any earlier reports on the same condition to which the examining party has access.

Because the normal result of an examination will be a request by the examinee for the report, the requesting party should consider the potential impact prior to requesting the examination. Careful preparation, including a thorough review of available medical records and other information, should be done in advance of any examination. The examination and the report should be structured by the examining party to eliminate information not relevant to the condition in controversy to avoid unnecessarily prejudicing the examining party's position in the litigation.

The failure or refusal of the physician or psychologist to make a detailed written report does not excuse the obligation as the rule provides that the court may, in that event, exclude the testimony if offered at the trial.[80] Rule 35(b)(1) also provides that the court on motion may make an order against a party "requiring delivery of a report on such terms as are just."[81] Once the examinee has requested the report and it has been delivered, the examining party can request any "like report of any examination, previously or thereafter made, of the same condition."[82]

Rule 35(b)(2) establishes that by requesting and obtaining a report of the examination or by taking the deposition of the examiner, the party examined waives any privilege the party may have in that action or any other involving the same controversy, regarding the testimony of *any* examiner as to the same physical or mental condition. A party involved in a case which puts in issue his physical or mental condition ordinarily has waived any privilege. A request for the examiner's report under Rule 35(b) is *also* a waiver. This is particularly useful where the matter is "in controversy" but has not been put

---

[79] Fed. R. Civ. P. 35(b)(3).

[80] Fed. R. Civ. P. 35(b)(1).

[81] *Id.*

[82] Fed. R. Civ. P. 35(b)(1). The only exception is in the case of a report of examination of a person not a party where the party shows that such party is unable to obtain it.

OTHER METHODS OF DISCOVERY

in issue by the examinee. In such cases, the examined party may wish to consider whether it is in his best interest to waive the physician/patient privilege.

The exchange of reports under Rule 35(b)(1) is not the only avenue for their discovery. Rule 35(b)(3) expressly states that discovery of a report of an examining physician or psychologist or the taking of a deposition of the physician or psychologist in accordance with the provisions of any other rule is not precluded.[83] The Advisory Committee notes recognized that "if the report is privileged, then discovery is not permissible under any rule other than Rule 35(b) and it is permissible under Rule 35(b) only if the party requests a copy of the report of examination made by the other party's doctor."[84] If the report is not privileged, it is discoverable by making a document request under Rule 34 or by making the requisite showing under Rule 26(b)(3) or (4) without regard to whether the person examined has demanded a copy of the report.

D. Sanctions

If a party fails to comply with a court order requiring submission to a physical or mental examination, the sanctions of Fed. R. Civ. P. 37(b)(2), other than contempt, are available. The sanctions which may be imposed include: (1) precluding a party from introducing at trial evidence of the party's physical or mental condition; (2) deeming the opponent's contentions as to the condition as admitted; (3) dismissing the action; and/or (4) requiring the party or the attorney or both to pay reasonable expenses, including attorney's fees caused by the failure to submit to the examination, unless the court finds the failure to be substantially justified or other circumstances make the award of expenses unjust.[85] A refusal to produce an examiner's report may cause the court to exclude the examiner's testimony at trial.[86]

IV. REQUESTS FOR ADMISSION

A. Purposes, Advantages, Disadvantages and Abuses

Rule 36, Fed. R. Civ. P., is intended to serve "two vital purposes, both of which are designed to reduce trial time": (1) to facilitate proof with respect to issues that cannot be eliminated from the case; and (2) to narrow the issues by

---

83 Fed. R. Civ. P. 35(b)(3).

84 Advisory Committee note to Fed. R. Civ. P. 35(b)(3) (1970).

85 Fed. R. Civ. P. 37(b)(2).

86 Fed. R. Civ. P. 35(b)(1).

eliminating those that can be.[87] For this reason, some commentators point out that because Rule 36 responses are conclusive evidence at trial, unless withdrawn, Rule 36 is more of a trial practice rule than a device for the discovery of facts.

Requests for admission permit a party to require another party to admit or deny the truth of any matters within the scope of Rule 26(b)—in other words, any relevant, nonprivileged matter. Admissions are binding on the party making them unless the court on motion permits withdrawal or amendment, but may only be used in the pending action. Requests may relate to statements or opinions of fact or to the application of law to fact or the genuineness of any documents.

To the extent that Rule 36 requests for admission facilitate the parties in narrowing the issues which will have to be tried and afford a "short cut" in the proof of certain matters which if admitted are considered "conclusively established," they fulfill some of the issue identification and narrowing goals of Rule 16. Rule 36 admissions may also be effectively used as a basis for a motion for summary judgment or partial summary judgment. If obtained early in the pretrial process Rule 36 admissions can narrow the scope of discovery. Rule 36 admissions can facilitate trial preparation by eliminating issues, dispensing with the need to introduce proof on certain issues and serving as effective trial evidence.

To a great extent, however, Rule 36 is a good idea that has never lived up to its promise. Parties by and large do not easily make admissions, especially not early in the course of a litigation, so Rule 36 tends to be used relatively infrequently or only with respect to generally noncontroversial issues such as ascertaining the genuineness of documents.[88]

To be effective, Rule 36 requests must be carefully and skillfully drafted and the responding party must answer candidly. As the imposition of Rule 26(g) sanctions becomes more routine for failure to respond appropriately, use of Rule 36 may become more common.

Abuses can be found in Rule 36 requests as well as in the responses to the requests. Requests can become burdensome if they are "so voluminous and so framed that the answering party finds the task of identifying what is in

---

[87] Advisory Committee note to Fed. R. Civ. P. 36 (1970). *See also Moosman v. Joseph P. Blitz, Inc.*, 358 F.2d 686 (2d Cir. 1966); *Keen v. Detroit Diesel Allison*, 569 F.2d 547 (10th Cir. 1978).

[88] One study indicated that only 10 percent of attorneys surveyed used Rule 36. 8 C. Wright & Miller, *Federal Practice & Procedure* § 2252 at 704 n.16. *See also* Shapiro, *Some Problems of Discovery in the Adversary System*, 63 Minn. L. Rev. 1055, 1078 (1979) ("The request for admission is among the least used of the principal discovery devices.")

dispute and what is not unduly burdensome."[89] Requests are sometimes inappropriately used in an attempt to establish the requester's legal or factual contentions or arguments. A particular request may be inappropriate at an early stage of the litigation and proper at a later stage.

B. Requirements under Fed. R. Civ. P. 36

1. Timing

Rule 36 requests for admission may, without leave of the court, be served upon the plaintiff after the commencement of the action and upon any other party with or after service of the summons and complaint upon that party. The matter is admitted unless, within 30 days after service of the request, unless modified by the court, a written answer or objection addressed to the matter is served upon the requesting party.[90] A defendant, however, is not required to serve answers or objections before 45 days after service of the summons and complaint.[91]

2. Information Obtainable

Rule 36 requests may only be addressed to parties in a litigation. A Rule 36 request may seek the admission of the "truth of any matters within the scope of Rule 26(b)"[92] that relate to:

(a) statements or opinions of fact;

(b) the application of law to fact; or

(c) the genuineness of any documents.

The rule specifically eliminates any requirement that the matters be "of fact" and resolved conflicts in earlier court decisions as to whether a request to admit "opinions" and matters involving "mixed law and fact" is proper under the rule.[93] As the Advisory Committee note to Rule 36(a) points out, it is difficult as a practical matter to separate "fact" from "opinion" and, in any event, an admission on a matter of opinion may facilitate proof or narrow

---

[89] Advisory Committee note to Fed. R. Civ. P. 36(a) (1970).

[90] *But see, e.g., Szatanek v. McDonnell Douglas Corp.*, 109 F.R.D. 37 (W.D.N.Y. 1985) (court has discretion to permit party to file answers after 30-day period when delay not occasioned by lack of good faith, filing would facilitate proper determination of merits and untimely response will not unduly prejudice requesting party).

[91] Fed. R. Civ. P. 36(a).

[92] Fed. R. Civ. P. 36(a).

[93] Advisory Committee note to Fed. R. Civ. P. 36(a) (1970).

the issues or both.[94] A question as to whether an employee was acting within the scope of his employment or whether the defendant occupied or controlled the premises where an accident occurred involves a "mixed question" of law and fact but if an admission is obtained will remove an important issue from the lawsuit and reduce the proof required at trial.[95] Requests for admissions of law unrelated to facts are not authorized. The court does, however, have express power to defer decisions as to whether a request must be answered or has been answered sufficiently until a pretrial conference is held or until some other designated time.[96] Although judges should not routinely defer requests, the rule recognizes that there are some disputes where the judge's intervention is necessary or desirable.

In addition to seeking admissions as to facts and opinions, Rule 36 can be particularly useful with respect to facilitating proof as to documents. A party may establish by Rule 36 requests the authenticity or genuineness of documents, whether particular documents are originals or copies, the foundation for introducing documents into evidence at trial or anything else within the scope of Rule 36(b). Similar use can be made of admissions regarding nondocumentary evidence or other types of trial exhibits. Rule 36 requests are often used to eliminate confusion in deposition transcripts and to clarify minor, peripheral matters to avoid a need for proof at trial.[97]

C. Form of Rule 36 Requests for Admission

Like other papers filed in federal court, Rule 36 requests should include a caption, title, docket number and signature line in addition to the substantive request.[98] The signature of the attorney on a Rule 36 request now carries with it the certification required under Fed. R. Civ. P. 26(g) that counsel has read the request and, after a reasonable inquiry, believes it to be consistent with the discovery rules, and warranted by existing law or a good faith argument for the extension, modification or reversal of existing law, not interposed for an improper purpose and not unreasonable, unduly burdensome or expensive within the context of the litigation and given the discovery already had.

---

94 *Id.*

---

95 *Id.*

---

96 Fed. R. Civ. P. 36(a).

---

97 The same thing can be done in a joint pretrial order or joint exhibit list, but if done by Rule 36 request it can be done earlier.

---

98 Fed. R. Civ. P. 7(b)(2) provides that the rules applicable to captions and other matters of form of pleadings apply to all papers, including discovery requests.

As with other types of discovery requests, a preface, definitions and instructions may be useful.[99] Some districts outside the Second Circuit limit the number of requests for admissions, similar to restrictions on the number of interrogatories. Local rules or individual judge's standing orders may impose additional requirements or supplement the requirements of the federal rules.

Rule 36(a) requires that "each matter of which an admission is requested shall be separately set forth."[100] Requests are generally drafted in the form of affirmative statements rather than questions.[101] Generally requests should be formed to elicit "yes" or "no" answers. Compound, complex and vague requests increase the likelihood that the response will be an objection or an inability to answer. Combining separable items makes it more likely that the respondent will, properly or not, deny the whole paragraph. Ambiguities should be avoided and the request framed as specifically, explicitly and simply as possible.

D. Responding to Rule 36 Requests for Admissions

1. Effect of Failure to Respond or Object

A party who has been served a Rule 36 request has several options. The least desirable is doing nothing because a failure to respond, either to the entire request or to a particular request, is deemed to be an admission of the matter set forth in the request. Even though such an admission may still be subject to pertinent objections at trial or the court may permit a belated answer or allow the admission to be withdrawn, the party is taking a real risk. No motion to compel a response is required. If additional time to respond is required, the answering party should make a motion for an extension of time under Rule 29.

2. Objections

A party may seek a protective order under Rule 26(c) if the request will subject it to annoyance, embarrassment, oppression or undue burden or expense. If a party objects, it must state the reasons for the objection. The available grounds for objections are essentially the same as those appropriate for interrogatories and document requests. Proper objections include:

---

99 In the Southern and Eastern Districts of New York Joint Civil Rule 47 establishes uniform definitions and rules of construction to be used for all discovery requests, including Rule 36 requests.

---

100 Fed. R. Civ. P. 36(a).

---

101 *See* Official Form 25.

(1) Not within the scope of discovery as defined in Fed. R. Civ. P. 26(b), *i.e.*, that the information sought is not relevant to the subject matter involved in any claim or defense in the action, and does not appear to be reasonably calculated to lead to the discovery of admissible evidence. (Because the scope of discovery under Rule 26(b) is so broad, this is a difficult objection to successfully advance).

(2) Attorney-client privilege or work product immunity.

(3) Annoyance, embarrassment, oppression or undue burden or expense. (These generally would provide grounds for a motion for a protective order under Fed. R. Civ. P. 26(c).)

(4) The request is vague and ambiguous.

(5) The response would disclose confidential business information or trade secrets. (These generally would be the basis for a protective order motion under Fed. R. Civ. P. 26(c).)

Rule 36(a) expressly states that a request is not objectionable merely because the responding party considers that the matter as to which an admission has been requested presents a genuine issue for trial; rather, the party must deny the matter or state the reasons why the party cannot admit or deny it.

3. Answers

If a party answers a Rule 36 request, it is like a pleading in that it may make specific admissions, deny, or set out the reasons why it cannot truthfully admit or deny. A denial must "fairly meet the substance" of a requested admission.[102] The rule permits a responding party, as with a pleading, to qualify an answer or deny only a part of the matter as to which an admission is requested. The answering party cannot give lack of knowledge or information as a basis for a failure to admit or deny unless the respondent states that a reasonable inquiry has been made and that the information known or readily available is insufficient to permit admitting or denying the request. This obligation to make a "reasonable inquiry" is akin to that required in preparing interrogatory answers and is a separate inquiry from that certified by signing pursuant to Rule 26(g). The response as well as the request is subject to Rule 26(g) and the attorney's signature certifies that he has made a reasonable inquiry, reasonably believes that the response is consistent with the discovery rules, warranted by existing law or a good faith argument for the extension, modification or reversal of existing law, and that it is not interposed for an improper purpose.

---

[102] Fed. R. Civ. P. 36(a).

Any matter admitted in response to a request for admission is "conclusively established" unless the court, on motion, permits withdrawal or amendment of the admission.[103] The effect is therefore like an admission made in pleadings or a stipulation by counsel for use at trial; it is not evidence but it makes the introduction of evidence unnecessary. Subject to the Rule 16 provisions regarding amendment of the pretrial order, the court may permit withdrawal or amendment of admissions (1) when the presentation of the merits of the action will be subserved thereby and (2) the party who obtained the admission fails to satisfy the court that withdrawal or amendment will prejudice that party in maintaining the action or defense on the merits.[104] The court is more likely to permit withdrawal or amendment if the party who obtained the admission cannot demonstrate reliance on the admission, as by deferring or forgoing discovery. A motion to amend or withdraw an admission is likely to be denied if the movant has delayed without cause in seeking that relief.[105] Courts are generally cautious in permitting withdrawal.

E. Motion to Determine the Sufficiency of Answers or Objections

The burden is on the requesting party to make a motion to determine the sufficiency of answers or objections. If the claim is that the respondent's answers are evasive or otherwise insufficient and an admission should have been made, it is a difficult burden to meet. In addition to monetary sanctions, however, if the court agrees that an answer or objection is insufficient, the court can compel a proper response or order the matter admitted. On a motion to determine the sufficiency of answers or objections, the prevailing party is entitled to its expenses, including attorney's fees, unless the judge finds the unsuccessful motion or opposition was substantially justified.[106]

The court also has the option under Rule 36(a) to defer final disposition of a request until the pretrial conference or other designated time before trial. This is most likely to occur where the responding party would need additional time to make a detailed investigation.

F. Use Made of Admissions

Subject to any appropriate evidentiary objections raised by any party admissions can be used at trial, except that a party may not use its own admis-

---

[103] Fed. R. Civ. P. 36(b).

[104] Fed. R. Civ. P. 36(b). *See, e.g.*, *Warren v. International Brotherhood of Teamsters, Chauffeurs, Warehousemen and Helpers of Am.*, 544 F.2d 334 (8th Cir. 1976).

[105] *See, e.g.*, *999 v. C.I.T. Corp.*, 776 F.2d 866 (9th Cir. 1985).

[106] Fed. R. Civ. P. 36(a) and 37(c).

sions at trial. Admissions may only be used in the pending proceeding and may not be used in any subsequent proceeding between the same or different parties.[107]

An amended or withdrawn admission may still "haunt" the maker if it is introduced at trial as a prior inconsistent statement. If an admission is denied at trial, the admission may be used for impeachment purposes like any other discovery response and may preclude the denying party from introducing contrary evidence. If the denial of a prior admission is unjustified and the party who had obtained the admission has to prove the matter at trial, the responding party may be required to pay for the costs of proof.[108]

Admissions may be used to support substantive pretrial motions such as a motion for summary judgment or to dismiss. Admissions useful for this purpose might include an admission of fact that would deprive the court of jurisdiction, an admission of the genuineness of a written agreement, an admission of facts establishing tort immunity or the applicability of workers' compensation or an admission which establishes the availability of a *res judicata,* collateral estoppel or statute of limitations defense. A request for admission not properly denied can be deemed admitted for purposes of a motion for summary judgment.[109]

---

[107] Fed. R. Civ. P. 36(a).

[108] Fed. R. Civ. P. 37(c).

[109] *See, e.g., Goodman v. Mead Johnson & Co.*, 534 F.2d 566 (3d Cir. 1976), *cert. denied*, 429 U.S. 1038 (1977).

CHAPTER SIXTEEN

MOTION PRACTICE AND DISMISSAL WITHOUT TRIAL

by Robert L. Haig, Esq.*

I. GENERAL STRATEGY AND TACTICS IN MOTION PRACTICE

A. Whether to Make a Motion

Motions constitute a very important and effective part of an attorney's arsenal. Among other things, they may be used to control the timing of litigation, to strike irrelevant or prejudicial claims or defenses, to clarify issues, to obtain or prevent discovery, to educate the court, or to dispose of a lawsuit altogether. However, while motions can have very advantageous results, before making a motion one should always carefully consider whether it is advisable to do so under the circumstances.

First, one should consider the feasibility and desirability of seeking relief through some other means. Perhaps a simple telephone call to opposing counsel will resolve the matter without the effort, expense, and possible delay of motion practice. Similarly, one may be able to resolve the matter through a conference with the court. In fact, many judges require a conference or some other communication with chambers before a motion may be made.

Second, one should carefully evaluate the prospects of succeeding on the motion. An unsuccessful motion that had little or no chance of success from

---

* The valuable assistance of Steven P. Caley and Lynn Hollenbeck Kuo in the preparation of this chapter is gratefully acknowledged.

the start not only wastes the client's money and the attorney's time, but it may result in legal rulings in the court's decision that prejudice, rather than help, the movant's case.

Even if a motion is likely to succeed, an attorney should consider what the motion will really accomplish. For example, a motion by a defendant for a more definite statement of a complaint may only result in educating the plaintiff in how better to present the case. Similarly, some motions may have the effect of alerting the adversary to facts or issues in the case which he previously may have been oblivious to. *See, e.g.*, the discussion on motions *in limine, infra*.

B. Timing

Once an attorney decides that it is in the client's interest to make a motion, another crucial tactical decision is the timing of the motion. The attorney must first determine whether there are any statutes or rules restricting when such a motion may be made. For example, if a party makes a pre-answer motion to dismiss under Rule 12(b) and omits a defense of lack of jurisdiction over the person, improper venue, insufficiency of process or insufficiency of service of process, the party is barred from making any subsequent motion asserting that defense. Fed. R. Civ. P. 12(g), (h).

Assuming some flexibility as to when to make a motion, an attorney must carefully consider the effect, if any, that the timing of the motion will have on the likelihood of the motion's success or on other aspects of the litigation. On the one hand, one should be careful not to make a motion prematurely. Thus, for example, a motion for summary judgment made in the early stages of discovery will likely be vulnerable to an argument by the opposing party that there has not been adequate opportunity to conduct discovery to rebut the motion. *See* Fed. R. Civ. P. 56(f). If the judge agrees with that argument and either denies the motion or orders a continuance so that further discovery may be taken, the movant probably accomplished nothing by making the motion at that time, and may have educated the opponent as to weaknesses in the opponent's case or provided a "road map" to the movant's own thinking and strategy.

On the other hand, a motion made after it reasonably could have been made may be denied on a theory of laches or waiver or because of the suspicion that it has been made for purely tactical reasons. For example, a judge is likely to look with disfavor on a motion to disqualify opposing counsel made on the eve of trial if the facts upon which the motion is based have been known to movant for some time.

C. Affidavits

Evidentiary matter in support of a motion is generally submitted in the form of affidavits, with pertinent documents, if any, attached. *See* Fed. R. Civ. P. 43(e). One important decision a movant must make about the affidavit or affidavits to be submitted on the motion is the identity of the affiant or affiants. This may depend in large measure on the type of relief sought.

If one is making a discovery motion or some other type of motion in which the material facts pertain to the proceedings in the litigation, or are few and largely undisputed, an attorney's affidavit generally will not only be sufficient, but also advisable, for several reasons. First, the attorney is more likely than the client to have knowledge of the proceedings in the litigation. Second, the client is spared the inconvenience and disruption that active participation in the preparation of affidavits might entail. Third, and perhaps most important, are the advantages that may accrue to the opposition if a party submits its own affidavit or the affidavit of an employee or other representative. For example, submission of such an affidavit may elicit a demand by the adversary for an opportunity to cross-examine the affiant through deposition. In addition, the affidavit is a sworn statement by or on behalf of the party submitting it which will have the practical effect of binding the party to the statements therein—statements which the opposing party later may be able to make use of in other contexts, including impeachment of the witness at trial.

An attorney's affidavit, however, is inadequate for some purposes. For example, if the motion is one for summary judgment, the Fed. R. Civ. P. requires that:

> Supporting and opposing affidavits shall be made on personal knowledge, shall set forth such facts as would be admissible in evidence, and shall show affirmatively that the affiant is competent to testify to matters stated therein.

Fed. R. Civ. P. Rule 56(e).

An affidavit by a party's attorney on a summary judgment motion is likely to be insufficient because the attorney rarely will have personal knowledge of the material facts. Similarly, in most instances where a party makes a dispositive or other substantive motion which is based upon facts known to the party, or in the case of a corporation, its officers, employees or other representatives, attorney affidavits simply are not adequate.

In instances where an attorney's affidavit is insufficient, the attorney should exercise great care in selecting an affiant or affiants. In determining the identity and the number of affiants, the attorney must make sure that the affidavits include all necessary proof on the motion, but are not needlessly duplicative.

If there is available a nonparty witness with personal knowledge who is willing to submit a supporting affidavit, such an affiant is sometimes preferable because of the risks inherent in submitting a party's affidavit, as discussed above. However, it is frequently necessary to negotiate the language of such an affidavit with the affiant and to prepare a number of drafts. If the affiant is a nonparty, the attorney should keep in mind the possibility that the opposing party may seek and obtain discovery of both the attorney's discussions with the affiant about the contents of the affidavit and the earlier drafts themselves.

If the attorney's client is a corporation, there may be multiple individuals having the requisite knowledge. In evaluating each such potential affiant, the attorney should consider such factors as the individual's availability, position within the company, degree of knowledge, the likelihood that the individual will remain with the company in the future, whether the individual has already been deposed or is likely to be deposed in the future, and the impression the individual is likely to make upon the trier of fact if called to testify at trial.

There is a substantial likelihood that the submission of an affidavit will focus attention on the affiant in subsequent discovery and other proceedings in the litigation. If the potential affiant is not likely to perform satisfactorily in those proceedings, or will be too busy to devote the necessary time to them, the attorney should consider whether another affiant may be available who has the requisite knowledge to sign the affidavit and who also has the time and ability to handle the remainder of the litigation. Some attorneys make the mistake of selecting as an affiant a high ranking officer of their corporate client in hopes that the officer's title will impress the court. The court is unlikely to be impressed. The primary impression upon the officer, after his selection as an affiant has subjected him to multiple days of depositions, is likely to be one of dissatisfaction with his own attorney.

The affidavit should begin with an identification of the affiant and should explain in general terms the basis for his knowledge and information. The affidavit should generally also state at or near its beginning the purpose of the motion, as well as the nature of the action and, where appropriate, its procedural posture. The body of the affidavit should set forth in a complete but succinct manner the material facts. Headings and subheadings in the affidavit often improve organization and facilitate ease of reading. Although an affidavit is not generally as argumentative as a memorandum, in order to maximize clarity and persuasiveness, the affidavit ordinarily should include some explanation of the significance of the facts and why the facts entitle the movant to the relief sought.

MOTION PRACTICE AND DISMISSAL WITHOUT TRIAL

In general, the affidavit should recite only those facts that are necessary to the motion. Otherwise, the affidavit may unduly burden the court and may also provide the opposition with statements and information that can be used to the opposition's advantage outside the context of the motion.

Difficult issues are frequently presented while the movant decides whether to anticipate in the moving affidavit arguments which the opposing party may make in the opposing affidavit. Judges look with disfavor upon litigants who deliberately hold back their most significant arguments for their reply papers. Such a presentation raises the suspicion that the movant is attempting to "sand bag" an adversary and thereby deprive the adversary of an opportunity to respond to crucial arguments. Such tactics are frequently unsuccessful because the court often gives the opposing party a further opportunity to be heard in response to significant material presented for the first time in a reply affidavit.

On the other hand, it is clearly not necessary or desirable for the movant to attempt to anticipate every argument which the opposing party may conceivably make in opposing papers. Such an approach not only unduly extends the length of the moving papers, it may also present the opposing party with helpful arguments which he never would have thought of had the arguments not been set forth in the moving papers. Each case is different and the moving party must exercise common sense.

Additional tactical issues are presented when the movant considers the submission of reply papers. The movant should resist the temptation to repeat in the reply affidavit that which has already been stated in the moving affidavit. Although it is frequently useful to bring the court's attention in reply papers to the fact that the opposing party has failed to respond to material facts in the moving affidavit, it is not necessary to repeat all of those material facts in the reply affidavit. It is usually sufficient to cite the page or paragraph number where the facts appear in the moving affidavit.

If the reply affidavit is lengthy, the court may believe that the movant has simply repeated in the reply affidavit that which was already presented in the moving affidavit. Under these circumstances, it is possible that the court will devote less attention to the moving affidavit than to the reply affidavit.

D. Memoranda of Law

A movant may be required to submit a memorandum of law in support of his motion. *See, e.g.*, S.D.N.Y./E.D.N.Y. Civ. Rule 3(b); N.D.N.Y. Gen. Rule 10(c). Even if a memorandum is not required, however, it is usually to the attorney's advantage to buttress the arguments supporting his client's position with relevant statutes and/or case law.

For the convenience of the judge, and in order to make the presentation as readily comprehensible and persuasive as possible, it is usually advisable to organize the memorandum into separately headed sections such as the following: Preliminary Statement or Introduction, Statement of Facts, Argument (which in turn should be broken down into subsections for each separate issue), and Conclusion. As always, one should check the pertinent local rule or individual judge's rules in order to determine if there are any special requirements of form. Rule 3(b) of the Civil Rules of the Southern and Eastern Districts of New York, for example, specifically requires that moving and opposing memoranda be "divided, under appropriate headings, into as many parts as there are points to be determined." S.D.N.Y./E.D.N.Y. Civ. Rule 3(b).

The relative emphasis placed upon the facts and the law will depend upon the particular circumstances of the case and the motion. These will also affect the nature of the legal argument. For example, where there is controlling legal authority supportive of movant's position which is directly on point, the argument should focus on analysis of that authority. Where a party's legal position is uncertain or weak but there are strong reasons of equity or public policy supporting the party's position, the attorney would be wise to emphasize those equitable and policy arguments in the memorandum.

Generally, one should make sure that the most significant matter in the affidavits is also mentioned in some form in the memorandum, and vice versa. This not only serves to emphasize the important points but also protects against the possibility that the judge may read only one or the other. Under most circumstances, however, repetition may not be necessary, and one may, for example, choose simply to refer the court to the affidavits rather than to repeat the facts in a separate section of the memorandum. Reliance on such references may be particularly appropriate where the motion is not especially complex, or where circumstances compel the attorney to prepare motion papers in an expedited manner, or where one has reason to believe that the judge hearing the motion prefers that motion papers be kept to a minimum.

E. To Argue or Not to Argue

Oral argument on a motion may be required or permissive. The attorney should check the local rules of the district court and the individual rules of the judge involved to see if the court requires or permits oral argument on the motion. *See* discussion, *infra.*

If given a choice, the attorney should carefully consider whether it would be advantageous to orally argue the motion or to simply submit it on the papers. Much depends on the particular circumstances of the case. Factors that a movant should consider include whether there has been an opportunity to submit a written reply, the relative strengths of the client's position on the law and on the equities, the adversary's abilities as a writer and an oral advocate, and the personality, practices and abilities of the judge who will decide the motion. For example, if the movant has not had an opportunity to prepare reply papers and it is uncertain whether there will be an opportunity to do so, the movant should almost certainly request oral argument in order to rebut arguments raised in opposition to the motion and, if necessary, to explain to the judge why submission of further papers is necessary. In contrast, if the movant knows there will be a full opportunity to submit papers, and the opponent is eloquent and articulate in oral presentation but does not generally submit effective papers, the movant may be better off without oral argument. One should, however, carefully analyze and weigh all of the relevant factors in determining whether to request oral argument.

II. RULES GOVERNING MOTION PRACTICE

A. Sources of Rules

An attorney engaged in motion practice in federal court must consult multiple sources of rules in order to ensure compliance with all applicable requirements. These include not only the Federal Rules of Civil Procedure, but also the local rules of the district court in which the action is pending and the individual rules, if any, of the judge who will determine the motion. Because these rules go through a continuing process of supplementation and revision, the importance of verifying that the version consulted is up-to-date cannot be overemphasized.

1. Federal Rules of Civil Procedure

a. General Rules

Several rules contained in the Fed. R. Civ. P. pertain to motion practice generally. The attorney should be aware of these provisions in reference to all motions. The following can serve as a checklist of general provisions in the Fed. R. Civ. P. relating to motions:

Rule 5	Service and Filing of Papers
Rule 6(d)	Time for Service of Motions-Affidavits
Rule 7(b)	Form of Motions
Rule 11	Signing of Motions
Rule 43(e)	Evidence on Motions
Rule 54	Judgments
Rule 77	District Courts and Clerks

Rule 78   Motion Day

b. Specific Rules

The Fed. R. Civ. P. also contain rules which govern specific types of motions. An attorney planning to make a motion must determine whether there are any rules specifically governing the particular type of motion to be made and, if there are, should be certain to comply with these as well as the Rules relating to motion practice generally. The following is a list of some such specific Rules.

Rule 12	Defenses and Objections by Motion
(b)	Defenses Which May be Presented by Motion
(c)	Motion for Judgment on the Pleadings
(d)	Preliminary Hearings of Motions Under Rule 12(b) and (c)
(e)	Motion for More Definite Statement
(f)	Motion to Strike
(g)	Consolidation of Defenses in Motion
(h)	Waiver or Preservation of Certain Defenses
Rule 21	Motion to Drop or Add Parties
Rule 24	Motion to Intervene
Rule 25	Motion for Substitution of Parties
Rule 26(c)	Motion for a Protective Order
Rule 30(d)	Motion to Terminate or Limit Oral Examination
Rule 37(a)	Motion for Order Compelling Discovery
Rule 41	Motion for Voluntary or Involuntary Dismissal
Rule 50	Motion for Directed Verdict and Judgment N.O.V.
Rule 55	Motion for Default Judgment
Rule 56	Summary Judgment Motion
Rule 59(a)-(d)	Motion for a New Trial
(e)	Motion to Alter or Amend a Judgment
Rule 60	Relief from Judgment or Order
Rule 65	Injunctions and Temporary Restraining Orders

2. Local Rules of District Courts

In addition to the requirements of the Fed. R. Civ. P., each district court in New York has promulgated its own local rules, some of which also govern motion practice. These rules can be obtained from the court clerks. There are also several reference books containing local rules of the federal district courts in New York. These include: *Federal Rules Service* (Callaghan & Company), *Rules of the U.S. Courts in New York* (Clark Boardman Company, Ltd.), *McKinney's New York Rules of Court—State and Federal* (West Publishing Company), and the *Second Circuit Redbook* published by the Federal Bar Counsel.

The following are rules from each of the four districts in New York which relate to motion practice:

Western District of New York

Rule 11	Orders
Rule 12	Motion and Naturalization Days
Rule 13	Form of Papers
Rule 14	Service and Filing of Papers
Rule 15	Oral Argument
Rule 17	Cooperation of Counsel (on discovery motions)

Northern District of New York

Gen. Rule 6	Clerk to Sign Certain Orders
Gen. Rule 7	Form of Papers
Gen. Rule 9	Service and Filing of Papers
Gen. Rule 10	Motions
Gen. Rule 43.1 through 43.5 and 44	U.S. Magistrates

Southern and Eastern Districts of New York (Joint Rules)

Civil Rule 1	Filing Papers
Civil Rule 3	Motions
Civil Rule 6	Orders
Civil Rule 7	Form of Orders, Judgments and Decrees
Civil Rule 8	Submission of Orders, Judgments and Decrees
Civil Rule 9	Preparation and Entry of Judgments, Decrees and Final Orders

3. Rules of Individual Judges

Finally, before making a motion, the practitioner should always check to see if the particular judge handling the case has promulgated any individual rules that may be applicable.

An attorney practicing in the Southern and Eastern Districts of New York should be particularly careful, because many judges in those districts have promulgated wide-ranging and detailed individual requirements. Individual rules are not as prominent a feature of motion practice in the Northern and Western Districts, and in the case of most judges such rules consist primarily of forms of orders. Nevertheless, an attorney practicing in one of these courts should familiarize himself with any individual rules that may be applicable. Helpful reference sources for keeping abreast of individual rules include the *New York Law Journal* and *Individual Judges' Rules, Procedures and Forms in United States District Courts for the Southern, Eastern, Northern and Western Districts of New York* (2nd edition 1986; compiled by the Committee on Federal Courts of the New York State Bar Association).

When in doubt as to the existence or substance of rules for a particular judge, some attorneys call the judge's chambers or courtroom deputy for information. However, before making such a call, one should make sure to exhaust all of the foregoing sources. Neither the judge nor the judge's clerk are likely to look favorably upon one who makes demands on their time for information that is readily available from public sources.

B. Form of Motion

Fed. R. Civ. P. 7(b) requires that all motions be reduced to writing, except when made during a hearing or a trial. Rule 7(b) also mandates that the motion state with particularity the grounds thereof, and that it specify the relief or order sought. The writing requirement will be satisfied if the motion is stated in a written notice of the motion hearing. Rule 7(b) also incorporates the caption and other form requirements of Rule 10.

The signing requirements of Fed. R. Civ. P. 11 are incorporated by Fed. R. Civ. P. 7(b)(3). Thus, every motion must be signed by at least one attorney of record and must state the address of the signing attorney. The signature of the attorney attests that he has read the motion and that to the best of his knowledge, information or belief, formed after reasonable inquiry, it is (1) "well-grounded in fact and is warranted by existing law or a good faith argument for the extension, modification or reversal of existing law," and (2) that it has not been interposed for any improper purpose such as harassment or to cause unnecessary delay or increase costs without justification. Fed. R. Civ. P. 11.

Local rules of the district courts also include requirements as to the form of motion papers. *See, e.g.*, W.D.N.Y. Rule 13; N.D.N.Y. Gen. Rule 7.

C. Service, Notice and Filing of Papers

Fed. R. Civ. P. 5(a) requires that all parties must be served with every written motion other than one which may be heard *ex parte*. Where a party has appeared by attorney, service should be made upon the party's attorney, unless service upon the party is ordered by the court. Service may be made by delivery or by mail. Fed. R. Civ. P. 5(b).

With respect to notice requirements, Fed. R. Civ. P. 6(d) requires that the motion and notice of the hearing be served not later than five days before the hearing date, unless a different period is fixed by the Fed. R. Civ. P. or by order of the court. However, this notice period has been varied by local rules in each of the federal district courts in New York. Thus, the Southern and Eastern Districts generally require at least ten days notice for motions, with certain specified exceptions. These exceptions include discovery motions, for which only five days notice is required. S.D.N.Y./E.D.N.Y. Civ. Rule 3(c). The Northern District of New York requires twenty-one days notice. N.D.N.Y. Gen. Rule 10(e). The Western District provides for ten days notice. W.D.N.Y. Rule 14(c).

These same local rules also include requirements as to when answering papers must be served. Thus, in the Southern and Eastern Districts, answering papers must be served at least three days before the return date, where the motion has been made on at least ten days notice. If the motion has been made on five days notice, answering papers are to be served not later than noon of the day preceding the return date. S.D.N.Y./E.D.N.Y. Civ. Rule 3(c). The Northern District requires that answering papers be served not later than fourteen days prior to the return date. N.D.N.Y. Gen. Rule 10(e). In the Western District, answering papers must be served three days prior to the return date. W.D.N.Y. Rule 14(c). In all cases, the judge's individual rules, if any, should also be consulted.

Every written motion must also be filed with the clerk of the court, "either before service or within a reasonable time thereafter," unless the judge permits the papers to be filed in chambers. Fed. R. Civ. P. 5(d) and 5(e). The local rules of the Northern and Western District Courts, however, specifically require that moving papers and answering papers be filed with the clerk not later than the last day by which the papers may be served. N.D.N.Y. Gen. Rules 9(c) and 10(e); W.D.N.Y. Rule 14(c).

D. Orders to Show Cause

An order to show cause may be appropriate where the urgency of the situation would prevent compliance with the usual notice requirements, or where a temporary restraining order or other emergency relief is sought.

Although the Federal Rules of Civil Procedure contain no specific rule explicitly authorizing orders to show cause, two rules imply such authority. Fed. R. Civ. P. 5(a) excepts motions which may be heard *ex parte* from the service requirement. In addition, Fed. R. Civ. P. 6(d) provides that the court may order a notice period other than the standard five days and that "[s]uch an order may for cause shown be made on *ex parte* application."

Some of the district courts have rules specifically governing orders to show cause. For example, in the Southern District and Eastern Districts of New York, Civil Rule 3(c)(4) states that "[n]o order to show cause to bring on a motion will be granted except upon a clear and specific showing by affidavit of good and sufficient reasons why procedure other than by notice of motion is necessary." S.D.N.Y./E.D.N.Y. Civ. Rule 3(c)(4). Similarly, Civil Rule 6(b) further requires that an application for an *ex parte* order be based upon an affidavit showing cause therefor and stating whether a prior application for similar relief has been made. S.D.N.Y./E.D.N.Y. Civ. Rule 6(b).

The Northern District of New York also requires that an order to show cause be granted only "upon a clear and specific showing by affidavit of good and sufficient reasons why a procedure other than notice of motion is necessary." N.D.N.Y. Gen. Rule 10(1).

In addition, some judges have individual rules governing aspects of order to show cause procedure.

E. Oral Argument

Fed. R. Civ. P. 78 provides for each district court to adopt a schedule for hearing and deciding motions, "unless local conditions make it impracticable." However, the judge is not constrained to such a schedule and may order hearings on motions at any time or place, on such notice as the judge deems reasonable. Fed. R. Civ. P. 78. The court may also provide for the submission and determination of motions without oral hearing. *Id.* Given the flexibility of Fed. R. Civ. P. 78, whether a motion will be argued or submitted is a matter governed primarily by the local rules, see N.D.N.Y. Gen. Rule 10(i), W.D.N.Y. Rule 15, and by the rules of individual judges.

F. Form and Submission of Orders

Requirements as to the form and submission of orders are also largely governed by the local rules of the district courts.

The Southern and Eastern Districts of New York have several rules governing orders. Civil Rule 6(a) provides that a "memorandum signed by the judge concerning a decision on the motion that does not finally determine all claims for relief shall constitute the order unless the memorandum directs the submission or settlement of an order in more extended form." Civil Rule 7 sets out the form of the order. Civil Rule 8 requires proposed orders to be submitted to the clerk, rather than directly to the judge, and sets forth requirements for settlement of orders. Civil Rule 8 also provides that "[t]he attorneys causing the entry of an order of judgment shall attend to or endorse upon it a list of the names of the parties entitled to be notified of the entry thereof and the names and addresses of their respective attorneys." S.D.N.Y./E.D.N.Y. Civ. Rule 8. Civil Rule 9 deals with the preparation and entry of judgments, decrees and final orders. S.D.N.Y./E.D.N.Y. Civ. Rule 9.

General Rule 10 of the Northern District of New York requires that every motion be accompanied by a form of order. Such form of order should ordinarily simply provide for the grant of the relief requested in the motion. Likewise, every response in opposition to the motion must be accompanied by a form of order which will deny or amend the relief sought by the motion if the court approves it. N.D.N.Y. Gen. Rule 10.

The Western District of New York requires that "[o]rders of discontinuance or dismissal, whether on consent or otherwise, shall be presented to the presiding judge for signature." Local Rule of Practice 11. Other types of orders which may be signed by the clerk without submission to the judge are specified. W.D.N.Y. Rule 11.

III. MOTIONS DIRECTED TO THE PLEADINGS

A. "Corrective" Motions

Corrective motions seek to require the amendment of an adverse pleading in some regard. In contrast, "dispositive" motions seek the dismissal of all or part of an adverse pleading.

One major disadvantage of corrective motions is that their practical effect is often to educate the other party about defects in its pleading and legal theories, and to provide its attorney with the opportunity to cure those defects. Also, corrective motions are often time-consuming and expensive to make. Many such motions result in Pyrrhic victories; they often provide fewer benefits for the moving party than for opponent, even when the moving party "wins" the motion.

1. Motion for a More Definite Statement

Fed. R. Civ. P. 12(e) provides for a motion for a more definite statement. Such relief will be granted if the pleading is not only "vague or ambiguous" but so vague or ambiguous that a response cannot reasonably be made. Fed. R. Civ. P. 12(e). As this rule is interpreted, this means that the pleading must be unintelligible. 2A *Moore* ¶ 12.18(1).

a. Purpose

The purpose of the motion is to aid to the *preparation for responsive pleading* rather than preparation for trial. If the moving party wants to prepare for trial, the attorney "is properly relegated to the various methods of examination and discovery provided in the rules for that purpose." Note of the Advisory Committee on Federal Rules of Civil Procedure, regarding the 1946 Amendment to Fed. R. Civ. P. 12(e).

b. Availability

The motion is available as to all pleadings for which a responsive pleading is either required or permitted by court order. Fed. R. Civ. P. 12(e). *See* Fed. R. Civ. P. 7(a) (responsive pleadings permitted by court order).

c. Timing of Motion

The period in which such a motion may be made is the answering period. Fed. R. Civ. P. 12(e). The answering period is usually 20 days, *see* Fed. R. Civ. P. 12(a), but it may be longer. *See* Fed. R. Civ. P. 4(e).

d. Timing of Responsive Pleading

Service of a motion for a more definite statement alters the movant's time for making a responsive pleading as follows: If the court either denies the motion or postpones its deposition until trial, the responsive pleading must be served within ten days after notice of the court's action. Fed. R. Civ. P. 12(a). If the court grants the motion, an amended pleading containing a more definite statement must be served within ten days after notice of the order granting same or within such other time as the court may fix. Fed. R. Civ. P. 12(e). Thereafter, the responsive pleading must be served within ten days after service of the more definite statement. Fed. R. Civ. P. 12(a).

e. Waiver

If any other motion provided by Rule 12 is made before serving a responsive pleading, a motion for a more definite statement must be consolidated with it as required by Rule 12(g) or it is "waived." *FRA S.P.A. v. Surg-O-Flex of America, Inc.*, 415 F. Supp. 421 (S.D.N.Y. 1976).

2. Motion to Strike Matter

Fed. R. Civ. P. 12(f) provides for a motion to strike certain objectionable matter. A motion to strike matter is more widely available than the motion for a more definite statement; it may be brought against matter in any pleading, regardless of whether a responsive pleading is required or permitted.

a. Standard for Granting Relief

The court may order stricken any allegation that is "scandalous," "redundant," "immaterial," or "impertinent." Fed. R. Civ. P. 12(f).

"To strike material as scandalous [under the Fed. R. Civ. P.], it must be obviously false and unrelated to the subject matter of the action." *Gateway Bottling, Inc. v. Dad's Rootbeer Co.*, 53 F.R.D. 585, 588 (W.D. Pa. 1971).

"In deciding whether to [grant] a Rule 12(f) motion on the ground that the matter is impertinent and immaterial, it is settled that the motion will be denied, unless it can be shown that no evidence in support of the allegation would be admissible." *Lipsky v. Commonwealth United Corp.*, 551 F.2d 887, 893 (2d Cir. 1976). Further, allegations that are redundant, immaterial, or impertinent generally are not stricken in the absence of a clear showing of prejudice to the movant. *E.g.*, *Leas v. General Motors Corp.*, 278 F. Supp. 661 (E.D. Wis. 1968) (respecting redundant matter); *United States v. Southern Motor Carriers Rate Conference*, 439 F. Supp. 29 (N.D. Ga. 1977) (respecting immaterial matter). Indeed, "where the [impertinent or immaterial] allegations cannot harm the defendants, . . . they should be allowed to remain in the pleadings." *Pessin v. Keeneland Ass'n*, 45 F.R.D. 10, 13 (E.D. Ky. 1968).

In deciding whether the allegations in question are prejudicial, the courts often consider them against other allegations in the complaint. *E.g.*, *Fuchs Sugars & Syrups, Inc. v. Amstar Corp.*, 402 F. Supp. 636, 638 (S.D.N.Y. 1975) (court refused to strike a reference to an earlier court decree, though arguably immaterial, because "the mention of the decree is no more prejudicial than much of the rest of the amended complaint").

b. Timing of Motion

Fed. R. Civ. P. 12(f) requires that the motion to strike matter be brought (1) before responding to the pleading, or (2) within twenty days of its service, if no responsive pleading is permitted.

c. Timing of Responsive Pleading

Under Fed. R. Civ. P. 12(a), if the court either denies the motion or postpones its disposition until the trial, the responsive pleading must be served within ten days after notice of the court's action.

B. "Dispositive" Motions

Such motions seek to dispose of one or more claims or defenses, or of an entire pleading, on the basis of insufficiency or other defect as a matter of law. Such motions are directed solely to the contents of the challenged pleading. However, in certain circumstances, the Federal Rules provide for "converting" a motion to dismiss into a motion for summary judgment. *See* discussion *infra*.

1. Rule 12(b) Motion to Dismiss

With such a motion, the movant seeks to obtain a judgment dismissing all or part of a pleading.[1] Fed. R. Civ. P. 12(b)(6) does not expressly so provide, but the courts have construed the rule as allowing a challenge to part of the complaint, such as a single count. *See, e.g., Drewett v. Aetna Casualty & Surety Co.*, 405 F. Supp. 877, 878 (W.D. La. 1975); *Magnotta v. Leonard*, 102 F. Supp. 593 (M.D. Pa. 1952). *See generally* 5 Wright § 1358 (1969); Report of the Advisory Committee on Federal Rules of Civil Procedure Recommending Amendments, 5 F.R.D. 339, 344 (1946). Fed. R. Civ. P. 12(b) provides that the motion may be made by a party defending against any claim(s) asserted in any pleading.[2]

a. Grounds

Fed. R. Civ. P. 12(b) provides seven grounds for the motion to dismiss. Three grounds cannot be waived and may be raised virtually at any time:

---

[1] Fed. R. Civ. P. 12(b)(c).

[2] Distinct provision is made in the Fed. R. Civ. P. for a motion to strike or dismiss a defense. *See* Fed R. Civ. P. 12(f).

MOTION PRACTICE AND DISMISSAL WITHOUT TRIAL

(b)(1) - lack of subject matter jurisdiction; (b)(6) - failure to state a claim upon which relief can be granted; and, (b)(7) - failure to join an indispensable party. Fed. R. Civ. P. 12(h)(2).[3]

The remaining four grounds are waived if omitted from a motion to dismiss upon any other Fed. R. Civ. P. 12(b) ground(s), or if not raised by motion or responsive pleading: (b)(2) - lack of personal jurisdiction; (b)(3) - improper venue; (b)(4) - insufficiency of process; and, (b)(5) - insufficiency of service of process. Fed. R. Civ. P. 12(h)(1). In other words, these defenses must be raised in the defendant's first responsive paper, whether the response is a motion under Rule 12, or an answer.

b. Evidence Outside the Pleadings

The Fed. R. Civ. P. provides that if matters outside the pleading are presented relative to a Rule 12(b)(6) motion to dismiss for failure to state a claim, and if the court does not exclude such material, "the motion shall be treated as one for summary judgment. . . ." *See* Fed. R. Civ. P. 12(b)(6). The parties must be given notice that the Rule 12(b)(6) motion will be disposed of in that manner, and that they will be given reasonable opportunity to be heard on the motion on that basis. *Id.*

c. Restrictions and Timing of Motion

There is no explicit limit to the number of motions to dismiss that may be made under Fed. R. Civ. P. 12(b), except that the defenses provided by Fed. R. Civ. P. 12(b)(2)-(5) must all be raised in one motion. If a responsive pleading is permitted, a motion to dismiss must be brought before the responsive pleading is required to be served by the movant. Fed. R. Civ. P. 12(b).

d. Timing of Responsive Pleading

Service of a motion to dismiss alters the movant's time for making a responsive pleading as follows: if the court either denies the motion or postpones its disposition until trial on the merits, the movant must serve a responsive pleading within ten days after notice of the court's action. Fed. R. Civ. P. 12(a).

---

[3] Fed. R. Civ. P. 120(h)(2) expressly authorizes these defenses to be raised via motion to dismiss, in any permitted pleading, or at trial on the merits. Fed. R. Civ. P. 12(h)(3) implicitly authorizes the defense of lack of subject matter jurisdiction to be raised at any time during the case throught the time of exhaustion of direct appeal. *Valex v. Crown Life Ins. Co.* 599 F.2d 471, 472 (1st Cir. 1979).

2. Motion to Dismiss/Strike Defense

The motion to strike or dismiss a defense provided by Fed. R. Civ. P.[4] is analogous in function to a motion to dismiss for failure to state a claim under Fed. R. Civ. P. 12(b)(6). *See* the motion to strike an insufficient defense, Fed. R. Civ. P. 12(f).

a. Grounds

The Federal Rules provide one ground for striking a defense: that the defense is legally "insufficient." Fed. R. Civ. P. 12(f). "Courts are generally reluctant to strike a defense [as "insufficient"] in the absence of a showing of prejudice to the moving party."[5] *United States v. 18.2 Acres of Land*, 442 F. Supp. 800, 813 (E.D. Cal. 1977). *See also Coca-Cola Co. v. Howard Johnson Co.*, 386 F. Supp. 330, 333 (N.D. Ga. 1974); *Ryer v. Harrisburg Kohl Bros., Inc.*, 53 F.R.D. 404, 408 (M.D. Pa. 1971).

b. Evidence Outside the Pleadings

Some federal courts have held that matters outside the pleadings may not be considered in support of a motion to strike a defense for insufficiency under Fed. R. Civ. P. 12(f). *E.g., Carter-Wallace, Inc. v. Riverton Laboratories, Inc.*, 47 F.R.D. 366 (S.D.N.Y. 1969); *U.S. Oil Co. v. Koch Refining Co.*, 518 F. Supp. 957 (E.D. Wis. 1981); *Krauss v. Keibler-Thompson Corp.*, 72 F.R.D. 615 (D. Del. 1976). These courts did not consider the motions before them as motions for summary judgment.

c. Timing of the Motion

The timing for a motion to strike an insufficient defense under Fed. R. Civ. P. 12(f) is the same as for a motion to strike objectionable matter under that rule. That is, the claimant must make the motion before responding to the pleading raising such a defense, or within twenty days of its service if no responsive pleading is permitted. *See* discussion *supra*.

---

[4] Fed. R. Civ. P. 12 (f) provided for *two* analytically distinct motions: the motion to strike redundant, immaterial, impertinent or scandalous matter *see* discussion *supra*, and the motion to strike an insufficient defense. We discuss here the latter.

---

[5] We find no reported decisions where an otherwise insufficient defense has been allowed to stand solely because plaintiff failed to demonstrate prejudice, but the want of prejudice is often listed among other justifications for denying a Rule 12(f) motion to strike a defense. *See, e.g., Lopez v. Resort Airlines, Inc.*, 18 F.R.D. 37, 41 (S.D.N.Y. 1955) ("the court(s) [have] been [un]willing to determine disputed and substantial questions of law or the legal consequences of pleadings on motion to strike"); *Fox v. Trans World Airlines Inc.*, 20 F.R.D. 565, 567, (E.D. Pa 1957) (the matter "can better be resolved at the trial on the merits of the case").

d. "Searching the Record"

In considering a motion to dismiss a defense under Fed. R. Civ. P. 12(f), the court may "search the record" and decide to dismiss all or part of the movant's own pleading for failure to state a claim. See 2A Moore ¶ 12.21 (3).

e. Tactical Consideration

Seeking to eliminate insufficient defenses through a motion under Fed. R. Civ. P. 12(f) may be particularly advisable in complex litigation, because it may result in better delineation of the issues and thereby simplify discover and trial on the merits. See *Louisiana Sulphur Carriers, Inc. v. Gulf Resources & Chem. Corp.*, 53 F.R.D. 458, 460 (D. Del. 1971); *Commonwealth Edison Co. v. Allis-Chalmers Mfg. Co.*, 245 F. Supp. 889, 892 (N.D. Ill. 1965).

IV. MOTIONS *IN LIMINE*

A. Introduction

A "motion *in limine*" is a pretrial motion which seeks a ruling on the admissibility of certain evidence. Generally, a motion *in limine* seeks to exclude evidence which is potentially damaging. This type of motion *in limine* is referred to as "prohibitive." More rarely used is the "permissive" motion *in limine*, which is made by the party proposing to offer sensitive evidence and seeking a pretrial determination that the evidence is admissible.

A ruling on a motion *in limine* is interlocutory in nature, and does not function as a final ruling on the admissibility of the evidence at issue. Rather, a motion *in limine* order serves as an "advisory opinion subject to change as events at trial unfold." *Sales v. State Farm Fire & Casualty Co.*, 632 F. Supp. 435, 436 (N.D. Ga. 1986).

B. Legal Authority

Although they do not use the phrase "motion *in limine*," several statutes and rules provide authority for such motions in the federal courts. Rule 16 of the Federal Rules of Civil Procedure, which governs the pretrial conference, empowers the judge to make preliminary evidentiary rulings. Specifically, it provides that: "[t]he participants at any conference under this rule may consider and take action with respect to . . . (3) . . . advance rulings from the Court on the admissibility of evidence. . . ." Fed. R. Civ. P. 16(c)(3).

Furthermore, Rule 103(c) of the Federal Rules of Evidence specifically provides that proceedings in all jury trials "shall be conducted, to the extent practicable, so as to prevent inadmissible evidence from being suggested to the jury by any means. . . ." Fed. R. Evid. 103(c). Rule 104(c) mandates that hearings on all preliminary matters be conducted out of the hearing of the jury "when the interests of justice require." Fed. R. Evid. 104(c). In addition, Rule 403 authorizes the exclusion of evidence where "its probative value is substantially outweighed by the danger of unfair prejudice, confusion of the issues, or misleading the jury, or by considerations of undue delay, waste of time, or needless presentation of cumulative evidence." Fed. R. Evid. 403.

C. Purposes and Advantages

The motion *in limine* offers a significant advantage in that it permits a ruling on admissibility of evidence *outside* the jury's presence. If granted, the motion reduces the risk of exposing the jury to prejudicial or irrelevant evidence. The motion also avoids the necessity of objecting before the jury, which may be perceived by the jury as an attempt to hide or obfuscate the truth. The motion may also avoid cautionary instructions to the jury, which often serve to emphasize the sensitive evidence in the jurors' minds rather than to erase it.

Another key advantage of obtaining an advance ruling through use of the motion *in limine* is that it affords the lawyer more certainty in the planning of trial strategy. For example, if the motion is denied, the proponent of the motion can prepare a "fall-back" plan to rebut the potentially harmful testimony. If the motion is granted, the proponent can plan accordingly, and may save the unnecessary expense of calling a witness or preparing special exhibits.

In addition, the motion *in limine* may preserve the point for appeal by providing a written record of one's position for appellate review, thus obviating the need to object in front of the jury. *See, e.g., American Home Assur. Co. v. Sunshine Supermarket, Inc.*, 753 F.2d 321 (3d Cir. 1985) (contemporaneous objection at trial not required to preserve the issue for review where trial court made definitive ruling on motion *in limine*, specifying conditions under which sensitive evidence could be admitted). However, some federal courts have held that a motion *in limine* to prohibit evidence, absent a contemporaneous objection at trial, will not preserve the issue for appeal. *See, e.g., Northwestern Flyers, Inc. v. Olson Bros. Mfg. Co.*, 679 F.2d 1264 (8th Cir. 1982).

Another advantage of the motion *in limine* is that it allows the court more time to consider the issue, and therefore should reduce the likelihood of an erroneous decision.

D. Disadvantage

The potential drawback to bringing a motion *in limine* is the risk that the motion will alert the opposing party to a weakness in movant's case which the opposing party may never have focused on in the absence of the motion, but

MOTION PRACTICE AND DISMISSAL WITHOUT TRIAL

which may now be exploited. If the motion is denied, the attempt to exclude evidence harmful to the client might well result in strengthening the opponent's case. Accordingly, before making a motion *in limine*, one should thoroughly review the case file in order to determine as best one can the adversary's state of knowledge with respect to the evidence at issue at that time, and likely state of knowledge by the time of trial.

E. Recent Examples of Motions *in Limine* Granted and Denied by Federal Courts

1. Motions Granted

a. Subsequent Remedial Measures

Koonce v. Quaker Safety Prod. & Mfg. Co., 798 F.2d 700 (5th Cir. 1986) (grant of motion to exclude evidence of repairs subsequent to accident affirmed in wrongful death action based on strict liability in tort).

b. Prior Contracts

SCNO Barge Lines, Inc. v. Anderson Clayton & Co., 745 F.2d 1188 (8th Cir. 1984) (grant of motion seeking to exclude evidence of prior contracts affirmed in breach of contract action).

c. Prior Bad Acts

Crimm v. Missouri Pac. R.R. Co., 750 F.2d 703 (8th Cir. 1984) (in age discrimination action in which the defendant employer asserted that the plaintiff employee's termination was due to charge against him of sexual harassment, the Eighth Circuit affirms grant of motion by defendant seeking to prevent cross-examination of witness who had charged sexual harassment regarding (1) failure to list shop-lifting conviction on employment application and (2) marijuana use two to three years prior to sexual harassment incident).

d. Statements Made in Remote Past

Wilson v. North American Reinsurance Corp., No. 86-4968, slip. op. (E.D. Pa. 1988) (grant of plaintiff's motion seeking to exclude evidence of statements made by plaintiff eight to ten years prior to plaintiff's action for defamatory falsehood).

e. Evidence in Eminent Domain Proceeding

Nat'l R.R., Passenger Corp. v. One 25,900 Square Foot More or Less Parcel of Land in the City of New London, 766 F.2d 685 (2d Cir. 1985) (district court's denial in eminent domain proceeding of motion by plaintiff railroad seeking condemnation of land to exclude evidence of parcel's access to public road, held by Court of Appeals to be in error).

f. Prior Judgment in Unrelated Matter

In re Catanella and E.F. Hutton and Co., Inc., Securities Litigation, No. MDL No. 546, Civ. A. No. 82-3176, slip. op. (E.D. Pa. 1988) (grant of defendant's motion in suit brought under 10(b) of the Securities Exchange Act of 1934 to exclude evidence of prior judgment in unrelated matter).

g. Expert Testimony

Moorehead v. Clark Equip. Co., No. 86 C 1442, slip op. (N.D. Ill. 1988) (in strict liability action against manufacturer of forklift based on theory that forklift was defectively designed because it lacked a seatbelt, the district court granted plaintiff's motion to exclude expert testimony as to studies concluding that seatbelts are ineffective).

h. Oral Agreements

Bower v. Weisman, 674 F. Supp. 113 (S.D.N.Y. 1987) (grant of defendant's motion to preclude plaintiff from introducing evidence of certain oral agreements between the parties modifying written agreements in an action for breach of contract).

2. Motions Denied

a. Insurance Coverage

Maggard Truck Line, Inc. v. Deaton, Inc., 573 F. Supp. 1388 (N.D. Ga. 1983) (denial of plaintiff's motion seeking to prohibit mention of plaintiff's insurance coverage in shipping broker's action against motor carrier to recover for loss of goods).

b. EEOC Opinion of Probable Cause for Lawsuit

Strickland v. American Can Company, 575 F. Supp. 1111 (N.D. Ga. 1983) (denial of defendant employer's motion seeking to exclude letter plaintiff employee received from EEOC stating that probable cause existed for age discrimination lawsuit).

c. Conduct of Employer or Fellow Employees

Moore v. General Motors Corp., 684 F. Supp. 220 (S.D. Ind. 1988) (denial of plaintiff's motion seeking to preclude defendant from introducing evidence of conduct of decedent's employer or fellow employees in negligence action).

d. Subsequent Design Changes

Dixon v. Int'l Harvester Co., 754 F.2d 573 (5th Cir. 1985) (denial of defendant's motion to prohibit reference to subsequent design changes by non-defendant affirmed in defective and negligent design action).

e. Expert Testimony

Center v. K-Mart Corp., No. Civ-83-833E, slip op. (W.D.N.Y. 1987) (denial of plaintiff's motion to exclude as irrelevant testimony by defendant's statistical expert witness in employment discrimination action).

f. Defendant's Financial Condition

Bower v. Weisman, 674 F. Supp. 113 (S.D.N.Y. 1987) (denial of defendant's motion to preclude testimony relating to defendant's great wealth in breach of contract action).

g. Effect of Future Income Tax Liability on Decedent's Future Earnings

Morgan Guar. Trust Co. v. Texasgulf Aviation, Inc., 604 F. Supp. 699 (S.D.N.Y. 1985) (denial of plaintiff executor's motion in wrongful death action to prohibit introduction of evidence as to effect of future income tax liability on decedent's future earnings).

F. Procedure for Motion *in Limine*

1. Time for Motion

In many cases the recommended time for bringing a motion *in limine* is likely to be after discovery is complete. The facts will be more fully developed than they are at earlier stages of a litigation and the court can make a more informed decision on the motion. In addition, the opposing party is less likely to be able to contend successfully that it requires more discovery in order to respond to the motion.

However, where the evidence is such that a decision on its admissibility is likely to have a major impact on the course of discovery or upon the eventual outcome of the case, it may make sense to make the motion earlier, perhaps as early as the beginning of discovery. In that way, the party making the motion will be able to conduct discovery and shape its overall case strategy in a more informed and efficient manner.

2. Form of Motion *in Limine*

Although some courts permit the use of an oral motion *in limine*, use of a written motion is usually advisable because it provides a written record that will be useful in the event of an appeal. In addition, where the evidentiary issues are complex, a clearly written, carefully organized motion enhances counsel's argument and can be used to refresh the judge's memory later in the proceeding.

When the motion is filed, the opposing party should be served with a copy of the notice of motion and supporting papers, which should conform to the general motion requirements of the Federal Rules and such local and individual judge's rules as may be applicable. The motion papers should state the basic issues in the trial, and should describe the potentially harmful evidence and explain why that evidence is prejudicial and/or irrelevant. The supporting papers should almost always include a memorandum of law setting forth the legal authority for the position that the evidence should be excluded. The motion papers should also show that the prejudicial effect of the sensitive evidence cannot be repaired by any remedial action taken by the court. The motion should expressly seek an order stating that *all* parties, witnesses and attorneys shall be prohibited from referring to the sensitive matter before the jury.

Generally speaking, the more specific and limited the motion, the greater the likelihood that the court will grant it and be sustained on appeal. An overbroad or vague motion risks being denied because of the difficulty of enforcing it. Furthermore, even if such a motion is granted, it may be reversed on appeal. The motion, however, should request relief broad enough to ensure that no room is left for the opposing party to indirectly introduce prejudicial evidence or otherwise frustrate the purposes for which the motion was made.

V. VOLUNTARY OR INVOLUNTARY DISMISSAL UNDER RULE 41

A. Voluntary Dismissal

1. Without Court Order

Rule 41(a)(1) of the Federal Rules of Civil Procedure permits a plaintiff to voluntarily dismiss an action without court order subject to certain exceptions and provided that the proper procedures are followed.

a. Voluntary Dismissal Without Court Order Unavailable in Some Cases

While voluntary dismissal by the plaintiff without court order is permissible in most cases, in certain instances it is unavailable. Rule 41(a)(1) is limited by Fed. R. Civ. P. 23(e), which requires court approval for dismissal or compromise of a class action, and by Fed. R. Civ. P. 66, which requires a court order for dismissal of an action where a receiver has been appointed. Other rules which take precedence over Rule 41(a)(1) include Fed. R. Civ. P.

MOTION PRACTICE AND DISMISSAL WITHOUT TRIAL

23.1, which requires court approval for dismissal or compromise of a shareholder derivative action, and Fed. R. Civ. P. 23.2, which requires court approval for dismissal or compromise of a class action by or against an unincorporated association.

b. Reasons for Voluntary Dismissal

Voluntary dismissal has been used by plaintiffs in situations where discovery has shown a lack of sufficient evidence to prove their claims. Dismissal without prejudice permits a plaintiff additional time to locate new evidence. Voluntary dismissal may also be desired where the plaintiff in a removed action wishes to file anew in state court, *see, e.g., Stevenson v. Missouri Pac. R.R. Co.*, 53 F.R.D. 184 (E.D. Ark. 1971), although some courts refuse to allow dismissal for this reason. See *Wall v. Connecticut Mut. Life Ins. Co.*, 2 F.R.D. 244 (S.D. Ga. 1941).

c. How and When Done

Rule 41(a)(1) permits the claimant to dismiss by filing a notice of dismissal with the clerk of the court before service of an adverse party's answer or motion for summary judgment, whichever occurs first. However, once the defendant serves his answer or motion for summary judgment, the plaintiff loses his right to voluntarily dismiss in this manner. At that point, the plaintiff can dismiss only with the consent of all of the parties or the court.

A claimant may also voluntarily dismiss by filing a stipulation signed by all parties who have appeared in the action. While a written stipulation is preferable, a verbal stipulation of dismissal in open court satisfies Rule 41(a)(1)(ii) even where no formal stipulation has been signed by the parties. See *Oswalt v. Scripto, Inc.*, 616 F.2d 191 (5th Cir. 1980). There is no time limit for dismissal by stipulation.

d. Effect of Dismissal

The filing of a notice or stipulation of dismissal under Rule 41(a)(1) automatically terminates the lawsuit; no action by the court is necessary. The first voluntary dismissal under 41(a)(1), unless otherwise stated in the notice or stipulation, is without prejudice. The plaintiff is left in the same position as if the lawsuit had not been filed.

However, Rule 41(a)(1) has a special provision for the plaintiff who twice dismisses an action based on or including the same claim. The "two dismissal rule" provides that the second dismissal operates as an adjudication on the merits and prohibits the plaintiff from filing another action on the same claim. The rule was intended to prevent harassment by the plaintiff's use of the unilateral right to dismiss an action before defendant files a responsive pleading. The "two dismissal rule" does not apply where the first dismissal was by stipulation of the parties. *Poloron Prod., Inc. v. Lybrand Ross Bros. & Montgomery*, 534 F.2d 1012 (2d Cir. 1976).

2. By the Court

Rule 41(a)(2) provides for a discretionary voluntary dismissal by order of the court. In contrast to voluntary dismissal by notice under Rule 41(a)(1), this procedure is not limited to the period prior to the adverse party's answer or motion for summary judgment. Furthermore, a voluntary dismissal under 41(a)(2) is not at the plaintiff's option, but is at the court's discretion, "upon such terms and circumstances as the court deems proper." Factors that a court will generally consider in ruling on a plaintiff's motion for voluntary dismissal include: plaintiff's motive for seeking dismissal, the burden and expense of litigating in another forum, fairness to the defendant, plaintiff's choice of forum, the stage of the proceeding at the time dismissal is requested, and the extent to which a judgment in the subsequent action would be conclusive.

Generally, courts favor granting plaintiffs' motions to dismiss under Rule 41(a)(2), either unconditionally or with stipulated conditions designed to minimize prejudice or inconvenience to the defendant. *But see Ockert v. Union Barge Line Corp.*, 190 F.2d 303 (3d Cir. 1951) (Court of Appeals affirms district court's denial of plaintiff's motion made on day of trial seeking dismissal of case without prejudice where case had been pending for two years and defendant had called witnesses from various parts of the country); *see also Rollison v. Washington Nat'l Ins. Co.*, 176 F.2d 364 (4th Cir. 1949) (Court of Appeals affirms district court's denial of plaintiff's motion to dismiss where plaintiff was given full opportunity to present his case but his pleadings failed to state cause of action after third attempt and after facts had been developed by pretrial conference and answers to interrogatories).

A dismissal under Rule 41(a)(2) is without prejudice "[u]nless otherwise specified in the order. . . . " Generally, courts will grant the dismissal without prejudice "unless the defendant will suffer some plain prejudice other than the mere prospect of a second lawsuit." *Le Compte v. Mr. Chip, Inc.*, 528 F.2d 601, 604 (5th Cir. 1976). Additionally, the court has discretion to condition the dismissal in order to protect the defendant's interests. Often payment of the defendant's costs and expenses are stipulated as a condition of dismissal without prejudice. *See, e.g., Stevenson v. Missouri Pac. R.R. Co.*, 53 F.R.D. 184 (E.D. Ark. 1971). The court may also condition dismissal on other terms, such as production of certain documents or other evidence by the plaintiff. *See, e.g., Eaddy v. Little*, 234 F. Supp. 377 (E.D.S.C. 1964).

Violation of the conditions for dismissal by the plaintiff may result in an order of dismissal with prejudice. *See, e.g.*, *Davis v. McLaughlin*, 326 F.2d 881 (9th Cir. 1964), *cert. denied*, 379 U.S. 833.

B. Involuntary Dismissal

1. Generally

Fed. R. Civ. P. 41(b) provides that the defendant may bring a motion to dismiss a case involuntarily for failure of the plaintiff to prosecute, or for failure of the plaintiff to comply with the Federal Rules of Civil Procedure or any order of the court. Since this sanction is so drastic, it is generally only used in extreme circumstances. Thus, in one case, even though plaintiff had delayed serving the summons and complaint on the defendant for over two years without justification, the court declined to dismiss the case, noting the harshness of this procedure. *Lyford v. Carter*, 274 F.2d 815, 816 (2d Cir. 1960). In addition, Rule 41(b) empowers the court to dismiss an action *sua sponte*.

Rule 41(b) also contains a special provision for nonjury actions. In such cases, a defendant may make a motion to dismiss after the presentation of plaintiff's evidence on the ground that plaintiff has demonstrated no basis for relief. If denied, the defendant has not waived the right to present favorable evidence. The court may grant the motion and render judgment against the plaintiff or may abstain from judgment until both sides have presented evidence.

2. Effect of Dismissal

Generally, a Rule 41(b) involuntary dismissal operates as an adjudication on the merits unless the court otherwise specifies. However, a dismissal based on lack of jurisdiction, improper venue, or the lack of an indispensable party does not operate as an adjudication on the merits.

C. Dismissal of Counterclaim, Cross-Claim or Third-Party Claim

Pursuant to Fed. R. Civ. P. 41(c), Rule 41 may also be used to dismiss a counterclaim, cross-claim or third-party claim. However, under Rule 41(a)(2), if a counterclaim has been pleaded by a defendant prior to service upon the defendant of the plaintiff's motion to dismiss, the action will not be dismissed against the defendant's objection unless the counterclaim can remain pending for independent adjudication by the court. This situation is probably rare, however, and the Rule does not prohibit voluntary dismissal of the action if the counterclaim has an independent jurisdictional basis.

D. Costs of Previously Dismissed Claims

Where a party dismisses, and subsequently files another action based upon or including the same claim, the court is authorized by Fed. R. Civ. P. 41(d) to impose against that party the costs of the previously dismissed action. While the language of Rule 41(d) refers only to the situation in which a plaintiff voluntarily dismissed the prior action, a motion for payment of costs may also be appropriate where the previous action was dismissed involuntarily. *See Gainey v. Brotherhood of R. & S.S. Clerks*, 34 F.R.D. 8, 12 (E.D. Pa. 1963). The motion for payment of costs should be made as soon as possible after commencement of the new action.

VI. DEFAULT JUDGMENTS UNDER RULE 55

A. When and Against Whom Entry of Default is Appropriate

Entry of default by the court clerk is appropriate where a party against whom a judgment for affirmative relief is sought has failed to plead or otherwise defend as provided by the Fed. R. Civ. P.[6] and where the court is made aware of that fact by affidavit or otherwise. Fed. R. Civ. P. 55(a). The entry of default by the clerk, essentially a ministerial task, is the first step of a two-step process provided by Fed. R. Civ. P. 55 for the taking of a default.[7] This first step is merely an interlocutory procedure and does not constitute a final judgment. The second step, the entry of the actual default judgment, may be carried out by the court clerk or by the court, depending upon the circumstances.

B. Granting of Judgment by Default

1. By the Clerk

In limited circumstances, the clerk of the court, upon the plaintiff's request and upon affidavit of the amount due, is required to enter judgment for the amount of the plaintiff's claim and costs against the defendant. Two conditions must be satisfied for the entry of default judgment by the court clerk: (1)

---

[6] The provisions of Rule 55 governing defaults "apply whether the party entitled to the judgment by default is a plaintiff, a third-party plaintiff, or a party who has pleaded a cross-claim or counterclaim." Fed. R. Civ. P. 55(d).

[7] However, courts have permitted motions for a default judgment in the absence of the initial step of a default entry. *See Meehan v. Snow*, 652 F.2d 274 (2d Cir. 1981) (Court of Appeals finds that even though entry of default had been omitted, the hearing on a motion for default judgment ordered by the district court judge allowed defendants the same opportunity to present mitigating circumstances that they would have had if a default had been entered and they had then moved under Rule 55(c) to set it aside); *see also Traguth v. Zuck*, 710 F.2d 90, 94 (2d Cir. 1983) (second Circuit rules htat district court's permitting a motion for default judgment "was functionally equivalent to an entry of default").

the plaintiff's claim against the defendant must be for a sum certain or for a sum which can be made certain by computation, and (2) the defendant cannot be an infant or an incompetent person. Fed. R. Civ. P. 55(b)(1).

2. By the Court

In cases where the amount of the plaintiff's claim is not for a sum certain or for a sum which can be made certain by computation, and in cases where the defendant is an infant or an incompetent person, the party seeking a judgment by default must apply to the court. Furthermore, Fed. R. Civ. P. 55(b) prohibits the entry of judgment by default against an infant or incompetent person unless such persons are represented by a general guardian, committee, conservator, or other such representative who has appeared.

If the party against whom judgment by default is sought has already appeared in the action, either personally or by a representative, Rule 55 requires that the party be served with written notice of the application for judgment at least three days before the hearing on the application for default judgment. Fed. R. Civ. P. 55 (b)(2).

Fed. R. Civ. P. 55 (b)(2) empowers the court to hold hearings at its discretion when, in order to enter or carry out a judgment, it is necessary to "take an account or to determine the amount of damages or to establish the truth of any averment by evidence or to make an investigation of any other matter." Fed. R. Civ. P. 55 (b)(2) also provides for the right of the parties to trial by jury for such a hearing when and as required by any United States statute.

Fed. R. Civ. P. 55 contains a special provision for the situation in which judgment by default is sought against the United States or any officer or agent of the United States. Under such circumstances, the party seeking entry of default judgment must demonstrate "a claim or right to relief by evidence satisfactory to the court." Fed. R. Civ. P. 55 (e).

C. Setting Aside an Entry of Default

1. Grounds for Setting Aside an Entry of Default

Fed. R. Civ. P. 55(c) delineates different standards for setting aside an entry of default and setting aside a judgment by default.

The court may set aside an entry of default "for good cause shown." Fed. R. Civ. P. 55(c). Factors which courts consider in determining whether good cause has been shown under Fed. R. Civ. P. 55(c) include "whether the default was willful, whether setting it aside would prejudice the adversary, and whether a meritorious defense is presented." *Meehan v. Snow*, 652 F.2d 274, 277 (2d Cir. 1981). Courts also take into consideration the promptness or lack thereof with which the defaulting party moves to correct the default.

See Chandler Leasing Co. v. UCC, Inc., 91 F.R.D. 81 (N.D. Ill. 1981) (motion to vacate a default denied, in part because defaulting party waited almost two months before filing petition to vacate and where opponent had relied on default).

Generally, federal courts disfavor default judgments, preferring to resolve cases on the merits, and accordingly tend to liberally construe the "good cause" standard when considering a motion to set aside an entry of default. *See, e.g., Kearney v. New York State Legislature*, 103 F.R.D. 625 (E.D.N.Y. 1984) (entry of default set aside where defendants claimed they believed in good faith that they were never served process); *Kennerly v. Aro, Inc.*, 447 F. Supp. 1083 (E.D. Tenn. 1976) (motion to set aside entry of default granted where counsel honestly but mistakenly believed that a timely answer had been earlier filed).

However, some courts have held that mere carelessness on the part of a party's attorney is not sufficient cause to set aside an entry of default. *See, e.g., Aberson v. Glassman*, 70 F.R.D. 683 (S.D.N.Y. 1976) (fact that defendant's attorney never informed him of scheduled depositions does not constitute sufficient cause to set aside default since defendant voluntarily chose the attorney as his agent and an attorney's knowledge is imputed to his client); *but see Lutwin v. City of New York*, 106 F.R.D. 502, 504 (S.D.N.Y. 1985), *aff'd*, 795 F.2d 1004 (2d Cir. 1986) (district court holds that "[w]here the attorneys and not the defendants are responsible for the mistakes leading to a default, relief from a default is especially appropriate" but assesses sanctions against defendants pursuant to Fed. R. Civ. P. 16(f) for failure to obey a scheduling order).

2. Time for Motion

The Fed. R. Civ. P. set no definitive time limits on a motion to set aside an entry of default. Obviously, however, the more prompt the motion, the greater the likelihood of success. *See, e.g., Singer Co. v. Greever & Walsh Wholesale Textile, Inc.*, 82 F.R.D. 1, 2 (E.D. Tenn. 1977) (default entry set aside where "[d]efense counsel demonstrated his good faith by moving to set aside his client's default . . . on the first working day after he returned to this jurisdiction and was met with the surprise of the previous entry of a default").

D. Setting Aside a Default Judgment

1. Grounds for Setting Aside a Default Judgment

The grounds for setting aside a default judgment are more limited than those for setting aside an entry of default. The justification for this distinction is that a default judgment constitutes a final judicial action, while an entry of default is merely an interlocutory procedure. Fed. R. Civ. P. 55(c) limits the court's power to set aside an entry of a judgment by default to the grounds provided for in Fed. R. Civ. P. 60(b). Rule 60(b) provides that a party may make a motion for relief from judgment for the following reasons:

> (1) mistake, inadvertence, surprise, or excusable neglect; (2) newly discovered evidence which by due diligence could not have been discovered in time to move for a new trial under Rule 59(b); (3) fraud (whether heretofore denominated intrinsic or extrinsic), misrepresentation, or other misconduct of an adverse party; (4) the judgment is void; (5) the judgment has been satisfied, released, or discharged, or a prior judgment upon which it is based has been reversed or otherwise vacated, or it is no longer equitable that the judgment should have prospective application; or (6) any other reason justifying relief from the operation of the judgment.

Fed. R. Civ. P. 60(b).

2. Proceedings

a. By Motion or Independent Action

Under Fed. R. Civ. P. 60(b) the party seeking relief from a default judgment may do so by motion in the pending action, or may commence an independent action. Typically, a party will initiate an independent action to set aside a judgment where the one-year limitation period on making a 60(b) motion to set aside the judgment has already run. *See, e.g., Averbach v. Rival Mfg. Co.*, 809 F.2d 1016 (3d Cir. 1987), *cert. denied*, 107 S. Ct. 3187, 96 L. Ed. 2d 675 (1987), *cert. denied*, 108 S. Ct. 83, 98 L. Ed. 2d 45 (1987) (independent action for relief from judgment based on fraud not untimely although filed over one year from judgment).

b. Time for Motion

Motions to set aside default judgments are also governed by the provisions of Fed. R. Civ. P. 60(b). Rule 60(b) mandates that the motion be made within a "reasonable time." If the ground for the motion is one of the first three grounds listed in Rule 60(b), the motion must be made not more than one year from the entry of the judgment. Obviously, the longer the defaulting party delays in making the motion, the more difficult it will be to convince the court that the delay was "reasonable." *See, e.g., Planet Corp. v. Sullivan*, 702 F.2d 123 (7th Cir. 1983).

c. Effect of Making Motion

A motion to set aside a default judgment, under Fed. R. Civ. P. 55(c) and Fed. R. Civ. P. 60(b), does not affect the finality of the judgment or suspend its operation. Fed. R. Civ. P. 60(b). Furthermore, such a motion does not limit the "power of the court to entertain an independent action to relieve a party from a judgment."

CHAPTER SEVENTEEN

SUMMARY JUDGMENT UNDER RULE 56

by Harry P. Trueheart, III, Esq.
and Jon O. Webster, Esq.*

I. INTRODUCTION

A. Nature of Summary Judgment

Summary judgment can be an efficient method for disposing of actions in which there is no genuine issue of any material fact. According to the Supreme Court, "[s]ummary judgment procedure is properly regarded not as a disfavored procedural shortcut, but rather as an integral part of the Federal Rule as a whole, which is designed 'to secure the just, speedy and inexpensive determination of every action.' " *Celotex Corp. v. Catrett*, 477 U.S. 317, 327 (1986) (*quoting* Fed. R. Civ. P. 1) (citation omitted). A successful motion for summary judgment demonstrates that one or more of the essential elements of a claim or defense is not in doubt, and therefore judgment should be entered as a matter of law. *Fontenot v. Upjohn Co.*, 780 F.2d 1190, 1194 (5th Cir. 1986). Summary judgment can be used to dismiss factually insufficient claims or defenses prior to trial. *Celotex, supra*, 477 U.S. at 327; *Parillo v. Sura*, 652 F. Supp. 1517, 1519 (D. Conn. 1987).

If used properly, summary judgment enables a court to "streamline the process for terminating frivolous claims and to concentrate its resources on meritorious litigation." *Knight v. U.S. Fire Ins. Co.*, 804 F.2d 9, 12 (2d Cir. 1986), *cert. denied*, 480 U.S. 932 (1987); *see also Quinn v. Syracuse Model*

---

* The authors gratefully acknowledge the valuable assistance of Andrea C. Farney in the preparation of this chapter.

Neighborhood Corp., 613 F.2d 438, 445 (2d Cir. 1980) ("summary judgment is a useful device for unmasking frivolous claims and putting a swift end to meritless litigation"). One function of summary judgment is to pierce the pleadings and determine from the proof whether there is a need for a trial. *Matsushita Elec. Indus. Co., Ltd. v. Zenith Radio Corp.*, 475 U.S. 574 (1986); *Cumberland Oil Corp. v. Thropp*, 791 F.2d 1037, 1043 (2d Cir. 1986).

B. Overview of Fed. R. Civ. P. 56[1]

Rule 56 is divided into seven major subparts dealing with various aspects of summary judgment in the federal courts.[2] Rule 56(a) and 56(b) regulate procedural aspects, establishing the timing of motions. Under 56(a), a claimant, counterclaimant, or declaratory judgment applicant may move for summary judgment 20 days after commencement of the action. Rule 56(b) provides that a party defending a claim may move for summary judgment at any time after commencement of a claim, counterclaim or declaratory judgment.

Rule 56(c) requires that the motion be served upon the nonmovant at least 10 days prior to the hearing on the motion. Opposing papers must be served upon the movant at least one day before such hearing or decision. Although Rule 56(c) uses the word "hearing" to determine when moving and opposing papers are to be served, it does not specify the type of hearing that is necessary. Section II, A, 7 *infra*.

Rule 56(c) also specifies that summary judgment as to liability only is interlocutory in nature, and hence, does not constitute a final order that would be appealable as a matter of right. *See* 28 U.S.C. § 1291 (only final orders are appealable as of right unless injunctive relief is involved). The balance of Rule 56(c) provides the substantive standard for granting the motion for summary judgment. Rule 56(c) precludes the grant of summary judgment unless there is no genuine issue as to any material fact and unless the movant is entitled to summary judgment as a matter of law. *Grand Union Co. v. Cord Meyer Dev. Corp.*, 735 F.2d 714, 717 (2d Cir. 1984).

Partial summary judgment as to discrete facts or claims is provided for in Rule 56(d). Part of Rule 56(e) outlines the proper requirements and format for the submission of affidavits and other documents in support or opposition to the motion for summary judgment. Rule 56(e) also contains rules concerning the nonmovant's obligation to respond to a properly supported motion by

---

[1] Rule 56 is set forth in its entirety in Appendix A.

[2] *See generally* Stempel, *A Distorted Mirror: The Supreme Court's Shimmering View of Summary Judgment, Directed Verdict, and the Adjudication Process*, 49 Ohio St. L.J. 95, 130, and n.194 (1988).

setting forth the specific facts demonstrating there is a genuine issue for trial. A court is empowered, under Rule 56(f), to grant the nonmovant additional time and discovery if it appears that the nonmovant cannot present facts in support of its opposition to the summary judgment motion. Rule 56(g) provides that a party who submits affidavits made in bad faith or solely for the purpose of delay may be held in contempt or required to reimburse the other party for all expenses incurred due to such bad faith, including attorney's fees.

C. The Second Circuit's View of Summary Judgment

Both the movant and nonmovant can cite authority regarding whether courts are receptive or hostile to motions for summary judgment. In a trilogy of cases decided in 1986, the Supreme Court intimated that summary judgment is now viewed more favorably than formerly. *Celotex, supra* (products liability claim); *Matsushita, supra* (antitrust claim); *Anderson v. Liberty Lobby, Inc.*, 477 U.S. 242 (1986) (libel claim). While noting that a motion for summary judgment must be considered with due regard for the right of parties asserting adequately supported claims and defenses to have those claims and defenses tried to the jury, the Supreme Court also emphasized that the right to a swift and inexpensive conclusion to claims and defenses lacking a factual basis cannot be ignored. *See, e.g., Celotex, supra*, 477 U.S. at 327.

Prior to these Supreme Court decisions, the Second Circuit had a reputation of being unreceptive to summary judgment motions. *See* New York Bar Association Report, *Summary Judgment in the Second Circuit*, 1-2, March, 1987 ("NYSBA Report"); *Knight, supra*, at 12 ("It appears that in this circuit some litigants are reluctant to make full use of the summary judgment process because of their perception that this court is unsympathetic to such motions and frequently reverses grants of summary judgment."). The Second Circuit sought to dispel that perception, stating that whatever accuracy that view held in the past, it is inaccurate in the present. *Knight*, at 12 (*citing* Final Report of the Second Circuit Committee on the Pretrial Phase of Civil Litigation, 16-17, June 1986).

In an effort to encourage use of Rule 56, the *Knight* court commented that it hoped that the discussion concerning the high affirmance rate on appeals from grants of summary judgment "dispels the misperception so that litigants will not be deterred from making justifiable motions for summary judgment." *Id.* New York District Courts are likely to embrace *Knight's* position on the efficacy of summary judgment. *See, e.g., Stanley-Fizer Associates, Inc. v. Sport-Billy Productions*, 685 F. Supp. 61, 64 (S.D.N.Y. 1988); *Benson v. RMJ Sec. Corp.*, 683 F. Supp. 359, 365 (S.D.N.Y. 1988) (summary judgment, properly utilized, permits courts to terminate frivolous claims and to concentrate its resources on meritorious litigation).

Nevertheless, even after the Supreme Court trilogy and *Knight*, the Second Circuit advised caution in granting summary judgment motions. While stating that the courts have a duty to "vigilantly weed out those cases that do not merit further judicial attention," the Second Circuit went on to warn that

> [t]he procedural tool of summary judgment enables courts to terminate meritless claims, but this potent instrument must be used with the precision of a scalpel. The courts must take care not to abort a genuine factual dispute prematurely and thus deprive a litigant of his day in court.

Donahue v. Windsor Locks Bd. of Fire Commissioners, 834 F.2d 54, 55 (2d Cir. 1987). Despite recognizing that both the Supreme Court and the Second Circuit have tended to encourage summary judgment even in complex cases, the Second Circuit has also instructed that such motions should not be considered a substitute for trial. *Apex Oil Co. v. DiMauro*, 822 F.2d 246, 252 (2d Cir.), *cert. denied*, 108 S. Ct. 488 (1987); *see also Belfiore v. New York Times Co.*, 826 F.2d 177, 180 (2d Cir. 1987), *cert. denied*, 108 S. Ct. 1030 (1988) (*quoting Apex Oil, supra*). In *Donahue*, the court admonished that too frequently summary judgment had been improvidently granted and must be used selectively to avoid trial by affidavit. *Donahue, supra*, 834 F.2d at 57-58. It should be remembered that the Second Circuit regards summary judgment as a drastic remedy because, if granted, it prevents a party's right to present his or her case to the jury. *Eastway Constr. Corp. v. City of New York*, 762 F.2d 243, 249 (2d Cir. 1985); *Heyman v. Commerce & Indus. Ins. Co.*, 524 F.2d 1317, 1320 (2d Cir. 1975).

The Supreme Court trilogy of *Celotex*, *Anderson* and *Matsushita* as well as *Knight* signals a new era for recognizing the proper role of summary judgment in eliminating issues and claims that should not go to trial. Movants routinely cite the favorable language in these cases when bringing motions for summary judgment. Thus, the courts are becoming sensitized to the trend of granting such motions, even in areas that traditionally had not been considered appropriate for summary judgment. The nonmovant can remind the court, using cases like *Donahue* and *Apex Oil*, that summary judgment is a drastic remedy which should be used sparingly and cautiously so as to ensure the nonmovant's right to have its genuine claims or defenses tried to a jury.

II. BASIC PROCEDURAL REQUIREMENTS

A. Federal Civil Practice

1. Who May Make the Motion

Any party to an action may move for summary judgment on the entire action or any issue within the action. *See* Fed. R. Civ. P. 56(a), (b) and (d).

SUMMARY JUDGMENT UNDER RULE 56

Even though Rule 56(a) specifically refers to a party seeking to recover "upon a claim, counterclaim, or cross-claim or to obtain a declaratory judgment," this is not an exhaustive listing. The rule is also applicable to all claimants, including third-party claimants, *Schwartz v. Compagnie General Transatlantique*, 405 F.2d 270, 272-73 (2d Cir. 1968); intervenors, *F. Palicio y Compania, S.A. v. Brush*, 256 F. Supp. 481, 483 (S.D.N.Y. 1966), *aff'd*, 375 F.2d 1011 (2d Cir.), *cert. denied*, 389 U.S. 830 (1967); and claimants in interpleader, *First Nat'l Bank of Cincinnati v. Pepper*, 454 F.2d 626, 629 (2d Cir. 1972).

Rule 56(b) permits defendants to bring summary judgment motions. Any party against whom a claim, counterclaim, or cross-claim is asserted or a declaratory judgment is sought may move for summary judgment in its favor.

2. When a Party May Bring the Motion

a. Claimant

A claimant may move for summary judgment after 20 days have elapsed from the commencement of an action, or subsequent to the opposing party serving a summary judgment motion. Fed. R. Civ. P. 56(a). The purpose of the 20-day waiting period is to allow a defendant an opportunity to secure counsel, plead or otherwise object, and determine its strategy. *See* 6 J. Moore, *Moore's Federal Practice* ¶ 56.07 (2d ed. 1988) ("Moore"); 10 C. Wright, A. Miller & M. Kane, *Federal Practice and Procedure* § 2717 (2d ed. 1983) ("Wright, Miller & Kane") and cases cited therein. A prematurely filed motion for summary judgment may be inappropriate for consideration. *Southern Pac. Transp. Co. v. National Molasses Co.*, 540 F.2d 213, 214 & n.1 (5th Cir. 1976) (summary judgment is not appropriate until 20 days after suit is filed; when defendant has not filed an answer, the appropriate motion is dismiss under Rule 12(b)(6)); *Local Union No. 490, United Rubber, Cork, Linoleum & Plastic Workers of Am., AFL-CIO v. Kirkhill Rubber Co.*, 367 F.2d 956, 958 (9th Cir. 1966).

If the defendant moves for summary judgment within the 20-day time period, that waiting period no longer is applicable. Fed. R. Civ. P. 56(a). Moreover, the time period may be waived if the defendant moves to dismiss for lack of subject matter jurisdiction and failure to state a claim pursuant to Rule 12(b)(6). *Stein v. Oshinsky*, 348 F.2d 999 (2d Cir.), *cert. denied*, 382 U.S. 957 (1965) (claimant's motion not premature). The claimant's motion for summary judgment brought 20 days after commencement of the action but prior to the defendant's responsive pleading is generally held timely. *Electro-Catheter Corp. v. Surgical Specialties Instrument Co., Inc.*, 587 F. Supp. 1446, 1456 (D.N.J. 1984); *Justice v. Fabey*, 541 F. Supp. 1019, 1025 (E.D. Pa. 1982); *First Am. Bank, N.A. v. United Equity Corp.*, 89 F.R.D.

81, 87 (D.D.C. 1981) (although an answer is not a prerequisite to the consideration of claimant's summary judgment motion, court has discretion to postpone decision on motion to consider further pleadings).

Although the claimant may move for summary judgment after the expiration of the 20 days from the commencement of the action and any time thereafter, excessive delay in making and prosecuting the motion may result in a denial. *See, e.g., Williams v. Howard Johnson's, Inc. of Washington*, 323 F.2d 102 (4th Cir. 1963).

b. Defendant

Rule 56(b) permits the defendant to move for summary judgment in its favor at any time. *Kistner v. Califano*, 579 F.2d 1004, 1005 (6th Cir. 1978). The phrase "at any time" has been interpreted to mean that the defendant may seek summary judgment after a claim is served on it. *See United States v. William S. Gray & Co.*, 59 F. Supp. 665, 667 (S.D.N.Y. 1945). The defendant may move for summary judgment before pleading to the action. *First Nat'al Bank of Ariz. v. Cities Services Co.*, 319 U.S. 253 (1968); *Investment Fin. Group, Inc. v. Chem-Nuclear Sys., Inc.*, 815 F.2d 391, 404 (6th Cir. 1987); *Hubicki v. ACF Indus., Inc.*, 484 F.2d 519, 522 (3rd Cir. 1973). Alternatively, the defendant may make the motion simultaneously with, or after it serves, a responsive pleading, such as an answer. *Beary v. West Publishing Co.*, 763 F.2d 66, 68 (2d Cir. 1985), *cert. denied*, 474 U.S. 903 (1986).

As with the claimant, the defendant should not belatedly move for summary judgment lest it be considered untimely. *See Management Investors v. United Mine Workers of Am.*, 610 F.2d 384, 389 (6th Cir. 1979). Waiting too long in seeking summary judgment could lead a court to deny the motion or to impose sanctions if it believes the motion is filed to cause delay. *See Cabarga-Cruz v. Fundacion Educativa Ana G. Mendez, Inc.*, 609 F. Supp. 1207, 1210 (D. Puerto Rico 1985), *aff'd*, 822 F.2d 188 (1st Cir. 1986) (although sanctions not imposed due to unusual procedural history, court would not hesitate to impose sanctions where defendant's late motion was unwarranted given previous rulings and advanced stage of action).

3. Timing for Filing Motion Papers and Supporting Affidavits

Pursuant to Rule 56(c), a motion for summary judgment "shall be served at least 10 days before the time fixed for the hearing" so that the nonmovant has sufficient notice of the request and adequate opportunity to respond. *Hancock Indus. v. Schaeffer*, 811 F.2d 225, 229 n.1 (3d Cir. 1985); *Dillard v. Blackburn*, 780 F.2d 509, 515 (5th Cir. 1986); *Gutwein v. Roche Labs.*, 739 F.2d 93, 95 (2d Cir. 1984). Failure to follow this advance notice rule can vitiate the entry of summary judgment. *Winbourne v. Eastern Air Lines,*

Inc., 632 F.2d 219, 223 (2d Cir. 1980). This 10-day period for service of the motion and supporting affidavits distinguishes it from all other motions, which must be served only five days before the hearing under Rule 6(d). When service is made by mail three days should be added to the 10-day period. Fed. R. Civ. P. 6(e).

A motion to dismiss pursuant to Rule 12(b)(6) for failure to state a cause of action that is accompanied by evidentiary material may be treated as a motion for summary judgment. *Crawford v. United States*, 796 F.2d 924, 927 (7th Cir. 1986); *Quantum Overseas, N.V. v. Touche Ross & Co.*, 663 F. Supp. 658, 662 n.2 (S.D.N.Y. 1987) (since court relied on factual allegations outside the complaint, it treated issue as motion for summary judgment). The court has discretion in determining whether to convert a motion to dismiss into a motion for summary judgment. *Morris v. Gilbert*, 649 F. Supp. 1491, 1493-94 (E.D.N.Y. 1987); *American Fed'n of States County & Municipal Employees, AFL-CIO v. Nassau Co.*, 609 F. Supp. 695, 700 (E.D.N.Y. 1985). A court considering documents other than the pleadings should convert a Rule 12(b)(6) motion into a Rule 56 motion, give the nonmovant notice of its intention to treat the motion as one for summary judgment and an opportunity to submit material showing a genuine issue of material fact. *Chandler v. Coughlin*, 763 F.2d 110, 113 (2d Cir. 1985); *Goldman v. Belden*, 754 F.2d 1059, 1065-67 (2d Cir. 1985); *Ryder Energy Distribution Corp. v. Merrill Lynch Commodities, Inc.*, 748 F.2d 774, 779 (2d Cir. 1984).

If a motion to dismiss is converted into a summary judgment motion by the introduction and consideration of evidence outside the pleadings, the nonmovant is entitled to the 10-day notice. *Donaldson v. Clark*, 819 F.2d 1551, 1555 (11th Cir. 1987); *Marine Coatings of Ala., Inc. v. United States*, 792 F.2d 1565, 1568 (11th Cir. 1987). For instance, it was held that a motion to dismiss for failure to state a claim which was converted to a motion for summary judgment where the argument was heard four days after service of the papers was invalid because it did not comport with Rule 56(c). *Tele-Communications of Key West, Inc. v. United States*, 757 F.2d 1330, 1334 (D.C. Cir. 1985) (since 10-day requirement was not complied with, motion to dismiss could not be recast as a motion for summary judgment).

Notice of the conversion of a motion to dismiss into a motion for summary judgment is required so that each side may supplement the filed pleadings and papers. *United States v. One Colt Python. 357 Cal. Revolver, S/N 703461 w/ Holster*, 845 F.2d 287, 289 (11th Cir. 1988); *Davis v. Bryan*, 810 F.2d 42, 45 (2d Cir. 1987). Indeed, it may be reversible error for a court to grant a summary judgment motion it converted from a motion to dismiss without providing all the parties a reasonable opportunity to present relevant evidence regarding the motion. *See Colt Python, supra,* 845 F.2d at 289; *Mack v. South Bay Beer Distributors, Inc.*, 798 F.2d 1279, 1282 (9th Cir. 1986).

Failure to give the parties the requisite notice of converting a motion to dismiss into a summary judgment motion can result in the motion not being evaluated under Rule 56 and hence the affidavits will be disregarded. *Baptiste v. Sennet & Krumholz*, 788 F.2d 910, 911 (2d Cir. 1986). However, a party cannot claim inadequate notice and lack of reasonable time when evidence has been submitted in support of or in opposition to a motion to dismiss since the court, by accepting such evidence, places the parties on notice that the motion may be treated as one for summary judgment. *Darlak v. Robear*, 814 F.2d 1055, 1064-65 (5th Cir. 1987); *Clark v. Tarrant County*, 798 F.2d 736, 745-46 (5th Cir. 1986), *reh. denied*, 802 F.2d 455; *In re G. & A. Books, Inc.*, 770 F.2d 288, 295 (2d Cir. 1985), *cert. denied sub nom. M.J.M. Exhibitors, Inc. v. Stern*, 475 U.S. 1015 (1986).

Unless the nonmovant objects that the service is untimely, however, the defect will be considered waived. *McCloud River R.R. Co. v. Sabine River Forest Prods., Inc.*, 735 F.2d 879, 882-83 (5th Cir. 1984); *Reilly v. Doyle*, 483 F.2d 123, 125 n.2 (2d Cir. 1973); *Feng Yeat Chow v. Shaughnessy*, 151 F. Supp. 23, 25 (S.D.N.Y. 1957). Even when the 10-day notice requirement is not complied with, a grant of summary judgment may be proper if such failure to comply does not prejudice the nonmovant or otherwise constitutes harmless error. *Hancock Indus., supra*, 811 F.2d at 229; *Moody v. Town of Weymouth*, 805 F.2d 30, 31 (1st Cir. 1986); *Denis v. Liberty Mut. Ins. Co.*, 791 F.2d 846, 850 (11th Cir. 1986); *Kaestel v. Lockhart*, 746 F.2d 1323, 1324 (8th Cir. 1984); *Winborne, supra*, 632 F.2d at 223 (court also noted that nothing in Rule 56(c) suggests that the 10-day notice is a discretionary procedural mechanism to be heeded or ignored as the district court deems appropriate).

A party which wants a motion to dismiss treated as one for summary judgment should clearly inform the court and the other parties. It is good practice to remind the court of the procedural requirements which result from such a change in order to protect the court's decision from a later reversal.

4. Filing of Opposing Papers and Affidavits

Rule 56(c) provides that the nonmovant must file and serve its papers at least one day prior to the hearing. Failure to file or submit opposing affidavits until or after the hearing date may result in their being held inadmissible. *Beaufort Concrete Co. v. Atlantic States Const. Co.*, 352 F.2d 460, 462 (5th Cir. 1965), *cert. denied*, 384 U.S. 1004 (1966); *Nestle Co., Inc. v. Chester's Market, Inc.*, 571 F. Supp. 763, 772-73 (D. Conn. 1983), *vacated as moot*, 609 F. Supp. 588 (D. Conn. 1985) (failure to offer any explanation or justification for not filing opposing affidavits until one month after oral argument resulted in affidavit being held inadmissible). Nevertheless, the court may, in its discretion pursuant to Fed. R. Civ. P. Rule 6(b) and (d), consider such untimely affidavits. *Beaufort Concrete, supra*, 352 F.2d at 462; *see Hooks v. Hooks*, 771 F.2d 935, 946 (6th Cir. 1985) (court would consider untimely opposing papers where opposing affidavit indicated genuine issue of material fact and nonmovant offered acceptable reason for not complying with 56(c) and filed timely motion for reconsideration). A prudent practitioner will strive to comply with the rule, however. In addition, the nonmovant's counsel should review local court rules, which may provide for service more than one day prior to the hearing. *See* Section II, B, *infra*.

5. Cross-Motions

Since any party may move for summary judgment, there are times when both parties may claim that there is no genuine issue of material fact that necessitates a trial. That both parties seek summary judgment does not, however, mean that the court must grant the motion to one party or the other. *Eastman Mach. Co., Inc. v. United States*, 841 F.2d 469, 473 (2d Cir. 1988) (fact that both sides move for summary judgment does not guarantee that there is no material issue of fact to be tried); *Bank of Am. Nat'l, Trust & Sav. Assoc. v. Gillaizeau*, 766 F.2d 709, 716 (2d Cir. 1985); *Benson, supra*, 683 F. Supp. at 365 (cross-motions for summary judgment do not warrant the granting of summary judgment unless court finds that one of the moving parties is entitled to judgment as a matter of law upon facts that are not genuinely controverted); *Frouge Corp. v. Chase Manhattan Bank, N.A.*, 426 F. Supp. 794, 796 (S.D.N.Y. 1976). Instead, the court should evaluate each side's motion on its own merits, in each instance drawing all inferences in favor of the nonmoving party. *Schwabenbauer v. Board of Educ. of City School Dist. of City of Olean*, 667 F.2d 305, 313-14 (2d Cir. 1981).

6. Summary Judgment Without a Motion

In *Celotex*, the Supreme Court noted that it is widely acknowledged that district courts have the power to enter summary judgment *sua sponte*, so long as the losing party is on notice that it has to come forward with all its evidence. *Celotex, supra*, 477 U.S. at 326; *Portsmouth Square Inc. v. Shareholders Protective Comm.*, 770 F.2d 866, 869 (9th Cir. 1985); *Adams v. United States*, 673 F. Supp. 1249, 1251 n.2 (S.D.N.Y. 1987) (court invoked its discretionary power to enter summary judgment *sua sponte* in the interest of judicial economy). A court may grant summary judgment to the nonmovant in certain limited situations, such as when the movant seeks summary judgment and, after the hearing, the court determines that no genuine issue of material fact exists as to the movant's claim or defense and as a matter of law the nonmovant is entitled to judgment. *British Caledonian Airway v. First State Bank*, 819 F.2d 593, 595 (5th Cir. 1987); *Landry v. G.B.A.*, 762 F.2d 462, 464 (5th Cir. 1985); *Morrissey v. Curran*, 423 F.2d 393, 399 (2d Cir.), *cert. denied*, 399 U.S. 928 (1970); *Aldrich v. Upstate Auto Wholesale of*

Ithaca, 564 F. Supp. 390, 394 (N.D.N.Y. 1982); *Commissioner on Indep. Colleges & Universities v. New York Temporary State Comm'n*, 534 F. Supp. 489, 501 (N.D.N.Y. 1982); *Moss v. Ward*, 450 F. Supp. 591, 594 (W.D.N.Y. 1978).

A court may grant the nonmovant's request to search the record and grant summary judgment even though the nonmovant has not formally moved for summary judgment. *Morrissey, supra*; *LeMon v. Zelker*, 358 F. Supp. 554, 555 (S.D.N.Y. 1972). However, the court must exercise great care in granting summary judgment to a nonmovant who has not made a motion so that the movant has sufficient notice of the request and adequate opportunity to respond. *Puro Int'l of N.J. Corp. v. California Union Ins. Co.*, 672 F. Supp. 129, 130-131 and n.3 (S.D.N.Y. 1987).

7. Summary Judgment Hearings

Rule 56(c) contains language which implicitly suggests a hearing is necessary before a decision is rendered. *See Season-All Indus., Inc. v. Turkiye Sise Ve Cam Fabrikalari, A.S.*, 425 F.2d 34, 39-40 (3d Cir. 1970) (usually appropriate to set a motion for summary judgment down for hearing). However, most circuits hold that courts may determine a summary judgment motion without a hearing. *See, e.g., Donaldson, supra*, 819 F.2d at 1555; *Langham-Hill Petroleum, Inc. v. Southern Fuels Co.*, 813 F.2d 1327 (4th Cir. 1987), *cert. denied*, ___ U.S. ___, 108 S. Ct. 99 (1987); *Bratt v. International Business Machs. Corp.*, 785 F.2d 352 (1st Cir. 1986); *Grigoleit Co. v. United Rubber, Cork, Linoleum & Plastic Workers of Am., Local No. 270*, 769 F.2d 434 (7th Cir. 1985) (oral argument is not mandated by Rule 56(c)); *Clark Equip. Credit Corp. v. Martin Lumber Co.*, 731 F.2d 579 (8th Cir. 1984); *Hamman v. Southwestern Gas Pipeline*, 721 F.2d 140 (5th Cir. 1983) ("hearing" requirement of Rule 56(c) need not consist of oral argument); *Cool Fuel, Inc. v. Connett*, 685 F.2d 309 (9th Cir. 1982).

Pursuant to Rule 78, each district court may consider a summary judgment motion without oral argument provided that neither party requests such a hearing. Therefore, local rules should always be consulted to determine whether oral argument or some other hearing device may be utilized without specifically requesting it, or whether a formal request is necessary to avoid having the motion automatically determined on submitted papers. *See* Section II, B, *infra*.

B. Local Rules in New York Federal Courts

Each New York federal district court promulgates rules governing motion practice in general and motions for summary judgment in particular. In addition, individual judges issue rules regarding motion practice in their courts. Local rules are available from the district court clerks and individual

SUMMARY JUDGMENT UNDER RULE 56 513

judges. Attorneys may also consult several reference books. *See, e.g., Federal Local Court Rules* (Callaghan & Company); *McKinney's New York Rules of Court—State and Federal* (West Publishing Company); *District Court Individual Judge Rules* (NYBSA). The following discussion will involve only selective local rules pertinent to summary judgment motions. See Chapter 27, Section II, *supra*, for a detailed treatment of local court motion practice in conjunction with the Federal Rules of Civil Procedure.

1. Form of Motion Supporting Papers

a. Southern and Eastern Districts

The Southern and Eastern Districts of New York do not have specific rules governing the form of the motion. However, the movant and nonmovant are required to serve and file with the motion papers a memorandum of law setting forth the points and authorities relied upon in support or in opposition to the motion. S.D.N.Y./E.D.N.Y. Civ. Rule 3(b). The memorandum should be divided into as many parts as there are points to be resolved, each part having an appropriate heading. The Court may deny the motion or grant the motion by default if one of the parties fails to comply with this provision. *Id.*

b. Western District

Rule 13 of the Western District Court provides for the form of motions, including ones for summary judgment. All papers shall be written and contain the court's name, case name, proper docket number and the name or nature of the paper so that it can be identified. W.D.N.Y. Rule 13(a), (b). Furthermore, all papers shall be signed by the attorney and contain the attorney's name, address and telephone number. W.D.N.Y. Rule 13(b). The papers must be dated. *Id.* Papers failing to comply with this Rule can only be filed with the court's permission. W.D.N.Y. Rule 13(d).

c. Northern District

As with the Western District Court, the Northern District Court requires that motion papers contain the court's name, the title of the action, the name or nature of the motion sufficient for identification, and the name and address of the party's attorney. N.D.N.Y. Gen. Rule 7(b). Papers not conforming to the local rule shall not be filed without the court's permission. N.D.N.Y. Gen. Rule 7(d). A memorandum of law and an affidavit must be filed and served in support of or in opposition to the motion. N.D.N.Y. Gen. Rule 10(c). The affidavits cannot contain legal arguments. *Id.* A motion for summary judgment must indicate that it is predicated on Rule 56. *Id.* Additionally, each motion and response in opposition to the motion shall be accompanied by a form of order granting or denying the relief sought by the motion. N.D.N.Y. Gen. Rule 10(d).

2. Notice and Filing of Papers

a. Southern and Eastern Districts

The Southern and Eastern District Courts require 10 days' notice for a motion for summary judgment. S.D.N.Y./E.D.N.Y. Civ. Rule 3(c)(2). The nonmovant's answering papers must be served at least three days before the return date. *Id.* If the movant serves its motion 10 days before the hearing date, the nonmovant must respond with its opposition papers seven days later rather than nine days later as Rule 56(c) permits.

With respect to filing, the Southern and Eastern District Courts follow Rule 5, which requires that motions be filed with the clerk of the court "either before service or within a reasonable time thereafter," unless the court allows the papers to be filed directly with it. Fed. R. Civ. P. 5(d), (e).

b. Western District

The Western District Court requires 10 days' notice for summary judgment motions. W.D.N.Y. Rule 14(c). A party that desires to shorten the 10-day notice requirement must make a written application to the courts indicating by affidavit good and sufficient reasons why procedure other than by notice of motion is necessary. W.D.N.Y. Rule 14(d). Serving opposition papers and counter-affidavits must be accomplished three business days prior to the return date. W.D.N.Y. Rule 14(c).

Unlike Rule 5(d) and (e), the Western District Court local rules require that moving papers and answering papers be filed with the court clerk not later than the last day by which the papers may be served. *Id.* Accordingly, the movant must file its motion papers 10 days prior to the hearing while the nonmovant must file its opposition papers not later than one day before the hearing.

c. Northern District

A party seeking summary judgment must give 21 days' notice prior to the hearing date. N.D.N.Y. Gen. Rule 14(e). The nonmovant must respond at least 14 days prior to the hearing. *Id.* Because the intent of this rule is to provide for the submission of all papers regarding the motion at least 14 days before the date set for oral argument, the movant does not have to select the earliest possible hearing date. *Id.*

3. Oral Argument

a. Southern and Eastern Districts

Pursuant to Civil Rule 3(i), the court may direct the parties to submit the motion for summary judgment without a hearing.

b. Western District

There may be oral argument on a summary judgment motion if any party requests such argument or upon court order. W.D.N.Y. 15. However, the court may determine that there will be no oral argument on the motion. *Id.* "A request for oral argument shall be separately stated by the moving party at the conclusion of the motion or by any party, either in answering papers or by filing a separate pleading state the request." Prior to any oral argument, the court may request written briefs. *Id.*

c. Northern District

Parties are expected to appear for oral argument on a motion for summary judgment on the hearing date. N.D.N.Y. Gen. Rule 10(i). Nevertheless, the court may, in its discretion, and upon the parties' request, render a decision on the motion without oral argument. *Id.* In the event that there will be no oral argument, the parties will be so informed prior to the hearing date. *Id.* The parties are cautioned to be prepared for having their papers and memorandum serve as the only method of argument. *Id.*

III. CONTENTS OF THE MOTION PAPERS

A. The Motion

Generally, the motion for summary judgment should be in writing unless it is made during a hearing or a trial. Fed. R. Civ. P. 7(b). A motion stated in a written notice of the motion hearing satisfies the writing requirement. *Id.* Pursuant to Rule 7(b), which incorporated the form requirements of Rule 10(a), the motion must have a caption setting forth the name of the court, the title of the action, the file number, and the designation of the motion, *e.g.*, "Notice of Motion for Summary Judgment." *Accord* W.D.N.Y. Rule 13; N.D.N.Y. Gen. Rule 7. To comply with Rule 7(b), the notice of motion for summary judgment shall state with particularity the grounds thereof. The movant's motion must give the nonmovant notice to present evidence to defeat summary judgment. *John Deere Co. v. American Nat'l Bank*, 809 F.2d 1190, 1192 (5th Cir. 1987). Moreover, the notice of motion is required to state the relief or order sought. *Accord* N.D.N.Y. Gen. Rule 10(c). For example, the movant may specifically request "an order awarding Summary Judgment to movant for each and every count set forth in the Complaint." The body of the motion may also include references to the attached exhibits, such as affidavits and statement of uncontested material fact. At the end of the motion the date should be indicated. Finally, an attorney of record is required to sign the motion, and that attorney's address and telephone number must be stated on the motion. Fed. R. Civ. P. 7(b)(3), 11; W.D.N.Y. Rule 13(b).

B. Statement of Uncontested Material Facts

Local rules for the Southern, Eastern and Western District Courts of New York provide that

> there shall be annexed to the notice of motion a separate, short and concise statement of the material facts as to which the moving party contends there is no genuine issue to be tried.

S.D.N.Y./E.D.N.Y. Civ. Rule 3(g); W.D.N.Y. Rule 13(a)(1); *see, e.g.*, *Dusaneko v. Maloney*, 726 F.2d 82, 83 (2d Cir. 1984). The Northern District Court local rules also mandate the inclusion of statement of uncontested material facts. N.D.N.Y. Gen. Rule 10(j) (omitting the phrase "to be tried"). Each of these local rules states that the movant's failure to submit such a statement constitutes grounds for denying the summary judgment motion. *See Zeno v. Cropper*, 650 F. Supp. 138, 139 (S.D.N.Y. 1986); *Harvey Cartoons v. Columbia Pictures Indus., Inc.*, 645 F. Supp. 1564, 1571 n.10 (S.D.N.Y. 1986); *Gear, Inc. v. L.A. Gear California, Inc.*, 637 F. Supp. 1323, 1333 (S.D.N.Y. 1986); *George v. Hilaire Farm Nursing Home*, 622 F. Supp. 1349, 1353 (S.D.N.Y. 1985). A court may nevertheless exercise its discretion to grant summary judgment even when the movant fails to submit a statement of uncontested material facts with its motion papers. *Salahuddin v. Coughlin*, 674 F. Supp. 1048, 1051-52 n.6 (S.D.N.Y. 1988) (court considered affidavits and other exhibits provided by movant in lieu of statement of uncontested material facts); *Adams, supra*, 673 F. Supp. at 1251 n.2. The nonmovant's failure to controvert material facts in the statement will result in those facts being deemed admitted. *Carlton v. Interfaith Medical Center*, 612 F. Supp. 118, 123 (E.D.N.Y. 1985).

The statement of uncontested material facts should be structured so that the court is convinced that there is no need for a trial. As with affidavits and statements of facts in a memorandum of law or appellate brief, one method of organizing the statement is to have separate sections with a heading indicating the content of the section. The early sections may be used to introduce the parties and the parties' actions in connection with the underlying claims. Each chronologically significant event can constitute a separately headed section reflecting that event. Within each of these sections, the headings can be expanded by setting forth pertinent facts. Towards the end of the statement, the movant can describe each of the claims, illustrating indirectly why they are either valid and hence merit the relief sought, or invalid and should

SUMMARY JUDGMENT UNDER RULE 56

be dismissed. A final section can demonstrate the absence of injury if the movant is the defendant, or the presence of injury if the movant is the plaintiff. In each of the sections, references can be liberally made to supporting evidence, such as "Exhibit ___" or "Appendix ___."[3] Thought should be given to numbering each page of the documents relied on, so that references in the statement, as well as in affidavits or memoranda of law, can be to a specific page. This increases the court's ability to locate the relevant portion of a document, increasing the probability that it will be reviewed.

While it may be appropriate to provide the court with background and collateral facts to aid its understanding of the case, it is important to clearly identify those facts which are material to the motion. The fewer material facts necessary to the court's decision the better. Fewer facts reduce the opportunity for the opposing party to create issues to be tried and allow the court to focus on the important issues and arguments in the moving papers.

C. Supporting Evidence

1. Acceptable Materials in Support of Summary Judgment

The party seeking summary judgment has the initial burden of informing the court of the basis for its motion and identifying those portions of its supporting evidence which demonstrate the absence of a genuine issue of material fact. *Celotex, supra,* 477 U.S. at 325; *Eastman Mach., supra,* 841 F.2d at 473; *Apex Oil, supra,* 822 F.2d at 252; *State of New York v. Bowen,* 655 F. Supp. 136, 145. To prevent parties from abusing the summary judgment procedure, courts mandate that the movant present specific, affirmative evidence which adequately supports the motion. *Slaughter v. Allstate Ins. Co.,* 803 F.2d 857, 860 (5th Cir. 1986).

The movant is not required to support its motion with materials that negate the nonmovant's claim. *Celotex, supra,* 477 U.S. at 325. The movant's burden is discharged if it can demonstrate that on all the facts before the court, including those which the nonmovant is required to supply, there is an absence of evidence to support the nonmovant's case. *Anderson, supra,* 477 U.S. at 249; *Puro Int'l, supra,* 672 F. Supp. at 133.

The movant can base its summary judgment motion on the pleadings, affidavits, depositions, answers to interrogatories, and admissions. Fed. R. Civ. P. 56(c); *see Celotex, supra,* 477 U.S. at 324; *Fontenot, supra,* 780 F.2d at 1195. Affidavits may be supplemented or opposed by depositions, answers to interrogatories, or further affidavits in the court's discretion. Fed. R. Civ.

---

[3] Excerpts from the statement of uncontested material facts are contained in *Dusaneko, supra,* 726 F.2d at 83.

P. 56(e); *see Michigan State Podiatry Assoc. v. Blue Cross and Blue Shield of Mich.*, 681 F. Supp. 1239, 1243 (E.D. Mich. 1987) (providing parties with opportunity to present supplemental evidence of the hearing). Case law demonstrates Rule 56 does not provide the exclusive method of presenting material in support of the motion. For instance, oral testimony under Rule 43(e) may be used for summary judgment purposes although it is not explicitly provided for in Rule 56. *Argus v. Eastman Kodak Co.*, 801 F.2d 38, 42 n.2 (2d Cir. 1986), *cert. denied*, 479 U.S. 1088 (1987).

Supporting evidence need not be in a form that would be admissible at trial. *Celotex, supra*, 477 U.S. at 324. However, in deciding a motion for summary judgment, the court may only consider facts that would be admissible in evidence. *Kamen v. American Tel. & Tel. Co.*, 791 F.2d 1006, 1011 (2d Cir. 1986) (evidence submitted outside the pleadings must be competent); *Burtnieks v. City of New York*, 716 F.2d 982, 985 (2d Cir. 1983); *Anderson v. City of New York*, 657 F. Supp. 1571, 1577 (S.D.N.Y. 1987). Thus, for example, a party's affidavit or that of its attorney which contains only hearsay will be given little or no weight.

a. Pleadings

A summary judgment motion may be made entirely on the pleadings, which renders it equivalent to a motion to dismiss for failure to state a claim under Rule 12(b)(6) or a motion for judgment on the pleadings under Rule 12(c). *See* Fed. R. Civ. P. 56(a) (party may bring summary judgment without affidavits); Fed. R. Civ. P. 56(c) (pleadings can serve as basis for motion); *Sellers v. M.C. Floor Crafters, Inc.*, 842 F.2d 639, 642 (2d Cir. 1988); *Falls Riverway Realty v. City of Niagara Falls*, 754 F.2d 49, 53 (2d Cir. 1985). The Court must deem uncontradicted facts set forth in the pleadings as true.

One of the purposes of summary judgment is to pierce the pleadings so as to assess whether the proof requires a trial. *Matsushita, supra*, 475 U.S. at 586; *Cumberland Oil, supra*, 791 F.2d at 1043. Thus, it is generally appropriate for the movant to provide evidentiary support that goes beyond the pleadings to establish the absence of any genuine issue of material fact. If the movant possesses such extra-pleading material which demonstrates summary judgment should be in its favor, that material should be made part of the motion papers. Otherwise, the court may determine a valid claim has been stated and deny the motion even though the movant might have furnished materials sufficient to warrant a grant of summary judgment.

b. Affidavits under Rule 56(e)

(1) Necessity of Affidavits

Rule 56(e) sets forth the requirements for evidentiary affidavits supporting and approving summary judgment that the court may utilize in making its determination. While Rule 56 does not contemplate a trial by affidavit in place of a trial, the court may grant summary judgment if the affidavits establish there is no triable issue of material fact. *Greco v. ABC Transnational Corp.*, 623 F. Supp. 104, 106 (E.D. Mo. 1985); *see Donahue, supra*, 834 F.2d at 58; *Kennedy v. Josephthal & Co.*, 635 F. Supp. 399, 405 (D. Mass. 1985), *aff'd*, 814 F.2d 798 (1st Cir. 1987) (summary judgment should not be a trial by affidavit).

The use of affidavits to support a summary judgment motion is permissive rather than mandatory. Analyzing Rule 56(a), (b) and (c), the Supreme Court stated

> [t]he import of these subsections is that, regardless of whether the moving party accompanies its summary judgment motion with affidavits, the motion may, and should, be granted so long as whatever is before the district court demonstrates that the standard for the entry of summary judgment, as set forth in Rule 56(c), is satisfied.

Celotex, supra, 477 U.S. at 323. Accordingly, the absence of affidavits should not preclude granting the motion if the movant has provided materials sufficient to satisfy the requirements for granting the summary judgment. Although the movant's affidavits are not required, they are typically included in the motion papers since affidavits provide an effective means of piercing allegations contained in the pleadings as well as introducing other evidentiary material. Despite the fact that the affiant is not subject to cross-examination and his demeanor cannot be viewed, the movant may establish that there is no triable genuine issue of material fact through affidavits. *See, e.g., In re Teletronics Services, Inc.*, 762 F.2d 185, 192 (2d Cir. 1985).

(2) Requirements for Affidavits

Rule 56(e) contains three requirements for summary judgment affidavits:

1. they shall be made only on personal knowledge;
2. they shall set forth only such facts as would be admissible in evidence; and
3. they shall show affirmatively that the affiant is competent to testify to the matters stated therein.

If made on personal knowledge and containing admissible evidence, affidavits are probative under Rule 56(e). *Applegate v. Top Associates*, 425 F.2d

92, 97 (2d Cir. 1970); *Schneider v. Og & C Corp.*, 684 F. Supp. 1269, 1274 (S.D.N.Y. 1988). However, affidavits not based on personal knowledge may be deemed insufficient to grant summary judgment. *See, e.g., Sellers, supra,* 842 F.2d at 643; *Kamen, supra,* 791 F.2d at 1011. Accordingly, the court is not required to rely on affidavits which contain matters set forth therein which are only based on "information and belief" in determining a summary judgment motion. *Chandler, supra,* 763 F.2d at 113-14; *Gatling v. Atlantic Richfield Co.*, 577 F.2d 185, 188 (2d Cir. 1978), *cert. denied,* 439 U.S. 861 (1979); *L. Orlik, Ltd. v. Helme Products, Inc.*, 427 F. Supp. 771, 778 (S.D.N.Y. 1977). As courts require that evidence submitted outside the pleadings be competent, the affidavit must affirmatively show that the affiant is competent to testify as to the contents of the affidavit. *See, e.g., Kamen, supra.* An affidavit that recites it was made on personal knowledge and contains material which demonstrates that the affiant has personal knowledge of the facts stated comports with Rule 56(e). *Schneider, supra,* 684 F. Supp. at 1271 n.6.; *Brueggemeyer v. American Broadcasting Corp.*, 684 F. Supp. 452, 463 (N.D. Tex. 1988).

Rule 56(e) also applies to attorney's affidavits. Attorney's affidavits not based on personal knowledge have long been held not to comply with Rule 56(e) so as not to be entitled to any consideration by the court in determining the motion. *Beyah v. Coughlin,* 789 F.2d 986, 989-90 (2d Cir. 1986); *In re Teletronics, supra,* 762 F.2d at 192; *Wyler v. United States,* 725 F.2d 156, 160 (2d Cir. 1983). Where a material fact is one within the attorney's personal knowledge, an attorney's affidavit is appropriate to support a motion for summary judgment. *Sitts v. United States,* 811 F.2d 736, 741-42 (2d Cir. 1987) (procedural fact within attorney's personal knowledge). Attorney's affidavits are usually part of a summary judgment motion and are used to establish procedural facts and introduce and martial evidence obtained from discovery. Statements of ultimate facts and conclusions of law should not be included in affidavits since they do not reflect the affiant's personal knowledge. *Galindo v. Precision Am. Corp.*, 754 F.2d 1212, 1216 (5th Cir.), *reh. denied,* 762 F.2d 1004 (1985); *Donnelly v. Guion,* 467 F.2d 290, 293 (2d Cir. 1972); *AFSCME, AFL-CIO, supra,* 609 F. Supp. at 700 (affidavit should be confined to statements of fact based on personal knowledge, and legal arguments raised in affidavit should be raised in briefs and memorandum of law).

Because the affidavit must set forth only admissible evidence, *see American Key Corp. v. Cole Nat'l Corp.*, 762 F.2d 1569, 1579 (11th Cir. 1985); *Union Ins. Soc'y v. William Gluckin & Co.*, 353 F.2d 946, 952 (2d Cir. 1965), the affidavit should be constructed as if the affiant were testifying in court. For instance, hearsay material not admissible under any hearsay exception does not comport with Rule 56(e). *Sellers, supra,* 842 F.2d at 643; *Leonard v. Dixie Well Serv. & Supply, Inc.*, 828 F.2d 291, 295 (5th Cir.

1987); *Miller v. Solem*, 728 F.2d 1020, 1026 (8th Cir. 1984), *cert. denied*, 469 U.S. 841 (1985); *Bambu Sales, Inc. v. Sultana Crackers, Inc.*, 683 F. Supp. 899, 910 (E.D.N.Y. 1988) (" '[h]earsay testimony and opinion testimony that would not be admissible if testified to at the trial may not properly be set forth in an affidavit.' 6-Pt. 2 *Moore's Federal Practice*, ¶ 56.22[1]"); *Anderson v. City of New York*, 611 F. Supp. 481 (S.D.N.Y. 1985). Averments in the affidavit that are admissible in evidence under the Federal Rules of Evidence if the affiant were testifying in court may be considered by the court in deciding the motion. *See, e.g., Battery Steamship Corp. v. Refineria Panama, S.A.*, 513 F.2d 735, 738 (2d Cir. 1975) (parol evidence in the affidavit permitted under parol evidence rule exception).

The contents of the affidavit should be restricted to facts relevant and material to the issues involved in the motion since only such statements are admissible in court. Although the affidavit contains some inadmissible statements, the entire affidavit is not required to be disregarded or stricken, but rather the court may disregard the inadmissible portions and consider the affidavit's remaining parts. *United States v. Alessi*, 599 F.2d 513, 515 (2d Cir. 1979); *New York State Energy Research & Dev. Auth. v. Nuclear Fuel Services, Inc.*, 561 F. Supp. 954 (S.D.N.Y. 1983). Affidavits which contradict prior deposition testimony may be disregarded by the court on a motion for summary judgment. *Mack v. United States*, 814 F.2d 120 (2d Cir. 1987); *Miller v. International Tel. & Tel. Corp.*, 755 F.2d 20, 24 (2d Cir.), *cert. denied*, 468 U.S. 841 (1985); *Reitmeier v. Kalinoski*, 631 F. Supp. 565, 574 (D.N.J. 1986).

The limited relevant case law suggests that defects in Rule 56(e) affidavits, whether because of inadmissible evidence or improper form, may be considered waived where the nonmovant fails to make a motion to strike before the district court. *Sellers, supra*, 842 F.2d at 643; *In re Teletronics, supra*, 762 F.2d at 192; Wright, Miller & Kane, *supra*, at § 2738 and cases therein. According to one commentator, however, the nonmovant may object to evidence in some other method; although not stated by the commentator, this might include objecting in opposing papers to inadmissible or improper material in the affidavit. Moore, *supra*, ¶ 56.22(1) and cases cited therein. If the practitioner chooses to object without moving to strike, such objection should be in a document that becomes part of the record, such as an affidavit. Because courts closely examine papers supporting summary judgment to ensure that they comply with Rule 56(e), the movant should strive to see that its affidavits satisfy all of that Rule's requirements.

c. Depositions

The court may consider depositions in determining whether to grant a summary judgment motion. Fed. R. Civ. P. 56(c); *Colan v. Cutler-Hammer*,

Inc., 812 F.2d 357, 365 (7th Cir.), *cert. denied*, ___ U.S. ___, 108 S. Ct. 79 (1987). This includes both oral depositions taken pursuant to Rule 30 and written depositions taken under Rule 31. As with affidavits, depositions used in the summary judgment motion must contain admissible evidence, in other words competent, relevant and material. *Samuels v. Doctors Hosp., Inc.*, 588 F.2d 485, 489 (5th Cir. 1979); *Sires v. Luke*, 544 F. Supp. 1155, 1160 (S.D. Ga. 1982). Therefore, only those portions of the deposition that are admissible should be considered by the court. An uncertified deposition may be utilized in deciding the motion if the opposing party does not move to suppress the deposition. *See* Moore, *supra*, ¶ 56.11[4].

Depositions are excellent forms of evidence in motions for summary judgment since they not only include spontaneous responses taken under oath but they also provide for cross-examination. A careful practitioner will consider the possibility of a summary judgment motion in planning and conducting depositions. For example, foundational requirements should be carefully established where particular testimony or documents will be important to a motion.

d. Answers to Interrogatories

In 1963 Rule 56(c) was amended to specifically permit the use of answers to interrogatories on a motion for summary judgment. To be considered on the motion, answers to interrogatories must satisfy the admissibility requirements of Rule 56(c). If those requirements are met, summary judgment may be granted based on answers to interrogatories. *Fontenot, supra*, 780 F.2d at 1194-96; *Rea v. Wichita Mortgage Corp.*, 747 F.2d 567, 574 n.6 (10th Cir. 1984).

e. Admissions

Pursuant to Rule 56(c), any admissions "on file" may be considered on a summary judgment motion. Rule 5(d) provides that the court may order depositions, interrogatories, requests for admissions, and answers and responses thereto not be filed unless on order of the court or for use in the proceeding. Local and individual judge's rules must be reviewed to determine when such material may be filed. For instance, the Western District Court of New York permits the filing of admissions "for use in a specific motion or proceeding," or by court order. W.D.N.Y. Rule 14(a)(1). In the Northern District Court, admissions are filed in accordance with Rule 5(d). N.D.N.Y. Gen. Rule 9(a). Under S.D.N.Y./E.D.N.Y. Civ. Rule 18(a), however, discovery material, including admissions, cannot be filed with the clerk's office except by court order. If the movant requires certain material containing admissions germane to the summary judgment motion, it may have to seek a court order mandating that the admissions be filed depending on which district court the action is in. As a practical matter, it is good practice for the parties to clarify with the court precisely how to file admissions, including whether original copies or the entire document must be filed.

Admissions may be demonstrated in a variety of ways. For instance, Rule 36 permits a party to serve a request to admit the genuineness of relevant documents or any part thereof. Unless the party specifically denies or objects in writing within 30 days, material contained in the requested admissions is considered admitted. Fed. R. Civ. P. 36. Other forms of admissions, such as stipulations, pretrial statements, discovery responses, depositions, and oral or written arguments by counsel, may also be used. Moore, *supra*, at ¶ 56.11[6]; Wright & Miller, *supra*, at § 2722. Requests for admissions that are unanswered or not timely responded to can serve as the basis for summary judgment. *Donovan v. Porter*, 584 F. Supp. 202 (D. Md. 1984).

f. Oral Testimony

Although Rule 56(c) does not discuss the issue, Rule 43(e), which authorizes the use of oral testimony on motions, generally, can be used to hear summary judgment motions. *Argus, supra*, 801 F.2d at 42 n.2; *Stewart v. RCA Corp.*, 790 F.2d 624, 628-29 (7th Cir. 1986); *State of Utah v. Marsh*, 740 F.2d 799, 801 n.2 (10th Cir. 1984); *Walters v. City of Ocean Springs*, 676 F.2d 1317, 1322 (5th Cir. 1980). Testimony given in an evidentiary hearing is no different from testimony given in a deposition, and may be treated the same in summary judgment proceedings. *Hancock Indus., supra*, 811 F.2d at 230. If there is no contradictory evidence, facts testified to in a hearing, as with affidavits and deposition testimony, may be accepted as true for summary judgment purposes without an assessment of the witness's credibility. *Id.* at 230-31.

Utilizing its discretionary power to hear oral testimony is especially appropriate for the court when the record consists of an enormous mass of documents; this allows the court to expeditiously and accurately assess the record. *Argus, supra*; *Davis v. Costa-Gavras*, 654 F. Supp. 653, 654-55 (S.D.N.Y. 1987). Oral testimony may provide the court an opportunity to elicit information more quickly as well as to indicate omissions and weaknesses without the need for an extended series of counter-affidavits and sur-replies. *Stewart, supra*, 790 F.2d at 628. One of the principal advantages of oral testimony, assessing the credibility of witnesses, is unavailable on a summary judgment motion. This is because the court may not evaluate the witness's credibility on the motion. *Id.* at 629. Rule 43(e) hearings on motions for summary judgment are not used routinely. *Id.*

g. Documentary Evidence

Documents submitted in support or opposition to a motion for summary judgment must be admissible in evidence in order to be considered. Affidavits, depositions, interrogatories or requests to admit must provide the foundation requirements for documents. Thus, for example, documents containing business records which are often used in summary judgment motions must be supported by authenticating testimony and testimony establishing the bases for the business records exception to the hearsay rule. Interrogatory answers or admissions may also be used to provide the necessary foundation. An attorney expecting to use documents in making a summary judgment motion at some stage in a lawsuit, should be careful to obtain necessary foundational facts during discovery.

Sworn or certified copies of all admissible documents or material parts thereof referenced in the affidavit are required to be attached to or served with the affidavit. Fed. R. Civ. P. 56(e); *Flaherty v. Coughlin*, 713 F.2d 10 (2d Cir. 1983). Documents that are not sworn to or certified in lieu of oath raise a question as to whether the court should consider them on a summary judgment motion. *Margrave v. British Airways*, 643 F. Supp. 510, 514 n.4 (S.D.N.Y. 1986).

IV. CONTENTS OF OPPOSITION PAPERS

A. Statement of Contested Material Facts

Local rules for the Southern, Eastern and Western District Courts of New York provide that

> [t]he papers opposing a motion for summary judgment shall include a separate, short and concise statement of the material facts as to which it is contended that there exists a genuine issue to be tried.

S.D.N.Y./E.D.N.Y. Civ. Rule 3(g); W.D.N.Y. Rule 13(a)(1). The Northern District Court rules also require the inclusion of contested material facts. N.D.N.Y. Gen. Rule 10(j) (omitting the phrase "to be tried"). Each of these local rules state that the nonmovant's failure to submit such a statement will result in all material facts contained in the movant's statement of uncontested material facts to be deemed admitted. *See, e.g., Dusaneko, supra*, 726 F.2d at 84 (plaintiffs' failure to serve statement of contested material facts pursuant to local Rule 3(g) to set forth a material fact as to which they contended genuine issues of fact remained to be tried resulted in the facts set forth in defendant's Rule 3(g) statement being admitted); *Weg v. Macchiarola*, 654 F. Supp. 1189, 1191 n.3 (S.D.N.Y. 1987); *Stanley-Fizer, supra*, 685 F. Supp. at 61. A statement of contested material facts which merely quotes the contentions in the complaint may be insufficient to satisfy the local rules regarding the contents of the statement. *L & L Started Pullets, Inc. v. Gourdine*, 762 F.2d 1, 4 (2d Cir. 1985). Failure of the nonmovant to furnish a statement of contested material facts does not, however, mandate granting summary judgment. *Schneider, supra*, 684 F. Supp. at 1270. Rather, the court must decide in such circumstances whether the admitted facts in the movant's statement are sufficient to warrant summary judgment. *Id.* at 1271.

In constructing a statement of contested material facts, the attorney must focus on stressing and highlighting evidence which compels the conclusion that a trial is necessary. The statement should point out and discuss elements of the case which demonstrate the presence of genuine issues of material fact, referring to and including pertinent evidence supporting the statement.

B. Opposing Evidence

1. Necessity of Opposing Evidence

Rule 56(e) states that

> [w]hen a motion for summary judgment is made and supported as provided by this rule, an adverse party may not rest upon the mere allegations or denials of the adverse party's pleading, but the adverse party's response, by affidavits or as otherwise provided in this rule, must set forth specific facts showing that there is no genuine issue for trial. If the adverse party does not so respond, summary judgment, if appropriate, shall be entered against the adverse party.

Thus, once the movant satisfies its initial burden of demonstrating the absence of a genuine issue as to any material fact,[4] the nonmovant must go beyond the pleadings and by its affidavits, depositions, answers to interrogatories, and admissions on file, provide specific facts showing that there is a genuine issue for trial. *Celotex, supra*, 477 U.S. at 324; *Anderson, supra*, 477 U.S. at 247; *Meyers v. M/V Eugene C.*, 842 F.2d 815, 817 (5th Cir. 1988) (after adequate opportunity for discovery, the nonmovant must, if it bears the burden of proof, adduce some evidence of fact that, if proved, would justify a judgment in its favor); *Salahuddin v. Coughlin*, 674 F. Supp. 1048, 1052 (S.D.N.Y. 1987) (burden shifts to nonmovant to show that there is a genuine issue of fact); *State of New York v. Bowen*, 655 F. Supp. 136, 145 (S.D.N.Y. 1987). Where movant meets its initial burden, the nonmovant

---

4 *American Int'l Group, Inc. v. London American Int'l Corp.*, 664 F.2d 348, 351 (2d Cir. 1981); *Heyman, supra*, 524 F.2d at 1319-20. The nonmovant cannot make a secret of its evidence until trial, otherwise it risks the court will grant summary judgment. *Donnelly, supra*, 467 F.2d at 293; *Anderson v. City of New York*, 657 Supp. 1571 1580 n.8 (S.D.N.Y. 1987).

must do more than merely "show that there is mere metaphysical doubt as to the material facts." *Matsushita Elec. Indus. Co. v. Zenith Radio, supra,* 475 U.S. at 586; *Washington v. Armstrong World Indus., Inc.,* 839 F.2d 1121, 1123 (5th Cir. 1988); *Argus, supra,* 801 F.2d at 42; *Bambu Sales, supra,* 683 F. Supp. at 903.

To avoid summary judgment, the nonmovant must proffer significant probative evidence tending to support the complaint. *Anderson, supra; First Nat'l Bank of Arizona v. Cities Serv. Co.,* 391 U.S. 253 (1968). The nonmovant may not defeat the summary judgment motion simply by relying on the contentions of the pleadings or on mere speculation or conjecture as to the true nature of the facts to overcome the motion. *Knight, supra,* 804 F.2d at 12; *Quarles v. General Motors Corp.,* 758 F.2d 839, 840 (2d Cir. 1985); *First City Fed. Sav. Bank v. Bhogaonker,* 684 F. Supp. 793, 798 (S.D.N.Y. 1988); *Jacobson v. John Hancock Mut. Life Ins. Co.,* 662 F. Supp. 1103, 1106 (D. Conn. 1987) ("one against whom summary judgment is sought cannot rely on factually unsubstantiated conclusory allegations to sustain a claim that questions of fact exist"); *Costa-Gavras, supra,* 654 F. Supp. at 655 (a prolix and cloudy paper response will not suffice to defeat a motion for summary judgment to dismiss a public figure libel claim). Thus, the nonmovant cannot simply set forth conclusions, statements or contentions that the evidence in support of the motion is not credible. *L & L Started Pullets, supra,* 762 F. Supp. at 3-4. Bare assertions that evidence to support a fanciful allegation lies within the exclusive control of the movant, and can be obtained only through discovery, are also insufficient to defeat the summary judgment motion. *Washington, supra,* 839 F.2d at 1123; *Eastway Constr. Corp., supra,* 762 F.2d at 251; *Silver Air v. Aeronautic Dev. Corp., Ltd.,* 656 F. Supp. 170, 177 (S.D.N.Y. 1987). *See* Section IV, C, *infra.* Isolated self-serving statements of the nonmovant or its officers cannot serve to defeat a motion for summary judgment. *Argus, supra,* 801 F.2d at 42.

The party opposing summary judgment may not stand mute in reliance solely upon its allegations when facing an evidentiary submission refuting its claim, nor can it use disputes over irrelevant facts to obscure the lack of a material issue of fact. *Burlington Coat Factory Warehouse Corp. v. Esprit De Corp.,* 769 F.2d 919, 923 (2d Cir. 1985). Rather, summary judgment is mandated where the nonmovant fails to establish the existence of an essential element of its case and on which it has the burden of proof. *Washington, supra,* 839 F.2d at 1122. This obligation arises only if the movant brings a "properly supported" motion for summary judgment. Fed. R. Civ. P. 56(e); *Celotex, supra; Anderson, supra.* A careful nonmovant should meet its burden in opposing a summary judgment motion, even if it appears that the

SUMMARY JUDGMENT UNDER RULE 56

movant has not brought a viable motion to avoid the risk that the court will nevertheless deem the movant's summary judgment motion properly supported.

2. Acceptable Materials in Opposition to the Motion

Rule 56(e) permits a proper summary judgment motion to be opposed by any of the kinds of evidentiary materials listed in Rule 56(c), except for pleadings by themselves, and it is from this list that the movant normally obtains its material to meet its burden of establishing genuine issues of material fact. *Celotex, supra*, 477 U.S. at 324. To withstand the motion, the nonmovant's materials must identify an issue of fact germane to the legal dispute, that is raised by more than mere speculation, conjecture or conclusory allegation. *Celotex, supra*; *Argus, supra*, 801 F.2d at 42; *Cook v. Pension Ben. Guarantee Corp.*, 652 F. Supp. 1085, 1089 (S.D.N.Y. 1987). Except for the special rule regarding affidavits in Rule 56(e), the materials need not be in a form that is admissible at trial. *Celotex, supra* (although evidence must be admissible, nonmovant is not required to produce such evidence in a *form* admissible at trial in order to avoid summary judgment). For example, affidavits are not themselves normally admissible in evidence at trial. However, the information contained in such documents is considered in deciding the motion provided that the information itself would be admissible if given as testimony in court.

a. Pleadings

In contrast to the movant's pleadings, the nonmovant's pleadings, taken alone, are insufficient to defeat a properly supported summary judgment motion. *Cumberland Oil Corp., supra*, 791 F.2d at 1044-45; *United States v. Potamkin Cadillac Corp.*, 689 F.2d 379, 381 (2d Cir. 1982) (genuine issue for trial not created by mere allegations in the pleadings); *Rosenthal v. Kingsley*, 674 F. Supp. 1113, 1127 (S.D.N.Y. 1987) (nonmovant's complaint alone is insufficient to meet its burden in response to the motion).

b. Affidavits

As with affidavits supporting the summary judgment motion, affidavits opposing the motion must meet the three requirements in Rule 56(e); *Bhogaonker, supra*, 684 F. Supp. at 798; *Seltel, Inc. v. North Florida 47, Inc.*, 683 F. Supp. 337, 340 (S.D.N.Y. 1987) (affidavits in opposition to the motion must be made on personal knowledge and set forth facts that would be admissible in evidence). Hence, affidavits based on belief or opinion alone do not satisfy the requirement, and will be disregarded since belief or opinion is not the equivalent of personal knowledge. *Bambu, supra*, 683 F. Supp. 910. Affidavits predicated on either hearsay for which there is no exception or which indicate no personal knowledge of the affiant are insufficient to meet the movant's burden. *Seltel, supra,* 683 F. Supp. at 340; *Austracan (U.S.A.), Inc. v. Neptune Orient Lines, Ltd.*, 612 F. Supp. 578, 587 (S.D.N.Y. 1985) (affidavit here did not comply with Rule 56(e) since such an affidavit must be made on personal knowledge and show affirmatively that affiant is competent to testify). Unsupported assertions in an affidavit by the nonmovant's attorney who lacks personal knowledge of the facts does not create genuine issues of material fact to preclude summary judgment. *Hansen v. Prentice-Hall, Inc.*, 788 F.2d 892, 893-94 (2d Cir.), *cert. denied,* 479 U.S. 850 (1986); *Potamkin Cadillac, supra,* 689 F.2d at 381; *Bhogoanker, supra,* 684 F. Supp. at 798. Moreover, an affidavit that simply repeats allegations from the nonmovant's pleadings and fails to substantiate the allegations with any documentary or other evidence is inadequate. *Stanley-Fizer, supra,* 685 F. Supp. at 64. An affidavit in opposition to the motion that contains statements based on personal knowledge deserves to be generously construed by the court. *Federal Deposit Ins. Corp. v. Arcadia Marine, Inc.*, 642 F. Supp. 1157, 1160 (S.D.N.Y. 1986). A document that is signed by the nonmovant's attorney who does not have personal knowledge of the document's contents and is not signed or sworn to by the nonmovant is insufficient to controvert the movant's materials. *United States v. One 1984 Ford Bronco,* 674 F. Supp. 424, 425 (E.D.N.Y. 1987).

Factual claims in the nonmovant's affidavit may be disregarded where they contradict affiant's prior deposition testimony. *Schwimmer v. Sony Corp. of Am.*, 637 F.2d 41, 45 (2d Cir. 1980); *Perma Research & Dev. Co. v. Singer Co.*, 410 F.2d 572, 578 (2d Cir. 1969); *Halloran v. Ohlmeyer Communications Co.*, 618 F. Supp. 1214, 1220 (S.D.N.Y. 1985). Therefore, the nonmovant cannot rely on an affidavit contradicting affiant's deposition testimony as sufficient to raise an issue of fact sufficient to defeat summary judgment. *Martin v. City of New York,* 627 F. Supp. 892 (E.D.N.Y. 1985).

c. Depositions

Transcripts of depositions may be used to oppose a motion for summary judgment. Fed. R. Civ. P. 56(c); *see* Section III, C, 1, c, *supra; Donovan v. Diplomat Envelope Corp.*, 587 F. Supp. 1417, 1426 (E.D.N.Y. 1984), *aff'd,* 760 F.2d 253 (2d Cir. 1985).

d. Answer to Interrogatories

The nonmovant may use answers to interrogatories to oppose a motion for summary judgment. Fed. R. Civ. P. Rule 56(c); *see* Section III, C, 1, d, *supra.*

e. Admissions

Admissions may be used to defeat a summary judgment motion. Fed. R. Civ. P. Rule 56(c); *see* Section III, C, 1, e, *supra*.

f. Oral testimony

Although not specifically provided for in Rule 56(c), courts have considered oral testimony taken pursuant to Rule 43(e); *see* Section III, C, 1, f, *supra*.

C. Obtaining Unavailable Evidence Via Rule 56(f)

Rule 56(f) provides that if it appears "from the affidavits of a party opposing the motion that he cannot for reasons stated present by affidavit facts essential to justify the party's opposition," the court may order a continuance to permit discovery. *Celotex, supra,* 477 U.S. at 326; *Hancock, supra,* 811 F.2d at 229; *Fontenot, supra,* 780 F.2d at 1194. Thus, if facts essential to support opposition to the summary judgment motion are unavailable, the nonmovant may seek a continuance under Rule 56(f) to allow affidavits to be obtained or discovery to be had. *L & L Started Pullets, supra,* 762 F.2d at 3. As the use of "may" rather than "shall" in Rule 56(f) indicates, the determination of the adequacy of the nonmovant's Rule 56(f) affidavits and the decision to grant a continuance thereon rests in the sound discretion of the court. *Walters, supra,* 676 F.2d at 1321.

The nonmovant who claims to be unable to furnish evidence in opposition to the motion must file an affidavit describing the nature of the requested discovery, its relevance to genuine issues of material fact, what attempts the affiant has undertaken to obtain the discovery and why those attempts were not successful. *Belfiore, supra,* 826 F.2d at 184. Where Rule 56(f) affidavits have been filed setting forth specific reasons why the movant's affidavits cannot be responded to, and the facts are in the movant's possession, a continuance of the motion should be routinely granted. *J.E. Mamiye & Sons, Inc. v. Fidelity Bank,* 813 F.2d 610, 618 (3d Cir. 1987) (trial court can abuse its discretion if nonmovant shows it is entitled to discovery which could demonstrate evidence of genuine issues of material fact); *Mid-South Grizzlies v. National Football League,* 720 F.2d 772, 779 (3d Cir. 1983), *cert. denied,* 467 U.S. 1215 (1984); *Temple Univ. v. Saffa Bros., Inc.,* 656 F. Supp. 97, 110 (E.D. Pa. 1986). If the nonmovant makes a timely application to discover specifically identified relevant material reasonably believed to exist, the denial of that discovery request may be an abuse of discretion. *VISA v. Bankcard Holders,* 784 F.2d 1472 (9th Cir. 1986).

However, the nonmovant's right to discovery is not unqualified since a court may conclude that there has been adequate opportunity for discovery prior to filing the summary judgment motion and thus decline to delay in deciding the motion. *Belfiore, supra,* 876 F.2d at 184 (where nonmovant offered its amended complaint 14 months after movant brought summary judgment motion, asserted as newly discovered material facts and did not explain delay, no abuse of discretion in denying further discovery); *Mid-South Grizzlies, supra,* 720 F.2d at 779-80; *Caravan Mobile Home Sales v. Lehman Bros. Kuhn Loeb,* 769 F.2d 561, 564 (9th Cir. 1985) (where nonmovant had ample opportunity to conduct discovery, no abuse of discretion to deny further discovery); *Pfeil v. Rogers,* 757 F.2d 850, 857 (7th Cir. 1985), *cert. denied,* 475 U.S. 1107 (1986); *Walters, supra,* 626 F.2d at 1321-22.

The nonmovant must file an affidavit under Rule 56(f) to request additional discovery time. A Rule 56(f) motion is procedurally defective if the nonmovant does not submit a Rule 56(f) affidavit. *Hancock, supra,* 811 F.2d at 230 (even if a 56(f) motion is considered a Rule 56(f) affidavit, the motion must explain the need for further discovery and what material facts nonmovants hoped to uncover to support their claim); *Cumberland Oil, supra,* 791 F.2d at 1045 (nonmovant made no effort to justify its failure to inform the court of the reasons why it failed to provide affidavits to support essential element in its case). Although the nonmovant's failure to comply with Rule 56(f) procedure does not preclude consideration of granting further discovery, "some equivalent statement, preferably in writing or at least at the hearing of the motion, is expected." *Fontenot, supra,* 780 F.2d at 1194. If the nonmovant neither files a Rule 56(f) affidavit nor states any facts that require a continuance, however, there may be no abuse of discretion in denying the continuance. *Id.* Thus, the Rule 56(f) affidavit should describe with specificity the nonmovant's efforts to obtain material facts.

The proposed discovery must be shown to be directed at material bearing on the outcome of the summary judgment motion. *United States v. Light,* 766 F.2d 394, 397-98 (8th Cir. 1985). If allowing the nonmovant further discovery would not result in material that could establish a genuine issue of fact, the court may properly deny the Rule 56(f) motion. *Cumberland Oil, supra,* 791 F.2d at 1037; *Taylor v. Gallagher,* 737 F.2d 134, 137 (1st Cir. 1984); *Gieringer v. Silverman,* 731 F.2d 1272, 1277-79 (7th Cir. 1984). The nonmovant cannot simply state "information is known to us, that simply must be pursued via discovery and deposition before [it is] in a position to respond" since that is insufficient to disclose what material facts it expects to uncover. *Hancock, supra,* 811 F.2d at 230; *see also Fontenot, supra,* 780 F.2d at 1194 (insufficient for nonmovant to state only that it has not yet had sufficient time or resources to complete discovery and that the facts creating genuine issues for trial are within the movant's control, but fails to indicate what material facts it hopes to obtain through further discovery).

V. STANDARDS FOR GRANTING OR DENYING SUMMARY JUDGMENT

A. The Basic Standard for Deciding the Summary Judgment Motion

Pursuant to Rule 56(c), summary judgment shall be rendered if the supporting evidence "show[s] that there is no genuine issue of material fact and that the moving party is entitled to a judgment as a matter of law." *See, e.g., Knight, supra*, 804 F.2d at 9; *Falls Riverway Realty, supra*, 754 F.2d at 57; *R.G. & Group, Inc. v. Horn & Hardart Co.*, 751 F.2d 69, 77 (2d Cir. 1984); *Orderline Wholesale Dist. v. Gibbons, Green, Van Amerongen, Inc.*, 675 F. Supp. 122, 125 (S.D.N.Y. 1985). In *Celotex*, the Supreme Court enunciated the standard the movant must meet to be awarded summary judgment:

> a party seeking summary judgment always bears the initial responsibility of informing the district court of the basis for its motion, and identifying those portions of "the pleadings, depositions, answers to interrogatories, and admissions on file, together with the affidavits, if any," which it believes demonstrate the absence of a genuine issue of material fact . . . [there] is no requirement in Rule 56 that the moving party support its motion with affidavits or other similar material *negating* the opponent's claim . . . regardless of whether the moving party accompanies its summary judgment motion with affidavits, the motion may, and should be granted so long as whatever is before the district court demonstrates that the standard for the entry of summary judgment, as set forth in Rule 56(c), is satisfied [emphasis in original].

Celotex, supra, 477 U.S. at 323.[5] The movant may therefore satisfy its initial burden by simply pointing out that the plaintiff failed to present any evidence to establish a necessary element of the claim. *Id.*; *Apex Oil, supra*, 822 F.2d at 252; *Rosenthal v. Kingsley*, 674 F. Supp. 1113, 1115 (S.D.N.Y. 1987); *Puro Int'l, supra*, 672 F. Supp. at 132-33. Accordingly, to meet its initial burden of going forward, the movant may either affirmatively negate the nonmovant's claim or demonstrate to the court that the nonmovant is unable to establish an essential element of its claim. In effect, *Celotex* reduces the initial burden of going forward to the movant who does not have the burden of proof at trial since it may simply indicate to the court a lack of any evidence to support the plaintiff's case.

---

5 The Second Circuit has rejected any distinciton in the standard governing summary judgment in a jury trial as opposed to a bench trial. *United States v. J.B. Williams Co., Inc.*, 498 F. 2d 414, 430 n.19 (2d Cir 1974).

Once a motion for summary judgment is properly made, the burden then shifts to the nonmovant, which "must set forth specific facts showing that there is genuine issue for trial." Fed. R. Civ. P. 56(e); *Celotex, supra,* 477 U.S. at 321 & n.3; *Anderson, supra,* 477 U.S. at 256; *Ackerman v. Oryx Communications, Inc.*, 810 F.2d 336, 343 (2d Cir. 1987); *Bowen, supra,* 655 F. Supp. at 145. The nonmovant cannot defeat a properly supported summary judgment motion without offering any significant probative evidence tending to support the claim. *Anderson, supra,* 477 U.S. at 256; *Jacobson, supra,* 662 F. Supp. at 1103. A complete failure of proof regarding an essential element of the nonmovant's claim renders all other facts immaterial, thereby mandating entry of summary judgment upon a properly supported motion. *Celotex, supra; Washington, supra,* 839 F.2d at 1122; *Orderline, supra,* 675 F. Supp. at 126; *Perillo, supra,* 652 F. Supp. at 1519; *Spannaus v. Federal Election Comm.*, 641 F. Supp. 1520, 1526 (S.D.N.Y. 1986).

The burden to be met by the nonmovant opposing summary judgment is set forth in *Anderson*:

> There is no issue for trial unless there is sufficient evidence favoring the nonmoving party for a jury to return a verdict for that party. If the evidence is merely colorable or is not significantly probative, summary judgment may be granted.

Anderson, supra, 477 U.S. at 249-250 (citations omitted); *Ackerman, supra,* 810 F.2d at 343; *Weg, supra,* 654 F. Supp. at 1192. In essence, the inquiry is

> whether the evidence presents a sufficient disagreement to require submission to a jury or whether it is so one-sided that one party must prevail as a matter of law. . . . The question here is whether a jury could reasonably find *either* that the plaintiff proved his case by the quality and quantity of evidence required by the governing law *or* that he did not [emphasis in original].

Anderson, supra; Ackerman, supra; Orderline, supra, 675 F. Supp. at 126. Consequently, the standard for summary judgment

> mirrors the standard for a directed verdict under Federal Rule of Civil Procedure 50(a), which is that the trial judge must direct a verdict if, under the governing law, there can be but one reasonable conclusion as to the verdict.

Anderson, supra; Rosenthal, supra, 674 F. Supp. at 1115.

From *Anderson*, it is evident that the standard in determining summary judgment is whether a jury could reasonably find for the nonmovant on the evidence presented, viewed in light of the substantive evidentiary burden. It must be remembered that unless the nonmovant proffers evidence pertaining

SUMMARY JUDGMENT UNDER RULE 56

to an element of its action, summary judgment will be granted against it, provided that the movant has met its initial burden. Counsel should note that the standards set forth in *Celotex, Anderson* and their progeny reflect a desire to encourage summary judgment by lessening the movant's burden while increasing the nonmovant's burden. Under *Celotex*, the movant need not negate the nonmovant's claim but merely demonstrate the absence of any essential element of that claim in the record. The nonmovant, on the other hand, must come forward with evidence sufficient to avoid a directed verdict.

Apex Oil, Ackerman and other Second Circuit opinions intimate that the "slightest doubt standard" which was previously applied in summary judgment cases, is no longer viable. Under that standard summary judgment was denied even if there was only the least or slightest doubt as to whether the nonmovant would not reach the jury at trial. *Bozant v. Bank of New York*, 156 F.2d 787 (2d Cir. 1946). The nonmovant plaintiff could, pursuant to the slightest doubt standard, delay in having to establish the essential elements of its claim until trial. *Celotex* and *Anderson* now require the nonmovant to present affirmative evidence demonstrating its claim to avoid summary judgment. Thus, the slightest doubt test should no longer be viable.

B. Determining What Constitutes a Genuine Issue of Material Fact

Rule 56(c) provides that the existence of an alleged factual dispute between the parties is insufficient to defeat a summary judgment motion; rather, there must be a genuine issue of material fact. *Anderson, supra*, 477 U.S. at 247; *Quarles, supra*, 758 F.2d at 840 ("mere existence of factual issues—where those issues are not material to the claims before the court—will not suffice to defeat a motion for summary judgment"); *Butler Foods, Inc. v. Trailer Marine Transport Corp.*, 680 F. Supp. 472, 473 (D. Puerto Rico 1988). In *Anderson*, the Supreme Court stated that a disputed fact is material only if it might affect the lawsuit's outcome under the governing law and thereby preclude granting summary judgment. *Anderson, supra; Hancock, supra*, 811 F.2d at 231; *Katz v. Gladstone*, 673 F. Supp. 76, 79 (D. Conn. 1987); *Scan-Plast Indus., Inc. v. Scanimport Am. Inc.*, 652 F. Supp. 1156, 1160 (E.D.N.Y. 1987) (genuine issue of material fact exists if there is a factual issue in dispute which might affect the outcome of the litigation and there is sufficient evidence on both sides of the issue that it could reasonably be resolved in favor of either party). The court must use the substantive law governing the case to decide which facts are material. *Anderson, supra* (the substantive law will identify which facts are material); *Puro Int'l, supra*, 672 F. Supp. at 132. An issue is material for purposes of Rule 56, therefore, if it may make a difference in the action's final determination. Consequently, factual disputes that are irrelevant or unnecessary to such a determination will not be deemed material. *Anderson, supra.* Materiality is only a criterion for categorizing factual disputes, not a criterion for assessing the evidentiary standards applicable to such disputes. *Anderson, supra.*

To determine what constitutes a genuine issue of fact, the court will apply the same test as it does in deciding whether to grant a directed verdict. *Anderson, supra; Hancock, supra,* 811 F.2d at 231; *Katz, supra,* 673 F. Supp. at 79; *Silver Air, supra,* 656 F.2d at 176. A genuine dispute over material facts exists if the evidence is such that a reasonable jury could return a verdict for the movant. *Anderson, supra.* Therefore, only when reasonable jurors could disagree does a genuine issue of material fact exist. *Margrave, supra,* 643 F. Supp. at 513. If the court determines that a rational trier of fact could not return a verdict in favor of the nonmovant, summary judgment should be denied. *Anderson, supra.* Where the entire record cannot lead a rational trier of fact for the nonmovant, there is no genuine issue for trial and hence summary judgment should be granted. *Matsushita, supra,* 475 U.S. at 587; *Weg, supra,* 654 F. Supp. at 1192.

C. Weighing the Evidence

In considering a summary judgment motion, the court's function is not to resolve disputed issues of fact but only to assess whether there are any genuine issues of material fact to be tried. *Anderson, supra,* 477 U.S. at 248; *Eastman Mach. Co., supra,* 841 F.2d at 473; *Knight, supra,* 804 F.2d at 11; *Rosenthal, supra,* 674 F. Supp. at 1115; *Salahuddin, supra,* 674 F. Supp. at 1052.[6] Thus, in ruling on the motion the court may not try issues of fact, but rather is limited to deciding whether there are issues of fact which mandate a trial. *Donahue, supra,* 834 F.2d at 58; *R.G. Group, supra,* 751 F.2d at 77; *Schneider, supra,* 684 F. Supp. at 1274.

To rule on the motion, the court is required to view the evidence "presented through the prism of the substantive evidentiary burden of the action." *Anderson, supra,* 477 U.S. at 254; *Orderline, supra,* 675 F. Supp. at 129. The court is required in deciding each motion to view the evidence submitted by the parties in the light most favorable to the nonmovant. *United States v. Diebold, Inc.,* 369 U.S. 654 (1962); *Eastman Mach. Co., supra; Burtnieks, supra,* 716 F.2d at 985. Accordingly, the court shall resolve all ambiguities and draw all reasonable inferences against the movant. *Anderson, supra;*

---

[6] As previously discussed, Rule 56(c) provides that the court shall grant a summary judgment motion if it determines that "there is no genuine issue as to any material fact and the moving party is entitled to a judgment as a matter of law." *Schwabenbauer v. Board of Educ.,* 667 F.2d 305, 313 (2d Cir. 1981); *Stanley-Frizer, supra,* 685 F. Supp at 61; *Bhogaonker, supra,* 684 F. Supp. at 796. Thus the court's weighing of the evidence determines whether the standard has been met.

Matsushita, supra, 475 U.S. at 588; *Wakefield, supra,* 813 F.2d at 540-41; *Knight, supra,* at 11; *Seltel, supra,* 683 F. Supp. at 341; *Stanford v. Kuwait Airways Corp.,* 648 F. Supp. 1158, 1160 (S.D.N.Y. 1986).

Anderson restricts the extent a court can weigh the evidence to determine whether sufficient evidence exists upon which a jury could base a verdict for the nonmovant. The *Anderson* Court clearly stated that its holding

> does not denigrate the role of the jury. It by no means authorizes trial on affidavits. Credibility determinations, the weighing of the evidence, and the drawing of legitimate inferences from the facts are jury functions, not those of a judge, whether he is ruling on a motion for summary judgment or for a directed verdict.

Anderson, supra, 417 U.S. at 255.

The Second Circuit has held that only a limited assessment of the evidence is appropriate in order to decide what inferences are reasonable and therefore permissible. It is clear that the issue of what weight should be accorded to competing permissible inferences remains within the province of the factfinder. *Apex Oil, supra,* 822 F.2d at 253; *accord Belifore, supra,* 826 F.2d at 180.

D. Expert Evidence

Expert evidence may be considered on a motion for summary judgment. It can be submitted on the motion in any form other evidence can be submitted. The court has broad discretion to rule on the admissibility of the expert's evidence unless "manifestly erroneous." *Washington, supra,* 839 F.2d at 1123. The court may inquire into the reliability and foundation of any expert's opinion to determine its admissibility. *Id.*; *In re Agent Orange Prod. Liab. Litig.,* 611 F. Supp. 1223, 1258-59 (S.D.N.Y. 1985), *aff'd,* 818 F.2d 187 (2d Cir. 1987). As with any evidentiary material submitted on a summary judgment motion, the expert's opinion must be based on a review of the relevant material and provide specific facts on which the opinion is based so as to avoid being deemed inadmissible because it lacks foundation and is, therefore, unreliable. *Viterbo v. Dow Chem. Co.,* 826 F.2d 420, 422 (5th Cir. 1987); *Evers v. General Motors,* 770 F.2d 984, 986 (11th Cir. 1985); *Duplar Corp. v. Deering Milliken, Inc.,* 370 F. Supp. 769, 786 n.27, 787 (D.S.C. 1973) (expert testimony amounting to legal conclusions need not be considered). If the expert's evidence does not meet this Rule 56 standard, it may be properly excluded from the party's papers. *Washington, supra*; *Bruggemeyer v. American Broadcasting Co.,* 684 F. Supp. 452, 465 (N.D. Tex. 1988). Thus, conclusory expert opinions are not sufficient to defeat a summary judgment motion. *Merit Motors, Inc. v. Chrysler Corp.,* 569 F.2d 666, 673 (D.D.C. 1977); *In re Agent Orange, supra,* 611 F.2d at 1258.

VI. APPEALABILITY AND STANDARD OF REVIEW ON APPEAL OF SUMMARY JUDGMENT MOTIONS

A. Appeal From an Order Granting Summary Judgment

The following is a brief discussion of appeals of decisions on motions for summary judgment. Pursuant to 28 U.S.C. § 1291, "[t]he court of appeals shall have jurisdiction of appeals from all final decisions of the district courts. . . ." No further proceedings may take place in a case after complete summary judgment has been granted. Consequently, an appeal is proper where summary judgment is entered in a two-party, one-claim action. Fed. R. Civ. P. 54(a). Furthermore, if the granting of summary judgment in a multiple-party or multiple claims action resolves all of the claims involving each of the parties, summary judgment may be appealable. Fed. R. Civ. P. 54(b).

Rule 54(b) governs whether summary judgment as to less than all of parties or claims is interlocutory or final. The rule allows the entry of a final partial judgment when there are other unresolved claims "upon an express determination that there is no just reason for delay and upon an express direction for the entry of judgment." In the absence of such determination and direction, however, any order which adjudicates less than all the claims or the rights and liabilities of less than all the parties does not terminate the action as to any of the claims or parties. Fed. R. Civ. P. Rule 54(b). Consequently, the grant of summary judgment on less than all of the action is not generally appealable unless the court designates its order final pursuant to Rule 54(b). *St. Mary's Health Center of Jefferson City v. Bowen*, 821 F.2d 493, 497-98 (8th Cir. 1987); *Aaro, Inc. v. Daewo Int'l (America) Corp.*, 755 F.2d 1398, 1400 (11th Cir. 1985) citing Wright, Miller & Kane, *supra*, at § 2715. The court of appeals may review the district court's decision to determine if in fact it is final or actually a partial adjudication and dismiss the appeal if it finds that the order is interlocutory. *Spencer, White & Prentis, Inc. v. Pfizer, Inc.*, 498 F.2d 358, 362, 363 n.17, 364 (2d Cir. 1974). The court of appeals may also review the district court's finding under 54(b). *Sears, Roebuck & Co. v. Mackey*, 351 U.S. 427, 437-38 (1956).

A partial summary judgment that is entered under Rule 56(d) determining some, but not all, issues as to a party or parties is an interlocutory order. *Leasing Service Corp. v. Graham*, 646 F. Supp. 1410, 1414 (S.D.N.Y. 1986) (summary judgment, interlocutory in nature, may be rendered on issue of liability alone even though there is a genuine issue regarding the amount of damages). Consequently, partial summary judgment deciding that a particular matter is established for trial of the action is generally not appealable until after the case has been tried. *See, e.g., Leasing Service, supra,* 646 F. Supp. at 1414. Under Rule 54(b) though, partial summary judgment that resolves completely the rights or liabilities of a single party in a multi-party case is appealable.

A partial summary judgment that is within the ambit of a statutory or common law exception to the 28 U.S.C. § 1291 requirement of a final judgment will generally be appealable. *See* Wright, Miller & Kane, *supra*, § 2715.

B. Appeal From an Order Denying Summary Judgment

The movant's failure to demonstrate that there are no genuine issues of material fact means that a trial is required to determine the action. *Ackerman, supra,* 810 F.2d at 339 (denial of summary judgment does not constitute a disposition on the merits, thereby mandating that the issues be resolved at trial). Thus, there are few, if any, appeals from orders denying summary judgment due to the interlocutory character of the order. *Knight, supra,* 804 F.2d at 12 n.1. Generally, therefore, an appeal of a denial of summary judgment must wait until the entry of judgment subsequent to the trial.

C. Standard of Review on Appeal

The Second Circuit has held that

> the standard applied by a reviewing court to determine whether summary judgment was properly granted is the same as that applied in the district court initially under Rule 56(c) . . . . The party who defended against the motion has the benefit of the court's reading of the record in the light most favorable to him.

Burtnieks v. City of New York, supra, 716 F.2d at 985; *accord Walters, supra,* 626 F.2d at 1322. This *de novo* review suggested in *Burtnieks* was subsequently applied by the Second Circuit. *Donahue, supra,* 834 F.2d at 58 (upon a *de novo* review of the entire record, court concluded summary judgment was inappropriate).[7]

---

[7] It should be noted that the appellate court need not affirm the trial court's summary judgment order for the same reasons that convinced the trial court to grant the motion. *Cumberland Oil, supra,* 791 F.2d at 1043.

VII. SOME STRATEGIC AND TACTICAL CONSIDERATIONS REGARDING SUMMARY JUDGMENT[8]

A. Considerations in Bringing the Motion

Summary judgment is a powerful tool for terminating all or part of a lawsuit. A successful motion on all issues results in a final judgment and terminates the action. While partial summary judgment is not final and does not terminate an action it can eliminate issues and reduce the scope of further discovery and trial.

A party should consider seeking summary judgment even if it concludes that the motion may not be granted. For example, the motion allows the movant to educate the court about the action as well as to gauge the court's view of the legal and factual merits of the action. It forces the nonmovant to come forward with its evidence. Even if the motion is denied in its entirety

> the invocation of Rule 56 may streamline and shorten the future course of the action if the district court accepts the invitation of Rule 56(d) to "make an order specifying the facts that appear without substantial controversy," which fact "shall be deemed established, upon the trial of the action."

NYSBA Report, *supra*, at 17. A prospective movant should not, however, make a frivolous motion which would expose it to the risks of Rule 11 and Rule 56(g) sanctions.[9]

Before making the motion, a party should analyze the "downside" of seeking summary judgment. In preparing and supporting a motion for sum-

---

[8] For further suggestions regarding strategic and tactical considerations concerning this topic, see Stempel, *supra*, at 172, Wallance *Summary Judgment Ascending*, 14 Litigation 6, 8 (Winter 1988); Childress, *A New Era For Summary Judgments: Recent Shifts at the Supreme Court*,116 F.R.D. 183, 191-193 (1987).

[9] *See, e.g., Calloway v. Marvel Entertainment Group*, 854 F.2d 1452 (2d Cir. 1988) (imposing sanctions under Rule 11 against nonmovant's attorney and law firm due to attorney's failure to make a reasonable investigaiton before repeatedly putting forward an untrue claim in his affidavit opposing summary judgment); *Eastway Constr. Corp. v. City of New York*, 726 F.2d 243, 253-54 (2d Cir. 1985) ("sanctions shall be imposed against an attorney and/or his client when it appears that a pleading has been interposed for any improper purpose, or where, after reasonable inquiry, a competent attorney could not form a reasonable belief that the pleadng is well-grounded in fact and is warranted by existing law or a good faith argument for the extension, modification or reversal of existing law"). Rule 11 applies to all papers filed in a lawsuit; the signer's conduct should be judged at the time a paper is signed. *Oliveri v. Thompson*, 803 F.2d 1265 (2d Cir. 1986), *cert. denied*, 480 U.S. 918 (1987). It should be noted, however, that Rule 11 is not meant to chill an attorney's enthusiasm or creativity in pursuing factual or legal theories. *Kamen, supra*, 791 F.2d at 1071-12.

mary judgment, the movant may spend nearly as much time as it would in readying for trial. Only if summary judgment is granted does it usually save time and costs. A motion that is denied generally increases the amount of pretrial preparation without correspondingly decreasing the effort at and after the trial. Using summary judgment to educate the court may be futile, if made too early in a case or to an overburdened court. Just as a successful motion places the nonmovant in a position of facing a trial where the court has already found that certain issues did not present genuine issues of material fact, an unsuccessful motion may result in the court being predisposed against the movant's case at trial.

B. When to Bring the Motion

While Rule 56(a) provides that a complainant may move for summary judgment any time after 20 days from commencing the action and Rule 56(b) provides the defending party to move for summary judgment at any time after the claim is asserted, significant tactical considerations will dictate the actual timing of the motion.

1. Prior to Discovery

An obvious advantage to moving for summary judgment before discovery is that it can eliminate time and expense of unnecessary discovery on immaterial matters. Moving before discovery has the advantage of limiting the nonmovant's opportunity to produce and develop evidence showing that there are indeed genuine issues of material fact that necessitate a trial.

If the movant meets its initial burden of demonstrating that no genuine issue of material fact exists, the burden shifts to the nonmovant to establish that such a genuine factual dispute does exist. The movant should support its motion with as much acceptable evidence in the form of affidavits and other documentary evidence that enable it to satisfy its initial burden. Under *Celotex*, however, the movant need not negate the nonmovant's claim but rather simply show that the movant is unable to prove an essential element of its claim. Thus, the movant's initial burden is easily satisfied.

The nonmovant must then come forth with specific facts demonstrating the existence of genuine issues. It must offer probative evidence supporting its claim. *Anderson, supra*, 477 U.S. at 256. Consequently, a motion for summary judgment brought prior to discovery forces the nonmovant to furnish much of its supporting evidence. The movant obtains significant material without having to go through discovery, enabling it to assess the strength and weaknesses of both the nonmovant's and its own case. Weighing against an early motion is the possibility of educating the nonmovant about the factual and legal position of the movant before nonmovant's position has been pinned down through discovery. Another factor to be considered is the extra effort entailed in a motion compared to some discovery devices.

Bringing summary judgment before discovery entails some risk. For instance, if the nonmovant establishes via a Rule 56(f) affidavit that it cannot present facts essential to justify its opposition prior to discovery, the court may deny rather than defer the motion. The court may view a second summary judgment motion less favorably if brought after the denial of the first motion. The movant should be confident that it can support its position without discovery. Otherwise, an early motion raises the possibility that judgment may be granted against it. Generally, early motions are useful only on cases with narrow factual issues and clear and narrow legal issues.

2. During or Subsequent to Discovery

Summary judgment motions are more commonly made at some point during or after the discovery phase. Discovered material may either conclusively negate the nonmovant's claim or defense, or demonstrate that the nonmovant is unable to make a showing sufficient to establish the existence of an essential element of the nonmovant's case. *Celotex, supra.* Moreover, the court may be more inclined to grant summary judgment after discovery in light of possible 56(f) claims by the nonmovant. Bringing the motion during discovery can serve to focus and limit remaining discovery. Courts often deny such motions without prejudice or defer a ruling while the nonmovant is allowed to take only focused discovery on its Rule 56(f) material.

Summary judgment motions may also be more effectively made at the end of discovery after the opposing party has responded to contention and expert interrogatories and its claims are more clearly focused and disclosed. The nonmovant's ability to recast its claim in response to a summary judgment motion is substantially reduced by careful discovery.

C. Planning for the Motion

A case should be analyzed for summary judgment potential at the earliest possible stage and investigation and discovery planned accordingly. If an early motion appears to be available, all possible defenses and factual disputes should be considered. Limited discovery or requests for admission may bolster a motion. If broader discovery will be necessary it should be planned in an effort to provide as much support as possible from the opposing party's own records and testimony. Future evidentiary requirements for the motion, such as foundational requirements for documents, should be considered. Adverse witnesses' testimony should be taken as definitively as possible so as to prevent or limit an adversary's use of supplemental or explanatory affidavits. Questions should be carefully phrased in light of anticipated use in the motion and answers clarified with follow-up questions where appropriate.

SUMMARY JUDGMENT UNDER RULE 56   541

Interrogatories and requests to admit may be used to provide foundational requirements for documents, to establish collateral or material facts and to focus issues.

D. Presentation of the Motion

The practical burden for the movant is to simplify the legal and factual issues and to present the evidence supporting the facts in the briefest, most accessible format. In complicated cases organization of the evidentiary materials, including careful labeling, highlighting and abstracting of evidence, may be crucial to success. Summary evidence under Fed. R. Evid. 1006 may even be used provided a proper foundation has been previously laid. *Wallance, supra*, at 8. Finally, careful annotation of arguments in the briefs to the evidence will assist the court. The movant must also take the necessary steps to insure that any discovery material relied on is on file with the court either as part of the moving papers or separately. This is particularly important now that depositions and discovery responses are not routinely filed.

E. Partial Summary Judgment

Partial summary judgment motions as to some, but not all, issues involving parties as to which a trial will still be necessary are most likely to be effective in very complicated cases. Any such motion meets the natural judicial reaction that since a trial is necessary in any event it would be prudent to try all issues, deferring a ruling on the sufficiency of the evidence until the close of proof or after verdict. This may be particularly true where the court concludes that many of the same facts must be developed at trial in support of other claims in the action. In a more complicated case a court may welcome the opportunity to reduce the burden of trial by disposing of claims on motion. Partial summary judgment motions which may eliminate a party from the trial of a case also may be viewed more favorably from the standpoint of judicial economy. Because a partial judgment without a Rule 54(b) finding allowing entry of judgment brings only limited peace to a party, it is important to analyze the likelihood of persuading the court to enter a judgment in considering whether to make the motion.

F. Opposing the Motion

In the wake of *Celotex*, the party bringing a claim must prepare and develop at the very earliest stages of litigation evidence supporting each of the elements of the case. The nonmovant must be able to come forward with evidence sufficient to support its claim or explain why it needs the opportunity under Rule 56(f) to discover that information from the movant and has not done so already. For the opposing party, complication and proliferation of supporting evidence is a frequent and frequently effective tactic. However, the lesson of *Matsushita* and its offspring are that the court is able to sift through even the most complicated case to focus on its material elements. Effective and focused marshalling of the controverting facts is necessary to defeat a motion. Organizing the opposing papers in a manner which assists the court in identifying the material factual dispute is important. As with the movant, the nonmovant must avoid submitting opposition papers that are not reasonably investigated or that are used for improper purposes.[10]

The movant's evidence should be scrutinized for admissibility and motions to strike or other objection clearly made as part of the record. Credibility issues should be raised where possible. The movant's legal arguments should be analyzed to determine if they are premised on mixed questions of law and fact which are for a jury. All material elements of the movant's legal theories should be analyzed for the possibility of underlying factual deficiencies.

The question of whether to cross-move for summary judgment should be carefully considered. Cross-motions obviously take away the basic argument in opposition, that a trial is necessary. Although courts can and often do ignore the parties' position that the case is ripe for summary judgment and find questions of fact for trial, a cross-motion may be a riskier strategy unless the nonmovant's position is very persuasive. Rarely is a cross-motion an effective way to present conflicting factual positions. It is generally better practice to carefully craft the statement of contested material facts required by most courts.

Practical considerations play an important role in a court's decision concerning partial summary judgment. Thus, opposing the grant of partial summary judgment in part on the basis of judicial economy can be effective. The thrust of the argument for the nonmovant is that many of the underlying facts will be presented at trial in connection with other claims or that the movant will necessarily participate in the trial on other issues and that a prudent court will defer a definitive ruling on all claims until the facts have been fully developed at trial. The argument, of course, depends on the nonmovant's ability to raise at least a strong potential for disputed material facts.

---

[10] *Id.*

APPENDIX

Rule 56. Summary Judgment

(a) *For Claimant.* A party seeking to recover upon a claim, counterclaim, or cross-claim or to obtain a declaratory judgment may, at any time after the expiration of 20 days from the commencement of the action or after service of a motion for summary judgment by the adverse party, move with or without supporting affidavits for a summary judgment in the party's favor upon all or any part thereof.

(b) *For Defending Party.* A party against whom a claim, counterclaim, or cross-claim is asserted or a declaratory judgment is sought may, at any time, move with or without supporting affidavits for a summary judgment in the party's favor as to all or any part thereof.

(c) *Motion and Proceedings Thereon.* The motion shall be served at least 10 days before the time fixed for the hearing. The adverse party prior to the day of hearing may serve opposing affidavits. The judgment sought shall be rendered forthwith if the pleadings, depositions, answers to interrogatories, and admissions on file, together with the affidavits, if any, show that there is no genuine issue as to any material fact and that the moving party is entitled to a judgment as a matter of law. A summary judgment, interlocutory in character, may be rendered on the issue as to the amount of damages.

(d) *Case Not Fully Adjudicated on Motion.* If on motion under this rule judgment is not rendered upon the whole case or for all the relief asked and a trial is necessary, the court at the hearing of the motion, by examining the pleadings and the evidence before it and by interrogating counsel, shall if practicable ascertain what material facts exist without substantial controversy and what material facts are actually and in good faith controverted. It shall thereupon make an order specifying the facts that appear without substantial controversy, including the extent to which the amount of damages or other relief is not in controversy, and directing such further proceedings in the action as are just. Upon the trial of the action the facts so specified shall be deemed established, and the trial shall be conducted accordingly.

(e) *Form of Affidavits; Further Testimony; Defense Required.* Supporting and opposing affidavits shall be made on personal knowledge, shall set forth such facts as would be admissible in evidence, and shall show affirmatively that the affiant is competent to testify to the matters stated therein. Sworn or certified copies of all papers or parts thereof referred to in an affidavit shall be attached thereto or served therewith. The court may permit affidavits to be supplemented or opposed by depositions, answers to interrogatories, or further affidavits. When a motion for summary judgment is made and supported as provided in this rule, an adverse party may not rest upon the mere allegations or denials of the adverse party's pleading, but the adverse party's response, by affidavits or as otherwise provided in this rule, must set forth specific facts showing that there is a genuine issue for trial. If the adverse party does not so respond, summary judgment, if appropriate, shall be entered against the adverse party.

(f) *When Affidavits are Unavailable.* Should it appear from the affidavits of a party opposing the motion that the party cannot for reasons stated present by affidavit facts essential to justify the party's opposition, the court may refuse the application for judgment or may order a continuance to permit affidavits to be obtained or depositions to be taken or discovery to be had or may make such other order as is just.

(g) *Affidavits Made in Bad Faith.* Should it appear to the satisfaction of the court at any time that any of the affidavits presented pursuant to this rule are presented in bad faith or solely for the purpose of delay, the court shall forthwith order the party employing them to pay the other party the amount of the reasonable expenses which the filing of the affidavits caused the other party to incur, including reasonable attorney's fees, and any offending party or attorney may be adjudged guilty of contempt.

(Amended August 1, 1987.)

CHAPTER EIGHTEEN

SETTLEMENT

by Alan Mansfield, Esq.

I. INTRODUCTION

This chapter considers the settlement process in federal practice. Administrative offices of the federal courts substantiate the fact that most cases settle. The vast majority settle before trial but a substantial number of cases settle during the trial, post-trial and appellate stages.[1] Given the likelihood of negotiated pretrial dispositions, counsel should consider each case from a settlement perspective at its inception. Unlike other components of federal practice, the settlement process is governed by few substantive and procedural rules. Reaching an amicable settlement is often the product of counsel's experience and skill in negotiation coupled with the reasoned business judgment of his client. Effective settlement techniques cannot be reduced to checklists. However, certain approaches to settlement are likely to enhance a successful negotiated resolution of a dispute. This chapter will address how counsel should evaluate a case for settlement purposes and various mechanisms which are available to further the settlement process. In addition, this chapter will consider various procedural, substantive and ethical rules which relate to settlements.

II. EVALUATING THE CASE

In view of the high probability of pretrial disposition, it is undoubtedly the case that claims for monetary damages have a "range" in which they should

---

[1] For example, under the Second Circuit's Civil Appeals Management Plan, preargument conferences have been successful in promoting settlement of docketed appeals. E.g., *Judicial Conference-Federal Circuit*, 108 F.R.D. 465, 494 (1985).

settle. To ascertain the "range," parties and their counsel must assess the realistic amount of recoverable damages, the risks inherent in litigation, the likelihood of liability, the costs of litigation (including attorney's fees, expert fees, routine stenographic fees, filing fees, and so forth), the present and discounted value of money, tax consequences, the collectibility of any judgment and specific concerns relating to the parties' actual circumstances. These circumstances can vary from age and ability to withstand the expensive and often intrusive litigation process to a party's concerns about confidentiality, publicity, exposure of damaging evidence and commercial advantage or disadvantage attendant to settling claims. Of course, the evaluation of a claim varies with its complexity. Academic literature is replete with elaborate analytical systems designed to determine the amount for which a claim should settle. *E.g.*, Note, *An Analysis of Settlement*, 22 Stan. L. Rev. 67 (1969); Schweitzer, 1 Cyclopedia of Trial Practice § 136 (2d ed. 1970).

Counsel's first step in taking on a matter ordinarily should be the development of a prelitigation record. Federal Rules of Civil Procedure ("Federal Rules" or "Fed. R. Civ. P.") Rule 11, of course, requires reasonable inquiry to show that a complaint is well grounded in fact and warranted by existing law or good faith arguments to extend existing law. As a preliminary matter, in addition to learning the client's version of the controversy, counsel should locate and review relevant files and documents. Witnesses should be interviewed and relevant secondary source material (such as media reports) should be collected. Depending on the nature of the dispute, it may be useful or even essential to retain investigators or experts (such as accountants, engineers, physicians and the like) properly to explore the nature of the claim and damages. Often appraisals and market analyses are critical to determining the true value of a claim. Counsel must also identify potential parties and consider whether deep-pocket or insured defendants exist.

As counsel develops the factual record, he must also formulate and research legal theories. The legal analysis must address substantive law in addition to jurisdictional and evidentiary points, which together should provide counsel with a reasoned judgment about the likelihood of a liability finding.

Assessment of damages entails both legal and practical components. Applicable statutory and case law may significantly impact on the magnitude of recoverable damages. For example, civil-RICO, 18 U.S.C. §§ 1961 *et seq.*, and Sherman Act, 15 U.S.C. §§ 1 *et seq.*, claims provide for treble damages; copyright violations are subject to statutory damage formulae; wrongful death and certain Uniform Commercial Code cases are often subject to recovery limitations. Indefinite losses and lost profits claims are subject to an independent body of the law of damages. The availability of attorney's fees in

SETTLEMENT 547

civil-RICO and civil rights cases, among others, punitive damages, and, to a lesser extent, prejudgment interest also fit into the assessment calculus.

Counsel must also evaluate practical matters with respect to damage awards. The dispute must be viewed from the perspective of the applicable jury pool. In personal injury cases, in particular, experienced trial counsel should be familiar with ranges of recoveries based on analogous circumstances. Resort to private jury reporters[2] and services such as BNA Civil Trial Manual can also be useful. Counsel must also consider whether particular facts relating to the proposed proof and witnesses as well as the nature of the claim are likely to impact favorably or unfavorably on the jury.

III. JUDICIAL INVOLVEMENT IN THE SETTLEMENT PROCESS

In light of crowded federal dockets and empirical evidence that early judicial intervention fosters more efficient dispositions of cases, the 1983 amendments to the Federal Rules explicitly provide for settlement conferences and the use of extrajudicial processes to further a negotiated resolution of the dispute. Fed. R. Civ. P. Rule 16(a)(5) specifically points to the facilitation and promotion of settlement as an appropriate objective of discretionary pretrial conferences. Moreover, Fed. R. Civ. P. Rule 16(c) provides that at any conference, the participants "may consider and take action with respect to . . . (7) the possibility of settlement or the use of extrajudicial procedures to resolve the dispute. . . ." While settlement conferences are not intended to be mandatory, the Federal Rules envision that the presence of a neutral forum may further the negotiation process.[3]

As a matter of practice, the settlement conference may be presided over by the judge assigned generally to the case, another member of the court assigned solely to the conference, an informal master or a court-appointed master under Fed. R. Civ. P. Rule 53 or a magistrate. Thus, for example, the

---

[2] These services include the ATLA Law Reporter and data published by Jury Verdict Research Inc. and Verdict and Settlements.

[3] Federal appellate courts have repeatedly observed that, while district courts may encourage settlement, they may not coerce it. In *Kothe v. Smith*, 771 F.2d 667 (2d Cir. 1985), the Second Circuit reversed a contempt fine levied against a defendant who failed to make a settlement offer in the amount recommended by the judge and for which the case actually settled after one day of trial. The Second Circuit observed: "[a]lthough the law favors the voluntary settlement of civil suits, it does not sanction efforts by trial judges to effect settlements through coercion." 771 F.2d at 669. Similarly, in *Hess v. New Jersey Transit Rail Operations, Inc.*, 846 F.2d 114 (2d Cir. 1988), the Second Circuit vacated a contempt judgment based on a defendant's refusal to follow a district judge's directive that it make a "bonafide" pretrial settlement offer.

Rules for the Division of Business Among District Judges, which apply to the Southern and Eastern Districts of New York, specifically provide:

> After a case has been assigned, the judge may direct the attorneys for each party to meet with said judge to discuss the case informally, to entertain oral motions and, to the extent desirable, to discuss settlement or to set a schedule for the case, including for discovery, pre-trial and trial.

Experienced counsel and members of the judiciary voice disparate views about whether an assigned judge (or any judge at all) should preside over settlement conferences. *See generally* 6 C. Wright & A. Miller, *Federal Practice and Procedure* § 1522 (1971 and 1987 Supp.). Although the assigned judge may be familiar with the facts and legal issues, otherwise inadmissible or prejudicial evidence is often significant in settlement conferences. Counsel may have concerns that the actual or perceived impartiality of a judge who will make decisions on dispositive motions or *pendente lite* equitable relief applications will be impaired by "frank" discussions. The concerns are exacerbated in nonjury trial settings, where the judge will be fact-finder in the event a settlement is not achieved. *See generally* Will, Merhige & Rubin, *The Role of the Judge in The Settlement Process*, 75 F.R.D. 203 (1976); Brazil, *What Lawyers Want From Judges in the Settlement Arena*, 106 F.R.D. 85 (1985).

There is virtually no substantive law which governs the conduct of the judicially-supervised settlement conference. While the privilege attendant to settlement discussions under Federal Rules of Evidence Rule 408 and applicable ethical precepts govern the interchange among the participants, *see infra* "Evidentiary Issues" and "Ethical Issues," settlement conference agendas vary according to the needs of the participants and style of the presiding officials. Generally, counsel for the respective parties make oral presentations and rebuttal arguments to justify their offers and counteroffers. Especially where the presiding judge or magistrate is not assigned generally to the case, the preparation of written settlement memoranda may be required. These memoranda may be exchanged or submitted on an *ex parte* basis, if the parties agree.

Depending on the size, complexity and stage of the proceeding, judicially-supervised settlement conferences are often more efficacious if principals are included in the process. Unless the case was initiated by hearings for injunctive relief or the like, the settlement conference may be the party's first exposure to the judicial system. Skepticism or encouragement raised by an impartial judicial officer may refocus a party's assessment of the case. Furthermore, attorneys who believe that their settlement proposals are not effectively communicated (if at all) to the opposing party can be assured that each side is properly educated at the settlement conference. Some presiding officials prefer to assume an aggressive role in settlement discussions: weaknesses in legal and factual positions may be articulated, and specific recommendations with respect to a settlement package may be proposed. Others limit their roles to providing a structured and neutral forum to the litigants.

On consent of the parties, the judge or magistrate can preside over *ex parte* oral presentations of the participants to consider specific legal or factual matters which, as a matter of strategy, would not be revealed to the other side at a pretrial stage of the proceeding. While the judicially-supervised settlement conference will not eliminate an advocate's "posturing," an experienced neutral observer is in a position meaningfully to disaggregate fact from fiction in assessing the real value of a case.

Judicially-supervised settlement conferences are not necessarily effective for every kind of case, and early intervention may be entirely inappropriate where the discovery process promises to lead to probative evidence—eyewitnesses, dispositive expert analyses and so forth—which can shift inordinately the worth and risks in a case. Similarly, pretrial motions addressed to jurisdictional matters or venue may significantly influence the value of a case: deep pockets in multi-party litigation may be dismissed or the case may be transferred to a forum which will significantly affect the costs of litigation. Dispositive and evidentiary motions can, of course, determine liability or provide a meaningful indication of whether liability will be found.

The settlement process can also be useful in curtailing the litigation. Often in complex, multi-party cases, settlement agreements can narrow the scope of discovery and the matters to be tried. Partial settlement can eliminate parties and issues altogether and thereby lessen the costs and risks of litigation.

As a practical matter, the commonly echoed concept, "what's good for my adversary must be bad for me," does not automatically apply to participation in settlement conferences. Most cases do settle, and a supervised settlement conference can be advantageous to both sides. However, counsel must consider whether the settlement value of a case may be adversely impacted by a party's exposing various weaknesses in his case too early.[4]

In addition to the settlement conference, Rule 16 expressly recognizes the potential advantages of extrajudicial techniques in achieving a settlement.

---

4 Various substantive rules may impact on the timing of settlement discussions. For example, settlement offers may be relevant to a party's right to an award of prejudgment interest under applicable state law. *E.g., Jarvis v. Johnson*, 668 F.2d 740 (3d Cir. 1982). Federal courts have also sanctioned counsel for waiting until the trial date to settle. *White v. Raymark Industries, Inc.*, 783 F.2d 1175 (4th Cir. 1986).

Among these techniques are the use of summary jury trials, minitrials, arbitrations and masters or experts—including those appointed by the court under Fed. R. Evid. Rule 706.

A. Summary Jury Trials

Pursuant to a 1984 U.S. Judicial Conference Resolution the experimental use of summary jury trials was endorsed "as a potentially effective means of promoting the fair and equitable settlement of potentially lengthy civil jury trials." *See generally* Lambros, *The Summary Jury Trial and Other Alternative Methods of Dispute Resolution*, 103 F.R.D. 461 (1984); Jacoubovitch & Moore, *Summary Jury Trials in the Northern District of Ohio* (FJC 1982). The summary jury trial is an alternative dispute resolution technique which utilizes trial by jury. The summary jury trial may be conducted by a judge or magistrate and involves jurors from the district court jury pool. The summary jury trial is commenced after the completion of discovery and the resolution of dispositive motions. A pretrial conference and rulings on *in limine* motions sets the stage for the summary trial. Three days before the summary trial, counsel must submit a trial brief and proposed jury instructions. The proceedings are not open to the public and, unless the court directs otherwise, they are not transcribed. Evidence is presented through counsel; no testimony is adduced through sworn witnesses, although anticipated testimony and exhibits are presented to the jury. Opening and closing arguments are consolidated to provide an overview of the trial evidence.

Courts may schedule summary jury trials under Fed. R. Civ. P. Rule 16(a) and (c). However, in keeping with the principle that settlement is not mandatory, a district judge may not force parties to participate. For example, in *Strandell v. Jackson County*, 838 F.2d 884 (7th Cir. 1987), the Seventh Circuit vacated a contempt order based on plaintiffs' counsel's refusal to cooperate in a summary jury trial. On appeal, counsel challenged the trial court's authority to mandate the procedure and argued that he should not have been compelled to reveal trial strategy and case preparation prior to trial. The Seventh Circuit agreed and reasoned that although Rule 16 was intended to foster settlement through extrajudicial devices, "it was not intended to require that an unwilling litigant be sidetracked from the normal course of litigation." The Court continued: "While the drafters intended that the trial judge 'explor[e] the use of procedures other than litigation to resolve the dispute,'—including '*urging* the litigants to employ adjudicatory techniques outside the courthouse,'—they clearly did not intend to *require* the parties to take part in such activities." 838 F.2d at 887.

Litigants faced with a summary jury trial prospect should carefully weigh its advantages and disadvantages in the given case. The revelation of trial strategy could prejudice a litigant. Moreover, because of the absence of witnesses, credibility assessments and probing cross-examination, the process can distort the merits of a case and, to that extent, actually impair a reasonable settlement. *See, e.g., Perspective*, 4 BNA Civil Trial Manual 96 (March 23, 1988) (collecting academic and judicial criticism of summary jury trials).

B. Minitrials, Arbitration, Masters and Experts

Unlike summary jury trials which utilize the judicial system, the minitrial is a voluntary, private and non-binding process in which lawyers and experts make summary presentations and rebuttal arguments. Along with management representatives of each party, the minitrial is conducted by a neutral advisor. The advisor may, if the parties agree, advise each party of its relative strengths and weaknesses. *See generally* Green, *Growth of the Minitrial*, 9 Litigation 12 (1982). Non-binding arbitration and proceedings before masters are similiar to the minitrial in that the parties are provided with an objective assessment of their positions. Depending upon the circumstances of the case, it may be useful for the arbitrators or masters to be experts in particular fields or former judges or magistrates who have been trained in the adjudicatory system. Binding arbitration, based on the parties' agreement, provides another method of alternative dispute resolution. Whether governed by the Federal Abitration Act, 9 U.S.C. §§ 1 *et seq.*, or applicable state law, arbitration is designed to afford an economical and efficient resolution of disputes. Counsel should carefully consider, however, whether to forego the tools of federal court practice, including discovery, motion practice and appellate review, in favor of binding arbitration. Whereas summary jury trials, minitrials and non-binding arbitration are devices which, if they fail, will leave litigants to the trial process, once parties agree to arbitrate their dispute, the opportunity for judicial review is highly circumscribed. 9 U.S.C. § 10 (limiting the grounds on which arbitral awards can be vacated).

IV. THE NEGOTIATION PROCESS

Without doubt, effective negotiation technique is an art, and any effort to reduce the negotiation process to a mechanical formula would be of no practical significance. During the past decade, law schools have added the discipline of negotiation to their curriculae; more recently, academic and professional literature on the topic has proliferated. *See, e.g.*, Peck, *Cases and Materials on Negotiation* (1980); Nolan, *Settlement Negotiations*, 11 Litigation 17 (1985). Indeed, works such as Fisher & Fry, *Getting To Yes: Negotiating Agreements Without Giving In* (1981), reached wide-ranging audiences comprising the business as well as the legal worlds.

Perhaps one common ground in the various approaches to the subject is the principle that prerequisite to an effective compromise is counsel's formulation of a realistic objective. Absent a reasoned goal, settlement negotiations will not be promising. The conduct of the negotiations will necessarily vary in accordance with the styles and experiences of the adversaries. Various age-old conceptions of negotiations are not readily subject to empirical verification. Some believe that the first side to raise settlement is showing weakness; others discount the notion as inconsistent with contemporary practice. Especially in simple cases or those where liability is apparent, initiation of settlement talks can hardly be disadvantageous. The effectiveness of high offers, low counter-offers, artifical deadlines, "good guy-bad guy" approaches, artificial client constraints, take-it-or-leave-it demands and the like necessarily corresponds to the nature of the dispute and the credibility and skill of counsel. Outlandish proposals are generally of little value in furthering settlement opportunities. Experienced counsel often conclude that any offer or counter-offer should be founded on an articulable rationale, whether addressed to legal positions, amount of loss, equities involved in the dispute or realistic assessment of what the fact-finder will determine after trial. For this reason, negotiations should not begin until counsel has sufficiently investigated the case with respect to both damage and liability issues. *See generally* Peck, *Cases and Materials on Negotiation* (1980).

Counsel should also be cognizant of collateral uses and abuses of the settlement process. Negotiations may serve as a vehicle for "free" discovery; settlement discussions may also divert counsel from the aggressive prosecution or defense of a matter. In addition, counsel must make certain that the adversary is authorized to make and accept offers. Accordingly, counsel must continually evaluate the progress of negotiations from the overall perspective of the litigation.

V. SUBSTANTIVE LAW GOVERNING SETTLEMENTS

A. Evidentiary Issues

The Federal Rules of Evidence explicitly recognize a settlement "privilege." Fed. R. Evid. 408, as a matter of public policy, has expanded the common law rule which governs the settlement process and provides:

> Evidence of (1) furnishing or offering or promising to furnish, or (2) accepting or offering or promising to accept, a valuable consideration in compromising or attempting to compromise a claim which was disputed as to either validity or amount, is not admissible to prove liability for or invalidity of the claim or its amount. Evidence of conduct or statements made in compromise negotiations is likewise not admissible. This rule does not require the exclusion of any evidence otherwise discoverable merely because it

is presented in the course of compromise negotiations. This rule also does not require exclusion when the evidence is offered for another purpose, such as proving bias or prejudice of a witness, negativing a contention of undue delay, or proving an effort to obstruct a criminal investigation or prosecution.

See generally 2 *Weinstein's Evidence* ¶¶ 408 [1] et seq. (1986).

Counsel should be aware that despite the fact that settlement discussions are generally inadmissible, under certain circumstances, third-parties or non-settling parties may, upon a showing of need, seek to discover the substance of settlement negotiations on the ground that it may lead to admissible evidence. Compare *Manufacturing Systems, Inc. v. Computer Technology, Inc.*, 99 F.R.D. 335, 336 (E.D. Wis. 1983) (requiring reasonable likelihood that information relating to settlement negotiations will lead to discovery of admissible evidence), with *Bottaro v. Hatton Associates*, 35 F.R.D. 158 (E.D.N.Y. 1982) (requiring a particularized showing that admissible evidence will be generated). Accordingly, counsel should be careful in protecting highly confidential information during the course of negotiations.

Because of public policies favoring settlement and a recognition that the range of possible motivations underlying efforts to compromise undercut their probative value, a settlement privilege will also apply to formal offers of judgment under Fed. R. Civ. P. Rule 68. See generally 2 *Weinstein's Evidence* ¶ 408 [7]. Fed. R. Civ. P. Rule 68 serves as a cost-shifting mechanism pursuant to which a plaintiff will be liable for costs—and, depending on the language of the statute on which his claim is based, attorney's fees—incurred after rejecting an offer of judgment if he loses at trial or recovers less than the amount offered. See *Marek v. Chesny*, 473 U.S. 1 (1985). See generally 12 C. Wright & A. Miller, *Federal Practice and Procedure* §§ 3001 et seq. (1973 and 1987 Supp.). Accordingly, Fed. R. Civ. P. Rule 68 provides that: "An offer not accepted shall be deemed withdrawn and evidence thereof is not admissible except in a proceeding to determine costs."

B. Agency Issues

A final settlement of a controversy is largely governed by contract law. Principals involved in a dispute ultimately have the authority to effectuate the settlement. However, under familiar agency principles, counsel in a litigated matter may be authorized to enter into a settlement on behalf of his client. See generally *Compromise - Attorney's Authority*, 30 A.L.R.2d 944. Thus, an attorney may have actual authority (whether express or implied) based on the principal's words or conduct which would reasonably cause the agent to believe that the principal desires the agent to act on his account. Restatement (Second) of Agency § 26 (1958). Further, an attorney may have apparent authority if, by words or conduct, a third party reasonably believes that the principal consents to have an act done on his behalf by a person purporting to act for him. *Id.* § 27. The Third Circuit has recognized that enforcing settlements on the basis of apparent authority "is consistent with the principles of agency law, the policies favoring settlement generally, and the notions of fairness to the parties in the adjudicatory process." *Edwards v. Born, Inc.*, 792 F.2d 387, 390 (3rd Cir. 1986). Where a client, informed of settlement conferences, advised counsel that arriving at a "settlement figure" was counsel's task, implied actual authority may have been conferred. *Id.* Further, as counsel of record, a lawyer's execution of a stipulation of settlement may be binding under the vicarious admission provisions of Fed. R. Evid. 801(d)(2)(c). *See* Mansfield, *Lawyers' Admissions*, 12 Litigation 39, 42 (1985).

Accordingly, counsel should raise the issue of settlement with his client and determine whether he is, in fact, authorized to participate in or reach a settlement on his client's behalf. To avoid potential misunderstandings, counsel should obtain specific instructions on the amount and terms of settlement which the client has authorized.

VI. PROCEDURAL LAW GOVERNING SETTLEMENTS

A. Judicial Approval

Pursuant to the Federal Rules, certain kinds of cases cannot be settled without judical approval. For example, Fed. R. Civ. P. Rule 23 (e), which governs class actions, provides:

> A class action shall be not dismissed or compromised without the approval of the court, and notice of the proposed dismissal or compromise shall be given to all members of the class in such manner as the court directs.

See, e.g., U.S. Trust Co. of New York v. Executive Life Ins. Co., 791 F.2d 10 (2d Cir. 1986). Similarly, shareholder derivative actions and cases brought by or against members of unincorporated associations as a class cannot be dismissed or compromised absent judically directed notice to affected parties of the proposed settlement and judicial approval. Fed. R. Civ. P. 23.1 and 23.2. *See, e.g., Mokhiber v. Cohn*, 783 F.2d 26 (2d Cir. 1986). The purpose of these rules is to assure that the settlement is fair. *See, e.g., Ficalora v. Lockheed California Co.*, 751 F. 2d 995 (9th Cir. 1985).

Rules promulgated by the various district courts also impact on settlement. For example, in the Southern and Eastern Districts of New York, actions filed by or on behalf of incompetents or infants cannot be settled or otherwise terminated without leave of court embodied in an order, judgment

SETTLEMENT

or decree. Moreover, the proceeding attendant to an application to settle on behalf of incompetents or infants should conform to New York State practice, unless for good cause shown the court decides otherwise. Southern and Eastern Districts of New York Rule 28. Similarly, in wrongful death actions with respect to which substantive law would require apportionment of the recovery, settlements must be approved by the court. Rule 29. *See also* N.D.N.Y. Rules 36 and 37; W.D.N.Y. Rule 25.

B. Formal Matters

Once a case has been settled, the parties may terminate the action or embody the terms of the settlement in a formal judgment.

With the exception of class action cases and proceedings in which the federal court has appointed a receiver, civil actions may be dismissed: (1) unilaterally by a plaintiff without court order prior to the joinder of issue or the filing of a summary judgment motion; or (2) by stipulation of all parties who have appeared. Fed. R. Civ. P. Rule 41. Unless the plaintiff had previously dismissed an action in any court based on the same claim or if the stipulation expressly provides otherwise, the dismissal is without prejudice. A Rule 41 dismissal need only provide the caption and file number of the case, a statement that it is dismissed and signature of counsel of record. *See generally* 9 C. Wright & A. Miller, *Federal Practice and Procedure* §§ 2361 *et seq.* (1971); 3 *Bender's Federal Practice Forms* Form 3108 (1988). Aside from dismissal of a settled matter, the parties can enter into a stipulation for the entry of judgment which would take the form of all other judgments filed in a federal court.

Various district courts have promulgated court rules which govern both the content and timing of stipulations for the entry of judgment or dismissal. For example, the Western District of New York requires that signed agreements for judgment or dismissal must be filed within ten days after a case settles unless the time is enlarged by the court. Western District of New York Rule 25(b). The failure to do so may result in the court's entering "an order dismissing the case as settled, without costs, and on the merits." *Id.*

Depending on the nature and complexity of a case, settlement often requires formal documentation including settlement agreements and the exchange of releases. Settlement agreements and releases need not be incorporated in the stipulation of dismissal or judgment; nevertheless counsel may agree to do so for purposes of expanding the vehicles for redressing defaults.

1. Settlement Agreements

Settlement agreements are no more than contracts executed by the parties.[5] *See, e.g., Miller v. Fairchild Industries, Inc.*, 797 F.2d 727 (9th Cir. 1986). The settlement agreement may be "ordered" or "adjudged" by the court in which event its breach is governed both by contract principles and the contempt power of the court. *See, e.g., Janus Films, Inc. v. Miller*, 801 F.2d 578 (2d Cir. 1986).

Typically, settlement agreements address matters such as: payment and other obligation terms, releases of claims, covenants not to sue, denial of liability, indemnification, case dismissal, choice of law, default, notice and cure periods, most favored-nation protection, authority, confidentiality, construction, integration, severability, assignment, written amendments, return or destruction of documents produced in discovery, approval of counsel, party signature and notarization. *See* Lindsey, *Documentation of Settlements*, 27 Ark. L. Rev. 27 (1973). Parties may also want to consider detailed structured payment provisions[6] and an array of guaranty provisions. In multiparty litigation, settling counsel must consider indemnification and contribution issues under applicable law. *See, e.g.,* Dewey, *Traps in Multitortfeasor Settlements*, 13 Litigation 41 (1987).

2. Releases

Although a dismissal of a case with prejudice precludes a new action based on the same claims, because of the uncertainty of whether the recharacterization of the underlying facts or legal theory may survive *res judicata* challenge, the party paying for the settlement may wish to have a general release of claims. Counsel may elect to use any number of "form" releases which, although often archaic and repetitive, nevertheless have withstood legal challenge. It is critical, however, that counsel carefully define who the releasors and releasees will be and consider precisely what the scope of the release will be. Reference to state law is necessary in that some states have specific rules

---

5 The terms of a settlement agreement may be governed by applicable state law. Accordingly, counsel must ascertain whether it must be in writing or set forth on a court record to be effective. *See, e.g.,* N.Y. Civ. Prac. L. & R. 2104; *Pugh v. Super Fresh Food Markets, Inc.*, 640 F. Supp. 1306 (E.D. Pa. 1986) (settlement agreement voluntarily entered into is binding regardless of writing); *Vari-O-Matic Machine Corp. v. New York Sewing Machine Attachment Corp.*, 629 F. Supp. 257 (S.D.N.Y. 1986) (failure to complete a formal stipulation does not mean that settlement in unenforceable).

6 In structured settlements, a part of the settlement fund is invested in annuities, trusts or similar vehicles to pay future benefits to the plaintiff. Structured settlements are particularly useful in settlements on behalf of minors and incompetents. They can also have beneficial tax consequences because of the payout feature. *See generally* BNA Civil Trial Manual Trial Practice Series 51:701.

with respect to the enforceability of release provisions. *See, e.g.*, California Civil Code § 1542 (release of unknown claims unenforceable).

3. Setting Aside Settlement Agreements and Releases

Because settlement agreements and releases are governed by contract law principles, counsel should consider whether traditional contract defenses might impair the enforceability of the settlement provisions. Case law is replete with settlement provisions being set aside on grounds of fraud, *e.g.*, *Rothenberg v. Kamen*, 735 F.2d 753 (2d Cir. 1984), misrepresentation, *e.g.*, *Saunders v. General Services Corp.*, 659 F. Supp. 1042 (E.D. Va. 1987) and mutual mistake, *e.g.*, *Reid v. Graybeal*, 437 F. Supp. 24 (W.D. Okl. 1977). Additionally, defenses based on lack of capacity or authority are particularly relevant to settlements on behalf of minors, incompetents and estates.

VII. ETHICAL ISSUES

A lawyer's conduct during the settlement process is, of course, governed by applicable standards of ethics. The Model Rules of Professional Conduct ("MRPC") and the ABA Model Code of Professional Responsibility ("CPR") are the primary sources of rules addressing counsel's relationship with a client, his adversary and the tribunal. *See generally* Rubin, *A Causerie on Lawyer's Ethics in Negotiation*, 35 La. L. Rev. 577 (1975).

A. Responsibilities to Client

MRPC Rule 1.2 outlines a lawyer's responsibilities and obligations during the course of representation and provides, in relevant part:

> (a) A lawyer shall abide by a client's decision concerning the objectives of representation . . . and shall abide by a client's decision whether to accept an offer of settlement of a matter.

See also CPR EC 7-7 ("In certain areas of legal representation not affecting the merits of the cause or substantially prejudicing the rights of a client, a lawyer is entitled to make decisions on his own. But otherwise the authority to make decisions is exclusively that of the client . . .")

MRPC Rule 1.4 provides:

> (a) A lawyer shall keep a client reasonably informed about the status of a matter and promptly comply with reasonable requests for information.
>
> (b) A lawyer shall explain a matter to the extent reasonably necessary to permit the client to make informed decisions reagarding the representation.

The Official Comment to Rule 1.4 emphasizes a lawyer's obligation to keep his client abreast of the matter, and observes that "[a] lawyer who receives from opposing counsel an offer of settlement in a civil controversy . . . should promptly inform the client of its substance unless prior discussions with the client have left it clear that the proposal will be unacceptable."

A lawyer's failure to inform a client of settlement offers or to settle on terms acceptable to the client may not only violate ethical standards but may also constitute malpractice. Similiarly, counsel's settlement of a case without authority of the client may give rise to malpractice exposure.

B. Responsibilities to Adversary Counsel

Although negotiation pervades a lawyer's practice, the Code of Professional Responsibility is remarkably silent in establishing ethical precepts to govern the negotiation process. While the CPR does prescribe knowingly making a false statement, CPR DR 7-102(A)(5), participating in the creation or presentation of false evidence, CPR DR 7-102(A)(6), assisting a client or otherwise engaging in illegal or fraudulent conduct, CPR DR 7-102(A)(7) & (8), it does not speak directly to the boundaries of proper negotiation. Of course, counsel may not communicate with a represented adverse party. CPR DR 7-104(A)(1). In addition, ethics opinions have held that an attorney cannot condone or assist in party to party negotiations if the direct purpose of those negotiations is to exclude the presence of counsel. *E.g.*, ABA Ethics Opinion 323 (Opinion No. 75).

The MRPC echoes the CPR in providing that: "In the course of representing a client a lawyer shall not knowingly: (a) make a false statement of material fact or law to a third person. . . ." MRPC Rule 4.1. The Official Comment to Rule 4.1 explicitly analyzes prohibitions against mispresentations in the context of practical day-to-day negotiations:

> This Rule refers to statements of fact. Whether a particular statement should be regarded as one of fact can depend on the circumstances. Under generally accepted conventions in negotiation, certain types of statements ordinarily are not taken as statements of material fact. Estimates of price or value placed on the subject of a transaction and a party's intentions as to an acceptable settlement of a claim are in this category. . . .

Material misrepresentation during the course of settlement negotiations, apart from ethical considerations, may constitute a basis to set aside the settlement agreement.

CPR DR 7-105 provides that a lawyer may not present or threaten to present criminal charges solely to gain an advantage in a civil matter. *See generally* Annot., *Initiating or Threatening to Initiate Criminal Prosecution* as a Ground for Disciplining Counsel, 42 A.L.R. 4th 1000. Ethics opinions of various bar associations have expanded this concept to prohibit threats to prosecute unrelated civil claims for purposes of obtaining a more advantageous settlement. *E.g.*, Association of the Bar of the City of New York Ethics Opinion 447.

C. Responsibilities to the Tribunal

Consistent with CPR DR 7-102 (A)(5), MRPC Rule 3.3 prohibits a lawyer from making a false statement of material fact or law to a tribunal. While it is unusual for an attorney to have personal knowledge of the facts set forth in documents prepared for litigation, statements made in a lawyer's affidavit or in open court "may properly be made only when the lawyer knows the assertion is true or believes it to be true on the basis of a reasonably diligent inquiry." MRPC Rule 3.3, Comment. This provision should apply to judicially-supervised settlement conferences.

Undoubtedly settlements based on illegal or against-public-policy provisions violate both the Code and the Model Rules. While illegal provisions are readily ascertainable, public policy issues are not necessarily apparent. For example, until 1986, it was debatable whether counsel in a civil rights case could negotiate for a waiver of attorney's fees in a settlement agreement. The Supreme Court, in *Evans v. Jeff D.*, 475 U.S. 717 (1986), held that such a provision was enforceable, although fee waiver issues continue to be troublesome. *See, e.g., Ebbinghouse v. Clark*, 844 F.2d 1506 (11th Cir. 1988). Similarly, in *Town of Newton v. Rumery*, 480 U.S. 386 (1987), the Supreme Court reversed the First Circuit and held as not *per se* invalid release-dismissal agreements pursuant to which civil rights plaintiffs agree not to sue public officials for alleged constitutional violations in exchange for the government's promise not to bring criminal charges against them.

Currently, courts and ethics committees take divergent approaches to "Mary Carter" agreements, pursuant to which settlements are concealed from non-settling parties. *See generally* BNA Civil Trial Manual Trial Practice Series, 51:650. Counsel must take care to assure that extraordinary provisions in a negotiated settlement agreement are consistent with applicable substantive as well as ethical rules.

CHAPTER NINETEEN

JURY TRIALS

by Frederic Block, Esq.*

I. INTRODUCTION

This chapter will examine the right to a jury trial in the federal courts, how the right is asserted and protected, and the role of the lawyer and the court in selecting the jury, instructing the jury on the law, and eliciting the jury's verdict. In keeping with the focus of this book, the chapter is confined to civil actions and citations of authority are primarily to United States Supreme Court, Second Circuit Court of Appeals and New York Federal District Court cases. From time to time comparisons are made to New York State law and, in particular, to those sections of the CPLR which are at variance with the federal rules. As always, the presentation of the material has been designed to assist the practitioner in the practical understanding and application of the law, but references frequently have been made to the principal treatises, Moore's and Wright's, for in-depth analyses.[1]

II. THE ORIGIN AND RIGHT OF JURY TRIAL[2]

The seventh amendment provides that (1) "[i]n suits at common law, where the value in controversy shall exceed twenty dollars, the right of trial

---

* David Yaffe, Mechel Bertholet and Lane T. Maxson have provided valuable research assistance for this chapter.

---

[1] Moore refers to J. Moore, *Moore's Federal Practice* (2d ed. 1948 & Supp. 1987), and Wright refers to C. Wright & A. Miller, *Federal Practice and Procedure* (1971 & Supp. 1984). They are hereafter referenced as "_____ Moore _____" and "_____ Wright _____," respectively.

---

[2] *See generally* 9 Wright §§ 2301-2307 and 5 Moore Par. 38.04.

by jury shall be preserved," and (2) "[n]o fact tried by a jury shall be otherwise re-examined in any Court of the United States, than according to the rules of the common law."[3]

Because the amendment simply preserves the common law right to a jury trial, Congress is free to expand the right whenever it chooses to do so. Thus, Fed. R. Civ. P. 38(a) provides that in addition to the seventh amendment, the right of jury trial "as given by a statute of the United States" shall also "be preserved to the parties inviolate." Therefore, in determining whether a cause of action carries with it the right to a jury trial in federal court the practitioner should ask whether:

1) The cause of action had its origin or existed at common law;

2) The cause of action was created by statute and the right to jury trial was extended to that cause of action be express statutory provision;

3) The cause of action is one which was created by statute, but the statute does not state whether the right to a jury trial attaches.[4]

In the first scenario, the seventh amendment creates an historical test. Since at common law jury trials only attached to actions at law,[5] there was no right to a trial by jury of claims that historically were "equitable." *Beacon*

---

[3] The right of trial by jury is embedded in the history of both English and American law. In criminal law, its roots go back to the Magna Carta of 1215 where it was declared that "[n]o Freeman shall be taken, or imprisoned, or [dispossessed], . . . or be outlawed, or exiled, or [in any way] destroyed; . . . [except] by [the] lawful Judgment of his Peers, or by the Law of the Land." 17 John (Magna Carta) CAP XXIX (1215). In reflecting on the right, Justice Story noted that "the Constitution would have been justly obnoxious to the most conclusive objection if it had not recognized and confirmed it in the most solemn terms." 2 Story, Commentaries on the Constitution, 1833, § 1779.

[4] In New York State the right to a trial by jury is constitutionally guaranteed "in all cases in which it had been used at the time of the adoption of the State Constitution in 1777 and, additionally, in actions where the right had been created by statute between 1777 and 1894." *Murphy v. American Home Products Corp.*, 136 A.D.2d 229, 231, 527 N.Y.S.2d 1 (1st Dep't 1988). In addition, the Legislature has statutorily provided that issues of fact shall be tried by a jury, unless jury trial is waived, in the following actions: (1) "an action in which a party demands and sets forth facts which would permit a judgment for a sum of money only"; (2) "an action of ejectment; for dower; for waste; for abatement of and damages for a nuisance; to recover a chattel; or for determination of a claim to real property under article fifteen of the real property actions and proceedings law," and (3) "any other action in which a party is entitled by the constitution or by express provision of law to a trial by jury." N.Y. Civ. Prac. L. and R. § 4101 (McKinney 1963) (hereafter "CPLR"). The limitation of "a sum of money only" will preclude a jury trial where equitable relief and monetary damages are sought in the same action. *See Murphy*, 527 N.Y.S.2d at 3-4.

[5] For a full explanation of the basis of this principle, *see* 9 Wright §§ 2302, 2316.

Theaters, Inc. v. Westover, 359 U.S. 500 (1959).[6] If the nature of the action was one which sought monetary damages, it was invariably considered to be an action at law to which the right to a jury trial attached.[7] By contrast, equitable actions were those seeking nonmonetary relief.[8]

In the second scenario, resort need only be had to a particular statute, and Congress is free to expand the right to jury trial, even in actions that were historically equitable.[9]

The troublesome area is in the third scenario, where new actions have been created by statute but Congress has not provided for the mode of trial. Here the court must look to the nearest historical analogue, and if the substance of the cause of action has a common law parallel the Seventh Amendment nonetheless will attach even though the action did not exist as such at common law. *Pernell v. Southall Realty*, 416 U.S. 363 (1974).

Finding the common law analogue is not always a simple matter. In all cases, the test is whether the nature of the cause of action is one impacting *legal* rights or *equitable* rights. As the Supreme Court explained in *Ross v. Bernhard*, 396 U.S. 531 (1970):

> The Seventh Amendment preserves to litigants the right to jury trial in suits at common law—
>
> "Not merely suits, which the *common* law recognized among its old and settled proceedings, but suits in which *legal* rights were to be ascertained and determined, in contradistinction to those where equitable rights alone were recognized, and equitable remedies

---

[6] *See* 9 Wright §§ 2302, 2308, 2309. In *Parsons v. Bedford, Breedlove & Robeson*, 28 U.S. 433 (3 Pet. 1830), Justice Story wrote "it is well known that in civil cases, in courts of equity and admiralty, juries do not intervene, and that courts of equity use the trial by jury only in extraordinary cases to inform the conscience of the court." *Id.* at 446.

[7] Examples of such actions were damages for assault, battery and false imprisonment (known at common law as "trespass to the person"); negligence, fraud, slander, nuisance and malicious prosecution (known at common law as "trespass on the case"); wrongful detention of personal property (known at common law as "detinue" and "replevin"); conversion (known at common law as "trover"), and breach of contract (known at common law as "assumpsit"). *See* 5 Moore Par. 38.11[5].

[8] Common law examples of such actions are those for specific performance, injunctions, quieting of title, rescission and cancellation, reformation, setting aside of fraudulent conveyances, accountings and breach of fiduciary duties. *See* 5 Moore Par. 38.11[6].

[9] For example, 29 U.S.C. § 626(c)(1) (1985) provides that any person who has been the subject of age discrimination may bring a civil action "for such legal or equitable relief as will effectuate the purposes of this chapter," and subdivision (c) (2) of § 626 provides that a "person shall be entitled to a trial by jury of any issue of fact in any such action for recovery of amounts owing as a result of a violation of this chapter, regardless of whether equitable relief is sought by any party in such action."

were administered. * * * In a just sense, the Amendment then may well be construed to embrace all suits, which are not of equity and admiralty jurisdiction, whatever may be the peculiar form which they may assume to settle legal rights."

Id. at 533, quoting from *Parsons v. Bedford, Breedlove & Robeson*, 28 U.S. 433 (3 Pet. 1830).

As a general proposition, where the statutory cause of action allows for the recovery of compensatory damages the court will allow the case to be tried by a jury. *See, e.g., Curtis v. Loether*, 415 U.S. 189 (1974). Where, however, the statute looks primarily towards equitable remedies, the action will undoubtedly be tried by the court. *Nobile v. Pension Comm. of Pension Plan*, 611 F. Supp. 725 (S.D.N.Y. 1985); *see also O'Brien v. King World Productions, Inc.*, 669 F. Supp. 639 (S.D.N.Y. 1987).[10] In making this assessment, the court will analyze both the nature of the action as well as the nature of the relief. *See Tull v. United States*, 481 U.S. 412 (1987).[11]

III. THE JOINING OF LEGAL AND EQUITABLE ISSUES IN ONE LITIGATION

In 1938, the Federal Rules of Civil Procedure effected the merger of law and equity.[12] Litigants were now required to present their case in one "civil action" even if it contained both legal and equitable claims. While the federal courts would now hear both types of issues in one case, Fed. R. Civ. P. 38 preserved the right to a jury trial for those issues triable of right by a jury.

---

[10] At issue in *Nobile* was whether a right to jury trial exists under the ERISA statute, 29 U.S.C. § 1001 (1985), which is silent on the issue. The historical analogue that was invoked by the Court in *Nobile*, a suit for pension benefits, drew on the law of trusts, and therefore the Court held that the case was one for the court and not for the jury. *See also Pollock v. Castrovinci*, 476 F. Supp. 606 (S.D.N.Y. 1979).

[11] Thus, while a suit to determine and adjudicate the amount of fees owing to a lawyer by a client under a retainer agreement is a traditional action at law for damages, subject to jury trial, *Simler v. Conner*, 372 U.S. 221, 223 (1963), an action to enforce an attorney's lien pursuant to statute is considered to be equitable in nature since it more closely resembles a foreclosure action than an action on contract. *See Rosenman, Colin, Freund, Lewis & Cohen v. Richard*, 656 F. Supp. 196 (S.D.N.Y. 1987).

[12] *See* Fed. R. Civ. P. 1 and 2. New York State law is to the same effect. Thus, CPLR § 103(a) provides that "[t]here is only one form of civil action. The distinctions between actions at law and suits in equity, and the forms of those actions and suits, have been abolished."

JURY TRIALS

Notwithstanding the merger of legal and equitable issues into one litigation, the court and counsel are required to separate the "legal" from the "equitable" in order to determine which issues are jury issues. The process is not always a simple one.[13]

If a single claim is presented and a single remedy demanded, it is usually a simple matter to determine whether the issue is legal or equitable. In practice, however, one of three situations is likely to exist: (1) where a party has a single claim, but demands various remedies, some available at law and some available only in equity; (2) where a party, by joining several claims and/or counterclaims, asserts several claims for relief or demands several remedies arising out of a single claim for relief; (3) where a party seeks relief that would be legal in nature but invokes a procedural device that historically has been available only in equity.

A. Mixing of Legal and Equitable Remedies with a Single Claim

A typical case of this nature is where a party seeks both damages and injunctive relief. The right to a jury does not depend on whether the claim seeks basically equitable or legal relief; rather, if a legal issue can be identified the right to jury trial attaches even though the resolution of that legal issue may entitle the successful party to the fashioning of an equitable remedy by the court. Thus, in the same action a jury can resolve the issue of fact common to the legal and equitable requests for relief, fixing monetary damages where indicated, while leaving to the court the fashioning of any equitable remedies. *Dairy Queen, Inc. v. Wood*, 369 U.S. 469 (1962); *cf.* CPLR § 4101(1) and *see* n.4, *supra*.

The same principle applies regardless of the number of claims or causes of action asserted by a party in a particular action.

B. Defenses and Counterclaims

When the whole panoply of integrated litigation is considered, numerous avenues exist for the commingling of legal and equitable issues in one litigation. Thus, "legal" counterclaims and defenses may be interposed in an equitable action and, conversely, equitable counterclaims and defenses may be interposed in legal actions.

Initially, a party's right to a jury trial cannot be adversely affected by the nature of his adversary's answer, nor, conversely, does a party lose his right to a jury trial by raising legal issues in a counterclaim. It "is the issues, not

---

13 Consistent with the principle that all issues should be resolved in one litigation, Fed. R. Civ. P. 18 permits the joinder of wholly unrelated claims, be they legal or equitable.

the form of case," which determines the method of trial. *Beaunit Mills, Inc. v. Eday Fabric Sales Corp.*, 124 F.2d 563, 566 (2d Cir. 1942).[14]

Where legal and equitable issues relate to separate factual matters, it makes no difference which issues are first resolved because no possible prejudice can come to pass.[15]

Where, however, equitable and legal claims share the same common factual aspects, the sequence of the trial becomes important since the same set of facts cannot both be presented to a jury and to the court for separate determination. This type of situation is likely to happen with compulsory counterclaims, which are claims arising "out of the transaction or occurrence that is the subject matter of the opposing party's claim." Fed. R. Civ. P. 13(a). Under Rule 13(a), such claims must be interposed as counterclaims, whether the action, as initiated, is essentially equitable or legal or contains both legal and equitable claims. In these types of cases, where there is an overlap of factual issues, the legal claims must be tried first, even if they appear for the first time in a counterclaim, in order to avoid depriving the party who asserts a legal claim of a determination by a jury on the common fact issue. *Beacon Theaters, Inc. v. Westover*, 359 U.S. 500 (1959); *see* 9 Wright § 2338.

Thus, under the *Beacon Theaters* rule, all legal claims must be determined prior to any final court determination of the equitable claims.

C. Procedural Devices at Variance with Relief

Consistent with the principle that the substance of the action rather than the form of the litigation governs the right to jury trial, nothing turns upon the procedural devices employed by the parties in bringing their litigation into court. Thus, procedural devices such as an interpleader, a class suit, a derivative action or intervention, that historically have been available only in equity, do not defeat the right to a jury trial on issues which are legal in nature. *Ross v. Bernhard*, 396 U.S. 531 (1970).[16]

In a similar vein, where Congress has created new remedies, such as the declaratory judgment action, 28 U.S.C. 2201 (1982 & Supp. 1988), which

---

[14] *See also Dairy Queen, Inc. v. Wood*, 369 U.S. 469 (1962), where the Court stressed that "the constitutional right to trial by jury cannot be made to depend upon the choice of words used in the pleadings." *Id.* at 477.

[15] While the order of trial will not here be a factor in preserving the integrity of the jury trial, the court will as a matter of practice invariably first allow for the resolution of the jury trial issues before resolving the equitable issues.

[16] *See* 7 Wright § 1718 (interpleader); 7A Wright § 1801 (class actions); 7A Wright § 1837 (derivative suits); 7A Wright § 1910 (intervention). *See also* 5 Moore Par. 38.38(1) (interpleader), 5 Moore Par. 38.38(2) (class actions), 5 Moore Par. 38.38(3) (intervention).

has neither legal nor equitable historical roots, the form of litigation cannot obscure the essential nature of the action. Hence, when the questions involved in a declaratory judgment action are traditionally common law issues, such issues must be submitted to a jury.[17] *Simler v. Conner*, 372 U.S. 221 (1963); *see also* Fed. R. Civ. P. 57.

D. Facts Affecting Jurisdiction and Venue

Matters dealing with the court's jurisdiction and the place of trial are the subject of preliminary hearings under Fed. R. Civ. P. 12, and contested facts which must be resolved to determine whether the court has jurisdiction of a particular case and whether the venue is proper are generally considered to be issues of fact for the court. *Land v. Dollar*, 330 U.S. 731 (1947).[18]

However, as suggested by the Court in *Land*, if the jurisdictional factual issue also impacts upon the merits of the case, the court would have to withhold its determination on the jurisdictional issue until the jury resolved the factual issue if the merits entitle the party to a jury trial.

E. Impact of State Law

The right to a jury trial in federal courts is purely a federal matter and, therefore, is never governed or controlled by state law.[19] *Simler v. Conner*, 372 U.S. 221 (1963). Hence, it makes no difference whether the issue to be tried is in the federal court by reason of diversity, pendent jurisdiction or removal,[20] since no matter how the case comes to court the right to a jury trial

---

17 For a full discussion of the advent of the declaratory judgment action and its effect upon jury trials, *see* 10A Wright §§ 2751-2771 and 5 Moore Par. 38.29.

18 Since the court has the inherent power to always determine whether it has jurisdiction over an action, it could, if it chooses, determine to exercise this power by having a jury resolve a particular jurisdictional fact issue. *Gilbert v. David*, 235 U.S. 561 (1915); *Romero v. Int'l Terminal Operating Co.*, 142 F. Supp. 570 (1956), *aff'd*, 244 F.2d 409 (2d Cir. 1957), *rev'd on other grounds*, 358 U.S. 354 (1959).

19 The courts have rejected the application of the *Erie* doctrine, *Erie R. R. v. Tompkins*, 304 U.S. 64 (1938), under which the "substantive" rules of common law are governed by state law in diversity cases, while the "procedure" to be used is subject to federal rule. Hence, the courts liken the issue to be more closely aligned to "procedure." *See generally* 19 Wright §§ 4503-4513 and 5 Moore Par. 38.09.

20 The procedures for the removal of cases from state court are set forth in Fed. R. Civ. P. 81(c). The grounds for removal are governed by 28 U.S.C. § 1441 (1983 & Supp. 1988). In general, actions which may have originally been brought in federal court may be removed to the federal forum. For a full analysis of the removal statutes *see* 14 Wright §§ 37-21 through 37-29.

is determined solely by reference to federal law.[21] Similarly, where state law provides for a trial by jury on an issue which is normally the subject of a bench trial in the federal forum, the issue need not be tried by jury in the federal court. *Herron v. Southern Pacific Co.*, 283 U.S. 91 (1931).[22]

Tactical Consideration

Since the right to a jury trial can depend, therefore, upon whether an issue will be litigated in either the state or federal forum, the practitioner should select his choice of forum with this consideration in mind.[23]

IV. ASSERTING, PROTECTING AND REGULATING THE RIGHT TO JURY TRIAL

A. The Demand

In order to assert the right to jury trial in a federal court a demand must be made in accordance with Fed. R. Civ. P. 38(b), which provides:

> Demand. Any party may demand a trial by jury of any issue triable of right by a jury by serving upon the other parties a demand therefor in writing at any time after the commencement of the action not later than 10 days after the service of the last pleading directed to such issue. Such demand may be indorsed upon a pleading of the party.

By contrast, under New York State law, the demand need only be asserted upon the filing of a note of issue, CPLR § 4102(a), which normally does not take place until all pretrial proceedings have been completed.[24]

---

21 Thus, where state law denies a jury trial on an issue which would be subject to jury trial in federal court, the right to jury trial attaches in the federal forum by reason of the seventh amendment even though the case originated in state court. *See Simler v. Conner*, 372 U.S. at 222. Even where the issue is not governed by the seventh amendment, the federal court may, but is not compelled to, allow for a jury trial. *See Byrd v. Blue Ridge Royal Elec. Coop.*, 356 U.S. 525 (1958).

22 In *Herron*, the Supreme Court held that the district court could direct a verdict on the ground of contributory negligence despite a state constitutional provision that the defense "shall, in all cases whatsoever, be a question of fact and shall, at all times, be left to the jury." 283 U.S. at 95; *see also* 9 Wright § 2525.

23 A good example of where the choice of forum would make a difference is portrayed in *Tobin v. Greenberg*, 659 F. Supp. 959 (S.D.N.Y. 1987), a diversity case, where the court ruled that the issue of whether a plaintiff sustained a "serious injury" supporting a claim for pain and suffering under the New York State no-fault law required a jury trial in federal court even though New York State law was to the contrary.

24 Under New York State law, a Certificate of Readiness certifying to the completion of all pretrial proceedings must accompany the Note of Issue. *See* McKinney's 1988 New York Rules of Court § 202.21 (22 NYCRR § 202.21).

JURY TRIALS

Rule 38(b) must be read in conjunction with Fed. R. Civ. P. 38(c), which allows a party to specify which issues he wishes tried by a jury. This allows for some jury trial issues to be tried by a jury and others by the court. It provides:

> Same: Specification of Issues. In the demand a party may specify the issues which the party wishes so tried; the party shall be deemed to have demanded trial by jury for all the issues so triable. If the party has demanded trial by jury for only some of the issues, any other party within 10 days after service of the demand or such lesser time as the court may order, may serve a demand for trial by jury of any other or all of the issues of fact in the action.[25]

Viewed collectively, these two rules require the practitioner who seeks a jury trial as to issues to which the right attaches to make the following decisions: (1) which issues are for the jury; (2) when should the jury demand be asserted; (3) in what manner and form should the demand be made.

1. Identification of Issues for Jury Resolution

A general demand is all that is needed to preserve the right to a jury trial on all of the issues raised by a party in his pleading that are subject to trial by jury, and all that need be stated in the demand is that the plaintiff or defendant "demands trial by jury."[26] If a jury trial is only desired for particular issues, then the demand must so state.[27]

Once a jury trial is demanded, be it for all or some of the issues, Rule 39(a) provides that "the action shall be designated upon the docket as a jury action," and even though nothing in Rule 38(b) or 39(c) expands the substantive right to a jury trial, all issues in the case will nonetheless then be subject to jury trial unless "the court upon motion or of its own initiative finds that a right of trial by a jury of some or all of those issues does not exist under the Constitution or statutes of the United States." Fed. R. Civ. P. 39(a)(2).[28]

Therefore, to avoid nonjury issues being tried by a jury, the practitioner, when faced with either a general demand in a case which entails both jury and

---

25 The New York State rule is the same. CPLR § 4102(b).

26 *See* Bender, 3 *Bender's Federal Practice Forms*, Form 3091 (Demand for Trial by Jury).

27 *See* Bender, 3 *Bender's Federal Practice Forms*, Form 3092 (Demand for Trial by Jury - Specification of Issues). Note, also, that Fed. R. Civ. P. 39(a)(1) provides that the parties may consent to trial by the court of any issue, the mechanism being a written stipulation filed with the court or an oral stipulation made in open court on the record.

28 *See* 5 Moore Pars. 38.11[4] and 38.41.

nonjury issues, or with a specification of issues for jury trial to which the right to trial by jury does not attach, must move to strike the jury demand.[29] If this is not done, and if the court does not on its own initiative act, the nonjury issues will blossom into a jury trial. *Kelly v. Shamrock Oil & Gas Corp.*, 171 F.2d 909 (5th Cir. 1948), *cert. denied*, 337 U.S. 917 (1949).[30] When faced with a motion to strike, the court will not strike the demand altogether "but should limit it to issues on which a jury trial was properly sought." *Damsky v. Zavatt*, 289 F.2d 46, 48 (2d Cir. 1961); *see also Ring v. Spina*, 166 F.2d 546, 550 (2d Cir.), *cert. denied*, 335 U.S. 813 (1948).

a. The Effect of a General Demand

Since a general demand embraces all issues in an action that are triable by jury, no further demands need be made by any of the parties to the original action to preserve the right to jury trial on any issues raised by any of the original parties affecting the demandant, even if they be new issues. *Rosen v. Dick*, 639 F.2d 82, 91 (2d Cir. 1980). Stated otherwise, all parties have the right to rely upon the general demand of the initial pleader as to any issue that affects that party.[31] If, however, a third party is brought into the action and new issues applicable only to that new party are raised which do not affect the initial demandant, the party bringing in such third party must demand a jury trial as to any such new issues which affect such third party.[32]

Where litigation is complex, with multiple cross-claims, third-party complaints and issues affecting in various degrees many different parties, law-

---

29 *See* Bender, 3 *Bender's Federal Practice Forms*, Form 3095 (Motion to Strike Demand for Jury Trial), and Form 3097 (Motion to Strike Demand for Jury Trial as to Particular Issues).

---

30 Except as to collateral issues such as jurisdiction, venue and *forum non conveniens*. *Meeropol v. Nizer*, 505 F.2d 232 (2d Cir. 1974).

---

31 It should be noted that once a general demand is timely made, it attaches to all amended pleadings against the same parties and hence no new demand is required. *See* 5 Moore Par. 38.41.

---

32 The following example is provided by Professor Moore:
    If the demand does not pertain to certain issues then one of the parties concerned with those issues should make demand therefor. Thus, assume that A sues X; X answers and also files a third-party complaint against Y. If A makes a timely general demand, the demand embraces all the issues between A and X, and X may rely thereon and need not make a demand for those issues. It is rather strained, however, to say that A's general demand embraces the third-party issues between X and Y, with which A is not concerned. And it would seem that either X or Y should make a timely demand as to the third party issues if a jury trial is desired as to those issues. If we vary the facts and assume that A has made no demand, but that X makes a general demand at the time he serves both his answer on A and the third-party complaint on Y, then it should follow that X has demanded jury trial for the issues between him and A and between him and Y, and that both A and Y may rely thereon and need make no demand. 5 Moore Par. 38.45.

yers would be well advised to heed the court's advice in *Rosen* by being "more careful in protecting [their clients'] jury trial rights and in sparing the courts and themselves avoidable expense, effort and delay by expressing their intention clearly and in a timely fashion." 639 F.2d at 100.

b. The Effect of Specifying Particular Issues

The advantages of specifying particular jury trial issues are essentially twofold: (1) it will avoid a motion under Rule 39(a)(2) to strike any nonjury issues which might be subsumed by a general demand; (2) it will allow the practitioner to select which jury issues he wishes to have tried by a jury and which he prefers to have tried by the court.[33]

For the party receiving a jury demand specifying particular issues, it must be first decided whether that issue is properly the subject of a jury trial, and if not, a motion to strike under Fed. R. Civ. P. 39(a)(2) must be made to ensure that the issue will not be tried by the court. Next, it must be decided whether there are any other issues in the action which the party wishes to have tried by a jury, and if so a timely demand must be made for a jury trial as to such issues. If counsel specifies an issue to which the right to jury trial does not attach, his adversary must then move to strike or run the risk of losing the right to trial by the court should the court choose not to act on its own initiative.

2. The Time of the Demand

A party seeking a jury trial on any or all issues where a jury demand is required must make the demand by either (a) making a proper indorsement upon the pleading which first sets forth the issue or issues for which he seeks a jury trial, or (b) serving a separate written demand upon all of the parties in the action not later than 10 days after the service of "the last pleading directed to such issue." Fed. R. Civ. P. 38(b). The decision is obvious. It should be the common practice to utilize the indorsed pleading, and the practitioner who does not get into this habit runs the risk of jeopardizing the client's jury trial rights should he fail to serve the jury demand within 10 days from the date of service of the last pleading. Thus, while a party can wait until all responsive pleadings are served before making the jury demand, the fail-safe approach of indorsing the pleading is clearly the preferred practice.

When the jury demand only specifies some of the issues for jury trial the burden then shifts to the other party, who must then take action under Fed. R. Civ. P. 38(c) within 10 days from the date of service of the demand if he

---

[33] As previously noted, *supra*, pp. 569-70, in the absence of a motion to strike, it will also serve to require a jury trial as to issues specified that would otherwise be tried by the court unless the court under Fed. R. Civ. P. 39(a)(2), strikes the specification on its own initiative.

wishes a jury trial on any of the other issues. It should be remembered that since nothing in the federal rules precludes a party from demanding a jury trial on a nonjury issue, any party can attempt to convert a nonjury issue into a jury trial by specifying such issue for jury trial, and it would thereafter be incumbent upon his adversary or the court to thwart this effort.

When a party specifies issues for trial by the indorsement method, Fed. R. Civ. P. 38(c), as literally read,[34] requires the other party to make his counter demand prior to the 20 days permitted for his responsive pleading under Fed. R. Civ. P. 12.[35] When the indorsement method is not used, Rule 38(c) provides that the court may nonetheless order a party to respond to a demand made after the last pleading within a lesser time than the 10-day time frame otherwise allowable.

Finally, it should be noted that since the 10-day time provisions of Rules 38(b) and (c) are measured from the date of *service* of the pleading or demand, these time provisions are affected by Fed. R. Civ. P. 6(e), which allows for three additional days if service is made by mail.[36] It should also be remembered that under Rule 5(d) all papers required to be served upon a party "shall be filed with the court either before service or within a reasonable time thereafter." This includes the demand for a jury trial. However, while the better practice would be to effect both service and filing within the time constraints of Rules 38(b) and (c), filing after the time limits is obviously permissible provided, as explicitly stated in Rule 5(d), it occurs "within a reasonable time thereafter."

3. The Manner and Form of the Demand

a. The Indorsed Pleading

The best place for the indorsement is on the face of the pleading under its title. It should not be on the summons, since the summons is not the pleading, nor should it be in the body of the pleading. Indeed, placing the demand in the body of the pleading in lieu of indorsement has been determined by at least

---

[34] Rule 38(c) provides, in pertinent part:
If the party has demanded trial by jury for only some of the issues, any other party within 10 days after service of the demand or such lesser time as the court may order, may serve a demand for trial by jury of any other or all of the issues of fact in the action.

[35] To be sure, this is the safer practice, but at least one commentator has suggested that the counter demand nonetheless need not be made where the demand is made before the pleadings are closed until 10 days after service of the last pleading. See 5 Moore Par. 38.42.

[36] Presumably, Fed. R. Civ. P. 6(b)(1), which allows for court-ordered extensions either upon the court's own motion or upon proper and timely motion by a party, would also serve to extend the time.

one court to be insufficient to satisfy the notice requirement of Rule 38(b). *Whitman Elec., Inc. v. Int'l Brotherhood of Elec. Workers, AFL-CIO*, 398 F. Supp. 1218, 1223 (S.D.N.Y. 1974).[37]

The form of the indorsement, as previously stated, need simply be a statement that the party "demands jury trial" if a general demand is sought. If specific issues are to be identified for jury trial, the indorsement must clearly specify those issues. Usually each issue will be the subject of a separate cause of action, and it is sufficient to simply identify the cause of action, such as "plaintiff demands jury trial as to the Second, Third and Fifth causes of action."

b. The Separate Demand

In the absence of an indorsed pleading, the demand must be in writing on a separate paper which should contain the caption of the action. Thus, an oral application for permission to file a written demand for a jury trial is insufficient, *Ward v. Brown*, 301 F.2d 445, 447 (10th Cir. 1962), as is simply checking the "Jury Demand" box on the civil cover sheet, *Omawale v. WBZ*, 610 F.2d 20 (1st Cir. 1979), even if the clerk thereafter dockets the case for jury trial, *Biesenkamp v. Atlantic Richfield Co.*, 70 F.R.D. 365 (E.D.N.Y. 1976).[38]

Conversely, if a jury trial is properly demanded, it cannot be adversely affected by incomplete or improper notations by the clerk on the court's docket sheet. *See Rosen v. Dick*, 639 F.2d 82, 89 (2d Cir. 1980).

Since the demand must be served upon all parties, an affidavit of service must accompany the document when it is filed with the court. The failure to serve one of the parties could be fatal since Rule 38(c) and (b) require that all parties be served. Service is to be made in the same manner as a pleading in accordance with the requirements of Fed. R. Civ. P. 5(b).

c. Withdrawal of Demand

Under Rule 38(d) a party who makes a jury demand may not thereafter rescind it without the consent of all of the parties. *McAndrews v. United States Lines Co.*, 167 F. Supp. 41 (S.D.N.Y. 1958); *see also State Mut. Life*

---

[37] There are cases, however, where the courts have honored a demand placed in the body of a pleading, *Allstate Ins. Co. v. Cross*, 2 F.R.D. 120 (E.D. Pa. 1941), and Moore suggests that indorsement is merely the better practice. *See* 5 Moore Par. 38.40. However, the court in *Whitman Electric* takes issue with this less literal interpretation. 398 F. Supp. at 1223, n.2.

[38] Such manifestation of a party's desire for a jury trial may, however, bear upon the exercise of a court's discretion to nonetheless relieve a party's waiver under Fed. R. Civ. P. 39(b). *See Pinemont Bank v. Belk*, 722 F.2d 232 (5th Cir. 1984).

Assurance Co. of Am. v. Arthur Andersen & Co., 581 F.2d 1045 (2d Cir. 1978). As stated therein, "[a] demand for trial by jury made as herein provided may not be withdrawn without the consent of the parties." Furthermore, where a withdrawal is made with such consent, the party withdrawing the jury demand cannot thereafter change his mind and revive his jury rights. *Bellmore v. Mobil Oil Corp.*, 783 F.2d 300 (2d Cir. 1986).

4. Removal from State Court

In recognition that the jury trial rules under state law may be at variance with Rules 38(b) and 39(a), separate provision has been made for jury demands when an action has been removed from state court. Thus, under Fed. R. Civ. P. 81(c), the following is set forth:

(1) Repleading is not necessary unless the federal court so orders.

(2) If prior to removal a party has made an express demand for trial by jury, in accordance with state law, he need not make a further demand after removal.

(3) "If at the time of removal all necessary pleadings have been served, a party entitled to trial by jury under Rule 38 shall be accorded it," even if he has failed to previously demand it, provided: (a) he serves his demand within 10 days after the petition for removal is filed if he is the one who has petitioned for removal, or (b) he files his demand within 10 days after service upon him of the notice of the filing of the petition for removal if he is not the party who petitioned for removal.[39]

Curiously, Rule 81(c) does not address the situation where a jury demand has not been made but the last pleading has yet to be served prior to removal. Accordingly, in this gray area the 10-day time frame under this rule does not apply, and the time to make the jury demand is governed by Rule 38(b). *Cascone v. Ortho Pharmaceutical Corp.*, 702 F.2d 389 (2d Cir. 1983); *South African Airways v. Tawil*, 658 F. Supp. 889, 890 (S.D.N.Y. 1987). Thus, the outer operative time frame is here measured from the date of service of the last pleading rather than from the date of the filing of the petition for removal or the service of notice of such filing.

---

[39] The Rule also provides that "if state law applicable in the court from which the case is removed does not require the parties to make express demands in order to claim trial by jury, they need not make demands after removal unless the court directs that they do so within a specified time if they desire to claim trial by jury." This part of Rule 81(c) would not be applicable in New York since CPLR § 4102(a) requires jury demand.

JURY TRIALS

Caveat

Because under New York State law a jury demand cannot be asserted until the filing of the note of issue, CPLR § 4102(a), which takes place only after all pretrial discovery has been completed and the case is ready for trial, *see* 22 NYCRR § 202.21, the state practitioner who is unfamiliar with the federal rules governing jury demands may not realize that the removal of his action into federal court requires him to demand a jury trial within the time constraints set forth in Rules 38(b) or 81(c).

Tactical Considerations

Since the right to jury trial in federal court is a matter always to be determined by federal law, where an issue if tried in state court would not carry with it the right to jury trial but would be the subject of jury trial if tried in federal court, the removal of such an action would allow for the conversion of a nonjury trial into a jury trial. *See Simler v. Conner*, 372 U.S. 221, 222 (1963); *Byrd v. Blue Ridge Royal Elec. Coop., Inc.*, 356 U.S. 525 (1958).

Further, since removal will invoke the shorter time constraints of Rules 38(b) and 81(c) rather than the longer time frame under CPLR § 4102(a), a party can determine at the earliest stages of the litigation which issues will be subject to jury trial.

B. Waiver

The failure to comply with the time constraints of Rules 38(b) and 81(c) results in a waiver of the right to a jury trial. In this respect, subdivision (d) of Rule 38 provides in part:

> Waiver. The failure of a party to serve a demand as required by this rule and to file it as required by Rule 5(d) constitutes a waiver by the party of trial by jury.

While this provision does not refer to removals under Rule 81(c), caselaw establishes that waiver also attaches under Rule 38(d) for non-compliance with the time requirements of that Rule. *See Lewis v. Time, Inc.*, 710 F.2d 549 (9th Cir. 1983).

1. Effect Upon Amended Pleadings

a. Amendments Made Before Responsive Pleading

Under Rule 15(a) an amendment of a pleading may be made as of right (1) at anytime before a responsive pleading is served, or (2) where no responsive pleading is permitted, within 20 days after service of the pleading sought to be amended. In the first situation, even if no jury demand has been made by the time of amendment, the demand can then be made under Rule 38(b) at anytime within 10 days from the date of the service and filing of the responsive pleading to the amended pleading, and jury trial can be preserved as to all issues raised in the complaint and the amended complaint. See *Bereslavsky v. Caffey*, 161 F.2d 499 (2d Cir.), *cert. denied*, 332 U.S. 770 (1947). However, in the second situation, where no responsive pleading is permitted, the amended pleading will not revive the right to a jury trial as to issues contained in the pleading unless it is made within the 10-day time frame under Rule 38(b). *Berisford Capital Corp. v. Syncom Corp.*, 650 F. Supp. 999 (S.D.N.Y. 1987).

b. Amendments Made After Responsive Pleading

Once a responsive pleading has been served to an original pleading which does not contain a jury demand, the right to jury trial will be waived as to all issues in that pleading unless, pursuant to Rule 38(b), a jury demand is served within 10 days thereafter. An amendment of the pleading after service of the responsive pleading will not serve such purpose. However, a jury trial may thereupon be demanded as to any new issue raised by the amended pleading, and the provisions of Rule 38(b) will once again come into play with respect to such new issues. *Rosen v. Dick*, 639 F.2d 82 (2d Cir. 1980); *Unique Concepts, Inc. v. Brown*, 659 F. Supp. 1008, 1010 (S.D.N.Y. 1987).

In ascertaining whether the issues raised in the amended pleading are truly "new issues," "[t]he court will look to the underlying essence of the two (pleadings) to see if they differ, rather than focusing on the fine-tuning of legal theories or the artful sharpening of allegations." *Berisford Capital Corp.*, 650 F. Supp. at 1002; *see Rosen v. Dick*, 639 F.2d 82.

2. Effect Upon Subsequent Trials

a. Retrial of Same Case

As long as the issues in the new trial are the same, nothing can be changed, and accordingly once the right to a jury trial is waived, the waiver remains. *Western Geophysical Co. v. Bolt Assoc., Inc.*, 440 F.2d 765 (2d Cir. 1971). However, if new issues surface, the right to a jury trial as to such issues can be asserted. *In re Zweibon*, 565 F.2d 742 (D.C. Cir. 1977).

b. Collateral Estoppel

Collateral estoppel effect can be given to an issue which was previously resolved in a nonjury trial, even though in the subsequent lawsuit a jury trial was demanded for such issue. *Whitman Elec., Inc. v. Local 363, Int'l Brotherhood of Elec. Workers, AFL-CIO*, 398 F. Supp. 1218, 1223 (S.D.N.Y. 1974). However, in recognition of the importance of the right to a jury trial, the court will stay a pending nonjury trial involving an issue which might collaterally estop the subsequent exercise of the right to have the issue decided by a jury. *See, e.g., Parklane Hosiery Co. v. Shore*, 439 U.S. 322 (1979); *also Goldman, Sachs & Co. v. Edelstein*, 494 F.2d 76 (2d Cir. 1974).

C. Relief from Waiver

Rule 39(b) allows the court in its discretion to relieve a party from a waiver. It provides:

> By the Court. Issues not demanded for trial by jury as provided in Rule 38 shall be tried by the court; but notwithstanding the failure of a party to demand a jury in an action in which such a demand might have been made of right, the court in its discretion upon motion may order a trial by a jury of any or all issues.

Unlike subdivision (a)(2) of Rule 39 which authorizes the court on its own initiative to order a nonjury trial on an issue where a jury trial does not exist as of right, subdivision (b) of Rule 39 does not give the court the right on its own initiative to order a jury trial where the right has been waived. Thus, once the right to a jury trial is waived, whether intentionally or otherwise, trial will be by the court unless a Rule 39(b) motion for relief from the waiver is made and granted.

While Rule 39(b) does not expressly refer to waivers resulting from removals under Rule 81(c), it nonetheless also applies to such cases. *See Marvel Entertainment Group, Inc. v. ARP Films, Inc.*, 116 F.R.D. 86, 88 and cases cited in n.5 (S.D.N.Y. 1987). In practice, however, different standards to guide the courts in the exercise of its discretion to relieve a party from waiver have emerged in the caselaw when relief from waiver has been sought in actions removed from New York State courts.

1. Actions Brought in Federal Court in the First Instance

Where the action has been brought in a New York federal court in the first instance, a party must show more than *mere inadvertence* to invoke the court's discretion to relieve the waiver. *Noonan v. Cunard Steamship Co.*, 375 F.2d 69 (2d Cir. 1967).

As explicitly held in *Noonan*, this principle is so strong that its violation by a district court judge is reversible error "because the settled course of decision had placed a gloss upon the Rule which a judge could no more disregard than if the words had appeared in the Rule itself." *Id.* at 70.[40] Thus, not even a *pro se* party will be relieved from his inadvertent waiver. *Washington v. N.Y.*

---

[40] This strict New York rule seems to be the minority view since a majority of circuits have held that absent compelling reasons to the contrary the jury demand should be granted. *See Printers II, Inc. v. Professionals Publishing Inc.*, 596 F. Supp. 1051, 1052 (S.D.N.Y. 1984), citing *Swofford v. B & W, Inc.*, 336 F.2d 406 (5th Cir. 1964), *cert. denied*, 379 U.S. 962 (1965).

City Bd. of Estimate, 709 F.2d 792 (2d Cir.), *cert. denied*, 464 U.S. 1013 (1983). Therefore, relief from waiver is hardly for the asking. Unless a compelling reason is offered, the court has no discretion other than to enforce the waiver.[41]

2. Actions Removed from State Court

In removal actions from New York State's courts, a more liberal approach is applied primarily because under New York law a jury demand need not be made until the filing of a note of issue, and relief from waiver may always be granted pursuant to CPLR § 4102(e) in the absence of "undue prejudice." *Higgins v. Boeing Co.*, 526 F.2d 1004 (2d Cir. 1975); *Cascone v. Ortho Pharmaceutical Corp.*, 702 F.2d 389, 391 (2d Cir. 1983). Thus, as stated by the Second Circuit in *Cascone*, "[a]lthough we may not overlook lack of compliance with the federal procedural rules in removed cases, there is nonetheless some 'play in the joints' for accomodating a removed party who may not be as at ease in the new surroundings imposed upon him." *Id.* at 392.

a. The Factors to be Weighed in Removal Cases

In *Cascone*, the Court gave its approbation to the following view expressed by Wright & Miller in their treatise: "The court ought to approach each application under Rule 39(b) with an open mind and an eye to the factual situation in that particular case, rather than with a fixed policy against granting the application or even a preconceived notion that applications of this kind are usually denied." *Id.* at 392, quoting from 9 C. Wright & A. Miller, *Federal Practice & Procedure*, § 2334 at 116 (1971). With this overview, the courts have looked with favor upon the following factors: (1) If the case is one which is traditionally tried by a jury, such as one for personal injury; (2) If the parties had proceeded on the assumption that the matter would not be a bench trial; (3) If there is an absence of prejudice; (4) If the party who was the subject of the removal was represented by counsel who was essentially a state court practitioner having greater familiarity with New York State practice than with the gray areas in Rule 81(c); (5) If the removal occurred prior to the filing of a note of issue. *Cascone*, 702 F.2d at 391-393; *Catapano v. W.*

---

[41] An example of such a compelling reason would be a lawyer's disability because of severe physical injuries. *Board of Educ., Cent. School Dist. No. 2 v. Aetna Casualty & Sur. Co.*, 48 F.R.D. 402 (S.D.N.Y. 1969).

JURY TRIALS

Airlines, Inc., 105 F.R.D. 621 (E.D.N.Y. 1985); *Sherwood Apartments v. Westinghouse Elec. Corp.*, 101 F.R.D. 102 (W.D.N.Y. 1984).[42]

D. Jury Demand Chart

The following chart groups together most of the situations counsel is likely to confront in respect to the making of jury demands and the consequences of counsel's action or inaction.

Action By Plaintiff	Reaction By Defendant	Result
(A) Timely general demand upon commencement of action containing only jury trial issues	No action	Jury trial on all issues
	Answer with counter-claim raising new jury trial issue. No jury trial demanded	Jury trial on all issues
	Answer with counter-claim raising new jury trial and nonjury trial issues. No jury trial demand	Jury trial on all issues unless plaintiff moves to strike as to nonjury trial issue or court acts on its own motion
	If co-defendants, cross-claims	Defendants can rely upon plaintiff's demand unless cross-claims raise new issues to which plaintiff is not connected
	Defendent initiates third-party action	Defendant must consider himself as a new plaintiff and cannot rely on

---

[42] By contrast, for example, where these factors do not dominate and the party seeking relief from waiver has failed to assert the demand for jury trial for an unexplained, protracted period of time after causing the removal, the court will not grant a jury trial. *South African Airways v. Tawil*, 658 F. Supp. 889 (S.D.N.Y. 1987).

		original plaintiff's demand
	Answer with equitable affirmative defenses No jury trial demand	Jury trial on all issues unless plaintiff moves to strike as to the equitable issues or court strikes on its own motion
(B) Timely general demand upon commencement of action containing jury trial and nonjury trial issues	No action	Jury trial on all issues unless court on own initiative strikes nonjury aspect of demand
	Motion to strike	Will be granted by court as to nonjury issues
(C) Timely general demand upon commencement of action followed by amendment of complaint as of right adding new issues, without renewal of general demand	No action	Jury trial on all issues, including new issues in amended complaint, unless court acts on own motion to strike nonjury issues
	Motion to strike	Will be granted by court as to any new issues to which right to trial by jury does not attach
(D) Timely general demand upon commencement of action followed by amendment of complaint by leave of court or consent, after right to amend has expired, adding new issues without new jury demand	No action	No jury trial as to new issues. Motion for relief from waiver necessary

JURY TRIALS 581

(E) Timely specific demand upon commencement of action for some, but not all, jury issues	No action	Jury trial only on issues set forth in specific demand
	Answer with jury demand for all issues	Jury trial on all issues
	Answer with counterclaim raising new jury trial issue. No jury trial demand	Jury trial on all issues set forth in plaintiff's specific demand, but no jury trial on new issues. Motion for relief from waiver necessary
	If co-defendants, cross-claims	Defendants can rely upon plaintiff's demand as to specific issues, but must request jury trial on cross-claims if not covered by plaintiff's specific demand
	Defendant initiates third-party action	Defendant must consider himself as a new plaintiff and must make a new jury demand
(F) Timely specific demand upon commencement of action specifying some jury trial and some nonjury trial issues	No action	Jury trial on all issues specifically delineated unless court on its own initiative strikes nonjury aspect of demand
	Motion to strike	Will be granted by court as to non jury issues
	Answer with general jury demand	Trial on all issues raised by all pleadings unless plaintiff moves to

> strike as to non
> jury issues or court
> strikes nonjury
> issues on its own
> motion

E. Advisory Jury

Rule 39(c) provides that "[i]n all actions not triable of right by a jury the court upon motion or of its own initiative may try any issue with an advisory jury." Thus, the court can use an advisory jury in an equity case and even when there has been a jury waiver. *(American) Lumbermens Mut. Casualty Co. of Ill. v. Timms & Howard, Inc.*, 108 F.2d 497 (2d Cir. 1939); *Stissi v. Interstate and Ocean Transp. Co.*, 765 F.2d 370 (2d Cir. 1985).[43]

The advisory jury acts to enlighten the conscience of the court and the jury's verdict has no binding effect upon the court. Thus, the trial remains a bench trial because the jury acts merely as an aid to the judge who must make his own findings of fact and conclusions of law. Therefore, the court is free to disregard the advisory verdict. Review on appeal is always from the court's judgment, as if no jury had been present. *Mallory v. Citizens Util. Co.*, 342 F.2d 796 (2d Cir. 1965); *see also Skoldberg v. Villani*, 601 F. Supp. 981 (S.D.N.Y. 1985).

V. SELECTING THE JURY

A. Creating the Jury Pool

1. Qualifications and Exemptions

The requisite qualifications for jury service are delineated by statute. Under 28 U.S.C. § 1865(b) (1966 & Supp. 1988), a person does not qualify if: (1) not a citizen of the United States, at least 18 years old and a resident within the judicial district for at least one year; (2) unable to speak the English language and read, write and understand the English language with a degree of proficiency sufficient to fill out satisfactorily the juror qualification form; (3) incapable by reason of mental or physical infirmity to render satisfactory jury service; or (4) the subject of a charge pending against him for the commission of, or having been convicted in a state or federal court of record of, a crime punishable by imprisonment for more than one year and his civil rights have not been restored.

---

[43] The Tenth Circuit, however, has held that the trial court cannot on its own initiative have an advisory jury when the parties have waived their jury rights. *Hargrove v. American Cent. Ins. Co.*, 125 F.2d 225 (10th Cir. 1942).

JURY TRIALS

In addition to these mandatory personal qualifications, 28 U.S.C. § 1863(b)(6) (1966 & Supp. 1988) provides that those in the following occupational categories shall be exempt: (1) members in active service in the United States Armed Forces; (2) firemen and policemen of any state, district, territory or possession; (3) public officers in the executive, legislative or judicial branches on both the federal and state levels who are actively engaged in the performance of official duties.

In addition, each district can fix by local rule the standards to be employed in the granting of individual requests to be excused from serving.[44]

2. Random Selection

Under 28 U.S.C. § 1863 (1966 & Supp. 1988), each district is charged by statute to formulate a plan for establishing its own pool of jurors in accordance with the following guidelines: (1) the district must either provide for a jury commission or delegate to the clerk of the court the task of preparing a list of names to be placed in a master jury wheel; (2) the list may be taken from voter lists or other appropriate sources; (3) the list must be made up under procedures "designed to insure a random selection of a fair cross section of the persons residing in the community in the district" and must reflect "substantial" proportional representation of the political subdivisions within the district. *See* 28 U.S.C. §§ 1863(b)(1)-(4) (1966 & Supp. 1988).[45]

The number of names placed into the master jury wheel must be at least 1,000, and either the clerk of the court or a judge must draw at random from the wheel sufficient names necessary to provide an appropriate complement of prospective jurors. 28 U.S.C. § 1863(b)(4) (1966 & Supp. 1988).

B. Determining the Size of the Jury

Under Fed. R. Civ. P. 48 "[t]he parties may stipulate that the jury shall consist of any number less than twelve." This does not mean, however, that

---

44 For example, a local rule of the Southern and Eastern Districts of New York provides that a prospective juror shall be excused upon request if: (1) over 70 years of age; (2) an active member of the clergy; (3) responsible for the active care and custody of a child under 10 years of age whose health and/or safety would be jeopardized by the custodian's absence for jury service; (4) needed to care for an aged or infirm person; (5) an actively practicing attorney, physician, dentist or registered nurse; (6) so essential to the operation of a business, commercial or agricultural enterprise that it must close if the person were required to perform jury duty; (7) the prospective juror had served as a grand or petit juror in either state or federal court within the preceding two years. Rules of U.S. Dist. Cts. for Southern and Eastern Dists. of N.Y., Gen. Rule Appendix B(7).

---

45 Accordingly, each district has sufficient flexibility to tailor its own plan to the unique characteristics of its component political subdivisions. Thus, the Eastern District of New York has established a separate jury wheel for its Long Island Division. Rules of U.S. Dist. Cts. for Southern and Eastern Districts of N.Y., Gen. Rule Appendix B(11).

in the absence of such a stipulation a party is entitled to a jury of twelve since the court may, by local rule, set a different number. *Colgrove v. Battin*, 413 U.S. 149 (1973).[46] The majority of federal district courts have done so, and in New York each of the four districts has fixed the number at six.[47]

Rule 47(b) provides that "[t]he court may direct that not more than six jurors in addition to the regular jury be called and impanelled to sit as alternates."[48] The court will, therefore, fix the number of alternates in each case from one to six. The common practice is to set the number at two.

C. Examining the Jury: The *Voir Dire*

Fed. R. Civ. P. 47(a) provides that "[t]he court may permit the parties or their attorneys to conduct the examination of prospective jurors or may itself conduct the examination." If the court decides to conduct the examination, the Rule further provides that it "shall permit the parties or their attorneys to supplement the examination by such further inquiry as it deems proper or shall itself submit to the prospective jurors such additional questions of the parties or their attorneys as it deems proper." The court often delegates the conducting of the *voir dire* to a federal magistrate. In *United States v. Garcia*, 849 F.2d 1468 (2d Cir. 1988), the Second Circuit construed the Federal Magistrates Act, 28 U.S.C. §§ 631-639 (1982 & Supp. III 1985), as implicitly authorizing such delegation, even in criminal trials, and upheld its constitutionality.

Thus, the course and extent of *voir dire* rests in the sound discretion of the court. *Parento v. Palumbo*, 677 F.2d 3 (1st Cir. 1982). However, while the court's discretion is broad, it is not without limits, and hence counsel must be afforded the opportunity to make reasonable inquiries. *Kiernan v. Van Schaik*, 347 F.2d 775 (3d Cir. 1965).

In practice, counsel will find that each court has its own particular notion as to how *voir dire* should be conducted. In most cases, however, the court will not be inclined to allow counsel to directly pose any questions to the prospective jurors, and counsel will be relegated to submitting proposed

---

[46] As explained in *Colgrove*, while the number of jurors at common law was twelve, this is to be viewed as simply an historical fact unrelated to the jury's purpose, and hence not absorbed as a substantive right under the seventh amendment.

[47] Rules of U.S. Dist. Ct. for Northern Dist. of N.Y., Gen. Rule 45; Rules of U.S. Dist. Cts. for Southern and Eastern Districts of N.Y., Civil Rule 22(a); Rules of U.S. Dist. Ct. for Western Dist. of N.Y., Local Rule 22(a). New York State courts are also composed of six jurors. CPLR § 4104.

[48] By comparison, under CPLR § 4106 "unless the court, in its discretion, orders otherwise," one or two additional jurors may be requested by a party as alternate jurors.

questions for the jurors to the court. Counsel should be prepared, therefore, to have a list of key questions to give to the court prior to the commencement of *voir dire*, and should not be timid in pressing the court to ask the jurors questions which counsel believes to be important to the case.[49]

Tactical Consideration

The rigid control by the court over *voir dire* in the federal forum is in sharp contrast to the procedure and practice under New York State law where a judge may be present at the examination of the jurors only at the insistence of a party, CPLR § 4107, and it is counsel, and not the court, who conducts the *voir dire*. *See* CPLR § 4107, J.J. Cunningham and W.J. Sullivan, *Practice Commentary* (McKinney 1963). Because the role of counsel is so circumscribed under the federal system, whenever there is a choice of forums the practitioner should consider whether the nature of the case is one which best lends itself to the latitude allowed by state law or the more streamlined and sterile process under federal law.

D. Challenges

There are no limits to the number of challenges a party may assert for cause. Curiously, on the federal level there are no statutes or rules that define "cause,"[50] the issue being one for the court to determine during the course of *voir dire*. 28 U.S.C. § 1870 (1966). Counsel may always ask the court to excuse a juror for cause whenever it is believed that the juror's responses to the *voir dire* reflects a bias or impartiality against counsel's client. *Swain v. Alabama*, 380 U.S. 202 (1965).

As for peremptory challenges to regular jurors, 28 U.S.C. § 1870 (1966) provides that each party shall have three,[51] and further provides that when there are multiple plaintiffs or defendants the court has the discretion to either treat each group as a single party, thereby restricting the challenges to

---

49 Local rules should always be examined. For example, Rules of U.S. Dist. Ct. for Western Dist. of N.Y., Local Rule 22(b) allows counsel to submit written questions to the court "prior to or during the *voir dire* examination," and further provides that "[t]he court in its discretion also may permit questions to be submitted orally." Subdivision (e) affords counsel an opportunity to seek a jury of more than six persons, provided that such a request is filed at least 30 days prior to the trial date.

50 By contrast, CPLR § 4110 specifies numerous situations which require removal for "cause."

51 The number of peremptories provided by 28 U.S.C. § 1870 (1966) remains the same regardless of the size of the jury.

three for all plaintiffs and three for all defendants, or to allow for a suitable number of additional challenges to be exercised either separately or jointly.[52]

As for the alternate jurors, Rule 49(b) allows for one peremptory challenge if one or two alternate jurors are to be impanelled, two challenges if there are to be three or four alternates, and three peremptories for five or six. It further provides that such challenges can only be used against an alternate juror and that the number of such challenges cannot be augmented by leftover challenges from the regular jurors.

Tactical Considerations

It is not sufficient for counsel to know the number of peremptory challenges at his disposal; he must also have an appreciation of the manner by which such challenges are to be exercised, which is to be governed either by local rule or the trial judge's discretion. *St. Clair v. United States*, 154 U.S. 134 (1894). The court will first look to the plaintiff, and counsel must then decide how many challenges to use. Whatever the decision, it should be made out of the earshot of the jury, lest any prospective juror's sensibilities be offended.

In making the decision counsel should not feel pressured or constrained to exercise the full complement of challenges at one time. While the common practice in the Second Circuit is to consider the failure to exercise and peremptory challenges at all as a waiver of one such challenge, the court cannot compel counsel to use all of his challenges at once. *Carr v. Watts*, 597 F.2d 830 (2d Cir. 1979).[53] Thus, counsel can, and should, husband the challenges so that he is not left at the mercy of the adversary.

VI. INSTRUCTING THE JURY

Instructions to the jury consist primarily of the court's explanation of the applicable law and the type of verdict the jury is to render. Each of these is governed by express rules.

---

[52] New York State law also provides for three peremptory challenges for each party, but unlike the federal statute, does not provide that the court may treat multiple parties as single parties. CPLR § 4109. This statute does provide, however, that "[w]here there are more parties on one side than on the other, the court may, before the examination of jurors begins, grant additional challenges to the side with the smaller number of challenges."

[53] By contrast, in New York State courts a party may peremptorily challenge a juror anytime before the jury is sworn, and hence a statement by plaintiff that he is content with the jury does not preclude him from changing his mind. *See Sorensen v. Hunter*, 268 A.D. 1078, 52 N.Y.S.2d 872 (4th Dep't 1945); Annotation, *Peremptory Challenge After Acceptance of Juror*, 3 A.L.R. 499 (1949).

Rule 51 addresses the process entailed in charging the jury as to the substantive aspects of the case.[54] Rule 49(a) governs the form of the jury's verdict where the court determines that a special verdict, rather than a general verdict, should be rendered.[55] Rule 49(b) allows for a general verdict to be accompanied by the answers to interrogatories posed by the court.[56] Collectively these rules contain the primary considerations governing the process that leads to a jury's verdict after all parties have rested.[57]

These rules assign varying responsibilities to the court and counsel, and the practitioner should have a clear appreciation of the separate roles.

---

[54] Rule 51. Instruction to Jury: Objection
At the close of the evidence or at such earlier time during the trial as the court reasonably directs, any party may file written requests that the court instruct the jury on the law as set forth in the request. The court shall inform counsel of its proposed action upon the requests prior to their arguments to the jury. The court, at its election, may instruct the jury before or after argument, or both. No party may assign as error the giving or the failure to give an instruction unless that party objects thereto before the jury retires to consider its verdict, stating distinctly the matter objected to and the grounds of the objection. Opportunity shall be given to make the objection out of the hearing of the jury.

[55] Rule 49. Special Verdicts and Interrogatories
(a) Special Verdicts. The court may require a jury to return only a special verdict in the form of a special written finding upon each issue of fact. In that event the court may submit to the jury written questions susceptible of categorical or other brief answer or may submit written forms of the several special findings which might properly be made under the pleadings and evidence; or it may use such other method of submitting the issues and requiring the written findings thereon as it deems most appropriate. The court shall give to the jury such explanation and instruction concerning the matter thus submitted as may be necessary to enable the jury to make its findings upon each issue. If in so doing the court omits any issue of fact raised by the pleadings or by the evidence, each party waives the right to a trial by jury of the issue so omitted unless before the jury retires he demands its submission to the jury. As to an issue omitted without such demand the court may make a finding; or, if it fails to do so, it shall be deemed to have made a finding in accord with the judgment on the special verdict.

[56] Rule 49. Special Verdicts and Interrogatories
(b) General Verdict Accompanied by Answer to Interrogatories. The court may submit to the jury, together with appropriate forms for a general verdict, written interrogatories upon one or more issues of fact the decision of which is necessary to a verdict. The court shall give such explanation or instruction as may be necessary to enable the jury both to make answers to the interrogatories and to render a general verdict, and the court shall direct the jury both to make written answers and to render a general verdict. When the general verdict and the answers are harmonious, the appropriate judgment upon the verdict and answers shall be entered pursuant to Rule 58. When the answers are consistent with each other but one or more is inconsistent with the general verdict, judgment may be entered pursuant to Rule 58 in accordance with the answers, notwithstanding the general verdict, or the court may return the jury for further consideration of its answers and verdict or may order a new trial. When the answers are inconsistent with each other and one or more is likewise inconsistent with the general verdict, judgment shall not be entered, but the court shall return the jury for further consideration of its answers and verdict or shall order a new trial.

[57] The New York State rules are similar. See CPLR § 4111.

A. The Jury Charge

1. The Court's Role

Rule 51 requires the court: (1) to allow any party to submit to the court written requests to charge at the close of the evidence or, if the court directs, during the trial; (2) to inform counsel of its proposed action in respect to such requests prior to summation; (3) to determine whether to instruct the jury before or after argument, or both; and (4) to allow counsel an opportunity to object to its charge outside of the hearing of the jury.

The court's overriding obligation under this Rule "is to permit counsel to argue intelligently upon the evidence, within the framework of the applicable law, and also, by reason of advance advice as to the disposition of requests for instructions, to alert him to take appropriate exceptions following delivery of the charge." *Tyrill v. Alcoa Steamship Co.*, 185 F. Supp. 822, 824-825 (S.D.N.Y. 1960).

However, the court is not bound to charge in the manner requested by counsel, *United States v. Heyward-Robinson Co.*, 430 F.2d 1077, 1085 (2d Cir. 1970), *cert. denied*, 400 U.S. 1021 (1971), to write out the charge in advance and submit it to counsel for editing and exceptions, *Puggioni v. Luckenbach Steamship Co., Inc.*, 286 F.2d 340, 344 (2d Cir. 1961), to use a particular format in ruling on the requests, it being sufficient, for example, to rule "denied except as charged," nor to incorporate every proposition of law suggested in counsel's requests, provided that the court cover the specific principles necessary for the jury's guidance and advise counsel accordingly. *See City of N.Y. v. Pullman, Inc.*, 662 F.2d 910, 917 (2d Cir. 1981).

While not therefor bound to any particular structure or format, the court must nonetheless let counsel know the particular substantive principles of law applicable to the case upon which it intends to instruct the jury, and it must do so with sufficient clarity and sufficiently in advance of summation to allow counsel to effectively sum up. *Frederic P. Wiedersum Assoc. v. Nat'l Homes Constr. Corp.*, 540 F.2d 62, 65-67 (2d Cir. 1976).

The court, therefore, need not be concerned about specific structure so long as it affords counsel fair opportunity to know the fundamental aspects of the court's contemplated instructions so that counsel can effectively argue to the jury their application to the facts of the case. The thrust of the court's responsibility in ruling on counsel's requests to charge and advising counsel of the nature of the intended jury instructions is to avoid surprise so that summation will be focused on the relevant issues. In aid of this, Rule 51 was amended in 1987 to allow the court the discretion to instruct the jury before summation.[58]

a. Failure to Observe the Rule

The court's failure to comply with its obligations under Rule 51 is not necessarily fatal. Regardless of whether counsel interposes objections to the court's non-compliance, a new trial will not be ordered unless material prejudice is shown, and "[w]hether prejudice has been visited upon a litigant in consequence of nonobservance of the Rule must be tested against its objectives." *Tyrill v. Alcoa Steamship Co., Inc.*, 185 F. Supp. 822, 824 (S.D.N.Y. 1960).[59] Accordingly, counsel has the burden of establishing that he would have presented the case differently to the jury.[60]

Thus, counsel has no vested interest in the precise manner by which the court deals with his requests to charge, nor the particular form of the court's charge.

b. Presenting the Charge to the Jury

The precise language of the jury's instructions is always for the court to determine, *Beard v. Mitchell*, 604 F.2d 485 (7th Cir. 1979), *cert. denied*, 469 U.S. 825 (1984), and they need not be in writing, *Lincoln v. Power*, 151 U.S. 436 (1894).

As for its responsibility to properly charge the jury, the court's obligation is satisfied if it appears that the jury has been fairly and adequately instructed. Thus, the test is not whether the instructions are faultless in every respect,

---

[58] The exercise of the court's discretion in presenting the case to the jury will invariably be supported by the appellate courts whenever the trial judge seeks to ensure that the jury will be fairly and properly informed of the law. Thus, a trial judge may *suo motu* recall a jury for further instruction when he thinks them needed. *Miscione v. Pennsylvania R.R., Co.*, 284 F.2d 428, 430 (2d Cir. 1960). Similarly, the court would undoubtedly have discretion to allow for further summation in such a situation.

[59] Thus, in *Vitarelle v. Long Island R.R., Co.*, 415 F.2d 302 (2d Cir. 1969), the Second Circuit held that while the trial court's failure to rule on counsel's properly presented requests prior to summation was "a cavalier ignoring of the requirements of Rule 51," the failure would not require reversal in the absence of prejudice. For an example of when such a failure, required a new trial because it prejudiced counsel's summation, *see Frederic P. Wiedersum Assoc. v. Nat'l Homes Constr. Corp.*, 540 F.2d 62 (2d Cir. 1976).

[60] Thus, by way of example, while the trial court should always afford counsel the opportunity to pose objections to the charge outside of the jury, the failure to do so does not constitute reversible error where the charge is unobjectionable and there are no aggravating prejudicial circumstances. *Swain v. Boeing Airplane Co.*, 337 F.2d 940; (2d Cir. 1964), *cert. denied*, 380 U.S. 951 (1965). *But see Bentley v. Stromberg-Carlson Corp.*, 638 F.2d 9, 12 (2d Cir. 1981), where requiring counsel to state objections in the presence of the jury was relied upon as one of a number of reasons for ordering a new trial.

but, rather, considering the charge as a whole, whether the jury was misled. *Mid-Texas Communications Sys., Inc. v. American Tel. & Tel. Co.*, 615 F.2d 1372 (5th Cir.), *reh. denied*, 449 U.S. 912 (1980).

The trial judge's role is not limited to instructing the jury on the law. He may also comment on the evidence. *Radiation Dynamics, Inc. v. Goldmuntz*, 464 F.2d 876, 888-889 (2d Cir. 1972). In so doing, the judge is to be guided by the following principles laid down by the Second Circuit in *United States v. Tourine*, 428 F.2d 865, 869 (2d Cir. 1970):

> So long as the trial judge does not by one means or another try to impose his own opinions and conclusions as to the facts on the jury and does not act as an advocate in advancing factual findings of his own, he may in his discretion decide what evidence he will comment upon. His fairness in doing so must be judged in the context of the whole trial record, particularly the evidence and the arguments of the parties.

2. The Lawyer's Role

a. Making Requests to Charge

It is decidedly in a party's interest to obtain the best possible charge, and therefore counsel should take an active part in assisting the court, even if not required by any particular rule. Thus, counsel should not wait until the court directs the submission of requests or until the close of the evidence, unless there is a tactical reason for not educating the adversary prior to the end of the trial.[61] Rather, counsel should prepare his requests in advance of trial and submit them to the court at the beginning of the trial. Not only will this help to orient the court to the key aspects of the case from counsel's point of view, but it will undoubtedly also help to discipline counsel to focus on the specific elements of the case throughout the trial. *See Ivy v. Sec. Borge Lines, Inc.*, 585 F.2d 732 (5th Cir. 1978), *reh'g granted*, 593 F.2d 20 (1979), *cert. denied*, 446 U.S. 956 (1980).

The requests should not contain the usual standard instructions common to all trials but should focus on the special aspects of the case. They should be in the form of specific, numbered points so that they may be affirmed or refused point by point.[62] Care should also be taken in drafting requests to assure

---

[61] Counsel should always be familiar with the court's local rules. For example, on the manner and time for submission of requests to charge, the rules of the Western District of New York provide that: "Two copies of any request to charge shall be submitted to the court, and a copy to opposing counsel at the earliest possible time prior to the anticipated close of proof. Each request should be numbered and on separate pages." Rules of Dist. Ct. for Western Dist. of N.Y., Local Rule 22(C).

[62] *See* Bender, 3 *Bender's Federal Practice Forms*, Form 3176 (Requests for Instructions).

accuracy and simplicity of presentation and thereby enhance the prospects of their verbatim adoption by the court. Each request should be followed by citation of authority and, if the law appears unsettled, with an appropriate memorandum.

If for some unfortunate reason timely written requests are not made, they should nonetheless be made after the close of evidence since the court has inherent discretion to consider a late request prior to presenting the case to the jury. Indeed, at least one court has held that a "trial court's discretion to refuse a charge because untimely requested should be sparingly and cautiously exercised." *Wilson v. Southern Farm Bureau Casualty Co.*, 275 F.2d 819, 822 (5th Cir.), *cert. denied*, 364 U.S. 817 (1960); *see* 5A Moore Par. 51.06, n.6. And if circumstances do not allow for time to put a request in writing, as required by Rule 51, the request should orally be made since the courts have the inherent discretion to overlook the strictures of form in order to do justice to the substantive presentation of the case to the jury.

b. Ascertaining the Court's Charge Prior to Summation

Since the court's failure to rule on counsel's requests to charge prior to summation does not necessarily constitute grounds for a retrial, counsel should be firm in pressing the court for its rulings. Further, even though Rule 51, as literally read, only requires the court to rule on counsel's requests, counsel should not so limit his inquiries but should make every reasonable effort to ferret out the court's intended charge. While Rule 51 does not require the court to supply counsel with a copy of its intended instructions, counsel is nonetheless entitled to be informed of the general content of the court's charge prior to summation. *Beimart v. Burlington N., Inc.*, 726 F.2d 412 (8th Cir.), *cert. denied*, 467 U.S. 1216 (1984). Where the court's charge is written, counsel should request the opportunity to read it and, in any event, should always press the court to inform counsel of the nature of the charge in sufficient time to allow for effective preparation of summation. *Hetzel v. Jewel Co., Inc.*, 457 F.2d 527 (7th Cir. 1972).

Counsel should also be vigilant to those situations where, having rejected a request to charge, the court nonetheless subsequently includes the request in its charge after summation. In keeping with the spirit of Rule 51, counsel would be entitled to request the right to argue the particular matter to the jury, and additional summation in such a situation is appropriate. *Terminal R.R. Ass'n of St. Louis v. Staengel*, 122 F.2d 271 (8th Cir.), *cert. denied*, 314 U.S. 680 (1941).[63]

---

[63] Thus, oral requests have been honored where counsel's contention was clearly articulated to the court. *Swiderski v. Moodenbaugh*, 143 F.2d 212 (9th Cir. 1944); *Haynes v. Coolidge*, 336 F.2d 736 (D.C. Cir. 1964).

Finally, counsel should be mindful of the 1987 amendment to Rule 51 permitting the court to elect to allow summation to follow its charge, and where counsel is unsure of the nature of the court's intended charge, it might be wise for counsel to request the court to first charge the jury so that he may have effective knowledge of the charge before summation.

c. Objecting to the Charge

The failure to submit requests to the court does not mean that counsel has waived the right to object to the court's charge. While he may have lost the opportunity to influence the charge and to educate himself before summation on the instructions the court intends to give the jury, counsel nonetheless can always object to an erroneous charge. Moreover, if counsel fails to do so, Rule 51 provides that he may not thereafter "assign as error the giving or the failure to give an instruction." The Rule further provides that objections must be made before the jury retires to consider its verdict, *see, e.g.*, *Clark v. John Lamula Investors, Inc.*, 583 F.2d 594 (2d Cir. 1978), and that the grounds of the objection must be distinctly stated.[64]

The purpose of the objection is to alert the court to errors in its charge, and therefore no particular form need be adhered to so long as that purpose is served. In this respect, Rule 51 is to be read in conjunction with Rule 46 which eliminates the need for formal exceptions to rulings or orders of the court.[65] Accordingly, if a request to charge has been previously denied, the matter is at once preserved and counsel need not object to the court's failure to give the requested charge after the court has presented its full charge to the jury. *Cohen v. Franchard Corp.*, 478 F.2d 115, 122 (2d Cir.), *cert. denied*, 414 U.S. 857 (1973).

However, the better practice dictates that counsel use every reasonable opportunity presented to influence the charge, and accordingly the court's

---

64 *See* Bender, 3 *Bender's Federal Practice Forms*, Form 3177 (Objections to Proposed Instructions).

65 Rule 46. Exceptions Unnecessary
Formal exceptions to rulings or orders of the court are unnecessary; but for all purposes for which an exception has heretofore been necessary it is sufficient that a party, at the time the ruling or order of the court is made or sought, makes known to the court the action which the party desires the court to take or the party's objection to the action of the court and the grounds therefor; and, if a party has no opportunity to object to a ruling or order at the time it is made, the absence of an objection does not thereafter prejudice the party.

failure to charge as previously requested should be objected to after the charge has been given unless the court has instructed counsel otherwise.[66]

The need to object is not limited to the initial charge, but applies as well to any further instructions which the court may give the jury during its deliberations. *Coleman v. City of Omaha*, 714 F.2d 804 (8th Cir. 1983); *see also Polara v. Trans World Airlines, Inc.*, 284 F.2d 34 (2d Cir. 1960).

Although formality is not required, counsel should not thereby be misled into believing that it is sufficient to interpose a general objection. Thus, the Supreme Court has specifically held that a mere general objection is insufficient "where a party might have obtained the correct charge by specifically calling the attention of the trial court to the error." *Palmer v. Hoffman*, 318 U.S. 109, 119 (1943). In general, counsel should be guided by the Second Circuit's advice in *Curko v. William Spencer & Son, Corp.*, 294 F.2d 410, 412-413 (2d Cir. 1961):

> Fed. R. Civ. P. 51, 28 U.S.C.A., requires more than an objection to a charge; the grounds of objection must be stated. The elaboration demanded depends upon the nature of the objection. When the reason is obvious on its face, little, if anything, need be said. Rule 51 was not intended to compel the superfluous. But if the reason for an objection is not apparent, then the demand of the rule must be substantially met and the objector must supply the court with an explanation for his objection if he desires to subject the court's action to appellate review.

Absent the requisite objection in the district court, an appellate court is precluded under Rule 51 from considering alleged errors in the court's charge unless the failure to do so would result in a "substantial miscarriage of justice." *Cohen*, 478 F.2d at 124. This judicially created exception, commonly known as the "plain error doctrine," does not demand that an error on a significant aspect of the case requires reversal. Rather, its application is limited "to the exceptional case where the error has seriously affected the fairness, integrity, or public reputation of judicial proceedings." *Cohen*, 478 F.2d at 125, quoting from 9 Wright & Miller, *Federal Practice and Procedure*, § 2588, at 675 (1971); *see also Schaafsma v. Morin Vt. Corp.*, 802 F.2d 629 (2d Cir. 1986).

---

[66] Typically, however, the court will spread its rulings on counsel's requests to charge on the record and advise counsel that further objection is not needed. The written requests are deemed automatically to be part of the record in the case since Rule 51 provides that they be *filed* with the court, and thus they are automatically preserved for subsequent judicial review.

B. Eliciting the Verdict

The jury's verdict can be either a general verdict, a special verdict whereby it simply responds to specific questions of fact posed to it by the court, or a mixture of the two, in which case the jury will be required to answer questions of fact in conjunction with its general verdict. Fed. R. Civ. P. 49(a)(b).[67]

1. The Court's Role

It is for the court to decide, in the exercise of its discretion, which option to utilize. *Chiarello v. Domenico Bus Serv., Inc.*, 542 F.2d 883 (2d Cir. 1976).[68]

a. Special Verdicts and Interrogatories

If the court decides to opt for a special verdict based upon the submission to the jury of interrogatories, Fed. R. Civ. P. 49(a) requires the court: (1) to submit to the jury questions covering all of the material issues of fact in the case; (2) to require the jury to make its findings in writing; (3) to submit the question in a form susceptible of categorical or brief answer; (4) to explain the questions to the jury and give proper instructions concerning the facts applicable to each question.

The formulation of the questions rests in the court's discretion and will only be disturbed by an appellate court if the factual issues are inaccurately framed or are misleading and confusing. *Cann v. Ford Motor Co.*, 658 F.2d 54, 58 (2d Cir. 1981), *cert. denied*, 456 U.S. 960 (1982). The questions should be framed, however, in simple and direct terms, each confined to a single factual issue, and should be fairly few in number.[69]

While the proper procedure is for the court to set forth the interrogatories in written form, "the manner by which the questions are submitted to the jury remains merely a matter of form rather than of substance, which, like other

---

[67] New York State law is essentially the same. CPLR § 4111.

[68] This discretion can only be reviewed for "gross abuse," and hence is virtually unfettered. *See Skidmore v. Baltimore & O. R.R., Co.*, 167 F.2d 54 (2d Cir.), *cert. denied*, 335 U.S. 816 (1948).

[69] For a good listing of the various factors which the trial judge should consider in formulating special interrogatories, *see Dreiling v. General Elec. Co.*, 511 F.2d 768, 774 (5th Cir. 1975).

procedural matters, may be waived by failure to make timely objection." *Turchio v. D/S A/S Den Norske Afr.*, 509 F.2d 101, 105 (2d Cir. 1974).[70]

The use of the special verdict obviates the need for the court to charge the jury on the law, and therefore has particular utility where the operative legal principles are complex and not susceptible to facile comprehension by the layman.[71]

While Rule 49(a) is silent as to whether the court is obliged to show counsel the interrogatories or to allow counsel to pose objections outside of the hearing of the jury, it is to be read in conjunction with Rule 51. Accordingly, the court should afford counsel the same rights which apply under Rule 51 to jury instructions. Thus, prior to summation, counsel should be allowed an opportunity to submit proposed interrogatories to the court, to elicit the court's ruling on the submissions, and be informed of the final version of the interrogatories. *Cutlass Prod., Inc. v. Bregman*, 682 F.2d 323, 330 (2d Cir. 1982).[72] Similarly, counsel should be given the opportunity to object to the interrogatories out of the presence of the jury. *Cann v. Ford Motor Co.*, 658 F.2d at 58.[73]

If the court fails to submit all of the material factual issues to the jury, Rule 49(a) provides that in the absence of objection by counsel the court *may* make any missing finding, the effect being that the parties will be deemed to have

---

[70] Thus, in *Turchio*, "the court's failure to submit written interrogatories to the jury . . . was waived by the parties' clear acquiescence in the court's submission of oral questions." 509 F.2d at 105. While *Turchio* dealt with a situation where the Court submitted interrogatories in conjunction with a general verdict, pursuant to Rule 49(b), the same reasoning would obviously apply to the submission of interrogatories under Rule 49(a).

[71] Where, however, a question entails a mixture of law and fact, the factual aspect cannot be submitted as an interrogatory to the jury unless the court explains the applicable legal principle which must be applied in evaluating the facts. *See, e.g.*, *Landy v. Federal Aviation Admin.*, 635 F.2d 143 (2d Cir. 1980), *cert. denied*, 464 U.S. 895 (1983).

[72] While in *Cramer v. Hoffman*, 390 F.2d 19, 23 (2d Cir. 1968), the Second Circuit held that the decision not to supply counsel with special interrogatories before closing argument was within the trial court's discretion, it subsequently stated in *Cutlass* that "[w]e believe it is the better practice under Rule 49(a) to submit special interrogatories to counsel prior to summation." 682 F.2d at 330. The court therefore limited *Cramer* to situations where, unlike *Cann*, 658 F.2d 54, no prejudice resulted.

[73] Where, therefore, the trial judge refuses to allow objections to the interrogatories to be made outside of the hearing of the jury, such objections can be raised for the first time on appeal. As the Court in *Cann* stated: "It is well settled in this Circuit that when a trial court errs by refusing to permit a party's objection to a charge to be made out of the hearing of the jury, the party's failure to object before the jury retires is excused and his objections may be raised on appeal." *Id.* at 58.

thereby waived their right to a jury resolution of omitted issues.[74] If the court fails to make the missing finding, the Rule provides that it may nonetheless enter judgment based upon the interrogatories which it did submit to the jury if such finding can fairly be implied from the jury's verdict. *Cullen v. Margiotta*, 811 F.2d 698, 731 (2d Cir. 1987).[75]

If a jury's findings appear to be inconsistent with each other, the court is obliged to determine whether there is any view of the case which can support such findings and, if so, the court must adopt that view and enter judgment accordingly. *Atlantic & Gulf Stevedores, Inc. v. Ellerman Lines, Ltd.*, 369 U.S. 355 (1962). If reconciliation is not possible, the court may resubmit the case to the jury before it has been discharged and may pose additional interrogatories so that the jury may have the opportunity to resolve the inconsistency. *Morrison v. Frito-Lay, Inc.*, 546 F.2d 154 (5th Cir. 1977).[76] If reconciliation is not possible, a new trial is required. *Bernardini v. Rederi A/B Saturnus*, 512 F.2d 660 (2d Cir. 1975).

b. General Verdict Accompanied by Interrogatories

Fed. R. Civ. P. 49(b) authorizes the court to "submit to the jury, together with appropriate forms for a general verdict, written interrogatories upon one or more issues of fact the decision of which is necessary to a verdict." Its purpose is to allow the court in its discretion to require the jury to focus on particular crucial questions of fact as a means of ensuring that the jury's general verdict will reflect its consideration of the key factual elements of the case, and is therefore particularly useful in the more complex trial. *See, e.g., Industries, Investments, Etc. v. Panelfab Int'l Corp.*, 529 F.2d 1203 (5th Cir. 1976). It differs from the special verdict in that all the issues of fact need not be submitted as interrogatories and, therefore, more readily lends itself to those cases where the quantity of factual issues are prolix and too unwieldy to warrant full submission of all facts under Rule 49(a).

---

[74] Just as in a nonjury trial, such court findings would be reviewable under the "clearly erroneous" standard of Fed. R. Civ. P. 52(a). *Murtagh v. University Computing Co.*, 490 F.2d 810 (5th Cir.), *cert. denied*, 419 U.S. 835 (1974).

[75] *See Gough v. Rossmoor Corp.*, 585 F.2d 381 (9th Cir. 1978), *cert. denied*, 440 U.S. 936 (1979), for an example where such a finding could not be implied from the jury's verdict, requiring, therefore, a new trial.

[76] While Fed. R. Civ. P. 49(a) does not provide for resubmission, those circuits which have been required to rule on the issue have afforded the trial court such discretion in order to minimize the prospects of a retrial. *See*, in addition to the Fifth Circuit's decision in *Morrison*, the Third Circuit's decision in *Stanton by Brooks v. Astra Pharmaceutical Products, Inc.*, 718 F.2d 553 (3d Cir. 1983). However, while authorizing the practice, the Fifth Circuit would not require counsel to request resubmission at the risk of losing the right to complain of the inconsistency on appeal. *Alverez v. J. Ray McDermott & Co.*, 674 F.2d 1037 (5th Cir. 1982); *see also* 5A Moore Par. 49.03(4).

When the general verdict and the answers to the interrogatories are harmonious, Rule 49(b) simply provides for entering judgment accordingly. However, the risk involved in mixing a general verdict with interrogatories is the heightened potential for inconsistent verdicts. Rule 49(b) identifies the two inherent possibilities and instructs the court as to how these inconsistencies are to be resolved.

First, when the answers to the interrogatories are consistent with each other but one or more is inconsistent with the jury's general verdict, the court may: (1) enter judgment in accordance with the answers, notwithstanding the general verdict;[77] (2) return the jury for further consideration of its answers and general verdict; (3) order a new trial.

Second, when the answers to the interrogatories are inconsistent with each other and one or more is also inconsistent with the general verdict, the court may not enter judgment and must either (1) return the jury for further consideration, or (2) order a new trial.

Since retrials are disfavored, the court will try to harmonize answers which appear to be inconsistent with a general verdict and thus may indulge in any reasonable interpretation of the evidence that will support the general verdict. *Gallick v. Baltimore & O.R.R.*, 372 U.S. 108 (1963). Indeed, "the terms of Rule 49(b) make it the responsibility of a trial judge to resolve the inconsistency even when no objection is made." *Schaafsma v. Morin Vt. Corp.*, 802 F.2d at 634.

If such reconciliation is not possible, the court will undoubtedly resubmit the case to the jury before deciding whether to enter judgment based on the answers or to order a new trial. It will undoubtedly also resubmit the case where answers are inconsistent with each other.

The court, therefore, has a host of weapons it may deploy in order to dispose of a case short of retrial since there is only one scenario where Rule 49(b) mandates a new trial, namely, where multiple answers are inconsistent with each other and at least one of the answers is also inconsistent with the general verdict. *See, e.g., Turchio v. D/S A/S Den Norske Afr.*, 509 F.2d 101.[78]

---

[77] A good example of the exercise of this particular option is depicted by *Elston v. Morgan*, 440 F.2d 47 (7th Cir. 1971), where the jury returned a general verdict for the plaintiff in his negligence case, but also, in answers to the Court's interrogatories, found that plaintiff was contributorily negligent and that his negligence was the proximate cause of the accident. Accordingly, the Court properly entered judgment for the defendant. *See also Julien J. Studley, Inc. v. Gulf Oil Corp.*, 407 F.2d 521 (2d Cir. 1969).

[78] As shown in *Turchio*, the trial judge is given ample latitude to first resubmit the inconsistencies before being obliged to order a retrial, provided it does not confuse the jury. *Id.* at 106.

Where the jury renders a general verdict but fails to answer all of the interrogatories its failure will not necessarily be considered fatal since the court need not, in the first instance, have submitted all of the factual issues in the case to the jury. *Cf.* Fed. R. Civ. P. 49(a). Thus, so long as the general verdict can factually be supported by the evidence, neither the failure by the court to submit a particular fact issue to a jury nor the failure by the jury to make a factual finding in response to an interrogatory will impair the general verdict. *Bolan v. Lehigh Valley R.R.*, 167 F.2d 934 (2d Cir. 1948) (failure to submit fact to jury); *Kissell v. Westinghouse Elec. Corp., Elevator Div.*, 367 F.2d 375 (1st Cir. 1966) (failure to make factual finding).

If reversal of a general verdict is required because the court improperly instructed the jury on the applicable law, the parties will nonetheless be bound on the retrial by the answers given by the jury to the interrogatories in the first trial. *Green v. American Tobacco Co.*, 325 F.2d 673 (5th Cir. 1963); *see also* 5 Moore Par. 42.03.

2. The Lawyer's Role

a. Shaping and Formulating the Form of the Verdict

While neither Rule 49(a) nor (b) addresses the role of counsel in the shaping and formulation of the verdict, the courts have generally accorded counsel the same rights provided under Rule 51. Accordingly, while Rule 49 does not obligate counsel to do so, he may nonetheless submit proposed interrogatories to the court, *Sakamoto v. N.A.B. Trucking Co.*, 717 F.2d 1000 (6th Cir. 1983), and, in any event, is entitled to disclosure of the court's questions prior to summation, *Kushner v. Hendon Constr., Inc.*, 81 F.R.D. 93 (M.D. Pa.), *aff'd*, 609 F.2d 501, 502 (3d Cir. 1979).

The failure of the court to make such disclosure or to advise counsel of its intention to submit interrogatories will not, however, constitute reversible error in the absence of demonstrated prejudice. *Smith v. Danyo*, 585 F.2d 83 (3d Cir. 1978). However, once interrogatories are presented to the jury, counsel should be given the opportunity to raise any objections outside of the hearing of the jury. *Cann v. Ford Motor Co.*, 658 F.2d at 58.[79]

Tactical Considerations

Since the court is given virtually unfettered discretion to determine whether to present interrogatories to the jury, counsel should determine well in advance of closing argument where his client's best interests lie. If inter-

---

[79] As the Second Circuit stated in *Cann*, after acknowledging that Rule 49 is silent on the issue, "there is no reason to give parties less protection when they object to the phrasing of a special verdict question than when they object to the phrasing of general instructions." *Id.* at 58.

rogatories are indicated, counsel should timely present them to the court in clear, concise written form, and should press for the adoption of his language at every opportunity. Too often counsel loses sight of the significance of this part of the jury trial. From a plaintiff's point of view, a lengthy number of interrogatories will invariably be deadly. From a defendant's perspective, lengthy and complicated interrogatories will usually be a welcomed obstacle course for the plaintiff to surmount. Counsel should also realize that by focusing the jury on specific questions of fact, interrogatories will tend to sanitize the intangibles and take from the jury the opportunity to do "substantial justice."[80]

If the court decides to submit interrogatories, counsel should make every effort to have them at his disposal during summation. Moreover, he should not hesitate to read them to the jury and argue for the answers that will lead to victory. Shaping the summation to the manner by which the verdict will be elicited is a critical component of effective lawyering.

b. The Necessity for Objections

(1) The Use of Interrogatories

While it is the rare case when the trial judge's discretion to employ interrogatories will be reversed on appeal, counsel must nonetheless timely object to the court's decision to forgo the general verdict if the issue is to be preserved. *Great Coastal Express, Inc. v. Int'l Brotherhood of Teamsters*, 511 F.2d 839 (4th Cir. 1975), *cert. denied*, 425 U.S. 975 (1976).[81]

---

[80] Different judges will undoubtedly have their own individual philosophical views on the subject, and the matter is the province of ubiquitous debate. As Wright aptly explains:
> The use of special verdicts is always in the discretion of the trial judge. The use he makes of this procedure is likely to depend on his view of its utility, and his conception of the role of the jury. At one extreme, the late Judge Jerome N. Frank, a brilliant and outspoken critic of the jury system, hailed the special verdict as "usually preferable to the opaque general verdict," and urged that the use of Rule 49 be made compulsory in all civil cases. At the other extreme, those who look on the jury as a means by which the law is made to speak the voice of the man in the street urge that the special verdict should be used rarely. Indeed Justices Hugo L. Black and William O. Douglas call Rule 49 "but another means utilized by courts to weaken the constitutional power of juries" and argue for its repeal. C. Wright, *Handbook of the Law of Federal Courts* 466 (3d ed. 1976).

[81] While the objection should obviously be made prior to the presentment of the interrogatories to the jury, counsel should not hesitate to renew the objection during jury deliberations since the court can, in an appropriate case, change its mind and withdraw the interrogatories provided the court acts before any verdict is returned. *Turchio v. D/S A/S Den Norske Africa*, 509 F.2d at 106.

(2) The Form of the Interrogatories

Objections must also be interposed to the form of the interrogatories. *J. C. Motor Lines, Inc. v. Trailways Bus Sys., Inc.*, 689 F.2d 599 (5th Cir. 1982).[82] Not only must counsel take issue with any particular language not to his liking, but if the case is to be submitted under Rule 49(a), counsel must also request the submission of omitted interrogatories if he believes that the court's questions do not cover all of the factual issues in the case. *Ribeiro v. United Fruit Co.*, 284 F.2d 317, 319 (2d Cir. 1960). As previously noted, *supra*, p. 595, counsel's failure to do so will constitute a waiver of the right to jury resolution on the omitted issue, and the court will then be permitted to make the finding. Here, counsel's objection will ensure the right to have the jury resolve the omitted factual issue since the court has no discretion to withdraw a valid jury issue from the jury's consideration over counsel's protestation. *Cutlass Prod., Inc. v. Bregman*, 682 F.2d at 328-329.[83]

Counsel may also propose additional submissions under Rule 49(b). Here, however, the court's refusal to submit every factual issue to the jury will not necessarily have the same consequences as under Rule 49(a) since the court is not bound to submit all factual matters to the jury in its interrogatories where it asks the jury to return a general verdict. *See supra*, p. 596; *Bolan v. Lehigh Valley R.R.*, 167 F.2d 934 (2d Cir. 1948); *Kissell v. Westinghouse Elec. Corp., Elevator Div.*, 367 F.2d 375 (1st Cir. 1966).

(3) Inconsistent Verdicts

If counsel believes that the jury's verdict is inconsistent, unclear or ambiguous, an objection must be raised before the jury is discharged so that the court may have the opportunity to return the jury for further consideration. If no such objection is made, counsel will be deemed to have acquiesced in the jury's discharge and will not be heard to complain on appeal. *United States Football League v. Nat'l Football League*, 644 F. Supp. 1040, 1049 (S.D.N.Y. 1986).

---

82 Thus, in *Turchio*, the parties could not complain of the use of oral interrogatories when they did not object to the Court's failure to submit the interrogatories in writing. 509 F.2d at 105.

---

83 As also noted in *Cutlass*, counsel will not be deemed to have waived his jury trial rights if he is not given a fair opportunity to object to the court's interrogatories before the jury retires. *Id.*

It is not entirely clear, however, whether counsel is under an obligation to specifically request that the case be resubmitted to the jury, but it is clearly best that this be done.[84]

VII. THE RENDERING OF THE VERDICT

A. The Need for Unanimity

The jury's verdict must be unanimous unless, as provided under Fed. R. Civ. P. 48, the parties stipulate to a "stated majority." This federal unanimity rule, which perpetuates the common law rule, *Patton v. United States*, 281 U.S. 276 (1930), applies to all federal trials and therefore is not affected by contrary state statutes. *Masino v. Outboard Marine Corp.*, 652 F.2d 330 (3d Cir.), *cert. denied*, 454 U.S. 1055 (1981).[85]

B. Polling the Jury

There is no statute or rule which governs the manner and form of the jury's verdict. It is understood, however, that the verdict must first be written and sealed by the jury, and then read aloud in open court in the presence of all parties. *California Fruit Exch. v. Henry*, 89 F. Supp. 580, 588 (W.D. Pa.), *aff'd*, 184 F.2d 517 (3d Cir. 1950).[86] Any party can then request that the jury be polled, which will usually entail the clerk calling the roll and inquiring from each juror whether the juror agrees with the verdict.[87] If there is dissent or confusion "it is permissible for the judge to inquire as to the true intent of a juror and as to the existence of unanimity among the jury, so long as such inquiry does not have a coercive effect towards a unanimous verdict." *Curry*

---

[84] Since resubmission is not provided for under Rule 49(a), the failure to their request resubmission has been held not to constitute a waiver, even though the court is deemed to have the power to resubmit. *See Alverez v. J. Ray McDermott & Co.*, 674 F.2d 1037 (5th Cir. 1982). By contrast, since Rule 49(b) expressly authorizes resubmission, at least one court has held that the failure of a party to move for resubmission of inconsistent verdicts results in a waiver of any such objections. *Barnes v. Brown*, 430 F.2d 578 (7th Cir. 1970).

[85] Under New York law, unanimity is not required, and a 5/6ths rule applies. N.Y. Const. art. I, § 2; CPLR § 4113. Thus, when a state action is brought into federal court by reason of diversity or pendent jurisdiction, or when a federal action is removed from state to federal court, the degree of difficulty in achieving a verdict is, at least in a theoretical sense, increased.

[86] Usually the sealed verdict is handed to the judge and the foreman then announces the verdict at which time the clerk officially records it.

[87] The right to have the jury polled will be deemed waived if not asserted by counsel in open court before the jury is discharged. *Baker v. Sherwood Constr. Co., Inc.*, 409 F.2d 194 (10th Cir. 1969).

v. Moore-McCormack Lines, Inc., 51 F.R.D. 301, 303 (S.D.N.Y. 1970). If the court is not satisfied with the elicited answers it has the discretion to return the jury for further deliberations.

It is not permissible for counsel to question the jury. *Bruce v. Chestnut Farms-Chevy Chase Dairy*, 126 F.2d 224 (D.C. Cir. 1942). If counsel is not satisfied that the jury's verdict properly reflects the unambiguous assent of each juror, objection must be raised prior to the jury's discharge in order to allow the court to clarify any perceived confusion or to require additional jury deliberation. Once the jury is discharged it cannot be reconvened for any purpose, and the trial is then concluded. *Baker v. Sherwood Constr. Co., Inc.*, 409 F.2d 194 (10th Cir. 1969).

CHAPTER TWENTY

OPENING STATEMENTS

by E. Stewart Jones, Jr., Esq.

I. INTRODUCTION

We do not get a second chance to make a good first impression, and that first impression is often the most lasting impression.

A variety of jury studies have concluded that a substantial majority of jurors have a view of the case at its conclusion that is consistent with the impressions of the case formed following the Opening Statements. It is also known that jurors' recollections tend to be selective, that they react more to impressions than details; and that they are more likely to recall and accept factual proof and arguments which are consistent with and reinforce their first formed beliefs, and reject those that cannot be reconciled with those first-formed beliefs.

Mock jury studies have also shown that jurors often forget the source of information presented to them but, nonetheless, will rely upon that information in their deliberations. These jury deliberation studies illustrate that information referred to in the Opening Statement but never proven at trial will, if the omission between statement and proof is not brought to their attention in summation, recall that information even though its source is forgotten, and will consider it along with evidence actually presented at trial.

In short, the Opening Statement is a vital tool of persuasion and will significantly influence the tone of the trial, the jury's perceptions, recollections and judgments and the ultimate result.

In Federal Court, where our opportunity for participation in the jury selection process may either be absent or severely restricted, the Opening Statement provides the trial lawyer's first significant opportunity for meaningful interaction with the jury.

At no other time during the trial is the jury likely to be as fresh, as expectant, as receptive and as attentive. The jurors are more than ready to finally get down to the business of listening to, evaluating, and deciding the case that has brought them there. Never again in the course of that trial are the jurors as likely to be so open to persuasion.

When your Opening Statement is concluded, each juror should have a clear understanding of your case, the central issue or issues as you have defined them, the theme or theory of the case as you have defined it, and why the facts, law and the jurors' collective sense of justice require that their verdict be in your client's favor.

The legal parameters of the Opening Statement have been described by the United States Supreme Court as follows:

> An Opening Statement has a narrow purpose and scope. It is to state what evidence will be presented, to make it easier for the jurors to understand what is to follow, and to relate parts of the evidence and testimony to the whole; it is not an occasion for argument. To make statements which will not or cannot be supported by proof is, if it relates to significant elements of the case, professional misconduct. Moreover, it is fundamentally unfair to an opposing party to allow an attorney, with the standing and prestige inherent in being an officer of the court, to present to the jury statements not susceptible of proof but intended to influence the jury in reaching a verdict. (*United States v. Dinitz*, 424 U.S. 600, 612 (1976))

While technically accurate, the Supreme Court's bland and fainthearted statement hardly conveys the tactical value of a positive, forceful and clear Opening Statement; nor does it accurately suggest the manner in which it should be presented in order to maximize its legitimate use as a vitally important vehicle for persuasion.

II. THE PSYCHOLOGY OF THE OPENING STATEMENT

A. The Principles of Primacy and Recency

An understanding of the principles of primacy and recency and application of those principles throughout the entire trial are essential weapons in the arsenal of the trial lawyer.

The principle of primacy demonstrates the importance of first impressions and confirms that first impressions are often lasting impressions. The principle of primacy holds that the first belief about a subject is the most deeply believed and resists change most strongly. It refers to the intensity of belief and illustrates that the first points to be made in an Opening Statement should be your best points and should be the points on which you want the jury to decide the case. The principal and most compelling strengths of the case should be stated early in the opening.

The principle of recency refers to ease of recollection and holds that you will remember most easily that which you heard last. For Opening Statement purposes, it demands that counsel, at the close of his opening, reiterate the evidentiary points on which counsel wants the case to turn and which will require the jury to do what you are asking of them.

In practical terms then, the principles of primacy and recency mean that the Opening Statement should begin and end dramatically and compellingly.

B. Order of Information

Psychologists and social scientists have also determined the type of information that is remembered best by jurors.

Information presented first to jurors will be best remembered in terms of the emotional or general content; information presented last will be remembered best for detail.

This research suggests that in the opening minutes you should describe the broad theme or themes of your case and define the central issues which you want the jurors to determine, issues on which your proof is strongest. There is both a factual and emotional basis for any case and it is important to convey both in broad strokes in the first moments of your presentation.

The trial is, in large measure, an exercise in impression creation and management. Jurors will first remember the impression of a given witness's appearance and testimony and the impressions formed during a lawyer's argument. It is important that the Opening Statement be crafted so that the jury can respond emotionally to it, as the emotional message will be remembered and first decisions and first impressions are, in substantial part, premised on emotion. Therefore, the theme or each one of the themes of your case must have some moral force to it.

As what we first believe resists change, jurors will tend to be selectively receptive to facts, incorporating those that support the position taken emotionally in the first instance and rejecting those that conflict. What we hear first and believe, therefore, influences our interpretation of future facts and events. Those that are consistent with our beliefs are more likely to be considered credible than those that are not. Having first established and then reiterated the themes and supporting facts in your opening, you must reaffirm them through the proof, trying to begin each day and each witness with proof that connects to those themes.

C. The "Halo" Effect

As the Opening Statement influences the way jurors process subsequent information, the lawyer should not be bashful about promising jurors favorable evidence. The favorable evidence described in the opening gives the jurors a thematic framework into which they will fit the proof introduced later in the trial. While unfulfilled promises are very dangerous and must be cogently explained in the closing argument, the mere fact that an item of evidence may be challenged should not dissuade us from making the strongest, most extensive statement plausible with respect to it, as that statement will provide a favorable framework for use by the jurors in later interpreting the evidence that relates to that statement. The influence a forceful, positive statement about the evidence to come has on the jury's perception of and interpretation of all other evidence that relates to that same issue is known psychologically as the "halo effect." That principle underscores the need to be positive in your presentation and illustrates the means by which the weaknesses in your case or the strength in your adversary's may be neutralized. Talk about the good things in your case before you talk about the bad.

D. Simplicity

Simplifying the case should be the goal of any lawyer in every case. Narrowing the issues, explaining technical terms, defining medical terms, using simple words, short and plain sentences and avoiding legalese all go a long way toward making the case easier to understand for the jury and, therefore, more interesting to them. Studies have shown that people lose interest in the task before them if it appears to be a complicated one. The process of simplification of the trial is recognized and appreciated by jurors and will serve to build rapport between the lawyer who engages in it and the jury who benefits from it. The opening is the lawyer's first and best opportunity to make the case understandable and to make it understandable in the client's favor.

III. THE PURPOSE OF THE OPENING STATEMENT

When the opening is completed, the jurors should know basically what the case is about, what your position is, how you will prove your position, what you are asking them to do, and why they should do what you are asking them to do.

It should be used to emphasize your theme of the case, your concept of the central issues in the case, your facts, and the moral force and justice of what you are asking them to do. The opening should prepare the jury for particularly critical witnesses and proof, reduce the element of surprise for them, and neutralize weaknesses in your case by sandwiching them between strengths, softening them by explanation and reducing their relevance.

The opening should fulfill the jurors' need to know about the process, the case and your client.

To the extent that you can help the jurors understand the process, the case and what is expected of them, it will create a reciprocal obligation running from them to you.

When you sit down, you should have sufficiently personalized your case and your client so that the jurors like your client and consider you credible, sincere, competent and one on whom they can rely and to whom they can look for "help." If you are perceived as a credible information source by the jury, then in the case of evidentiary conflict or irreconcilable arguments, your version is more likely to be credited.

IV. THE STRUCTURE OF THE OPENING STATEMENT

A. Introduction

The structure of the Opening Statement must be designed to grab the jury's attention and sustain their interest.

You cannot waste time or words.

The first four minutes are vital and should not be allotted to a discussion of the purpose of the opening, the process of the trial or the introduction of parties. The first four minutes should capture the emotional, factual and moral essence of the case, describe its themes and define its issues. Having done that, you can then tell them what you have done, what the Opening Statement is and quickly rid yourself of whatever other "boiler plate" obligations you feel you have.

B. Brevity

Brevity is important. With the American attention span conditioned by television, the persuasive force of your opening must be accommodated to the roughly 20-minute interest span inculcated in us by television and its advertisers. Of course, that interest span is renewable and therefore it is important to use "transitions" where the subject matter of the trial requires significantly more time for the opening to be complete. While we should be brief, we should not sacrifice thoroughness to brevity. Do not, for the sake of brevity, fail to touch upon all important aspects of the case.

C. Transitions

A transition may take the form of silence, movement to a different location in the courtroom, gestures or a change in vocal tone, intensity or pace.

Transitions should be employed in order to mark different topics within your opening as well as to recapture or rekindle the jury's interest.

D. Construction

In analyzing the construction of an Opening Statement, you must assure that it meets at least six (6) basic requirements. It must tell the jury the story of *what* happened. It must tell the jury *why* it should reach a verdict for your client and *how* the jury is to reach that vedict for your client. It must give the jury a feeling for your client so that they will *want* to find a verdict in your client's favor. The "what," "why," "how" and "want" functions must be accomplished with a presentation that is clear, informed and informative, simple and consistent with the proof that you will develop.

Once you have dramatized your case, established your theme and defined your issues in the opening moments of your presentation, the balance of the Opening Statement is generally best delivered as a chronological story. It is easier for the jury to understand a story that is presented in order and it is also easier to present a story in that way.

E. The Story Order

Of course, in opening your Opening Statement, you will have seized out of context and out of sequence certain dramatic highlights of your case, but these should be repeated in the course of your chronological story. Repetition is a necessary psychological tool when attempting to persuade, and certainly the opening should utilize repetition for the proof highlights which most dramatically support your claim. Illustratively, an Opening Statement is often begun utilizing the flashback technique in which the end of the story, the consequences of the conduct which is the subject of the lawsuit, e.g., the damages, are first described and then the most aggravated events leading to those consequences are highlighted. Thereafter, the story of the case is told in chronological sequence and the events and elements which made up the dramatized beginning are repeated in chronological context, thereby re-emphasizing them and the theme and issue to which they relate.

F. Elements of the Opening

1. Beginning

The structure of any opening contains certain basic elements.

Its introduction should be dramatic and clearly stated. It should contain not only a statement of facts which cry out to the jury for redress but that statement of facts should lead naturally to a theme for the case.

OPENING STATEMENTS

2. Theme

It is important to strike a theme for your case in order to elevate it in the eyes of the jury to something more than a contest between lawyers or a quarrel over money. Before the jury retires to deliberate and reach its verdict, they must be made to understand that there is a moral justification for what it is being asked to do and that its verdict will not only fulfill your client's needs but will also serve a greater societal purpose. Any case can have a theme broader than the individuals involved and that theme must be stated in the opening and reiterated in summation. In a products liability case, the theme may be consumer safety; in a medical negligence case, the right of a patient to an informed choice; in an industrial accident case, the right of laborers to safe working conditions. The theme of the case should be well settled by the time you stand to make your Opening Statement and it must be linked to what you will be arguing in your summation.

3. Issues

Related to the case theme element of the opening is the definition of issues component. Defining the issues during the Opening Statement is necessary if the jury is to have a clear understanding of what the case is about and is to understand how the factual proof and the law require the verdict that you want. Most importantly, the lawyer who first defines the issues establishes the agenda regarding the issues on which the case will be decided. In a products liability case, the plaintiff would want the issue to be the character of the product and not the conduct of the plaintiff. In an industrial accident case, the injured worker would want the issue to be who is better able to bear the burden of adequate precautions rather than the worker's own conduct or knowledge. In an infant-pedestrian knockdown case, the infant would want the issue to be unsafe speed in a residential neighborhood rather than his or her own culpable conduct in running into the street.

There is always a relationship between the broad theme and the more specific issue. The theme of consumer safety in the products liability case directly relates to the issue of the product's character. In the industrial accident case, the theme of a safe work place is directly tied to the more specific issue of who is in the better position to provide the precautions necessary to protect the worker. The issue of unsafe speed in a residential neighborhood in the infant-pedestrian auto collision case would be tied to the broader theme of keeping neighborhoods safe for playing children.

4. The Story

The next element would be the story itself. This is an appropriate point for you to assure the Court that you know that the law considers an Opening Statement a promise and not proof. A simple statement to the effect that "the evidence will show" or "the proof will be" or "the evidence that will be presented will prove that" should suffice. A statement in this form need only be said once and should always be said forcefully and positively. To be equivocal in defining what you are about to tell the jury undermines the persuasive force of what you are about to relate to them and is a clear signal to the jury that you do not have much confidence in what you expect to be able to develop in the course of the trial. Therefore, never say "I expect the evidence will be" or "I believe the proof will show."

The story itself contains a number of elements.

The lawyer must introduce the jury to the client in a way that personalizes and humanizes the client and ultimately will lead the jury to identify with and feel for the client. All of the facts and background material that is relevant to the client and his position in this lawsuit should be presented.

The character and role of the other parties to the lawsuit must also be described. However, once you have introduced your opponent, there is no longer any need to refer to your adversary by name. You personalize your client by using his or her name whenever possible. You depersonalize your adversary by characterizing the opponent as "the defendant," "the corporate defendant," "the defense lawyer," "the defense team," "my opponents," "they," or other similar terms, rather than by name. To the extent that you can keep your opponent depersonalized, you maximize the psychological distance between the jury and your opponent.

Where the lawsuit has a physical scene, that should be described in its relevant particulars.

Where there are other physical facts that are relevant to the case, such as time, distance or weather, those should be described.

Any instrumentality such as the product in a products liability case or industrial equipment in an industrial accident case should be described fully.

In Federal Court, we have the advantage of generally being required to stipulate to the admissibility of exhibits in advance of trial and to have all exhibits premarked. Where it is conceded that a given exhibit is coming into evidence and that that exhibit or those exhibits demonstrate a physical scene or instrumentality, then you should seek permission from the Court to use that demonstrative evidence in your Opening Statement. Illustrating through the exhibit what you are saying aids understanding.

The courtroom itself furnishes a species of demonstrative evidence which can be used to describe a physical scene. Simply ask the jury to assume that they are facing a particular direction, then take the jury to the scene involved using counsel table, chairs, the jury rail, or other contents of the courtroom as props.

Where there are technical terms from specialized disciplines such as engineering, medicine or the components or workings of a particular product those terms should be explained and made understandable. This demonstrates not only your preparation and professionalism, and, therefore, enhances your credibility, but also builds your rapport with the jury as one they perceive to be helpful and a reliable information source. It is important in the opening to simplify the complex. If you have defined the technical jargon and explained the expert proof, then the expertise and expert testimony of professional specialists will be less threatening to the jury, and the jury more accepting of such proof. You need not display your knowledge in an ostentatious or pompous way thereby alienating the jury. In dealing with the explanation of the technical language and scientific proof, you should explain to the jury that you have been living with this case for some time and as a result of your exhaustive study and preparation of the "scientific" issues, and consultation with the experts, you have been able to learn what you are about to tell them. You are doing nothing more than teaching them what you have been taught.

Before you reach the damages elements of your story, the opening should have established the entitlement of your client to be compensated for whatever the consequences were of the defendant's conduct. It is a sound psychological principle that in order to avoid the appearance of overreaching, it is best to demonstrate your entitlement to what you have asked for, before you ask for it. The chronology of your factual story should naturally lead you to the events and acts which brought about the harm and the loss, and should have fixed forever in the respective minds of the jurors the unforgiveable responsibility of the defendant for those acts and events.

Leading from your discussion of the liability aspects of the case to the damages aspects, it is helpful to recapitulate for the jury the central liability facts and themes upon which you rely for their verdict. In doing so, make sure that the recapitulation comprehends the elements of your cause of action.

Reiteration of the principle factual strengths of your case is important to your persuasive effort. We indoctrinate by repetition. The liability strengths may be restated in highlight fashion as you conclude your discussion of the liability facets of the case and then again summarized in the fabric of your concluding remarks on the damages components in your case.

5. The Damages

The structural elements of the damages story will vary widely depending upon the nature of the damages inflicted and the presence or absence of issues relating to causation. The discussion of damages in the opening generally should be understated. At the same time, each item or element should be segregated and discussed independently rather than run together and discussed collectively.

In a personal injury or wrongful death case, each item of special damage should be identified and discussed separately and the items of special damage should be segregated from the general damages. Again, the items of general damage should be individualized without overstating them.

The University of Chicago's jury studies demonstrated that jury verdicts were higher where separate verdicts were returned on each item of damage than where a lump sum verdict was returned. In individualizing the different items of damage in your opening, you should tell the jury to consider each item you have identified, separately and distinctly and, in essence, to consider that item of damage as its own case and to calculate a separate monetary verdict for that and each element of damage.

The significance of some types of harm is apparent. What it means to be an amputee, or paralyzed, or brain damaged need not be elaborated upon in the opening. There will be ample opportunity in summation to discuss all of the implications, many of which will not have occurred to anyone who has not lived with such an injury. Similarly, with other types of harm, the full significance and entire scope of the consequences of that harm should not be stated in the opening. At the time of the opening, before the jury has heard any proof, a full statement of all of the implications of the harm may be viewed as overstatement or overreaching. The jury does not yet know either you or your client well enough. It could be misconstrued by them as a base appeal to their emotions, designed to obscure another issue in the case. At the very least, it will drown them in detail, take any element of anticipation or surprise out of the damages proof and unnecessarily prolong the opening. While the injury and its consequences must be highlighted dramatically, every nuance and detail need not and should not be spelled out. It is best to leave the jury with something to look forward to and you can tell them that proof is coming that they can look forward to. For example, "You will learn all about the structure and function of the spine"; or, "You will hear what it means to John Smith to be paralyzed, to have no use of his legs"; or, "You will hear and see and learn what it has meant and will mean for Mrs. Brown and her children to have lost her husband and their father." This does not suggest that you should sacrifice thoroughness to preserve the jury's interest. However, it does suggest that understatement has its place in this component of the opening and that you may better avoid an excess of detail in discussing damages than in discussing liability.

The technique of telling the jury that they will learn something about something without telling them what it is they will learn may, of course, be used in connection with any anticipated witness or item of proof where you can spare the details without reducing the persuasive force of your opening.

Of course, if you are trying a case where liability is not seriously contested and where the true battleground is the extent of the damages, the damages presentation should be more detailed.

In discussing the damages, do not forget to define and interpret the language of the specialists who will testify.

6. Confronting Problems

There are few perfect cases and, consequently, in the Opening Statement of virtually every case, you will have to explain a weakness in the case, confront a problem in the proof or defuse a defense to the claim. This element of the opening is generally best dealt with in the context of your factual story. By weaving the problem and its explanation into the fabric of your narrative you are putting it in the context in which you want it considered by the jury. In controlling where the jury hears about the problem and how it hears about the problem, you can minimize its impact. It is generally best to integrate the problem and its explanation into the story between points on which your claim is particularly strong. By "sandwiching" problems and their explanation between strong points, you are implementing one of the practical implications of the "halo" effect psychological principle. Describe the "good" in your proof before you confront and characterize the bad. In confronting your weaknesses, anticipating the defenses and recasting them in the light that you want the jury to see them, you blunt their impact and at the same time show the jury that they can trust you to be honest and candid with them about all facets of the case.

Where your adversary's contentions or proof deserve belittling rather than defusing then you might consider isolating them and discussing them in their own context. "As against all this proof, what does the defendant offer?"

7. Language of the Law

You want to incorporate the understandable language of the law into your opening.

The judge is generally perceived as the authority figure in the courtroom and to the extent that you can apparently align yourself with his authority in using some of the same language that they will later hear from him in his instructions to them, you will have enhanced your credibility and the jury's perception of your professionalism and expertise. Therefore, some of the commonly understood legal terms that are part of the legal vocabulary of your case should be sprinkled into your Opening Statement and more generously used in your summation.

For example, in a case involving a claim of negligence in any setting, you will want to use the word "duty" and the word "negligence" and equate "negligence" with the standard in that particular case. Similarly, each type of case has its own legal language, some of which is even used by lay people, or if not used at least capable of being understood.

The term "departed from acceptable standards of medical practice," routinely used in medical negligence cases particularly when establishing the applicable standards of practice and the breach thereof by the defendant, should certainly be used in any medical negligence case.

While you may not discuss the applicable law in detail, you can, without characterizing it as the applicable law, use the language of the law applicable to that case by simply incorporating it into your sentence structure as you discuss the case. Moreover, where the case has a statutory basis such as a case brought under a Wrongful Death statute or a Dram Shop or Labor Law statute, you may explain the statutory basis for bringing the suit.

If you wish to mention the burden of proof in the case, it is best done after you have recited for the jury the outline of the overwhelming proof that will be presented against the defendant. In mentioning it at the conclusion of your discussion of liability or at the conclusion of your discussion of liability and damages, you diminish the importance of the burden of proof and also put it into a factual context which permits you to implicitly state to the jury, "see how easy it was, is and will be to meet my obligation of proof." The important thing is that you not allow your adversary to convey to the jury the sense that the burden of proof is more than it is or that you are afraid of the burden of proof and that fear caused you to shy away from discussing it during your opening.

8. Closing the Opening

The theme of your case should be repeated at the close of the Opening Statement, the highlights of your proof recapitulated and again related to the issues on which you want the case to turn. The jury should be reminded again what you want them to do and how and why they should do it. In your requests for relief be as specific as the law and your trial strategy allow.

You should talk to the jury in terms of the debt created by the defendant's wrongdoing; and of the need to shift the burden of the defendant's wrongdoing from the innocent plaintiff who has borne it up to this point in time to the defendant who caused the harm, loss and debt.

The power of the jury should be identified and the jurors thereby flattered. The jury should be told that only they have the power to compel payment of that debt, to shift the burden of that loss. They should be reminded that what they do here they do for all time as this is your client's only day in court, the only opportunity he or she will ever have, and the only opportunity the jurors will ever have to do justice on such a grand scale.

OPENING STATEMENTS 615

The call for personal and societal justice is a recurrent theme stated in many different ways and should always find its way into the concluding remarks of an Opening Statement.

9. Forcing Your Adversary's Hand

In the context of the closing, you may wish to embarrass your adversary by suggesting that if he has anything to say in defense of the defendant, he should be as candid and forthcoming, as thorough and as detailed, as you have been. This may force him to do something that he had not wanted to nor intended to do, or will underscore his failure to do that.

In the same vein, you may want to remind the jury, if it has not been done by the court in its preliminary instructions, of the sequence of the case and of the defendant's opportunity to present a case. Should your adversary fail to provide a thorough and detailed opening, it will serve to diminish whatever proof was later presented by the defense and certainly permit the inference that the defense was still evolving at the time of the opening, and, consequently, the defense lawyer could not identify what the defense would be. The absence of detail in an adversary's Opening Statement followed by a detailed defense provides a fertile opportunity in summation for challenge to the credibility of that defense.

10. The Opening Must Relate to the Summation

In structuring the Opening Statement you must remember that there has to be a correlation between it and the summation. Each must be talking about the same case and each must be relying upon the same central facts, themes and issues. If the case has gone well, then the summation will permit you to expand on what was promised in the opening but there still must be a consistency between the two in order to sustain credibility.

There are many who feel you should frame the structure of your summation and then prepare your opening and outline your proof. At the very least, you must know what you would like to be able to argue in summation and how you would like to argue that and support it. Having determined what the thrust of your case should be, the themes, issues and facts which evolve from your concept of the case then become the fabric of your Opening Statement and the outline for your proof.

You should never lose an opportunity to remind the jury how consistent, candid, prepared and professional and, therefore, credible you have been. Credibility projection is critical to impression creation and management. Credibility projection requires that you be able to demonstrate in summation how well you have delivered on the promises implicit in what you told them about the case in your Opening Statement. If you do not prepare both the structure of the summation and the opening before you deliver the opening, you may not be able to do that.

V. THE PRESENTATION OF THE OPENING

A. Be Positive

The opening is a promise that you intend to keep. The summation is the fulfillment of the Opening Statement and a reminder of how well you have kept the promises you made in that Opening Statement.

In delivering your Opening Statement, there must be no hint of a doubt about your ability to deliver on what you are promising. The language used should be positive and affirmative. "The proof will be" and "the evidence will show" are affirmative and unequivocal phrases that convey confidence in your cause.

In the book *The Art of Persuasion*, the author described as a basic principle of persuasion the need to project sincerity and to convey the impression that what you are saying you genuinely believe.

To convey confidence, you must be enthusiastic and energetic in your presentation. Enthusiasm and energy naturally translates into forcefullness which in turn is perceived by a jury to reflect a strong belief in the cause you are representing.

B. Be Specific

Your factual presentation should be specific and concrete. Studies have shown that the persuasive force of any theme, argument or statement is enhanced by details. Illustratively, it is more persuasive to state that "the defendant ran a red light" than to state "the defendant was negligent"; similarly, the statement "John's leg was fractured in three separate places" is more forceful than simply saying "John was seriously injured."

While first decisions and impressions are generally made on emotion, jurors require facts and the details of facts to then support the position emotionally.

Detailed stories are perceived as credible and persuasive, but do not submerge the broad themes of the case in excessive detail and do not detail the opening to the point of interest loss or jury confusion.

C. Develop Psychological Identification Between the Jury and You, Your Client and the Client's Case

By personalizing your client and your case, you begin the process of securing the jury's identification with your cause.

Psychological identification is facilitated with the use of names and first person references.

D. Personalize Your Client

Stand by your client when you talk about him. Place your hand on his shoulder as you discuss how he or she has coped with the harm inflicted by the defendant.

In the course of the trial, show concern and care for your client.

If the jury has a sense that you are not interested in or do not really care for or about your client, then why should they.

E. Use the Courtroom

Studies have demonstrated that up to 85 percent of our knowledge is gained visually; and that information that is both seen and heard is much more likely to be retained than information that is only heard.

In the opening and in the course of the trial, it is necessary to try to bridge the gap between the visual orientation of jurors and the verbal orientation of trials. That is done most effectively by demonstrative exhibits, visual aids or word pictures.

In the opening, the courtroom itself and its contents may be used demonstratively. The jury itself may be asked to assume it is in a given location and the jury rail, counsel tables, chairs, books, briefcases, water pitchers, cups may all be used to fulfill a role, define a point or measure a distance.

Space usage within the courtroom will also give a visual orientation to an opening.

F. Use of Physical Space

If permitted by the court, you should break down any physical barriers between you and the jury. A lectern is a physical barrier and if you do not need it and the court does not require that you use it, move it out of the way. The absence of a physical barrier between you and the jury creates, psychologically, an openness and a sense of free flow between you and they.

When you move during the opening, move for emphasis and move purposely and energetically. Do not walk on your lines. Do not move in the middle of an important statement. Move before the statement in order to isolate it and mark it. Movement in the courtroom should have purpose and meaning. Avoid random or nervous pacing.

Do not violate the personal physical space of the jurors. At the time of the opening, particularly in Federal Court where there has been no or very little personal *voir dire*, you and the jurors are still relative strangers to one another.

You have not yet earned the right to invade their personal physical space, which is generally considered to be an area extending out from them for approximately three (3) feet. Certainly, during the opening you should not hover over them or lean across the jury rail.

You should range generally between three and six feet from the first row of jurors during your opening, but for the purpose of emphasis or transition can range beyond the six feet. To distance yourself too far from them throughout the entire opening will suggest to them a lack of comfort with them and it is likely to prohibit the development of any personal rapport, trust or identification.

G. Use of Pleadings and Exhibits

In Federal Court where pleadings are required to be marked and exhibits stipulated to and premarked, the foundation for a request to use such exhibits or refer to the factual statements in such pleadings during the Opening Statement has been laid. Prior to opening, you should request permission to use a pleading or exhibit which will serve to visualize and, therefore, simplify statements you are going to make.

You may not use the pleadings for the purpose of reciting legal contentions. You may use them for the purpose of narrating facts or reciting admissions that are created by your adversary's pleading.

H. Depositions

Where you know you will be using depositions in the course of the trial, the depositions should be referred to in the opening and an explanation of the deposition process and the purpose and use of the deposition should be given.

The jury should be told that the deposition testimony was taken under oath, in the presence of the witness's lawyer or your adversary or both, under essentially the same rules as apply in the courtroom.

By the time you conclude your discussion of the deposition, the jury should understand that what you read to them from it must be considered by them as though it were given in the courtroom, under oath, in their presence.

I. Make the Jurors "Experts"

Define and make understandable the technical, scientific, medical and anatomical proof that is to come. You not only establish your role as helper and teacher, but in making the complex simple and understandable the jury will be more receptive to and accepting of the expert proof when it comes. We are fearful of that which we do not comprehend and are likely to have little interest in or acceptance of that which makes no sense to us.

J. Word Choice

Words that have the same essential meaning may convey much different impressions and impact. "Fault" is a better trigger word than "negligence." Jurors are more receptive to the term "professional negligence" than the term "medical malpractice." "Collision" or "crash" suggests something more than "accident."

"The defective ladder collapsed beneath him hurtling him to the ground" is certain to create a different impression and word picture than "He fell to the ground when the ladder broke."

A plaintiff's lawyer would want to characterize a fall down case in terms of the fault associated with the failure to properly maintain the property, while a defense lawyer would describe it as a slip and fall by a needlessly distracted plaintiff.

"The evidence will show that John Smith deserves and is entitled to monetary compensation. . . . " is more effective than "We are suing for. . . . . "

The words selected to convey a message, the way in which something is said, significantly influences the impression formed by the listener. Take time before your Opening Statement to review the words and phrases you want to use to maximize the impressions you desire to create by the stated fact.

Use plain words, short sentences and action verbs.

Avoid depersonalizing or incomprehensible legalese such as "administrator," "the subject occurrence," "plaintiff," in discussing your case. While there will be words and phrases that must be used and then explained and clarified, those should be the exception. If a juror is trying to figure out what you just said then he or she will not hear what you next say.

K. Do Not Overreach

Do not argue how big or how serious your case is until you demonstrate how good the case is.

You overreach if you ask the jury to do something for you where there is no showing of your client's entitlement to the relief you request.

You overreach where you overstate. A lawyer caught in overstatement loses credibility.

If the jury senses that you are overreaching on behalf of your client, you will no longer be perceived as their source of reliable information, or as sincere.

This should not be misconstrued to suggest that you should be bashful about promising jurors favorable evidence. Studies have shown that the promise of favorable proof influences the way jurors process information presented later on, and consequently their verdict. A statement of favorable proof to come gives the jurors a thematic framework into which they will then "fit" the evidence and testimony later introduced. It is important to provide the jurors with a favorable framework that they will then use to interpret later evidence. In the unfortunate event that a promise goes unfulfilled, it will have to be explained in the closing argument. A reasonable explanation may blunt the effect of your adversary's comments on the discrepancy.

L. Emotion

While controlled emotion is important to the Opening Statement and to the moral force of your case, remember that too much emotion will make the jury uncomfortable, particularly in the early stages of the trial. You ultimately will have to earn the right to share a jury's emotions, and to have them trust you in order for them to accept the sincerity of your emotions. The full emotional argument is more likely to be accepted from someone whom the jury has come to know.

While there must be passion and energy, enthusiasm and force in the opening, full-scale emotional fireworks should usually be preserved for the closing argument, lest the jury treat your overemotional statement as a form of overreaching.

M. Vocal Tone

You should avoid a slow delivery or long pauses. The Opening Statement should have good momentum.

Rapid speakers can hold attention better than slow speakers without a loss of comprehension.

However, you want to vary the speed of your speech for emphasis and for interest retention.

While much of your Opening Statement will be in a conversational tone, it would be a mistake not to raise your voice in outrage, or for emphasis of certain high points in the statement, and drop your voice dramatically at other intervals, particularly when discussing damages.

The vocal range should be used for emphasis, for transition and for interest retention.

N. Use Transitions

The jury must hear the topical shifts in your Opening Statement and their interest must be retained.

When you move from one point to another or one subject area to the next, it is best to create a transition from one to the other. The transition will isolate that area and give it a more memorable life of its own. The transition from one topic to another can be accomplished by the use of preparatory remarks, a change in vocal pace or tone, silence, physical movement within the courtroom, or dramatic gestures. The important thing is to mark the topical shift for the jury.

In order to anchor certain themes or factual highlights in the jury's consciousness, you should use the same transition technique whenever you discuss that theme or those facts. Illustratively, by standing in the same place or using the same gestures or the same vocal pace and tone each time you refer to a given theme or factual highlight, the synthesis of word content, voice and "body language" reinforces and anchors the message for the jury.

Key points must be reinforced throughout the Opening Statement by repetition, utilizing the principles of primacy and recency, and that reinforcement is facilitated by repetition of the non-word cues as well.

According to Dr. Albert Nehrabian, a highly respected Research Psychologist, only 7 percent of the total persuasive message in a courtroom reflects the content of the words used; 38 percent reflects vocal pitch, volume, intonation, speed and inflection; while the remaining 55 percent of the total message is non-verbal and non-vocal and includes posture, body movements, facial expressions, stance, dress and eye contact.

O. Maintain Eye Contact

You cannot persuade if you do not look at the object of your persuasion.

In the course of your Opening Statement, you should focus occasionally on each juror; do not leave anyone out and do not pay undue attention to any single juror.

Eye contact is the most potent tool for bringing passive receivers into active roles for communication.

P. Levity

The representation of a person in a lawsuit is serious business and levity has no place in that exercise unless it is spontaneous, natural and non-disruptive. Certainly, forced humor or joke telling should be avoided.

While lighthearted banter is often used to break down barriers and reduce tension in the course of the jury selection process, it should not find its way into your Opening Statement.

Q. Avoid Objections

You want your opening to be forceful, clear and undisturbed by objections from opposing counsel. If the opening draws objections, it will interfere with the flow of the story and distract the jury's attention; if the objection draws a ruling adverse to you from the judge, it will identify you at the very outset of the trial as someone who was caught attempting to break the rules.

R. Do Not Promise a Witness by Name or Link Precise Details of Testimony to a Specific Witness

The danger is obvious. If you cannot deliver the witness or if the witness cannot deliver the precise details you promised he would, you have lost credibility. It is best to promise facts, not witnesses by name.

S. Opening the Opening

Examples:

Elevator Failure - Products Liability Case:

> At 7:00 a.m. on October 12, 1988, John Smith kissed his wife, Anne, and nine (9) year old daughter, Susan, goodbye and headed off to work to a job that he had held for 23 years.
>
> John Smith was 51 years of age, healthy, productive and happy. He led a full life, a vital and active life, a proud life as the father, husband and breadwinner.
>
> At 7:30 a.m. he checked in at work.
>
> Five (5) minutes later, he boarded an elevator and began his ascent to the top of a silo.
>
> Two (2) minutes later as a result of a series of failures and malfunctions, that elevator was hurtling toward earth, out of control with John Smith in it.
>
> Seconds later, the shattered body of John Smith lay crumpled on the floor of that elevator.
>
> John Smith will never work again, will never walk again without braces and crutches and will never be the father or the husband he was and would have been.
>
> What happened, how it happened, why and how these defendants could have prevented it and who must bear the financial responsibility for the catastrophic consequences to John Smith, his wife and child is what this case is all about.

Medical Neligence-Wrongful Death Case:

> On September 12, 1988, John Smith walked into the Doctors and Nurses Hospital for minor surgery on his left foot.
>
> One month later, he left, on his back in a coffin. He was dead.
>
> He was 30 years old.
>
> Together we shall investigate the cause of and responsibility for his death and the value of his life to his now widow and two children.

OPENING STATEMENTS

Commercial Contract Case:

> This is a case about a broken promise. It is a case about trust and a violation of that trust.

Often in capsulizing the case in the opening paragraphs, your broader theme will not naturally be incorporated. If not, then it should be in the next paragraph. Illustratively, in the elevator failure products liability case referred to above, the theme of consumer safety was struck:

> This case is a tragic illustration of the harm done by the failure to make a safe elevator, by the failure to test and inspect it to make sure it was safe after installing it and by the failure to correct and repair that unsafe elevator in order to make it safe.

T. Use Contrast

Example:

Infant-Pedestrian Knockdown:

> This is a story of an uneven contest between a 45 pound little boy and a three (3) ton truck; between a six (6) year old child and a 38 year old adult.

In a products liability case, you may contrast the corporate designer and manufacturer with the lay consumer. That, too, is an uneven contest. You may incorporate the technique of contrast and rhetorical question in asking the jury, "Who knew the product best?" "Whose product was it?" "Who was best able to prevent this product from failing?" With each question, the answer is the corporate defendant designer and manufacturer, as the proof will show.

U. Use Rhetorical Questions

Example:

Elevator Failure Product Liability Case:

> "When the cables began to free wheel did the slack cable safety brake device work?"
>
> "No."
>
> "Should it have worked?"
>
> "Yes."
>
> "If it had worked, would the elevator have stopped?"
>
> "Yes."
>
> "Was the safe and proper functioning of that safety device the duty and responsibility of this defendant?"

"Yes."

"Was the failure malfunction of that safety device the fault of this defendant?"

"Yes."

Infant-Pedestrian Knockdown:

"When he saw that little boy, did he slow down?"

"'No."

"Did he blow his horn?"

"No."

"Did he swerve?"

"No."

"Did he stop?"

"No."

Medical Negligence:

"Did they read the *Physicians Desk Reference* before administering the drug?"

"No."

"When John became obviously sicker, did they call the defendant-doctor?"

"No."

"When the defendant-doctor was finally called did he come?"

"No."

V. Do Not Tell the Jury that What You are Telling Them is Not Evidence

They will hear that from the judge and more likely than not from your adversary. There is no reason for you to reaffirm it and by reaffirming it, cheapening and diminishing what you are doing.

W. Pre-Empt the Defense

You must confront your problems and neutralize your adversary's strengths. The jury must not hear for the first time from your adversary about the problems in your case or strengths in his. That reflects adversely on your candor and also takes from you the opportunity to have recast those problems in their best possible light in your opening.

Problems such as a pre-existent condition, a criminal record, an inconsistent statement, an adverse eyewitness, a negative panel in a medical negligence case, or an absent product in a products liability case may always be explained and diminished by the explanation but not if your adversary first brings it to the jury's attention, undoubtedly in a way that suggests that you were trying to conceal it from them.

Researchers say that lawyers can "inoculate" jurors against the other side's point of view by presenting opposing arguments first in weakened form and then demolishing them.

It is also important to leave your adversary with as little as possible to say. Your Opening Statement should be sufficiently thorough to render redundant an opening of any length by your adversary.

X. Concluding the Opening

In closing, alert the jury to the fact that you are ready to conclude. The level of attention is heightened when there is an expectation that a talk is coming to a close. If the jury's interest has been flagging, the knowledge that you are about to conclude will rekindle that interest. You do not want to waste your closing on jurors who are not paying close attention because they did not realize that you were "summing up."

The closing may be introduced as simply as stating "in closing" or by forging a link between opening and summation by stating, "I am about to sit down but I will have another opportunity to discuss with you the proof in this case and the promises that I have made to you about that proof in my summation at the end of this case. Before I sit down, however, let me summarize . . . " The important thing is that jury know well that you are about to conclude the opening.

In closing, you should again express confidence in your cause and confidence that the proof will require the jurors to return the verdict you want for your client.

In concluding, restate the broader theme which you will tell the jury their verdict will address, such as consumer safety.

Example:

An injustice has been done to John Smith.

A wrong has been committed by these defendants.

We are here to ask you to right that wrong, to correct that injustice.

You have the power, the opportunity, the privilege and the responsibility on the proof in this case to do what we ask of you, to shift the burden of these catastrophic losses from John Smith and his family who continue to suffer them to these defendants who caused them.

Your verdict in this case will speak to the issues of product safety and consumer rights. I am confident that John Smith has no reason to fear your verdict for on the proof in this case, the only right verdict, the only fair verdict, the only just verdict, is the verdict I ask for on behalf of John Smith.

Thank you.

At that point, you may want to consider involving the authority figure in the courtroom, the judge, by turning to him and saying:

"That, Your Honor, will be the case and the proof on behalf of John Smith."

That serves to reaffirm your confidence in your cause and certifies your commitment to the proof you will have just discussed.

Y. Do Not Present the Jury with Too Many Dominant Themes or Alternative Theories

The themes you present to a jury must have a relationship and be internally consistent. Always remember that while you have lived with the case, the jurors are brand new to it. To present too many themes serves only to confuse them. Research suggests that no case should have more than three dominant themes.

Similarly, alternative theories serve not only to confuse but also to diminish the force of any single given theory. The hydra-headed approach to case presentation generally suggests that you have little confidence in either or any of the alternative theories. If you find yourself in a position where you have to say to a jury, in essence, "if you don't like this theory, then try this alternative one," neither theory will have much credibility.

The exception is where the facts which govern the theory to be applied are in dispute, but either set of facts to be found by the jury to be true, compels the result you seek. You argue alternative theories not from weakness but only where either or any of the theories and the facts upon which they are predicated leave your adversary with no escape.

Z. Notes

Speakers gain prestige by being well prepared and by carefully choosing and organizing their presentation.

There is a direct correlation between prestige, credibility and favorable audience response.

The advocate who delivers an opening without notes will be perceived as better prepared and more conversant with the facts of the case than the advocate who must rely extensively on his notes.

The absence of notes will also permit better eye contact with the jury and will eliminate the "note barrier" between the speaker and the jury.

VI. THE LAW OF OPENING STATEMENTS

An action may be dismissed or a directed verdict may be granted on admissions made by counsel during an Opening Statement. *See Best v. District of Columbia*, 291 U.S. 411 (1934). Although a party whose claim or defense has been terminated based upon his Opening Statement should have the right to reopen where the omission or admission was inadvertent, counsel must be able to assure that the deficiency made evident in the Opening Statement will be cured. *Oscanyan v. Arms Co.*, 103 U.S. 261 (1881); *Morgan v. Koch*, 419 F.2d 993 (7th Cir. 1969).

It is, however, not necessary to allude to every fact counsel hopes to prove. *Hanley v. United States*, 416 F.2d 1160 (5th Cir. 1969). The Opening Statement is a road map not a doctoral dissertation. Failure to make reference in the Opening Statement to facts intended to be proved does not justify subsequent exclusion of these facts as long as they are comprehended by the pleadings. *Butler v. National Home for Disabled Volunteer Soldiers*, 144 U.S. 64 (1892).

The Opening Statement is required to be a statement of facts not argument. *Best v. District of Columbia*, 291 U.S. 411 (1934).

A. Avoiding Mistrials and Reversals

While the excesses that may be committed in the course of an Opening Statement are beyond the scope of any list, the indiscretions listed below are common.

1. Inflammatory Statements

United States v. Signer, 482 F.2d 394 (6th Cir. 1973) (characterizing a defendant as Aesop's fabled "fox in the chicken coop"); *Hallinan v. United States*, 182 F.2d 880, 885 (9th Cir. 1950) (intemperant language used in discussing the veracity of adverse witnesses).

2. Personal Opinions

See Annotation, *Propriety and Prejudicial Effect of Comments by Counsel Vouching for Credibility of Witnesses*, 81 A.L.R.2d 1240 (1962).

3. Blatant Appeals to Sympathy of Jury

Lazofsky v. Sommerset Bus, Inc., 389 F. Supp. 1041 (E.D.N.Y. 1975) (Counsel's choking and showing of emotion during Opening Statement held improper).

4. The Golden Rule Argument

Leathers v. General Motors Corp., 546 F.2d 1083 (4th Cir. 1976) (asking jurors to put themselves in the place of the plaintiff in Opening Statement constituted reversible error requiring new trial); *see also* 70 A.L.R.2d 935 (1960).

5. References to Inadmissible or Irrelevant Matter

Maxworthy v. Horn Elec. Serv., 452 F.2d 1141, 1143-44 (4th Cir. 1972).

6. Mistating or Characterizing Evidence in a Way That Cannot be Proved is Unethical, Model Rules of Professional Responsibility DR 7-102 (1980).

7. The Law

Generally, detailed discussions of the law in Opening Statement are not allowed. *Murphy v. L.J. Press Corp.*, 558 F.2d 407 (8th Cir. 1977).

B. The Need to Object

You must object to opposing counsel's indiscretions during the Opening Statement and should do it contemporaneously with the indiscretion. This is necessary in order to identify the breach and to preserve the issue for objection, motion or subsequent appeal. *Patriarca v. United States*, 402 F.2d 314, 318-22 (1st Cir. 1968).

Curative instructions will generally be held to correct any potential prejudice flowing from the misstatement. *Affleck v. Chicago and N. W.RY.*, 253 F.2d 249 (7th Cir. 1958); *United States v. Modica*, 663 F.2d 1173 (2nd Cir. 1981).

Of course, a mistrial is appropriate if the error realistically cannot be cured.

BIBLIOGRAPHY

Carlson, *Successful Techniques for Civil Trials: Opening Statements*, Section 6.9, et seq. (The Lawyers Cooperative Publishing Company, 1983).

Decof, *The Art of Advocacy—Opening Statement* (Matthew Bender and Company, 1982).

Figg, McCullough, Underwood, *Civil Trial Manual II*, Joint project of the American College of Trial Lawyers and the ALI-ABA Joint Committee on Continuing Legal Education.

Fisher, *Federal Trial Procedure Handbook*, Chapter 6, *Opening Statements* (Wiley, 1985).

Frederick, *The Psychology of the American Jury* (The Michie Company, 1987).

Hunter *Federal Trial Handbook II*, Chapter 21, *Opening Statements* (The Lawyers Cooperative Publishing Company 1984).

Jeans, *Trial Advocacy* (West Publishing Company).

Julien, *Opening Statements* (Callaghan & Company).

Mauet, *Fundamentals of Trial Techniques* (Little, Brown and Company).

Minnick, *The Art of Persuasion* (Houghton, Mifflin, 1957).

Pyszczynsti, Greenburg, Mock and Wrightsman, *Opening Statements in a Jury Trial: The Effect of Promising More Than The Evidence Can Show*, 11 Journal of Applied Social Psychology, 434, 442 (1981).

Pyszczynsti and Wrightsman, *The Effects of Opening Statements on Mock Jurors, Verdicts and Criminal Trial*, 11 Journal of Applied Social Psychology, 301, 309 (1981).

Rasicot, *Winning Jury Trials*, Chapter 5, *Opening Statements* (A.B. Publications, 1983).

Sonsteng, Haydock, Boyd, *The Trial Book*, Chapter 5, *Opening Statements* (West, 1985).

Vinson, *Social Science Research Methods for Litigation*.

CHAPTER TWENTY-ONE

SUMMATION

by Philip H. Magner, Jr., Esq.

Since civil trial practice is conducted under an adversary system, the object, of course, is to win. An advocate will win his case if he persuades the jury under appropriate legal instructions to adopt his position and to act upon it by their verdict. It follows, therefore, that every part of trial—opening statement, direct examination, cross-examination, and summation—should have persuasion as its sole objective.

During a competent opening statement, the primary tool of persuasion is instruction; that is, the transmission of relevant information in a clear and attractive manner well-calculated to persuade. So, too, in the course of direct examination does the skillful advocate try to elicit relevant and helpful evidence, and the artful cross-examiner, while extracting information destructive of or debilitating to the direct examination, attempts also to elicit new facts persuasive to his cause. In each of these tasks the trial lawyer functions primarily as a teacher, providing the jury with relevant information designed to persuade and to convince.

Finally, however, when trial counsel rises to begin summation, he is permitted for the first time to employ the ultimate weapon of the advocate—argument. Indeed, because persuasive advocacy in summation is so often decisive in close cases, final argument is widely regarded as the ultimate test of the trial lawyer's art.

I. PURELY PRACTICAL ASPECTS

It is axiomatic that the trial lawyer should always be herself or himself, no matter the place of trial, and should always avoid any semblance of artificiality in speech, dress, or personal mannerisms. Ostentatious or excessive use of personal jewelry, lotions, or hairstylings are to be avoided under any circumstances. The careful advocate will endeavor, in both dress and speech, to identify with the community in the district in which trial is held, and obviously, to avoid actions which are or might be offensive. Inquiry about and attention to local customs, practices, and sensitivities are always worthwhile and enable the trial lawyer to avoid giving even the most unintentional offense. In a district where a majority of the jurors will be drawn from economically depressed areas, for example, wearing extremely luxurious clothing or operating an expensive automobile may provoke at least subliminal resentment and present a handicap to the most competent of professional efforts. Similarily, the use of slang or excessive idiom in a district where the educational level is high is likely to have a grating effect.

The attention span of even the most dedicated juror has limitations, no matter how effective the summation. Reasonable regard for the comfort of the members of the jury is certainly in order, and it is appropriate and sensible for trial counsel to request reasonable recesses and adequate ventilation for the courtroom, to avoid drowsiness or discomfort occasioned by jurors' personal needs. For the trial lawyer who has occasion, as this writer frequently does, to try cases in other jurisdictions far removed from his home base and to find himself largely in the hands of unfamiliar court personnel utilizing different court rules than those which prevail at home, a tactful accommodation to those circumstances is certainly desirable, and creates a good and often rewarding working relationship throughout the trial.

This writer, at the very beginning of summation in an unfamiliar district, almost invariably finds an opportunity to compliment the courthouse staff on their effectiveness and hospitality, and to tell the jurors that they are well served as taxpayers by the court personnel of their community. Almost everyone is happy to hear this estimate and compliment from a stranger, and the good feeling is usually returned in one way or another.

II. IMMEDIATE LEGAL PREPARATION

Since final argument cannot be really effective if regularly interrupted, it behooves the careful advocate to prepare for summation in such a way as to limit the occasions for interruptions, and to leave as little as possible to chance.

Accordingly, motions *in limine* having to do with summation, if not made previously, should be made immediately preceding or during the precharge conference. Counsel should secure a ruling determining what evidence can be referred to, as well as the parameters of permissible argument. This preparation will allow the summation to proceed without unnecessary interruption.

Similarly, counsel must prepare and present to the court requests and objections to charge as early in the trial as possible, and certainly not later than the precharge conference. It is utterly impossible to give an effective summation without a thorough knowledge of the law that will be charged and, in fact, the language in which it will be couched. Heavy reliance on form jury instructions is in order, although reasonable differences of opinion as to which charges ought to be given are fairly common. Additionally, almost every case will have some unique features which will cause counsel to prepare and urge, or to argue against, special charges. A thorough airing and argument of requests and objections will enable the court to advise trial counsel before summation exactly the law on which the jury will be instructed, and usually the language that will be employed. Thus informed, counsel can prepare for summation confidently and without the risk of ultimate embarrassment from a charge of the court which was unanticipated.

If summations are not ordinarily recorded by the court reporter in the district as a matter of course, a request to have an opponent's summation or to have all of the summations taken ought to be made adequately in advance, and the opposition so advised. When blackboards are to be employed for the purpose of tabulations or freehand drawings, a request to the court for that privilege should be made early and upon notice, as should arrangements to photograph the unerased blackboard following summation, so that the contents can be preserved in the record of the trial. If counsel desires to use physical objects not in evidence for purposes of illustration during summation, a timely request should be made to the court upon notice to all opponents. If this request is granted, these articles should be marked and preserved. Finally, counsel ought to know before commencing final argument which of the exhibits marked in evidence will be allowed into the jury room. The trial judge has a good deal of discretion on this issue. Many judges will not permit some exhibits, though received in evidence, to be taken to the jury room. If counsel is interested in having a particular exhibit go to the jury room, counsel should make the request on the record, adequately argued and briefed, no later than the precharge conference.

III. IMMEDIATE PHYSICAL PREPARATION

Just as counsel will want to have legal rulings firmly settled before final argument commences, care should also be taken that the physical tools to be employed are marshalled and ready to avoid fumbling, delay, and interruption.

If counsel intends to quote testimony from the record during summation, it should be done accurately by having the desired testimony typed in advance, readily available and suitably underlined for use during argument. Exhibits should be selected and marshalled in order of intended use. Depositions and records from which reading is planned must be available close at hand with pages tabbed and the language to be quoted underlined.

If a blackboard, display board, X-ray view box, magnifying equipment, or projector is to be used during summation, it ought to be in place and ready for immediate use so that continuity of counsel's summation is not impaired.

Complicated tabulations and computations, as for example, complaints of pain, records of drug purchases, or chronologies of stock transfers must be made, preferably on an adding machine, and the tapes submitted to opposing counsel for verification in advance of summation.

If counsel intends to use an outline or notes during summation, they should be prepared and organized for easy reference, and illustrative quotations from literature or especially important phraseology committed to memory for best effect.

Attention to these seemingly inconsequential details in preparation for final argument will enable the advocate to sustain a much higher level of jury interest and attention, and to emphasize the important points without distraction or delay.

IV. PHILOSOPHY OF TRIAL AND PSYCHOLOGY OF SUMMATION—THE PLAINTIFF

Many cases which fill the federal courts of this state pit an individual plaintiff or family against an experienced business defendant, insurer, or governmental entity.

Because the plaintiff has generally only one case and the defendant or the insurer has many, the considerations which motivate and control each side are likely to be dramatically different, involving dissimilar approaches and tactics.

Because the plaintiff in a tort action has ordinarily only one case, he always wants and often needs a complete victory to make him whole, especially since he must generally pay a percentage of his recovery to his attorney. That plaintiff, unless otherwise affluent, cannot afford to sustain a serious loss in litigation, since he has no other cases from which to recoup. His bargaining position is relatively weak because the outcome of his one case, especially if it is a major one, will have a great deal to do with the quality of the remainder of his life, and even the lives of the members of his family.

The plaintiff, therefore, wants and needs to obtain a verdict against all financially responsible defendants, to avoid comparative negligence, and to obtain full and uncompromised damages. The burden of proof which the plaintiff has on most issues is balanced by the advantage of the final summation.

Plaintiff's counsel will often be aided implicitly, though not expressly, by sympathy for the victim, especially in a serious damage case, and will probably paint with a broad brush, avoiding technicalities, details, particularizations, and finite points. He will prefer to stress right and wrong, to contrast victim and perpetrator, unless references to specifics are both clear and helpful.

Usually the plaintiff, bearing the burden of proof, will be less likely to stress the applicable law, except in situations clearly to his advantage, such as violations of the Labor Law or cases in strict liability.

The plaintiff's counsel should try always to emphasize the positive, and may elect to skim lightly over defendant's questions and arguments, unless an answer is either vital to success or can be extremely effectively made.

Almost always, plaintiff's counsel will choose to discuss liability first in his summation, and to spend enough time on that subject to insure a plaintiff's verdict. Indeed, if he fails to obtain a verdict in his client's favor, it matters little how eloquent on the subject of damages his argument may have been.

Ordinarily, then, the difficulty of plaintiff's cause will determine the amount of time counsel devotes to the subject of liability during summation, so that the more difficult the case for the plaintiff, the greater the emphasis on liability will be. Cases of clear or excellent liability are usually settled, and it is not often that plaintiff's counsel has the great luxury of quickly reviewing well-established liability on the part of the defendant, and then proceeding to an extensive and exhaustive argument on damages.

For the skilled plaintiff's attorney in the more difficult case, however, the mandate of the circumstances is clear—a cause verdict *must* be obtained and, if necessary, damages must be allowed to take care of themselves. Obviously, a full and adequate verdict is desirable, and counsel must strive to obtain one if at all possible, but even an inadequate verdict for the plaintiff is better than no verdict at all. Morever, if based upon competent liability evidence, there remains always the possibility of a successful appeal on the issue of adequacy only.

On the subject of damages, plaintiff's counsel will want to give careful thought in preparation to the organization and phraseology of the argument he intends to make, culminating with some suggestion, within the parameters of existing law and the court's anticipated rulings, of an appropriate total verdict. Counsel should try to give the jury some sort of target or standard against which to measure its own thinking, and to do so in a way that neither exaggerates nor offends.

V. PHILOSOPHY OF TRIAL AND PSYCHOLOGY OF SUMMATION—DEFENDANT

To a major extent, the psychology with which defense counsel approaches trial and summation depends upon who the defendant is and who is the real party in interest. The insurance company or large corporation which has many actions to defend is in a very different category than the plaintiff who has only one case. The large corporate defendant, insurer or governmental entity has experience with many cases and anticipates many more, and is interested less in the results of any one particular case than in its experience over an extended time period. A particularly good or bad result in a single case is unlikely to be decisive of the insurance company or corporation's financial future, because the outcome of other cases bears upon that subject as well, and a single case may well turn out to be an abberation in terms of overall experience and results.

The small uninsured or underinsured corporation can soften the blow of a particularly bad result in a single case through a tax write off. Even an uninsured or underinsured individual can often claim a similar advantage, particularly if the loss is incurred in connection with the taxpayer's business.

Obviously, any insurance company or large corporate defendant would find a complete victory in any individual case desirable, but its need for unqualified success is not comparable to that of the plaintiff. The experienced defendant or insurer may view a number of possible verdicts as fairly satisfactory in terms of its overall experience, ranging from total victory by reason of a no-cause-of-action to various types of partial victory.

For example, a defendant which is quite clearly liable to the plaintiff may be delighted if a substantial percentage of liability is found against a co-defendant, and some contribution thus obtained, or a right of indemnification established, or if a plaintiff's verdict is significantly reduced by a finding of comparative negligence, or if the damage award is substantially less than might have been expected, or if the jury returns what is tantamount to a compromise verdict.

Such defendants and their insurers need only a reasonable result in any individual case because, unlike the plaintiff, they expect and plan for some losses. The aim of such defendants is for satisfactory statistics and averages, and the concern is for the bottom line. They can afford a loss, even a grievous one, far better than the plaintiff, and thus are in a vastly superior bargaining position.

There are, however, some notable exceptions to this rule, including newspapers, magazines, and broadcast media who regard any verdict in any amount against them for libel or slander as a catastrophe, and professionals such as physicians, accountants and attorneys charged with malpractice, fraud, securities violations or RICO violations, who believe their reputations are at stake in such trials. In the field of product liability, a single case or a class-action suit may be largely determinative of the outcome of all such claims, and of the manufacturer's financial stability, and thus such cases are also exceptions.

In certain situations, defendants may find themselves at odds with their insurers who, in this author's view, may not be as sensitive to the reputations of their insured as in their overall claims experience. It is remembered, however, that defense counsel's first duty is to his client, and not to its insurance carrier. His judgments and tactics must be formed and carried out in accordance with that obligation, even though the interests of the insurer may be different.

Corporations, which are frequently defendants, and casualty insurance companies ordinarily do not take big risks, preferring to keep results under reasonable control and to effect outcomes which are within the limits of their expectations. They will generally play the percentages, and be guided heavily by their experiences of the past. Their defense attorneys will rely implicitly, but not expressly, on natural suspicion and skepticism, and on the exacting requirements of the law.

Defense counsel in final argument will emphasize that the advancement of a claim is not proof of its validity, and raises no inference of fault, will hammer repeatedly on plaintiff's burden of proof on most issues, and will be quick to point out any failure of proof. Defense counsel will try to show that conflicting inferences are equally probable, and that there are acceptable alternative explanations to the one urged by the plaintiff. Any untruth or exaggeration in the plaintiff's case will be employed to undermine plaintiff's case on both liability and damages.

Since the plaintiff generally has the burden of proof, defense counsel will tend to be specific in his treatment of the issues and demand the same of the plaintiff. The defense lawyer will insist on proof of each element of each cause of action, and, in anticipation of plaintiff's summation, will raise as many questions as possible in order to create doubt, to distract plaintiff's counsel and the jury, and to require plaintiff's counsel to spend his summation answering defendant's points and questions.

Some experienced defense counsel who face particularly serious or aggravated cases of injury will choose to ignore the subject of damages completely, preferring not to argue the unarguable, to maintain their credibility, and to concentrate their time and attention on liability.

If the subject of damages is to be treated, however, defense counsel will argue that they are unproven or overstated, that there is no causal connection to the incident of which complaint is made, or that the same outcome was to be anticipated from an entirely different cause. Defense lawyers will generally discuss damages first to the extent that they are discussed at all, then proceed to the subject of liability. Unlike plaintiff's counsel, the defense lawyer summing up will be able to devote the largest part of his time to the subject on which he is strongest, since any one of a variety of possible verdicts is likely to be reasonably satisfactory to his client.

Even in cases of clear liability, few defense lawyers choose to advance a figure on damages for jurors to consider. It is suggested, however, that in a proper case, good sense may require counsel to do so, and a fair figure may be highly credible to a jury, especially if plaintiff's request is exaggerated or unreasonable. Defense counsel must use his best judgment under all the circumstances but should at least consider the subject.

VI. PREREQUISITES TO EFFECTIVE FINAL ARGUMENT

In order to structure a summation likely to accomplish its intended objective, it is important for the advocate to realize the purpose and limitations of final argument. Summation is not a substitute for proof unprepared and unpresented, and is unlikely to succeed, no matter the eloquence of the advocate, unless it is thoroughly grounded in the evidence actually received during trial. Summation is not an opportunity to speculate or to fantasize, but rather to marshal evidence, and from it, argue reasonable inferences and conclusions. As noted, successful final argument is virtually impossible unless it is based upon definitive knowledge of the law to be charged, or without substantive evidence clearly presented and well understood. Equally important to success is a jury estimate of counsel gained over the course of the entire trial as a person of stature and integrity, honorable, fair, dedicated, and reliable. If these prerequisites have been met, and if summation has been carefully prepared, counsel can rise to begin final argument with a well-founded confidence in its ability to persuade.

VII. PREPARING THE ARGUMENT

The time to begin thinking about summation it is not after the evidence has been closed, but well before the trial commences. A careful trial lawyer will have examined, tested, molded, and shaped the theory of the case during the process of preparation, thinking *then* about what to say during final argument. In early preparations, the lawyer must identify the main thrust of the case and the evidence ultimately used during summation.

At the close of the evidence, counsel should reconsider the state of the proof—what are its strengths and weaknesses—what points need to be made to obtain the desired result. It is then that counsel can begin to consider the composition of the jury and their behavior during trial, as well as the locality where the case has been tried, in order to select arguments and phraseology which will be most likely to persuade.

In the process of preparing summation, the careful advocate will want to anticipate and be ready to meet arguments expected to be advanced by the opposition. This process involves far more than guesswork or surmise. Some of the opposition's points will be quite obvious from the facts adduced at trial, while others can be gleaned from the arguments during various motions and from requests to charge. In reflecting on an opponent's probable arguments and questions, counsel should decide in advance, at least provisionally, which to answer and how, subject always to last minute revisions based on preceding summations.

Similarly, in structuring a summation, astute counsel will consider all of the possible arguments, identifying, shaping, and expanding the strongest, and discarding the weakest. Summation time is valuable, and must be wisely and economically used, and weak arguments that will expose themselves or will be easy to refute are better not made at all.

Counsel will want to give careful thought to the organization of final argument before deciding which testimony to discuss and how, and which exhibits to utilize. While a neophyte may be tempted to follow in summation the chronological order of proof during trial, that is not necessarily the most persuasive and compelling presentation. Indeed, there is no summation drearier or more painful to the listener than a witness-by-witness, note-by-note, exhibit-by-exhibit rehearsal of the evidence received. Such a performance does not rise to the stature of argument, but is little more than a tedious recital.

The skilled advocate will often choose to match conflicting items of evidence against each other, suggesting and then soundly refuting the opposition's arguments first, proceeding then to advance the client's case, and ending on a strong and positive note. If the advocate, by effective argument, can persuade the jury to reject totally the opponent's positions or conclusions, the advocate will have created a vacuum which the client's positive arguments will be able to fill, thus completing the process of persuasion.

VIII. CREDIBILITY

The principal reason that juries are still extensively used in this country is that they are thought to have a special ability to resolve issues of credibility. It is a rare trial, indeed, in which some issues do not arise regarding the truth or accuracy of testimony or even of exhibits. While the jury may be totally unskilled and may require substantial in-trial education on technical matters which are the subject of proof, jurors require no such training to determine credibility. Their various experiences in life prepare them well for this task, to which they bring the skills of life itself. Trial lawyers will find jurors finely tuned and sensitive to issues of truth and falsity, accuracy and mistake, and likely to base their determinations largely, if not entirely, on the resolution of those issues. For that reason, the wise advocate in preparation for summation will carefully consider how to treat issues of credibility.

Fair-minded jurors may well be extremely hard on any party or advocate believed to have produced testimony which is knowingly false. Conversely, however, the same fair-minded jurors are likely to react unfavorably to unfounded accusations of forgery or perjury. Thus, if counsel intends to charge deliberate falsehood in testimony or proof in the course of summation, counsel had best be sure it has been proven. Otherwise, an unsubstantiated or unbelieved accusation will more than probably be turned against the client's case by a righteous opponent or an outraged jury.

If there is reason for suspicion but no clear proof of deliberate falsification, it is better not to make a frank charge of chicanery, but rather to gently invite the jurors to wonder about the quality of the suspected evidence.

Instead of indulging in serious, but unproven, accusations it is wiser to argue the basic unlikelihood of the suspected testimony, based on such factors as the demeanor, interest, or motives of the witness, the witness's ability to observe or remember, the physical impossibility or absurdity of the testimony, or a prior inconsistent statement. Similarly, the proof may contain other evidence which may be fairly and effectively argued, such as a relevant and fairly recent criminal conviction, or other conflicting testimony or documents.

Experienced counsel will have attempted during the course of the trial to make some objective appraisal of the impact of each witness, and of the jury's reaction to his or her testimony. Except in the most extreme circumstances when no other course is open, the seasoned advocate will not attempt a frontal assault in summation on a witness who has made a good impression and withstood cross-examination well, but will prefer to use more peripheral approaches to show that there are good reasons why the witness may be honestly mistaken.

IX. MATTERS OF STYLE AND TECHNIQUE

It is virtually impossible for any lawyer to instruct others on the manner and style that ought to be employed in addressing the jury during final argument, partly because it is axiomatic that one needs to be oneself; partly because each case is different from the last and the next, and may require a slightly or even significantly different approach; and finally, because subjectivity is involved to such a great extent there can be no single "right way" to sum up.

The writer has not included quotations or exerpts from his own summations or those of other advocates because effective techniques or arguments do no exist in the abstract, but only in relation to the evidence itself and to the time, the place, the personalities, the problems, and the circumstances of a particular trial. It is only when all of those factors are fully perceived and understood that the effectiveness of a particular argument or approach will become apparent.

Beyond that, summation is oral argument meant to be heard and seen, and to be experienced and felt in the highly charged atmosphere of the courtroom itself. It necessarily loses much of its impact when reduced to the printed page in the quiet of an office or study.

SUMMATION

Within this century, the style of public speaking has changed greatly, and the florid bombast of William Jennings Bryan has long since given way to the gentler persuasion of Franklin Delano Roosevelt. The reasons are many, but high on the list must be the significantly higher educational level of today's jurors, and the evolution of a less docile population.

There was a day not all that long ago when the appearance of a college graduate on a jury was a notable rarity; when some had graduated high school, but most had not. Jurors were exclusively male, and minorities were lightly represented, if at all. The trial lawyer's summation was an authoritarian statement of a better educated man, and the most verbose approach was often the successful one.

The modern trial lawyer will do well to study and reflect upon changing mores and differing attitudes among age groups and segments of the population if he is to be able to present arguments which will be well received and effective. Jurors of these days are exposed to all sorts of experiences and influences largely unknown to their parents and grandparents, and their attitudes and approach to life are fashioned to a large degree by the rapidly changing environment in which they live. For better or for worse, prudery has virtually disappeared from the courtroom, subject matter is explicit within reasonable bounds of taste, and jurors are largely inured to shock and horror by two generations of graphic films and books. Consumerism and skepticism flourish, old values are questioned and often rejected, and submissiveness has almost totally disappeared among jurors under 40.

To all of these generalizations, there are, of course, exceptions, and the thoughtful advocate will reflect carefully on individual jurors to find the approach most likely to persuade.

While it is mandatory to address any jury in clear and understandable English, it is important to talk neither above nor beneath the common denominator of jury intelligence. The trial lawyer who "talks down" to jurors makes the most egregious error of all by insulting their intelligence, while the advocate whose choice of language or phraseology is on too high a plane runs a risk that he will not be understood at all.

It is a serious mistake these days to attempt to tell jurors in the course of summation what they must or are bound to do, or what conclusions are required by the evidence. Especially these days, the advocate will do far better to employ the language of suggestion, persuasion, or exhortation in summation, and avoid any appearance of an attempt to command or enforce a favorable verdict.

Only the case itself and all its attendant circumstances can determine the appropriate length of final argument, but, except in the most unusual circumstances, it ought to bear some rough relationship to the length and complexity of the proof, and the issues to be decided. In a particularly long and complicated case, selectivity is clearly required in order to make the most compelling arguments while at the same time retaining jury attention, but the truly skillful advocate will often be able to reduce a seemingly complex issue to a simple and obvious conclusion through the use of illustration, anecdote, or comparison. If an extended summation is really required by the circumstances, it ought to be broken by a recess and airing of the courtroom. Counsel will more likely retain the attention of the jurors if in the course of argument regular eye contact is maintained with the jurors. Tone of voice, position, and gestures should be varied often enough to avoid monotony. While large courtroom audiences are flattering, it is only the jurors who will decide the case and it is entirely to them that everything must be directed. Special attention, of course, must be paid to those readily identifiable "leader jurors" who are likely to have more than average influence in determining the outcome, and arguments should be tailored in such a manner as to appeal especially to them without appearing to slight less assertive jurors.

Movement and gestures for the purpose of attention and emphasis are entirely appropriate, but only auxiliary to the persuasive force of the argument itself, and will not be an effective substitute for slipshod organization or faulty reasoning.

Humor, emotion, quotations, dramatics, and even tears may have a proper place in final argument, depending upon the subject matter of the case, the atmosphere of the trial, and the personality of the advocate, but only if they are thoroughly consistent with the carefully conceived and consistently followed objectives of the argument. It is not the task of trial counsel to cut a fine figure, to entertain hearers, or to impress with eloquence, but soley and entirely to persuade. It does little good to perform an exercise in showmanship if a favorable verdict is not achieved.

Jurors, virtually without exception, no matter their derivation, background, or personalities, take their obligations as jurors very seriously, and approach their tasks in good conscience and with a determination to do what is right. They view the courtroom as a hall of justice, the home of a hallowed process of which they are an integral part. Counsel must never do anything to discourage those feelings, and ought to be in every respect an honorable advocate and an instrument of justice. Counsel must always adopt the high road, acting, urging, and persuading in such an ethical and responsible manner as to obtain and deserve the confidence and respect of the jury. The summation's appeal ought to be always to the finest and best instincts that govern human behavior, to the fairness and decency with which one human being ought to treat another, and to the cause of justice, of which counsel is but the dedicated servant.

CHAPTER TWENTY-TWO

DIRECT AND CROSS-EXAMINATION

by Walter Barthold, Esq.

I. INTRODUCTION

Direct and cross-examination have opposing goals. What direct examination tries to build, cross-examination seeks to destroy. What the cross-examiner attacks, the direct examiner endeavors to defend.

In almost every case, the trial lawyer must play both parts. He or she must tear down what the other side has built up, and do what can be done to protect what he or she has constructed.

Yet mastery of both roles requires many of the same skills. This chapter has as its purpose the development of those skills.

II. DIRECT EXAMINATION

A. Non-Leading Questions

With too many trial lawyers, direct examination remains a neglected science. With so much to do as the trial approaches, many a practitioner sketches a general outline and anticipates composing questions *ex tempore*. That attitude can represent a fatal mistake.

The avoidance of leading questions ranks as the most elementary skill of direct examination. Nothing distinguishes the professional from the amateur more readily than the presence or absence of this talent. No one who has not mastered it belongs in any federal courtroom. No one can master it without thinking out individual questions beforehand.

The leading authority on federal practice defines a leading question thus, 10 *Moore's Federal Practice*, 2d Ed. 1948 and 1988 ¶ 611.31:

A leading question is a question framed in such a manner that it suggests or indicates to the witness the answer which the interrogator wants.

The Federal Rules of Evidence take a permissive attitude on the matter of leading questions. Subparagraph (c) of Rule 611 says:

> Leading questions. — Leading questions should not be used on the direct examination of a witness except as may be necessary to develop the witness' testimony. Ordinarily leading questions should be permitted on cross-examination. When a party calls a hostile witness, an adverse party, or a witness identified with an adverse party, interrogation may be by leading questions.

This text, especially the words "should not" at its beginning, reflects the long-standing attitude that the trial judge may allow or exclude leading questions without fear of reversal either way.

In *United States v. DeFiore*, 720 F.2d 757, 764 (2d Cir. 1983), *cert. denied*, 466 U.S. 906 (1984), the Court of Appeals quoted the words "should not be used" from Rule 611(c), above, and said, "These are words of suggestion, not command." Then quoting the Advisory Committee on Rules of Evidence, the court continued:

> An almost total unwillingness to reverse for infractions has been manifested by appellate courts.

DeFiore was a criminal action, but the language just quoted has the same validity in civil cases.

The astute trial lawyer refuses to take advantage of liberality that the above authorities suggest. He realizes that leading questions tolerated can do as much damage to his case as the gaps left by their exclusion.

Leading questions on direct examination create a bad impression. To the trier of the facts, especially a jury, they suggest that the witness, instead of giving his own version of the facts, is acquiescing in a story that his lawyer has developed.

Leading questions can lead both court and jury to draw invidious comparisons. If your adversary pops up every few questions with an objection, it makes little difference whether outright exclusion or gentle admonitions result. You have created the impression that the other side knows more about the rules of the game than you do.

Thorough preparation of the witness stands as an essential element of avoiding the leading question. Before he takes the stand, the witness should know what each of your questions is aimed at. If you and he have gone over every step of his testimony, questions such as "What happened next?" or "What if anything did you do then?" will not puzzle him.

The lawyer's own preparation counts, too. A detailed outline, with all but the most routine questions written out, will free the direct examiner's mind of puzzling over how to get each item of information from the witness. He can better cope with the unexpected developments that occur in every trial and take advantage of any new ideas that occur to him.

A danger exists in over-preparation on the part of a witness. If the witness goes on for too long without the interruption of a question, he will appear rehearsed. Maintain the question-and-answer format even if it means from time to time breaking into otherwise satisfactory testimony.

Some lawyers believe that preceding a statement with "State whether or not" provides insurance against the disallowance of a question as leading. The technique unquestionably works in making a relatively simple point, but is of dubious utility in a more complicated context. For example, this question would surely survive an objection as leading:

> State whether or not you recognize the signature at the end of Plaintiff's Exhibit A as your own.

This, in contrast, might not work out as well:

> State whether or not you conferred with Mr. Jennings on February 12, 1988, and told him that you had decided to terminate the contract with Webster on the following day.

A measured dialogue between counsel and witness, with each playing his proper part with assurance, will enhance any line of testimony. The absence of long pauses and repeated objections will have the same effect. Both lie within the reach of the trial lawyer who knows what leading questions are and how to avoid them.

B. Laying the Foundation

A direct examination cannot proceed smoothly without knowledge of how to lay a proper foundation when that is necessary. As with leading questions, the presence or absence of the technique helps brand trial counsel as master of his craft or as beginner.

Laying a foundation means supplying the evidentiary predicate before offering a given item of evidence, be it testimony or an exhibit. Principles of logic as much as rules of evidence govern the adequacy of a foundation.

If you expect the court to receive in evidence a letter from the defendant to the plaintiff, you must prove at least that the defendant wrote and mailed it if not also that the plaintiff received it. You cannot start questioning a witness about a conversation without locating him at the place of the conversation and showing who else was there. No court will receive a photograph without testimony as to who took it, from where and when. A physical object that played a part in an accident or other occurrence will never get into evidence without a showing that it is in fact the identical thing about which testimony has been or will be given.

These are elementary examples. Laying a foundation can become exceedingly complex when, for example, scientific or technical matters or involved fact situations arise. The principle, however, remains the same. If you do not supply every detail essential to the evidentiary validity of an element of your case, you can count that element as missing.

By their nature, questions of foundation must usually be dealt with before the trial. This truth provides another item in the long list of reasons for thorough preparation. The practitioner who fails to realize, until he is on his feet in the midst of direct examination, that none of the witnesses on his list can authenticate the document he regards as crucial to his case, may never be able to rescue himself.

In federal practice, discovery provides in many instances a short-cut to laying a foundation. Rule 32 of the Federal Rules of Civil Procedure provides for the use of deposition testimony at the trial. Rule 33(b) applies in the same way to answers to interrogatories. Rule 36 ("Requests for Admissions") makes available a technique too often overlooked in trial preparation. Admissions pursuant to this provision constitute in many instances the simplest and least expensive way to obtain, in admissible form, the components of a proper foundation.

Astute counsel make every effort to have the foundation laid before the time comes to offer a given piece of evidence. This makes for a logical flow of the proof, ordinarily more convincing than presenting the trier of the facts with pieces of a puzzle that he or they must try to put together in their heads. Yet the ideal does not always prove possible. A means exists of putting the cart before the horse when that becomes unavoidable.

"Subject to connection" serves as the password for the lawyer who must depart from logical order and provide a foundation after instead of before the introduction of a piece of evidence. Absent extraordinary circumstances, federal judges will accept counsel's representation that the necessary support for the testimony or exhibit will be forthcoming. If the foundation is not provided, the conditionally-received evidence must be stricken.

C. Introducing Exhibits

As a trial proceeds, the trier of the facts does more than weigh the evidence, evaluate credibility of evidence and ponder on whose side justice lies.

DIRECT AND CROSS-EXAMINATION

A judge, jury or both simultaneously observe the lawyers and formulate a mental report card. A post-trial interview of jurors, where permissible, will confirm this process.

The introduction of tangible evidence in the form of exhibits offers trial counsel another opportunity to classify himself as a bumbling beginner or a smooth professional. The rules to follow are few but can make a world of difference.

How many lawyers seem to shy away from the simple sentence, "I offer it in evidence." Circumlocutions and paraphrases abound, but none matches the simplicity and clarity of these plain words. One may, of course, vary them to specify the object being offered, for example, "I offer in evidence this letter dated October 2, 1988."

That brings to mind another essential step in the introduction of physical exhibits. The offering attorney must establish a fool-proof connection between what the court reporter's transcript refers to and the exhibit itself. Marking exhibits for identification represents the customary way of achieving that objective.

It seems to escape many lawyers that the sole point of marking for identification is that mentioned above, namely, to provide a reader of the transcript with a way to identify the exhibit he is reading about. The point can become crucial when counsel questions one witness about a physical object but does not offer it in evidence until he has another witness on the stand.

As an example of the simplest application of the technique, this hypothetical exchange will suffice:

COUNSEL: Your Honor, I ask the reporter to mark as Plaintiff's Exhibit 1 for identification this two-page letter dated October 2, 1988, on the letterhead of XYZ Tubing Corp. bearing what appears to be the signature of Leonard T. Smith, Vice President, and addressed to Mr. R. H. Clement, Purchasing Agent, Anderson Supply Co.

THE COURT: It may be so marked.

COUNSEL: Mr. Smith, can you tell us what Plaintiff's Exhibit 1 for Identification is?

A. Yes, it's a letter that I wrote to Bob Clement.

Q. Can you identify the signature that appears at the bottom of page 2?

A. That's my signature.

Q. Did you affix your signature to Plaintiff's Exhibit A for Identification and cause it to be mailed on or about the date that appears near the upper right-hand corner of its first page?

A. Yes, I did.

COUNSEL: Your Honor, I offer in evidence Plaintiff's Exhibit 1 for Identification.

(In most trials in federal courts, judges permit leading questions in the course of a routine authentication such as that which the above exchange is intended to represent.)

A court, counsel should remember, will always permit an object to be marked for identification. That step should be taken even where the attorney knows the exhibit will be excluded. An exhibit cannot otherwise be brought to the attention of an appellate court for a determination of the propriety of its exclusion.

In modern federal practice, courts commonly call for the pre-marking of exhibits. Legal stationers carry adhesive stickers made for this purpose. Pre-marking need not alter the procedure, as suggested above, for offering exhibits in evidence.

The deposition and other discovery procedures provide another way to mark exhibits for identification before trial. In a case that involves extensive documentary or other physical evidence, this can save a volume of time.

Knowing how properly to offer physical evidence helps to bring about a smooth-running, efficient trial. Such a result can only gratify all concerned, including judge and jury, and reflect credit on the attorney or attorneys responsible.

D. Offers of Proof

A trial lawyer must never cease to think ahead to the possibility of an appeal. For that purpose, he or she wants a record that will show the appellate court what went on below. As appellant, counsel will wish to show not only what improper material went into the record, but also what proper evidence the trial court kept out.

The offer of proof provides the means for accomplishing the latter objective. According to Rule 103 (*Rulings of Evidence*) of the Federal Rules of Evidence:

> (a) Effect of erroneous ruling.—Error may not be predicated upon a ruling which admits or excludes evidence unless a substantial right of the party is affected, and

DIRECT AND CROSS-EXAMINATION

(2) Offer of proof.—In case the ruling is one excluding evidence, the substance of the evidence was made known to the court by offer or was apparent from the context within which questions were asked.

Exceptions exist, especially where the appellate court can see for itself what the excluded testimony would have shown, but the attorney who fails to make an offer to prove what the trial judge has refused to hear may find the door shut to review on appeal. *Moss v. Hornig*, 314 F.2d 89 (2d Cir. 1963).

This chapter has shown how to make an offer of proof when documentary or other physical evidence is in issue. One simply marks this document or object for identification and makes it a part of the record.

With respect to oral testimony, a somewhat more elaborate procedure is called for. The lawyer must show the appellate court what a witness would say if an objection to a particular segment of testimony had not been sustained. Depending on the matter excluded, this can be a simple or a complex task.

Typically, the offer of testimonial proof consists of a summary by counsel of the excluded testimony. It hardly needs explanation here that the summary must be thorough. If any doubt exists of its importance to the proponent's case, an explanation, not necessarily argumentative, should precede or follow the offer.

The court, however, according to subparagraph (b) of Rule 103, "may direct the making of an offer [of proof] in question and answer form." This may include, especially where the excluded testimony is complex, having the witness himself or herself give that testimony from the stand. Such a procedure is especially recommended where the excluded testimony arises on cross-examination. Counsel who attempts to summarize or paraphrase the testimony of an adverse witness risks an accusation of unfairness.

All of this, of course, happens out of the hearing of the jury. Federal Rule of Evidence 103(c) codifies thus the policy underlying that necessary precaution:

> In jury cases, proceedings shall be conducted, to the extent practicable, so as to prevent inadmissible evidence from being suggested to the jury by any means, such as making statements or offers of proof or asking questions in the hearing of the jury.

The offer of proof represents one of the innumerable details that beset counsel as the trial progresses. Overlooking it, however, can spell defeat on what otherwise might prove a successful appeal.

E. Expert Witness

No competent lawyer will prepare expert testimony without first reviewing Article VII of the Federal Rules of Evidence. As a codification, it has changed many of the traditions of that area. Most of these changes appear to smooth the way for the party who calls the expert. At the same time they create opportunities for the cross-examination, opportunities that the direct examiner will do his best to foresee and eliminate.

One retains and calls an expert, of course, for opinion evidence. Only a physician can diagnose a set of symptoms, only a civil engineer can explain why a bridge collapsed, and only a jeweler can appraise a precious stone. Yet not all opinions require experts. Federal Rule of Evidence 701 provides:

> If the witness is not testifying as an expert, the witness' testimony in the form of opinions or inferences is limited to those opinions or inferences which are (a) rationally based on the perception of the witness and (b) helpful to a clear understanding of the witness' testimony or the determination of a fact in issue.

Application of this broad, dual standard, which prevailed long before the Federal Rules of Evidence came into being, poses a question essentially of the trial court's discretion. Appellate courts rarely if ever disturb the receipt or exclusion of non-expert opinion evidence. *Central R.R. Co. v. Monahan*, 11 F.2d 212, 214 (2d Cir. 1926); 11 *Moore's Federal Practice* (2d Ed., 1948 and 1988) ¶ 701.20.

Drawing the line between permissible lay opinion evidence and the area deemed appropriate for experts amounts to a difficult if not impossible job. The Federal Rules of Evidence avoid the morass by using the same kind of pragmatic test for both realms. Rule 701, governing lay testimony, has been quoted above. Rule 702 speaks thus of expert testimony:

> If scientific, technical, or other specialized knowledge will assist the trier of fact to understand the evidence or to determine a fact in issue, a witness qualified as an expert by knowledge, skill, experience, training, or education, may testify thereto in the form of an opinion or otherwise.

The simplicity and breadth of this single sentence astonish many veterans at the bar who for years have struggled in case after case to compose and organize lengthy hypothetical questions and then spent sometimes hours defending them against nitpicking objections. In fact, not all of those practicing in the federal courts realize and take advantage of the liberality that now governs expert testimony.

DIRECT AND CROSS-EXAMINATION 651

Note, for example, that the Rule does not require testimony in hypothetical form. It does not even require expert testimony to take the form of an opinion.

No one should make the mistake of concluding that the liberality of Rule 702 makes the presentation of expert testimony easy. On the contrary, the availability of so much latitude presents counsel with the imperative of concentrating on the development of expert testimony that will prove effective, not just permissible.

The testimony of every expert can be divided into three principal parts. First comes the witness's qualifications. Second comes the work that he or she did in studying or investigating the subject or matter as to which testimony is to be given. Last comes the opinion or other conclusions or observations that counsel hopes to elicit. Each of these categories presents a myriad of considerations and problems, most of them unique to the specific witness whom one is preparing.

F. The Forgetful or Mistaken Witness

It happens to everyone. Now and then a witness, on direct examination, gets something wrong or forgets something that counsel had reason to remember. Such a development can provide a disappointment, even a jolt. It need not always, however, cause despair.

Before deciding what to do about such a failure on the part of his or her own witness, the trial lawyer must decide whether the slip has done any damage to the case. Correcting or changing testimony will itself detract from the strength of that testimony. So a weighing must take place, often on the spur of the moment, of the harm done by the error or lapse against the inevitably weakening effect of the remedy.

With a decision made that something must be done, counsel has a number of choices. First comes refreshing the witness's recollection. Nothing prohibits using this technique to help out one's own witness. It may be used by resort to a document, whether or not in evidence. The alternative involves the examining attorney's making a statement himself.

If a writing of any sort is available, it provides the better, less embarrassing way of refreshing the memory of an errant or forgetful witness. Suppose, as an example, your own witness has just said that he first met the defendant in the spring of 1985. You know from trial preparation that in fact the parties' first encounter took place a year later. Suppose, moreover, that the date of the meeting makes a difference to the substance of your case. If you have a suitable document, say, a letter confirming an understanding reached at the meeting, you should encounter no difficulty with a question such as:

Q. Mr. Bradley, I hand you your letter of May 9, 1985, to Mr. Fields, Defendant's Exhibit B for Identification, and ask you if it refreshes your recollection as to when you had your first meeting with him.

Use of this device requires keeping in mind an evidentiary consideration. To begin, do not forget that Rule 612 of the Federal Rules of Evidence requires you to give your adversary access to any writing used to refresh a witness's testimony "while testifying." This can make a difference, since such access is required to documents used for that purpose "before testifying" only "if the court in its discretion determines it is necessary in the interests of justice."

In the use a document to refresh the recollection of one's own witness, therefore, it is essential first to have it marked for identification. Most federal judges, once the paper has served its purpose, will receive it in evidence as a matter of course. If that probability threatens the divulgence of extraneous matter of a prejudicial character, counsel should read with care the entirety of Rule 612. It provides for, among other things, excision of "matters not related to the subject matter of the testimony."

Perhaps no suitable writing exists. Perhaps, if one does exist, the damage that disclosure will do outweighs its value as help to the witness. In that case, a question such as this may be asked, assuming the same set of facts that underlay the suggested use, above, of a document.

Q. If I say the spring of 1985, does it refresh your recollection as to when you had your first meeting with Mr. Fields?

The disadvantage of this technique requires only the briefest discussion. It can create the impression that counsel is putting words in the mouth of the witness. An objective source such as a piece of paper makes a more authoritative basis for correction than does the unsupported assertion by counsel.

Other means exist to correct a witness's error or fill a gap in his memory. Asking the same question of another witness may work in appropriate circumstances. It may prove effective then to ask the second witness why he is certain that he is right and his predecessor wrong. To make the correction stronger, it may seem worthwhile to recall the first witness and ask him or her whether the corrective testimony has brought about a refreshing of his or her recollection.

When all else fails, remember that Rule 611(c) of the Federal Rules of Evidence permits leading questions, even on direct examination, when "necessary to develop the witness' testimony." Do not, however, expect every federal judge to exercise in applying this clause the same liberality as its draftsmen employed in writing it.

DIRECT AND CROSS-EXAMINATION

Making a correction or filling a gap in memory has dangers. This chapter has mentioned some. Others include providing the opposition both with material for cross-examination and with argument as to the witness's unreliability. Counsel also runs the risk of a judge's applying to the effort at correction the most misunderstood principle in the law of evidence, namely, the prohibition against impeaching a party's own witness, a rule that has no place in the present context.

A lawyer who has employed, successfully or otherwise, any of the techniques discussed in this section knows that an exhaustive preparation of the witness has far greater value than any of them. Yet in the best-prepared case, things go wrong. Blunders or lapses by witnesses happen. Every lawyer who litigates must have within his grasp the means to deal with such eventualities.

G. Redirect

Too often the trial lawyer who sees his or her witness emerge from cross-examination, lets it go at that. The easy words "No redirect" can signify the surrender of an opportunity to undo some of the harm, be it little or great, of cross-examination. The decision whether to conduct redirect belongs on the list of those instantaneous judgments that too often mean the difference between a successful and an unsuccessful trial.

Not that redirect qualifies as a "must" in every instance. Passing it up may appear to the trier of the facts as a signal that counsel sees his witness as unscathed by cross-examination and that the situation calls for neither repair nor rehabilitation. Remember, on the other hand, that renunciation may also stand out as a gesture of hopelessness, an indication that the cross-examiner has wounded the witness beyond hope of recovery.

In fact, the opportunity to conduct redirect presents not one but several decisions, one for each topic or each episode into which the cross-examiner has inquired. Every one of these sub-decisions as one might call them represents the same opportunity and the same risks that preceding paragraphs have mentioned concerning the basic decision whether to conduct redirect at all.

Looked at broadly or narrowly, redirect requires an immediate assessment of the damage, if any, that cross-examination has done. Where a witness has stood up, either in the entirety of his or her testimony or as to a particular topic, it makes no sense to embark on redirect just for the sake of getting in the last word on a key point. Too many risks arise. The witness may stumble or hesitate the second time around. The reiteration may give the cross-examiner ideas that did not occur the first time. In the border-line case, wisdom calls for forgoing redirect.

Yet an outright repetition of direct testimony has its place. It can provide the hope of rescue when all seems lost.

Assume a situation where cross-examination has inflicted serious damage on a witness's testimony. Say that doubt has been cast on his opportunity to observe a physical event, that he has been shown to have an interest in a transaction about which he testified or that peripheral aspects of his recollection have been shown to have flaws. Assume further, however, that the cross-examination has not brought about a recantation of the direct testimony on a crucial point.

In such circumstances, a simple restatement of the point on redirect can undo much of the damage. Where, for example, the cross-examiner has shown a witness seriously confused about events in which he participated on a particular occasion, redirect might consist of no more than this single question:

Q. Now, Ms. Matthews, please give the jury your best present recollection of the events on the afternoon of last January 14.

A witness who has kept his or her self-possession through cross-examination will welcome such a question. It enables the witness to tell the essence of his or her story as a coherent whole, without the interruptions, challenges, distractions and insinuations of cross-examination. The lawyer who put the witness on the stand can usually do no more than hope that the witness will make the most of the opportunity. If, however, the possibility of damage on cross-examination is foreseeable, the witness can be told that the chance to set things straight may arise.

Redirect examination raises few questions of law that do not arise on direct. Most federal judges limit redirect to subjects dealt with on cross-examination. Counsel, in other words, will not often get away with trying to use redirect to fill in gaps that he left in his direct questioning.

Where the cross-examiner has sought to impeach a witness by means of a prior inconsistent statement, may opposing counsel on redirect bring out prior statements consistent with the witness's direct testimony? Most federal judges answer the question in the affirmative, at least where the prior consistent statement originated early enough to stand as evidence negating a recent contrivance. Federal Rule of Evidence 801(d)(1)(B) exempts prior consistent statements from the hearsay rule in these terms:

> A statement is not hearsay if —
>
> . . . The declarant testifies at the trial or hearing and is subject to cross-examination concerning the statement, and the statement is . . . (B) consistent with the declarant's testimony and is offered to rebut an express or implied charge against the declarant of recent fabrication or improper influence or motive. . . .

An exhaustive discussion of the question appears in *United States v. Pierre*, 781 F.2d 329 (2d Cir. 1986), a criminal case. Its reasoning, like the language of Rule 801(d)(1)(B), above, appears to apply as well to civil litigation. *See Felice v. Long Island Railroad Co.*, 426 F.2d 192, 197-198 (2d Cir.), *cert. denied*, 400 U.S. 820 (1970).

Redirect examination, in conclusion, is a weapon in the arsenal of every lawyer on trial. To maximize the help that the weapon can give, however, the lawyer must recognize its limitations and risks.

III. CROSS-EXAMINATION

A. "Whether," a Crucial Question

As an exception to the practice of filling manuals on cross-examination with anecdotal material and examples, often autobiographical, of successful interrogation, this section of a book intended for the working lawyer will concentrate on principles. If applied correctly, they will enable the reader to accumulate and retell his own collection of courtroom triumphs.

First among these principles comes the commandment, do not cross-examine automatically. The conclusion of the direct testimony of an opposing witness represents a time for decision, not the time for reflex action.

Once again, in fact, the opportunity to cross-examine presents not one but a plurality of decisions. Each topic, each event into which the direct examiner inquired should be studied separately to determine whether what is to be gained by cross-examination outweighs its risks.

To decide for or against cross-examination, counsel must ask himself three questions. First, how much harm has the direct testimony done? Secondly, how much of a chance does cross-examination stand of undoing that harm? Thirdly, what risks does cross-examination run?

Every trial differs from every other. That truism illustrates the folly of trying to establish formulae for answering these crucial questions. Generalizations in this area emerge too often in the form of abstractions whose application to specific situations begs the questions sought to be answered.

On the other hand, a few rules may provide guidance. A thorough familiarity with every aspect of the case ranks as an imperative to successful cross-examination. Less obvious but equally valuable is the availability of clues from the delivery itself of direct testimony. The potential cross-examiner who occupies himself so intensively with taking notes of the direct testimony may deprive himself of what can be learned from the demeanor of the witness.

"Sizing up" a witness in the usually brief time during which he or she appears on the stand is an art. Learning it from a book may seem impossible, but the awareness that the possibility of such an appraisal exists stands as the first step in mastering a skill that can pay almost limitless dividends.

Each of us, whatever his or her background, engages in daily life in the evaluation of what others say. The imperfections of human perception, recollection and truthfulness require us to determine as a matter of course whether what we are hearing at a given moment deserves acceptance as the truth.

The successful cross-examiner, in addition to preparing his case thoroughly, has perfected this universal human faculty and applies it to the person to whose direct examination he or she is listening. A nervous gesture or the clearing of the throat or shifting position in the chair may signal the approach of a soft spot in the testimony. The emphatic assertion of a fact that appears to call for a matter-of-fact recital may betray insecurity. The pitch of a witness's voice or the focus of his or her gaze may change at a point that the cross-examiner will thereupon perceive as sensitive. Making a mental note of the place in his testimony where the witness gains a "time out" by reaching for the water pitcher will probably amount to wasted effort nine times out of ten. It may pay off on a large scale the tenth time.

This section has not tried to construct a formula for when to cross-examine and when not to. It has sought only to show that the question whether to cross-examine must be asked with respect to each witness that an opposing party puts on the stand, indeed with respect to each topic with which the direct examiner deals. If some techniques that help in answering that question have emerged, so much the better.

B. Leading Questions

The right to ask leading questions provides the cornerstone of cross-examination. Not every trial lawyer makes the most of this tool.

Federal Rule of Evidence 661(c), which says that "Ordinarily leading questions should be permitted on cross-examination," codifies a long tradition in federal as well as state practice. See *Ewing v. United States*, 77 App. D.C. 14, 135 F.2d 633, 639 (1942), *cert. denied*, 318 U.S. 776 (1943). The right to lead, however, should mean more than freedom to be careless in framing one's questions.

A series of leading questions, uttered with authority and confidence, tells both the witness and the trier of the facts that the cross-examiner knows the case and knows where he or she is going. It avoids the impression that counsel is just probing, hoping that something will turn up.

It is crucial, of course, to live up to the initial impression that a vigorous line of leading questions can create. Counsel must in fact be marching toward a goal, not just pretending to be. A later section of this chapter will stress the importance of an organized, selective cross-examination. The style of the questioning forms part of it.

The skilled trial lawyer, then, knows how not to lead his or her own witness on direct examination. He or she knows also how to make the most of the right to lead the other side's witnesses on cross.

C. Blanket Cross: A Blunder

Nothing dulls the sharp edge of cross-examination more quickly or more thoroughly than using the weapon on every single item of a witness's direct proof. In the great majority of cases, the exhaustive cross-examination dilutes the effectiveness of the technique.

Federal Rule of Evidence 611(b) says as to "Scope of cross-examination":

> Cross-examination should be limited to the subject matter of the direct examination and matters affecting the credibility of the witness. The court may, in the exercise of discretion, permit inquiry into additional matters as if on direct examination.

It does not follow that the cross-examiner should take up with the witness everything within "the subject matter of the direct examination."

Typically, alas, the cross-examiner rises to his feet, turns back to the beginning of his copious notes and proceeds to pick away at the direct testimony, item by item, in the same order as that in which his adversary presented the proof. Judges in federal courts often crack down on this approach, but too often it proceeds to its wearying conclusion.

The errors in this all-too-prevalent approach should not require much by way of exposition. To begin, the exhaustive cross-examination gives the witness the chance to reaffirm and strengthen such testimony as the cross-examiner fails to shake. Secondly, any but the most sensational points scored in that kind of cross-examination tend to get lost in the mass of fruitless questioning. Finally, unless the witness has given totally or predominantly worthless testimony, the encyclopedic cross-examination soon begins to impress the trier of the facts as a contest between witness and examiner, a contest that the witness is winning on points.

This chapter has already pointed out that taking the voluminous notes necessary to conduct a comprehensive cross-examination deprives counsel of the opportunity to observe facets of demeanor that may provide immense help.

Dean Wigmore accurately called cross-examination "the greatest legal engine ever invented for the discovery of truth." 5 *Wigmore on Evidence*

(Chadbourn Rev. 1974) § 1367. It does not work out that way in every case. All-encompassing, point-by-point questioning provides one reason for the failures that occur.

D. Selectivity: The Right Way

Successful cross-examination is pragmatic cross-examination. It concentrates on points that matter, as to which at least the hope of vulnerability exists and in which excessive risk is not present. Picking out such points is a topic on which generalization seems futile, but recognizing the soundness of the approach means taking the first step to mastery of the art.

The wise cross-examiner does not seek to trip a witness up on every item in his or her testimony. Such a cross-examiner will not bother with matters that make no difference even if he or she feels confident of being able to prove the witness wrong. One of the great trial lawyers of this century, Emory R. Buckner, as quoted in Wellman, *The Art of Cross-Examination* (4th Ed. 1936) said:

> A cross-examiner should limit himself to the vital points of the story he is seeking to discredit or to reduce to its proper proportions. A witness makes an unimportant error,—the train he took, the floor on which he got off, the route he drove in his car. The truth, if developed, will neither help nor hurt either side. Time is consumed, the evidence marshalled, the admission of error finally triumphantly wrung from the witness, all to no purpose. In the meantime, the cross-examiner has lost momentum, the high spots of his case are forgotten.

The benefits of the selective cross-examination call for only the briefest enumeration. Such a technique holds the attention of the trier of the facts. It saves time. It isolates and emphasizes what the cross-examiner sees as important in the case. Not to be disregarded is the manner in which a concise, purposeful cross-examination enhances the stature of counsel who has delivered it.

In choosing items for cross-examination, an attorney should not forget that his goal will not always consist of destroying or impeaching direct testimony. Sometimes the cross-examiner will wish to confirm or underscore testimony given on direct. He or she may wish to pin a witness down on a point as to which he or she expects to introduce irrefutable contradictory proof. He or she may wish to bring out an attitude on the part of the witness that will provide ammunition for the cross-examiner's closing argument. Other possibilities will come to the mind of even the relatively inexperienced advocate.

Using cross-examination to aim at and hit specific points rather than to scatter fire over the whole of a direct examination will not guarantee devastating results with every opposing witness in every trial. It will, however, if pursued with a background of thorough preparation and careful observation, improve results.

E. The Sequence of Cross

No rule of evidence, written or unwritten, says that a cross-examiner must take up topics in the order that his or her adversary introduced those topics on direct. On the contrary, the cross-examiner, with a totally different goal, must arrange his or her own agenda.

If the guiding principles of the order of cross-examination could be summarized in one sentence, that sentence would read thus: Begin strong, and finish strong. The freedom to arrange the questioning as he or she wishes gives every cross-examiner the opportunity to profit from this precept.

A cross-examination that starts by scoring a real point focuses the attention of the trier of the facts. It tells the judge or jury that cross-examiner knows what he or she is about and deserves to be listened to.

A previous section of this chapter has propounded a corollary to the principle just enunciated. Beginning cross-examination with a vigorous, purposeful series of leading questions cannot fail to enhance the chances of success.

Ending with a telling blow may qualify as even more important. It conveys an impression that the cross-examiner has got what he or she set out after and is satisfied with the results of the effort expended. Perceiving confidence in this way will have an effect. The final point, moreover, will tend to linger in the mind or minds of the fact-trier.

The skillful cross-examiner arranges his or her topics with these goals in mind. He or she will begin by placing the two strongest lines of questioning at the beginning and at the end of the list. Topics less strong or less certain can be explored in between. Yet flexibility must be preserved. If a question deemed of limited importance surprises counsel with an extraordinarily helpful answer, he or she may decide, for the sake of ending on a strong note, to terminate the cross even though it means eliminating subject-matter previously classified as worthwhile.

The cross-examiner who knows what he or she wants and works toward that goal gets results far more often than the slave to routine who tries to break down every word of a witness's testimony. Arranging questions plays almost as important a part in such successes as does selecting those questions.

F. The Witness

Cross-examination does not take place in a vacuum. It involves a human being on the other side. To make the most of the opportunity to question the other side's witness, counsel must fashion his approach with the character, appearance and personality of the witness in mind.

The witness, for example, who appears most vulnerable on an issue may represent a dangerous target for that very reason. The trier of the facts may resent seeing someone "picked on" by one who enjoys the advantages of the cross-examiner. If it becomes necessary to undermine the testimony of a person who, for any reason, seems likely to generate sympathy, subtlety often proves the most desirable approach. The job can be done without a direct confrontation.

On the other hand, a witness may have impressed the trier of the facts as deserving a knocking down. Sometimes a jury yearns to see the testimony of a witness demolished but feels constrained to accept that testimony if impeachment does not happen.

One of the burdens of trial practice is deciding into which of the two categories each witness falls. Probably the majority belong in neither but fit somewhere in between. Yet a seemingly damaging cross-examination may have in fact damaged the cross-examiner more than the witness if the judge or jury resents the severity of the questioning. Correspondingly, counsel may have missed a prime opportunity by taking it easy on a witness whom the trier of the facts thought should be and could be destroyed.

Since the present chapter does not purport to stand as a treatise on the substantive law of evidence, the rules governing impeachment of a witness's character and reputation will not be gone into here. The reader should remember, however, that nowhere do the principles just discussed have greater relevance than in the decision whether to discredit a witness by resort to something out of his or her background.

G. Prior Inconsistent Statements

No objective tool proves more helpful to the cross-examiner than the availability of an earlier utterance, oral or written, that contradicts what the witness has said on the stand. An innovation makes that tool easier to use.

The rule long prevailed that before questioning the witness about a prior statement in writing, the cross-examiner must first show the statement to the witness. All that changed on July 1, 1975, the effective date of the Federal Rules of Evidence. Rule 613(a) provides:

> (a) Examining witness concerning prior statement.—In examining a witness concerning a prior statement made by the witness,

whether written or not, the statement need not be shown nor its contents disclosed to the witness at that time, but on request the same shall be shown or disclosed to opposing counsel.

The final passage of this provision is intended to prevent unscrupulous counsel from confronting a witness with a supposed statement of which in fact no proof exists. This concession is made in return for the freedom that the cross-examiner enjoys, by virtue of the main part of sub-paragraph (a), not to let the witness know the basis of a question concerning a prior statement.

Another safeguard protects the witness. Sub-paragraph (b) of Rule 613 provides:

> (b) Extrinsic evidence of prior inconsistent statement of witness.—Extrinsic evidence of a prior inconsistent statement by a witness is not admissible unless the witness is afforded an opportunity to explain or deny the same and the opposite party is afforded an opportunity to interrogate the witness thereon, or the interests of justice otherwise require. This provision does not apply to admissions of a party-opponent as defined in Rule 801(d)(2).

In the use of prior inconsistent statements as in all aspects of cross-examination, discretion must be used. It does no good to show a witness contradicting himself or herself on a trivial issue. In fact, it often does harm by making the cross-examiner look foolish, ineffectual or both.

Similarly, a prior inconsistent statement does no good if it does not in fact contradict what the witness has said on the stand. Rest assured that if the prior statement you plan to use can be even arguably reconciled with the testimony, your adversary or the witness himself under Rule 613(b), above, will attempt that reconciliation. The better course, in short, is to limit the use of prior inconsistent statements to out-and-out contradictions on crucial or at least significant points.

IV. CONCLUDING OBSERVATIONS

At the outset of this chapter, the author noted that the trial lawyer must master the dual skills of building and destroying evidence. The intervening pages have sought to demonstrate that proposition. It provides the foundation of the adversary system upon which our society and its predecessors have depended for centuries in endeavoring to ascertain the truth and do justice. Scholars may debate whether that system achieves its goals better than others that might be devised to replace it, but such explorations do not concern the working lawyer. To survive professionally, he or she must master both of the mentioned skills.

CHAPTER TWENTY-THREE

ALTERNATIVES TO TRIAL

by Loretta A. Preska, Esq.

This section will describe some of the methods by which a litigant might avoid the formality and expense of a full-blown trial on all issues before a federal judge while still obtaining a finding of fact or, in the case of advisory juries, obtain a jury trial where it might not otherwise be warranted. A litigant must consent, either expressly or constructively, to some of these methods of fact determination, *viz.*, trial before a magistrate and arbitration, while others can be imposed by the court, either on its own motion or upon a litigant's motion.

I. CONSENT TO TRIAL BEFORE MAGISTRATES

A. Consent

1. Fed. R. Civ. P. 73(a)

As an alternative to trial before a district judge, litigants in the Southern, Eastern and Western Districts of New York have the option of consenting to trial before a United States Magistrate.[1] The authority to do so originates in 28 U.S.C. § 636(c)(1) which provides, in part, that:

> [u]pon the consent of the parties, a full-time United States magistrate or a part-time United States magistrate who serves as a full-time judicial officer may conduct any or all proceedings in a jury or nonjury civil matter and order the entry of judgment in the case, when specially designated to exercise such jurisdiction by the district court or courts he serves.

This power is made part of the Federal Rules of Civil Procedure in Rule 73(a) which provides that:

> [w]hen specially designated to exercise such jurisdiction by local rule or order of the district court and when all parties consent

---

[1] The Northern District of New York has not adopted a local rule authorizing trial before magistrates.

thereto, a magistrate may exercise the authority provided by Title 28 U.S.C. § 636(c) and may conduct any and all proceedings, including a jury or non-jury trial, in a civil case.

As noted both in the statute and in Rule 73(a), trial before a magistrate can only be had upon the consent of the parties, and both rules have rather specific provisions regarding consent. Section 636(c)(2) provides that the clerk of the court shall "at the time the action is filed" notify the parties of their right to consent to trial by magistrate. Both the statute and Rule 73 provide that neither the district judge nor the magistrate shall attempt to persuade the parties to consent to trial by magistrate, and the Rule prohibits informing the judge or the magistrate of the parties' responses unless all parties have consented to the referral.

Accompanying Rule 73 are forms of notice of the right to consent to trial by magistrate (Form 33) and of the parties' consent to such referral (Form 34). Also included in the official form (but not mentioned in the statute or the Rule) is the district court's order referring the matter to the district court for all further proceedings—a matter of theoretical rather than practical significance.

2. Local Rules

Local rules governing trial before magistrates generally coincide with 28 U.S.C. § 636 and can be found in the SDNY and EDNY Rules for Proceedings Before Magistrates and in WDNY General Rule 35. The less sweeping powers delegated to magistrates in the Northern District of New York can be found in that court's Rules 43.1-43.5.

B. Appeals

Two routes of appeal are available from the entry of judgment following trial before a magistrate; the first directly to the Court of Appeals, and the second to the district court. 28 U.S.C. § 636(c); Fed. R. Civ. P. 73(c) and (d). The parties are to designate the method of appeal they desire on the form on which they consent to the reference. *See* Form 33.

1. Appeal to the Court of Appeals

Unless the parties choose the optional appeal route provided in Fed. R. Civ. P. 73(d), appeals from a trial by a magistrate "will lie to the court of appeals as it would from a judgment of the district court." Fed. R. Civ. P. 73(c). This is hardly surprising since the magistrate is sitting as a district court judge. As with any appeal from a judgment of the district court, appeals pursuant to Fed. R. Civ. P. 73(c) are governed by the Federal Rules of Appellate Procedure.

2. Appeal to the District Court

If at the time of consenting to refer the matter to a magistrate for trial the parties chose the optional method of appeal provided by Fed. R. Civ. P. 73(d), an appeal from the magistrate's judgment will lie to the district court with further appeal to the court of appeals by petition only. The procedure applicable to such appeals is set out in Fed. R. Civ. P. 74 through 76 and is intended to provide a relatively quick, inexpensive method of appeal.

An appeal to the district court will lie from any final judgment of the magistrate or any interlocutory decision or order which, if made by a district court judge, is appealable. Fed. R. Civ. P. 74(a). Appeal from a final order may be taken by filing with the clerk of the district court a notice of appeal within 30 days of the date of entry of the judgment appealed from (60 days if the United States is a party) or within 15 days of the entry of an appealable interlocutory order. *Id*. In contrast to the strict time limit for filing a notice of appeal to the court of appeals, "upon a showing of excusable neglect, the magistrate may extend the time for filing a notice of appeal upon motion filed not later than 20 days after expiration of the time otherwise proscribed . . . ." *Id*.

Fed. R. Civ. P. 74(a) also provides that the time for filing a notice of appeal is stayed pending disposition of post-trial motions (1) for judgment under Fed. R. Civ. P. 50(b); (2) granting or denying a motion pursuant to Fed. R. Civ. P. 52(b) to amend or make additional findings of fact; (3) granting or denying a motion under Fed. R. Civ. P. 59 to alter or amend the judgment; or (4) denying a new trial under Fed. R. Civ. P. 59.

The notice of appeal is filed with the clerk of the court who mails it to the other parties. Fed. R. Civ. P. 74(b). It should specify the party taking the appeal (the better practice being to list each such party specifically by name), the judgment or order appealed from (or the particular part of such judgment or order) and the statement that the appeal is to the district judge. *Id*.[2] Counsel need not specify the grounds for the appeal or otherwise make specific assignments of error.

All judgments, including those following trial by a magistrate, are effective after ten days unless stayed. Fed. R. Civ. P. 62(a). Thus, Fed. R. Civ. P. 74(c) provides that:

> [u]pon a showing that the magistrate has refused or otherwise failed to stay the judgment pending appeal to the district judge under Rule 73(d), the appellant may make application for a stay to the district

---

[2] *See* 7 Moore's Federal Practice ¶ 74.03[3] for a form of notice of appeal pursuant to Fed. R. Civ. P. 73(d).

judge with reasonable notice to all parties. The stay may be conditioned upon the filing in the district court of a bond or other appropriate security.

Finally, Fed. R. Civ. P. 74(d) provides that the appeal may be dismissed by the district court for a variety of reasons, including a party's failure to comply with the Federal Rules of Civil Procedure on any local rule or order.

II. SUMMARY TRIALS

A summary jury trial is just what its name describes—a "summarized" jury trial consisting of counsel's presentation of anticipated evidence and argument to a jury which, after a truncated charge, renders an advisory verdict. Summary jury trials often facilitate settlements giving counsel and the parties the benefit of a real jury's view of the case. Such a proceeding also fulfills some litigant's need to have their "day in court" and permits counsel and the litigants to see the strengths and weaknesses of their respective cases more clearly. The summary jury trial procedure was initated by Judge Thomas D. Lambros of the Northern District of Ohio. His *Report to the Judicial Conference of the United States* on *The Summary Jury Trial and Other Alternative Methods of Dispute Resolution*, reprinted at 103 F.R.D. 461 (1984) (*"Lambros"*), contains a full description of the process as well as a summary jury trial handbook, a juror profile form, a jury opinion form and the like.

A. Procedure

In order to reap the benefits of the summary jury trial process, the case must be ready for trial. Discovery should be closed and motions, including motions *in limine*, determined. Trial briefs and requests to charge should be submitted.

The summary trial should be presided over by a judge or magistrate, and clients should attend. Evidence is summarized (with argument incorporated) by counsel. No testimony is taken through witnesses, and the evidence summarized by counsel must be based on discovery materials or reasonably anticipated testimony. To the extent possible, objections should be anticipated and ruled on in connection with motions *in limine* so as not to take up "trial" time.

Following an abbreviated charge, the jury retires to reach a verdict. Depending upon counsel's preference, this can be a consensus verdict or individual verdicts covering various specific issues.[3]

---

[3] Suggested forms for verdicts are contained in *Lambros* at Appendix D, 103 F.R.D. at 492.

B. Basis in the Federal Rules

Although not specifically mentioned in the Federal Rules of Civil Procedure, summary jury trials are certainly within the admonition of Rule 1 that the Rules "shall be construed to secure the just, speedy, and inexpensive determination of every action." More specifically, Rule 16(a) permits the court, in its discretion, to direct the attorneys and unrepresented parties to appear for conferences for such purposes as "(1) expediting disposition of the action . . . and (5) facilitating the settlement of the case." Rule 16(c)(7) and (11) also provide that "[t]he participants at any conference under this rule may consider and take action with respect to . . . (7) the possibility of settlement of the use of extrajudicial procedures to resolve the dispute . . . and (11) such other matters as may aid in the disposition of the action."

It is important to note that although the court can direct the attorneys to appear at a settlement conference, any action by the participants with respect to settlement or extrajudicial means to resolve the dispute are purely volitional. Indeed, the Seventh Circuit reversed a district court's finding of criminal contempt against an attorney who refused to participate in a summary jury trial, finding that Rule 16 "was not intended to require that an unwilling litigant be sidetracked from the normal course of litigation."[4] Thus, it appears for the moment,[5] at least, summary jury trials are a voluntary alternative to trial.

III. ADVISORY JURIES

Fed. R. Civ. P. 39(c) provides in relevant part:

> In all actions not triable of right by a jury the court upon motion or of its own initiative may try any issue with an advisory jury . . .

A. Availability

The meaning of "actions not triable of right by a jury" remains in dispute. Does it mean that advisory juries are not available in cases which were originally triable by a jury but where the parties waived that right? In New

---

[4] *Strandell v. Jackson County, Illinois*, 838 F.2d 884, 887 (7th Cir. 1988); *contra*, *McKay v. Ashland Oil, Inc.*, 120 F.R.D. 43 (E.D. Ky. 1988) (upholding mandatory summary jury trial); *Arabian American Oil Co. v. Scarfone*, 119 F.R.D. 448 (M.D. Fla. 1988) (same); *but cf.*, *Rhea v. Massey-Ferguson, Inc.*, 767 F.2d 266, 269 (6th Cir. 1985) (upholding local rule authorizing mandatory mediation).

[5] Legislation has been introduced in the past which would permit the district courts to sanction parties which unreasonably refuse to agree to some method of alternative dispute resolution (which, of course, includes summary jury trials). *See* H.R. 473, 100th Cong., 1st Sess., 133 Cong. Rec. H.157 (daily ed. Jan. 7, 1987) ("Alternative Dispute Resolution Promotion Act of 1987"); S. 2038, 99th Cong., 2d Sess., 132 Cong. Rec. S. 848 (daily ed. Feb. 3, 1986) ("Alternative Dispute Resolution Promotion Act of 1986"). It is expected that such legislation will be re-introduced in the coming session.

York, it has long been the law that advisory juries are available in cases where a jury trial was originally available but was thereafter waived, *(American) Lumbermen's Mutual Casualty Co. of Illinois v. Timms & Howard, Inc.*, 108 F.2d 497 (2d Cir. 1939), as well as in cases where there is no right to a jury trial. *See, e.g., Birnbaum v. United States*, 436 F. Supp. 967 (E.D.N.Y. 1977) (Federal Tort Claims Act case).

It is within the discretion of the trial judge (not the motion judge),[6] whether or not to utilize an advisory jury, and the judge may act *sua sponte* or upon motion.

B. Effect of Verdict

Since the jury is sitting in an advisory capacity, the court is free to accept or reject the jury's verdict. In either event, the court should proceed to make its own findings of fact and conclusions of law since Fed. R. Civ. P. 52(a) provides that in:

> all actions tried upon the facts without a jury or with an advisory jury, the court shall find the facts specially and state separately its conclusions of law thereon. . . .

The appellate court's review will be based on these findings and conclusions, not on the jury's verdict. For this reason, it should not logically be necessary to move to reject the jury's verdict, although there is some rather aged authority to that effect.[7]

IV. ARBITRATION

A. Introduction

Arbitration proceedings are generally governed by the Federal Arbitration Act, 9 U.S.C. § 1 *et seq.* and CPLR Article 75. Counsel may find it useful to review these statutes to put the arbitration process into context, *e.g.*, to recognize the federal policy favoring arbitration, *see, e.g., Southland Corp. v. Keating*, 465 U.S. 1, 10 (1984), and to become familiar with certain procedural devices, *e.g.*, service of a notice of intent to arbitrate, CPLR 7503(c), compelling arbitration, CPLR 7503(a); 9 U.S.C. § 4, vacating, modifying or confirming an award, CPLR 7510, 7511; 9 U.S.C. §§ 9-11.

In New York, the primary established arbitral fora are the American Arbitration Association and the various securities Self-Regulatory Organizations ("SROs"), *viz.*, the New York Stock Exchange ("NYSE"), the National

---

[6] *Strelitz v. Surrey Classics, Inc.*, 7 F.R.D. 101 (S.D.N.Y. 1946).

[7] *Mahon v. Bennett*, 81 F. Supp. 901 (W.D. Mo. 1948).

ALTERNATIVES TO TRIAL

Association of Securities Dealers ("NASD") and the American Stock Exchange. There has been a marked increase in the number of securities industry arbitrations as a result of the Supreme Court's decisions in *Dean Witter Reynolds Inc. v. Byrd*, 470 U.S. 213 (1985) (finding a plaintiff's state law claims to be arbitrable pursuant to an arbitration agreement although federal securities claims remained in federal court) and *Shearson/American Express Inc. v. McMahon*, 107 S. Ct. 2332 (1987) (finding claims under Section 10(b) and Rule 10b-5 of the Securities Exchange Act of 1934 and under the Racketeer Influenced and Corrupt Practices Act ("RICO") to be arbitrable pursuant to an arbitration agreement).

The procedures for the arbitration process itself are, of course, set out in the rules of the different arbitral fora. The AAA has different rules for different types of cases, *e.g.*, Commercial Arbitration Rules, Securities Arbitration Rules. Arbitration rules for the SROs can be obtained from each directly,[8] and the NYSE Arbitration Rules and the NASD Code of Arbitration Procedure are published by Commerce Clearing House in its NYSE Guide and NASD Manual, respectively. Also, both the NYSE and the NASD provide rules for simplified arbitration of disputes involving $5,000 or less.

B. Agreements to Arbitrate

As noted above, a litigant generally arrives in arbitration by agreement, either express or "constructive."

1. Express Agreements

Parties have wide latitude in fashioning arbitration agreements tailored to their own particular situation. They can specify which issues are subject to arbitration, *e.g.*, all issues arising out of or related to the contract at hand or only particular issues such as compensation, certain computations or the like.

---

8   New York Stock Exchange
    20 Broad Street
    Fifth Floor
    New York, NY
    (212) 623-3000

    National Association of Securities Dealers
    Two World Trade Center
    98th Floor
    New York, NY 10048
    (212) 839-6251

    American Stock Exchange
    86 Trinity Place
    New York, NY 10006
    (212) 306-1000

The parties can draft or otherwise designate rules to be applicable to the arbitration and often do so by incorporating those of one of the established fora. The parties can also choose individual arbitrators *in futuro*, but more often set out an agreed method of choosing arbitrators, should the need arise. *E.g.*, each side chooses an arbitrator, and those two arbitrators agree on a third.

2. Constructive

In some instances, a litigant can be compelled to arbitrate in the absence of an express agreement in a particular contract. For example, the Rules of the NYSE and NASD require that certain controversies arising out of the business of a member *shall* be arbitrated upon the demand of a member against a member or a customer against a member. *E.g.*, NYSE Constitution, Sec. 1; NYSE Rule 600; NASD Code of Arbitration Procedure, Sec. 8, 12. Thus, a member firm can compel another member firm, merely by virtue of SRO membership, to arbitrate certain issues, and customers can compel member firms to arbitrate certain issues—even in the absence of a separate arbitration agreement.

3. Determining the Validity of an Arbitration Agreement

No lesser authority than the Supreme Court of the United States has spoken on the issue of determining the validity of an arbitration agreement. In *Prima Paint Corp. v. Flood & Conklin Mfg. Co.*, 388 U.S. 395 (1967), the Court noted the language of Section 4 of the Federal Arbitration Act which instructs the federal courts "to order arbitration to proceed once it is satisfied that 'the making of the agreement for arbitration . . . is not in issue.' " *Id.* at 403. Thus, the Court concluded that if the issue presented is whether the arbitration clause itself (as opposed to the entire agreement wherein the arbitration clause appears) was fraudulently induced, then that is a matter for the federal court to determine. "Statutory language does not permit the federal court to consider claims of fraud in the inducement of the contract generally." *Id.* at 404.[9]

---

9 If counsel anticipates a question concerning the validity of or compliance with an arbitration agreement, service of a notice of intention to arbitrate under CPLR 7503(c) might be considered. That section provides that:
    A party may serve upon another party a demand for arbitration or a notice of intention to arbitrate, specifying the agreement pursuant to which arbitration is sought and the name and address of the party serving the notice, or of an officer or agent thereof if such party is an association or corporation, and stating that unless the party served applies to stay the arbitration within twenty days after such service *he shall thereafter be precluded from objecting that a valid agreement was not made or has not been complied with* and from asserting in court the bar of a limitation of time. (emphasis added).

ALTERNATIVES TO TRIAL

C. Pleadings

Not surprisingly, parties to an arbitration set forth their positions in documents which correspond generally to a complaint, answer, counterclaim and the like in state and federal practice.

1. Statement of Claim

The claimant's position is set out in a statement of claim. Just as in a judicial forum, counsel should take care to ensure that the proceeding is properly commenced pursuant to either a specific agreement, *e.g.*, notice is timely and sent to the correct party, or pursuant to the rules of the AAA or an SRO, *e.g.*, the AAA generally requires that the notice of intent to arbitrate (including a statement of the nature of the dispute, amount involved and remedy sought) be served on the respondent and filed with the AAA together with copies of the arbitration agreement and the appropriate fee. The AAA, in turn, then formally notifies the respondent. The NYSE and NASD generally require filing with the SRO of the required number of copies of the statement of claim, a Uniform Submission Agreement (available from the SRO) executed by the claimant and the required fee, and the SRO then serves respondent.[10]

The statement of claim should be less formal than a judicial complaint. It should be rather chatty in style and tell a persuasive story. Like a good story, it need not have numbered paragraphs, and some experienced counsel prefer a letter format addressed, for example, to the Director of Arbitration of the particular SRO.

Counsel should also attach to the statement of claim as many of the documents to be introduced on direct examination as possible. This presents all of claimant's material in a single package and permits the arbitrators to refer to whichever documents they choose in their pre-hearing review of the statement of claim. Since the panel generally admits the statement of claim (and any attached exhibits) into evidence at the outset, attaching desired documents saves the time and potential problems involved in proffering documents for admission into evidence.

---

10 For example, the AAA levies administrative fees based on the amount in dispute, fees for the arbitrators after the first day of service and adjournment fees. *See, e.g.*, AAA Securities Arbitration Rules 48-50, and accompanying fee schedules. The NASD and NYSE levy fees based on the amount in dispute, a nominal fee for withdrawing a matter after submission and other associated fees (generally lower than the AAA fees).

2. Statement of Response

The respondent's position is set forth in the statement of response, and the same considerations discussed with respect to the statement of claim are applicable here.

Contrary to the practice in judicial litigation where extensions of time are arranged by counsel with little or no intervention by the court, extensions in the established arbitration fora are arranged through arbitration counsel assigned to the matter. While it is helpful to have an adversary's consent to the desired extension, such consent is neither necessary nor sufficient to obtain an extension. For example, NASD arbitration counsel routinely grant a single two-week extension. Regardless of the forum involved, a call to arbitration counsel in advance of the expiration of the time to respond is the recommended practice. The final decision as to requested extensions and adjournments rests with the panel.

3. Counterclaims and Third-Party Claims

In general, counterclaims are permitted in the established fora so long as the counterclaim is within the scope of the properly arbitrable issues. Similar to judicial pleading, counterclaims are presented in the respondent's statement of response.

While the filing of third-party claims in arbitration involve the same types of jurisdictional considerations as in judicial pleading, *viz.*, does subject matter jurisdiction over the controversy exist and is it possible to obtain jurisdiction over the desired party in the desired forum, the practical limitations on jurisdiction of arbitral fora complicate the matter substantially. Unless the intended third-party respondent is subject to an express or constructive arbitration agreement, that party generally cannot be compelled to submit to the arbitration process.[11] That party can either move in state court pursuant to CPLR 75 to stay arbitration as to himself or simply not appear. Thus, unless all the parties are bound by the same contract or otherwise subject to the same arbitration agreement, arbitration is not well suited to multi-party disputes.

---

11 An arbitration agreement, express or constructive, may not always be necessary to permit a party to enjoy the benefits of such an agreement. For example, several courts have held that the agent of a party to the arbitration agreement is entitled to enforce it even though the agent was not a party to the agreement. *E.g.*, *Phillips, et al. v. Merrill Lynch, Pierce, Fenner & Smith, Inc., et al.* [1984 Transfer Binder] CCH Fed. Sec. L. Rptr. ¶ 91,650 at 99,294, n.5 (D. Minn. 1984); *Brown v. Dean Witter Reynods, Inc.*, 601 F. Supp. 641, 644 (S.D. Fla. 1985); *Ross v. Mathis*, [1985-1986 Transfer Binder] CCH Fed. Sec. L. Rptr. ¶ 92,343 at 92,246 (N.D. Ga. 1985); *Berman v. Dean Witter & Co., Inc.*, 119 Cal. Rptr. 130, 133 (Cal. App. 1975).

D. Discovery

One of the major differences between judicial litigation and arbitration is the relative dearth of discovery devices in arbitration. While, as with all aspects of arbitration, the parties can agree otherwise, discovery in arbitration generally consists of document exchange only, with no depositions, interrogatories, etc. The AAA panels monitor document exchange, while the NYSE and NASD leave that process largely to the parties with disputes resolved by the panel. Recently, the NYSE has required that the parties exchange documents no later than ten days before the hearing, NYSE Rule 638, rather than at any time prior to the first hearing session (often interpreted in practice as on the way to the hearing).

Witnesses can be subpoenaed to appear either by an arbitrator or by any attorney of record, CPLR 7505; 9 U.S.C. § 7,[12] although the NYSE and NASD Rules admonish the parties to "produce witnesses and present proofs to the fullest extent possible without resort to the subpoena process." NASD Rules, Sec. 32(a); NYSE Rule 619(a).

E. Hearing

1. Panel Members

Whether or not a hearing is held is determined by the parties' agreement or the rules of the forum. For example, at the NYSE and NASD, a hearing is required unless waived by the parties, and even then, the panel can require a hearing.[13] NASD Codes of Arbitration Procedure, Sec. 14(a); NYSE Rules 602. Similarly, unless the parties have agreed otherwise, panel members are chosen pursuant to the rules of the forum, generally by reviewing lists of proposed arbitrators and striking the names of members deemed undesirable in accordance with the applicable rules as to challenges.

In the established fora, the number of panel members varies. For example, the AAA Commercial Arbitration Rules provide that if the arbitration agreement does not specify the number of arbitrators, the dispute shall be heard by one arbitrator unless the AAA determines otherwise (Rule 17), while the AAA Securities Arbitration Rules provide for three arbitrators for claims involving over $20,000 (Rule 17). Similarly, the NYSE Rules provide for three arbitrators for claims up to $100,000 and five for claims exceeding $100,000. NASD Code of Arbitration Procedure, Sec. 19. *See also* NYSE

---

[12] Counsel should note the possibility of different territorial limits on subpoenas issued pursuant to the state and federal statutes.

[13] In simplified arbitration involving claims under $5,000, no hearing is required unless demanded by a customer or arbitrator. NASD Code of Arbitration Procedure, Sec. 13(f); NYSE Rule 601(f).

Rule 607(a) providing for three arbitrators for matters involving $500,000 or less and five for matters over that amount (unless the parties agree otherwise).

Under the AAA Securities Rules and in the securities SROs, panels will generally consist of a majority of public members, *i.e.*, persons not employed in the securities industry, unless a public customer demands otherwise. *See* NASD Code of Arbitration Procedure, Sec. 9; NYSE Rule 607(a). In the established fora, the panel is assisted by arbitration counsel who coordinates pre-hearing activities (*e.g.*, service of pleadings, extensions, scheduling) and at the hearing acts as a combination bailiff-law clerk-courtroom deputy.

In contrast to judicial trials, arbitration hearings are rather informal. The panel, arbitration counsel, the parties, counsel and the witness testifying generally sit around a large table or tables. Counsel and the witness usually remain seated during the examination. In the established fora, proceedings are private with attendance of nonparties determined by the panel. *E.g.*, AAA Securities Arbitration Rule 25. Also, decisions or arbitral panels are private and are not published.

2. Evidence

In keeping with the informality of arbitration generally, the panel is not bound by the rules of evidence. *E.g.*, NYSE Rule 621. Admissibility is at the panel's discretion, and, in practice, most arbitrators are rather liberal in receiving evidence "for what it's worth."

3. Award

Although the panel's decision is usually written, it rarely appears in a form similar to a judicial opinion. *See, e.g.*, NYSE Rule 628(a). In practice, the award is usually a single sentence either granting or denying recovery. Since arbitrators are often business people rather than lawyers, they often tend to divide the losses between the parties rather than award damages strictly according to the letter of the contract. Thus, it is frequently the case that a litigant is unable to determine how a particular damage figure was arrived at.

4. Motions to Confirm, Modify or Vacate

A litigant can move pursuant to CPLR 7510 to confirm the award within one year after its delivery. *See also* 9 U.S.C. § 9 regarding motions to confirm where the arbitration agreement provides that a judgment of a specified court shall be entered upon the award. Counsel may wish to confirm if, for example, it appears unlikely that the party obligated to pay the award will do so voluntarily. Confirmation of an award converts it into a judgment which can then be judicially enforced, if necessary.

An application to vacate or modify an award in state court must be made within ninety days of the delivery of the award to the movant. CPLR 7511(a). The award shall be vacated only if the court finds the movant's rights to have been prejudiced by

> (i) corruption, fraud or misconduct in procuring the award; or (ii) partiality of an arbitrator appointed as a neutral, except where the award was by confession; or (iii) an arbitrator, or agency or person making the award exceeded his power or so imperfectly executed it that a final and definite award upon the subject matter submitted was not made; or (iv) failure to follow the procedure of this article, unless the party applying to vacate the award continued with the arbitration with notice of the defect and without objection.

CPLR § 7511(b), or, in addition, in the case of one who was neither served with notice of intention to arbitrate nor participated in the arbitration if

> (i) [one of the grounds listed in 7511(b) exists]; (ii) a valid agreement to arbitrate was not made; or (iii) the agreement to arbitrate had not been complied with; or (iv) the arbitrated claim was barred by limitation under subdivision (b) of section 7502.

CPLR § 7511(b).

The award will be modified only if:

> 1. there was a miscalculation of figures or a mistake in the description of any person, thing or property referred to in the award; or
>
> 2. the arbitrators have awarded upon a matter not submitted to them and the award may be corrected without affecting the merits of the decision upon the issues submitted; or
>
> 3. the award is imperfect in a matter of form, not affecting the merits of the controversy.

CPLR § 7511(c).

If the party seeking vacatur or modification otherwise can establish subject matter jurisdiction in the federal courts, that party can move pursuant to § 10 of the Federal Arbitration Act. A federal court's power to vacate an arbitration award is "confined" to the grounds specified there, *viz.*:

> (a) Where the award was procured by corruption, fraud or undue means.
>
> (b) Where there was evident partiality or corruption in the arbitrators, or either of them.

(c) Where the arbitrators were guilty of misconduct in refusing to postpone the hearing, upon sufficient cause shown, or in refusing to hear evidence pertinent and material to the controversy; or of any other misbehavior by which the rights of any party have been prejudiced.

(d) Where the arbitrators exceed their powers or so imperfectly executed them that a mutual, final, and definite award upon the subject matter submitted was not made.

9 U.S.C. § 10(a)-(d), and to a judicially created addition allowing vacatur when arbitrators show "manifest disregard" for the law in making awards. *Dundas Shipping & Trading Co., Ltd. v. Stravelakis Brothers, Ltd.*, 508 F. Supp. 1000, 1003 (S.D.N.Y. 1981).

Modification can be sought in the federal court under 9 U.S.C. § 11 on the following grounds:

(a) Where there was an evident material miscalculation of figures or an evident material mistake in the description of any person, thing, or property referred to in the award.

(b) Where the arbitrators have awarded upon a matter not submitted to them, unless it is a matter not affecting the merits of the decision upon the matter submitted.

(c) Where the award is imperfect in matter of form not affecting the merits of the controversy.

With reference to 9 U.S.C. § 10, Judge Pollack has stated that:

Vacatur is, possible under this section only if the arbitrator's decision is fundamentally irrational, *Swift Industries, Inc. v. Votany Industries, Inc.*, 466 F.2d 1125 (3d Cir. 1972), does not draw its essence from the contract between the parties, *United Steelworkers v. Enterprise Wheel & Car Corp.*, 363 U.S. 593, 597 (1960) or constitutes a manifest disregard of the law, *Sobel v. Hertz, Warner & Co.*, 469 F.2d 1211 (2d Cir. 1972). The fact that the arbitrator's expressed reasoning may not be entirely satisfactory or that he may have made a single mistaken interpretation of the law will not alone support vacatur.

Local 771, I.A.T.S.E., AFL-CIO v. RKO General, Inc., 419 F. Supp. 553, 558 (S.D.N.Y. 1976).

The court may not overturn an arbitration award for errors of fact or law. *Orion Shipping & Trading Co., Inc. v. Eastern States Petroleum Corporation of Panama, S.A.*, 312 F.2d 299, 300 (2d Cir.), *cert. denied*, 373 U.S. 999 (1963) (manner of computation of damages in arbitration agreement is to be determined solely by arbitrator and thus motion to vacate on the ground that damages were improperly calculated was denied; that portion of the award finding liability as to a nonparty exceeded arbitrator's powers and, accordingly, was vacated).

The burden of proof falls on the party seeking vacatur, *Saxis Steamship Co. v. Multifacs International Traders, Inc.*, *supra*, 375 F.2d 577, 582 (confirming arbitration award in favor of shipowner for breach of time charter) and, as is apparent from the above, it is a heavy burden indeed.

F. Advantages and Disadvantages to Arbitration

The major advantages to arbitration and the reason most parties choose it over a judicial forum are the simplicity, efficiency and speed of the process, and thus its economy, relative to judicial litigation. Each advantage, however, mirrors what some at least find to be a disadvantage. For example, the process is relatively simple and efficient because discovery is extremely limited and because the rules of evidence are not applicable to the hearing. In some cases, however, the loss of the opportunity for depositions of the adversary's witnesses or the loss of the protection afforded by the rules of evidence will be a significant disadvantage. Efficiency also obtains in the arbitral process because there is little motion practice similar to that under Fed. R. Civ. P. 12(b)(6) or 56. This can be a disadvantage, especially where a respondent is forced to proceed through hearing on a meritless claim either because it cannot make a motion under Fed. R. Civ. P. 12(b)(6) or cannot obtain deposition testimony to permit a motion under Fed. R. Civ. P. 56.

Similarly, the arbitration process is concluded quickly in part because of the limited appellate review available. In some cases, usually by hindsight, this turns out to be a significant disadvantage, particularly in light of the courts' reluctance to disturb an award even for errors of fact or law.

In cases where the facts are particularly egregious, the arbitrators' inability to award punitive damages in New York under *Garrity v. Lyle Stuart, Inc.*, 40 N.Y.2d 354, 353 N.E.2d 793, 386 N.Y.S.2d 831 (1976) (holding that punitive damages are to be awarded only for "evil and reprehensible" conduct and therefore should be left to the State to award through the courts) is viewed (by claimant's counsel, at least) as a significant disadvantage. Needless to say, respondent's counsel may feel differently.[14]

---

14 Undecided as yet is the question of whether treble damages under RICO claims (now arbitrable under *McMahon*) are punitive, and thus not within the panel's power to award, *e.g.*, *Summers v. FDIC*, 592 F. Supp. 1240 (W.D. Okla. 1984), or merely remedial and thus recoverable in arbitration, *e.g.*, *State Farm, Fire and Casualty Co. v. Caton*, 540 F. Supp. 673 (N.D. Ind. 1982).

At the SROs and pursuant to the AAA Securities Rules, at least one member of a multi-person panel will be familiar with the securities industry. This generally simplifies the presentation of pleadings and evidence immensely in that, for example, counsel need not explain what a margin account is or why options are risky. The industry member is familiar with these and other common matters in the industry and generally shares that knowledge with any non-industry members on the panel.

Such industry members also know what is good procedure and what is not and, in practice, do not hesitate to punish conduct which does not meet industry standards, even if the evidence on that point is not presented in the most effective manner.

The public press has recently commented on what it believes to be a disadvantage of the arbitration process at the SROs, *viz.*, a pro-industry bias on the part of the arbitrators. *E.g.*, *The New York Times*, March 29, 1987, section 3, page 1, column 3. In this writer's view, such comment is unwarranted. Precisely *because* of the securities expertise available to the panels, they are more likely than juries to see through a smoke screen laid down by *either* side and, thus, to arrive at a fair result. Also, the Supreme Court's reliance in *McMahon* on the SEC's supervision of the arbitration process has engendered new vigor in the SEC's supervision and movement within the industry to examine and improve the arbitration process.

In sum, the arbitration process, particularly at the SROs, provides an opportunity for a quick and efficient resolution of the facts without much of the burden and expense and some of the protections afforded in judicial litigation.

G. Open Issues

The increase in arbitrations and in litigation surrounding arbitration is likely to resolve some of the open questions surrounding the process. For example, with the *McMahon* and *Byrd* decisions at least opening the possibility of concurrent judicial litigation of federal securities claims and arbitration of 10b-5 and state claims arising out of the same facts, and of an earlier resolution of the arbitration proceeding, the question arises of what is the preclusive effect of the arbitration award on the federal action. Will the same issues be tried both by the arbitrators and later by the court if claims under the Securities Act of 1933 are held not to be arbitrable or will the usually earlier arbitration award preclude relitigation of the entire claim or of certain issues raised in the claim? *See, e.g.*, *Greenblatt v. Drexel Burnham Lambert, Inc.*, 736 F.2d 1352 (11th Cir. 1985) (relitigation of issues decided in arbitration prohibited because arbitration proceedings were adequate to protect the rights of the parties); *Artman v. Prudential-Bache Securities Inc.* [1987 Transfer Binder] Fed. Sec. L. Rep. (CCH) ¶ 93,346 (S.D. Ohio May 29,

1987) (permitting relitigation of issues because preclusion would circumvent policy under which jurisdiction over federal securities claims in federal court); Friedman, *The Preclusive Effect of Arbitral Determinations in Subsequent Federal Securities Litigation*, 60 Fordham L. Rev. 655 (1987).

As more claims can be brought to arbitration, it might be anticipated that more customers will argue that an arbitration agreement which is included in a standard form contract is a contract of adhesion. Although courts have generally rejected this view, *e.g.*, *Nesslage v. York Securities, Inc.*, 823 F.2d 231, 234 (8th Cir. 1987), the argument may well be renewed. Perhaps in anticipation, it has been suggested that the standard customer agreement contain a separate signature line with respect to the arbitration clause.

Although it is perhaps more of a transitory issue because of the enormous change in the law wrought by *McMahon*, waiver of a party's right to arbitration will be frequently raised. In general, courts have permitted parties who, because of pre-*Byrd*, pre-*McMahon* law, failed to press their right to arbitration to revive those rights after these rulings. *E.g.*, *Gilmore v. Shearson/ American Express, Inc.*, 668 F. Supp. 314 (S.D.N.Y. 1987). More generally, following the Second Circuit's decision in *Rush v. Oppenheimer*, 779 F.2d 885 (2d Cir. 1985) (litigant who moved to dismiss federal complaint pursuant to Fed. R. Civ. P. 9(b) and 12(b)(6), answered the amended complaint (including several affirmative defenses, but not the arbitration) and thereafter moved to compel arbitration had not waived his right to arbitrate), litigants seem to have substantial breathing space with respect to possibly waiving their rights to arbitrate by engaging in federal court proceedings.

H. Other

Counsel should also be aware that the United States District Court for the Eastern District of New York has adopted a Plan for Court-Annexed Arbitration which provides for compulsory arbitration of all civil cases (except social security and prisoners' civil rights cases) seeking monetary damages only in an amount not in excess of $50,000. Sec. 3. Pretrial discovery may be supervised by a magistrate. Sec. 4(a).

Unless the parties agree to a single arbitrator, the matter is tried before a panel of three arbitrators chosen from a list of certified arbitrators. Sec. 4(c); Sec. 1.

Following the award, any party may demand a trial *de novo* in the district court, from which trial evidence as to the arbitration is barred. Sec. 7.

CHAPTER TWENTY-FOUR

TRIAL AND POST-TRIAL MOTIONS

by Lawrence Mentz, Esq.

I. INTRODUCTION

Motions during and after a civil trial are the subject of this chapter. Not discussed here are motions to dismiss for lack of subject matter jurisdiction, which can be made at any time before, during or after trial, and even while a case is on appeal,[1] and any other motions permitted by Fed. R. Civ. P. 12(b). Some of the post-trial motions discussed herein can extend the time to appeal, but not all do so. If an appeal is contemplated, counsel must take great care in determining whether the post-trial motion that is made does, or does not, extend the time. An appeal taken either prematurely or too late is subject to possible dismissal by a Court of Appeals or the Supreme Court.[2]

The permissible trial and post-trial motions that can be made in a jury trial are not identical to those that can be made in a nonjury trial. Even where the motions are identical in the sense that they are made pursuant to the same rule of civil procedure, the standard governing determination of the motion can vary depending on whether a jury or nonjury trial is involved. Because this book is intended to be practical, and because a practitioner is more likely to try a particular case before a judge or before a jury, but not before both at the same time, this discussion of trial and post-trial motions treats the jury trial and bench trial separately. Motions relating to a jury trial are discussed first. In

---

1 *See* Fed. R. Civ. P. 12(h)(3).

2 *Budinich v. Becton Dickinson & Co.*, 108 S. Ct. 1717 (1988).

those instances where discussion of the same motion or topic in a nonjury trial would be duplicative, the practitioner is referred to the appropriate discussion under jury trial.

II. JURY TRIAL

A. Motions for Consolidation or for Separate Trials—Rule 42

Rule 42(a) specifies the circumstances under which separate actions pending in the same district may be consolidated for trial.[3] When a common question of law or fact exists, the court may order a joint hearing or trial on any one or all of the issues in those actions. Fed. R. Civ. P. 42(a). The prerequisite for consolidation is a "common question of law or fact." That threshold question is not always answered easily. *See Bank of Montreal v. Eagle Assoc.*, 117 F.R.D. 530 (S.D.N.Y. 1987). The purpose of consolidation is to promote judicial economy and convenience and to avoid possible conflicting results from separate actions. *Id.* Consolidation is not appropriate despite the presence of a common question of law or fact and increased judicial efficiency where it would result in prejudice to a party, however. *Arnold v. Eastern Air Lines, Inc.*, 712 F.2d 899 (4th Cir. 1983) (en banc), *cert. denied*, 464 U.S. 1040 (1984).

It would be a highly unusual situation to wait until trial to make a motion to consolidate two or more actions. The motion should normally be made before trial is commenced. The party seeking consolidation has the burden of persuading the court to exercise its discretion and order consolidation. *McCrae v. Pittsburgh Corning Corp.*, 97 F.R.D. 490, 492 (E.D. Pa. 1983). The court may order consolidation *sua sponte*. *Miller v. United States Postal Service*, 729 F.2d 1033, 1036 (5th Cir. 1984).

Once consolidated, the actions do not lose their separate identity or change the rights of the parties. *Stacey v. Charles J. Rogers, Inc.*, 756 F.2d 440, 442 (6th Cir. 1985); *Zdanok v. Glidden Co.*, 327 F.2d 944 (2d Cir.), *cert. denied*, 377 U.S. 934 (1964).[4] Under Rule 42(a) the court does have the power, however, to issue orders that may minimize unnecessary costs or delay including, for example, orders appointing lead counsel and restricting the activities

---

[3] When the actions are pending in different districts, a party desiring consolidation should first seek transfer of all actions to one district under the appropriate statute. *See* 28 U.S.C. §§ 1404, 1406, 1407. *See also* Chapter 3.

[4] The time to appeal any one of the consolidated actions can be affected by a motion made in another of the consolidated actions, however. The utmost care must be exercised to preserve the right to appeal or avoid dismissal of a premature appeal. *Compare Harcon Bridge Co. v. D & G Boat Rentals, Inc.*, 746 F.2d 278 (5th Cir. 1984), *aff'd on reh'g*, 784 F.2d 665 (5th Cir. 1986), *with Stacey v. Charles J. Rogers, Inc.*, 756 F.2d 440 (6th Cir. 1985).

TRIAL AND POST-TRIAL MOTIONS

of other counsel representing a party in a consolidated action. *Vincent v. Hughes Air West, Inc.*, 557 F.2d 759 (9th Cir. 1977); *In re Richardson-Merrell, Inc. "Benedictin" Products Liab. Litig.*, 624 F. Supp. 1212, 1246 (S.D. Ohio 1985).

A motion for separate trials is governed by Rule 42(b). It empowers the court to authorize a separate trial of any one or more claims, cross-claims, counterclaims, third-party claims or any separate issues. Fed. R. Civ. P. 42(b).[5] A court may order such separate trials when to do so will promote convenience and economy or avoid prejudice to a party. *Id.* In doing so, however, the Rule specifically states that the right to trial by jury as guaranteed by the seventh amendment or by statute must be preserved. *Id.*

Whether a separate trial of any claim or issue is desirable often cannot be determined at the outset of the litigation when it is impossible to tell from the pleadings if judicial economy will be served or prejudice avoided by an order for a separate trial. Consequently, a motion for separate trial may, under appropriate circumstances, be timely if made at the final pretrial conference, *see Fairchild Stratos Corp. v. General Electric Co.*, 31 F.R.D. 301 (S.D.N.Y. 1962), or even during trial, *Helminski v. Ayerst Laboratories*, 766 F.2d 208, 212 (6th Cir.), *cert. denied*, 474 U.S. 981 (1985).

The discretion of the court is invoked when a motion is made under Rule 42(b). Because in most cases a single trial will best promote economy and avoid delay, the party seeking a separate trial of any claim or issue must establish to the satisfaction of the court that such relief may result in substantial economy of time or expense and will avoid the likelihood of prejudice to a party. *Ropfogel v. Wise*, 112 F.R.D. 414 (S.D.N.Y. 1986).

The issue or claim sought to be tried separately must be truly distinct from the remaining claims or issues. Should the evidence relevant to the claims or issues pending in a single action overlap to any significant degree, there is scant likelihood a separate trial of a separate claim or issue will be granted or upheld. *See Witco Chemical Corp. v. Peachtree Doors, Inc.*, 787 F.2d 1545, 1549 (9th Cir.), *cert. dismissed*, 479 U.S. 877 (1986). The probability of separate trial being ordered is increased if there is little or no overlap in the evidence relevant to one set of claims or issues present in the action and in the evidence relevant to the issue or claim sought to be tried separately.

Separable issues whose determination may either result in early resolution of a critical threshold matter clearing the way for further progress in the case,

---

5 A motion for separate trial must not be confused with severance of a claim under Rule 21. Any such confusion may lead to harsh consequences. *United States v. O'Neil*, 709 F.2d 361 (5th Cir. 1983) (no timely appeal from judgment on claim severed from counterclaims pursuant to Rule 21 rather than Rule 42(b)).

or result in early termination of the case are likely to warrant favorable consideration for Rule 42(b) treatment. Included in this category are affirmative defenses such as statute of limitation, statute of fraud, lack of personal jurisdiction, collateral estoppel and res judicata. Also included are issues such as subject matter jurisdiction and venue. 9 C. Wright & A. Miller, *Federal Practice And Procedure*, § 2388 (1971); *see United States v. American Tel. & Tel. Co.*, 83 F.R.D. 323, 335 (D.D.C. 1979).

Among the issues most frequently tried separately are liability and damages. This is particularly true in personal injury actions. Although some authority exists for the proposition that bifurcation should not be ordered as a matter of course,[6] there are now some districts that provide for bifurcation routinely in local rules.[7] An order of bifurcation is needed where no local rule exists. Such an order may be obtained under Rule 42(b) either by a motion or by the court acting *sua sponte*. *See Helminski v. Ayerst Laboratories*, 766 F.2d 208, 212-13 (6th Cir.), *cert. denied*, 474 U.S. 981 (1985).

Seventh amendment concerns are implicated when different juries determine facts in separate trials. If the issues and facts are distinct, then no problem arises. *See Smith v. Aleyeska Pipeline Service Co.*, 538 F. Supp. 977, 984-85 (D. Del. 1982), *aff'd*, 758 F.2d 668 (Fed. Cir. 1984). If the same facts would be presented to different juries with a risk of conflicting findings, however, the seventh amendment would prohibit separate trials. *See Gasoline Products v. Champlin Refining Co.*, 283 U.S. 494 (1931); *United Air Lines, Inc. v. Wiener*, 286 F.2d 302 (9th Cir.), *cert. denied*, 366 U.S. 924 (1961).

B. Involuntary Dismissal—Rule 41(a)(2)

Motions by a plaintiff for an involuntary dismissal under Rule 41(a)(2) are discussed in detail in Chapter 16. Although rare, plaintiff may make such a motion during trial: the Rule does not prohibit such a motion even then. *See Cone v. West Virginia Pulp & Paper Co.*, 330 U.S. 212, 217 (1947). In *Cone* the Supreme Court noted that it was an appropriate use of Rule 41(a)(2) to permit plaintiff to dismiss without prejudice where there had been a failure of proof and the trial court believed a meritorious claim nevertheless existed. Of course, terms and conditions can be imposed by the court including payment of defendant's attorney's fees.[8] *See Taragan v. Eli Lilly and Co.*, 838 F.2d 1337, 1339-40 (D.C. Cir. 1988). Under the appropriate circumstances, therefore, a

---

[6] *See* 9 C. Wright & A. Miller, *Federal Practice And Procedure*, § 2390, at 300 (1971).

[7] *See, e.g.*, N.D.N.Y. Gen. R. 40.

[8] For the various factors considered by the court *see* Note, *Voluntary Dismissal by Order of Court—Federal Rules of Civil Procedure Rule 41(a)(2) and Judicial Discretion*, 48 N.D. Lawyer 446 (1972).

motion under Rule 41(a)(2) for involuntary dismissal without prejudice may be a useful trial tool for a plaintiff.[9] If the plaintiff chooses not to comply with the terms and conditions imposed by the court, the plaintiff may withdraw the motion, or the dismissal will be with prejudice. *See Lau v. Glendora Unified School Dist.*, 792 F.2d 929 (9th Cir. 1986).

C. Motion to Amend Pleadings to Conform to Evidence— Rule 15(b)

Amendment of the pleadings to conform to the evidence is not often thought of as an important part of the trial process. Under Rule 15(b) of the Federal Rules, a failure to seek such an amendment can have no adverse consequences to the successful litigation of a particular case because if issues not raised by the pleadings are actually tried, "failure . . . to amend does not affect the result of the trial of these issued." Fed. R. Civ. P. 15(b).

Failure to amend the pleadings when warranted can substantially affect future litigation, however. There are circumstances when it may be important to establish that an issue not reflected in the original pleading was tried. For example, the doctrine of collateral estoppel requires a finding that an issue actually was litigated in a prior case before determination of that issue can be used offensively or defensively in another litigation. A review of the pleadings in the first case can sometimes be a helpful factor in resolution of that question. *See Melikian v. Corradetti*, 791 F.2d 274 (3d Cir. 1986). An understanding, therefore, of the circumstances under which an amendment of the pleadings to conform to the evidence can be obtained is important. *See* 6 C. Wright & A. Miller, *Federal Practice And Procedure*, §§ 1491, 1493 (1971).

1. When There is No Objection to Introduction of Evidence

If a party does not object to the introduction of evidence at a hearing or trial on an issue which is arguably outside the scope of the pleadings, the first two sentences of Rule 15(b) delineate under what circumstances the pleadings may be amended or treated as if they had been amended.

> When issues not raised by the pleadings are tried by express or implied consent of the parties, they shall be treated in all respects as if they had been raised in the pleadings. Such amendment of the pleadings as may be necessary to cause them to conform to the evidence and to raise these issues may be made upon motion of any party at any time, even after judgment; but failure so to amend does not affect the result of the trial of these issues.

---

[9] Voluntary dismissal with prejudice is another alternative to consider. *See Lapierre v. Executive Indus., Inc.*, 117 F.R.D. 328 (D. Conn. 1987).

Fed. R. Civ. P. 15(b). The primary requirement is that the issues which are not raised by the pleadings actually be tried "by express or implied consent of the parties." *Id.*

Express consent to try issues not raised by the pleadings may be evidenced by a stipulation or by a pretrial order agreed to by the parties. Implied consent to the trial of such issues is not easily inferred, however. *See Wesco Mfg., Inc. v. Tropical Attractions of Palm Beach, Inc.*, 833 F.2d 1484, 1486-87 (11th Cir. 1987); *Esquire Radio & Elec., Inc. v. Montgomery Ward & Co., Inc.*, 804 F.2d 787, 795 (2d Cir. 1986). Although it is not necessary for the parties to recognize that the issue was not raised by the original pleadings, the parties must have tried the issue and either have, or should have, been aware that the issue was tried. *See Pershern v. Fiatallis North America, Inc.*, 834 F.2d 136, 139 (8th Cir. 1987); *Esquire Radio & Electronics, supra.* The admission of evidence on an issue not encompassed by the pleadings, but claimed by a party to have been tried by implied consent, is not conclusive if the evidence was also admissible on an issue within the scope of the pleadings. *See Wesco Mfg. Co., Inc., supra.* Admission of such evidence with knowledge of its bearing on a new issue without objection or introduction of such evidence by the party objecting to amendment are factors considered by courts in determining whether to infer consent.[10] *See Luria Brothers & Co. v. Alliance Assurance Co., Ltd.*, 780 F.2d 1082, 1088-90 (2d Cir. 1986); 6 C. Wright & A. Miller, *Federal Practice And Procedures*, § 1492 (1971).

If an issue beyond the scope of the pleadings was tried by express or implied consent, then the court must treat the issue as if it "had been raised in the pleadings." Fed. R. Civ. P. 15(b). Having been tried and not been resolved as a matter of law, therefore, the issue must be submitted to the jury for determination with appropriate instructions on the law. *See Securities & Exch. Comm'n v. Rapp*, 304 F.2d 786, 790 (2d Cir. 1962); *Slavitt v. Kauhi*, 384 F.2d 530, 532-34 (9th Cir. 1967); 6 C. Wright & A. Miller, *Federal Practice And Procedures*, § 1493, at 469 (1971). Amendment may be made at any time, even in an appellate court. *See Brandon v. Holt*, 469 U.S. 464, 471 (1985).

2. When There is Objection to Introduction of Evidence

Additional factors must be taken into consideration by the court when a party objects to introduction of evidence on an issue not raised by the pleadings. Rule 15(b) permits the pleadings to be amended to cure the objection and directs that the court

---

10 Determining whether the issue was tried by express or implied consent is a matter of discretion for the trial court. *United States v. Van Diviner*, 822 F.2d 960, 964 (10th Cir. 1987). It will be reviewed for an abuse of discretion. *See Pershern v. Fiatallis North America, Inc.*, 834 F.2d 136, 139 (8th Cir. 1987).

shall do so freely when the presentation of the merits of the action will be subserved thereby and the objecting party fails to satisfy the court that the admission of such evidence would prejudice the party in maintaining the party's action or defense upon the merits.

Fed. R. Civ. P. 15(b). In the absence of prejudice to the opposing party, therefore, the court should permit amendment of the pleadings. *Hillburn v. Maher*, 795 F.2d 252, 264 (2d Cir. 1986).

The "prejudice" referred to in the rule is not merely that of being placed at some tactical or monetary disadvantage. Rather, it is the type of prejudice arising from an inability to counter the new issue sought to be introduced at a late stage of the proceedings. *See Richardson v. United States*, 841 F.2d 993, 999-1000 (9th Cir. 1988); *Cunningham v. Quaker Oats Co.*, 107 F.R.D. 66, 71 (W.D.N.Y. 1985). A claim of surprise must be real, not technical, and if actual notice had been given that the issue was likely to be raised at trial, such a claim will not avoid amendment of the pleadings. *See Esquire Radio & Elec., Inc. v. Montgomery Ward & Co., Inc.*, 804 F.2d 787, 795 (2d Cir. 1986). On the other hand, when amendment would result in an inability of a party to meet the new issue with opposing evidence, prejudice exists of the type warranting denial of the motion. Thus, for example, where an equitable remedy is added by amendment and the opposing party had no opportunity either to have discovery on or to present equitable defenses, amendment is improper. *Luria Brothers & Co. v. Alliance Assurance Co., Ltd.*, 780 F.2d 1082, 1090 (2d Cir. 1986).

When the nature of the claimed prejudice is surprise and an inability to counter the new issue raised by the evidence, Rule 15(b) empowers the court, in its discretion, to "grant a continuance to enable the objecting party to meet such evidence." Fed. R. Civ. P. 15(b). If a party fails to request a continuance it cannot later claim that no opportunity was given to obtain evidence relevant to the new issue. *See Dalbec v. Gentleman's Companion, Inc.*, 828 F.2d 921, 929 (2d Cir. 1987). A continuance may be unavailing when, through the passage of time, witnesses can no longer be found or the newly asserted claim is stale. Under such circumstances amendment may be denied by the court. *See Johnson v. Trueblood*, 629 F.2d 287, 294-95 (3d Cir. 1980), *cert. denied*, 450 U.S. 999 (1981).

D. Motion for Directed Verdict—Rule 50(a)

A motion for directed verdict is provided for under Rule 50(a) of the Federal Rules of Civil Procedure. Normally the motion is made by defendant at the close of plaintiff's evidence and by both parties at the close of all the evidence.

A party who moves for a directed verdict at the close of the evidence offered by an opponent may offer evidence in the event that the motion is not granted without having reserved the right to do so and to the same extent as if the motion had not been made. A motion for a directed verdict which is not granted is not a waiver of trial by jury even though all parties to the action have moved for directed verdicts. A motion for directed verdict shall state the specific grounds therefor. . . .

Fed. R. Civ. P. 50(a).

Making the motion at the close of all the evidence is a prerequisite to a motion for judgment notwithstanding the verdict under Rule 50(b). Fed. R. Civ. P. 50(b). Moreover, if a party fails to make a motion for a directed verdict at the close of all the evidence both the trial and appellate courts refuse to review whether the evidence adduced at trial was sufficient to submit the case to the jury. *See, e.g., Bartholomew v. CNG Producing Co.*, 832 F.2d 326, 329 (5th Cir. 1987).

1. Time for Making Motion

Although not specifically provided for in Rule 50(a), a motion for directed verdict may be made by defendant after plaintiff's opening statement and by plaintiff after defendant's opening. *Morfeld v. Kehm*, 803 F.2d 1452, 1454 (8th Cir. 1986); 5A J. Moore, *Moore's Federal Practice* ¶ 50.02[1] (1988). At that stage, the motion presents the court with the issue of whether the opening revealed either that there was no fact which could give rise to a valid claim, *i.e.*, "no cause of action exists," or that there was no fact which could possibly support any valid defense to the claim. Such motions are made infrequently and even less frequently granted. The court should normally provide an opportunity to supplement the opening statement to the extent any real defect existed and only grant the motion if warranted as a matter of law when a party cannot or will not cure the defect. *Morgan v. Koch*, 419 F.2d 993, 999 (7th Cir. 1969).

2. Requirements for Motion

Any motion "for directed verdict shall state the specific grounds therefor." Fed. R. Civ. P. 50(a). It is not necessary that the motion be made in writing, although this appears to be preferable. Handing the motion to the court may not be sufficient unless some indication that the motion was made appears in the record. *See DeMarines v. KLM Royal Dutch Airlines*, 580 F.2d 1193, 1195 n.4 (3d Cir. 1978). *But see Freeman v. Franzen*, 695 F.2d 485, 488 (7th Cir. 1982). The motion may be made orally in open court as long as it is done on the record. Fed. R. Civ. P. 7.

In the absence of stating the grounds for the motion, the party making it cannot argue on appeal that the motion was improperly denied. *Stewart v. Thigpen*, 730 F.2d 1002, 1006 n.2 (5th Cir. 1984). Detailed specificity is not required so long as the court and the adverse party understand the position urged. *Id.* Knowing the grounds for the motion, the adverse party will then be able to argue it should be permitted to submit additional evidence relevant to the ground stated and the court can determine whether any such additional evidence should be heard. *Virginia-Carolina Tie & Wood Co. v. Dunbar,* 106 F.2d 383, 385 (4th Cir. 1939); *see Hinojosa v. City of Terrell, Texas,* 834 F.2d 1223, 1228 (5th Cir. 1988). Merely arguing that the evidence as a whole is insufficient to submit the case to the jury does not meet the rules requirement, however, except in certain limited circumstances. *See Herrington v. Sonoma County,* 834 F.2d 1488, 1500 n.11 (9th Cir. 1987). It must be pointed out in what respect the evidence is insufficient, for example, no proof of causation, no proof of breach or no proof of antitrust injury. *See* 9 C. Wright & A. Miller, *Federal Practice And Procedure,* § 2533 (1971).

3. Standard Governing Determination of Motion

The court must consider all evidence and any reasonable inference to be drawn therefrom in the light most favorable to the party opposing the motion. If the evidence submitted creates an issue of fact relevant to the claim upon which reasonable minds could differ, then the motion must be denied. The question is:

> whether the evidence is such that without weighing the credibility of the witnesses or otherwise considering the weight of the evidence, there can be but one conclusion as to the verdict that reasonable men could have reached.

Simblest v. Maynard, 427 F.2d 1, 4 (2d Cir. 1970); *see Grogg v. Missouri Pac. R.R.,* 841 F.2d 210, 212 (8th Cir. 1988).

The standard does not vary in diversity cases where, pursuant to *Erie R.R. v. Tompkins,* 304 U.S. 64 (1938), state substantive law governs. The standard is seen not as a matter of state substantive law but of Federal procedure, at least where state law arguably requires less evidence to warrant submission of an issue to the jury.[11] *Hurd v. American Hoist & Derrick Co.,* 734 F.2d 495, 498 (10th Cir. 1984); *McHann v. Firestone Tire & Rubber Co.,* 713 F.2d 161, 164 (5th Cir. 1983). The question of which law governs the issue of sufficiency of the evidence should not be confused with that of whose law determines the factual elements necessary to establish a claim to relief, however. State law

---

[11] There are instances where the state standard governing sufficiency of the evidence is more stringent than the Federal standard and would require that a verdict be directed while a Federal court would submit the issue to the jury. Whether a state or Federal standard is the appropriate one to apply in such a case has not yet been decided definitively. *Mercer v. Theriot,* 377 U.S. 152, 156 (1964), and the decisions in the circuits are not always consistent. *Compare Mehra v. Bentz,* 529 F.2d 1137 (2d Cir. 1975), *cert. denied,* 426 U.S. 922 (1976), *with Wratchford v. S.J. Groves & Sons Co.,* 405 F.2d 1061 (4th Cir. 1969).

under the *Erie* doctrine definitely governs the latter issue and a Federal court must look to state substantive law to determine what elements are required to make out a *prima facie* case. *See Toner v. Lederle Laboratories*, 779 F.2d 1429 (9th Cir. 1986).

There is no waiver either of the right to offer evidence or of the right to a jury trial in the event a motion for directed verdict is denied. Fed. R. Civ. P. 50(a). When the motion is made by defendant at the close of plaintiff's case, the court will consider the evidence elicited both by plaintiff and by defendant upon cross-examination of plaintiff's witnesses. Should the court deny the motion at the close of plaintiff's case or reserve decision, defendant is then permitted to offer evidence. Fed. R. Civ. P. 50(a). If defendant does so, the right to later object to denial of the motion for directed verdict at the close of plaintiff's case is waived.[12] *See Karns v. Emerson Elec. Co.*, 817 F.2d 1452, 1455-56 (10th Cir. 1987). In determining a motion for directed verdict at the close of all the evidence, the court will consider all the evidence admitted either during plaintiff's case-in-chief or defendant's case. *Trustees of Univ. of Pennsylvania v. Lexington Ins. Co.*, 815 F.2d 890, 903 (3d Cir. 1987).

E. Motion for Judgment Notwithstanding the Verdict—Rule 50(b)

Rule 50(b) of the Federal Rules provides an important tool for the courts and litigants. It is essentially the last opportunity a trial court has to correct a jury verdict and have judgment entered in accordance with the court's view of the law.[13]

1. Time for Making Motion

The Rule provides that the motion must be made within 10 days of entry of the judgment referred to in Rule 58. If no verdict was returned by the jury, within 10 days after discharge of the jury a party can move to have "judgment in accordance with [the party's] motion for a directed verdict." Fed. R. Civ. P. 50(b). The 10-day time period is one which the court and the parties cannot enlarge. Fed. R. Civ. P. 6(b).

Whether a motion is "made" at the time it is served or at the time of filing has sometimes given rise to the question of timeliness of a motion for judgment notwithstanding the verdict. *United States v. Valdosta/Lowndes County Hosp.*

---

[12] Only by resting without offering any evidence could defendant preserve a right to argue on appeal that the motion was improperly denied at this stage of the proceedings. In view of the tendency of courts to submit cases to the jury despite some doubts as to the soundness of plaintiff's claims, a defendant obviously takes a substantial risk of an adverse jury verdict by choosing not to offer any evidence.

---

[13] What the trial court's views of the facts are is irrelevant except to the extent it holds in any particular case that a reasonable person could not find as the jury did.

Auth., 91 F.R.D. 521 (M.D. Ga. 1981). Rule 7 provides little or no guidance on this point and the safer practice is to both serve and file the motion within the 10-day period.

2. Requirements for Making Motion

A prerequisite for making the motion is that the movant must have made a "motion for directed verdict at the close of all the evidence." Fed. R. Civ. P. 50(b). A motion for directed verdict at the close of plaintiff's case will not suffice. *Mark Seitman & Assoc. v. R. J. Reynolds Tobacco Co.*, 837 F.2d 1527, 1531 (11th Cir. 1988).

As with any other motion, Rule 7 governs its formal requirements. Inasmuch as the motion for judgment notwithstanding the verdict seeks "judgment in accordance with [a party's] motion for a directed verdict," the same grounds specified in the motion for a directed verdict serve as the basis for a motion under Rule 50(b). New grounds, not asserted in the Rule 50(a) motion for directed verdict, cannot be advanced for the first time in a motion for judgment notwithstanding the verdict. *See Lifschitz v. Walter Drake & Sons, Inc.*, 806 F.2d 1426, 1428-30 (9th Cir. 1986); *Baskin v. Hawley*, 807 F.2d 1120, 1129-30 (2d Cir. 1986). This requirement is somewhat liberally construed, however, and, for example, if a party properly raised a question as to the sufficiency of the evidence in the motion for directed verdict, *e.g.*, no evidence of proximate cause, that ground can be reasserted in the motion for judgment notwithstanding the verdict even if not precisely identical, *e.g.*, insufficient evidence of negligence.

Failure to make the motion can have serious consequences in both the trial and appellate courts. Neither court can enter judgment notwithstanding the verdict if a party has not actually made a motion requesting the court to do so. *Cone v. West Virginia Pulp & Paper Co.*, *supra*. This requirement is carried to technical extremes. *Globe Liquor Co. v. San Roman*, 332 U.S. 571 (1948). In *Globe Liquor* the Supreme Court held that defendant's failure to make the motion for judgment notwithstanding the verdict, when it would clearly have been unavailing because the trial court had directed a verdict for plaintiff, prevented the appellate court from ordering entry of judgment for defendant despite defendant's timely motion for a directed verdict which the appellate court held should have been granted as a matter of law. The Supreme Court said that the only course available to the appellate court was to order a new trial. *Id.*; *see Mark Seitman & Associates v. R. J. Reynolds Tobacco Co.*, 837 F.2d 1527, 1531 (11th Cir. 1988). In the absence, therefore, of a motion for judgment notwithstanding the verdict, appeal of denial of a motion for a directed verdict if successful will only result in a new trial on remand, not judgment. *See Smith v. Trans-World Drilling Co.*, 772 F.2d 157, 162 (5th Cir. 1985). *But see Ebker v. Tan Jay Int'l, Inc.*, 739 F.2d 812 (2d Cir. 1984).

The only way in which a party's rights on appeal can be fully protected is to move for judgment notwithstanding the verdict.

3. Standard Governing Determination of Motion

Because the motion for judgment notwithstanding the verdict is, in effect, based upon a renewal of the motion for a directed verdict, the standard used by the court in considering whether to grant judgment notwithstanding the verdict is identical to that used for directed verdict motions. *U.S. Industries, Inc. v. Blake Constr. Co.*, 671 F.2d 539, 549-50 (D.C. Cir. 1982). The party seeking judgment must demonstrate to the court it is entitled to judgment either as a matter of law or because the evidence was insufficient to permit reasonable jurors to return the verdict sought to be set aside. *Id.* For a fuller discussion of the standard, *see* Part II, D, 3, *supra*.

4. Alternative Motion for New Trial—Rule 50(b)

"A motion for a new trial may be joined with this motion [for judgment notwithstanding the verdict], or a new trial may be prayed for in the alternative." Fed. R. Civ. P. 50(b). In virtually all cases where a party seeks judgment notwithstanding the verdict it should also take advantage of the quoted language and move, alternatively, for a new trial. There are circumstances when a court may be unable to order judgment, for example, failure to move for directed verdict at the close of all evidence, but is willing to order a new trial.

The standard on a motion for new trial is not the same as for judgment notwithstanding the verdict. *See Landes Constr. Co. v. Royal Bank of Canada*, 833 F.2d 1365, 1371 (9th Cir. 1987). Whereas the motion for judgment raises a question of law for determination by the court, a motion for new trial asks the court in the exercise of its discretion to order a new trial for some perceived unfairness or because it is against the weight of the evidence. *Id.*

Rule 50(c) specifies the duties of court when it grants a motion made under Rule 5C(b). If judgment notwithstanding the verdict

> is granted, the court shall also rule on the motion for new trial, if any, by determining whether it should be granted if the judgment is thereafter vacated or reversed, and shall specify the grounds for granting or denying the motion for new trial.

Fed. R. Civ. P. 50(c). The reason for the requirement that the court rule on the motion for new trial is obvious. Should the appellate court reverse the grant of the motion for judgment notwithstanding the verdict, the court can also consider whether the motion for new trial was properly decided. Subdivision (c) of the Rule provides further guidance to the appellate court:

> In case the motion for new trial is conditionally granted and the judgment is reversed on appeal, the new trial shall proceed unless the

appellate court has otherwise ordered. In case the motion for a new trial has been conditionally denied, the appellee on appeal may assert error in that denial; and if the judgment is reversed on appeal, subsequent proceedings shall be in accordance with the order of the appellate court. *Id.*

When the motion for judgment notwithstanding the verdict is denied, Rule 50(d) delineates the rights on a subsequent appeal of the party who prevailed on the motion. As appellee that party may "assert grounds entitling [the party] to a new trial in the event the appellate court concludes that the trial court erred in denying the motion for judgment notwithstanding the verdict." *Id.* The subdivision empowers the appellate court, if it reverses the judgment in the trial court, to determine whether appellee is entitled to a new trial or to remand for such a determination by the trial court. Fed. R. Civ. P. 50(d).

F. Motion for New Trial—Rule 59(a)(1)

Rule 59 provides the procedural basis for seeking a new trial and specifies in general terms the grounds on which such relief may be obtained. After a jury trial any party or parties may seek a new trial "on all or part of the issues . . . for any of the reasons for which new trials have heretofore been granted in actions at law in the courts of the United States." Fed. R. Civ. P. 59(a). The grounds specified in Rule 59(a) for a new trial apply not only to motions made under that Rule but also to motions made under Rules 50(b) and 50(c)(2).

1. Time for Making Motion

The motion for new trial must be served within 10 days after the entry of the judgment referred to in Rule 58. Fed. R. Civ. P. 59(b). The time specified may not be enlarged either by order of the court or by stipulation. Fed. R. Civ. P. 6(b).

Unlike Rule 50(b), which only specifies that a party must move for judgment not withstanding the verdict within 10 days but does not mention "service" or "filing" within that time, Rule 59(b) requires "service" within 10 days. Filing of the motion within the 10-day time period is not also required.[14] *E.g., Clayton v. Douglas*, 670 F.2d 143 (10th Cir.), *cert. denied*, 457 U.S. 1109 (1982). The motion must, however, be filed within a reasonable time after service. Fed. R. Civ. P. 5(d).

One party cannot rely on a motion for new trial made by another party. Moreover, attempting to join in another party's motion for new trial after the

---

14 Filing of the motion within the 10-day period but serving it afterwards, which is permitted for any paper by Rule 5(d), would be untimely under Rule 59(b). *Kruse v. Zenith Radio Corp.*, 82 F.R.D. 66 (W.D. Pa. 1979).

10-day time period has expired is equally unavailing. *Tarlton v. Exxon*, 688 F.2d 973 (5th Cir. 1982). When a new trial is granted which necessarily requires retrial of other parties, the failure to make the motion will not prevent a new trial with respect to those other parties, however. *Ryan v. McDonough Power Equipment, Inc.*, 734 F.2d 385 (8th Cir. 1984).

Within 10 days after entry of judgment the court on "its own initiative may order a new trial for any reason for which it might have granted a new trial on motion of a party." Fed. R. Civ. P. 59(d). If the court does not order a new trial on its own initiative within the 10-day time period it cannot do so at all because the time period is jurisdictional in nature. *Peterman v. Chicago, R.I. & Pac. R.R.*, 493 F.2d 88 (8th Cir.), *cert. denied*, 417 U.S. 947 (1974).

If a timely motion for a new trial has been made by a party, the court may grant the motion on a ground not presented by the moving party, but only if it has given "the parties notice and an opportunity to be heard" of its intention to do so. Fed. R. Civ. P. 59(d). When a timely motion for new trial has been made but the court grants the motion on a ground not stated after the 10-day time period has expired without providing notice to the parties as required by Rule 59(d), some appellate courts have implied that the order for a new trial is a nullity. *See Harkins v. Ford Motor Co.*, 437 F.2d 276, 277 (3d Cir. 1970). *But see* C. Wright & A. Miller, *Federal Practice & Procedure*, § 2813, at 91 (1973). Failure of the court to specify the grounds on which it acted on its own initiative should not render it a nullity inasmuch as such a deficiency may be easily cured. *Cherokee Laboratories, Inc. v. Pierson*, 415 F.2d 85 (10th Cir. 1969), *cert. denied*, 396 U.S. 1059 (1970).

If the "motion for a new trial is based upon affidavits they shall be served with the motion." Fed. R. Civ. P. 59(c). Opposing papers must be served within 10 days, but that time period may be extended for no more than another 20 days by order of the court or by written stipulation. In addition, the "court may permit reply affidavits." *Id.*

2. Standard Governing Determination of Motion

Parties to litigation in the Federal courts are not entitled to perfect trials. *McDonough Power Equip., Inc. v. Greenwood*, 464 U.S. 548, 553 (1984). Mere error by the trial court in the conduct of the trial does not entitle the losing party to a new trial under every circumstance. The error must be prejudicial to the losing party:

> No error in either the admission or the exclusion of evidence and no error or defect in any ruling or order or in anything done or omitted by the court or by any of the parties is ground for granting a new trial or for setting aside a verdict or for vacating, modifying, or otherwise disturbing a judgment or order, unless refusal to take such action

appears to the court inconsistent with substantial justice. The court at every stage of the proceeding must disregard any error or defect in the proceeding which does not affect the substantial rights of the parties.

Fed. R. Civ. P. 61. In determining whether the "substantial rights of the parties" have been affected by an error at the trial such as to warrant a new trial, the court's discretion is invoked. "The authority to grant a new trial . . . is confided almost entirely to the exercise of discretion on the party of the trial court." *Allied Chem. Corp. v. Daiflon, Inc.*, 449 U.S. 33, 36 (1980).

The discretion to order a new trial, although broad, is not exercised routinely. "Courts do not grant new trials unless it is reasonably clear that prejudicial error has crept into the record or that substantial justice has not been done." 11 C. Wright & A. Miller, *Federal Practice & Procedure*, § 2803, at 32 (1973) (footnotes omitted). *See Overpeck v. Chicago Pneumatic Tool Co.*, 634 F. Supp. 638, 639 (E.D. Pa. 1986). An order denying a new trial is subject to reversal only for an abuse of discretion.[15] *E.g., Wilhelm v. Blue Bell, Inc.*, 773 F.2d 1429, 1433 (4th Cir. 1985), *cert. denied*, 475 U.S. 1016 (1986).

Inasmuch as the question of whether to grant a new trial is procedural rather than substantive, Federal law governs even in diversity cases.[16] 11 C. Wright & A. Miller, *Federal Practice And Procedure*, § 2802 (1973). *See Donovan v. Pen Shipping Co., Inc.*, 429 U.S. 648, 649 (1977).

The grounds a party can assert in moving for a new trial are numerous. They include, among others, claims that the verdict was against the weight of the evidence, excessive damages and inadequate damages. *Thompson v. Int'l Ass'n of Machinists & Aerospace Workers*, 614 F. Supp. 1002, 1010 (D.D.C. 1985) ("other reasons" supporting a Rule 59 motion may include substantial errors in admission or rejection of evidence or jury instructions, jury misconduct, inconsistency in the verdict, denial of the proper mode of trial or belated discovery of evidence, to name a few").

Essentially any prejudicial occurrence or error in the conduct of the trial can be asserted as a ground warranting a new trial. If a party establishes an error of

---

15 An order granting a new trial is not appealable as of right and mandamus is only available in exceptionable circumstances which are rarely occasioned by an order granting new trial. *Allied Chem. Corp. v. Daiflon, Inc.*, 449 U.S. 33, 36 (1980). The order is reviewable upon an appeal from an adverse judgment in the second trial. *Id.*

16 It is not settled whether a Federal court in a diversity case should look to state law when determining whether a verdict is excessive. *Compare* 11 C. Wright & A. Miller, *Federal Practice and Procedure*, § 2802 (1973), and *Johnson v. Parrish*, 827 F.2d 988 (4th Cir. 1987), *with T.D.S., Inc. v. Shelby Mut. Ins. Co.*, 760 F.2d 1520, 1530 n.8 (11th Cir. 1985), *and Martell v. Boardwalk Enter., Inc.*, 748 F.2d 740, 750, 754 (2d Cir. 1984).

law either in a ruling on the admissibility of evidence or an instruction to the jury, then the question confronting the court is whether such error was prejudicial or harmless. Fed. R. Civ. P. 61.

When presented with an assertion that the verdict is against the weight of the evidence, the trial court is free to and, in fact, must weigh the evidence and assess the credibility of the witnesses. *See Landes Constr. Co. v. Royal Bank of Canada*, 833 F.2d 1365 (9th Cir. 1987). It is not sufficient for the grant of a new trial that the court merely disagree with the jury's verdict, however. The standard required is that the court be convinced that the verdict is against the "great" or "clear" weight of the evidence.[17] *Id.*; *Isaksen v. Vermont Castings, Inc.*, 825 F.2d 1158, 1163 (7th Cir. 1987), *cert. denied*, 108 S. Ct. 1728 (1988).

In reviewing the size of a verdict for either inadequacy or excessiveness, a new trial is only required when the verdict "shocks the conscience" of the court or when it is the result of passion, prejudice, or gross mistake. *T.D.S., Inc. v. Shelby Mut. Ins. Co.*, 760 F.2d 1520, 1530 (11th Cir. 1985); *Martell v. Boardwalk Enter., Inc.*, 748 F.2d 740, 750 (2d Cir. 1984). Where a verdict is excessive, the court may conditionally grant a new trial unless the plaintiff accepts a remittitur in a stated amount.[18] *See Donovan v. Penn Shipping Co.*, 429 U.S. 648 (1977). Calculation of the remittitur can vary depending upon the theory applied. In some courts the damages are reduced to the maximum amount a jury could have awarded, and in other cases damages are reduced to a minimum permissible amount. Under a third theory, the judge determines a reasonable amount. It is unsettled which of these theories is appropriate. *See* 6A J. Moore, *Moore's Federal Practice* ¶ 59.08[7], at 59-193 to -198 (1987); 11 C. Wright & A. Miller, *Federal Practice & Procedure*, § 2815, at 104-05 (1973). When the verdict results from jury passion or prejudice or an improper instruction on damages a new trial is required, and remittitur is improper. *Baskin v. Hawley*, 807 F.2d 1120, 1135 (2d Cir. 1986); *Wells v. Dallas Indep. School Dist.*, 793 F.2d 679, 683 (5th Cir. 1986).

The court may order a partial new trial either of damages or liability, or any other issue, as long as they are separable and distinct and there is no persuasive

---

17 Even "substantial" evidence in support of the verdict does not prevent the trial court from exercising its discretion to order a new trial if it is convinced the verdict is against the great weight of the evidence. *Landes Construction Co.*, 833 F.2d 1365, 1371. If the trial court refuses to grant a new trial, however, an appellate court cannot "weigh evidence or assess the credibility of witnesses" and will only order a new trial in very limited circumstances. *Landes Construction Co.*, 833 F.2d 1365, 1372.

18 Additur is not permitted having been held to be in violation of the seventh amendment. *Dimick v. Schiedt*, 293 U.S. 474 (1935).

indication that the factual finding on one influenced that of the other. *See Continental Casualty Co. v. Howard*, 775 F.2d 876, 883 (7th Cir. 1985), *cert. denied*, 475 U.S. 1122 (1986).

G. Motion to Alter or Amend Judgment—Rule 59(e)

Motions directed to a judgment that has become a final one are treated elsewhere. A judgment is not necessarily final when entered, however, because of the power given to the trial court by Rule 59(e) of the Federal Rules to alter or amend a judgment.

1. Time for Making Motion

The rule provides that a "motion to alter or amend the judgment shall be served not later than 10 days after entry of the judgment." Fed. R. Civ. P. 59(e). If a motion is made pursuant to Rule 59(e) it "suspends the finality" of the judgment and extends the time to take an appeal. *See* Fed. R. App. P. 4(a)(4). The court has no power to and cannot enlarge the time to make a motion under Rule 59(e). Fed. R. Civ. P. 6(b). Filing of the motion within the 10-day time period is insufficient because the rule prescribes service,[19] *Rivera v. M/T Fossarina*, 840 F.2d 152, 154 (1st Cir. 1988), and, moreover, an untimely Rule 59(e) motion does not extend the time to appeal. *Id.* A notice of appeal filed by any party either while a timely Rule 59(e) motion is pending in the district court or even before service of a timely Rule 59(e) motion is premature and ineffective.[20] *Acosta v. Louisiana Dep't of Health & Human Resources*, 478 U.S. 251 (1986).

2. Grounds for Motion

A motion to alter or amend a judgment provides the procedural means for correcting a judgment which contains, or is based upon, some legal error, *Appeal of Sun Pipe Line Co.*, 831 F.2d 22, 24 (1st Cir. 1987), or omits matter to which a party is entitled. *See Boyd v. Bulala*, 678 F. Supp. 612 (W.D. Va. 1988), or includes too much.[21] Thus, for example, in response to a motion made under Rule 59(e) a court may amend a judgment in favor of a plaintiff by

---

19 Filing after the 10-day limit is of no consequence as long as service is within the 10-day time period. *Nichols v. Asbestos Workers Local 24 Pension Plan*, 835 F.2d 881, 887 n.51 (D.C. Cir. 1987).

20 A motion by the prevailing party for costs is not a Rule 59(e) motion. *Buchanan v. Stanships, Inc.*, 108 S. Ct. 1130 (1988). Likewise a motion by the prevailing party for attorney's fees permitted by statute is not a Rule 59(e) motion suspending finality of the judgment or extending the time to take an appeal. *See Budinich v. Becton Dickson & Co.*, 108 S. Ct. 1717 (1988); *White v. New Hampshire*, 455 U.S. 445 (1982).

21 Rule 59(e) is not used to correct clerical errors, however. *See* Rule 60(a). Unlike Rule 59(e), a motion under Rule 60 does not affect the finality of the judgment or the time to appeal.

reducing it in order to reflect amounts previously received in settlement from a joint tortfeasor. *Boyd, supra.* Similarly, a Rule 59(e) motion is the appropriate procedure to be followed when seeking reconsideration of the grant of summary judgment. *See Northern Cheyenne Tribe v. Hodel,* 842 F.2d 224, 227 (9th Cir. 1988); *Kadane v. Hofstra Univ.,* 682 F. Supp. 166, 171 (E.D.N.Y. 1988), or for reconsideration of an order granting a preliminary injunction, *Financial Services Corp. v. Weindruch,* 764 F.2d 197 (7th Cir. 1985).

III. NONJURY TRIAL

A. Motion for Involuntary Dismissal—Rule 41(b)

Rule 41(b) of the Federal Rules of Civil Procedure delineates two grounds for making a motion under the Rule. The first ground, which is for "failure of plaintiff to prosecute or to comply with these rules or any order of court," will not be discussed in this chapter. Such a motion under Rule 41(b) is usually made before trial commences and normally is considered by defense counsel when plaintiff delays, hinders or procrastinates progress toward trial.

The second ground specified is "that upon the facts and the law the plaintiff has shown no right to relief," and is the subject of this section. A motion for involuntary dismissal on this ground is the procedural equivalent of a motion for directed verdict under Rule 50(b) made at the close of plaintiff's evidence in a jury trial. The standards used in deciding such motions are totally different, however. *United States v. General Dynamics Corp.,* 246 F. Supp. 156, 159 (S.D.N.Y. 1965). Because there can be no verdict in a nonjury trial, Rule 50(b) is inapplicable.

A Rule 41(b) motion is only available to a defendant. *See DuPont v. Southern Nat'l Bank,* 771 F.2d 874, 879 (5th Cir. 1985), *cert. denied,* 475 U.S. 1085 (1986). It is applicable to a counterclaim, cross-claim or third-party claim. Fed. R. Civ. P. 41(c). Should defense counsel in a bench trial inadvertently denominate a motion made at the close of plaintiff's evidence as one for directed verdict under Rule 50(b), the court will generally consider it as one for involuntary dismissal under Rule 41(b). *See Central Maine Power Co. v. Foster Wheeler Corp.,* 116 F.R.D. 339, 340 (D. Me. 1987).

1. Time for Making Motion

The Rule provides that the motion is made "[a]fter the plaintiff, in an action tried by the court without a jury, has completed the presentation of evidence." As a practical matter, the defendant is not restricted to waiting for plaintiff to rest. When it becomes manifestly clear that plaintiff will not be able to prove his case, a Rule 41(b) motion may be granted, *D.P. Apparel Corp. v. Roadway Express, Inc.,* 736 F.2d 1 (1st Cir. 1984); *Erie Conduit Corp. v. MAPA,* 102

F.R.D. 877 (E.D.N.Y. 1984), even at the completion of plaintiff's opening statement, *Stone v. Millstein*, 804 F.2d 1434, 1437-38 (9th Cir. 1986).

On the other hand, grant of a Rule 41(b) motion may be premature even after plaintiff has rested its case-in-chief. If during the case-in-chief plaintiff is not given an opportunity to rebut an alleged affirmative defense or is not required to do so until after defendant's case, a dismissal pursuant to Rule 41(b) is premature and subject to reversal. *See CMS Software Design Sys., Inc. v. Info Designs, Inc.*, 785 F.2d 1246, 1248-59 (5th Cir. 1986); *Mitchell v. Baldrige*, 759 F.2d 80, 87-89 (D.C. Cir. 1985).

As a general proposition, trial courts are reluctant to grant a Rule 41(b) motion and the preferred practice is to deny the motion or reserve decision. *Central Maine Power Co. v. Foster Wheeler Corp.*, 116 F.R.D. 339, 341 (D. Me. 1987); *see D.P. Apparel Corp., supra*. If the court does not grant the motion at the close of plaintiff's case and defendant proceeds to put in its case, for which the Rule specifically provides, the defendant waives any right to appeal denial of the motion. Only by refusing to put on evidence can defendant preserve a right to appeal denial of a Rule 41(b) motion. *See DuPont v. Southern Nat'l Bank*, 771 F.2d 874, 881 (5th Cir. 1985).

2. Standard Governing Determination of Motion

In considering a Rule 41(b) motion, a court is free to weigh the evidence and judge the credibility of witnesses. *Continental Casualty Co. v. DLH Services, Inc.*, 752 F.2d 353, 355-56 (8th Cir. 1985). The court is not required either to view the evidence in the light most favorable to plaintiff, *Romain v. Kurek*, 836 F.2d 241, 245 (6th Cir. 1987), or to draw any inferences in plaintiff's favor, *Central Maine Power Co. v. Foster Wheeler Corp.*, 116 F.R.D. 339, 340 (D. Me. 1987).

The standard for grant of a Rule 41(b) motion has been expressed in various terms. For example, some cases state that the motion may be granted once it is "manifestly clear that plaintiff will not prove his case," *D.P. Apparel Corp. v. Roadway Express, Inc.*, 736 F.2d 1, 3 (1st Cir. 1984), or "provided the court is convinced that the evidence preponderates against the plaintiff," *Johnson v. United States Postal Serv.*, 756 F.2d 1461, 1464 (9th Cir. 1985), even though plaintiff has made out a prima facie case, *id.*, or if the court "determines that the plaintiff has failed to offer persuasive evidence regarding the necessary elements of his case," *DuPont v. Southern Nat'l Bank*, 771 F.2d 874, 879 (5th Cir. 1985). *See Romano v. Merrill Lynch, Pierce, Fenner & Smith*, 834 F.2d 523, 530 (5th Cir. 1987), *cert. denied*, 108 S. Ct. 2846 (1988); *CMS Software Design Sys., Inc. v. Info Designs, Inc.*, 785 F.2d 1246, 1248 (5th Cir. 1986). Essentially, these various expressions of the standard suggest the proposition that the court should grant the motion when the appropriate law is applied to the facts as found by the court at the close of plaintiff's case and the court is convinced either that plaintiff has not made out a case or that defendant has established a defense.[22]

Rule 41(b) requires that when granting a motion for involuntary dismissal the court make findings of fact and conclusions of law as provided by Rule 52(a). *See* Fed. R. Civ. P. 41(b). If the factual findings are incomplete or inadequate, *Municipal Leasing Corp. v. Fulton County*, 835 F.2d 786, 788-91 (11th Cir. 1988); *Denofre v. Transp. Ins. Rating Bureau*, 532 F.2d 43, 45 (7th Cir. 1976), or absent altogether, *Schlitt v. Florida*, 749 F.2d 1482 (11th Cir. 1985), dismissal will be vacated and the case remanded for supplemental findings and conclusions. *Id.* As in any other case where the court makes factual findings, they are reviewable under a clearly erroneous standard. *Romain v. Kurek*, 836 F.2d 241, 245 (6th Cir. 1987). But the clearly erroneous rule does not apply to review of the trial court's legal determinations. *Johnson v. United States Postal Serv.*, 756 F.2d 1461, 1464 (9th Cir. 1985). Where so-called mixed questions of fact and law are involved, the appellate court will conduct a *de novo* review. *Id.*

B. Motion to Amend Findings or Make Additional Findings—Rule 52(b)

After a trial by the court either without a jury or with an advisory jury, any party may move, pursuant to Rule 52(b) of the Federal Rules of Civil Procedure, to amend the "findings or make additional findings." Fed. R. Civ. P. 52(b). The motion may be joined with a motion for a new trial under Rule 59(a)(2). *See* Fed. R. Civ. P. 52(b).

1. Time for Motion

A motion under Rule 52(b) must be "made not later than 10 days after entry of judgment." Fed. R. Civ. P. 52(b). That time period may not be enlarged by the court. Fed. R. Civ. P. 6(b). A timely motion pursuant to Rule 52(b) extends the time to take an appeal. Fed. R. App. P. 4(a)(4). *See Gribble v. Harris*, 625 F.2d 1173 (5th Cir. 1980). A notice of appeal filed before disposition of a timely motion under Rule 52(b) is ineffective and a nullity, Fed. R. App. P. 4(a)(4), and another notice of appeal must be timely filed after disposition of the motion. *Id.* Upon appeal from denial of a timely motion, the underlying judgment is brought up for review. *Ercolani v. Excelsior Ins. Co.*, 830 F.2d 31, 35 (3d Cir. 1987).

---

[22] In Title VII discrimination cases, dismissal may be inappropriate once plaintiff has presented a *prima facie* case. *See Lucas v. Dole*, 835 F.2d 532 (4th Cir. 1987); *Mitchell v. Baldridge*, 759 F.2d 80 (D.C. Cir. 1985).

TRIAL AND POST-TRIAL MOTIONS

2. Standard Governing Determination of Motion

The ground recognized to support a motion to amend the court's findings or to make additional findings are "(1) that the trial court has made a manifest error of fact or law, (2) that there is newly discovered evidence, or (3) that there has been a change in the law." *Dow Chem. Pacific Ltd. v. Rascator Maritime S.A.*, 609 F. Supp. 451, 452-53 (S.D.N.Y. 1984). Only in limited situations may the moving party present newly discovered evidence in support of the motion, however. *Fontenot v. Mesa Petroleum Co.*, 791 F.2d 1207, 1219 (5th Cir. 1986); *Burzynski v. Travers*, 111 F.R.D. 15, 16-17 (E.D.N.Y. 1986). The motion lies "even if the modified or additional findings in effect reverse the judgment." *Fontenot v. Mesa Petroleum Co.*, supra at 1219.

Whether a motion to amend or make supplemental findings of fact based upon newly discovered evidence should be granted is within the sound discretion of the trial court. *Solmitz v. United States*, 640 F.2d 1089, 1091 (9th Cir. 1981). A motion under Rule 52(b) may not be used to relitigate old matters or present some new theory to the court. *United States v. Carolina E. Chem. Co., Inc.*, 639 F. Supp. 1420, 1423 (D.S.C. 1986); *Adams v. James*, 526 F. Supp. 80, 86 (M.D. Ala. 1981); *Filner v. Shapiro*, 83 F.R.D. 630 (S.D.N.Y. 1979). A Rule 52(b) motion may, however, be used to delete findings inadvertently included in an order. *Ross v. Pennsylvania State Univ.*, 445 F. Supp. 147, 156 (M.D. Pa. 1978).

C. Motion to Amend Pleadings to Conform to the Evidence—Rule 15(b)

As in jury trials, a motion to amend the pleadings to conform to the proof under Rule 15(b) of the Federal Rules of Civil Procedure may be made at any time, *see Brandon v. Holt*, 469 U.S. 464, 471 (1985), during or after a non-jury trial, and lies within the sound discretion of the court. *Hillburn v. Maher*, 795 F.2d 252, 264 (2d Cir. 1986). The motion "may be granted if the party against whom the amendment is offered will not be prejudiced by the amendment and it should be granted in the absence of prejudice if the interests of justice so require. . . . " *Id.* Such a motion may serve to enlarge the capacity in which a party sues or is sued, *Oppenheimer Mendez v. Acevedo*, 512 F.2d 1373, 1374 n.1 (1st Cir. 1975), add an additional theory upon which recovery is based, *Silver v. Nelson*, 610 F. Supp. 505, 520-21 (E.D. La. 1985), or add a party to the lawsuit, *Brandon v. Holt*, 469 U.S. 464, 471 (1985).

D. Motion for New Trial—Rule 59(a)(2)

A motion for a new trial in an action tried by the court without a jury is governed by Rule 59(a)(2). The court may grant such a motion "for any of the reasons for which rehearings have heretofore been granted in suits in equity in the courts of the United States." Fed. R. Civ. P. 59(a)(2).

1. Time for Making Motion

Any such motion must "be served not later than 10 days after entry of judgment." Fed. R. Civ. P. 59(b). The time limit cannot be enlarged by the court, Fed. R. Civ. P. 6(b), and failure to timely serve the motion will result in its dismissal, except for extraordinary circumstances. *See Agola v. Hagner*, 678 F. Supp. 988, 991-92 (E.D.N.Y. 1987). A timely motion for new trial will extend the time to take an appeal. Fed. R. App. 4(a)(4)(iv). A notice of appeal filed while a timely motion for new trial is pending is ineffective and a new notice of appeal must be filed after disposition of the motion. *Id.*

2. Standard Governing Determination of Motion

The number of grounds recognized as providing the basis for a new trial in an action tried to the court are substantially less than the number available in a nonjury trial. *See* 6A J. Moore, *Moore's Federal Practice and Procedure* ¶ 59.07 n.6 (1987). "Three grounds have been recognized in non-jury cases as a basis for granting a new trial: 1) manifest errors of law, 2) manifest errors of fact, and 3) newly discovered evidence." *Agola v. Hagner*, 678 F. Supp. 988, 991 (E.D.N.Y. 1987); *United States v. Carolina Eastern Chem. Co., Inc.*, 639 F. Supp. 1420, 1423 (D.S.C. 1986). But the motion cannot serve as a vehicle to relitigate old matters. *See Coastal Transfer Co. v. Toyota Motor Sales, U.S.A.*, 833 F.2d 208, 210 (9th Cir. 1987).

In a nonjury action, the court ruling on a motion for a new trial has options that are not available in an action tried to a jury.[23] Rule 59(a)(2) specifically provides that "the court may open the judgment if one has been entered, take additional testimony, amend findings of fact and conclusions of law or make new findings and conclusions, and direct the entry of a new judgment." Fed. R. Civ. P. 59(a)(2). *See Wimbley v. Bolger*, 642 F. Supp. 481, 483 (W.D. Tenn. 1986).

Although the remedy of additur is unconstitutional when a jury is involved, *Dimick v. Schiedt*, 293 U.S. 474 (1935), it has been used by an appellate court in ordering a new trial before the court on apportionment of fault unless plaintiff consented to an additur, *Davis v. United States*, 716 F.2d 418, 430 (7th Cir. 1983).

---

[23] The court must order a new trial before a jury if it determines one is warranted, although it can be a partial new trial. *See Treadwell v. Kennedy*, 680 F. Supp. 1275 (S.D. Ill. 1988)

CHAPTER TWENTY-FIVE

JUDGMENTS

by Frank Gulino, Esq.

I. DEFINITION; REQUIREMENT OF "SEPARATE DOCUMENT"

A judgment is the document issued by the court, upon its decision or the verdict of a jury, that defines the rights of the parties in a litigation. Rule 54(a) states that a judgment includes a decree and any order of the court from which an appeal lies.[1] Thus, a judgment may be a final judgment, usually disposing of an entire action,[2] or an appealable interlocutory order that grants only partial relief.[3] Under Rule 54(c), a final judgment—except a judgment by default—that grants relief to a party must grant *all* of the relief to which that party is entitled, even if the party failed to demand the relief in his pleadings.[4]

The Rules require that a judgment be set forth in writing "on a separate document"—separate, for example, from the opinion that embodies the court's

---

[1] Fed. R. Civ. P. 54(a).

[2] It is possible to have a final judgment that does not finally determine an entire action. Rule 54(b) sets forth the standard for finality of judgments in actions involving multiple claims or parties where the court has adjudicated fewer than all of the claims or the rights of fewer than all of the parties. *See infra* notes 20-21 and accompanying text.

[3] With certain exceptions, a final judgment is a prerequisite to appeal. *See Cobbledick v. United States,* 309 U.S. 323 (1940). The most notable statutory exceptions are set forth in 28 U.S.C. § 1292. Section 1292(a) grants appeals as of right from certain enumerated interlocutory orders, and section 1292(b) grants a permissive right of appeal from interlocutory orders not otherwise appealable under section 1292(a) where (i) the district court makes a required certification of the question sought to be resolved by the court of appeals and (ii) the court of appeals permits the appeal. *See* Chapter 26 for a discussion of appellate review.

[4] Fed. R. Civ. P. 54(c). *See* Chapter 16 for a discussion of default judgments.

rationale for the judgment to follow.[5] The Supreme Court has held, however, that the requirement that a judgment be set forth on a separate document may be waived.[6]

II. FORM AND ENTRY OF JUDGMENT

A. Preparation of the Judgment

The rendition of judgment—the pronouncement of the court's adjudication—is the act of the court.[7] The Supreme Court has held that for a judicial act to constitute a judgment, it must constitute a present adjudication clearly evidencing the court's intention that it be its final act in the case.[8] It is a ministerial act of the clerk of the court, however, to prepare the written judgment required by Rule 58.

When the judgment is based upon a general jury verdict or upon a court decision that a party shall recover only a sum certain in money damages or costs (or, conversely, that a party is to be denied all relief), the Rules call for the clerk to prepare, sign and enter the judgment without awaiting any direction by the court.[9] When a judgment is based upon a special verdict or a general verdict accompanied by interrogatories, or upon a decision of the court granting relief other than a determinate sum of money, the court must first "promptly approve" the form of judgment before entry of the judgment by the clerk.[10]

The Rules do not require that a judgment be set forth in any particular form. On the contrary, as to form, Rule 54(a) states only what a judgment may *not* contain (*i.e.*, a recital of pleadings, the report of a master, or the record of prior proceedings).[11]

---

[5] *See* Fed. R. Civ. P. 58.

[6] *See Bankers Trust Co. v. Mallis*, 435 U.S. 381 (1978) (per curiam).

[7] *Comm'r v. Estate of Bedford*, 325 U.S. 283 (1945).

[8] *United States v. F. & M. Schaefer Brewing Co.*, 356 U.S. 227, 232 (1958).

[9] Fed. R. Civ. P. 58. For a discussion of entry of judgments by the clerk, *see infra* notes 14-19 and accompanying text.

[10] *Id.*

[11] Fed. R. Civ. P. 54(a).

B. Sample Forms

Official Forms 31 and 32 were promulgated in 1963 to be illustrative of the judgments to be entered, respectively, upon the general verdict of a jury and upon a decision of the court:

Form 31. — JUDGMENT ON JURY VERDICT

UNITED STATES DISTRICT COURT
FOR THE SOUTHERN DISTRICT OF NEW YORK

Civil Action, File Number . . . . .

A.B., PLAINTIFF
V.   *Judgment*
C.D., DEFENDANT

This action came on for trial before the Court and a jury, Honorable John Marshall, District Judge, presiding, and the issues having been duly tried and the jury having duly rendered its verdict,

It is Ordered and Adjudged
[that the plaintiff A.B. recover of the defendant C.D. the sum of . . . . ., with interest thereon at the rate of . . . percent as provided by law, and his costs of action.]

[that the plaintiff take nothing, that the action be dismissed on the merits, and that the defendant C.D. recover of the plaintiff A.B. his costs of action.]

Dated at New York, New York, this . . . day of . . . ., 19 . . .

Clerk of Court

Form 32. — JUDGMENT ON DECISION BY THE COURT

UNITED STATES DISTRICT COURT
FOR THE SOUTHERN DISTRICT OF NEW YORK

Civil Action, File Number . . . . .

A.B., PLAINTIFF

V.   *Judgment*

C.D. DEFENDENT

This action came on for [trial] [hearing] before the Court and the Honorable John Marshall, District Judge, presiding, and the issues having been duly [tried] [heard] and a decision having been duly rendered.

It is Ordered and Adjudged

[that the plaintiff A.B. recover of the defendant C.D. the sum of . . . . ., with interest thereon at the rate of . . . percent as provided by law, and his costs of action.]

[that the plaintiff take nothing, that the action be dismissed on the merits, and that the defendant C.D. recover of the plaintiff A.B. his costs of action.]

Dated at New York, New York, this . . . day of . . . ., 19 . . .

                                                          Clerk of Court

Forms 31 and 32 provide simple, brief examples of the judgments that are to be prepared and entered by the clerk immediately, without direction from the court, under Rule 58. Even in situations involving more complex judgments that require prior court approval as to form, the Rules make clear that simplicity and speed are the order of the day, directing the court to "promptly" approve the form of the judgment, upon which approval the judgment is to be immediately entered by the clerk.[12] The Rules make clear, too, that attorneys "shall not submit forms of judgment except upon direction of the court," which direction, the Rules state further, "shall not be given as a matter of course."[13]

---

12 Fed. R. Civ. P. 58.

---

13 *Id.* Indeed, it was contemplated by the Advisory Committee that submission of forms of judgment by counsel would be limited to "special cases where counsel's assistance can be of real value." Advisory Committee Note to 1963 Amendment of Rule 58.

C. Entry by the Clerk

Even after a judgment is rendered and set forth in an appropriate form, it is not effective until it is entered by the clerk as provided in Rule 79(a).[14] That Rule provides for the entry of all papers in a civil action, including judgments, in a book known as the "civil docket" to be kept by the clerk of the court.[15] The entry of judgment is a brief description of the substance of the judgment and must show the date that the entry was made.[16]

Once it is properly entered, a judgment becomes effective, and it is from the date of entry of judgment that the time begins to run for

(a) the making of post-trial motions;[17]

(b) issuance of executions of judgment;[18] and

(c) the taking of an appeal from the judgment.[19]

D. Multiple Claims and Parties

When there are multiple claims for relief, or when multiple parties are involved in an action, the court may direct entry of a final judgment as to fewer than all of the claims or parties only upon an express determination that there is no just reason for delay and upon an express direction for entry of judgment.[20] Absent such an express determination and direction by the court, an order or decision of the court—no matter how it is designated—which purports to

---

[14] Fed. R. Civ. P. 58. Rule 58 also provides that entry of judgment shall not be delayed for the taxing of costs, which are routinely allowed to a prevailing party and taxed by the clerk on notice under Rule 54(d).

[15] Fed. R. Civ. P. 79(a). Entry of judgment is ordinarily but one of the many entries made by the clerk in the civil docket during the course of a particular litigation. As Rule 79(a) states, "[a]ll papers filed with the clerk, all process issued and returns made thereon, all appearances, orders, verdicts, and judgments shall be entered chronologically in the civil docket on the folio assigned to the action and shall be marked with [the] file number [of the action]."

[16] *Id.*

[17] *See* Fed. R. Civ. P. 50(b), 52(a), 59(b), 59(d), 59(e) and 60(b). *See also* Chapter 24, "Trial and Post-Trial Motions" and *infra* notes 89-110 and accompanying text.

[18] *See* Fed. R. Civ. P. 69(a). *See also infra* notes 41-50 and accompanying text.

[19] *See* Fed. R. App. P. 4(a).

[20] Fed. R. Civ. P. 54(b). The Second Circuit, however, generally discourages Rule 54(b) certification. *See Ansam Associates, Inc. v. Cola Petroleum, Ltd.*, 760 F.2d 442 (2d Cir. 1985) (district court should grant certification under Rule 54(b) only when there is some danger of hardship or injustice through delay exists which could be alleviated by immediate appeal).

adjudicate fewer than all of the claims or the rights and liabilities of fewer than all of the parties shall *not* terminate the action as to any of the claims or parties.[21]

E. Notice of Entry

Rule 77(d) provides that the clerk shall serve a notice of the entry of an order or judgment "by mail in the manner provided for in Rule 5 upon each party who is not in default for failure to appear."[22] Such mailing by the clerk is sufficient notice for all purposes for which notice of entry of an order is required by the Rules, although any party may also serve notice of entry pursuant to the provisions of Rule 5 for the service of papers.[23] The Rule makes quite clear, however, that any failure by the clerk to provide a party with notice of entry will not affect the time period within which to take an appeal; it is the date of entry, and not notice of entry as in New York state practice, that starts the running of the time for the taking of an appeal.

F. Registration of Judgments

Under section 1963, Title 28, United States Code, a litigant may register a final judgment for money or property in any district other than that in which it was renderd by filing a certified copy of the judgment in such other district.[24] A judgment registered in this manner is treated as though it was rendered by and entered in the district court of the district in which it is registered.

III. DECLARATORY JUDGMENTS

A. Statutory Basis

The power of the federal courts to render declaratory relief is founded upon the Declaratory Judgment Act (the "Act"),[25] which states in part that

> [i]n a case of actual controversy within its jurisdiction, except with respect to Federal taxes, any court of the United States, upon the

---

[21] *Id.* Indeed, absent the required determination and direction, an order or decision that purports to adjudicate fewer than all of the claims or the rights and liabilities of fewer than all of the parties may be revised at any time prior to the entry of a judgment that adjudicates all of the claims or the rights and liabilities of all of the parties.

[22] Fed. R. Civ. P. 77(d).

[23] *Id. See* Fed. R. Civ. P. 5.

[24] 28 U.S.C. § 1963.

[25] 28 U.S.C. § 2201.

filing of an appropriate pleading, may declare the rights and other legal relations of any interested party seeking such declaration....

Morever, the Act provides that a declaration obtained thereunder "shall have the force and effect of a final judgment" and is reviewable as such.[26]

B. When Declaratory Relief Appropriate

As clearly set forth in its language, the Act creates the remedy of declaratory relief but does not itself confer jurisdiction on the federal courts. Declaratory relief will lie only in cases "of actual controversy" which, the Supreme Court has made clear, means a "controversy" in the sense of Article III of the Constitution;[27] such relief, however, will *not* lie in cases "with respect to Federal taxes."[28] Rule 57, governing the procedure for obtaining a declaratory judgment under the Act, also makes clear that such a judgment may be had only "in cases where it is appropriate."[29]

Declaratory relief, the granting of which is within the discretion of the court,[30] is appropriate

(1) when it will terminate and afford relief from the uncertainty and the controversy giving rise to the declaratory judgment action, and

(2) when it will serve a useful purpose in clarifying and settling the legal relations in issue.[31]

---

26 *Id.*

27 *See Aetna Life Ins. Co. v. Haworth*, 300 U.S. 227 (1937); *see also* U.S. Const. art. III, § 2.

28 28 U.S.C. § 2201. *But see Nelson v. Regan*, 731 F.2d 105 (2d Cir.), *cert. denied, Manning v. Nelson*, 469 U.S. 853 (1984) (prohibition against declaratory relief in cases "with respect to Federal taxes," designed to protect Government in collection of taxes with minimum of pre-enforcement judicial interference, inapplicable in case brought after collection of taxes).

29 *See* Fed. R. Civ. P. 57.

30 28 U.S.C. § 2201. *See, e.g., Doe v. Randall*, 314 F. Supp. 32 (Minn. 1970), *aff'd sub nom. Hodgson v. Randall*, 402 U.S. 967 (1971).

31 *See* E. Borchard, *Declaratory Judgments* 299 (2d ed. 1941); *see also Aetna Casualty & Surety Co. v. Quarles*, 92 F.2d 321 (4th Cir. 1937).

On the other hand, where the underlying uncertainty would not be terminated, the courts will usually refuse to grant declaratory relief when they deem that further proceedings would be necessary to enable the plaintiff to obtain needed relief.[32]

C. Procedure

Rule 57 provides that the procedure for obtaining a declaratory judgment under the Act is governed by the Federal Rules of Civil Procedure.[33] Indeed, since the Act provides that declaratory judgments shall have the force and effect of a final judgment and be reviewable as such,[34] the Rules that apply to judgments in general apply to declaratory judgments as well. Thus, whether declaratory relief is pleaded in an action as a claim, counterclaim, cross-claim or third-party claim, declaratory judgments are governed by the provisions of Rule 54.

Rule 57 also provides that, in declaratory judgment actions, the right to a trial by jury may be demanded under the circumstances and in the manner provided in Rules 38 and 39.[35] It is also clear from Rule 57 that declaratory relief is a cumulative remedy and may be pleaded in the alternative, since "[t]he existence of another adequate remedy does not preclude a judgment for declaratory relief" in appropriate cases.[36]

Finally, Rule 57 provides that the court may order a "speedy hearing" of an action for declaratory judgment and may advance it on the court's calendar.[37] And the Declaratory Judgment Act empowers the court to grant "[f]urther necessary or proper relief based on a declaratory judgment," after notice and a hearing, against any adverse party whose rights have been determined by such judgment.[38]

---

[32] See Declaratory Judgments, supra note 31, at 300.

[33] Fed. R. Civ. P. 57.

[34] 28 U.S.C. § 2201.

[35] Fed. R. Civ. P. 57. See Fed. R. Civ. P. 38 ("Jury Trial of Right") & 39 ("Trial by Jury or by the Court").

[36] Fed. R. Civ. P. 57.

[37] Id.

[38] 28 U.S.C. § 2202.

Since the Act also provides that declaratory judgments have the force and effect of final judgments,[39] it is clear that this power to grant "further relief" on such a judgment after hearing does not affect the finality or effectiveness of a declaratory judgment rendered by the court and entered by the clerk. Rather, the power of the courts to grant "further relief" is meant to allow a court, once it has declared the rights of the parties before it, to effectuate its judgment by providing for affirmative relief or negative injunctive relief as against a party adverse to the successful proponent of declaratory relief.

IV. ENFORCEMENT OF JUDGMENTS

Normally, a party in whose favor a judgment was rendered must *enforce* the judgment in order to obtain the relief granted by it.[40] The Rules provide for the enforcement of both judgments for the payment of money and judgments directing a party to perform specific acts.

A. Enforcement of the Money Judgment: The Writ of Execution

1. Governing Procedure

Rule 69(a) provides that, unless the court directs otherwise, the process for enforcement of a money judgment is a "writ of execution"[41] issued by the court.[42] The Rule further provides that the procedure to be followed on execution of the writ, in proceedings supplementary to and in aid of a judgment, and in proceedings on and in aid of execution "shall be in accordance with the practice and procedure of the state in which the district court is held . . . ."[43]

---

39 28 U.S.C. § 2201.

---

40 This is so because, in the vast majority of cases, the judgments rendered by the courts are not self-executing. Rather, as already noted, a judgment merely sets forth a definition of the rights of the parties, including the relief to which the parties are entitled. The obvious exception to the need for enforcement is when a judgment is one that grants only declaratory relief. When a party has sought and obtained nothing more than a "definition of rights"—in the form of a declaratory judgment—the judgment *is* self-executing, making enforcement unnecessary.

---

41 Fed. R. Civ. P. 69(a).

---

42 The court that rendered the judgment usually issues the writ of execution. When a judgment has been registered in another district, *see supra* note 24 and accompanying text, the court in the district of registration may issue the writ of execution. *See* 28 U.S.C. § 1963.

---

43 Fed. R. Civ. P. 69(a). The Rule makes clear that the state law to be applied is the law for enforcement of judgments "existing at the time the remedy is sought." *Id.*

This is subject, however, to the proviso that the procedure for execution, and on proceedings in aid of a judgment or execution, shall be governed by *federal law* whenever there is an applicable statute.[44]

2. Service of the Writ

Like other forms of process, a writ of execution must be served in the manner provided by Rule 4.[45] Thus, the writ is to be served by a marshal, a deputy marshal, or another person specifically appointed by the court for that purpose.[46] It may be served anywhere in the state in which the district court is held and, if permitted by federal statute, may be served beyond the territorial limits of that state.[47]

3. Execution of the Writ

Generally, execution of the writ may be had only in the state in which the district court is held, since, as already noted, Rule 69(a) provides that state law for the enforcement of judgments shall govern proceedings on execution.[48] However, a judgment creditor may enforce a judgment outside of the state in which the district court that rendered the judgment is held. When a judgment is registered in a district other than that in which it was rendered,[49] the judgment may be enforced in any district where it is so registered. In addition, a writ of execution issued in favor of the United States may be executed in any state or territory or in the District of Columbia.[50]

---

[44] *Id.* Among the many federal statutes that may govern execution are the Foreign Sovereign Immunities Act, 28 U.S.C. §§ 1602-11 (execution against property of foreign state), and 28 U.S.C. § 2006 (execution against revenue officer).

[45] *See* Fed. R. Civ. P. 4.

[46] Fed. R. Civ. P. 4(c)(1) ("[p]rocess, other than a subpoena or a summons and complaint, shall be served by a United States marshal or deputy United States marshal or by a person specifically appointed for that purpose").

[47] *See* Fed. R. Civ. P. 4(f).

[48] *See supra* note 43 and accompanying text.

[49] *See* 28 U.S.C. § 1963. *See also supra* note 24 and accompanying text and note 42.

[50] 28 U.S.C. § 2413.

4. Enforcement Against Certain Public Officers

Rule 69(b) prohibits the issuance of a writ of execution against certain public officers or their property.[51] Specifically, the Rule provides that

> [w]hen a judgment has been entered against a collector or other officer of revenue under the circumstances stated in [28 U.S.C. § 2006], or against an officer of Congress in an action mentioned in [2 U.S.C. § 118], and when the court has given the certificate of probable cause for the officer's act as provided in those statutes, execution shall not issue against the officer or the officer's property but the final judgment shall be satisfied as provided in such statutes.[52]

If the court certifies that the officer against whom judgment was entered acted with probable cause, or that the officer acted under the directions of a proper Government officer,[53] the amount of the judgment shall be paid out of a proper appropriation by the Treasury.[54]

---

51 Fed. R. Civ. P. 69(b).

---

52 *Id*. The statutes mentioned in Rule 69(b) provide as follows:

28 U.S.C. § 2006. Execution against revenue officer

Execution shall not issue against a collector or other revenue officer on a final judgment in any proceeding against him for any of his acts, or for the recovery of any money exacted by or paid to him and subsequently paid into the Treasury, in performing his official duties, if the court certifies that:
  (1) probable cause existed; or
  (2) the officer acted under the directions of the Secretary of the Treasury or other proper Government officer.

When such certificate has been issued, the amount of the judgment shall be paid out of the proper appropriation of the Treasury.

2 U.S.C. § 118. Actions against officers for official acts

In any action brought against any person for or on account of anything done by him while an officer of either House of Congress in the discharge of his official duty, in executing any order of such House, the United States attorney for the district within which the action is brought, on being thereto requested by the officer sued, shall enter an appearance in behalf of such officer; and all provisions of the eighth section of the Act of July 28, 1866, entitled "An Act to protect the revenue, and for other purposes," and also all provisions of the sections of former Acts therein referred to, so far as the same relate to the removal of suits, the withholding of executions, and the paying of judgments against revenue or other officers of the United States, shall become applicable to such action and to all proceedings and matters whatsoever connected therewith, and the defense of such action shall thenceforth be conducted under the supervision and direction of the Attorney General.

---

53 *See* 28 U.S.C. § 2006.

---

54 *Id*.

B. Enforcement of Judgments for Specific Acts

The Rules also provide for enforcement of judgments other than money judgments. When a judgment requires the performance of specific acts—including the conveyance of real property or the delivery of deeds or other documents—Rule 70 empowers the courts to compel performance of the ordered acts.[55]

The Rule, operative only after judgment is entered,[56] is clearly intended to prevent recalcitrant parties from frustrating judgments for the performance of specific acts:

(1) The court may appoint "some other person" to carry out its judgment when a party fails or refuses to do so. The court may direct that an ordered act be done, at the cost of the disobedient party, by the person so appointed, and the act so performed will have "like effect" as if it had been done by the disobedient party.

(2) The clerk, on application of the party entitled to performance, shall issue a writ of attachment or sequestration against the property of the disobedient party to compel obedience to the judgment.

(3) The court may adjudge the disobedient party in contempt.

(4) The court, in lieu of directing a conveyance of real or personal property within the district, may enter a judgment divesting the title of any party to that property and vesting such title in any other parties. Such a judgment shall have the effect of a duly executed conveyance of the property.

(5) The clerk shall issue a writ of execution or assistance on application of a party in whose favor is entered an order or judgment for the delivery of possession of property.[57]

C. Enforcement Against Nonparties

Rule 71 provides for enforcement of orders by or against a person who is not a party to the action.[58] Specifically, the Rule provides that when an order is made in favor of a nonparty, "that person may enforce obedience to the order

---

[55] *See* Fed. R. Civ. P. 70.

[56] *See De Beers Consolidated Mines v. United States*, 325 U.S. 212 (1945). Thus, Rule 70 confers neither jurisdiction nor venue to enforce liens on property located in the district in which the court is held under 28 U.S.C. § 1655.

[57] Fed. R. Civ. P. 70.

[58] Fed. R. Civ. P. 71.

by the same process as if a party . . . ."[59] By the same token, when obedience to an order may be lawfully enforced against a nonparty,[60] the nonparty "is liable to the same process for enforcing obedience to the order as if a party."[61]

D. Discovery in Aid of Execution

A judgment creditor or the creditor's successor in interest, when that interest appears of record, may obtain discovery from any person, including the judgment debtor, in aid of the judgment or execution.[62] The discovery thus available includes all of the discovery devices provided by the Rules as well as by the practice of the state in which the district court is held.[63]

E. Stay of Enforcement of Judgments

Proceeedings to enforce a judgment are subject to stay under the provisions of Rule 62.[64] That Rule provides as follows:

(a) *Automatic Stay*: No execution shall issue upon a judgment, nor shall proceedings be taken for its enforcement, until the expiration of ten days after its entry, except in actions for injunctions, receiverships or accountings in patent infringement actions;[65]

(b) *Stay on Motion for New Trial or for Judgment*: The court, in its discretion, may stay the execution of any proceeding to enforce a judgment pending the disposition of motions made pursuant to

   (i) Rule 59 (for a new trial or to alter or amend a judgment);

   (ii) Rule 60 (for relief from a judgment or order);

---

59 *Id*. A nonparty may use Rule 71 to enforce an order that was not made in the nonparty's favor. *See, e.g.*, *Gautreaux v. Pierce*, 743 F.2d 526 (7th Cir. 1984); *Wang v. Gordon*, 715 F.2d 1187 (7th Cir. 1983).

60 *See, e.g.*, Fed. R. Civ. P. 37(b) (provides for sanctions by court against nonparties in connection with taking of depositions).

61 Fed. R. Civ. P. 71.

62 Fed. R. Civ. P. 69(a).

63 *Id*. A creditor who seeks to enforce a judgment that it has registered in another state, pursuant to 28 U.S.C. § 1963, may avail itself of the federal discovery rules, Fed. R. Civ. P. 26-37, or the rules for discovery in the state where the judgment is so registered.

64 Fed. R. Civ. P. 62.

65 Fed. R. Civ. P. 62(a).

(iii) Rule 50 (for judgment in accordance with a motion for a directed verdict); or

(iv) Rule 52(b) (for amendment to findings or for additional findings);[66]

(c) *Injunction Pending Appeal*: The court may, in its discretion, suspend, modify, restore or grant an injunction during the pendency of an appeal from a judgment involving an injunction;[67]

(d) *Stay Upon Appeal*: An appellant may obtain a stay, when an appeal is taken, by the giving of a supersedeas bond;[68]

(e) *Stay in Favor of the United States or Agency Thereof*: When an appeal is taken by the United States or one of its officers or agencies, no supersedeas bond is required as a prerequisite for a stay of judgment or enforcement thereof;[69]

(f) *Stay According to State Law*: A judgment debtor is entitled to such stay of execution as would be accorded if the action had been maintained in the courts of the state in which the district court rendering judgment is held;[70]

(g) *Power of Appellate Court Not Limited*: Rule 62 does not limit the power of an appellate court, including an individual judge or justice thereof, to

---

[66] Fed. R. Civ. P. 62(b). For a discussion of motions made pursuant to Rules 50, 52(b) and 59, *see* Chapter 24, "Trial and Post-Trial Motions." For a discussion of motions made pursuant to Rule 60 for relief from judgments, *see infra* notes 81-88 & 93-110 and accompanying text.

[67] Fed. R. Civ. P. 62(c). This subdivision enables the court, in its discretion, to suspend, modify, restore or grant the injuction pending appeal "upon such terms as to bond or otherwise as it considers proper for the security of the rights of the adverse party." *Id*. In addition, Rule 62(c) provides that, if the judgment appealed from was rendered by a three-judge district court constituted pursuant to federal statute, no order under the Rule shall be made except (1) by such court sitting in open court, or (2) by the assent of all the judges of such court, evidenced by their signatures on the order. *Id*.

[68] Fed. R. Civ. P. 62(d). The bond may be given at or after the time of filing the notice of appeal or procuring the order permitting the appeal, as the case may be. The stay is effective when the bond is approved by the court. *Id*. A district court may authorize a stay pending appeal without requiring a supersedeas bond to be filed. *See Federal Prescription Service, Inc. v. American Pharmaceutical Ass'n*, 636 F.2d 755 (D.C. Cir. 1980). When the appeal is taken "by the United States or an officer or agency thereof or by direction of any department of the Government" and the operation or enforcement of the judgment is stayed, no bond, obligation or other security shall be required of the appellant. Fed. R. Civ. P. 62(e).

[69] Fed. R. Civ. P. 62(e). *See* note 68 *supra*.

[70] Fed. R. Civ. P. 62(f). This provision is applicable "[i]n any state in which a judgment is a lien upon the property of the judgment debtor and in which the judgment debtor is entitled to a stay of execution . . . " *Id*.

(i) stay proceedings during the pendency of an appeal;

(ii) suspend, modify, restore or grant an injunction during the pendency of an appeal; or

(iii) make any order appropriate to preserve the status quo or the effectiveness of the judgment to be entered;[71]

(h) *Stay of Judgment as to Multiple Claims or Parties*: When a court has ordered a final judgment as prescribed in Rule 54(b),[72] the court may stay enforcement of that judgment until the entering of a subsequent judgment or judgments on any conditions as may be necessary to secure the benefit of the judgment to the party in whose favor it is entered.[73]

V. RELIEF FROM JUDGMENTS

A. Overview

Rule 60 prescribes the procedure for obtaining relief from judgments without resort to the appellate process.[74] Rule 60(a) governs the procedure for the correction of clerical mistakes in judgments, either by the court, *sua sponte*, or on motion of a party.[75] Rule 60(b) permits relief from final judgments on motion, and "upon such terms as are just," for a variety of reasons, ranging from "mistake" and "fraud" to "any other reason justifying relief . . . ."[76]

The provisions of Rule 60 are not a substitute for the taking of an appeal, nor is the Rule intended to correct errors of law made by the trial court in the

---

[71] Fed. R. Civ. P. 62(g). *See Application of President and Directors of Georgetown College, Inc.*, 331 F.2d 1000 (D.C. Cir.), *rehearing en banc denied*, 331 F.2d 1010 (D.C. Cir.), *cert. denied*, *Jones v. President & Directors of Georgetown College, Inc.*, 377 U.S. 978 (1964) (circuit judge, relying on 28 U.S.C. § 1651 (All Writs Act), Rule 62(g) and Circuit and Supreme Court rules, issued order permitting hospital to administer emergency blood transfusions).

[72] *See* Fed. R. Civ. P. 54(b). *See also supra* notes 20-21 and accompanying text.

[73] Fed. R. Civ. P. 62(h).

[74] Fed. R. Civ. P. 60. In addition to the vehicles for relief available under Rule 60, Rule 59(e) provides for motions to alter or amend a judgment. *See* Fed. R. Civ. P. 59(e). *See also infra* notes 89-92 and accompanying text; Chapter 24.

[75] Fed. R. Civ. P. 60(a). *See infra* notes 81-88 and accompanying text.

[76] *See* Fed. R. Civ. P. 60(b). *See also infra* notes 93-106 and accompanying text.

decision that resulted in the judgment at issue.[77] Moreover, the making of a motion under Rule 60 neither tolls the time to appeal from a judgment nor affects the judgment's finality.[78]

B. Harmless Error

Not every error or defect in a ruling or order will provide a ground for disturbing a judgment rendered by the court. Indeed, Rule 61 directs that "[t]he court at every stage of the proceeding must disregard any error or defect in the proceeding which does not affect the substantial rights of the parties."[79] That Rule makes clear that (i) no error in the admission or exclusion of evidence, and (ii) no error or defect in any ruling, order, or, indeed, in *anything* done or omitted by the court or any party, is a ground for vacating, modifying, or otherwise disturbing a judgment or order unless refusal to do so would appear to the court "inconsistent with substantial justice."[80] In short, it is within the discretion of the court to determine whether an error is substantial, prejudicing the substantial rights of a party, or "harmless error" to be disregarded.

C. Obtaining Relief from Clerical Mistakes

Rule 60(a) permits a court to correct clerical mistakes in judgments, orders or other parts of the record as well as errors therein arising from "oversight or omission."[81] The Rule provides that the court may correct such mistakes or errors "at any time" and may do so either on its own initiative or on the motion of any party, on such notice as the court may require.[82]

The provisions of Rule 60(a) do not apply to errors of a serious nature affecting substantial rights of the parties.[83] Such errors are properly the subject

---

[77] *See McKnight v. United States Steel Corp.*, 726 F.2d 333 (7th Cir. 1984).

[78] *See* Fed. R. Civ. P. 60(b); *Browder v. Director, Dep't of Corrections of Illinois*, 434 U.S. 257 (1978).

[79] Fed. R. Civ. P. 61.

[80] *Id.*

[81] Fed. R. Civ. P. 60(a).

[82] *Id. But see infra* notes 87-88 and accompanying text.

[83] *See, e.g., In re Galiardi*, 745 F.2d 335 (5th Cir. 1984).

JUDGMENTS

of motions under either Rule 59(e)[84] or Rule 60(b).[85] Rather, Rule 60(a) is meant to afford relief from truly "clerical" mistakes, such as typographical errors in a judgment or a trial transcript, and from errors, caused by "oversight or omission," that have resulted in an order not reflecting the true intentions of the court.[86]

Where an appeal is pending, the court may correct mistakes under Rule 60(a) at any time before the appeal is docketed in the appellate court.[87] After the appeal is docketed, and while the appeal is still pending, the district court can utilize Rule 60(a) to correct clerical mistakes only with leave of the appellate court.[88]

D. Motion to Alter or Amend a Judgment

Although it is Rule 60 that nominally governs the procedure for obtaining "Relief from [a] Judgment or Order," motions to alter or amend a judgment are provided for by Rule 59(e).[89] Under that Rule, a party may move to alter or amend a judgment, provided that such motion is made not later than 10 days after entry of the judgment.[90] Under Rule 6(b), the time within which to move to alter or amend may not be enlarged by the court.[91] As do other Rule 59 motions, a motion timely made pursuant to Rule 59(e) tolls the time for taking an appeal. The full time for an appeal begins to run again from the entry of an order that grants or denies the timely Rule 59 (e) motion.[92]

---

84 *See* Fed. R. Civ. P. 59(e) ("Motion to Alter or Amend a Judgment)." *See also infra* notes 89-92 and accompanying text.

85 *See infra* notes 95-106 and accompanying text.

86 *See, e.g., Jones & Guerrero Co. v. Sealift Pacific*, 650 F.2d 1072 (9th Cir. 1981) (Rule 60(a) may be used to correct order to reflect court's true intentions by remanding case erroneously removed).

87 Fed. R. Civ. P. 60(a). *See* Fed. R. App. P. 12(a) ("Docketing the Appeal"); Rules of the Supreme Court, Rule 12 ("Docketing Cases").

88 Fed. R. Civ. P. 60(a).

89 Fed. R. Civ. P. 59(e).

90 *Id.*

91 *See* Fed. R. Civ. P. 6(b).

92 For a discussion of other motions pursuant to Rule 59, *see* Chapter 24, "Trial and Post-Trial Motions."

E. Obtaining Relief from Final Judgments: Rule 60(b) Motion

Under Rule 60(b), "[o]n motion and upon such terms as are just," the court may grant relief to "a party or a party's legal representative" from a final judgment, order or proceeding.[93] A 1946 amendment to the Rule made clear that it was intended to afford relief only from *final* judgments, orders or proceedings. Thus, relief from an interlocutory judgment is left to the discretion of the court that rendered it and is not subject to the restrictions governing motions pursuant to Rule 60(b).[94]

1. Grounds for Rule 60(b) Motion

Rule 60(b) empowers the court to grant relief from a final judgment, order or proceeding for the following reasons:

(a) *Mistake, inadvertence, surprise or excusable neglect.*[95] On its motion, a party would have to demonstrate to the court that the mistake or related ground justifies disturbance of a final judgment. Mere carelessness or ignorance of the law will not suffice to warrant relief from a judgment. However, a client's reliance upon statements of counsel has been held to constitute "excusable neglect" to warrant affirmance of an order granting the client's Rule 60(b)(1) motion to vacate dismissal of his action for failure to prosecute.[96]

(b) *Newly discovered evidence.*[97] Under Rule 60(b)(2), a party may obtain relief from a judgment based upon newly discovered evidence which, by due diligence, could not have been discovered in time to move for a new trial under Rule 59(b). (Under the latter Rule, a party has only until 10 days after entry of judgment within which to make a motion for a new trial.) Of course, a party must still convince the court both that

---

[93] Fed. R. Civ. P. 60(b). Rule 60(b) abolishes the ancient common law writs of coram nobis, coram vobis and audita querela and common law bills of review, all vehicles by which a party could seek review of and relief from a judgment. The motion procedure provided by Rule 60(b) expressly replaces these writs and bills as the method of obtaining relief from a judgment.

[94] *Cf.* Moore and Rogers, *Federal Relief from Civil Judgments*, 55 Yale L.J. 623, 641-43 (1946) ("The principle of *[John Simmons Co. v. Grier Brothers Co.*, 258 U.S. 82 (1922)]* is sound: so long as the court has jurisdiction over an action, it should have complete power over interlocutory orders made therein and should be able to revise them when it is 'consonant with equity' to do so.").

[95] Fed. R. Civ. P. 60(b)(1).

[96] *See Thompson v. Kerr-McGee Refining Corp.*, 660 F.2d 1380 (10th Cir. 1981), *cert. denied*, 455 U.S. 1019 (1982).

[97] Fed. R. Civ. P. 60(b)(2).

the evidence could not have been discovered in time to make a Rule 59(b) motion and that the evidence warrants disturbing the final judgment.[98]

(c) *Fraud, misrepresentation, or other misconduct of an adverse party.*[99] The court may grant relief from a judgment where a fraud or other misconduct has been perpetrated against the party moving for such relief pursuant to Rule 60(b)(3).[100] This provision also eliminates the distinction between "intrinsic" and "extrinsic" fraud. Thus, relief may be granted upon the commission of any fraud or misrepresentation, whether collateral to or related to the subject matter of the action.

(d) *The judgment is void.*[101] Rule 60(b)(4) codifies the inherent power of the court to grant relief from a judgment that is null and void because the court that rendered it lacked jurisdiction over the subject matter or the parties. In fact, the court has no discretion in such circumstances: once it is determined that the court had no jurisdiction, the void judgment must be vacated.[102]

(e) *The judgment has been satisfied, released, or discharged or a prior judgment upon which it is based has been reversed or otherwise vacated, or it is no longer equitable that the judgment should have prospective application.*[103] Rule 60(b)(5) provides for relief from any judgment by reason of satisfaction, release or discharge. If a judgment debtor has satisfied the debt underlying the judgment, or has been otherwise released or discharged from that debt, there is obviously no need for continued existence of the judgment. In addition, clause (5) of Rule 60(b) permits relief where a prior judgment, relied upon by the court for purposes of claim or issue preclusion, has been reversed or

---

98 *See Vicon, Inc. v. CMI Corp.*, 657 F.2d 768 (5th Cir. 1981) (newly discovered evidence did not warrant setting aside judgment where evidence would not have produced different result).

99 Fed. R. Civ. P. 60(b)(3).

100 *See, e.g., Square Construction Co. v. Washington Metropolitan Area Transit Auth*, 657 F.2d 68 (4th Cir. 1981).

101 Fed. R. Civ. P. 60(b)(4).

102 *See, e.g., Watts v. Pinckney*, 752 F.2d 406 (9th Cir. 1985).

103 Fed. R. Civ. P. 60(b)(5).

vacated.[104] Finally, this clause provides for relief where the interests of justice would no longer be served by continued application of the judgment, such as where the conditions that gave rise to a consent judgment no longer exist.[105]

(f) *Any other reason justifying relief from the operation of the judgment.*[106] Rule 60(b)(6) provides a "catch all" basis upon which the court, in its discretion, may grant relief from a judgment when no other ground under Rule 60(b) is appropriate. A motion based upon this clause is clearly addressed to the court's exercise of its equity power to advance the interests of justice.

2. Timing of Rule 60(b) Motion

Rule 60(b) provides that a motion thereunder must be made "within a reasonable time" after the judgment, order or proceeding was entered or taken.[107] The Rule further provides, however, that a motion made pursuant to clauses (1), (2) or (3)—for mistake, newly discovered evidence or fraud—must be made within one year after the judgment, order or proceeding.[108] Thus, the "reasonable time" requirement applies only to motions brought pursuant to clause (5) (for satisfaction, release or discharge, etc.) or the catch all clause (6).[109] Motions made pursuant to clause (4)—seeking relief from a void judgment—may be made at any time, since no amount of delay can make valid a judgment that is void.[110]

---

[104] *Id.* This portion of the Rule does not apply to reversal or vacatur of a prior judgment relied upon as precedent by the court. *See Title v. United States,* 263 F.2d 28 (9th Cir.), *cert. denied,* 359 U.S. 989 (1959).

[105] Fed. R. Civ. P. 60(b)(5). *See, e.g., System Federation No. 91 Railway Employees' Dep't v. Wright,* 364 U.S. 642 (1961).

[106] Fed. R. Civ. P. 60(b)(6). *See Seven Elves, Inc. v. Eskenazi,* 635 F.2d 396 (5th Cir. 1981).

[107] Fed. R. Civ. P. 60(b).

[108] *Id.*

[109] It has been held that a motion made pursuant to Rule 60(b)(6) must be made within a reasonable time that should not exceed the time for taking an appeal. *See Scola v. Boat Frances, R., Inc.,* 618 F.2d 147 (1st Cir. 1980). *See also infra* note 110 and accompanying text.

[110] *See, e.g., Misco Leasing, Inc. v. Vaughn,* 450 F.2d 257 (10th Cir. 1971).

F. Other Methods of Obtaining Relief from Judgments to Rule 60(b)

Rule 60(b) expressly provides that it does not limit the power of the court to grant relief from judgments by three methods other than the prescribed motion:

First, the court has the power to entertain an independent action to relieve a party from a judgment, order or proceeding.[111]

Second, the court can grant relief to a defendant not "actually personally notified as provided in Title 28, U.S.C., § 1655 . . . ."[112] That statute provides that, in *in rem* actions, any defendant not personally served with an order to appear or plead may, at any time within one year after final judgment, enter an appearance. The court thereupon shall set aside the judgment and permit the defendant to plead and defend on payment of costs as the court deems just.[113]

Finally, the court is not limited by the procedural constraints of Rule 60(b) from exercising its inherent power to set aside a judgment because of a fraud perpetrated upon it.[114]

---

[111] Fed. R. Civ. P. 60(b). Where a party resorts to an independent action, it will be bound by applicable statutes of limitation and the doctrine of laches. *See, e.g., M.W. Zack Metal Co. v. Int'l Navigation Corp.*, 675 F.2d 525 (2d Cir.), *cert. denied*, 459 U.S. 1037 (1982); *Simons v. United States*, 452 F.2d 1110 (2d Cir. 1971).

[112] Fed. R. Civ. P. 60(b).

[113] *See* 28 U.S.C. § 1655.

[114] Fed. R. Civ. P. 60(b). *See Universal Oil Products Co. v. Root Refining Co.*, 328 U.S. 575 (1946).

CHAPTER TWENTY-SIX

APPELLATE REVIEW

by Edward W. Keane, Esq.

Any party aggrieved by a final decision of a district court in a civil case is entitled to appeal that decision to a court of appeals or, in a few instances, directly to the Supreme Court. Appellate review of some non-final district-court decisions may also be available, either as a matter of right or in the exercise of judicial discretion. All decisions of the courts of appeals are subject to discretionary review by the Supreme Court. Whether, when, and how to obtain appellate review is the subject of this chapter.

I. WHETHER TO SEEK APPELLATE REVIEW

The availability of appellate review does not of course mean that review should be sought in a particular case. Whether to seek review is a decision calling for careful consideration of all pertinent factors, including the anticipated expense of an appellate proceeding, the importance of the interests at stake, and, above all, the prospect of a favorable outcome.

The expense of obtaining appellate review may be substantial, especially if the record is lengthy and the issues are complex. Printing or otherwise producing the briefs and appendix may cost thousands of dollars. Even if appellate counsel has tried the case and is thus already familiar with it, a properly conducted appellate proceeding will usually require a considerable amount of additional work; the appellate briefs, for example, may be different in nature and more extensive in scope than those filed in the district court. That additional work will ordinarily be reflected in the attorneys' fees.

Because of the expense, review is usually warranted only when the potential appellant has a substantial interest at stake. Obviously an order or judgment awarding or refusing to award a large sum of money or granting or denying significant injunctive relief is likely to encourage the disappointed litigant to take his chances in the appellate court. Even when the interests involved in the immediate case are small, however, the district court's decision may have effects—such as collateral estoppel in other cases— that will induce the losing party to seek appellate relief.

Whether there is a reasonable chance of obtaining a favorable decision from the appellate court may depend not only on the evidence in the record and the applicable substantive law, but on the limitations of appellate review. Among the most important of those limitations are these:

1. The record must show that each contention to be made on appeal was properly raised and preserved in the district court. For example, evidence admitted without a timely objection cannot usually be complained of on appeal, Fed. R. Evid. 103(a); certain defenses are generally waived unless raised either by motion to dismiss or in a responsive pleading, Fed. R. Civ. P. 12(h)(1); and claims and defenses raised in the pleadings or by motion may have been waived if omitted from the pretrial order, which "supersedes the pleadings and becomes the governing pattern of the lawsuit," *Case v. Abrams*, 352 F.2d 193, 195 (10th Cir. 1965); *see* Fed. R. Civ. P. 16(e). The appellate court will usually not consider an argument unless it was first presented to the district court.

2. Rulings made in the exercise of the district court's discretion can be overturned only if the appellate court finds that this discretion was abused; any party making an abuse-of-discretion contention faces an uphill battle.

3. In a nonjury case, the district court's findings of fact, whether based on oral or documentary evidence, cannot be set aside unless the appellate court finds them to be "clearly erroneous." Fed. R. Civ. P. 52(a). The Supreme Court has emphasized that "review of factual findings under the clearly-erroneous standard—with its deference to the trier of fact—is the rule, not the exception." *Anderson v. City of Bessemer*, 470 U.S. 564, 575 (1985). Jury verdicts are of course given equivalent deference.

4. Even if there were errors or defects in the district court proceedings, the appellate court will reverse only if it is persuaded that "substantial justice" affecting "the substantial rights of the parties" so requires; "harmless error" will be disregarded. Fed. R. Civ. P. 61.

For these and other reasons, most district-court decisions that are appealed are affirmed. It is hardly surprising that most such decisions are not appealed at all.

II. WHAT DISTRICT-COURT DECISIONS ARE REVIEWABLE BY THE COURT OF APPEALS

Reviewable decisions are of two basic types: (1) those reviewable as of right and (2) those reviewable as a matter of judicial discretion. There is a long-standing federal policy that, with limited exceptions, an appeal lies only from a final judgment. In general, the exceptions to the final-judgment rule are construed narrowly.

A. Review as of Right

"Final" decisions, certain kinds of interlocutory orders, and so-called "collateral" orders of the district court may be appealed as a matter of right.

1. "Final" Decisions

The courts of appeals have jurisdiction over appeals from all "final decisions" of the district courts except where direct review may be had in the Supreme Court. 28 U.S.C. §§ 1291, 1295(a). A "final" decision for this purpose is one that adjudicates all claims and the rights and liabilities of all parties to the action. *See* Fed. R. Civ. P. 54(b). As the Supreme Court said in *Catlin v. United States*, 324 U.S. 229, 233 (1945), "a 'final decision' generally is one which ends the litigation on the merits and leaves nothing for the court to do but execute the judgment." By definition, such a decision is a "judgment." Fed. R. Civ. P. 54(a). To minimize uncertainty, a judgment must be "set forth on a separate document" and becomes effective "only when so set forth and when entered as provided in Rule 79(a)." Fed. R. Civ. P. 58.

Determining whether and when a final judgment has been entered usually presents little difficulty. In a few circumstances, however, a judgment may be "final" and appealable even though potentially significant rulings have yet to be made, such as taxing costs, Fed. R. Civ. P. 58, awarding attorneys' fees, *Budinich v. Becton Dickinson & Co.*, 108 S. Ct. 1717 (1988), and determining the details of an antitrust divestiture, *Brown Shoe Co. v. United States*, 370 U.S. 294, 308-309 (1962). The guiding principle is that "a question remaining to be decided after an order ending litigation on the merits does not prevent finality if its resolution will not alter the order or moot or revise decisions embodied in the order." *Budinich v. Becton Dickinson & Co., supra*, 108 S. Ct. at 1720.

As *Budinich* illustrates, failure to take a timely appeal from "an order ending litigation on the merits" results in the loss of the right to a "merits appeal"; if an appeal is taken from a subsequent order not affecting the merits, the court of appeals will have jurisdiction to review only the non-merits order. *See* 108 S. Ct. at 1719, 1722.

2. Certain Interlocutory Decisions

The courts of appeals have jurisdiction to entertain appeals from three kinds of interlocutory orders of the district courts: (1) orders "granting, continuing, modifying, refusing or dissolving injunctions, or refusing to dissolve or modify injunctions," except where direct review may be had in the Supreme Court; (2) certain orders relating to receiverships; and (3) certain decrees in admiralty cases. 28 U.S.C. § 1292(a), (c)(1). In civil patent-infringement actions the Court of Appeals for the Federal Circuit also has jurisdiction over appeals from judgments that are final except for an accounting. 28 U.S.C. § 1292(c)(2).

3. "Collateral" Orders

Certain kinds of district court orders, generally referred to as "collateral orders," are appealable as "final" orders even though they do not terminate the litigation. The Supreme Court first delineated the contours of the "collateral order" doctrine in *Cohen v. Beneficial Industrial Loan Corp.*, 337 U.S. 541 (1949), a stockholder's suit in which the Court permitted an appeal from an order denying the defendant's motion to require the plaintiff to post security for costs pursuant to applicable state law. The Court viewed the order as being within "that small class which finally determine claims of right separable from, and collateral to, rights asserted in the action, too important to be denied review and too independent of the cause itself to require that appellate consideration be deferred until the whole case is adjudicated." *Id.* at 546. The Court indicated, however, that such an order is nevertheless not appealable if it is "tentative, informal or incomplete" or if it does not present "a serious and unsettled question." *Id.* at 546-547.

Coopers & Lybrand v. Livesay, 437 U.S. 463 (1978), illustrates the Court's more recent application of the "collateral order" doctrine. In holding that an order decertifying a class action under Fed. R. Civ. P. 23 cannot be appealed, the Court said that to be appealable "the order must conclusively determine the disputed question, resolve an important issue completely separate from the merits of the action, and be effectively unreviewable on appeal from a final judgment." *Id.* at 468. Other cases illustrating the Supreme Court's application of the "collateral order" doctrine include *Swift & Co. Packers v. Compania Colombiana Del Caribe*, 339 U.S. 684, 688-689 (1950) (allowing appeal from order vacating attachment in an admiralty case); *Eisen v. Carlisle & Jacquelin*, 417 U.S. 156, 169-172 (1974) (allowing appeal from order requiring defendants to pay most of class-notification costs); *Firestone Tire & Rubber Co. v. Risjord*, 449 U.S. 368, 373-378 (1981) (disallowing appeal from an order refusing to disqualify opposing counsel); *Mitchell v. Forsyth*, 472 U.S. 511, 524-530 (1985) (allowing appeal from order denying claim of qualified immunity from suit); *Van*

Cauwenberghe v. Biard, 108 S. Ct. 1945 (1988) (disallowing appeal from order denying motions to dismiss on grounds of immunity from civil process and *forum non conveniens*).

B. Review by Permission

Appellate review of non-final district-court orders may be obtained in three ways requiring permission of the district court itself, the court of appeals, or both.

1. Orders Certified Under 28 U.S.C. § 1292(b)

In making an interlocutory order that is not otherwise appealable, the district court may "state in writing in such order" that the order "involves a controlling question of law as to which there is substantial ground for difference of opinion and that an immediate appeal from the order may materially advance the ultimate termination of the litigation." Upon application made to it within ten days after entry of such an order, the court of appeals having appellate jurisdiction of the action (that may be the Court of Appeals for the Federal Circuit in appropriate cases) "may thereupon, in its discretion, permit an appeal to be made from such order." 28 U.S.C. § 1292(b). An appeal under Section 1292(b) thus requires permission of both the district court and the court of appeals.

Although Section 1292(b) requires the appellant to file an application in the court of appeals within ten days after entry of the district court's order bearing the requisite certification, the district court may supply that certification at any time during the pendency of the action by amending a previously entered order.

The parties are under no compulsion to proceed under Section 1292(b). If an order is not certified, or if the order is certified but the appeal is not allowed, that order is still subject to review on appeal from the final judgment under 28 U.S.C. § 1291.

2. Orders Entered Pursuant to Rule 54(b)

In actions involving multiple claims or multiple plaintiffs or defendants, Rule 54(b) of the Federal Rules of Civil Procedure empowers the district court, on the basis of an "express determination that there is no just reason for delay," to "direct the entry of a final judgment as to one or more but fewer than all of the claims or parties." The district court thus acts as a "dispatcher," determining when an order that would otherwise be interlocutory is "ready for appeal." *Sears, Roebuck & Co. v. Mackey*, 351 U.S. 427, 435 (1956). The determination authorized by Rule 54(b) is within the district court's discretion, although any abuse of that discretion is reviewable by the court of appeals. *Id.* at 437. In the Second Circuit, a Rule 54(b) determination is proper only to alleviate "hardship or injustice" and must be accompanied by a "reasoned explanation" so that its propriety can be reviewed on appeal. *Ansam Associates, Inc. v. Cola Petroleum, Ltd.*, 760 F.2d 442, 445 (2d Cir. 1985).

Once a judgment has been properly entered pursuant to Rule 54(b), it is immediately appealable as a matter of right. If it is not appealed within the prescribed time, the right of appeal is lost. In the absence of the determination and direction permitted by Rule 54(b), however, an order that does not adjudicate all claims and the rights and liabilities of all parties is not final and not appealable, although such an order may of course be reviewed on appeal from the final judgment under 28 U.S.C. § 1291.

3. Review Under the All Writs Act (28 U.S.C. § 1651)

In exceptional circumstances a non-final order may be reviewed by mandamus, prohibition, or other writ authorized by 28 U.S.C. § 1651. Such writs are not "substitutes for appeals" but are "extraordinary remedies ... reserved for really extraordinary causes." *Ex parte Fahey*, 332 U.S. 258, 260 (1947). "The power to issue them is discretionary and it is sparingly exercised. . . . [T]hey may not be used to thwart the congressional policy against piecemeal appeals." *Parr v. United States*, 351 U.S. 513, 520-521 (1956). A writ is justified only by "exceptional circumstances, amounting to a judicial usurpation of power." *Allied Chemical Corp. v. Daiflon, Inc.*, 449 U.S. 33, 35 (1980).

For examples of situations in which mandamus has been held proper, see *La Buy v. Howes Leather Co.*, 352 U.S. 249 (1957) (requiring district court to vacate order appointing a master to conduct trial); *Beacon Theatres, Inc. v. Westover*, 359 U.S. 500 (1959) (requiring district court to permit trial by jury); *Thermtron Products, Inc. v. Hermansdorfer*, 423 U.S. 336 (1976) (requiring district court to vacate order remanding case to state court).

III. WHERE DISTRICT-COURT DECISIONS ARE REVIEWABLE

In most cases, an appeal from a reviewable decision of a district court must be taken "to the court of appeals for the circuit embracing the district." 28 U.S.C. § 1294(1). The Court of Appeals for the Second Circuit, for example, has jurisdiction to hear appeals from decisions of the district courts in New York, Connecticut, and Vermont. See 28 U.S.C. § 41.

There are two exceptions to this arrangement. First, orders of three-judge district court's granting or denying interlocutory or permanent injunctions are appealable directly to the Supreme Court. 28 U.S.C. § 1253. Second, the

Court of Appeals for the Federal Circuit has exclusive jurisdiction over appeals from final and certain interlocutory district-court decisions whenever the jurisdiction of the district court was based, in whole or in part, on certain provisions of 28 U.S.C. §§ 1338 and 1346 (principally cases arising under the patent laws and certain actions against the United States). 28 U.S.C. §§ 1292(c), 1295(a)(1), (2). Whether the district court's jurisdiction was based on these provisions is to be determined on the basis of the "well-pleaded complaint" without reference to defenses or issues that may in fact have been determined by the district court. *Christianson v. Colt Industries Operating Corp.*, 108 S. Ct. 2166 (1988).

Although in most cases there is little room for doubt as to where an appeal should be taken, close questions occasionally arise. If a court of appeals finds that it lacks jurisdiction over a particular appeal, it is empowered, "in the interest of justice," to transfer that appeal to the court of appeals that does have jurisdiction. 28 U.S.C. § 1631. The transferor court's determination of the jurisdictional issue ordinarily becomes the law of the case and is not subject to re-examination by the transferee court. *Christianson v. Colt Industries Operating Corp.*, supra, 108 S. Ct. at 2179.

IV. HOW AN APPEAL TO A COURT OF APPEALS IS TAKEN

The Federal Rules of Appellate Procedure, which together with the various local court rules generally govern procedure on appeal, prescribe different methods for appeals as of right, Fed. R. App. P. 3, 4, appeals by permission, Fed. R. App. P. 5, and petitions for mandamus, prohibition, and other extraordinary writs, Fed. R. App. P. 21.

A. Appeals as of Right

An appeal from a district court to a court of appeals "as of right" is taken by filing a notice of appeal with the clerk of the *district* court. Fed. R. App. P. 3(a). The notice must (a) specify the party or parties taking the appeal, (b) designate the judgment, order, or part thereof appealed from, and (c) name the court to which the appeal is taken. Fed. R. App. P. 3(c). (Fed. R. App. P. Form 1 is a sample notice of appeal.) Failure to file a notice of appeal in accordance with the specificity requirements of Fed. R. App. P. 3(c) presents a jurisdictional bar to the appeal. *Torres v. Oakland Scavenger Co.*, 108 S. Ct. 2405 (1988). Certain fees must be paid at the time the notice of appeal is filed. Fed. R. App. P. 3(e). The clerk is responsible for mailing copies of the notice to counsel for all other parties and, together with the docket entries, to the clerk of the court of appeals; the clerk's failure to do so, however, does not affect the validity of the appeal. Fed. R. App. P. 3(d).

If two or more parties are entitled to take an appeal "and their interests are such as to make joinder practicable," they may file a joint notice of appeal or, if they have filed separate notices, may "proceed on appeal as a single appellant." Fed. R. App. P. 3(b). Appeals may be consolidated either by order of the court of appeals (on motion of a party or on the court's own motion) or by stipulation of the parties. *Id.*

A notice of appeal must be filed within thirty days after entry of the judgment appealed from; but if the United States or an officer or agency thereof is a party, a notice of appeal may be filed *by any party* within sixty days after such entry. Fed. R. App. P. 4(a)(1). If any party files a timely notice of appeal, any other party may file a notice of appeal within fourteen days thereafter or within the time otherwise prescribed for filing a notice of appeal. Fed. R. App. P. 4(a)(3). The district court, on a showing of excusable neglect or good cause, may extend the time for filing a notice of appeal in the manner and to the extent set forth in Fed. R. App. P. 4(a)(5).

The time for filing a notice of appeal is automatically extended by the making of a timely motion under Rules 50(b), 52(b), or 59 of the Federal Rules of Civil Procedure (*i.e.*, a motion for judgment n.o.v., amended or additional findings of fact, amendment of the judgment, or a new trial). When such a motion has been made, "the time for appeal for all parties shall run from the entry of the order denying a new trial or granting or denying, any other such motion." Fed. R. App. P. 4(a)(4). A notice of appeal filed before disposition of such a motion "shall have no effect"; a new notice must be filed within the prescribed time after the motion has been decided. *Id.* A notice of appeal filed after the announcement of a decision but before entry of the judgment or order, however, "shall be treated as filed after such entry and on the day thereof." Fed. R. App. P. 4(a)(2).

B. Appeals by Permission under 28 U.S.C. § 1292(b)

An appeal from an interlocutory order certified by the district court pursuant to Section 1292(b) is taken by filing a petition for permission to appeal, together with proof of service on all parties, with the clerk of the court of appeals within ten days after entry of the order. Fed. R. App. P. 5(a). A notice of appeal is unnecessary. Fed. R. App. P. 5(d).

A Section 1292(b) petition must set forth (i) the facts necessary to an understanding of the controlling question of law the district court has certified; (ii) the question itself; (iii) a statement of the reasons why there is a substantial basis for difference of opinion as to that question; and (iv) a statement showing why an immediate appeal may materially advance the termination of the litigation. The order sought to be appealed, together with any related findings of fact, conclusions of law, and opinion, must be either included in the petition or attached to it. Fed. R. App. P. 5(b).

Within seven days after service of the petition, any adverse party may file an answer in opposition. The petition and answer in opposition (the rules make no provision for reply papers) may be typewritten, and three copies must be filed with the original. Fed. R. App. P. 5(c). In the Second Circuit the petition is submitted without oral argument. 2d Cir. R. 27(e).

Within ten days after entry of an order granting permission to appeal, the appellant must pay the requisite fees to the clerk of the district court and also file a bond for costs if the district court requires such a bond. Fed. R. App. P. 5(d), 7. Upon receiving notification that such fees have been paid, the clerk of the court of appeals will docket the appeal. Fed. R. App. P. 5(d).

C. Extraordinary Writs

An application for mandamus, prohibition, or other extraordinary writ is made by filing a petition with the clerk of the court of appeals with proof of service on all parties to the action and, in the case of a petition for mandamus or prohibition, on the respondent judge or judges. Fed. R. App. P. 21(a), (c). The petition must state (i) the facts necessary to an understanding of the issues presented; (ii) the issues presented and the relief sought; and (iii) the reasons why the writ should issue. The petition must also contain copies of any order, opinion, or parts of the record that may be necessary for an understanding of the matters set forth in the petition. *Id.* The petition may be typewritten, and three copies must be filed with the original. Fed. R. App. P. 21(d).

After receiving the prescribed docket fee, the clerk will docket the petition and submit it to the court. Fed. R. App. P. 21(a). The court may either deny the petition or order the respondents to answer it within a prescribed time. The clerk will advise the parties of the dates on which briefs are to be filed, if briefs are required, and of the date for oral argument. Fed. R. App. P. 21(b).

All parties below, other than the petitioner, are deemed respondents for all purposes. If the judge or judges named as respondents do not desire to appear in the proceeding, they may so inform the clerk and all parties by letter. *Id.* The rules of the Second Circuit provide that a petition for mandamus or prohibition "shall not bear the name of the district judge, but shall be entitled simply, In re . . ., Petitioner." Unless otherwise ordered, a district judge from whom relief is sought "shall be represented pro forma by counsel for the party opposing the relief, who shall appear in the name of the party and not that of the judge." 2d Cir. R. 21.

V. CIVIL APPEALS MANAGEMENT PLAN

In the Second Circuit, civil appeals are governed by a Civil Appeals Management Plan ("CAMP"), which supplements and, in important respects, displaces the Federal Rules of Appellate Procedure.

The Plan requires the appellant, within ten days after filing the notice of appeal, to docket the appeal by (a) serving and filing a pre-argument statement, in a form prescribed by the Court (CAMP Form C), describing the nature of the action, the result below, and the issues on appeal, and providing certain other information; (b) ordering a transcript from the court reporter (CAMP Form D); (c) certifying that satisfactory arrangements have been made for paying for the transcript; and (d) paying the docket fee. At the same time the appellant must also file copies of each judgment, order, decision, and opinion of the district court relevant to the appeal. CAMP 3. If the appellant fails to take these steps within the prescribed ten-day period, the clerk may dismiss the appeal without further notice. CAMP 7(a).

As soon as practicable after the filing of the pre-argument statement, staff counsel for the Court of Appeals will issue a scheduling order establishing the dates by which the record on appeal, the appellant's brief and appendix, and the appellee's brief are to be filed and designating the week during which counsel shall be ready to present oral argument. Staff counsel may defer the scheduling order until the pre-argument conference, if one is to be held; in that event, the scheduling order may be incorporated in the pre-argument conference order. CAMP 4. Failure to comply with the scheduling order may result in sanctions, including, in the case of the appellant, dismissal of the appeal. CAMP 7(b).

At the discretion of staff counsel, a pre-argument conference may be held to consider possible settlement, simplification of the issues, and any other matters that may aid in the handling or disposition of the appeal. At the conclusion of the conference, staff counsel will enter a pre-argument conference order "which shall control the subsequent course of the proceeding." CAMP 5.

A motion for leave to file an oversize brief, to postpone the date on which a brief must be filed, or to alter the argument date shall be made at least two weeks before the brief is due or the argument is scheduled, "unless exceptional circumstances exist." Once the case has been put on the argument calendar, a motion to alter the argument date is "not viewed with favor and will be granted only under extraordinary circumstances." CAMP 8.

VI. THE RECORD ON APPEAL

The record on appeal consists of the original papers and exhibits filed in the district court, the transcript (if any), and a certified copy of the docket entries prepared by the clerk of the district court. Fed. R. App. P. 10(a). The parties may, however, exclude from the record any exhibits and portions of the transcript that they consider irrelevant to the issues on appeal. If the appellant intends to argue that a finding or conclusion is unsupported by or contrary to the evidence, the record must include a transcript of all evidence relevant to such finding or conclusion. Fed. R. App. P. 10(b)(2).

Within ten days after filing the notice of appeal, the appellant must order from the reporter, in writing (using CAMP Form D, in the case of a Second Circuit appeal), those portions of the transcript that are not already on file and that the appellant intends to include in the record on appeal. A copy of the transcript order must be filed with the clerk of the district court. Unless the appellant intends to include the entire transcript, he must also file a statement of the issues he intends to raise on appeal. If the appellant does not intend to order any portion of the transcript, he must file a certificate to that effect. Copies of the transcript order or certificate and of the statement of issues, if any, must be served on the appellee. Within ten days after such service, the appellee may file and serve on the appellant a designation of any additional portions of the transcript he deems necessary. If the appellee makes such a designation and is not notified by the appellant within ten days that those additional portions have been ordered, the appellee within the following ten days may either order those portions himself or move in the district court for an order requiring the appellant to do so. Fed. R. App. P. 10(b)(1), (3).

If the proceedings were not reported or if a transcript is unavailable, the appellant may prepare a statement of the evidence from the best available means, including his own recollection. He must serve that statement on the appellee, who may serve objections or proposed amendments within ten days. The appellant's statement, together with the appellee's objections and proposed amendments, must thereupon be submitted to the district court for settlement and approval. Fed. R. App. P. 10(c).

Trial exhibits may be, and frequently are, retained by the attorney for the party who introduced them. If there is an appeal, the attorney having custody of any exhibit to be included in the record on appeal must make it (or a true copy) available at the office of the clerk of the district court. 2d Cir. R. 11(c). The parties are encouraged to agree as to which exhibits are necessary for the appeal. Absent such agreement, the appellant must serve a designation of the exhibits to be included in the record within fifteen days after filing the notice of appeal, and the appellee may serve a cross-designation of other exhibits within ten days thereafter. 2d Cir. R. 11(b).

Disputes as to the contents of the record, if not resolved by agreement, must be submitted to the district court for resolution. Material omissions from or errors in the record may be corrected by stipulation of the parties, by the district court (either before or after the record is transmitted to the court of appeals), or by the court of appeals itself. All other questions as to the form and content of the record must be presented to the court of appeals. Fed. R. App. P. 10(e).

Before the record is transmitted to the court of appeals, the documents comprising the record must be numbered and indexed. Fed. R. App. P. 11(b). Although the district court clerk has nominal responsibility for this task, it is in practice performed by the appellant's counsel under the clerk's supervision.

The parties may stipulate, or the district court on motion may direct, that the clerk of the district court temporarily retain the record for use by the parties in preparing their appellate papers. Fed. R. App. P. 11(c). Usually, however, counsel for both parties will have copies of the complete record, or of the portions pertinent to the appeal, so it will rarely be necessary to have the original record retained in the district court.

VII. THE APPENDIX

The purpose of the appendix is to provide each member of the court, in compact form, a copy of those portions of the record on appeal that are of especial importance to the issues being raised on the appeal and to which the parties wish to direct the particular attention of the court. The parties are free to refer to parts of the record not included in the appendix. Extensive reference to the original record, however, will not be necessary if the appendix is adequate. Conversely, inclusion of extensive materials not referred to in the briefs not only causes needless expense but defeats the purpose of the appendix. Designation of unnecessary materials, if done "unreasonably and vexatiously," may lead to the imposition of sanctions. Fed. R. App. P. 30(b).

Certain portions of the record must be included in the appendix: the relevant docket entries in the court below; any relevant portions of the pleadings, charge, findings, or opinion; and the judgment, order, or decision from which the appeal is taken. Fed. R. App. P. 30(a). What is "relevant," and what additional materials should be included, are within the sound judgment of counsel.

The appendix must contain, in order, a table of contents showing the pages of the appendix at which each part begins; the relevant docket entries; and other parts of the record set out in chronological order. Page numbers of the original transcript must be indicated in brackets. Omissions must be shown by asterisks. Captions, acknowledgements, and other immaterial formal matters are omitted. Fed. R. App. P. 30(d). Ten copies of the appendix must be filed, and one copy must be served on each party separately represented. Fed. R. App. P. 30(a). Exhibits may be set forth in one or more separate volumes, only four copies of which need be filed. Fed. R. App. P. 30(e). The exhibit volume or volumes must be "suitably indexed," *id.*; in the Second Circuit the exhibit index "shall include a description of the exhibit sufficient to inform the court of its nature," 2d Cir. R. 30(3).

The parties are encouraged to agree on the contents of the appendix. Absent such agreement, the appellant must serve on the appellee, within ten days after the filing of the record (unless the deferred-appendix procedure is employed), a designation of the parts of the record the appellant intends to include in the appendix together with a statement of the issues he intends to raise on the appeal. Within ten days after receiving the appellant's designation, the appellee may serve a designation of additional parts of the record, and the appellant must include those parts in the appendix. Fed. R. App. P. 30(b). Unless the appendix is deferred pursuant to Fed. R. App. P. 30(c), the appellant must serve and file the appendix together with his brief. Fed. R. App. P. 30(a).

The Second Circuit permits use of a deferred appendix either by stipulation of the parties or by direction of the Court upon application. 2d Cir. R. 30(1). The purpose of the deferred appendix is to permit the parties to determine what parts of the record need to be reproduced in the appendix in light of the issues actually presented in the briefs. *See Notes of Advisory Committee on Appellate Rules*, Rule 30(c) (1967). Under the deferred appendix procedure, the appendix is not filed until twenty-one days after service of the appellee's brief. Because the briefs are prepared before the appendix, citations are handled in either of two ways: (1) The briefs may cite directly to pages of the original record, in which event the appendix must indicate the record page numbers in brackets; or (2) a party wishing to cite directly to the appendix may initially serve and file the brief in preliminary form (typewritten or in page proof) citing the original record, and fourteen days after the appendix is filed the party must then serve and file the brief in final form with citations to the appendix replacing citations to the record, no other changes (other than correction of typographical errors) being allowable. Fed. R. App. P. 30(c).

The appendix must be printed or otherwise produced in accordance with Fed. R. App. P. 32(a) and Section 32 of the Second Circuit Rules.

VIII. THE BRIEFS

Preparation of the brief will nearly always be the most demanding and time-consuming part of appellate counsel's task. The importance of a good brief cannot be overstated. When oral argument is not sought or permitted (as is frequently the case in some courts of appeals), the brief is counsel's only opportunity to state the client's position. Even when the court allows oral argument, the brief is usually the only statement of that position that is both detailed and complete.

A. Formal Requirements

Fed. R. App. P. 31(a) sets forth a general-purpose briefing schedule but authorizes each circuit to shorten that schedule either by rule or by order in particular cases. As already discussed, the Second Circuit's Civil Appeals Management Plan requires briefs to be filed in accordance with a scheduling order issued in each individual case. CAMP 4(b). Twenty-five copies of each brief must be filed, and two copies must be served on counsel for each party separately represented. Fed. R. App. P. 31(b).

Briefs may be produced either by standard typographic printing or by any other process (such as photo-offset and electrostatic reproduction) that produces a clear black image on white paper; carbon copies are allowed only with the court's permission except by parties proceeding in forma pauperis. Briefs must meet detailed requirements as to type of paper, page and type size, color of the cover (*e.g.*, blue for the appellant's brief, red for the appellee's brief, and gray for the reply brief), and other matters of format. Fed. R. App. P. 32(a); 2d Cir. R. 32(a). In patent cases, however, briefs may be large enough to accommodate patent documents. Fed. R. App. P. 32(a).

The front cover of each brief must contain (1) the name of the court and the number of the case (in the Second Circuit the number must be printed in the upper right-hand corner in type at least one inch high, 2d Cir. R. 32(b)); (2) the title of the case; (3) the nature of the proceeding (*e.g.*, appeal) and the name of the court below; (4) the title of the brief (*e.g.*, Brief for Appellant); and (5) the name and address of counsel for the party filing the brief. Fed. R. App. P. 32(a). Although not required, the name of the attorney who will argue the appeal may be printed on the cover so that the court will be able to address counsel by name.

B. Contents

The appellant's brief must contain, in the following order and under appropriate headings: (1) a table of contents and a table of authorities (alphabetically arranged), with page references; (2) a statement of the issues presented for review; (3) a statement of the case, including the nature of the case, the course of proceedings, the disposition below, and the relevant facts with citations to the appendix or record; (4) the argument, which may be preceded by a summary, setting forth the appellant's contentions with citations to the appendix or record and to the authorities relied on; and (5) a short conclusion stating the precise relief sought. Fed. R. App. P. 28(a). In the Second Circuit, the appellant's brief must also include a preliminary statement setting forth the name of the judge who rendered the decision appealed from and a citation for that decision if it has been reported. 2d Cir. R. 28(2).

The appellee's brief must contain the first four of these elements, except that a statement of the issues and a statement of facts may be omitted if the appellee is satisfied with the appellant's statement of these. Fed. R. App. P. 28(b). Ordinarily, however, the appellee will wish to provide his own statement of the issues and of the facts so as to emphasize his own point of view and to lay a proper foundation for his argument.

A reply brief may be filed by the appellant and, in the case of a cross-appeal, by the appellee, but further briefs are not allowed except by leave of court. Fed. R. App. P. 28(c). If, however, "pertinent and significant authorities" come to a party's attention after the filing of his brief and before decision, the party may so advise the court by letter addressed to the clerk with a copy to all counsel. The letter may refer to the point to which the newly discovered authorities pertain and state the reasons for the supplemental citations, but must do so "without argument." Any response to such a letter must be made promptly "and shall be similarly limited." Fed. R. App. P. 28(j).

If the appeal involves statutes, rules, or regulations, they must be reproduced in the body of the brief, in an addendum at the end, or in a separate pamphlet. Fed. R. App. P. 28(f).

C. Length of Briefs

Except by permission of the court or as allowed by local rule, principal briefs may not exceed fifty pages and reply briefs may not exceed twenty-five pages, exclusive of the table of contents, the table of authorities, and any addendum (such as a statutory addendum). Fed. R. App. P. 28(g). The fifty-page limit applies whether the brief is printed or produced by other permissible means. The Second Circuit has no local rule generally allowing briefs longer than as specified in Fed. R. App. P. 28(g), and any motion for leave to file an oversized brief must comply with Section 27(g) of the Court's Rules. In civil cases, such a motion must be made at least two weeks before the brief is due, must be accompanied by a statement of reasons, and must attach a copy of the page proofs. Subject to standing directions of the Court, such a motion may be disposed of by the clerk or referred to a judge. 2d Cir. R. 27(g).

Because of the tight briefing schedule frequently mandated by Second Circuit scheduling orders, compliance with Section 27(g) is often difficult. To minimize such difficulty, counsel should make every effort to keep his brief within the length provided by Fed. R. App. P. 28(g) and to ascertain at the earliest possible time whether a motion under Section 27(g) will be necessary. In any event, briefs should always be as short as possible, and a brief exceeding fifty pages is warranted only in exceptional cases.

D. Importance of the Brief

In the Second Circuit, as well as in most courts of appeals today, it is the court's practice to examine the briefs in advance of the oral argument. Many circuits, moreover, dispense with oral argument in many or even in most cases. The brief, therefore, is not only counsel's first step in the process of advocacy; it may well be his only opportunity to persuade the court of the correctness of the client's position.

It is not the function of this chapter to discuss the principles of effective brief-writing. It may be useful, however, to emphasize three precepts of fundamental importance and universal application:

Accuracy. The brief must give meticulous regard for the facts of the case, as established by the record, and must deal with legal authority in a careful, responsible manner. Candor in dealing with unfavorable facts and adverse authority is not only a professional responsibility but good tactics as well, for significant misstatements and omissions will invariably be pointed out by opposing counsel, often with telling effect. Accuracy should extend to small matters as well as large, for typographical errors, misspellings, grammatical lapses, and imprecisions of even a minor nature may diminish the brief's credibility in the eyes of the court.

Brevity. The Second Circuit wisely admonishes that briefs must be "compact," "concise," and free from "irrelevant" and "immaterial" matter. 2d Cir. R. 28(1). Counsel must evaluate each potential point stringently and objectively, and must expunge each one that is without substantial merit. Patently weak contentions may reduce the effectiveness of the strong ones. Counsel must then seek to state the remaining contentions as succinctly as possible. A long-winded brief is less likely to persuade than to annoy. A draft brief can often be improved by shortening it: substituting short, simple words for long ones, deleting unneeded words, and using direct rather than convoluted expressions.

Clarity. Persuasion requires understanding, and understanding springs from clarity. It is often useful to have the draft brief read by a colleague lacking detailed knowledge of the case. Such a colleague can often identify murky passages that need rewriting. Judicious use of headings facilitates understanding. Footnotes should be used sparingly, for they invariably interrupt the flow of the discussion. At least one Second Circuit judge has publicly said that he never reads footnotes in briefs. Hon. George C. Pratt, *Circuit Judge's Views on Appellate Process*, 199 N.Y.L.J. 5 (March 22, 1988).

IX. ORAL ARGUMENT

All appeals may be argued orally unless, pursuant to local rule, a panel of three judges, after examining the briefs and record, unanimously determines that argument is unnecessary. Fed. R. App. P. 34(a). The Second Circuit has such a rule, 2d Cir. R. 34(g), but it is rarely if ever employed; the Court encourages oral argument and will ordinarily hear argument by one party even if the opposing party chooses to submit. In this respect the practice of the Second Circuit differs from that of many other circuits.

In the Second Circuit, the judge scheduled to preside over the panel determines the time allowed for argument, and the clerk will notify counsel of the ruling. 2d Cir. R. 34(d). With certain exceptions, an appeal will be added to the general calendar as soon as the appellant's brief has been filed. 2d Cir. R. 34(a). Appeals will ordinarily be placed on the day calendar for argument in the same order in which they were added to the general calendar; subject to the clerk's approval, however, out-of-town counsel may stipulate a date for argument. 2d Cir. R. 34(b). The clerk will notify counsel of the argument date.

After a case has been set for argument, it may be continued only by order of the court for good cause shown; counsel's engagement in other courts (except the Supreme Court) will not be considered good cause. 2d Cir. R. 34(b). Except in the event of counsel's unforeseen illness, the Court will not ordinarily permit postponement of the argument unless application is made at least two weeks before the date set for argument or the date for filing appellee's brief, whichever date is later. 2d Cir. R. 34(e). A case scheduled to be heard on a designated day will be heard on that day; the panel will sit until it has heard all cases on its day calendar. The names of the judges who will sit during a particular week may be ascertained from the clerk's office during the previous week.

Except with the Court's permission, only one attorney will be allowed to argue for each party. 2d Cir. R. 34(c). Divided argument is usually not advisable in any event. If possible, parties having common interests should agree to have one counsel argue on their behalf even if they have submitted separate briefs.

Under current Second Circuit practice, each judge on the panel will ordinarily have examined the briefs prior to the argument. Counsel should therefore assume that each member of the panel has general familiarity with the facts and the general contentions of the parties, and should therefore concentrate on the essential facts and legal theories that he believes will support a decision in his favor. Questions from the bench are to be expected and should be welcomed, for they may provide valuable clues as to points in which the Court is particularly interested. Questions should be answered forthrightly and at once, with amplification later if time permits. It is not unusual for counsel to have to make an entire argument in response to questions from the bench. Improvisation, grounded on a thorough knowledge of the record and the pertinent authorities, is thus essential, and dogged adherence to a prepared argument is likely to be both useless and ineffectual. Except when referring to a statute or other document whose precise language is important, reading from a prepared script is universally disfavored. Counsel has no obligation to use all of his allotted time; once satisfied that he has adequately dealt with all points that he wishes to cover, or when the court indicates that it does not wish to hear more, he should promptly conclude the argument.

X. TEMPORARY RELIEF PENDING APPEAL

With certain exceptions, all district court judgments are automatically stayed for ten days after entry and may be further stayed pending appeal by the giving of a supersedeas bond approved by the court. Fed. R. Civ. P. 62(a), (d). An interlocutory or final judgment in an action for an injunction or in a receivership action and a judgment or order directing an accounting in an action for patent infringement, however, are effective immediately unless stayed by court order. Fed. R. Civ. P. 62(a).

Ordinarily, an application for a stay or other relief pending appeal, or for approval of a supersedeas bond, must be made in the first instance to the district court. Fed. R. App. P. 8(a). When an appeal is taken from an interlocutory or final judgment granting, dissolving, or denying an injunction, the court in its discretion may suspend, modify, restore, or grant an injunction during the pendency of the appeal upon such terms as it considers proper to secure the rights of the adverse party. Fed. R. Civ. P. 62(c).

A motion for a stay or other interim relief, or for approval of a supersedeas bond, may be made to the court of appeals only if the district court has previously denied such relief or if application to the district court was "not practicable." The motion must be made on reasonable notice to all parties and must be supported by appropriate papers. Ordinarily the motion will be referred to a panel of the court, but in cases of exceptional urgency it may be made to a single judge. Fed. R. App. P. 8(a).

In general, motions for temporary relief addressed to a court of appeals should conform to the procedure for motions, described below.

XI. MOTION PRACTICE

In the Second Circuit, a motion for an extension of time to file briefs or other papers, to dispense with printing, for leave to file an amicus brief, for permission to add, drop, or substitute parties, for consolidation, to intervene, for a preference, for postponement of the argument, or for other procedural relief will normally be determined by a single judge without oral argument. 2d Cir. R. 27(f). That determination may be reviewed by the court. Fed. R. App. P. 27(c).

A motion addressed to a previous decision or order of the court, for the stay, recall, or modification of any mandate or decision of the court, or to withdraw or dismiss an appeal that has been argued but not decided will be referred to the panel that heard the appeal, usually without oral argument. 2d Cir. R. 27(c). Petitions for rehearing, which are governed by Fed. R. App. P. 40, are discussed below. Other motions for substantive relief, such as dismissal, summary affirmance, or a stay or injunction pending appeal, will normally be determined by the panel sitting on the return date. Such motions should be noticed for a Tuesday, and the supporting and opposing papers must be filed on or before the times specified by Second Circuit Rule 27(b). The Court will hear oral argument on such motions. 2d Cir. R. 27(b).

If any party requests an expedited hearing of any motion and submits a written factual showing of urgency, the clerk will set the motion for hearing on any day the Court is in session. If the hearing is set within twenty-four hours (or for a Tuesday morning, in the case of applications made later than the previous Thursday), the clerk may direct the parties to maintain the status quo, and such a direction has the effect of a stay unless otherwise ordered by a judge on application. 2d Cir. R. 27(b).

On both procedural and substantive motions, the notice of motion must be in the form prescribed by the Court. *See* 2d Cir. R. 27(a)(1) and attached form. Affidavits should contain only factual information and not legal argument. Except by permission of the Court, memoranda of law must not exceed ten typewritten, double-spaced, 8-1/2-by-11-inch pages. If the moving party is seeking substantive relief, he must submit a copy of the district court's opinion as a separately identified exhibit to the motion papers. Unnecessary exhibits are not to be submitted. Sanctions may be imposed against any party whose papers do not meet these formal requirements. 2d Cir. R. 27(a).

XII. DECISION

In the Second Circuit, when the decision is unanimous and each judge believes that no purpose would be served by a formal opinion, the appeal may be disposed of by summary order to which the Court may append a brief written statement. Because such statements are not formal opinions and are unreported and not uniformly available to all parties, the Second Circuit's Rules provide that "they shall not be cited or otherwise used in unrelated cases before this or any other court." 2d Cir. R. 0.23. In recent years, more than half of all appeals in the Second Circuit have been disposed of by summary order.

XIII. PETITIONS FOR REHEARING

A petition for rehearing may be filed within fourteen days after entry of judgment. The petition must not exceed fifteen pages, must set forth "with particularity" the points of law or fact that it is claimed the court overlooked or misapprehended, must be in the form prescribed by Fed. R. App. P. 32(a), and must be served and filed in conformity with Fed. R. App. P. 31(b). Oral argument in support of the petition is not permitted. Fed. R. App. P. 40.

No answer to the petition will be received unless requested by the court, but in the absence of such a request a petition will "ordinarily" not be granted. If the petition is granted, the court may make a final disposition of the matter with or without reargument. Fed. R. App. P. 40(a).

Petitions for rehearing rarely result in outright reversal of the court's decision but on occasion induce the court to modify, clarify, or amplify its original opinion. In the Second Circuit, if the Court finds a rehearing petition to be "wholly without merit, vexatious and for delay," it may impose sanctions. 2d Cir. R. 40.

If a timely petition for rehearing is filed, the mandate, which otherwise issues twenty-one days after entry of judgment, will be automatically stayed until the petition is disposed of unless the court orders otherwise. If rehearing is denied, the mandate will issue seven days thereafter unless the court shortens or enlarges that time. Fed. R. App. P. 41(a).

The filing of a timely petition for rehearing also suspends the time for all parties (not just the party who filed the petition for rehearing) to file a petition for certiorari in the Supreme Court. In such circumstances, the time for filing a petition for certiorari runs from the date on which the petition for rehearing is denied or on which a judgment is entered on the rehearing. Sup. Ct. R. 20.4.

XIV. HEARINGS AND REHEARINGS *IN BANC*

Although a court of appeals ordinarily hears and determines cases in three-judge panels, a majority of the circuit judges in regular active service may order a hearing or rehearing *in banc*. 28 U.S.C. § 46(c); Fed. R. App. P.

35(a). A hearing or rehearing *in banc* "is not favored" and will ordinarily be ordered only when the case involves an issue of exceptional importance or when there is a conflict among different panels of the same circuit. Fed. R. App. P. 35(a). The Second Circuit sits *in banc* very rarely.

A party desiring to suggest that an appeal be heard initially *in banc* must do so by the date on which the appellee's brief is filed. A suggestion for rehearing *in banc*, which is customarily included in a petition for rehearing (although the suggestion may be made in a separate document), must be made within the time specified by Fed. R. App. P. 40(a) for filing a petition for rehearing, normally fourteen days after entry of judgment. Unlike a petition for rehearing, a suggestion for rehearing in banc does not stay the mandate or affect the time for filing a petition for certiorari in the Supreme Court. Fed. R. App. P. 35(c).

When a suggestion for hearing or rehearing *in banc* has been made, the clerk transmits the suggestion to members of the panel as well as to all judges of the court who are in regular active service. No response to the suggestion will be received unless directed by the court. A vote on the suggestion will be taken only if requested either by a judge in regular active service or by a member of the panel that rendered the decision sought to be reheard *in banc*. Fed. R. App. P. 35(b).

If the court grants a rehearing *in banc*, it may decide the case on the original briefs without additional oral argument, it may invite supplemental briefs, or it may set the case down for further argument with or without additional briefing.

XV. SUPREME COURT REVIEW

The Supreme Court has jurisdiction to review cases in a court of appeals either by writ of certiorari or on certified questions of law. 28 U.S.C. § 1254. Under legislation that became effective in September 1988, appeals can no longer be taken from the courts of appeals to the Supreme Court. Pub. L. No. 100-352 102 Stat. 662-644 (effective September 25, 1988, except as to cases pending in the Supreme Court on that date and judgments and decrees entered before that date). The only appeals that the Supreme Court is still required to determine are from certain orders of three-judge district courts. 28 U.S.C. § 1253.

A. Review by Certiorari

The Supreme Court may review a decision of a court of appeals on writ of certiorari upon the petition of any party, including the party that prevailed in the court of appeals. 28 U.S.C. § 1254(1). The Supreme Court is also empowered to review a case in the court of appeals before that court has rendered judgment, *id.*, although the Court exercises this power only in cases of extraordinary urgency and public importance, Sup. Ct. R. 18; *see, e.g., Youngstown Sheet & Tube Co. v. Sawyer*, 343 U.S. 579 (1952) (the steel-seizure case); *United States v. Nixon*, 418 U.S. 683 (1974) (the presidential-tapes case).

Review by certiorari is entirely a matter of the Supreme Court's discretion and will be granted only when there are "special and important reasons therefor," such as a conflict among the circuits on an important question of federal law. *See* Sup. Ct. R. 17.1(a). Ordinarily, the Supreme Court will grant certiorari only to resolve questions of federal law that are clearly presented by the record, that have been squarely passed on by the court below, and that at least four justices consider to be of general public importance.

Because certiorari is granted only as a matter of judicial discretion, the denial of certiorari has no precedential significance, nor does it establish the law of the case for purposes of any later petition for certiorari. If certiorari is denied at an interlocutory stage of the case (although the Supreme Court is empowered to review interlocutory decisions of a court of appeals, lack of finality is generally a factor militating against the grant of certiorari), the Court will entertain a further petition for certiorari from a final decision of a court of appeals even if the later petition raises the same questions as the earlier one.

A petition for certiorari in a civil case must be filed within ninety days after the entry of judgment in the court of appeals (not the issuance of the mandate), although a justice of the Supreme Court may extend that time for an additional sixty days for good cause shown. 28 U.S.C. § 2101(c). A court of appeals has no authority to grant such an extension. An out-of-time petition will be rejected by the clerk. Sup. Ct. R. 20.3.

A petition for certiorari need not be, and usually is not, accompanied by a copy of the record. The record should be filed only when it is essential to a proper understanding of the case. Sup. Ct. R. 19.1. The petition must comply with Supreme Court Rule 21 as to form and must be produced in accordance with Rule 33. The petition must be "as short as possible" and in any event may not exceed thirty pages exclusive of index, table of authorities, statutory addenda, and appendix. Sup. Ct. R. 21.4.

Within thirty days after receipt of a petition for certiorari (unless the time is extended), the respondent may file a brief in opposition, not exceeding thirty pages and in conformity with Rules 33 and 34, setting forth the reasons why the Court should not review the case. Any objections to the Court's jurisdiction must be included in the brief in opposition; a motion to dismiss the petition is not permitted. Sup. Ct. R. 22.3. The petitioner may file a reply brief, not exceeding ten pages, addressing any new matters raised in the brief in opposition, but the Court's consideration of the petition will not be delayed pending the Court's receipt of a reply brief. Sup. Ct. R. 22.5.

The Supreme Court may deny certiorari; grant certiorari and set the case down for full briefing and oral argument; or summarily dispose of the case on the merits without further action by the parties. Sup. Ct. R. 23. Counsel should be mindful of a possible summary disposition and frame their papers accordingly.

B. Review on Certified Questions

The Supreme Court is also empowered to review a case in which a court of appeals has certified a question of law as to which instructions are desired. In such a case, the Supreme Court "may give binding instructions or require the entire record to be sent up for decision of the entire matter in controversy." 28 U.S.C. § 1254(2). *See* Sup. Ct. R. 24.1.

The court of appeals' certificate must state the nature of the case and the facts on which the certified question arises. Questions of fact cannot be certified, but only questions of law, and such questions must be "distinct and definite." Sup. Ct. R. 24.1.

Certification under 28 U.S.C. § 1254(2) is at the discretion of the court of appeals, and it is the court that prepares the certificate, although the parties are free to ask the court to modify or supplement it. Certification may be made either before or after the court of appeals has decided the case. The Supreme Court determines whether a certified case is to be briefed and argued or whether the certificate is to be dismissed. Sup. Ct. R. 25.2. If the Court accepts the case for briefing and argument, further proceedings will be conducted in accordance with Supreme Court Rule 25.3 and 25.4.

Cases coming to the Supreme Court on certified questions are rare, and the Court's certification jurisdiction is generally viewed with disfavor by both the Supreme Court and the courts of appeals.

C. Review by Appeal

Although the Supreme Court now reviews decisions of the courts of appeals solely on writ of certiorari, the Court continues to have jurisdiction over appeals from orders of three-judge district courts granting or denying interlocutory and permanent injunctions. 28 U.S.C. § 1253. Three-judge district courts are convened to hear challenges as to the apportionment of congressional districts and state legislatures and for a few other specific purposes. *See* 28 U.S.C. § 2284(a). Appeals therefore constitute a relatively small part of the Supreme Court's business.

Selected Bibliography

Arthur A. Charpentier (ed.), *Counsel on Appeal* (1968).

Committee on Federal Courts of the Association of the Bar of the City of New York, *Appeals to the Second Circuit* (6th ed. 1988).

John W. Davis, *The Argument of an Appeal*, 26 A.B.A.J. 895 (1940).

James Wm. Moore, Bernard J. Ward, and Jo Desha Lucas, *Moore's Federal Practice*, Vol. 9 (2d ed. 1948 with supplements).

Robert L. Stern, *Appellate Practice in the United States* (1981).

Robert L. Stern, Eugene Gressman, and Stephen M. Shapiro, *Supreme Court Practice* (6th ed. 1986).

William Strunck, Jr. and E.B. White, *The Elements of Style* (3d ed. 1979).

Frederick Bernays Wiener, *Briefing and Arguing Federal Appeals* (1961).

Charles Alan Wright, *The Law of Federal Courts*, Chapts. 11 & 12 (4th ed. 1983).

CHAPTER TWENTY-SEVEN

PRECLUSION: *RES JUDICATA* AND COLLATERAL ESTOPPEL RECENT DEVELOPMENTS IN THE UNITED STATES SUPREME COURT WHAT PRACTITIONERS CAN EXPECT

by Bernice K. Leber, Esq.*

I. INTRODUCTION

This chapter considers practice and procedure in the Second Circuit concerning claim and issue preclusion, subjects about which the United States Supreme Court has written extensively recently.[1] "Claim Preclusion," or *res judicata*, is present where a final judgment on the merits bars further claims

---

* The valuable assistance of Chavie N. Kahn in the preparation of this chapter is gratefully acknowledged.

---

[1] *See, e.g., Marino v. Ortiz*, 108 S. Ct. 586 (1986); *reh'g denied*, 108 S. Ct. 1964 (1988); *University of Tennessee v. Elliott*, 478 U.S. 788 (1986); *Parsons Steel, Inc. v. First Alabama Bank*, 474 U.S. 518 (1986); *Marrese v. American Academy of Orthopaedic Surgeons*, 470 U.S. 373 (1985); *Cooper v. Federal Reserve Bank*, 467 U.S. 867 (1984); *Limbach v. Hooven & Allison Co.*, 466 U.S. 353 (1984); *McDonald v. City of West Branch*, 466 U.S. 284 (1984); *United States v. One Assortment of 89 Firearms*, 465 U.S. 354 (1984); *Migra v. Warren City School Dist. Bd. of Educ.*, 465 U.S. 75 (1984); *United States v. Mendoza*, 464 U.S. 154 (1984); *United States v. Stauffer Chem. Co.*, 464 U.S. 165 (1984); *Nevada v. United States*, 463 U.S. 110 (1983); *Haring v. Prosise*, 462 U.S. 306 (1983); *Arizona v. California*, 460 U.S. 605 (1983); *Kremer v. Chemical Constr. Corp.*, 456 U.S. 461 (1982); *Underwriters' Nat'l Assurance Co. v. North Carolina Life and Accident & Health Ins. Guar. Ass'n*, 455 U.S. 691 (1982); *Federated Dep't Stores Inc. v. Moitie*, 452 U.S. 394 (1981); *Allen v. McCurry*, 449 U.S. 90 (1980); *Thomas v. Washington Gas Light Co.*, 448 U.S. 261 (1980); *Sandefer v. United States*, 447 U.S. 10 (1980); *Brown v. Felsen*, 442 U.S. 127 (1970); *Montana v. United States*, 440 U.S. 147 (1979); *Parklane Hosiery Co. v. Shore*, 439 U.S. 322 (1979). *Cf. Dean Witter Reynolds, Inc. v. Byrd*, 470 U.S. 213 (1985) (though discussed in light of *McDonald v. City of West Branch*, 466 U.S. 284 (1984) (question of preclusive effect of prior arbitration proceeding was not before Court and was not decided)).

by parties or their privies on the same cause of action.[2] "Issue Preclusion," or collateral estoppel, is present where, once a court has decided an issue of fact or law that is necessary to its judgment, the decision is conclusive in a subsequent suit based on a different cause of action involving any party to the prior litigation.[3]

This discussion starts with the sources for and policies underlying the doctrines, followed by their application in a variety of contexts. Particular focus will be on (a) decisions of the Supreme Court and in the Second Circuit; (b) how a party can use preclusion to its advantage; and (c) pitfalls that may accompany its application. The discussion is confined to preclusion in the inter-system context, that is, preclusion by judgment when the second or subsequent action is brought in federal court.[4]

A. Policies Underlying Preclusion and Terminology

1. Claim Preclusion

Under Article IV, § 1 of the Constitution and its implementing statute, 28 U.S.C. § 1738, federal courts must give "full faith and credit" to judgments of state courts.[5] In determining the scope of "full faith and credit," the

---

[2] *Restatement (Second) of Judgments* §§ 17-29 (1982); *see also Parklane Hosiery Co. v. Shore*, 439 U.S. 322, 326 n.5 (1979); *Migra v. Warren City School Dist. Bd. of Ed.*, 465 U.S. 75, 77 n.1 (1984); 1B Moore's Federal Practice ¶ 0.4505[1] (2d ed. 1974).

[3] *Id.*

[4] Generally, intersystem preclusion refers to preclusion by judgment when the second or subsequent actions are brought in the courts of a jurisdiction different from that rendering the initial judgment, such as when the first suit is in state court and the second in the court of another state or in federal court. Intersystem preclusion is distinguished from intrasystem preclusion in that the latter refers to preclusion by judgment when the second or subsequent actions are brought in the courts of the same jurisdiction that rendered the initial judgment. The expression is attributed to Professor Robert C. Casad in his article, Casad, *Intersystem Issue Preclusion and the Restatement (Second) of Judgments*, 66 Cornell L. Rev. 510, 511 n.4 (1981).

[5] U.S. Const. art. IV, § 1 provides:
   Full Faith and Credit shall be given in each State to the public Acts, Records, & Judicial Proceedings of every other state.
28 U.S.C. § 1738 (1982) provides in pertinent part:
   The records and judicial proceedings of any court of any such State, Territory or Possession, or copies thereof, shall be proved or admitted in other courts within the United States and its Territories and Possessions by the attestation of the clerk and seal of the court annexed, if a seal exists, together with certificate of a judge of the court that the said attestation is in proper form.
   Such Acts, records and judicial proceedings or copies thereof, so authenticated, shall have the same full faith and credit in every court within the United States and its Territories and Possessions as they have by law or usage in the courts of such State, Territory or Possession from which they are taken. *Id.*

Supreme Court has observed that preclusion has three basic purposes: (1) "protecting litigants from the burden of relitigating an identical issue with the same party or his privy . . . (2) promoting judicial economy by preventing needless litigation";[6] and (3) ". . . by preventing inconsistent decisions, encourag[ing] reliance on adjudication."[7]

Balanced against the constitutional directives and policies is the constitutional requirement of due process: that the party to be adversely affected by preclusion have had a full and fair opportunity to be heard.[8] If, for example, a class action is brought in federal court pursuant to Title VII of the Civil Rights Act of 1964 alleging employment discrimination based on race and a general pattern or practice of discrimination (necessary to a Title VII class action) was not found to exist, the Supreme Court holds that an individual class member would still not be precluded from proving his claim of discrimination because the individual's claim focuses on a particular employment decision—not on a pattern of discriminatory decision making.[9]

The constitutional imperative of "a full and fair opportunity to be heard," does not, however, always protect a party from preclusion. If, in the initial litigation in state court, one of the parties raised or could have raised contentions that its federal statutory or constitutional rights were violated, such contentions may be relevant to subsequent suits in the federal courts of the same state.[10] Even if final judgment on the merits may have been decided wrongly or rests on a legal principle subsequently overruled in another case, *if unappealed*, preclusion mandates that the same parties cannot relitigate issues in federal court that were or could have been raised in the prior action.[11]

2. Fundamental Principles and Terminology

Of late, the trend is to favor issue preclusion, resulting not so much from an increased appreciation of the value of repose, as from a belief that improved procedures warrant broader preclusion and that courts need increased

---

[6] *Parklane Hosiery Co. v. Shore*, 439 U.S. 322, 326 (1979).

[7] *Allen v. McCurry*, 449 U.S. 90, 94 (1981).

[8] U.S. Const. Amend. V, *id.* amend. XIV, § 1.

[9] *Cooper v. Federal Reserve Bank of Richmond*, 467 U.S. 867, 876 (1984).

[10] Luneberg, *The Opportunity to Be Heard And the Doctrines On Preclusion: Federal Limits On State Law*, 31 Vill. L. Rev. 139 (1986).

[11] *Federated Department Stores, Inc. v. Moitie*, 452 U.S. 394, 398 (1981).

protection against the burdens of repetitious litigation.[12] The most obvious expansion has increased the opportunities of nonparties to take advantage of prior judgments.

a. Defensive Issue Preclusion

In *Blonder-Tongue Laboratories, Inc. v. University of Illinois Foundation*, 402 U.S. 313 (1971), the Supreme Court opened the gateway to using preclusion defensively, holding that the party sued for patent infringement may plead that the patent in issue had previously been held invalid against a different defendant, and thereby estopped the patentee from relitigating the patent's validity.[13] The Supreme Court noted that a misallocation of resources occurs where a defendant is forced to present a complete defense on the merits to a claim which plaintiff has fully litigated and lost in a costly prior action. As a safeguard, trial courts should require the party against whom preclusion is sought to demonstrate, if he can, that he did not have "a fair opportunity, procedurally, substantively and evidentially to pursue his claim the first time."[14] To summarize, defensive issue preclusion occurs when a defendant seeks to prevent a plaintiff from asserting an issue that plaintiff has previously litigated and lost against another party.

Since *Blonder-Tongue*, the Supreme Court has approved applying defensive issue preclusion to plaintiffs in § 1983 suits.[15] In *Allen v. McCurry*, 449 U.S. 90 (1980), the Supreme Court decided that federal actions challenging constitutional violations by persons acting under color of state law, 42 U.S.C. § 1983, following a state court criminal proceeding that did deal or could have dealt with fourth amendment claims are not exempt from preclusion.[16] In *Allen v. McCurry*, the plaintiff had asserted in state court that his fourth amendment rights had been violated by an improper search and seizure, had lost that issue, been convicted and then tried to sue local police officers in federal court under 42 U.S.C. § 1983 for the same fourth amendment violations. In affirming the dismissal of the suit, the Supreme Court stated that the possible exceptions to preclusion are where state law did not

---

[12] 18 C. Wright *Federal Practice And Procedure* § 4493 at 21 (1981).

[13] *Blonder-Tongue Labs., Inc. v. University of Illinois Foundation*, 402 U.S. 313 (1971). *But see Amalgamated Sugar Co. v. NL Industries, Inc.*, 667 F. Supp. 87 (S.D.N.Y. 1987).

[14] *Id.* at 328, 333. The Supreme Court expressly stated that the case did not involve due process considerations or the offensive use of preclusion. *Id.* at 330.

[15] *See Allen v. McCurry*, 449 U.S. 90 (1980).

[16] *Id.* at 97 n.7.

provide fair procedures for the litigation of constitutional claims, or where the state failed to acknowledge the existence of a constitutional principle on which a litigant based his claim.[17] In *Allen*, however, the court was convinced that Missouri state courts had given plaintiff "a full and fair opportunity to litigate" his federal claim by means of the suppression motion.

b. Offensive Issue Preclusion

Ever widening the net of preclusion, the Supreme Court also permits offensive collateral estoppel (offensive issue preclusion) to be applied, that is, when a plaintiff seeks to foreclose a defendant from relitigating an issue that defendant litigated unsuccessfully with another party.[18] In *Parklane Hosiery Co. v. Shore*, 439 U.S. 322 (1979), the Supreme Court decided that class action stockholder-plaintiffs could use offensive collateral estoppel against a corporation, its officers, directors and stockholders for preparing a materially false and misleading proxy statement in violation of the federal securities laws.[19] In a prior suit, the SEC sued the same defendants for a declaratory judgment that the proxy statement was materially false and misleading and won. Using the SEC judgment offensively in the second suit, the stockholder-plaintiffs moved for partial summary judgment in order to halt the defendants from relitigating the issues previously resolved against them.

Reversing the Second Circuit, which had reversed the district court granting plaintiffs partial summary judgment, the Supreme Court allowed the preclusion. It also issued guidelines instructing district courts when not to apply offensive collateral estoppel: (1) when plaintiffs in the second suit could have joined in the earlier action such that the application of offensive collateral estoppel would be unfair to defendants; (2) when defendants had no incentive to litigate the first action fully and vigorously; (3) when the judgment relied on was itself inconsistent with one or more prior judgments in favor of the defendants; and (4) when the second action gives defendants procedural opportunities unavailable to them in the first action that could cause a different result.[20]

The Supreme Court's guidelines in *Parklane* differ from its "opportunity to be heard" approach taken in *Allen v. McCurry*, a defensive issue preclu-

---

17 *Id.* at 100-01 (citations omitted).

18 *See Parklane Hosiery Co., Inc. v. Shore*, 439 U.S. 322 (1979).

19 Sections 14(a), 10(b) and 20(a) of the Securities Exchange Act of 1934, various rules and regulations promulgated by the Securities Exchange Commission.

20 *Parklane Hosiery Co., Inc. v. Shore*, 439 U.S. at 331-332 (1979).

sion case. In *Parklane*, the Supreme Court emphasized the procedures applicable in the first SEC action as compared to those in the second district court action and concluded they were not so different as to cause a difference in result. It appears that since the party against whom issue preclusion is to be applied offensively did not choose the forum, the Supreme Court wanted to ensure that the defendant had a full and fair opportunity to be heard. By contrast, with defensive issue preclusion, the same consideration is not given because the plaintiff was the party who initially chose the forum.

Despite varying approaches, preclusion is favored, leading to the conclusion that parties can use the doctrine most effectively in motion practice which, in the case of defensive issue preclusion, may result in the dismissal of the complaint or, as regards offensive issue preclusion, the dismissal or preclusion of a defense.

II. APPLICATION OF DOCTRINES

A. Effect of State Court Judgment in Federal Court

1. Developments since *Allen v. McCurry*

Since *Allen v. McCurry*, the Supreme Court has examined preclusion in the context of three important civil rights cases: *Haring v. Prosise*, 462 U.S. 306 (1983); *Migra v. Warren City School District Bd. of Educ.*, 465 U.S. 75 (1984); and *Parsons Steel, Inc. v. Alabama Bank*, 474 U.S. 518 (1986). The significance of these decisions is that the Court may bar the party who waits until the outcome of the prior state court action on the merits from pursuing federal claims.

At issue in *Haring* was whether plaintiff's § 1983 action to redress an alleged fourth amendment violation was barred by a prior judgment of conviction for manufacturing drugs entered in Virginia state court following a guilty plea.[21] *Allen v. McCurry* specifically left open that question, concluding only that the doctrine of collateral estoppel applies to § 1983 suits against police officers to recover for fourth amendment violations.[22]

The first principle enunciated in *Haring* was that since the estoppel effect of a state court judgment was at issue, a federal court should apply the rules of preclusion that would be applied by the state (here, Virginia) courts, to determine whether a judgment of conviction based on a guilty plea foreclosed

---

[21] *Haring v. Prosise*, 462 U.S. 306, 312 (1983).

[22] *Allen v. McCurry*, 449 U.S. at 105, n.25.

the party in the subsequent civil action from challenging the legality of a search which had produced inculpatory evidence.[23] Under Virginia preclusion rules, the Supreme Court found that Virginia would bar the action if the issue had (a) been actually litigated and (b) determined to be necessary to support the judgment entered.[24]

The second principle decided in *Haring* was that the doctrine of offensive issue preclusion would not be applied when a prior conviction was founded on a guilty plea because (1) the legality of the search of the plaintiff's apartment for drug manufacturing had not actually been litigated; (2) the criminal proceedings did not actually decide against plaintiff any issue to be determined in his subsequent § 1983 claim; and (3) none of the issues he raised in federal court could have been "necessarily" determined because a finding as to whether the police violated plaintiff's fourth amendment rights would not have been essential or even relevant to the trial court's acceptance of his plea.[25]

Another issue which *Allen v. McCurry* left open was the possibility that the preclusive effect of a state-court judgment might be different as to a federal issue that a § 1983 litigant could have raised but did not raise in the earlier state-court proceeding.[26] *Migra v. Warren City School District Bd. of Education*, 465 U.S. 75 (1984), resolved that question in the negative.

In *Migra* the issue was whether a teacher's § 1983 action to redress first, fifth and fourteenth amendment violations was barred by a previous judgment which she obtained in Ohio state court against the same defendant, which found defendant Board of Education had first agreed to renew plaintiff's employment as a teacher but then terminated her.[27] Plaintiff had not asserted any constitutional claims in state court. After an Ohio state court awarded her judgment, plaintiff went to federal court, suing on the theory that the Board's objection and opposition to her role in fashioning a voluntary plan of desegregation in the district schools resulted in her termination and violated her first, fifth and fourteenth amendment rights.[28] The Board raised claim preclusion as a defense.

---

[23] *Haring*, 462 U.S. at 312, 440 U.S. at 96.

[24] *Id.* at 314.

[25] *Id.* at 315.

[26] *Id.* at 316.

[27] *Migra v. Warren City School Dist. Bd. of Education*, 465 U.S. 75, 83 (1984).

[28] *Id.*

Writing for the majority, Justice Blackmun established the principle that for purposes of § 1983 there was no distinction between the issue and claim preclusion effects of a state-court judgment.[29] He decided that the rule in *Allen v. McCurry* (state-court judgments can have preclusive effects in § 1983 suits), applied to issues that actually were decided as well as to those that could have been. He pointed out that plaintiff never argued that the state court would not have adjudicated her federal claims had she pleaded them in her state court complaint. Finally, he chided the unwary plaintiff that she could easily have preserved her § 1983 claims if she had proceeded first in federal court.[30]

Preclusion can have far-reaching significance: even nonparties may be affected by the *Migra* case. Recently the Supreme Court affirmed the Second Circuit's holding that nonparties who choose not to intervene in a lawsuit, the settlement of which may deprive them of equal protection, cannot wait until the conclusion of the action (entry of a consent decree) and collaterally attack the consent decree; rather, they must intervene and present their constitutional claims at the objectors' hearing on the settlement or be barred thereafter from objecting to the decree. *Marino v. Ortiz*, 108 S. Ct. 586 (1988).

In *Parsons Steel, Inc. v. First Alabama Bank*, 474 U.S. 518 (1986),[31] the Supreme Court decided that a federal court is not empowered to issue an injunction to halt enforcement of a state court judgment under the Anti-Injunction Act where the state court had already ruled on the merits of a *res judicata* defense and rejected it. The plaintiffs had sued defendant bank in Alabama state court for fraud. Three months later, plaintiffs sued defendant bank in federal court, alleging the same conduct by the bank violated a federal law (the Bank Holding Company Act). The trial in federal court which preceded the state court trial resulted in a judgment notwithstanding the verdict for the defendant bank. The federal court judgment was affirmed on appeal. The defendant bank then amended its state court pleading and asserted preclusion as a defense in the state action. The state court ruled that the federal court judgment did not bar the state court fraud action. Ultimately, a general verdict was rendered for plaintiffs.

---

29 *Id.* at 84.

30 *Id.* at 85, n.7. Should the federal court abstain from passing on the federal claims, directing plaintiff to go to state court to address state law (contract) issues, all plaintiff had to do to preserve her right to a federal forum was to inform the state court of her intention to return to federal court following litigation of her state court claims.

31 *Parsons Steel, Inc. v. First Alabama Bank*, 474 U.S. 518 (1986).

Having lost in state court, the defendant bank returned to federal court and filed an injunction action against plaintiffs to halt enforcement of the state court judgment. The district court decided that plaintiffs should have raised the state claims in federal court as pendent claims, and having failed to do so, the prior federal judgment n.o.v. against plaintiffs barred the state claims under *res judicata*. The court then enjoined plaintiffs from enforcing the state court judgment on the theory that under an exception to the Anti-Injunction Act, 28 U.S.C. § 2283, it was empowered to be the final adjudicator as to the *res judicata* of its prior judgment on a subsequent state action. The district court decision was affirmed by the circuit court.[32]

The Supreme Court in *Parsons Steel* reminded litigants that under the Full Faith and Credit Act, 28 U.S.C. § 1738, a federal court must give the same preclusive effect to a state-court judgment as another court of that state would give.[33] Neither the Circuit Court of Appeals nor the district court had considered the possible preclusive effect of the state-court judgment under Alabama law, which it found was error.[34] Absent a later statute containing an express repeal of 28 U.S.C. § 1738, the Supreme Court stated that the relitigation exception under the Anti-Injunction Act was limited to those situations in which the state court has not yet ruled on the merits of the *res judicata* issue. Once the state court does rule and rejects the defense of preclusion, the federal court must turn to state law to determine the preclusive effect of the state court decision.[35] Thus, the Supreme Court in *Parsons Steel* reversed the Circuit Court, stating the latter erred by not applying Alabama law on the preclusive effect of the state-court judgment, which did not justify "the highly intrusive remedy of a federal-court injunction against the enforcement of the state-court judgment."[36]

2. Second Circuit Decisions and New York State Preclusion Rules

The Second Circuit has followed the Supreme Court's lead in favoring the use of both offensive and defensive preclusion. At times, though, it has recognized that preclusion can produce harsh results, but even in those instances it has applied it and harshly criticized the party against whom preclusion was applied, as having caused the problem.

---

[32] 747 F.2d at 1376 (11th Cir. 1984) (footnote omitted).

[33] *Parsons Steel*, 474 U.S. at 520.

[34] *Id.*

[35] *Id.*

[36] *Id.*

LaRocca v. Gold, 662 F.2d 144 (2d Cir. 1981), is a noteworthy case that illustrates the Second Circuit's willingness to apply preclusion. The plaintiff was a priest who was also licensed to practice law in New York, and sought, but was not allowed, to wear his clerical collar while trying cases for clients brought on criminal charges before a jury. In the course of three trials, he consistently yet unsuccessfully argued that his first and fourteenth amendment rights were violated. He appealed the rulings and lost.

The priest then filed a §§ 1983 and 1985 civil rights complaint predicated on the same constitutional violations in federal court[37] which was dismissed on the merits.[38] On appeal, the Second Circuit decided the case not on its merits but on issue preclusion grounds. It first found that the issue preclusion doctrine applies not only to § 1983 actions but to § 1985 suits as well. Second, it analyzed how a New York state court would apply the rules of preclusion to the subject of his federal court action. "For a party to be precluded from relitigating an issue two requirements must be met. First, the party must have had a 'full and fair opportunity to contest the decision said to be dispositive of the present controversy' . . . Second, the issue must be identical to the issue in the prior action."[39]

The approach New York state courts have adopted is that of the *Restatement (Second) of Judgments* and the Second Circuit, adhering to that approach, had no trouble finding both requirements were met in *LaRocca*.[40] *LaRocca* is significant because the court applied offensive collateral estoppel, recognized that under New York law the requirement of mutuality of parties has been eliminated and easily extended issue preclusion to a § 1985 civil rights case.[41] Consequently, it barred the action. *Cf. Cameron v. Fogarty*, 806 F.2d 380 (2d Cir. 1986).

---

37 *LaRocca v. Gold*, 662 F.2d at 144 (2d Cir. 1981).

---

38 *Id.* at 145.

---

39 *Id.* at 148 (*citing Gramaton Home Investors Corp. v. Lopez*, 46 N.Y.2d 481 (1979)). Since *LaRocca*, the Second Circuit in *Cameron v. Fogarty*, 806 F.2d 380 (2d Cir. 1986), has added a third requirement: "the issue [was] necessarily decided in the prior proceeding," *citing Capital Telephone Co. v. Pattersonville Telephone Co.*, 56 N.Y.2d 11 (1982).

---

40 *Id.* at 149 (*citing Parklane Hosiery Co., Inc. v. Shore*, 439 U.S. 322 (1979)); *see Blonder-Tongue Laboratories, Inc. v. University of Illinois Foundation*, 402 U.S. 313 (1971) and *Schwartz v. Public Administrator*, 24 N.Y.2d 65 (1969). The Court also relied on *Restatement (Second) of Judgments* § 68, comment C (Tent. Draft No. 4, 1977), for an analysis of whether the issue plaintiff raised had he been allowed to *voir dire* the jury on the possible bias caused by his continuing to wear the collar at trial created a different issue for collateral estoppel purposes. The Court found that it did not. *See also Reilly v. Reid*, 45 N.Y.2d 24 (1978).

---

41 *Id.*

Two later cases, *Gargiul v. Tompkins*, 790 F.2d 265 (2d Cir. 1986), and *Golkin v. Abrams*, 803 F.2d 55 (2d Cir. 1986), show the Second Circuit's inclination to find preclusion in different contexts. *Gargiul v. Tompkins* involved a teacher who was terminated on the grounds of incompetency and suspended without pay. In state administrative proceedings and in a separate state court proceeding under Article 78, she unsuccessfully challenged her suspension. In a second Article 78 proceeding, she tried again unsuccessfully to raise the propriety of her suspension and, for the first time, challenged her dismissal.[42] The Appellate Division affirmed the denial of relief.

Plaintiff then brought a § 1983 action challenging the constitutionality of both her termination and suspension of pay. The Second Circuit affirmed the district court's dismissal of the termination claim but refused to bar her claim for suspension of pay based on denial of procedural due process because that claim had not been litigated in either state court action. It reached the merits, held that the Board had acted arbitrarily in suspending plaintiff and remanded for determination of damages.

While the defendants were appealing the Second Circuit ruling to the Supreme Court, *Migra v. Warren City School District Bd. of Educ.*, *supra*, was decided. In its wake the Supreme Court remanded the *Gargiul* case to the Second Circuit for reconsideration.[43] The Second Circuit was instructed to consider the claim preclusive effect of the prior state court litigation on plaintiff's federal claim for suspension of pay based on denial of procedural due process. *Migra* had held that state-court judgments can have preclusive effects in § 1983 suits as to issues that actually were decided as well as to those that could have been.

The Second Circuit addressed the issue thus "we cannot ignore the reality that the critical facts underlying Gargiul's claim were available for presentation in court at the time of *Gargiul I* [the first state court Article 78 proceeding] as at any time thereafter."[44] The Court then hypothesized that had the Appellate Division directly considered the point, it would have found the claim was also barred by the preclusive effect of the first Article 78 petition.[45] It concluded that New York state courts would have required plaintiff to join in the first Article 78 petition all her available challenges to the

---

[42] *Gargiul v. Tompkins*, 739 F.2d 34, 36 (2d Cir. 1984), *aff'd*, 790 F.2d 265 (2d Cir. 1986).

[43] *Tompkins v. Gargiul*, 465 U.S. 1016 (1984).

[44] 790 F.2d at 270.

[45] *Id.*

decision to suspend her without pay.[46] It rejected plaintiff's argument that she lacked a full and fair opportunity to be heard, finding nothing in the record to support the argument.[47] Indeed, as a final blow to a teacher who had been litigating her suspension-without-pay claim for ten years, the Second Circuit sharply criticized plaintiff for having been unable to have "any body, administrative or judicial, state or federal, effectively adjudicate the merits of her constitutional claim" by her "own untimeliness and the multiplicity of her challenges to a single transaction."[48]

In an election case, *Golkin v. Abrams*, 803 F.2d 55 (2d Cir. 1986), the Second Circuit similarly criticized the plaintiffs, two candidates excluded from the primary ballot, for failing to raise all of their claims (including federal constitutional claims) in their prior state court action and applied the rule of offensive issue preclusion to dismiss their federal suit. The State Supreme Court, as affirmed by the Appellate Division, had previously found that both had failed to comply with New York Election Laws requiring a separate designating petition for each candidate with a cover sheet listing each candidate separately. (They had filed one joint petition and one joint cover sheet.)

3. Practical Considerations

(a) Under cases interpreting the Full Faith and Credit Clause and § 1738, a state-court judgment's preclusive effect will be applied by a federal district court in the same manner as it would by a state court.

(b) Under New York law, the state preclusion test is whether: (1) the party to be precluded had a full and fair opportunity to contest the decision/issue said to be dispositive of the later action; (2) the issue was identical to the issue in the prior action; and (3) the issue was necessarily decided in the prior proceeding. It is the identical test that a state court will apply if presented with the issue. *See, e.g., Gargiul, supra.*

(c) Parties should consider very early on (before commencing an action or administrative proceeding) whether they have constitutional or federal claims and defenses to raise and if so, whether they ought to be asserted at the

---

46 *Id.* at 271. The Second Circuit also reviewed the nature of plaintiff's legal challenge as to her claim for suspension pay in the first Article 78 petition. Plaintiff had advanced both a statutory right to her pay but also due process right to compensation. It was a claim "necessarily challenging the lawfulness of the suspension itself" which went to the merits. *Id.*

47 *Id.* at 273-74.

48 *Id.* at 274. In dissent, Judge Oakes defended plaintiff's litigation tactics and decided that under New York law state courts would not agree with the all-inclusive claim preclusive effect of the majority. *Id.* at 276.

same time or in the same forum. A review of the federal compulsory counterclaim rule is advised. If parties do not assert all claims or defenses, but await the outcome of a state court action, they risk being precluded from litigating them at a later date in federal court. *See, e.g., Migra, supra; LaRocca, supra.*

(d) Parties are not discouraged from bringing proper federal claims to federal court—the issue is when to do so. The Supreme Court in *Migra, supra,* chided plaintiff for not presenting her civil rights claims sooner by filing her federal constitutional claims in federal court first, followed by a state court action. It suggested one method to preserve federal claims is to ask a federal court to abstain from deciding them until the parties fully litigate state claims in state court. Another obvious alternative is to bring all claims in federal court. *But see Murphy v. Gallagher, infra* and discussion which follows *infra* (B).

(e) If a party takes the *Migra* approach, commences a federal action based solely on federal constitutional claims and begins a state suit premised on state common law causes of action, the party also ought to compare the breadth of the federal allegations with the state causes so as to avoid, if possible, an overlap in issues presented and related fact-finding. A party should also inform the state court of its intention to return to federal court following litigation of the state court claims. For further suggestions, *see* discussion *infra*.

B. The Effect of Failure to Raise Exclusively Federal Claims in State Court

1. Supreme Court Decisions

Suppose an aggrieved party has an exclusively federal claim, such as an antitrust claim and at the same time, has a state common law claim based on the same facts. If the party commences the state court suit first based solely on the common law claim, will it be precluded thereafter from pursuing its federal court claim, given the exclusively federal nature of an antitrust claim? The answer turns on whether the preclusion law of New York has recognized or would recognize the theory of the case or the remedy sought in the later federal court action.

In *Marrese v. American Academy of Orthopaedic Surgeons*, 470 U.S. 373 (1985), the Supreme Court addressed the issue under Illinois law in the context of an antitrust claim. Orthopaedic surgeons, who were excluded from membership in the American Academy of Orthopaedic Surgeons, initially filed state court actions in Illinois, alleging that the denial of membership violated their common law right to association.[49] The court dismissed the suits for failure to state a cause of action. The surgeons then filed a federal antitrust suit, alleging the Academy had "monopoly power," that they were denied membership in order to discourage competition and that their exclusion constituted a boycott in violation of § 1 of the Sherman Act.[50] The Supreme Court decided that the federal antitrust suit was not barred, reversing the Seventh Circuit.[51]

The Supreme Court found that the federal court had not referred to the preclusion law of Illinois in which the judgment of dismissal had been issued, contrary to the requirements of 28 U.S.C. § 1738.[52] Citing two examples of exclusively federal actions,[53] the Supreme Court indicated it was possible to have issue preclusive effect of a state court judgment in a subsequent patent suit or claim of employment discrimination under Title VII of the Civil Rights Act of 1964, even though those claims could not have originally been brought in state court. The converse was also true. If the state law of preclusion did not direct preclusion in federal court of the federal claim, then a federal court is not barred from entertaining the action. Although it was clear that a state court will not have decided the specific issue raised in *Marrese* (whether a state judgment has preclusive effect of the exclusively federal antitrust claim), nevertheless, the federal court was instructed to rely on state preclusion principles to determine the extent to which an earlier state judgment bars subsequent litigation.[54]

The test whether a state judgment has preclusive effect is that expressed in the *Restatement (Second) of Judgments* § 26(1)(c): "claim preclusion generally does not apply where the plaintiff was unable to rely on a certain theory of the case or seek a certain remedy because of the limitations on the subject matter jurisdiction of the courts."[55] If Illinois law paralleled the Restatement, then the earlier state court judgment would have no preclusive effect on the

---

[49] *Marrese v. American Academy of Orthopaedic Surgeons*, 470 U.S. 373, 375 (1985).

[50] *Id.* at 376.

[51] *Id.* at 378.

[52] *Id.* at 380.

[53] *Id.* at 381.

[54] *Id.* at 382.

[55] *Id.*

surgeons' antitrust claim in federal court.[56] Only if state law did provide the theory of the case or remedy sought, would the first action bar the subsequent federal claim and the issue of whether there is an exception to § 1738 would arise.[57] In *Marrese* the Supreme Court never articulated what the exception might be.

Since the majority opinion gave no guidance as to how the district court should proceed if Illinois state preclusion law were silent or indeterminate on the claim preclusion issue, Chief Justice Burger suggested an approach in his concurring opinion.[58] If Illinois state law provided a cause of action that is virtually identical with the federal antitrust claim, he said, the surgeons should be barred from suing in federal court, as they would have been provided a "full and fair opportunity" in state court to litigate their rights.[59]

It is worthy of attention that in *Marrese*, the majority rejected the facile approach suggested by the Seventh Circuit that the surgeons be encouraged to sue in federal court alleging pendent state claims in one tidy forum.[60] "We have parallel systems of state and federal courts, and the concerns of comity reflected in § 1738 generally allow states to determine the preclusive scope of their own courts' judgments."[61]

2. Second Circuit Decisions

Thus far, the Second Circuit has considered under New York state court preclusion rules whether the antitrust and Securities Exchange Act of 1934 are exclusively federal remedies and, hence, not barred by a prior state court judgment. See *Andrea Theatres, Inc. v. Theatre Confections, Inc.*, 787 F.2d 59 (2d Cir. 1986); *Murphy v. Gallagher*, 761 F.2d 878 (2d Cir. 1985).

Since *Marrese v. American Academy of Orthopaedic Surgeons, supra*, was decided, the Second Circuit has not addressed any other areas of exclusively federal jurisdiction with respect to that issue. The gap obviously leaves some uncertainty; in the absence of Second Circuit cases, reference to other Circuit Court decisions is necessary.

---

[56] *Id.*

[57] *Id.* at 383.

[58] *Id.* at 388.

[59] *Id.* at 391.

[60] *Id.* at 385.

[61] *Id.*, citing *Allen v. McCurry*, 449 U.S. at 96.

a. Securities Laws

In *Murphy v. Gallagher*, the Second Circuit decided that federal securities laws are not exclusive remedies, and, therefore, it precluded a later federal action predicated on the same facts and issues decided against the plaintiffs in a state court corporate dissolution proceeding. Interestingly, plaintiffs had initially tried to bring all of their claims to federal court and failed. The minority stockholders, who claimed they were prevented from purchasing shares of stock in a closely-held corporation, filed a federal court action alleging violations of § 10(b) of the Securities and Exchange Act of 1934 and Rule 10b-5. They charged that the corporation's directors, stockholders and related corporations had engaged in a scheme to defraud them in connection with the sale of the corporation's stock.[62] The complaint included thirteen pendent state claims.[63]

On the defendants' Rule 12(b)(6) motion, the district court initially dismissed the pendent state claims because (1) they substantially predominated the federal claim and (2) some fifteen pendent parties substantially outnumbered the five defendants to the federal claim. Additionally, the court narrowed the federal § 10(b)-5 claim to one theory—an alleged conspiracy to seize control of the family corporation.[64] The minority stockholders then filed a state court proceeding for corporate dissolution, alleging illegal, fraudulent and oppressive actions toward them, along with waste and mismanagement of corporate assets.[65] The state court decided after trial that there had been no illegal, fraudulent or oppressive actions by the directors or those in control toward the minority stockholders and dismissed the suit.[66] When the district court learned about the dismissal, it decided the federal securities action was barred and dismissed the complaint.[67]

---

[62] *Murphy v. Gallagher*, 761 F.2d 878, 880 (2d Cir. 1985).

[63] The thirteen claims alleged corporate waste and mismanagement, improper exclusion of one of the plaintiffs from the management of and wrongful discharge from the corporation, and breach of the shareholder agreements. Six of the state causes of action were asserted only against the corporate defendants. *Id.* at 880.

[64] *Id.*

[65] *Id.* at 881.

[66] *Id.*

[67] *Id.*

On appeal, the Second Circuit closely followed Chief Justice Burger's suggested approach in *Marrese*.[68] It referred to the preclusion law of New York in which the judgment of dismissal had been issued and asked: first, was there an identity of issue which had necessarily been decided in the prior action and was decisive in the federal action, and, second, whether there had been full and fair opportunity to contest the decision said to be controlling.[69]

The Second Circuit determined that the plaintiffs had asserted in the state court dissolution petition the narrow and precise issues that the federal court delineated be alleged in the federal court.[70] It also found that the plaintiffs had their day—in state court.[71]

Importantly, the Second Circuit found in the record no proof that the parties had, as plaintiff urged on appeal, met with the state judge informally in his chambers and had agreed—because of the pending federal action—not to litigate the issues concerning the stock sale. It also found no agreement by the parties to do so in the record and underscored plaintiffs' failure to amend the state court petition to preserve their federal claim as well as eliminate that issue from the state court trial.[72]

Having found plaintiffs were barred under state law principles of preclusion from litigating their federal claims, the Second Circuit then reviewed the federal securities laws to determine whether they gave exclusively federal remedies and provided an exception to or repeal of the Full Faith and Credit Statute, 42 U.S. § 1738. The Court decided that Congress was aware of the long-established state securities laws and common law fraud in enacting the federal Securities Acts. Moreover, Congress did not intend to render the federal securities laws exclusively federal.[73] Rather, the legal principles governing the application of § 10(b) and Rule 10b-5 (components such as intent, scienter, fraud and deceit) actually involve issues regularly adjudicated in state courts, resulting in a "fair overlap between the state and federal claims"

---

[68] *Marrese v. American Academy of Orthopaedic Surgeons*, 470 U.S. 373, 375 (1985).

[69] *Murphy v. Gallagher*, 761 F.2d 878, 882 (citing *Schwartz v. Public Administrator*, 24 N.Y.2d 65, 71 (1969)).

[70] *Id.*

[71] *Id.*

[72] *Id.* at 884.

[73] *Id.* at 885.

when the focus is on narrow issues.[74] Had the plaintiffs prevailed on their state common law fraud causes of action, they would have obtained the same relief as that sought in federal court.[75] The Second Circuit, therefore, affirmed the district court judgment and barred plaintiffs from relitigating them in federal court.

b. Antitrust Laws

The Second Circuit has decided that federal antitrust laws do provide exclusively federal remedies, so that a prior state court judgment does not bar a later federal suit for treble damages. *Andrea Theatres, Inc. v. Theatre Confections, Inc.*, 787 F.2d 59 (2d Cir. 1986) *(citing Lyons v. Westinghouse Elec. Corp.*, 222 F.2d 184, 189 (2d Cir.), *cert. denied*, 350 U.S. 825 (1955)).[76] The suits alleged violations of §§ 1, 2 of the Sherman Act, §§ 1, 2, 3 of the Clayton Act and § 13 of the Robinson-Patman Acts. In both suits, the Second Circuit found that a party may raise antitrust defenses to a state court action but must resort to federal court to obtain affirmative relief (*i.e.*, treble damages).[77] Thus, even if a state court rejected a federal antitrust defense, it is doubtful whether the state defendant would be precluded from exerting it as a basis for affirmative relief in the federal suit: "The grant to the district courts of exclusive jurisdiction over the action for treble damages should be taken to imply an immunity of their decisions from any prejudgment elsewhere."[78] The implication is that since an antitrust claim cannot be adjudicated except in federal court, a state court action cannot bar it.[79]

c. Copyright Laws

In the absence of Second Circuit precedent, it is necessary to turn to other circuit decisions for guidance. At present, only the Sixth Circuit has considered the question of whether the federal copyright laws provide exclusively federal claims or theories of the case, summarily concluding that they do.

---

[74] *Id.*

---

[75] *Id.*

---

[76] *Andrea Theatres, Inc. v. Theatre Confections, Inc.*, 787 F.2d 59 (2d Cir. 1986), *Lyons v. Westinghouse Electric Corp.*, 222 F.2d 184 (2d Cir.), *cert. denied*, 350 U.S. 825 (1955).

---

[77] *Andrea Theatres, Inc.*, 787 at 63; *Lyons*, 222 F.2d at 189.

---

[78] *Lyons*, 222 F.2d at 189. Other circuit courts are in accord. *Marrese v. Academy of Orthopedic Surgeons*, 628 F. Supp. 918 (N.D. Ill. 1986) [on remand from Supreme Court, 470 U.S. 373 (1985)] citing *Marrese v. American Academy of Orthopedic Surgeons*, 726 F.2d at 1155-1156 (7th Cir. 1984).

---

[79] *Id.*

Forry, Inc. v. Neundorfer, Inc., 837 F.2d 259, 265 (6th Cir. 1988). The Circuit Court never reached the issue, however, whether the federal copyright laws constitute an exception to the Full Faith and Credit Statute, 42 U.S.C. § 1738, primarily because on the facts which the case presented, it did not have to do so.[80] Following the reasoning of *Marrese*, the Circuit Court applied Ohio preclusion law and determined that the second federal suit did not involve the same facts or infringing product as the prior state court suit.[81] Therefore, although the court considers copyright remedies exclusively federal, *Forry* is not as helpful as it might be.

d. Patent Suits

The Federal Circuit has followed *Marrese* and decided that although a federal court has exclusive jurisdiction of patent suits, a prior state court judgment finding of non-infringement in a contract dispute involving the nonpayment of royalties barred relitigation in federal court of a claim of patent infringement, under the doctrine of defensive collateral estoppel. *MGA, Inc. v. General Motors Corp.*, 827 F.2d 729 (Fed. Cir. 1987). If collateral estoppel is asserted defensively, as did General Motors in *MGA*, then the party sued who previously prevailed in state court against the patentee because of non-infringement could bar the later patent suit.[82] Again, the Circuit Court did not address whether federal patent suits (*e.g.*, which may involve validity and infringement) by virtue of their exclusively federal nature, constitute exceptions to the Full Faith and Credit Statute. However, the reasoning of the court on the question of "identity of issues" in a prior infringement action, indicates the answer is no.

3. Practical Considerations

(a) Before commencing a suit or asserting a defense to one, parties should determine whether they have exclusively federal claims to raise or defenses to assert besides state claims and counterclaims.

(b) Particularly where the federal securities laws are implicated, consider whether and the extent to which there may be an overlap in the factual allegations, the theories of the case or the relief sought by the federal and state claims or defenses.

(c) Simultaneously analyze the possible preclusive effect of the exclusively federal claim, first by applying state law principles of preclusion, and

---

80 837 F.2d at 265.

81 *Id.*

82 827 F.2d at 734-35.

second by examining whether there is an exception or partial repeal of the Full Faith and Credit Statute, 28 U.S.C. § 1738, under the existing case law.

(d) Make a record in writing acknowledging to your adversary and to the court(s) of the concerns you have about and plans for dealing with preclusion. Make certain that the pleadings (complaint or answer) and amendments to pleadings reflect your concerns. If necessary, protect your record during oral conferences by arranging for a transcript so as to avoid a result similar to *Murphy v. Gallagher, supra.*

(e) Act on the position taken. If possible, move to dismiss claims which are possibly precluded by earlier court determinations. The motion, if successful, may narrow discovery and the issues for trial. Alternatively, consider moving to dismiss the defense of preclusion if you believe it is not well-founded or weak.

(f) If you are litigating in state court on only state claims, take special care when presenting a charge to the jury so that it is not phrased broadly enough to later undercut, subserve or decide any federal issues or claims you are asserting or may wish to assert in a separate action.

C. Effect of State Court Agency Judgment in Federal Court

In *Kremer v. Chemical Construction Corp.*, 456 U.S. 461 (1982), the Supreme Court decided to preclude a Title VII claim of employment discrimination brought in federal court after the New York State Division of Human Rights dismissed a state law discrimination claim for lack of probable cause.[83] The dismissal by the Division of Human Rights, which was affirmed by its Appeal Board, was also upheld by the Appellate Division of the New York State Supreme Court.[84] When Kremer's employer was sued under Title VII in federal court, it moved to dismiss on the grounds of claim preclusion. Despite the exclusive federal subject matter jurisdiction of a Title VII action, the Supreme Court affirmed the Second Circuit's bar of the district court action.

The Supreme Court decided that by enacting Title VII, Congress did not intend to repeal existing state antidiscriminatory legislation, allow an exception to the Full Faith and Credit Statute, or provide an absolute right to relitigate in federal court an issue resolved by state court. It applied a two-prong test to Kremer's Title VII claim. First, it analyzed whether the issue to be resolved by the district court was identical to the issue already decided by

---

[83] *Kremer v. Chemical Construction Corp.*, 456 U.S. 461 (1982).

[84] *See id.* at 470-72; *see also id.* at 472 n.10 (petitioner failed to make an affirmative showing of a clear and manifest congressional intent to repeal § 1738 by implication).

the Division of Human Rights.[85] The Court reasoned that the state agency decided the same issue of discrimination as the District Court would need to determine in the plaintiff's Title VII claim.[86] Second, the Court concluded that Kremer had had a full and fair opportunity to litigate the merits of his employment discrimination charge before the state courts.[87] In this regard, *Kremer* is significant not only because the Supreme Court decided that a federal court must apply state court standards as to whether there was "full and fair opportunity to be heard," but also because litigants who do not appeal an adverse agency determination are not precluded from seeking *de novo* review in a later Title VII action but those who do so appeal, as Kremer did, are precluded.[88]

1. Second Circuit Decisions

In contrast to *Kremer*, in *Hill v. Coca Cola Bottling Company*,[89] the Second Circuit was presented with a prior state agency determination on an issue that differed from the issue to be determined in a subsequent Title VII action. As may be expected, the Circuit Court held that a finding by a state unemployment insurance proceeding that an employee violated company policy did not collaterally estop the employee from relitigating a racial discrimination issue in a subsequent Title VII action.[90]

---

[85] 456 U.S. at 477.

[86] *Id.* The Court also ruled that the comity and federalism interests furthered by § 1738 are not compromised by applying *res judicata* and collateral estoppel in Title VII cases. *Id.* at 478. Instead, the Court reasoned that excepting federal courts in Title VII actions from applying *res judicata* and collateral estoppel will be "stripping State court judgments of finality," and will deter petitioners from seeking State court review. *Id.* at 477.

[87] *Id.* at 479-80.

[88] *Id.* In his dissent, Justice Blackmun criticized the majority's analysis as ignoring the dictates of Title VII. *Id.* at 493 (Blackmun, J., dissenting). Justice Blackmun reasoned that the Appellate Division did not review the merits of Kremer's discrimination claim; rather, the state court held that the ruling of the Appeal Board of the New York Human Rights Division was not arbitrary or capricious. Thus, he asserted that the majority had not held that a federal court must give a state court judgment preclusive effect, but rather that the petitioner's claim was barred based on the administrative agency's no-probable-cause ruling. *Id.* at 492-93. Justice Blackmun argued that the Court disregarded the mandate under Title VII that an adverse state agency decision will not bar a petitioner's subsequent Title VII claim. *Id.* at 493.

[89] 786 F.2d 550 (2d Cir. 1986).

[90] *Id.* at 553.

Hill was an employee who resigned after he could not explain to his employer his approval of sample gifts.[91] Hill protested the resignation in three ways: (1) he filed with the New York State Department of Labor for unemployment insurance benefits, (2) he filed claims under 42 U.S.C. §§ 1981, 1983 and Title VII in federal court, and (3) he filed a complaint with the Human Rights Division alleging that he had been treated discriminatorily.[92]

Hill was denied unemployment insurance benefits by the New York State Department of Labor on the ground that he violated company policy by approving sample gifts. An administrative law judge affirmed the agency's denial of insurance benefits. His affirmance was upheld by the Unemployment Insurance Appeal Board.[93] Hill sought further review (Article 78 proceeding) in state court. The Third Department affirmed the Supreme Court's approval of the Unemployment Insurance of the Appeal Board.[94]

Meanwhile Hill filed a racial discrimination claim under 42 U.S.C. §§ 1981, 1983 and Title VII in federal district court. At the same time, he filed a complaint with the Human Rights Division on the same grounds, which he withdrew, deciding instead to pursue his remedy in federal court.[95]

The Second Circuit was asked by Judge Weinstein, pursuant to certification under 28 U.S.C. § 1292(b), to address his denial of defendants' motion for summary judgment on the grounds that Hill was estopped by the state unemployment insurance proceeding from pursuing his Title VII claim.[96] The Second Circuit applied New York law on preclusion and found that since the plaintiff did not have a "full and fair opportunity" to litigate his discrimination claim before the state insurance agency proceeding, the plaintiff was not collaterally estopped from relitigating his discrimination claim in federal court. Having made that determination, the court did not reach or address either the identity-of-issues element or the necessarily decided element of collateral estoppel.[97]

---

91 *Id.* at 551.

92 *Id.*

93 *Id.*

94 *Id.* at 552.

95 *Id.* at 552.

96 *Id.*

97 *Id.* at 553.

In reaching this conclusion, the Circuit Court adopted the rationale of the Appellate Division, Second Department in *Board of Educ. v. New York State Human Rights Appeal Board*.[98] The court held that since New York State has two separate state agencies for hearing discrimination and unemployment insurance complaints, a claimant could not have foreseen that an application for unemployment benefits would bar a subsequent antidiscrimination complaint.[99] Hill's having filed simultaneously with both agencies did not bar his present suit because they "barely touched on the discrimination claim."[100]

Hill is significant because it shows that when issues decided by one state agency differ from those of a later federal action, the later suit will not be barred. *Hill* also teaches litigants to choose their forums wisely. Had Hill pursued his remedy before the Human Rights Division, he would clearly have been in a *Kremer* situation and been precluded from bringing the federal suit.

In *Fay v. South Colonie School District*, 802 F.2d 21 (2d Cir. 1986), the Second Circuit held that a plaintiff who litigated in a state agency his right under federal law to receive notices from his children's school was not thereafter precluded in a § 1983 action from relitigating a federal statutory claim.[101]

In *Fay*, a father with joint custody of his children demanded that the school superintendent mail him all school-related notices.[102] Although he advised the school that under the Family Educational Rights and Privacy Act ("FERPA")[103] it was required to mail a parent the education records of his children, the school refused. He appealed to the New York Commissioner of Education,[104] who dismissed Fay's appeal for timeliness, but who also opined that mailing all school-related notices to him would place an unrea-

---

98 106 A.D.2d 364, 482 N.Y.S.2d 495 (2d Dep't 1984).

---

99 786 F.2d at 554.

---

100 *Id.*

---

101 802 F.2d 21 (2d Cir. 1986).

---

102 *Id.* at 24.

---

103 20 U.S.C. § 1232(g) (1982).

---

104 *See id.* at 25; N.Y. Educ. Law § 310 (McKinney 1969 & Supp. 1986).

sonable burden on the school district.[105] An Article 78 proceeding was then dismissed, and the dismissal affirmed by the Appellate Division.

Fay then commenced a § 1983 action in the district court, alleging that the school district had violated his rights under FERPA, his due process right to control the upbringing of his children, his right to equal protection, and his state law right as a joint custodial parent, seeking compensatory damages. The district court granted plaintiff summary judgment and denied the school district's motion that plaintiff be precluded from pursuing his claim based on the judgment of dismissal of the Commissioner of Education.[106]

The Second Circuit ruled that it could not decide whether the Commissioner's dismissal of plaintiff's appeal on procedural grounds was rational and supported by the record or even whether the Commissioner's additional comments on the merits of plaintiff's action (*i.e.*, the burden on the school district to mail all school-related notices) were rational.[107] The Second Circuit also found it impossible to conclude from the subsequent, vague decision dismissing Fay's Article 78 petition that "substantive issues raised by Fay [were] necessary to reach the decision to dismiss the case."[108] *Cf. Bray v. New York Life Insurance*, No. 87-7963, slip. op. at 4632 (2d Cir. June 28, 1988). Accordingly, it affirmed summary judgment for plaintiff and denied defendant's preclusion motion.

2. Practical Considerations

(a) Parties who obtain an ambiguous decision on the merits of their state court proceeding, or its appeal, should consider pursuing fresh relief in federal court, particularly as in *Fay, supra*, where there is no finding on the merits that could preclude counsel from relitigating the issue. The discrimination issue that Fay raised had not been "finally resolved" in the sense dictated by state court preclusion principles so as to bar his later suit.

(b) In determining whether to seek review of a state agency decision by Article 78 in state court, a party should analyze its possible preclusive effect on a subsequent federal court claim. Under *Kremer, Hill* and *Fay, supra*, a district court will determine whether the identical factual or legal issue to be decided was already, in fact, decided by the state court. The review of an

---

105 802 F.2d at 25.

106 *Id.* at 24.

107 *Id.* at 30.

108 *Id.*

agency decision in state court is narrow: whether the agency's decision was "arbitrary and capricious." That very limited appellate inquiry may not provide a party with a meaningful, "fair and full opportunity to litigate" the merits of the issue.

D. Effect of Unreviewed State Agency Decision in Federal Court

From the discussion *supra*, one area untouched by preclusion seems to involve a federal suit instituted after an unappealed state agency decision. *McDonald v. City of West Branch*, 466 U.S. 284 (1984), initially set that as the outer limits of preclusion. Of late, however, even unappealed agency decisions can have marked preclusive effect.

In *McDonald*, when plaintiff was discharged from the city police force, he arbitrated the cause for his termination as provided under a collective bargaining agreement. Instead of appealing the finding that there had been "just cause" for his discharge, he sued in federal court pursuant to 42 U.S.C. § 1983, alleging that he had been discharged for exercising his first amendment rights of freedom of speech, of association and to petition the government for redress.[109] The Sixth Circuit reversed judgment in plaintiff's favor but the Supreme Court reversed the Sixth Circuit, holding that a federal court should not give preclusive effect to an arbitration award because an arbitration is not a "judicial proceeding" within the meaning of the Full Faith and Credit Statute, 28 U.S.C. § 1738, and, therefore, the statute does not apply to arbitration awards.[110]

The Supreme Court considered when it was appropriate for a court to fashion the rule that arbitrations were not "judicial proceedings," citing two cases where it had previously rejected the suggestion.[111] Since Congress intended Title VII actions or claims for minimum wages under the Fair Labor Standards Acts, for example, to be judicially enforceable, the Court decided that an arbitrator should not usurp the role of the courts or substitute for judicial proceedings.[112] Moreover, § 1983 created a "cause of action," specifically placing the courts in the position of defending people's federal

---

[109] *McDonald v. West Branch*, 466 U.S. 284, 287 (1984).

[110] *Id.* at 287-388. The statute does apply to acts of state legislatures and records of state courts—but arbitration "obviously falls into neither of these categories." *Id.* at 288 n.7.

[111] *Alexander v. Gardner-Denver Co.*, 415 U.S. 36 (1974) and *Barrentine v. Arkansas-Best Freight System, Inc.*, 450 U.S. 728 (1981).

[112] *McDonald v. West Branch*, 466 at 289.

rights.[113] The Supreme Court also did not consider an arbitrator necessarily having the expertise needed to resolve complex legal questions that arise under § 1983 actions. As creature of contract, an arbitrator was not a factfinder and lacked authority to invoke public laws in order to decide a claim presented by an employee (as opposed to one asserted by the union at arbitration on behalf of that employee).

Two years later, the Supreme Court had occasion to revisit the subject of the preclusive effect of an unreviewed arbitration award in *University of Tennessee v. Elliott*, 106 S. Ct. 3220 (1986), and cut back on its holding in *McDonald*. Elliott, a black employee discharged for inadequate work performance, initially requested an administrative hearing but before trial also filed suit in federal court pursuant to Title VII and the Reconstruction civil rights statutes. The district court allowed the administrative hearing to proceed and then gave preclusive effect to the university administrator's later finding of "no racial motivation in the discharge." On review from the Court of Appeals, the Supreme Court reaffirmed the *McDonald* rule that the Full Faith and Credit Statute does not require the determination that plaintiff was not discriminated be given preclusive effect to a Title VII claim, but also curiously concluded that a district court *may give* preclusive effect to the findings of a university administrator and bar a federal civil rights action brought under the Constitution, the Reconstruction Civil Rights Statutes and 42 U.S.C. § 1983.[114]

Contrary to the opinion of the majority, three Justices (Stevens, Brennan and Blackmun) dissented. They sharply criticized the majority's schizophrenic approach, *i.e.*, ruling that state administrative findings may establish preclusion as to the claims under the civil rights acts, at the same time as the same issues are relitigated under a Title VII claim.[115] "Litigants will presumably forego state administrative determinations in order to protect their entitlement to a federal forum."[116] As acerbic as the dissent is, the *University of Tennessee's* holding nevertheless stands; *Elliott* will compel a party to choose a federal forum in the first instance for the litigation of all claims brought under the Constitution and the Reconstruction civil rights statutes to avoid any possible negative administrative fact-finding.

---

[113] *Id.* at 290.

[114] *University of Tennessee v. Elliott*, 106 S. Ct. 3220, 3227 (1986).

[115] *Id.* at 3227, n.1.

[116] *Id.* at 3228.

1. Second Circuit Decision

In *Kirkland v. City of Peekskill*, 651 F. Supp. 1225 (S.D.N.Y. 1987), the Southern District of New York closely adhered to the teachings of *Elliott*, and dismissed a police commissioner's complaint of racial discrimination brought under 42 U.S.C. §§ 1983, 1985 and 2000e. As in *Elliott*, plaintiff Kirkland had first proceeded to air his complaint with the New York State Division of Human Rights, lost, but did not appeal.[117] The Southern District distinguished the case from one brought under Title VII, and held that the Division of Human Rights functioned in a "quasi-judicial capacity." The court also found the issues of fact were identical to his federal constitutional claims of discrimination and that plaintiff had an adequate opportunity to litigate.[118] Additionally, for that matter, *Kirkland* parallels the analysis and holding of *Kremer, supra*.

2. Practical Considerations

(a) On civil rights claims brought under 42 U.S.C. §§ 1983, 1985, 1986, 2000e, the Constitution, and Reconstruction Civil Rights Statutes, litigants get one bite of the apple. They cannot litigate that claim in two courts or forums. Parties should, therefore, choose carefully whether their claim should proceed in a state administrative agency followed by state appellate review or federal courts.

(b) If a party has a Title VII claim, an unreviewed administrative award will not preclude *de novo* federal court review.

E. How Does the Government Fare?

The Supreme Court has excepted the government as a litigant from the onus of offensive issue preclusion, an exception which the Second Circuit had even previously recognized. In *Olegario v. U.S.*, 629 F.2d 204 (2d Cir. 1980), *cert. denied*, 450 U.S. 980 (1981), plaintiff was a Philippine citizen who had served in the U.S. Army during World War II. Although expressly eligible to apply for naturalization by statute due to his service in the U.S. Army, he failed to apply in a timely fashion, probably because he was unaware of the law. When he did try to apply, there was no U.S. Consular Official then assigned to the Philippines who could accept his petition. Years later, he brought suit in federal court, contending that his constitutional rights had been violated by the absence of a U.S. representative in the Philippines. He relied on a case entitled *In re Naturalization of 68 Philippino War Vet-*

---

[117] *Kirkland v. City of Peekskill*, 651 F. Supp. 1225 (S.D.N.Y. 1987) (Lasker, J.).

[118] *Id.* at 1231.

erans, 406 F. Supp. 931 (N.D. Cal. 1975), in which the Government previously brought a suit on the identical facts by 68 other Philippino war veterans who were similarly situated. In that action, the Government had also failed to appeal the judgment ordering it to offer citizenship to the 68 Philippinos.

The Second Circuit reversed the grant of relief and decided that the doctrine of offensive collateral estoppel could not be invoked against the Government which failed to appeal an adverse decision. Distinguishing *Parklane Hosiery Co. v. Shore*, 439 U.S. 322 (1979), the Second Circuit was guided by far different policy considerations; here, the Government's decision not to appeal may result from a variety of factors—scarcity of resources, potential impact, public interest—which were unrelated to the issues of the case.[119] It denied plaintiff Olegario the right to use offensive issue preclusion against the Government.

U.S. v. Mendoza, 464 U.S. 154 (1984), followed shortly thereafter with a different plaintiff but the identical facts. A Philippine national, Mendoza, applied for naturalization asserting that the Government's administration of the Nationality Act denied him due process of law.[120] Neither the district court or the Ninth Circuit ever reached the merits of his claim because they held the Government was collaterally estopped from litigating that constitutional issue in view of *In re Naturalization of 68 Philippino War Veterns*, supra, 406 F. Supp. at 931 (N.D. Cal. 1975). The Supreme Court decided the case exactly as the Second Circuit did in *Olegario, supra*, holding that for the same policy reasons, the doctrine of nonmutual offensive collateral estoppel does not apply to the Government.[121] The Government is not in a position identical to that of a private litigant[122] such that applying the rule strictly would thwart its development of important questions of law by freezing the first final decision rendered on a particular issue. The Government would be barred from using a "test case approach" to litigation, as it must do, in order to function properly.

Decided the same day as *Mendoza, supra*, was *U.S. v. Stauffer Chemical Co.*, 464 U.S. 165 (1984), in which the Supreme Court held that the doctrine of defensive issue preclusion is applicable against the Government.[123] There

---

[119] 629 F.2d 204, 215.

---

[120] *U.S. v. Mendoza*, 464 U.S. 154 (1984).

---

[121] *Id.* at 158.

---

[122] *Id.*

---

[123] *U.S. v. Stauffer Chemical Co.*, 464 U.S. 165 (1984).

the Government was precluded from relitigating whether a group of private contractors were authorized representatives under the Clean Air Act for the purpose of conducting inspection on premises subject to regulation under the Act. The private contractors contended that a decision in another Circuit Court of Appeals involving the same parties had been decided in their favor and against the Government.[124] Here there was no reason to allow the Government to litigate twice with the same party, an issue arising in both cases from virtually identical facts. The Court said that the Government was free to litigate the same issue in the future with other litigants and, thus, there would be no chilling effect in its ability to develop the law.[125]

III. CONCLUSION

Of late, on balance, the Supreme Court and Second Circuit favor preclusion. It is viewed as a means to relieve the burdens of a burgeoning federal docket and conserve judicial resources.[126] With the advance of preclusion, though, come some harsh and sometimes unfair results.[127] Given the restrictions preclusion brings on relitigating issues, parties would be wise to consider, analyze and reflect on their procedural choices before deciding which court or administrative agency should decide the merits of their claims or defenses.

---

[124] *Id.* at 168.

[125] *Id.* at 173-74.

[126] *Allen v. McCurry*, 449 U.S. at 94.

[127] *University of Tennessee v. Elliott*, 106 S. Ct. at 3220.

CHAPTER TWENTY-EIGHT

SPECIAL CONSIDERATIONS IN CASES INVOLVING FOREIGN PARTIES

by Lawrence W. Newman, Esq.*
and
David Zaslowsky, Esq.**

I. INTRODUCTION

This chapter discusses the special considerations applicable to federal civil cases involving foreign parties, and focuses on: (1) motions to dismiss, (2) discovery abroad and (3) the enforcement of judgments, including the use of prejudgment attachments.*** Moreover, since foreign parties may sometimes be foreign states or instrumentalities of foreign states, the special impact of their participation is also discussed.

---

* Partner, New York Office of Baker & McKenzie.

** Partner, New York Office of Baker & McKenzie.

*** We are indebted to various of our colleagues in other offices of Baker & McKenzie for their advice regarding foreign law concerning enforcement of judgments and prejudgment attachments. The following lawyers provided advice: Ignace Maes (Brussels—Belgian law), Kevin Mundie (Rio de Janiero—Brazilian law), Harold Margles (Toronto—Canadian law), Gijsbert Loos (Amsterdam—Dutch law), David Frazer and John Leadley (London—English law), Stephan Haimo (New York—French law), Franco Macconi (Rome—Italian law), Hiroshi Kinoshita (Tokyo—Japanese law), Sae Ree Yun (New York—Korean law), Maneul A.J. Teehankee (New York—Phillippine law), Jose' Arcila (Barcelona—Spanish law) Heinz Scharer (Zurich—Swiss law) and Franz J. Waltermann (Frankfurt—West German law).

II. MOTIONS TO DISMISS

A foreign party wishing to escape litigation in the United States will first consider whether the case against him may be dismissed on the grounds of improper service or lack of jurisdiction, or whether it may be dismissed for reasons of convenience (*forum non conveniens*).

A. Service of Process

Service on parties located in foreign countries is often time-consuming, difficult and expensive. Service made may not comport with applicable law and, thus, may be challenged as ineffective. The Federal Rules of Civil Procedure ("Fed. R. Civ. P.") address the problem of serving foreign parties in two different provisions of Rule 4.

Fed. R. Civ. P. 4(e)[1] provides that service on a party not an inhabitant of, or found within, the state shall be made pursuant to the terms set forth in any applicable statute of the United States[2] or order of the court. If no statute is applicable, or the court has not issued an order, Rule 4(e) goes on to provide that service may be made in any manner set forth in the other provisions of Rule 4.[3]

Dissatisfied with the general vagueness of Rule 4(e), and spurred on by the suggestions of numerous commentators,[4] the Supreme Court in 1963 approved a new paragraph known as 4(i) as an addition to Rule 4. Entitled

---

[1] Rule 4(e) states:
Summons: Service Upon Party Not Inhabitant of or Found Within State. Whenever a statute of the United States or an order of court thereunder provides for service of a summons, or of a notice, or of an order in lieu of summons upon a party not an inhabitant of or found within the state in which the district court is held, service may be made under the circumstances and in the manner prescribed by the statute or order, or, if there is no provision therein prescribing the manner of service, in a manner stated in this rule. Whenever a statute or rule of court of the state in which the district court is held provides (1) for service of a summons, or of a notice, or of an order in lieu of summons upon a party not an inhabitant of or found within the state, or (2) for service upon or notice to such a party to appear and respond or defend in an action by reason of the attachment or garnishment or similar seizure of the party's property located within the state, service may in either case be made under the circumstances and in the manner prescribed in the statute or rule.

---

[2] Examples of statutes which specify how service is to be made include 28 U.S.C. § 2361 (Interpleader) and 28 U.S.C. § 1655 (Lien enforcement).

---

[3] These provisions include Rule 4(c)(2)(C)(i) (pursuant to the law of the state in which the district court sits), Rule 4(c)(2)(C)(ii) (discussed *infra*) and Rule 4(i)(discussed *infra*).

---

[4] *See, e.g*, Smit, *International Aspects of Federal Civil Procedure*, 61 Colum. L. Rev. 1031 (1961), Jones, *International Judicial Assistance: Procedural Chaos and a Program for Reform*, 62 Yale L.J. 515 (1953).

"Alternative Provisions for Service in a Foreign Country," it provides for five methods of service in addition to those listed in Rule 4(e). These methods are the following: (1) in such manner as prescribed by the law of the country in which service is to be made; (2) as directed by a foreign authority in response to a letter rogatory; (3) by making personal service; (4) by any form of mail requiring a signed receipt which has been sent by the clerk of the court in which the action is proceeding; or (5) as directed by the court.

Of the five methods provided for in Rule 4(i), only one represented a real change from previous practice but that one—service by mail—subsequently created questions for U.S. courts when the Hague Service Convention entered into force in the United States on February 10, 1969. Known officially as the Convention on the Service Abroad of Judicial and Extrajudicial Documents in Civil or Commercial Matters (the "Hague Service Convention"), its purpose is to facilitate the service of judicial documents in foreign countries by creating a uniform regime for the service of such documents.[5] Under Article I, the Convention applies to civil or commercial cases "where there is occasion to transmit a judicial or extrajudicial document for service abroad." The Supreme Court recently defined this scope in a narrow manner, holding that the Hague Service Convention did not apply to service upon a foreign party (West German) where, under the law of the forum (Illinois), service was completed without documents having to be transmitted abroad.[6]

The cornerstone of the Hague Service Convention is the Central Authority that is designated by each country to receive requests for service from other contracting parties.[7] After receiving a request conforming to the model annexed to the Convention and determining that the request complies with the Convention, the Central Authority sees to it that the document is served by a method prescribed by its internal law or by a particular method requested by the applicant, unless the requested method is inconsistent with the law of the

---

5 Done at The Hague on November 15, 1965; *entered into force for the United States* February 10, 1969; *codified at* 20 U.S.T. 361, T.I.A.S. 6638, 658 U.N.T.S. 163. The signatories to the Hague Service Convention are: Antigua & Barbuda, Barbados, Belgium, Botswana, Cyprus, Czechoslovakia, Denmark, Egypt, Federal Republic of Germany, Finland, France, Greece, Israel, Italy, Japan, Luxembourg, Malawi, Netherlands, Norway, Portugal, Seychelles, Spain, Sweden, Turkey, United Kingdom and United States. Department of State, *Treaties in Force—January 1, 1988*, 317 (1988). The Preamble to the Hague Service Convention states that one of the goals of the convention is to "ensure that judicial and extrajudicial documents to be served abroad shall be brought to the notice of the addressee in sufficient time . . ."

6 *Volkswagenwerk Aktiengesell Schaft v. Schlunk*, 108 S. Ct. 2104 (1988).

7 Hague Service Convention, Article 2.

state in which service is to be made.[8] A state may require that the documents to be served be written in, or translated into, one of the official languages of the state.[9] Each contracting state may also effect service directly through its diplomatic or consular agents.[10]

Under Article 10 of the Hague Service Convention, service may also be accomplished by mail.[11] While Article 10 and Rule 4(i)(D) are consistent with each other, many of the countries which have ratified the Hague Service Convention have objected to Article 10 and—as they are entitled to do under the terms of the Convention—have opted out of Article 10 in ratifying the Convention.[12]

Parties from those countries which adhere to the Hague Service Convention but do not adhere to Article 10 have successfully challenged service by mail in United States federal courts. Thus, in *Vorhees v. Fischer & Krecke*,[13] the Fourth Circuit Court of Appeals held that, although service by mail would otherwise have been proper under Rule 4(i), the Rule had been superseded by the Hague Service Convention because it had entered into force in 1969, six years after the adoption of Rule 4(i).[14] The court went on to con-

---

[8] Hague Service Convention, Articles 3-5.

[9] Hague Service Convention, Article 5.

[10] Hague Service Convention, Article 8. A state may, however, declare that it is opposed to such service within its territory, unless the documents are to be served upon a national of the state in which the documents originate.

[11] Article 10 of the Hague Service Convention states:
   Provided the State of destination does not object the present Convention shall not interfere with —
   (a) the freedom to send judicial documents, by postal channels, directly to persons abroad,
   (b) the freedom of judicial officers, officials or other competent persons of the State of origin to effect service of judicial documents directly through the judicial officers, officials or other competent persons of the State of destination,
   (c) the freedom of any person interested in a judicial proceeding to effect service of judicial documents directly through the judicial officers, officials or other competent persons of the State of destination.

[12] Countries which have objected to all or part of Article 10 include: Botswana, Czechoslovakia, Denmark, Egypt, Finland, Israel, Japan, Luxembourg, Norway, Seychelles, Sweden, Turkey, the United Kingdom and West Germany.

[13] *Vorhees v. Fischer & Krecke*, 697 F.2d 574 (4th Cir. 1983).

[14] *Id.* at 575-576. The Court relied on the principle that the latter act of the sovereign controls if there is a conflict between two statutes or a statute and a treaty citing *Cook v. United States*, 288 U.S. 102 (1933) and *Whitney v. Robertson*, 124 U.S. 190, 194 (1888).

clude that, as between the United States and the foreign jurisdiction in question, West Germany, the Hague Service Convention had to be interpreted in accordance with that country's reservation to Article 10, and that the attempt to serve the defendant by mail was ineffective because it was contrary to the reservation.[15] Two district court decisions have reached similar results.[16] There is, however, also authority to the contrary. For example, the Court of Appeals for the Second Circuit has stated in dictum that "there is much to be said in support of the view that, even if the terms of the Convention were applicable, the Convention was not intended to abrogate the methods of service prescribed by Fed. R. Civ. P. 4."[17]

The relatively new provisions of Rule 4(c)(2)(C)(ii) set forth a specific mechanism for service by mail, but also permit the same type of problem to arise. This rule provides that the primary method of serving process is by sending, via first-class mail, a copy of the summons and complaint to the defendant. If the defendant does not respond to the summons and complaint by signing and returning the accompanying acknowledgment form within 20 days of receipt, the serving party must then effect personal service. Although the courts have had to resolve cases involving this rule in international contexts, they have not yet addressed the question of whether Rule 4(c)(2)(C)(ii) has greater authority than the Hague Service Convention with respect to service on a national of a signatory that has opted out of Article 10.[18]

---

[15] The United States could, of course, have chosen not to accept West Germany's reservation at the time West Germany deposited its ratification of the Convention. The United States, however, did not make any such objection.

[16] *Brown v. Bellaplast Maschinenbau*, 104 F.R.D. 585 (E.D. Pa. 1985); *Harris v. Browning-Ferris Industries Chemical Services, Inc.*, 100 F.R.D. 775 (M.D. La. 1984), *aff'd*, 806 F.2d 259 (5th Cir. 1986).

[17] *International Controls Corp. v. Vesco*, 593 F.2d 166 (2d Cir. 1979).

[18] In one case, for example, *Akzona, Inc. v. E. I. DuPont de Nemours & Co.*, 607 F. Supp. 227 (D. Del. 1984), the District Court of Delaware held that service in the case was governed by Delaware state law and that, therefore, Rule 4(c)(2)(C)(ii) was inapplicable. The court chose not to address the question of whether the rule could be used for service abroad. In a second case, *CeCom, Inc. v. Micro Tempus, Inc.*, Civ. No. 4-84-608 (D. Minn. Nov. 5, 1984) (Slip Opinion), the District Court of Minnesota denied defendant's motion to dismiss the case on grounds of insufficient service or lack of personal service and granted its motion to have the matter submitted to arbitration as called for in the contract. In discussing the insufficiency of process, the court held *sub silentio* that Rule 4(c)(2)(C)(ii) could be used to serve parties in foreign countries. *See also Zisman v. Sieger*, 106 F.R.D. 194 (N.D. Ill. 1985). *But cf. A.I.M. International, Inc. v. Battenfeld Extrusion Systems, Inc.*, 116 F.R.D. 633 (M.D. Ga. 1987) (holding that service by mail on defendants in Germany (which opted out of Article 10) was not technically considered service under the Hague Service Convention but—in order to avoid the time necessary to serve process under the Convention, and in light of the attorney's return of the Acknowledgments—requesting that the defendants not dispute service, and assessing costs against the defendants for not returning the Rule 4(c)(2)(C)(ii) Acknowledgment on time).

Since the courts have yet to determine whether Rule 4(c)(2)(C)(ii) requires or permits American courts to ignore reservations to Article 10 of the Hague Service Convention by foreign countries, litigants face uncertainty in deciding how to serve notice on adversaries abroad. Given that the original impetus behind Rule 4(c)(2)(C)(ii) was to reduce the burden on federal marshals, who under the earlier version of the rule did not effect service on parties in foreign countries, that Congress did not consider carefully all of the ramifications of the final product,[19] and that the "last-in-time" rule of construction employed by the Fourth Circuit in *Vorhees* was not intended to force the United States to violate its treaty relationships with countries that have entered reservations concerning Article 10 of the Hague Service Convention, it would appear doubtful that American courts will be required or even permitted to ignore such reservations.

Reservations to Article 10 of the Hague Service Convention are not the only factor complicating service abroad. A number of countries will not recognize foreign judgments, particularly those obtained by default, if the defendant was not served in his home country according to its local service rules.[20] Another factor to bear in mind is the position taken by some federal courts that service pursuant to Rule 4(c)(2)(C)(ii) will not be sustained in diversity cases if the state in which the federal court sits does not allow service by mail.[21] Therefore, in determining how to serve notice on a party abroad, it is necessary to consider rules governing service both in the appropriate foreign country and in the state in which the contemplated action will be heard.

B. Jurisdiction Over Foreign Parties

Successfully serving notice on a foreign party, be it according to the Fed. R. Civ. P. or the Hague Service Convention, is but the first step toward resolving the dispute. Foreign parties, much like their domestic counterparts, may also seek dismissal on other grounds, including lack of personal or subject-matter jurisdiction.

---

19 *See* Comment, *Civil Procedure—Service of Summons and Complaint under State Law Subsequent to Attempted Service Under Rule 4(c)(2)(C)(ii)*, 14 Mem. St. U.L. Rev. 565, 577 (1984).

---

20 This is true in the case of Germany. See German Code of Civil Procedure, art. 328(I)(2).

---

21 Cases which have so held include *Reno Distributors, Inc. v. West Texas Oil Field Equipment, Inc.*, 105 F.R.D. 511, 513 (D. Kan. 1985) and *Epstein v. Wilder*, 596 F. Supp. 793, 796-97 (N.D. Ill. 1984). These cases, in turn, rely on *William B. May Co., Inc. v. Hyatt*, 98 F.R.D. 569, 570 (S.D.N.Y. 1983). Contra *McDougald v. Jenson*, 786 F.2d 1465 (11th Cir. 1986); *Boggs v. Darr*, 103 F.R.D. 526 (D. Kan. 1984); *A.I.M. Int'l, Inc. v. Battenfeld Extrusion Systems, Inc.*, 116 F.R.D. 633 (M.D. Ga. 1987).

1. Personal Jurisdiction

Personal jurisdiction over a foreign party may be obtained either under the traditional jurisdictional basis or under long-arm statutes. In New York, for example, jurisdiction may be obtained over a foreign individual who is served within the state of New York.[22] In the case of foreign corporations, however, there are other means to obtain personal jurisdiction.

Every state has set forth conditions that must be satisfied if corporations chartered elsewhere are to do business regularly within its borders. One of these conditions is that the corporation consent to the jurisdiction of that state's courts and designate an agent to receive process. If a foreign corporation has not taken the formal steps to qualify to conduct business within a state, but nonetheless is doing so, jurisdiction over it may be obtained on the basis of "doing business" statutes. The jurisdiction derived from these statutes may be reconciled with the traditional bases of jurisdiction by means of "presence" analysis[23] or implied consent to jurisdiction.[24] Presence analysis maintains that a corporation is deemed to be present wherever it is conducting business and may be sued in the courts of a state where it is conducting business just as a nonresident individual found in that state could be sued there.[25] The theory of implied consent is premised on the contention that conducting business within a state implies consent to its jurisdiction.[26] Moreover, since the foreign corporation is benefiting from doing business within the state, subjecting it to the jurisdiction of the state courts by implication is equitable.

In addition to jurisdiction secured by personal service, consent and doing business statutes, long-arm jurisdiction may also be invoked over foreign parties under "long-arm" statutes. The same two-part inquiry applied to potential American defendants is applied to potential foreign defendants: (1) does the defendant's conduct bring him within the statute; and (2) would jurisdiction over the defendant for the particular cause of action be consistent

---

[22] Weinstein Korn & Miller, *New York Civil Practice* ¶ 301-11 (Supp. 1988). Jurisdiction over a corporation, on the other hand, may not be obtained solely by service of process on a corporate officer within the forum state. Restatement (Second) Conflicts of Law, § 42, comment e.

[23] *See Philadelphia & Reading R.R. Co. v. McKibbin*, 243 U.S. 264 (1917).

[24] *See Lafayette Ins. Co. v. French*, 59 U.S. 404 (1856).

[25] *Philadelphia & Reading R.R.*, supra, 243 U.S. at 265.

[26] *Lafayette Ins.*, supra, 59 U.S. at 407.

with the Due Process Clause? The latter question must be answered in the context of the "minimum contacts"[27] standard that has developed in *International Shoe*[28] and its progeny.

The manner in which American courts define minimum contacts for jurisdictional purposes may be of particular concern to foreign parties engaged in manufacturing. Such parties may sell their products directly to end-use consumers or to distributors and retailers. Once the foreign manufacturer places his product into the stream of commerce, he has little, if any, control over its final use. This limited control notwithstanding, a manufacturer may find itself hauled into court under the "commits a tortious act" provision of a state long-arm statute if its product causes injury or damage in that state.[29] Such a scenario is not too far-fetched, as the defendants in the leading cases of *Gray v. American Radiator and Standard Sanitary Corp.*[30] and *Asahi Metal Industry Co. v. Superior Court of California*[31] discovered.

In *Asahi*, however, the United States Supreme Court set forth limits on the ability of plaintiffs to pursue claims against foreign manufacturers with limited contacts with the forum state. The Court reaffirmed its holding in *World-Wide Volkswagen Corp. v. Woodson*[32] that the foreseeable unilateral action of consumers bringing a product into the forum state was an insufficient basis for personal jurisdiction.[33] The minimum contacts required for jurisdiction had to be the result of an action of the defendant purposefully directed toward

---

[27] An issue arises as to whether, in actions arising under federal law, the "minimum contacts" must be with the forum state or whether they can be with the United States as a whole. In general, if the federal law at issue provides for nationwide service, the courts have employed the national contacts standard, but, in the absence of such a provision, the courts have been split. *See* Casad, *Jurisdiction in Civil Actions* (1983) § 4.06[5].

[28] *International Shoe Co. v. State of Washington*, 326 U.S. 310 (1945). *International Shoe* and its progeny are discussed in detail in Chapter 2.

[29] For example, the New York "long-arm" statute provides, in part:
As to a cause of action arising from any of the acts enumerated in this section, a court may exercise personal jurisdiction over any non-domiciliary, or his executor or administrator, who in person or through an agent:
(2) commits a tortious act within the state . . .
N.Y. Civ. Prac. L. & R. Law § 302 (McKinney 1988).

[30] 22 Ill.2d 432, 176 N.E.2d 761 (1961).

[31] 480 U.S. 102 (1987).

[32] 444 U.S. 286 (1980).

[33] *Asahi, supra*, 480 U.S. at 110.

the forum state.[34] Moreover, in the case of a foreign defendant, the court noted that the procedural and substantive interests of other nations in an American state court's assertion of jurisdiction over their nationals, as well as federal foreign policy interests, would be best served by "a careful inquiry into the reasonableness of the assertion of jurisdiction in the particular case, and an unwillingness to find the serious burdens on an alien defendant outweighed by minimal interests on the part of the plaintiff or the forum State."[35]

Generally speaking, then, the bases for obtaining personal jurisdiction over foreign parties is little different from that on which jurisdiction is obtained over domestic parties from a state other than the forum state. For a more detailed discussion of the general basis of personal jurisdiction, see Chapter 2.

2. Subject-Matter Jurisdiction

In certain areas of the law in which statutes give rise to causes of action, the courts have imposed limits on the extent to which claims under those laws may extend to persons and conduct outside the territory of the United States. Of particular importance to private litigants are judicial interpretations of the antitrust, securities and commodities statutes.

Section 1 of the Sherman Act[36] refers to restraint of trade involving "foreign commerce." The courts, however, have limited the extraterritorial application of the antitrust laws. As Judge Hand stated, in *United States v. Aluminum Corporation of America*,[37] "we should not impute to Congress an intent to punish all whom its courts can catch, for conduct which has no consequences within the United States." The rule generally followed is one of "substantial effects" on the foreign commerce of the United States, and was codified by the Congress in 1982 in the Foreign Trade Antitrust Improvement Act (the "FTAIA").[38]

The provisions of the FTAIA prohibit private antitrust actions under certain sections of the antitrust laws unless the conduct in question has a "direct, substantial and reasonably foreseeable effect" on certain types of foreign trade or commerce. The Court of Appeals for the Ninth Circuit introduced a

---

34 *Id.* at 104.

35 *Id.* at 106.

36 15 U.S.C. § 1 *et seq.*

37 148 F.2d 416, 443 (2d Cir. 1945).

38 Pub. L. 97-290, Title IV, §§ 401-403, Oct. 8, 1982, 96 Stat. 1246 (15 U.S.C. §§ 6(a)(1), 45(a)(3)(A)).

balancing test for the application of the "substantial effects" test in 1976 in *Timberlane v. Bank of America*.[39] The court listed certain factors which it said should be taken into account, such as the nationality or allegiance of the parties, the degree of conflict with foreign law or policy, the relative significance of the effects on the United States as compared with those elsewhere, and the extent to which there is explicit purpose to harm or affect American commerce.[40]

Many other cases have discussed the balancing test applicable to determining whether subject-matter jurisdiction exists over acts by persons outside the United States that would be regarded as violating the antitrust laws if they occurred in the United States.[41] For purposes of this chapter, however, it is sufficient to call attention to the potential for dismissal of an antitrust complaint on this ground and to suggest that, with respect to the particular complaint, careful analysis of the facts and circumstances should be applied to the various cases discussing whether there is a direct, foreseeable and substantial effect on United States commerce.

The commodities and securities laws,[42] particularly those relating to fraudulent activity, have often been applied to foreign nationals and to their activities abroad. Although these laws do not, on their face, refer to the activities of foreigners, they have been held to apply to such activities that may have had a significant impact on trading activities in the United States or when activities in furtherance of an allegedly fraudulent scheme have taken place, to a significant extent, in this country.

Under the tests of the proposed Restatement of Foreign Relations Law,[43] the securities laws of the United States are said to be properly applied to activities of persons abroad when (1) they concern transactions in which a national or resident of the United States is a party and are carried out on or affect United States securities exchanges or markets or (2) they involve

---

39 549 F.2d 597 (9th Cir. 1976).

---

40 *Id.* at 614. *See also Mannington Mills, Inc. v. Congoleum Corp.*, 595 F.2d 1287, 1297 (3d Cir. 1979); Restatement of Foreign Relations Law of the United States (Revised) § 415 (Tent. Draft No. 6, 1985).

---

41 *See, e.g., Laker Airways v. Sabena, Belgian World Airlines*, 731 F.2d 909 (D.C. Cir. 1984); *Industrial Investment Development Corp. v. Mitsui & Company*, 671 F.2d 876 (5th Cir. 1982), *vacated on other grounds*, 460 U.S. 1007 (1983); *National Bank of Canada v. Interbank Card Association*, 666 F.2d 6 (2d Cir. 1981); *Montreal Trading Limited v. AMAX, Inc.*, 661 F.2d 864 (10th Cir. 1981).

---

42 The Commodity Exchange Act of 1922, 7 U.S.C. § 13a-1; the Securities Act of 1933 and the Securities Exchange Act of 1934, 15 U.S.C. §§ 77i(a), 78aa.

---

43 Restatement of Foreign Relations Law of the United States (Revised) § 416 (Tent. Draft No. 7, 1986).

representations or negotiations in the United States.[44] These tests—broadly stated here—endeavor to codify case law as it has been developed over the past 20 years.[45] As with cases under the antitrust laws, the facts of the particular case must be analyzed to determine if the securities or commodities laws of the United States are properly applicable to the transaction complained of. Although the securities and commodities laws of the United States do have broad reach, particularly where U.S. securities markets are concerned, the courts have occasionally dismissed such cases for lack of subject-matter jurisdiction.[46]

C. *Forum Non Conveniens*

A foreign defendant that has been properly served and over whom a federal court has jurisdiction may still be able to obtain the dismissal of the case against him on the grounds of *forum non conveniens*. Under this doctrine, even if a court has both personal and subject-matter jurisdiction, and venue is properly laid, the court can dismiss a suit if there exists another forum so much more convenient for the parties and the courts that the plaintiff's privilege of choosing the forum is outweighed. Within the United States, the doctrine of *forum non conveniens* has been displaced to a large extent by transfer to a more convenient federal court under 28 U.S.C. § 1404(a).[47] If the more convenient court is outside the United States, however, transfer is impossible and a dismissal on *forum non conveniens* grounds will be granted if the circumstances warrant.[48]

---

[44] *Id.*

[45] *See Schoenbaum v. Firstbrook*, 405 F.2d 200 (2d Cir.), *rev'd in part, en banc, on other grounds*, 405 F.2d 215 (1968), *cert. denied*, 395 U.S. 906 (1969); *IIT v. Cornfeld*, 619 F.2d 909 (2d Cir 1980); *SEC v. Kasser*, 548 F.2d 109 (3d Cir. 1977), *cert. denied sub nom. Churchill Forest Industries (Manitoba) Ltd. v. SEC*, 431 U.S. 938 (1977); *Bersch v. Drexel Firestone, Inc.*, 519 F.2d 974 (2d Cir.), *cert. denied*, 423 U.S. 1018 (1975); *IIT v. Vencap, Ltd.*, 519 F.2d 1001 (2d Cir. 1975); *AVC Nederland B.V. v. Atrium Investment Partnership*, 740 F.2d 148 (2d Cir. 1984).

[46] *Fidenas AG v. Compagnie Internationale Pour L' Informatique CII Honeywell Bull S.A.*, 606 F.2d 5 (2d Cir. 1979); *Recaman v. Barish*, 408 F. Supp. 1189 (E.D. Pa. 1975); *F. O. F. Proprietary Funds, Ltd. v. Arthur Young & Co.*, 400 F. Supp. 1219 (S.D.N.Y. 1975). *Finch v. Marathon Securities Corp.*, 316 F. Supp. 1345 (S.D.N.Y. 1970); *Kook v. Crang*, 182 F. Supp. 388 (S.D.N.Y. 1960).

[47] 28 U.S.C. § 1404a provides: "For the convenience of parties and witnesses, in the interest of justice, a district court may transfer any civil action to any other district or division where it might have been brought."

[48] *Piper Aircraft Co. v. Reyno*, 454 U.S. 235 (1981); *In re Union Carbide Corp. Gas Plant Disaster at Bhopal*, 809 F.2d 195 (2d Cir.), *cert. denied, Executive Committee Members v. Union of India*, 108 S. Ct. 199 (1987); *Transunion Corp. v. Pepsico, Inc.*, 811 F.2d 127 (2d Cir. 1987); *Overseas Nat'l Airways, Inc. v. Cargolux Airlines Int'l, S.A.*, 712 F.2d 11 (2d Cir. 1983); *Alcoa S.S. Co. v. M/V Nordic Regent*, 654 F.2d 147 (2d Cir. 1980).

Initially, a district court must find that there exists an adequate alternative forum for the litigation. The circumstances considered by the courts were first set forth in *Gulf Oil Corp. v. Gilbert*[49] and *Koster v. Lumbermens Mutual Casualty Co.*[50] and more recently recapitulated in *Piper Aircraft v. Reyno*.[51] Beginning with the general presumption that a plaintiff's choice of forum should be respected,[52] the court weighs both private and public interests to determine whether this choice should be respected in the case before it. Although the Supreme Court in *Gilbert* stated that, "[w]isely, it has not been attempted to catalogue the circumstances which will justify or require"[53] dismissal on *forum non conveniens* grounds, the court listed the following private interests of the litigant as factors to be considered:

(1) The relative ease of access to sources of proof;

(2) The availability of a compulsory process for securing the attendance of uncooperative witnesses;

(3) The costs of obtaining the attendance of witnesses;

(4) The possibility of viewing the relevant premises;

(5) Other practical problems which will allow the trial to be easy, expeditious, and inexpensive; and

(6) The enforceability of a judgment if obtained.[54]

Among the public interests weighed are:

(1) The administrative difficulties that arise when litigation is piled up in congested centers instead of being handled at the origin;

(2) Imposing jury duty on the people of a community which has no relation to the litigation;

(3) The desire to have localized controversies decided at home; and

---

[49] 330 U.S. 501 (1947).

[50] 330 U.S. 518 (1947).

[51] *Piper Aircraft, supra*, 454 U.S. 235.

[52] In recent decisions, the courts have stated that "less deference" will be given to the choice of foreign plaintiffs. *Piper Aircraft, supra,* 454 U.S. at 256. *In re Union Carbide Corp. Gas Plant Disaster at Bhopal*, 634 F. Supp. 842 (S.D.N.Y. 1986), *aff'd in part and modified in part on other grounds*, 809 F.2d 195 (2d Cir. 1987).

[53] *Gilbert, supra*, 330 U.S. at 508.

[54] *Id.*

(4) Not burdening courts with complex conflicts of law problems and with applying a law that is foreign to them.[55]

The courts balance these and other factors to determine which available forum is the most appropriate for trial and resolution of the issues.

When deciding a motion to dismiss based on *forum non conveniens*, the courts look to the difficulties which the application of a foreign law may entail[56] and beyond. Another forum will be treated as an alternative if the defendant is amenable to process and the other forum offers a remedy for the plaintiff's claims. While a change in law which would be caused by a change of forum will not ordinarily be weighed in the balance, "if the remedy provided by the alternative forum is so clearly inadequate or unsatisfactory that it is no remedy at all," the unfavorable change in law may be given substantial weight and, thus, if relevant, should be brought to the court's attention by the party opposing the motion.[57] The foreign law in question need only be such that "there is no danger that [the plaintiff] will be deprived of any remedy or treated unfairly" for the court to grant a *forum non conveniens* dismissal; the foreign law need not treat the plaintiff in the same manner as would American law.[58]

In *Piper Aircraft v. Reyno*,[59] for example, the plaintiff argued that his inability to rely on strict liability in Scotland rendered the law of the alternative forum less favorable to his claim than Pennsylvania law and that, therefore, the defendants' motion to dismiss on *forum non conveniens* grounds should be denied. The United States Supreme Court concluded that the availability to plaintiff under Scottish law of the right to recovery under a negligence theory accorded him sufficient opportunity to secure an adequate remedy and granted the motion to dismiss.[60] Similarly, in *Transunion Corp. v. Pepsico, Inc.*,[61] the Second Circuit dismissed on *forum non conveniens* grounds a civil RICO action, despite the fact that the RICO claim would not be available to the plaintiff in the more convenient forum—the Philippines.

---

55 *Id.* at 508-509.

56 *See, e.g., Piper Aircraft, supra,* 454 U.S. at 254-255.

57 *Id.* at 254.

58 *Id.* at 254-55.

59 *Id.*

60 *Id.*

61 811 F.2d 127 (2d Cir. 1987).

The court stated that it was sufficient that the plaintiff would be able to assert the three fraud counts that made up its RICO claims and that dismissal would not be denied simply because the plaintiff would not be entitled to treble damages for proving its fraud claims as it might be if it proved its RICO claims.[62]

Defendants seeking dismissal of cases against them on *forum non conveniens* grounds face conflicting pressures as to timing. There is considerable pressure to file such motions promptly. Several state court decisions suggest that a defendant's delay may be a sufficient reason for denying dismissal.[63] Such pressure notwithstanding, it may be necessary in a given case for a defendant to conduct a certain amount of discovery before determining whether to seek dismissal on *forum non conveniens* grounds. Given the difficulties and delays associated with obtaining pretrial discovery in foreign jurisdictions, a considerable period of time may elapse before a defendant seeks this type of dismissal. In such cases, the defendant would be advised to set forth in his motion papers not only the specific delays due to discovery procedures abroad, but also the link between the information so obtained and the decision to seek a dismissal on these grounds.

Given the courts' concern with the adequacy of the remedy provided by foreign law, a motion to dismiss on *forum non conveniens* grounds is frequently accompanied by an affidavit by a recognized expert in the relevant foreign law attesting that the remedies available under such law are adequate. In the same vein, papers in opposition to such motions often include affidavits by foreign law experts that the remedies available in the alternative forum may leave the plaintiff with no remedy at all.

III. DISCOVERY ABROAD

Litigators in this country have grown accustomed to gathering evidence according to the liberal rules of discovery which prevail in the federal and state courts. Although the United States has made available the full range of its discovery system to those seeking evidence for use abroad, American litigators continue to face obstacles when attempting to conduct U.S.-style discovery in foreign jurisdictions. The Hague Convention on the Taking of Evidence Abroad in Civil or Commercial Matters (the "Hague Evidence

---

62 *Id.* at 129.

---

63 *Bell v. Louisville & Nashville, R.R.*, 106 Ill. 2d 135, 478 N.E.2d 384 (1985); *Arthur v. Arthur*, 452 A.2d 160 (D.C. App. 1982); *Dietrich v. Texas Nat'l Petroleum Co.*, 56 Del. 435, 193 A.2d 579 (Del. Sup. 1963). *But see Bongards' Creameries v. Alfa-Laval, Inc.*, 339 N.W.2d 561 (Minn. 1983) (appellate court raised issue *sua sponte* for first time on appeal).

Convention")[64] has somewhat simplified and liberalized the system of international judicial assistance among its signatories by providing for a system of "letters of request" to appropriate governmental authorities abroad.[65] Nevertheless, the quest for evidence abroad for use in the United States remains an involved and often frustrating adventure.

The main obstacles to obtaining evidence abroad (aside from the ordinary difficulties posed by distance and language barriers) arise from international resistance to three fundamental characteristics of discovery in this country. These are: first, the "extrajudicial" nature of discovery under the Fed. R. Civ. P. according to which private parties organize and virtually control the discovery process; second, the availability in the United States of "pretrial" discovery; and third, the requirement that evidence be taken in a fashion which creates an admissible record.

The first obstacle arises whenever U.S. litigants desire information located in civil-law jurisdictions. The inquisitorial role of the civil-law judge is fundamentally different from the common-law practice of placing the burden of obtaining and presenting evidence on adverse parties. Further, even many common-law nations are uncomfortable with the unusual freedom and responsibility accorded to the litigants themselves under the Fed. R. Civ. P.

The second obstacle is more nearly universal—few countries outside the United States allow the discovery of evidence or the taking of testimony which is not necessarily to be used at trial. Fed. R. Civ. P. 26(b)(1), on the other hand, allows the discovery of all nonprivileged information which is "relevant to the subject matter" and is "reasonably calculated to lead to the discovery of admissible evidence."

The third obstacle—the difficulty in gathering evidence in a form useful for trial—is more technical but, nonetheless, presents a significant problem. While all nations have formal and substantive requirements regarding the proper collection of testimony, the rules of evidence used in the United States tend to be technical and, at times, uncompromising. The problem is most severe in civil-law countries where testimony is frequently taken directly by the presiding judge without the administration of an oath, without the creation of a verbatim transcript and without cross-examination by counsel.

---

64 Done at The Hague March 18, 1970, *entered into force for the United States* October 7, 1972, *codified at* 23 U.S.T. 2555, T.I.A.S. 7444, 847 U.N.T.S. 231; *reprinted in* 28 U.S.C.A. § 1781 (Supp. 1988).

---

65 At present, the following countries are, with various reservations, parties to the Hague Evidence Convention: Argentina, Barbados, Cyprus, Czechoslovakia, Denmark, Finland, France, Federal Republic of Germany, Israel, Italy, Luxembourg, Monaco, Netherlands, Norway, Portugal, Singapore, Spain, Sweden, United Kingdom and United States. 28 U.S.C.A. § 1781 (Supp. 1988).

When Americans seeking evidence abroad are forced to accept such procedures, the evidence so obtained may not be useful for trial purposes.

While the Hague Evidence Convention has not succeeded in liberalizing the international quest for evidence to the satisfaction of most American litigators, it has helped expedite the process of obtaining evidence among the signatory nations, and has to some extent bridged the gap between the civil law and common law systems.[66] Article 15, for example, permits diplomatic officers to take evidence from nationals of the country they represent. Article 16 goes even further. It allows diplomatic officers to take evidence from nationals of the country in which he exercises his functions and from nationals of third countries. The appointment of commissioners by the requesting court is provided for in Article 17. Finally, Article 18 allows a foreign state in which evidence is to be taken to declare the availability of compulsion under local law. Probably the greatest advantage for U.S. litigants offered by the Hague Evidence Convention is its ninth article, which provides that judicial authorities executing letters of request *"will* follow a request of the requesting authority that a special method or procedure be followed, unless this is incompatible with the internal law of the State of execution or is impossible of performance . . . " (emphasis added). This provision has allowed American courts to request American-style procedures even from civil-law courts.

The Hague Evidence Convention, though, has its drawbacks and a number of restrictions on evidence-gathering methods. For example, Article 12(b) of the Convention permits a foreign state to refuse to execute a Letter of Request if "the state addressed considers that its sovereignty or security would be prejudiced thereby." Under Article 21(d), diplomatic and consular officers or agents and private commissioners may obtain evidence in the manner set forth in a discovery request from a U.S. court only if "such manner is not forbidden by the law of the state where the evidence is taken." These obstacles to discovery may be raised often in signatory countries that have blocking statutes. In addition, Article 23 of the Convention permits signatories to declare that they "will not execute Letters of Request issued for the purpose of obtaining pretrial discovery of documents as known in Common Law countries." Several signatory countries have made declarations under Article 23 of the Convention either prohibiting or restricting pretrial discovery of

---

[66] The Hague Evidence Convention provides three methods for obtaining evidence abroad: (1) a U.S. judicial authority may send a Letter of Request or "letter rogatory" to the competent authority in the foreign state—the Letter of Request must specifically request the evidence sought, (2) by an American or foreign diplomatic or consular officer or agent after permission is obtained from the foreign state, and (3) by a private commissioner duly appointed by the foreign state.

documents.[67] Furthermore, most signatories require parties to apply for permission from local authorities prior to conducting extrajudicial discovery.[68] And, only a handful of signatories will compel unwilling witnesses to attend depositions under these articles.[69]

A. Enforceability of the Hague Evidence Convention

Some litigants have argued, that, among its signatories, the Hague Evidence Convention pre-empts the use of discovery methods available under the Fed. R. Civ. P. The case most frequently cited to support this contention

---

[67] The following table summarizes the reservations taken by the signatory states with respect to various provisions of the Hague Evidence Convention.

	Article 15 (Nationals)	Article 16 (Others)	Article 17 (Commissioners)	Article 18 (Compulsion)	Article 23 (Pretrial)
Argentina	Y	P	P	N	N
Barbados	Y	P	P	N	Y
Cyprus	Y	P	P	N	Y
Czechoslavakia	Y	w/oP[1]	w/oP[1]	Y	Y
Denmark	P	P	N	N	N
Finland	Y	w/o P	w/o P	N	N
France	Y	P w/c	P w/c	N	N
Germany (West)	Y	P[2]	P w/c	N	N
Israel	Y	P	P	N	Y
Italy	Y	P	P	Y	N
Luxembourg	Y	P w/c	P w/c	N	N
Monaco	Y	P w/c	P w/c	N	N
Netherland	Y	w/o P	P w/c	N	N
Norway	P	P	P	N	N
Portugal	P	N	N	N	N
Singapore	N	N	N	N	N
Spain	Y	w/oP[3]	w/oP[3]	N	N
Sweden	P	P	P	N	N
U.K.	Y	w/oP[1]	w/o P	Y	N
U.S.A.	Y	w/o P	w/o	P	Y

w/o P = No permission required
P = Permission required
P w/c = Permission required, conditions specified
Y = Yes (available upon request)
N = No (not available)
(1) On the condition reciprocity is applied.
(2) Applies only to nationals of third states—no permission required for German nationals.
(3) Evidence may be taken without prior permission in the premises of the diplomat or consular representative of the requesting state.

---

[68] See table in footnote 67, *supra*.

---

[69] See table in footnote 67, *supra*.

is *Volkswagenwerk, A. G. v. Superior Court, Alameda County,*[70] in which the court required an American party to obtain evidence from a foreign party under the Hague Evidence Convention prior to seeking enforcement measures available under the Fed. R. Civ. P. The trend in judicial decisions, however, is in the direction of reducing the extent to which American litigants are obliged to rely, wholly or partially, on the Hague Evidence Convention.

In June 1987, a five-member majority of the Supreme Court held, in *Societe Nationale Industrielle Aerospatiale v. United States District Court for the Southern District of Iowa,*[71] that the Hague Evidence Convention does not prescribe exclusive procedures for obtaining pretrial discovery of documents and other information located in the territory of a signatory to the Hague Evidence Convention. The Supreme Court held that the text and legislative history of the Hague Evidence Convention "unambiguously supports the conclusion that it was intended to establish optional procedures that would facilitate the taking of evidence abroad."[72] Parties, therefore, are free to seek discovery from foreign litigants (parties and third parties)[73] under either the Hague Evidence Convention or the Fed. R. Civ. P. (or pertinent state court rules of procedure).

In each case, a judicial determination must be made by the trial court as to whether discovery must be sought under the Hague Evidence Convention prior to the service of discovery requests under the Fed. R. Civ. P. The determination is to be based on an international comity analysis that requires "prior scrutiny in each case of the particular facts, sovereign interests and likelihood that resort to [the convention] procedures will prove effective."[74] The Supreme Court refused to "articulate specific rules to guide [the lower courts in] this delicate task,"[75] but noted that "[t]he nature of the concerns

---

[70] 123 Cal. App. 3d 840, 176 Cal. Rptr. 874 (1st Dist. 1981).

[71] 482 U.S. 522 (1987).

[72] *Id.*, 96 L. Ed. 2d at 480.

[73] *Id.* at 482.

[74] *Id.* at 484.

[75] *Id.* at 485.

that guide a comity analysis are suggested by the Restatement of Foreign Relations Law of the United States (Revised) § 437(1)(c) (Tent. Draft No. 7, 1986)."[76]

Since the Supreme Court's decision in *Aerospatiale*, there have been at least five reported federal district court cases in which the applicability of the Hague Evidence Convention procedures has been addressed: *Hudson v. Hermann Pfauter GmbH & Co.*; *Benton Graphics v. Uddeholm Corp.*; *Haynes v. Kleinwefers*; *John Jenco v. Martech Int'l Inc.*; and *Rich v. Kis California, Inc.*[77]

The first four of these cases demonstrate that there are at least three critical inquiries that courts are likely to make in determining whether, in a particular case, pretrial discovery of foreign litigants in United States courts is to be obtained under the Hague Evidence Convention or under the Fed. R. Civ. P. (or local state rules). The first inquiry is: What sort of comity analysis is to be used in determining whether the Hague Evidence Convention should be followed? The second is: Which party has the burden of demonstrating whether the Hague Evidence Convention procedures are appropriate in a given case? The third is: Which type of discovery is being requested of the foreign party? The answers to these three inquiries will have a significant impact on a court's determination of the pretrial discovery procedures to be utilized in cases involving foreign litigants.

If the "case-by-case comity analysis" employed in *Benton Graphics*, *Haynes* and *John Jenco* is utilized by the courts,[78] with its emphasis on, in addition to sovereign interests, the facts of the case, the interests of the individual litigants, the Restatement's articulation of relevant concerns, and on whether Hague Evidence Convention procedures will prove effective, the

---

[76] *Id.* at 484, n.28. According to the Restatement, the factors relevant to any comity analysis include: "(1) the importance to the . . . litigation of the documents or other information requested; (2) the degree of specificity of the request; (3) whether the information originated in the United States; (4) the availability of alternative means of securing the information; and (5) the extent to which noncompliance with the request would undermine important interests of the United States, or compliance with the request would undermine important interests of the state where the information is located." Restatement of Foreign Relations Law of the United States (Revised) § 437(1)(c) (Tent. Draft No. 7, 1986).

[77] *Hudson v. Hermann Pfauter GmbH & Co.*, 117 F.R.D. 33 (N.D.N.Y. 1987); *Benton Graphics v. Uddeholm Corp.*, 118 F.R.D. 386 (D.N.J. 1987); *Haynes v. Kleinwefers*, 119 F.R.D. 335 (E.D.N.Y. 1988); *John Jenco v. Martech Int'l, Inc.*, No. 86-4229 (E.D. La. May 19, 1988) (LEXIS, Genfed library, Dist. file); *Rich v. Kis California, Inc.*, 121 F.R.D. 254 (M.D.N.C. 1988).

[78] The "case-by-case comity analysis" was recently cited with approval in *In re Anschuetz & Co. GmbH.*, 838 F.2d 1362, 1363-64 (5th Cir. 1988). *See also Sandsend Fin. Consultants, Ltd. v. Wood*, 743 S.W.2d 364, 365 (Tex. App. - Houston [1st Dist.] 1988).

result should often be the application of the Fed. R. Civ. P. (or local state rules) for discovery from foreign party litigants that are nationals of signatories to the Hague Evidence Convention.[79]

As to the burden of persuasion, if, as in *Benton Graphics* and *Haynes*, the party seeking to utilize the Hague Evidence Convention procedures has the burden of demonstrating appropriate reasons for use of those procedures and that they will prove effective, it will be difficult in most cases to convince a court that the Hague Evidence Convention procedures should be followed. If, on the other hand, the burden is placed on the party opposing the use of the Hague Evidence Convention procedures to demonstrate that they will be ineffective, as was done in *Hudson*, it will be more likely that courts increasingly will require parties to resort first to the Hague Evidence Convention. It appears likely, however, that most courts will place the burden of persuasion on the party seeking to utilize the Convention procedures, and discovery will proceed under the Fed. R. Civ. P. (or local state rules).[80]

A review of the cases decided since *Aerospatiale* also reveals that the type of discovery requested of the foreign party can be a significant factor in determining whether the Hague Evidence Convention procedures must be followed. Interrogatories appear to be most compatible with Hague Evidence Convention procedures. Document requests, on the other hand, may, in a number of cases, be incompatible with the Hague Evidence Convention procedures, in view of the large number of Article 23 declarations or reservations by the signatory states relating to the pretrial discovery of documents. Lastly, a court may be more willing to resort to Convention procedures if the discovery is sought in the context of a jurisdictional dispute raised by a foreign party litigant.

---

[79] With respect to the production of documents, the "case-by-case comity analysis" should ordinarily result in the use of the discovery provisions of the Federal Rules of Civil Procedure since 15 of the signatory states of the Hague Convention have made declarations under Article 23 of the Convention restricting pretrial discovery of documents in their countries. *Aerospatiale, supra,* 96 L. Ed. 2d at 479, n.22.

[80] *Cf. Rich v. Kis California, Inc.*, 121 F.R.D. 254 (M.D.N.C. 1988) ("The proponent of using the Hague Evidence Convention bears the burden of demonstrating the necessity for using those procedures"); *S & S Screw Mach. Co. v. Cosa Corp.*, 647 F. Supp. 600, 618, n.34 (M.D. Tenn. 1986) ("The requesting party . . . would be required to make a prima facie showing that the particular request [under the Convention] would not be honored in meaningful fashion. The burden then would shift to the requested foreign party to show a substantial likelihood of successful use of Convention procedures. Placing the burden of persuasion on the requested party would follow the established approach of allocating the burden to a party who possesses 'readier access to knowledge about the fact in question'" (citations omitted)).

B. Depositions Abroad

The Fed. R. Civ. P. provide three basic methods by which testimony can be taken abroad without the involvement of foreign officials: deposition by stipulation (Rule 29), deposition on notice (Rule 28(b)(1)), and deposition by commission (Rule 2B(b)(2)). The first two methods differ more in name than in practice. Both rely on the voluntary presence of the witness, since neither contemplates judicial compulsion. Rule 29 states that the parties may agree to a deposition at any time and place, and in any manner determined by the parties. Rule 28(b)(1) requires (while Rule 29 only allows) notice of the deposition and the taking of testimony before an officer authorized to administer oaths. Since parties will rarely forego the opportunity to take sworn testimony, the choice between these types of depositions may be largely academic. Under either rule, parties may choose to have a U.S. consular or diplomatic officer (authorized by 22 C.F.R. 92.4[a]) preside over the deposition, thereby assuring the presence of an officer who has at least some familiarity with United States procedure.

The main advantage of these methods is that testimony may be taken in the form most suitable for use at trial. Further, it may be possible to obtain some "pretrial" discovery otherwise not available in the country where evidence is sought. Unfortunately, deposition by these methods is still sometimes considered a usurpation of sovereignty and some countries have laws specifically prohibiting such activity by consular officers. In some civil-law countries, such as Switzerland, it is a crime for anyone, other than a judicial officer, be he or she a consular officer or not, to conduct a deposition.[81] Criminal penalties have been levied against lawyers trespassing on the sovereignty of civil judiciaries.[82]

The third method by which depositions may be taken abroad without the involvement of foreign authorities—deposition by commission—requires the party seeking testimony to request a U.S. court to appoint a commissioner empowered to administer oaths and take evidence. While commissioners will most often be U.S. consular officers, Fed. R. Civ. P. 28(b)(2) allows the court to appoint any individual. The principal drawback of this method is that it requires an application for a court order appointing a commissioner. The advantage is that certain measures of compulsion may be available. For

---

[81] Swiss Penal Code, Art. 271.

---

[82] For example, the celebrated case of the two Dutch attorneys jailed on charges of economic espionage for taking testimony in Switzerland. *See* Jones, *International Judicial Assistance: Procedural Chaos and a Program for Reform*, 62 Yale L.J. 515, 520 (1953).

example, when U.S. nationals or residents are to be deposed, commissioners may be appointed in conjunction with subpoenas under 28 U.S.C. § 1783.[83]

Among its signatories, the Hague Evidence Convention provides for improved procedures for deposition by notice and commission. The benefits of the Hague Evidence Convention, however, may be more apparent than real since several signatories have entered reservations as to some of these provisions.[84]

Where evidence is sought from an uncooperative witness who is beyond the reach of U.S. subpoena power, and who does not reside in a country which is a signatory to the Hague Evidence Convention, the only means to compel testimony or the production of documents remains the traditional letter rogatory. The issuance of letters rogatory is specifically provided for

---

[83] 28 U.S.C. 1783 states:

(a) A court of the United States may order the issuance of a subpoena requiring the appearance as a witness before it, or before a person or body designated by it, of a national or resident of the United States who is in a foreign country, or requiring the production of a specified document or other thing by him, if the court finds that particular testimony or the production of the document or other thing by him is necessary in the interest of justice, and, in other than a criminal action or proceeding, if the court finds, in addition, that it is not possible to obtain his testimony in admissible form without personal appearance or to obtain the production of the document or other thing in any other manner.

(b) The subpoena shall designate the time and place for the appearance or for the production of the document or other thing. Service of the subpoena and any order to show cause, rule, judgment, or decree authorized by this section or by section 1784 of this title shall be effected in accordance with the provisions of the Federal Rules of Civil Procedure relating to service of process on a person in a foreign country. The person serving the subpoena shall tender to the person to who the subpoena is addressed his estimated necessary travel and attendance expenses, the amount of which shall be determined by the court and stated in the order directing the issuance of the subpoena.

[84] See footnote 67 and accompanying text.

by Fed. R. Civ. P. 28(b)[85] and 28 U.S.C. § 1781,[86] but federal courts have also found it among their inherent powers to issue such requests on the basis of comity.[87] While diplomatic channels are often used for the transmittal of letters rogatory (some nations insist on it) many such requests for international judicial assistance move directly from tribunal to tribunal.[88]

The major drawback of traditional letters rogatory, aside from the delays in their execution, is that the recipient court usually collects the requested evidence according to its own procedure. In civil-law countries this practice often leads to the creation of a record inadmissible in U.S. courts. Two of these formalistic problems—the failure to administer an oath and the dictation of a summary in lieu of a verbatim transcript—have been somewhat offset by the 1963 amendment to Fed. R. Civ. P. 28(b)(3) which provides that "[e]vidence obtained in response to a letter rogatory need not be excluded

---

[85] Rule 28(b) provides:
In Foreign Countries. In a foreign country, depositions may be taken (1) on notice before a person authorized to administer oaths in the place in which the examination is held, either by the law thereof or by the law of the United States, or (2) before a person commissioned by the court, and a person so commissioned shall have the power by virtue of the commission to administer any necessary oath and take testimony, or (3) pursuant to a letter rogatory. A commission or a letter rogatory shall be issued on application and notice and on terms that are just and appropriate. It is not requisite to the issuance of a commission or a letter rogatory that the taking of the deposition in any other manner is impracticable or inconvenient; and both a commission and letter rogatory may be issued in proper cases. A notice or commission may designate the person before whom the deposition is to be taken either by name or descriptive title. A letter rogatory may be addressed "To the Appropriate Authority in [here name the country]." Evidence obtained in response to a letter rogatory need not be excluded merely for the reason that it is not a verbatim transcript or that the testimony was not taken under oath or for any similar departure from the requirements for depositions taken within the United States under these rules.

[86] 28 U.S.C. § 1781 states:
(a) The Department of State has power, directly, or through suitable channels—
  (1) to receive a letter rogatory issued, or request made, by a foreign or international tribunal, to transmit it to the tribunal, officer, or agency in the United States to whom it is addressed, and to receive and return it after execution; and
  (2) to receive a letter rogatory issued, or request made, by a tribunal in the United States, to transmit it to the foreign or international tribunal, officer, or agency to whom it is addressed, and to receive and return it after execution.
(b) This section does not preclude—
  (1) the transmittal of a letter rogatory or request directly from a foreign or international tribunal to the tribunal, officer, or agency in the United States to whom it is addressed and its return in the same manner; or
  (2) the transmittal of a letter rogatory or request directly from a tribunal in the United States to the foreign or international tribunal, officer, or agency to whom it is addressed and its return in the same manner.

[87] *See, e.g., De Villeneuve v. Morning Journal Ass'n*, 206 F. 70 (S.D.N.Y. 1913).

[88] *See, e.g., In re Petition to Compel Arbitration between Trade & Transport, Inc.*, No. 78 Civ. 1180 (S.D.N.Y. June 22, 1979).

merely for the reasons that it is not a verbatim transcript or that the testimony was not taken under oath." Indeed, even in a recent *criminal* matter,[89] the Second Circuit Court of Appeals held admissible the deposition testimony of a witness whose deposition was taken in France while in custody of French authorities. Because, according to the court, French law does not permit those accused to take oaths, the magistrate presiding over the deposition was only permitted to ask the witness if she would tell the truth. The Second Circuit said that there is no rule that a witness must be sworn but only that the witness agree to tell the truth.

Nevertheless, since courts are the ultimate arbiters of admissibility in individual cases, the problems caused by unsworn summarized testimony continue. A more persistent and substantive problem has been the absence of cross-examination in many civil-law proceedings since the courts have been insistent regarding the rights of parties to question hostile witnesses.

C. Blocking Legislation

Its shortcomings notwithstanding, the Hague Evidence Convention has liberalized international rules for the gathering of evidence. At the same time, however, there have been legislative moves in various countries, some of them signatories to the Hague Evidence Convention, to frustrate the efforts of American litigators to obtain evidence within their jurisdictions. While the initial "blocking legislation" arose in response to the extraterritorial facets of United States antitrust laws, they since have developed into a general resistance to American efforts to conduct "pretrial" discovery abroad.

The first set of blocking legislation was passed after the litigation arising out of the uranium price rise of the mid-1970s. As the uranium litigation subsided and the Hague Evidence Convention began to take effect, countries such as England and France became concerned with the "threat" of American pretrial discovery techniques. They, therefore, passed anti-discovery laws couched in terms of protecting sensitive national commercial and industrial data.[90]

---

[89] *United States v. Salim*, 855 F.2d 944 (2d Cir. 1988).

---

[90] Law 80-538 of July 16, 1980 protects French firms from having to provide information to foreign public authorities and prevents the taking of depositions within France other than those authorized by the Hague Evidence Convention. The British equivalent is the Protection of Trading Interests Act of 1982. A similar statute was enacted in Ontario in 1980, the Business Records Protection Act, which prohibits the removal pursuant to subpoenas of authorities outside Ontario from Ontario of business records including "any record, statement, report, or material in any way relating to any business carried on in Ontario" unless such disclosure is made pursuant to regular company reporting practices or as required under Ontario law.

For some time, United States courts showed deference to foreign laws which conflicted with American discovery requests. Since 1958, however, courts have been increasingly willing to ignore the possible liabilities that may be incurred by a disclosing party abroad and have ordered disclosure despite the conflict with local laws.[91]

IV. JUDGMENTS AND PREJUDGMENT ATTACHMENTS

The ultimate, if not primary, concern of litigators is to assist their clients in enforcing whatever award or judgment the clients may get, and conversely, to avoid incurring an adverse judgment or award. Opportunities exist for judgments to be enforced against foreign parties both in this country and abroad, depending on the location of the parties' assets. It is therefore important that American litigators be aware of such opportunities, as well as of the constraints imposed by foreign countries' laws on the recognition and enforcement of foreign judgments.

The initial decision with which a foreign party is faced is whether to make a special appearance to contest jurisdiction, to make a general appearance to contest the merits, or to accept a default judgment in the United States and then try to contest the enforceability of the judgment in his home territory. Which of these alternatives a foreign party will select will depend on the laws relating to the enforcement of judgments in whatever country he may have assets.

There are obvious advantages for a creditor in the United States if he obtains a prejudgment attachment of the foreign party's assets in this country, or elsewhere. If prejudgment attachments are not available or advisable in certain circumstances, one should give consideration in the early stages of any litigation to the enforceability abroad of judgments obtained against foreign defendants. This consideration should also be given when attachments are obtained abroad, because those attachments will be of no value if the expected judgments which they secure are not enforceable under local foreign law.

A. Prejudgment Attachments

Enforcing an American judgment abroad is a difficult and uncertain process. Foreign jurisdictions may not accord the judgment the status of a lien against the defendant's assets. Alternatively, these jurisdictions may have

---

[91] *See Societe Nationale Industrielle Aerospatiale v. U.S. Dist. Court for Southern Dist. of Iowa*, 482 U.S. 522 (1987); *Societe Internationale Pour Participations Industrielles et Commerciales, S.A. v. Rogers*, 357 U.S. 197 (1958); *United States v. First Nat'l City Bank*, 396 F.2d 897 (2d Cir. 1968).

property conveyance laws which may enable defendants to transfer assets in such a way as to evade the judgment. Thus, the enforcement of an American judgment abroad may turn on the claimant's ability to secure a prejudgment attachment (or its equivalent) of the defendant's assets, either in the U.S. or in a foreign jurisdiction.

In the United States, an attachment is obtained by a motion, usually *ex parte*, made as part of an action on the merits. *In personam* and subject-matter jurisdiction must exist, generally speaking, independent of the attachment itself.[92] As a result, it is not always a simple matter to attach a defendant's assets in whatever part of the United States they may be found. The defendant may not be doing business where his assets happen to be, and that place may lack sufficient transactional contacts to permit an attachment.[93]

Countries outside the United States which permit attachments or the equivalent tend to do so through either of two different philosophical approaches. First, there are jurisdictions that are like the United States in their requirement that attachments be part of proceedings on the merits.[94] There are also jurisdictions in which attachments are brought as separate proceedings from those in which the merits of the underlying controversy are determined.[95] In countries where attachments are independent proceedings, the action on the merits, or main proceeding, may be brought in the same or another country. The main proceeding on the merits may already have been started or may not have yet begun. The main proceeding may even be in arbitration. There is sometimes a reciprocity condition, however, requiring

---

[92] *Shaffer v. Heitner*, 433 U.S. 186 (1977), all but eliminated quasi-in-rem jurisdiction under which courts previously had jurisdiction over a defendant to the extent of the amount of his property attached, even in the absence of any other contacts with the jurisdiction.

---

[93] The situation is different, however, with attachments sought under Rule B(1) of the Supplemental Rules for Certain Admiralty and Maritime Claims. Under Rule B, a plaintiff with an *in personam* maritime claim may obtain an attachment of the defendant's assets within the forum district "[i]f the defendant shall not be found within [that] district." Most courts that have considered the issue have held that the mere presence of assets in a district is sufficient to support a maritime attachments there because the "minimum contacts" requirement of *Shaffer v. Heitner* does not apply to maritime attachments. *See, e.g.*, *Grand Bahama Petroleum Co. v. Canadian Transportation Agencies, Ltd.*, 450 F. Supp. 447, 455-56 (W.D. Wash. 1978); *Amoco Overseas Co. v. Compagnie Nationale Algerienne de Navigation*, 459 F. Supp. 1242, 1248-49 (S.D.N.Y. 1978), *aff'd*, 605 F.2d 648 (2d Cir. 1979).

---

[94] Examples are England, Australia, Canada and the Philippines. (Citations for many of the foreign law provisions referred to have been omitted since such provisions are not of direct use to, or available to, any but a few readers. In any event, any use of foreign law would involve counsel in the foreign countries concerned.)

---

[95] Examples are Belgium, France, Japan, Germany, Italy, Korea, and Switzerland and, in some cases, the Netherlands.

SPECIAL CONSIDERATIONS IN FOREIGN PARTY CASES 805

that the main proceeding be in a country whose judgments or arbitral awards would be enforceable in the courts of the country where the attachment was obtained.

Legal systems which treat attachments as separate proceedings often permit jurisdiction over defendants on grounds which extend considerably further than our courts consider permissible for *in personam* jurisdiction under such cases as *International Shoe* and *Shaffer v. Heitner*.[96] Thus, the mere presence of moveable goods in The Netherlands is sufficient to permit a plaintiff having no transactional or other contacts there to obtain an attachment of the assets of a defendant having no other connection with that country, aside from the fact that its assets are there. Belgium's laws are similar in this respect, as are the laws of France, Germany, Italy and Switzerland.[97]

Jurisdictions which permit attachments without a main proceeding and based only on the presence of assets can be extremely useful to U.S. litigants suing foreign defendants. Often, actions against foreign defendants initially appear unattractive because, although there may be jurisdiction in the United States over such foreign defendants, those defendants may have no assets here. In addition, later enforcement of a U.S. judgment in the defendant's home country may be difficult, expensive, or, as a practical matter, unrealistic. In such situations, the plaintiff's lawyer may be able to take advantage of a third jurisdiction's attachment laws to obtain security for enforcement of the judgment. Indeed, the plaintiff may be able to bring pressure upon the foreign defendant by attaching that defendant's assets in the third country even before the lawsuit is commenced in the United States.

Other countries, especially those which do not separate attachment proceedings from proceedings on the merits, have requirements for attachment jurisdiction which are similar to our own. Some of those jurisdictions do not look with much favor on the idea of prejudgment attachments. Such a jurisdiction is England, where, aside from *in rem* admiralty actions against vessels, the only relief resembling an old prejudgment attachment is what is known as the *Mareva* injunction, which restrains the defendant from removing his assets from the jurisdiction pending the trial of the action against

---

96 *International Shoe, supra,* 326 U.S. 310 (1946); *Shaffer v. Heitner, supra,* 433 U.S. 186 (1977).

97 Belgian Judicial Code Art. 633; French Code of Civil Procedure, ant. 48-57; Civil Procedure Code of the Federal Republic of Germany (Zivilprozessordnung, hereinafter referred to as the "ZPO"). Art. 916 *et seq.* Italian Code of Civil Procedure §§ 670-671; Art. 271 *et seq.* of the Swiss Federal Statute on Execution of Debts and Bankruptcy of April 11, 1889, as amended.

him.[98] This type of injunction is issued as part of a proceeding on the merits in which the usual requirements for jurisdiction over the defendant have been satisfied.

Although the criteria for obtaining attachments outside the United States vary, they generally require a showing by the plaintiff that he has a *prima facie* case on the merits, and that, on the basis of plaintiff's *ex parte* presentation, it appears likely that he will prevail. Jurisdictions differ, however, in the degree of detail required to be shown concerning the underlying claim. Courts in Belgium and France, for example, are relatively easy to satisfy, since the plaintiff need only show that a certain and material claim exists against the defendant and that its amount can be determined or estimated provisionally.[99] In practice, this requirement may be satisfied through summary affidavits accompanied by such documentary proof as copies of unpaid invoices. Dutch and Swiss courts are also generally favored to plaintiffs seeking attachment.[100] German courts, on the other hand, require considerable detail and documentation if the posting of substantial security is to be avoided.[101]

Since attachments are generally provided to protect the plaintiff against the eventuality that enforcing a judgment will be impossible, or at least difficult, most countries require, in addition to proof of a *prima facie* case on the merits, a satisfactory showing as to the need for the attachment. However, it is generally not necessary—as it often is in the United States—that the defendant be a foreigner or nonresident. Two exceptions are Switzerland,

---

[98] *Mareva Compania Naviera S.A. v. Int'l Bulk Carriers S.A.*, [1975] 2 Lloyd's Rep. 509.

[99] Belgian Judicial Code, §§ 1445, 1447; French Code of Civil Procedure, art. 48-57 (*Ancien*).

[100] Articles 271 and 272 of the Swiss Federal Statute on Execution of Debts and Bankruptcy of April 11, 1889, as amended.

[101] ZPO (German Civil Procedure Code), Article 916, *et seq.*

SPECIAL CONSIDERATIONS IN FOREIGN PARTY CASES 807

where the principal basis for obtaining an attachment is the defendant's non-residence,[102] and Spain, which has similar requirements.[103]

In some jurisdictions, such as England, the plaintiff must present evidence that the defendant has assets in the country. He is not, however, because of a plaintiff's usually limited knowledge of the extent of a defendant's assets, obliged to show where the assets may be found, although he may be assisted in identifying assets through orders for discovery, interrogatories and disclosure of assets by affidavits, which are commonly granted in aid of a *Mareva* injunction. Broader "fishing expeditions"—under attachment orders which allow levies on a variety of possible garnishees—are permitted in the Netherlands, Italy and Belgium, just as they are in New York.[104] On the other hand, under Swiss law, plaintiffs have to comply with certain minimum standards as to the specification of the assets to be attached. The Federal Supreme Court still holds a mere generic description of the assets as sufficient.[105] Based on a long-standing practice that attachment may not be abused as a measure to search for assets of debtors, however, in a recent decision, the Zurich Appelate Court ruled that the existence of certain assets has to be substantiated if there are indications that the attachment is sought in order to search for assets of the debtor.[106] In such countries as Japan and Korea, although not required by law, the generally accepted practice is that the assets to be attached be identified.[107] In most countries, however, the plaintiff may obtain an attachment order without presenting evidence as to the identity or location of the defendant's assets.

---

[102] Other bases for attachment in Switzerland are (1) that the defendant is absconding in an attempt to evade payment, (2) that he has no fixed residence, (3) that earlier compulsory debt collections against him were totally or partially unsuccessful, or (4) if the debtor is in transit and the claim for which the attachment is sought is due.

[103] The debtor must either be a non-naturalized foreigner in Spain, or a Spaniard or a naturalized foreigner in Spain without a known domicile, properties, or industrial or mercantile establishment located where proceedings against him could be initiated. An attachment may be available also when the defendant is a resident, but (i) has no real estate assets or (ii) there is a reasonable threat that the defendant will dispose of his assets in prejudice to his creditors. Spanish Law of Civil Procedure, Art. 1400.

[104] Italian Code of Civil Procedure §§ 670-671; Belgian Judicial Code Art. 1447; Philippine Revised Rules of Court Rule 57 § 2; N.Y. Civ. Prac. L. & R. §§ 6201, 6212, 7502(c) (McKinney 1988).

[105] Decision of the Swiss Federal Supreme Court ("BGE") 103 II 86 and 51.

[106] Decision of the Zurich Appelate Court March 13, 1986; ZR 85 (1986) No. 95.

[107] Japanese Code of Civil Procedure §§ 744-747.

One of the most important considerations in obtaining attachments abroad is the security which the plaintiff may be required to provide to protect the defendant against the consequences of an attachment that ultimately proves not to have been warranted. In some countries, such as France and Belgium, no security is required,[108] while in England a court will normally require the plaintiff to give an undertaking not to use, without the leave of court, information obtained in asset-related discovery. In other countries, security requirements are more burdensome—sometimes an almost insurmountable obstacle. In Germany, for example, if the showing made by the plaintiff is not sufficiently persuasive as to the probability of success on the merits, the court may, at its discretion, require the posting of a bond or a similar guarantee that may equal the full amount of the damages sought by the plaintiff.[109]

The extent to which an attachment may be worth the time and expense required depends, in significant part, on what the attaching plaintiff obtains as a result of the attachment. If plaintiffs are able to obtain a lien that is superior to the rights asserted by creditors who may come later, they will be willing to expend more effort than they would if the best they can obtain is a right that is subject to later defeasance by other claimants against the same assets.

In New York, once an order of attachment is served, the garnishee, frequently a bank, is obliged to report what assets are affected by the order.[110] This information is made available to the plaintiff, who may also, when there are numerous creditors seeking security, obtain information as to where his attachment stands in relation to attachments and liens obtained by others, including the amounts of those other liens.[111]

The plaintiff is in quite a different position in many jurisdictions outside the United States. In Switzerland, for example, the majority of the banks—the most likely garnishees—still refuse to reveal what, if anything, was attached. A bank that has its own claim against the attached assets must, however, make disclosure to the bankruptcy office or risk losing its right against the assets. Under the law in The Netherlands, the plaintiff only finds out what he has attached at the completion of the hearing on the merits, when he enforces his judgment against the bank.

---

108 French Code of Civil Procedure, art. 48-57 (*Ancien*); Belgian Judicial Code, Arts. 1413, 1447.

---

109 *See* note 101, *supra.*

---

110 N.Y. Civ. Prac. L. & R. § 6219 (McKinney 1988). The garnishee may limit its statement to the amount of the attachment, even if the garnishee holds property or money in excess of that amount.

---

111 N.Y. Civ. Prac. L. & R. §§ 6220 and 6221 (McKinney 1988).

SPECIAL CONSIDERATIONS IN FOREIGN PARTY CASES   809

In other countries, disclosure is obtained by the parties directly or through the courts. Thus, in Belgium[112] and Germany,[113] the garnishee must provide to the plaintiff, within two weeks of service of the attachment order, information concerning the nature of the assets attached and about other attachments against the same property. In such countries as Brazil, France, Italy, Japan, Korea and the Philippines,[114] disclosure is made to the court or a court official, either on application by the plaintiff, or as a matter of course. The information so provided is ordinarily available to the plaintiff.

In New York, the existence of other attachments and the order in which they are obtained are of crucial importance to the attaching plaintiff, because the race is to the swift—the earliest attachments have priority over those filed later.[115] If the assets attached are insufficient to satisfy the claims of the latecomers, those too late are left without protection since there is no proration among claimants as in bankruptcy.

Surprising as it may seem to American lawyers, an attaching creditor outside the United States does not always obtain a priority lien over the assets he attaches. In England, for example, the courts do not assume control over the assets; they issue *"Mareva* injunctions" under which the defendant is restrained from removing his assets from the jurisdiction pending the trial of an action on the merits.[116] The *Mareva* injunction does not give the plaintiff any priority over other creditors. Similarly, Belgian law does not create a priority lien in the attaching creditor.

In France, the attached assets are not removed or transferred from the control of the garnishee, but are simply frozen where they are.[117] Attachment creditors obtain, through their attachment, no priority over other creditors. Therefore, although the attached assets remain out of the defendant's control, they may be executed on by the first creditor with a judgment, regardless of

---

[112] Belgian Judicial Code Art. 1447.

[113] German Code of Civil Procedure, § 840.

[114] Brazilian Code of Civil Procedure, arts. 646-679 (Decree-Law 5.869 of Jan. 11, 1973); French Code of Civil Procedure, arts. 48-57 (*Ancien*); Italian Code of Civil Procedure, art. 670; Japanese Code of Civil Procedure, arts. 737, 738, 744-747; Philippine Revised Rules of Cout, Rule 57, § 10.

[115] The priority among two or more orders of attachment against the same defendant is in the order in which they were delivered to the officer who levied upon the property or debt. N.Y. Civ. Prac. L. & R. §§ 6226 (McKinney 1988).

[116] *See* note 98, *supra*.

[117] French Code of Civil Procedure, art. 48-57 (*Ancien*).

whether he obtained a prejudgment attachment. If the debtor has gone into bankruptcy, however, bankruptcy rules will apply to the disposition of assets. A similar approach is taken under the laws of Italy, Japan, Korea, The Netherlands and the Philippines.[118]

The bases on which attachments are vacated in countries outside the United States are generally similar to one another and to the procedures followed in New York.[119] Generally, when a defendant can establish that the grounds for the issuance of an attachment order no longer exist—or never did exist—a court will vacate the attachment. In some jurisdictions a garnishee may also apply to the court for the *vacatur* of an attachment. The garnishee may deny, for example, that he has any property of the defendant in his possession or owes any money to the defendant. In many countries, courts will require, if they did not in granting the attachments, the establishment of security for damages which might be caused by the attachment if it turns out not to have been warranted. The security is often in the form of a bond and frequently covers consequential damages as well as attorneys' fees and court costs.

B. Enforcement of Judgments

Generally speaking, judgments in which the foreign defendant has appeared in a United States court and defended on the merits will be recognized and enforced by foreign courts. The enforcement of judgments abroad often involves both the obtaining of a court order of attachment to secure the ultimate award of judgment and the commencement of recognition, or *exequatur*, proceedings. In many respects, the enforcement of arbitral awards in countries which are signatories to the New York Convention for the Recognition and Enforcement of Foreign Arbitral Awards[120] is procedurally easier than is enforcement of court judgments obtained here. Generally, arbitral awards under the New York Convention are enforced in more simplified proceedings than are foreign judgments.[121]

---

[118] Italian Code of Civil Procedure, art. 670 and Royal Decree No. 267 of March 16, 1942; Japanese Code of Civil Procedure, arts. 737, 738 and Bankruptcy Law, arts. 17, 59; Korean Bankruptcy Law, arts 16, 50, 84-88; Philippine Insolvency Law §§ 29 and 59.

---

[119] *See* generally N.Y. Civ. Prac. L. & R. §§ 6223 (McKinney 1988) (describing the procedures for vacating attachments in New York).

---

[120] Done at New York June 10, 1958; *entered into force for the United States* December 29, 1970; *codified* at 21 U.S.T. 2517, T.I.A.S. 6997, 330 U.N.T.S. 3.

---

[121] A.J. van den Berg, *The New York Arbitration Convention of 1958*, 236-37 (1981).

SPECIAL CONSIDERATIONS IN FOREIGN PARTY CASES 811

Since the United States is not a party to any treaties or conventions on the recognition of foreign judgments, the judgments of courts of the United States are reviewed for recognition and enforcement in accordance with provisions of the laws of the foreign country where such recognition and enforcement are sought. Greater scrutiny is given to judgments obtained by default than to those obtained in proceedings in which there has been an appearance by the defendant, although, theoretically, it should not matter that a judgment is obtained by default, providing due process has been accorded to the defendant.

In many countries, such as West Germany, the procedure for the recognition and enforcement of a foreign judgment is often combined with an attachment of the defendant's local property based on the judgment obtained outside the country, followed by or contemporaneous with the commencement of *exequatur*, or recognition, proceedings. Finally, there is the execution of that judgment, once recognized, against the attached assets.[122]

Swiss law provides a typical example of the conditions under which foreign judgments will be enforced. In the absence of a treaty,[123] foreign judgments and foreign arbitral awards are enforced and recognized under Swiss law if the following three conditions are satisfied:[124] (1) the foreign court which rendered the judgment must have had jurisdiction over the defendant according to Swiss law standards of jurisdiction; (2) the foreign judgment must be final and enforceable according to the law of the foreign country where the judgment was rendered; and (3) the enforcement of the foreign judgment must not violate Swiss public policy.

Of these three conditions, the first may be the most difficult to satisfy. For example, if the courts of the United States would not, under the German civil

---

122 Articles 723, 917 of the ZPO.

123 Currently, no treaty exists between the United States and Switzerland. If a treaty applies, federal and cantonal rules on the enforcement of judgments are overridden by treaty standards. Decisions of the Swiss Federal Supreme Court, BGE 53 I 219 and 76 I 345.

124 Up to December 31, 1988, enforcement and recognition of foreign judgment was governed by cantonal law. *See, e.g.*, § 302 of the Code of Civil Procedure of the Canton of Zurich (most of the civil procedure codes of the other cantons contain the same conditions). On January 1, 1989, the new Federal Private International Law ("IPRG") will be enacted; it includes a comprehensive set of rules on enforcement of foreign judgment in Switzerland (Art. 25 *et seq.* IPRG). These rules will replace all the rules on enforcement of foreign judgments at the cantonal level. However, the IPRG will not supersede conflicting provisions in treaties on enforcement of judgments to which Switzerland is a party.

procedure code or the Swiss cantonal codes of civil procedure,[125] have jurisdiction, the United States judgment will not be recognized in West Germany or Switzerland.[126] Thus, an American judgment obtained on the bases of "long-arm" jurisdiction will not be enforced in these two countries unless there is independent bases in the facts for jurisdiction under their respective laws.

As to default judgments, some civil-law jurisdictions, such as West Germany, will recognize such judgments only if service of process was made on the defendant personally outside their home country or in their home country according to its service rules.[127] Care should be taken not only as to service of process, but also as to the legal definition of a default judgment. Under West German law, for example, any type of participation in foreign judicial proceedings, even if only a special appearance to challenge jurisdiction, renders the judgment a contested one rather than one obtained by default.[128]

In a common-law jurisdiction, such as England, the enforcement of American judgments will be governed by common-law rules rather than by statute since the United States is not a party to a convention on the enforcement of foreign judgments. Under these rules, a foreign judgment is not directly enforceable by execution or any other process. Such judgments instead are considered a debt between the parties which is enforceable through an ordinary lawsuit.

At common law, an English court will recognize a foreign judgment only if the foreign court had jurisdiction under English conflict of law rules. According to these rules, jurisdiction is proper if: (1) the defendant was resident or present in the foreign country on the date the proceedings commenced; (2) where the defendant is a corporation, it was carrying on business in the foreign country at a definite and reasonably permanent place on the date the proceedings commenced; or (3) the defendant submitted or agreed to submit to the jurisdiction of the foreign court.

---

[125] Article 59 of the Swiss Federal Constitution confers on solvent debtors domiciled in Switzerland the privilege of being sued at their domicile. U.S. money judgments based on "long-arm" statutes are, therefore, enforceable against solvent Swiss-domiciled debtors only if those persons have waived (*e.g.*, through a carefully worded forum selection clause) their Article 59 rights; *see also* Art. 26, 143 para. 2 and 165 IPRG.

---

[126] Article 328 of the ZPO; Section 302 of the Code of Civil Procedure of the Canton of Zurich.

---

[127] Article 328(I)(2) of the ZPO.

---

[128] Article 328(I)(2) of the ZPO n.151f.

Under § 33 of the Civil Jurisdiction and Judgments Act of 1982 (which reversed the common law rule), an appearance to contest the foreign court's jurisdiction does not constitute submission to that court's jurisdiction. However, if the defendant appears in the foreign court to contest the merits, even if he is at the same time challenging the court's jurisdiction, submission to its jurisdiction will be found. The jurisdiction of a foreign court will also be found if there is an express contractual agreement by the defendant that all disputes are to be referred exclusively to that court. Moreover, under any of the above situations, there are differing rules depending upon whether the judgment sought to be enforced is *in personam* or *in rem*. Generally, a judgment *in personam* will be enforced only if it is for a definite monetary sum and, thus, for example, a court will not enforce an order for specific performance.

V. CASES INVOLVING FOREIGN SOVEREIGNS

Foreign governments are increasingly entering the commercial marketplace. Today, state-owned oil, banking and trading companies are active participants in commercial markets. Disputes involving state-owned companies and enterprises are governed by a special statute, the Foreign Sovereign Immunities Act of 1976 (the "FSIA").[129]

Before the FSIA went into effect on January 19, 1977, determinations of sovereign immunity were usually made on the basis of advice from the State Department. Under the Supreme Court's 1943 decision in *Ex Parte Republic of Peru*,[130] suggestions by the executive branch to the courts for immunity in a particular case were dispositive of the immunity issue. Moreover, even if a foreign state were not entitled to immunity, no machinery existed for effecting personal service upon the foreign state. The result was that plaintiffs often resorted to prejudgment attachments to obtain *quasi-in-rem* jurisdiction over the foreign state. Not only were such attachments regarded as an irritant to foreign relations, but they were also useless to secure judgments because the general practice in the United States was to accord a foreign state absolute immunity from execution.[131]

---

129 The Foreign Sovereign Immunities Act of 1976, Pub. L. No. 94-583, 90 Stat. 2891-97 (*codified at* 28 U.S.C. Sections 1330, 1332(a), 1391(f), 1441(d), 1602-1611). All Section references throughout the balance of this chapter, unless otherwise indicated, are to Title 28.

130 318 U.S. 578 (1943).

131 See H.R. Rep. No. 1487, 94th Cong., 2d Sess. 1, 7-8 (1976), reprinted in [1976] *U.S. Code Cong. & Ad. News.*, 6604 (hereinafter cited as the "House Report").

In order to bring the United States into alignment with the general practice of other developed countries, to provide a comprehensive scheme for resolving issues of sovereign immunity and to take away from the executive branch the responsibility of acting, in effect, as the judge of such issues, Congress enacted the FSIA.[132] The FSIA broadened the bases for obtaining *in personam* jurisdiction over foreign states[133] and permitted for the first time execution against certain of their property.[134] In exchange for these rights against foreign states, however, Congress eliminated the availability of jurisdictional prejudgment attachments[135] and prescribed limitations on prejudgment attachments for security purposes.[136] Issues of importance under the FSIA include jurisdiction, service of process and attachment and execution against property of a foreign state.

A. Jurisdiction

The FSIA proceeds on the premise[137] that a foreign state is immune from the jurisdiction of the courts of the United States (federal and state)[138] unless it is party to a case that comes within one of the exceptions enumerated in the FSIA.[139] As the House Judiciary Committee noted:

> Stating the basic principle in terms of immunity may be of some advantage to foreign states in doubtful cases, but, since sovereign immunity is an affirmative defense which must be specially

---

[132] *Id.*

[133] Sections 1605-1607. See discussion, *infra*.

[134] Sections 1610-1611.

[135] Sections 1609, 1910(d). See discussion, *infra*.

[136] Under Section 1610(d), a foreign state's property used for commercial activity in the United States may be subject to prejudgment attachment only if such attachment (1) is for the purpose of securing satisfaction of a judgment and (2) the foreign state has "explicitly waived its immunity from attachment prior to judgment."

[137] Section 1604.

[138] The FSIA sets forth the "sole and exclusive standards to be used in resolving questions of sovereign immunity raised by foreign states before Federal and State courts in the United States," and is, thus, clearly "intended to preempt any other State or Federal law." House Report at 12.

[139] The FSIA has been interpreted so as to be broad enough to cover cases brought in the courts of the United States by foreign plaintiffs against foreign states. *Verlinden B.V. v. Central Bank of Nigeria*, 488 F. Supp. 1284 (S.D.N.Y. 1980), *aff'd on other grounds*, 647 F.2d 320 (2d Cir. 1981), *rev'd on other grounds*, 461 U.S. 480 (1983).

SPECIAL CONSIDERATIONS IN FOREIGN PARTY CASES 815

pleaded, the burden will remain on the foreign state to produce evidence in support of its claim of immunity. Thus, evidence must be produced to establish that a foreign state or one of its subdivisions, agencies or instrumentalities is the defendant in the suit and that the plaintiff's claim relates to a public act of the foreign state— that it is, an act not within the exceptions in Sections 1605-1607. Once the foreign state has produced such prima facie evidence of immunity, the burden of going forward would shift to the plaintiff to produce evidence establishing that the foreign state is not entitled to immunity. The ultimate burden of proving immunity would rest with the foreign state.[140]

Section 1605 contains the exceptions to sovereign immunity. The exception relied on most often provides that a foreign state shall not be immune in any case:

> [1] In which the action is based upon a commercial activity carried on in the United States by the foreign state; or [2] upon an act performed in the United States in connection with the commercial activity of the foreign state elsewhere; or [3] upon an act outside the territory of the United States in connection with the commercial activity of the foreign state elsewhere and that act causes a direct effect in the United States.[141]

Crucial to each of these three clauses is the phrase "commercial activity," a term through which the drafters adopted the long-recognized distinction between "commercial" and "governmental" activity—the latter for which the foreign state is entitled to immunity.[142] Section 1603(d) provides the following definition of "commercial activity":

> A "commercial activity" means either a regular course of commercial conduct or a particular commercial transaction or act. The commercial character of an activity shall be determined by refer-

---

[140] House Report at 17.

[141] Section 1605(a)(2).

[142] *Texas Trading & Milling Corp. v. Fed. Republic of Nigeria*, 647 F.2d 300 (2d Cir. 1981), *cert. denied*, 454 U.S. 1148 (1982).

ence to the nature[143] of the course of conduct or particular transaction or act, rather than by reference to its purpose.[144]

The term "commercial," however, is nowhere defined in the FSIA and it has been left to the courts to describe the commercial activity jurisdictional exception.[145] As one court has stated, the FSIA "did little more than produce . . . a statutory skeleton from which the federal judiciary has been left to create, through a case-by-case decisional process, a fully developed body of sovereign immunity law."[146] In *Texas Trading*,[147] the Second Circuit sought to define "commercial activity." The court referred to the legislative history of the FSIA, case law on the subject prior to enactment of the FSIA, and, because the FSIA contained a reference to international law, standards of international law, as the sources for defining "commercial activity."[148] The court stated that if the activity was one in which a private person could

---

[143] This language sought to settle a dispute over whether a "nature" or "purpose" test should be applied. The fact that goods or services to be procured through a contract are to be used for a public purpose is irrelevant; it is the commercial nature of an activity that is critical. Thus, a contract by a foreign government to construct a government building constitutes a commercial activity and should be considered to be a commercial contract, even if its ultimate activity is to further a public function. House Report at 16.

[144] Section 1603(d) (footnote added).

[145] Indeed, the draftsmen of the FSIA described it as providing only "very modest guidance" on issues of preeminent importance. Congress deliberately left the meaning open and "decided to put [their] faith in the U.S. courts" to answer the difficult questions. *Hearings on H.R. 11315 Before the Subcommittee on Administrative Law and Governmental Relations of the House Committee on the Judiciary*, 94th Cong., 2d Sess. 53 (1976) (testimony of Monroe Leigh, Legal Adviser, Dep't of State).

[146] *Gibbons v. Udaras na Gaeltachta*, 549 F. Supp. 1094, 1106 (S.D.N.Y. 1982).

[147] *Texas Trading, supra*, 647 F.2d 300.

[148] *Id.* at 309-10.

SPECIAL CONSIDERATIONS IN FOREIGN PARTY CASES 817

engage, the sovereign would not be entitled to immunity.[149] Nevertheless, despite attempts by the courts to define "commercial activity," as commentators have noted, the courts have been unable to agree as to the meaning of the jurisdictional criteria and the resulting ambiguity has been criticized as threatening the important uniformity policy which underlies the FSIA.[150]

A second category of cases from which the protection of immunity has been removed comprises those in which the sovereign has waived its immunity.[151] Waivers may be explicit, such as those found in treaties and in specific contractual provisions, or they may be implied. According to the section-by-section analysis of the Judiciary Committee:

> [T]he courts have found [implied] waivers in cases where a foreign state has agreed to arbitration in another country or where a foreign state has agreed that the law of a particular country should govern a contract. An implicit waiver would also include a situation where a foreign state has filed a responsive pleading in an action without raising the defense of sovereign immunity.[152]

Many questions, however, have been raised about this comment.

The courts have had little difficulty in holding that foreign states waive immunity by responding on the merits to a suit without raising immunity as a defense.[153] Also, Section 1607 specifically provides that there is no immunity

---

[149] *Texas Trading* also sought to build a concrete foundation for analyzing whether a case falls within the "commercial activity" exception by setting forth the following five-prong test:
  1) Does the conduct the action is based upon or related to qualify as "commercial activity?"
  2) Does that commercial activity bear the relation to the cause of action and to the United States described by one of the three phrases of § 1605(a)(2), warranting the Court's exercise of subject matter jurisdiction under § 1330(a)?
  3) Does the exercise of this congressional subject matter jurisdiction lie within the permissible limits of the "judicial power" set forth in Article III?
  4) Does subject matter jurisdiction under § 1330(a) and service under § 1608 exist, thereby making personal jurisdiction proper under § 1330(b)?
  5) Does the exercise of personal jurisdiction under § 1330(b) comply with the due process clause, thus making personal jurisdiction proper?
  Id. at 308.

[150] *E.g.*, Dellappena, *Suing Foreign Governments and Their Corporations* (1988) at 157-160 in which the author collects cases with similar fact patterns but in which courts reached opposite results.

[151] Section 1605(a)(1).

[152] House Report at 18.

[153] *Sea Lift, Inc. v. Refinadora Costarricense de Petroleo, S.A.*, 601 F. Supp. 457 (S.D. Fla. 1984), *rev'd on other grounds*, 792 F.2d 989 (11th Cir. 1986); *Aboujdid v. Singapore Airlines, Ltd.*, 67 N.Y.2d 450, 494 N.E.2d 1055, 503 N.Y.S.2d 555 (1986).

with respect to counterclaims arising out of the transaction or occurrence that is the subject matter of the claim or to the extent that the counterclaim does not seek relief exceeding an amount or differing in kind from that sought by the foreign state. However, the Judiciary Committee's second suggestion, that a sovereign impliedly waives immunity by agreeing to arbitrate in another country, has not been as readily accepted. The courts have had no difficulty in holding that a party may compel a foreign state to arbitrate (or may enforce an arbitral award against it) when the parties have agreed to arbitrate in the United States.[154] Where the arbitration is to take place abroad, however, some courts have expressed an unwillingness to conclude that the foreign state has implicitly waived its immunity from suit in the United States.[155]

In an attempt to clarify this issue, the Congress, in the closing hours of the 100th Congress, passed an amendment to the FSIA.[156] The amendment, S.2204, which was promoted by the American Bar Association, specifically provides that there is no immunity in actions to enforce an agreement to arbitrate or to confirm an award made pursuant to such an agreement to arbitrate if:

(A) the arbitration takes place or is intended to take place in the United States,

(B) the agreement or award is or may be governed by a treaty or other international agreement in force for the United States calling for a recognition and enforcement of arbitral awards,

(C) the underlying claim, save for the agreement to arbitrate, could have been brought in a United States court under [Sections 1605 or 1607], or

(D) paragraph [1] of [Section 1605] is otherwise applicable

As soon as the bill is signed into law,[157] this exception to immunity will be codified as the sixth exception in Section 1605.

---

[154] See Birch Shipping Corp. v. Embassy of United Republic of Tanzania, 507 F. Supp. 311 (D.D.C. 1980); Ohntrup v. Firearms Center, Inc., 516 F. Supp. 1281, 1285 (E.D. Pa. 1981), aff'd, 760 F.2d 259 (3d Cir. 1985).

---

[155] See, e.g., Ohntrup, 516 F. Supp. at 1285, Verlinden B.V. v. Central Bank of Nigeria, 488 F. Supp. 1284, 1300-01 (S.D.N.Y. 1980), aff'd on other grounds, 647 F.2d 320 (2d Cir. 1981), reversed on other grounds, 461 U.S. 480 (1983).

---

[156] See 134 Cong. Rec. 17209 (Oct. 21, 1988).

---

[157] In all likelihood, by the time of the publication of this book, S.2204 will have already been signed into law.

SPECIAL CONSIDERATIONS IN FOREIGN PARTY CASES 819

The Judiciary Committee's third suggestion, that an implied waiver may be found from a choice-of-law provision, has also been questioned by the courts[158] and appears contrary to the judicial principle that choice-of-law provisions cannot be relied upon in and of themselves to create jurisdiction.[159] Nevertheless, at least one court has followed the committee's suggestion.[160] Thus, although implied waivers of immunity may be inferred by the courts, the situations in which implied waivers will be found need further to be developed in judicial decisions.

A third exception to sovereign immunity is in suits over property rights improperly taken in violation of international law.[161] The first clause of section 1605(a)(3) authorizes jurisdiction if the property (or property exchanged for it) is found in the United States in connection with a commercial activity carried on in the United States by the foreign state. The second clause provides for jurisdiction if the property (or property exchanged for it) is owned or operated by an agency or instrumentality of a foreign state and that agency or instrumentality is engaged in commercial activity in the United States. This section represents an effort by the Congress to narrow the application of the Act of State doctrine, under which the courts of the United States have refrained from ruling on actions by foreign states with respect to property within their own borders.[162] The doctrine has been primarily applied to deny relief in United States courts to persons whose property was expropriated by a foreign state within its own territory.[163] Discussion of the Act of State doctrine—described by one commentator as in "a state of utter confusion"[164]—is beyond the scope of this chapter and is referred to only as a

---

158 *Verlinden B.V.*, 488 F. Supp. at 1301-1302.

159 *McShan v. Omega Louis Brandt Et Frere*, 536 F.2d 516 (2d Cir. 1976); *Baron & Company, Inc. v. Bank of New Jersey*, 497 F. Supp. 534 (E.D. 1980).

160 *Marlowe v. Argentine Naval Comm'n*, 604 F. Supp. 703 (D.D.C. 1985).

161 Section 1605(a)(3).

162 Following is the classic formulation of the Act of State doctrine:
Every sovereign state is bound to respect the independence of every other sovereign state, and the courts of one country will not sit in judgment on the acts of the government of another, done within its own territory. Redress of grievances by reason of such acts must be obtained through the means open to be availed of by sovereign powers between themselves.
Underhill v. Hernandez, 168 U.S. 250, 252 (1897).

163 The leading case is *Banco Nacional de Cuba v. Sabbatino*, 376 U.S. 398 (1964).

164 Dellapenna, *Suing Foreign Governments and Their Corporations* (1988) at 268.

reminder that the doctrine should be borne in mind in expropriation cases, or even in cases in which governmental acts of foreign states within their own territory may be involved.

The fourth exception denies immunity to a foreign state in cases in which rights and property located in the United States are acquired by succession or gift, or rights in immovable property situated in the United States are at issue.[165] This section expresses the general agreement on this issue in international practice and effectuates a strong judicially stated policy for local authority over real property.[166]

A fifth exception to sovereign immunity is for cases in which "money damages are sought against a foreign state for personal injury or death or damage to or loss of property, occurring in the United States and caused by the tortious act or omission" of a foreign state or its officials or employees acting within the scope of their office or employment.[167] Immunity remains intact, however, for claims arising out of the performance of discretionary functions—regardless of whether the discretion is abused—and for claims arising out of malicious prosecution, abuse of process, libel, slander, misrepresentation, deceit or interference with contractual rights.[168] According to the Judiciary Committee, since no case relating to a traffic accident could be brought against members of diplomatic missions who enjoy diplomatic immunity, the purpose of this exception is to permit the victim of a traffic accident or other noncommercial tort to maintain an action against the foreign state, to the extent otherwise permitted by law.[169]

The sixth exception denies immunity to a foreign state in a suit brought to enforce a maritime lien against the foreign state's vessel or cargo if the "lien is based upon a commercial activity of the foreign state."[170] Although the purpose of this section was to allow plaintiffs to pursue their claims, Congress also sought to avoid the friction caused by arresting the vessel of a

---

[165] Section 1605(a)(4).

[166] House Report at 20.

[167] Section 1605(a)(5).

[168] Section 1605(a)(5)(A)-(B).

[169] House Report at 21.

[170] Section 1605(b).

foreign state.[171] Accordingly, Section 1605(b), in essence, converts maritime liens from *in rem* claims against the vessel to *in personam* claims against the foreign state owning the vessel.

Regardless of which of the exceptions is relied on, "[i]n view of the potential sensitivity of actions against foreign states and the importance of developing a uniform body of law in this area,"[172] Congress has encouraged the bringing of actions against foreign states in federal courts. This goal was effectuated by providing that cases involving foreign states may be brought in federal courts without regard to the amount in controversy.[173] In addition, at the request of a foreign state, any civil action brought against it in state court may be removed to federal court.[174]

B. Service of Process

Prior to the enactment of the FSIA, attachment of a foreign state's property was a common method of informing the foreign state of the initiation of a suit against it. This method of notice was explicitly abolished under the FSIA[175] and replaced by specific provisions relating to the service of process.

Section 1608 distinguishes between service upon "a foreign state or political subdivisions" on the one hand and upon "an agency or instrumentality of a foreign state" on the other, although the methods of service upon both groups are similar. The structure of Section 1608 is hierarchical; that is, the methods prescribed in succeeding subsections can only be used if the methods in the preceding subsections prove unavailing.

For service upon a foreign state or a political subdivision, the preferred method is by delivery of a copy of the summons and complaint in accordance with whatever "special arrangement" exists between the parties.[176] A provision in a contract for the sale of airplanes which provided that "all notices, requests, demands, or other communications to or upon the respective par-

---

[171] Indeed, Congress was so intent on preventing a foreign state's vessel from being arrested that Section 1605(b) provides that a plaintiff will lose his *in personam* remedy and the foreign state will be entitled to immunity if an arrest is made with knowledge that the vessel belongs to a foreign state. House Report at 22.

[172] House Report at 32.

[173] Section 1330.

[174] Section 1441.

[175] Sections 1609, 1610(d).

[176] Section 1608(a)(1).

ties shall be deemed to have been given or made when deposited in the mail . . . [to the] respective addresses set forth below," was held to be a special arrangement under Section 1608(a)(1).[177] The court declined to accept the sovereign's argument that the contractual provision was not a "special arrangement *for service*" and held that service by mail in accordance with the contract constituted valid service.[178]

If no such special arrangement exists, service upon a foreign state or political subdivision may be made by delivering a copy of the summons and complaint in accordance with an applicable international convention.[179] At present, the only applicable international convention that has been ratified by the United States is the Hague Service Convention,[180] which has been ratified by only 23 countries.

The next most preferred method of service is by registered mail or some equivalent form requiring a signed receipt. The plaintiff is required to dispatch by mail through the clerk of the court a copy of the summons, complaint and notice of suit, together with a translation of each into the official language of the foreign state, to the head of the ministry of foreign affairs of the foreign state.[181]

If the first three methods fail and 30 days have passed without confirmation of receipt of service by registered mail, the plaintiff may seek to serve a foreign state or political subdivision through diplomatic channels. The plaintiff must send by return receipt mail, through the clerk of the court, to the United States Secretary of State, two copies of the summons, complaint and notice of suit, together with a translation of each into the official language of the foreign state. The Secretary of State then transmits one copy of the papers through diplomatic channels to the foreign state and returns to the clerk of the

---

[177] *Marlowe v. Argentine Naval Comm'n*, 604 F. Supp. 703 (D.D.C. 1985), *but see Mendik Realty Company, Inc. v. Permanent Mission of Libya to the United Nations*, Civ. No. 81-5410 slip op. (S.D.N.Y. Nov. 16, 1981).

[178] *Id.* at 708.

[179] Section 1608(a)(2).

[180] Convention on the Service Abroad of Judicial and Extrajudicial Documents in Civil or Commercial Matters. 20 U.S.T. 361, T.I.A.S. 6638, 658 U.N.T.S. 163. See footnotes 6-8, *supra*, and the accompanying text, which describes how service is made through a Central Authority designated for the receipt of process from abroad.

[181] Section 1608(a)(3). A "Notice of Suit" is meant to provide the foreign state with an explanation of the significance of the summons and complaint and to indicate the steps available or required under U.S. law in order to defend the action. House Report at 24-25.

court a certified copy indicating when the papers were transmitted.[182] Problems can arise under this method, however, if service is required upon a foreign state with which the United States does not maintain diplomatic relations.

Somewhat different rules apply for service of process upon "an agency or instrumentality of a foreign state." The first method is through any special arrangement which may exist.[183] The second method, if the first is unavailable, is in accordance with an applicable international convention. However, as an additional method in this second level of service methods (and which is not available for service on a foreign state), service may be accomplished by delivering a copy of the summons and complaint to an officer, managing agent or any other agent authorized by appointment or by law to receive process in the United States.[184]

The third level for service upon an agency or instrumentality is similar to the third method of service upon a foreign state in that it permits service by a form of mail of a copy of the summons and complaint (but not a notice of suit), together with a translation of each into the official language of the foreign state, to be dispatched by the clerk of the court, requiring a signed receipt, to the agency or instrumentality to be served.[185] There are, however, two additional methods under this third level. One alternative is delivery of a copy of the summons and complaint (and translations) as directed by an authority of the foreign state or political subdivision in response to a letter rogatory.[186] The second is for delivery to be made of the summons and complaint (and translations) as directed by an order of a United States court "consistent with the law of the place where service is to be made."[187] In choosing among these three alternatives, it is important to bear in mind that the method chosen must also be "reasonably calculated to give actual notice."[188]

---

[182] Section 1608(a)(4).

[183] Section 1608(b)(1).

[184] Section 1608(b)(2).

[185] Section 1608(b)(3)(B).

[186] Section 1608(b)(3)(A).

[187] Section 1608(b)(3)(C).

[188] Section 1608(b)(3).

For purposes of responsive pleadings by the foreign state and default judgments against the foreign state, the foreign state is treated similarly to the United States government in suits against it. Thus, the foreign state has 60 days after service of process to answer or otherwise plead,[189] and no default judgment may be taken unless the claimant establishes the claim or right to relief by evidence satisfactory to the court.[190]

C. Attachment and Execution

Prior to the enactment of the FSIA, prejudgment attachments of a foreign state's property were a common method of commencing lawsuits against foreign states although the courts did not permit execution against the property of a foreign state to satisfy final judgments.[191] The FSIA abolished attachments for the purpose of obtaining jurisdiction but permitted, under specified circumstances, prejudgment attachments for security purposes and attachments for the enforcement of judgments.[192]

As with the general immunity rule, the FSIA proceeds on the premise that the property of a foreign state, located in the United States, is immune from attachment and execution except as otherwise specifically provided for in the FSIA.[193] Furthermore, the rules relating to prejudgment attachment and execution are both "subject to existing international agreements to which the United States is a party at the time of enactment."[194]

Prejudgment attachments are available only for the purpose of securing satisfaction of a judgment and only if the foreign state has explicitly waived its immunity from attachment prior to judgment.[195] If these two requirements are met, a prejudgment attachment may be obtained against property that is "used for a commercial activity in the United States."[196]

---

189 Section 1608(d).

190 Section 1608(e).

191 House Report at 8.

192 Section 1610.

193 Section 1609.

194 Section 1609.

195 Section 1610(d).

196 Section 1610(d).

The Second Circuit has stated that, in determining whether there is an explicit waiver, it is not necessary that the words "prejudgment attachment" appear *in haec verba*.[197] Courts, however, have been reluctant to find express waivers of prejudgment attachment. Thus, in a case in which a plaintiff argued that the Treaty of Amity between Iran and the United States[198] included an express waiver, the Southern District of New York disagreed, stating, "it is hard to imagine that a sovereign nation, in entering a treaty supposedly to promote commerce, would at the same time even suggest that it would evade a lawful judgment arising out of commercial activities."[199]

And in a similar case construing a trade agreement between Romania and the United States, the Second Circuit seemed to limit its earlier decision in *Libra Bank Ltd. v. Banco Nacional de Costa Rica* to the "all-inclusive" waiver in that case.[200] The court pointed out:

> [A] waiver of immunity from prejudgment attachment must be explicit in the common sense meaning of that form: the asserted waiver must demonstrate unambiguously the foreign State's intention to waive its immunity from prejudgment attachment in this country. We do not take lightly the congressional demand for explicitness.[201]

The court held that the waiver of immunity "from suit or execution of judgment or other liability" was not an explicit waiver, stating that "in view of the delphic character of the phrase 'other liability,'" the defendants did not explicitly waive their immunity from prejudgment attachment.[202] Thus, as a practical matter, parties to contracts with foreign states who envision a future

---

[197] *Libra Bank Ltd. v. Banco Nacional de Costa Rica*, 676 F.2d 47, 49 (2d Cir. 1982).

[198] Treaty of Amity, Economic Relations, and Consular Rights between the United States of America and Iran, 8 U.S.T. 899, 909, T.I.A.S. No. 3853 (signed August 15, 1955). Article XI(4) thereof provides: No enterprise of either High Contracting Party . . . shall, if it engages in commercial, industrial, shipping or other business activities within the territories of the other High Contracting Party, claim or enjoy, either for itself or its property, immunity therein from taxation, suit, execution of judgment *or other liability* to which privately owned and controlled enterprises are subjected therein. [Emphasis supplied]

[199] *Reading & Bates Corp. v. Nat'l Iranian Oil Co.*, 478 F. Supp. 724, 729 (S.D.N.Y. 1979).

[200] *S&S Machinery Corp. v. Masinexportimport*, 706 F.2d 411, 418 (2d Cir.), *cert. denied*, 464 U.S. 850 (1983).

[201] *Id.* at 416.

[202] *Id.* at 418.

need for an attachment are well advised to negotiate for provisions specifically providing that the foreign state waives its immunity from prejudgment attachment.

In an apparent attempt to circumvent the restrictions on prejudgment attachments, at least one plaintiff sought a temporary restraining order or preliminary injunction against the removal of a foreign state's assets.[203] However, since the restriction against jurisdictional attachments is meant, *inter alia*, to eliminate the friction in foreign relations that was said to have been caused by jurisdictional attachments,[204] the court did not permit the use of injunctions or restraining orders to circumvent the purposes of the FSIA.

The standards and restrictions regarding postjudgment executions are much less stringent. A foreign state's property used for commercial activity in the United States is not immune from execution or from attachment in aid of execution if: (i) The foreign state has waived its immunity either explicitly or implicitly; (ii) The property is or was used in commercial activity upon which the claim is based; (iii) Execution relates to a judgment establishing rights in property taken in violation of international law; (iv) Execution relates to a judgment establishing rights in property acquired by succession or gift or which is immovable (with the exception of diplomatic or consular property); or (v) The property consists of proceeds under a liability or casualty insurance policy covering claims which were merged into judgments.[205]

In addition, with respect to an agency or instrumentality of a foreign state engaged in commercial activity in the United States, its property in the United States is not immune from execution or from attachment in aid of execution if it has waived its immunity from execution, either explicitly or implicitly, or the judgment relates to a claim from which the agency or instrumentality is not immune under Sections 1605(a)(2) (commercial claims), 1605(a)(3) (expropriation claims), 1605(a)(5) (tort claims), or 1605(b) (maritime claims), regardless of whether the property was used for the activity upon which the claim is based.[206]

---

[203] *Id.*

[204] House Report at 26-27.

[205] Section 1610(a). Under S.2204, passed during the closing hours of the 100th Congress, a sixth category was added which removes property from immunity from execution (or attachment in aid of execution) upon a judgment that "is based on an order confirming an arbitral award rendered against the foreign state, provided that attachment in aide of execution, or execution, would not be inconsistent with any provision in the arbitral agreement." By the time of the publication of this book, S.2204 will, in all likelihood, have already been signed into law.

[206] Section 1610(b).

SPECIAL CONSIDERATIONS IN FOREIGN PARTY CASES 827

No execution or attachment in aid of execution is, however, permitted until a court has ordered such attachment or execution, after determining that a reasonable period of time has elapsed following entry of judgment.[207] Among the factors to be considered by the court in determining whether a reasonable period of time has elapsed are: procedures which may be necessary for payment of a judgment by a foreign state, representations by the foreign state of steps being taken to satisfy the judgment, and evidence that the foreign state is about to remove assets from the jurisdiction to frustrate satisfaction of the judgment.[208]

Finally, notwithstanding the other provisions of the FSIA, the following three categories of property are immune from attachment or execution: (1) property of certain international organizations which disburse funds to, or on the order of, a foreign state, (2) property of a foreign central bank held for its own account (unless such bank has explicitly waived its immunity), and (3) property of a military character or under the control of a military authority which is used or intended to be used in connection with a military activity.[209]

Thus, in suits against foreign sovereigns and their instrumentalities it is the special rules of the FSIA which determine whether suit can be brought, how service of process must be accomplished and in what manner execution of judgment may be carried out.

---

[207] Section 1610(c).

[208] House Report at 30.

[209] Section 1611.

CHAPTER TWENTY-NINE

JURISDICTION AND PROCEDURE IN BANKRUPTCY

by John F. Scheffel, Esq.

I. INTRODUCTION

This chapter skims the highlights of bankruptcy practice in the Federal Courts. The United States Bankruptcy Courts are divisions of the United States District Courts 28 U.S.C. § 157. Practitioners are urged always to refer to the local rules of the bankruptcy court for the district in which the matter they are handling is (or will be) pending. Practitioners also are cautioned that due to the complexities and sophistication of bankruptcy practice and the limitation of space in this book, the following is by no means exhaustive. This chapter is intended only as a general guide for practitioners who do not regularly specialize in bankruptcy practice. Therefore, where a substantial involvement is required, practitioners are urged only to use this chapter as a starting point and to research further and/or call in a qualified bankrutpcy specialist.

Generally, it should be noted that to qualify as a bankrupt (now referred to as a "debtor"), a person (including corporation, partnership, individual, 11 U.S.C. § 101(35)) need not be insolvent; the only requirement is that the debtor not be generally paying its debts as they mature. Further, the bankruptcy court primarily is a court of equity which applies the most fundamental public policies embodied in the bankruptcy code. These include equal treatment of all creditors of each class of creditor and the debtor's right to a fresh start (with all or most past financial woes wiped away).

As a division of the Federal District Court, the bankruptcy court's procedures mesh into those of the Federal District Court. However, in bankruptcy the debtor's assets are the res central to all proceedings. The entire process is geared toward marshalling the debtor's assets and adjudicating the rights of all parties in and to that res. This is so even in reorganization cases not involving the liquidation of the debtor's assets. As the estate and interests in it are the central concerns, a bankruptcy case is comparable to a degree to a probate case.

A practitioner always should bear in mind that the issues and the procedural rules in bankruptcy practice are oriented to the practical and equitable result. For this reason delaying tactics and procedural calisthenics, although available within the Bankruptcy Rules, are not favored in bankruptcy courts and, in fact, are quite frankly frowned upon by most bankruptcy judges in most cases. A practitioner who indulges in such practices without a clearly practical or equitable reason other than delay and obstruction likely will meet with disfavor and, at the bottom line, will not have provided his client with the best possible representation.

II. BANKRUPTCY JURISDICTION

A. Bankruptcy Reform Act/*Northern Pipeline Construction Co. v. Marathon Pipe Line Co.*

With the Bankruptcy Reform Act of 1978, the old bankruptcy statute of 1898 as amended was repealed and major reforms were instituted in the bankruptcy laws of the United States. The 1978 Act sought to vest in the bankruptcy courts national jurisdiction covering virtually all aspects of the bankruptcy case and virtually all civil matters pertaining to the debtor or his estate. The sweeping changes and expanded jurisdiction quickly were challenged, however, most notably in *Northern Pipeline Construction Co. v. Marathon Pipe Line Co.*, 458 U.S. 50 (1982) (*"Marathon"*).

In *Marathon*, the United States Supreme Court found that the sweeping jurisdiction vested in the bankruptcy courts by the 1978 Act was not constitutional in that it violated Article III of the Constitution due, in large part, to the lack of lifetime tenure of bankruptcy judges. Considerable confusion ensued and bankruptcy practice was cast into considerable disarray until remedial legislation ultimately was passed into law. Of the bankruptcy statutes passed since *Marathon*, the most generally significant are the Bankruptcy Amendments and Federal Judgeship Act of 1984, Pub. L. No. 98-353, and the Bankruptcy Judges, United States Trustees and Family Farmer Bankruptcy Act of 1986, Pub. L. No. 99-554.

B. 28 U.S.C. § 1334

The key provision pertaining to bankruptcy jurisdiction is Title 28 U.S.C. § 1334. Section 1334 of Title 28 vests in the United States District Courts original and exclusive bankruptcy jurisdiction. The bankruptcy courts are, in essence, divisions of the United States district courts to which primary responsibility for bankruptcy cases is referred. 28 U.S.C. § 1334 provides:

(a) Except as provided in subsection (b) of this section, the district courts shall have original and exclusive jurisdiction of all cases under title 11.

(b) Notwithstanding any Act of Congress that confers exclusive jurisdiction on a court or courts other than the district courts, the district courts shall have original but not exclusive jurisdiction of all civil proceedings arising under title 11, or arising in or related to cases under title 11.

1. Abstention

While the district courts are vested with "original and exclusive jurisdiction of all cases under Title 11," they have only original but not exclusive jurisdiction over civil proceedings arising within or under Title 11 (bankruptcy) cases.[1]

28 U.S.C. § 1334(c) provides that the district court may abstain from exercising its non-exclusive jurisdiction in respect to any proceeding arising within or related to a bankruptcy case:

> (c) (1) Nothing in this section prevents a district court in the interest of justice, or in the interest of comity with State courts or respect for State law, from abstaining from hearing a particular proceeding arising under title 11 or arising in or related to a case under title 11.

Where a proceeding is based upon a state law cause of action relating to a bankruptcy case (but not arising in the bankruptcy) and could not have been brought in a United States court but for the pendency of the bankruptcy, the district court *must* abstain from hearing it if (a) such case is commenced and can be timely adjudicated in a state forum and (b) a motion to abstain is filed, 28 U.S.C. § 1334(2). This provision most frequently is invoked by practitioners representing defendants or respondents in actions brought before a bankruptcy court where the cause of action is grounded in state law and could not be brought in the district court but for the pendency of the bankruptcy case. Abstention is applied for by motion. See Bankruptcy Rule 5011. Any decision to abstain "is not reviewable by appeal or otherwise." 28 U.S.C. § 1334(c)(2). However, a decision *not* to abstain may be reviewable. *Collier* 1: 3.01, p. 3-67, Fifteenth ed.

28 U.S.C. § 1334(c) should not be confused with the abstention provision contained in Title 11 of the U.S. Code at § 305 which relates to abstention

---

[1] The filing of a petition under Title 11 of the United States Code commences a bankruptcy *case*. Within the *case*, *proceedings* arise, including motions and adversary proceedings (commenced by the filing and service of summonses and complaint).

from hearing entire bankruptcy cases, not merely proceedings within cases. That is to say, under 11 U.S.C. § 305, the court may abstain from presiding over an entire bankruptcy case. The abstention provision in Title 28 of the U.S. Code at § 1334(c) relates to specific matters within a bankruptcy case which is before the court. (Note distinction addressed in footnote 1 hereto between bankruptcy cases and proceedings.)

2. Core vs. Non-Core Proceedings

Central to the matter of abstention *within a bankruptcy case* is the less than crystal clear distinction between core and non-core proceedings. 28 U.S.C. § 157(a) provides that each district court may refer all bankruptcy cases "and any or all proceedings arising under Title 11 or arising in or related to a case under Title 11" to the bankruptcy court in the district. This provision is designed to avoid constitutional problems raised in *Marathon*. The section therefor continues, in subsections (b), (c) and (d), to define the powers of the bankruptcy judges and in so doing creates the distinction between "core" and "non-core" proceedings. 28 U.S.C. § 157(b)(1) provides:

> (b) (1) Bankruptcy judges may hear and determine all cases under title 11 and all core proceedings arising under title 11, or arising in a case under title 11, referred under subsection (a) of this section, and may enter appropriate orders and judgments subject to review under section 158 of this title.

The statute continues by defining by example what a core proceeding is:

> (2) Core proceedings include, but are not limited to
>
> (A) matters concerning the administration of the estate;
>
> (B) allowance or disallowance of claims against the estate or exemptions from property of the estate, and estimation of claims or interests for the purposes of confirming a plan under chapter 11, 12, or 13 of title 11 but not the liquidation or estimation of contingent or unliquidated personal injury tort or wrongful death claims against the estate for purpose of distribution in a case under title 11;
>
> (C) counterclaims by the estate against persons filing claims against the estate;
>
> (D) orders in respect to obtaining credit;
>
> (E) orders to turn over property of the estate;
>
> (F) proceedings to determine, avoid, or recover preferences;
>
> (G) motions to terminate, annul, or modify the automatic stay;

JURISDICTION AND PROCEDURE IN BANKRUPTCY

(H) proceedings to determine, avoid, or recover fraudulent conveyances;

(I) determinations as to the dischargeability of particular debts;

(J) objections to discharges;

(K) determinations of the validity, extent, or priority of liens;

(L) confirmations of plans;

(M) orders approving the use or lease of property, including the use of cash collateral;

(N) orders approving the sale of property other than property resulting from claims brought by the estate against persons who have not filed claims against the estate; and

(O) other proceedings affecting the liquidation of the assets of the estate or the adjustment of the debtor-creditor or the equity security holder relationship, except personal injury tort or wrongful death claims.

28 U.S.C. § 157(b)(2)

A core proceeding therefore may be conceptualized as, generally, any proceeding in a bankruptcy case that directly relates to the administration of the bankruptcy case or is centered upon property of the bankruptcy estate. For example, a proceeding brought by a Chapter 11 debtor to enjoin an equity committee and one of its members from pursuing a state court action to compel a meeting of debtor's shareholders was a "core proceeding" within the meaning of the Bankruptcy Code, "where there is a basis for concluding that rehabilitation, the very purpose for the bankruptcy proceedings, might be undone by the other action." *Manville Corp. v. The Equity Sec. Holders Comm.*, 801 F.2d 60, 64 (2d Cir. 1986). Non-core proceedings, conversely, are those which relate to the debtor or its estate but are not concerned primarily with the assets of the estate or the administration of the bankruptcy case.

Practitioners should not, however, assume that non-core proceedings may not be heard by the bankruptcy judge. The mandatory abstention requirements of 28 U.S.C. § 1334(c)(2) refer only to related matters, not to non-core proceedings. That is to say, a proceeding may be non-core and yet be determinable by the district court even absent the pendency of the bankruptcy case. The court may but is not required to abstain from hearing non-core matters and is only required to do so where the tests of 28 U.S.C. § 1334(c)(2) are met. Further, personal injury tort and wrongful death cases will be heard in the appropriate district court and not in the bankruptcy court. 28 U.S.C. § 157(b)(5). However, a proof of claim still must be filed in a bankruptcy proceeding in order for collection of a district court judgment on a pre-petition claim against the debtor to continue. *White Motor Credit v. White Motor Corp.*, 761 F.2d 270 (6th Cir. 1985). Where a bankruptcy judge hears a non-core proceeding, the judge shall submit proposed findings of fact and conclusions of law to the district court which then will consider the matter and enter a final order or judgment, unless the parties agree to a referral for actual decision to the bankruptcy judge.

Whether a matter is core or not is determined by the bankruptcy judge *sua sponte* or on motion of a party. The decision that a proceeding is not core "shall *not* be made solely on the basis that its resolution may be affected by state law." 28 U.S.C. § 157(b)(3) (emphasis added).

As can be seen, after *Marathon*, Congress attempted to retain as much jurisdiction in the bankruptcy courts as it constitutionally could. Congress, in light of *Marathon*, left the door open, however, for parties to seek abstention or removal to the district court itself in appropriate situations.

C. Venue

1. The Bankruptcy Case

Proper venue for a bankruptcy case is the district court for the district in which "the domicile, residence, principal place of business in the United States, or principal assets in the United States, of the person or entity that is the subject of such case have been located for the one hundred and eighty days immediately preceding such commencement, or for a longer portion of such one-hundred-and-eighty-day period . . ." than in any other district; or "in which there is pending a case under Title 11 concerning such person's affiliate, general partner, or partnership." 28 U.S.C. § 1408.

The intent is that the bankruptcy case should be filed in the district with the closest contacts to the debtor or its assets. Where related cases are to be filed (*e.g.*, a parent company and its subsidiary), the intent is that all the related cases should be disposed of in the same district (where under applicable rules the related cases almost certainly will pend before the same judge). However, as may be seen, some room is left for forum shopping. The venue of the first of more than one affiliate's cases will be determinative of the venue of all others. For example, a corporation headquartered in another state may plan to become the subject of a Chapter 11 reorganization and may desire venue in the Southern District of New York. A subsidiary or other affiliate for which venue in the Southern District of New York is proper can be made the subject of a Chapter 11 reorganization in that district first, thereby opening the doors of the Southern District of New York's bankruptcy court to the parent company and other affiliates which file later.

2. Proceedings Arising Under Title 11 or Arising In or Related To the Bankruptcy Case

Once the bankruptcy case is filed, proceedings arising in the case or related to it generally belong in the same bankruptcy or district court. There are limits, however. For example, where a bankruptcy trustee would sue to recover money or property worth less than $1,000 or a consumer debt of less than $5,000, he may sue only in the district in which the defendant resides. 28 U.S.C. § 1409(b). Before *Marathon*, a Maine trustee, for example, could sue a Hawaiian for, say, $350. Even if the Hawaiian had good defenses, he would be economically and geographically pressured to allow a default. However, 28 U.S.C. § 1409(d) excepts from the limitation in 28 U.S.C. § 1409(b) proceedings "arising under Title 11 or arising in or related to a case under Title 11 based on a claim arising *after* the commencement of such case from the operation of the business of the debtor" (emphasis added), stating that such claims may be pursued "only in the district court for the district where a state or federal court sits in which, under applicable non-bankruptcy venue provisions, an action on such claim may have been brought." Conversely, the trustee or other representative of the estate may be sued in such a district court on claims arising from the operation of the debtor's business after the bankruptcy case is commenced. 28 U.S.C.§ 1409(c).

The practitioner must bear in mind that the above provisions relate solely to proceedings "arising in" or "related to" bankruptcy cases. "Foreign proceeding" and "foreign representative," as referred to in 11 U.S.C. § 304, are defined in 11 U.S.C. § 101(22) and (23) respectively. 11 U.S.C. § 306 provides for limited appearances by foreign representatives. It should be noted that, while discussion of same is beyond the scope of this discussion, specific venue provisions relative to cases ancillary to foreign proceedings, 11 U.S.C. § 304 are contained in 28 U.S.C. § 140.

D. Jury Trials

The statute provides that the district court may order that the issues arising relative to the filing of an involuntary bankruptcy petition be tried without a jury. However, the statute also provides that bankruptcy does not affect "any right to trial by jury that an individual has under applicable nonbankruptcy law with regard to a personal injury or wrongful death tort claim." 28 U.S.C. § 1411. While the district court has discretion to permit a jury trial relative to the issues arising in respect to the filing of a contested involuntary petition, jury trials are generally the exception rather than the rule in bankruptcy cases and proceedings. Nevertheless, Bankruptcy Rule 9015 had been cited as conferring a right to jury trial on other matters before bankruptcy judges. In light of the clear mandate on 28 U.S.C. § 2075 that the "Rules shall not abridge, enlarge, or modify any substantive right," Rule 9015 is abrogated.

It should be noted that trustees and debtors-in-possession in bankruptcy cases may be sued with respect to "any of their acts or transactions in carrying on business connected with" property of the estate without leave of the court and without loss of any right to a jury trial. 28 U.S.C. § 959(a).

E. Power of the Court in Bankruptcy Cases

Bankruptcy practice is marked, generally, more by practicality than nicety. The situation generally boils down to the inability of a debtor to pay its debts and the need for creditors to realize as much as they can in that negative situation. The court, in bankruptcy, therefore has broad power to assure that the case and all of the issues within it are disposed of finally, effectively and economically. 11 U.S.C. § 105 provides:

> (a) The court may issue *any* order, process, or judgment that is *necessary or appropriate* to carry out the provisions of this title. No provision of this title providing for the raising of an issue by a party in interest shall be construed to preclude the court from, sua sponte, taking any action or making *any* determination *necessary or appropriate to enforce or implement court orders or rules, or to prevent an abuse of process* (emphasis added).

The quoted section frequently is referred to as embodying the bankruptcy court's equity powers. For example, "This provision includes the authority to enjoin litigants from pursing actions pending in other courts that threaten the integrity of a bankrupt's estate." *In re Davis*, 730 F.2d 176, 184 (5th Cir. 1984). In invoking the section, the practitioner generally should weigh the practical effect of what is sought, looking at the requested result from as many points of view as he or she is able. The court's power under 11 U.S.C. § 105 does not, however, include the power to appoint a receiver in bankruptcy, 11 U.S.C. § 105(b); nor does it include, of course, the power to ignore or contradict other provisions of the law.

III. BANKRUPTCY PROCEDURE

A. Appeals

1. Generally

Appeals from bankruptcy court orders generally are taken to the District Court. 28 U.S.C. § 158. Appeals from final judgments, orders and decrees

JURISDICTION AND PROCEDURE IN BANKRUPTCY

are of right except where, for example, a statute precludes review of even a final order.[2] Appeals from interlocutory orders and decrees "in cases and proceedings referred to bankruptcy judges under section 157 of this title," 28 U.S.C. § 158(a), may be heard by the district court with leave of the court in which the bankruptcy judge sits.

The circuit court may establish a panel of bankruptcy judges from the districts within the circuit to which appeals may be taken, by-passing the district court, if all of the parties consent and if a majority of the district judges have voted to authorize such referrals. 28 U.S.C. § 158(b). Such consent and such appeals are extremely rare.

2. Procedure

Procedurally, 28 U.S.C. § 158(c) provides that appeals from bankruptcy courts "shall be taken in the same manner as appeals in civil proceedings generally are taken to the courts of appeals from the district courts and in the time provided by Rule 8002 of the Bankruptcy Rules." Bankruptcy Rule 8002 provides generally that an appeal must be taken within ten days of the date of entry of the order, judgment or decree appealed from.

The date of entry is the date upon which the bankruptcy court clerk enters the order, judgment or decree on the docket—it is *not* the date the order, judgment or decree is signed. Many practitioners overlook the distinction between the dates of entry and of signing an order and, by so doing, are in danger of assuming that the deadline to take an appeal has lapsed before in fact it has. The time difference may be substantial due to the workload in recent years in the bankruptcy courts.

3. Bankruptcy Rules Regarding Appeals

Part VIII of the the Bankruptcy Rules sets forth the procedure for taking an appeal. Part VIII of the Bankruptcy Rules includes Bankruptcy Rules 8001 through 8019. The Part VIII Rules clearly and explicitly guide the practitioner through the appellate procedure. An appeal is commenced as provided in Bankruptcy Rule 8001. Appeals of right are taken by the filing of a simple notice of appeal with "the clerk." The "clerk" so referred to is *not* the District Court clerk, but the Bankruptcy Court clerk. Official Form No. 35 is the form of Notice of Appeal to be used.

The rules are clear and should be referred to directly. It need only be mentioned here that all time periods should be strictly observed. Also, it

---

[2] 11 U.S.C. § 305(c) provides, for example, that an order under 11 U.S.C. § 305(a) "dismissing a case or suspending all proceedings in a case, or a decision not so to dismiss or suspend, is not reviewable by appeal or otherwise."

should be pointed out that once an appeal is taken, jurisdiction leaves the bankruptcy court and rests in the district court *per se*.

4. Stay Pending Appeal

As substantial economic rights or interests frequently are disposed of by Bankruptcy Court decisions and orders, stays pending appeal often have substantial practical and tactical importance.

Where a stay pending appeal is desired, the party desiring the stay must apply first to the bankruptcy judge. This may be done by formal motion. However, at least in the Southern District of New York, due to the pressure of time frequently involved, parties have been known simply to make oral application to the deciding bankruptcy judge (or in his absence, any other bankruptcy judge in the district), preferably with the opposing parties present after due notice to them which, in practice, may be by telephone. If the stay is denied by the bankruptcy judge, the applicant applies to the district court in accordance with its rules. In applying to the district court for a stay pending an appeal from the Bankruptcy Court, the applicant must make the representation that application first has been made to the Bankruptcy Court and denied.

Very frequently a bond must be posted when a stay pending an appeal from the Bankruptcy court is granted. Any party who may be adversely affected by the stay has the right to request a bond and to be heard regarding the appropriate amount thereof. Stays and bonds pending appeal are the subject of Bankruptcy Rule 8005.

Stays pending bankruptcy appeals can be tactically very critical. The Bankruptcy Code not only recognizes the precept that an order or judgment is valid until reversed or modified but specifically so provides where a sale or lease of property of the debtor's estate is authorized pursuant to 11 U.S.C. § 363. Subsection (m) of 11 U.S.C. § 363 provides:

> (m) The *reversal* or modification on appeal of an authorization under subsection (b) or (c) of this section of a sale or lease of property *does not affect* the validity of a sale or lease under such authorization to an entity that purchased or leased such property in good faith, *whether or not such entity knew of the pendency of the appeal, unless such authorization and such sale or lease were stayed pending appeal* (emphasis added).

As can be seen, an appeal of an order authorizing the sale or lease of property can be mooted where the opposing party fails to seek and obtain a stay pending appeal and the sale or lease is consummated before the appeal is completed.

B. United States Trustee

With the passage of the present bankruptcy code, one major objective of reform was to remove the bankruptcy judge from what had been the added traditional role of, in effect, administering the bankruptcy case. Under the former Bankruptcy Act, particularly in Chapter XI reorganizations, the presiding judge participated actively in the entire case on the business level. The 1978 revisions sought to enhance and confine the bankruptcy judge's judicial role and limit the judge to it. Hence, for example, while the first meeting of creditors formerly was presided over by the bankruptcy judge, the judge now not only does not participate but is specifically barred from even attending. 11 U.S.C. 341, which provides for meetings of creditors and equity security holders, mandates in subsection (c):

> (c) The court may not preside at, and may not attend, any meeting under this section including any final meeting of creditors.

In addition, Bankruptcy Rule 9003 proscribes *ex parte* contact with the bankruptcy judge "concerning matters affecting a particular case or proceeding . . . Except as otherwise permitted by applicable law . . . ."

Congress, in streamlining the role of the bankruptcy judge to its judicial side (while also increasing the court's jurisdiction), recognized that someone is needed for such functions as, for example, calling meetings of creditors, selecting creditors' committees, bringing parties together to try to precipitate settlements, monitoring the case on behalf of all parties and the community at large, and seeing that cases be moved through the court to appropriate and expeditious conclusion. To fill such functions as these, the office of the United States Trustee was established by the enactment of Chapter 39 of Title 28 U.S.C. §§ 581 through 589a.

Pursuant to 28 U.S.C. 581(a), the Attorney General is charged with the duty of appointing one United States Trustee for each of 21 defined areas. One United States Trustee serves the entire State of New York as well as Connecticut and Vermont. Located in the U.S. Customs House, One Bowling Green, New York, New York 10004-1408 (fifth floor), the Trustee has satellite offices located in Buffalo, Rochester, Albany and Garden City, New York, as well as in New Haven, Connecticut. Vermont cases are handled by the United States Trustee's Albany office.

The duties of the United States Trustee are enumerated in 28 U.S.C.§ 586:

> (a) Each United States trustee, within the region for which such United States trustee is appointed, shall—
>
> > (1) establish, maintain, and supervise a panel of private trustees that are eligible and available to serve as trustees in cases under chapter 7 of title 11;

(2) serve as and perform the duties of a trustee in a case under title 11 when required under title 11 to serve as trustee in such a case;

(3) supervise the administration of cases and trustees in cases under chapter 7, 11, or 13 of title 11 by, whenever the United States trustee considers it to be appropriate

(A) monitoring applications for compensation and reimbursment filed under section 330 of title 11 and, whenever the United States trustee deems it to be appropriate, filing with the court comments with respect to any of such applications;

(B) monitoring plans and disclosure statements filed in cases under chapter 11 of title 11 and filing with the court, in connection with hearings under sections 1125 and 1128 of such title, comments with respect to such plans and disclosure statements;

(C) monitoring plans filed under chapters 12 and 13 of title 11 and filing with the court, in connection with hearings under sections 1224, 1229, 1324, and 1329 of such title, comments with respect to such plans;

(D) taking such action as the United States trustee deems to be appropriate to ensure that all reports, schedules, and fees required to be filed under title 11 and this title by the debtor are properly and timely filed;

(E) monitoring creditors' committees appointed under title 11;

(F) notifying the appropriate United States attorney of matters which relate to the occurrence of any action which may constitute a crime under the laws of the United States and, on the request of the United States attorney, assisting the United States attorney in carrying out prosecutions based on such action;

(G) monitoring the progress of cases under title 11 and taking such actions as the United States trustee deems to be appropriate to prevent undue delay in such progress; and

(H) monitoring applications filed under section 327 of title 11 and, whenever the United States trustee deems it to be appropriate, filing with the court comments with respect to the approval of such applications;

(4) deposit or invest under section 345 of title 11 money received as trustee in cases under title 11;

(5) perform the duties prescribed for the United States trustee under title 11 and this title, and such duties consistent with title 11 and this title as the Attorney General may prescribe; and

(6) make such reports as the Attorney General directs.

A practitioner will find that most U.S. Trustee's offices are willingly helpful in giving basic direction in matters relative to cases pending in their jurisdictional area. For example, they often will be helpful in calling meetings among the parties to see if a consensual settlement of a controversy can be worked out. The practitioner representing a debtor or a trustee who is operating the debtor's business also is advised to contact the United States Trustee's office to ascertain what the requirements are in respect to the filing of monthly operating reports.

C. Bankruptcy Rules and Forms

28 U.S.C. § 2075 charges the United States Supreme Court with "the power to prescribe by general rules, the forms of process, writs, pleadings, motions and the practice and procedure in cases under Title 11."

1. Bankruptcy Rules

The Rules of Bankruptcy Procedure (generally referred to as the Bankruptcy Rules) are organized generally to follow as well as practical the organizational scheme of the Bankruptcy Code itself. They are broken down into ten parts. These begin with Rules (Part I) 1002 through 1019 dealing with the commencement of a bankruptcy case and proceedings relating to the petition and order for relief. (Part I) Rules 2001 through 2019 deal with officers and administration of cases, notice, meetings, examinations, elections, and attorneys and accountants. Part III (Rules 3001 through 3022) deals with claims, creditors and plans of reorganization. Part IV (Rules 4001 through 4008) relates to the duties and benefits of the debtor, touching on such significant areas as relief from the automatic bankruptcy stay, the debtor's use of cash collateral and discharge of debts. Part V (Rules 5001 through 5011) pertains to the courts and clerks. Part VI (Rules 6001 through 6010) pertains to the collection and liquidation of the estate and refers to such matters as the use, sale and lease of property and the disbursement of money of the estate. Adversary proceedings (*i.e.*, the commencement and prosecution of lawsuits with summons and complaint within a bankruptcy case) are governed by Part VII (Rules 7001 through 7087). Appeals (as noted above) are the subject of Part VIII (Rules 8001 through 8019). Part IX (Rules 9001 through 9033) contains a miscellany of necessary rules to fill in between the other parts. The Part X rules pertain to the United States Trustee.

a. Bankruptcy Rules vs. Fed. R. Civ. P.

In promulgating the Bankruptcy Rules, it is apparent that effort was made to conform where possible to the Federal Rules of Civil Procedure and to deviate only when the vagaries of bankruptcy law and policy so require. Therefore, Bankruptcy Rule 7002 provides that whenever a Federal Rule of Civil Procedure that is made applicable in an adversary proceeding refers to another such rule, "the reference shall be read as a reference to the Federal Rule of Civil Procedure as modified in this Part VII." Not suprisingly, 37 of the 53 rules contained in Part VII of the Bankruptcy Rules (controlling adversary proceedings) simply incorporate a corresponding rule of the Federal Rules of Civil Procedure. For example, Bankruptcy Rule 7056, referring to summary judgment, reads, "Rule 56 Fed. R. Civ. P. applies in adversary proceedings" and Bankruptcy Rule 7014, referring to third-party practice, reads, "Rule 14 Fed. R. Civ. P. applies in adversary proceedings." In addition, a number of the other rules state that a correspondent rule of Fed. R. Civ. P. applies "except that . . . ."

However, not all of Fed. R. Civ. P. is incorporated by reference even in respect to adversary proceedings. Practitoners representing parties in bankruptcy will be remiss if they do not first refer to the Bankruptcy Rules and get a clear fix on the exceptions and differences. This is especially true in respect to Part VII, adversary proceedings. As Rule 7002 states, the Bankruptcy Rules in Part VII modify Fed. R. Civ. P.

b. Adversary Proceedings

Bankruptcy Rule 7001 defines what an adversary proceeding is:

> It is a proceeding in a bankruptcy court (1) to recover money or property, except a proceeding under § 554(b) or § 725 of the Code, Rule 2017, or Rule 6002, (2) to determine the validity, priority, or extent of a lien or other interest in property, other than a proceeding under Rule 4003(d), (3) to obtain approval pursuant to § 363(h) for the sale of both the interest of the estate and of a co-owner in property, (4) to object to or revoke a discharge, (5) to revoke an order of confirmation of a chapter 11 or chapter 13 plan, (6) to determine the dischargeability of a debt, (7) to obtain an injunction or other equitable relief, (8) to subordinate any allowed claim or interest, except when subordination is provided in a chapter 9, 11, or 13 plan, (9) to obtain a declaratory judgment relating to any of the foregoing, or (10) to determine a claim or cause of action removed to a bankruptcy court.

Any proceeding that does not seek the specific types of relief included among those enumerated in Bankruptcy Rule 7001 is not and may not be the subject of an adversary proceeding. All other types of relief are to be sought by motion.

Bankruptcy Rule 9002 provides that when words "action" or "civil action" are used in Federal Rules of Civil Procedure made applicable to bankruptcy cases by the Bankruptcy Rules, unless inconsistent with the text, they mean an adversary proceeding "or, when appropriate, a contested petition, or proceedings to vacate an order for relief or to determine any other contested matter."

(1) Summons and Complaint

Other than the type of relief sought, the main characteristic of any adversary proceeding is that it is commenced by the filing of a summons and complaint. Bankruptcy Rule 7003 states, simply, "Rule 3 Fed. R. Civ. P. applies in adversary proceedings."

(2) Service

Rule 7004 does incorporate much, but not all, of Fed. R. Civ. P. Rule 4 and it clearly and explicitly sets forth the procedure for service. Perhaps its most notable provisions are those contained in subdivisions (d) and (f). These provide for nationwide service of process (except subpoenas) and require service of a summons within ten days of issuance and adds that if a summons is not served within ten days "another summons shall be issued and served."

(3) Pleadings

Bankruptcy Rule 7010 states that Fed. R. Civ. P. Rule 10 applies in adversary proceedings "except that the caption of each pleading in such a proceeding shall conform substantially to Official Form No. 34."

FORM NO. 34

Caption of Adversary Proceedings

UNITED STATES BANKRUPTCY COURT

... DISTRICT OF ...

_____x

In re Case No. . . . . :

. . . . :

   Debtor,:

. . . . ,:ADV. PRO. NO....

   Plaintiff,:

v. :

. . . . ,:

   Defendant.:

_____-x

Complaint [or other Designation]
Advisory Committee Note

Rule 7010 requires the caption of a pleading in an adversary proceeding to conform substantially to this form.

(4) Defenses and Objections

Bankruptcy Rule 7012 sets forth procedures applicable in adversary proceedings relative to defenses and objections stating when and how presented (time limits and whether by pleading or motion).

(5) Counterclaims and Cross-Claims

Rule 7013 modifies Fed. R. Civ. P. Rule 13 in respect to counterclaims and cross-claims.

(6) Legibility

Last, but not least, it should be noted that in *any* proceeding, adversary or not, the Bankruptcy Rules provide that neatness counts; Bankruptcy Rule 9004(a) reads:

> Legibility; Abbreviations. All petitions, pleadings, schedules and other papers shall be clearly legible. Abbreviations in common use in the English language may be used.

The Southern District of New York's local Rule 9(b) provides:

> (b) Form of Papers. Unless a judge of this court otherwise directs, no paper shall be received for filing unless (1) it is plainly written, a typed ribbon copy, printed, or an identical facsimile without erasures or interlineations which materially deface it, (2) it bears the title, initials of the judge to whom the case has been assigned and the index numbers, if any, assigned to the case and the adversary proceeding, (3) it bears endorsed on the cover the name, office and post office address and telephone number of the attorney of record, if any, for the party filing the same, and the name and address of the local attorney, if any, designated pursuant to Local Bankruptcy Rule 4(a), and (4) it is signed by an attorney of record, if any, in accordance with Civil Rule 1(b) of the District Rules.

c. Motion Practice/Contested Matters

Basically stated, any litigation to resolve a dispute in a bankruptcy case not seeking a form of relief included in the ten categories specifically designated by Rule 7001 as the subjects of an adversary proceedings is a "contested matter." As such, Bankruptcy Rule 9014 controls and the "relief shall be requested by motion." Bankruptcy Rule 9014 must be referred to as the starting point by the practitioner. As in respect to adversary proceedings, service and notice and time limitations spelled out in the Bankruptcy Rules must be adhered to.

Bankruptcy Rule 9013 states the following:

A request for an order, except when an application is authorized by these rules, shall be by written motion, unless made during a hearing. The motion shall state with particularity the grounds therefor, and shall set forth the relief or order sought. Every written motion other than one which may be considered ex parte shall be served by the moving party on the trustee or debtor in possession and on those persons specified by these rules or, if service is not required or the persons to be served are not specified by these rules, the moving party shall serve the persons the court directs.

In addition, local bankruptcy rules in effect for the district in which the bankruptcy case is pending also must be referred to. For example, in the Southern District of New York, orders to show cause are not favored, the use of that device having in the past been somewhat abused. Local Rule 13(d) for the Southern District of New York states:

(d) *Order to Show Cause.* No order to show cause to bring on a motion will be granted except upon a *clear and specific showing by affidavit of good and sufficient reasons why procedure other than by notice of motion is necessary*, and shall also state whether a previous application for similar relief has been made (emphasis added).

Southern District of New York local Rule 13 also requires that a brief or memorandum of law be submitted with any motion:

Unless the court orders otherwise, the moving party shall serve and file with *any* motion *a memorandum setting forth the points and authorities relied on in support of the motion*, divided under appropriate headings into as many parts as there are points to be determined. Unless the court orders otherwise, *the opposing party shall serve and file* with its papers in opposition to the motion *an answering memorandum*, similarly divided, setting forth the points and authorities relied on in opposition. Failure to comply may be deemed sufficient cause for the denial of the motion or the granting of the motion by default (emphasis added).

Motion practice also is greatly streamlined in bankruptcy practice in certain situations specified by the statute and in other situations where relief is sought but it is not presumed that there will be sufficient opposition to require a hearing. In such cases, a simple notice of the explicit relief sought, accompanied normally with a proposed order, is sent to all interested parties stating that on a given date the relief will be requested of the court and/or the order will be presented for signature. Upon such a motion, the relief will be

JURISDICTION AND PROCEDURE IN BANKRUPTCY 847

granted and an order signed, unless a party in interest files an objection and requests a hearing. The basis for this efficient procedure is found in 11 U.S.C. § 102(1) which provides:

(1) "after notice and a hearing," or a similar phrase—

(A) means after such notice as is appropriate in the particular circumstances, and such opportunity for a hearing as is appropriate in the particular circumstances; but

(B) authorizes an act without an actual hearing if such notice is given properly and if—

(i) such a hearing is not requested timely by a party in interest; or

(ii) there is insufficient time for a hearing to be commenced before such act must be done, and the court authorizes such act; . . .

The bankruptcy code in various sections provides that specific relief may be had "after notice and a hearing." The type of relief so sought can be very important. For example, relief from the stay of actions and proceeding against the debtor which automatically is triggered by the filing of a bankruptcy petition, 11 U.S.C. § 362, can be sought by this method, 11 U.S.C. § 362(d). The main point to be remembered is that even though sections like § 362 track the language of 11 U.S.C. § 102 and specifically state "after notice *and a hearing*" (emphasis added), no hearing is required and none will be had unless a party requests one by objecting to the relief referred to in the notice and requesting that a hearing be had.

2. Official Forms

Bankruptcy Rule 9009 provides as follows:

The Official Forms prescribed by the Judicial Conference of the United States shall be observed and used with alterations as may be appropriate. Forms may be combined and their contents rearranged to permit economies in their use. The Director of the Administrative Office of the United States Courts may issue additional forms for use under the Code.

Thirty-five official forms have been made available. Like the Bankruptcy Rules, they are arranged in a numbered sequence generally following the normal general progress of events in a bankruptcy case. Thus, Official Form No. 1 is the standard form of the voluntary bankruptcy petition. There is neither time nor space here to address or describe the various forms—they speak for themselves and, generally, are very clear. Suffice it to say here, the bankruptcy forms published by reputable legal publishers generally follow the Official Forms quite closely.

D. Title 11—The Chapters Defined; *i.e.*, Types of Bankruptcy Cases

1. Chapter 7—Liquidation

Chapter 7 of Title 11 governs the standard liquidation in which a trustee is appointed from the panel of trustees maintained by the United States Trustee. Such a trustee is an interim trustee appointed pursuant to 11 U.S.C. § 701, who may be superceded by a trustee elected by creditors pursuant to 11 U.S.C. § 702.

a. Chapter 7 Trusteeship

(1) Duties of Trustee

The trustee's job basically is to locate, liquidate and account for the assets of the debtor's estate and to distribute the proceeds in accordance with the priorities established by the Bankruptcy Code. The trustee also has other powers and duties, such as to investigate and make information available to interested parties. The duties of a trustee are set forth in 11 U.S.C. § 704:

(1) collect and reduce to money the property of the estate for which such trustee serves, and close such estate as expeditiously as is compatible with the best interests of parties in interest;

(2) be accountable for all property received;

(3) ensure that the debtor shall perform his intention as specified in section 521(2)(B) of this title;

(4) investigate the financial affairs of the debtor;

(5) if a purpose would be served, examine proofs of claims and object to the allowance of any claim that is improper;

(6) if advisable, oppose the discharge of the debtor;

(7) unless the court orders otherwise, furnish such information concerning the estate and the estate's administration as is requested by a party in interest;

(8) if the business of the debtor is authorized to be operated, file with the court, with the United States trustee, and with any governmental unit charged with responsibility for collection or determination of any tax arising out of such operation, periodic reports and summaries of the operation of such business, including a statement of receipts and disbursements, and such other information as the United States trustee or the court requires; and

(9) make a final report and file a final account of the administration of the estate with the court and with the United States trustee.

(2) Record Keeping

Bankruptcy Rule 2015 elaborates on the trustee's record keeping, notice and reporting duties.

(3) Qualification of Trustee

The sections pertaining to qualification of a trustee, role, compensation, and other factors pertaining to the office pro se are found, generally, in 11 U.S.C. §§ 321 through 331 and §§ 701 through 704.

b. Stockbroker and Commodity Broker Liquidations

The Bankruptcy Code, recognizing the special problems attendant upon the liquidation of stockbrokers and commodity brokers, contains specific provisions relative to such liquidation. These are the subjects of Subchapter III of Title 11 (Stockbrokers), 11 U.S.C. §§ 741 through 752, and Subchapter IV (Commodity Brokers), 11 U.S.C. §§ 761 through 766.

c. Chapter 9: Adjustment of Debts of a Municipality

Chapter 9 of Title 11 contains the law specific to the bankruptcy of municipalities. Chapter 9 includes Sections 901 through 946 of Title 11. Municipal adjustments in bankruptcy are so rare and esoteric that no further comment will be made here.

d. Chapter 11: Reorganization

Other than the Chapter 7 liquidation, the most widely known and used chapter of the Bankruptcy Code in respect to commercial endeavors is, of course, the Chapter 11 reorganization. What is not so widely recognized is that Chapter 11 is available in proper cases to individuals as well as to incorporated and other commercial companies.

(1) Who May Be a Chapter 11 Debtor

In respect to all chapters of the Bankruptcy Code, 11 U.S.C. § 109 is determinative of who may be a debtor under the various chapters. 11 U.S.C. § 109(d) provides that, "Only a person that may be a debtor under chapter 7 of this title, except a stockbroker or a commodity broker, and a railroad may be a debtor under chapter 11 of this title." 11 U.S.C. § 109(c) limits the Chapter 13 wage earner reorganization to a person who individually (or with his or her spouse) owes less than $100,000 of noncontingent, liquidated, unsecured debts and less than $350,000 of noncontingent, liquidated secured debts and who has a regular income. Conversely, a person engaged in business with too much of the types of debt enumerated is considered eligible for a Chapter 11 reorganization proceeding.

It would seem that, in fact, any individual engaged in business would be eligible for Chapter 11 but it generally is perceived that Chapter 11 is available to an individual only when his indebtedness cannot be effectively managed in a Chapter 13 or 7 case. It has been held, however, that Chapter 11 is available to petitioners who are not engaged in business. *See In re Moog*, 774 F.2d 1073 (11th Cir. 1985) (*"Moog"*), wherein the court said, "we see nothing in the current Bankruptcy Code or its legislative history or the prior Bankruptcy Act that would support that a consumer debtor may not seek relief under chapter 11," p. 1075. However, if an individual is not engaged in business, upon a motion, he or she may not be allowed to remain in Chapter 11. *See, e.g., Wamsganz v. Boatmen's Bank of De Soto*, 804 F.2d 503 (8th Cir. 1986), which held that persons not engaged in business may not seek relief under Chapter 11 and refused to follow *Moog*.

While an individual may qualify for a Chapter 11 reorganization proceeding, the individual presumably must be engaged in business and must have more than a Chapter 13 debtor's debt load, although neither the statute nor cases are crystal clear on the subject. In fact, it is quite rare for an individual to file under Chapter 11 but such cases do occur and sometimes are successful. Even under the old Chapter XI arrangement proceeding under the old Bankruptcy Act, the debtor sometimes was an individual business person.

(2) Genesis of Chapter 11

The Chapter 11 reorganization represents an amalgamation of what Congress believed to be the best of the old Chapters X, XI and XII of the Bankruptcy Act. Those chapters were intended to be tailored generally to the publicly held corporation (Chapter X), the less complex business corporation (Chapter XI) and real property owners (Chapter XII). While the original intent held fairly fast in respect to the real property reorganization of old Chapter XII, Chapter X rarely was invoked voluntarily by a public corporation and Chapter XI was used by businesses ranging in size and complexity from "mom and pop" operations through major corporations such as Dynamics Corporation of America and W.T. Grant (later in Chapter 7). Chapter X was shunned because it entailed such a complex and expensive proceeding that a succcessful Chapter X reorganization was rare—most companies subjected to it ended in liquidation and/or with creditors receiving less than they would have had Chapter XI been used. Chapter XII was little used for many years but came into substantial vogue in the 1970s.

JURISDICTION AND PROCEDURE IN BANKRUPTCY

(3) Railroad Reorganizations

In reforming the bankruptcy laws, as noted above, an objective was to incorporate the best features of Chapters X, XI and XII in the present Chapter 11. In so doing, a special subchapter was incorporated to address the unique problems and public policy considerations attendant upon the reorganization of railroads. Subchapter IV; 11 U.S.C. §§ 1161 through 1174.

e. Family Farmer Debt Adjustments; Chapter 12

Chapter 12, 11 U.S.C. §§ 1201 through 1231, governs the adjustment of debts of family farmers "with regular annual income." This chapter was written bearing in mind the unique situation of the farmer including, for example, the fact that while the family farm may be a substantial capital intensive enterprise, it also is a home and not just a business. It should be noted that 11 U.S.C. § 109(f) states that "Only a *family* farmer with *regular annual income* may be a debtor under chapter 12 of this title" (emphasis added). This seems to exclude the large corporate farmer and also is intended, we believe, to withhold benefits of the chapter from the tax shelter or gentleman farmer to avoid abusive use. 11 U.S.C. (17) (18) (19) and (20) define "family farmer," "family farmer with regular income," "farmer" and "farming operation" respectively.

When a family farmer case arises, Chapter 12 should be reviewed with care. While space does not permit intensive analysis of Chapter 12 here, a couple of provisions are noted to exemplify the uniqueness of the chapter.

11 U.S.C. § 1201 provides the farmer with protection by way of an automatic stay (within limits) of actions to collect consumer debt of the debtor from co-obligors.

11 U.S.C. § 1205 is a separate "adequate protection" provision tailored to the family farmer situation and, as such, it supercedes 11 U.S.C. § 361 in Family Farmer cases. As noted, the chapter requires careful study by the practitioner and is intended to address the needs of the family farmer in distress. Before referring to Chapter 12, however, it is urged that the terms of the act defined in 11 U.S.C. § 101 (17) (18) (19) and (20) be studied and thoroughly understood.

f. Adjustment of Debts of an Individual With Regular Income; Chapter 13

In essence, Chapter 13 is the working person's version of the Chapter 11 reorganization. As noted above, pursuant to 11 U.S.C. § 109(c) Chapter 13 is available only to an individual (or married couple) with regular income who owes noncontingent, liquidated debt that is not secured of less than $100,000 and that is secured of less than $350,000. Chapter 13 is an alternative to the Chapter 7 liquidation. It enables the individual or couple with regular income to propose a plan within available financial means to pay out a portion of owed debt without losing all that is owned (over and above property that is exempt from execution as provided pursuant to 11 U.S.C. § 522). As the chapter provides for a reasonable payment over time of all or a portion of the wage earner's debts, 11 U.S.C. § 1306 includes in the property of the estate some property which would not be included in a Chapter 7 liquidation, such as earnings and property acquired after filing in bankruptcy and before the case is closed, dismissed or converted to Chapter 7, 11 or 12.

E. Commencing a Case

1. Voluntary Petitions

A bankruptcy case is commenced by the filing of a petition. Official Form No. 1 is the form of voluntary petition which may be modified to suit the chapter under which a voluntary filing is being made, as shown therein. Forms published by reputable publishers are available through legal stationers.

A voluntary case is filed pursuant to 11 U.S.C. § 301, which provides that the filing of the petition not only commences the case but also constitutes an order for relief. A petition in bankruptcy, be it voluntary or involuntary, is an application for an order for relief. An order for relief is, in effect, an order adjudicating the debtor as a bankrupt (referred to as a "debtor" under Title 11) under the chapter under which the petition has been filed. As the debtor obviously will not contest a voluntary petition, the filing of the petition itself constitutes the order for relief. Hence, a copy of a voluntary petition bearing the stamp of the bankruptcy court noting that it has been filed is evidence of the bankruptcy denoting that the debtor is (or became) a debtor pursuant to the relevant chapter. Where a more explicit verification is desired, Official Form No. 5 is a form of Certificate of Commencement of Case which may be presented to the court for signature as evidence that the debtor has become the subject of a bankruptcy case. The use of such certificates is rare in the Southern District of New York and many other districts but can be helpful in some situations, such as to stop a foreclosure.

A voluntary petition may be filed by anyone eligible to be a debtor. 11 U.S.C. § 109(a) specifies that "only a person that resides or has a domicile, a place of business, or property in the United States, or a municipality, may be a debtor under this title." The section then goes on to state who may be a debtor pursuant to the various chapters. It should be noted that Chapter 7 (and therefore Chapter 11, 11 U.S.C. § 109(d)) is not available to insurance companies, Federal Deposit Insurance Act insured institutions, banks and similar institutions, 11 U.S.C. § 109(b). In other words, Chapters 7 and 11

JURISDICTION AND PROCEDURE IN BANKRUPTCY

generally are not available to regulated businesses when liquidations and/or reorganizations are governed by other state or federal laws except that railroads, while not eligible for Chapter 7 liquidation, may be the subject of subchapter IV reorganizations under Chapter 11.

2. Involuntary Petitions

An involuntary bankruptcy case is commenced by the filing of a petition pursuant to 11 U.S.C. § 303. Only Chapter 7 and 11 cases may be filed involuntarily, 11 U.S.C. § 303(a), and even those chapters may not be invoked involuntarily against a farmer, a family farmer (as those terms are defined in 11 U.S.C. § 101(19) and (17) respectively), "or a corporation that is not a managed business, or commercial corporation . . . ." Generally, therefore, farmers and non-financial, non-business corporations are exempt from involuntary filings. These include, for example, not-for-profit, religious and charitable corporations. Note also, however, that pursuant to 11 U.S.C. § 303(k), in the proper circumstances an involuntary Chapter 7 can be filed against a foreign bank.

Official Forms Nos. 11 and 12 should be used in filing involuntary petitions along with Official Form 13 which is the form of summons to the involuntary debtor.

a. Who May File an Involuntary Petition

11 U.S.C. § 303(b) provides who may file an involuntary petition:

> (b) An involuntary case against a person is commenced by the filing with the bankruptcy court of a petition under chapter 7 or 11 of this title—
>
> (1) by three or more entities, each of which is either a holder of a claim against such person that is not contingent as to liability or the subject of a bona fide dispute, or an indenture trustee representing such a holder, if such claims aggregate at least $5,000 more than the value of any lien on property of the debtor securing such claims held by the holders of such claims;
>
> (2) if there are fewer than 12 such holders, excluding any employee or insider of such person and any transferee of a transfer that is voidable under section 544, 545, 547, 548, 549, or 724(a) of this title, by one or more of such holders that hold in the aggregate at least $5,000 of such claims;
>
> (3) if such person is a partnership—
>
> (A) by fewer than all of the general partners in such partnership; or

(B) if relief has been ordered under this title with respect to all of the general partners in such partnership, by a general partner in such partnership, the trustee of such a general partner, or a holder of a claim against such partnership; or

(4) by a foreign representative of the estate in a foreign proceeding concerning such person.

The general rule, therefore, is that one creditor may file an involuntary petition against a debtor which has less than twelve creditors, otherwise three petitioning creditors are needed. As the would-be petitioning creditor often does not know as a certainty how many creditors the debtor has, he should as the creditor (a) try to find out and (b) try to get two others to join in on the involuntary petition. As a pragmatic consideration, the petitioning creditor may assume that an entity or person owing debt to less than twelve entities in today's world is the exception rather than the rule. The practitioner should be sure also to adhere to the requisites in 303(b) relative to the amount of debt and status of debt.

b. Risks of Filing Involuntary Petitions

Any practitioner advising a would-be petitioning creditor will be remiss if he or she fails to take particular notice of subsections (e) and (i) of 11 U.S.C. § 303. Obviously, the filing of an involuntary petiton in bankruptcy is a powerful and potentially very damaging act against the debtor. Therefore, subsection (e) of 11 U.S.C. § 303 empowers the court to, for cause, require the petitioning creditor(s) to file a bond indemnifying the debtor "for such amounts as the court may later allow under subsection (i) of this section." Subsection (i) of 11 U.S.C. § 303 provides:

(i) If the court dismisses a petition under this section other than on consent of all petitioners and the debtor, and if the debtor does not waive the right to judgment under this subsection, the court may grant judgment—

(1) against the petitioners and in favor of the debtor for—

(A) cost; or

(B) a reasonable attorney's fee; or

(2) against any petitioner that filed the petition in bad faith, for—

(A) any damages approximately caused by such filing; or

(B) punitive damages.

c. Gap Period Between Filing and Adjudication

When an involuntary petition is filed, obviously the debtor has the right to contest it. During the period between the filing and the entry of an order for

JURISDICTION AND PROCEDURE IN BANKRUPTCY

relief, the debtor's business may continue unless the court orders otherwise. 11 U.S.C. § 303(f). But the statute also makes provision for the appointment of an interim trustee. 11 U.S.C. § 303(g). If and when an order for relief is granted, Official Form 14 (Order For Relief) may be used.

d. Miscellaneous

It should be noted that the petitioning creditor(s) may be required to file schedules of the debts and assets of the involuntary debtor when the debtor fails to do so as required by 11 U.S.C. § 521. This situation usually arises where the involuntary petition is filed against an entity that has ceased doing business and the petition is not contested. Bankruptcy Rule 1007(k) provides:

> (k) Preparation of List, Schedules, or Statements on Default of Debtor. If a list, schedule, or statement, other than a statement of intention, is not prepared and filed as required by this rule, the court may order the trustee, a petitioning creditor, committee, or other party to prepare and file any of these papers within a time fixed by the court. The court may approve reimbursement of the cost incurred in complying 001276 with such an order as an administrative expense.

3. Petition—Number of Copies to File

In filing either a voluntary or involuntary petition, the local rules of the bankruptcy court in which the petition is to be filed should be consulted as to the number of copies that must be filed and any other formalities that may require observance. *See also* Bankruptcy Rules 1002 and 1003 and the Advisory Committee Notes thereto.

4. Filing Fees

The amounts of the filing fees required in connection with the filing of bankruptcy petitions and notices of appeal is dictated by 18 U.S.C. § 1930. The entire section (which also goes to the awarding of costs upon dismissal of a case or proceeding) is reproduced here:

> (a) Notwithstanding section 1915 of this title, the parties commencing a case under title 11 shall pay to the clerk of the district court or the clerk of the bankruptcy court, if one has been certified pursuant to section 156(b) of this title, the following filing fees:
>
> (1) For a case commenced under chapter 7 or 13 of title 11, $90.
>
> (2) For a case commenced under chapter 9 of title 11, $300.

(3) For a case commenced under chapter 11 of title 11 that does not concern a railroad, as defined in section 101 of title 11, $500.

(4) For a case commenced under chapter 11 of title 11 concerning a railroad, as so defined, $1,000.

(5) For a case commenced under chapter 12 of title 11, $200.

(6) In addition to the filing fee paid to the clerk, a quarterly fee shall be paid to the United States trustee, for deposit in the Treasury, in each case under chapter 11 of title 11 for each quarter (including any fraction thereof) until a plan is confirmed or the case is converted or dismissed, whichever occurs first. The fee shall be $150 for each quarter in which disbursements total less than $15,000; $300 for each quarter in which disbursements total $15,000 or more but less than $150,000; $750 for each quarter in which disbursements total $150,000 or more but less than $300,000; $2250 for each quarter in which disbursements total $300,000 or more but less than $3,000,000; $3,000 for each quarter in which disbursements total $3,000,000 or more. The fee shall be payable on the last day of the calendar month following the calendar quarter for which the fee is owed.

An individual commencing a voluntary case or a joint case under title 11 may pay such fee in installments. For converting, on request of the debtor, a case under chapter 7, or 13 of title 11, to a case under chapter 11 of title 11, the debtor shall pay to the clerk of the court a fee of $400.

(b) The Judicial Conference of the United States may prescribe additional fees in cases under title 11 of the same kind as the Judicial Conference prescribes under section 1914(b) of this title.

(c) Upon the filing of any separate or joint notice of appeal or application for appeal or upon the receipt of any order allowing, or notice of the allowance of, an appeal or a writ of certiorari $5 shall be paid to the clerk of the court, by the appellant or petitioner.

(d) Whenever any case or proceeding is dismissed in any court for want of jurisdiction, such court may order the payment of just costs.

(e) The clerk of the court may collect only the fees prescribed under this section.

JURISDICTION AND PROCEDURE IN BANKRUPTCY

With respect to the provision in 28 U.S.C. § 1930(a) relative to the payment of bankruptcy filing fees by individuals in installments, see Official Forms Nos. 2 and 3.

5. List of Creditors and Schedules of Assets and Liabilities and Statement of Affairs

A list of all known creditors, as complete and accurate as possible, must be filed with the court with the petition. This requirement is very important as the list provided will be used by the court to give notice to all creditors of the bankrupt and invite them to the first meeting of creditors pursuant to 11 U.S.C. 341. Bankruptcy Rule 1007 should be read and carefully adhered to.

In Chapter 11 cases (as well as Chapter 9—Municipalities) a list of the 20 largest creditors also must be filed. Bankruptcy Rule 1007(d). This list is used by the United States Trustee's office to designate the creditors committee.

Debtors in every chapter of the bankruptcy code are required to file schedules of their assets and liabilities. Such schedules are necessary to enable trustees, creditors and other parties in interest to know with what they are dealing. From the debtor's point of view, it is essential that all creditors be included on the schedules to assure that all debts are finally disposed of. The first duty of a debtor mandated by 11 U.S.C. § 521 is that of filing a list of creditors, and "unless the court orders otherwise" (which would be very rare), "a schedule of assets and liabilities" as well as a statement of financial affairs and current income and expenditures. Official Forms Nos. 6 and 6A or their equivalent should be used.

Where the debtor is an individual and the schedule of assets and liabilities includes consumer debt secured by property of the estate, the individual debtor also must file a statement of intent as to the retention or surrender of such property and, within 45 days thereafter, perform said intention. 11 U.S.C. § 521(2). Official Form No. 8A is a Chapter 7 individual debtor's statement of intention.

The Statement of Affairs includes a list of questions designed to provide a road map for the trustee and creditors as to relevant transactions and facts for use in finding assets, identifying voidably preferential transfers, and in generally investigating the debtor's affairs and relevant financial activities. Official Form No. 7 is a statement of affairs designed for use by a debtor not engaged in business. Official Form No. 8 is a statement of affairs for a debtor engaged in business.

Bankruptcy Rule 1007 sets forth in detail what lists, schedules and statements are required by debtors in the various chapters. The time limitations for filing same also are specified.

The list of creditors referred in 11 U.S.C. § 521 and Bankruptcy Rule 1007 is filed with the petition in a voluntary case. Bankruptcy Rule 1007(a)(1).

In Chapter 13 wage earner cases, Official Form No. 10 shall be filed, unless the court orders otherwise, as provided in Bankruptcy Rule 1007(b)(2). This form may be the most important document filed in a Chapter 13 case and it should be prepared with particular attention to detail.

F. Trustees

The United States Trustees maintain panels of qualified persons to act as trustees in bankruptcy cases. 11 U.S.C. § 701(a)(1) provides: "Promptly after the order for relief" the United States Trustee "shall appoint one disinterested person that is a member of the panel of private trustees established under section 586(a)(1) of title 28 or that is serving as trustee in the case immediately before the order for relief . . . to serve as interim trustee." The interim trustee serves until a trustee is elected pursuant to 11 U.S.C. § 702 and qualifies as provided in 11 U.S.C. § 322.

11 U.S.C. § 702 provides for the election of a trustee by creditors holding "allowable, undisputed, fixed, liquidated, unsecured" claims and who do not "have an interest materially adverse" to the interest of other creditors. The term "claim" is defined in 11 U.S.C. § 101(4). To the extent its claim is under-secured, a secured creditor holds an unsecured claim 11 U.S.C. § 506(a).

In representing a trustee, Official Form No. 25 should be used with respect to bonding the trustee and obtaining approval of the bond.

The duties of the trustee are set forth in 11 U.S.C. §§ 704, 1302, 521, 1146 and 1106. Eligibility to act as a trustee is governed by 11 U.S.C. § 324.

1. Chapter 11 Trustees and Debtors in Possession

While trustees act in Chapter 7 liquidation cases and Chapter 13 adjustment cases and others, the Bankruptcy Code contemplates that in Chapter 11 reorganizations, the incidence of trusteeships should be limited. In Chapter 11 cases, it is contemplated that existing management should in most cases continue to operate the debtor's business. The code, however, is written in terms of trustees (due in large part to the fact that in most non-Chapter 11 cases, trustees are normally used). The very first subsection in Chapter 11, therefore, defines a debtor in possession as follows:

(1) "debtor in possession" means debtor except when a person that has qualified under section 322 of this title is serving as trustee in the case.

11 U.S.C. § 1101(1).

11 U.S.C. § 1101(1) keys into 11 U.S.C. § 1107 which sets forth the rights, powers and duties of a debtor-in-possession which are, generally that "a debtor in possession shall have all the rights . . . and powers, and shall perform all the functions and duties . . . of a trustee serving in a case under this chapter" with certain exceptions. Hence, the debtor normally remains in possession and control of the Chapter 11 estate and, as debtor-in-possession, has essentially the same duties and powers as a trustee would. As such, the debtor-in-possession acts in a fiduciary capacity for the benefit of creditors and other interested parties.

While it is the rule that the debtor should remain in possession in Chapter 11 cases, the exception is provided for. Thus, 11 U.S.C. § 1103(c) in outlining powers of creditors' committees in Chapter 11 cases provides that, among other things, the committee may "(4) request the appointment of a trustee or examiner under section 1104 of this title. . . ." 11 U.S.C. § 1104(a) provides:

> (a) At any time after the commencement of the case but before confirmation of a plan, on request of a party in interest or the United States trustee, and after notice and a hearing, the court shall order the appointment of a trustee—
>
> (1) for cause, including fraud, dishonesty, incompetence, or gross mismanagement of the affairs of the debtor by current management, either before or after the commencement of the case, or similar cause, but not including the number of holders of securities of the debtor or the amount of assets or liabilities of the debtor; or
>
> (2) if such appointment is in the interest of creditors, any equity security holders, and other interests of the estate, without regard to the number of holders of securities of the debtor or the amount of assets or liabilities of the debtor.

Note that *cause* must be demonstrated before the debtor-in-possession will be superceded by a Chapter 11 trustee to operate the business and hold the assets. Also note that the word "including" used in 11 U.S.C. § 1104(a)(1) is *not* limiting, *see* 11 U.S.C. § 102(3); therefore, the examples given are just examples and any "cause" may be used as the basis of a motion for the appointment of a Chapter 11 trustee.

2. Examiners in Chapter 11

Where a trustee is not appointed in a Chapter 11 case, 11 U.S.C. § 1104(b) provides that in appropriate circumstances, an examiner may be appointed to investigate the affairs of the debtor. The examiner's report sometimes includes facts forming the basis for a motion to appoint a Chapter 11 trustee.

Appointment of a trustee in a railroad reorganization is mandated by 11 U.S.C. § 1163. Chapter 13 trustees are appointed as provided in 11 U.S.C. § 1302.

G. Chapter 11 Plans and Disclosure

Space does not permit more than cursory discussion of the reorganization process under Chapter 11. It is widely understood, however, that Chapter 11 reorganizations are bankrupty cases in which the debtor remains in business and seeks to work out a compromise with its creditors. That compromise is embodied in a plan of reorganization which, if accepted by creditors and confirmed by the court, will provide for the disposition of the debtor's liabilities.

Before votes can be solicited for a proposed plan of reorganization, a disclosure statement must be approved by the court after notice. Said disclosure statement will accompany the proposed plan when it is sent to creditors and equity security holders in an effort to solicit votes (proxies) to have the plan accepted. In this connection Official Form Nos. 28 and 29 are useful. *See* 11 U.S.C. § 1125. Official Form No. 30 is a form of ballot for use in seeking acceptances of a proposed plan of reorganization and Official Form No. 31 is a form of order confirming an accepted plan. 11 U.S.C. §§ 1121 through 1124 generally control who may file a plan, the classification of claims and interests, the contents of a plan of reorganization and impairment of claims and interests. Acceptance of the plan is governed by 11 U.S.C. § 1126, modifications of a plan by 11 U.S.C. § 1127, and confirmation of a plan by 11 U.S.C. §§ 1128 and 1129.

Chapter 11 reorganization practice is a sophisticated area of specialization which requires a solid understanding of the relevant law. When a debtor, creditors or equity security holders committee, or a trustee or examiner is to be represented in connection with a Chapter 11 case, non-specialist practitioners will proceed at their own (as well as their clients') risk unless they are prepared to study in depth the relevant law or, preferably, call in an accomplished specialist who may be retained either to handle the case entirely or as co-counsel or special counsel.

H. Creditors

"Creditors" is defined by 11 U.S.C. § 101(9) as follows:

(A) entity that has a claim against the debtor that arose at the time of or before the order for relief concerning the debtor;

(B) entity that has a claim against the estate of a kind specified in section 348(d), 502(f), 502(g), 502(h) or 502(i) of this title; or

(C) entity that has a community claim.

JURISDICTION AND PROCEDURE IN BANKRUPTCY

1. Equity Security Holders

Similar to the creditor, and subordinate to it is the equity security holder. "Equity security holder" is defined in 11 U.S.C. § 101(16):

> (16) "equity security holder" means holder of an equity security of the debtor.

"Equity security" is defined by 11 U.S.C. § 101(15):

> (A) share in a corporation, whether or not transferable or denominated "stock", or similar security;
>
> (B) interest of a limited partner in a limited partnership; or
>
> (C) warrant or right, other than a right to convert, to purchase, sell, or subscribe to a share, security, or interest of a kind specified in subparagrah (A) and (B) of this paragraph . . . .

As noted, equity security holders' claims are subordinated to those of general creditors. Little attention need be given them here as they commonly do not receive any pay-out in a bankruptcy case because insufficient assets exist to pay general creditors in full. They do have rights, however, and in appropriate cases do realize a return; often, for example, shareholders of a Chapter 11 corporation retain shares in the reorganized debtor. The scope of this chapter, however, is too limited to deal with them further.

2. Claims

Official Forms No. 19, 20 and 21 are useful in respect to filing claims. The law provides that where the debtor includes a creditor's claim on its schedules of liabilities as not contingent, unliquidated or disputed, the claim is deemed filed on behalf of the creditor. Good practice, however, dictates that the creditor file its claim for itself. Further, when the claim is taken or sent to the Bankruptcy Court clerk for filing, a duplicate should be included (with a self-addressed stamped envelope when dealing by mail) along with a request that the duplicate be stamped by the clerk with the time and date of filing and returned to the creditor. Should the original claim then be lost or misplaced, the receipted copy will be useful as proof that the claim was timely filed if and when the claim is objected to.

In preparing a proof of claim, any security securing the claim should be declared. Failure to file a secured claim as such constitutes (according to certain case law) a waiver of the security. Therefore, even where there is no known security, it is prudent to include on the face of the proof of claim a statement to the effect that to the extent any security may exist, it is not waived.

Official Form Nos. 17 and 18 are forms of power of attorney useful where a creditor wishes to have counsel act on its behalf in connection with its claim.

The filing of a proof of claim is *prima facie* evidence of its truth and validity.[3] 11 U.S.C. § 502(a) provides:

> (a) A claim or interest, proof of which is filed under section 501 of this title, is deemed allowed, unless a party in interest, including a creditor of a general partner in a partnership that is a debtor in a case under chapter 7 of this title, objects.

Objections to claims are a subject of motion practice (see above) and the objection may be (and usually is) made by mere notice. As 11 U.S.C. § 502(b) includes the phrase "after notice and a hearing," as noted above, the objection will be successful without any hearing unless the claimant whose claim is objected to responds and requests a hearing. Objections to claims are controlled generally by 11 U.S.C. § 502. As an unanswered objection to a claim prevails unless the claimant responds, it should be noted that claimants (and their attorneys) should be diligent in assuring that any change in address is filed with the court and the debtor's or trustee's counsel as well as counsel to any creditors' commitee active in the case.

When an objection to a claim is noticed, it frequently is done as part of an omnibus motion to which are annexed schedules of claims being objected to. As a practical matter, a large proportion of objections are resolved through correspondence and telephonic communication between the objectant's counsel and counsel to the holders of the objected-to claims. Where a defense to the objection is to be pursued, always contact opposing counsel and note that response will be made and request an adjournment of the hearing on the objection so that settlement negotiations can be pursued. Always verify in writing and create a "paper trail." In most cases, objections are settled upon consent of the parties. Where the defense is proper, the objection may, of course, be settled by its withdrawal. In any case, once a disposition of the objection is agreed to between counsel, the creditor's lawyer should be sure to obtain a court order accurately disposing of the objection.

3. Creditors Meetings

11 U.S.C. § 341 provides for the convening of meetings at which, pursuant to 11 U.S.C. § 343, creditors and other parties in interest may question the debtor. Similarly, Bankruptcy Rule 2004 provides that on motion of a

---

[3] Filing of a false claim is subject to the imposition of fines of not more than $5,000 plus up to five years in prison. 11 U.S.C. § 152.

JURISDICTION AND PROCEDURE IN BANKRUPTCY

party in interest, "the court may order the examination of *any* entity" (emphasis added) in respect to a wide scope of relevant activities of the debtor.

a. Committees

At the § 341 meeting, creditors eligible to vote for a trustee pursuant to 11 U.S.C. § 702(a), *supra*, may elect a committee of creditors of "not fewer than three, and not more than eleven, creditors. . . ." 11 U.S.C. § 705(a). 11 U.S.C. § 705(b) provides:

> (b) A committee elected under subsection (a) of this section may consult with the trustee or the United States trustee in connection with the administration of the estate, make recommendation to the trustee or the United States trustee respecting the performance of the trustee's duties, and submit to the court or the United States trustee any question affecting the administration of the estate.

It should be remembered that, as noted above, a debtor-in-possession stands in the shoes of a trustee in Chapter 11 cases where no trustee has been appointed. Therefore, in Chapter 11 cases, the references to "trustee" in 11 U.S.C. § 705(b) may be read to include the debtor-in-possession. While 11 U.S.C. § 705 provides for the election of a creditors' committee, most frequently, committees are not active in Chapter 13 and Chapter 7 cases. The United States Trustee normally appoints committees in Chapter 11 cases, drawing from information filed by the debtor, most notably the list of 20 largest creditors. A creditor wishing to participate on a creditors' committee should contact the United States Trustee responsible for cases filed in the district where the case is pending.

At the first meeting of the creditors' committee, it is normal and advisable for the committee to adopt operating rules (such as the number required for a quorum) and appoint a chairman, vice chairman and secretary. Counsel to the committee also should be selected. Counsel selected by the committee should take charge. Such counsel must be appointed on application of the committee by the court if said counsel is to be paid from the bankrupt's estate. Counsel to the committee, like counsel to the debtor, counsel to the trustee and counsel to other committees appointed may apply to the court for payment of reasonable fees and out-of-pocket expenses. 11 U.S.C. § 330 goes to compensation of attorneys, accountants, trustees and examiners. 11 U.S.C. § 331 provides that during the pendency of a case, trustees, examiners, debtor's attorneys and other professionals employed in the case may apply for and receive interim compensation "not more than once every 120 days . . . or more often if the court permits." A trustee's fees are limited pursuant to 11 U.S.C. § 326; the trustee's counsel's are not.

b. Powers and Duties of Committee

11 U.S.C. § 705(b), quoted above, outlines powers and duties of committees.

In Chapter 11 cases, the committee as well as any other party in interest specifically has the right to "raise . . . appear and be heard on any issue in a case under this chapter." 11 U.S.C. § 1109(b).

The United States Trustee is charged with the responsibility of appointing committees of creditors in Chapter 11 cases. 11 U.S.C. § 1102(a)(1). The number of committees in Chapter 11 cases and who shall comprise them also are subjects of 11 U.S.C. § 1102. Once appointed, a committee in a Chapter 11 case has all of the powers and duties set forth in 11 U.S.C. § 1103 which provides:

> (a) At a scheduled meeting of a committee appointed under section 1102 of this title, at which a majority of the members of such committee are present, and with the court's approval, such committee may select and authorize the employment by such committee of one or more attorneys, accountants, or other agents, to represent or perform services for such committee.
>
> (b) An attorney or accountant employed to represent a committee appointed under section 1102 of this title may not, while employed by such committee, represent any other entity having an adverse interest in connection with the case. Representation of one or more creditors of the same class as represented by the committee shall not per se constitute the representation of an adverse interest.
>
> (c) A committee appointed under section 1102 of this title may
>
> (1) consult with the trustee or debtor in possession concerning the administration of the case;
>
> (2) investigate the acts, conduct, assets, liabilities, and financial condition of the debtor, the operation of the debtor's business and the desirability of the continuance of such business, and any other matter relevant to the case or to the formulation of a plan;
>
> (3) participate in the formulation of a plan, advise those represented by such committee of such committee's determinations as to any plan formulated, and collect and file with the court acceptances or rejections of a plan;
>
> (4) request the appointment of a trustee or examiner under section 1104 of this title; and
>
> (5) perform such other services as are in the interest of those represented.

JURISDICTION AND PROCEDURE IN BANKRUPTCY

(d) As soon as practicable after the appointment of a committee under section 1102 of this title, the trustee shall meet with such committee to transact such business as may be necessary and proper.

I. Automatic Stay

Upon the filing of a bankruptcy case most actions and proceedings to collect upon claims against the debtor are stayed by action of law. 11 U.S.C. § 362. The scope of the stay is contained in 11 U.S.C. § 362(a) and (b), which read:

(a) Except as provided in subsection (b) of this section, a petition filed under section 301, 302, or 303 of this title, or an application filed under section 5(a)(3) of the Securities Investor Protection Act of 1970 (15 U.S.C. 78eee(a)(3)), operates as a stay, applicable to all entities, of

(1) the commencement or continuation, including the issuance or employment of process, of a judicial, administrative, or other action or proceeding against the debtor that was or could have been commenced before the commencement of the case under this title, or to recover a claim against the debtor that arose before the commencement of the case under this title;

(2) the enforcement, against the debtor or against property of the estate, of a judgment obtained before the commencement of the case under this title;

(3) any act to obtain possession of property of the estate or of property from the estate or to exercise control over property of the estate;

(4) any act to create, perfect, or enforce any lien against property of the estate;

(5) any act to create, perfect, or enforce against property of the debtor any lien to the extent that such lien secures a claim that arose before the commencement of the case under this title;

(6) any act to collect, assess, or recover a claim against the debtor that arose before the commencement of the case under this title;

(7) the setoff of any debt owing to the debtor that arose before the commencement of the case under this title against any claim against the debtor; and

(8) the commencement or continuation of a proceeding before the United States Tax Court concerning the debtor.

(b) The filing of a petition under section 301, 302, or 303 of this title, or of an application under section 5(a)(3) of the Securities Investor Protection Act of 1970 (15 U.S.C. 78eee(a)(3)), does not operate as a stay—

(1) under subsection (a) of this section, of the commencement or continuation of a criminal action or proceeding against the debtor;

(2) under subsection (a) of this section, of the collection of alimony, maintenance, or support from property that is not property of the estate;

(3) under subsection (a) of this section, of any act to perfect an interest in property to the extent that the trustee's rights and powers are subject to such perfection under section 546(b) of this title or to the extent that such act is accomplished within the period provided under section 547(e)(2)(A) of this title;

(4) under subsection (a)(1) of this section, of the commencement or continuation of an action or proceeding by a governmental unit to enforce such governmental unit's police or regulatory power;

(5) under subsection (a)(2) of this section, of the enforcement of a judgment, other than a money judgment, obtained in an action or proceeding by a governmental unit to enforce such governmental unit's police or regulatory power;

(6) under subsection (a) of this section, of the setoff by a commodity broker, forward contract merchant, stockbroker, financial institutions, or securities clearing agency of any mutual debt and claim under or in connection with commodity contracts, as defined in section 761(4) of this title, forward contracts, or securities contracts, as defined in section 741(7) of this title, that constitutes the setoff of a claim against the debtor for a margin payment, as defined in section 741(5) or 761(15) of this title, or settlement payment, as defined in section 741(8) of this title, arising out of commodity contracts, forward contracts, or securities contracts against cash, securities, or other property held by or due from such commodity broker, forward contract merchant, stockbroker, financial institutions, or securities clearing agency to margin, guarantee, secure, or settle commodity contracts, forward contracts, or securities contracts;

(7) under subsection (a) of this section, of the setoff by a repo participant, of any mutual debt and claim under or in connection

with repurchase agreements that constitutes the setoff of a claim against the debtor for a margin payment, as defined in section 741(5) or 761(15) of this title, or settlement payment, as defined in section 741(8) of this title, arising out of repurchase agreements against cash, securities, or other property held by or due from such repo participant to margin, guarantee, secure or settle repurchase agreements;

(8) under subsection (a) of this section, of the commencement of any action by the Secretary of Housing and Urban Development to foreclose a mortgage or deed of trust in any case in which the mortgage or deed of trust held by the Secretary is insured or was formerly insured under the National Housing Act and covers property, or combinations of property, consisting of five or more living units;

(9) under subsection (a) of this section, of the issuance to the debtor by a governmental unit of a notice of tax deficiency;

(10) under subsection (a) of this section, of any act by a lessor to the debtor under a lease of nonresidential real property that has terminated by the expiration of the stated term of the lease before the commencement of or during a case under this title to obtain possession of such property; or [sic]

(11) under subsection (a) of this section, of the presentment of a negotiable instrument and the giving of notice of and protesting dishonor of such an instrument;

(12) under subsection (a) of this section, after the date which is 90 days after the filing of such petition, of the commencement or continuation, and conclusion to the entry of final judgment, of an action which involves a debtor subject to reorganization pursuant to chapter 11 of this title and which was brought by the Secretary of Transportation under the Ship Mortgage Act, 1920 (46 App. U.S.C. 911 et seq.) (including distribution of any proceeds of sale) to foreclose a preferred ship or fleet mortgage, or a security interest in or relating to a vessel or vessel under construction, held by the Secretary of Transportation under section 207 of title XI of the Merchant Marine Act, 1936 (46 App. U.S.C. 1117 and 1271 et seq., respectively), or under applicable State law; or

(13) under subsection (a) of this section, after the date which is 90 days after the filing of such petition, of the commencement or continuation, and conclusion to the entry of final judgment, of an action which involves a debtor subject to reorganization pursuant

to chapter 11 of this title and which was brought by the Secretary of Commerce under the Ship Mortgage Act, 1920 (46 App. U.S.C. 911 et seq.) (including distribution of any proceeds of sale) to foreclose a preferred ship or fleet mortgage in a vessel or a mortgage, deed of trust, or other security interest in a fishing facility held by the Secretary of Commerce under section 207 of title XI of the Merchant Marine Act, 1936 (46 App. U.S.C. 1117 and 1271 et seq. respectively).

The § 362 stay remains in effect generally until the case is completed, 11 U.S.C. § 362(c), unless a party successfully moves for relief from the stay as provided in 11 U.S.C. § 362(d), (f) and (g) or the stay, after motion, is lifted pursuant to 11 U.S.C. § 362(e). To ignore the stay is to risk being held in contempt of court and, where the violation of the stay is willful, punitive as well as actual damages may be awarded to an "individual" injured by such willful violation of the stay. 11 U.S.C. § 362(h).

Where the stay is not modified or relieved upon an 11 U.S.C. § 362 motion by a secured creditor, if said creditor shows a lack of "adequate protection," 11 U.S.C. § 362(d)(1), such "adequate protection" may be provided pursuant to 11 U.S.C. § 361. A secured creditor that can demonstrate that its security is diminishing in value during the pendency of the automatic stay, normally moves for relief from the stay and alleges, among other things, that it is not adequately protected due to depreciation continuing while such creditor is stayed from executing on its collateral. In such cases, if the collateral is needed by the debtor or the trustee in the course of the debtor's business, relief from the stay normally will be denied but such creditor will receive adequate protection pursuant to 11 U.S.C. § 361. Both sections 361 and 362 of Title 11 should be studied.

It also should be noted that while, pursuant to 11 U.S.C. §§ 361 and 362, a creditor is entitled to compensation by way of adequate protection of the value of its depreciating collateral, a secured creditor is *not* entitled to adequate protection of the value of its "lost opportunity" to immediately execute upon its collateral (*i.e.*, the present value of money). The leading case is *United Savings Association of Texas v. Timbers of Inwood Forest Assoc., Ltd.*, 108 S. Ct. 626 (1988) ("*Timbers*"). Valuable discussion of the law and underlying considerations respecting adequate protection also is found in the circuit court opinion affirmed by the United States Supreme Court in *Timbers*, 793 F.2d 1380 (5th Cir. 1986).

As to the procedure when relief from the stay is sought, note again the use in 11 U.S.C. § 362(d) of the phrase "after notice and a hearing" (defined in 11 U.S.C. § 102(1) and discussed *supra*).

J. Executory Contracts and Leases

One other key provision of the Bankruptcy Code that should be noted is 11 U.S.C. § 365. Section 365 of Title 11 provides that a debtor or trustee may assume or reject executory contracts and leases—even in some cases where on the face of the contract or lease consent appears to be required. Generally, a contract or lease may be rejected when the debtor or trustee demonstrates that it would be good business to do so.[4] The key factors to recall procedurally are (a) that no lease or contract is assumed or rejected without a court order (except as provided in 11 U.S.C. § 365(d)), (b) assumption and rejection of leases and other contracts are subjects of motion practice (unless affirmative relief of a kind specified in Bankruptcy Rule 7001 also is sought), and (c) a lease or other contract may not be assumed unless defaults (other than technical defaults such as pursuant to a bankruptcy clause) are cured. Once assumed, a lease or contract may be assigned pursuant to 11 U.S.C. § 363. There can be no assignment of a lease or contract unless it is assumed and, therefore, there can be no assignment without the curing of all except technical defaults unless the other side of the contract agrees to waive such defaults. Assumption, rejection and assignment of contracts is another area where consultation with specialized expertise is particularly advised.

Note also should be given to the automatic rejection of contracts and leases contained in 11 U.S.C. § 365(d). Counsel to landlords of debtors should take particular note of that subsection.

IV. CONCLUSION

The above discussion is intended as a guide to bankruptcy practice for practitioners not frequently engaged in the area. The practitioner is invited to use it as his or her entree into what otherwise might appear to be a jurisdictional and procedural maze. Where substantial issues are involved, the practitioner is advised to research thoroughly or to call in an experienced specialist.

Special thanks is given to the Honorable Prudence B. Abram, United States Bankruptcy Judge, S.D.N.Y., for her review of this chapter and her many helpful suggestions.

---

[4] This discussion will not address the matter of rejection of union contracts due to the limited scope of this chapter. The rejection of collective bargaining agreements is specifically addressed in and governed by 11 U.S.C. § 1113.

CHAPTER THIRTY

MULTIDISTRICT LITIGATION

by Leonard L. Rivkin, Esq.*

I. INTRODUCTION

The multidistrict litigation statute, 28 U.S.C. § 1407 (1982), permits cases brought in federal courts nationwide to be consolidated in a single court for discovery and other pretrial purposes. If the cases are not settled or disposed of by summary judgment, they may eventually be transferred back to the districts where they were first brought for trial. They also may stay in the transferee court for trial.

The procedures for transferring related federal cases for coordinated pretrial proceedings allow for substantial efficiencies in conducting federal civil litigation. This chapter, which draws upon the author's involvement in four multidistrict dockets,[1] describes multidistrict procedure.

II. THE STATUTE

Congress enacted the Multidistrict Litigation Act, 28 U.S.C. § 1407 (1982), in 1968. The statute was prompted by the federal courts' efforts in coordinating almost two thousand treble damages actions that were filed in the 1960s against electric equipment manufacturers which had been convicted of price-fixing. The experience gained in coordinating those cases indicated that centralized coordination of related actions would be a valuable managerial tool

---

* Counsel and Founding Partner, Rivkin, Radler, Dunne & Bayh, Uniondale, New York. The assistance of Eugene S. R. Pagano, Associate, Rivkin, Radler, Dunne & Bayh, and the editorial advice of Leslie R. Bennett, Partner, Rivkin, Radler, Dunne & Bayh, are gratefully acknowledged.

1 *In re Texas Eastern Transmission Corp. Polychlorinated Biphenyl Pollution Insurance Coverage Litigation*, MDL Docket No. 764; *In re The Dow Chemical Company "Sarabond" Products Liability Litigation*, MDL Docket No. 711; *In re "Agent Orange" Product Liability Litigation*, MDL Docket No. 381; *In re Franklin National Bank Securities Litigation*, MDL Docket No. 196.

to have available on a permanent basis. Herndon & Higginbotham, *Complex Litigation—An Overview of 28 U.S.C.A. § 1407*, 31 Baylor L. Rev. 33, 35-37 (1979); Note, *The Experience of Transferee Courts Under the Multidistrict Litigation Act*, 39 U. Chi. L. Rev. 588, 588 (1972).

The statute establishes the Judicial Panel on Multidistrict Litigation ("Panel"), and gives it the authority to transfer civil actions involving one or more common questions of fact to any district court for coordinated or consolidated pretrial proceedings. 28 U.S.C. § 1407(a) (1982). The Panel is composed of seven circuit and district judges designated by the Chief Justice. *Id.*, § 1407(d).

There are only two specific restrictions on the Panel's authority to transfer civil actions. It cannot transfer civil actions brought by the United States to enforce the antitrust laws. *Id.*, § 1407(g). In addition, no equitable action brought by the Securities and Exchange Commission ("SEC") to enforce the securities laws can be transferred without the SEC's consent. 15 U.S.C. § 78u(g) (1982). The Panel can transfer any other civil action pending in a federal court. 15 C. Wright, A. Miller & E. Cooper, *Federal Practice and Procedure* § 3862 at 509-11 (2d ed. 1986).

The Panel is also explicitly authorized to transfer specific claims, cross-claims, counterclaims and third-party claims within pending civil actions. 28 U.S.C. § 1407(a) (1982); *see, e.g.*, *In re Equity Funding Corp. Securities Litigation*, 385 F. Supp. 1262 (J.P.M.L. 1974). It cannot, however, separate and transfer particular issues. *In re Plumbing Fixture Cases*, 298 F. Supp. 484, 489-90 (J.P.M.L. 1968).

III. TRANSFER OF ACTIONS

A. Criteria for Transfer

The Panel can transfer civil actions pending in federal court if they share common questions of fact and if transfer would serve the convenience of parties and witnesses and promote the just and efficient conduct of the actions. 28 U.S.C. § 1407(a)(1982). The Panel is reluctant to consider anything other than these factors, such as dissatisfaction with the current judge. *See In re Motion Picture "Standard Accessories" and "Pre-Vues" Antitrust Litigation*, 339 F. Supp. 1278, 1280 (J.P.M.L. 1972).

The party moving for transfer bears the burden of persuasion on whether the statutory criteria are satisfied. The Panel has characterized the burden as a heavy one. *In re 21st Century Productions, Inc. "Thrilsphere" Contract Litigation*, 448 F. Supp. 271, 273 (J.P.M.L. 1978); *see also In re Buffalo Valley Gas Authority Litigation*, 429 F. Supp. 1029, 1032 (J.P.M.L. 1977).

The Panel is aware that transfer involves inconveniences and costs of its own, even though it believes that transfer often creates a net savings in convenience and cost. *See In re Motion Picture Licensing Antitrust Litigation*, 468 F. Supp. 837, 842 (J.P.M.L. 1979). Because of this potential for increased cost, the moving party's burden becomes especially heavy when only a minimal number of actions are involved. *In re Raymond Lee Organization, Inc. Securities Litigation*, 446 F. Supp. 1266, 1268 (J.P.M.L. 1978); *In re Scotch Whiskey*, 299 F. Supp. 543, 544 (J.P.M.L. 1969). Nonetheless, on several occasions, the Panel has transferred as few as two cases. *See, e.g., In re Haven Industries, Inc. Securities Litigation*, 415 F. Supp. 396 (J.P.M.L. 1976); *In re Cross-Florida Barge Canal Litigation*, 329 F. Supp. 543 (J.P.M.L. 1971).

The Panel can transfer cases even though potentially dispositive motions may be pending in some of the transferred actions, because the transferee judge can decide those motions. *In re Data General Corp. Antitrust Litigation*, 510 F. Supp. 1220, 1227 (J.P.M.L. 1979); *In re Commonwealth Oil/Tesoro Petroleum Securities Litigation*, 458 F. Supp. 225, 230 (J.P.M.L. 1978). Indeed, in one recent decision, the Panel ordered transfer where there were only two actions, and where there were pending motions to dismiss both cases. *In re Texas Eastern Transmission Corp. Polychlorinated Biphenyl Pollution Insurance Coverage Litigation*, MDL No. 764 (J.P.M.L. May 31, 1988) (Appendix A).

B. Motions to Transfer

The party seeking to transfer related cases must move before the Panel for transfer. The chief documents are the notice of motion, the supporting brief, and a schedule giving the following data for each action:

    a) the complete name;

    b) the district court where the action is pending;

    c) the civil action number; and

    d) the assigned judge, if known.

R.J.P.M.L. 10(a).[2]

The motion is unlike the notice of motion familiar to practitioners in this state. It consists of numbered paragraphs, with each paragraph limited, as far as possible, to stating only one factual averment. R.J.P.M.L. 9(a). Its format is much like that of a pleading. *See* Appendix B for a sample form.

---

[2] The Panel's Rules, which were recently revised and renumbered, are published at 120 F.R.D. 251 (1988).

The brief, in contrast to the motion, is a familiar document. The maximum length is 20 pages, unless the Panel grants permission to file a longer one. R.J.P.M.L. 9(f).

Any opponent of transfer must file a "response" within 20 days after the filing of the motion. A party who does not file a response is deemed to acquiesce to the action requested in the motion. *Id.*, R. 10(c). The response, like the motion, must be made in numbered paragraphs. Each numbered paragraph in the response must respond to the paragraph in the motion bearing the same number, and admit or deny, in whole or part, the averment in the corresponding paragraph of the motion. If the response denies anything, it must state the opponent's version of the denied subject matter. *Id.*, R. 9(b).

Practice point: Writing a motion with paragraphs as specific and focused as possible takes advantage of this requirement of a specific response to denied matter. The opponent will be forced to follow and respond to your presentation and may have to admit averments damaging to its position.

The moving party can file a reply brief within five days after the deadline for filing responses. *Id.*, R. 10(d).

Sometimes there is no opposition to transfer. All parties may perceive it to be advantageous. *See, e.g., In re Fire Disaster at DuPont Plaza Hotel*, 660 F. Supp. 982 (J.P.M.L. 1987). At other times a party may support transfer, but urge selection of a different transferee court. A party can also oppose a motion for transfer, yet alternatively urge selection of a different transferee district than the one urged by movants should the Panel order transfer.

The Panel has stated that it can order transfer over the opposition of all parties. *In re Asbestos & Asbestos Insulation Material Products Liability Litigation*, 431 F. Supp. 906, 910 (J.P.M.L. 1977). Nevertheless, it is reluctant to order transfer when all parties oppose it. *See, e.g., id.* This writer is not aware of any case where the Panel transferred cases over the opposition of all parties. In at least one docket, however, the Panel ordered transfer where the defendants in a group of products liability cases moved for transfer but were opposed by all the plaintiffs. *In re Dow Chemical Company "Sarabond" Products Liability Litigation*, 650 F. Supp. 187 (J.P.M.L. 1986).

C. Orders to Show Cause

The Panel has the power to consider transfer of litigation on its own initiative. 28 U.S.C. § 1407(c)(i) (1982). *See, e.g., In re Asbestos & Asbestos Insulation Products Liability Litigation*, 431 F. Supp. 906, 909 (J.P.M.L. 1977). The Administrative Office of the United States Courts informs the Panel of potentially transferable actions. In addition, several district courts

MULTIDISTRICT LITIGATION 875

also inform the Panel of such cases. Howard, *A Guide to Multidistrict Litigation*, 75 F.R.D. 577, 581 (1977). Such sources enable the Panel to obtain the information necessary for such initiatives.

If the Panel decides to act on its own initiative, the Clerk will file an order to show cause why the litigation should not be transferred. Parties who are engaged in more than one of the actions covered by the order to show cause must notify the Clerk of any additional related actions, including those filed after issuance of the order to show cause. R.J.P.M.L. 11(a). Any party can respond to the order within 20 days after its filing. Failure to respond is deemed acquiescence to the action proposed by the order. *Id.*, R. 11(b). Any party can file a reply to a response within 5 days after the end of the 15-day period for filing responses. *Id.*, R. 11(c).

D. Papers: Format, Filing and Service

The Panel Rules require papers to be unfolded, on letter size paper and bound on the left. Each paper must bear a descriptive title and an identification in the form "MDL Docket No. ___." The title on the first page must begin at least three inches from the top margin. *Id.*, R. 9(d).

An original and 11 copies of all papers on a motion to transfer must be filed with the Panel. *Id.*, R. 7(a). In addition, a copy of the motion to transfer must be filed in every district court in which an underlying action is pending. *Id.*, R. 7(c).

Each paper must be served on each party in each action. The proof of service on a motion to transfer must state that a copy of the motion has been filed in each District Court where any action is pending. The proof of service on any paper must be sent to each person listed in the proof of service. *Id.*, R. 8(a), (b).

Within 10 days after the filing of a motion to transfer, each party must notify the Clerk, in writing, of the one attorney designated to receive papers on its behalf. *Id.*, R. 8(c). The Clerk will then prepare an official Panel Service List of the designated attorneys and of unrepresented parties. *Id.*, R. 8 (d).

Important Note on Time: The automatic three-day extension of time after service by mail provided by Fed. R. Civ. P. 6(e), does not apply in Panel proceedings. Although the Panel Rules do not explicitly so provide, the Panel's staff firmly takes this position.

E. Panel Hearings and Decisions

The sessions at which the Panel considers motions are called "hearings." *Id.*, R. 16. Oral testimony, however, is to be avoided as much as possible. *Id.*,

R. 16(g). The proceedings are more like oral arguments on motions. Hearings occur approximately every two months, in different cities around the country rather than at a fixed location.

In a new docket which is being considered for transfer, the Panel will allow only one-half hour total argument. *Id.*, R. 16(f). Based upon the author's extensive personal experience, few lawyers receive more than five minutes. The Panel decides cases quickly, often issuing decisions in only a few weeks.

The Panel, of course, may deny transfer. As noted subsequently, such a denial of transfer is unreviewable.

If the Panel orders transfer, the transfer takes effect when the transfer order is filed with the transferee court. 28 U.S.C. § 1407(c) (1982). Most cases hold that transfer strips the transferor court of all jurisdiction. *Glasstech, Inc. v. AB Krno OY*, 769 F.2d 1574, 1576 (Fed. Cir. 1985) (collecting cases); *accord Manual for Complex Litigation (Second)* § 31.121 at 252 (1985). The Eighth Circuit, however, reviewed on the merits an order entered by a transferor court subsequent to transfer. *Meat Price Investigators Association v. Spencer Foods, Inc.*, 572 F.2d 163, 167 (8th Cir. 1978). It implicitly determined that the transferor court had retained jurisdiction to issue the order. However, this case is apparently unique.

If the Panel orders transfer, it must also select a transferee court. The Panel is not limited by venue statutes. Thus, cases can be transferred to a district where they could not have been commenced. *See, e.g., In re New York City Municipal Securities Litigation*, 572 F.2d 49, 51-52 (2d Cir. 1978).

The Panel has not established any definite rules on choosing the transferee court. The Panel's Executive Attorney has described the selection of the transferee court as "essentially a balancing test based on the nuances of a particular litigation." Cahn, *A Look at the Judicial Panel on Multidistrict Litigation*, 72 F.R.D. 211, 214 (1976). He lists a number of the factors considered:

1. The district in which the pretrial proceedings are most advanced.
2. The judge with the greatest familiarity with the litigation's subject matter.
3. The district where a related Government action is pending.
4. The district where relevant grand jury records are located.
5. The district where the majority of witnesses and documents are located.
6. The district in which the most actions are pending.
7. The district where a common disaster (*e.g.*, an airplane crash) occurred.
8. Central location for litigation national in scope.
9. Backlog of a district's civil docket.

10. Accommodation of discovery with a state court where similar actions are pending.

11. The preferences of the parties.

Id. at 214-15.

F. Tag-Along Actions

After a transfer is ordered, additional cases presenting the same common questions of fact may be filed. The Panel's Rules label such cases "tag-along actions," R.J.P.M.L. 1, and establish a procedure to transfer them to join the previously transferred actions. Any party to a previously transferred action or to an action under Panel consideration must notify the Panel of any potential tag-along action to which it becomes a party. *Id.*, R. 13(e).

A potential tag-along action filed in the transferee district does not require Panel action. Parties can request the transferee court to assign it to the transferee judge pursuant to the local rules for case assignments. *Id.*, R. 13(a).

If a potential tag-along action is filed in a district other than the transferee one, Panel action is required. Upon learning of the case, the Clerk of the Panel enters a conditional transfer order and serves it on the parties, but does not send it to the clerk of the transferee court until at least 15 days after the entry of the conditional transfer order. If any party to the case opposes transfer, he or she must file a notice of opposition with the Clerk during the 15-day period. If a notice of opposition is filed, the Clerk will not send the conditional transfer order to the transferee court. *Id.*, R. 12(a), (c).

The party who filed the notice of opposition must file a motion to vacate the conditional transfer order and a supporting brief within 15 days after filing the notice. The Clerk will then schedule the motion for argument before the Panel. If the opponent does not timely file the motion to vacate, the Clerk will send the conditional transfer order to the transferee court. *Id.*, R. 12(a). If the motion is timely filed, the Panel will consider the motion. If the motion is denied, the Clerk sends the order to the transferee court. Once the transferee court files the conditional transfer order, the order becomes effective and the action is transferred. *See id.*, R. 12(e).

The Panel can also use its order to show cause procedure to raise the question of transferring tag-along actions. *Id.*, R. 13(b).

IV. AFTER THE PANEL DECISION

A. Appellate Review of the Panel

Appellate review of the Panel's decisions is extremely limited, and is available only by a petition for "extraordinary writ," *i.e.*, mandamus. Mandamus to review an order to transfer a case and orders entered after transfer (*e.g.*, orders with respect to remand) are reviewable only in the court of appeals having jurisdiction over the transferee district. Orders denying transfer are not reviewable in any court. Orders to set a transfer hearing and other orders made prior to the order granting or denying transfer are reviewable only in the Court of Appeals with jurisdiction over the district in which the hearing is to be held. 28 U.S.C. § 1407(e) (1982).

Mandamus is an extremely limited remedy. *See Allied Chemical Corp. v. Daiflon, Inc.*, 449 U.S. 33 (1980). Because of the limited scope of review in mandamus, and the great discretion which the Panel has in implementing the criteria for transfer, review is virtually unavailable.

B. Proceedings in the Transferee Court

Once a transfer order is entered, the transferee court has full control over all proceedings prior to trial. *In re "Agent Orange" Product Liability Litigation*, 597 F. Supp. 740, 751-52 (E.D.N.Y. 1984), *aff'd*, 818 F.2d 145 (2d Cir. 1987), *cert. denied, Pinkney v. Dow Chemical Co.*, 108 S. Ct. 695 (1988). The Panel has repeatedly stated that its power is limited to granting and refusing transfer orders. *E.g., In re Uranium Industry Antitrust Litigation*, 458 F. Supp. 1223 (J.P.M.L. 1978); *In re Equity Funding Corp. Securities Litigation*, 375 F. Supp. 1378, 1384 (J.P.M.L. 1974).

Nonetheless, the Panel's rules provide that parties to a transferred action do not need to retain local counsel in the transferee district, thus overriding the local counsel requirements of those districts. R.J.P.M.L. 6. In addition, the Panel has offered advice to transferee judges, and Panel staff members have taken part in post-transfer proceedings. Levy, *Complex Multidistrict Litigation and the Federal Courts*, 40 Ford. L. Rev. 41, 59-60 (1971). The Panel also holds annual conferences for transferee judges.[3] Lauter, *Who Gets the Most Cases? Specific Judges Win MDL Assignments*, Nat'l. L.J., Nov. 21, 1983, at 24.

C. Power of the Transferee Court

The transferee court's power extends to all pretrial proceedings. The author's experience in *In re "Agent Orange" Product Liability Litigation* bears this out. Judge Weinstein, in that single docket, certified a class action, approved a settlement of the class action, and granted summary judgment dismissing on the merits actions brought by those who had opted out of the class.

---

[3] Two of the papers presented by Panel members at those conferences have been published in *Federal Rules Decisions*. Weigel, *The Judicial Panel on Multidistrict Litigation, Transferor Courts and Transferee Courts*, 78 F.R.D. 575 (1977); Caffrey, *The Role of the Transferee Judge in Multidistrict Litigation*, 69 F.R.D. 289 (1975).

See In re *"Agent Orange" Product Liability Litigation*, 818 F.2d 145, 154-59 (2d Cir. 1987) (summarizing these rulings), *cert. denied*, 108 S. Ct. 695 (1988).

A major feature of the transferee judge's power over the case is his or her control over discovery. This power can even be exercised outside the district, because the transferee judge

> may exercise the powers of a district judge in any district for the purpose of conducting pretrial depositions in such coordinated or consolidated pretrial proceedings.

28 U.S.C. § 1407(b)(1982). *See Manual for Complex Litigation (Second)* § 31.122 (1985).

When the transferee judge exercises this power with respect to a deposition outside his or her own circuit, the question arises which circuit hears appeals from the transferee judge's orders. Four different circuits addressed this question in *In re Corrugated Container Antitrust Litigation*, which had been transferred to a judge in the Southern District of Texas (in the Fifth Circuit). The judge chose to exercise his power over depositions outside his district. Nonparty witnesses who were deposed in New York (Second Circuit), Illinois (Seventh Circuit) and the District of Columbia (District of Columbia Circuit) were all held in contempt after the transferee judge overruled their claims of the privilege against self-incrimination. The witness who was deposed in New York appealed to both the Second and Fifth Circuits. The Fifth Circuit ruled that it lacked jurisdiction and that the appeal should go to the Second Circuit. *In re Corrugated Container Antitrust Litigation*, 620 F.2d 1086, 1090-91 (5th Cir.), *cert. denied*, 449 U.S. 1102 (1981). The Second Circuit then heard the appeal, although it expressed concern that allowing appeals to several circuits would not serve the efficiency which 28 U.S.C. § 1407 sought to achieve. *In re Corrugated Container Antitrust Litigation*, 644 F.2d 70, 74 n.6 (2d Cir. 1981). In the case of the witness who was examined in Illinois, the Seventh Circuit ruled that it had jurisdiction to hear the appeal. *In re Corrugated Container Antitrust Litigation*, 655 F.2d 748, 750 n.2, *rehearing en banc*, 661 F.2d 1145 (7th Cir. 1981), *aff'd sub nom. Pillsbury Co. v. Conboy*, 459 U.S. 248 (1983). Finally, the District of Columbia Circuit similarly held that it had jurisdiction to hear an appeal from a contempt order issued to a nonparty witness who invoked the fifth amendment during a deposition taken in the District of Columbia. *In re Corrugated Container Antitrust Litigation*, 662 F.2d 875, 879-81 (D.C. Cir. 1981).

The Supreme Court later reviewed the Seventh Circuit's decision on the merits. Interestingly, it did not address the issue of appellate jurisdiction, although it did comment that the transferee judge expressly exercised the powers of the District Court for the Northern District of Illinois pursuant to 28 U.S.C. § 1407(b).

459 U.S. at 251 n.3. This statement can be read to suggest that the transferee judge was acting as a judge sitting in the Northern District of Illinois and that his decision was therefore reviewable in the Seventh Circuit.

D. Choice of Law After Transfer

The Panel has long assumed that the law of the transferor forum would accompany a case to the transferee district. *In re Plumbing Fixtures Litigation*, 342 F. Supp. 756, 758 (J.P.M.L. 1972). This is well-settled with respect to state law. *See, e.g., In re Nucorp Energy Securities Litigation*, 772 F.2d 1486, 1492 (9th Cir. 1985); *In re Air Crash Disaster Near Chicago, Illinois*, 644 F.2d 594 (7th Cir.), *cert. denied*, 454 U.S. 878 (1981) (applying choice-of-law rules of five transferor states and Puerto Rico).

The adoption of the transferor forum's state law is premised upon *Van Dusen v. Barrack*, 376 U.S. 612 (1964), which requires the application of the transferor forum's state law after a transfer of venue pursuant to 28 U.S.C. § 1404(a) (1982).

There is some disagreement as to whether *Van Dusen* applies where federal law is involved and the federal caselaw of the transferor court's circuit differs from that of the transferee court. Some courts have ruled that the caselaw of the transferor court's circuit applies after transfer. *See, e.g., Berry Petroleum Co. v. Adams & Peck*, 518 F.2d 402, 408 n.7 (2d Cir. 1975); *In re Dow Co. "Sarabond" Products Liability Litigation*, 666 F. Supp. 1466, 1468-70 (D.C. Colo. 1987). The Third Circuit questioned this approach in *In re Pittsburgh & Lake Erie R.R. Co. Securities and Antitrust Litigation*, 543 F.2d 1058, 1065 n.19 (3d Cir. 1976).

The District of Columbia Circuit recently ruled that each federal court has its own independent duty to analyze and interpret federal law, even in cases transferred from other circuits, and can reject decisions of the transferor court's circuit. *In re Korean Air Lines Disaster*, 829 F.2d 1171, 1173-76 (D.C. Cir. 1987), *cert. granted sub nom. Chan v. Korean Air Lines, Ltd.*, 108 S. Ct. 1288 (1988). *See also* Marcus, *Conflict Among Circuits and Transfers Within the Federal Judicial System*, 93 Yale L.J. 677 (1984) (strong argument that *Van Dusen* does not apply to issues of federal law). The Supreme Court's decision in *Korean Air Lines* may resolve the issue.

E. Law of the Case

The principle of law of the case generally precludes relitigation within a case of a question already decided. Steinman, *Law of the Case: A Judicial Puzzle in Consolidated and Transferred Cases and in Multidistrict Litigation*,

135 U. Pa. L. Rev. 595, 597-98 (1987). A major question in multidistrict practice is whether transferee judges must adhere to transferor judges' pre-transfer rulings under that doctrine. There is no clear consensus on this issue. For example, *In re Upjohn Co. Antibiotic Cleocin Products Liability Litigation*, 664 F.2d 114 (6th Cir. 1981), ruled that a transferee judge could vacate a protective order which a transferor judge had entered prior to transfer. In contrast, a panel of the Eighth Circuit, in *In re Exterior Siding and Aluminum Coil Antitrust Litigation*, 696 F.2d 613 (8th Cir. 1983), ruled that a transferee judge could not overturn a transferor judge's refusal to certify a class action unless changed circumstances warranted a reconsideration of the question. On rehearing *en banc*, however, the court divided evenly and failed to resolve the issue. *In re Exterior Siding and Aluminum Coil Antitrust Litigation*, 705 F.2d 980 (8th Cir.), *cert. denied*, 464 U.S. 866 (1983).

The issue is far from settled and probably should not receive a categorical answer that law of the case never applies to a transferred case or that it always applies. Multidistrict litigation presents too many variables and complexities to allow such simple answers. This is especially true because law of the case is discretionary. *See Crane Co. v. American Standard, Inc.*, 603 F.2d 244, 248-49 (2d Cir. 1979). One area where the doctrine of law of the case generally should not apply is pretrial management of the transferred cases. Conflicting ground rules from different transferor courts concerning discovery deadlines, protective orders and so forth would impede the transferee judge's power to manage the pretrial work. *See* R. Marcus & E. Sherman, *Complex Litigation: Cases and Materials on Advanced Civil Procedure* 230-31 (1985).

F. The Anti-Injunction Act

The breadth of the transferee court's authority may extend to the power to enjoin state court litigation, a power normally denied federal courts by the Anti-Injunction Act, 28 U.S.C. § 2283 (1982). In *In re Corrugated Container Antitrust Litigation*, 659 F.2d 1332 (5th Cir. 1981), *cert. denied*, 456 U.S. 936 (1982), the Fifth Circuit affirmed the grant of an injunction against a state court action brought by some members of the federal plaintiff class against some of the federal defendants. Although the court stated several grounds for its decision that the Anti-Injunction Act was inapplicable, the one which is relevant to this chapter is the one that the injunction was permissible under the Anti-Injunction Act's exception for injunctions which are necessary in aid of the federal court's jurisdiction because it aided the district court in disposing of the complex litigation. *Id.*, at 1334-35. Major commentators have endorsed this argument. 17 C. Wright, A. Miller & E. Cooper, *Federal Practice and Procedure* § 4225 at 531 n.10 (2d ed. 1988).

G. Appeals in Transferred Actions

The question of appeals from orders concerning out-of-circuit depositions has been previously discussed. Two circuits have expressly held that other appeals from the transferee court go to the circuit which includes the transferee district. *FMC Corp. v. Glouster Engineering Co.*, 830 F.2d 770 (7th Cir. 1987), *petition for cert. dismissed*, 108 S. Ct. 2838 (1988); *Astarte Shipping Co. v. Allied Steel & Export Service*, 767 F.2d 86, 87 (5th Cir. 1985). This does appear to be the clear consensus. As an example of this consensus, all parties to the many appeals in *In re "Agent Orange" Product Liability Litigation*, recognized that the appeals from decisions of the transferee court, the Eastern District of New York, were to be filed with the Second Circuit. However, the Eighth Circuit has expressed a minority view that appeals can go to the transferor district's circuit. *Meat Price Investigators Association v. Spencer Foods, Inc.*, 572 F.2d 163, 167 (8th Cir. 1978).

For the practitioner, the hazard of appealing to the wrong circuit is alleviated by 28 U.S.C. § 1631 (1982), enacted in 1982. This provision states that if a civil action or appeal is filed in a federal court which finds that it lacks jurisdiction, it can transfer the case to any other federal court which could have heard it, if it is in the interest of justice to do so. *See FMC Corp.*, 830 F.2d at 772-73.

H. Transfer for All Purposes—28 U.S.C. §§ 1404 (a), 1406

One of the overriding realities of multidistrict litigation is that a transfer for pretrial purposes often becomes a transfer for all purposes. Although the Panel can transfer cases only for pretrial purposes, the transferee judge can then transfer the action to the transferee or other district pursuant to 28 U.S.C. §§ 1404(a), 1406 (1982). Weigel, *supra, The Judicial Panel*, 78 F.R.D. at 581; *see, e.g., Pfizer, Inc. v. Lord*, 447 F.2d 122 (2d Cir. 1971). Jurisdiction and venue, however, must be proper in the transferee court. *See, e.g., In re Penn Central Commercial Paper Litigation*, 62 F.R.D. 341, 344-45 (S.D.N.Y. 1974), *aff'd mem.*, 515 F.2d 505 (2d Cir. 1975).

I. Termination and Remand

Most transferred actions either terminate before trial in the transferee court or are transferred there for all purposes, including trial. Few cases are ever remanded to the transferor court. Weigel, *supra, The Judicial Panel*, 78 F.R.D. at 583.

Only the Panel can remand a case. *Id.* It can do so at the end of pretrial proceedings. 28 U.S.C. § 1407(a) (1982). The Panel can consider remand on a party's motion, the transferee court's recommendation or on its own initiative. It also can act on its own initiative by issuing an order to show cause or a conditional remand order. R.J.P.M.L. 14(c). An opponent of remand can move to vacate the conditional remand order. The procedure for such a motion is identical to that for motions to vacate conditional transfer orders. *Id.*, R. 14(b).

The Panel generally accepts the recommendation of a transferee judge whether a case should be remanded. *In re Richardson-Merrell, Inc. "Bendectin" Products Liability Litigation*, 606 F. Supp. 715 (J.P.M.L. 1985). Any party urging the Panel to remand a case "bears a strong burden of persuasion" if the transferee judge has not recommended remand. *In re Data General Corp. Antitrust Litigation*, 510 F. Supp. 1220, 1226 (J.P.M.L. 1979); *In re Air Crash Disaster Near Chicago, Illinois*, 476 F. Supp. 445, 450 n.6 (J.P.M.L. 1979).

V. CONCLUSION

The *Agent Orange* litigation illustrates how early multidistricting can drastically reduce the expenses which are otherwise inevitable in litigating multiple cases. Over 550 actions, involving the claims of 20,000 individual *Agent Orange* plaintiffs, were transferred from courts all over the country to the Eastern District of New York. Although the litigation was eventually certified as a class action, the initial multidistrict treatment of the case was the crucial tactical move in unifying the litigation and keeping costs under control.

While it may not always be possible to achieve the same high degree of consolidation in mass tort situations and other instances of multiple related cases, there will often be enough common issues and a sufficient basis for federal jurisdiction in such situations to justify some degree of multidistricting or consolidation. In this connection, it should not be forgotten that cases brought in state court may often be removed to federal court to take advantage of the multidistrict proceedings. The easiest situation is when diversity jurisdiction exists. If there is no diversity, however, the complaint can be construed to raise issues under federal law which would be sufficient to support federal question jurisdiction.

The utilization of multidistrict litigation in a group of only two cases, *e.g.*, *In re Texas Eastern Transmission Corp. Polychlorinated Biphenyl Pollution Insurance Coverage Litigation*, MDL No. 764 (J.P.M.L. May 31, 1988), or over 550 cases, *i.e.*, *In re "Agent Orange" Product Liability Litigation*, or of any number in between must be considered in any litigation where duplicative or overlapping cases are pending in more than one federal district.

SELECTIVE BIBLIOGRAPHY

Books:

Manual for Complex Litigation (Second), ch. 31 (1985).

15 C. Wright, A. Miller & E. Cooper, *Federal Practice & Procedure* §§ 3861-3868 (2d ed. 1986).

Articles:

Cahn, *A Look at the Judicial Panel on Multidistrict Litigation*, 72 F.R.D. 211 (1976).

Herndon & Higginbotham, *Complex Multidistrict Litigation — An Overview of 28 U.S.C.A. § 1407*, 31 Baylor L. Rev. 33 (1979).

Howard, *A Guide to Multidistrict Litigation*, 75 F.R.D. 577 (1977).

Weigel, *The Judicial Panel on Multidistrict Litigation, Transferor Courts and Transferee Courts*, 78 F.R.D. 575 (1977).

APPENDIX A

Transfer Order in *In re Texas Eastern Polychlorinated Biphenyl Pollution Insurance Coverage Litigation*, MDL Dkt. No. 764 (J.P.M.D.L. May 31, 1988).

DOCKET NO. 764

BEFORE THE JUDICIAL PANEL ON MULTIDISTRICT LITIGATION

IN RE TEXAS EASTERN TRANSMISSION CORP. PCB CONTAMINATION INSURANCE COVERAGE LITIGATION

TRANSFER ORDER

This litigation presently consists of two actions pending in two federal districts: one action each in the Northern District of Texas and the Eastern District of Pennsylvania. Before the Panel is a motion by the two plaintiffs in the Pennsylvania action to centralize the two actions in this litigation, pursuant to 28 U.S.C. § 1407, in the Eastern District of Pennsylvania for coordinated or consolidated pretrial proceedings.[1] One defendant in the Pennsylvania action joins in the Section 1407 motion. Texas Eastern Transmission Corporation (Texas Eastern), a defendant in the Pennsylvania action and the sole defendant in the Texas action, opposes centralization. In the alternative, Texas Eastern would favor transfer of both actions to the Southern District of Texas.

On the basis of the papers filed and the hearing held, the Panel finds that these two actions involve common questions of fact and that centralization under Section 1407 in the Eastern District of Pennsylvania will best serve the convenience of the parties and witnesses and promote the just and efficient conduct of the litigation. These common factual questions arise because the issue presented in both actions is whether Texas Eastern is entitled to liability insurance coverage for contamination of waste sites along its pipeline system. Centralization under Section 1407 is thus necessary in order to eliminate duplicative discovery, prevent inconsistent pretrial rulings, and conserve the resources of the parties, their counsel and the judiciary. Texas Eastern contends that the Section 1407 motion is premature and that the Panel should make no

---

[1] One other related action is pending in Texas state court in Harris County, Texas.

decision in this matter until motions to dismiss or stay that are pending in both actions have been resolved. We disagree. Such motions can be presented to and decided by the transferee judge after transfer. *See In re Commonwealth Oil/ Tesoro Petroleum Securities Litigation*, 458 F. Supp. 225, 230 (J.P.M.L. 1978).

In designating the Eastern District of Pennsylvania as transferee forum, we note that 1) the Pennsylvania action, of the two federal court actions, has by far the more comprehensive roster of parties; 2) more of the contaminated waste sites are located in Pennsylvania than in any other state; and 3) Texas Eastern's estimated cleanup cost for Pennsylvania is higher for any other state.

IT IS THEREFORE ORDERED that, pursuant to 28 U.S.C. § 1407, the action listed on the attached Schedule A and pending in the Northern District of Texas be, and the same hereby is, transferred to the Eastern District of Pennsylvania and, with the consent of that court, assigned to the Honorable Donald W. VanArtsdalen for coordinated or consolidated pretrial proceedings with the action pending in that district and listed on Schedule A.

FOR THE PANEL:

Andrew A. Gaffrey
Chairman

SCHEDULE A

MDL-764 — In re Texas Eastern Transmission Corp. PCB Contamination Insurance Coverage Litigation

   Northern District of Texas

The Fidelity & Casualty Company of New York v. The Texas Eastern Transmission Corporation, C.A. No. CA3-87-2925-T

   Eastern District of Pennsylvania

Associated Electric & Gas Insurance Services Ltd., et al. v. Texas Eastern Transmission Corporation, et al., C.A. No. 88-2126

APPENDIX B

[Note: the top margin on the first page must be at least three inches.]

BEFORE THE JUDICIAL PANEL
ON MULTIDISTRICT LITIGATION

―――――――――――――――― X

IN RE TEXAS EASTERN TRANSMISSION
CORP. POLYCHLORINATED BIPHENYL   MDL Docket No. ____
POLLUTION INSURANCE COVERAGE
LITIGATION

―――――――――――――――― X

MOTION BY ASSOCIATED
ELECTRIC & GAS
INSURANCE SERVICES, LTD.
AND NATIONAL SURETY CORPORATION
FOR TRANSFER OF ACTIONS FOR
COORDINATED OR CONSOLIDATED

PRETRIAL PROCEEDINGS

Associated Electric & Gas Insurance Services, Ltd. ("Aegis") and National Surety Corporation ("National Surety") move, pursuant to 28 U.S.C. § 1407, for an order transferring the actions described in the attached Schedule of Actions ("Schedule") to the United States District Court for the Eastern District of Pennsylvania for coordinated or consolidated pretrial proceedings. In support of the motion, Aegis and National Surety allege as follows:

1. The two similar actions both involve disputes as to whether Texas Eastern Transmission Corp. ("Texas Eastern") is entitled to liability insurance coverage with respect to its pollution of hazardous waste sites along its pipeline system. Texas Eastern has contaminated 89 such sites in 14 states with polychlorinated biphenyls ("PCBs"). Aegis and National Surety are among Texas Eastern's insurance carriers.

2. The two similar actions listed upon the Schedule involve many common questions of fact, including, but not limited to the following:

a. whether Texas Eastern intended or expected the PCB pollution;

b. whether Texas Eastern failed to disclose to its insurers its practices in handling and disposing of PCBs;

c. whether Texas Eastern failed to timely notify its insurers of the claims for which it seeks coverage;

d. whether the pollution was the result of regular and continuous polluting activity by Texas Eastern;

e. whether Texas Eastern intentionally caused the pollution;

f. whether the pollution was the result of Texas Eastern's intentional noncompliance with environmental statutes and/or regulations; and

g. whether any property damage resulting from the pollution was to property owned by, or in the custody or control of, Texas Eastern.

3. There is an overall issue, common to both actions, as to whether there is coverage for Texas Eastern's pollution, which in turn requires examination of many issues of fact common to both actions.

4. Transfer of these actions for coordinated or consolidated pretrial proceedings will promote the just and efficient conduct of the litigation and will be in the interest of the parties and witnesses.

5. The related actions are in early stages of litigation. The pleadings are not yet complete in either action, and discovery is in the early stages in both actions.

6. Each action has almost all pretrial proceedings remaining to be performed. Transfer will provide considerable efficiencies and avoid wasteful duplication of effort.

7. The cases on the Schedule should be transferred to the Eastern District of Pennsylvania as the most appropriate forum.

8. Texas Eastern's pipeline has contaminated more waste sites in Pennsylvania than in any other state along its pipeline system. Texas Eastern has estimated that it will cost more to clean up the waste sites in Pennsylvania than the sites in any other state.

9. The case pending in the Eastern District of Pennsylvania has been assigned to Judge Donald W. VanArtsdalen. Judge VanArtsdalen is experienced in handling complex, multiparty federal litigation. He has been informed of this motion.

WHEREFORE, Aegis and National Surety respectfully request that the Panel order transfer of the actions listed in the attached Schedule of Actions to the United States District Court for the Eastern District of Pennsylvania for coordinated or consolidated pretrial proceedings on the docket of Judge Donald W. VanArtsdalen.

Dated: Uniondale, New York
March 31, 1988

      Respectfully submitted,

      RIVKIN, RADLER, DUNNE & BAYH
      Attorneys for Moving Parties
      ASSOCIATED ELECTRIC & GAS
      INSURANCE SERVICES, LTD. and
      NATIONAL SURETY CORPORATION

      By: _____ /s/ _____
       Leonard L. Rivkin
      EAB Plaza
      Uniondale, N.Y.
      11556-0111
      (516) 357-3000

INDEX

ABSTENTION
  Arbitration clauses in state insurance liquidations 22
  Bankruptcy
    jurisdiction of district courts over bankruptcy cases 830
  Pretrial management of complex litigation
    abstention in multiple cases 307
  When federal courts abstain generally 21
ACCIDENT REPORTS
  Availability 111
  Coast guard search and rescue reports 111
  Police reports of accidents 111
  Public transportation accident reports 111
  Tape recordings of 911 emergency calls 111
ACTIONS
  Actions against U.S.
    see ACTIONS AGAINST THE UNITED STATES
  Civil rights actions
    see CIVIL RIGHTS ACTIONS
  Class actions
    see CLASS ACTIONS
  Commencement
    see COMMENCEMENT OF ACTION
  Consolidation
    see CONSOLIDATION OF ACTIONS
  Criminal actions
    see CRIMINAL ACTIONS
  Implied rights of action
    attachment of jurisdiction 23
  Limitation of actions
    see STATUTE OF LIMITATIONS
  Multidistrict litigation
    see MULTIDISTRICT LITIGATION
  Personal injury actions
    see PERSONAL INJURY ACTIONS
  Removal
    see REMOVAL
  Shareholder derivative actions
    see SHAREHOLDER DERIVATIVE ACTIONS
  Tag-along actions 877
ACTIONS AGAINST THE UNITED STATES
  Removal

civil or criminal proceedings against federal officers 92
Venue 70
ADMINISTRATIVE AGENCIES
Permissive intervention
    waiver of sovereign immunity 262
Preclusion
    effect of unreviewed state agency decisions in federal court 773
Removal to federal court 85
United States agencies
    permissive intervention 262
    service on 40
ADMIRALTY
Impleader procedures 269
Subject matter jurisdiction
    complaints invoking 146
Venue
    special venue rules 74
ADMISSIONS
Failure to deny averment 183
Opening statements
    dismissal of action on admissions during 627
Requests for admissions
    abuses 463
    advantages and disadvantages 463
    answers 468
    failure to respond or object 467
    form of requests 466
    generally 326
    information obtainable 465
    motion to determine sufficiency of answers or objections 469
    objections 467
    purposes of rules 463
    summary judgment motions 522
    timing of requests 345,465
    use made of admissions 469
Summary judgment
    opposing motion 527
    requests for admissions 522
ADVISORY JURIES
Availability 667
Basis in rule 39 667
Effect of verdict 668
Use generally 582
AFFIDAVITS
Motions
    attorney's affidavits 473
    evidentiary matter in support of 473
Preliminary injunctions
    motion supported by affidavit 165

INDEX

Summary judgment
    affidavit in support of opposition to motion 527
    attorney's affidavits 520
    failure to file opposing affidavits 510
    necessity 519
    requirements for affidavits 519
    statements of ultimate facts and conclusions of law 520
    time for filing supporting affidavits 508
    waiver of defects 521

AFFIRMATIVE DEFENSES
Answers
    burden of proof 185
    generally 185
    specificity 184
    waiver 186
Lack of personal jurisdiction 58

***AGENT ORANGE* LITIGATION**
Multidistricting 883

AGENTS
Labor unions
    service on agents 39
Service of process
    corporations or partnerships 38
    labor unions 39
    public officials appointed to receive process 38
Summons
    delivery to authorized agents 36

ALIENS
Diversity jurisdiction
    disputes between citizens and aliens 13
Venue
    residency for venue purposes 69

ALTERNATIVE DISPUTE RESOLUTION
Minitrials 551
Nonbinding arbitration 551
Summary jury trials 550

ALTERNATIVES TO TRIAL
Advisory juries
    see ADVISORY JURIES
Alternative dispute resolution
    see ALTERNATIVE DISPUTE RESOLUTION
Arbitration
    see ARBITRATION
Magistrates
    see MAGISTRATES
Summary trial
    see SUMMARY TRIAL

AMENDED PLEADINGS
    see PLEADINGS

AMOUNT IN CONTROVERSY
  Diversity jurisdiction
    failure to recover more than minimum amount 12
    generally 10
    removed actions 87,88
  Federal question jurisdiction
    no minimum amount required 9
  Interpleader
    rule interpleader 273
    statutory interpleader cases 271
  Removal
    diversity cases 87,88
ANCILLARY JURISDICTION
  Compulsory and permissive counterclaims...20
  Impleaded parties 268
  Intervenor's rights...263
  Joinder
    necessary parties regardless of citizenship..................................258
ANSWERS
  Admissions
    failure to deny averment 183
  Affirmative defenses
    burden of proof...185
    generally 185
  Amendments
    when permitted 189
  Counterclaims
    generally
      see COUNTERCLAIMS
    inclusion in answer 186
  Cross-claims
    see CROSS-CLAIMS
  Excess matters 184
  Failure to deny averment 183
  Form of answer 181
  Interrogatories 436
  Jury demand...181
  Multiple parties 184
  Requests for admissions 468
  Responses to individual averments 183
  Specificity...184
  Supplemental answers 189
  Third party claims 188
  Timing
    generally 182
    government as defendant...182
    motions addressed to complaint..183
    service under rule 4(e)...182
  Venue

INDEX

   objections to venue raised by 76
ANTITRUST
  Civil investigation demands 109
  Foreign parties
    limits on extraterritorial application 787
  Preclusion
    effect of prior state court judgments 766
  Venue
    special venue provisions 74
APPEALS
  All writs act
    review by permission 730
  Appeals as of right
    procedure 731
  Appendix
    purpose 736
    table of contents 736
  Attachment 176
  Availability of appellate review 725
  Bankruptcy
    procedure 837
    right of appeal generally 836
    rules regarding appeals 837
    stay pending appeal 838
  Briefs
    accuracy, brevity and clarity 740
    contents 738
    cover requirements 738
    examination in advance of oral argument 740
    formal requirements 738
    length 739
    printing 736
    reply briefs 739
  Choice of law
    Erie doctrine applicability 200
  Civil appeals management plan 734
  Collateral orders
    appeal as of right 727
  Depositions
    appealing discovery orders 371
    pending appeal 356
  En banc hearings and rehearings 744
  Exhibits
    custody 735
    exclusion from record 735
  Expenses 725
  Extraordinary writs
    contents of petition 733
    procedure 733

Fees 731
Final decisions
    jurisdiction of courts of appeals 725
Hearings and rehearings en banc 744
Impleader 269
Interlocutory orders
    appeals as of right 727
    review by permission 728
Interpleader 275
Intervention 264
Limitations on appellate review 725
Magistrates
    appeals to court of appeals 664
    appeals to district courts 665
    entry of judgment following trial 664
    review of decisions 316
Motions
    determination without oral argument 743
Multidistrict litigation
    appellate review of panel decisions 877
    transferred actions 882
Multiple claims or parties
    review of orders entered pursuant to rule 54(b) 729
Notice
    appeals as of right 731
    fees 731
    time for filing 731
Oral argument
    continuances 741
    divided arguments 741
    necessity for 741
    time allowed for 741
Orders
    disposition by summary order 743
Petitions for rehearing
    answers to petition 744
    effect of filing 744
    formal requirements 744
    when filed 744
Preliminary injunctions
    expedited appeals 170
    procedure 169
    standard of review 171
    stays pending appeal 170
    when order appealable 168
Receivers
    orders appointing or refusing appointment 179
Record on appeal
    appendix 736

INDEX

    contents 735
    disputes as to contents 736
    exclusion of exhibits and transcript portions 735
    statement of evidence 735
Removal
    orders granting or denying remand 105
Review as of right 727
Review by permission
    all writs act 730
    orders certified under 28 U.S.C. 1292(b) 728
    orders entered pursuant to rule 54(b) 729
    procedure for appeals 732
Stays
    temporary relief pending appeal 742
Summary judgment
    orders denying motion 537
    orders granting motion 536
    standard of review 537
Supersedeas bonds
    temporary relief pending appeal 742
Supreme court
    jurisdiction generally 745
    review by appeal 747
    review by certiorari
        effect of denial 746
        generally 745
    review on certified questions 747
Temporary relief pending appeal 742
Temporary restraining orders
    when orders appealable 168
Three judge district courts
    direct appeal to supreme court 730
Transcripts
    exclusion of irrelevant portions 735
    orders 735
Venue
    dismissal of actions on *forum non conveniens* grounds 81
Where district court decisions reviewable 730

ARBITRATION
Advantages and disadvantages 677
Agreements to arbitrate
    choice of law clauses 216
    constructive agreements 670
    express agreements 669
    foreign sovereign immunity in actions to enforce 817
    validity 670
Alternative dispute resolution
    nonbinding arbitration 551
Awards

898 FEDERAL CIVIL PRACTICE

    form 674
    grounds for overturning. 674
    motions to confirm or vacate 674
Choice of law 216
Counterclaims 672
Discovery. 673
Evidence
    applicability of rules of evidence 674
Foreign sovereign immunity
    immunity in actions to enforce arbitration agreements. 817
Grounds for overturning award 674
Hearings
    conduct generally 673
    when required 673
Insurance liquidation clauses
    abstention by federal courts. 22
Motions
    confirming, modifying, or vacating awards. 674
Panel members
    composition of panel 673
    number of members 673
Plan for court-annexed arbitration 679
Pleadings
    statement of claim 671
    statement of response 672
Statutory authority 668
Third party claims 672
Waiver of right 679
Witnesses
    power to subpoena. 673
ARMED FORCES
  Removal
    civil or criminal actions against federal officers. 92
  Service of process
    affidavit showing defendant not in service 46
ASSIGNMENT
  Diversity jurisdiction
    invoking by fictitious assignment. 14
ATTACHMENT
  Appeals 176
  Burden of proof 176
  Complaints. 172
  Counterclaims 174
  Debts or property subject to 174
  Ex parte applications 174
  Foreign parties
    see FOREIGN COUNTRIES AND PARTIES
  Grounds 172
  Hearings. 176

INDEX

```
    Motions . . . . . . . . . . . . . . . . . . . . . . . . . . . . . . . . . . . . . . . . . . . . . . . . . . . . . . . . . 174
    Order to show cause . . . . . . . . . . . . . . . . . . . . . . . . . . . . . . . . . . . . . . . . . . . . . 174
    Prejudgment attachment against foreign parties
        see FOREIGN COUNTRIES AND PARTIES
    Quasi in rem jurisdiction
        see QUASI IN REM JURISDICTION
    Required showings . . . . . . . . . . . . . . . . . . . . . . . . . . . . . . . . . . . . . . . . . . . . . 172
    State procedures . . . . . . . . . . . . . . . . . . . . . . . . . . . . . . . . . . . . . . . . . . . . . . 172
    Surety bonds
        motion for order of attachment . . . . . . . . . . . . . . . . . . . . . . . . . . . . . . . . 175
ATTORNEY GENERAL
    Service of process on United States . . . . . . . . . . . . . . . . . . . . . . . . . . . . . . . . . 40
ATTORNEYS
    Affidavits . . . . . . . . . . . . . . . . . . . . . . . . . . . . . . . . . . . . . . . . . . . . . . . . . . . 473
    Complaints
        predrafting preparation checklist . . . . . . . . . . . . . . . . . . . . . . . . . . . . . . 142
        signatures by attorneys . . . . . . . . . . . . . . . . . . . . . . . . . . . . . . . . . . . . 145
    Depositions
        preparing the deponent . . . . . . . . . . . . . . . . . . . . . . . . . . . . . . . . . . . . 378
    Determining client's grievance . . . . . . . . . . . . . . . . . . . . . . . . . . . . . . . . . . . 140
    Direct examination
        see DIRECT EXAMINATION
    Discovery
        privileged information excluded from scope . . . . . . . . . . . . . . . . . . . . . . 327
    Fees
        see ATTORNEYS' FEES
    Identifying client's objectives . . . . . . . . . . . . . . . . . . . . . . . . . . . . . . . . . . . . 141
    Interrogatories
        certification by counsel . . . . . . . . . . . . . . . . . . . . . . . . . . . . . . . . . . . . 431
    Interviews
        adverse parties . . . . . . . . . . . . . . . . . . . . . . . . . . . . . . . . . . . . . . . . . . 104
        client interviews . . . . . . . . . . . . . . . . . . . . . . . . . . . . . . . . . . . . . . . . 104
        ethical problems . . . . . . . . . . . . . . . . . . . . . . . . . . . . . . . . . . . . . . . . 104
        nonparty witnesses . . . . . . . . . . . . . . . . . . . . . . . . . . . . . . . . . . . . . . 104
    Jury trial
        instructing the jury . . . . . . . . . . . . . . . . . . . . . . . . . . . . . . . . . . . . . . 590
    Multidistrict litigation
        retaining local counsel in transferee court . . . . . . . . . . . . . . . . . . . . . . . 878
    Opening statements
        see OPENING STATEMENTS
    Service of process
        responsibility for service . . . . . . . . . . . . . . . . . . . . . . . . . . . . . . . . . . . 29
    Settlement
        authority as agent . . . . . . . . . . . . . . . . . . . . . . . . . . . . . . . . . . . . . . . 553
        responsibilities to adversary counsel . . . . . . . . . . . . . . . . . . . . . . . . . . . 558
        responsibilities to client . . . . . . . . . . . . . . . . . . . . . . . . . . . . . . . . . . . 557
        responsibilities to court . . . . . . . . . . . . . . . . . . . . . . . . . . . . . . . . . . . 559
    Special masters
        appointment of attorneys as . . . . . . . . . . . . . . . . . . . . . . . . . . . . . . . . 320
```

Summation
    see SUMMATION
Verdicts
    role in formulating form of verdict 598
Work product
    immunity from discovery 328
ATTORNEYS' FEES
    Choice of law effects 212
    Class actions..288
    Removal
        levying sanctions by federal judges 106
BAILMENT
    Representatives of interested parties
        capacity to sue or be sued 255
BANKRUPTCY
    Abstention 831
    Adversary proceedings..842
    Appeals
        procedure 837
        right of appeal generally 836
        rules regarding 837
        stay pending appeal 838
    Chapter 7 liquidation
        duties of trustee...848
    Chapter 11 reorganizations
        closure statements 860
        debtors 849
        examiners 860
        plan of reorganization 860
        purpose 849
        railroad reorganizations...851
    Claims
        forms...861
        objections to 862
    Complaints
        form of pleading 843
    Composition of court 5
    Core and non-core proceedings 832
    Counterclaims and cross-claims 845
    Creditors
        committees 863
        defined 860
        form of claims..861
        meetings 863
    Debtors
        chapter 11 debtors...849
        debtors in possession...858
        qualification as bankrupt 829
    Defenses

INDEX

    rules for raising 845
Equity security holders
    defined 861
    subordination of claims 861
Executory contracts 869
Family farmer debt adjustments 851
Filing fees 855
Forms
    claims 861
    official forms 847
Individuals with regular income
    chapter 13 debt adjustments 851
Investigation of cases
    court records 114
Jurisdiction
    abstention 831
    bankruptcy reform act of 1978 830
    core and non-core proceedings 832
    provisions of 28 U.S.C. section 1334 830
Jury trials 835
Landlord and tenant
    assumption or rejection of leases 869
Leases
    assumption or rejection by debtor or trustee 869
List of creditors
    filing with petition 857
Motions 845
Municipalities
    chapter 9 debt adjustments 849
Objections
    claims 862
    rules for raising in adversary proceedings 845
Order to show cause 846
Petitions
    commencement of action 852
    involuntary petitions 852
    list of creditors 857
    number of copies filed 855
    statement of affairs 857
    voluntary petitions 852
Pleadings
    caption 843
    complaints 843
    legibility 845
Powers of court generally 836
Railroad reorganizations 851
Removal
    claims within exclusive jurisdiction 94
Rules of procedure

    conformity with federal rules of procedure 842
    scheme of rules generally 841
Schedules of assets and liabilities
    filing with petition 857
Service of process
    rules providing for 843
Statement of affairs
    filing with petition 857
Stays
    appeals 838
    automatic stay upon commencement of action 865
Stockbroker and commodity broker liquidations 849
Summons and complaint 843
Trustees
    appointment 858
    bonds 858
    chapter 11 trustees 858
    U.S. trustees 839
Venue
    generally 834
    title 11 proceedings 835

BOARDS AND COMMISSIONS
Service of process on 40

BRIEFS
Appeals
    see APPEALS
Class actions
    briefs in support of settlement 296

BURDEN OF PROOF
Affirmative defenses 185
Attachment 176
Removal 99
Summary judgment
    evidence in support of motion 517
    standards for meeting initial burden of going forward 531

BUSINESS RECORDS
Interrogatories
    option to designate and produce 438

CASES OR CONTROVERSIES
Constitutional limitations on federal jurisdiction 3

CENTERS FOR DISEASE CONTROL
Sources for investigative information 137

CERTIORARI
Appeals generally
    see APPEALS
Review by supreme court 745

CHOICE OF FORUM CLAUSES
Agreements by parties as to venue 66
Transfer of venue for convenience 79

INDEX

CHOICE OF LAW
- Arbitration 216
- Attorneys' fees
  - effect of choice on recovery 212
- Borrowing statutes 208
- Contract actions
  - act of state doctrine 252
  - corporate considerations 249
  - express choice of law provisions 233
  - foreign arbitral awards 250
  - foreign law, countries, and citizens 250
  - foreign sovereign immunities act.......................................251
  - law of the place of making contract 237
  - law of the place of performance..237
  - most significant relationship method 241
  - N.Y. modern methods..238
  - no express choice of law provisions....................................237
  - presumed intent of parties 237
  - property interests...246
  - statute of frauds considerations 243
  - uniform commercial code actions 241
  - usurious interest rates 245
  - Warsaw convention 251
- Corporations..249
- Damages
  - effect of choice of law on recovery 212
  - federal courts sitting in N.Y. 213
  - N.Y. state courts 213
- Determining which state law applies......................................202
- *Erie* doctrine
  - constitutional basis 192
  - federal common law applicability 196
  - federal procedural statutes..201
  - federal question applicability...196
  - federal rules of appellate procedure applicability.....................200
  - federal rules of evidence applicability 201
  - federal rules of procedure applicability 198
  - generally 191
  - outcome determinative test 194
  - purpose 191
  - substantive versus procedural test 194
- Foreign law, countries, and citizens
  - act of state doctrine 252
  - foreign arbitral awards 250
  - foreign sovereign immunities act......................................251
  - Warsaw convention 251
- *Forum non conveniens* *217*
- Interest
  - effect of choice on recovery 212

     usurious interest rates under state law 245
  Laches 210
  Multidistrict litigation 215
  Neutral or unprovided for case 205
  Public policy exception 211
  Renvoi 207
  Statute of frauds 243
  Statutes of limitations
     borrowing statutes 208
     federal courts sitting in N.Y. 210
     laches 210
     N.Y. state courts 209
  Substance of applicable state law 205
  Tort actions
     basic methods 222
     better rule of law/choice influencing considerations 232
     comparative impairment method 232
     interest analysis method 223
     lex loci delecti 222
     most significant relationship method 231
  Transferred actions 214
  True and false conflicts 203
  Uniform commercial code provisions 241
CITIZENSHIP
  Diversity jurisdiction
     actions between citizens of different states 12
     corporate citizenship 14
     disputes between aliens and citizens 13
CIVIL APPEALS MANAGEMENT PLAN
  Procedure for docketing appeals 734
CIVIL COVER SHEETS
  Submission with complaint 160
CIVIL RIGHTS ACTIONS
  Preclusion
     defensive issue preclusion in section 1983 actions 752
  Removal
     statutes permitting 93
CLAIMS FOR RELIEF
  Adoption by reference 148
  Alternate or hypothetical pleading 148
  Complaints
     see COMPLAINTS
  Counterclaims
     see COUNTERCLAIMS
  Cross-claims
     see CROSS-CLAIMS
  Interpleader
     see INTERPLEADER
  Pleading on information and belief 149

INDEX

Preclusion
    see PRECLUSION
Separation of paragraphs and counts...148
CLASS ACTIONS
    Actions maintainable 277
    Advantages to defendants..289
    Attorneys' fees..297
    Certification standards 292
    Class representatives 290
    Complaints
        particularity in pleading...156
    Complexity of litigation 286
    Cost burdens...286
    Credibility of claimant 283
    Delay in litigation..287
    Derivative actions by shareholders 279
    Discovery...285
    Dismissal or compromise..279
    Diversity jurisdiction
        exceptions to complete diversity rule.................................13
    Due process considerations...281
    Election to opt out 294
    Exclusion of class members 294
    Expense allocation 285
    Fiduciary relationship of plaintiff and class members 288
    Introduction 280
    Jury trial
        procedural devices at variance with relief 566
    Magistrates
        motions for class certification 315
    Motions
        class certification motion..291
    Notice to absent class members
        form of notice 294
        identifying class members 293
        paying for notice 293
        settlement 296
        when notice required...293
    Orders in conduct..279
    Pendent parties..20
    Pleadings
        particularity in pleading...156
        sample allegations 290
    Prerequisites...277
    Rules applicable to 277
    Settlement
        briefs in support of 296
        hearings..296
        judicial approval 554

notice of settlement and hearing date 296
preliminary hearings 295
stipulations 295
Size of individual claims. 283
Smell test 284
Statute of limitations. 285
Stipulation of settlement 295
Subject matter jurisdiction
    use of rule 23 to broaden jurisdiction. 282
Subordination of individual claims 288
Unincorporated associations
    actions under rule 23.2 280,298
Venue
    residence of parties 70
CLAYTON ACT
Venue provisions 74
CLERKS OF COURT
Default judgments
    granting by clerk 498
Judgments
    entry by clerk 707
    relief from clerical mistakes 718
Summons
    issuance by clerk. 27
CLOSING ARGUMENT
    see SUMMATION
COAST GUARD
Boating safety law violations 115
Search and rescue reports 111
COLLATERAL ESTOPPEL
Jury trial
    issues previously resolved in nonjury trial 576
Preclusion generally
    see PRECLUSION
COLLECTIVE BARGAINING AGREEMENTS
Venue
    where actions brought under agreements. 75
COMMENCEMENT OF ACTION
Complaints
    see COMPLAINTS
Depositions
    before or after commencement 354
Generally 139
COMMON CARRIERS
Investigation of cases
    reports of delays or incidents. 116
Removal of cases involving 94
COMPLAINTS
Admiralty

INDEX

subject matter jurisdiction 146
Agents
    service on agents 36
Alternate or hypothetical pleading 148
Antitrust
    particularity in pleading 157
Appearance 145
Attachment 172
Attorneys
    signatures by attorney of record 145
Bankruptcy
    form of pleading 843
Captions
    information contained in 145
Certificates of corporate identification 160
Civil cover sheet 160
Claims for relief
    adoption by reference 148
    alternate or hypothetical pleading 148
    generally 145
    pleading on information and belief 149
    separation of paragraphs and counts 148
Class actions
    particularity requirements 156
    pleading requirements 290
Constitutional right violations
    court-imposed particularity 157
Corporations
    certificate of identification to accompany 160
Covers 145
Declaratory judgments 151
Default judgments
    amendment of complaint 150
Demand for judgment
    declaratory judgments 151
    default judgments 150
    form of demand 149
    money damage demands 150
    subsequent modification 150
Determining client's grievance 140
Diversity jurisdiction
    methods of invoking jurisdiction 146
    particularity of pleading of state law claims 155
Drafting checklists 151
Federal question jurisdiction
    claims based on state law 147
    methods for invoking 146
Filing fees 161
Fraud

pleading fraud 153
Function of civil complaint 139
Identifying client's objectives 141
Independent investigation of facts 141
Information and belief 149
Introductory sentence 145
Jurisdiction
    pleading subject matter jurisdiction 146
Jury trial
    demand for 145
Legal research prior to drafting 141
Mail service 31
Mistake
    pleading claims of mistake 154
Money damage demands
    particularity required 150
Particularity in pleading
    antitrust complaints 157
    class actions 156
    constitutional rights violations 157
    court-imposed particularity 156
    fraud 153
    intellectual property 158
    mistake 154
    racketeer influenced corrupt organizations 157
    rule 9 pleading provisions 154
    securities complaints 157
    shareholder derivative actions 156
    state law claims in diversity actions 155
Personal jurisdiction 147
Predrafting preparation 142
Preliminary injunctions
    money damage allegations 164
    where filed 165
Reconstituting the case 141
Rule 9 pleading provisions 154
Securities
    particularity in pleading 157
Service of process
    agents for 36
    how made 30
    summons and complaint served together 28
    who serves 30
Special damages 151
State law claims in diversity actions
    particularity of pleading 155
Statement of facts 145
Statute of limitations
    effect of filing generally 161

INDEX

Summons
    issuance by clerk upon filing 161
    Temporary restraining orders 165
    Theory of modern pleading 142
    Third party claims
        service of complaint 188
    Venue 148
COMPROMISE
    Arbitration
        see ARBITRATION
    Class actions 279
    Settlement
        see SETTLEMENT
COMPULSORY COUNTERCLAIMS
    see COUNTERCLAIMS
COMPULSORY JOINDER
    see JOINDER
COMPUTERS
    Production of documents and things
        term "document" to include electronic data 446
    Sources of information for investigations 119
CONFLICTS OF LAW
    see CHOICE OF LAW
CONGRESS OF THE UNITED STATES
    Federal courts
        power to reduce jurisdiction 3
CONSENT
    Personal jurisdiction 26
CONSERVATORS
    Service of process
        methods of serving incompetent persons 37
CONSOLIDATION OF ACTIONS
    Motions for consolidation 682
    Multidistrict litigation
        see MULTIDISTRICT LITIGATION
    Venue
        transfer of venue for convenience 78
CONSTITUTION OF THE UNITED STATES
    Case or controversy requirement 3
    Due process
        see DUE PROCESS
    Federal question jurisdiction
        cases arising under constitution 9
    Judicial power 2
    Jury trial
        seventh amendment origin of right 561
CONSUMER PRODUCTS SAFETY COMMISSION
    Product information 117
    Sources of information for investigation 133

CONTEMPT
  Service of process. 48
CONTRACTS
  Bankruptcy
    assumption or rejection of executory contracts 869
  Choice of law
    act of state doctrine 252
    corporate considerations 249
    express provisions in contract 233
    foreign arbitral awards 250
    foreign law, countries, or citizens 250
    foreign sovereign immunities act 251
    law of place of making contract 237
    law of place of performance 237
    most significant relationship method 241
    N.Y. modern methods 238
    no express choice of law provisions 237
    presumed intent of parties 237
    property interests 246
    statute of frauds considerations 243
    uniform commercial code actions 241
    usurious interest rates 245
    Warsaw convention 251
  Investigation of cases 125
  Motions *in limine*
    prior contracts 491
  Production of documents and things
    requests for documents in contract actions 444
  Statute of frauds
    choice of law considerations 243
COPYRIGHTS
  Preclusion
    exclusivity of federal remedies 766
  Venue
    where actions may be brought 74
CORPORATIONS
  Agents for service on 38
  Choice of law
    federal courts sitting in N.Y. 250
    generally 249
    internal matters of corporation 249
    N.Y. state courts 249
  Complaints
    certificate of identification to accompany 160
  Depositions
    testifying through officers, directors, or agents 352
  Derivative actions
    justification 298
    procedural devices defeating right to jury trial 566

INDEX

    requirements under rule 23.1..279
    residence of parties for venue purposes..................................70
    venue..71,75
Diversity jurisdiction
    corporate citizenship...14
    invoking by creation of sham corporation.................................14
Dual citizenship
    diversity jurisdiction problems..14
Investigation of cases
    corporate filings...113
Residence
    determination for venue purposes...69
Service of process
    agent for service..38
    federal rules methods..38
    state law methods...38
Venue
    doing business test..69
    minimum contacts test...69
    residence of corporation...69
    shareholder derivative actions..70,75

COSTS
Dismissal
    previously dismissed claims...498
Diversity jurisdiction
    denial or imposition on plaintiff..12
Removal
    levying sanctions by federal judges....................................106

COUNTERCLAIMS
Amended pleadings..309
Ancillary jurisdiction
    compulsory and permissive counterclaims................................20
    intervenor's rights...263
Arbitration...672
Attachment...174
Bankruptcy...845
Claims against United States..188
Compulsory counterclaims
    defined..186
    exceptions...187
    jurisdiction...187
    transaction or occurrence defined.....................................186
Inclusion in answer...186
Intervenor's rights...263
Jurisdiction
    compulsory counterclaims...187
Jury trial
    commingling legal and equitable issues in single action.................564
    Limitations on damages...186

Parties
  counterclaims adding additional parties 186
Permissive counterclaims
  defined 186
Removal 91
  Summary judgments 506
  Transaction or occurrence defined 186
COUNTIES
  Service of process 40
COURT OF INTERNATIONAL TRADE
  Current composition 5
COURT RECORDS
  Appeals
    see APPEALS
  Investigation of cases
    prior litigation information 114
  Removal
    transfer of state court records 101
COURTS OF APPEAL
  Current composition 5
  Magistrates
    appeal of judgment 664
CRIMINAL ACTIONS
  Removal
    actions against federal officers 92
    civil rights actions 93
    generally 85
CROSS-CLAIMS
  Asserting against co-parties 188
  Dismissal 497
  Intervenor's rights 263
  Removal 91
  Summary judgments 506
CROSS-EXAMINATION
  Blanket cross 657
  Leading questions 656
  Prior inconsistent statements 660
  Scope 657
  Selectivity 658
  Sequence 659
  When to conduct 655
DAMAGES
  Amount in controversy
    see AMOUNT IN CONTROVERSY
  Choice of law
    effect on recovery 212
    federal courts sitting in N.Y. 213
    N.Y. state courts 213
  Complaints

INDEX

    particularity in demanding money damages.................................150
Settlement
  see SETTLEMENT
Special damages
    mode of pleading...151
DEATH CERTIFICATES
  Contents..112
  Suspicious deaths...112
DECLARATORY JUDGMENTS
  Actual controversies
    when relief appropriate..709
  Complaints..151
  Procedure for obtaining...710
  Speedy hearings of actions..710
  Statutory basis...709
  Summary judgments..506
  When relief appropriate...709
DEFAULT JUDGMENTS
  Against whom entry appropriate......................................498
  Amendment of complaint..150
  By court..499
  Clerks of court granting..498
  Setting aside
    entry of judgment...499
    grounds..499,500
    motions or independent actions....................................501
  When entry of default appropriate...................................498
DEFENSES
  Affirmative defenses
    see AFFIRMATIVE DEFENSES
  Bankruptcy
    rules for raising defenses..845
  Jury trial
    commingling legal and equitable issues in single action...........564
  Personal jurisdiction
    raising lack of jurisdiction as defense............................58
  Pleadings
    purposes for permitting amendment.................................309
  Service of process
    remedies for improper service......................................46
DEMAND FOR JUDGMENT
  Declaratory judgments...151
  Form of demand..149
  Money damage demands
    particularity in complaint..150
  Subsequent modification...150
DEMAND FOR JURY TRIAL
  see JURY TRIAL
DEPARTMENT OF HEALTH AND HUMAN SERVICES

Sources of investigative information ... 133
DEPARTMENT OF JUSTICE
Sources of investigative information ... 133
DEPARTMENT OF TRANSPORTATION
Sources of investigative information ... 133
DEPOSITIONS
   see DISCOVERY
DIRECTED VERDICT
  Diversity cases
    standards for determining motion ... 689
  Effect of denial ... 690
  Failure to make motion ... 687
  Grounds ... 687
  Requirements ... 688
  Standards governing determination of motion ... 689
  Time for making motion ... 688
DIRECT EXAMINATION
  Evidence
    offers of proof ... 648
  Exhibits
    methods of introducing tangible evidence ... 646
  Expert witnesses
    categories of testimony ... 650
    opinion evidence of experts ... 650
  Forgetful or mistaken witnesses ... 651
  Laying the foundation
    defined ... 645
    discovery as means of ... 645
    subject to connection ... 645
  Leading questions
    defined ... 643
    discretion of trial judge ... 643
    when permissible ... 656
  Opinion evidence ... 650
  Redirect ... 653
  Refreshing recollection ... 651
DISCOVERY
  Access to materials by nonparties ... 339
  Appeals
    depositions pending ... 356
  Arbitration ... 673
  Class actions ... 285
  Corporations
    testifying through officers, directors, or agents ... 352
  Depositions
    adjournment ... 411
    administration of oaths ... 360
    administrative matters ... 383
    after commencement of action ... 354

INDEX

appeal of discovery orders...371
before commencement of action 354
breaks in testimony 390
certification..414
concluding the deposition 411
copies 414
corporations 352
correcting transcripts..413
costs 362
credibility and demeanor of witnesses 379
defects preserved without objection.................................405
defending depositions 403
directing witness not to answer 408
disadvantages 348
documents in connection with 363
etiquette...380
exhausting witness's knowledge and recollection...........397
exhibits 386
experts..330
failure to attend 387
fielding questions...381
follow-up to witness answers...402
foreign countries or parties.......................................331,799
goals of 376
judicial intervention...412
knowing the deponent 375
knowing the facts 373
knowing the law 378
letters rogatory 800
mode of examination...393
nonparty depositions 346
notice 364
oaths 390
objections 403
objectives in using...348
opening statement use 618
opposing motion for summary judgment........................528
oral examination 324
outlines 376
parties attending 384
partnerships...352
pending appeal 356
persons before whom taken...360
preparation..372,378
priorities in taking...357
prisoners 354
privileged matters 391
protection orders 368
purpose 348

recording..361
scope of examination...391
sealing transcript...390
seating arrangements...386
service..386
signatures...413
stipulations..350,388
subpoenas..387
summary judgment motions...521
supervision by courts..412
telephone depositions..359
timing...345,354,383
using documents..402
waiver of objections...404
where to take..357
who may be deposed...351
who may take...351
work product doctrine..392
written questions..325
Expert witnesses
   depositions of experts..330
   generally...127
   non-testifying experts..329
   purposes..328
   testifying experts..329
   treating physicians in personal injury actions..........................330
Hague evidence convention
   applicability...335,792
   blocking legislation..27-23
   diplomatic and consular officers and commissioners......................334
   enforceability..27-17
   exclusivity of procedures...27-17
   letters of request..334,794
   limitations...334
   provisions..334
Initial discovery..344
Insurance agreements
   scope of discovery..327
International discovery
   blocking legislation..802
   civil law countries...333
   depositions under federal rules of procedure............................799
   letters rogatory..800
   nondisclosure laws..333
   obstacles to obtaining evidence abroad..................................793
   provisions of federal rules generally...................................331
   provisions of rule 28...331
   provisions of rule 29...331
   subpoenas under rule 45...332

INDEX

Interrogatories
    advantages 425
    answers 436
    authority for 325
    business records 438
    certification by counsel 431
    compelling responses 440
    contention interrogatories 345
    disadvantages 425
    first served 344
    form of 431
    general verdicts on 596
    objections 434
    opinion or contention interrogatories 427
    opposing motion for summary judgment 528
    procedure for service 426
    purposes 425
    responses to 434
    restrictions on content 345
    scope of discovery 427
    service 426
    special verdicts on 594
    summary judgment 522
    supplementing and amending responses 439
    timing 344
    types 427
    use made of 441
Judgments
    discovery in aid of execution 715
Laying the foundation
    using discovery as means of 645
Limitations on discovery
    generally 327
    privileged information 327
    work product 328
Methods generally 323
Motions
    good faith requirement 339
    grounds for motion to compel discovery 341
    orders compelling discovery 340
    responding to motions to compel discovery 342
    types of motions 339
Multidistrict litigation
    powers of transferee court 343
Order among parties 343
Orders compelling discovery
    available relief 341
    grounds for motion 341
    procedure in making motion 340

```
    responding to motions ................................................342
    sanctions for violations of .............................................342
Personal jurisdiction
    lack of jurisdiction as defense ..........................................58
Physical and mental examinations
    conditions for ......................................................549
    generally ..........................................................326
    good cause showing..................................................459
    in controversy requirement ............................................458
    kind of examination..................................................459
    orders .............................................................459
    persons conducting ..................................................460
    persons present during................................................461
    procedural requirements ..............................................457
    sanctions for failure to comply with order ................................463
    where conducted ....................................................460
    who may be examined................................................458
Preliminary injunctions
    motion for expedited discovery .........................................166
Pretrial management of complex litigation .....................................304
Privileged information ....................................................327
Production of documents and things
    see PRODUCTION OF DOCUMENTS AND THINGS
Protective orders
    applicable rules of procedure...........................................335
    confidentiality and trade secrets........................................337
    grounds............................................................337
    local rules of court...................................................337
    undue burden or expense..............................................338
Purposes................................................................323
Requests for admissions
    abuses .............................................................463
    advantages and disadvantages .........................................463
    answers............................................................468
    failure to respond or object ............................................467
    form of ............................................................466
    generally ..........................................................326
    information obtainable................................................465
    motion to determine sufficiency of answer or objection.....................469
    objections .........................................................467
    purposes of rule.....................................................463
    summary judgment motions ..........................................522
    timing of requests...............................................345,463
    use made of admissions ..............................................469
Scope of discovery generally ...............................................326
Sequence among discovery devices .........................................344
Work product ...........................................................328
DISMISSAL
    Class actions........................................................279
```

INDEX 919

Costs
    previously dismissed claims 498
Counterclaims 497
Cross-claims...497
Foreign parties
    see FOREIGN COUNTRIES AND PARTIES
Improper service 46
Involuntary dismissal
    effect..497
    motion in nonjury trial..698
    motion made during trial 684
    when permitted 497
Magistrates
    purposes for referring cases to..315
Motion to dismiss 486,698
Personal jurisdiction
    raising lack of jurisdiction as defense 58
Summary judgment
    treatment of motion to dismiss as motion for 507
Third party claims 497
Two dismissal rule 495
Venue
    authority to dismiss action generally 75
    dismissal under *forum non conveniens*......................................81
Voluntary dismissal
    by order of court 496
    effect..495
    filing notice..494
    reasons for use 495
    two dismissal rule 495
    without court order 494

DISTRICT COURTS
Current composition..4
Magistrates
    appeal of judgment 665
Original jurisdiction 16

DIVERSITY JURISDICTION
Aliens
    disputes between citizens and aliens 13
Amount in controversy
    failure to recover more than required amount 12
    pleading amount required 11
    statutory requirement 11
Assignment
    invoking jurisdiction by fictitious assignment 14
Choice of law
    common law in diversity actions 197
    outcome determinative test 194
    substantive versus procedural test 194

Citizenship
　　actions between citizens of different states................................13
　　actions by real parties in interest 256
　　corporate citizenship 14
　　requirements for jurisdiction 13
Class actions
　　exceptions to complete diversity rule.....................................13
Complaints
　　particularity of state law claims 155
　　requirements for invoking jurisdiction....................................146
Considerations in obtaining 15
Corporations
　　citizenship of..14
　　dual citizenship problems 14
　　invoking by creation of sham corporation 14
Defeating..14
Denial or imposition of costs 12
Directed verdict
　　standard for determining motion 689
Exception to complete diversity rule...13
Forms
　　pleading jurisdiction under form 2(a).......................................15
Forum non conveniens 15
Grounds for exercise of judicial power...4
Impleader..268
Insurance companies
　　citizenship of insured..14
Interpleader
　　rule interpleader requirements..272
Joinder
　　defeating jurisdiction by joining nonparty 15
　　restrictions on power to join 257
Joint and several liability 14
Maintaining 14
Multiple parties 13
Partnerships
　　diversity requirements..14
Pendent parties..20
Real parties in interest
　　jurisdiction determined by citizenship 256
Removal
　　amount in controversy..87
　　avoiding removal...15
　　improperly joined defendants 89
　　John Doe defendants..89
　　requirements for removal 87
Residence
　　actions between citizens of different states................................12
Statute of limitations

INDEX

    state law applicability 162
Statutory provisions 10
Venue
    plaintiff's residence proper venue 67
    where claim arose 67
DOING BUSINESS TEST
Foreign parties
    obtaining personal jurisdiction 785
Jurisdiction over out-of-state entities 50
Venue
    corporations doing business in state 69
DUE PROCESS
Class actions 281
Preclusion
    adverse affects 751
Quasi in rem jurisdiction 56
ECONOMISTS
Use as expert witnesses 127
ELECTRONIC EAVESDROPPING
Consensual recordings 121
Use by private investigators 121
EMINENT DOMAIN
Motions *in limine* 491
Venue
    local actions involving United States 73
EMPLOYMENT DISCRIMINATION
Venue provisions 74
EMPLOYMENT RECORDS
Use of in investigations 112
EMPLOYMENT RETIREMENT INCOME SECURITY ACT (ERISA)
Venue of actions 75
ENCYCLOPEDIAS
Sources for legal theories 141
ENTRY FOR INSPECTION
Types of rule 34 information obtainable 447
ENVIRONMENTAL PROTECTION AGENCY (EPA)
Availability of investigation records 116
Records of grants 116
Sources of investigative information 133
EQUITY
Interpleader practice 275
***ERIE* DOCTRINE**
    see CHOICE OF LAW
ETHICS
Settlement
    see SETTLEMENT
EVIDENCE
Arbitration
    applicability of rules of evidence 674

Choice of law
   Erie doctrine applicability..201
Final pretrial orders
   scope of evidence at trial...302
Hague evidence convention
   see DISCOVERY
Motions *in limine*
   see MOTIONS *IN LIMINE*
Newly discovered evidence
   grounds for rule 60(b) motions 720
Offers of proof...648
Opinion evidence
   expert witnesses 650
   lay opinion evidence 650
Pleadings
   amendments to conform to evidence 311, 685, 701
   introducing evidence outside scope of 685
Requests for admissions
   use made of admissions at trial 469
Requests for production of documents and things
   use of documents produced 456
Settlement
   offers to compromise claims 552
Summary judgment
   documents submitted in support or opposition to motions 524
   evidence opposing motion...525
   obtaining unavailable evidence under rule 56(f)............................529
   standards for granting or denying motion 534
   supporting evidence..517

EXAMINATIONS
Physical and mental examinations as method of discovery
   conditions for 459
   generally..326
   good cause showing..459
   in controversy requirement 458
   kinds of...459
   orders...459
   persons conducting 460
   persons present during...461
   procedural requirements 457
   sanctions for failure to comply..463
   where examination conducted 460
   who may be examined...458

EXECUTIONS
Attachment
   see ATTACHMENT
Enforcement of writ against public officers 713
Execution of writ 712
Procedure governing writs 710

INDEX

Service of writs 712
EXECUTORS AND ADMINISTRATORS
  Representatives of interested parties
    capacity to sue or be sued 255
EXHIBITS
  Appeals
    custody during appeal 735
  Depositions 386
  Introducing tangible evidence 645
  Marking for identification 645
  Opening statements
    use of demonstrative exhibits, visual aids or word pictures 618
  Record on appeal
    exclusion of exhibits 735
  Summation 633
EXPERT WITNESSES
  Accountants 127
  Categories of testimony 650
  Delay in hiring 127
  Determining type of expert needed 127
  Discovery
    non-testifying experts 329
    purposes 328
    testifying experts 329
    treating physicians in personal injury actions 330
    under federal rules 127
  Economists 127
  Evaluation by professional societies 127
  Experience 127
  Human factors experts 127
  Motions *in limine*
    denial of motion 492
    exclusion of expert testimony 492
  Opening statements
    making jury more receptive to expert proof 618
  Opinion evidence 650
  Respect among peers in field 127
  Summary judgment
    consideration of expert evidence upon motion 535
  Written reports 127
EXTRATERRITORIAL JURISDICTION
  Constitutional limitations 53
  Federal statutes authorizing 48
  Federal statutes not expressly authorizing 49
  Foreseeability test 53
  Long-arm statute
    see LONG-ARM STATUTE
  Minimum contacts standard 53
  National contacts theory 54

New York federal court jurisdiction under state law 50
Purposeful direction theory. 54
Statutory authorization 48
Stream of commerce theory 53
EYEWITNESS INTERVIEWS
   see WITNESSES
FEDERAL AVIATION ADMINISTRATION (FAA)
   Sources of investigative information. 133
FEDERAL COMMON LAW
   Erie doctrine applicability. 196
FEDERAL COURTS
   Abstention
      see ABSTENTION
   Bankruptcy courts
      current composition. 5
   Circuit courts of appeal
      appeals from magistrates' judgments. 664
      current composition. 5
   Congress of the United States
      power to reduce jurisdiction 3
   Court of international trade
      current composition. 5
   Courts of limited jurisdiction
      jurisdiction of limited by congress. 2
   District courts
      appeals from magistrates' judgments. 665
      current composition. 4
   Inferior federal courts
      current make-up 4
   Injunctions
      staying state court proceedings 23
   Investigation of cases
      prior litigation information 114
   Judicial panel on multidistrict litigation
      current composition. 5
   Option of bringing action in state or federal court. 6
   Preclusion
      see PRECLUSION
   Supreme court
      see SUPREME COURT
   Temporary courts 5
   United States claims court
      current composition. 5
   United States tax court
      current composition. 5
FEDERAL DEPOSIT INSURANCE CORPORATION (FDIC)
   Removal of actions. 94
FEDERAL OFFICERS
   Permissive intervention 262

INDEX

    Service of process upon 40
FEDERAL QUESTION JURISDICTION
  Amount in controversy
      minimum amount not conditioned to jurisdiction. 9
  Cases arising under constitution, laws and treaties 9
  Choice of law
    Erie doctrine applicability. 196
  Complaints
      methods of invoking jurisdiction 146
  Considerations in obtaining 10
  Grounds for exercise of federal judicial power 4
  Implied rights of action. 23
  Pendent parties 20
  Pleadings
      specific reference to statute or constitution 9
  Price-fixing conspiracy
      jurisdictional allegations 10
  Private rights of action 23
  Removal to federal court 86
  Statute of limitations
      rule 3 applicability. 161
  Statutory provisions 8
  Venue
      generally 67
      where claim arose 67
FEDERAL RULES OF CIVIL PROCEDURE
see **RULES OF CIVIL PROCEDURE**
FIDUCIARIES
  Class actions
      responsibility of plaintiff to absent members of class 288
FINDINGS
  Motion to amend or make additional findings in nonjury trial 700
FOOD AND DRUG ADMINISTRATION (FDA)
  Product information 117
  Sources of investigative information 133
FORECLOSURE
  Removal of actions against United States 94
FOREIGN ARBITRAL AWARDS CONVENTION
  Choice of law considerations 250
  Removal of actions 94
FOREIGN CORPORATIONS
  Doing business test 51
FOREIGN COUNTRIES AND PARTIES
  Act of state doctrine. 252,819
  Antitrust law applicability. 787
  Arbitration
      immunity in actions to enforce agreements to arbitrate 817
  Attachment
      foreign sovereign immunity act provisions 824

Choice of law
    act of state doctrine 252
    foreign arbitral awards 250
    foreign sovereign immunities act. 251
Warsaw convention. 251
Commercial activity
    foreign states entitled to immunity 814
Discovery
    see DISCOVERY
Doing-business statutes
    obtaining personal jurisdiction. 785
Enforcement of judgments
    arbitral awards 810
    common-law jurisdictions 812
    default judgments 812
    exequatur proceedings. 811
Foreign sovereign immunities act
    actions in violation of international law 819
    act of state doctrine 819
    agreements to arbitrate 817
    attachment and execution. 824
    choice of law considerations 251
    commercial activity jurisdictional exception 815
    enactment 813
    exceptions to sovereign immunity 815
    jurisdictional issues 814
    maritime liens against vessels or cargo 820
    service of process 821
    waiver of immunity. 817
Forum non conveniens
    applicability of doctrine. 789
    factors considered by court 790
International discovery
    see DISCOVERY
Jurisdiction
    foreign sovereign immunities act provisions 814
    personal jurisdiction 785
Long-arm statutes
    obtaining personal jurisdiction. 785
Maritime liens against vessels of foreign states 820
Minimum contacts 786
Motions to dismiss
    forum non conveniens grounds 789
    improper service grounds 780
    jurisdictional grounds 780
Prejudgment attachments
    criteria for obtaining outside U.S. 803
    disclosure of assets affected 808
    foreign sovereign immunities act provisions 824

INDEX

    mareva injunctions 809
    security 808
    systems treating attachment as separate proceeding 804
    vacation of 810
Removal
    actions against 92
Securities law applicability 788
Service of process
    by mail 782
    defendants in foreign countries 43
    foreign sovereign immunities act provisions 821
    generally 43
Hague convention procedures 781
Subject matter jurisdiction 787
Venue
    civil actions against 69
Warsaw convention
    choice of law provisions 251

FORMS

Bankruptcy
    claims 861
    official forms 847
Diversity jurisdiction
    form of pleading 15
Judgments
    official forms 31 and 32 705
Service of process
    notice and acknowledgement form 31
Summons
    requirements of rule 4(b) 28

FORUM NON CONVENIENS

Appealing dismissals 81
Burden of proving 81
Choice of law
    federal courts sitting in N.Y. 218
N.Y. state courts 217
Common law doctrine generally 75
Dismissal 81
Foreign parties
    dismissal based on 789
Restrictions on common law doctrine in federal court 80

FRAUD

Elements of 153
Pleadings
    particularity required 153
Relief from final judgments
    grounds for rule 60(b) motions 720

FREEDOM OF INFORMATION

Advantages over discovery 108

```
Exemptions under statutes .................................................. 108
Federal and state statutes .................................................. 108
Workers' compensation and social security records .......................... 113
FUGITIVES
  Service of process
    state law methods of serving ............................................ 37
FULL FAITH AND CREDIT
  Preclusion
    basic purposes ......................................................... 750
GARNISHMENT
  Attachment
    see ATTACHMENT
  State procedures .......................................................... 172
GUARDIANS
  Representatives of interested parties
    capacity to sue or be sued ............................................. 255
  Service on infants ........................................................ 37
HABEAS CORPUS
  Court-imposed particularity in pleading ................................... 158
  Magistrates
    review of petitions .................................................... 315
HAGUE CONVENTION
  Convention on taking of evidence abroad
    see DISCOVERY
  Service on defendants in foreign countries ............................. 44,781
HALO EFFECT
  Opening statements to jury ................................................ 606
HAZARDOUS MATERIALS TRANSPORTATION
  Safety violation records .................................................. 116
HEARINGS
  Class action settlement hearings .......................................... 296
  Multidistrict litigation
    hearing on motion to transfer .......................................... 875
  Preliminary injunctions
    when hearing required .................................................. 168
  Summary judgment
    see SUMMARY JUDGMENT
HOSPITAL RECORDS
  Consent forms ............................................................. 109
  Discharge summaries ....................................................... 109
  Medical history of patients ............................................... 109
  Nurses' notes ............................................................. 109
  Outpatient records ........................................................ 109
  Surgical records .......................................................... 109
  Test reports .............................................................. 109
HUSBAND AND WIFE
  Discovery
    privileged information excluded from scope ............................. 327
IMPLEADER
```

INDEX

Admiralty practice 269
Appeals 269
Claims allowed to be impleaded 265
Jurisdiction 268
Jury trial
    admiralty practice 270
Objections to venue 269
Procedure 265
Purpose 265
Rights of plaintiffs 267
Rights of third party defendants 267
Venue
    objections prohibited 269
    transfer for convenience 78
IMPLIED RIGHTS OF ACTION
Attachment of jurisdiction 23
INCOMPETENT PERSONS
Methods of serving process on 37
INJUNCTIONS
Interpleader
    staying state and federal court proceedings 273
Jury trial
    mixing legal and equitable with single claim 564
Magistrates
    purposes for referring cases 315
Multidistrict litigation
    enjoining state court actions 881
Preliminary injunctions
    see PRELIMINARY INJUNCTIONS
State court proceedings
    when federal courts may grant 23
Temporary restraining orders
    see TEMPORARY RESTRAINING ORDERS (TRO'S)
IN PERSONAM JURISDICTION
    see PERSONAL JURISDICTION
INSTRUCTIONS TO JURY
    see JURY TRIAL
INSURANCE
Arbitration clauses in state insurance liquidations
    abstention by federal courts 22
Discovery
    contents of agreements 327
Motions *in limine*
    mention of insurance coverage prohibited 492
INSURANCE COMPANIES
Diversity jurisdiction
    citizenship of insured 14
Service of process
    public officials designated to receive process 38

INTANGIBLE PROPERTY
Quasi in rem jurisdiction
    exercise for attachment 56
INTELLECTUAL PROPERTY
Particularity of pleading 158
INTERNAL REVENUE SERVICE (IRS)
Venue
    civil actions for collection of taxes. 75
INTERPLEADER
Adjudication of claims among litigants 273
Adverse claimants
    generally 270
    U.S. as 276
Amount in controversy
    rule interpleader 273
    statutory interpleader. 271
Appeals
    dismissed actions. 275
    injunctions. 275
Defined 270
Deposits
    rule interpleader 273
    statutory interpleader. 273
Discharge of stakeholder 273
Equitable doctrines. 275
Independent liability 274
Injunctions
    state and federal proceeding stays 274
Jurisdiction
    rule interpleader 272
    statutory interpleader. 271
Jury trial
    generally 274
    procedural devices at variance with relief 566
Rule interpleader
    amount in controversy. 273
    deposits or surety bonds 273
    jurisdiction 272
    service. 273
    venue. 273
Service of process
    rule interpleader 273
    statutory interpleader. 272
Statutory interpleader
    amount in controversy. 271
    by United States 276
    deposits of funds 273
    jurisdiction 271
    venue. 272

INDEX

Substantive law applied 274
Surety bonds 273
Types of actions 270
United States
    as adverse claimant 276
    statutory interpleader by 276
Venue
    generally 75
    rule interpleader 273
    statutory interpleader 272

INTERROGATORIES
    see DISCOVERY

INTERVENTION
Absolute right
    federal statutes conferring 261
    jurisdictional requirements 262
    nonstatutory right 261
Appeals 264
Counterclaims
    rights of intervening parties 264
Cross-claims
    rights of intervening parties 264
Defined 261
Jurisdiction
    challenges by intervenor 264
    grounds generally 262
Motions for leave to intervene 262
Permissive intervention
    federal or state officials or agencies 262
    jurisdictional basis 262
    limitations on court discretion 262
Rights of intervenors 264
Types 261
Venue
    waiver of objections to 262

INTERVIEWS
Client interviews 104
Eyewitness interviews
    accident reports 105
    accuracy of observations 105
    identifying eyewitnesses 105
    prior expectations and subsequent exposures 105
    witness recall 105
    written reports 105
Nonparty witnesses 104
Parties to actions 104

INVESTIGATION OF CASES
Accident reports
    availability 111

```
    coast guard search and rescue reports ................................... 111
    public transportation reports ........................................... 111
Bankruptcy filings ........................................................... 114
Centers for Disease Control
    sources for medical information ........................................ 137
Civil investigation demands .................................................. 109
Common carrier reports ....................................................... 116
Computer records ............................................................. 119
Consumer Product Safety Commission
    generally .............................................................. 133
    product information .................................................... 117
Contract cases ............................................................... 125
Corporate filings ............................................................ 113
Court records ................................................................ 114
Death certificates
    suspicious deaths ...................................................... 112
Department of Health and Human Services
    sources of information for investigations .............................. 133
Department of Justice
    sources of investigative information ................................... 133
Department of Transportation
    sources of investigative information ................................... 133
Directory of federal government agencies ..................................... 133
Disease associations ......................................................... 137
Employment records ........................................................... 112
Environmental Protection Agency
    availability of records ................................................ 116
    sources of investigative information ................................... 133
Expert witnesses
    see EXPERT WITNESSES
Federal Aviation Administration
    sources of investigative information ................................... 133
Food and Drug Administration
    sources of investigative information ................................... 133
Freedom of Information requests
    advantages over discovery .............................................. 108
    exemptions under statutes .............................................. 108
    federal and state statutes ............................................. 108
Governmental and institutional records
    accident reports ....................................................... 111
    common carrier reports ................................................. 116
    computer records ....................................................... 118
    corporate filings ...................................................... 113
    court records .......................................................... 114
    death certificates ..................................................... 112
    freedom of information requests ........................................ 108
    generally .............................................................. 108
    government funding records ............................................. 117
    government regulations violations ...................................... 115
```

INDEX

government standards and statistical information	118
medical records	109
product information	117
public facility maintenance records	116
school and employment records	112
United States postal service	118
weather information	118
workers' compensation and social security records	113
Government funding records	117
Government regulations violations	115
Government standards and statistical information	118

Hazardous materials transportation
    records of regulation violations 116

Hospital records
    categories of information 109
    consent forms 109
    discharge summaries 109
    medical history of patient 109
    nurses notes 109
    outpatient records 109
    surgical records 109
    test reports 109

Interviews
    see INTERVIEWS

Introduction to chapter 103

Jurisdiction
    pre-complaint investigations 7

Medical associations
    sources for medical information 137

Medical malpractice 123

Medical records
    categories of information 109
    medical malpractice cases 123

National Climatic Data Center
    sources of investigative information 133

National Highway Traffic Safety Administration
    sources of investigative information 133

National Injury Information Clearing House
    sources of investigative information 133

National Library of Medicine
    sources for medical information 137

National Technical Information Service
    sources of investigative information 133

National Transportation Safety Board
    sources of investigative information 133

Occupational Safety and Health Administration
    sources of investigative information 133

Physicians records 111

Private investigators

see PRIVATE INVESTIGATORS
Product information 117
Products liability 122
Public facility maintenance records 116
School records 112
Securities and Exchange Commission
    sources of investigative information 133
Social Security records
    freedom of information requests 113
United States Postal Service
    address information 118
    sources of investigative information 133
Veterans Administration
    sources of investigative information 133
Weather information 118
Workers' compensation
    freedom of information requests 113
    office of workers' compensation programs 133
    sources of information 125

IRREPARABLE HARM
Obtaining preliminary injunctions 164

ISSUE PRECLUSION
  see PRECLUSION

JNOV
  see JUDGMENT NOTWITHSTANDING VERDICT

JOINDER
Compulsory joinder
    conditionally necessary parties 258
    criteria for under rule 19 258
    indispensable parties 258
    necessary parties 258
Defined 256
Diversity jurisdiction
    defeating by joining nonparty 15
    restrictions on joinder 260
Interpleader
  see INTERPLEADER
Intervention
  see INTERVENTION
Jurisdiction
    restrictions on joinder 260
Necessary parties
    compulsory joinder 258
Pendent jurisdiction
    joinder of state law claims 17
Permissive joinder
    criteria for permitting 257
    objections to 257
    severance 257

INDEX 935

Removal
    identification and joinder of nondiverse necessary parties 6
Venue
    joinder defeating venue 260
JOINT AND SEVERAL LIABILITY
  Diversity jurisdiction
    action against diverse defendants...15
  Grounds for permissive joinder 257
JONES ACT
  Removal under act prohibited...95
  Special venue statute...74
JUDGES
  Pretrial conference role 547
JUDGMENT NOTWITHSTANDING VERDICT
  Failure to make motion..691
  Requirements for making motion 691
  Standards governing determination of motion.................................692
  Time for making motion...690
JUDGMENTS
  Amendments
    motion to alter or amend judgment 697
  Clerks of court
    entry by clerk 707
    relief from clerical mistakes 718
  Declaratory judgments
    see DECLARATORY JUDGMENTS
  Default judgments
    see DEFAULT JUDGMENTS
  Defined 703
  Demand for judgment
    see DEMAND FOR JUDGMENT
  Discovery
    discovery in aid of judgment or execution 715
  Enforcement
    discovery in aid of execution..715
    money judgments 711
    nonparties 714
    performance of specific acts 714
    stays 715
  Entry
    duties of clerk 707
    notice of entry 708
  Foreign parties
    see FOREIGN COUNTRIES AND PARTIES
  Forms
    official forms 31 and 32..705
  Fraud
    grounds for rule 60(b) motions 720
  General verdicts on interrogatories

```
    approval of judgment form ................................................705
Judgment notwithstanding verdict
    see JUDGMENT NOTWITHSTANDING VERDICT
Mistake
    grounds for rule 60(b) motions ...........................................720
Motions
    altering or amending judgment.......................................697,719
Multiple claims and parties...................................................707
Newly discovered evidence
    grounds for rule 60(b) motions ...........................................720
Notice of entry ..............................................................708
Performance of specific acts..................................................714
Preparation...................................................................704
Registration of final judgment................................................708
Relief from judgments
    clerical mistakes ........................................................718
    harmless error ...........................................................718
    motions to alter or amend ................................................719
Rule 60(b) motions............................................................719
Special verdicts on interrogatories
    approval of judgment form ................................................705
Stays
    enforcement of judgments .................................................715
Summary judgment
    see SUMMARY JUDGMENT
Void judgments
    grounds for rule 60(b) motions ...........................................720
Writs of execution
    enforcement against public officers.......................................713
    execution of writ.........................................................712
    procedure governing ......................................................711
    service...................................................................712
JUDICIAL CODE
    Diversity jurisdiction
        statutory provisions...................................................10
    Federal question jurisdiction
        statutory provisions....................................................8
    Section 1331
        federal question jurisdiction...........................................8
        implied rights of action ...............................................23
    Section 1332
        disputes between citizens and aliens ...................................13
        diversity jurisdiction provisions.......................................10
        failure to recover more than minimum amount ............................12
JUDICIAL DISTRICTS
    Multidistrict litigation
        see MULTIDISTRICT LITIGATION
    Venue
        actions against multiple defendants residing in different districts ....71
```

INDEX

JUDICIAL PANEL ON MULTIDISTRICT LITIGATION
  Current composition of federal courts. 5
JUDICIAL POWER
  Congressional power to limit 4
  Constitutional provisions 2
  Grounds for exercise of 4
JURISDICTION
  Amount in controversy
    see AMOUNT IN CONTROVERSY
  Ancillary jurisdiction
    see ANCILLARY JURISDICTION
  Bankruptcy
    see BANKRUPTCY
  Case or controversy requirement 3
  Counterclaims
    ancillary jurisdiction 20
    compulsory counterclaims 187
  Diversity jurisdiction
    see DIVERSITY JURISDICTION
  Exclusive jurisdiction
    statutes conferring 16
  Extraterritorial jurisdiction
    see EXTRATERRITORIAL JURISDICTION
  Federal question jurisdiction
    see FEDERAL QUESTION JURISDICTION
  Foreign sovereign immunities act 814
  Impleader 268
  Injunctions
    state court proceedings enjoined by federal courts 23
  Interpleader
    amount in controversy 271
    original jurisdiction in statutory interpleader cases 271
    rule interpleader 272
  Intervention
    jurisdictional grounds required 262
  Jury trial
    resolution of jurisdictional issues 567
  Long-arm statute
    see LONG-ARM STATUTE
  Original jurisdiction
    statutes conferring on districts courts 16
  Pendent jurisdiction
    joinder of state law claims 17
    pleadings 19
  Pleadings
    failure to properly plead 7
    grounds to be affirmatively pleaded 7
    grounds to be expressly pleaded 2
    pendent jurisdiction 19

Pre-complaint investigations...7
Quasi in rem jurisdiction
    see QUASI IN REM JURISDICTION
State courts
    statutes conferring parallel jurisdiction 16
Subject matter jurisdiction
    see SUBJECT MATTER JURISDICTION
Supreme Court
    original jurisdiction of...3
JURY TRIAL
    Advisory juries
        see ADVISORY JURIES
    Answers
        demand for jury trial 181
    Attorneys
        instructing the jury 590
    Bankruptcy cases 835
    Challenges
        for cause 585
        peremptory challenges..585
    Choice of forum
        tactical considerations 568
    Closing argument
        see SUMMATION
    Collateral estoppel
        issues previously resolved in nonjury trial 576
    Commingling legal and equitable issues
        legal and equitable remedies 564
        procedural devices at variance with relief 566
    Common law
        preservation of right at common law 561
    Complaints
        demand for jury trial 145
    Consolidation motion 682
    Constitutional origin of right...561
    Counterclaims
        commingling legal and equitable issues in one litigation 564
    Defenses
        commingling legal and equitable issues in one litigation 564
    Demand
        effect of general demand 570
        identification of issues for jury resolution 569
        indorsed pleadings...572
        jury demand chart 579
        manner and form..572
        provisions of rule 38 568
        removed actions from state court..574
        separate demand 573
        service...573

INDEX 939

    specifying particular issues 571
    time. 571
    withdrawal 573
Directed verdict
    right to jury trial not waived by denial of motion. 690
Dismissal
    motion for involuntary dismissal during trial 684
Exemptions from jury service. 582
Instructing the jury
    attorney's role in charge 590
    court's charge prior to summation 591
    jury charge 586
    objections to charge. 592
    presenting charge to jury 589
    rules governing 586
Interpleader
    generally. 274
    procedural devices at variance with relief 566
Jurisdiction
    resolution of factual issues by jury. 567
Jurors
    challenges 585
    number of 583
    qualifications and exemptions 582
    random selection 583
    voir dire 584
Motions for consolidation. 682
New trial
    see NEW TRIAL
Objections
    charge to the jury. 592
Opening statements
    see OPENING STATEMENTS
Pleadings
    amended pleadings waiving right. 575
    indorsed pleading 572
    motion to amend pleadings to conform to evidence 685
Polling the jury. 601
Procedural devices at variance with relief. 566
Qualifications for jury service. 582
Removal
    demanding jury trial in removed actions. 101,574
    relief from waiver 577
Separate trials
    motions under rule 42(b) 682
Service of process
    demand for jury trial 573
Size of jury. 583
State law

940 FEDERAL CIVIL PRACTICE

  impact on right to jury trial in federal court 567
 Summation
  see SUMMATION
 Unanimous verdicts 601
 Venue
  resolution of factual issues. 567
 Verdicts
  see VERDICTS
 Voir dire
  examination of prospective jurors 584
 Waiver
  actions brought in federal court in first instance. 577
  amendments made after responsive pleading 576
  amendments made before responsive pleading 575
  collateral estoppel 576
  provisions of rule 38 575
  relief from waiver 577
  removed actions from state court. 578
  retrial of same case 576
LABOR UNIONS
 Capacity to sue and be sued. 39
 Collective bargaining agreements
  venue of actions coming under 75
 Service of process
  service on agents or officers 39
LACHES
 Choice of law considerations 210
LANDLORD AND TENANT
 Bankruptcy
  assumption or rejection of leases. 869
LIMITATION OF ACTIONS
  see STATUTE OF LIMITATIONS
LOCAL RULES
 Discovery
  protective orders 337
 Interrogatories
  form of interrogatories 431
 Magistrates
  rules governing trial before 664
 Motions
  form and submission of orders 483
  generally 479
 Orders to show cause 482
 Production of documents and things 449
 Settlement
  see SETTLEMENT
 Summary judgment
  see SUMMARY JUDGMENT
LONG-ARM STATUTE

INDEX

Doing business test 51
Due process clause
    constitutional limitations on extraterritorial jurisdiction 53
Foreign parties
    obtaining personal jurisdiction 785
Framework 51
Grounds for exercise of jurisdiction 50
New York federal court jurisdiction under state law 51
Service on out of state defendants 33
Special purpose provisions 53
Substantial revenue criterion 52
Telephone, telex or mail communications into state 52
Transaction of business criterion 52

MAGISTRATES
Additional duties 316
Appeals
    entry of judgment following trial 664
    to court of appeals 664
    to district court 665
Class actions
    motions for certification 315
Consent of parties 663
Habeas corpus
    review of petitions 315
Injunctions
    purposes for referring cases to magistrates 315
Jurisdiction
    consent to 318
Local rules governing 664
Motions to dismiss
    purposes for referring cases to magistrates 315
Objections
    failure to file in timely fashion 317
    procedures for making 317
Objections to reports 316
Pretrial hearings 315
Prisoners
    challenges to conditions of confinement 315
Referral of case to magistrate 314
Reports
    adoption by district court 318
Review of decisions 316
Special masters
    distinguished from magistrates 320
Statutory source of authority 314
Summary judgments
    purposes for referring cases 315
Trial
    consent of parties 318

942 FEDERAL CIVIL PRACTICE

    constitutional challenges to consent trials...................................318
    Types of cases 315
    Withdrawal by district court 318
MAIL
    Long-arm statute
        communications into state constituting transaction of business...................52
    Service by mail..31
MANDAMUS
    Multidistrict litigation
        review of panel decisions...877
    Removal...85
MASTERS
    see SPECIAL MASTERS
MCCARRAN-FERGUSON ACT
    Arbitration clauses in state insurance liquidations
        abstention by federal courts..22
MEDICAL ASSOCIATIONS
    Sources for medical information...137
MEDICAL EXAMINERS
    Death certificates in cases of suspicious death....................................112
MEDICAL MALPRACTICE
    Investigation of cases 123
    Medical records 123
    Opening statements
        examples of opening 622
        examples of rhetorical questions 623
    Removal of actions against federal employees 94
    Statute of limitations...123
MEDICAL RECORDS
    Hospital records
        see HOSPITAL RECORDS
    Medical malpractice cases 123
    Physicians' records...111
MILITARY SERVICE
    Service of process
        affidavit showing defendant not in military service 46
MINIMUM CONTACTS TEST
    Constitutional limitations on extraterritorial jurisdiction 53
    Corporations
        venue of actions involving..69
    Foreign parties...786
    Quasi in rem jurisdiction 56
MINITRIALS
    Alternative dispute resolution techniques 551
MINORS
    Service of process on 37
MISTAKE
    Pleadings 154
    Relief from final judgments

INDEX 943

    grounds for rule 60(b) motions 720
MOTIONS
  Affidavits
    attorney's affidavit. 473
    evidentiary matter in support of motions 473
  Appeals
    determination without oral argument 743
  Arbitration
    motion to confirm, modify, or vacate award 674
  Attachment 174
  Bankruptcy 845
  Class actions
    certification motion 291
  Corrective motions
    generally 483
    motions for more definite statement. 484
    motion to strike matter 485
  Default judgments
    setting aside. 500
  Directed verdict
    see DIRECTED VERDICT
  Discovery
    see DISCOVERY
  Dismissal
    foreign parties
      see FOREIGN COUNTRIES AND PARTIES
    generally 486
    involuntary dismissal in nonjury trial. 698
  Dispositive motions 486
  Filing 481
  Form of motion
    local rules governing. 483
    signing requirements. 480
    writing requirement. 480
  General strategy and tactics 471
  Involuntary dismissal
    making motion during trial 684
  Judgments
    altering or amending judgments 697, 719
  Jury trial
    alternative motion for new trial 692
    consolidation. 682
    consolidation or separate trial 682
    directed verdict 687
    involuntary dismissal. 684
    judgment notwithstanding verdict 690
    motion for separate trial. 682
    motion to amend pleadings to conform to evidence 685
    new trial 693

Local rules
    form and submission of orders 483
    generally 479
Memoranda of law
    organization 475
    submission in support of motion 475
More definite statement 484
Motions *in limine*
    see MOTIONS *IN LIMINE*
New trial
    see NEW TRIAL
Nonjury trial
    amend findings or make additional findings 700
    amend pleadings to conform to evidence 701
    generally 701
    involuntary dismissal 698
    new trial 701
Notice 481
Oral argument
    schedule for hearings and deciding motions 483
    strategy and tactical considerations 483
Pleadings
    amending pleadings to conform to evidence 685
    motion to amend 308
Rules of civil procedure
    general rules pertaining to motion practice 477
    specific rules 479
Rules of individual judges 480
Service of process
    generally 481
    remedies for improper service 46
Summary judgment
    see SUMMARY JUDGMENT
Timing
    strategy and tactics 472
Venue
    objections to venue raised by 76
    transfer for convenience 77

MOTIONS *IN LIMINE*
Advantages 490
Appeals
    preserving issue for 490
Authority for 489
Design changes 493
Disadvantages 490
Eminent domain actions 491
Employers and employees
    conduct of employer or fellow employees 492
    EEOC opinion of probable cause for lawsuit 492

INDEX

Expert testimony 492
Financial condition of parties 493
Form of motion 493
Future income tax liability 493
Insurance coverage 492
Introduction 489
Oral agreements 492
Prior bad acts 491
Prior contracts 491
Prior judgments in unrelated matters 492
Statements made in remote past 491
Subsequent remedial measures 491
Summation 632
Time for motion 493

MULTIDISTRICT LITIGATION
Agent Orange litigation 883
Appeals
    review of panel's decisions 877
    transferred actions 882
Attorneys
    retaining local counsel in transferee court 878
Choice of law 215
Choice of law after transfer 880
Discovery
    power of transferee court 878
Injunctions against state court actions 881
Law of the case 880
Mandamus
    appellate review of panel decisions 877
Multidistrict litigation act 871
Panel
    appellate review 877
    composition 872
    establishment 872
    powers generally 872
    remands 882
    restrictions on authority 872
Proceedings in transferee court 878
Remands 882
Tag-along actions 877
Termination of transferred actions 882
Transfer of actions
    burden of persuasion 872
    choice of law after transfer 880
    criteria for transfer 872
    decisions of panel 875
    denial of transfer 876
    documents 873
    hearings 875

946   FEDERAL CIVIL PRACTICE

    law of the case 880
    motions for 872
    opposition to 874
    orders 879
    orders to show cause 874
    papers 875
    power of transferee court 878
    proceedings in transferee court 878
    retaining local counsel 878
    termination of transferred action 882
    transfer for all purposes 882
MUNICIPALITIES
  Bankruptcy
    chapter 9 debt adjustments 849
  Service of process on 40
NATIONAL BANKS
  Special venue statutes 73
NATIONAL CLIMATIC DATA CENTER
  Sources of investigative information 133
NATIONAL CONTACTS THEORY
  Constitutional limitations on extraterritorial jurisdiction 54
NATIONAL LIBRARY OF MEDICINE
  Sources for medical information 137
NEW TRIAL
  Motions
    alternative rule 50(b) motions 692
    amending judgments 696
    determination 694
    grounds for 694
    nonjury trial 701
    time for making 693
  Partial new trial of damages or liability 696
  Procedural basis under rule 59 693
  Review of verdicts 696
NONRESIDENTS
  Extraterritorial jurisdiction
    see EXTRATERRITORIAL JURISDICTION
  Long-arm statute
    see LONG-ARM STATUTE
  Service of process
    infants or incompetents in another state 37
    jurisdiction based on federal law 42
    service on out of state defendants 33
    state law basis 42
NOTICE
  Appeals
    failure to file 731
  Class actions
    generally

INDEX

    see CLASS ACTIONS
       notice of settlement and hearing date 296
  Depositions
     contents of notice 365
     nonparties 366
     parties 364
  Motions 481
  Removal
     filing petition for removal 100
  Temporary restraining orders
     notice of application 167

OATHS
  Depositions 390

OBJECTIONS
  Bankruptcy
     rules for raising in adversary proceedings 845
  Depositions 403
  Evidence
     introducing outside scope of pleadings 685
  Interrogatories
     grounds for objecting 434
  Intervention
     waiver of objections to 262
  Jury trial
     objections to charge 592
  Opening statements 621
  Permissive joinder of parties 257
  Requests for admissions 467
  Requests for production of documents and things 451
  Subject matter jurisdiction
     when lack of jurisdiction raised 7

OPENING STATEMENTS
  Admissions
     dismissal of action on admission by counsel 627
  Alternate theories 626
  Appealing to sympathy of jury 628
  Avoiding mistrials and reversals 627
  Brevity 607
  Closing the opening 614
  Concluding the opening 625
  Confronting problems 613
  Construction 608
  Contracts
     examples of openings 622
  Contrast 623
  Courtrooms
     demonstrative use of contents 617
  Depositions
     use during opening 618

Discussing law in opening statement..628
Elements of opening...608
Emotion...620
Evidence
    misstating or characterizing in unethical way..............................628
    referring to inadmissible or irrelevant matter..............................628
    telling jury statement not evidence.......................................624
Examples of openings..622
Exhibits
    use of demonstrative exhibits, visual aids, or word pictures....................618
Expert testimony
    making jury more receptive..618
Eye contact..621
Forcing adversary's hand...615
Golden rule argument..628
Halo effect..606
Inflammatory statements..627
Language of the law...613
Legal parameters...603
Levity..621
Medical negligence
    examples of openings...622
    examples of rhetorical questions..623
Notes...627
Objections...621
Opening the opening...622
Opinions..628
Order of information presented...605
Overreaching case...619
Personalization of client..617
Physical space...617
Pleadings used during..618
Preempting defense...624
Presentation...616
Primacy...604
Product liability
    examples of rhetorical questions..623
Psychological identification...616
Purpose...606
Recency..604
Relation to summation...615
Rhetorical questions...623
Simplicity...606
Story order..608
Structure
    brevity..607
    construction...608
    damage story..608
    elements of opening...608

INDEX 949

    introduction..607
    story order..608
    transitions..607
Themes
    presenting jury with multiple dominant themes..............626
Transitions..607, 620
Vocal tone..620
Witnesses
    linking details of testimony to specific witness..............622
    promising witness by name................................622
Word choice...619
Wrongful death
    examples of opening......................................622
ORDERS
  Appeals
    disposition by summary order..............................743
  Compelling discovery
    see DISCOVERY
  Final pretrial orders..302
  Form and submission
    local rules governing.....................................483
  Multidistrict litigation
    transfer order..879
  Preliminary injunctions
    form and scope..165
  Pretrial orders
    see PRETRIAL MANAGEMENT
  Protective orders
    see DISCOVERY
  Scheduling orders..301
  Show cause
    see ORDERS TO SHOW CAUSE
  Temporary restraining orders
    see TEMPORARY RESTRAINING ORDERS (TRO'S)
ORDERS TO SHOW CAUSE
  Attachment..174
  Bankruptcy..846
  Local rules..482
  Multidistrict litigation
    transfer of actions..874
  Preliminary injunctions..165
  When use appropriate..482
PARTICULARITY IN PLEADING
  Antitrust complaints..157
  Checklist..158
  Class actions..156
  Constitutional right violations
    court-imposed particularity................................158
  Court-imposed particularity....................................156

Fraud 153
Intellectual property 158
Mistake 154
Racketeer Influenced Corrupt Organizations Act
    court-imposed particularity 157
Rule 9 requirements 153
Securities complaints 157
State law claims in diversity actions 155

PARTIES
  Capacity to sue or be sued
    rule 17 summary 255
  Citizenship of represented parties 256
  Cross-claims against co-parties 188
  Diversity jurisdiction
    actions by representative parties 256
    multiple parties 13
  Foreign parties
    see FOREIGN COUNTRIES AND PARTIES
  Impleader
    see IMPLEADER
  Indispensable parties
    compulsory joinder 258
  Interpleader
    see INTERPLEADER
  Intervention
    see INTERVENTION
  Joinder
    see JOINDER
  Necessary parties
    compulsory joinder 258
  Pendent parties
    class action applicability 20
    diversity cases 20
    when joinder permitted 19
  Pretrial management of complex litigation
    multiple parties 307
  Real parties in interest
    actions by parties not 253
    citizenship of parties represented 256
    claims derived from others 253
    defined 253
    representatives 255
  Removal
    identification and joinder of nondiverse necessary party 6
  Representatives
    categories 255
  Venue
    all plaintiffs/all defendants rule 67
    multiple parties 67

INDEX

```
    sham parties ............................................68
    subsequently added parties ..............................71
PARTNERSHIPS
  Depositions
    testifying through officers, directors, or agents .......352
  Diversity jurisdiction
    diversity requirements of parties .......................14
  Residence
    determination for venue purposes ........................69
  Service of process
    federal rules methods ...................................38
    state law methods .......................................38
  Venue
    residence for venue purposes ............................69
PATENTS
  Preclusion
    exclusive federal court jurisdiction ...................767
  Venue
    where action for infringement brought ...................74
PENDENT JURISDICTION
  Joinder of state law claims ...............................17
  Pleading requirements .....................................19
PENDENT PARTIES
  Class actions .............................................20
  Diversity cases ...........................................20
  Joinder permitted .........................................19
PERMISSIVE JOINDER
    see JOINDER
PERSONAL INJURY ACTIONS
  Discovery
    treating physicians ....................................330
  Motion for separate trial ................................682
  Production of documents and things .......................444
PERSONAL JURISDICTION
  Complaints ...............................................147
  Consent ...................................................26
  Defenses
    raising lack of jurisdiction as defense .................58
  Discovery
    lack of personal jurisdiction ...........................58
  Doing business test ...................................51,785
  Extraterritorial jurisdiction
    see EXTRATERRITORIAL JURISDICTION
  Foreign corporations
    doing business test .....................................51
  Foreign countries and parties
    Foreign Sovereign Immunities Act provisions ............814
    long-arm or doing business statutes ....................785
  Ignoring complaint
```

raising lack of jurisdiction as defense 59
Long-arm statute
    see LONG-ARM STATUTE
Obtaining following removal 101
Pendant personal jurisdiction
    extraterritorial service under federal statute................................. 49
Quasi in rem jurisdiction
    see QUASI IN REM JURISDICTION
Removal
    obtaining following removal 101
Service of process
    see SERVICE OF PROCESS
Statutory authorization 48
Summons
    see SUMMONS
PERSONAL PROPERTY
Choice of law
    intangible property 248
    tangible property 247
PETITIONS
Bankruptcy
    involuntary petitions 853
    list of creditors and schedules of assets and liabilities......................... 857
    number of copies filed... 855
    statement of affairs 857
    voluntary petitions.. 852
Certiorari to supreme court.. 746
Rehearings
    effect of filing 744
    filing requirements 744
Removal
    see REMOVAL
PHYSICIANS
Discovery
    treating physicians in personal injury actions............................... 330
Physical and mental examinations as method of discovery
    persons conducting examination 460
PLEADINGS
Alternate or hypothetical pleading 148
Amendments
    conformity to evidence.. 311,685
    counterclaims or defenses 309
    delay in seeking relief 309
    identity of interest test 313
    motions to amend 308
    multiple parties 308
    permitted purposes 309
    relation back doctrine 312
    requirements of rule 15 generally 308

INDEX 953

```
    right to amend ................................................308
    sufficiency of proposed amendment ..............................309
    timeliness .....................................................308
Amount in controversy
    jurisdictional amount in diversity case to be pleaded ...........11
Answers
    see ANSWERS
Arbitration
    statement of claim .............................................671
    statement of response ..........................................672
Bankruptcy
    caption ........................................................843
    complaints .....................................................843
    legibility .....................................................845
Claims for relief
    see CLAIMS FOR RELIEF
Class actions
    sample allegations .............................................290
Complaints
    see COMPLAINTS
Diversity jurisdiction
    requirements of pleadings .......................................15
Evidence
    introducing evidence outside scope of ..........................685
Federal question jurisdiction
    specific reference to statute or constitution ....................9
Field code .........................................................142
Fraud
    particularity in pleading ......................................153
Implied rights of action
    federal question jurisdiction ...................................23
Information and belief ............................................149
Intellectual property
    court-imposed particularity ....................................158
Jurisdiction
    failure to properly plead ........................................7
    grounds to be affirmatively pleaded ..............................7
    grounds to be expressly pleaded ..................................2
Jury trial
    amended pleadings waiving right ................................575
    demand for jury trial by indorsed pleading .....................572
Mistake
    pleading claims of .............................................154
Motions
    more definite statement ........................................484
    striking matter ................................................485
Notice pleading ...................................................145
Opening statements
    use of pleadings during ........................................618
```

Particularity in pleading
    checklist 158
    class actions. 156
    constitutional right violations 158
    court-imposed particularity 156
    fraud 153
    intellectual property cases 158
    mistake 154
    Racketeer Influenced Corrupt Organizations act 157
    rule 9 requirements 153
    securities complaints 157
    state law claims in diversity actions 155
Pendent jurisdiction 19
Pleading practice 142
Price-fixing conspiracies
    jurisdictional allegations 10
Relation back doctrine 312
Removal
    prior pleadings in state court actions 101
    procedure following removal. 101
Requirements 15
Special damages 151
Statute of limitations
    failure to properly plead jurisdiction 7
Summary judgment
    motions on the pleadings 518
    pleadings in opposition to motion 527
Supplemental pleadings
    filing by leave of court. 314
    relation back doctrine 314
Theory of modern pleading 142
Theory of pleadings in state practice. 142
POLICE REPORTS
Request for aided/accident reports 111
PRECLUSION
Antitrust
    effect of prior state court judgments 766
Civil rights actions
    defensive issue preclusion in 1983 actions 752
Claim preclusion
    defined 750
    purposes 750
Copyrights
    exclusivity of federal remedies 766
Defensive issue preclusion 752
Due process aspects 751
Failure to raise federal claims in state court 761
Issue preclusion
    defined 751

INDEX

Offensive issue preclusion
    generally 753
    U.S. government as litigant 777
Patents
    exclusive jurisdiction of federal courts 767
Securities
    remedies under federal securities laws 764
State agency decisions 769
State court judgments in federal court 754
State preclusion test 760

PREEMPTION
State law claims preempted by congressional enactment 21

PREJUDGMENT ATTACHMENTS
Judgments against foreign parties
    see FOREIGN COUNTRIES AND PARTIES

PRELIMINARY INJUNCTIONS
Affidavits
    motion supported by 165
Appeals
    expedited appeals 170
    procedure for 169
    standard of review 171
    stays pending 170
    when order appealable 168
Complaints
    money damage allegations 164
    where filed 166
Discovery
    motions for expedited discovery 166
Elements of proof 165
Hearings
    when required 168
Irreparable harm 164
Legal memoranda 165
Notice 165
Orders
    form and scope 165
    show cause orders 165
Security 166
Stays 170
Tender offer cases 163

PRETRIAL MANAGEMENT
Alternative dispute resolution
    see ALTERNATIVE DISPUTE RESOLUTION
Complex litigation
    abstention in multiple cases 307
    defined 304
    discovery 305
    multiple cases 307

multiple issues..305
multiple parties...307
Final pretrial orders
    approval by court...302
    binding nature..302
    creation...302
    functions..302
    scope of evidence determined by................................302
Magistrates
    pretrial hearings conducted by.................................315
Premotion conferences..300
Pretrial conferences
    objectives..547
    obligation to participate......................................300
    presiding judges..547
    purposes...300
    scope..300
Pretrial proceedings
    requirements under rule 16....................................299
Scheduling orders
    contents...301
    failure to seek...301
    modification...302
    sanctions for violations......................................301
PRISONS AND PRISONERS
Depositions
    orders for deposing prisoners.................................354
Magistrates
    challenges to conditions of confinement........................315
PRIVATE INVESTIGATORS
Control by attorney..120
Electronic eavesdropping by......................................121
Illegal or unethical behavior....................................120
Invasions of privacy...120
Licenses...121
Relationship with client...121
Sources of information...120
Surveillance role..120
Telephone abuse..121
Wiretaps...121
Witness statements...120
PRIVATE RIGHTS OF ACTION
Implied rights under federal statutes.............................23
PRIVILEGES
Discovery
    matters excluded from scope...............................327,391
PRODUCTION OF DOCUMENTS AND THINGS
Abuses...442
Advantages and disadvantages of rule 34..........................442

INDEX

Document defined	.442
Electronic data	.446
Entry and inspection on property	.447
Form of requests	.449
Local rules	.449
Locating documents	
obligations of responding party	.453
Motion to compel response	.456
Objections to requests	.451
Obligations of responding party	.453
Procedure under rule 34	.444
Purpose of rule 34	.442
Requests for	.326
Responses to rule 34 requests	.450
Review by requesting party	.455
Scope of rule 34 discovery	.445
Segregation of responsive documents	.454
Types of information obtainable	.445
Use of documents at trial	.456

PRODUCTS LIABILITY
  Investigation of cases 122
  Opening statements
    examples of rhetorical questions .... .623

PROTECTIVE ORDERS
  see DISCOVERY

PROVISIONAL REMEDIES
  Attachment
    see ATTACHMENT
  Garnishment
    see GARNISHMENT
  Preliminary injunctions
    see PRELIMINARY INJUNCTIONS
  Purpose generally 163
  Receivers
    see RECEIVERS
  Temporary restraining orders
    see TEMPORARY RESTRAINING ORDERS (TRO'S)

PUBLIC POLICY
  Choice of law exceptions .... .211

PURPOSEFUL DIRECTION THEORY
  Constitutional limitations on extraterritorial jurisdiction .... .54

QUASHING SERVICE
  Effect on pending action .... .46

QUASI IN REM JURISDICTION
  Attachment
    procedure in state court .... .56
  Basis .... .56
  Intangible property .... .56
  Minimum contacts test .... .56

Nature of property attached 56
QUIETING TITLE
  Removal of actions against United States 94
RACKETEER INFLUENCED AND CORRUPT ORGANIZATIONS ACT (RICO)
  Pleading fraud 153
RAILROADS
  Bankruptcy
    chapter 11 reorganizations 851
  Removal
    statutes prohibiting 94
REAL PROPERTY
  Choice of law 246
RECEIVERS
  Actions by and against 179
  Appeals
    orders appointing receivers 179
  Appointment 177
  Bonds 178
  Equity receivers
    defined 176
    rights, duties and liabilities, ... 177
  Evidence
    manner of presenting 178
  Jurisdiction
    power of district court to appoint 179
  Notice of appointment 179
RECORDS
  Appeals
    see APPEALS
  Business records
    option to designate and produce 438
  Court records
    see COURT RECORDS
  Employment records
    use in investigations 112
  Hospital records
    see HOSPITAL RECORDS
  Medical records
    see MEDICAL RECORDS
  Prior litigation as sources of information 114
  Removal
    transfer of state court records 101
  School records
    use in investigations 112
RELATION BACK DOCTRINE
  Amended pleadings raising new allegations 312
REMAND
  Removal
    appeal of order granting or denying 105

INDEX

    grounds for remand..103
    motion for remand..103
REMOVAL
    Actions against federal officers
        statutes permitting removal..................................92
    Actions which may be removed
        grounds for removal..84
    Administrative proceedings..85
    Amount in controversy
        diversity cases...87
    Appeals
        orders granting or denying remand............................105
    Arbitration agreements or awards..................................94
    Armed forces members
        actions against federal officers................................92
    Attorneys' fees
        levying sanctions by federal judges...........................106
    Bankruptcy
        claims within exclusive federal jurisdiction....................94
    Bonds
        required with petition..100
    Burden of proof..99
    Civil action requirement...85
    Civil rights actions..93
    Collateral or incidental claims.....................................91
    Common carriers
        removal of actions against prohibited..........................94
    Costs
        levying sanctions by federal judges...........................106
    Counterclaims..91
    Criminal actions
        actions against federal officers................................92
        generally..85
    Cross-claims...91
    Defined..83
    Diversity actions
        amount in controversy...87
        avoiding removal..15
        generally..87
        improperly joined defendants..................................89
        John Doe defendants..89
    Federal Deposit Insurance Corporation.............................94
    Federal question cases...86
    Federal Tort Claims Act
        actions against federal employees..............................94
    Foreclosure actions against United States..........................94
    Foreign countries
        actions against...92
    Granny Goose doctrine

validity of state court orders in removed case 102
Grounds for removal 84
Interlocutory orders by state court 102
Joinder of claims 90
Jury trial
    demand for jury trial in actions removed from state court 574
    demanding jury in removed action..103
    relief from waiver 577
Mandamus actions 85
Medical malpractice claims 94
Necessary parties
    identification and joinder of nondiverse parties 6
Notice
    filing petition for removal 100
Parties
    who may remove generally 95
Personal jurisdiction
    obtaining following removal 101
Petition for removal
    amendments 99
    bond to accompany 100
    contents...98
    nominal or fraudulently joined defendants..................................96
    notice for filing 100
    place of filing 97
    procedure for removal generally 83
    removal effective upon filing..100
    required signatures 96
    time for filing 97
    verification 98
Pleadings
    prior pleadings in state court action 102
    procedure following removal..101
Post-removal procedure
    service of process 101
    transfer of state court record 101
Practical considerations 105
Quieting title
    actions against United States 94
Railroads
    statutes prohibiting removal...94
Remand
    appeal of order granting or denying......................................105
    grounds for remand...103
    motion for remand..103
Rules of Civil Procedure
    actions governed by after removal.......................................101
Securities
    removal of actions under securities act prohibited 94

INDEX

Separate and independent claims
    actions asserting removable and nonremovable claims 90
Service of process
    obtaining personal jurisdiction following removal 101
State court record
    transfer following removal 101
Statutes prohibiting removal 94
Statutory right to remove 83
Taxation
    actions challenging state taxes 95
Third party claims 91
Vacation of state court orders 100
Venue
    actions removed from state courts 75
    generally 97
Waiver
    actions in state court waiving right to remove 99
When removal effective 100
Who may remove 96
Workers' compensation
    removal of actions against employees under state laws prohibited 95

RENVOI
    Choice of law considerations 207

REPORTS
  Accident reports
    see ACCIDENT REPORTS
  Police reports
    requests for aided/accident reports 111

REPRESENTATIVE ACTIONS
  see CLASS ACTIONS

REQUESTS FOR ADMISSIONS
  see ADMISSIONS

RESIDENCE
  Diversity actions
    requirements for jurisdiction 13
  Nonresidents
    see NONRESIDENTS
  Venue
    see VENUE

RES JUDICATA
  Preclusion generally
    see PRECLUSION

RULES OF CIVIL PROCEDURE
  Advisory juries 582
  Answers
    amendments 189
  Appeals
    notice (FRAP 3) 731
    review of orders entered pursuant to rule 54(b) 729

Attachment
    actions pursuant to rule 64 172
Bankruptcy
    conformity of bankruptcy rules 842
Choice of law
    Erie doctrine applicability 198
Class actions
    exclusion of class members 294
    notice to absent class members 293
    prerequisites 277
    settlement 554
Complaints
    captions 145
    demand for judgement 149
    particularity of pleadings 156
    pleading subject matter jurisdiction 146
Costs of previously dismissed claims 498
Counterclaims
    assertion under rule 13 186
Cross-claims
    assertion against co-parties 188
    assertion under rule 13 186
Default judgments
    against whom entry appropriate 498
    by court 499
    grounds for setting aside 500
    grounds for setting aside entry of default 499
    motion or action to set aside judgment 501
Depositions
    discovery pending appeal 356
    failure to attend or serve subpoena 387
    notice of oral examination 324
    protection orders 368
    sealing transcript 390
    superseding rules by stipulation 350
Derivative actions 298
Discovery
    access to materials by nonparties 339
    depositions of experts 330
    depositions upon written questions 325
    insurance agreements 327
    international discovery 331
    non-testifying experts 329
    order among parties 343
    orders compelling 340
    physical and mental examination of persons 326
    privileged information 327
    production of documents and things 326
    protective orders 336

INDEX

    requests for admissions 326
    sanctions for violating orders compelling discovery........................342
    scope of permissible discovery 326
    sequence among discovery devices 344
    testifying experts 329
    treating physicians in personal injury actions 330
    types of motions 339
    work product......................................328
Dismissal
    involuntary dismissal.................................497
    voluntary dismissal without court order......................494
Expert witnesses
    discovery of experts 127, 330
Fraud
    particularity in pleading................................153
Impleader
    rights of third party defendants 267
Interpleader
    right generally.....................................270
    rule interpleader 272
Interrogatories
    authority for 325
    compelling responses 440
    option to designate and produce business records 438
    procedure for service.................................426
    responses to......................................434
    use made of......................................441
Intervention 260
Joinder
    grounds for compulsory joinder 258
    grounds for permissive joinder 257
Judgments
    notice of entry 708
Jurisdiction
    affirmative pleading 7
Jury trial
    demand 568
    instructing the jury 586
    jury *voir dire*......................................584
    motion for separate trial...............................682
    motions for consolidation or for separate trials 682
    peremptory challenges of alternate jurors 585
    preservation of right 561
    relief from waiver 577
    time for demand 571
    waiver of right.....................................575
    withdrawal of demand................................573
Magistrates
    appeals to district court 665

964   FEDERAL CIVIL PRACTICE

    consent to trial..663
Motions
    class action certification motion...291
    dismissal..486
    form of motion..480
    more definite statement..484
    notice requirements..481
    oral argument..482
    rules pertaining to motion practice generally................................477
    service..481
    specific rules..478
    striking matter...485
New trial
    alternative motion for new trial under rule 50(b).............................692
    rule 59 motions..693
Orders to show cause...482
Parties
    capacity to sue or be sued...253
Pendent jurisdiction
    joinder of state law claims..17
Persons present during examination..461
Pleadings
    alternate or hypothetical pleading..148
    amending pleadings to conform to evidence................................685
Preliminary injunctions
    notice to adverse parties..167
    security...166
Pretrial conferences
    settlement at pretrial conference...547
Production of documents and things......................................326,442
Protective orders...336
Quasi in rem jurisdiction..56
Receivers
    rights, duties and liabilities of equity receivers..............................177
Removal
    demanding jury trial..103
    rules governing action after removal.......................................101
Rule 3
    statute of limitations on federal question claims.............................161
Rule 4
    alternative provisions for service in foreign country..........................781
    corporations or partnerships..38
    defendants outside forum state..42
    federal officers or agencies..40
    foreign countries...42,780
    form of summons...28
    how summons served...30
    infants or incompetent persons..37
    issuance of summons..27

INDEX

methods of serving individuals 35,781
one hundred mile bulge rule 48
quasi in rem jurisdiction 56
return of service 46
service on state or local governmental organizations 40
summons and complaints served together 28
territorial limits of effective service 34,48
time limit for service 45
timing of answer 182
who serves summons 30

Rule 5
access to discovery materials by nonparties 339
orders to show cause authorized 482
service of motion 481
summary judgment motions
    requests for admissions 522

Rule 6
notice of motions 481
orders to show cause authorized 482

Rule 7
form of motions 480

Rule 8
alternate or hypothetical pleading 148
demand for judgment 149
grounds for federal question jurisdiction 9
grounds for jurisdiction affirmatively pleaded 7
pleading subject matter jurisdiction 146

Rule 9
admiralty and maritime claims 155
pleading fraud with particularity 153
pleading provisions 154
pleading time and place 155
specificity in answers 184

Rule 10
captions 145

Rule 11
independent investigation of facts 141

Rule 12
improper service 46
motion for more definite statement 484
motion to dismiss 486
motion to strike matter 485
objections to venue 76
raising lack of subject matter jurisdiction 7
time after service to appear and defend 29
treatment as motion for summary judgment 507
waiver of objections to improper venue 76

Rule 13
assertion of counterclaims and cross-claims 186

    counterclaims against United States..188
    cross-claims against co-parties..188
    exceptions to compulsory counterclaims.......................................187
Rule 14
    permissive claims of third party defendants...................................267
    third party complaints...188
Rule 15
    amended answers...189
    amended pleadings to conform to evidence...............................311,685
    introducing evidence outside scope of pleadings...............................685
    procedure for amending or supplementing pleadings............................308
    purposes for permitting amended pleadings....................................309
    relation back of new allegations..312
    supplemental pleadings..314
Rule 16
    pretrial conferences..547
    pretrial proceedings..299
Rule 17
    capacity of parties to sue or be sued..255
    representatives deemed real parties in interest................................255
    service on unincorporated associations..38
Rule 18
    joinder of state law claims..17
    pendent parties..19
Rule 19
    criteria for compulsory joinder..258
Rule 20
    grounds for permissive joinder..257
Rule 22
    right to interplead...270,272
Rule 23
    class action certification motions...291
    exclusion of class members..294
    notice to absent class members..293
    prerequisites to class action..277
    settlement of class actions...554
Rule 23.1
    class action pleadings...156,294
    derivative actions by shareholders...298
Rule 23.2
    class actions against unincorporated associations.............................298
Rule 24
    intervention..260
Rule 26
    depositions of experts...330
    discovery of expert witnesses..127
    discovery of insurance agreements...327
    discovery of non-testifying experts...329
    discovery of physicians in personal injury actions.............................330

INDEX

    methods of discovery...323
    motions...339
    motion to establish priority in discovery..............................339
    order of discovery among parties......................................343
    privileged information..327
    protective orders...336, 369
    scope of permissible discovery..326
    sequence among discovery devices......................................344
    testifying experts..329
    work product..328

Rule 28
    depositions in foreign countries......................................331

Rule 29
    international discovery...331
    stipulations regarding depositions....................................350

Rule 30
    depositions upon oral examination.....................................324
    failure to attend deposition or serve subpoena........................387
    order of discovery among parties......................................344
    sealing deposition transcript...390

Rule 31
    depositions upon written questions....................................325

Rule 33
    interrogatories to parties..325
    option to designate and produce business records......................438
    procedure for serving interrogatories.................................426
    response to interrogatories...434
    use made of interrogatories...441

Rule 34
    depositions pending appeal..356
    production of documents and things...............................326, 442

Rule 35
    conditions for examinations...459
    exchange of medical reports...461
    good cause showing..459
    in controversy requirement..458
    persons conducting examination..460
    physical and mental examination of persons............................326
    procedural requirements...457
    who may be examined...458

Rule 36
    abuses..463
    advantages and disadvantages..463
    answers...468
    failure to respond or object to request...............................467
    form of requests..466
    information obtainable..465
    motion to determine sufficiency of answers or objections..............469
    purposes..463

requests for admission generally 326
timing of requests 465
Rule 37
    compelling responses to interrogatories................................. 440
    motion for orders compelling discovery 340
    motion to compel response 456
    types of discovery motions 339
    violations of orders compelling discovery 342
Rule 38
    demand for jury trial 568
    preservation of right to jury trial 561
    time for demand 571
    waiver of right to jury trial 575
    withdraw of demand for jury trial 573
Rule 39
    advisory juries 582,667
    identification of issues for jury resolution 569
    relief from waiver of jury trial... 577
Rule 41
    costs of previously dismissed claims 498
    dismissal for improper service.. 46
    dismissal of counterclaims, cross-claims or third party claims............ 497
    involuntary dismissal 497,684
    motion for involuntary dismissal in nonjury trial........................ 698
    voluntary dismissal by order of court................................... 495
Rule 42
    motion for consolidation or for separate trial........................... 682
    motion for separate trial.. 682
Rule 43
    oral testimony on summary judgment motions 523
Rule 45
    subpoenas 332
Rule 47
    jury *voir dire*.. 584
Rule 49
    general verdicts on interrogatories..................................... 596
    peremptory challenges of alternate jurors 585
    verdict options... 594
Rule 50
    alternative motion for new trial 692
    extending time for filing notice of appeal............................... 732
    motion for directed verdict 687
    motion for judgment notwithstanding verdict........................... 690
Rule 51
    failure of court to comply 589
    instruction to the jury.. 586
Rule 52
    extending time for filing notice of appeal............................... 732
    motion to amend findings or make additional findings in nonjury trial... 700

INDEX

Rule 53
    appointment of special masters 320
    authority of magistrates 314

Rule 54
    appeal of orders entered pursuant to 729
    definition of judgment 703

Rule 55
    default judgment by court 499
    entry of default judgments 498
    grounds for setting aside entry of default 499

Rule 56
    see SUMMARY JUDGMENT

Rule 57
    procedure for obtaining declaratory judgement 710
    when declaratory relief appropriate 709

Rule 59
    extending time for filing notice of appeal 732
    motion for new trial 693
    motion for new trial in nonjury trial 701
    motion to alter or amend judgment 697

Rule 60
    grounds for rule 60(b) motions 719
    motions to alter or amend judgments 719
    obtaining relief from final judgments 720
    relief from clerical mistakes 718
    setting aside default judgments 501
    timing of rule 60(b) motion 722

Rule 61
    judgments rendered in harmless error 718

Rule 62
    stay of enforcement of judgment 715

Rule 64
    attachment 172
    attachment for exercise of quasi in rem jurisdiction 56

Rule 65
    notice of preliminary injunction 167
    security for preliminary injunctions 166

Rule 66
    equity receivers 177

Rule 69
    issuance of writs of execution against public officers 713
    procedure for writs of execution 711

Rule 70
    enforcement of judgments by performance of specific acts 714

Rule 71
    enforcement of judgments against nonparties 714

Rule 72
    objections to magistrate decisions 317

Rule 73

consent to trial before magistrates 663
Rule 74
   appeal of judgments of magistrates 665
Rule 77
   notice of entry of judgment 708
Rule 78
   hearings on motions 482
   summary judgment motions without oral argument 512
Rule 81
   jury trial in removed actions 102
   removal 101
Service of process
   corporations or partnerships 38
   defendants in foreign countries 43,780
   defendants outside forum state 42
   federal officers or agencies 40
   generally 27
   infants or incompetents 37
   mail service 31
   methods of serving individuals 35
   remedies for improper service 46
   return of service 46
   state or local governmental organizations 40
   summons and complaints served together 28
   territorial limits of effective service 34,48
   time limit for service 45
   time to appear and defend 29
   unincorporated associations 38
Statute of limitations
   federal question claims 161
Subject matter jurisdiction
   when lack of jurisdiction may raised 8
Summary judgment
   see SUMMARY JUDGMENT
Summons
   form of summon 28
   how service made 30
   issuance 28
   who serves summons 30
Temporary restraining orders
   applications 167
Venue
   objections raised by answer or motion 76
   waiver of objections 76
Voluntary dismissal without court order 494
SCHOOL DISTRICTS
   Service of process upon 40
SCHOOL RECORDS
   Use of in investigations 112

INDEX

SECURITIES
  Foreign parties
    applicability of U.S. securities laws..788
  Preclusion
    remedies under federal securities laws......................................764
  Production of documents and things
    requests for production in securities fraud action............................444
  Removal
    actions under section 12 of securities act....................................94
  Venue
    actions under Securities Exchange Act......................................74

SECURITIES AND EXCHANGE COMMISSION (SEC)
  SEC filings as source of investigative information..............................133

SERVICE OF PROCESS
  Agents
    corporations or partnerships...38
    delivery of summons and complaint to authorized agent......................36
    public officials as agents..38
  Bankruptcy
    rules providing for service...843
  Boards and commissions
    personal service on...40
  Civil contempt orders..48
  Conventional service..34
  Copies of summons...28
  Corporations
    federal rules methods...38
    state law methods...38
  Counties...40
  Courts
    personal service on...40
  Defenses
    remedies for improper service...46
  Dismissal of action..46
  Evading service...36
  Extraterritorial service
    constitutional limitations..53
    federal statutes not expressly authorizing...................................49
    foreseeability test...53
    implied authorization..50
    mail service on extraterritorial defendants...................................33
    minimum contacts standard...53
    national contacts theory...54
    New York federal court jurisdiction under New York law.....................50
    pendant personal jurisdiction..49
    purposeful direction theory..54
    statutory authority..48
    stream of commerce theory..53
    time for response...29

United States statutes authorizing 48
Federal officers or agencies 40
Foreign countries
    foreign sovereign immunities act provisions 821
    motions to dismiss based on improper service 780
    service on defendants in 43
Foreign states 42
Forms
    notice and acknowledgment form 32
Fugitives
    state law methods of service 36
Guardians
    service on infants under 14 37
Hague convention
    service on defendants in foreign countries 44, 781
How service made 30
Impleader 269
Improper service
    remedies 46
Incompetent persons
    methods of service 37
Individuals 36
Insurance
    public officials designated to receive process 38
Interpleader
    rule interpleader 273
    statutory interpleader cases 272
Interrogatories 426
Issuance of summons
    provisions of rule 4(a) 27
Jury trial
    demand 573
Labor unions
    service on officers or agents 39
Leave and mail service 36
Leaving summons at dwelling house 36
Long-arm statute
    see LONG-ARM STATUTE
Mail service 32
Military service
    affidavit showing defendant not in military service 46
Minors
    method of serving infants 37
Motions 481
Multidistrict litigation 875
Municipalities 40
Nail and mail service 36
Nonresidents
    Hague convention procedures 44

INDEX

  infants or incompetents in another state 37
  jurisdiction based on federal law 42
  service on out of state defendants 33
  state law basis 42
 Notice and acknowledgment form 32
 One hundred mile bulge rule 48
 Partnerships
  federal rules methods 38
  state law methods 38
 Personal delivery to individuals 36
 Process servers
  qualifications 30
 Proof of service 46
 Quashing service 46
 Removal
  obtaining personal jurisdiction following 101
 Return of service 46
 Rule for generally 27
 School districts 40
 State law methods
  corporations or partnerships 38
  evading service 36
  leave and mail service 36
  mail service 33
  nail and mail service 36
  unincorporated associations 38
 State or local governmental organizations 40
 Territorial limits 34
 Third party claims 188
 Time limit for service 45
 Time to appear and defend 29
 Towns and villages 40
 Treaties
  service on defendants in foreign countries 44
 Unauthorized methods 34
 Unincorporated associations
  actions under common name 38
 United States
  methods of serving U.S. as party 40
 United States marshals
  when marshals used for service 30
 Who serves summons 30
 Writs of execution 712
SETTLEMENT
 Agency
  authority of attorney 553
 Agreements
  matters addressed by 556
  setting aside 557

Alternative dispute resolution
 minitrials..551
 nonbinding arbitration..551
 summary jury trials...550
Arbitration
 see ARBITRATION
Attorneys
 authority as agent..553
 responsibilities to adversary counsel...............................558
 responsibilities to client..557
 responsibilities to court...559
Class actions
 briefs in support of..296
 hearings..296
 judicial approval...554
 notice of settlement and hearing date...............................296
 preliminary hearings..295
 stipulations..295
Damages
 assessment..547
 range...545
Ethical issues
 Mary Carter agreements..559
 responsibilities of attorney to client..............................557
 responsibilities to adversary counsel...............................558
 responsibilities to court...559
Evidence
 offers to compromise claims...552
Expert witnesses..545
Formal documentation..555
Investigators...545
Judgments
 terms of settlement in..554
Judicial involvement
 approval..554
 presiding judges..547
 procedure...547
Local rules
 actions by or on behalf of incompetents or infants..................554
 stipulations for entry of judgment or dismissal.....................555
 wrongful death actions..554
Minitrials..551
Negotiation process...551
Prelitigation record..545
Pretrial conferences..547
Releases
 generally...556
 setting aside...557
Settlement conferences

INDEX

    ex parte oral presentations 547
    inclusion of principals 547
  Summary jury trials 550
SHAREHOLDER DERIVATIVE ACTIONS
  Justification for 298
  Requirements under rule 23.1 279
  Venue
    residence of parties 70
    where actions prosecuted. 75
SHERMAN ANTITRUST ACT
  Applicability to foreign parties 787
  Venue 74
SOCIAL SECURITY
  Requests for records 113
SOVEREIGN IMMUNITY
  Foreign sovereigns
    see FOREIGN COUNTRIES AND PARTIES
  Permissive intervention
    waiver of immunity 262
SPECIAL MASTERS
  Appointment 320
  Compensation 320
  Distinguished from magistrates 320
  Reports 320
STANDING
  Case or controversy requirements 3
  Subject matter jurisdiction
    objection to jurisdiction on grounds of standing 3
STATE COURTS
  Abstention by federal courts
    see ABSTENTION
  Injunctions
    federal injunctions staying state court proceedings 23
  Jurisdiction
    federal statutes conferring parallel jurisdiction 16
  Option of bringing action in state or federal court 6
  Preclusion
    see PRECLUSION
  Records
    transfer upon removal to federal court 101
STATUTE OF FRAUDS
  Choice of law considerations 243
STATUTE OF LIMITATIONS
  Choice of law
    borrowing statutes 208
    federal courts sitting in N.Y. 210
    laches 210
    N.Y. state courts 209
  Class actions 285

Diversity jurisdiction
    state law applicability in diversity cases....................................162
Effect of filing on limitations generally...161
Failure to properly plead 7
Federal question jurisdiction
    rule 3 applicability..161
Medical malpractice...123

STAYS
Bankruptcy
    automatic stay upon commencement of action..............................865
    stay pending appeal 838
Judgments
    staying enforcement 715
Preliminary injunctions..170
Temporary relief pending appeal...742

STIPULATIONS
Depositions
    provisions of rule 29 350
    usual stipulations governing..388

STREAM OF COMMERCE THEORY
Constitutional limitations on extraterritorial jurisdiction 54

SUBJECT MATTER JURISDICTION
Abstention
    arbitration clauses in state insurance liquidations...........................22
    when federal courts abstain from exercise of jurisdiction.....................22
Ancillary jurisdiction
    jurisdictional basis...20
Basis of 4
Class actions
    use of rule 23 to broaden jurisdiction....................................282
Complaints
    methods of invoking 146
Foreign parties
    statutory limitations..787
Grounds for exercise of federal judicial power 4
Impleader...268
Implied rights of action
    generally...23
    pleadings..23
Interpleader
    jurisdiction under rule interpleader 272
Objections
    when lack of jurisdiction may be raised...................................8
Pendent jurisdiction
    joinder of state law claims...17
    pleading requirements..19
Pendent parties
    diversity cases..20
    generally..19

INDEX

Preemption 21
Standing
    objections on grounds of lack of 4
Statutory provisions 8,11,16
Venue
    transfer for convenience 77
    transfer for improper venue 76
When absence of may be raised 2
SUBPOENAS
Depositions
    failure to attend or to serve subpoena. 387
Service of process
    see SERVICE OF PROCESS
SUBSTANTIAL REVENUE TEST
Exercising jurisdiction under long-arm statute 52
SUMMARY JUDGMENT
Admissions
    opposing motion 529
Affidavits
    attorney's affidavits 520
    failure to file 510
    necessity 519
    opposition to motions 527
    requirements for 519
    statements of ultimate facts and conclusions of law 520
    time for filing supporting affidavits 508
    waiver of defects 521
Answers to interrogatories 522
Appeals
    orders denying motion. 537
    orders granting motion 536
    standard of review 538
Burden of proof
    evidence in support of motion 517
    standards for meeting initial burden of going forward 531
Claimants
    when party may bring motion 507
Counterclaims 506
Cross-motions 511,542
Declaratory judgments 506
Defendants
    when parties may bring motion 508
Depositions
    opposition to motion 528
    use by court in granting motion 521
Discovery
    motions prior to discovery. 539
    obtaining unavailable evidence 529
Entry of judgment *sua sponte* 511

Evidence
    documents submitted in support or opposition to 524
    obtaining unavailable evidence under rule 56(f). 529
    opposing evidence. 525
    standards for granting or denying motion 534
    supporting evidence. 517
Expert witnesses
    consideration on motion 535
Functions 503
Genuine issue of material fact
    standards for determining 533
Hearings
    consideration of motions without oral argument 512
    determination of motion without hearing 512
    local rules in New York federal courts 514
    oral testimony in opposition to motion. 529
    when required 512
Interrogatories
    answers. 522
    answers opposing motion 528
Local rules in New York federal courts
    form of motion supporting papers 513
    notice and filing of papers 514
    oral argument 515
    statement of uncontested material facts. 516,524
Magistrates
    purposes for referring cases to. 315
Motions
    cross motions 511,542
    delay in moving. 507
    documentary evidence submitted in support or opposition to 524
    during or subsequent to discovery 540
    entry of judgment *sua sponte*. 511
    evidence in support of 517
    grounds. 515
    local rules in New York federal courts 513
    on the pleadings. 518
    oral argument 513
    oral testimony 523
    parties making motion. 507
    planning for. 540
    presentation. 541
    prior to discovery 539
    signature by attorney. 515
    statement of uncontested material facts 516
    time for filing motion papers 508
    twenty-day waiting period. 507
    when to bring motion 507,539
    writing requirement. 515

INDEX

Motion to dismiss
    treatment as motion for summary judgement 507
Nature generally 503
Notice
    local rules in New York federal courts 514
Opposition to motion
    admissions 529
    affidavits 527
    answers to interrogatories 528
    depositions 528
    materials acceptable in opposition 527
    obtaining unavailable evidence 529
    opposing evidence 525
    oral testimony 529
    pleadings 527
    statement of contested material facts 524
    strategic and tactical considerations 541
Oral testimony on motions 523
Overview of rule 56 504
Partial summary judgment 541
Pleadings
    motion on 518
    opposition to motions 527
Requests for admissions
    consideration on motion 522
Second circuit's view 505
Service of process
    failure to file opposing papers 510
Standards for granting or denying motion
    basic standard 531
    expert evidence 535
    genuine issue of material fact 533
    slightest doubt standard 533
    weighing evidence 534
Statement of uncontested material facts
    inclusion with motion 516
Strategic and tactical considerations
    considerations in bringing motion 538
    cross motions 541
    motion during or subsequent to discovery 540
    motions prior to discovery 539
    opposing the motion 541
    partial summary judgment 541
    planning for motion 540
    presenting motion 541
    when to bring motion 539
SUMMARY TRIAL
    Alternative dispute resolution techniques 550
    Authority in federal rules 666

Defined 666
Procedure... 666
Settlement.. 666
SUMMATION
   Anticipating arguments of opposition 638
   Credibility issues 639
   Defendant's psychological approach... 635
   Exhibits 633
   Legal preparation 632
   Local customs and practices 632
   Motions *in limine* 632
   Organization.. 639
   Physical preparation 633
   Plaintiff's psychological approach... 634
   Practical aspects of delivery 631
   Purpose of 638
   Recording.. 633
   Slang or idioms.. 632
   Style and technique... 640
SUMMONS
   Agents
      delivery to authorized agents 36
   Bankruptcy
      summons and complaint in adversary proceeding 843
   Clerks of court
      issuance of summons... 27
   Complaints
      issuance by clerk 161
      simultaneous service 28
   Copies 28
   Corporations
      service on 38
   Forms
      requirements of rule 4(b)... 28
   How service made 30
   Issuance
      provisions of rule 28
   Leaving at dwelling house or residence 36
   Mail service 31
   Order to show cause
      order performing function of summons...................................... 29
   Partnerships
      service on 38
   Purpose of 27
   Qualifications of recipients 36
   Temporary restraining orders
      order as substitute for summons 29
   Who may serve 30
SUPERSEDEAS BONDS

Temporary relief pending appeal..742
SUPREME COURT
  Judicial power of United States vested in 3
  Jurisdiction
    generally..745
    original jurisdiction...3
  Review by appeal..747
  Review by certiorari
    effect of denial...746
    petitions...746
    when review granted...745
  Review on certified questions
    contents of certificate..747
    discretion of court of appeals.......................................747
SURETY BONDS
  Attachment
    motion for order of attachment 175
  Interpleader actions 273
  Removal
    bond to accompany petition..100
TAG-ALONG ACTIONS
  Multidistrict ligation..877
TAXATION
  Composition of U.S. tax court 5
  Removal of actions challenging state taxes 95
TELEPHONES
  Electronic eavesdropping
    abuses by private investigators 121
  Long-arm statute
    communications into state constituting transaction of business........52
TEMPORARY RESTRAINING ORDERS (TRO'S)
  Appeals
    when orders appealable...168
  Applications..167
  Complaints
    where filed 166
  Duration..168
  Ex parte orders...167
  Judges' assignments 166
  Notice
    application for..167
    generally...165
  Preliminary injunctions
    see PRELIMINARY INJUNCTIONS
  Security..166
  Summons
    order as substitute for 29
THIRD PARTY CLAIMS
  Ancillary jurisdiction 21

Arbitration 673
Dismissal 497
Intervenor's rights..264
Removal..91
Service of complaint..188
TORTS
  Choice of law
    basic methods 222
    better rule of law/choice influencing considerations........................232
    comparative impairment method 232
    Federal Tort Claims Act actions 233
    interest analysis method..223
    lex loci delecti 222
    most significant relationship method 231
  Federal Tort Claims Act
    choice of law considerations 233
    removal of actions...94
  Long-arm statute
    grounds for exercise of jurisdiction 50
TOWNS AND VILLAGES
  Service of process on 40
TRADE SECRETS
  Grounds for protective orders...337
TRANSACTION OF BUSINESS TEST
  Exercise of jurisdiction under long-arm statute..............................52
TRANSFER OF ACTIONS
  Choice of law 214
  Multidistrict litigation
    see MULTIDISTRICT LITIGATION
  Removal
    see REMOVAL
TREATIES
  Federal question jurisdiction
    cases arising under treaty 9
  Service of process
    service on defendants in foreign countries 44
TRIAL
  Alternatives to trial
    advisory juries
      see ADVISORY JURIES
    arbitration
      see ARBITRATION
    magistrates
      see MAGISTRATES
    summary trial
      see SUMMARY TRIAL
  Cross-examination
    see CROSS-EXAMINATION
  Direct examination

INDEX

    see DIRECT EXAMINATION
Jury trial generally
    see JURY TRIAL
Motion for new trial
    see NEW TRIAL
Opening statements
    see OPENING STATEMENTS

TRUSTS
Representatives of interested parties
    capacity to sue or be sued 255

UNIFORM COMMERCIAL CODE
Choice of law considerations 241

UNINCORPORATED ASSOCIATIONS
Capacity to sue or be sued 38
Class actions
    actions under rule 23.2 298
    generally 280
Service of process
    actions under common name 39
Venue
    residence for venue purposes 69

UNITED STATES
Actions against
    civil or criminal actions against federal officers 92
    venue 70
Agencies
    permissive intervention 262
    service on 40
Counterclaims against government 188
Interpleader
    statutory interpleader by U.S. 276
    U.S. as adverse claimant 276
Service of process
    agencies of U.S. government 40
    methods of service on 40
Venue
    local actions involving United States 73
    residence for venue purposes 70

UNITED STATES ATTORNEYS
Service of process
    delivery of summons and complaint 40

UNITED STATES CLAIMS COURT
Current composition 5

UNITED STATES CONSTITUTION
    see CONSTITUTION OF THE UNITED STATES

UNITED STATES MARSHALS
Service of process by 30

UNITED STATES POSTAL SERVICE
Address information 118

984 FEDERAL CIVIL PRACTICE

Sources of investigative information..133
UNITED STATES TAX COURT
Current composition...5
VENUE
Admiralty actions
    special venue rules 74
Aliens
    residence for venue purposes...69
All plaintiffs/all defendants rule 67
Answers
    raising objections by 76
Antitrust
    special venue provisions 74
Appeals
    dismissal of actions on *forum non conveniens* grounds 81
Bankruptcy
    generally...834
    title 11 proceedings...835
Burden of proof
    dismissal under *forum non conveniens*....................................81
    transfer of venue for convenience 79
Calendar congestion
    transfer for convenience 78
Choice of forum clauses
    agreements by parties as to venue 66
    transfer of venue for convenience 79
Class actions
    residence of parties 70
Collective bargaining agreements
    actions brought under agreements 75
Complaints...147
Consolidation of actions
    transfer for convenience 78
Copyright and patent infringement actions
    where actions under copyright laws may be brought 74
Corporations
    doing business test..69
    minimum contacts test..69
    residence of corporations...69
    shareholder derivative actions 70,75
Dismissal
    authority of court generally 75
Diversity jurisdiction
    plaintiff's residence 67
    where claim arose 67
Eminent domain
    local actions involving United States 73
Employment discrimination actions 74
Employment retirement income security act

INDEX

```
        special venue statute ................................................. 75
Federal question jurisdiction
        generally ............................................................. 67
        where claim arose ..................................................... 67
Foreign countries
        civil actions against ................................................. 69
Forum non conveniens
        appealing dismissal of action ......................................... 81
        burden of proof ....................................................... 81
        common law doctrine generally ......................................... 75
        dismissal under doctrine .............................................. 81
        restriction of common law doctrine in federal court ................... 80
General federal venue statute ................................................. 65
Impleader
        objections to venue prohibited ....................................... 269
Internal Revenue Service
        civil actions for collection of taxes ................................. 75
Interpleader ............................................................. 75, 272
Intervention
        waiver of objections to .............................................. 263
Joinder defeating venue ...................................................... 260
Jones Act
        special venue provisions .............................................. 74
Judicial districts
        non-local civil actions against multiple defendants ................... 71
Jury trial
        resolution of factual issues ......................................... 567
Local actions
        generally ............................................................. 65
        special rules for actions involving U.S. .............................. 73
Motions
        transfer for convenience .............................................. 77
Multiple parties ............................................................. 67
National banks
        special venue statutes ................................................ 73
Objections
        generally ............................................................. 75
        pleadings ............................................................. 76
        raising by motion ..................................................... 76
        waiver ................................................................ 76
Parties
        all plaintiffs/all defendants rule .................................... 67
        multiple parties ...................................................... 67
        sham parties .......................................................... 68
        subsequently added parties ............................................ 71
Partition actions involving U.S.
        special venue statute ................................................. 73
Partnerships
        residence for venue purposes .......................................... 69
```

Personal privilege of defendants 66
Removal
    actions removed from state courts 75
    venue requirements in federal court. 97
Residence of parties
    aliens. 69
    class actions 70
    corporations 69
    determination of 68
    federal officials sued in official capacity 68
    general concepts in choosing forum. 67
    individuals. 68
    judicial districts 71
    partnerships. 69
    shareholder derivative actions 70
    special rules for residence 70
    state officials sued in official capacity 68
    subsequently added parties 71
    unincorporated associations. 69
    United States 70
Securities actions
    special venue provisions 74
Shareholder derivative actions
    residence of parties 70
    where actions prosecuted. 75
Special venue statutes
    actions against national banks 73
    admiralty actions. 74
    antitrust actions 74
    collective bargaining agreements. 75
    conflict with general venue statute. 73
    copyright and patent infringement actions 74
    employment discrimination actions 74
    ERISA actions. 75
    federal laws containing venue provisions. 65
    internal revenue service actions 75
    interpleader. 75
    Jones Act actions. 74
    local actions involving United States 73
    partition. 73
    removal from state courts 76
    securities actions 74
    stockholder derivative suits 75
Subject matter jurisdiction
    transfer for convenience 77
Transfer for convenience
    access to sources of proof 77
    appeal of motions 79
    burden of proof 79

INDEX

calendar congestion 78
choice of forum clauses 79
consolidation of actions 78
courts familiar with substantive law 78
factors in deciding motion 77
impleading necessary third parties 78
motion to transfer 77
process compelling reluctant witnesses 78
Transfer for improper venue
    interest of justice standard 76
    objections 76
    statutory authority generally 76
    subject matter jurisdiction required 76
Unincorporated associations
    residence for venue purposes 69
    United States
    actions against United States 70
Waiver
    objections to improper venue 76
Where claim arose
    claims arising in more than one district 71
    determination 71
    diversity and federal question cases 67
    venue gap in multi-party cases 71

VERDICTS
Advisory juries
    effect of verdict 667
Attorneys
    role in formulating form of verdict 598
Directed verdict
    see DIRECTED VERDICT
Discretion of court 594
General verdict
    options generally 594
General verdicts on interrogatories
    approval of judgment form 705
    authority of court 596
    objections to use or form 599
Inconsistent verdicts 600
Judgment notwithstanding verdict
    see JUDGMENT NOTWITHSTANDING VERDICT
Objections
    special or general verdicts on interrogatories 599
Options available 594
Polling the jury 601
Special verdicts on interrogatories
    approval of judgment form 705
    discretion of court in formulation 594
    failure to submit material factual issues to jury 594

    objection to use or form..599
    requirement of rule 49...594
    rights of counsel 594
  Unanimity 601
WAIVER
  Answers
    failure to plead affirmative defense 186
  Arbitration 679
  Jury trial
    actions brought in federal court in first instance...........................577
    actions removed from state court...578
    amendments made after responsive pleading...............................576
    amendments made before responsive pleading 575
    collateral estoppel 576
    provisions of rule 38 575
    relief from waiver 577
    retrial of same case 576
  Removal
    actions in state court waiving right to remove 99
  Venue
    objections to improper venue...76
WEATHER INFORMATION
  Sources of information 118
WITNESSES
  Arbitration
    power to subpoena..673
  Cross-examination
    see CROSS-EXAMINATION
  Direct examination
    see DIRECT EXAMINATION
  Expert witnesses
    see EXPERT WITNESSES
  Eyewitness interviews
    accident reports...105
    accuracy of observations 105
    identifying eyewitnesses 105
    prior expectations and subsequent exposures of eyewitness....................105
    recall time..105
    written reports of witnesses 105
  Opening statements
    linking precise details to specific witnesses 622
    promising witness by name 622
  Prior inconsistent statements
    use in cross-examination 660
  Refreshing recollection..651
WORKERS' COMPENSATION
  Investigation of cases
    sources of information...125
  Office of workers' compensation programs

INDEX

    sources of investigative information 133
Removal
    actions against employees under state laws 95
    Request for information 113
WORK PRODUCT
    Discovery of 328,392
WRITS OF EXECUTION
    Enforcement against public officers 713
    Execution of writ 712
    Procedure governing 711
    Service 712
WRONGFUL DEATH
    Opening statements
        examples of opening 622

TABLE OF AUTHORITIES

Cases

	Page
ABCKO Music, Inc. v. Beverly Glen Music, Inc.	269
ABKCO Industries, Inc. v. Apple Films, Inc.	174
ACLI Intern. Commodity Services, Inc. v. Banque Populaire Suisse	338
A.I.M. International, Inc. v. Battenfeld Extrusion Systems, Inc.	783;784
A/S Krediit Pank v. Chase Manhattan Bank	270
A/S L. Ludwig Mowinckels Rederi v. Dow Chem. Co.	217
A.S. Rampell, Inc. v. Huster Co.	236
A.T. & T. v. Milgo Electronic Corp.	72;74
AVC Nederlands B.V. v. Atrium	221;789
Aaro, Inc., v. Daeus Int'l Corp.	536
Aberson v. Glassman	500
Abonjrd v. Singapore Airlines, Ltd.	817
Abraham v. Volkswagen of America, Inc.	196;257
Ackerman v. Oryx Communications, Inc.	532;533
Acosta v. Louisana Health & Human Resources (Dep't of)	697
Adams v. Heckler	319-20
Adams v. James	701
Adams v. United States	511;516
Aetna Casualty & Surety Co. v. Flowers	101
Aetna Casualty & Sur. Co. v. General Time Corp.	207
Aetna Casualty & Sur. Co. v. Quarles	709
Aetna Life Ins. Co. v. Haworth	709
Agent Orange Prod. Liab. Litig., In re	197;215-16;338; 362;535;871; 878-79;882-883
Agola v. Hagner	702
Agor v. Stormont Hosp. & Training School for Nurses	330
Agrashell, Inc. v. Sirotta Co., Bernard	52
Air Crash Disaster at Warsaw, In re	251-52
Air Crash Disaster Near Chicago, Illinois, In re	880;883
Akzona Inc. v. E.J. DuPont de Nemours & Co.	783
Alcoa S.S. Co. v. M/V Nordic Regent	789
Aldinger v. Howard	19
Aldrich v. Upstate Auto Wholesale of Ithaca	511
Alexander v. Unification Church of Am.	47
Alexander v. Gardner-Denver Co.	773

Allen & Co. v. Occidental Petroleum Corp.	413
Allen v. Canadian Gen. Elec. Co.	52
Allen v. McCurry	749;751;752;754;755; 756;763;777
Allied Chem. Corp. v. Daiflon, Inc.	695;730,878
Allstate Ins. Co. v. Hague	212
Almenares v. Wyman	20
Amalgamated Packaging Indus. Ltd. v. National Container Corp.	257
Amalgamated Sugar Co. v. NL Industries, Inc.	752
Amburn v. Forster, Indus., Ltd. Harold	55
American Dredging Co. v. Federal Ins. Co.	253
Amercian Federation of States Co. v. Mun. Employees v. Nassau Co.	509
American Fire & Casualty Co. v. Finn	80;86
Amercian Home Assur. Co. v. Sunshine Supermarket,Inc.	490
American Industrial Contracting, Inc. v. Johns-Manville Corp.	333
American Int'l Group, Inc. v. London American Int'l Corp.	525
American Jerex Co. v. Universal Aluminum Extrusions, Inc.	173;174
American Key Corp. v. Cole Nat'l Corp.	520
(American) Lumberman's Mut. Cas. Co. v. Times & Howard, Inc.	582
American Optical Co. v. Curtiss	253
American Pipe and Construction Co. v. Utah	285
American Tel. & Tel. Co. v. Grady	339
Amoco Overseas Co. v. Campagnie Nationale Algerienre de Navigation	804
Anderson v. City of Bessemer	726
Anderson v. Liberty Lobby, Inc.	505;506;517
Anderson v. City of New York	518;521;525;532;535
Andover Realty, Inc. v. Western Elec. Co.	244-45
Andrea Theatres, Inc. v. Theatre Confection, Inc.	763;766
Ansam Associates, Inc. v. Cola Petroleum, Ltd.	707;730
Anschuetz & Co., Grumblt v. Mississippi River Bridge Authority	332
Anschuetz & Co., In re	332;335;797
Antone v. General Motors Corp.	209
Apex Oil Co. v. DiMauro	506;517;531;533
Applegate v. Top Assocs., Inc.	85;519
Archie v. Christian	319
Architectural League of New York v. Bartos	413
Argonaut Insurance Co. v. Italvanon Insurance Co.	178
Argus v. Eastman Kodak Co.	518;526
Arizona v. California	749
Arley v. United Pacific Ins. Co.	64
Armco, Inc. v. Penrod-Stauffer Bldg. Sys., Inc.	32
Armstrong v. McAlpin	179
Arnold v. Eastern Air Lines, Inc.	682
Arthur Young & Co. v. Leong	218;236
Arthur v. Arthur	792

TABLE OF AUTHORITIES 993

Artman v. Prudential-Bache Securities Inc.	678
Asahi Metal Indus. Co. v. Superior Court	54;55;786
Asbestos & Asbestos Insulation Material Products Liability Litigation, In re	874
Associated Metals and Minerals Corp. v. Sharon Steel Corp.	243
Astarte Shipping Co. v. Allied Steel & Export Service	882
Atlantic and Gulf Stevedores, Inc. v. Ellerman Lines, Ltd.	596
Atlantic Coastline R.R. v. Locomotive Engineers, Brotherhood of	23
Austin v. Unarco Industries, Inc.	15
Austracan (U.S.A.) Inc. v. Neptune Orient Lines Ltd.	528
Auten v. Auten	238
Avco Corp. v. Aero Lodge No. 735	83
Averbach v. Rival Mfg. Co.	501
Ayers v. Watson	93
Baas v. Elliot	102
Babcock v. Jackson	204;222-24;230
Bache and Co., Inc. v. Int'l Controls Corp.	243
Backo v. Local 281, United Bhd. of Carpenters & Joiners	29
Bader v. Purdom	204;212-213;229;231
Baker v. Sherwood Constr. Co., Inc.	601-02
Baki v. B.F. Diamond Constr. Co.	330
Balestrieri v. Bell Asbestos Mines, Ltd.	93
Baltimore Gas & Electric Co. v. United States Fidelity & Guaranty Co.	87
Bambu Sales, Inc. v. Sultana Crackers, Inc.	521;526-27
Bamco 18 v. Reeves	256
Banco Nacional de Cuba v. Sabbatino	252;819
Banco Ambrosiano v. Artoc Bank & Trust Ltd.	50;56;57
Bank of America v. Parnell	198
Bank of America Nat., Trust and Sav. Assoc. v. Gillaizeau	511
Bank of Montreal v. Eagle Assoc.	682
Bankers Trust Co. v. Mallis	704
Baptiste v. Sennet & Krumholz	510
Barco Arroyo v. Federal Emergency Management Agency	45
Baron Bros. Co. v. Stewart	272
Baron & Company, Inc. v. Bank of New Jersey	819
Barrentine v. Arkansas-Best Freight System, Inc.	773
Barrick Group, Inc. v. Mosse	372
Bartholomew v. CNG Producing Co.	688
Baskin v. Hawley	691;696
Battery Steamship Corp. v. Refineria Panama, S.A.	521
Bayersdorfer v. Secretary of Health and Human Sevices	316
Beacon Theaters, Inc. v. Westover	274;562-63;566;730
Beacon v. R.M. Jones Apartment Rentals	385
Beard v. Mitchell	589
Beary v. West Publishing Co.	508
Beaufort Concrete Co. v. Atlantic States	510-11
Beaunit Mills, Inc. v. Eday Fabric Sales Corp.	566
Beaunit Mills, Inc. v. Industries Reunides F. Matarazzo	188
Beech Nut, Inc. v. Warner-Lambert Co.	101

Beimart v. Burlington N., Inc.	591
Belfiore v. New York Times Co.	506
Belknap v. Leary	169
Bell v. Louisville & Nashville, R.R.	792
Bellmore v. Mobil Oil Corp.	576
Benson v. RMJ Securities	505
Benton Graphics v. Uddeholm Corp.	335;797;798
Bereslavsky v. Caffey	576
Berger v. Winer Sportswear, Inc.	266
Berisford Capital Corp v. Syncom Corp.	576
Berman v. Dean Witler & Co. Inc.	672
Bernard v. U.S. Lines, Inc.	270
Bernardine v. Rederi A/B Saturnus	596
Bernhard v. Harrah's Club	232-33
Bernhardt v. Polygraphic Co. of Am., Inc.	192;207;216
Berry Petroleum Co. v. Adams & Peck	880
Bersch v. Drexel Firestone, Inc.	797
Best v. District of Columbia	627
Beyah v. Coughlin	520
Biesenkamp v. Atlantic Richfield Co.	573
Billy v. Ashland Oil, Inc.	32
Birch Shopping Corporation v. Embassy of United Republic of Tanzania	818
Birnbaum v. United States	668
Biscup v. New York	93
Blank v. Ronson Corp.	433
Block v. First Blood Assocs.	85
Blonder-Tongue Laboratories, Inc. v. University of Illinois Foundation	752;758
Blossom Farm Products Co. v. Amtraco Commodity Corp.	310
Blue Chip Stamps v. Manor Drug Stores	153
Blum v. Stenson	297
Board of Education of New York v. City-Wide Comm. for Integration of Schools	100
Board of Education v. New York State Human Rights Appeal Board	771
Boeing v. VanGemert	284
Boggs v. Darr	33;784
Bolan v. Lehigh Valley R.R.	598;600
Boland v. Bank Sepah-Iran	94
Bomze v. Nardis Sportswear, Inc.	96;97
Bongards' Creameries v. Alfa-Laval, Inc.	792
Bottaro v. Hatton Associates	553
Bournias v. Atlantic Maritime Co.	210
Bower v. Weisman	492-93
Bowers v. Buchanan	367
Boyd v. Bulala	697-98
Boyle v. United Technologies Corp.	197
Bozant v. Bank of New York	533
Bradford v. Harding	92
Branch v. Reynolds Metals Co.	285

TABLE OF AUTHORITIES 995

Brandon v. Holt	701
Brastex Corp. v. Allen Int'l.	176
Bratt v. IBM	512
Bray v. New York Life Insurance	772
Breslerman v. American Liberty Ins. Co.	86;87
Bridge C.A.T. Scan Associates v. Technicare Corp.	336
British Caledonian Airway v. First State Bank	511
Brock v. Tolkow	182
Brotherhood of R.R. Trainmen v. Baltimore & Ohio R.R.	264
Browder v. Director, Illinois Dep't of Correction	718
Brown v. Bellaplast Maschinenbau.	783
Brown v. Dean Witter Reynolds, Inc.	672
Brown v. Felsen	749
Brown Shoe Co. v. United States	727
Browne Bros. Cypen Corp. v. Carner Bank of Miami Beach Fla.	92
Bruce v. Chestnut Farms-Chevy Chase Dairy	602
Brueggemeyer v. American Broadcasting Corp.	520;535
Brunett Machine Works Ltd. v. Kockum Industries, Inc.	65
Bruns, Nordeman & Co. v. American National Bank & Trust Co.	61
Bryant v. Finnish Nat'l Airline	51
Bryant v. Ford Motor Co.	85
Buchanan v. Stanships, Inc.	697
Budinich v. Becton Dickinson & Co.	697;727
Buffalo Courier-Express, Inc. v. Buffalo Evening News, Inc.	171
Buffalo Forge Co. v. Ampco-Pittsburgh Corp.	164
Buffalo Valley Gas Authority Litigation, In re	872
Bulova's Will, In re	247
Burford v. SunOil Co.	21
Burger King Corp. v. Rudzewicz.	54
Burlington Northern R.R. Co. v. Woods	200;201;214
Burlington Coat Factory Warehouse Corp. v. Espirit DeCorp.	526
Burnett v. New York Cent. R.R. Co.	72
Burt Printing Co. v. Middle East Media Corp.	174
Burtnieks v. City of New York	518;537
Buryan v. Max Factor & Co.	338
Butler Foods, Inc. v. Trailer Marine Transport Corp.	533
Butler v. National Home for Disabled Volunteer Soldiers	627
Butler v. Polk	82
Butterworth v. Hill.	64
Byrd v. Blue Ridge Rural Electric Coop.	193;193-94;568;575
C.E. Bickfor & Co. v. M.V. "Elly"	302
C.I.T. Leasing Corp. v. Manth Machine & Tool Corp.	32
CBS Inc., v. Ahern.	336
CF&I Steel Corp. v. Mitsui & Co.	367
CMS Software Design Sys., Inc. v. Info. Designs, Inc.	699
Cabarga-Cruz v. Fundacion Educativa Ana.	508
Calder v. Jones	54
Caldwell v. Wheeler.	363
California Fruit Exch. v. Henry	601

Calloway v. Marvel Entertainment Group	538
Cameron v. Fogarty	758
Camp v. Gress	64
Canadian Javelin, Ltd. v. SEC	108
Cann v. Ford Motor Co.	594-95;598
Capital Nat'l Bank of N.Y. v. McDonald's Corp.	248
Capital Telephone Co. v. Pattersonville Telephone Co.	758
Caravan Mobile Home Sales v. Lehman Bros.	530
Cargill, Inc. v. Sabine Trading & Shipping Co., Inc.	188
Carlenstolpe v. Merck & Co.	77;220-21
Carlsberg Resources Corp. v. Cambria Sav. & Loan Ass'n	256
Carlton v. Interfaith Medical Center	516
Carlton v. Bawn, Inc.	260
Carnegie-Mellon Univ. v. Cohill	88;100
Carr v. Monroe Mfg. Co.	385
Carr v. Watts	586
Carter Products, Inc. v. Eversharp, Inc.	371
Carter Wallace Inc. v. Riverton Laboratories, Inc.	488
Carter Wallace, Inc. v. Davis-Edwards Pharmacal Corp.	168
Cascone v. Ortho Pharmaceutical Corp.	574
Cascone v. Ortho Pharmaceutical Corp.	98;578
Case v. Abrams	726
Castillo v. Shipping Corp. of India	74
Catalyst Energy Dev. Corp. v. Iron Mountain Mines, Inc.	33
Catapano v. Western Airlines, Inc.	578;579
Caterpillar v. Williams	82;83
Catlin v. United States	727
Cavuoto v. Smith	385
CeCom, Inc. v. Micro Tempus, Inc.	783
Celanese Corp. of America v. Vandelia Warehouse Corp.	258
Celotex Corp. v. Catrett	503;505-06;511;517-19; 525-27;531-33
Celton Man Trade, Inc. v. Utex, S.A.	52
Center v. K-Mart Corp.	493
Central R.R. Co. v. Monahan	650
Central Maine Power Co. v. Foster Wheeler Corp.	698-99
Centronics Data Computer Corp. v. Mannesmann, A.G.	54
Certain Complaints Under Investigation by an Investigating Comm., In re	371
Champion Spark Plug Co. v. Karchmar	64
Chan v. Korean Air Lines, Ltd.	880
Chandler Leasing Co., v. UCC, Inc.	500
Chandler v. Coughlin	509;520
Chapman v. Dow Chem. Co.	197;215
Chardon v. Soto	285
Chartener v. Kice	210
Chase & Sanborn Corp., In re	55
Cheeseman v. Carey	64
Cherokee Laboratories, Inc. v. Pierson	694
Chiarello v. Domenico Bus Serv., Inc.	594
Chicago R.I.P. Ry. Co. v. Martin	92

TABLE OF AUTHORITIES

Chicago v. Stude	92
Chicago, Rock Island & Pac. R.R. v. Stude	92
Childs v. Brandon	210
Chodos v. F.B.I.	309
Christianson v. Colt Industries Operating Corp.	731
Chronister v. Sam Tanksley Trucking, Inc.	33
Church of Scientology International v. Elmira Mission	164
Churchill Forest Industries (Manitoba) Ltd. v. SEC	789
Citicorp v. Interbank Card Ass'n	317
Clark v. John Lamula Inv., Inc.	592
Clark v. Paul Gray, Inc.	11
Clark v. South Central Bell Tel. Co.	288
Clark v. Tarant County	510
Clark v. United States	182
Clark Equipment Credit Corp. v. Martin Lumber Co.	512
Clarkson Co. v. Shaheen	166;168
Clayton v. Douglas	693
Clearfield Trust Co. v. United States	197
Clem v. Allied Van Lines Int'l Corp.	358
Coastal Transfer Co. v. Toyota Motor Sales, U.S.A.	702
Cobbledick v. United States	703-04
Coca Cola Co. v. Howard Johnson Co.	488
Cohen v. Franchard Corp.	592-93
Cohen v. Beneficial Industrial Loan Corp.	169;176;728
Cohen v. Uniroyal	285
Colan v. Cutler-Hammer, Inc.	521
Coleman v. City of Okla	593
Colgrove v. Batlin	584
Collins v. Foreman	318-19
Colonial Realty Corp. v. Bache & Co.	84
Colorado River Water Conserv. Dist. v. United States	21;308
Colorado v. Symes	88
Combs v. Nick Garin Trucking	32
Comm'r v. Estate of Bedford	704
Commissioner on Indep. Colleges and Univs. v. N.Y. Temporary State Comm'r	512
Commonwealth Edison Co. v. Allis-Chalmers Mfg. Co.	489
Commonwealth Oil/Tesoro Petroleum Securities, Litigation, In re	873
Compagnie Francaise d'Assurance Pour Le Commerce Exterieur v. Phillips Petroleum Co.	430;447
Competex, S.A. v. La Bow	206;208
Computer Strategies Inc. v. Commodore Business Machines, Inc.	174
Concession Consultants, Inc. v. Mirisch	62
Cone v. West Virginia Pulp & Paper Co.	684;691
Conley v. Gibson	142;373
Connecticut General Life Ins. Co. v. Cohen	10
Continental Casualty Co. v. DLH Services, Inc.	699
Continental Casualty Co. v. Howard	697
Contra La Chemise LaCoste v. The Alligator Co.	82

Cook v. Pension Ben Guarantee Corp.	527
Cook v. United States	782
Cool Fuel, Inc. v. Connett.	512
Cooper v. Welch Foods, Inc.	336;352
Cooper v. Federal Reserve Bank.	749;751
Cooper Industries, Inc. v. British Aerospace	447
Coopers & Lybrand v. Livesay	728
Corbin v. FDIC	182
Corcoran v. Ardra Ins. Co.	23
Corke v. Sameiet M.S. Song of Norway	72
Corporation of Lloyd's v. Lloyd's U.S.	371
Corporation of New Orleans v. Winter.	13
Corrugated Container Antitrust Litigation, In re	879;881
Cowan v. United States	272
Crane Co. v. American Standard	881
Crawford v. United States	509
Crimm v. Missouri Pac. R.R. Co.	491
Crisafuli v. Childs	246
Cross v. United States Trust Co.	247
Cross-Florida Barge Canal Litigation, In re	873
Cryomedics, Inc. v. Spembly, Ltd.	54
Cullen v. Margiotta	596
Cumberland Oil Corp. v. Thropp	504;518;526;536
Cunningham v. Quaker Oats Co.	314;687
Curko v. Wiliam Spencer & Sons Corp.	593
Curry v. Moore-McCormack Lines, Inc.	601
Curtis v. Loether	564
Cutco Industries, Inc. v. Naughton.	58;234-35
Cutlas Prods., Inc. v. Bregman	595;600
Dairy Queen, Inc. v. Wood	565-66
Dalbec v. Gentleman's Companion, Inc.	687
Daley v. ALIA	33
Damsky v. Zavatt.	570
Darlak v. Robear.	510
Data General Corp. Antitrust Litigation, In re.	873;883
Data Digests, Inc. v. Standard & Poor's Corp.	310
Davenport v. Webb.	213
Davenport v. Proctor & Gamble Mfg. Co.	81
Davis, In re	836
Davis v. Baer.	93
Davis v. Bryan.	509
Davis v. Buffalo Psychiatric Center	313
Davis v. Costa-Gavras	523
Davis v. Fendler.	434
Davis v. McLaughlin	310
Davis v. Musler	31;33;42
Davis v. Smith	310
Davis v. United States	702
Day Zimmerman, Inc. v. Challoner	205
Dayco Corp. v. Foreign Transactions Corp.	176
Dean Witter Reynolds Inc. v. Byrd	669;749

TABLE OF AUTHORITIES 999

Deats v. Joseph Swantak, Inc.	99
DeBeers Consolidated Mines v. U.S.	714
Delicata v. Bowen	45
Del Raine v. Carlson	32
Delta S.S. Lines, Inc. v. Albano	32
DeMarines v. KLM Royal Dutch Airlines	688
DeMelo v. Toche Marine, Inc.	26
Denis v. Liberty Mut. Ins. Co.	510
Dennis v. BASF Wyandotte Corp.	330
Denofre v. Transp. Ins. Rating Bureau	700
Denver & Rio Grande Western R.R. Co. v. Bhd. of R.R. Trainmen	65
Deposit Guarantee Nat'L Bank v. Roper	284
Dery v. Wyer	267-68
DeSeversky v. Republic Aviation Corp.	413
DeSylva v. Ballentino	196
Detection Systems, Inc. v. Pitt Way Corp.	317
Detroit, City of v. Grinnell Corp.	297
Detsch & Co. v. American Products	388
DeVillenve v. Morning Journal Ass'n	801
DeVore & Sons, Inc. v. Aurora Pacific Cattle Co.	315
DeWeerth v. Baldinger	206;207;210
Dietrich v. Texas Nat'l Petroleum Co.	792
Diamond Shamrock Chemical Co., In re	215
Dienstag v. Bronsen	182
Dillard v. Blackburn	508
Di Meglio v. Italia Crociere Internazionale	93
Dimick v. Schiedt	696;702
D'Ippolito v. Cities Service Co.	254
Dixon v. Int'l Harvester Co.	493
Dobelle v. National R.R. Passenger Corp.	214
Doe v. Randall	709
D'Oench, Duhme & Co. v. Federal Deposit Ins. Corp.	197
Dolgow v. Anderson	302;497
Donahue v. Windsor Locks Bd. of Fire Com'rs	506;519
Donaldson v. Clark	509;513
Donnelly v. Guion	520
Donovan v. Bierwirth	171
Donovan v. Diplomat Envelope Corp.	528
Donovan v. Pen Shipping Co.	695-96
Donovan v. Porter	523
Dopp v. Franklin National Bank	168;172
Doran v. Salem Inn., Inc.	171
Dow Chemical Company "Sarabond" Products Liability Litigation, In re	871;874;880
Dow Chemical Pacific Ltd. v. Rascator Maritime S.A.	701
Dow Corning Corp. v. General Electric Co.	310
Downs v. Am. Mot. Liab. Ins. Co.	240
D.P. Apparel Corp. v. Roadway Express, Inc.	698-99
Dr. Franklin Perkins School v. Freeman	12
Drewett v. Aetna Casualty & Surety Co.	486

Drexel Burnham Lambert, Inc. v. D'Angelo	57
Dreyfus v. Von Finck	9
Dri Mark Products, Inc. v. Meyercord Co.	95
DuPont v. Southern Nat'l Bank	698-99
Duke v. University of Texas	285
Dundas Shipping & Trading Co. Ltd. v. Stravelaks Bros. Ltd.	676
Duplar Corp v. Deering Milliken, Inc.	535
Dusoneko v. Maloney	516;524
Dziwanoski v. Ocean Carriers Corp.	461
EEOC v. Sage Realty Corp.	311
Eaddy v. Little	496
Eastman Machine Co., Inc. v. United States	510;517
Eastway Constr. Corp. v. City of New York	506;526;536
Ebbinghouse v. Clark	559
Ebker v. Tan Jay Int'l, Inc.	691
Eden Foods, Inc. v. Eden's Own Prods., Inc.	32
Edwards v. Born	554
Eisen v. Carlisle & Jacquelin	728
Eisenhardt v. Coastal Indus., Inc.	87
El Cid, Ltd. v. N.J. Zinc. Co.	246
Electro Catheter Corp. v. Surgicial Specialties Instrument Co. Inc.	507
Electronic Data Systems Corp. v. Kinder	87
Elfand v. Widman	11
Elton Leather Corp. v. First General Resources Co.	176
Employee Savings Plan of Mobil Oil Corp. v. Vickery	311;314
Empressa Hondurena de Vapores, S.A. v. McLeod	171
Encoder Communications, Inc. v. Telegen, Inc.	84
Entron, Inc. v. Affiliated FM Ins. Co.	206;213
Environmental Defense Fund Inc. v. Andrus	169
Epstein v. Wilder	33;784
Equity Funding Corp. Securities Litigation, In re	872;878
Ercolani v. Excelsior Ins. Co.	700
Erie Conduit Corp. v. MAPA	698
Erie R.R. Co. v. Tompkins	162;191-92;196;198-99; 201-02;205;237;274;567
Errion v. Connell	36
Esquire Radio & Elec., Inc. v. Montgomery Ward & Co., Inc.	686-87
Evans v. Jeff D.	559
Evans v. Syracuse City School District	311
Evers v. General Motors	535
Ewing v. United States	656
Ex Parte Republic of Peru	813
Executive Committee Members v. Union of India	789
Executive Financial Services, Inc. v. Heart Chec, Inc.	20
Exterior Sliding and Aluminum Coil Antitrust Litigation, In re	881
FMC Corp. v. Glouster Engineer Mg. Co.	882
F.O.F. Propriety Funds, Ltd., v. Arthur Young & Co.	789
FRA S.P.A. v. Surg-O-Flex of America, Inc.	485
FTC v. Carter	368
FTC. v. Compagnie de Saint-Gobain-Pont-a-Moussan	368

TABLE OF AUTHORITIES 1001

FTC v. Owens-Corning Fiberglas Corp.	108
Factors Etc. Inc. v. Prol Arts, Inc.	75;206
Fahey, Ex parte	730
Fair (the) v. Kohler Die & Specialty Co.	82
Fairchild Stratos Corp. v. General Electric Co.	683
Falls Riverway Realty v. City of Niagara Falls	518;531
Farmland Dairies v. Barber	212
Fay v. South Colonie School District	771-72
Feder v. Turkish Airlines	57
Federal Aviation Administration v. Landy	336
Federated Dep't Stores Inc. v. Moitie	749; 751
Federal Deposit Inc., Corp. v. Arcadia Marine Inc.	528
Federal Deposit Ins. Corp v. Ernst & Ernst	339
Federal Prescription Service, Inc., v. American Pharmaceutical Ass'n.	716
Federman v. Empire First and Marine Ins., Co.	187-88
Felice v. Long Island Railroad Co.	655
Felix Cinematografica S.R.I. v. Penthouse Intern, Ltd.	260
Fellman v. Fireman's Fund Insurance Co.	319
Feng Yeat Chow v. Shavohnessy	510
Ferguson v. Ford Motor Co.	368
Ferguson v. Tabah	178
Ficalora v. Lockhead California Co.	554
Fidenas AG v. Compagnie Internatinale Pour L'Informatique CII Honeywell Ball S.A.	789
Filner v. Shapiro	701
Financial Services Corp. v. Weindruch	698
Finch v. Marathon Securities Corp.	789
Fino v. McCullum Mining Co.	388
Fire Disaster at DuPont Plaza Hotel, In re	874
Firestone Tire & Rubber Co. v. Coleman	108;728
First American Bank N.A. v. United Equity Corp.	507
First City Federal Sav. Bank v. Bhogaonker	526
First Colonial Corp. of America, In re	264
First Tennessee Bank v. Federal Deposit Ins. Corp.	409
First National Bank of Arizona v. Cities Serv. Co.	508;526
First National Bank of Cincinnati v. Pepper	507
First Nat'l Bank & Trust Co. of Okla.City v. Port Lavaca Vending Mach., Inc.	87
Fisher v. Harris, Upham & Co.	320
Fishgold v. Sullivan Drydock & Repair Corp.	264
Flaherty v. Coughlin	524
Folding Carton Antitrust Litigation, In re	409;444
Foman v. Davis	310
Fontenot v. Mesa Petroleum Co.	701
Fontenot v. Upjohn Co.	503;522
Ford v. Estelle	316
Ford Motor Co. v. Bryant	85
Ford Motor Co. v. Ryan	76
Forry, Inc. v. Neundorfer,Inc.	767
Fort Howard Paper Co. v. William D. Witter, Inc.	203;214;245

Forts v. Ward	168
Foster v. Boise-Cascade, Inc.	288
Foster v. Litton Industries	74
Foster-Milburn Co. v. Knight	73;74
Four Keys Leasing & Maintenance Corp. v. Simithis	102
Fourco Glass Co. v. Transmirra Products Corp.	69
Franchise Tax Bd. of Cal. v. Constr. Laborers Vac. Trust For S. Cal	82
Frank B. Hall & Co. v. Rushmore Ins. Co.	97;98
Franklin National Bank Securities Litigation, In re	871
Frederic Weindersum Assos. v. National Homes Constr. Corp.	589
Freeman v. Bee Mach. Co.	97
Freedman v. Chemical Const. Corp.	235;244
Freeman v. Franzen	688
French v. Banco Nacional de Cuba	252
French v. Hay	97
Fritzlen v. Boatmen's Bank	100
Frouge Corp. v. Chase Manhattan Bank, N.A.	511
Fuchs Sugars & Syrups, Inc., v. Amstar Corp.	485
Fugard v. Thierry	94
Fustok v. Conticommodity Services Line, Inc.	190
G. & A. Books, Inc., In re	510
Gainey v. Brotherhood of R. & S.S. Clerks	498
Galef v. Alexander	250
Galella v. Onassis	336;385
Galiardi, In re	718
Galindo v. Precision American Corp.	520
Gallick v. Baltimore & O. R.R.	597
Glasstech Inc. v. ABKno OY	876
Gamble v. Central of GA. Ry. Co.	90
Gardner and Florence Call Cowles Found. v. Empire, Inc.	86;99
Gardner v. United States	265
Gargiul v. Tompkins	759-60
Garrity v. Lyle Stuart, Inc.	677
Gasoline Products v. Champlin Refining Co.	684
Gateway Bottling, Inc. v. Dad's Rootbeer Co.	485
Gatling v. Atlantic Richfield Co.	520
Gautreaux v. Pierce	715
Gear, Inc. v. L.A. Gear Calif., Inc.	516
General Inv. Co. of Conn., Inc. v. Ackerman	257
General Electric Credit Corp. v. Toups	75
George v. Hilaire Farm Nursing Home	516
Georgia v. Rachel	89
Gerety v. Inland Newspaper Representatives, Inc.	94
Gerlach v. Michigan Bell Telephone Co.	183
Ghandi v. Police Dep't.	371
Gibbons v. Udaras noz Gaeltachta	816
Gibson-Homans Co. v. New Jersey Transit Corp.	13
Gieringer v. Silverman	530
Gilbert v. Burnstine	236
Gilmore v. Shearson/American Express, Inc.	679

TABLE OF AUTHORITIES 1003

Gladrow v. Weisz	371
Globe Liquor Co. v. San Roman	691
Goetschius v. Brightman	247
Goldbaum v. Bank Leumi Trust Co. of New York	303
Goldey v. Morning News	96
Goldlawn, Inc. v. Heiman	72
Goldman v. Belden	339;509
Goldman Sachs & Co. v. Edelstein	577
Goldschmidt, v. Smith	335
Golkin v. Abrams	759-60
Gonsalves v. AMOCO Shipping Co.	90;91
Gonzalez v. Progressive Tool & Die Co.	254
Goodman v. Mead Johnson & Co.	470
Gordon v. Hunt	45
Gordon v. Washington	177
Grace v. Carroll	259
Grace & Co. v. City of Los Angeles	441
Graef v. Graef	82
Graham Eng'g Corp. v. Kemp Prods., Ltd.	55
Gramatan-Sullivan, Inc. v. Koslow	258
Gramaton Home Investors Corp. v. Lopez	758
Grand Bahama Petroleum Co. v. Canadian Transportation Agencies, Ltd.	804
Grand Union Co. v. Cord Meyer Develop. Corp.	505
Granfinanciera, S.A. v. Nordberg	55
Granny Goose Foods, Inc. v. Bhd. of Teamsters & Auto Truck Drivers	98
Grant v. United States	169
Gray v. Am. Radiator and Standard Sanitary Corp.	786
Great Coastal Express, Inc. v. International Brotherhood of Teamsters	599
Great N. Ry. Co. v. Alexander	82
Great Southern Fire Proof Hotel Co. v. Jones	14
Greco v. ABC Transnational Corp.	519
Green v. American Tobacco Co.,	598
Green v. Humphrey Elevator & Truck Co.	32
Green v. Zuck	93
Greenblatt v. Drexell Burnham Lambert, Inc.	687
Greenfield v. Villager Industries	288;296
Greenspun v. Lindley	249-50
Greenwood City of, Miss. v. Peacock	89
Greenwood v. Dittmer	388
Gribble v. Harris	700
Griffin v. McCoach	275
Griffin v. Red Run Lodge, Inc.	12
Grigoleit Co. v. United Rubber, Cork, Linoleum & Plastic Workers of America,	512
Grogg v. Missouri Pac. R.R.	689
Guaranty Trust Co. v. York	194
Guerrino v. Ohio Casualty Insurance Co.	14
Guilloz v. Falmouth Hospital Ass'n, Inc.	330

Guiterrez v. Vegari	311
Gulf Oil Corp. v. Gilbert	76;77;220;790
Gutwein v. Roche Labs	508
Guy v. Citizens Fidelity Bank & Trust C. v. Byrne	275
Haar v. Armendaris Corp.	52;58
Haelan Laboratories, Inc. v. Topps Chewing Gum, Inc.	99
Hages v. Aliquippa & So. R.R. Co.	90
Hales v. Winn-Dixie Stores, Inc.	11
Hall v. Sharpe	316
Hallinan v. United States	627
Halloran v. Ohlmeyer Communications Co.	528
Hamman v. Southwestern Gas Pipeline	512
Hancock Industries v. Schaeffer	508;510;523
Handley v. Indiana & Michigan Elec. Co.	50
Hanley v. United States	627
Hanlin v. Mitchelson	410
Hanna v. Plumer	155;193;195-96;198-99; 201
Hansberry v. Lee	281-82
Hansen v. Prentice-Hall, Inc.	528
Hanson v. Denckla	53
Hanson Trust PLC v. MLSCM Corp.	171
Hanson Trust PLC v. MLSCM Acquisition, Inc.	171
Harcon Bridge Co. v. D & G Boat Rentals, Inc.	682
Hargrave v. Oki Nursery, Inc.	49
Haring v. Prosise	749;754-55
Harkins v. Ford Motor Co.	694
Harlem River Produce Co. v. Aetna Casualty & Surety Co.	95
Harper v. Sonnabend	87
Harris v. Steinem	187
Harris v. Browning-Ferris Industries Chemicals Services, Inc.	783
Harris v. G.C. Servs. Corp.	87
Harris, In re	95
Harrison v. Prather	368
Harrison v. Flota Mercante Grancolombiana, S.A.	270
Harrisonville v. W.S. Dickey Clay Manufacturing Co.	164
Harry Rich Corp. v. Curtiss-Wright Corp.	73
Hart v. General Motors Corp.	250
Harvey Cartoons v. Columbia Pictures Indus., Inc.	516
Haven Industries, Inc. Securities Litigation, In re	873
Haymes v. Columbia Pictures Corp.	358
Haynes v. Kleinwefers	335;797-98
Hearst Corp. v. Shopping Center Network, Inc.	94
Heifetz v. Tugendrajch	81
Helminski v. Ayerst Laboratories	683-84
Hensley v. Eckerhart	297
Hepburn v. Ellzey	13
Hercules Inc. v. Dynamic Export Corp.	257
Herman & MacLean v. Huddleston	23
Herrington v. Sonoma County	689
Herron v. Southern Pacific Co.	568

TABLE OF AUTHORITIES 1005

Hess v. Gray	257
Hess v. New Jersey Transit Rail Operations, Inc.	547
Hetzel v. Jewel Cos., Inc.	591
Heyco, Inc. v. Heyman	74;75
Heyman v. Commerce & Indust. Ins. Co.	506
Hickman v. Taylor	328;392
Higgins v. Boeing Co.	98;578
Hill v. Coca Cola Bottling Company	769;771-72
Hillburn v. Maher	687;701
Hipp v. United States	266
Hodgson v. Randall	709
Hoffman v. Charnita, Inc.	285
Hoffman v. Blaski	72;73;74
Hoffritz For Cutlery, Inc. v. Amajac, Ltd.	58
Hoh v. Pepsico, Inc.	168
Holding Capital Group, Inc. v. A.P. and Co.	245
Home Ins. Co. v. Dick	193
Honeywell, Inc. v. Metz Apparate-Werke	54
Honojosa v. Terrell, Texas, City of	689
Horizons Titanium Corp. v. Norton Co.	371
Horton v. Moore-McCormack Lines, Inc.	267
Housman v. Buckley	207
Hubicki v. ACF Industries, Inc.	508
Hudson v. Hermann Pfauter GmbH & Co.	797-98
Humana, Inc. v. Jacobson	32
Humble Oil & Ref. Co. v. Sun-Oil Co.	262
Hunter v. Greene	203;240;245
Hunter v. H.D. Lee Co., Inc.	153
Hurd v. American Hoist & Derrick Co.	689
Hurn v. Oursler	17
Hutchinson v. Ross	248
Hyman v. American Export Lines, Inc.	358
IIT v. VenCap, Ltd.	789
ITT v. Cornfield	373;789
Illinois v. City of Milwaukee	9
Incontrade, Inc. v. Oilburn International, S.A.	174
Index Fund, Inc. v. Hagopian	189;265-66
Industrial Consultants, Inc. v. H.S. Equities, Inc.	205
Industrial Inv. Development Corp. v. Mitsui & Company	788
Industries, Inv. Etc. v. Panelfab Int'l	596
Ingram v. Kumar	314
Ins. Corp. of Ireland v. Compagnie des Bauxites de Guinee	58
Intercontinental Planning Ltd. v. Daystrom	240;244-45
Intermeat, Inc. v. American Poultry, Inc.	57
Int'l Controls Corp. v. Vesco	49;783
Int'l Shoe Co. v. State of Washington	53;786;805
Int'l Union of Elec. Radio and Mach. Workers AFL/CIO v. Westinghouse Elec. Corp.	409-10
Invst Financial Group, Inc. v. Chem-Nuclear Systems, Inc.	508
Ionian Shipping Co. v. British Law Ins. Co.	264
Iran Islamic, Republic of v. Pahlavi	218-20

Isaksen v. Vermont Castings, Inc.	696
Isbrandtsen Co. v. National Marine Eng'rs Beneficial Assoc.	40
Istituto per lo Sviluppo Economico Dell' Italia Meridionale v. Sperti Prods., Inc.	98
Ivy v. Security Borge Lines, Inc.	590
J.C. Motor Lines, Inc. v. Trailways Bus System, Inc.	600
J.E. Mamive & Sons, Inc. v. Fidelity Bank	529
Jackson Dairy Inc. v. H.P. Hood & Sons, Inc.	164
Jacobson v. John Hancock Mut. Life Ins. Co.	526
Jaffe v. Dolan.	67
James River Flood Control Ass'n v. Watt	170
James v. Powell	203;213;246
Janus Films, Inc. v. Miller	556
Jarvis v. Johnson	549
Jean v. Nelson	170
Jefferson Standard Ins. Co. v. Craven	274
John Jenco v. Martech Int'l Inc.	797
John Deere Co. v. American Nat'l. Bank	515
John Hancock Mut. Life Ins. Co. v. Kraft	275
John Simmons Co. v. Grier Brothers Co.	720
Johnson v. Parrish.	695
Johnson v. Unites States Postal Serv.	699-700
Johnson v. Mississippi	89
Johnson v. Trueblood.	687
Jones Knitting Corp. v. A.M. Pullen & Co.	258
Jones & Guerrero Co. v. Sealift Pacific	719
Jones v. New York City Human Resources Administration.	309
Justice v. Fabey.	507
Kadane v. Hofstra University	698
Kaestel v. Lockhart	510
Kahane v. Carlson.	64
Kamen v. American Tel & Tel. Co.	518;520
Kamens v. Horizon Corp.	409
Karns v. Emerson Elec. Co.	690
Katz v. Gladstone.	533
Kearney v. New York State Legislature	500
Keen v. Detroit Diesel Allison.	464
Keeton v. Hustler Magazine, Inc.	54
Keil Lock Co., Inc. v. Earle Hardware Manufacturing Co.	188
Kelleam v. Maryland Casualty Co.	177
Kelly v. Shamrock Oil & Gas Corp.	570
Kennedy v. Josephthal & Co.	519
Kennerly v. Aro, Inc.	500
Kentucky v. Powers	89
Kerschbaumer v. Bell	385
Key West, Inc. v. United States	509
Kicklighter v. Nails by Jannee, Inc.	269
Kiernan v. Van Schaik	584
King v. Order of United Commercial Travelers	206
Kinney v. Columbia Savings & Loan Ass'n.	95
Kirkland v. City of Peekskill	775

TABLE OF AUTHORITIES

Misco Leasing, Inc. v. Vaughn	722
Mississippi Publishing Corp. v. Murphree	27;48
Miss Universe, Inc. v. Patricelli	373
Mitchell, In re	457
Mitchell v. All-States Business Products Corp.	321
Mitchell v. Baldrige	699;700
Mitchell v. Forsyth	728
Mokhiber v. Cohn	554
Monarch Indus. Corp. v. American Motorists Inc. Co.	267
Montalbano v. Easco Hand Tools, Inc.	45;47;54
Montana v. United States	749
Montreal Trading Limited v. AMAX, Inc.	788
Moody v. Town of Weymouth	510
Moog, In re	850
Moor v. County of Alameda	19
Moore v. General Motors Corp.	492
Moorehead v. Clark Equip. Co.	492
Moosman v. Joseph P. Blitz	464
Morfeld v. Kehm	688
Morgan Guar. Trust Co. v. Texasgulf Aviation, Inc.	493
Morgan v. Koch	627,688
Morning Telegraph v. Powers	168-69
Morris v. Gilbert	509
Morrison v. Frito-Lay Inc.	896
Morrissey v. Curran	511-12
Morse v. Elmira Country Club	32
Moses H. Cone Memorial Hosp. v. Mercury Construction Corp.	21
Moss v. Hornig	649
Moss v. Ward	512
Motion Picture Licensing Antitrust Litigation, In re	873
Motions Picture "Standard Accessaries" and "Pre-Vues" Antitrust Litigation, In re	872
Mullane v. Central Hanover Bank & Trust Co.	37,295
Municipal Leasing Corp. v. Fulton County	700
Murphy v. Gallagher	761;763-66;768
Murphy v. L.J. Press Corp.	628
Nader v. General Motors Corp.	120
Napolitano v. Compania Sud Americana de Vapores	303
National Am. Corp. v. Fed. Republic of Nigeria	263
National Automotive Publications, Inc. v. United States Lines, Inc.	317
National Bank of Canada v. Interbank Card Ass'n	788
National Bank & Trust Co. of N. Am. Ltd. v. J.L.M. Int'l, Inc.	173
National Life Ins. Co. v. Hartford Accident and Indem. Co.	371
National R.R., Passenger Corp. v. One 25,900 Square Foot Land in the City of New London.	491
National S.S. Co. v. Tugman	96
National Upholstory Co. v. Corley	85
Naturalization of 68 Philippine War Veterans, In re	775;776
Naylor v. Case & McGrath, Inc.	95

Neal v. Butler Aviation Int. Inc.	208
Neirbo Co. v. Bethlehem Shipbuilding Corp.	62
Neizer v. Sheet Metal Workers Int'l Ass'n.	300
Nelson v. Greenspoon	263
Nelson v. Regan	709
Nelson v. Smith	316
Nesslage v. York Sec.	679
Nestle Co., Inc. v. Chester's Market, Inc.	510
Nettles v. Wainwright	316
Neumeier v. Keuhner	205;224;226;229;230; 231
Nevada v. Hall	212
Nevada v. United States	749
New England Apple Council v. Donovan	108
New York v. Bowen	517,525
New York v. Nuclear Regulatory Comm'n	164
New York Ass'n. for Retarded Children v. Carey	256,260
New York, Board of Educ. of v. City-Wide Comm. for Integration of Schools	100
New York City Municipal Securities Litigation, In re	876
New York, City of v. Pullman, Inc.	588
New York Life Ins. Co. v. Connecticut Dev. Auth.	270
New York Shipping Ass'n v. Int'l Longshoremen's Ass'n, AFL-CIO	83
New York State Energy Research & Dev, Auth. v. Nuclear Fuel Serv., Inc.	521
Newman v. Piggie Park Enter.	284
Newmark v. Abeel	364
Newton, Town of v. Rumery	559
Nichols v. Asbestos Workers Local 24 Pension Plan	697
Niles-Bement-Pond Co. v. Iron Moulders' Union Local 68.	15
999 v. C.I.T. Corp.	469
Nobile v. Pension Comm. of Pension Plan	564
Noonan v. Cunard Steamship Co.	577
Nordlicht v. New York Tel.	100
Norlin Corp. v. Rooney, Pace, Inc.	205;250
Northern Cheyenne Tribe v. Hodel	698
Northern Ill. Gas Co. v. Airco Indus. Gases	92
Northern Pipeline Construction Co. v. Marathon Pipe Line Co.	830;832;834;835
Northwestern Flyers, Inc. v. Olson Bros. Mfg. Co.	490
Novak v. World Bank	36
Nucorp Energy Sec. Litigation, In re	880
O'Brien v. King World Prods., Inc.	564
Oceana Int'l., Inc., In re	264
Ockert v. Union Barge Line Corp.	496
O'Connor v. Western Freight Ass'n.	254
Odette v. Shearson, Hamill & Co.	149
Oetiker v. Jurid Werke, G.M.B.H.	49
Office of Personnel Mang. v. Am. Fed. of Gov. Employees.	168
Ohntrup v. Forearms Center, Inc.	818

TABLE OF AUTHORITIES 1013

Olberding v. Illinois Cent. R.R. Co.	62
Olegario v. United States	775;776
Olinick, A & Sons v. Demster Bros.	73;75
Oliver v. McBride's Industries, Inc.	312
Oliver v. Thompson	538
Olympic Corp. v. Societe Generale.	268
Olympus Corp. v. Dealer Sales & Serv., Inc.	33
Omawale v. WBZ.	573
Omega Importing Corp. v. Petri-kine Camera Co.	171
Omni Capital Int'l v. Rudolf Wolff & Co.	47;49;53;55
O.P.M. Leasing Serv., Inc., In re	169
Oppenheimer Fund, Inc. v. Sanders	293
Oppenheimer Mendez v. Acevedo	701
Orderline Wholesale Dist. v. Gibbons, Green, Van Amerongen, Inc.	531
Orion Shipping & Trading Co. v. E. States Petroleum Corp. of Panama, S.A.	676
Orlik, L., Ltd. v. Helme Products Inc.	520
Ortiz v. General Motors Acceptance Corp.	93
Osage Oil Exploration, In re.	311
Osborn v. Directors of Bank of United States.	8
Oscanyan v. Arms Company	627
Ouarles v. General Motors Corp.	526
Overpeck v. Chicago Pneumatic Tool Co.	695
Overseas Nat'l Airways, Inv. v. Cargolux Airlines Int'l, S.A.	789
Overseas Programming Companies, Ltd. v. Cinematographische Commerzanstalt.	76
Owen Equip. & Erection Co. v. Kroger	20,267,269
Owen v. City of Independence.	23
P.H. Glatfelter Co. v. Thomas A. Galante & Sons, Inc.	11
Paliaga v. Luckenbach Steamship Co.	269
Palicio, F. v. Comoania S.A. v. Brush.	507
Palmer v. Hoffman.	593
Palmieri v. New York.	339
Pan American Petroleum Corp. v. Superior Court of Del.	82
Paone v. Aeon Realty Corp.	265
Paparelli v. Prudential Ins. Co. of Am.	409
Parento v. Palumbo.	584
Parillo v. Sura	503
Parke-Bernet Galleries, Inc. v. Franklin	52
Parker v. Mack	47
Parklane Hosiery Co. v. Shore	577,749-51,753-54, 758,776
Parr v. United States.	730
Parrett v. Ford Motor Co.	447
Parsons Steel, Inc. v. First Alambama Bank	749;754;756;757
Parsons v. Bedford, Breedlove & Robeson.	563
Patrick v. Beasley	266
Patton v. United States	564
Pecherski v. General Motors Corp.	85
Penn Central Commercial Paper Litigation, In re	882

Pennoyer v. Neff	601
Pennsylvania, Trustees of Univ. of v. Lexington Ins. Co.	690
Pennzoil Co. v. Texaco, Inc.	21
Peralta v. Heights Medical Center	37
Percell's Inc. v. Central Tel. Co.	93
Perma Research & Dev. Co. v. Singer Co.	528
Pernell v. Southall Realty	281
Pershern v. Fiatallis North America, Inc.	686
Pesin v. Goldman, Sachs & Co.	74
Pessin v. Keeneland Ass'n	485
Peter Pan Fabrics, Inc. v. Kay Windsor Frucks, Inc.	269
Peterman v. Chicago, R.I. & Pac. R.R.	694
Petition to Compel Arbitration between Trade & Transport, Inc., In re	801
Pfeil v. Rogers	530
Pfizer Inc. v. Lord	882
Pfotzer v. Aqua Systems, Inc.	349
Philadelphia & Reading R.R. Co. v. McKibbin	785
Philadelphia Gear Corp. v. Am. Pfauter Corp.	335
Philippines, Republic of the v. Marcos	178
Phillips Petroleum Co. v. Shutts	202;205;216
Phillips Petroleum Co. v. Texaco, Inc.	9
Phillips v. Levie	373
Phillips, et al v. Merrill Lynch, Pierce, Fenner & Smith, Inc., et al	672
Photometric Products Corp. v. Radtke	254
Piambino v. Bailey	178
Pierburg GmbH & Co. v. Superior Court	335
Pilkinton v. Pilkinton	9
Pillsbury Co., v. Conboy	879
Pinkney v. Dow Chem. Co.	216,878
Piper Aircraft Co. v. Reyno	15,220,789-91
Pittsburgh Terminal Corp. v. Mid Allegheny Corp.	33
Pittsburgh & Lake Erie R.R. Co. Sec. and Antitrust Litig., In re	880
Plaintiffs v. Union Carbide Corp.	221
Planet Corp. v. Sullivan	501
Plumbing Fixture Cases, In re	872
Plumbing Fixtures Litig., In re	880
Poland v. Atlantis Credit Corp.	274
Polara v. Trans World Airlines	593
Polaroid Corp. v. Polarad Elec. Corp.	373
Polizzi v. Cowles Magazine, Inc.	71
Pollux Marine Agencies, Inc. v. Louis Dreyfus Corp.	310
Poloran Prod., Inc. v. Lybrand Ross Bros. & Montgomery	496
Portsmouth Square, Inc. v. Shareholders	511
Postal Tel. Cable Co v. Alabama	13
Powell v. Ward	320
Powers v. Chesapeake & O. Ry. Co.	84
Prescription Plan Serv. Corp. v. Franco	9

TABLE OF AUTHORITIES 1015

President & Directors of Georgetown College, Inc.,
   Application of 717
Prima Paint Corp. v. Flood & Conklin Mfg. Co., ... 670
Pritchard v. Norton 238
Procario v. Ambach. 64
Proseus v. Anchor Line, Ltd. 352
Prudential Ins. Co. v. Glasgow. 274
Prudential Oil Corp. v. Phillips Petroleum Co. 14
Puerto Rico Aqueduct and Sewer Auth v. Clow Corp. 330
Puerto Rico v. Cordeco Dev. Corp. 82
Puggioni v. Luckenbach Steamship Co., Inc. 588
Pullman Co. v. Jenkins 92
Pure Oil Co. v. Suarez. 69
Puro Int'l of N.J. Corp. v. California Union Ins. Co. 513
Quaker Chair Corp. v. Litton Business Systems, Inc. 337
Quantum Overseas, N.V. v. Touche Ross & Co. 509
Quarantillo v. Consol. Rail Corp. 331
Quarles v. General Motors Corp. 526
Quinn v. Aetna Life & Casualty Co. 84;98
Quinn v. Syracuse Model Neighborhood Corp. 503
R.G. Barry Corp. v. Mushroom Makers, Inc. 94
R.G. & Group Inc. v. Horn & Hardart Co. 531
Radiation Dynamics Inc. v. Goldmuntz 590
Radio Corp. of Am. v. Rauland Corp. 365
Ragen v. Merchant's Transfer & Warehouse Co. 162
Railroad Commission of Texas v. Pullman 21
Ralston Purina Co. v. McFarland. 409
Range Oil Supply Co. v. Chicago, Rock Island & P.R. Co. 81
Rank v. Krug 262
Rankel v. Town of Greenburgh 47
Raymond Lee Organization, Inc. Securities Litigation, In re .. 873
Rea v. Wichita Mortgage Corp. 522
Reading & Bates Corp v. National Iranian Oil Company 825
Recaman v. Barish. 789
Reger v. Nat'l. Ass'n. of Bedding Mgf. Group Ins. Trust Fraud 208
Reid v. Graybeal 557
Reiken v. Nationwide Leisure Corp. 92
Reilly v. Doyle 510
Reilly v. Reid 758
Reiter's Beer Distributors, Inc. v. Christian Schmidt Brewing
   Co. 189
Reitmeier v. Kalinoski 521
Reno Distrib., Inc. v. West Texas Oil Field Equip., Inc. 33,784
Republic of China v. American Express Co. 272,275
Republic of the Philippines v. Marcos 178
Retail Software Services, Inc. v. Lashlee 53;54
Reynolds v. United States 45
Rhea v. Massey-Ferguson, Inc. 667
Ribeiro v. United Fruit Co. 600
Rich v. Kis California, Inc. 797;798
Richards v. United States 233

Richardson Greenshields Securities, Inc. v. Lan	301
Richardson Merrell, Inc., In re	683
Richardson v. United States	686-87
Richardson-Merrell, Inc. "Benedictin" Products Liab. Litig., In re	683,883
Ring v. Spina	570-71
Risher v. United States	300
Riso Kagaku Corp. v. A.B. Dick Co.	75
Rivera v. M/T Fossarina	697
Rivoli Trucking Corp. v. New York Shipping Ass'n	261
Robinson v. Penn Cent. Co.	49
Rogers v. Roth	413
Rollison v. Washington Nat'l Ins. Co.	496
Romain v. Kurek	699;700
Romano v. Merrill Lynch, Pierce, Fenner & Smith	699
Rondeau v. Mosinee Paper Corp.	165
Roorda v. American Oil Co.	310
Ropfogel v. Wise	683
Rorick v. Devon Syndicate, Ltd.	98
Rosen v. Dick	570;571;573;576
Rosenberg v. Martin	312
Rosenblum v. Dig Felder	254
Rosenthal v. Kingsley	527;531
Ross v. Mathis	672
Ross v. Bernhard	563;566
Ross v. Pennsylvania State Univ.	701
Rothenberg v. Kamen	557
Royal School Laboratories, Inc. v. Town of Watertown	275
Ruiz Varela v. Sanches Velez	45
Ruppert, In re	447
Rush Presbyterian St. Luke's Medical Center v. Safeco Insurance Co.	14
Rush v. Oppenheimer	679
Russian Reinsurance Co. v. Stoddard	250
Ryan v. McDonough Power Equipment, Inc.	694
Ryder Energy Distribution Corp. v. Merrill-Lynch Commodities, Inc.	509
Ryer v. Harrisburg Kohl Bros., Inc.	488
S & H Grossinger, Inc. v. Hotel & Restaurant Employees & Bartenders Int'l Union	40
S & S Machinery Corp. v. Masinexportimport	825
S & S Screw Mach. Co. v. Cosa Corp.	798
Sadowy v. Sony Corp.	309
Sagamore Corp. v. Diamond West Energy Corp.	207
Sakamoto v. N.A.B. Trucking Co.	598
Salahuddin v. Coughlin	516
Salahuddin v. Harris	302
Salem Trust Co. v. Manufacturers' Finance Co.	84
Sales v. State Farm Fire & Casualty Co.	489
Sally Beauty Co. v. Nexxus Prods., Co.	32
Sam Fox Publishing Co. v. United States	264

TABLE OF AUTHORITIES

Saminsky v. Occidental Petroleum Corp.	75
Sampson v. Murray	164;168
Samuels v. Doctors Hosp., Inc.	522
San Miguel & Compania, Inc. v. Int'l Hauester Export Co.	33
Sandefer v. United States	749
Sander v. Mayo Clinic	461
Sanders v. Thrall Car. Mfg. Co.	310;311
Sandsend Financial Consultants, Ltd. v. Wood	797
Sarnoff v. American Home Products Corp.	11
Saunders v. General Services Corp.	557
Saxe, Bacon & Bolan, P.C. v. Martindale-Hubbell, Inc.	84
Saxis Steamship Co. v. Multifact International Traders Inc.	677
Scan-Plast Indus., Inc. v. Scanimport America, Inc.	533
Scarton v. Charles	33
Schaafsma v. Morin Vt. Corp.	593;597
Schaffer v. Heitner	57
Schertenleib v. Traum	76
Schiavone v. Fortune	313;314
Schlagenhauf v. Holder	457;458
Schlesinger v. Reservists Committee	3
Schlitt v. Florida	700
Schneider v. Sears	73
Schneider v. Og & C Corp.	520
Schneider's Estate, In re	208;247
Schoenbaum v. Firstbrook	789
Schroeder v. Lufthansa German Airlines	335
Schultz v. Boy Scouts of Am.	211;212;213;223;229; 230;231;334
Schwabenbauer v. Olean Board of Education	511;534
Schwartz v. Compagnie General Transatlantique	507
Schwartz v. Public Administrator	758;765
Schwimmer v. Sony Corp. of America	528
S.C.N.O. Barge Lines, Inc. v. Anderson Clayton & Co.	491
Scola v. Boat Frances, R., Inc.	722
Scotch Whiskey, In re	873
Sea Colony, Inc. v. Continental Ins. Co.	330
Sealift Inc. v. Refinadora Costarricense de Petrolio	817
Sears, Roebuck & Co. v. Enco Association, Inc.	236
Sears, Roebuck & Co. v. Mackey	526;729
Season All Industries, Inc. v. Turkiye Sise Ve Cam Fabrikalari, A.S.	513
SEC v. Am. Bd. of Trade, Inc.	180
SEC v. Banca Della Svizzera Italiana	447
SEC v. Everest Management Corp.	262
SEC v. Frank	168
SEC v. Kasser	789
SEC v. Kingsley	391,392
SEC v. Republic Nat'l Life Ins. Co.	177;178
Securities Investor Protection Corp. v. Vigman	55
Security Nat'l Bank v. Ubex Corp., Ltd.	189
Sedima, S.P.R.L. v. Imrex Co., Inc.	158

Segal v. Gordon	339
Seitman, Mark, & Assoc. v. Reynolds R. J.	691
Sellers v. M.C. Floor Crafters, Inc.	518;520;521
Seltel Inc. v. North Florida 47, Inc.	527
Sequoyah Feed & Supply Co. v. Robinson	87
Seven Elves, Inc. v. Eskenazi	722
Severnoe Sec. Corp. v. London & Lancashire Inc., Co.	247;248
Shaffer v. Heitner	804;805
Shamrock Oil & Gas Corp. v. Sheets	80;87
Shapiro v. Freeman	409,410
Shapiro v. Merrill Lynch	293
Shaw v. Gaurdy	149
Shaw v. Munford	260
Shawmut, Inc. v. American Viscose Corp.	371
Shearson American Express, Inc. v. McMahon	669
Shearson Hayden Stone, Inc. v. Scrivener	174
Sheeran v. General Elec. Co.	101
Shephard v. Swatling	385
Sherwood Apartments v. Westinghouse Electric Corp.	579
Shields v. Barrow	259
Shopping Carts Antitrusts Litigation, In re	434
Siegelman v. Cunard White Star, Ltd.	237
Sierra Club v. Hardin	289
Silver Air v. Aeronautic Dev. Corp., Ltd.	526
Silver v. Nelson	701
Simblest v. Maynard	689
Simler v. Conner	564;567;568;575
Simmons v. United States	723
Simonson v. Int'l Bank	51;52
Singer Co. v. Greever & Walsh Wholesale Textile, Inc.	500
Sires v. Luke	522
Sitts v. United States	520
Skelly Oil Co. v. Zimmerman	269
Skoldberg v. Villani	582
Slade v. Transatlantic Fin. Corp.	358
Slaughter v. Allstate Ins. Co.	517
Slavitt v. Kauhi	686
Slavitt v. Kavhi	686
Smiga v. Dean Witter Reynolds, Inc.	310
Smith v. Aleyeska Pipeline Service Co.	684
Smith v. Am. Fed'n. of Musicians	260
Smith v. Apple	23
Smith v. Danyo	598
Smith v. Murchison	64
Smith v. Trans-World Drilling Co.	691
Smithers v. Smith	11
Sobel v. Hertz, Warner & Co.	676
Societe Inernationale Pour Participations Industrielles et Commerciales v. Rogers	331
Societe Nationale Industrielle Aerospatiale v. U.S.D.C. for the for the Southern District of Iowa	44;335;796-98;803

TABLE OF AUTHORITIES 1019

Sola Elec. Co. v. Jefferson Elec. Co.	197
Soler v. G. & U., Inc.	190;314
Solmitz v. United States	701
Soltex Polymer Corp. v. Fortex Indus., Inc.	26;49
Somerville v. Major Exploration, Inc.	153
Soo Line R.R. Co. v. City of Harvey	91
Sounds Express Int'l, Ltd., v. American Themes & Tapes, Inc..	313
South Afr. Airways v. Tawil	574;579
Southern California Edison Co. v. Westinghouse Elec. Corp...	372
Southern Int'l. Sales Co. v. Potter & Brumbield Div. of AMF, Inc.	237
Southern P. Co. v. Haight	84
Southern Pac. Transp. Co. v. National Molasses Co.	507
Southland Corp. v. Keating	217;668
Spannaus v. Federal Election Comm.	532
Spencer, White & Prentis, Inc. v. Pfizer, Inc.	536
Spevack v. Klein.	182
Spirt v. Teachers Ins. and Annuity Ass'n.	262,263
Spring Mills, Inc. v. Ultracashmere House, Ltd.	373
Square Constr. Co. v. Washington Metro. Area Transit Auth...	721
St. Clair v. United States.	586
St. Mary's Health Center v. Bowen.	536
St. Paul Mercury Indem. Co. v. Red Cab Co.	85
Stacy v. Rogers	682
Staggers v. Otto Gerdau	254
Standard & Poor's Corp. v. Commodity Exch.	373
Stanford v. Kuwait Airways Corp.	535
Stanley-Fizer v. Sport-Billy Productions	505;524
State Farm v. Caton.	677
State Farm v. Tashire.	270,271
State Mut. Life Assurance Co. of Am. v. Arthur Anderson	573;574
Stein v. Oshinsky	507
Stevens v. Nichols	84
Stevenson v. Missouri Pac. R.R. Co.	495;496
Stewart v. RCA Corp.	523
Stewart v. Thigpen.	688
Stewart Org., Inc. v. Ricoh Corp.	63;75;201;215;221; 237
Stewart-Warner Corp. v. Westinghouse Electric Corp.	263,264
Stimler v. Yoshida Shoji Co.	97
Stissi v. Interstate and Ocean Transp. Co.	582
Stokes v. Merrill Lynch	87
Stone v. Millstein.	699
Stormy Clime Ltd. v. Progroup, Inc.	164
Strait v. Mehlenbacher	338
Strandell v. Jackson County	550
Stratton Group, Ltd. v. Sprayregen	265,266
Strawbridge v. Curtiss.	13
Strelitz v. Surrey Classics Inc.	668
Strickland v. American Can Co.	492
Stringfellow v. Concerned Neighbors in Action	264

FEDERAL CIVIL PRACTICE

Sugarhill Records, Ltd. v. Motown Record Corp.	352,358
Sullivan v. American Airlines, Inc.	310
Sullivan v. Sturm, Ruger & Co.	371
Summers v. FDIC.	677
Sun Oil Co. v. Wortman.	208
Superior Coal Co. v. Ruhrkohle, A.G.	55
Supine v. Compagnie Nationale Air France	253
Supreme Tribe of Ben-Hur v. Cauble	13
Swain v. Alabama	585
Swift v. Swift	255;461
Swift v. Tyson.	192
Swift & Co. Packers v. Compania Colombiana Del Caribe	728
Swift & Co. v. Wickham	6
Swift Industries Inc. v. Votany Industries, Inc.	676
Swiss Bank Corp. v. Eatessami.	174
System Federation No.91, Etc. v. Wright	722
Szatanek v. McDonnell Douglas Corp.	465
T.D.S., Inc. v. Shelby Mut. Ins. Co.	695;696
Taca Int'l Airlines, S.A. v. Rolls-Royce, Ltd.	44
Tampimex Oil Ltd. v. Latina Trading Corp.	173
Taragan v. Eli Lilly and Co.	684
Tarlton v. Exxon.	694
Tauza v. Susquehanna Coal Co.	51
Taylor v. Gallagher	530
Tel. Co. v. Delta Communications Corp.	190
Tele-Communications of Key West v. United States	509
Teletronics Services, Inc., In re.	519;521
Telex Corp. v. IBM.	169
Temple Uinv. v. Saffa Bros., Inc.	529
Terminal R.R. Ass'n of St. Louis v. Staengel	591
Terry v. Raymond Int'l, Inc.	50
Texas Eastern Transmission Corp., In re	55;871;873;883
Texas Trading & Milling Corp. v. Fed. Rep. of Nigeria.	815;816;817
Textile Workers Union of Am. v. Lincoln Mills of Alabama	197
Thermtron Products, Inc. v. Hermansdorfer	99;100
Thomas v. Arn	318
Thomas v. Washington Gas Light Co.	749
Thompson v. Int'l Ass'n of Machinists & Aerospace Workers	695
Thompson v. Kerr-McGee Refining Corp.	720
Thorpe v. Erb.	213
Timberlane v. Bank of America.	788
Times Newspaper, Ltd. (Gr. Brit.) v. McDonnell Douglas Corp.	385
Toner v. Lederle Laboratories.	690
Torres v. Oakland Scavenger Co.	731
Touche Ross & Co. v. Redington.	23
Townsel v. County of Contra Costa.	45
Tracy, In re.	367
Trans World Airlines, Inc. v. Civil Aeronautics Board.	263
Trans World Metals, Inc. v. Southwire	243

TABLE OF AUTHORITIES

Transcontinental Motors, Inc. v. NSU Moterenwerke Aktiengesellschaft 352
Transunran Corp v. Pepsico, Inc. 789;791
Transvision, Inc., In re 261
Travelers Indem. Co. v. Isreal 275
Travelers Indemnity Co. v. Sarkisian 82;212
Treadwell v. Kennedy 702
Treines v. Sunshine Mining Co. 13
Triangle Industries, Inc. v. Kennecott Copper Corp. 310
Truck Drivers Local Union No. 807 v. Bohack Corp. 168-69
Tull v. United States 564
Turchio v. D/S A/S Den Norske Afr. 595;597;599;600
Turick v. Yamaha Motor Corp 434
Turner v. Bank of North America 2
Turner v. Parsons 364
21st Century Productions, Inc. "Thrilsphere" Contract Litigation, In re 872
20th Century Wear, Inc. v. Sanmark-Stardust, Inc. 373
Tyrill v. Alcoa Steamship Co. 588;589
U.S. Fidelity & Guar. Co. v. Smith Co. 210
U.S. Industries, Inc. v. Blake Constr. Co. 692
U.S. Industries, Inc. v. Gregg 90
U.S. Oil Co. v. Koch Refining Co. 488
U.S. Trust Co. of New York v. Executive Life Insurance Co. ... 554
Ulichny v. General Electric Co. 82
Underhill v. Hernandez 819
Underwriters at Interest v. Fed'l Express Corp. 429
Underwriter's Nat'l. Assurance Co. v. North Carolina Ins. Guar. Ass'n 749
Unico Indutrial Corp. v. S.S. Andros City 74
Unicon Management Corp. v. Koppers Co. 171
Union Carbide Corp. Gas Plant Disaster, In re 76;77;221
Union Carbide Corp. Gas Plant Disaster at Bhopal, In re .. 789-90
Union Ins. Soc. v. William Gluckin & Co. 520
Unique Concepts, Inc. v. Brown 414;576
United Airlines v. McDonald 285
United Airlines Inc. v. Wiener 684
United Artists Corp. v. Fields Productions, Inc., ... 275
United Mine Workers v. Gibbs 17;19
United Nations Korean Reconstruction Agency v. Glass Prod. Meth 64
United Savings Ass'n of Texas v. Timbers of Inwood Forest ... 868-69
United States v. Alessi 521
United States v. Allegheny County 197
United States v. Aluminum Corp. of Am. 787
United States v. American Tel. & Tel. 684
United States v. Anchor Line, Ltd. 258
United States v. Carolina E. Chem., Co., Inc. 701;702
United States v. Coumantaros 273
United States v. DeFiore 644
United States v. Diebold, Inc. 534

United States v. Dinitz	604
United States v. 18.2 Acres of Land	488
United States ex. rel. Echevarria v. Silberglitt	96
United States ex Rel. United Brotherhood of Carpenters & Joiners Local Union No. 2028 v. Woerfel Corp.	255
United States v. F & M Schaefer Brewing Co.	704;708
United States v. 58.16 Acres of Land	434;435
United States v. First Nat'l City Bank	331;803
United States v. Garcia	584
United States v. General Dynamics Corp.	698
United States v. Heyward-Robinson Co.	588
United States v. Hooker Chem. & Plastics Corp.	330;336
United States v. IBM Corp.	336;364
United States v. J. B. Williams Co., Inc.	531
United States v. Joe Grasso & Sons, Inc.	266
United States v. Light	530
United States v. Mendoza	749;776
United States v. Modica	628
United States v. Morelock	354
United States v. Nixon	371;746
Unites States v. One Assortment of 89 Firearms	749
United States v. One Colt Python, 357 Cal. Revolver, S/N 703361 w/Holster	509
United States v. One 1984 Ford Bronco	528
United States v. O'Neil	683
United States v. Pierre	655
United States v. Potamkin Cadillac Corp.	527
United States v. Raddatz	316
United States v. Reliable Transfer Co., Inc.	197
United States v. Salim	802
United ex rel. Sero v. Preiser	66
United States v. Singer	627
United States v. South-Eastern Underwriters Ass'n	3
United States v. Southern Motor Carriers Rate Conference	485
United States v. Standard Oil Co.	197
United States v. Stauffer Chem. Co.	749;776;777
United States v. Tourine	590
United States v. 216 Bottles	436
United States v. Union Indem. Ins. Co.	27
United States v. Valdosta/Lowndes County Hosp. Auth.	690
United States v. Van Diviner	686
United States v. Vetco Inc.	333
United States v. William S. Gray & Co.	508
United States v. Yazell	198
United States v. Yonkers Bd. of Educ.	257
United States Catholic Conference v. Abortion Rights Mobilization, Inc.	3
United States Football League v. National Football League	600
United Steelworkers v. Enterprise Wheel & Car Corp.	676
Universal Motors Group of Cos. v. Wilkerson	93
Universal Oil Prod. Co. v. Root Refining Co.	723

TABLE OF AUTHORITIES 1023

Universe, Miss, Inc. v. Patricelli 373
University of Tennessee v. Elliot 749;774;775;777
UpJohn Co. v. United States 327
*Upjohn Co. Antibrotre Cleocm Products Liability Litigation,
In re.* 881
Uranium Industry Antitrust Litigation, In re. 878
Usiak v. New York Tank Barge Co. 413
Utah v. Marsh 523
Valdan Sportswear v. Montgomery Ward & Co. 311
Van Cauwenberghe v. Biard 77;220;729
Vandenbark v. Owens-Illinois Glass Co. 206
Van Dusen v. Barrack 75;214,215,216,880
Vasallo v. Neidermeyer 74
Vaughn v. American Basketball Ass'n 74
Verlinden v. Central Bank of Nigera 814;818;819
Verschell v. Fireman's Fund Ins. Co. v. 87
Vicon, Inc. v. CMI Corp. 721
Victrix S.S. Co., S.A. v. Salem Dry Cargo, A.B. 213;214;251
Video Connection of Am., Inc. v. Priority Concepts, Inc. 99
Vincent v. Ateliers de la Moto be cane, S.A. 335
Vincent v. Hughes Air West, Inc. 683
VISA v. Bankcard Holders 529
Virginia-Carolina Tie & Wood Co. v. Dunbar 689
Viterbo v. Dow Chem. Co. 535
Volkswagenwerk, A.G. v. Superior Court, Alamedon County .. 796
Volkswagenwerk Aktiengesellschaft v. Beech Aircraft Corp. 44
Volkswagenwerk Aktiengesellschaft v. Schlunk 44;787
Volvo v. M/V Atlantic Saga 313
Von Bulon v. Von Bulon 255
Vorhees v. Fischer & Krecke 782;784
Vulcan Soc'y v. Fire Dept. of City of White Plains 258
Waco v. United States Fidelity & Guar. Co. 101
Waldron v. Skelly Co. 94
Walker v. Armco Steel Corp. 28;162;198-201;210
Wall v. Connecticut Mut. Life Ins. 495
Walter E. Heller & Co. v. James Godbe Co. 62
Walters v. City of Ocean Springs 523
Wamsganz v. Boatmen's Bank of DeSoto 850
Wang v. Gordon 715
Ward v. Brown 573
*Warren v. Int'l. Bhd. of Teamsters, Chauffeurs, Warehousemen
and Helpers of Am.* 469
Warrick v. Brode 461
Washburn v. Corcoran 23
Washington v. Armstrong World Indus. Inc. 526
Washington v. New York City Bd. of Estimate 578
Wasserman v. Perugini 260
Watters v. Ralston Coal Co. 10
Watts v. Pinckney 721
Wehling v. CBS 182
Weinberger v. Romero-Barcelo 164

Weiner v. Bache Halsey Stuart, Inc.	330
Weiss v. Chrysler Corp.	435
Weissman v. Banque De Bruxelles	247
Wells v. Dallas Indep. School Dist.	696
Wells v. Simonds Abrasive Co.	205
Wells Fargo & Co. v. Wells Fargo Express Co.	55
Weo v. Macchiarola	524
Wesco Mfg., Inc. v. Tropical Attractions of Palm Beach, Inc.	686
West v. Conrail	161
Westchester Rockland Newspapers, Inc. v. Marbach	385
Western Geophysical Co. of Am. v. Bolt Assoc., Inc.	576
Westinghouse Elec. Corp. v. City of Burlington	371
Westinghouse Elec. Corp. Uranium Contracts Litig., In re	447
Westmoreland v. CBS, Inc.	371
Wetzel v. Liberty Mut. Inc.	288
White v. Hughes	87
White v. New Hampshire	697
White Motor Credit v. White Moter Corp.	834
Whitman Elec., Inc. v. Local 363 Int'l Bhd. of Elec. Workers, AFL-CIO	573;576
Whitney v. Robertson	782
Wilhelm v. Blue Bell, Inc.	695
William B. May Co., Inc. v. Hyatt	33;784
Williams v. Allen	45
Williams v. Howard Johnson's, Inc. of Washington	508
Willingham v. Morgan	88
Wilson v. North Am. Reinsurance Corp.	491
Wilson v. Southern Farm Bureau Casualty Co.	591
Wilson & Co. v. United Packinghouse Workers	40
Wimbley v. Bolger	702
Wimmer v. Cook	316
Winbourne v. Eastern Air Lines, Inc.	508
Windsor Indus., Inc. v. EACA Int'l Ltd.	243
Winn, In re	99
Winters v. Teledyne Movible Offshore, Inc.	45
Witco Chem. Corp. v. Peachtree Doors, Inc.	683
WIXT Television, Inc. v. Meredity Corp.	311
Wolff v. Wolff	320
Women in Science, Association for v. Califano	109
Woodling v. Garrett Corp.	237
World Arrow Tourism Enters., Ltd v. Trans World Airlines, Inc.	309
Worldwide Carriers, Ltd. v. Aris S.S. Co.	173
Worldwide Volkswagen v. Woodson	53;54;786
Wratchford v. Groves, S.J. & Sons Co.	689
Wuchter v. Pizzutti	34
Wyatt v. Fulrath	247
Y4 Design, Ltd. v. Regensteiner Publishing Enter., Inc.	74
Yannitelli v. Navieras de Puerto Rico	301
Yates v. Buscaglia	337
Yonkers Racing Corp. v. City of Yonkers	92

TABLE OF AUTHORITIES

Yonkers Comm'n on Human Rights v. City of Yonkers	253
Younger v. Harris	21
Youngstown Sheet & Tube Co. v. Sawyer	746
Zack Metal Co. v. International Navigation Corp.	723
Zahn v. International Paper Co.	11;13;20;86
Zdanok v. Glidden Co.	682-83
Zeno v. Cropper	516
Zerman v. Ball	237;245
Zisman v. Sieger	783
Zittman v. McGrath	177

STATUTES
Federal

Bankruptcy
Section 4	845
554	725,842
1002	841,855
1003	855
1007	855-58
2001	841
2004	863
2015	849
2017	842
3001	841
4001	841
4003	842
5001	831,841
6001	841-42
7001	842-45,869
7002	842
7003	843
7004	843
7010	843-44
7012	845
7013	845
7014	842
7056	842
8001	837,842
8002	837
8005	838
9001	842
9002	843
9003	839
9004	845
9009	847
9013	846
9014	845
9015	836

Rules of Appellate Procedure
Rule

3	731-32
4	169,697,700,702,707,731, 732
5	731-33
7	733
8	170,171,742
10	735,736
11	736
12	719
21	731,733
25	170
27	170,743
28	739,740
30	736,737
31	169,738,744
32	737-38,744
34	741
35	745
37	214
38	200,214
40	743-45

Rules of Civil Procedure
Rule

1	503-04
3	28,195-96,200,843
4	26-40,42-48,50,53-54, 57,162,182,269,273,313, 484,712,780,782-84,843
5	146-47,181,263,268,339, 431,449,477,481-82,514, 572-73,575,693,708
6	45,146,183,317,477, 481-82,509-10,572,690,693, 700,7027-19,875
7	46,186,431,449,466,477, 480-81,484,688,691
8	2,7,9,10,15,58,139, 142-143,146-50,152,184
9	147,150,152,154-55,184-85
10	145,148,181,480,843
11	94,102,140-41,146,149,181, 185,340,477,481,546
12	2,7,28,46,58-9,72, 140,182-83,186,259,268, 472,478,484-89,507,509, 567,572,651,681,726
13	186-89,264-69,566,845
14	48,188-89,264-70,842
15	113,150,182,189-90, 308,314,575,685-87,701

TABLE OF AUTHORITIES

16	299,300,304,340,430-31, 464,469,489,547,54950,667, 726
17	6,39,253-56
18	17,19,189,565
19	6,15,48,64,258-59
20	19,257-58,272
21	258,478,683
22	271-76
23	146,156,216,277,279-82, 286-87,290-96,298,554
24	260-62,266
25	478
26	128,143,330,323,326-30, 336-37,339-41,343-44, 427-28,430-40,444,446-47, 449,451-54,456-57,459, 463-65,467-68,478,793
28	331,799,801
29	331,342,450,467,799
30	166,324-25,330-31,340, 344,346,478
31	325,331
32	345,646
33	325,344,426-27,430-32, 434,436,438-42,646
34	324,326,344,442-50,453, 456,463
35	326,329,457,60,461-63
36	326,344-45,428,465-70
37	339-42,440,452,456,463, 469-70,478,715
38	176,182,562,468-69,564, 571-77,710
39	569,571,573-74,577-78,582, 667,710
41	46,343,478,494-98,555, 684-85,698-700
42	308,682-84
43	473,477
45	332,444
46	592
47	584
48	583,601
49	587,594-98
50	478,665,687,688,690-93, 707,716,732
51	587-89,591,593,595
52	166,171,665,700,704, 707,716,726,732
53	315,320-21,54⁷

Rule	Pages
54	150,477,703,707,710,717, 727,729,269,275,730
55	59,478,498,499,501
56	442,472-73,504-14,677,842
57	151,567,709-10
58	690,693,704,706-07,727,
59	478,501,665,693-94,697-98, 700-02,707,715-16,719,720, 732
60	59,154,478,501-02,697, 715-21,722-23
61	718,726,795-96
62	170,665,715-17,742
64	56,172,214
65	98,165-68,478
66	177,179,494
68	553
69	707,711-15
70	714
71	714,715
72	316-17
73	663-65
74	665
77	477,708
78	478,482,483
79	707,727
81	96-98,198,567,574,575,577
82	282
83	430
84	28,143

Rules of Evidence

Rules	Pages
103	489,648-49,726
104	307,489,490
302	201
401	201,202
403	490
501	327
601	201
611	644,652,657
612	652
613	660-61
661	656
701	650
702	650,651
	441,654,661
	201
	201
	201

TABLE OF AUTHORITIES

United States Code

Title	Section	
2	118	713
5	552	108
9	1	157,216,551,668
	2	157
	10	551,676
	205	90
10	1089	90
11	101	829,835,851,853,858,860-61
	102	847,859,869
	105	836
	109	849,851-52
	152	862
	158	832
	301	852-53,865-66
	303	855
	303	853-54
	304	835
	305	831-32,839
	306	834
	321	849
	322	858-59
	324	858
	326	864
	327	841
	330	840,863
	331	863
	341	839,857,863
	343	863
	345	841
	348	861
	361	851,868
	362	847,865,868-69
	363	838,869
	365	869
	501	862
	502	861-62
	506	585
	521	848,855,857,858
	522	852
	544	853
	546	866
	547	853,866
	701	848-49,858,863
	705	863
	724	853
	741	849,866-67
	761	849,866-67
	901	849
	1101	859

United States Code (Continued)

Title	Section	
	1102	864-65
	1103	859, 864
	1104	859-60, 865
	1106	859
	1107	859
	1109	864
	1113	869
	1121	860
	1125	840, 860
	1127	860
	1128	860
	1129	860
	1146	858
	1161	851
	1163	860
	1201	851
	1224	840
	1302	858, 860
	1306	852
12	94	69
	1819	90, 92
15	1	10, 546, 787
	4	146
	5	48
	6	787
	10	48
	15	10
	22	70
	25	48
	45	787
	77	48, 90, 146, 788
	78	2, 48, 70, 865, 866, 788
	751	6
	771	90
	1011	3, 22
	1012	22
	1311	109
	2072	147
18	156	855
	1914	856
	1915	855
	1930	855
	1961	153, 546
	1964	157
	1965	48
22	2699	90
	4215	331
25	375	49

TABLE OF AUTHORITIES

United States Code (Continued)

Title	Section	
28	140	835
	1406	682
	1602	712
	41	5,730
	46	744
	81	4
	112	4
	151	5
	157	832-34,837
	158	836,837
	171	5
	251	5
	346	208
	581	839,858
	631	314
	636	315-20,663-64
	959	177,836
	1252	5
	1253	5,730,747
	1254	745,747
	1291	169,504,537,727,729-30
	1292	73,101,275,703,728-32,770
	1294	730
	1295	5,731
	1330	16,813
	1331	8,23,146
	1332	10-14,146,256,813
	1333	16
	1334	16,830,831,832,833
	1335	16,271-72,276
	1337	10,16
	1338	731
	1341	91
	1343	16
	1346	233,266,731
	1350	13
	1351	13
	1359	14,256
	1391	63,66,273,813
	1392	67
	1393	67
	1396	71
	1397	71,271-72
	1399	69
	1400	70
	1401	71
	1402	66
	1403	69

United States Code (Continued)

Title	Section	
	1404	71-77,201,214-15,221-22, 308,682,789,880
	1407	215-16,871-80,886
	1408	834
	1409	835
	1411	835
	1441	71,79-81,83,85-88, 90-94,567,813
	1443	88,89,92,100
	1444	89,92
	1445	90,91
	1446	79,81,91-94,96
	1447	84,96-97,99-101
	1448	96
	1449	96,97
	1450	96,98
	1452	89
	1602	251,813
	1603	11,80,88
	1608	29,42
	1631	731,882
	1651	92,717,730
	1652	192,201
	1653	95
	1655	714,723,780
	1696	332
	1738	750,757,760-63,768-69,773
	1781	332-33,793,801
	1783	332,800
	1784	333,800
	1863	583
	1865	582
	1870	585
	1915	30
	1916	30
	1921	57
	1927	340
	1930	857
	1963	708,711-12,715
	2006	712,713
	2072	198,201
	2075	836,841
	2101	746
	2201	151,708-11
	2202	710
	2254	158
	2283	23,274,757,881
	2284	6,747
	2321	49

United States Code (Continued)

Title	Section	
	2361	48,271-74,780
	2403	261
	2410	89,276
	2413	712
	2679	89
29	160	161,261
	161	49
	185	39,71,83
	201	147
	626	563
	657	125
	1132	71,83
	2000	70
33	1365	261
35	293	48
38	445	276
	784	49
	4116	90
42	233	90
	1738	765,767
	1981	770
	1983	752-59,770-75
	1985	758,775
	1986	775
	2000	261,775
	2458	90
45	51-60	90
	701	6
	1301	6
46	688	69,70,91
	801	261
50	520	46

Court Rules

Supreme Court

Rule		
	17.1	746
	18	746
	19.1	746
	20.3	746
	20.4	744
	21.4	746
	22.3	747
	22.5	747
	23	747
	24.1	747
	25.2	747
	25.3	747
	25.4	747

Second Circuit
Rule	11	735
	21	733
	27	733,739,740,743
	28	739,740
	30	737
	32	737,738
	34	741
	40	744

N.D.N.Y.
Rule	6	479
	7	513
	7	145,146
	7	479,481
	9	161
	9	479
	9	482
	10	165,337,440,456,475,479, 481-83,513-14
	14	514
	19	329
	21	320
	31	158
	36	555
	37	555
	40	684
	43	315,479
	44	479
	45	584

S.D.N.Y./E.D.N.Y.
Rule	1	145-46,181,480,514
	3	165,188,337,440,456, 475-76,480-82,513
	4	156
	6	480,482-83
	7	480,483,845
	8	480,483
	9	480,483
	13	846
	18	339,431,449
	19	320
	22	584
	25	95
	28	555
	29	555
	32	158
	46	305,306,329,345,428-30, 432,436-37,439
	47	433,443,450,467

TABLE OF AUTHORITIES

W.D.N.Y.
Rule 8 156
         11 479,483
         12 479
         13 145,479,481,513
         14 339,479,481-82,514
         15 479,483
         16 329
         17 337,440,456,479
         21 158
         22 584-85,590
         25 555
         35 315

State

Business Corporation Law
Section 304 38
         306 38
         307 38

Civil Practice Law and Rules
Section 103 564
         202 209
         205 47,162
         301 50,56
         302 50-52,57,58,786
         304 28,93
         305 28,93
         307 41
         308 36,37,46
         309 37
         310 38
         311 38,41
         312 41
         313 29,43
         314 43
         320 29
         320 29,182,218
         621 175
         1002 86
         2103 30
         3013 144
         3016 155-56
         3017 150
         3021 146
         3103 336
         3213 97
         3214 183
         4002 98
         4102 568-69,574-75,578
         4104 584

4106	584
4107	585
4109	586
4110	585
4111	587,594
4113	601
4501	327
4502	327
4503	327
4504	327
4505	327
4506	327
4507	327
4508	327
5201	74
6201	28,172,174-75
6202	174
6210	57,174
6211	57,176
6212	28,173-75
6219	808
6220	808
6221	808
6222	176
6223	176,808
6226	809
7501	217
7502	28
7511	668

General Associations Law
Section 13	39

General Business Law
Section 686	53,38

General Obligations Law
Section 5-1401	235,242
5-1402	218,221,235,242

Insurance Law
Section 7401-36	22
1212	38

Mental Hygiene Law
Article 77	37
78	37

Public Officers Law
Section 66	111
84-90	108
87	108

Vehicle and Traffic Law
Section 253	52,36